P9-BHV-975

THE GREAT GAMBLE

ALSO BY DUDLEY POPE

non-fiction

Flag 4
The Battle of the River Plate
73 North
England Expects
At 12 Mr Byng Was Shot
The Black Ship
Guns

fiction (the 'Ramage' series)

Ramage
Ramage and the Drum Beat
Ramage and the Freebooters

Dudley Pope

THE
GREAT GAMBLE

WEIDENFELD AND NICOLSON
5 Winsley Street London W1

Copyright © The Ramage Company Limited 1972

All rights reserved. No part of this publication
may be reproduced, stored in a retrieval system,
or transmitted, in any form or by any means,
electronic, mechanical, photocopying, recording
or otherwise, without the prior permission of the
Copyright owner.

ISBN 0 297 00484 0

Printed by C. Tinling & Co Ltd,
London and Prescot

For Henry and Bet

CONTENTS

	Introduction	1
1	The Fortune . . .	5
2	. . . And the Fame	15
3	Naples – and the Nile	31
4	The Mad Czar	46
5	The New Grand Master	53
6	The Fate of Neutrals	67
7	The Lonely Fight	77
8	The Social Whirl	85
9	The Open Secret	90
10	'Fools and Madmen'	99
11	'The Champion of England'	109
12	The Sword and the Olive	125
13	Changing the Helmsman	135
14	An Olive Branch?	143
15	Storm in a Mustard Pot	153
16	The Fretful Lover	161
17	'By a Side Wind . . .'	190
18	Divided Command	202
19	'The Fire of England'	217
20	The Horse-drawn Ultimatum	243
21	By the Sound or the Belt?	259
22	Squandering Victories	284
23	The Sight of the Sound	290
24	'. . . In Copenhagen Roads'	303
25	The Eve of Battle	327
26	Maundy Thursday	345
27	Into Battle	361

CONTENTS

28 Signal Number 39   404
29 Another Battle?   431
30 The Truce Expires   449
31 The Swedish Fleet Sails   474
32 The Czar's Overture   492
33 Strawberries for Nelson   507

Epilogue   512
Appendices   514
Bibliography and Notes   531
Sources   560
Index   567

ILLUSTRATIONS

between pages 68 and 69

1 Lord Nelson, painted by Sir William Beechey *(On loan to the National Portrait Gallery from Leggatt Trustees)*
2 Sir Hyde Parker *(National Maritime Museum)*
3 Captain Edward Riou *(Photo: John R. Freeman)*
4 Captain Thomas Fremantle *(Commander The Hon. John Fremantle; photo: A. C. Cooper)*
5 Captain Thomas Foley *(National Portrait Gallery)*
6 Colonel the Hon. William Stewart *(Photo: John R. Freeman)*
7 Nicholas Vansittart *(Christ Church, Oxford)*
8 Lady Emma Hamilton by Romney *(National Portrait Gallery)*

between pages 132 and 133

9 A contemporary plan of Copenhagen *(Rigsarkivet, Copenhagen)*
10 The final plan providing three sea forts to protect Copenhagen – Stubben, Trekroner and Provesteen *(In the private library of HM the King of Denmark)*
11 Trekroner Fort *(Painting by H. Kramer in the private library of HM the King of Sweden)*
12 The Danish Crown Prince (later Frederick VI) *(The King's Library, Copenhagen)*
13 Commodore Olfert Fischer *(The King's Library, Copenhagen)*

between pages 196 and 197

14 Count Bernstorff *(The King's Library, Copenhagen)*
15 Captain Hans Lindholm *(The King's Library, Copenhagen)*
16 The *Monarch* leads the British Fleet through the Sound *(Original drawing by Robinson Kittoe owned by Acton Bjørn, Copenhagen)*

17 The entrance to the Sound, looking north (*The King's Library, Copenhagen*)

18 The British Fleet sails down under topsails to anchor north of Copenhagen (*Original drawing by Robinson Kittoe owned by Acton Bjørn*)

19 A page from Robinson Kittoe's notebook showing Copenhagen and its defences before the Battle (*Original owned by Acton Bjørn*)

between pages 260 and 261

20 A rough sketch by Robinson Kittoe during the Battle shows how he visualized the Danish view from the shore to the north of Castellet (*Original owned by Acton Bjørn*)

21 The Battle, looking northwards across Nyeholm (*Engraved by I. F. Clemens from the painting by C. A. Lorentzen; Frederiksborg Museum, Denmark*)

22 The Danish defences from another angle, drawn by Robinson Kittoe (*Original owned by Acton Bjørn*)

23 Kittoe's rough plan of the positions of Fischer's and Nelson's ships in the Battle (*Original owned by Acton Bjørn*)

between pages 324 and 325

24 A page from Kittoe's notebook describing the British ships (*Original owned by Acton Bjørn*)

25 Kittoe's notes for the Danish line, describing each of the ships (*Original owned by Acton Bjørn*)

26 On board Floating Battery No. 1 at the height of the Battle (*Painting in Assens Museum, Denmark*)

27 A British shot embedded in a piece of oak beam from the Danish *Indfødsretten* (*Navy Museum, Copenhagen*)

28 The pocket telescope traditionally reputed to have been the one Nelson put to his blind eye (*National Maritime Museum*)

between pages 388 and 389

29 Nelson's letter to the Danish Crown Prince proposing a truce (*Rigsarkivet, Copenhagen*)

30 Nelson's seal, bearing his coat of arms (*National Maritime Museum*)

31 Captain Thesiger brings Nelson's truce letter to the Crown
    Prince *(Painting by C. A. Lorentzen in the Frederiksborg Museum)*

32 Robinson Kittoe's panoramic drawing of the Battle *(Original
    owned by Acton Bjørn)*

33 A letter, and two medals, which Nelson sent to Captain Hans
    Sneedorff, Commandant of the Naval Academy in Copenhagen,
    shortly after the Battle *(Original letter and medals in the possession
    of the Danish Admiralty)*

The author and publishers are grateful to the copyright owners for
permission to reproduce the pictures.

MAPS

page

The track of Sir Hyde Parker's Fleet from Lowestoft to the   218
    entrance of the Skagerrak

The approach from the North Sea to Copenhagen and the Baltic   264

Copenhagen Roads   310

The position of the Danish and British ships during the Battle   415

INTRODUCTION

It has not previously been possible for an historian to make a full-scale study of all aspects of the Battle of Copenhagen and the gradual slide into war because the whereabouts of many important documents was not known, and this has resulted in one-sided accounts which have given distorted views of both the Battle and the diplomatic exchanges. These documents recently came to light, and I am fortunate in being the first person to be able to make use of them.

Since I am a Briton who has a great love for Denmark, I hope I have succeeded in being as detached and impartial as an historian should be. From the British point of view, Sir Hyde Parker's signal recalling Nelson's division has in the past caused much controversy. This has arisen mainly because few people have read the Signal Book, and others have quoted out of context only a few of the accounts that were in fact available.

With all the facts now given, I hope the controversy is finally settled. From the Danish point of view, Nelson's motives in offering a truce have been questioned by several earlier historians, who have failed to take into account the written views of the Danish Crown Prince, the battle situation at the time Nelson made it, and – very relevant – Nelson's character. Again, I hope this book will finally settle that controversy.

Fortunately, long before I began my research into the Battle I had sailed my boat from England to Denmark and – since it had no engine – faced many of the problems which beset Sir Hyde Parker and his fleet owing to the vagaries of wind and current. Having sailed more than once over the waters of the Cattegat that gave Sir Hyde so many sleepless nights, I feel my judgments of him are fair, particularly since my boat at that time was considerably smaller than the smallest carried on board his flagship.

Research on the scale necessary to write a book such as this depends on the willing and patient help of many people. I would particularly like to thank Commander Jørgen Teisen, of the Historical Section of the Danish Admiralty, and Admiral E. J. Saabye, an authority on the Battle – and on many other aspects of Danish naval history – who not only gave me much help but introduced me to Mr Acton Bjørn, the architect. He owns the remarkable drawings and paintings made by Robinson Kittoe during and immediately after the Battle, and has allowed me to reproduce them.

His Royal Highness King Frederik of Denmark gave permission for me to use material from his own library; the Rigsarkivet, Copenhagen, gave me every assistance in going through the considerable number of documents concerning the Battle which have not previously been used by historians.

His Royal Highness the King of Sweden has allowed me to use material from his private library. The Danish Admiralty, and particularly the Marine Library, have given me enormous help. The late Captain H. P. Kiær, then head of the Historical Section of the Danish Admiralty, and the King's Librarian, discovered many of the scores of documents used in this book and, with Commander Jørgen Teisen, listed them and helped my wife and myself go through them. Commander Teisen has subsequently patiently answered the written questions I have sent him from various places, often half way round the world.

Through him, Admiral Saabye became involved in helping me, and his friendship with Mr Acton Bjørn has resulted in Mr Bjørn making available to me his collection of hitherto unpublished drawings and paintings by Robinson Kittoe, secretary to Nelson's second-in-command, which were made during and immediately after the Battle. They confirm material in the documents mentioned above, and at last the positions of the British and Danish ships can be fixed with some accuracy.

Major Sir Richard Proby, Bt, MC, has allowed me to use documents concerning the Earl of Carysfort, Lord Grenville and Lord Hawkesbury, kept at Elton Hall. Letters to and from Captain Thomas Fremantle are used by permission of Lord Cottesloe.

Professor Paul Lassen spent many days translating the old and fading Danish script into modern English for us; Mrs Tanja Grønning translated much printed material.

Our old friend Mr Eggert Benzon made us welcome guests at his home while we were doing research in Copenhagen, provided us with a car to visit many towns and villages, and lent us his yacht to resail the Sound, which I had visited many years earlier in my own yacht. (We had crewed for him in a race round Saelland, and a navigational error on my part near Sjaellands Rev – a reef which claimed one of Sir Hyde Parker's ships – cost him first prize!)

To Lt. Colonel Harold Wyllie, OBE, the marine artist and a valued friend, we owe a great deal: for many years he has been a constant source of information and advice, and we treasure the days spent with him at Hillhead of Dunkeld. Rear-admiral A. H. Taylor, CB, OBE, DL, JP, an authority on the Battle, extended us both help and hospitality as we began the research.

I have made extensive use of documents at the Public Record Office and they are published by courtesy of the Keeper of Public Records; those in the British Museum are used by permission of the Trustees; and those in the National Maritime Museum are also used by permission of the Trustees.

Commander Peter Kemp, Head of Historical Section, Admiralty, once again allowed me to make use of the Admiralty Library, where Mr Young was unfailingly patient.

As always, my greatest debt is to my wife: for more than a year she transcribed many of the quarter of a million words from old documents upon which this book is based, took dictation from translators, and has acted as secretary, editor and friendly critic while this MS was written – as well as acting as mate of the yacht which is our home.

1
THE FORTUNE...

Two British admirals returned to England in the autumn of 1800. One of them had been in the West Indies for four years and the other in the Mediterranean and off the coasts of Spain for seven. Each reported his arrival to the Board and went to London to await a letter from their Lordships – as the Lords Commissioners of the Admiralty were collectively known – which would begin with the time-honoured phrase, 'You are hereby required and directed . . .' and tell him of his next appointment. The junior of the two admirals waited with ill-concealed impatience; the other, a much older man, was in no hurry to go back to sea.

During the long war against Revolutionary France (which had already lasted more than seven years and was to go on for another fifteen) many an admiral returned to England to wait in vain for the letter. There were many reefs and shoals on which a flag officer's career could be wrecked – too many mistakes for their Lordships to overlook, lack of sufficiently powerful influence to help in his present rank (often the result of a patron ageing or dying), playing too openly at politics with a party now out of favour, or simply being one of the odd men out because there were too few appointments for all the admirals in the Navy List.

It now contained more than 120 names, each admiral being listed in descending order of seniority and entitled to hoist a special flag afloat – hence 'flag officer' and 'flagship'. Dating from the time the ships of a fleet were first divided into three divisions (van, centre and rear) there were three grades of flag officer (admiral, vice-admiral and the rear-admiral). Each grade was again divided into three for the purpose of seniority and distinguished by the colour of the ensign an admiral was entitled to hoist – red, white or blue. Thus a vice-admiral of the red was senior to one of the white, with the blue the junior.

But fame, fortune and skill had little to do with seniority; with two exceptions the dozen best flag officers were all well below the halfway mark in the Navy List. Below the flag officers was a long list of captains, each knowing that almost his only – and certainly his best – chance of reaching flag rank was the ability to outlive the rest of the captains on the List above him until he reached the top. Merit, influence, chance and ability – all these played a part, but a high mortality rate among one's seniors was the surest way to promotion.

The elder of the two admirals, Sir Hyde Parker, was the first to arrive back in England, and the Navy List showed him to be the eleventh of eighteen admirals of the blue and twenty-eighth in the complete list of five score flag officers. Landing at Plymouth in the middle of September, he found London cold but bustling after four years spent in the tropical heat and languor of the Caribbean as Commander-in-Chief of 'His Majesty's ships and vessels employed . . . at and about Jamaica'. Nevertheless he was thankful that the First Lord of the Admiralty's letter of recall had arrived in time for him to leave Jamaica before the most dangerous weeks of the hurricane season, from mid-August to the end of September, when the Trade winds dropped and the humidity brought mildew, frayed tempers and sickness.

Sir Hyde was sixty-one years old and a widower with three sons. Waiting for his return to London was an eighteen-year-old girl who, within a few weeks, was to be his bride. Sir Hyde's prospective father-in-law, Admiral Sir Richard Onslow, was eleven years younger than his future son-in-law although his name was three places higher in the Navy List.

But from a father-in-law's point of view, what Sir Hyde lacked in youthfulness he more than made up in recently acquired fortune; moreover it was in hard cash, not inherited estates which might be entailed, kept afloat on mortgages, or costly to run. The sea had yielded Sir Hyde more wealth than was dreamed of by any avaricious privateer captain though it had been harvested in much the same way.

'In consequence of some new arrangements,' Lord Spencer, the First Lord of the Admiralty, had written in a revealing letter to Sir Hyde in Jamaica the previous April, 'it is not unlikely that we may be under the necessity of recalling you from the station where you now are, and on which I have been much pleased to find you have derived so much advantage in point of prize money.'

Nor did Spencer – who was used to wealth and trying to soften the order to a very touchy man – exaggerate in his assessment. In four years on the station Sir Hyde had 'derived' a fortune estimated to be at least £200,000 – more than a million pounds at today's values. He had become richer in those four years than many nabobs who had spent twenty in their own offices or in the counting houses of the Honourable

East India Company; and a great deal richer than the majority of planters after half a lifetime in the West Indies transmuting rum and spices into money.[1] Working among the hills and valleys of Caribbean islands – which were plagued with yellow fever and reckoned among the unhealthiest places in the world – such men gambled with high stakes, betting they would accumulate a fortune before the black vomit killed them or a hurricane ripped up the nutmeg trees and torrential rain washed sugar plantations into the sea, for the rich soil is spread thin on hard rock.

Sir Hyde's wealth came with little or no effort and risk to himself, apart from writing orders and reading and making reports. More important, as far as his acceptance by London society was concerned, his fortune did not derive from 'trade': no one would or could label him with the single word 'nabob', which was the social death sentence of the day. Richness through trade allowed a man to rise socially just so far – probably a knighthood, perhaps even an Irish peerage; with a large estate it would be enough to ensure that with judicious entertaining he could be on first-name terms with members of some famous families. But the ultimate test was, could his sons marry into the 'true' aristocracy? His daughters, suitably endowed, would be welcome: such girls saved many an old and famous family whose fortune had been eroded by lethargy or gambling from financial ruin.[2]

Riches from the spoils of war, however, carried no stigma: they were merely something tangible that went with the orders and decorations received by an admiral. Ironically enough, most of the money did come from 'trade', since the fortune arose because one-eighth of all prize money went to the Commander-in-Chief of the station, and the majority of prizes were enemy merchantmen or privateers, not warships.

Nor did Lord Spencer exaggerate when he wrote to Parker a month after the letter already quoted that 'I trust you will not look upon your recall in any other light than as is meant, namely as a change of service, which may naturally be looked for after so long a term as you have enjoyed of the most lucrative station in the service. . . .'

Just how lucrative it was, and why it was now someone else's turn, is shown by the prize list. From the beginning of 1797 until Sir Hyde received his recall in July 1800, ships of the Royal Navy on stations as

[1] George III, seeing the luxurious carriage of a Jamaica planter driving along a London street with liveried outriders, demanded of his Prime Minister: 'Sugar, sugar, eh? All that sugar! How are the duties, eh Pitt, how are the duties?'

[2] But whatever his social background the West Indian merchant was never able to make rum or coffee, two of his major products, popular in Britain, whose people remained loyal to whisky, gin and tea. The Royal Navy was one of the best customers for rum.

far apart as the North Sea and the Indian Ocean, the Cape of Good Hope and the Caribbean, captured 453 French privateers. Of these, 158 were captured in the West Indies, and that proportion, a third, also applies to French and Spanish merchantmen. This means that for nearly four years Sir Hyde was probably receiving his share of a third of all the prize money won by the Royal Navy during that period. It is hardly surprising that the Jamaica station was much sought after by a certain type of admiral: it was as good as a royal warrant to print money.

Much of Sir Hyde's subsequent behaviour, both before and after the Battle of Copenhagen, can be better understood by realizing the significance of the fact that a command such as Jamaica made an admiral rich without, in Sir Hyde's case, any responsibility for handling a fleet in action. Since it gave him enormous powers of patronage, he could also rapidly promote his young favourites. Promotion to fill vacancies was, of course, routine but there was such a high death rate among officers on this station because of sickness that he had much more patronage at his disposal than other admirals. And, perhaps more important, he had the power to make his favourite young captains rich – at no cost to himself – by letting them cruise for weeks on end in the areas where they were most likely to find prizes. Indeed, far from costing him anything it increased his share in the proceeds.

The West Indian islands lie like a sickle (Cuba forming the handle, and the blade comprising Hispaniola, the Virgin, Leeward and Windward Islands, with Trinidad as the point resting on South America) and cover a distance of 2,200 miles, farther than from Gibraltar to the Arctic Circle.

The Royal Navy's two major tasks in the Caribbean at this time were safeguarding British merchantmen by keeping out enemy warships and privateers, and blockading the French and Spanish islands and the Spanish Main (the northern coast of South America). Since the Commander-in-Chief at Jamaica normally never had enough ships to form a line of battle, it was assumed by the Admiralty that he would not be called upon to tackle a French or Spanish fleet arriving from Europe: if one managed to escape the British blockade it would be pursued by a fleet from the eastern side of the Atlantic (as happened before Trafalgar).

So the basic functions of the Commander-in-Chief on the Jamaica station were that he ensured that the merchantmen, laden with their cargoes from the various islands, collected at specified ports at specified times, so the convoys for the United Kingdom could sail punctually; and that he kept frigates on patrol at key points, guarding against the arrival of enemy warships and at the same time capturing any merchantmen trying to break the blockade by entering or leaving the Caribbean.[1]

Frigates were the key: they were used to escort convoys and to maintain the blockade. But convoy work was tedious for the frigate captain and unrewarding: the merchantmen were slow and, since the convoy system relieved them of the need to be first at the market place to ensure a high price for their cargoes, they usually reduced sail at night, which allowed the masters to have smaller crews. If a frigate was always on convoy work, it was a sure sign that her captain found no favour with Sir Hyde. On the other hand, his favoured captains spent most of their time cruising in search of prizes, providing a rare example of patriotism and private profit going hand in hand, since cruising in search of enemy merchantmen was part of the Navy's role. When the court condemned a captive as a prize, the money was divided into eight parts, the captain receiving two eighths, his officers and the ship's company sharing five eighths and the Commander-in-Chief being paid an eighth (which he had to share with a junior flag officer if he had one).

Sir Hyde's favourite young captain – the chief of many, since Sir Hyde was notorious for his use (and misuse) of patronage even in an age when an ounce of influence was worth a ton of ability in getting promotion, and carried no stigma – was Robert Waller Otway, who provides a good example of one of the fortunate beneficiaries of prize money and favouritism and was to play an important role in the Battle of Copenhagen.

Otway commanded a frigate on the Jamaica station and with certain other favoured young frigate captains[2] spent most of his time cruising. According to one contemporary source, in his last year in the West Indies – he returned to England with Sir Hyde – Otway 'made as many captures as ever fell to the lot of one vessel in the same space of time'. A privately-printed memoir says that in six years in the West Indies he captured two hundred privateers and merchantmen. If the ships averaged only £1,000 each in prize money, Otway would have received £50,000 and the Commander-in-Chief £25,000 (a third of this would have gone to a junior flag officer if there was one on the station).

[1] British convoys usually left England in October, arriving in the West Indies before Christmas, and left the Caribbean before June to avoid the hurricane season. Insurance rates, doubled for a ship still in the Caribbean in July, usually lapsed automatically if she had not sailed by the first day of August.

[2] Among them Hugh Pigot, commanding the *Hermione*, and one of the most brutal and sadistic officers in the Navy. After Sir Hyde had sent him cruising in the autumn of 1797 many of his men mutinied, murdering Pigot and most of the officers, and sailed the frigate to La Guaira (in what is now Venezuela) where they handed her over to the Spanish. For a full account of this, the worst single ship mutiny in the Royal Navy, see the author's *The Black Ship* (London and New York, 1963).

Clearly the basic requirement for the Commander-in-Chief at Jamaica was that he be a good organizer, keeping the men of his fleet fit (a difficult task), arranging and escorting the convoys and having his frigates cruising. He had to be an admiral who fought the enemy with pen and paper, not a fleet; an administrator, not a strategist or tactician, since it was more important he kept well up to windward of the clerks at the Admiralty and the Navy Board than the enemy's line of battle.

Sir Hyde fitted the specification perfectly; probably better than any other admiral available when the appointment became vacant. Fussy and obsessive over detail, too touchy and jealous of his authority to work with other flag officers or the Army, Sir Hyde combined a complete lack of detachment with a complete inability to delegate work or make decisions. He loved routine; the mere thought of any departure from it was blasphemy.

In fairness to Sir Hyde, he was a product of his times: his early years had been spent at sea in wartime, followed by a long period of peace which kept him unemployed in middle age and left him mentally ill-equipped for the demands of initiative, decisiveness and leadership forced on an active admiral in the present war. Promotion came too late; his personality had been moulded and set rock hard in those long years of peace spent in England before he became a flag officer, and it was the colourless yet inflexible personality so useful in a senior secretary of an unimportant government office.

First going to sea in a ship commanded by his father, Parker became a lieutenant at eighteen and served in three more ships with his father before getting his first command at the age of twenty-three. Sent to the North America station when he was twenty-eight, he spent the next thirteen years on that side of the Atlantic. Four of them were spent serving under Commodore Hood (later a powerful figure in the Navy). He was thirty-seven and commanding the *Phoenix* when Lord Howe sent him with a small squadron to occupy the North River, which had been closed by blockships and devices invented by Benjamin Franklin. Parker forced his way through, carried out his orders, and was rewarded with a knighthood. After taking part in a highly successful expedition to Savannah, Parker was sent home in the *Phoenix*, and when she was caught in a hurricane and ran ashore in Cuba he managed to get most of his men to safety, landed some guns, had trenches built and sent to Jamaica for help.

At this point Parker was forty-one and had been active enough, although he had commanded nothing larger than a frigate. His father was commanding a squadron in the North Sea and one would have expected Parker, at his age and backed by his knighthood, the recommendations of Howe and Hood, and his father's influence, to have been given command of a ship of the line. Significantly he was given a frigate, joined his father's fleet in the North Sea and was present at the Battle of the Dogger Bank – an ineffectual affair with no losses on either side. Later he was with Howe at the relief of Gibraltar, and he was forty-four when peace in 1783 saw him put on the half-pay list – although his name rose steadily in the Navy List as his seniors died. When he was forty-eight, and again when he was fifty-one, he was given command of a ship of the line as Britain hurriedly rearmed in the face of a threat of war which never came, and on neither occasion did he go to sea.

Eventually on 1 February 1793, the day that the French National Convention declared war on Britain, Parker became a rear-admiral after ten years on shore. At this point his past service helped – Lord Hood chose him as his captain of the fleet in the Mediterranean. From then on Parker methodically did his job: all the required returns were sent in punctually to Commander-in-Chief, Admiralty, Navy Board, Sick and Hurt Board, and Board of Ordnance. . . . Parker obeyed orders; he conformed. *Si non fa, non falla* – if you don't do anything you don't make mistakes. He was at the capture of Toulon (aged fifty-five) and in 1795 when promoted to vice-admiral, became third-in-command in the Mediterranean under a notoriously cautious temporary Commander-in-Chief, Admiral Hotham, for whom the doctrine of *si non fa, non falla* might well have been created.

The lessons learned during this period of service were ultimately to prove disastrous for Parker. It gave him his first experience as a flag officer in a fleet action and also gave him his first sight of a young captain, Horatio Nelson, in action, impatient and goading the Commander-in-Chief. From it all, Parker drew only one conclusion – it paid an admiral to be cautious. Hotham had thirteen sail of the line, including Parker's flagship, the 98-gun *St George* (commanded by Captain Thomas Foley[1]) and the 64-gun *Agamemnon*, commanded by Captain Nelson (a 64-gun ship was the smallest to stand in the line of battle).

Hearing a French fleet was at sea, Hotham steered to intercept and sighted it to windward on the afternoon of 11 March, fifteen sail of the line. At daylight next day it was still in sight but the wind was light with a heavy swell, and the fleets could not get into action. When the French were sighted next morning and showed no sign of bearing down to engage, Hotham made the signal for a general chase. The weather was squally and as the French turned away the 80-gun *Ça Ira* accidentally ran foul of the *Victoire*. She was taken in tow by a French frigate,

---

[1] By coincidence the *St George* was to be Nelson's flagship on the Copenhagen expedition, although he shifted his flag to the *Elephant*, commanded by Foley, for the battle.

but Captain Thomas Fremantle – another officer to become famous at Copenhagen and commanding the leading British frigate, the *Inconstant* – promptly attacked, tacking back and forth across the *Ça Ira*'s stern to keep out of the arcs of fire of her broadside guns.

Captain Nelson in the *Agamemnon* had, with a few other ships, managed to get well ahead of the rest of the Fleet and took over the attack, using the same tactics. The French admiral then sent back ships of the line to protect the *Ça Ira* but Nelson still continued attacking until Hotham, instead of sending reinforcements at once, finally hoisted a signal recalling him.

It was past two o'clock in the afternoon; as far as Hotham was concerned the action was over for the day. Next morning, since the French Fleet was still in sight and separated from the *Ça Ira* (which was then being towed by the 74-gun *Censeur*) Hotham sent the *Captain* and *Bedford* to capture them. The *Captain* arrived first and was so badly damaged by the combined fire of the two ships that she could not help the *Bedford*, which was also badly damaged. Finally reinforcements arrived, including the *Agamemnon*, and the two French ships were captured before the French Fleet – which had in the meantime turned back to cover them – could help.

With the French Fleet in sight Hotham once again decided to call it a day. Nelson went on board Hotham's flagship, hoping to persuade him to leave behind the *Captain* and the *Bedford* with the two French prizes and continue the chase. 'We must be content,' Hotham told him. 'We have done very well.' That two French sail of the line had been captured out of fifteen may have left Hotham content but Nelson, one of his junior captains, wrote to a friend, 'Sure I am that had I commanded our Fleet . . . that either the whole French Fleet would have graced my triumph, or I should have been in a confounded scrape.' Even Sir William Hamilton (who had met Nelson for the first time a few months earlier) wrote from Naples that 'I can, *entre nous*, perceive that my old friend Hotham is not quite awake enough for such a command as that of the King's Fleet in the Mediterranean; although he appears the best creature imaginable.'

For young Captain Nelson, salt was rubbed in a few weeks later: sent by Hotham with four smaller ships to cruise off Genoa, Nelson sighted the French Fleet which immediately gave chase. Nelson led them to San Fiorenzo, in Corsica, where Hotham's fleet was at anchor, and raised the alarm. The British Fleet sailed, sighting the French on 13 July. Hotham formed his line of battle, saw the French had no intention of fighting, and far too late made the signal for a general chase. A wind shift put one of the French ships at the mercy of three British sail of the line and, after a gallant fight, she surrendered to the *Cumberland* which, without stopping, carried on to attack the next French ship. Four more British ships, including the *Agamemnon*, had by now got into action, and the *Cumberland* was alongside her chosen second opponent. It was now 2.42 p.m. – and Hotham made the signal to discontinue. It had to be repeated to the *Cumberland*, whose captain at first ignored it.

Thus ended an action when twenty-one British and two Portuguese sail of the line were opposed to the Toulon Fleet of seventeen. One French ship had been captured, and the British casualties totalled eleven killed and twenty-seven wounded. Forty years earlier Admiral Byng had been court martialled and shot for allegedly 'not doing his utmost' when commanding a British fleet not far from where Hotham had now twice thrown away a chance of destroying the Toulon Fleet. Hotham was not even reprimanded. 'In the forenoon,' commented Nelson, 'we had every prospect of taking every ship in the Fleet, and at noon it was almost certain we should have had the six near ships. . . .'

In the short term, Hotham's failure to destroy the Toulon Fleet was to lead to the British Fleet being forced to leave the Mediterranean. In the long term, his third-in-command, Vice-admiral Sir Hyde Parker, then fifty-six years old, saw once again that *si non fa, non falla*; a policy which would eventually lead to him being virtually sacked, to end his days a puzzled and bitter man.

From the Mediterranean Sir Hyde was later sent to command the Jamaica station, and his correspondence with Lord Spencer, the First Lord of the Admiralty, shows better than anything else his negative attitude. These letters reveal someone who constantly magnified difficulties which would have gone unremarked by most men; who had no flexibility of mind, so that if he received orders from the Admiralty which were not routine he regarded them as impossible to carry out. Nor can he be entirely blamed: the short outline of his career given above is enough to show he had no opportunity after his frigate days for exercising initiative because he never bore responsibility. Until he went to Jamaica he was always led; always the follower, never the leader.

'I cannot but perceive the very difficult and delicate situation in which I am placed . . .' he wrote to Lord Spencer on 21 July 1796 within six days of being told he was to be the new Commander-in-Chief at Jamaica, and a few weeks later hoped that 'the particular delicate situation in which I am placed, and where so much has been left to [my] discretion will, if any errors have arose, I trust plead for me. . . .' Within a month this was followed by, 'I am well aware, my Lord, by these measures and ideas, great responsibility attaches to me, but trusting to your Lordship's candour and support.'

The particular circumstances leading Parker to write such weak letters are irrelevant, particularly when they are compared with those of such men as St Vincent and Nelson. But the correspondence goes on, month after month: complaints to Spencer of Army generals slighting him and junior flag officers either failing to carry out their duties, or doing too much. . . . Spencer's patient and understanding replies are equally revealing. 'I have not had an opportunity of seeing General Simcoe since his return, but I can scarce conceive there can be any grounds for your thinking that you have been ill-treated intentionally by him, or by General Forbes,' he wrote on one occasion.

When Parker had quite wrongly sent home his second-in-command, Vice-admiral Richard Rodney Bligh, virtually in disgrace, Spencer wrote (in a letter referring to Parker's own recall), 'though in the course of your command a few circumstances have occurred in which I could have wished you to have acted differently from what you did, especially with regard to the business of Vice-admiral Bligh, I can, however, assure you that it is not on that account that this arrangement [Parker's recall] is made.'

Yet Parker's original letter to Lord Spencer about the Bligh affair had begun with words which would have been suitable for his own epitaph – 'I cannot help feeling most sensibly the inactivity and want of judgment of Vice-admiral Bligh; and although he may not be criminally guilty. . . .' The letter was dated 4 June 1799. Almost exactly two years later to the day, after the Battle of Copenhagen, Parker's own name could have been substituted for Bligh's with complete justification.

So Vice-admiral Sir Hyde Parker returned to London, to a house in Cumberland Place, near Marble Arch. In one of its rooms there was a full-length portrait of him painted much earlier by Romney, the artist who delighted in painting Emma Hamilton. Romney had portrayed a slim, handsome naval officer, but the succeeding years had changed the subject. Sir Hyde's cheeks were now flabby and red, from good living rather than tropical sun, and the once almost aquiline nose was bulbous, while several chins overlapped his stock. The corners of his mouth revealed a querulous nature and the slim figure had grown portly. But installed with his Romney, comforted by his fortune, still in excellent health at the age of sixty-one and with Miss Frances Onslow, aged eighteen, making arrangements for their wedding, Sir Hyde was certainly in no hurry to go back to sea.

2

...AND THE FAME

The second admiral returning to England was so different from Sir Hyde Parker that if some vindictive wit had set down all of Parker's material, mental and spiritual resources, characteristics and deficiencies and then created his complete opposite, he would have produced the man whose name was the eleventh of the fifteen rear-admirals of the red, and was printed in the current Royal Kalendar as 'Duke of Bronté (Lord Nelson) K.B.'.

If Sir Hyde had recently acquired the substance without the fame, Nelson certainly had the fame without the substance. Parker returned to London from the West Indies without the newspapers bothering to devote more than a couple of lines to the fact. Nelson landed at Yarmouth from Naples to a hero's welcome with bands playing and many cities, including London, anxiously waiting to bestow their freedom upon him. While Parker could raise more than £100,000 without effort, Nelson could have been bankrupted for less than £10,000.

Whereas for eighteen years Sir Hyde had hardly heard a shot fired in anger, Nelson had more than two years earlier written in a memorial[1] to the King that

During the present war your memorialist has been in four actions with fleets of the enemy ... in three actions with frigates; in six engagements against [shore] batteries; in ten actions in boats employed in cutting out [enemy ships from] harbours; in destroying vessels and taking three towns ... served on shore with the army four months, and commanded the batteries at the sieges of Bastia and Calvi ... assisted in the capture of seven sail of the line, six frigates, four corvettes, and eleven privateers ... and taken and destroyed near fifty sail of merchant vessels ... and ... had actually been engaged against the enemy upwards of 120 times, in which service [he has]

[1] Pensions (in effect, compensation) for wounds received were often granted to *serving* officers, unlike today, and the applicant had first to present a 'memorial' to the King listing his service, wounds and disabilities. Although Nelson would never have passed the medical examination to enter a twentieth-century navy, he would certainly have been invalided after losing an eye or an arm.

lost his right eye and arm, and been severely wounded and bruised in his body.

When he wrote that, Nelson had just celebrated his thirty-ninth birthday, and ten months later won a great victory which brought his present fame but, more important – though few realized it at the time – changed naval warfare.

Previously it had been enough to break the enemy's line, capture a few of his ships and call it a day, the Commander-in-Chief being assured of an earldom or viscountcy and his subordinates a scattering of lesser honours. In the previous fleet actions of this war Howe, with twenty-five ships, had captured six of twenty-six French sail of the line in a battle in 1794 – such a victory resulting in it being called 'The Glorious First of June' and the flag officers receiving two peerages and three baronetcies. Then came the Battle of Cape St Vincent on Valentine's Day, 1797, when Sir John Jervis with fifteen ships captured four of a Spanish fleet of twenty-seven (two of these being captured by Nelson), and Jervis received an earldom, becoming Earl of St Vincent. This was followed in October by Admiral Duncan's action at Camperdown, sixteen British against fifteen Dutch, when eight enemy ships were captured. Duncan received a viscountcy.

In the following May Rear-admiral Sir Horatio Nelson was in command of a detached squadron of thirteen sail of the line when late one afternoon he found a French squadron of thirteen sail of the line at anchor in Aboukir Bay. By dawn next day two of the thirteen French ships were destroyed and nine more captured. Only two had managed to escape in the darkness – a fact which made Nelson angry. There had never before been such a great British sea victory as the Battle of the Nile nor, perhaps more important, such anger on the part of the admiral that two ships had escaped him.

The importance of the revolution that Nelson had wrought in naval warfare was not only in the actual figures (the like of which had not been seen before in a battle between two evenly matched fleets) but in his objective. From his very first command in action as a junior captain he always aimed at the total destruction or capture of each and every enemy ship. Today this would be the obvious aim of every Commander-in-Chief; but until Nelson it was most certainly not the case.

From the time each of the more advanced nations organized its navy as a regular force (earlier, privately owned ships were hired or chartered) naval warfare had become increasingly formalized until, at the time of Cape St Vincent, it resembled a stately dance, where one side's move produced a specific response from the other. The most important reason for this was the very rudimentary method of signalling; once the battle began, each Commander-in-Chief was, for all practical purposes, gagged. This, in combination with the need to have one's fleet in the best position (usually to windward of the enemy) and in good formation, naturally led admirals to take great care to have their ships in the most suitable formation before beginning the battle. A sudden change in the direction of the wind, or failure of the enemy to manoeuvre as expected (particularly if he did not intend to fight, trying to use his mere presence to frighten off or deter his opponent) meant many opportunities were lost.

Over the years the formalized manoeuvres were set down in writing as the Fighting Instructions. At first they were issued by individual Commanders-in-Chief; later they became permanent, and were as effective as trying to use one type of hook and bait to catch every kind of fish in the sea. Rodney in the Battle of the Saintes in 1782 had, almost unintentionally, departed from the Instructions and met with a measure of success – enough to make some people wonder about their rigidity. But the Instructions were backed by the Articles of War, a set of rules governing the conduct of the Navy, whether an admiral 'failing to do his utmost' to attack the enemy or a seaman getting drunk.

The effect of all this was predictable: the object of the Commander-in-Chief was to break the enemy's line and attempt to capture four or five ships by orthodox tactics rather than try for a dozen by unorthodox means. Orthodox success brought honours; a failure due to unorthodoxy was plain heresy with the certainty of a court martial. Admiral Byng was shot in 1757 by a firing squad ostensibly for just that (although there were political factors), and no admiral had that fact far from mind. And orthodoxy certainly paid dividends – St Vincent's four prizes had gained him an earldom, and Hotham's 'We have done very well' after capturing two and letting the French Fleet escape brought no court martial.

If Nelson's objective was different, so was his most important method of gaining it: instead of relying on signalling his wishes and intentions – the difficulties of which usually prevented a sudden manoeuvre which would take the enemy by surprise – he had an uncanny ability to describe his ideas to his captains so that, faced with an unexpected situation, any one of them could guess what Nelson would want him to do. This ability was in fact the real 'Nelson Touch'.

So much has been published about Nelson by romantically-minded writers, particularly in quoting remarks of his out of context, that the 'Nelson Touch' has been confused with recklessness and a disregard for the odds. But Nelson was neither reckless nor a gambler against heavy odds; in fact the 'Nelson Touch' involved the exact opposite.

Nelson was a supreme artist in the field of naval tactics at a time when it was an art rather than a science. Depending not only upon the vagaries of wind and sea and the seamanship, courage and ability of individual captains, it entailed a complete knowledge of the enemy's strength and weakness in ships, tactics, seamanship, leadership and courage. To this day the understanding of what makes a leader has (perhaps mercifully) not yielded to scientific study nor, to the regret of industry, political parties and the armed services, can even a few principles be taught from manuals.

Blended with Nelson's artistry was a happy combination of the precision of a scientist or skilled engineer and the cool calculation of a mathematician. Before going into battle he weighed up such matters as arcs of fire, the penetration of shot at different ranges and the effect of close range fire. These could be calculated. But the vagaries of the wind, the chances of his leading ships running aground on uncharted shoals – these were not predictable: these were the things on which he had to gamble. But he gambled only when he knew the exact odds: he never hesitated when a stake of ten shillings could win a hundred; he never gambled when a hundred could win him only ten. Although frequently impetuous and wrong in his private life, in the planning and execution of a battle he was always cool and calculating, leaving to chance only that which he could not control and, even more important, knowing the precise extent of what depended on chance.

Bearing in mind that Jervis received an earldom for capturing four ships and Duncan a viscountcy – one step lower in the peerage – for eight at Camperdown, it might be thought that Nelson would have received at least a viscountcy for the Nile. Instead he received the lowest of all, a barony. However, if his own country's ruler treated him shabbily, the King of the Two Sicilies showed his appreciation by making him Duke of Bronté and giving him the estate that went with it on the lower slopes of Mount Etna, while the ordinary people of Britain took him to their hearts: he was the kind of hero they understood; the hero.that, at this stage of the war, they and their country desperately needed.

Yet Nelson was far from being the accepted type of hero and even farther from being the type of hero that legend, with a helpful prod from romantic writers, has since portrayed him. He tended to be all things to all men: there was plenty for his enemies and rivals to jeer and sneer at; there was plenty to strain the patience of his real friends. But once a man had given him his loyalty nothing Nelson did in his public or private life could ever weaken it.

The complicated and interwoven incentives that led him constantly to seek a complete victory and at the same time glory in visible honours – the great stars pinned to the breast, or gold collars worn round the neck – are difficult to comprehend without an understanding of Nelson's equally complicated personality.

At first glance the man is an almost unbelievable mass of apparent contradictions. Although he fought his battles with an almost unique combination of precision engineering and highly skilled gambling, he also went into battle and came out of it surrounded by smoke and high-flown patriotic phrases liberally larded with 'King and Country' and 'Victory or Death'.

After his brilliant piece of disobedience at Cape St Vincent – where, merely a Commodore, he broke out of the line of battle to cut off the escaping Spanish – he used influence to have the baronetcy intended for him changed to a knighthood, a lower honour which was not hereditary but which carried a star the size of a saucer. 'If my services have been of any value, let them be noticed in a way that the public may know me – or them' he told an officer returning to England with the despatches. So he received the Order of the Bath, with its elaborate collar, a large eight-pointed star worn on the breast, and a jewel (in effect a medallion) worn round the neck on a ribbon.[1]

Vulgar ostentation? It was a convenient and easy label if you did not like him. Thirsting for glory? Perhaps – but he had already been in action more than 120 times. Although a flag officer, he had led the boarding party at St Vincent which captured the *San Nicolas* and the *San Josef* – a job for lieutenants, not the captain of a ship and certainly not the fourth-in-command of the Fleet. Nelson received his knighthood because his ship captured two prizes, not because he personally boarded the enemy; his knighthood would have been secure even if he had stayed on his own quarterdeck – indeed, he could be criticized for ever having left it.

If it was only glory he sought, then he was paying an overly high price – up to then he had only a knighthood to show for the loss of an eye and an arm, a head wound and various other injuries: poor exchange by any standards. Glory could be bought much more cheaply; indeed, he was lucky to have lived long enough to receive even the knighthood.

Clearly the two most obvious labels do not fit. Physically puny – he

---

[1] This was an instance where considerable trouble was taken to please a junior officer: the Order of the Bath, founded in 1399 and revived in 1725, was limited to the King and thirty-six Companions. Since there were already thirty-six, it was necessary to make Nelson an extra one.

was less than five feet tall – with a large nose and undistinguished features, Nelson had no physical 'presence'. Suffering from bad health for most of his life, his letters, written over a period of many years and to people as diverse as the First Lord of the Admiralty and Lady Hamilton, frequently grumbled that he was almost too ill or worn out to carry on. In his frequent bouts of depression he often pictured himself becoming a physical wreck, condemned to spend the rest of his years living in a house on half pay. He was obsessed with his health, and not without reason. The life of an admiral at sea is a lonely one. He can invite captains to dine; but he cannot discuss problems and decisions with them. Weeks and months at sea leave such a man with plenty of time for introspection; plenty of time for brooding over health.

Persistent coughs, sickness, sleeplessness, inability to keep food down (almost certainly a form of nervous dyspepsia), inflammation in his remaining eye which almost blinded him at times.... These were constant and real afflictions for Nelson but, even so, when read at random his letters seem to be the querulous complaints of a hypochondriac.

Yet if each is read carefully a distinct pattern emerges; a pattern as revealing of the man as the key to a cipher. The illnesses, real or imaginary, only occurred when he was inactive, and were worst when his wishes or ideas were being ignored or frustrated, particularly by superior officers in whose bellies the fire of battle did not burn as brightly as in his own. One thing alone always wrought a miraculous and rapid cure of every malady – the prospect of battle. Although often still protesting he was a sick man he would then perform feats of physical and mental endurance and take on enormous responsibilities (usually in excess of his own authority) that would have left a strong man forever broken in body and spirit.

Reading through all the Admiralty's correspondence with Nelson, from the time he was a young and unknown frigate captain until he became the most famous fighting admiral alive, one is constantly reminded on the one hand of the creative person who can rarely fit into the conventional patterns of life however he might try, and who exists in limbo, creating in spite of difficulties and setbacks undreamt of by the beneficiaries of his talents.

On the other hand there is authority, in this case the Admiralty, anxious to get the best out of the creator yet having certain rules which they insist must be obeyed; always trying to encourage conformity without crushing the creative spirit or inducing failure. Nelson was fortunate that for the last few years of his career – after Copenhagen – the Admiralty recognized that his genius could not be caged: indeed, that it was not in their own interests to attempt it.

It is obvious that although labels are invidious, there is one that fits: Nelson had what is called, in a much narrower sense, an 'artistic personality'. Although the phrase is generally used today to describe or excuse various writers, painters, composers and sculptors, this is to limit the very substance of creativity. An Einstein developing a theory of relativity, a naval architect designing a revolutionary ship, an engineer a new type of space rocket and the astrophysicist discovering and reducing to figures the precise trajectories, thrusts and orbits required to land that rocket on the moon, are all creating. Because of their insight, progress is made.

It is not an odd quirk of human nature that a truly creative person rarely fits into the ordered structure of Society, be he a Leonardo or a Nelson, a Chopin or a Shaw. He finds the very orderliness, the set patterns and timetables, the dislike of change, to be confining, irrelevant or a hindrance to his creativity; there are few occupations, for example, which benefit by being interrupted to answer some letter or form drawn up by a bureaucrat totally incapable of expressing himself clearly in writing, always resorting to safe clichés, and shocked if required to give his own opinion on a point where there was no precedent for a safe answer. To such people a creative man is dangerous; he cannot be categorized and does not conform; he is liable to do something unusual which would require a decision, and that situation must be avoided at all cost.

Yet a creative man's task involves taking accepted theories and either altering and advancing them or rejecting them entirely and substituting new ones. Thus scientists and engineers are as creative as writers or artists, and creative in the same way as an admiral with a complete grasp of strategy who trains his fleet and inspires his men by new methods, devises revolutionary and completely unorthodox tactics, and then combines them all to crush an enemy fleet on a scale never before seen.

Although allowances are made for the sometimes abrasive, touchy and unpredictable nature of the creator of something artistic, the same allowances are not for the most part made in people unconnected with the arts; certainly not in Nelson's case nor, for that matter, in Wellington's, a man who developed a new type of army and tactics which eventually defeated Napoleon's creation.

Originality in thoughts and ideas, coupled with the energy and strength of purpose to act on them, rarely if ever make a man popular; for a man seeking popularity – or trying to avoid unpopularity – the policy of *si non fa, non falla* is safer and more suitable, as many aspiring politicians soon learn. Few men can be forgiven for being right – and then usually only in old age and by a younger generation – and never for being both unorthodox and right.

Most creative people need encouragement, and most seek some sort of recognition. Depending upon the field in which they are working, this recognition takes many forms – a knighthood, honours from a famous university, and in modern times a Nobel prize, a star billing on theatre or film posters. . . . For an admiral with Nelson's personality it could only be honours conferred by the King since in those days there was no other form of recognition, and money meant little to him. A completely uncreative admiral like Sir Hyde Parker was more than satisfied to receive recognition in the form of hard cash, but it is unlikely that Nelson would have exchanged his knighthood or barony for £100,000 in prize money.

Being overly sensitive to actual or imagined criticism by other people is a common defect in a creative personality, and Nelson was no exception: if he thought he had been slighted by a superior or humbugged by a junior, he became as outraged, vicious and spiteful with his tongue or pen as a jealous woman. Yet although impatient with a fool, whether his senior or junior, he was generous with praise, patience and assistance for the less clever man who did his best. And one of the finest aspects of his personality was also occasionally a defect: his loyalty to anyone serving with him was often almost beyond reason and sometimes quite unjustified. The fact that a man was serving or had served with him was enough to bring Nelson to his defence. Each ship he commanded was always the best – his first ship of the line, the 64-gun *Agamemnon*, was, he told his parson brother William, 'without exception the finest sixty-four in the Service, and has the character of sailing most remarkably well'.

While Nelson demanded the best from every man and usually received it because he provided the inspiration and gained his loyalty, he sometimes confused the criticism of a subordinate with criticism of himself. At the same time, although pathetically quick to imagine he was being ignored, slighted or denigrated, he was equally quick to bask in praise and flattery, with sometimes disastrous effects on his private life.

This was an age when brave men were commonplace and very brave men almost legion; it is therefore significant that once a man had served with Nelson, he was a 'Nelson man' in both senses of the word, and the source of his loyalty was manifold. In many cases it was based on admiration of Nelson's extreme bravery and skill, whether as captain or admiral. In every case it was also based on genuine and deep affection. Since these men include some of the greatest fighting seamen among

Nelson's contemporaries – Troubridge, Berry, Hardy, Fremantle, Foley and dozens of others (some of whom were, like Lord St Vincent, his superior officers) it is obvious that men of this calibre were unlikely to have been misled in their judgment, mistaking showmanship for efficiency. In the case of St Vincent, for instance, it was based on a cool assessment of Nelson's tactical skill.

Yet Nelson was the complete opposite of his great predecessors in the Navy. Even though this was long before the British habit of understatement had become a vogue, it[1] was usual to present a stern face in times of stress and not display emotion publicly. The majority of the great admirals were by nature stern and sombre men and for the most part unapproachable to subordinates. Nelson, on the other hand, was highly emotional both in public and private, and although the men around him – whether senior officers or seamen – were usually suspicious of openly expressed emotion, one never finds them criticizing or even commenting upon it: an indication perhaps that they did not notice it because it was an integral part of the man himself.

Nor is it hard to understand this. At St Vincent he had, sword in hand, been among the first to board the Spanish *San Josef* and the *San Nicolas*, and it can be argued his post was on the quarterdeck of his ship, it not being the function of the fourth-in-command of a fleet to engage in hand-to-hand fighting with Spanish seamen and soldiers. But it was part of the man; he could no more have stayed on his own quarterdeck at such a time than he could have gone to bed. So although he often appeared to be an exhibitionist, it hardly needs pointing out that in situations like this even the most flagrant exhibitionist is usually able to control his weakness sufficiently to avoid needlessly risking his life.

It is also significant that it was the sea officers who, though privately regretting his association with Lady Hamilton, stood by Nelson when he returned to England. Many of these officers knew her well, and almost to a man they liked her, regretting her influence on Nelson only because it led him to behave foolishly in public.

The more vicious of the comments about Lady Hamilton's 'vulgar behaviour' and Nelson's childishness in her company were made by people who did not know either of them well and saw them only in public. Many of course were women, and since Nelson was the conquering hero of the day no woman in his company, even if she had been Lady Nelson transformed into the beauty of the century, would have received much mercy from their tongues and pens.

[1] However, at the Battle of Cape Passaro, in 1718, Sir George Byng reported tersely: 'We have taken and destroyed all the Spanish ships which were upon the coast; the number as per margin.'

Should Nelson be condemned for his liaison with Lady Hamilton? The point will be argued by those who consider it relevant for as long as history is written or read, and much depends on whether one takes the view of the moralist or the realist.

The historical realist can argue that Nelson's prime task was to fight and win sea battles, which he did with gusto, and Emma provided him with inspiration (although to an outsider it looked like gross flattery) which Nelson seemed to need and which was certainly not forthcoming from Lady Nelson. If victory should come only to men with irreproachable morals, it is interesting to speculate what would have been the outcome of the Nile, Copenhagen and Trafalgar if someone like St Vincent had commanded the fleets.

The historical moralist could point to the fact that Nelson was not only betraying his own wife by his relationship with Emma but cuckolding his close friend Sir William. In the eyes of the Church he was certainly guilty of the former; but at the time of the Nile, which was when the friendship ripened, Sir William was sixty-eight, Emma was thirty-one and Nelson within a month of forty. Sir William, one of the most sophisticated and worldly men of his time, had spent thirty-five years in the decadent atmosphere of Naples, and was past having any sexual desires. But he was worldly enough to know this was far from true for Emma, and if she wanted a lover then who better than Nelson, whom Sir William admired more than any man alive. With Nelson in Naples, Emma was bubbling with happiness and Sir William had the company of the guest he enjoyed more than any other. The trio was closely knit by friendship, and there is little doubt that from Sir William's point of view it was an ideal arrangement. If Emma had taken any other lover, that man might have broken up Sir William's household and would certainly have plagued the old Ambassador with signs of jealousy. Instead he still had Emma, whose beauty he enjoyed and of whom he was proud, and the firm friendship of Nelson.

As far as Lady Nelson was concerned, it is worth remembering plants will not grow on barren land. A happily married man has no use for a permanent mistress, and certainly would not fall deeply in love with her. When Nelson first arrived in Naples he had a wife, and that is about all that can be said of his marriage.

He had been a young captain commanding the *Boreas* frigate in the West Indies when he met Mrs Nisbet, a widow with a seven-year-old son. He met her at a time when he had grown to hate the indolence and corruption of the Caribbean and was thoroughly bored with the unavoidable company of minds sodden by too much hard liquor drunk for too long (Nelson himself drank hardly at all). He had, like most young officers on such a station – he was twenty-eight at the time – fallen desperately in love with a married woman. She had returned to England eight months later and took with her, as far as Nelson was temporarily concerned, everything that made life in Antigua not just bearable but idyllic.

Then, on a visit to the nearby island of Nevis, he was entertained at the house of the President of the island's council, Mr John Herbert, a wealthy widower possessed of many nieces. One of them, Fanny Nisbet, had lived with her uncle since her husband died but was away when Nelson made his first call. Fortunately one of her cousins was quick to write her a report which reveals much of Nelson and his future wife.

We have at last seen the Captain of the *Boreas*, of whom so much has been said. He came up, just before dinner, much heated, and was very silent; yet seemed, according to the old adage, to think the more. He declined drinking any wine; but after dinner, when the President as usual gave the following toasts, 'the King', 'the Queen and Royal Family', and 'Lord Hood', this strange man regularly filled his glass and observed that those were always bumper toasts with him; which having drunk he uniformly passed the bottle and relapsed into his former taciturnity. It was impossible . . . for any of us to make out his real character; there was such a reserve and sternness in his behaviour, with occasional sallies, though very transient, of a superior mind. Being placed by him, I endeavoured to rouse his attention by showing him all the civilities in my power; but I drew out little more than 'Yes' and 'No'. If you, Fanny, had been there, we think you would have made something of him; for you have been in the habit of attending to these odd sort of people.

And Nelson did appear odd, both in dress and behaviour. He wore his hair in a then unfashionably long queue; his uniform was of an old-fashioned cut; and, as his Commander-in-Chief, the Governor of Antigua, merchants, local shipowners, planters, masters of American merchantmen and Customs officials discovered a short time after the *Boreas* arrived, he had some old-fashioned ideas about maintaining maritime law – which is why Fanny Nisbet's cousin had heard so much about him.

American merchantmen had for a long time been loading and discharging cargoes in the islands, particularly at Antigua. This was, as the *Boreas*'s young captain sharply pointed out, in direct defiance of the Navigation Acts. Then he discovered that his Commander-in-Chief had waived sections of the Acts for American ships, although in fact the admiral had no such powers and had been gulled into signing it by the merchants, planters and Customs House men, all of whom made a handsome profit by the trade.

Although one of the junior captains on the station, Nelson would have none of it. Waiver or no waiver, it stank of corruption and was against the law. He gave the American ships forty-eight hours to sail. Very soon every one of consequence in Antigua, and subsequently the other British islands, was bellowing protests; funds were collected to pay lawyers to sue Nelson. Socially he was ostracized and the Commander-in-Chief, caught standing on one leg, was undecided whether to back Nelson or court martial him.

More important was that, on a matter of principle, Nelson had the courage to face up to his Commander-in-Chief, the Governor of Antigua, and the powerful commercial interests of all the Leeward Islands when, at no risk to himself, he could have carried out orders and let the law be broken.

'My name is probably unknown to your Lordship,' he wrote to the Secretary of State when the dispute was referred to London, 'but my character as a man I trust will bear the strictest investigation. I stand for myself, no great connexion to support me if inclined to fall.' Fortunately Whitehall upheld him and the Navigation Acts were once again enforced.

Nelson and Fanny Nisbet were married in March 1787, when Nelson was twenty-eight and Fanny a few months older. And the bride was given away by the distinguished captain of the *Pegasus* frigate – Prince William Henry, the King's son, who had served under Nelson as a midshipman. The Prince, who became a good friend to Nelson, noted the bride was a 'pretty and a sensible woman' while 'poor Nelson is over head and ears in love'. The future William IV could not refrain from adding a comment which proved prophetic: 'He is now in for it: I wish him well and happy, and that he may not repent the step he has taken.'

A few weeks later, a very sick man, Nelson was on his way back to England in the *Boreas* to begin five years of unemployment on half pay, during which time his young stepson Josiah was sent to a boarding school and Fanny spent the winters coughing and sneezing and frequently took to her bed. Nelson's attempts to get employment failed – he even appealed to Lord Hood, whom he regarded as a patron, and was shattered to learn that not only could he expect no help but, even worse, was told by the old Admiral that the King 'was impressed with an unfavourable opinion' of him. Nelson was too proud to ask why; but it was probably the result of distorted accounts of the Navigation Acts dispute.

Fanny naturally found life in a chilly England, existing on half pay, was vastly different from that in Nevis, where her uncle was a wealthy man and his word almost law, servants were numerous, the climate

perfect and entertaining a way of life. Nevertheless she made the best of
the long stays in Norfolk with her father-in-law at the rectory at
Burnham Thorpe. She embroidered while Nelson read Dampier's
Voyages, and her father-in-law noted that 'she does not openly complain.
Her attention to me demands my esteem, and to her good husband she
is all he can expect.' But the old rector guessed that time dragged for a
young woman used to West Indian luxury and hoped for 'a little
Society and an instrument, with which she could pass away an hour'.
It dragged not because Fanny had an active mind; on the contrary, it
dragged because she was unable to provide anything but small talk.

There were frequent visits to the rest of the family and Nelson, who
loved children, enjoyed them because his elder brother and younger
sister each had a son and daughter. The excited chatter caused by the
visits of their sailor uncle only served to emphasize that the years passed
and Fanny still did not bear him a child. At Christmas, Easter and for
the summer Josiah came to the rectory for school holidays, and
although Nelson was devoted to his stepson, the boy's presence only
drew attention to the fact that Fanny had succeeded in giving her first
husband an heir but had failed her second.

By the time Nelson's five years 'on the beach' ended in February 1793
with his appointment – just four days before the war with Revolutionary France began – to the command of the *Agamemnon*, there is
little doubt that although Nelson was still a dutiful husband he was not
an infatuated one; and the once pretty niece of Nevis's President had
become at the age of thirty-four drab in appearance, limited in her
interests, and wrapped up in her husband and her son and her own
health. Nelson devoted himself to Josiah, taking him to sea as a midshipman.

Fanny failed to keep Nelson as a husband in anything but name
because she failed to provide any inspiration or incentive, never understanding his mercurial temperament. She did everything that the wife
of an ordinary naval officer could be expected to do; but Nelson was
not an ordinary naval officer. However, he did not regard his marriage
as a failure: at this time he had no yardstick by which to measure
happiness.

Although Fanny did not understand him, a woman like Lady
Hamilton did, since she had that instinctive knowledge of men that
often goes with an easy virtue. And although Nelson understood men
better than most – this was part of his greatness as a leader – he certainly
did not understand women. It is only too obvious from all the scores of
letters he wrote that in this respect he was but a callow schoolboy.

By September Nelson, serving in the Mediterranean, was visiting

Naples in the *Agamemnon* and meeting the Hamiltons for the first time. The visit was brief – it lasted five days, and he did not see them again for five years – but it gave him a glimpse of another world: Naples was warm, gay and dissolute; a violent contrast with chilly, orderly and formal Norfolk. Moreover, the Palazzo Sessa, where the Hamiltons lived, was a luxurious haven; a remarkable example of graceful living.

Sir William, grandson of a duke on his father's side and an earl on his mother's, had been a playmate of George III, and was in the widest sense a highly civilized man. He had been the British Ambassador in Naples from the time Nelson was four years old. Described by William Beckford, the millionaire author, patron of the arts and man of the world, as 'the first of connoisseurs – not only in the fine arts but in the science of human felicity', he had spent those years collecting oil paintings and Greek vases. Among the latter was one which became known throughout the civilized world as the Portland Vase; among the former were works by Rubens, Velasquez, Titian and Leonardo, Rembrandt, van Dyck and Hals. Even his wife might well have stepped from a Rubens canvas: she was dark-eyed and vivacious, full-breasted and voluptuously beautiful in the romantic style, with a lively interest in everything that went on, be it gambling or diplomacy. Those who chose to criticize Emma often described her as plump and coarse-featured; but their opinions are of little consequence since Romney, one of the greatest portrait artists of the time, regarded her as the most beautiful woman he had ever seen and painted her more than a score of times, before she was famous.

If Sir Hyde Parker was the opposite in every way to Nelson, then Emma too was the complete opposite of Fanny: she was exuberant where Fanny was reserved; she was beautiful and ripe while Fanny was now drab and withering. While Fanny wrote her husband dutiful letters full of family news and sniffles, Emma flattered the young captain, fussed over his stepson Josiah, and when he was away wrote lively letters, and although they were ill-spelled they were warm, emphatic and unmistakably Emma's.

Ferdinand, the King of the Two Sicilies (a kingdom which, of course, included Naples) was a guest on board the *Agamemnon* during this first visit, although Queen Maria Carolina, about to be delivered of her sixteenth child, was indisposed. But Emma, firmly established as one of the Queen's favourites, regaled Nelson with plenty of stories about the Royal Household and, with Sir William, acted as Nelson's translator. Although her English had a Liverpool accent (particularly noticeable in her letters because she tended to spell words as she pronounced them) her Italian was excellent.

Nelson wrote to Fanny that 'Lady Hamilton has been wonderfully kind and good to Josiah. She is a young woman of amiable manners and who does honour to the station to which she is raised.'

It is unlikely at this stage that any reports of Lady Hamilton's background had reached Fanny. In fact Emma had been born Amy Lyon at Nesse, in Cheshire, and became a domestic servant until her beauty and ambition took her to London before she was sixteen. From then on her life for some time was like a few chapters from the adventures of Fanny Hill: she became the mistress of a friend of the Prince of Wales and then of Sir Harry Featherstonhaugh, who dropped her when she became pregnant. After the birth of a daughter she became the mistress of Charles Greville, a nephew of Sir William Hamilton, and Amy Lyon became Emma Hart. She was then seventeen and lived with Greville for the next four years, with her mother acting as the housekeeper. Greville, no mean judge of beauty, set about educating her, and through him she met George Romney and frequently posed for him. And then she met her lover's uncle, the courtly Sir William.

Greville was tiring of her and thought (incorrectly) that he had the chance of marrying Lord Middleton's daughter, who would bring a reasonable dowry with her – providing Greville could show he was an heir. Sir William obliged with a letter saying he had already named Charles in his will. During all this Emma and her mother went to stay in Naples with Sir William, who became enchanted with Emma. They arrived in March 1786. By 1791 they were all back in London on a visit and Emma and Sir William were married in Marylebone Church, the bride being twenty-six and the bridegroom sixty-one.

In Naples Emma, as a respectably married woman, could now be accepted officially by Neapolitan society. Her popularity was of long standing, and her acceptance was given a healthy shove by the Revolution in France because Queen Maria Carolina, daughter of the renowned Maria Theresa, sister of the previous Emperor of Austria and aunt of the present one, was the real ruler of the Two Sicilies. She saw that her most powerful ally against the Revolution would be Britain, whose representative in Naples had long been the faithful Sir William. Thus began the Queen's friendship with Emma. It began as a way of exerting royal pressure on the Ambassador and quickly developed into something much stronger and more genuine: Emma had learned a lot on the road from Nesse to Naples, and her sturdy commonsense meant the Queen received advice from the British Ambassador's wife which made up in honest intention what it may have lacked in finesse.

After his five-day visit to Naples Nelson sailed to rejoin Lord Hood, little dreaming he would not return to that turbulent city for five years.

Long after his death Lady Hamilton said there had been love at first sight, but there is little to back up the claim, although Sir William and Nelson began a correspondence which showed each had a mutual respect for the other and many interests in common.

During Nelson's absence the war took on the character of a game of musical chairs, with Britain's allies falling or quitting or changing sides. When at last Spain joined France and Bonaparte began to invade Italy, menacing the port of Naples, the British Government decided the Fleet should quit the Mediterranean, leaving the King of the Two Sicilies to make the best of it. 'Till this time it has been usual for the Allies of England to fall from her,' Nelson wrote to Sir William, 'but till now she never was known to desert her friends whilst she had the power of supporting them.'

3

NAPLES – AND THE NILE

Nelson's eventual return to Naples began more dramatically and
ended more sadly than the most adventurous of playwrights would have
dared to imagine. In the late Spring of 1798 reports reached England
of a large French fleet and transport ships assembling at Toulon. These
coincided with other reports of troops marching towards that great
port.

Lord St Vincent, commanding the British Fleet which was then
covering Cadiz, sent a small squadron into the Mediterranean to see
what was happening. The man put in command of it was Nelson, by
now a rear-admiral.

His orders from Lord St Vincent were 'to proceed in quest of the
armament preparing by the enemy at Toulon and Genoa' and whose
possible objectives appeared to be an attack on Naples or Sicily, the
landing of an army in Spain for an attack on Portugal, or to pass
through the Strait of Gibraltar to attack Ireland. Nelson could pursue
the French to 'any part of the Mediterranean, Adriatic, Morea [Greece],
Archipelago [the Aegean] or even into the Black Sea'.

Nelson and his squadron of three sail of the line arrived off Toulon to
find the French Fleet had already sailed southward – taking with it
dozens of transports carrying the army of General Bonaparte.[1] Their
destination was probably Naples, perhaps Sicily. More ships joined
Nelson in the search until he had thirteen sail of the line, but there was
no sign of the French. The weeks passed and Naples waited in dread
for Bonaparte to arrive while St Vincent was criticized for entrusting
such a junior admiral with so important a mission.

May gave way to June with Nelson still hunting the enemy; fear gave
a fair wind to every rumour. Then word came that the French Fleet
had captured Malta – which belonged to the Knights Hospitallers –

---

[1] Among his young generals were Berthier (whom Napoleon later created Prince of
Neuchatel), Davoust (Duke of Auerstadt and Prince of Eckmuhl), Junot (Duke of Abrantes),
Lannes (Duke of Montebello), Marmont (Duke of Ragusa) and Murat (King of Naples).

and Nelson went there, to find the island had indeed just been captured but the enemy fleet had gone (he had passed it on the night of 22 June). Nelson decided Egypt was now the only possible destination for Bonaparte's army, and turned his squadron eastward. But he arrived at Alexandria and, finding the harbour empty, sailed away again, little knowing he had in fact overtaken the enemy, who arrived there a few hours after he left.

The British squadron went back to Sicily for supplies and found itself unwelcome in the Kingdom of the Two Sicilies, which was now very anxious to remain neutral. That was of little interest to Nelson after two months at sea chasing Bonaparte, and his squadron took on food and water.

Some idea of the strain Nelson was under for all these weeks, and the difference between a natural leader and the led, is given by his second-in-command, Captain James de Saumarez, (later to become Admiral Lord Saumarez) who wrote that some time must elapse 'before we can be relieved from our cruel suspence,' but 'Fortunately I only act here *en second*; but did the chief responsibility rest with me, I fear it would be more than my too irritable nerves would bear. They have already been put to the trial in two or three instances this voyage.'

All the intelligence Nelson could collect – mostly from neutral ships – was negative: the French had not been sighted in the Aegean or the Adriatic, and they had not passed Sicily heading westward. They must therefore still be to the eastward. And eastward could only mean Egypt. Checking over the charts and going back over his flagship's log showed that the squadron had made a fast passage to Alexandria: probably faster than a French fleet shepherding a great convoy of slow transports. If he had been close in their wake after Malta he might have overtaken them and arrived in Alexandria first. . . . On 25 July the squadron weighed and steered once again for Egypt.

Naples heard nothing more for weeks; then came news of a great British victory in Aboukir Bay. Finally the badly-damaged *Vanguard* limped into Naples on 22 September with a worn-out Nelson on board, the scar from a head wound still a livid weal. Twelve of Nelson's thirteen sail of the line (one went aground) and which were all 74-gun ships, had attacked thirteen French and captured or destroyed eleven. Nor did the total tell the whole story – the *Orient*, which caught fire and blew up, was a 120-gun ship, and three others carried 80 guns. One French admiral and two captains had been killed; another admiral and six captains were wounded. And although most of the British ships were badly damaged, every one of them was able to get under way after repairs.

Naples, never a city to hide its feelings, went crazy with joy. A letter from Lady Hamilton, written in her typical breathless style, was sent off to meet him by a frigate.

My dear dear Sir how shall I begin what shall I say to you – tis impossible I can write for since last monday I am delerious with joy and assure you I have a fevour caus'd by agitation and pleasure. Good God what a victory – never never has their been any thing so glorious so compleat. . . . How shall I describe to you the transports of [Queen] Maria Carolina – tis not possible – she fainted cried kiss'd her Husband her children walked frantic with pleasure about the room cried kiss'd and embraced every person near her exclaiming *oh brave nelson oh God bless and protect our Brave deliverer oh nelson what do we not owe to you oh victor savour of itali oh that my swoln heart could now tell him personally what we owe to him.* You may judge my dear sir of the rest . . .

Sir William's letter was briefer but no less revealing.

History either ancient or modern does not record an action that does more honour to the Heroes that gained the Victory than the late one. . . . You have now completely made yourself, My Dear Nelson, *Immortal*, God be praised! . . . You may well conceive, my dear Sir, how happy Emma and I are in the reflection that it is *you, Nelson, our bosom Friend*, that has done such wonderous good in having humbled these proud robbers and vain boasters . . .

But there was something else to bother the young Admiral, besides his exhaustion. Josiah was proving a thoroughly unpleasant young man. Through Nelson's influence he had been promoted quickly and now commanded a frigate. He quarrelled with his officers, and his behaviour was often excused by his senior officers only because of their loyalty to Nelson. But Josiah showed his gratitude by rarely having a good word for his stepfather. The latest episode was reported to Nelson in a letter from his own Commander-in-Chief, Lord St Vincent. Josiah himself delivered it – a typical St Vincent touch – and the Commander-in-Chief told Nelson:

It would be a breach of friendship to conceal from you that he loves drink and low company, is thoroughly ignorant of all forms of service, inattentive, obstinate, and wrong-headed beyond measure, and had he not been your son-in-law [sic] must have been annihilated months ago. With all this, he is honest and truth telling, and, I dare say, will, if you ask him, subscribe to every word I have written.

Before receiving this, Nelson had written to Lord St Vincent that 'I trust my Lord in a week we shall all be at sea. I am very unwell and the miserable conduct of this Court is not likely to cool my irritable temper. It is a country of fiddlers and poets, whores and scoundrels.'
The week was a long one – it lasted from 30 September 1798 until

33

14 July the following year. Nelson's reasons for staying were ostensibly his own health and, more important, the safety of Naples, and there is no doubt he believed they were valid. What he did not see was that in the overheated atmosphere of Naples and the Palazzo Sessa, idolized by Emma, flattered by the Queen and regarded by Sir William as the only man who could save the Kingdom, his judgment was hardly detached. By now he was deeply in love with Lady Hamilton and despaired of by his officers, who worshipped him but hated seeing him make a fool of himself with her in the Neapolitan Court and providing gossip for every backbiter visiting the city. Hints and even outspoken letters from his friends had no effect. Yet there can be no doubt that Lady Hamilton did love him. Her love for him may have been no greater than Fanny's but it was displayed in different ways; in ways that mattered to a man of his temperament.

In the past century and a half the flagrantly vicious morals of Nelson's contemporaries, notably the Prince of Wales and his circle, have attracted plenty of comment but little actual criticism, whereas Nelson's single lapse is constantly under fire from moralists applying twentieth-century standards to eighteenth-century conditions. Sir John Acton, although a British subject, was the King of the Two Sicilies' Prime Minister. Just before Nelson and the Hamiltons left Naples, Acton, who was sixty-four, married his thirteen-year-old niece. The marriage caused little comment at the time: Sir John had received a special dispensation – from the Church, if not from Nature. Nelson had but one mistress whom he avowedly wished to make his wife on the death of Sir William and, but for the fact that he had a wife whom he no longer loved and Emma an old husband to whom she was too devoted to leave, they would have married. The Prince of Wales's mistresses were legion: indeed, in the weeks immediately preceding the Battle of Copenhagen Nelson was torn with jealousy because he knew the Prince was more than anxious to add Lady Hamilton to his lists of conquests.

Yet while in Naples Nelson's letters to his wife had continued all the time, and her replies were written in her usual placid, gossipy style. In April 1799 she told Josiah she had heard from 'my Lord Nelson' and he 'mentions your improvements with tenderness and kindness. His love for you is very great.' Nelson was told she had seen his brother William – never Fanny's favourite – and 'I cannot say his manners are better. The roughest mortal surely that ever lived.' In the autumn Nelson was told, 'Harvest is very backward. I have one piece of news to tell you which caused a few "is it possible?" Admiral Dickson is going to marry a girl of eighteen years, surely he has lost his senses.' Later, recording the visit of one of Nelson's officers with news, she wrote 'I long to hear of the arrival [in England] of Sir William and Lady Hamilton.' By November she was recording that the doctor had ordered her to Lisbon – 'he fears the winter will be too severe for me' – but she had refused, not knowing Nelson's plans. On Boxing Day 1799 she wrote that Captain Hardy 'told me you would be grateful if I sent Lady Hamilton anything, therefore I shall send her ladyship a cap and kerchief such as are worn this cold weather.' She added that 'I am clothed in two suits of flannel. I hope I shall be better for it.' Early the next spring she noted 'I have got the flower seeds you sent me' and a few weeks later, 'I can with safety put my hand on my heart and say it has been my study to please and make you happy, and I still flatter myself we shall meet before very long. I feel most sensibly all your kindnesses to my dear son, and hope he will add much to our comfort.' By then, March 1800, it seems Fanny, now forty-two, had heard the gossip, felt a twinge of fear, but trusted her husband.

Nelson's long stay in Naples finally drew letters from the First Lord. They were understanding and patient. The last was also firm:

I am quite clear, [wrote Lord Spencer] and believe I am joined in opinion by all your friends here, that you will be more likely to recover your health and strength in England, than in an inactive situation at a foreign court, however pleasing the respect and gratitude shown to you for your services may be; and no testimonies of respect and gratitude, from that court to you, can be, I am convinced, too great for the very essential services you have rendered it . . .

And so Nelson returned to England – by land. He had dawdled too long in Naples to be in favour at the Admiralty, and his relationship with Emma was a standard topic of conversation in fashionable drawing rooms.

The fact Nelson came back by land with the Hamiltons provided the gossips with a rich and easily-reaped harvest. Everywhere they stayed Nelson's adoration of Emma was not only obvious but eagerly noted by many hosts and hostesses who wined and dined them with sycophantic eagerness, basking in their reflected glory, and then, as their coaches left, hurriedly took up pens to write the more obvious kind of hypocritical letters to London. But all of them were ignorant of one thing: Emma was already carrying Nelson's child, conceived on board the *Foudroyant* in the early summer.

Queen Maria Carolina accompanied them as far as Vienna, where Nelson's old friend Lord Minto was the British Ambassador. And, with the genuine affection and candour of an old friend, Lady Minto wrote: 'I don't think him altered in the least. He has the same shock head, and

35

the same honest simple manners; but he is devoted to *Emma*, he thinks her quite an *angel*, and talks of her as such to her face and behind her back, and she leads him about like a keeper with a bear.' And he was a hero to the people of Austria: 'The door of his house is always crowded with people, and even the street, when his carriage is at the door. . . . On the road it was the same. The common people brought their children to *touch* him. . . .'

After Vienna came Prague, with Archduke Charles – himself a general and a popular hero – entertaining the party. At Dresden the British Minister was Hugh Elliot, brother of Lord Minto, but a vastly different type of man who had divorced and married again to a social inferior. This may have been one of the reasons why he affected a languid and would-be blasé manner which was to become fashionable in the twentieth century among the more ineffectual members of the Diplomatic Service who used it as an excellent cloak for ignorance and incompetence. Elliot had little liking for Nelson and the Hamiltons and was glad when they left for Hamburgh, referring to the departure of 'Antony and Moll Cleopatra'. Elliot was the kind of man who derived more satisfaction from delivering a subtle snub at a reception than writing an informative despatch to London, and three and a half years later he ran true to form: he had a large family and asked Nelson to take two of the boys as midshipmen in the *Victory* – a request Nelson gladly granted.

From Vienna Nelson had written to Fanny to take 'a house or good lodgings for the very short time I shall be in London, to which I shall instantly proceed and hope to meet you in the house'. Fanny was also told, 'You must expect to find me a worn out old man.'

When the mail packet brought Nelson and his party to Yarmouth his reception, which is described later, was to reveal the position he was to occupy in the hearts of the majority of the British people until his death off Cape Trafalgar five years and a few days later. To the ordinary people he was purely and simply a hero. To them, as to Nelson, the war was an uncomplicated affair: we had to beat the French, and the one-eyed, one-armed little sailor had shown he could do that superbly well. To them it mattered not at all that he had a mistress as well as a wife; indeed, the possession of a harem would probably have brought forth even more admiration since, being simple folk, they were too wise to confuse fighting and fornication and they knew their continued freedom depended on his prowess in battle, not in the bedroom.

But to Society – and here the word is used to describe the tightly-meshed aristocracy which then wielded the power and had the influence in Britain – Nelson had broken the rules. Yes, he was a brave sailor and even a great one; but not only had he let his private life become public, he was actually flaunting it. Society knew that public men and its own members had mistresses (indeed, these affairs provided much of its conversation) and all that Society required was that both man and mistress be discreet. According to the rules neither of them should expect the mistress to be accepted socially. But Nelson did, so Society treated him as a heretic, not a hero, never pausing to think that only conquest, not conformity, would defeat Bonaparte and bring Flanders lace and French brandy back to the shops.

When Nelson landed in England on Thursday, 6 November, from the *King George* mail packet, Yarmouth responded, for here was a true Norfolk man returning (admittedly somewhat tardily) to his own country after the great victory of the Nile. The *Naval Chronicle* records the scene:

> The populace assembled in crowds to greet the gallant Hero of the Nile; and, taking the horses from his carriage, drew him to the Wrestler's Inn amidst bursts of applause.
> The Mayor and Corporation immediately waited on his Lordship, and presented him with the Freedom of the Town. . . . The infantry in the Town paraded . . . with their regimental band, etc. firing *feux-de-joie* of musketry and ordnance till midnight.

For all the excitement, Nelson made sure a letter was sent off at once to Evan Nepean, the Secretary of the Board of Admiralty. Dated Yarmouth, 6 November, it said briefly,

> I beg you will acquaint their Lordships of my arrival here this day, and that my health being perfectly re-established, it is my wish to serve immediately; and I trust my necessary journey by land from the Mediterranean will not be considered as a wish to be a moment out of active service.

Nor did he forget that fame cost money: next day he wrote a brief note to his agents, '£50 for His Worship the Mayor [of Yarmouth], to be distributed by him [to the poor]. 5 guineas for the Town Clerk. 1 guinea for the officer. To be paid by Mr Warmington for Lord Nelson of the Nile.'

Next day, as Nelson and the Hamiltons prepared to enter their carriage to go to London, 'the Corps of Cavalry unexpectedly drew up, saluted, and followed the carriage, not only to the Town's end, but to the boundary of the County. All the ships in the harbour had their colours flying.'

News that the conquering hero had not only arrived in Ipswich, the next large town on the road to London, but was actually lunching at

Bamford's Hotel, spread rapidly and 'he was waited on by several gentlemen and congratulated on his arrival'. Then 'on getting into his carriage, the populace unharnessed the horses and drew him to the end of St Matthews Street amid repeated acclamations'.

For those who believed in omens, Nelson's arrival in London with the Hamiltons was significant: when the carriage was within a few miles of the city the worst storm for nearly a century broke over southern England, flooding streets, ripping off tiles and blowing down trees.

Reaching Nerot's Hotel in King's Street, St James's (the present site of the St James's Theatre) at 3.00 p.m. on Sunday, they were greeted by Lady Nelson and the admiral's father, the aged and ailing rector of Burnham Thorpe; but Nelson's seaman servant Tom Allen, secretary Francis Oliver, and Lady Hamilton's coloured maid[1] had hardly supervised the removal of the baggage before the first visitors began to arrive.

Their travelling companions, Emma's mother Mrs Cadogan, and Miss Ellis Cornelia Knight, an authoress and daughter of a rear-admiral, left to stay in a smaller hotel nearby. Miss Knight was a good example of a shrewd social opportunist. In Naples she had worked her way into the Hamiltons' circle and thus into the Neapolitan Court, and then had seized the chance of travelling to London with Nelson and the Hamiltons (at Nelson's expense), spending much of her time writing ahead to various friends in England and composing trite little poems and songs suitable for various public occasions during the journey. (A fellow authoress Mrs St George, who met her at Dresden, said significantly that she rarely spoke unless it was to flatter Nelson or the Hamiltons).

Charles Greville was the first visitor at Nerot's while the second was the Duke of Queensbury. Both men called, of course, to see their relative Sir William (who, although impoverished – indeed, he owed Nelson £2,000 – was a cousin of the Duke of Hamilton and Lord Abercorn, who were extremely wealthy, and numbered the Duchess of Atholl among his nieces and the Earl of Warwick as a nephew).

The next few days left Nelson with barely a spare moment. At his first meeting with Fanny (who was staying at 64, Upper Seymour Street, off Portman Square) he gave her the presents he had brought – among them some lace from Hamburgh and intended to be made into a Court dress. And, of course, Lady Nelson met Lady Hamilton for the first time.

The Hamiltons, the rector and Lord and Lady Nelson dined early on Sunday evening. Although there was no open breach between Nelson

---

[1] A Copt girl Nelson had brought back from Egypt as a present.

38

and his wife the atmosphere must have been strained, but the meeting was not described, apart from Lady Hamilton recording that Lady Nelson never asked Nelson about the Battle of the Nile, though this was of course their first meeting since then; an omission indicating her inability to participate in Nelson's life. After dinner, Nelson left for the Admiralty to see Lord Spencer.

Miss Knight soon had a visitor, Captain Sir Thomas Troubridge, who was on his way to join Lord St Vincent, then commanding the Channel Fleet. Troubridge was an old friend of Nelson's – indeed, one of his closest. Troubridge, who knew Miss Knight and her parents well from Mediterranean days, did not approve of Lady Hamilton nor, more important, her influence on Nelson. And he knew what Nelson did not yet even suspect – that Society was not going to accept Lady Hamilton. When Troubridge told her of this, Miss Knight needed no chart to plot her future course. The doors of European palaces may have opened to Nelson, the Hamiltons and Miss Knight during their journey from Naples; but in London much lesser doors were closed. . . . So next day Miss Knight packed her bags, said goodbye to Emma's mother, and moved once again to a socially inferior but nevertheless socially safer house, that of Evan Nepean, the highly respectable and influential Secretary of the Board of Admiralty. His wife welcomed Miss Knight as a guest and an invaluable and exclusive source of information about the woman of whom most of London's gossiping tongues were talking.

Although Miss Knight had abandoned her ship with alacrity before it struck the social reef, her role as a former passenger was displayed for all to see because a newspaper had published one of her songs on the day before they all arrived in London. It had the incriminating title of 'An Ode to Lady Hamilton on her Birthday'.

'Most of my friends were urgent with me to drop the acquaintance but, circumstanced as I had been,' Miss Knight wrote later, 'I feared the charge of ingratitude, though greatly embarrassed what to do, for things became very unpleasant.' One could feel more sympathy had she not managed to put the acquaintanceship to so much profit for so many months in Naples, and during the journey across Europe, enjoying the welcome and hospitality of kings and princes and the cheers of the multitude. But when she discovered that the woman to whom she had dedicated so many adoring poems was shunned by London Society she ran true to type.

Nevertheless she recorded that she was shocked to find that many of the people comprising London Society were completely defeatist in their attitude to the war, openly and loudly longing for peace on whatever terms could be gained from Napoleon. Their attitude was not governed by pacifist convictions or Revolutionary sympathies; the war was simply an inconvenience. They formed a proportion of the people who shunned Nelson – the man who had done more than most to give them and the nation the security against Napoleon from which they could safely voice their defeatism and applaud each other as they related the latest gossip surrounding him.

Yet one must not judge the whole of Society too harshly because, strongly woven into its shallow judgments, hypocrisy, and to some extent jealousy, there was a considerable and unique tradition of service. Many of its men devoted their lives to politics because it was a family tradition, and since many – though by no means all – were rich, there was no question of doing it for any considerable financial rewards, though jobbery was part of politics.

Others paid vast sums for commissions in the Army and subsequent promotions, and much of the cost of their regiments came out of their own pockets. They also served, in other words, and if they were married and had mistresses, they kept the mistresses in the background, and therefore Nelson's behaviour was, by their own code, in bad taste. One did not drink with one's butler nor take one's mistress to visit a maiden aunt.

Miss Knight had no sooner moved in than Nepean received, by coincidence, a curious letter from Admiral Lord St Vincent: a letter which indicates Nepean interpreted his duties widely, keeping certain of the more influential admirals informed of matters outside official business.

It is evident from Lord Nelson's letter to you on his landing, [St Vincent wrote] that he is doubtful of the propriety of his conduct. I have no doubt he is pledged to getting Lady Hamilton received at St James's and everywhere and that he will get into much *broullerie* about it. Troubridge says Lord Spencer talks of putting him in a two-decked ship. If he does, he cannot give him a separate command, for he cannot bear confinement to any object; he is a partisan; his ship always in the most dreadful disorder, and never can become an officer fit to be placed where I am [Commander-in-Chief of the Channel Fleet]. . . .

For once St Vincent, usually the most succinct of letter writers, obscured his real meaning. If Nelson was to have a separate command he would have to be given a three-decker. Since Spencer talked of only a two-decker (i.e. a smaller ship) he was obviously not proposing to give him a separate command. But St Vincent, making the point that Nelson was not a good subordinate and therefore needed a separate command, then says he could never be fit to be a Commander-in-Chief.

Although muddled and giving more than a hint of personal jealousy, the letter is not as vicious as it seems: Nepean knew his real opinion of Nelson, so St Vincent could make comments without qualification. In fact St Vincent had a very high professional regard for Nelson — he had of course given him command of the squadron which won at the Nile, and stood up to the resulting bitter protests of senior admirals. Nevertheless, the last sentence of the letter came ill from the pen of a man who had made such a potentially disastrous tactical mistake at the Battle of Cape St Vincent and was saved from its consequence only by Nelson's courage in disobeying the Fighting Instructions to bring about a victory. Had Nelson failed, incidentally, the disobedience would probably have resulted in a court martial. As it was, St Vincent's flag captain, Calder, did all he could to lessen the credit due to Nelson, and until Nelson's death remained his enemy.

Since Nelson, despite St Vincent's judgment that he 'can never become an officer fit to be placed where I am', had already proved himself considerably fitter than St Vincent to command a fleet in battle, St Vincent's letter shows either a resentment that an obligation might exist, or, consciously recognizing Nelson had the tactical genius that he lacked, subconsciously belittled him to others as a potential Commander-in-Chief. Stated simply, St Vincent was a great administrator and Nelson a great fighter. The trouble was St Vincent had had plenty of time to reflect on his shortcomings as a tactician before subsequently becoming First Lord of the Admiralty and achieving fame as an administrator.

After seeing Lord Spencer on Sunday evening, Nelson paid a formal visit to the Admiralty on Monday morning, seeing Nepean, and in the evening went to the Lord Mayor's banquet in his honour for the Nile victory, where he was presented with the ceremonial sword 'to the value of two hundred guineas' voted him by the City — a splendid example of the sword cutler's craft. The newspapers were, of course, full of Nelson. Special medals had been struck to commemorate his return — 'Hail Virtuous Hero' said the wording of one showing Britannia bestowing laurels on his ship.

Nelson spent a long time with the Duke of Clarence — as the young Prince William Henry, who had attended his wedding in Nevis, was now styled — because the future 'Sailor King' wanted to hear, in the victor's own words, all the details of the Battle of the Nile.

The next day Nelson was publicly snubbed by the King; a wounding episode for such a sensitive man who had been in action with the enemy 'upwards of 120 times', lost an arm and an eye in the King's service, and won the Battle of the Nile. Every Wednesday and Friday were the King's *levée* days, and it was natural enough that Sir William Hamilton, his boyhood playmate and former Ambassador to the King of the Two Sicilies, should attend the next one held at St James's Palace, and natural enough that Rear-admiral the Baron Nelson of the Nile and Burnham Thorpe, having just returned to England for the first time since the victory, should attend with him.

The *levée* was also attended by Cabinet Ministers, the Archbishop of Canterbury, the Diplomatic Corps and several other admirals, generals and the usual crowd of courtiers. Nelson wore full uniform but in addition to his British decorations, such as the Star of the Order of the Bath, he also wore the foreign decorations presented to him after the Battle of the Nile.

His old friend Captain Cuthbert Collingwood (who was to be his second-in-command at the Battle of Trafalgar) recorded in a letter: 'He gave me an account of his reception at Court, which was not very flattering, after having been the admiration of that of Naples. His Majesty merely asked him if he had recovered his health; and then, without waiting for an answer, turned to General ——, and talked near half an hour in great good humour. It could not be about his successes.'

It has been claimed that the King was offended at Nelson wearing foreign orders and decorations at the *levée*, but this is completely wrong: a year earlier Nelson had taken the precaution, on receiving his barony, of writing to Sir Isaac Heard, the Garter King of Arms, asking how he should sign his name, if the King approved him receiving the title of Bronté, and how he should wear his foreign decorations. 'I shall have much pleasure in putting myself in your management,' he concluded. At the time of this *levée*, the King of the Two Sicilies had already written requesting that Nelson be allowed to accept the title of Duke of Bronté 'with the fief of the Duchy annexed thereto, for himself and his heirs'. Permission was granted three weeks after the *levée*. There is little doubt that Nelson received and followed Heard's advice; but the King, even now verging on bouts of insanity, had little time for his eldest son's circle, and knew of Nelson's friendship for the Duke of Clarence, who was also out of favour with his father. The King's behaviour was thus petty and churlish, since Nelson's victory at the Nile had made his crown considerably more secure; it was behaviour more worthy of an ill-trained butler than a reigning monarch.

That evening Nelson and Lady Nelson dined at Admiralty House where their hostess, Lady Spencer, was a social dragon and a diligent gossip. She enjoyed having veteran admirals and captains at her mercy – for a word from her could blast any sea officer's career, at least while her husband was First Lord.

Lady Spencer described the dinner to Lady Shelley, who inaccurately recorded it for posterity in her diary:

Having, more than once, declined the invitation,[1] Nelson at last brought her [Fanny]. Such a contrast [with the previous occasion, several years earlier] I never beheld! A trifling circumstance marked it very strongly. After dinner, Lady Nelson, who sat opposite to her husband (by the way, he never spoke during dinner, and looked blacker than all the devils[2]), perhaps injudiciously, but with a good intention, peeled some walnuts, and offered them to him in a glass. As she handed it across the table Nelson pushed it away from him, so roughly that the glass broke against one of the dishes. There was an awkward pause; and then Lady Nelson burst into tears! When we retired to the drawing-room she told me how she was situated.

Even if the road to Hell is paved with good intentions, and even if Lady Nelson perpetually irritated him, such behaviour in public was unpardonable; but one might be excused for thinking that however upset Lady Nelson was, pouring her heart out to Lady Spencer was unwise and unnecessary since her situation was common knowledge. Lady Spencer was little more than an acquaintance and likely to use her husband's position to punish Nelson, which would be the last thing Fanny wanted.

Next day, Thursday, the Queen held her weekly 'Drawing Room' at St James's Palace, and Sir William Hamilton went with Nelson, who took Fanny with him. Emma, to no one's surprise, stayed at home. With Nelson were five officers who had been among his captains at the Nile and whom the Queen wished him to present. Since the Prince of Wales and the Duke of Kent were with the Queen, her interest in his former captains must have mollified the Admiral.

A letter from the Admiralty had been waiting in London for Nelson's arrival. Dated 7 November and addressed to 'Rear Adml Lord Nelson K.B., Nerots Hotel,' it said: 'I have received and communicated to my Lords Commissioners of the Admiralty your Lordship's letter to me of yesterday's date, acquainting me of your arrival at Yarmouth, and of your desire again to be employed', and was signed by Evan Nepean. Brief, impersonal, stylized, it was the standard reply.

[1] This is an example of the accuracy: Nelson arrived in London on the afternoon of Sunday, 9 November. On Sunday he visited Lord Spencer at Admiralty House: on Monday he was the guest at the Lord Mayor's Banquet; the *levée* was held on Wednesday and Nelson must have still been smarting from the Royal snub when he went to dinner with the Spencers that night.

[2] Presumably because of his treatment by the King at the *levée* a few hours earlier.

Thus two admirals waited to hear their Lordships' pleasure. The one, aged forty-two, who had been wounded several times and won a knighthood, a barony and a foreign dukedom in battle and was sufficiently anxious to get to sea again that the letter reporting his arrival reached London before he did; the other, aged sixty-one, was at his house in Cumberland Place preparing for his wedding.

In the late autumn Lord St Vincent had previously written with his customary directness to the First Lord:

My dear Lord, I see by the paper Sir Hyde Parker is arrived, and as he has had no work whatever, or responsibility to affect his mind or body, he is very well able to come out in the *Royal George* and give me a spell [of rest] . . . if he does not object to serve in the second post . . . Captain Domett will conduct the squadron under his direction with great ability . . . I am now entering into the fifth month [at sea] from Torbay and though I stand my ground better than most men, it is right your Lordships should know I am being much affected by damp weather, and I dread the approach of cold. . . .

Since St Vincent was by far the most powerful influence at the Admiralty and the First Lord was a highly competent man who knew him intimately, there was much for St Vincent to read between the lines of Lord Spencer's reply:

Sir Hyde Parker had no hesitation in expressing the utmost readiness to serve as second to your Lordship, but I am sorry to say I do not think at present his health in a fit state for an autumnal cruise off Brest, and unless it was absolutely and indispensably necessary that he should be called forth immediately I should strongly recommend letting him have a run on shore to recruit.

This brought a tart reply from St Vincent:

My dear Lord – I repeat with the utmost degree of solicitude and anxiety my request that I may be allowed to take rest ashore in Torbay during the five ensuing months; no instance will be found in the annals of naval history of a Commander-in-Chief going through the work I have done in different climes during the last seven years, the machine thus wrought cannot endure for ever.

A postscript to the correspondence is given by Troubridge, who wrote to St Vincent a few days later: 'Sir Hyde will expand this month [November] before he joins; the cold will perish him; he ought to exert himself, for he certainly has had all the sweets of this war, without trouble or weight.'

So, in the light of what was to follow within a matter of weeks, it is worth remembering that St Vincent and Troubridge had no illusions about Sir Hyde's past service in this particular war or his tenacity of purpose for future service, since both refer in almost contemptuous terms to the lack of physical and mental responsibilities attached to the West Indies command, and Spencer knew their views, even if he did not share them. But Spencer above all others knew, from years of tedious correspondence with him, that Sir Hyde was an old fusspot, his mind bedevilled with trivia, with no initiative, and no desire for responsibility. The responsibility of Spencer and St Vincent for Sir Hyde's next command is almost inexplicable, although the story of recent twentieth-century warfare shows that the politicians' skill in choosing the wrong man has not been lost.

4
THE MAD CZAR

While the British cheered their latest hero, so the people of Republican France were well pleased with theirs, Napoleon Bonaparte, having recently elected him First Consul. France had by conquest changed the map of Europe more rapidly and more radically than any country before and after her, until the German invasion which began in 1940.

Napoleon and the French were the most powerful enemy that Britain had ever faced – and now faced alone, bereft of any allies. But although neither he nor the French took any direct part in the Battle of Copenhagen, Napoleon's influence was sufficient to bring it about because one of Britain's former allies, a fanatical and absolute monarch totally opposed to republicanism, had recently fallen under his spell.

That man was Czar Paul I, Emperor and Autocrat of all the Russias,[1] descendant of Peter the Great (who had built a great new city among the Neva Marshes on the edge of the Gulf of Finland, called it St Petersburg and transferred the capital there from Moscow) and son of Catherine the Great. His nation stretched from the Arctic to the Black Sea; his people ranged from Tartars to Balts, Uzbeks to Slavs.

Nothing could equal Paul's heritage; no one man had such absolute power over so much land and so many people. But Paul was not only brutishly cruel and sadistic, perverted and dangerously unpredictable in his moods and actions but completely insane, as great a menace to his family, courtiers, servants and people as he was to his enemies and allies; particularly, as Britain was now discovering, to his allies.

A complete autocrat, he was not restrained by any innate humanity since he had the instincts and morals of a wild animal; nor, because of the constitution, was there the restraining influence of a government which could advise him: ministers were simply his tools. His mere whim or word took up or discarded an ally, brought death to thousands of his

---

[1] His full title ran to more than five score words, including Czar of Poland and Siberia, Grand Duke of Lithuania and Finland, Prince of Estonia, Lord and Sovereign of Armenia, Sovereign of the Circassian Princes and the Mountain Princes, Lord of Turkestan, etc.

people, introduced new laws or sated one of his perverted appetites. And against whim or word there was no appeal.

To understand why an arch-monarchist should suddenly ally himself with an arch-republican who had toppled more thrones and occupied more countries in a few years than most conquerors dreamed of doing in a lifetime, it is worth taking a brief look at Napoleon's earlier career, particularly since it had already been considerably influenced by Nelson.

The unemployed brigadier of artillery who was in Paris by chance in 1795 and saved the Directory from a royalist revolt with the famous 'whiff of grapeshot', had made good use of his reward from a grateful but wary Directory – a generalship and command of the Army of Italy.

He had crossed the Alps and driven the Austrians from the northern states, forcing them to sign an ignominious treaty. He had then gone on to capture all of Italy that was worth taking – including the Papal States – in a series of brilliant campaigns. He then made a disastrous mistake – but one which was eventually to make him the sole ruler of France.

In 1798, by which time the Mediterranean had become a Franco-Spanish lake with the withdrawal of the British Fleet, the Directory sent him to Toulon with his army with orders to sail for Egypt and more conquests. With his army landed and the French Fleet anchored in Aboukir Bay, Napoleon set off to bring reality to his dream of an Eastern empire – a dream suddenly turned into a nightmare by Nelson's arrival and the destruction of the French Fleet. Napoleon, who had never, and would never, understand the exercise of sea power, found himself trapped in Egypt, his plans brought to nought by a junior British admiral.

He had no choice but to try to fight his way back to France overland through Turkey; indeed, the fact that at one time he set up his head-quarters in Nazareth was the propaganda material the Directory used to cover up the extent of Nelson's victory and at the same time conjure up visions of a great Crusade in the old tradition.

Ironically enough, to keep itself in power the Directory – which had sent Bonaparte to Egypt to get him out of the way because it feared his growing popularity – had to wax lyrical about his successes, and once again Bonaparte was France's hero.

His campaign in the Eastern Mediterranean was lengthy – long enough for him to become a living legend in France; such a legend that when, in July 1799, he knew his campaign could never succeed, he was able to abandon his army, escape to France in a frigate, and reach Paris amid such popular acclaim that few realized his whole campaign had failed disastrously – because of Britain's sea power.

By November he had overthrown his erstwhile masters in a highly successful *coup d'état*, and a new constitution was drawn up giving him the title of First Consul, the sole ruler of France for the next ten years and answerable to no one. It showed him to be as clever a politician as he was a soldier, and when France voted on it a few months later the declared results were three million people for and one thousand five hundred against. Henceforth General Bonaparte called himself simply Napoleon.

In the meantime the British had not been sleeping. During the period Nelson was in Naples Pitt had – by backing his diplomacy with hard cash – managed to form the Second Coalition, so that Britain once again had allies, Austria and Russia. The Russian Army in the field was led by Marshal Suverov, an ancient but fiery Tartar general un-trammelled by the text-book tactics which had reduced other European armies to slow-moving mastodons trying to battle with a Bonaparte who moved like a tiger in the night. Suverov, too, moved swiftly: he led his army in a great sweep through Italy, scattering the puppet republics set up by Bonaparte as though they were but powdered snow on his boots.

But where his fast-moving and highly unorthodox tactics brought him victory, the armies of his Austrian allies were led by generals whose orthodoxy and advance-a-step-and-consolidate tactics brought him only frustration and led to bitter quarrels.

Finally Suverov's Italian victories were, thanks to his wilful royal master, completely wasted: the Czar quarrelled with Austria and Britain and in September 1799 withdrew his armies from the field, leaving Austria to fight France on land and Britain to fight her at sea. Two months earlier Napoleon had returned to France; two months later he staged his *coup d'état*.

Napoleon, son of a petty Genoese nobleman who became French when the French captured Corsica, knew that on the domestic front the whole future of France and his only hope of personal survival lay in gathering the nation's most brilliant men into every ministry, every regiment, and every battalion. He realized what no king of France had ever discovered or acknowledged: there was an enormous unquarried mine of talented men in the country: men who before the Revolution had no chance to develop or use their talents because of their political views or, more likely, the lack of the prerequisite for making the first step: noble birth.

So during his first few months of power Napoleon set about reorganizing France. There were new systems of taxation – which had been even more chaotic and absurd than those subsequently contrived by the taxation experts of the twentieth century – and civil and judicial administration.

Talleyrand, born an aristocrat, once a bishop and now, with his highly developed talent for survival, a revolutionary, headed the Foreign Office; Fouché, brilliant, devious and ruthless, was made the Minister of Police and thus, after Napoleon, the most powerful and certainly most feared man in France. Soldiers of ability – men who had proved themselves on the field of battle, not by the quarterings on their coats of arms – were rapidly promoted. Privates became captains; corporals became colonels; captains and majors became generals. Every man in the great citizen army knew that it needed only ability, even if he did not possess it himself, to gain a field marshal's baton. The pattern for total war on land was as well established by the French Army as total war at sea was by Nelson's activities.

Few people had any insight into Napoleon's long-term plans or, for that matter, his personality. Both were probably developing; certainly the contradictions were not yet apparent. For the moment he was a brilliant general who apparently loved peace. That he was a revolutionary who, after helping to overthrow one French monarchy, intended establishing another, a European one with his own family, sharing the crowns among his brothers, was not yet apparent; nor were the other contradictions – the dreamer and the ruthless and merciless politician; the flights of fancy in which he planned well-nigh impossible schemes for world conquest – yet he was a practical realist who could manipulate the erratic and insane Czar as if he was a puppet; the liberating general marching with slogans of equality and liberty and brotherhood who established worse tyrannies than those previously existing in the states he 'liberated'; an egalitarian yet as despotic as the Emperor of all the Russias. He was a curious mixture of Caesar and Czar, revolutionary and a new-style aristocrat, Dante and Machiavelli, patriot and charlatan. A personality, in fact, that a century and a half of study has by no means completely unravelled.

In the summer of 1800, as Sir Hyde Parker and Nelson were preparing to return to England, Napoleon was thus well established as First Consul and planning the strategy which would retain France's present borders. By this time France had either occupied or set up puppet republics so that within her new frontiers were Holland, Belgium, Germany and most of the individual states that formed Italy. Her eastern frontier stretched roughly north-south from neutral Denmark to beyond Rome. Holland became the Batavian Republic, Genoa the Ligurian Republic and Naples, Rome and Switzerland respectively the Parthenopean, Roman and Helvetian Republics.

But Napoleon was not yet ready to challenge his present enemy, Britain, because the only battleground open to him was one which was certainly not of his own choosing and one where France was very weak – the sea.

So he turned to finish off Britain's remaining ally and his only other opponent, Austria. At Marengo on 4 June 1800 he won a battle which, although it did not bring Austria to her knees, gave Bonaparte his first victory as First Consul. Militarily it was a lucky victory; but no-one, least of all the people of France and Czar Paul, looked close enough to see how near Bonaparte had been to defeat.

Austria began peace talks in Paris on 24 July, and found Bonaparte's main aim was to destroy her former alliance with Britain. But Britain had been a loyal ally and the Austrians stood firm on their agreement with her not to conclude a separate peace. Negotiations and threats continued for many weeks, involving proposals from Bonaparte to Britain for a naval armistice – and Austria obtained a respite until 28 November.

Soon after becoming First Consul, Napoleon had moved from the Luxembourg Palace to the airy graciousness of the former royal residence, the Tuileries, where his every appearance at a balcony made the gardens ring with cheers and an enthusiasm which had not been heard for a couple of centuries.

Most of Bonaparte's enemies dismissed his removal to the Tuileries as a piece of pretentiousness; but he had, of course, already made the first moves in restoring the monarchy to France, only instead of giving the Crown back to the Bourbons (Britain's reply to his overture had been that the best guarantee he could give of his desire for peace would be to recall France's legitimate sovereign) he proposed taking it for himself.

Meanwhile Czar Paul, having wilfully broken his treaties with Britain and Austria, watched and waited at St Petersburg. Catherine the Great had treated her son like a child so that when he succeeded to the throne on her death four years earlier he had received no training. As an absolute monarch his early views on the beginning of the French Revolution and the execution of France's Bourbon King are obvious: revolutions are contagious.

It is not clear what went on in his unstable mind after he had broken with Britain and Austria and recalled Marshal Suverov from the field of battle. It is unlikely he was realist enough to see that the Bourbons would never be restored to the French throne in the foreseeable future; but perhaps he recognized that Napoleon's new France was at least stable. Perhaps, more important, he divined Napoleon's intention to crown himself, and decided that a great soldier turned king ruling a well-ordered state was preferable to a republic run by revolutionaries. Whatever went on in his disordered mind, the result was that he made no secret of his growing admiration for Napoleon. And the First Consul was shrewd and quick enough to turn it to his own advantage. A neutral Russia would leave Austria as the only ally in the field with Britain, and he knew Austria's final defeat was only months away.

By chance he had an opportunity to make a handsome gesture to the Czar which cost him nothing. He still held five thousand Russian prisoners of war who had been, in effect, held to ransom. The Czar decided that they had been captured while in British service and demanded that Britain pay the ransom.

Britain refused, so Napoleon provided them with new uniforms (ensuring they were of the correct design for their respective regiments), restored their regimental standards, and sent them back to Russia, writing to the Russian Minister in Paris that he was 'unwilling to suffer such brave soldiers' to remain away from their homeland any longer 'on account of the English'.

The Czar saw in this shrewd move only an act of extreme courtesy, and a correspondence began between the autocratic monarch and the head of Revolutionary France.

Citizen Chief Consul [the Czar said in an early letter] I do not write to you to discuss the rights of men or citizens; every country governs itself as it pleases. Whenever I see at the head of a nation a man who knows how to rule and how to fight, my heart is attracted towards him.

I write to acquaint you of my dissatisfaction with England, who violates every article of the law of nations, and has no guide but her egotism and her interest. I wish to unite with you and put an end to the unjust proceedings of that government.

Soon after that a frantic Queen of Naples arrived in St Petersburg (having travelled for the first part of the journey with Nelson and the Hamiltons) pleading with the Czar to use his influence with Bonaparte over the French troops which were threatening her Kingdom.

The Czar, flattered by the plea, sent an envoy to the Tuileries, where he was received with sufficient pomp and circumstance to impress his royal master. Napoleon not only agreed to spare Naples; indeed, he assured the Czar, he would go further: he personally would assume the responsibility of the little Kingdom's safety. And he kept his word: all the ports of the twin Kingdoms of Naples and Sicily were closed to

British ships. Knowing the only point in invading the Kingdom of Naples was to stop the Royal Navy using the port, Napoleon was able to achieve this while leading the Czar to think he was doing him a favour.

Meanwhile, as Sir Hyde Parker and Nelson returned to England in the late autumn of 1800, two events took place which eventually led both men to Copenhagen and to battle. The events were unconnected; neither was regarded as particularly significant in London at the time it happened.

5

THE NEW GRAND MASTER

The two events were the long-awaited capture of Malta by the British and an incident between a Danish convoy and British frigates. Together they finally convinced the Czar that Britain was his enemy and Napoleon his ally; in his unbalanced mind they proved his cleverness in recognizing the perfidy of Britain and the integrity of the First Consul.

Malta had been owned and governed by the Order of St John of Jerusalem since 1530, when Charles v of Spain gave it to the Order (which had been homeless after being expelled from Rhodes four score years earlier) so that they 'could perform in peace the duties of their religion . . . and employ their forces and armies against the enemies of the Holy Faith'.[1] The Knights of the Order came from every nation in Europe and owed complete allegiance to the Pope. Although they took monastic vows these were, by Napoleon's time, a matter of form, and after serving a few years each knight usually returned to his estates. This meant that the Order had a wide influence at many of the courts of Europe, particularly in Catholic nations, but riches and luxury had sapped the crusading spirit and reduced it to the level of an exclusive club whose committee, the Grand Council, had flexible standards over its policy.

Although Napoleon had little or no idea of the fundamentals of sea power, he knew the importance of the Mediterranean to France, and he saw Malta as the lock of the door to the eastern end of it. A fleet based on Malta could control that door because the island sat four-square in the middle of the Sicilian Narrows, the ninety-mile-wide stretch of water between Sicily and North Africa. Malta had fine harbours for a fleet which, with one based on Toulon, could put all the ports of Italy, the Adriatic, the Aegean, Egypt and Arabia at its

[1] It was the last of the three military orders which achieved fame in the Crusades, the other two being the Templars and the Teutonic, and was mainly a nursing brotherhood.

mercy. 'I had rather see the English in the Faubourg St Antoine than in Malta,' Napoleon declared.

Although one might think a maritime nation like Britain would regard Gibraltar and Malta as at least of equal importance to bases like Jamaica, the facts contradict the legend of the strategic wisdom of Britain's rulers and the impregnability of 'The Rock'. Gibraltar was vulnerable only to attacks from its owners; the British Government had already tried to give it to Spain or exchange it six times between 1718 and 1783, although fortunately for the British people and the Royal Navy the Spanish refused on every occasion.[1] Its attitude towards the Mediterranean was little more than apathetic.

The younger Pitt and his War Minister Dundas, a typical opportunist politician who would sacrifice twenty battalions for a guaranteed cheer in the House of Commons and ten lines in the newspapers, based their strategy almost entirely on short-term and generally ill-conceived plans which would bring quick propaganda results. Losing 40,000 troops to sickness in two years in the West Indies, for instance, was effective strategy politically since the capture of some wretched sugar or spice island was always good for a Parliamentary cheer.

Pitt revealed his concept of the Mediterranean's role in a speech he made in 1803. In a debate on the Treaty of Amiens, which had brought a few months of peace with France, he said:

> The external trade of England is with the East Indies, the West Indies and the Mediterranean. It fortunately happens that the chief British conquests have been in the Mediterranean; they include Egypt, Malta, Port Ferrajo [in Elba] and Minorca. To give these up costs nothing; to retain them serves but to mortify the pride of France – a dangerous course.

This was the view of the man who had led Britain through much of the war; who had kept large armies rotting in the West Indies protecting the sugar islands when five hundred troops could not be spared to capture Malta. Pitt was obsessed with protecting trade, and certainly without trading Britain could not survive. But what he and Dundas never understood was that it was a completely unsound war policy

---

[1] The offers were: (1) In 1718 as a bribe to induce Spain to join the Quadruple Alliance to maintain the Treaty of Utrecht. (2) In 1720 in exchange for Florida or Hispaniola. (3) In 1721 when, after a request by the Spanish Government, George I offered to exchange it 'for an equivalent'. This was rejected because Spain would not barter. (4) Resulting from this rejection, George I on 1 June 1721 wrote to the Spanish King that he would arrange it with Parliament's approval at 'the first favourable opportunity' (Spain subsequently made an unsuccessful attempt to capture Gibraltar in 1727). (5) In 1757 the elder Pitt offered Gibraltar if Spain would help Britain capture Minorca from France. (6) In 1783 Shelburne offered it in exchange for Puerto Rico. Rebuffed yet again, the British Government resigned itself to the possession of the greatest overseas naval base in the world.

simply to try to safeguard only those British bases which protected her trading interests; Britain had to prevent the French capturing bases which would allow them to launch powerful attacks on Britain or her allies. If Malta, for example, was of no immediate use to Britain, it was potentially of vital interest to France. Because Dundas usually disregarded his advisers and plain commonsense, inventing wild schemes of his own, British strategy all too often looked as if it had been drawn up by tradesmen rather than in defence of trade.

Napoleon has often been blamed for underestimating British sea power when he sailed from Toulon for his attack on Malta and Egypt, an attack which was intended to end with the building of a Suez canal and a victory in India, the one place he could bring the British to battle on land. But in fairness did he? For two years, as described earlier, the Royal Navy had, on the orders of Pitt's Government, withdrawn completely from the Mediterranean. What had Napoleon to fear? Only France would benefit from Britain quitting the Mediterranean – a fact Napoleon saw at once and which Pitt never understood. In war it is often necessary to hold a position simply to deny it to the enemy who could make better use of it. Napoleon's own fleet, which would convoy the Army of Egypt, was large; that of his Spanish ally at Cadiz even larger. Napoleon had not made a mistake; he was unlucky because the man commanding the tiny British squadron that unexpectedly entered the Mediterranean and chased him was Rear-admiral Sir Horatio Nelson.

This brief outline of Malta's history and strategic significance helps explain why the island's fate was of absorbing interest to the Czar, who received reports from his warships which spasmodically operated in the Mediterranean and occasionally wanted to co-operate with the British, to the alarm of Nelson.

In planning the attack on Malta, the French left as little as possible to chance. Secret negotiations went on with the Grand Master of the Order and the more influential Knights so that, as General Caffarelli said afterwards, when Napoleon's fleet arrived on 16 June 1798, 'It was lucky that someone was inside to open the gates.'

General Vaubois was left behind with three thousand troops to garrison the island. The booty included six months' provisions, twelve thousand barrels of powder, and all the gold and silver plate and other treasure in the Church of St John. It did not take long for the Maltese people to find that the French, who had taken the credit for liberating them from the far from benevolent rule of the Order and talked loudly of liberty and equality for all men, were silent when it came to practising them. Instead they began levying contributions.

Soon after the French defeat at the Nile, but before Nelson could send help to the island, the Maltese rose against the French, although ill-armed and worse organized – among the French booty were thirty thousand muskets from Valetta's arsenal. A passing British and Portuguese squadron was surprised to find itself intercepted by a boat bringing out a deputation of Maltese with a letter to Nelson asking for help and requesting arms and ammunition. They were promptly given all that could be spared from the ships – enough to arm ten thousand men – and went back to lay siege to the French, who shut themselves up in the heavily-fortified capital of Valetta with little to fear.

Nelson did the best he could to blockade and besiege the French but was told by the Government that no troops were available and so had to use seamen and Marines from his own ships. Nor would the Neapolitans help with the task of feeding the 190,000 Maltese. Captain Thomas Troubridge told Nelson early in January 1799 that he had just saved thirty thousand Maltese from starving but could do no more, although there were two grain ships in Sicily which the Governor would not let him buy. Troubridge, however, then had second thoughts: telling Nelson he had taken some strong measures ('I trust your lordship will bear me out of this scrape') he had the two ships seized and taken to Malta. Nelson promptly gave him an order covering the action.

So the siege dragged on month after month, amounting to a blockade by British and Portuguese ships and what attacks five hundred British seamen and Marines and ten thousand ill-armed Maltese could make on Valetta. Napoleon's great army in Egypt first met with success, but by the following October it had been abandoned by Napoleon, who returned to France.

Meanwhile the French garrison held out in Malta, and in turn the island occupied the thoughts of the Czar. At the end of 1798 Pitt had managed to form the Second Coalition. More Russian warships came through to the Mediterranean as if to emphasize the Czar's interest in Homer's 'wine dark sea'; Britain made the Czar a down-payment of £225,000 and £75,000 a month for forty-five thousand soldiers.

Whether the Czar's interest in Malta was due to a whim or the realization of its strategic importance, we shall never know; but he wanted it and made it part of the price Britain would have to pay for Russia joining the Coalition. To begin with he had no possible claim to the island, but he quickly arranged one. He arranged for the few Knights of the Order of St John who lived in Russia to elect him Grand Master of the Order. He saw no contradiction in that the most powerful and perhaps most depraved member of the Orthodox Church should be elected Grand Master of a Roman Catholic order by a few members who were bound by oaths of chastity and owing complete allegiance to the Pope. He could certainly boast that the Cathedral of Our Lady of Kazan, one of the largest buildings in St Petersburg, was a copy of St Peter's in Rome. . . .

Whether the Czar's claim was sham or slender, it was recognized because, although Britain had no choice, Pitt's administration was not particularly concerned; they regarded Minorca, which had been captured the previous November, as a better base. The only problem facing Britain – a slight one, considering the Coalition was at stake – was that the King of the Two Sicilies regarded himself as Malta's rightful sovereign in the present situation, and this was one of the reasons why Nelson had such trouble in getting food for the Maltese people from Naples and Sicily.

By the summer of 1799 Nelson had found himself with a motley collection of ships: in addition to the Portuguese, who were helping blockade Malta, there were Russian and Turkish squadrons, and in September he warned Captain Alexander Ball, commanding at Malta, that 'The Russians are anxious to get Malta, and care for nothing else – therefore I hope you will get it before their arrival.' The First Lord of the Admiralty was told, 'the Russian Admiral has a polished outside, but the bear is close to the skin, he is jealous of our influence, and thinks whatever is proposed, that we are at the bottom [of it].'

A few days later, instructions arrived from the Admiralty which made it clear that his comments to Lord Spencer would not be very welcome, and Nelson's reply was masterly. He had received the Board's secret orders 'respecting the re-establishment of the Order of Malta, should we be so happy as to force it to surrender,' he wrote.

I am glad I can assure their Lordships that Captain Ball, who is named by His Sicilian Majesty (who is the undoubted Sovereign of that Island) at my request, and by the unanimous desire of the Maltese people, Chief of the Island of Malta, has had since last March my secret orders and instructions for a cordial cooperation with the Russians, should they arrive.

The better sort of people of Malta know that the Emperor of Russia is named Grand Master, yet the lower order have not an idea that the Island is to be under the Order again, or bad consequences might be expected, from the dread of, as they say, their former oppressors: the better sort hope, from the character of the Emperor Paul, to have their condition meliorated.

It was a forlorn hope, and Nelson knew it; but his orders were explicit. To an Army general he wrote more freely, saying that 'the Order is to be restored. It is the hobby horse of the Emperor of Russia; and England wishes of all things to please him.' At the same time he was begging for British troops from General Erskine, commanding at

Minorca, warning that otherwise 'We shall lose it, I am afraid, past redemption'.

This was followed on 28 October by more explicit orders to Ball because a Russian fleet had been sighted which, it was hoped, was bringing troops for Malta. Telling him once again to co-operate with the Russians, Nelson warned:

At the same time you will take care of the honour of our King and Country, and also of His Sicilian Majesty; and recollect that Russia, England and Naples, are the Allies of the Grand Master, that although one Power may have a few more men in the island than the other, yet they are not to have a preponderance. The moment the French colours are struck, the colours of the Order must be hoisted and no other. . . .

The Russian admiral had reported to the Czar several weeks earlier that the flag flown by the British seamen and the Maltese while besieging the French in Valetta was that of the King of the Two Sicilies. A protest was made to London, and after Lord Grenville, the Foreign Secretary, had absorbed it, Lord Spencer wrote to Nelson.

The letter, with other instructions, appears to have been delivered by Lord Elgin, who visited Nelson at Palermo on his way to Constantinople, where he was to be the British Ambassador. Elgin left Nelson in no doubt about the British Cabinet's position, and Spencer's letter warned him that

the utmost importance is attached by His Majesty's Government to the object of carefully avoiding to do anything which may raise any jealousies in the mind of the Emperor of Russia, who is particularly bent on this point of restoring under some new regulations the Order of Malta; and whose conduct ever on this subject, though one on which he may perhaps have been suspected by the world of entertaining more ambitious views, has been, as far as we are enabled to judge of it, of the most disinterested and honourable kind.

The last forty words – which could well have been the prototype of similar comments by various British politicians on another autocrat 139 years later – are a good indication that although the needs of the Second Coalition meant Malta had to be given up, the British Government had been hoodwinked by the Czar. To sacrifice Malta and the Maltese as the price of Russian entry into the Coalition was one thing; but to judge the Czar's behaviour as 'of the most disinterested and honourable kind' shows a political naiveté that would, by twentieth-century standards, have qualified the senior members of the Cabinet for immediate grants of earldoms and the rest the chairmanship of various state boards.

Nelson was sent a plan for the precise method of taking the surrender of the French, and through Lord Elgin was instructed to report directly to the Czar describing the present situation. He wrote:

Until it was known that you were elected Grand Master, and that the Order was to be restored in Malta, I never allowed an idea to go abroad that Great Britain had any wish to keep it. I therefore directed his Sicilian Majesty's flag to be hoisted as, I am told, had the Order not been restored, that he is the legitimate Sovereign of the Island. Never less than 500 men have been landed from the [British] Squadron, which, although with the volunteers, not sufficient to commence a siege, have yet kept posts and battery not more than 400 yards from the works. The quarrels of the Nobles, and the misconduct of the Chiefs, rendered it absolutely necessary that some proper person should be placed at the head of the island. His Sicilian Majesty, therefore, by the united request of the whole Island, named Captain Ball for their Chief Director, and he will hold it till your Majesty, as Grand Master, appoints a person to the Office.

A week later, writing to the Duke of Clarence, Nelson took little trouble in hiding his exasperation from the King's son.

All my anxiety is at present taken up with the desire of possessing Malta. But I fear, notwithstanding all my exertions, that I shall not get any British troops from Minorca, without which the business will be prolonged, perhaps till [the French are] relieved, when all the force we can collect would be of little use against the strongest place in Europe.

He explained he wanted a couple of regiments, and whereas in England or on the Continent they would 'be like a drop of water in the ocean', used against Malta 'they would liberate us from our enemy close to our door, gratify the Emperor of Russia, protect our Levant trade, and relieve a squadron of our ships from this service'.

Meanwhile the French, besieged in Valetta, had been fighting on but slowly losing heart. By January 1800, a year and a half after landing in Malta, General Vaubois received news which put fresh heart into his men: Napoleon was the new ruler of France. It was certain their old General had not forgotten them; soon Valetta could expect a French squadron to arrive and break the British blockade, bringing food, ammunition and reinforcements. And a month later a French squadron did arrive – only to be driven off. Spring came, and then summer. Rations were once again reduced, the blue Mediterranean sky parched the ground and the fresh-water cisterns began to dry up. By autumn there was not a living animal in Valetta – earlier even rats had been fetching a high price – and typhus was killing French soldiers faster than enemy fire, between a hundred and a hundred and fifty men a day.

Finally, on 4 September 1800, after a siege lasting more than two years, General Vaubois called his officers together in a council of war, a flag of truce was sent out, and next day Vaubois and Rear-admiral Villeneuve[1] surrendered to Major-general Pigot, who was commanding the allied forces on shore. Captain Alexander Ball, the man whose patience and tact as 'Chief of the Island' had led to him being idolized by the Maltese, was later appointed Governor.

In the meantime Pitt's carefully organized Second Coalition had collapsed: Russia was out of the war and Austria on the verge of defeat. And during the past year the Czar himself had finally persuaded the British Cabinet that his views on many things, not just Malta, were far from being of the 'most disinterested and honourable kind'. For the time being the British flag flew over the island, but before he knew about that the Czar was brooding over the second event, which had happened in the English Channel in July.

The church bells of the Kentish towns of Walmer, Deal and Sandwich were calling people to prayer on Sunday evening, 25 July 1800, as the Danish frigate *Freya* sailed past outside the Goodwin Sands, escorting a convoy of six Danish merchant ships. The news was bad; there was much for the British folk to pray for, including deliverance from the French, whose coastline was in sight on a clear day. They knew that ten months earlier the Czar had quarrelled with his allies, pulled his armies out of the field and deserted the Austrians; now, although the congregations did not know it, Austria had the day before begun armistice talks with Napoleon in Paris following their defeat at Marengo in June.

Even before the bell-ringers had finished their task the heavy drum-roll of gunfire from seaward sent the congregations rushing outside in alarm. The first shot in fact signalled the beginning of the other event which, with the fall of Malta in a few weeks' time, would send Sir Hyde Parker (who was on his way back to England from the West Indies) and Nelson (who had not yet left Italy) into battle off Copenhagen.

The *Freya*, commanded by Captain Peter Krabbe, and her convoy had been sighted by a squadron of three British frigates under the command of Captain Thomas Baker in the appropriately named *Nemesis*. Baker closed with the *Freya* and hailed Captain Krabbe, saying he was sending a boat to board the convoy. Krabbe's reply – since it was customary for nations at war to board and search neutral ships to ensure they were not carrying contraband – was both surprising and firm: if a boat was sent, he would fire on it.

Both Baker and Krabbe were, in their own view and that of their respective governments, in the right; the difference was that sailing

---

[1] Who five years later was destined to commit suicide after the combined French and Spanish fleet which he commanded was defeated by Nelson at Trafalgar.

neutral ships in convoys escorted by their own warships was a comparatively new idea.

The boat was sent, the *Freya* did fire into it, and within a matter of minutes found herself in action with three British frigates. She was, of course, so outnumbered that she had to surrender, with two men dead and several wounded.

Captain Baker ordered the *Freya* and the convoy into the Downs (the nearest safe anchorage, between Deal and Walmer) and reported to the Commander-in-Chief there, Admiral Skeffington Lutwidge. He in turn hurriedly sent a report to the Admiralty, but in admiration of the *Freya*'s determination ordered that her ensign and Captain Krabbe's pendant should be kept flying.

The strategic importance of the Baltic and its approaches was something the British Government understood well, and it acted swiftly, since there had already been similar trouble with a Danish convoy in the Mediterranean. Lord Whitworth was sent off to Copenhagen to discuss the whole affair with Count Bernstorff, the Danish Minister. It was not an ordinary diplomatic mission, however, since his Lordship sailed with an escort of ten sail of the line and several smaller warships.

By 29 August Whitworth and Bernstorff had agreed to a convention, the main points of which were: (1) Britain agreed to pay for repairs to the *Freya* and the convoy and release them; (2) Danish warships would convoy Danish merchant ships only in the Mediterranean (where there was a very real danger from the Algerine pirates) but the convoys could be searched by the British as before; (3) the whole question of the British right to search would be discussed later in London; (4) the convention would be ratified by both governments within three weeks.

So the *Freya* affair was settled, for the time being, in a way which satisfied both Britain and, apparently, Denmark. For Britain there was the satisfaction that her blockade of France still contained neither physical holes nor legal loopholes. As far as the Danes were concerned, they claimed their ships did not carry contraband, and in that case search by British ships of war was only a slight inconvenience.

But whatever the views of Denmark and Britain, the one person who was in no way involved, the Czar, was far from satisfied. He had been angry when he heard about the *Freya* episode; but when he heard that the British squadron (with Lord Whitworth on board) had sailed into the Sound – which he regarded as part of the Baltic and thus almost his own private sea – he became so enraged that at the beginning of September he threw aside every treaty obligation and ordered all British property in Russia to be seized and the Army and Navy to be mobilized. Three weeks later his temper cooled, and on 22 September the British merchants were given back their goods, warehouses and homes. Their relief was to prove short-lived.

For some months before Malta was captured on 5 September, the British had been cooling towards the Czar's claims while Napoleon, realizing his troops had no chance of holding out, had encouraged the Czar in his idea that he was the genuine Grand Master and that the island belonged to Russia. This was easy enough to do since he and the Czar had by then reached the stage of exchanging the friendly letters described earlier.

Britain did not make the obvious objection to the Czar's claim – that even though the island belonged to the Order it did not become the private property of the Grand Master, and if a Briton had become the Grand Master, no nation would expect the British Government to claim it. Instead, the British troops who had captured it remained as the garrison and the British flag flew over Valetta in place of the Tricolour.

On 5 November, when the Czar heard that Malta had finally been captured and the British did not intend handing it over to him, he once again went berserk, ordering all the British merchant ships in Russian Baltic ports to be seized – more than three hundred of them – and the crews marched off to prison camps in the snow-bound interior. All British property was again appropriated, and because some ships at Narva had escaped, he ordered those remaining in the port to be burnt.

From Britain's point of view she was justified in refusing the Czar's demands. She had recognized his curious claim to Malta as the price of his joining the Second Coalition; since then, however, the Czar had wilfully broken his treaties with Britain and Austria and, from reports reaching London, was well along the road to a personal friendship with Napoleon, if not an official one with France. Thus to let him have Malta would be the same as handing it back to the French. Restoring it to the Order, even with another Grand Master, would have amounted to the same thing since the Order was not strong enough to defend itself.

Apart from these considerations, in first seizing the British property the Czar had thrown aside a treaty between the two countries which said specifically that, in the event of a rupture, no embargo would be placed on each other's ships, and merchants would have a year in which to take away or dispose of their goods.

For a nation which has, quite deservedly, won an unenviable reputation in this century for awakening only just in time to win the last battle, and which has been generally badly served by a diplomatic service whose reports were in any case often ignored by the Government, the autumn and winter of 1800 and the spring of 1801 are a remarkable period in Britain's history.

Her diplomats in Europe were for once highly competent men; their reports were read and heeded by a Premier and a Foreign Secretary (though both changed halfway through), who were decisive in their reaction to them, and for once the British Government had the ships and seamen with which to act.

This seems in complete contradiction to the Government's handling of the events in the Mediterranean; but there had always been certain factors in Britain's basic strategy which were recognized by successive governments. A major one was the importance of the Baltic as a main source of much timber, rope and other material needed by the Navy. (Another was the threat to Britain if an enemy controlled the River Scheldt – from there an east wind could bring an invasion flotilla to the shores of Britain before the Channel Fleet could beat up from the west to intercept it.) The Mediterranean was not yet a factor because its importance was not yet understood or accepted. Thus trouble in the Baltic brought a specific response based on known requirements and a couple of centuries of hard-won experience; trouble in the Mediterranean brought a response which was vague and faltering and based on the whims and prejudices of the Government of the day.

A month after the *Freya* episode the British Government had heard that Russia and Prussia were intending to attempt to mediate between France and Britain and bring the war to an end. The first hint came from Berlin in a report by the Earl of Carysfort, the British Minister to the Court of Frederick III, the King of Prussia.

The relationship between the Secretary of State for Foreign Affairs and the envoy was a close and interesting one. Grenville as a young man at Trinity College, Oxford, had won the Chancellor's prize for Latin verse; Carysfort, four years older, wrote poetry as a hobby and later published *Dramatic and Narrative Poems*. And they were brothers-in-law.

'The principal object for Your Lordship's attention in the present moment, is, as you so rightly judged,' Grenville wrote to Carysfort on Sunday, 22 August, 'the negotiations between the Courts of Berlin and St Petersburg for the joint mediation between the belligerent powers.' Emphasizing that while there was every reason to believe that Prussia was much less keen than the Czar on adopting any 'active or vigorous measures for this purpose' nevertheless, Grenville pointed out, a desire for a closer union with Russia 'might induce Prussia to go farther than if it acted solely from its [own] more cautious and temporizing system of policy'. The British Government must know as soon as possible of all the steps taken, particularly anything indicating the terms of peace or the general basis of negotiation the two countries wanted to recommend or support.

For a few weeks the Cabinet waited, well aware that the talk of peace might be another of the Czar's whimsies but, like Napoleon, knowing full well the war was moving into something of a stalemate. Then suddenly a chill wind arrived from the north in the shape of a despatch from the British Minister in Copenhagen.

At the beginning of October the British envoy to Denmark, Mr William Drummond, wrote to Lord Grenville of a disturbing report that the Czar had made 'very pressing proposals' to the Danish Court to renew the Treaty of 1781, but he could get no confirmation from Count Bernstorff. This was more than a hint to the British Government that the Czar, so recently an ally, later apparently planning to be a mediator and possibly a neutral, now seemed to be adopting the role of a 'belligerent neutral'.

More important, of course, was that a few weeks earlier Lord Whitworth had received an assurance from the Danes that until further discussions took place in London they would convoy their ships only in the Mediterranean, and they could be searched by the British. Any mention of the Treaty of 1781 could only mean that the Danes were going back on the agreement.

Meanwhile Carysfort told Grenville that he had no doubts of Prussia's weak attitude in any negotiations or plans.

My private opinion is that nothing can be expected from hence in any conjuncture. A few nonsensical words from France, or the mere mention of the journey [to Berlin] of Louis Bonaparte [Napoleon's brother] who orders post-horses every week but never arrives is sufficient to keep everything here in suspense.

A fortnight later and ten days after the Czar seized the British ships – although before Carysfort knew of it – he wrote a cryptic comment on the Czar's sanity: 'The moon is certainly not near the change in Russia; I hear every day some new instance of extravagance.'

Then four days later, on 19 November, he was able to send the first substantial news of the Czar's real intentions: 'There is on foot not only a plot for renewing the Armed Neutrality against us, but also a League of the Northern Powers, Denmark, Sweden, Russia and Prussia, for a mediation of a general peace. . . .' But on 23 November, after hearing of the Czar's seizure of the British ships, he wrote 'I cannot but think the violent measures of the Emperor of Russia will check the scheme for an Armed Neutrality'.

And that was indeed the question which Grenville and Pitt pondered: there had been long-standing friendships with Denmark (whose Crown Prince was the British King's nephew) and Sweden, despite previous bickerings over their neutrality, and both Scandinavian nations regarded Russia as a constant threat. Would they become sufficiently alarmed at the violence of Russia to break off any proposed dealings with the Czar? Or would they be frightened into agreeing with him?

Whatever happened, Britain was violently against an Armed Neutrality, as Lord Grenville made clear to Carysfort. 'Nothing is more important,' he wrote in a carefully-worded letter on 2 December, 'than to convince the Cabinet of Berlin that the object of such a confederacy will not be attained but by a struggle in which Great Britain, contending for her very existence, will exert the utmost efforts,' and even if such a confederacy was successful it would be 'in the highest degree injurious to all the interests of Europe'.

The claims of Great Britain [he added] will never be relinquished, on her part, till her naval power be annihilated and consequently the same preponderance left to France by sea as she has been suffered to acquire by land; and when that shall happen it is not difficult to collect even from the transaction of the present war, what degree of advantage or security neutral nations will have acquired for carrying on their commerce. . . .

The last point was a good one: the United Provinces (Holland), Savoy, Sardinia, Piedmont, Milan, Lombardy, Genoa, Tuscany, the Papal States . . . all and more had been neutral; all and more were now puppet states of France. A nation stays neutral only as long as it suits an aggressor – a lesson still not understood in the twentieth century.

And the day after Grenville wrote, Napoleon finally brought Britain's sole ally to her knees: on 28 November Austria's armistice with France, following Marengo, had expired and Bonaparte and his armies marched, to win a crushing victory against the Austrians on 3 December at the Battle of Hohenlinden. The Austrians were forced yet again to sue for peace, and the armistice signed on Christmas Day meant the last of Britain's allies had been toppled, but Austria had fought hard; she had refused to turn against Britain as Russia had done and Prussia appeared likely to do.

So once again, Napoleon was supreme on the Continent of Europe. But his one remaining enemy, Britain, who stood between him and any and all dreams he had of ruling the world, remained supreme wherever there was sea or river deep enough to float a ship of war or her boats. Both nations had reached a stalemate – neither could challenge the other on a battlefield which would ensure the final and decisive victory.

As a result Britain was left with only one way in which she could use her sea power against France – a continental blockade. Napoleon, however, had several ways in which he could use his control of the Continent to evade or weaken the blockade, but each method depended on the degree of co-operation, willingly given or under coercion, that he could get from the Baltic powers; the only ones with whom he had to trade to get the supplies he urgently needed.

6

THE FATE OF NEUTRALS

The warning that the Czar was planning to break Britain's blockade of France and Spain reached London on 9 December, and the King's Messengers ready for duty were told to stand by while Lord Grenville drafted letters in his Downing Street office telling his envoys in Copenhagen, Berlin and Vienna to investigate the report.

He told Carysfort that the messenger was bringing intelligence, 'the accuracy of which cannot be doubted', that the Swedish King had sent full powers to his Minister in Russia to join a convention for establishing the principles of maritime law which had been adopted in 1780, and the Swedish Government also expected Denmark and Prussia to join. Carysfort was told to 'lose no time' in investigating the truth of it.

The intelligence appears to have been given to Grenville verbally by either the Swedish or Danish Minister in London: it did not come from any of the British ministers abroad. In any case it was accurate: five days later, on 14 December, the Convention of the Northern Powers, otherwise known as the 'Armed Neutrality', was signed by Sweden and Russia and on the 20th ratified by both Governments.

'In order that the freedom of navigation and the security of the merchandise of the neutral powers may be established, and the principle of the laws of nations be fully ascertained during the continuance of the present maritime war,' it said, the two countries were determined 'to give a new sanction to those principles of their neutrality,' and to show 'how sincerely it is the object of their hearts to restore, in its full independence, the general rights of all the nations to convoy their ships and merchantmen freely, and without being subject to the powers at war. . . .'

The two countries would 'strictly prohibit' the export of contraband by their merchants, and to prevent 'all doubts and misunderstandings' everything they regarded as contraband was listed: cannon, mortars, firearms, balls, flints, flint stones, matches (in effect fuses), gunpowder, saltpetre and sulphur (two of the three ingredients of gunpowder), helmets, pikes, swords, hangars (small swords), cartridge boxes, saddles and bridles. That was the complete list 'with the exception of such quantity of the above articles as may be necessary for the defence of the ships and their crew'.

More important, everything *not* on the list 'shall not be considered as war or naval stores', would not be liable to confiscation, and 'shall pass free without restraint'.

Had Napoleon written its terms the Convention could not have been more favourable to France and unfavourable to Britain. Food (particularly grain), timber for shipbuilding, naval materials such as sails and rope . . . none of these was contraband, yet they formed the major export trade from the Baltic; they were the vital supplies that both France and Britain wanted. Britain, France and Spain, the major maritime nations, all had in some degree the timber reeded for the hulls of their ships; but none could get enough *Pinus Silvestrias*, the Baltic fir, the straight-grained, durable and springy wood needed to make masts and spars and which came primarily from Russia and Sweden. Yet without masts and spars (which seldom lasted more than ten years without rotting, apart from damage caused by bad weather or battle) obviously a navy was completely helpless. One of Britain's main reasons for her Baltic blockade was to safeguard her own supply of mast and spar timber and prevent any reaching France or Spain.[1]

Even as the new Convention was being signed, many of France's and Spain's great ships in Brest, La Coruña, Cadiz and Toulon could not put to sea because the British blockade stopped them getting new masts or yards to replace those which were rotten. And this was how Britain's sea power made itself felt. Because the Royal Navy could stay at sea and the French Fleet could not sail from Toulon, for example, it had been impossible to supply or reinforce Napoleon's Army of Egypt.

Apart from timber, the Baltic was a major source of flax, which was used for making the sails, and rope. In other words the supply of masts, yards and booms, flax to make the sails to set on them, and the rope used for supporting the masts and yards and trimming the sails depended almost entirely on the Baltic. Without these the sailing ship of war was as helpless as its twentieth century counterpart when deprived of fuel. But quite apart from these items, ships required anchors; ropes had to be led through blocks; rigging was set up taut with dead-eyes and lanyards; copper and iron fastenings were needed to fasten planking

---

[1] Such timber ranged in lengths from 120 feet for a first-rate ship's mainmast (which had a maximum diameter of three feet) to seventy-two feet for a frigate's. It could not be transported by land and was carried from the forests by sea or river to such ports as Riga, Narva, St Petersburg, Revel and Gothenburg.

1 Nelson a few months after the Battle, as seen by one of the leading portrait artists of the day. Sir William Beechey was proud to paint the hero of the day for a fee of less than forty guineas.

2 Sir Hyde Parker, whose career ended abruptly when the Admiralty recalled him as the bells rang out for Nelson's victory.

3 A few minutes after being forced to obey Sir Hyde's signal to break off the battle, Captain Edward Riou was killed by a stray shot.

4 Captain Thomas Fremantle. His wife Betsey thoroughly approved of Pellegrini's portrait, noting it was 'very well done and excessively like' him.

5 Captain Thomas Foley, who was lucky enough to be commanding the *Elephant* when she was selected as Nelson's flagship for the Battle.

6 The best account of the Battle was written by the soldier at Nelson's side, Colonel the Hon. William Stewart.

7 Nicholas Vansittart, the young politician who had to become a diplomat overnight, was later created Lord Bexley, and this portrait shows him in middle age.

8 Emma. This was one of the artist Romney's favourite paintings of one of his favourite models.

when repairing old ships or building new. Yet none of these items was 'contraband'. In fact not one thing required to build and equip a new ship of war was contraband, apart from the guns and ammunition, which neither France nor Britain needed to import.

Nor were many important items of army equipment, among them an army itself, the tents the troops slept in, the uniforms they wore, the blankets keeping them warm, the field kitchens that prepared their meals, the carts carrying their equipment, cavalry and artillery horses, gun carriages. . . .

Having decided what was contraband, the Convention then settled down to define its real purpose.

Every ship could navigate freely from one harbour to another providing it was not blockaded, and along the coasts of nations at war. If it was carried in a neutral ship, anything belonging to the subject of one belligerent nation could not be seized by the other, unless it was something the Convention listed as 'contraband'.

When was a harbour blockaded? 'When the disposition and number of belligerent ships' was such as 'to render it apparently hazardous to enter'. Such a definition was ludicrous. To say that a country controls the seas does not mean she has big fleets always ranging every ocean, squadrons watching each enemy port, and frigates searching everywhere. It means she can concentrate her strength to control any area at the time she chooses. When Napoleon's army was stranded in Egypt because Nelson destroyed its fleet, the Royal Navy did not have ships watching every port and covering every square mile of the Mediterranean – but it could and did prevent more French ships from Toulon or Spanish from Cadiz sailing to his help.

Blockades take many forms. A close blockade, with a squadron near an enemy main base, was usually only maintained to stop an enemy fleet sailing, or to intercept it if it did. (Brest, for example, was blockaded for months and years on end.) A trade blockade usually worked differently, its aim being not to prevent a merchantman with much-needed supplies entering an enemy port but intercepting her before she arrived within hundreds (and often thousands) of miles of it. A few British frigates guarding the entrances and exits to the Caribbean cut Spain off, for example, from the Spanish Main – indeed, Spanish attempts to break the blockade had helped enrich Sir Hyde Parker and his frigate captains.

In the same way, merchantmen sailing from the Baltic for French and Spanish ports were usually caught in the North Sea, whether they were trying to get through the English Channel or going north round Scotland. It was irrelevant that there might not have been a British warship within a hundred miles of the merchantmen's destinations. To see the absurdity of the Convention's definition of a blockaded port we have only to look ahead five years. Before the Battle of Trafalgar, Nelson's fleet was intentionally fifty miles from Cadiz: only a single frigate watched the entrance, although inside all the admirals and captains of the Combined Fleet of France and Spain held a council of war to decide whether or not to sail. After much argument they sailed, and were defeated. Yet by the Convention's definition the single British frigate might not have spotted a small merchant ship sneaking into Cadiz in the darkness – the entrance is wide – and the Fleet was too far off 'to render it apparently hazardous to enter'. But not a French or Spanish admiral or captain would have denied the port was completely blockaded. . . .

In the case of Russian or Swedish convoys, the Convention stated, the declaration of the senior officer of the escorting warships 'that the convoy has no contraband goods on board' would be sufficient; no search of his ship, or other ships of the convoy, would be permitted.

To prove their 'sincerity and justice', both governments would give 'the strictest orders' to the captains of their warships and merchantmen not to carry 'or secretly to have on board, any articles . . . which may be considered contraband'. To make sure the belligerents accepted the terms of the Convention, both countries were equipping 'a number of ships of war and frigates, which shall be charged to see that object obtained'. But if, despite the observance of 'the most perfect neutrality', their merchant ships 'be insulted, plundered or taken up' by belligerent ships of war or privateers, the appropriate Swedish or Russian minister would 'demand due satisfaction', and both countries agreed they would back each other in the most energetic manner possible, and if because of the Convention either nation was attacked, they would mutually defend each other.

Finally the two nations announced that since the Convention was intended to 'assure the general freedom of commerce and navigation', any other neutral nation could join it. The Czar already had a plan for providing volunteers.

Obviously Britain could not accept any part of the Convention, and this would have been true for any nation with an effective navy. Under the terms of the Convention all Napoleon had to do, if he found his army trapped in Egypt again, was either to order the supplies from the Baltic or have them sent from French ports in neutral ships. Such ships could not be intercepted by the Royal Navy because they were not carrying anything on the Czar's list of contraband. Grain, potatoes, salt meat and fish, wine and spirits – nothing an army needed for its stomach was contraband. Indeed, if he wanted to turn his infantry into cavalry, Napoleon could have shipped out horses by the thousand although, since saddles and bridles were contraband, the men might have had to ride bareback.[1] The only problem for Napoleon would have been to get the ships unloaded at a port which was 'not hazardous to enter'. By using boats, any stretch of the beach would be sufficient.

Likewise, with the French fleets blockaded at Toulon and Brest and the Spanish at Cadiz, both countries could have new masts, spars, sails, cordage, anchors, blocks and timber for repairs brought from the Baltic in convoys escorted by Russian or Swedish warships, providing the port of arrival was 'not hazardous to enter'. There were many small ports open to merchantmen leaving a convoy under cover of darkness: ports from which the cargoes could later be transhipped.

If one of his fleets received severe damage in battle with the British and fled to, say, a Spanish port in South America, everything needed to repair the ships – except guns and ammunition – could be sent out in a neutral convoy subject only to the 'hazardous entry' reference to the port of arrival. Since the Convention allowed a neutral ship to navigate from one harbour to another without being stopped, providing she was not carrying the few items listed as contraband, Napoleon could in practice have all his supplies carried safely by neutral ships because the French and Spanish coasts are well provided with small ports. From Britain's point of view it would mean every neutral coasting vessel would have to be shadowed day and night by a British warship, since her presence was the only way of proving that entering a particular port would be 'hazardous'. Napoleon's merchant marine thus became, at the stroke of the Czar's pen, as numerous as there were neutral ships to carry his cargoes – providing the British Government accepted the Convention.

No reasonable person would expect any belligerent maritime power in Britain's position to accept it when loopholes like these, all to France's advantage, are pointed out. Yet, ironically enough, with only slight variations these were the claims and arguments put forward against the British blockade in, for example, the Second World War, by neutral nations, among them Denmark, Norway, Holland and Belgium (all of whom were subsequently attacked and occupied by Germany) and the United States.

The apparent safeguards were naive. 'The strictest orders' might well

---

[1] Had Napoleon not wished to risk capture by escaping from Egypt in a French corvette, he would have been able to charter a neutral vessel, load her with all the treasure he had looted, his favourite pieces of furniture and his best generals (providing they left their swords and pistols behind), and return to France knowing no British warship could interfere.

be given that no ship was to load contraband, but with the high profits to be made it was absurd to expect shipowners to obey, and the traders of the neutral nations would be the first to object if they did. That, of course, had much to do with the Czar's choice for his list.

It should be borne in mind that although Britain's island situation makes her comparatively safe from attack by continental armies, it also makes her extremely vulnerable to blockade, since she cannot feed her population without imports. (The most recent occasions when she came near to defeat was when Germany, in the two World Wars, was nearly successful in establishing a complete blockade with submarines.) Yet she has always been a firm upholder of the right of a belligerent to carry out a blockade.

The questions of contraband and blockade have been dealt with at length because they are not only vital factors in the events leading up to the Battle of Copenhagen, but because within a dozen years they were to lead the United States to go to war with Britain, and cause a great deal of friction and misunderstanding in the two World Wars more than a century later.

The Armed Neutrality in its renewed form, it can be argued, applied equally to France. This view is legalistic but hardly realistic. At the time the Convention was signed the Czar's intentions were obvious: he was angry with Britain; Napoleon was his new-found friend. The Convention could only harm a sea power and favour a land power. At no time between the original Convention of 1780 and the revised version of 1800 had France been other than a land power and Britain a sea power.

So whether viewed from the known motives of the Czar or the wording of its terms, the Convention was aimed at Britain. Since it cannot be claimed that Napoleon's conquests in Europe liberated previously enslaved people, or that he overthrew a corrupt or oppressive government to set up an enlightened one (though of course he did topple corrupt and oppressive governments, but those he set up in their place were usually no better, and often worse), one is left with the question of why the Swedes (and later the Danes) signed the Convention, since Britain's reaction should have been obvious and potentially dangerous to both countries.

Britain did not think at the time – and a full study of the whole situation a century and a half later leads to only one modification of the judgment – that Denmark (which included Norway) and Sweden signed because of any enmity towards Britain. Neither country dared risk a breach with Russia: each thought the Czar was too powerful and too near, and both knew the Czar was France's new friend. Had they defied him and been attacked by Russia, Britain's complete inability to give anything but naval aid seemed obvious. The Swedes and the Danes gave little consideration to the extent of this aid and decided they had but little choice. It was a curious mistake for two maritime nations to make.

The Armed Neutrality gave Britain two choices: to accept it meant freeing Napoleon from the blockade; to oppose it meant risking the total loss of vitally important naval supplies – apart from food, the most important supplies of all. That a maritime nation like Britain should ever have let herself get into the position where she depended upon the Baltic for mast timber is lamentable; but at a time when other sources (mainly America and Canada) were available, the British Government neglected them and several decades later, thanks to an insane Czar, faced the consequences.

But in early December 1800, although the British Government did not know the precise terms of the Convention and could only guess what was happening in St Petersburg, its guesses were accurate, the Czar's moves were anticipated, and Britain's countermoves were well thought out.

Nine days after receiving the first news of the Convention, Grenville wrote again to Carysfort in Berlin that Britain was sending to Copenhagen and Stockholm 'a categorical demand for a full explanation of any engagement or negotiations into which they may have entered with any other power, respecting the rights of Great Britain as a belligerent maritime state'.

Writing privately from his home in Cleveland Row, Grenville told Carysfort, 'I think the communication of the line we have taken towards Denmark may be very useful as a lesson at Berlin, but it is important not to let them know time enough to enable them to give Bernstorff [the Danish Minister] any advice as to the answer he is to make to our categorical demand.' For that reason he had ordered Drummond to send back the messenger on the fourth morning after his conference with Bernstorff, whether or not an answer had been received, and to warn Bernstorff those were his instructions.

In what was to prove a prophetic letter to Hugh Elliot in Dresden, Grenville commented: 'I think the thing must be drawing to its crisis, I cannot conceive how so manifest a madman [i.e. the Czar] can be permitted to go on even so long as he has. . . .'

Grenville's letter to Carysfort crossed with one from the envoy who summed up the situation in a few sentences:

I am entirely of opinion with you that the only way of dealing with these Northern Powers is by threatening them. The fear of England must be opposed to the fear of France, and I trust will be found the strongest. Sweden, perhaps, wishes to be detached from Prussia. Denmark, it is true, is in a hobble, but as the British fleet can always pass the Baltic many weeks before the Russian Fleet can put to sea[1] it seems as if even there the balance might be turned in our favour. I am glad you feel so bold, notwithstanding the scarcity [of food, particularly grain]. I had great fears it might oblige you to take a lower tone. . . .

Although so far the Convention was between Sweden and Russia, the British Government was more concerned with Denmark's intentions. The reason was simple: of the four Baltic powers – Russia, Sweden, Denmark and Prussia – Denmark was the greatest potential threat; her Navy was well trained, and geographically she was considered to be strategically well placed to challenge a fleet's entry into the Baltic since Elsinore Castle and Copenhagen itself guarded the Sound.

Bearing this in mind, the intelligence the British Minister in Copenhagen sent to the Admiralty at the end of December was not very reassuring: 'The Danes pretend they will have at least 20 ships of the line ready before Spring. The number may be about fifteen . . . with five frigates, three brigs and two cutters.'

Since the ships were already laid up 'in ordinary' for the winter in Danish ports, there was certainly no reason why they should not be ready by the spring: three months was ample time to commission a ship. And, more important, during that period the homecoming Danish merchantmen could be stripped of their prime seamen to man the warships, so there should be no shortage of men.

In the meantime Drummond had received the British 'categorical demand' note. The King's Messenger arrived on Boxing Day and Drummond went to see Bernstorff at the Foreign Office on 27 December, a few days after Russia and Sweden had ratified the Convention but before its existence was officially announced.

The British Note was uncompromising, beginning: 'The Court of London, informed that Denmark is carrying on with activity negotiation very hostile to the interest of the British Empire,' considered it necessary to demand 'a frank and satisfactory explanation'. It noted that

In all the Courts of Europe they speak openly of a confederacy between Denmark and some other powers, to oppose by force the exercise of those principles of maritime law on which the naval power of the British Empire

[1] Because the ice, closing the Russian ports of Revel and Cronstadt at the head of the Baltic for much of the winter, thawed later. The British Fleet could therefore sail from England, deal with Denmark and Sweden and then work its way up towards the Russian ports as the ice thawed, and be waiting for the Russian Fleet the moment it was able to sail.

in a great measure rests, and which in all wars have been followed by the maritime states, and acknowledged by their tribunals.

The British King, 'relying with confidence upon the loyalty of his Danish Majesty', had not previously demanded any explanation as he wished to wait for the moment when the Danish Court 'should think it its duty to contradict those reports, so injurious to its good faith'.

Lord Grenville, the note concluded, now found himself bound to demand 'a plain, open and satisfactory answer' on any obligations Denmark had contracted or negotiations being carried on which affected Britain. Bernstorff, on the last day of the time limit set by Grenville, replied that Britain must have received 'very incorrect' information to think Denmark had conceived projects hostile to it. 'The negotiation had no other object than the renewal of the agreements which in 1780 and 1781 were made by the same powers' for the safety of their navigation. . . .

When it was proposed by the Czar, Bernstorff continued, Denmark did not hesitate to agree because, far from ever having abandoned the principles adopted in 1780, she considered it her duty to maintain them. In a neat phrase he said that if Denmark 'wishes to shelter her innocent navigation from the manifest abuses and violence which the maritime war produces but too easily, she thinks she pays respect to the belligerent powers by supposing that, far from wishing to authorize or tolerate those abuses, they would, on their side, adopt measures best calculated to prevent or repress them'.

On the British charge that Denmark had been secretive – for Grenville's note merely said this politely – Bernstorff wrote, 'Denmark has not made a mystery' of the object of her negotiations, and had not departed from the usual procedure in waiting for the definitive result before sending an official account to the powers at war.

Having failed to present Britain with a *fait accompli*, Bernstorff was ready with a justification of his action – for his influence was strong. It is worth noting just how empty was one of diplomacy's usually empty phrases, 'having given an account to the King my Master', used by Bernstorff in his note. The Danish King, Christian VII, was fifty-one and by then completely and incurably insane following a life – which included thirty-four years on the throne – of drink and debauchery.

As a boy Christian was left in the charge of one of the King's friends, Ditlev Reventlow, a brutal man whose idea of educating the future king was to terrorize him. When Christian began to show signs of homosexuality he was hurriedly married to the English Princess Caroline Mathilda, sister of George III.

The years after Christian became King were years of tragedy, debauchery, deceit and finally brutality. His neglected Queen came under the influence of a court physician, Dr Johann Struensee, who soon gained so much influence that the King was in his power. Struensee had to fight the Danish nobility to get that power, and the reforms he brought in were long overdue and remarkable. Among them were revised and better tax laws; all men were made equal in the eyes of the law (previously nobles could not be jailed for debt); Copenhagen's streets were named; press censorship was stopped; and dozens of religious holidays were abolished. But before all his plans were completed there was a palace revolution in which Struensee was put in prison and secured in chains. The Queen was taken to Elsinore Castle and locked in a tiny and bare eight-sided room with no fire and only a straw mattress.[1]

The British Government was quick to warn the Danes of what would happen if their King's sister was harmed. Both Struensee (who was tortured) and Mathilda were trapped into writing 'confessions' – Mathilda being assured hers would save Struensee's life. After Struensee was executed, the Queen was divorced but kept in prison. The British King then warned his former brother-in-law that Britain would declare war unless Mathilda was freed, and she was allowed to board a British warship at Elsinore, though her baby was snatched from her at the last moment.

After that, Christian VII was kept in the background and power rested in the hands of such men as Bernstorff and, later, the King's eldest son, Crown Prince Frederick, who was thirty-two at the time Bernstorff wrote Denmark's reply to Drummond.

Christian VII on the throne of Denmark, as much a cipher as his seal 'cvII'; Paul Petrowitz, Emperor and Autocrat of all the Russias; George III, King of Great Britain and Ireland, and Elector of Hanover: three monarchs who had one thing in common apart from their crowns – insanity, though in George III's case it was at first periodic. Fortunately, even if they were crazy, Christian VII and George III were well served by their ministers and in any case their powers were limited; but the Czar was an autocrat both in title and action.

---

[1] The room, or cell, is unchanged to this day, and in the form of a cupola attached to the castle. Barred windows face the Sound to the east with batteries in the foreground. The ceiling, umbrella shaped, is painted with representations of Neptune, the Planets, Sun, Moon, Night and Dawn. Although the room has no means of heating it, the door opens into a very large room – used by her guards – which has an enormous ornate fireplace.

7

THE LONELY FIGHT

Britain's war against France had by Christmas 1800 lasted almost eight years. One by one her allies had fallen to France's armies or the intrigues of their own governments. And although each was defending itself, not one of the allies had sent a single soldier into battle without cash guarantees from Britain, who had to provide not only the leadership in the fight against France's determination to conquer Europe but also the cash.

Britain's position was such that it seemed too much even to hope the war would ever end, let alone end in victory. Napoleon indeed bestrode most of the European world like a greedy Colossus, with new conquests only increasing, not sating his appetite.

In a war which was to last twenty-two years, Britain eventually would be the only nation that fought from the first day until the last; but at the moment she had nothing to show for her huge investment in her allies except the highest rate of taxation her people had ever known. Although loans (mostly interest-free) and grants made to these allies between 1793 and 1815 eventually amounted to £52 million, already the total was impressive, bearing in mind that Britain's population was a scant fifteen million. There was, for instance, £4,500,000 paid to Austria and £1 million a year to Russia in 1795; £1,200,000 to Austria in 1796; and £225,000 down and £75,000 a month to the Czar at the signing of the Second Coalition in return for the promise of 45,000 troops. The most recent transaction had been a £2 million interest-free loan to Austria for an undertaking that she would not sign a separate peace with France. (But, unlike the loans the United States made to its allies in the Second World War, none of these was ever repaid.)

So finally Britain stood alone in Europe: there was not the slightest prospect of forming a new alliance against Napoleon. She did have one distant ally, the Sultan of Turkey: a few weeks after the Nile he had declared a Jihad, a Holy War against the infidel French and had, since then, co-operated with the British to the best of his ability.

Napoleon seemed at the height of his power: as Britain received the news of the Armed Neutrality, he controlled all of Europe that mattered; controlled (with the exception of those of Portugal, and the bases of Gibraltar, Minorca and Malta) every port from the Texel on the North Sea coast to the Adriatic: commercial and naval ports such as Antwerp, Dunkirk, Boulogne, Brest, Bordeaux, Ferrol and Cadiz, and in the Mediterranean Cartagena, Toulon, Genoa, Leghorn, Naples, Venice and Trieste. With the one-sided Convention coming into force it was likely his influence would stretch from the Arctic to the Adriatic.

To fight a land war, Britain's entire army numbered 200,000, both Regulars and auxiliaries. By comparison, in 1798 alone France had called up 200,000 conscripts between the ages of twenty and twenty-five. In terms of fighting Napoleon in properly-planned campaigns on the mainland of Europe, it was too much for sensible men even to dream, although politicians like Dundas occasionally went vote-catching with talk more suited to a boastful brewer's drayman in his cups. Yet although the British people were not for the moment nervous for their safety (though the time was to come) they were sick of war. More than six times in the previous hundred years they had fought France. Now the working people of Britain found the price of bread still rising and, from the end of January, the sale of fine wheaten flour was forbidden; only brown bread was to be used. There had been bad harvests for the first two of the eight years of war and grain had to be imported. Much of it came from the Baltic, and even that source was now threatened.

Yet perhaps Lord Romney summed up the nation's spirit when he told the House of Lords that it was time to test the sincerity of Napoleon's declaration that he was 'at all times ready to treat for peace', because it was 'in some measure necessary to convince the people that the war was unavoidable' and he believed Napoleon's assertions were merely a pretext to keep himself in power.

But while the British people were heartily sick of war Britain, although now alone, had by a strange irony never been in a stronger position: gone was the need to temporize, to be wary of offending neutrals, and forever raising millions of pounds in subsidies to keep her allies fighting for their own freedom. The Government could be firm, even harsh, in dealing with neutrals; it could, without being fettered in any way, continue the fight for the nation's survival by doing precisely what it considered necessary instead of compromising by adopting plans forced on it by circumstances.

Although Britain's attitude towards neutral ships carrying contraband had never changed, in earlier years and earlier wars she had often been forced to accept what she was too weak to prevent. Now she was strong enough at sea – and it was on the broad oceans that the power was needed – to insist on her terms being accepted. Then, as in the two succeeding world conflicts, war was regarded by the short-sighted commercial interests of neutral nations as good business yielding high and quick profits. Then, as later, the commercial interests were not concerned in the rights and wrongs of the war, or the fact that their trade might spread it to their own countries. Nor were they concerned in such abstract ideas as freedom: the highest bidder was the customer; there was no transgressor and no defender; simply a market, entries in ledgers and comforting balance sheets. Making money made it moral – yet in almost every case from 1793 until 1945 – with the notable exception of the United States after Pearl Harbor – those neutral commercial interests ended up at the feet of an invader.

Britain was now fighting Revolutionary France because she knew Napoleon intended to extend and keep all his conquests. French policy was aggressive; like Hitler's nearly a century and a half later it was a war policy whose only aim was seizing power and land with all the obsessive and unquenchable thirst of an alcoholic groping for a bottle.

Coming so quickly after the Revolution in France, the early conquests which had toppled corrupt monarchies gave the French armies the appearance of liberators. Cries of *'Liberté, Égalité, Fraternité'* and the setting up of a Tree of Liberty in every town square at first gave long-oppressed peoples a sense of hope. But quickly the Tree rusted – for it was usually made of iron – and a guillotine had been set up beside it whose blade remained bright. Towns were expected to feed the occupying armies; a citizen disagreeing in any way was executed; whole nations were looted, their treasuries emptied and their treasures carried to Paris. The new republics with high-sounding names that Napoleon set up were merely branch offices of a dictatorship based in Paris.

While Britain always saw France's aggressions as acquisitive and for the glory of France, not a wish to topple absolute monarchies and replace them with truly democratic republics, America was during this war generally pro-French – indeed by 1812 she had become a distant ally of Napoleon's by going to war with Britain. Two major factors in this, often ignored or not realized, are firstly that at this time she confused the new Revolutionary, aggressive France with the old Royalist France of decades earlier which had helped her gain her independence of Britain and set up a democratic, republican system. In the first flush of democratic independence it was not realized that the French King had no sympathy with revolution and republics; indeed, few monarchs viewed them with less favour. But by helping the colonists in their revolt he struck a hard blow at Britain yet ensured that revolutions and republican ideas remained – it seemed at the time – on the western shores of the Atlantic. Helping the colonists was quite incidental to harming Britain. The second factor is that the United States, having successfully set up a democratic republic in their own country, assumed that the overthrow of the French monarchy and the setting up of the Republic meant that France too now had a democratic government. The same assumption was made as France overthrew other European monarchies, particularly those in Italy, and any evidence that no democracy appeared was ignored or excused on the grounds that problems were always bound to follow a sudden change. By mistakenly equating their own republican system with that of Revolutionary France, the Americans could only see that Britain was again the villain of the piece; and we are still too close to events to understand fully how much this type of thinking subsequently affected the American people at the time of the Kaiser's attack on Belgium and Hitler's on Poland.[1]

After the Napoleonic, First and Second World Wars, Britain tried patiently to restore Europe in the shape of the old. This policy was often proved by history to have been mistaken, but it had the merit of being honest. Today it is fashionable to ignore the fact that had Napoleon, the Kaiser or Hitler been victorious, none would have relinquished an acre of his conquests. And ignoring this means that an important point is quietly pushed under the carpet: in each of these three wars the intentions of the aggressor nations should have been absolutely obvious to the governments of the neutral nations. Each, for its own reasons, chose to ignore them.

Some of the reasons are understandable; many are contemptible. A small nation's fear of a powerful and aggressive neighbour is forgivable; a larger nation whose government and businessmen deliberately blur or ignore all moral issues to confuse their people to leave the way open for enormous commercial gains can expect little sympathy when their turn comes to be attacked.

The main reason why Britain, at the very moment she stood alone in 1800, need compromise no more was the strength of her Navy. Her

---

[1] Norway, Denmark, Holland, Belgium, Greece, Yugoslavia, Albania, Russia and the United States were all neutral when Germany attacked Poland and Britain and France went to her help. All remained neutral; all were later attacked by Germany and her allies; all were, with the exception of the United States, occupied by the enemy for several years.

safety was in her island position; the English Channel was worth a couple of million men in defending her shores against Napoleon because it was there the Navy could sink an invasion flotilla.

The Royal Navy, the only weapon Britain could now use against Napoleon, had never been stronger; the morale of its men had never been higher. Victories – fortunate against the Spanish at Cape St Vincent, hard fought against the Dutch at Camperdown, brilliantly achieved at the Nile – had convinced the British sailor he was the equal of any three Frenchmen or Spaniards, and since high morale and good leadership are often more important in battle than fire power the Navy rarely need numerical equality to win and seldom had it anyway. Britain had started the war with fifty-four ships of the line in commission, 45,000 officers and men, 9,000 Marines and a Parliamentary vote of £4 million for the year 1793. Despite losses, by 1800 she had a hundred sail of the line, 100,000 seamen, 20,000 Marines, a vote of £13,133,000 and fifteen more sail of the line being built or ordered. France, on the other hand, had started the war with eighty-six sail of the line in commission; by 1800 she had only forty-eight.

The Royal Navy was not only the most powerful in size but also the most efficient: the finest of its young captains had emerged to secure the best commands; the more blatantly inefficient or aged admirals were, for the most part, being left aside and some of the younger ones, like Nelson, were slowly coming to the front. And for eight years of war, the ships and seamen had been kept at sea. Nelson was to say, 'Ships and seamen rot in harbour', and this was as true in the days of Drake as it is today.

By comparison, the ships of the navies of France and Spain spent most of their time in port. There were many reasons, ranging from lack of money and equipment to lack of leadership and the British blockade. The ships of France and Spain were extremely well designed and equally well built: their designers had the almost indefinable combination of art and science necessary to produce fine ships which sailed well and sailed fast (so much so that the British frequently copied the designs of those they captured). But the navies of France and Spain lacked leaders at almost every level.

The reason is not hard to find. To command a frigate needed a minimum of eight to ten years' training; the captain of a sail of the line needed ten to fifteen. An admiral, even a clever man of the most junior rank, needed several more years. Nelson, unique among them all, went to sea at thirteen and was thirty-nine when he became a rear-admiral. But the French Navy suffered its first and most important defeat even before France went to war: the Revolution purged the Navy of the 'aristocrats' or any men remotely connected with or resembling one. They had fled or been led to the guillotine. Because of the very structure of the Navy the officers, particularly senior captains and admirals, were generally either 'nobles' or regarded as such by the Revolutionaries. So France, in a matter of months, lost her best senior officers; men in whom the nation and its Navy had an investment it could ill afford to lose, since it was not an investment in money but in time; in years of training.

Ships are not like any other weapon of war: if left at anchor they deteriorate. Artillery, muskets, shot, bayonets, swords – these can be greased and stored indefinitely in arsenals. But ships – the wood of their hulls and spars, the cordage, rigging and sails – all decay with fearful rapidity if not constantly tended, mended or renewed. And the process of tending them means that dry docks, special timber, ropewalks and sail lofts must always be available, with shipwrights, sailmakers, rope-makers, coopers, smiths and riggers.

But Revolutionary France was desperately short of money and most of it was needed for the Army. The complicated structure of timber stores and dockyards which kept ships in commission and fit for sea collapsed under the triple attack of decay, neglect and corruption.

So at the time when Napoleon wanted it to destroy his last enemy but one (for Russia was always at his back, even if at present an ally) the Navy was badly led and worse manned, the ships in poor condition, the dockyards bereft of timber and cordage, sails, guns and skilled workmen. Mast timber, cordage and flax had to come from the Baltic, and were paid for with what little money was available. And between France and the Baltic stood the Royal Navy, snapping up any French merchantman trying to get to or return from the Baltic – or, indeed, leave or enter any port controlled by France.

It was against this background that the Czar dreamed up the Convention, and it was obviously in Napoleon's interest to do anything to encourage neutral nations to make sure their cargoes were not seized as contraband.

The war on land presented a vastly different situation for Britain, with a small, old-style army. Its officers bought their commissions as they bought their uniforms, and had no military training other than what they picked up or their own enthusiasm led them to learn. There were no standard manuals and the Army had its share of the Sir Hyde Parkers with closed minds. The young officers lacked nothing in courage but, with few exceptions, lacked all-round military skill. Promotion was also by purchase – a rich young man could buy himself a lieutenant-colonelcy at once or, if he was wise, start as a lieutenant and buy his way up as his knowledge increased.[1] Corruption and nepotism were common; indeed, in the third year of the war the Duke of York had written to every battalion in the Army demanding the names of all captains who were less than twelve years old and all colonels less than twenty.

The Duke, in an effort to reorganize the Army, issued orders which began a more systematic method of training; but his greatest enemy – and that of the Army, in one sense – was tradition: it was impossible to destroy the old tentacles which gripped administration, tactics and training – it could only be modified here and there with a sabre slash. And the brilliant young officers emerged only on the battlefield – dashing about over the Kentish hills from the barracks at Shornecliffe, for instance, merely indicated an officer's physical stamina. And yet, ironically, tradition and pride were vital, since many a man feared disgracing his regiment's tradition more than being killed.

Facing the British Army, the French Army was by contrast one of the first truly citizens armies ever to be created (and France's population was double that of Britain). Constant and often hard-won victories had raised its morale; the brilliant young men had been given their chances of leadership, seized them, and proved themselves, achieving victory as well as promotion. Events had shown private soldiers could become generals: several of Bonaparte's generals were former privates.

To the mass of people the Revolution had at first been the chance to snatch up any available weapon and fight for the freedom the leaders promised was there for the taking. And what an army those leaders – some of whom, heavily involved with politics, were to perish at the hands of their own comrades' plottings as the Revolution progressed – had produced: an entirely reverse process compared to the expansion of, for example, standing British, Austrian and Prussian armies.

In those countries the ponderous administrative machine and method were well entrenched: twenty copies of this form were required, ten of that. Expanding the size of these armies meant expanding the bureaucracy: they expanded from the administrative centres outwards, like octopuses whose crippling arms were red tape, and recruits came only by conscription or the lure of bounties.

The citizens' army of France sprang up in the opposite way: fifty enthusiastic French farm lads armed with pitchforks, stolen sporting guns and scythes formed themselves into a company. That within a year

[1] *The Times* of 6 January 1801 carried a typical advertisement: 'Two hundred guineas will be given for a commission appointing an ensign in one of His Majesty's regiments (an old established regiment) now serving, or to serve either in the East or West Indies.' Since each was notoriously an unhealthy spot, one is tempted to think the advertiser was a spurned suitor.

the company had grown into a proud regiment was due to the enthusiasm of subsequent recruits (and from 1798 onwards conscripts). But because of its very nature it was able to expand rapidly since administrative detail was alien to its spirit, and the bureaucrats were recruited only as necessary. They were not there at the beginning; indeed, had they existed there would have been no beginning because those inertia-producing 'No' men had scores of years of training in the art of prevarication.

That promotion in the new French Army was by merit, and those meriting it were promoted swiftly, is shown by Napoleon's own experience: he had risen from the artillery captain of 1790 to the First Consul of 1799.

Thus with scores of thousands of men under arms, the greatest and most truly national army ever seen, Napoleon knew that on the Continent of Europe he had nothing to fear. The weapon of his choice was his strongest – the Army. The battleground of his choosing was therefore the Continent of Europe. But the battleground of his choosing was just where he could not challenge the British who, with their comparatively feeble army, were secure beyond the Channel. And, in turn, the weapon of Britain's choosing was the Royal Navy. Would the Armed Neutrality break Britain's blockade, allow the French Fleet to re-equip, and tip the scales towards Napoleon?

8

THE SOCIAL WHIRL

After being snubbed by the King at the *levée* and adding to the gossip by knocking over a glass of walnuts at Lady Spencer's, the next few weeks for Nelson were both busy and, although he protested otherwise, enjoyable. The Hamiltons soon left Nerot's Hotel to stay at 22 Grosvenor Square, a house lent them by William Beckford, the eccentric millionaire whose fortune had come from the West Indies and who was an old friend sharing Sir William's love of antiquities. In the meantime Lady Nelson started to prepare 17 Dover Street, the house that Nelson's old friend Alexander Davison had rented for him.

In between calling on Lord Grenville in Downing Street to press for a pension and payment of his claim for compensation, and visiting his wealthy relatives, Sir William began negotiating to buy the lease of 23 Piccadilly. The only problem was money – his estate in the United Kingdom was heavily mortgaged, he owed his bankers more than £7,000, and apart from his collection, which had been shipped home earlier, he had lost all his possessions in Naples, for which he was claiming £10,000 compensation from the British Government.

It would seem hardly the time to buy a large house in one of the most fashionable parts of London, but Sir William knew that Society would drop him with a bang audible in Naples if they thought he was broke; the influential friends who might help get the pension granted and the claim paid would stay away; and the prices at the auction he was planning for some of his collection would be derisory if buyers thought he was desperate for money. Apart from that, living within his income was a difficult habit to start at his age. So Nelson lent him more than £2,250, Lady Hamilton sold her diamonds, the lease of the house was signed, and the auction arranged.[1]

On 19 November, a week after attending the *levée* at St James's, Nelson was guest of honour at Covent Garden's staging of 'The Mouth

[1] When an infuriated Nelson found that one of the items to be sold was Romney's portrait 'Lady Hamilton as Cecilia', he instructed Davison to buy it for him secretly.

of the Nile', a musical play specially written to celebrate Nelson's victory. The audience went wild, standing up and cheering, when they found Nelson sitting in the second box on 'The Prince's side of the stage', with Lady Nelson on his left and Lady Hamilton on his right. In the next box was the elegant Sir William, the bluff Captain Thomas Masterman Hardy, and Nelson's father, the ancient rector of Burnham Thorpe. While Nelson stood at the front of the box, bowing frequently, his father burst into proud and appreciative tears.

The interest with which Nelson's every move was noted is best shown by the newspaper accounts of this one evening: they reported every visible detail. Lady Nelson, 'in white with a satin head-dress and a small white feather', was described as 'of a very pleasing description: her features are handsome and exceedingly interesting, and her general appearance is at once prepossessing and elegant'. Lady Hamilton, in 'a blue satin gown and head-dress with a fine plume of feathers', was seen as 'rather *en bon point* but her person is nevertheless highly graceful and her face extremely pretty'. This was praise indeed since she was six months' pregnant with Nelson's child.

Next day Nelson (who had received a barony after the Nile) took his seat in the House of Lords for the first time, being introduced, as is the custom, with a peer on each side. Lord Grenville, the austere and scholarly Foreign Secretary was one; Lord Romney the other. Later Baron Nelson of the Nile and Burnham Thorpe took his place next to Lord Seaforth and for a short while listened to his fellow peers' speeches. The Directors of the Honourable East India Company held a banquet in his honour and the importance 'John Company' attached to it is shown by the guests, who included the Prime Minister and the Duke of York, son of the King and Commander-in-Chief of the Army. But although everywhere the Admiral showed himself the crowds gathered and cheered, behind whatever expression the moment required of him in public – stern, smiling, modest or determined – Nelson's private life was rapidly becoming a tragic turmoil.

By the time he took his seat in the Lords Nelson had heard privately from Lord Spencer that he was to hoist his flag in the *San Josef*, one of the two ships he had captured at Cape St Vincent, and he had asked for and been promised Thomas Masterman Hardy as his captain.

Until just before Christmas he had little time to himself. Old friends wrote – like Captain Sir Edward Berry (beside him when he boarded the *San Josef*) who sought a command and received a prompt reply. 'You know how I am fixed with Hardy, who could not get a ship. I wrote immediately to Lord Spencer, who says if the *Princess Charlotte* is good, you have a fair chance for her and that he shall be happy to show his regard for you.' He added, 'I hope we shall serve together and mine will not, I hope, be an *inactive* service,'[1] while a postscript told Berry, 'The Duke of Clarence spoke much of you this day'.

Midshipmen and lieutenants who had been fortunate to serve with the Admiral and their relatives needed letters, a typical one being to the Reverend Dixon Hoste saying, 'Your son deserved more than I could give him: he ought to have been Post [i.e. made a captain], and would long since, had I retained the command.'

Artists and sculptors were queuing up to get the Admiral to give them sittings. The artist S. De Koster arrived in Dover Street on 8 December to draw a small portrait of the Admiral and went away delighted with the result, which he handed over to the engraver Stow. Both Koster and the printer, wanting to profit by the present wave of popularity, worked swiftly and on 24 January *The Times* announced the engraving ('considered so excellent a likeness') had just been published by Mr Brydon at Charing Cross.

Mrs Damer, the fashionable sculptress, had been commissioned to do a bust of him for the Guildhall; Sir William Beechey painted one of the finest portraits of Nelson; Lemuel Abbott arrived to make more sketches to ensure his portraits were up to date. (Starting from a full-length portrait in 1797, Abbott had subsequently painted more half-length portraits, adding the appropriate new decorations and backgrounds.)

Nelson's last public appearance with Lady Nelson was disastrous. With the Hamiltons they went to see *Pizarro* at Drury Lane, and at the end of an impassioned outburst by the leading lady, Lady Nelson brought the curtain down with an unscripted scream and then fainted. Nelson, keeping a stiff upper lip, or being callous, depending on who relates the story, stayed on with Sir William and their guest, Princess Castelcicala, while his father and Lady Hamilton took Lady Nelson home to Dover Street.

Nelson's plans for Christmas did not include his wife, but although it may have been his secret wish it was probably not by design. William Beckford owned Fonthill, a large fake Gothic country seat he built in Wiltshire, and had invited the Hamiltons and Nelson to stay for Christmas for 'a few comfortable days of repose, uncontaminated by the sight and prattle of drawing room parasites'. The invitation did not include Lady Nelson.

[1] A reference – which Berry, who had been with him at the time, would recognize at once – to a phrase in a letter from Lord Spencer while Nelson was still in Palermo, which said: 'You will be more likely to recover your health and strength in England, than in an inactive situation at a foreign Court....'

They were due at Fonthill on the 20th and by leaving London on the 15th, Nelson was able to fit in other engagements on the way. At Salisbury, where his carriage was met outside the boundary by a cavalry escort, he was presented with its Freedom and the city, though thick with fog, rang with the cheers of an exultant crowd. Among them Nelson spotted some old shipmates – one a sailor who had been with him at the Nile, and had been at the abortive attack at Teneriffe, when Nelson lost an arm. The seaman said he had been in Nelson's boat and had torn a piece of lace from the bloodstained shirt sleeve and kept it ever since as a memento of his service with Nelson.

Christmas at Fonthill Park proved far from being 'a few comfortable days of repose' – beginning with the reception Nelson received as his carriage arrived at the park gates in the darkness of a December evening. Flambeaux were ready for the postillions; the Fonthill Volunteers presented arms as their band played 'Rule Britannia', and they then escorted the carriage to the house in a slow procession. There, as Beckford greeted them at the imposing entrance, the Volunteers gave a drill display on the lawn by the light of torches, and fired salutes.

Nelson wanted to be back in London for the closing session of Parliament on 31 December and left Fonthill on Boxing Day with Emma and Sir William. In London he stayed at Dover Street while the Hamiltons went back to Beckford's house in Grosvenor Square until their new home at 23 Piccadilly had been redecorated.

Nelson's return was saddened by a letter waiting for him saying that Captain William Locker had died the previous day at the age of seventy. Locker had been the captain of the frigate in which young Nelson, having just passed his examination for lieutenant, first served as a commission officer, and began a friendship and affection which lasted until the old man's death.

Early on New Year's Eve the Royal Family drove up from Windsor Castle, where they had spent Christmas, and while the Queen and the five princesses went to the Queen's House (better known now as Buckingham Palace) the King went to St James's to meet the Cabinet Ministers and discuss the speech he was to deliver from the Throne to close the present session of Parliament.

It was customary for two peers to escort the King from the Presence Chamber to the Throne, and later that afternoon, after Black Rod had summoned the Members to the Bar of the House, the onlookers were surprised to see Rear-admiral Lord Nelson walking in front of His Majesty and Admiral Lord Hood walking behind. It is not clear whether this was a tacit hint that the Royal snub at the *levée* was just a warning and that Nelson was now back in favour – as long as he left

Lady Hamilton out of it – or a warning to people like the Swedish Minister, who was among the listeners, that the King's Speech meant business.

After giving the Royal Assent to twenty-three public and private Bills the King delivered the Speech which had been carefully drawn up by his ministers in the light of the latest news of the Czar's activities.

The detention of property of my subjects in the ports of Russia, contrary to the most solemn treaties, and the imprisonment of British sailors in that country, have excited in me sentiments in which you and all my subjects will I am sure, participate. I have already taken steps as this occasion indispensibly required; and it will afford me great satisfaction if they prove effectual but [he warned] if it shall become necessary to maintain against any combination the honour and independence of the British Empire, and those maritime rights and interests on which both our prosperity and our security must always essentially depend, I enter no doubt either on the success of those means which, in such an event, I shall be enabled to exert, or the determination of my Parliament and my people to afford me a support proportioned to the importance of the interests which we have to maintain.

So the warning to the Czar was delivered. But in the Commons Mr John Nicholls, recently elected as one of the two representatives for Tregony, Cornwall, had sent the Members to the voting lobbies. He would decline entering on specific reasons, he told the House, and therefore would make no speech on the closing day of the session, but would move 'that an humble address be presented to His Majesty, beseeching him to take the earliest opportunity for entering on a negotiation for peace'.

The Members listened but did not agree; one vote was cast for the motion, forty-two against.

9
THE OPEN SECRET

The position of Denmark and Sweden at the beginning of 1801 was unenviable although neither nation fully realized the Baltic was now a powder magazine. For years, whether the rest of Europe was at war or peace, both nations had carried out a highly profitable trade, particularly with Britain. Their merchants had grown wealthy and their regimes remained stable amidst revolution and conquest elsewhere on the Continent. To live and trade in peace amid a warring Europe had become a habit; a way of life and a source of great profit for these hardworking northern people.

Certainly a powerful and feudal Russia always watched from the east; more recently Revolutionary France had advanced very close to the Danish frontier with her occupation of the Netherlands. But so far in this latest war, the Czar and Napoleon, the improbable bedfellows representing the extremes of autocratic monarchy and aggressive republicanism, had left them alone.

In the case of Sweden, Russia had taken all she wanted in the war which ended in 1721 with the Swedish empire smashed forever, Poland and most of Swedish Pomerania lost and Russia in possession of Riga and Revel – leading Peter the Great to exclaim during the decisive battle, 'Now by God's help are the foundations of St Petersburg laid for all time'.

Then, as 1800 drew to an end, Denmark's and Sweden's stable world suddenly seemed to be on the verge of collapse as the Czar produced his scheme for the Armed Neutrality. With this in force, most of Europe would be divided between a great northern group, headed by the Czar, and France which, having occupied most of Western Europe, covered the southern and western flank.

In his imagination the Czar saw the combination, each half ruled by a powerful man and bound by personal friendship, more than strong enough to enforce the type of stability he so much desired – for it was Napoleon's stabilizing influence on France that first impressed him –

and more than sufficient to cow Britain; more than sufficient to obtain Malta and salve his pride.

So, to fit into his plan, Sweden and Denmark had to stand up and cast their vote. The choice had been brutally simple. From the Danish and Swedish points of view, Britain's day had clearly passed. The decline had been rapid, beginning in an earlier war with the loss of North America. Admittedly she was powerful on the oceans – but what of Europe? Could any alliance of nations stand up to Napoleon and the Czar? Any alliance topple them?

The old order had changed; it was useless to ignore the fact. The present order in Europe was not a stalemate; it was a new order, a new and obviously permanent change of power, with Europe divided between France and Russia, both of whom were now friends. So Britain was left in isolation across the North Sea, her ships snapping at Napoleon's heels but apparently no more capable of preventing either the Czar or Napoleon from attacking Denmark or Sweden than of turning the rolling lands of France into an ocean to permit a seaborne assault on Paris. Cut off from Europe, particularly from Baltic supplies, Britain would wither like a tree whose roots were cut.

Yet, as Bernstorff's conversations with Drummond had shown, in Denmark's case there was a doubt, hard to explain and lying beyond sentimental or trade attachments to Britain. It is unlikely Bernstorff himself could have defined exactly what the doubt was, but it existed, like a half-remembered dream.

Sweden, unlike Denmark, had not hesitated when presented with the Czar's choice: Russia was too near. She knew her trade was going to suffer but the alternative was too perilous. The King of Sweden perhaps more than the Crown Prince of Denmark saw Russia as an enormous snowstorm, a terrifying great blizzard lying to the east that could engulf him overnight as she once had his predecessor.

The situation in Sweden was described by the British chargé d'affaires in Stockholm, Mr James Talbot, in despatches to Lord Grenville on 13 and 16 January. 'No batteries worth mentioning' were erected along the coast of the Skagerrak, his first report said, although Gothenburg was 'called a fortified town'. As for the Swedish Navy, his information was that Sweden could 'upon a great emergency' send eleven ships of the line to sea. Several of them were old 'but perhaps they might venture into the Baltic'.

His second despatch reported that the Swedish King was shortly expected to visit Carlskrona, the naval base in south-west Sweden, 'probably to make some preparations for the equipment of the Fleet'. Talbot added that he had just heard six ships of the line and a few frigates 'are immediately to be got ready' and stationed at Gothenburg.

Whether or no the number of good seamen necessary to man this Fleet are to be procured, I cannot pretend to say; I am assured that there never were during the winter months so few Swedish vessels in their own ports. . . . The Government sailors for the most part have not been exercised since the Russian War.

Talbot then turned to the other aspect of the situation.

The commercial interest is in the greatest consternation, and the ruin of the Swedish trade is foreseen in case of a rupture with England. The proprietors of the iron works (in which consists the wealth of Sweden) are already much distressed. The demand is so inconsiderable, and the price consequently so reduced that the sale of the iron scarcely defrays the expense of the charcoal consumed in the manufacture of it.

In Denmark, however, so little was happening to prepare the nation's defences it is quite clear that both Bernstorff and the Crown Prince assumed Britain would accept the Armed Neutrality and try to make the best of it, little dreaming that when Bernstorff's long reply to Britain's demand for a 'frank and satisfactory explanation' arrived in Downing Street it would have the effect of a grenade exploding.

Only one order was given which had anything to do with Denmark's security. This came from the Crown Prince and was addressed to Captain Johan Olfert Fischer, the man who was soon to play a leading role in the battle. Fischer's family was originally Dutch.[1] His grandfather, the master of a Dutch merchant ship, emigrated to Denmark in time for Olfert's father to be born in Copenhagen in March 1700. This son, who went into the Navy and became a vice-admiral, married twice, and by his second wife had fourteen children in twenty years. The oldest boy was Johan Olfert, who followed his father into the Navy.

By January 1801 Johan Olfert was fifty-three years old, a senior captain and 'Commander of the Defences of Copenhagen Roads' – the Roads being the stretch of sea forming the approaches to the city. On the first day of the year he received an order signed by Crown Prince Frederick and the Defence Commission: 'In consequence of this letter you will enter the Defence Commission in order to take part in its deliberations.' The Crown Prince's own files of correspondence with the Danish Admiralty and the Army, and the Admiralty's files, all show that for the next month, until 20 February, no preparations were made for defence or offence. The significance of this is already obvious.

---

[1] The Dutch influence on Danish life is particularly noticeable in the architecture of the older parts of Copenhagen and other towns due, to a large extent, to the fact that Dutch stonemasons and architects were frequently employed.

In their assumption that Britain would have to accept the Armed Neutrality, both Sweden and Denmark were repeating the mistake already made by the Czar: they saw the Royal Navy as Britain's defence. Neither nation saw it as Britain's most powerful *offensive* weapon, a long arm which could hold a cutlass at their throats. As far as they were concerned, Britain would not and could not take up the challenge the Czar had just thrown at her feet.

Having so far dealt with the diplomatic correspondence between Grenville and his envoys, and the position of Sweden and Denmark in the first half of January, we need to see what the people of Britain knew – for it was on their backs the ultimate burden would rest – and what the men who would lead them during the next critical fourteen weeks were thinking, saying and doing about Russia's challenge.

As New Year's Day ushered in the year 1801, much was happening in Britain. To begin with there was a new and fuller title for the King, and a new national flag, since Ireland now received representation in Parliament. The King's new title was, by proclamation, to be 'George the Third, by the Grace of God, of the United Kingdom and Great Britain and Ireland, King, Defender of the Faith.'

The original flag (combining the red cross on white of St George and the white diagonal cross on blue of St Andrew) now incorporated the red diagonal cross on white of St Patrick and was to retain its original name of the Union Flag.[1] Henceforth Ireland would be represented in Parliament by twenty-eight Lords temporal and four Lords spiritual.

Meanwhile the cost of living was rising fast: a few days earlier 'a very respectable meeting of merchants, bankers, traders and other inhabitants of the metropolis' at the London Tavern opened a subscription immediately to help the poor in the cities of London and Westminster and the borough of Southwark. And the men at this meeting, held on 23 December, knew prices would be rising again in the near future.

The King's proclamation, made on New Year's Day, for a general fast must have been received with mixed feelings in many quarters. 'We, taking into our most serious consideration the heavy judgments with which the Almighty God is pleased to visit the iniquities of this land, by a grievous scarcity and dearth of divers articles of sustenance and necessities of life,' the proclamation said, and taking into serious consideration the just and necessary war in which the country was

---

[1] Union 'Jack' is a wrong description of the national flag. A 'Jack' is a flag flown at the bow of a ship. This does not stop even ministers and ministries repeating the error in speeches and statements more than a century and a half after the new flag was adopted.

engaged, the King commanded that 'a public fast and humiliation be observed' on Friday, 13 February.

Yet a casual glance at the daily newspapers gave a contradictory impression of a capital city, if not a nation, which was 'carrying on as usual', to use a phrase that was to become famous in another war nearly one and a half centuries later.

Theatres were full, and Scott's shop at 417 Strand was advertising the new magic lantern, 'a pleasing family amusement well suited to all ages and sexes, ready in a few minutes for the entertainment of friends or family; in fact a cheerful house should never be without one'.[1]

The *Morning Post*'s correspondent, writing of 'The Fashionable World' in January, reported the prevailing colours were purple, puce, yellow and scarlet; that spangled nets were fashionable for the hair; and as usual the latest play was affecting fashion – the most popular item being the 'Le Brun's Pizarro hat made of wove silk, in all colours, augmented with Pizarro feathers'.

Indeed, in newspapers which did not use headlines, the juxtaposition of paragraphs of news was bewildering. On 2 January the *Morning Post* reported, 'Before the King of Sweden left Stockholm [for Russia] he gave orders to arm eight ships of the line and several frigates; a measure supposed to have the Armed Neutrality in view. Denmark is also preparing armaments.' And, on the same page: 'The female fashions are every day encroaching on the male costume. The ladies now wear the Pizarro Hat in addition to boots and buckles.'

The *Morning Post* did not neglect to report Sir Hyde Parker's wedding. He had married Miss Onslow on 23 December, and on 2 January the newspaper commented, 'Sir Hyde Parker's *honeymoon* is to last *three weeks* – we should not be surprised if it appeared but *a day*,' adding on 5 January, 'Sir Hyde Parker is just *eleven years* older than his father-in-law, Admiral Onslow'.

The *Post* had good informants in the Admiralty because Sir Hyde had written to his new Commander-in-Chief, St Vincent, the day after his wedding, and the Earl had replied on 31 December from his flagship, the *Ville de Paris*, in Torbay. Having forwarded to the Admiralty Sir Hyde's request for leave until 20 January, 'their Lordships have in reply been pleased to authorize me to grant you the said leave accordingly'. St Vincent's private thoughts can be imagined, bearing in mind his comments when he suggested to Lord Spencer that Sir Hyde might relieve him for a few weeks and was told that Sir Hyde was not well.

[1] Complete with twelve glass slides on which were painted 'sixty grotesque figures', the prices ranged from 12s. 6d. to a very large size at twelve guineas.

The Press, and thus the people, was well informed – not by correspondents well placed in the capitals of Europe but because it had good sources of news inside the Government itself and, perhaps more important, because influential people gossiped. Nor was there any form of voluntary or compulsory censorship to prevent the publication of secret information of use to the enemy. Politicians, admirals and generals made their plans and sent off their orders marked 'Secret' – and then all too often discussed them at dinner or in the drawing room after joining the ladies. It was almost impossible to launch a large-scale operation secretly against the enemy, so that surprise, the essential element of any attack, was almost always missing. The only thing that saved many expeditions from disaster was the fact that although the enemy had learned of British intentions, he had no chance – because of the blockade or the difficulties of transport – to make proper dispositions. Fortunately for Britain, the despatches reaching Lord Grenville from people like Drummond and Lord Carysfort show that other nations conducted their business in a similar way.

The *Morning Post* reported on 5 January: 'From the armaments carrying on in the Danish and Swedish ports, and the probability of a rupture with the Northern League, it is daily expected that orders will be issued for capturing the vessels of those nations.' This should have been a clear warning to any prudent master of a Danish or Swedish merchant ship in a British port to sail at once, whether or not his cargo was loaded or unloaded.

On the same day *The Times* reported:

The public will learn with great satisfaction that Lord Nelson is about to be employed on a SECRET EXPEDITION, and will hoist his flag in the course of a very few days. His instructions will not be opened until he arrives in a certain latitude. We shall only permit ourselves to observe that there is reason to believe his destination is to a distant quarter, where his Lordship's personal appearance alone would preponderate over the influence or the intrigues of any Court in Europe.

The prospect of the seizure of ships mentioned in the *Morning Post* and Nelson's forthcoming appearance somewhere in Europe ('influence and intrigues' mentioned in *The Times* pointed to the Baltic) could hardly have been lost on three men in London: Count de Wedel Jarlsberg, the Danish Envoy Extraordinary, who lived in Wimpole Street; Baron von Ehrensward, Sweden's Envoy Extraordinary and Minister Plenipotentiary, whose home was near by; and Baron de Jacobi Klvest, who represented Prussia. (Russia and Britain had earlier withdrawn their respective envoys.)

Having decided the Baltic was Nelson's obvious destination a naïve envoy might have been puzzled by *The Times* next day:

Vice Admiral Lord Nelson will hoist his flag in a few days for the supposed purpose of proceeding with a squadron to the Dardanelles, to chastise the insolence of the Russians in that quarter, should the amicable expedient had recourse to by His Majesty for adjusting the existing difference not be attended with the desired success.

However, it is unlikely these three envoys, all experienced men, were puzzled by the report. Three simple questions – what effect could Nelson have on the Czar by appearing at the Dardanelles? Why send him there when the Baltic offered a better place for 'chastizing'? Since Admiral Lord Keith was already in the Mediterranean, why not send him to the Dardanelles? – would have brought answers showing the report was probably a clumsy attempt by the British Government, following the Press revelations, to mislead the Northern League.

On 8 January the *Morning Post* was recording that 'Lord Nelson expects to leave Town tomorrow to hoist his flag at Portsmouth', while *The Times* added to the mystery by reporting on the 10th, 'Lord Keith is certainly coming home. It is believed Lord Nelson will have a detachment from the Mediterranean Fleet placed under his command.' Then on the 13th the same newspaper noted: 'Yesterday Lord Nelson took his leave of the Lords of the Admiralty, and this morning his Lordship will positively leave Town to hoist his flag. We have reason to know his destination is NOT the Baltic.'

Two days later the *Morning Post* reported, 'Sir Hyde Parker has not asked leave of absence from his fair bride. Before he leaves Town, he intends giving a *grand ball*.' But *The Times* on that same Thursday said

Lord Nelson left Town on Tuesday morning for Plymouth, and will proceed immediately to the Mediterranean, from whence Lord Keith has been recalled. . . . We have already observed that a particular expedition would be entrusted to Lord Nelson, the object of which would not transpire for a considerable period of time. We are led to believe his Lordship will visit Constantinople, where his presence cannot fail to be useful in confirming the British influence at that Court. Nor can the appearance of a British Fleet in the Dardanelles be without its effect upon that power of the Baltic whose ambitions extend to Byzantium.

The reference to Lord Keith, the Commander-in-Chief, being recalled would certainly have added a little to the confusion in the foreign envoys' minds; but again they must have realized that Lord Keith's reputation, backed by a few ships of the line, would be sufficient to rattle the bars along the Dardanelles and alarm the Russians: it was not a job that required Nelson, who would obviously be better employed in the Baltic.[1]

Up to 15 January the newspapers were reporting conjecture or stories given them by the Government deliberately to mislead, but the next day put an end to speculation.

The Admiralty, although gathering intelligence and making certain preparations, had been limited by the fact that forming a squadron or fleet meant using ships already serving in the Channel Fleet under Lord St Vincent and blockading Brest, or refitting in Plymouth, Portsmouth and the Medway to reinforce distant fleets in the Mediterranean, and the East and West Indies. Until the Government decided what to do and when, the Admiralty had to back and fill, refitting ships already in the dockyards but delaying the recall of those at sea.

The intelligence reports already passed to the Admiralty and filed included Drummond's note of 20 December, and the next relating to Denmark, early in January, said: 'Scarcely fifteen sail of the line can be fitted out, although eighteen may be put in a condition to defend the Sound. All the frigates and small vessels are supposed to be in a state of readiness.'

That was all that the Admiralty knew by mid-January, but it was enough: the original strength of the Danish Fleet was known, and many of the ships had been laid up and out of commission for a long time.

Among the first orders to British ships was one dated 19 December concerning the *St George*, a line of battle ship. The very short-barrelled cannon with a large bore, which fired either round or grape shot for a short range but with enormous destructive power, was at last being accepted by even the most conservative of captains. Called the 'carronade' – it was made by the Carron Company of Scotland, from whose foundry came a considerable amount of ordinary cast iron wares – it was made in various sizes. The Board of Admiralty, whose duties were in effect to operate the Navy, wrote to the Navy Board, who were charged with maintaining the ships and provisioning them, that: 'Judging it proper that His Majesty's ship *St George* at Spithead should be supplied with carronades of 32 pounders [sic] for her quarterdeck in lieu of the long 12-pounder guns at present on board her', the Board 'desire you will cause the said 32 pounder carronades to be supplied'.

As usual there was a promotion of flag officers on New Year's Day and Nelson, eleventh in seniority of the fifteen rear-admirals of the red, was promoted over the heads of several others to be a vice-admiral of

---

[1] Since Nelson was still a very junior admiral it is worth noting, in view of what was to follow, that the Press took it as a matter of course that the mere mention of his name was enough to alarm, if not terrorize, an enemy.

the blue. Apart from the one Admiral of the Fleet, there were now seventy-five admirals senior to him and nearly fifty junior.

The news of his promotion was sent to Nelson in the stylized but graceful way used for many years by the Admiralty. Dated 'Admiralty Office, 1st January 1801' the letter was signed by Evan Nepean, the extremely competent and influential Secretary to the Board (his salary was £4,000 a year, compared with £3,000 for the First Lord and £1,000 each for the members of the Board) and said:

His Majesty having been pleased to order a Promotion of Flag Officers of His Fleet; and my Lords Commissioners of the Admiralty having in pursuance thereof signed a commission appointing your Lordship Vice Admiral of the Blue, I have the honor [sic] to acquaint you therewith. . . .[1]

On the 9th, the First Lord and three other members of the Board met in the graceful and impressive Board Room at the Admiralty, and Mr Nepean made notes of their decisions in his 'Rough Copy' of the Board Minutes, which were later neatly entered in the Minute Book as:

Vice Adm[l] Lord Nelson – to proceed to Plymouth and hoist his flag on board the *St Joseph*.

Captain Hardy – *St Joseph*, Plymouth, to put himself under the command of Vice Adm[l] Lord Nelson.

The Board Minute was, of course, officially recording a decision made some time earlier and passed privately to Nelson by Spencer. The ship had been undergoing repairs for several months at Plymouth but his other St Vincent prize, the *San Nicolas*, was reduced to being a prison ship at Plymouth.

Spencer had proved very thoughtful in giving Nelson the *San Josef*, since he had last boarded her sword in hand. As early as 28 November he had written to St Vincent: 'Your Lordship has no doubt heard from Lord Nelson since his arrival in this country; it gave me very great satisfaction to find that he had no sooner set his feet in it than he applied in the most pressing manner for service; and expressed the strongest wish to serve under your Lordship's command.' Spencer sent Captain Hardy down to the *Namur* to 'get acquainted with that ship's company preparatory to their being turned over to the *San Josef*, which ship I consider (unless you had yourself wished for her) to be Nelson's peculiar right'. But Spencer was careful to add that he had told Nelson 'that if his services should be required in a smaller ship he will of course not think himself ill-treated by being removed into one'.

[1] A few days later Lord Grenville wrote to the Board: 'I have it in command from His Majesty to inform you that the King of the Two Sicilies having solicited His Majesty's consent to allow Rear Admiral Lord Nelson to accept of the Title of Duke of Bronté, with the Fief of the Duchy annexed thereto, for himself and his heirs, His Majesty has been graciously pleased to grant his consent.'

10
'FOOLS AND MADMEN'

Count Bernstorff's reply to Britain's categoric demand for an answer whether or not Denmark was joining in a Confederacy was dated 31 December and was not received in London until 13 January.

Six days after sending off Bernstorff's note, Drummond was again reporting on another meeting he had with the Count after hearing unofficially that the Convention had been signed in St Petersburg on 16 December.

Count Bernstorff began by confirming that Russia, Prussia, Sweden and Denmark had signed the Convention, Drummond wrote, and 'appeared very anxious to know in what light this measure would be construed' by Britain. Drummond said he could not speak officially but 'would venture to assure him that the principles of the treaty were such as England had [never] admitted, and certainly never would admit while she continued to consult either her dignity or her interest'.

Bernstorff said he was very far from supposing Britain would acknowledge the pretensions of neutral powers, but 'hoped that [the] joint declaration would not be productive of any more serious consequences [than] those which had followed the Convention of 1780'.

Drummond was quick to make the obvious answer, getting at the very crux of the whole matter, by telling Bernstorff that 'the circumstances of the times rendered the present alliance of the Northern Powers infinitely more hostile to England than that which had before taken place', and reminding him that when Denmark joined the Alliance of 1780 his father, the late Count Bernstorff, had expressly declared that Denmark's chief object was

to protect the Danish commerce from the violence of the Spaniards, who were then principally accused of infringing the rights of neutral nations.

But that now when England, of all nations of Europe engaged in war, might be considered rather as the sole, than as the chief maritime power, it seemed to me against her alone that the present confederacy had been formed.

Drummond was careful to tell Bernstorff these were his private views. A few minutes later Bernstorff began a discussion which led Drummond to report to Lord Grenville: 'I believe this Minister to be a man of probity, desirous of preserving peace, and one of the very few in this country sincerely attached to the ancient system of law and government in Europe.'

Bernstorff told Drummond that he had seen 'with the deepest regret the progress of the misunderstanding between Great Britain and Russia. Nothing was more contrary to the wishes of his Court, as nothing could be more contrary to the interests of Denmark, than a serious rupture between those two powerful nations.' Not only did Denmark wish to adhere faithfully to its engagements with Britain but, with Russia, 'equally desired to find the means of reconciliation with [the Court] of London'.

Drummond admitted that he was prompted to ask for more explicit details, 'but in the present situation of affairs I judged it better not to appear too solicitous about the friendship of Russia'. Continuing his despatch in cipher, Drummond reported: 'It is evident . . . that this Court is under the greatest dread and embarrassment, and already repents of its rash appeal to Russia last Autumn. The differences which were said lately to have existed in this Cabinet begin now to be more generally spoken of.' (The appeal to Russia followed Lord Whitworth's mission to Copenhagen.)

He went on to say that Fenwick, referred to in an earlier despatch as having been held up by bad weather, had reported from Elsinore that two French privateers, the *Marengo* and the *Chasseur*, were cruising off the coast of Norway and had taken two British prizes into the port of Tannanger [sic: Stavangar] while a third privateer, the *Voltigeur*, had captured a British merchantman on voyage from London to Riga and taken her into Christiansund.

As these were 'direct infringements of a treaty, lately established with Denmark, I mean tomorrow morning to make a strong remonstrance upon the subject to Count Bernstorff'. But Drummond was also a man of action, as the next paragraph showed. 'In the meantime I have given directions to Captain Sotheron [of the *Latona* frigate] who is still detained at Elsinor, to go in pursuit of these vessels as soon as the wind will permit him.'

Then, just before he sealed the despatch, he wrote a postscript saying he had just learned from Bernstorff that although the Convention followed that of 1780, 'there were some modifications'. He had tried to discover what they were and, although unable to vouch for the accuracy of his information, understood the new Convention stated that no treaty now existing between a neutral and a belligerent power should be broken, and that the contracting parties agreed not to enter into any new treaty 'without the signatories of the Convention being advised'.

This one despatch has been quoted at length because it emphasizes first the quandary in which Denmark found herself when Russia applied pressure and, second, the factor which Bernstorff seems not to have realized or was forced to ignore: that the new Convention, unlike its predecessor of 1780, could only be aimed at Britain and thus could only aid Napoleon.

Gathering speed like some great avalanche, events and reactions now began overtaking the despatches being carried between Copenhagen and London. Because of the frost and contrary winds delaying the messenger, Drummond's letter of 3 January and Bernstorff's reply on whether or not Denmark was involved in negotiations, had not left the city before Grenville was writing again to Drummond.

Dated 2 January, the Foreign Secretary warned Drummond that the Czar's seizure of British ships in Russian ports and his subsequent un-justifiable treatment of their crews and British subjects living in St Petersburg 'give but too much reason to believe that these hostile measures on the part of his Imperial Majesty must immediately lead to an open state of war between the two countries'.

'If this should happen,' Grenville wrote emphatically, 'it will be absolutely necessary that His Majesty's Government should be distinctly and immediately informed of the part which it is the intention of the Court of Denmark to take in this new contest.' Drummond was to write an official letter to Bernstorff 'to the effect of what I have here stated in order that the King's Government may receive in writing the sentiments of the Danish Government on a point so essentially affecting the interests of Great Britain, and the tranquillity of Northern Europe'.

Dundas, the Secretary of State for War, wrote to Grenville that from what the Prime Minister had told him the night before, 'there seems little doubt we shall soon order the Ministers of Denmark and Sweden to leave the country'. And at once Dundas's mind had turned to the Caribbean – 'I am making arrangements for the capture of Danish settlements in the West Indies'.

In Parliament a few weeks later – in a debate on the Government's handling of the war – he revealed the childish reasoning behind his sugar and spice islands strategy.

As Britain depended entirely on commerce and navigation for her existence, he said, the most important object was maritime. Trade depended on distant and colonial commerce, so cutting off an enemy's colonies was as important as cutting off an army's communications. Hence, he declared, in any war an enemy's colonial possessions should be the first objective of British forces, except for 'those needed to furnish security at home'. These captured colonies would provide markets for British manufacturers who had lost their markets in Continental Europe, he said.

No one pointed out the total population of the West Indian islands; no one pointed out that the West Indies took only a seventh of Britain's exports. And Dundas completely ignored the one vital strategic task in the Caribbean: destroying the effectiveness of enemy bases. It was of supreme importance that the French and Spanish Fleets should have no refuge on the western side of the Atlantic; no bases from which to harry the British islands.

The tragedy was that Dundas genuinely believed these forays in search of sugar and spice were substantial assaults against the enemy; part of a grand strategy which he and Pitt discussed, all too often in their cups, late into the night. Although poking at shadows, he convinced himself he was dealing body blows. But every soldier who died of an abominable disease while garrisoning islands captured at Dundas's behest was as dead as if he had been shot by Napoleon.

The Santo Domingo expedition of 1794, another of Dundas's ideas, is a typical example. Large and mountainous, it was of no naval, military or commercial value to Britain – or her enemies, particularly since Jamaica covered the whole area. Yet 11,000 troops died there that year, along with forty-six masters of transport ships.[1] The *Hannibal* lost two hundred men from sickness in six months (compared with fiifty-seven dead in the *Victory*, which suffered worst among the British ships at Trafalgar, where the total British casualties were 449 dead).

A week later, Drummond reported to Grenville that Bernstorff was anxious to know how Britain would view the Convention. He wrote again on 14 January, this time very hurriedly with a postscript saying 'Count Bernstorff has ordered the Post to be delayed for me', and confirmed 'to a certain extent' his previous reference to the extra articles in the Convention, the most important being that no existing treaties should be affected, so that 'all goods declared to be contraband by former treaties will continue to be so considered'.

---

[1] This story was repeated down the islands: at St Lucia in May 1796, the 31st Foot comprised 776 men, but seven months later only fifteen were still alive. In nine months of the next year the 57th lost fifteen officers and 605 men. In the year ending April 1796, sickness killed 6,480 of the 15,881 white troops in the West Indies, and in the next year 3,760 died out of 11,500. By comparison the total losses at the Battle of Waterloo were 6,932 killed, wounded and missing – a few more than yellow fever killed in a year.

Because of the delays in delivering despatches, it must be emphasized that none of these recent reports by Drummond had yet been received in London. However, on the day Drummond wrote this last despatch, Mr Fenwick finally arrived in London with Drummond's despatch and Bernstorff's written reply to Britain's demand for a 'frank and satisfactory explanation' of any obligations Denmark had contracted. But events were moving fast, and Grenville's earlier warning to Drummond – that open war was likely with Russia – still had not arrived in Copenhagen.

As soon as Fenwick delivered the diplomatic bag there was the usual ritual of breaking the seals and calling Edward Willes, the Decipherer of Letters, to write in the words above the three- and four-figure groups.

Drummond began by explaining the delay: he had sent Fenwick by sea because the heavy frosts meant 'it would have been in vain for him to have attempted going any other way', but no sooner had Fenwick left Copenhagen to board the ship than the wind changed. After that, Drummond wrote in cipher, and as soon as Willes filled in the words above the figures Lord Grenville read:

> Your Lordship will have
> 209   2227   1913   241
> seen that the Danish Ministry has
> at length avowed its intention
> 3365   3357   345   1417   3269
> with respect to the Armed Neutrality,
> 2368   3874   345   779   132
> I believe however I can safely
> 1447   1662   1447   1924   3755
> assure your Lordship that (there?)
> 1353   2076   1377   266   2498
> prevailed upon this subject
> 345   2695   4175   3315   1070
> considerable difference of opinion
> in the cabinet. Count Bernstorff
> 631   39   132   3749   2253
> does not even affect to conceal
> 529   2360   1268   2201   3356
> his alarm and inquietude.

As Grenville then went on to read Bernstorff's reply, given on page 75, there was no mistaking Denmark's intentions. It all boiled down to one thing: the right of a belligerent to search neutral vessels to make sure they were not carrying contraband, a right that had for centuries been exercised by all nations which had the power, was now denied by Denmark, Sweden, Russia and Prussia. . . . Any such attempt would be an attempt against their sovereign rights.

Although Grenville had been waiting for Bernstorff's reply to his second letter asking what Denmark's policy would be if Britain and Russia went to war, he saw that this one, although only answering his first referring to negotiations, was also an answer to the second. There was now no doubt what Denmark's policy would have to be, whether she wished it or not, if 'an open state of war' broke out between Britain and Russia.

So it was Bernstorff's letter, written on New Year's Eve and arriving in London two weeks later, that decided the British Government. Up to 13 January it was taking the more obvious precautions described earlier; but immediately after Fenwick arrived in Downing Street on that day with the delayed despatches, there was decisive action.

Grenville provides an example. In the morning, before Fenwick's arrival, he had written to Carysfort telling him to 'learn as accurately as possible' how the Prussian Court viewed the Convention – whether, in other words, Prussia was to be a passive ally of the Czar or an active enemy of Britain. Then, as soon as he received Bernstorff's reply, Grenville showed it to Pitt, who immediately called a cabinet meeting which discussed it at length, decided on Britain's policy, and called a meeting of the Privy Council for the next day.

Grenville's second letter to Carysfort tells the story. He wrote that because of the reply just received from Denmark, the Government had decided 'to recommend to His Majesty that such measures should forthwith be taken against the commerce and colonies of Denmark and Sweden' as were necessary to weaken their alliance with 'a power so decidedly hostile to His Majesty's interest as Russia has shown herself to be'.

In a private letter written from Cleveland Row that night, Grenville said that in his despatches:

I have there explained the past, the present and the future. But I fear the result will be that we shall meet much sooner than we foresaw when you left this country. It is in vain to reason with such fools and madmen, but really their want of all common sense does provoke one beyond all patience.

If you can persuade them [Prussia] that they have not agreed to act against us, and that they can do no better than sit still and enrich themselves by the profits of that neutrality which Denmark has made so abundant an harvest, you will do a fine thing. But I have no very great hopes that they will have even as much sense.

The Cabinet had drawn up a Proclamation which was placed before the Privy Council and the King signed it. The Councillors dispersed and the ministers returned to their offices to despatch written orders whose destinations ranged from other ministries a few yards from Whitehall to naval and army officers serving across the Atlantic.

The 'prime mover' was the Duke of Portland, the Secretary of State for the Home Department. A circular letter marked 'Secret' and addressed to 'The Governors of All His Majesty's Possessions in the Mediterranean, North America, Cape of Good Hope, St Helena, East Indies, West Indies', and written from Downing Street, said:

In the present state of affairs between this country and the Powers of Russia, Denmark and Sweden, His Majesty has judged it expedient that all Ships of War or vessels of any description belonging to those Powers . . . which are at present arrived, or which may arrive within the limits of your Government should be prevented from putting to sea until further orders, or if an opportunity should offer that they should be sent as ships detained in virtue of this order, to the ports of this country under a proper convoy.

Sending a copy to the Admiralty next day, Dundas told Their Lordships that they were to order all captains 'to detain and bring into the nearest port belonging to His Majesty' all ships belonging to Russia, Denmark and Sweden 'which they may meet with at sea'.

Lord Grenville had the task of warning his envoys. Drummond was sent a brief message in cipher saying, 'There being reason to apprehend that measures may immediately be adopted in Denmark for laying an embargo on British property there, you are immediately . . . to destroy all your ciphers and secret papers.' He could give to anyone he thought it would be of use 'such notice of this danger as you may be able to convey to them'.[1]

One of the King's Messengers, Nathaniel Vick, was waiting to leave London to catch the packet for Hamburgh, from where he would travel overland with these instructions, but at the last moment he was told he would be leaving next day, Friday, a hold-up which was to have grave consequences.

On the Thursday Grenville had given written warning of the embargo to the Danish and Swedish Ambassadors in London. De Wedel Jarlsberg promptly sent a messenger to Copenhagen to warn his Government – a journey which could be done overland in ten days.

Vick had been delayed because the British Government appears to have decided at the last moment either to give Denmark one more chance, or to justify the embargo. 'The accompanying despatch,' Grenville told Drummond, 'is written for the purpose of being read by you to

---

[1] Drummond's reply had a twentieth-century ring about it – '. . . I have destroyed all my secret letters; but, from the apparent omission of a cipher, I was thrown into some perplexity. Imagining, however, that your Lordship apprehended the forcible seizure of the archives I caused all the ciphers . . . to be burnt.'

Count Bernstorff', and he could give him a copy or the substance of it in a note.

Bernstorff's reply, the despatch said, went beyond the impressions already gained in London from various sources. Grenville pointed out that it was 'in a very high degree offensive', that considering the circumstances in which the *Freya* discussions had ended, Denmark should start negotiations for a convention 'with the other Northern powers' without notifying Britain.

The next point Grenville made was even more important: Britain would have even more cause to resent this conduct if it was based on an intention to revive the 1780 Convention, the terms of which had since been formally disavowed in treaties by some of the contracting parties 'and in practice abandoned by all'.

The whole situation 'is greatly aggravated indeed', he added, when Britain is told 'not only that this exploded system is again to be revived', but in the same form as in 1780 – '*sous leur forme primitive*' and imposed as law on nations 'which may not be disposed to sacrifice their rights and interests'.

This meant the King had to decide immediately whether to submit to this or 'adopt such measures as may be most effective to repel the aggression of this hostile confederacy'. There could be no doubt about the choice, Grenville wrote, and the Danish Minister in London had been told of the embargo. Bernstorff was asked to tell the Danish Government that the King intended to take all other measures necessary to put him in a position 'to resist the efforts of that hostile league which it now appears has been preparing against him ever since that period when the most unequivocal proof was given by him [i.e. the *Freya* episode] of his moderation and of his desire to avoid proceeding to extremities injurious to the interests of Denmark'.

The reference to 'all other measures' was no idle threat: orders for the capture of the Danish and Swedish islands in the West Indies were drawn up for Lt-general Thomas Trigge and Rear-admiral Duckworth, both of whom were in Martinique.

Dundas told Trigge that immediately he received the orders he was, with the admiral, 'to make every necessary preparation for proceeding in His Majesty's name to seize . . . the islands of St Thomas, St Croix and St John, and the Swedish island of St Bartholomew, together with all ships, stores or public property of any description, belonging to Russia, Denmark or Sweden, which may be found on the said islands'.

The first reaction to the embargo came from the Swedish Minister in London, Baron von Ehrensward, who expressed his King's astonish ment. As the dispute between Russia and Britain related to Malta, and the declaration of the Danish Court related to the Convention of 1780, the Baron said he could see no reason why Sweden – which had given Britain no cause for complaint and from whom no other declaration was required than that required in the Note of 31 December (asking for an explanation of Sweden's action in signing the Convention) – 'should be attacked in so hostile a manner before any answer has been given to the insinuations contained in that Note. . . .'

Formally protesting against the embargo, he demanded 'in the most forcible and expressive terms' that it should be lifted because continuing it 'can no other wise be considered than as a designed and premeditated declaration of war on the part of England'.

On the morning the Baron's protest was being delivered to Grenville in Downing Street, the *Morning Post* reported: 'Dover, January 15th. After receiving the orders on the 14th, ten Danish and/or Swedish ships were detained in this port.'

However, delivery of the Baron's protest was all that happened of any significance since it was a Saturday, and the English weekend had been sufficiently long established for the Northern Convention to be safe from any further moves at least until Monday.

From Berlin, Carysfort wrote in a private letter to Grenville:

I still think this Court will get out of the scrape if it can. Haugwitz persists in saying nothing is concluded and that, if there is war between us and Russia, the neutral league falls to the ground. . . . I know not whether the bad news from Austria will oblige you to lower your tone; I rather expect it will have a contrary effect, and I am sure if we temporise now, this Armed Neutrality will come upon us [again] in the summer with double force. . . . Everybody here, and private accounts from Petersburg confirm it, is of opinion that whoever will give a subsidy will have the Swede. The Dane, I trust, you will make sure of by other means. . . .

It is interesting – and significant – to compare the attitudes of informed men like Grenville, Carysfort and Drummond, all advocating the strongest possible action against the grave threat to Britain, with the clamour of peace at any price by certain people in London and referred to earlier.

The Marquis of Buckingham, a man of much influence, writing from the quietude of Stowe, told Grenville the day after hearing Bernstorff's reply:

Even in the midst of the tremendous difficulties of our French contest, I rejoice that the question avowed by the Northern Coalition comes so distinctly to issue. . . . All depends on a vigorous Baltic blow, and I trust you will not wait for the thaw before you strike where the ice certainly does not impede you. Denmark will pay the piper; but I wish I could see the prospect of shaking the Bear by the beard. . . .

The Marquis was not disappointed, and the naval activities of the preceding weeks show that although Sir Hyde Parker was occupied with his new bride, the Admiralty's plans were to shorten his honeymoon.

11

'THE CHAMPION OF ENGLAND'

Finding new employment for Nelson had not at first been an easy task for Lord Spencer who, better than most men, understood his temperament, potential and shortcomings. Before Christmas it seemed he would have no chance of using the old political trick of delaying in the hope that something would turn up because, whatever else Nelson had done since he was in London, he had not stopped badgering the Board for a new appointment.

To begin with there had been only one possibility for Spencer to consider. Since Lord St Vincent had been asking for a spell of rest and the newly-married Sir Hyde was showing no concern to get back to sea, sending Nelson to the Channel Fleet not only put him under St Vincent's command, but meant the old Admiral could go on leave knowing Nelson was quite competent to take the Fleet to sea if the French tried to quit Brest.

Since writing to St Vincent to this effect, he later had to consider the Mediterranean: Lord Keith was asking to be relieved, and few people knew the Mediterranean better than Nelson. So, in his talks with Nelson, Spencer had mentioned these two possibilities.

Before anything had been finally decided, however, the first real intelligence began coming in about the Czar's plans for the Armed Neutrality, and as soon as it became obvious that the Baltic was likely to be the next troubled sea, Spencer ruled out the Mediterranean for Nelson, deciding to send him to the Channel Fleet, where he would be near at hand if action had to be taken against the Northern Powers. At the same time, he began sounding out Nelson's views on a naval attack against the Danes since plans had to be made for every possible situation the Navy might meet. This attack would be aimed at securing the Sound, a geographical bottleneck which apparently controlled the whole Baltic.[1] At this time Nelson had more experience of combined land and sea operations than any other officer in the King's service; indeed, his wounds were visible evidence of successes and failures and lessons learned since he had lost the sight of an eye at the siege of Calvi and an arm at the abortive boat attack on Santa Cruz.

Spencer told Nelson it had been suggested that a squadron sent against the Danes should carry a large number of troops who would be landed at Copenhagen to capture the Royal Arsenal and to occupy the city itself, and also storm and capture the fortress at Elsinore (which is, of course, Cronborg Castle, and perhaps more famous for its association with Hamlet than as the guardian of the Sound).

Nelson was frank in giving his opinions – he had spent many anxious weeks and months at various times trying to persuade generals to use both initiative and troops for particular emergencies that the unpredictability of war often threw up without warning – the most recent occasion being the capture of Malta. He had also seen well-planned operations fail because clashing personalities led to Army and Navy officers refusing to co-operate with each other.

So he told Spencer that the main problem, if a large number of troops were carried, would be finding a general competent to command them and at the same time able and willing to work closely with the Navy. The First Lord agreed completely, no doubt remembering letters he had written to the touchy Sir Hyde Parker, among others, trying to smooth over complaints about generals.[2]

Spencer then hinted that Sir Hyde Parker was one of the admirals being considered 'for the chief command' in the event of a Baltic campaign; he also broadly hinted that there would be an important role for Nelson. In the meantime, as described earlier, he would fly his flag on board the *San Josef*.

As far as his private life was concerned, the first few weeks of the New Year were the most turbulent of Nelson's life. The year had begun with his promotion, and for a man who sought publicly-acclaimed honour and glory with the same single-minded fervour that ambitious and hard-headed businessmen seek hard cash, at the age of forty-one he might have felt a certain satisfaction with his progress so far. But his marriage – other than the outward legal bond – had only a few days to run.

---

[1] This was the accepted view at the time but one which had never in recent decades been put to the test, and certainly from his subsequent actions it is not likely that Nelson agreed with it.

[2] Parker had accused Generals Simcoe and Forbes of 'gross and dishonourable deception' and subsequently complained of Brig-gen. Sir Thomas Maitland, Maj-gen. Thomas Nesbitt and Brig-gen. Spencer.

To a man whose vanity was a bottomless bucket, with Lady Hamilton and a host of hangers-on pouring in fluent and adoring flattery, the attentions of Lady Nelson, although loving, must have seemed cloying. It was a time when, probably subconsciously, he reflected that at the height of the celebration of his victory at the Nile – when he had been created a peer, voted a pension of £2,000 a year, received the vote of thanks of both Houses of Parliament, £10,000 from the East India Company, a valuable silver cup from the Levant Company, the Dukedom of Bronté from the King of the Two Sicilies, jewels from the Sultan, the freedom of a dozen English cities, including London, and fame that made his name revered in Britain and feared in France – Lady Nelson's letters were mundane.

The fact was the young frigate captain serving unhappily in the West Indies should never have married the widowed Mrs Nisbet whom he met so soon after having fallen hopelessly in love with a married woman, the wife of the Commissioner at Antigua. Nevertheless the end came unexpectedly. Just before he left London to join the *San Josef* there were various matters to be dealt with before going to sea again, and Nelson invited his solicitor, William Haslewood, to breakfast.

Describing the scene many years later, Haslewood wrote that during he meal

. . . a cheerful conversation was passing on indifferent subjects, when Lord Nelson spoke of something which had been done or said by 'dear Lady Hamilton'; upon which Lady Nelson rose from her chair and exclaimed with much vehemence, 'I am sick of hearing of dear Lady Hamilton, and am resolved that you shall give up either her or me'.

Lord Nelson, with perfect calmness said: 'Take care, Fanny, what you say. I love you sincerely; but I cannot forget my obligations to Lady Hamilton, or speak of her otherwise than with affection and admiration'. Without one soothing word or gesture, but muttering something about her mind being made up, Lady Nelson left the room, and shortly after, drove from the house. They never lived together again.

Haslewood, as Nelson's solicitor, was hardly an unprejudiced observer and in recalling the scene many years later his memory was at fault at least to the extent of recording the breakfast as taking place in 'their lodgings in Arlington Street', whereas it was at the house Nelson had rented in Dover Street.

Nelson's immediate destination, following Lady Nelson's departure, was to the Hamiltons' new home, No. 23 Piccadilly, because as soon as they heard Nelson was now alone at Dover Street they invited him to stay.

On 7 January, after spending the previous day hunting deer on Ascot Heath, the King came up to St James's Palace from Windsor for his usual Wednesday *levée*, and among the five admirals present to kiss His Majesty's hand on promotion were Nelson and Sir Hyde Parker.

When Nelson received his written orders two days later he lost little time in packing: a note was sent round to the Duke of Queensbury cancelling 'a tour' the Duke had planned for Monday, and instead that day Nelson called at the Admiralty to take his leave of the Board. He had a high opinion of the effectiveness of carronades, and took the opportunity of asking the Board to order some to be fitted to his new flagship. The change in the Board's spelling from *St Joseph* to the original Spanish spelling, *San Josef*, was also probably due to Nelson's visit. Previously her name had been anglicized, although the *San Nicolas* and other Spanish prizes retained their original spelling.

On the same day *The Times*, in a report about Nelson, said: 'We have reason to know that his destination is NOT the Baltic.' After leaving the Admiralty Nelson said goodbye to Emma and Sir William and left for Plymouth, travelling with his brother William[1] and planning the journey so that he could call on various people on the way. The first stop was at Southampton, where they stayed the night and Nelson wrote his wife a letter which shows that they could not have parted with as much bitterness as Haslewood's description implied.

'My dear Fanny,' he wrote, 'We arrived and heartily tired, so tell Mrs [William] Nelson, and with kindest regards to my father and all the family. Believe me your affectionate Nelson.'

Next day they set off for Dorchester and, just before the coach arrived, William had a shock. As Nelson wrote to Emma, 'Anxiety for friends left, and various workings of my imagination, gave me one of those severe pains of the heart that all the windows were obliged to be put down, the carriage stopped, and the perspiration was so strong that I never was wetter, and yet dead with cold.'[2] And he told Captain Hardy when he eventually arrived at Plymouth, 'he thought he would have died in the carriage'.

After spending the night at Axminster the Nelson brothers set out for Torbay, where the Admiral was to call on Lord St Vincent. The Commander-in-Chief of the Channel Fleet had the Admiralty's per-

---

[1] A grasping clergyman who was, at Nelson's death at Trafalgar, to be created an earl as a mark of the King's belated gratitude to the admiral, and given a pension of £5,000 a year and £110,000 to buy an estate by Parliament.

[2] From the Baltic on 28 April Nelson wrote to Troubridge, 'Last night's attack almost did me up, and I can hardly tell you how I feel today . . . Whatever has again brought on my old complaint I cannot tell; the two last [attacks] I had was going down to Plymouth with my brother, and a little one in Yarmouth Roads.'

mission to live on shore for the worst of the winter, since he could make his headquarters at Torre Abbey, a large mansion above Torbay owned by a cousin, and from where he could look down and see his ships at anchor.

But first Nelson had a particular call to make at Honiton; one which reveals a thoughtfulness for other people which makes some of his other relationships even more puzzling. Captain George Westcott had commanded the 74-gun *Majestic* at the Battle of the Nile, and was killed by a musket shot from *L'Heureux*. But amid the welter of honours that Nelson had recently received – with more to follow: West Country cities such as Plymouth were still waiting to bestow their freedoms on him – he did not forget Westcott's family.

At Honiton, then, Nelson sought out the family and found Westcott's mother. She was the widow of a baker and 'except from the bounty of the country and Lloyds,[1] in very poor circumstances,' he wrote. 'The brother is a tailor, but had they been chimney sweeps, it was my duty to show them respect.'

He remembered to make sure that Mrs Westcott had the gold medal presented to all the Nile captains by Alexander Davison. When the old lady said she had not received it Nelson promptly took off his own – the medal was worn round the neck on a blue ribbon – and gave it to her, saying: 'You will not value it less because Nelson has worn it.'

Nelson's next stop was at Exeter, seventeen miles along the old Roman road. Two miles from the boundary, *The Times* reported, he was met by troops of cavalry who escorted his carriage into the city. As soon as they arrived in the crowded High Street amid the cheers of hundreds of people, 'the populace took the horses from the carriage and drew him to his hotel escorted by the Volunteer Corps in the City, with colours and bands'.

At the hotel the Admiral was met by the Mayor and Corporation, 'who requested him to come to the Guildhall'. Nelson donned his various orders and medals and, with the bands playing, walked with the Mayor to the Guildhall, where he received the Freedom of the City 'in an oak box'.

After breakfast with the Mayor he left at once in his carriage for Torre Abbey, less than twenty miles away. When he arrived there, tired from Exeter's reception and naturally still in full uniform, he was anxious about the prospect of meeting St Vincent since their respective

[1] The Committee of Lloyds granted pensions to certain dependants, as well as presenting swords for distinguished conduct. The 'bounty of the country' was equally meagre for dependent relatives after the First and Second World Wars, and administered to the disabled with a callousness so remarkable that occasionally even Parliament noticed it.

prize agents were in dispute over prize money, lawyers had been called in, and a court case seemed likely.

Describing the visit to Evan Nepean, St Vincent wrote:

Nelson was very low when he first came here . . . appeared and acted as if he had done me an injury, and felt apprehension that I was acquainted with it. Poor man. He is devoured with vanity, weakness, and folly; was strung with ribbons, medals etc., and yet pretended that he wished to avoid the honour and ceremonies he everywhere met with upon the road.

Once again St Vincent's ambivalent attitude towards Nelson manifests itself. In past years he had recognized Nelson's brilliance as a young captain; had helped him in his career; at Cape St Vincent had won a battle because of Nelson that would otherwise have been inconclusive; and had given Nelson the command which led to the victory at the Nile. Yet Nelson had more than justified all this, so it ill became him – in a letter he was able to sign 'St Vincent' instead of plain 'John Jervis' because of the earldom Nelson's brilliance had won him – to sneer at Nelson's 'ribbons and medals &c.', particularly without mentioning that they were worn following the Exeter ceremony three hours earlier. Most were worn for his own acts of bravery, in contrast to St Vincent's earldom for which the old man knew he had to thank Nelson.

However, Nelson was happily unaware of what his host and Commander-in-Chief was going to write, and enjoyed his brief stay. Soon after he arrived the post brought a letter to St Vincent from Sir Hyde Parker announcing Parker's appointment to command a squadron in the North Sea, and saying that Nelson would most likely be serving under him, probably in the *Windsor Castle*.

This left Nelson free to tell his old chief in confidence of the recent conversations with Lord Spencer about his future. St Vincent was told that, next to getting the Mediterranean command 'which I was a candidate for', Nelson would like to have served under him. But from what Lord Spencer had told him just before he left London, 'it is almost certain I shall go to the Baltic'.

Nelson later told Spencer that St Vincent 'was very handsome to me, and hoped that by a temporary absence of a few months I should not lose my *San Josef*, the finest ship in the world. . . .'[1] The Earl reckoned the *Formidable* would be 'the ship fittest for me, for real and active service', but he was scathing about the *Windsor Castle*, trying to persuade Nelson not to go in her because 'she was such a leewardly ship that he knew she would break my heart'.

---

[1] But, being a first-rate ship of 112 guns, reckoned too large for the shallow waters of the Cattegat.

Having discussed ships, the two men then talked of the Baltic, speculating on the Czar's final intentions. Neither doubted what Denmark's role would have to be nor her fate if Britain had to go to war with Russia and, Nelson wrote, the conversation 'naturally enlarged on the best means of destroying the Danes'.

St Vincent, perhaps surprisingly, was 'clearly of the opinion that 10,000 troops ought to be debarked to get at the Danish Arsenal'. Nelson told him that his proposal had already been made to Lord Spencer, 'but the difficulty was, where to find such a general as was fit for the service, to which he, of course, was forced to acquiesce; but General Simcoe seemed the only man....' Since both Nelson and St Vincent obviously ruled him out reluctantly, they must have known of Sir Hyde Parker's violent accusations against him in the West Indies.

The proclamation putting an embargo on all ships of the North Confederation was read on the day St Vincent and Nelson had their meeting, and *The Times*, reporting Nelson's departure from London, said that he 'will proceed immediately to the Mediterranean, from whence Lord Keith has been recalled'.

Letters from Lady Nelson arrived just as he was leaving for Plymouth, and he replied the same day. Although we do not know what Lady Nelson wrote, the letters were obviously not unfriendly because Nelson, dating his letter '5 o'clock, January 16', answered:

My Dear Fanny, This moment of the post's departure we arrived [in Plymouth]. Your letters I received this morning at Tor [sic] Abbey for which I thank you. I have only time to say God bless you and my dear Father and believe me, your affectionate Nelson.

On board the *San Josef*, which was in the Dockyard, Nelson sat down next morning, Saturday, 17 January, and wrote to the Secretary of the Admiralty, reporting in the time-honoured phrase that 'I have this day hoisted my flag on board His Majesty's ship *San Josef*, in obedience to their [Lordships'] order of the 9th inst'. Without a break he continued:

I have to request that their Lordships will not consider my necessary coming from Italy as a dereliction of the Service, but only as a remove from the Mediterranean to the Channel Fleet, and that consequently they will be pleas'd to give directions for my receiving full pay up to the present day.

(Nepean replied that his request 'could not be complied with'.)

A letter from St Vincent giving further views on the Baltic situation arrived just as Nelson was writing to the First Lord describing their conversation at Torre Abbey, and Nelson decided to enclose it with his own. A postscript showed he was far from pleased with the progress of the Dockyard.

The *San Josef*, as far as relates to Captain Hardy, is ready for sea, but the Dockyard have not done with her. My cabin is not yet finished, of course – not even painted; but that I do not care about: I shall live in Captain Hardy's. My wish is to get her to Torbay, and, in seven days alongside the *Ville de Paris* [St Vincent's flagship].

Nelson spent Sunday and Monday (the Queen's Birthday) in a state of ill-concealed rage over the Dockyard's tardiness in refitting the *San Josef* and over the way his personal possessions had either been left behind in London, badly packed, or broken on their way to Plymouth.

Plymouth and the rest of the country celebrated the Birthday with guns firing salutes and the new Union Flag flying from church towers and public buildings. At St James's Palace the Queen heard a birthday ode by the Poet Laureate lauding 'Albion and Erin's kindred race', and everyone admired the new crimson velvet canopy and throne which had been put up in the Great Council Chamber, the new 'Royal Arms of the Union being beautifully embroidered and decorated with diamonds'.

On Tuesday Nelson, who dealt with administrative work with the same promptness as his Commander-in-Chief, wrote to St Vincent,

May this day, my dear Lord, which I am told is your birthday, come round as often as life is comfortable, and may your days be comfortable for many, many years. Almost my only ungratified wish is, to see you alongside the French Admiral, and myself supporting you in the *San Josef*. We may be beat, but I am confident the world will believe we could not help it.

He went on to describe how 'the people in the [Dockyard] did not believe that I wished to get to sea till the winter was worn more away, and now all are bustle. . . . My cabin was finished yesterday. . . .' He mentioned that Hardy had not yet received Admiralty orders to complete the ship, nor were there any orders concerning her movements – she was still under Admiralty orders, not attached to a particular fleet.

Nelson was equally exasperated with his wife.

My dear Fanny, All my things are now breaking open for only one key can be found [he began without any preamble]. My steward says I have no one thing for comfort come [from London] but a load of useless articles from Burgess's and a large chest of green tea. I have been buying a few things just to make me *un*comfortable for in fact I have nothing usefull but two chairs. £100 I have paid for carriage, £20 would have bought me more than I could want from Mr Burgess. I know not where I shall be in a week, with my kindest regards to my father and Mrs Nelson, I am your affectionate Nelson.

By the next day, when more packing cases had been opened, Nelson wrote again:

Half my wardrobe is left behind and that butler, a French rascal, ought to be hanged, and I hope you will never lay out a farthing with Mr Burgess. Had the waste of money been laid out in Wedgewood's ware, knives, forks for servants or cooking utensils it would have been well, but I am forced to buy every thing, even a little *tea* for who would open a large chest? In short I find myself without any thing comfortable or convenient. In glasses of some kind the steward tells me he finds a useless quantity of decanters, as yet not one can be found, and if he cannot find them today I must buy. In short [he added in a typically Nelsonian burst of impatience] I only regret that I desired any person to order things for me. I could have done all in ten minutes and for a 10th part of the expense, but never mind I can eat off a yellow ware plate. It is now too late to send half my wardrobe, as I know not what is to become of me, nor do I care.

Two weeks later, when he received a reply from an aggrieved Lady Nelson, he wrote again giving enough detail to justify his wrath.

It was never my intention to find [fault] but the fact is I have nothing and every thing. If I want a piece of pickle it must be put in a saucer, if a piece of butter on an earthen plate. . . . The stands for the decanters I thought was to have been repaired and sent me [;] if they are not I shall desire Hancock to send me two. Not one thing that Mr Dods sent but is ruined, large nails drove through the mahogany table and drawers to fasten the packing cases. If they had been sent so to a gentleman's house and new, of course they would have been returned. Mr D has sent only 3 keys, of a small table and chest of drawers, not of the wardrobe, trunk, case of the Turkey Cup[1] &c., &c. By the by the trident of Neptune is bent double from ill package. I have six silver bottle stands but not one decanter to fit them, you told me six of the house ones should be sent. . . .

Since at this time Nelson was preoccupied with Baltic strategy and the tactics of any battles there, the refit of the *San Josef*, the constant claims on his patronage and purse by relatives, friends and friends of friends, and the fact that any day Lady Hamilton was expecting the birth of the child they had conceived on board the *Foudroyant* the previous year, most people will understand his irritation even though not everyone can forgive some of the reasons.

In the meantime, on Thursday, 22 January, he gave orders to Hardy that the *San Josef* was to move from the Hamoaze to Cawsand Bay. The last time he had been in the *San Josef* when she was under way was St Valentine's Day four years earlier, when he boarded her from the

---

[1] A silver cup presented to him by the Levant Company in commemoration of the Nile, and now in the National Maritime Museum, Greenwich.

Captain, sword in hand, amid the smoke and flame of the Battle of St Vincent. That the comparatively undistinguished commodore of those days was now a famous fighting admiral must have occurred to Nelson, and writing later in the day to the Secretary of the Admiralty asking him to 'acquaint their Lordships that I directed the *San Josef* to come from the Hamoze [sic] to this bay this morning', he added that 'I may truly congratulate their Lordships on the apparent good qualities of this noble ship'.

But with shipwrights, joiners and painters swarming through the cabins it was easier for a one-armed admiral to live on shore for the time being, and he went to join his brother William at an hotel.

To add to his physical discomfort, it snowed heavily the next day and his single eye began to show symptons of another attack of ophthalmia. Fortunately Cuthbert Collingwood, an old friend and former fellow captain, now a rear-admiral (and destined to be Nelson's second-in-command at Trafalgar), was flying his flag on board the 98-gun *Barfleur*, and they had dinner together and exchanged news, Nelson telling him of the King's behaviour in snubbing him at a *levée*.

Collingwood, who was expecting his wife Sarah to arrive any minute from Cumberland bringing their young daughter with her, was presiding at a court martial at two o'clock in the afternoon on Tuesday, 27 January, when from the Admiralty 'I received an express to go to sea immediately with all the ships that were ready'.

The reason for the departure of Collingwood and the small squadron was that the French squadron under Admiral Ganteaume had escaped the British blockade off Brest on 23 January by sailing in a strong gale and without being seen.

Nelson promptly wrote to Lord Spencer:

It is this moment reported and very generally believed that 14 sail of the line are got out of Brest. If this proves true consider me as ready and wishing to follow them; if they are bound to Egypt, by no means improbable if that force is actually sailed, I should hope they might be overtaken by a good sailing squadron, 8 or 10 sail of the line with *San Josef* at their head. . . . If they are gone either to the East or West Indies or not unlikely to take the Brazils, I am equally ready to follow them. . . .

Two days later, when there was still no word that Ganteaume's squadron had been sighted, he wrote to St Vincent: 'If you believe these damned French ships are escaped let me offer myself a willing candidate to follow.' Spencer refused the offer, noting however that it 'does you great credit'. So Nelson, left fretting in Plymouth and anxious to get away, had little to console him. No orders came from the Admiralty to man the *San Josef*, and his interest in her was waning now he knew he would (unless sent after Ganteaume) soon be hoisting his flag in another ship.

A few days earlier Spencer, replying to his long letter describing the conversation with St Vincent about the Baltic campaign, reassured him that 'it is by no means in contemplation for you to be put into the *Windsor Castle*, which was only mentioned cursorily one day in conversation with Sir Hyde as being one of the three-deckers which draws the least water. . . . As to troops, you know the objections in the way, and they certainly appear to be insurmountable.'

The last sentence is a curious commentary on the way operations sometimes had to be planned. Had a suitable general been available the British assault on the Danes would probably have been a major landing by 10,000 troops, with the Royal Navy's role secondary once the troops had been landed. But the one general competent to command the troops, Simcoe, had fallen foul of the admiral who was to command the British squadron. (A sudden landing on the low-lying coast immediately north or south of Copenhagen by such a force would, as this narrative will show later, have stood a very good chance of complete success.)

The Times reported on Saturday, 24 January,

Yesterday arrived the mail from Hamburgh. . . . All the intelligence brought by it breathes the language of war and preparation in the Baltic. From the tone and tenor of the answer of the Court of Copenhagen to the categorical memorial of Mr Drummond, there is no longer any room for hope from negotiation and adjustment. . . . Mr Drummond is probably on his way home.

While reading this item, which gave Nelson the latest and only news of the situation for some time, he would have seen another in the same issue which said that the new engraving of Nelson by Stow, 'which is considered so excellent a likeness' was now published by Mr Brydon of Charing Cross.

On Monday *The Times* was able to reveal that 'We are led to believe that Lord Nelson's destination has been changed. His Lordship is about to hoist his flag on board the *St Joseph* in the Channel Fleet, on which service he will continue till the opening of the Baltic, and act as second to Sir Hyde Parker. Lord Nelson will sail from Plymouth on Tuesday next.'[1]

The postal system in Britain at this time was remarkably good and cheap, the charge being proportional to the distance. A letter from London to Plymouth took two days, comparing favourably with about

---

[1] He had in fact hoisted his flag ten days earlier. The Board's orders, which he had not received at this time, were for him to sail on Wednesday.

the same time, using computers and trains, in the latter half of the twentieth century. Foreign mail to places like the West Indies was considerably faster than present-day surface mail. But although safe enough – apart from the occasional highwayman – the post was not secure from prying eyes and, in particular, no government was above having the mail watched and letters secretly opened.[1]

This was the reason for a subterfuge Nelson and Lady Hamilton now adopted. Their child was due to be born any day, and to allow them to write freely they had invented a young couple, Mr and Mrs Thompson, expectant parents whom they had befriended. Mr Thompson was supposedly with Nelson, and Mrs Thompson in London. They could, by writing on behalf of one or other, disguise from prying eyes the fact they were referring to themselves and their child. (Both were careless enough to call the name 'Thompson' or 'Thomson'.)

If you'll believe me [Nelson wrote in the first letter mentioning the fictitious characters] nothing can give me so much pleasure as your truly kind and friendly letters, and where friendship is of so strong a cast as ours, it is no easy matter to shake it – mine is as fixed as Mount Etna, and as warm in the inside as that mountain. . . .

Let her [Lady Nelson] go to Briton [sic: Brighton] or where she pleases, I care not; she is a great fool and, thank God, you are not the least bit like her.

I delivered poor Mrs Thompson's note; her friend is truly thankful for her kindness and your goodness. . . . Poor man! he is very anxious, and begs you will, if she is not able, write a line just to comfort him. He appears to me to feel very much her situation: he is so agitated, and will be so for 2 or 3 days, that he says he cannot write, and that I must send his kind love. . . .[2] What dreadful weather we have got: a deep snow. I wish I was just setting off for Bronté. I should then be happy.

Next day, 26 January, he wrote wistfully, 'When I consider that this day nine months [ago] was your birthday, and that, although we had a gale of wind, yet I was happy and sung "Come cheer up Fair Emma' ".[3]

But as if the prospect of a Baltic campaign, a ruined marriage, the first warnings of an attack of ophthalmia in his single eye, and the imminent birth of his child were not enough, he now had the depthless pain of jealousy beginning to jab him by day and by night.

'I own I wonder that Sir William should have a wish for the Prince of Wales to come under your roof; no good can come of it, but every harm,' he wrote. Nor was his judgment of the Prince's morals harsh; even in a

---

[1] Examples are given in the author's *At 12 Mr Byng was Shot*, London and Philadelphia, 1962, pp. 246-9.

[2] The agitation for the next two or three days was real enough: the baby was born within a day or two of Lady Hamilton receiving the letter.

[3] The first line of one of Miss Knight's poems.

century when it was accepted that each heir to the throne was gross in taste, behaviour and morals, the Prince's behaviour made *Honi Soit Qui Mal y Pense* seem a defiant excuse rather than a proud challenge.

You are too beautiful not to have enemies, [Nelson continued] and even one visit will stamp you as his *chere amie*, and we know he is dotingly fond of such women as yourself, and is without one [trace?] of honour in those respects, and would leave you to bewail your folly. But, my dear friend, I know you too well not to be convinced that you cannot be seduced by any prince in Europe. You are, in my opinion, the pattern of perfection. . . .

After grumbling he had received no orders from the Admiralty he declared:

I feel no loss in not going to these balls and assemblies. My thoughts are very differently engaged. I know nothing of my destination more than I did when in London, but the papers and reports of my being put in a bad ship which, although I can hardly credit, fills me with sorrow, which, joined to my private feelings, makes me this day ready to burst every moment into tears.

But even as Nelson lamented he had received no orders, they were being prepared and on Thursday, 29 January, he wrote to the Admiralty acknowledging them. Sent on Monday, they directed him to put himself under the command of Lord St Vincent – but, as he wrote crossly to Emma, 'as no order is arrived to man the ship, it must be Friday night or Saturday before she can sail for Torbay'. More irritating, though, was the knowledge that Emma's letters had been going to Brixham for the past few days, in anticipation of the *San Josef*'s arrival there.

But he had other troubles, too.

My eye is very bad [he told Emma in the same letter]. I have had the Physician of the Fleet [Dr Trotter] to examine me. He has directed me not to write (and yet I am forced this day to write to Lord Spencer, St Vincent, Davison about my lawsuit, Troubridge, Mr Locker &c., but you are the only female I write to), not to eat anything but the most simple food; not to touch wine or porter; to sit in a dark room; to have green eye shades for my eyes – (will you, my dear friend, make me one or two? – nobody else shall) – and to bathe them in cold water every hour. I fear it is the writing has brought on this complaint. My eye is like blood; and the film so extended that I only see from the corner farthest from my nose. What a fuss about my complaints! . . . I have this moment seen Mrs Thompson's friend. Poor fellow! he seems very uneasy and melancholy. . . .

At two o'clock that afternoon, soon after he finished writing the letter, orders came from St Vincent that as soon as the *San Josef* was 'in all respects ready for sea' he was to proceed to Torbay.

One of the people Nelson did meet in Plymouth was General Simcoe and, with the Baltic now the staple topic of conversation, Nelson had to listen to the general expounding with obvious knowledge and competence on the defences of Zealand (the island on which Copenhagen stands) and the fortifications of Copenhagen itself, without being able to reveal how closely Simcoe had come to being involved.

Nelson had written to Davison four days earlier because, as he wrote:

There are nonsensical reports here that you are going to buy a fine house for me. I do not believe Lady Nelson can have desired any such thing, for where am I to get the money, and if I had ever so much I should not think of a house at this time. The best thing for Lady N . . . is good lodgings, next to that to hire a very small ready-furnished house.

Saying the *San Josef* would soon be at Torbay he added he hoped he would see Davison there – 'I have a spare bed and plenty of room in the *San Josef*'.

Apparently commenting on some item of gossip Davison passed on, Nelson wrote, 'The Lady of the Admiralty [Lady Spencer] never had any just cause for being cool to me, either as a public or private [person]. I wish nothing undone which I have done.'

A long postscript showed that honours could be costly.

Pray tell Sir Isaac Heard [Garter King of Arms] that I cannot afford to pay for any honours conferred upon me; they are intended and do honour to this country, and to mark the gratitude of His Sicilian Majesty to his faithful ally our Gracious King in my person, his faithful servant. As far as relates to the personal trouble of Sir Isaac or any other friend I am not baward [sic: backward] in payment by thanks or money as the case requires, and for personal trouble I have already paid £41 and have had no answer relative to the Imperial Order of the Crescent, Sir Isaac is bound in honour to follow up this application for my wish is to have all my honours Gazetted together, but paying those fees to Secretaries of State, Earl Marshall [the Duke of Norfolk] &c., and without which I am told the *King's order* will not be obey'd it would in my opinion be very wrong in the[m] to do it. I could say more on this subject but I think I'd better not at present.[1]

The *San Josef* finally left Cawsand on 31 January, arriving at Torbay next morning at eight o'clock. Nelson reported at once to Lord St

[1] Nelson clearly had little idea how affairs were managed at Court, or why such posts as Heard's were so eagerly sought. The 'benefits' from fees and commissions were considerably in excess of the salary; indeed, they were so great that the salary was often nominal and the posts were a form of patronage dispensed by the Government or the King. A variation was for a senior civil servant in London to hold other appointments overseas, paying a deputy a nominal sum to do the work. Evan Nepean, for instance, the Board Secretary, augmented his salary of £4,000 a year by holding extra appointments such as Clerk of the Court at Jamaica, as well as being Member of Parliament for Queenborough, an 'Admiralty seat'.

Vincent at Torre Abbey, where he found fresh orders. It took two hours for his barge to pull back to the *San Josef* in a fresh breeze, and he was hoisted on board to find a letter awaiting him: he was the father of a baby girl.

I believe poor dear Mrs Thomson's friend will go mad with joy. He cries, prays and performs all tricks, yet dare not show all or any of his feelings, but he has only me to consult with [he wrote to Emma]. He swears he will drink your health this day in a bumper, and damn me if I don't join him in spite of all the doctors in Europe, for none regard you with truer affection than myself. . . . I cannot write, I am so agitated by this young man at my elbow. I believe he is foolish; he does nothing but rave about you and her. I own I participate of his joy and cannot write anything.

When the *San Josef* arrived that morning in Torbay, he told Emma, 'I found an order to hoist my flag in the *St George*, as Lord Spencer says I must go forth as the Champion of England in the North. . . . I trust I shall soon be at Portsmouth, and every endeavour of mine shall be used to come to town for three days. . . .'

Apart from the orders and letters already mentioned, the Admiralty's activities concerning the forthcoming Baltic expedition were, for the rest of January, comparatively few: final decisions had yet to be made by the Government. In the meantime it was a case of getting ready to get ready, and the routine work of keeping scores of ships at sea, in the East and West Indies, Cape of Good Hope and Indian Ocean, the Mediterranean, Atlantic and the Channel continued, and the orders sent out ranged from routine promotions and replacements to one noted in the Board Minutes on 22 January:

Circular letter to Commanders-in-Chief informing them that as there is reason to believe that the enemy have possession of both the private and public signals, it is judged proper to make an alteration in them, send to each admiral a sufficient number of copies of the private signals to distribute to the flag officers and captains.

Then, on 27 January (the day after *The Times* had reported Sir Hyde Parker was to command a Baltic squadron with Lord Nelson as his second-in-command), there was a spurt of activity at the Admiralty when a Board meeting was held, attended by Lords Spencer and Arden, and Admirals Gambier and Young. The minutes recorded: 'Admiral St Vincent [sic] not to employ any of the ships [listed] in the margin on service beyond Brest, as they may be wanted on a service which may require their suddenly being recalled into port. . . .' The ships, intended to form the backbone of Parker's squadron, were the

London, St George, Courageux, Russell, Warrior, Defiance, Saturn, Edgar, and *Bellona*.

The Board also took steps to ensure Parker's squadron could bombard the fortress of Elsinore and the Arsenal of Copenhagen and land detachments of troops: 'Navy Board to bring forward the bombs[1] which require repair at Sheerness as well as the fireships. . . . Navy Board to inform us what number of flat [bottom] boats there are at any of the ports.'

Next day *The Times* printed a short item of news from Elsinore. 'A [semaphore] telegraph has been already erected on one of the towers of Kronburg [Cronborg castle], to carry on a correspondence along the coasts as far as Gillelige [Gilleleje] on one side and Copenhagen on the other. The works at Kronburg are carried on every day with great activity and zeal for the purpose of putting the fortress in the best state of defence.' This telegraph is shown in illustration no. 16.

The *Morning Post*'s contribution to information about Sir Hyde Parker comprised two ribald items. The first, on the 28th, said: 'Sir Hyde Parker's appointment to a command in the North Sea has converted his *honeymoon* into a sort of *ague*; a complaint always attended with a sudden transition from a *hot* to a *cold* fit.' The other, on the 31st, noted: 'Should the gallant Admiral who late entered the Temple of Hymen be sent to sea again, he will leave his *sheet anchor* behind him.'

One of the reasons for the apparent tardiness of the Admiralty's preparations was reported by *The Times* on Monday, 2 February: 'Mr Ross, the messenger, who has been expected for some days past from Copenhagen, had not arrived yesterday. . . . His despatches [from Drummond] are looked for with great impatience.'

---

[1] Small vessels, usually ketch-rigged in a way that the bombs fired by the large mortars they carried did not foul the rigging. Most of them were appropriately named after volcanoes.

12

THE SWORD AND
THE OLIVE

While Nelson had been harrying the Dockyard to speed the commissioning of the *San Josef*, and Sir Hyde and Lady Parker continued their prolonged honeymoon, the British Government, in the last week of January and much of February, continued to watch for any change of heart in Denmark but only too conscious that, for once, time was an enemy of Britain and an ally of the Czar.

Until the end of March at the earliest – if past years were anything to go on – the Russian Fleet would be frozen in at its Baltic bases of Cronstadt and Revel, and Sweden and Denmark would probably present no great problem to the Navy. But once the thaw set in and they could join the Russian Fleet (many of whose officers were British-trained) the Northern Confederation could send a powerful combined force to cover the Baltic, Cattegat and Skagerrak.

If Britain had to destroy the three navies, then it would be easier for them to be dealt with one at a time, starting with Denmark, so that no enemy ships remained to cut the Fleet's communications with the United Kingdom.

The naval bases were Copenhagen for the Danes, Carlskrona for the Swedes, and Revel and Cronstadt for the Russians. The prevailing westerly winds could carry a British fleet from Copenhagen to Carlskrona, and then to Revel and Cronstadt (which was the main base), and because ice usually cleared at Revel a week before Cronstadt, it was vital that the Danes and Swedes were dealt with as soon as possible to allow the British to be waiting off Revel and Cronstadt for the last of the ice to thaw.

So at this stage the climate governed Britain's naval strategy and planning for the Baltic. Yet the one thing that was to delay the British Government at the very time when speedy decisions were needed everywhere if the Fleet was to arrive before the Danes had time to strengthen their fortifications and the ice freed the Russians, was not indecision over what to do, nor the fear of an enemy nation, but Ireland. . . .

The Act of Union, which became law on 1 January, had brought in Ireland, and Pitt had promised Catholic emancipation, which he considered vital to complete the Union. But George III, of sound German Protestant stock, great perseverance but little imagination, would not consider it. Whether right or wrong, his reason was genuine: in his opinion he would be violating his Coronation Oath by granting emancipation to the Catholics. Pitt's pressure on the King mounted throughout January; but as his pressure increased, so did the King's determination that he would have nothing of emancipation.

While despatches and instructions were sent back and forth between Downing Street and British envoys in Northern Europe, Drummond reported to Lord Grenville on 20 January that 'an extraordinary occurrence has happened here . . . which has given birth to many conjectures, and which may very probably have most important consequences'. A courier had arrived in Copenhagen from Russia with instructions for the Chevalier Lizakewitz, and as a result the whole Russian diplomatic mission was to quit Denmark. Drummond had also heard a report – which he believed – that the Danish Minister in Russia, de Rosencrantz, had already left St Petersburg to return home.

Drummond, admitting frankly that he had no idea what crisis had caused it all, said that on the few facts he knew 'it would be vain to pretend to reason with confidence', adding

. . . the facts themselves are, indeed, sufficiently wonderful. The Emperor of Russia had scarcely signed that famous alliance . . . when he drives the Minister of one of the Allied powers from his Court, and recalls his own. A luminous proof of the wisdom, consistency and unanimity of those coalesced Sovereigns who were to throw new lights upon the general laws [of] Europe, and who with the sword in one hand and the olive in the other, were to set examples to the world of justice and moderation.

It was generally pretended in Copenhagen that there was nothing more to the affair than 'a sudden dislike which his Imperial Majesty had taken to M. de Rosencrantz', but 'the character of M. de Rosencrantz is commonly esteemed and, if I be not mistaken, he originally went to Russia in compliance with the request of that Prince. . . .'

There could be other reasons, Drummond wrote. Some Danes blamed it on Denmark's refusal to back the Czar's claim to Malta, and her display of independence had angered him.

Lord Grenville would have heard from Stockholm of the Swedish

King's return from St Petersburg, and the Swedish Ambassador in Copenhagen

... assured me the object of his Majesty's journey to St Petersburg was to prevent the Emperor, if possible, from carrying things to too great a length with England. The Swedish and the Danes, phlegmatic as they are, feel very sensibly the danger of provoking a war which might be alike fatal to their commerce, their finances and their maritime powers.

Two days later Drummond was reporting that the hurried departure of Chevalier Lizakewitz was still the main topic of conversation in Copenhagen. A letter from St Petersburg said only that the Czar 'did not choose an intriguing minister such as M. de Rosencrantz to remain at his Court, and that Lizakewitz should retire to Germany until he received further orders'. In the meantime the Danish Government, 'extremely alarmed at the intelligence, has dispatched General Lowendal to St Petersburg with the ratification of the Convention for an Armed Neutrality'.

But Drummond had kept the bad news for the closing paragraphs of his despatch: 'I have very good reason to think that a proposal for an alliance between Russia and Holland has been made on the part of the Republic,[1] and has been acceded to by the Emperor'.

Meanwhile Grenville was sending further information to his brother-in-law, Lord Carysfort: 'Before this messenger can reach your Lordship, it is probable that steps will actually have been taken ... for the occupation of the island of Heligoland, as affording the means of material protection to the commerce of [British] subjects.'

A rocky island in the south-eastern corner of the North Sea near the mouths of the rivers Elbe and Weser, Heligoland has had a great fascination for British politicians in the last century and a half.[2]

Henry Dundas, fresh from his plans for the Danish and Swedish islands in the West Indies, was the instigator of this wild scheme. It is impossible to guess quite what object he had in mind, but up to then his schemes had been responsible for causing more British casualties than the French, and he was soon to be made a viscount (but ironically later impeached for peculation and acquitted on a technicality).

Fortunately for Britain the Helder Expedition to Holland, another costly scheme of Dundas's, was still fresh in people's minds and led to a

---

[1] The puppet government set up in Holland by Napoleon, who had renamed the country the Batavian Republic.
[2] In the First World War, after the completion of the Kiel Canal, which debouches into the Elbe, its apparent strategic value was that it lay athwart the German High Seas Fleet's route to the North Sea, but its value was greater on a chart than in reality because it would have been impossible to maintain.

more detailed study of the Heligoland proposal than might otherwise have been the case, and it was subsequently dropped. However, the blame should not fall entirely on Dundas. He was an energetic man brimming with ideas, and dangerous only because he was always backed by Pitt, who could have over-ridden him, but rarely did. Pitt chose to ignore his naval and military advisers – as he had a right to, and such advisers are frequently too conservative – but all too often it did not require a knowledge of naval or military strategy or tactics to know Dundas's schemes (often discussed when both men looked at them in the rosy reflection of a decanter of port) were utterly wrong. In the case of Den Helder, the decision not to allow an army of 40,000 to be landed in October for a winter campaign across the waterlogged fens and polders of Holland would have required no more knowledge than that possessed by an East Anglian poacher, who knew the difficulties of crossing a flooded dyke holding a brace of dead duck and a gun.

On 27 January Grenville wrote to Drummond what was in effect a recapitulation of Britain's attitude to the Northern Confederation, and for that reason it is worth examining in some detail. If it was true – as Count Bernstorff had stated – that the Danish Government was far from supposing Britain would accept 'the exploded pretensions' of the 1780 Convention, Grenville asked, 'what purpose but that of provoking war' can be ascribed to the renewing of a confederacy binding Denmark with other nations 'to use force against Great Britain in support of those very pretensions'?

Drummond was correct in pointing out that in 1780 the Northern Confederacy was 'ostensibly at least' directed against all the belligerents, whereas now 'the rights of the British Empire alone can at this moment be injured by such an aggression'.

Grenville pointed out that in 1780 Count Bernstorff's father kept Britain informed during the negotiations, while now his own son adopted the opposite course – 'observing a profound silence' on the whole thing. The father had resisted every step that might draw Denmark into an attack on 'a natural ally'.

As for the modifications now said to have been made in the latest Declaration 'to render it less offensive than that of 1780', Grenville said, this was contradicted by Bernstorff's statement that 'the engagements of 1780 and 1781 are to be re-established *sous leur forme primitive*'. Furthermore there was not one article of those two conventions which was not now directly at variance with subsequent treaties between Britain and Denmark.

It would be in vain for the British Government to attempt to reconcile those glaring contradictions; nor could it delay taking all necessary measures for the country's security.

His Majesty must therefore persist in measures which he considers as necessary under such circumstances for the safety of his people, left as His Majesty is to contend alone with France and looking for one of his principal means of defence in that very naval strength the destruction of which was in 1780, and is now, the object of these confederacies.

But the King did not want to prevent any nation offering explanations which gave him security against 'these insidious and hostile measures' made by other countries at 'every period of real or supposed embarrassment or danger to his Empire'.

Lord Grenville had, in one phrase, summed up the situation – 'left as His Majesty is to contend alone with France' and facing a threat by so-called neutral nations to his Navy, which was the main weapon at this time with which he could fight France. It was all so obvious, yet was so often ignored by neutral nations; indeed it is surprising Grenville had to restate it when France had already occupied much of Europe, attacked Egypt and the Levant, and Napoleon's only aim could be to dominate the rest of the world.

On the day Grenville wrote to Drummond, the latter was reporting from Copenhagen about the Danish reception of the embargo. In a very revealing private note, Drummond wrote:

You will see . . . the unpleasant language which, in the heat of passion, Count Bernstorff applied to me in our conversation. . . . This has certainly affected me, inasmuch as I really had a great regard for him, and believe him to be a man of integrity. I have no doubt, indeed, when he reflects he will be sorry for what he has said. If I had answered him [in a like manner] the consequences may have been disagreeable. . . . I am afraid I have stated my conversation with Count Bernstorff indistinctly. Indeed, it is not easy to recollect the language of passion, which is never consistent.

Like so many of his countrymen before and after him, Drummond had a sincere love and respect for Denmark, and lamented, 'Your Lordship must be sensible how painful my situation is become, and how anxiously I look forward to the day of my recall.' A postscript added that 'Count Bernstorff took particular notice of that part of your Lordship's letter . . . where you announce His Majesty's intention to pursue all such other measures *et cetera*. He asked what other measures. I told him I had no further instructions upon the subject.'

In the accompanying despatches that the messenger Vick eventually delivered to Downing Street on 7 February, Drummond described how he set about telling Bernstorff officially of the embargo. The appointment was arranged for the next morning and, 'knowing the temper and character of that Minister, I was not sorry to let one day elapse before I waited upon him'.

The reason for this was that Drummond had lost that essential of warfare and diplomacy – surprise. Vick had been delayed in leaving London, and the Danish messenger had beaten him and delivered to Bernstorff a copy of Grenville's official Note to de Wedel Jarlsberg announcing the embargo.

When I waited upon [Count Bernstorff] this morning [Drummond wrote] I found him as I expected, extremely agitated and in a state of irritation, which only served to put me more upon my guard. He had completely given way to the natural heat of his temper, which upon such occasions never leaves him in complete possession of a very good understanding. Upon my entering the room, he asked me abruptly if I had come to take leave.[1] I answered in the negative. He then poured forth a very long, a very angry, and a very incoherent declaration against the conduct of His Majesty's Government in laying an embargo. . . . I found no difficulty in making an answer.

Drummond told him that Denmark could never have been ignorant of the way Britain would consider the Armed Neutrality and 'as far as I could take it upon myself without the special authority of my superiors, I have never failed to warn him of the danger of entering into such a confederacy'.

Bernstorff replied 'with increased acrimony' that his Court had been deceived; that it had taken only defensive measures. At the time Britain complained of the Russian embargo on British ships, she was doing the same to Denmark. Finally, Bernstorff accused Drummond of deceiving him 'with respect to the intentions of Great Britain'.

'Your Lordship will easily imagine,' Drummond declared, 'that this personal apostrophe had nearly made me forget all the lessons of prudence which I had been giving myself. Happily for me, however, the eloquence of Count Bernstorff suddenly took another channel. . . .' He began 'an elaborate defence' of Denmark's conduct during the winter, 'when they had sought by all the means in their power to avoid giving umbrage to Great Britain'.

In answer to this harangue, the main point Drummond combated was Bernstorff's comparison between the British and the Russian embargoes. Bernstorff retorted that it was true – the comparison was

---

[1] One of the preliminaries to a declaration of war was a request by an envoy for his passport, which was simply a document allowing him to pass the frontier safely.

unjust because the British measure had been more violent than the Russian. In denying this, Drummond said that he was 'infinitely surprised, when the severities committed by the Emperor against the English were known to the Count, that he should pretend to hold such language'.[1]

This led to some altercation and, to avoid prolonging it, Drummond read aloud Grenville's Note, later reporting that he suspected Bernstorff's want of temper was because the part Drummond believed he had taken in the Cabinet 'will now expose him to the censure of his enemies, and may even risk his political influence'.

Nevertheless, even though the Danish Government had joined the Russians despite Bernstorff's efforts, and the pro-Russian party at last prevailed in Copenhagen, 'Count Bernstorff cannot be justified for the language which he has this day held.'

The second of Drummond's despatches concerned de Rosencrantz, an episode where comedy was nudging tragedy and both were jostling farce. A member of the Danish mission who had just returned to Copenhagen told Drummond that the Czar was inspecting some troops,

... and called to him a major of the Army upon the parade, and desired him to inform M. de Rosencrantz that he was to quit the Court of St Petersburg.

The major, very much astonished at this order, humbly represented to the Emperor that being a person of no authority, it was possible that M. de Rosencrantz would not obey him. 'Tell him, then,' said the Emperor, 'that you have my commands.'

The major repaired to the house of M. de Rosencrantz and told him the Emperor desired him to quit his Court.

The Minister, no less astonished at receiving this order than the major in delivering it, replied that without some other authority he could not quit his residence at St Petersburg.

The next day a more formal notice from Count Rastopchin [the Imperial Chancellor and Director of Posts] put the matter beyond doubt.

The cause of the King of Sweden's departure was said to have been nearly as singular. The Emperor sent one of his orders [of chivalry] to the King for the young Prince, his son. The King desired that in the diploma granting the investiture the words heir to the *Crown of Denmark* should be inserted. His Imperial Majesty, upon hearing of his demand, withdrew his Guards who attended the person of the King of Sweden, and the relays of [carriage] horses which had been ordered for the use of the King upon the road were countermanded. His Swedish Majesty immediately quitted St Petersburg in incognito.

[1] The crews of more than 300 ships had, in the depth of winter, been marched through thick snow to prison camps in the interior.

In Berlin Lord Carysfort was carrying on a spirited correspondence and having a series of meetings with the Prussian Foreign Minister, Count de Haugwitz. Prussia's reaction to recent events was of outraged indignation; even for a Prussian lady she protested too much. Bearing in mind the actual text of the treaty the Northern Powers had signed, Prussia had obviously completely misjudged Britain's ability and willingness to react strongly. De Haugwitz now complained to Carysfort that his policy had been misunderstood, declaring that the Northern Powers had resolved that their decision should be candidly communicated to the belligerent powers 'to prove the purity of their views and motives', but England would not allow them time. Had she waited for this confidential communication, 'she might have avoided those intemperate measures which threaten to spread still wider the flames of war. . . .'

Within the week Carysfort was reporting that he found the Danish chargé d'affaires in Berlin 'much more coaxing and communicative; very desirous of establishing a distinction between the case of Russia, as with respect to us, and that of Sweden and Denmark' and very full of hopes that Denmark might be able to give Britain 'full satisfaction as to the innocence of the engagements she had taken before we should have proceeded to the last extremities'. Carysfort understood that the Danes were most anxious to have Britain 'fairly embroiled with Russia upon the affair of Malta, and the [Russian] embargo, so that, in conjunction with the other powers, it may enter into explanations with us that may prevent the rupture into which Russia would precipitate them all'. At the same time he learned that Denmark was at the moment embarrassed 'by something untoward in the state of its own particular politics with Russia.'

The King opened the new session of Parliament on 2 February, speaking from the Throne in the House of Lords. The old tapestry had just been cleaned and, surrounded with the dark panelling, was 'well calculated to give effect to the lights in the respective representations of the different views of the English and Spanish Fleets in the memorable defeat of the Spanish Armada'. The tapestry, wrote an observer, 'lends an air of sober dignity to the room, which is extremely commodious but, we fear, not the most happily calculated to render the human voice distinct and audible.'

However, the King's words were intended to be heard not in this overheated atmosphere but in distant lands. He said that:

the representations which I directed to be made to the Court of St Petersburg, in consequence of the outrages committed against the ships,

9 Copenhagen in Nelson's day. This map, drawn sixteen years before the Battle,
shows: A the ramparts encircling the city; B the Castellet; C the harbour entrance
and boom; D the warship harbour; E Nyeholm; F the Sixtus Battery; G the Quintus
Battery; H the Naval Arsenal; I Merchant ship harbour and wharves; J Gammelholm
K the Asiatic Company warehouse; L the West Gate; M Christiansborg Palace;
N Holmen; O Nyboder, the seamen's quarters; P Amalienborg Palace, the Crown
Prince's residence; Q Friderich's Hospital; R Toldboden, the Custom's House quay;
S the Naval Cemetery.

11 Trekroner Fort from the eastern corner. Anyone standing here during the Battle would have seen the *Elephanten* in line with the guns on the right and the frigate *Iris* beyond those on the left. His back would be towards Fisher's Defence Line and the *Holsteen* and *Indfœdsretten*, in action with the *Monarch* and *Defiance*, would be immediately behind him.

10 The Danish Government intended that three sea forts should protect Copenhagen and the final plan was completed on 8 June, 1784, providing for the building of Stubben (*left*), Trekroner and Provesteen (*right*). The plan was approved on 27 October, 1786 and work began on building Trekroner the following year. Long years of peace meant the work was not hurried and only Trekroner was completed by 1801 and the other two had not been started. Had Provesteen been completed, Nelson would never have attempted an attack from the south. The lines drawn perpendicular to the walls show the fields of fire, and each fort was to have a small battery built each side whose guns would prevent attacks at night by boats coming from seaward and getting too close for the guns of the forts to be depressed to hit them. The small fort of Lynetten, between the harbour entrance and Trekroner, had been built many years before the plan was made. The blockship *Provesteenen* was moored during the Battle within a few hundred yards of the Provesteen fort's intended position.

12 The Danish Crown Prince (later Frederick VI). Although he made the mistake of not appointing a naval commander-in-chief, he subsequently negotiated a generous peace treaty with the British.

OLFERT FISCHER

13 Commodore Olfert Fischer: his motley Defence Line bore the brunt of Nelson's attack.

property and persons of my subjects, have been treated with the utmost disrespect; and the proceedings of which I have complained have been aggravated by subsequent acts of injustice and violence. . . .

As for the Northern Confederation:

I have taken the earliest measures to repel the aggression of this hostile confederacy, and to support those measures which are necessary to the maintenance of our naval strength. . . .

The debate that followed was noisy. Earl Fitzwilliam did not agree with the Government's plans: he warned the House to be cautious in case they should consolidate into one body nations whose interests were various; those of Denmark and Sweden were perfectly distinct from that of Russia. Defending himself and his colleagues against attacks on the handling of the war, the First Lord of the Admiralty said that although the plans of the Government might not always succeed to the utmost of their wishes, he contended the war had added to the glory of their country, for at no one period had the Navy acquired greater conquests; and we were now, after eight years of war, 'able to bid defiance' not only to the Fleets of France, Spain and Holland, but even to a confederacy which had been unjustly entered into by the Northern Powers.

The House of Commons debated the address the same day. Mr Charles Grey, one of the Members for Northumberland, said that although Russia's conduct was 'highly unjustifiable', he did not think the question sufficiently clear for the House to pledge itself to support a new war. The consequence would be, he warned, that 'we shall give to France, as allies, the fleets of our new enemies. From Archangel to the Tagus, and from the Tagus to the Gulf of Venice, there will not be a single friendly port out of our own possessions where a British Fleet can take shelter. . . . Will it then be possible for our Navy, with all its skill, to stretch along such an extent of coast?'

The news from Europe, summarized in the *Gentlemen's Magazine* for February, would certainly have depressed even a sober Falstaff, at least in the section headed 'Foreign Round-Up'. The armistice in Italy had been signed at Treviso on the 16th and many fortresses were to surrender as 'the purchase of the suspension of hostilities'. A week earlier the peace treaty was signed between France and Austria at Lunéville.

Nearer home, Holland was making the most vigorous preparations for getting a fleet to sea under the command of Admiral de Winter, 'destined, some say, to cooperate with the Fleets of Russia, Sweden and

Denmark; or, according to other reports, to join the combined Spanish and French Fleets in Brest Harbour.'

The Empire of the Turks seemed tottering under the menace of the Emperor of Russia who, the magazine reported, with a fleet in the Dardanelles and an immense land force on the Turkish frontiers, 'has caused it to be hinted to the Divan [Selim III] that the Ottoman Court must not permit a landing in Egypt of the English force under Sir Ralph Abercromby which, if allowed, will be looked upon as an act of hostility on the part of the Turks'.

It was hardly news to cheer a Briton, whether he was a peer of the realm or a weaver's apprentice, particularly with a very stiff Budget due to be presented to Parliament within a few days; but at least Britain was no longer paying out millions of pounds in subsidies to try to keep her former allies in the field of battle.

It seemed for a few days as if the nation, now it stood alone, had gained both strength and confidence. But a few lines in *The Times* on Saturday, 7 February, recording two rumours which had spread rapidly through the City of London on Friday, first sent Consols plunging down and then up as people tried without success to guess their significance. The report said, quite simply:

A very extraordinary rumour got into circulation yesterday afternoon in the City – that Mr Pitt has resigned, and that a negotiation for peace was instantly to be renewed. We understand the Consols rose to 58 and upwards.

13

CHANGING THE
HELMSMAN

For more than a month, while Grenville wrote detailed instructions to
his envoys and received their equally detailed reports, and Spencer
began assembling the ships for the Baltic operation, Pitt had continued
arguing and cajoling the King over the question of Catholic emancipation, but the King had remained adamant.

Stated in its simplest and briefest form, Pitt's view was that the Irish
had agreed to the Union because Pitt had given them hope for Catholic
emancipation. With the Union proclaimed and the King refusing to
agree to emancipation, Pitt declared he had no choice but to resign.

However in politics it is unusual and frequently unwise to assume any
decision is reached in a straightforward way since the shortest distance
between two political objectives is often a devious path. Lady Malmesbury knew this well enough and gave a sprightly if not entirely accurate
account to Lord Minto, Nelson's old friend and the British Minister in
Vienna.

You will, of course, have received an official account of the event of the
day [she wrote]. I (of course) know no more than the public; and as I never
get an answer I never ask a question. However my Dominie [Lord Grenville]
was induced to own this morning that Pitt had resigned, though whilst it
was between 200 or 300 *friends only* he would not have mentioned it to me for
the world.

He says the Speaker [of the House of Commons, Henry Addington] is to
be the successor, and it is perfectly evident to my mind that the whole *is a
farce*, for it is impossible that Pitt's friend and creature should be his real
successor, or more than a stop-gap till matters are settled and he may come
in again.

It certainly must appear incomprehensible to any common understanding
that in such a business as the Union and during the year elapsed since [the
negotiations were] settled, all parties should not have come to a clear
explanation, especially on such a major point as the Emancipation of the

Catholics. It therefore, I own, strikes me in this light – that Pitt always intended to give it up.

The story appears to me in the style of the Arabian Nights [she added, in an apt simile]. You know every now and then a man puts himself in a rage with his wife and divorces her; then wants her again; but according to the Asiatic laws she must marry another man and be divorced from him before she can take back her first husband. So England is the Bride and Addington the *Hullah*. I trust he will play Pitt the same trick that one gentleman did in the book and refuse to give up the lady. No subaltern resigns but Canning.[1]

Grenville had been telling the truth: Addington had been invited by the King to form a new government – on the previous Thursday, the day before the rumour of Pitt's resignation spread. He was, as Lady Malmesbury expressed so succinctly, 'Pitt's friend and creature'. Pitt had been responsible for his election as Speaker in 1789, and in the following eleven years he had been all that a Speaker should be – detached and above party politics. This was not difficult for a man completely lacking any leadership and endowed with a personality dreary enough to make him unpopular.

The choice had fallen on Addington because one of the very few subjects about which he had decided views was Catholic emancipation; and being firmly opposed to it he was acceptable to the King. But before accepting the King's invitation to form a new government he had to sound out various men to see if they would serve under him, and he reported to the King on 9 February that his progress had, with one exception, 'nearly equalled his wishes'. However, 'the difficulty of supplying, in an adequate manner, the vacancy which unfortunately will take place at the Admiralty cannot but have impressed itself forcibly on your Majesty's mind'. Addington had finally decided that Lord St Vincent would be the man to fill the post 'most beneficially to the country at the present crisis', later telling his biographer that Pitt had suggested St Vincent, 'and that Lord Hood had very nearly been selected'.

The day after he resigned, Lord Spencer had written a hurried note to St Vincent saying he was

. . . glad to find that our arrangements here [at the Admiralty] respecting the Baltic Fleet have as far as they have gone met with your approbation; it will be necessary more than ever to expedite the preparation and detachment of that Fleet, as the season is advancing and the Dane seems by the latest accounts likely to fight stout. . . .

It is now my duty to apprize your Lordship of what you are probably

[1] She was wrong: several ministers resigned, including Grenville and Spencer. George Canning, MP for Wendover, had been Joint Paymaster General of the Forces.

already apprized by less authentic means of my approaching retreat from this Board. I trust that you do too much justice to my earnest desire to serve my country . . . not to be persuaded that nothing short of indispensable necessity could have induced me to this measure at this time; but [he added, in a graceful compliment to St Vincent] if what I hear rumoured in the press today [that St Vincent would replace him] has really any foundation, all my regret (so far as it relates to my own situation) will be [assuaged?] in the certain expectation I shall feel that the detachment will be in the most decided manner essentially benefitted by the change.

Addington was not a politician for nothing: he wrote to St Vincent the same day not to offer him the post of First Lord but to request the admiral's 'immediate presence' in London to inform him 'on the affairs of the Navy'.

St Vincent, still at Torre Abbey, answered that he would

. . . set out for London the moment I have made a few necessary arrangements for carrying on the public service in my absence. All the knowledge and sense I possess on naval subjects shall be, as it always has been, devoted to the service and support of Government and [he added with his usual frankness] lamenting as I do most sincerely that any reverse in this arduous contest should make it necessary for Mr Pitt to retire from his situation, I deem it a most fortunate event for the country that His Majesty's choice has fallen upon you.

The old Earl's secretary and subsequent biographer, Jebediah Tucker, describes the next few hours.

He departed to London, with his secretary, on the evening after this communication reached him. They travelled till eight in the evening, rising nominally at five, which in reality was four, and at Newton, where they reposed on the first night, they left orders accordingly with the waiter at the inn.

Occupying the adjoining room to his Lordship, his secretary heard him stirring before four on the next morning, and he immediately arose, well knowing he should soon be summoned. Before he was half dressed he heard 'Tucker, Tucker,' and that his Lordship was violently ringing his bell; but there was no answer to it – the servants were all asleep.

Presently after, he heard his Lordship on the landing-place of the stairs, calling out 'Holloa! Holloa! Holloa!' as loud as, with his very powerful voice, he could possibly hollow [sic].

Mr Tucker ran out and found his Lordship in his [night] shirt, and many of the inmates of the house in theirs, each of these exclaiming on arrival, 'What's the matter? What's the matter?'

'I can get no answer to my bell,' said his Lordship.

'Why, my Lord, there's no one up yet,' said one of the naked alarmed.

'And so I perceive,' said his Lordship, sinking with laughter at the very ridiculous scene, and figures he had raised. 'But how then were you going to call me on time?' and then, 'By God, Mr Tucker, you West Country people sleep away all your senses; 'tis owing to the climate, I suppose.'

It may be imagined that now, his Lordship having called the servants to enable them to call himself, the carriage soon came round, and how gladly the folks at the inn got rid of such a restless animal. . . .

Addington was not, by calling in St Vincent, relying on the support of a man who was against Catholic emancipation. Comparing him with the King ('the bigotted, uncompromising, immovable opponent'), Tucker wrote that 'of religious tolerance Lord St Vincent was as firmly the advocate. His Lordship had full confidence in the loyalty of Ireland; at least, that the Catholic religion predominating there by no means tended to shake his assurance of her allegiance.'

In the capital enough had happened to keep tongues wagging for more than a week. Although the news would not reach London for several days, Austria signed the Treaty of Lunéville with Napoleon on the Monday, while on Tuesday there had been a Lords debate on an inquiry into the Government's conduct and Addington's resignation as Speaker, which signalled to Napoleon that at the very moment he had – with the Czar's help – completely isolated Britain, her leader, the one man he feared, had resigned as Prime Minister. . . .

On Wednesday, the *levée* at St James's Palace was 'very full' and among those attending were Sir Hyde Parker and his new father-in-law, Admiral Sir Richard Onslow. Next day by an unfortunate coincidence the Lord Mayor of London in full regalia and attended by aldermen and Members of the Court of Common Council arrived at St James's in a colourful procession to present the King with the Court's 'humble and dutiful address on the circumstances of the Union with Ireland'. In view of the events since the Court approved the address two days before the first rumour of Pitt's resignation, it was unlikely the irony of their visit was lost on the City worthies.

In the meantime, as Addington busied himself trying to form a new ministry, the ministers who had resigned with Pitt in fact continued running the country's day to day affairs. On Friday, the day appointed for the 'General Fast and Humiliation', the King and Queen attended a special service at the Chapel Royal. As if to emphasize the purpose, it was a bitterly cold day, and by the time the old King returned to the Palace he was shivering. Superstitious folk could point an accusing finger at those who chose the date for the fast, Friday the thirteenth, because by Saturday night the King was ill with a high fever and delirium.

Fortunately that Saturday morning the King, in a letter to Addington from the Queen's House dated 'Three minutes past 10 a.m.', wrote '. . . This is the anniversary of the Earl of St Vincent's victory [at Cape St Vincent]. I should think it would flatter him much if Mr Addington would desire him to call on me. Any hour this forenoon will be perfectly convenient, as I shall not stir from home. . . . George R.'

Fortunately Lord St Vincent had arrived in London in time to see the King before the illness worsened. Previously he dined with some friends – Evan Nepean, the Secretary of the Board, Sir Andrew Snape Hamond, Comptroller of the Navy, Lord Hobart and Tucker, who describes 'the after-dinner talk of the prospects of a new administration' headed by Addington. Hobart expressed strong doubts about their chances, but St Vincent was confident 'because the country did not see any occasion for reducing the Crown to an extremity'. To this Hobart replied, 'Our reliance is on you – your Lordship is our shield and back-bone'.

Telling the story against himself, Tucker wrote that as St Vincent was going to bed he saw from Tucker's face that the secretary had 'accepted office in a most unfashionable willingness', prompting St Vincent to warn: 'Mr Tucker, it is by no means certain as you and the gentlemen with whom we have dined today seem to think, that I shall take the Admiralty; however, I'll tell you more about it tomorrow, after I have seen the King.'

Next day, after returning from St James's, the old Admiral told his Secretary, 'Now, Mr Tucker, it is all settled, and I shall take office'. He had told the King, according to Tucker, that

. . . he should make but a bad return for all the honours and favours which His Majesty had most graciously bestowed upon him, and very ill discharge his duty, if he did not frankly and honestly tell His Majesty that having served nearly half a century with the Roman Catholics, and seen them tried in all situations, it was his decided and conscientious opinion that they were entitled to be placed upon the same footing in every respect as His Majesty's Protestant subjects; that he had been informed that the retiring Ministry had resigned upon that question, and that he could not accept office under such circumstances without first stating to His Majesty that upon his honour and upon his allegiance, he entirely agreed with them in opinion; that having now discharged this duty [of expressing his views] to His Majesty he would also add that his life and his utmost services were all at His Majesty's disposal, and that he was ready to return to the Fleet, or serve His Majesty on shore, as His Majesty might think proper to command.

The King's reply was, according to Tucker:

Lord St Vincent, you have in this instance, as you have in every other, behaved like an honest, honourable man. Upon the question of Catholic Emancipation my mind is made up, from which I *never* will depart; and therefore, as it is not likely to be a matter agitated or discussed between us, I can see no reason why you should not take the Admiralty, where I very much wish to see you, and to place the Navy entirely in your hands.

Thus St Vincent left the Channel Fleet, which he had commanded for almost a year. He had found it in comparatively poor shape, owing to the decrepitude of his predecessor, and restored its discipline as well as keeping a tighter blockade on Brest. The health of the Fleet – for this was a matter on which he had strong and, for the times, advanced views – had never been better.

He had needed to use a strong and stern hand to restore and enforce regular discipline after the great mutinies at the Nore and Spithead – yet there had been only two courts-martial. The reason was that he received the wholehearted co-operation of his officers, while the seamen admired 'old Jarvie' and, like all seamen, were happier under a stern but consistent disciplinarian. Lax admirals and captains inconsistent in discipline and punishment leave men at the mercy of officers who are either forced to be overly strict to make up for their seniors' shortcomings or allowed to be bullies if so inclined.

The Board of Admiralty he assembled was a good one. Unlike modern times, the naval members were by no means always admirals, nor did they always have specific duties.[1] His first choice was Captain Sir Thomas Troubridge, until then his Captain of the Fleet and the man who had done so much to help the Maltese, while the second was Captain John Markham, second son of a former Archbishop of York, an extremely competent officer who had served for several years under St Vincent, and for the past three years had been commanding the 74-gun *Centaur*.[2] The other three members were civilians. Sir Philip Stephens, who stayed on from Spencer's Board (and was a former Secretary of the Board), was MP for Sandwich – traditionally one of several 'safe' seats filled by Admiralty nominees – and had risen from a clerk in the Admiralty. His usefulness was in his remarkable knowledge of the workings of the Admiralty bureaucratic machine – and his ability to bend to the wishes of whoever was First Lord.

The Hon. William Eliot, also a member of the previous Board, was

[1] Lord Barham, First Lord at the time of Trafalgar, was the first to specify in detail the particular duties of the sea lords, naval and civil.
[2] Markham, then aged thirty-nine, was destined never to serve at sea again: he served on three Admiralty Boards, the last being in 1807, and was elected MP for Portsmouth (an 'Admiralty seat') in November 1801, representing the city almost continuously until 1826, by which time he was an Admiral of the White, by automatic promotion as his seniors died.

MP for St Germains and son of Lord Eliot. The third civilian, William Gartshore, MP for Weymouth, had been a fellow pupil of Captain Markham's at Westminster School and, at thirty-six, was three years younger. A brilliant man, he had been an MP for five years, but his public life was to be smashed when his wife died in 1804 and, driven insane by grief, he died in 1806.

The only person in the Administration of the Navy whom St Vincent disliked was the Comptroller, Sir Andrew Snape Hamond, who was head of the Navy Board. While the Board of Admiralty controlled the Royal Navy as a fighting force, the Navy Board gave contracts for every requirement of the Navy, from salt pork to timber for building ships, as well as controlling the dockyards and being responsible for the conditions of the ships. The opportunities for bribery, jobbery and peculation were enormous and few were missed. Sir Andrew was an obvious target for St Vincent, who had made no secret that if he ever became First Lord he intended to clean up the corruption and inefficiency.

While Addington spent the weekend completing his new ministry, we can look at the latest diplomatic correspondence. Two days after the messenger Vick left Copenhagen on 27 January with the despatches describing the angry interview with Bernstorff, Drummond wrote again to report that he had received a private note from Bernstorff repeating his earlier remarks but, Drummond emphasized, 'I must observe, and certainly with satisfaction, that the warm colouring of his answer has been very much mellowed by time.'

Grenville would see, however, the Danish Government 'now positively refused to declare what part it will take in case of an open rupture between Great Britain and Russia. The futility of the excuse must be obvious to all the world.' He decided that as things stood it would be wrong for him to write any more notes to Bernstorff, public or private.

This despatch arrived in London on 7 February and on that day Drummond wrote again that it was now confidentially reported in Copenhagen that there had been a reconciliation between Denmark and Russia. However, although he had no doubt of this 'being at length purchased by Denmark', he did not believe it had yet taken place.

Meanwhile in Berlin the Prussian Foreign Minister had told Lord Carysfort that his King 'cannot see without the utmost grief and concern the violent and hasty measures to which the Court of London has proceeded against the Northern Powers. Error alone can have given occasion to these measures'.

Since the Czar had approached Prussia in October it was a crude impertinence to accuse Britain in the second week of February of 'hasty measures'; but coming from Prussia (whose present King, Frederick William III, was notoriously indecisive, while his predecessor, Frederick William II, who died in 1797, had been feeble as well) it was pathetic; one of those notes written with an eye on the recipient of a copy – in this case the Czar.

A despatch from Drummond rounds off the week. Written on Saturday, 14 February, it reached London a week later. He had seen Bernstorff again, but the interview 'was a fruitless waste of words, where if nothing was lost, nothing was gained'. The Danish Government's determination to adhere to the Convention, Drummond wrote, obviously choosing his words very carefully, 'appears to me now so manifest from every circumstance that I have not the smallest hope of seeing Denmark relinquish that line of conduct which had already provoked those measures which his Majesty has judged it proper to take'.

However, one thing had emerged from their conversation: Bernstorff repeated to him that before the departure of de Rosencrantz from St Petersburg 'he had been led to hope that Russia would have acted differently towards England, and towards Europe, than she has done. He acknowledged that her declaration in favour of France was now pronounced'.

The tragedy, for Denmark, was that it had taken the Crown Prince and Bernstorff four months to realize it.

14
AN OLIVE BRANCH?

The King's chill worsened considerably over the weekend; but on Sunday Addington was able to announce the names of the members of his new Government, and the newspapers printed the list on Monday. But with few exceptions the names did not inspire the slightest martial spirit or confidence in anyone's breast, be he a weaver or a warrior: the new men achieved that high level of mediocrity which characterized Addington himself, making him an ideal Speaker of the House of Commons but an almost fatal choice – for Britain, anyway – as Prime Minister.

The new Lord Chancellor was the Earl of Elgin, a former ambassador to the Sultan and presently and more prosaically the Colonel of the Elgin Fencibles. The Duke of Portland, whose party had of course earlier joined Pitt's Government, remained Secretary of State for the Home Department; Lord Hawkesbury, MP for Rye and son of the Earl of Liverpool, became the new Foreign Secretary.

Henry Dundas was succeeded as the Secretary of State for War by Lord Hobart, and the two Joint Secretaries of the Treasury who resigned were replaced by Nicholas Vansittart and Charles Bragge. Vansittart, who was to play an important role in the events before the battle in the north, was thirty-four years old. He was called to the Bar in 1791, but first found the life of a gay blade in fashionable London more interesting. He soon tired of it and became interested in politics, backing Pitt's Government and making himself useful as a shrewd and sharp pamphleteer and winning a Parliamentary seat at Hastings in 1796.

Although the newspapers announced Addington's new Government on Monday, next day a brief announcement, 'The King is indisposed with a cold', prevented the new Administration taking office. In fact the King was seriously ill, and the time-honoured ritual of the outgoing ministers surrendering their seals of office and the incoming ministers receiving them at the hands of the King could not be carried out. In the meantime, it seemed, Pitt's ministers would have to continue in office until the King recovered....

The major difficulty resulting from the King's illness was in dealing with the diplomatic and naval aspect of Britain's policy towards Denmark. This was immediately complicated by a sudden hint received in London, and best described by Grenville in a private letter to Carysfort in Berlin.

The New Government, contrary to the prognostics of many, is formed, and though the materials are not in every instance exactly such as might be wished, I have very little doubt that they will establish themselves in Parliament and in the country.

He went on to suggest that Carysfort – who from the previous August had been asking to be allowed to come home – should stay in Berlin for the present because of 'some circumstances' about which he had just heard. That this was a remarkable understatement he soon made as clear as his dislike of it.

Upon a sort of overture from the Prince of Hesse, we are sending Mr Vansittart to Copenhagen on a secret mission to see if they will (as they seem to hold out to us) abandon at once their league and all its principles. But I am convinced our fleet will be the best negotiator there, and I trust it will not be long before its arguments are heard.

Clearly Grenville considered this 'sort of overture' was for an opera with no score, but he had to listen because the Prince concerned was father-in-law to the Danish Crown Prince. He would be an obvious choice for such delicate and dangerous negotiations.

Addington himself decided to send Vansittart: the young man's legal training would be useful and he was of just the right ministerial rank – senior enough if the Danes wanted the overture to be taken seriously; junior enough to be disavowed if anything went wrong and, equally important, without powerful 'interest' behind him to prevent it.

Grenville drew up his lengthy instructions, which were drafted the same day, Tuesday. Since they repeated much of British policy already covered in diplomatic correspondence, only the new points need be mentioned here.

Enclosing copies of the two letters received from Denmark in the last mails – the 'sort of overture' – Grenville was less certain about their origin than he had led Carysfort to believe. Vansittart was told 'there is every reason to believe they had been written by the Prince of Hesse', and the purpose of Vansittart's mission was that, as they contained 'express assurances' that the overtures they described came directly from the Crown Prince, the British Government 'judged it proper not to omit taking such steps' to ascertain whether satisfactory negotiations could result from them.

It was grasping at a slender straw when Britain had an enormous club to wield, but even at this stage the Government had not fully appreciated that its only strategic objective was Russia.

Vansittart was to go to Hamburgh in the *Blanche* frigate, find the Prince of Hesse 'wherever he may happen to be' and have a confidential conversation with him 'on the subject of these papers'. Vansittart was told in no uncertain terms that 'it is useless' to discuss the passages in the letters referring to Denmark's past conduct. But the mutual advantages of the new system they proposed were 'fully admitted', and Vansittart could negotiate on that basis, impressing on the Prince that there was no other hope of independence and safety for Denmark 'against the overwhelming power of Russia, except by the aid and protection of Great Britain: and that the maintenance of that independence cannot be indifferent to use'. Therefore, Britain agreed to the proposal for an alliance as set out in the letters 'if there were corresponding dispositions at Copenhagen and Stockholm'.

Whether or not Addington was being realistic or simply chasing after the writings of some anonymous pedlar of hope, it is significant that with the great battle only seven weeks away, the British Government even at this late stage was anxious to reach a peaceful solution with Denmark.

The first letter contained five articles. Of these, Grenville said, the first needed only slight alterations, the next two were 'entirely conformable' with existing treaties, the fifth could be adopted, and the fourth, dealing with convoys, presented no problems. Two other points in the letter – the definition of contraband and the detention of neutral property – also raised no problems.

'Seven articles thus framed,' Grenville wrote, 'would embrace all that Great Britain would wish to propose or stipulate for on the subject of the commerce of neutrals in time of war.' Vansittart was authorized 'conjointly with Mr Drummond to conclude a treaty in conformity with them'. The embargo on Danish ships would be lifted as part of the treaty, and the same would apply to Sweden's ships if she agreed to a similar treaty. Since Russia's conduct did not show any desire on the part of the Czar to be friendly, Britain's need of 'repelling by force the hostile aggression of Russia' would still remain, and she would have to claim free passage of the Sound for her ships of war.

At the same time, since the Danes had made a considerable armament in the past year, Denmark could not expect the British Fleet would go up the Baltic leaving this armament behind it and 'depending for security against its possible hostility on no better ground than that of the signature of such a treaty. . . .' There were only three alternatives –

the Danish armament must be reduced, or 'rendered decidedly and actively friendly, or destroyed'.

Destruction was the method to which 'His Majesty would be the least willing to recourse', and Britain left the decision to Denmark providing a treaty on the lines of the letters was signed. Furthermore the treaty alone would be sufficient providing it included a promise to disarm the Danish Fleet immediately and facilities were given to the British admiral in the Baltic 'to satisfy himself from time to time that such disarming is actually executed'.

However, the British Government was realistic enough to know that, even if Denmark wanted to come to terms with the deep blue sea, the Devil, in the form of the Czar, was lurking over the eastern horizon. If the Danes argued the danger from Russia precluded disarming, Grenville wrote, their fleet 'must then be used actively to ensure the success of the proposed system'.

Vansittart could discuss all the points freely with the Prince of Hesse, and if it led to his going on to Copenhagen he was to communicate with Drummond 'without the least reserve'. The last paragraph of the instructions warned him they had been drawn up on the assumption the letters *had* been written by the Prince with the authorization of the Crown Prince; but if they had not or the Prince of Hesse's political influence 'is now such that he cannot render any effective service' in the negotiations, Vansittart was to return without delay 'avoiding as much as possible everything that can create observation or attract attention'.

Vansittart's own account of the birth of his mission makes interesting reading. It was the practice of the Lord Chancellor and the Speaker to hold Saturday evening parties attended by members of the Bar and peers. 'At one of these I was present, and perceived . . . that something extraordinary had happened.' Vansittart was puzzled, and

. . . after some time Mr Perceval took me aside and said, 'You seem not to be aware of what has happened, and I wish you would let me take you home to Lincoln's Inn in my carriage.'

As soon as we were in the carriage together, he said, 'Mr Pitt has resigned, and the King has sent for the Speaker, who is to be Prime Minister, and who will send for you tomorrow morning. I am authorised by Mr Pitt to tell his friends that he wishes as many of them as think with the King on the Catholic question to accept office under the new administration, and I hope you will have no difficulty in doing so.'

I answered, that I thought the circumstances of the country were so critical, that every man who could make himself useful ought to accept any situation. . . .

On my arrival at my chambers. I found a note from Mr Addington, desiring to see me at eight the next morning.

Vansittart was offered and accepted the office of one of the Secretaries of the Treasury, and a few evenings later received a note telling him to go immediately to Lord Hawkesbury's.

When we met, Lord Hawkesbury told me that the Government had occasion to send a confidential minister to Denmark, and that Mr Addington had mentioned me as suited to that service. He said that the Government had received a secret communication from Prince Charles of Hesse, intimating that the Danish Government might be detached from the Northern Coalition ... if a confidential person with full powers and conciliatory instructions were sent to it. This communication from a brother-in-law of the King of Denmark appeared to the Government to be so important, that they wished to avail themselves of it as speedily as possible, and with the greatest secrecy.

1 answered that I should be ready to set out as soon as my instructions could be prepared; and the next morning I met Lord Hawkesbury and Mr Addington, with Lord Grenville (who, as well as Mr Pitt, still retained his office), at the Foreign Office. They explained to me the nature of the instructions I was to receive. . . .

At the last moment the Government changed Vansittart's travelling arrangements, probably to make his mission less conspicuous, so that instead of sailing in the *Blanche* frigate, he left next day for Harwich with his secretary, Dr Beeke, and

. . . embarked immediately on board the packet for Hamburgh. She was a miserable little vessel and we had a very rough and disagreeable passage of above a week to Cuxhaven, at the mouth of the Elbe, which we found enclosed with ice, by which a Swedish vessel had been cut in two the day before our arrival. We had an unpleasant scramble to get over the ice to the shore at Cuxhaven. . . .

On 23 February, just after Vansittart's departure, Count de Wedel Jarlsberg requested an audience with the Secretary of State. At this point Hawkesbury took over from Grenville, and the Note from Bernstorff that de Wedel Jarlsberg delivered caused an almost immediate change in Britain's policy.

Bernstorff had, it seems, at last unwittingly succeeded in persuading Addington and Hawkesbury to the view Grenville had earlier expressed to Lord Carysfort – 'Our fleet will be the best negotiator. . . .'

Coming within a few days of the olive branch apparently held out by the Prince of Hesse, the Danish Note caused a more violent reaction than would have otherwise been the case. It was a reply to the British Note of 16 January informing them of the embargo and, repeating points already made to Drummond, began by accusing Britain of confusing two unconnected issues, Russia's action against British interests, and the Convention. 'It is a subject of perfect notoriety', that the British occupation of Malta caused the Russian embargo on British ships. The Danish King requested the British embargo on Danish ships to be lifted at once, otherwise 'he will see himself with regret reduced to the urgent necessity of exerting those means which his dignity and the interests of his subjects will imperiously prescribe'.

The Note – read in conjunction with Drummond's despatches, which showed he had always been remarkably well-informed – indicated that the two mysterious letters certainly did not reflect the Danish Government's views or sympathies: the Danes were truculent, not conciliatory. Vansittart's instructions, with the plans for an alliance which fully covered the defence of Denmark against the Russian Fleet, were probably not worth the paper they were written on.

As far as Britain was concerned, the flaw in the Danish argument that Russia's quarrel with Britain was over Malta and therefore no concern of Denmark, and signing the Convention with Russia did not ally Denmark with Russia against Britain, was that the Convention itself *was* aimed against Britain. It was as serious as a declaration of war, and any nation carrying out its terms became one of Britain's enemies. In other words, if Denmark became an ally of one of Britain's enemies, then she could not continue calling herself a neutral.

Stripped of all the polite or defiant verbiage subsequently added by diplomats and historians, this was Britain's attitude from the first; and from the first it was the only attitude she could take. And she acted swiftly when the Note made it clear that short of a miracle the offer of a treaty or alliance that Vansittart had taken with him would come to nought.

On the same day the Note was received, Hawkesbury drew up new instructions for Drummond and orders were sent to the Admiralty and War Office for the Baltic expedition. There is no doubt the Danish reply was responsible, since the new and the old ministers were involved. Just as an earlier Note had sounded the alarm, so this Note sent the British ships of state to general quarters.

Hawkesbury's letter to Drummond contained, wrapped up in suitably vague language, a simple promise either to fight Denmark or to defend her against the Russians with a powerful British fleet of twenty sail of the line. New instructions he would get when the British Fleet arrived on the coast of Denmark would be 'suitable to the circumstances under which the two countries may at that time find themselves'.

There was no need for Hawkesbury to mention one of the main

reasons for haste: the ice would soon be melting in the Baltic, freeing the Russian Fleet as well as opening it to the British. The King 'has accordingly given orders to the Fleet destined for the Baltic to sail without delay,' he continued. Sir Hyde Parker would bring a duplicate of the despatch and 'upon the receipt of it you will require an explicit answer from the Government of Denmark in the course of forty-eight hours; and in case they should refuse to enter into a treaty . . . conformable to the above-mentioned instructions to Mr Vansittart . . . you will leave Copenhagen, together with all persons attached to your mission.' A copy of Sir Hyde's instructions was enclosed.

So much for the threat of war. In the last two paragraphs of his letter Hawkesbury gave yet another and more detailed assurance of Britain's offer for an alliance, and there is no question that Count Bernstorff did not receive it because there is a copy in the Danish State Archives. If Denmark agreed to the alliance, Hawkesbury wrote, Britain would keep a contingent naval force of not less than twenty sail of the line, with a proportionate number of frigates, in the Baltic for the defence of Denmark for as long as the season permitted, providing Denmark agreed to keep not less than ten sail of the line in the same area.[1]

Meanwhile Henry Dundas, the former Secretary of State for War in Pitt's administration, remained at his post to draw up the detailed orders to the Admiralty, assuring the Lords Commissioners that the King still hoped to avoid actual war with Denmark and Sweden.

However, he wrote, the season was now so far advanced and the preparations at Copenhagen and other Baltic ports were being carried out with so much activity that the King could not wait for the result of the new negotiation without taking steps 'calculated to give weight to the negotiation, and bring it to a speedy and satisfactory conclusion', or if it failed, 'to capture or destroy the [ships] and weaken as much as possible the maritime resources of Denmark in the port of Copenhagen, or wherever they may be found and can be attacked'.

To cover either alternative, to make sure the question was resolved immediately, and to remove 'in every quarter any doubt which may still remain of HM's fixed determination neither to relinquish nor compromise the naval rights of this country', a fleet of not less than twenty ships of the line, with appropriate frigates and smaller vessels, 'should forthwith be sent off to Copenhagen', and on arriving there the Commander-in-Chief should 'make such a disposition of the ships . . .

---

[1] Twenty sail of the line was a considerable fleet: St Vincent had fifteen sail of the line at Cape St Vincent, Nelson fourteen at the Nile, Duncan sixteen at Camperdown, and Nelson twenty-seven at Trafalgar.

as in his judgment may appear most likely to ensure the success of the attempt it will be his duty to make (should all proposals for conciliation fail) to destroy the Arsenal of Copenhagen with the whole of the shipping in that port'.

The Commander-in-Chief's first step after arriving in the Cattegat was to send the enclosed letter from Lord Hawkesbury to Drummond and to inform him of the Fleet's arrival. He was also to arrange with Drummond the quickest way of being told Denmark's decision. But if Drummond had already been ordered to quit the country, or no reply was received within forty-eight hours of Drummond's letter being delivered, 'he will . . . immediately proceed to vigorous hostilities, and use his utmost endeavour to accomplish the object above mentioned . . . and as far as may be consistent with his operation, to capture or destroy the trade and shipping of the Danes, Swedes or Russians within the Baltic, and to annoy or distress them in such other manner as may be in his power according to the Rights and Usages of War'.

Dundas then wrote a strict injunction which must be borne in mind when later considering the much-debated question of Nelson's letter of truce:

His Majesty is fully aware that it will probably be impossible to carry into execution the eventual instructions contained in this letter for destroying the Arsenal and shipping of Copenhagen without exposing that City also to great damage; if not to entire destruction. . . .

Next to the wish of avoiding a rupture altogether, there is nothing His Majesty would have more at heart than to prevent its calamitie [sic] being thus extended to the destruction and injury of unoffending individuals, and it will therefore be proper that your Lordships should direct the commanding naval officer to take an early opportunity after the actual commencement of hostilities, of explicitly making known to the persons charged with the defence of Copenhagen, and the inhabitants themselves if possible, that no injury or damage whatever will be done to the Town in case of all the shipping of every description then in the harbour or its immediate dependencies, together with all naval stores in the Arsenal, being delivered up to the Fleet under his command.

If this was refused, he would have to continue operations without regard to preservation of the town, in order to destroy the Arsenal and shipping, or to compel the surrender of the latter to the Fleet under his command.

There was no mention of Russia, other than a passing reference; yet Russia was the real enemy. . . . Furthermore it must have been clear to the British Government that the various provisions and alternatives in the instructions had so many permutations that successfully carrying them out, either by diplomatic or martial means, depended so much on the Commander-in-Chief himself that he must be clear-headed, calm, decisive, and equally competent whether manoeuvring his own fleet or a foreign diplomat. A skilfully turned phrase might have more effect than a thousand skilfully aimed broadsides.

Obviously they were not orders to be given to an admiral who shied from responsibility, whose indecision hypnotized him into inaction, or who quibbled over individual words in his orders without regard to the obvious intentions behind them. Since the man chosen as Commander-in-Chief was already known to suffer from each of these defects, and the orders were given to him without anyone voicing any doubts about him *at the time*, it is important to know who was responsible for a decision which, but for Nelson, would have wrecked the whole expedition as effectively as a storm sinking the Fleet at Spithead.

Taken in sequence, Parker was first chosen by Spencer (who, as First Lord, was not a member of the Cabinet) with the approval of the Prime Minister and Dundas (who was in the Cabinet). All three were in office; there was no hint of the resignation of Pitt's administration at the time Parker was chosen.

With the Government's resignation, the onus passed from Spencer to St Vincent, who had made no secret of his poor opinion of Sir Hyde. He knew better than anyone his professional ability, had been kept fully informed of the Baltic preparations by Spencer, and had approved the appointment. In his determination that the Navy should be efficient St Vincent was ruthless where the replacement of an inefficient officer was concerned, sparing no man and giving not a damn that it made him many enemies. But he did nothing about Parker's appointment. Although to have replaced Parker at this stage would certainly have been a blow to the man's pride, the Admiralty has always been more ruthless than, for example, the Foreign Service, in preferring to sacrifice a man's career than risk the nation's safety, and there is no doubt from the evidence of his own pen that at the time St Vincent was satisfied with Sir Hyde.

After writing the verbose collection of bureaucratic clichés which formed the ill-considered instructions to the Admiralty, Dundas sent off orders to the Commander-in-Chief of the Army, the Duke of York.[1]

---

[1] The modern political trick of changing a ministry's name as an alternative to giving it a policy is simply a new tune played on an old fiddle. The Duke's title is a good example. On 3 April 1798 he was appointed 'Commander-in-Chief in Great Britain'; on 4 September 1799 'Captain-General of the Forces in Great Britain and all Forces employed on the Continent of Europe'; and on 9 June 1801, 'Commander-in-Chief of the Forces of Great Britain and Ireland'. The only thing lacking was a definition of his duties.

'A Corps of about 600 men being wanted to embark and to attend a Division of His Majesty's Fleet now on the point of putting to sea for a particular service' Dundas wrote, he had to request that the Duke would 'direct them to embark forthwith at Portsmouth'. As the success of the highly important expedition 'may very much depend upon the exertion of this small body of land officers, it is very essential that they should consist of the most seasoned and experienced troops that the Army of this country can supply,' Dundas added, 'and that they should be commanded by an officer of acknowledged ability and enterprise.'

In sending a copy of this letter to the Admiralty, Dundas wrote: 'The officer appointed to command this detachment is Lt Col the Hon. W. Stewart of the Rifle Battalion', adding that the Admiralty should instruct Sir Hyde 'to communicate confidentially with him on everything that relates to the service in which it is intended he should be employed'.

Unlike the politicians, the Duke of York chose wisely in Colonel Stewart; not only was he a highly intelligent man and a fine soldier, but an excellent observer and reporter to whom historians owe a great debt.

15

STORM IN A MUSTARD POT

With the King's illness worsening and continuing to delay matters the Government resembled a game of musical chairs with too many players. In some cases new ministers took over, but it led to curious situations like the one at the Admiralty where St Vincent, beginning his duties as the new First Lord on Wednesday, 18 February, received on the following Monday the detailed instructions for the Baltic expedition from Dundas, who had resigned and been replaced by Lord Hobart.

However, the King's illness certainly did not slow up the Navy's preparations. St Vincent presided at his first Board meeting on Friday, 20 February, but naturally the Board had up to then been meeting regularly under Spencer, and the minutes describe the situation that St Vincent found.

At the end of January, as mentioned earlier, orders had been given to prepare the bomb ketches and fire ships and find out how many flat-bottom boats were available. Then on 3 February, Evan Nepean's rough minutes record, 'Inform the Ordnance Board that there are 21 flat boats at Deal and desire they would direct a proper number of carronades to be prepared for them as expeditiously as possible.'

By 12 February they were recording the detailed plans for assembling the ships for the Baltic Fleet.[1] The rough minute is worth quoting in full

---

[1] The way that everyone, from the Admiralty to Nelson, referred to the force as a 'fleet' on one occasion, and a 'squadron' on another needs explanation. Although in earlier times a squadron had been regarded as one of three divisions of a fleet (van, centre and rear), it had by now come to mean a group of ships, usually five or more sail of the line, detached from a fleet and commanded by a rear-admiral (thus at the Nile Rear-admiral Nelson commanded a squadron of thirteen sail of the line detached from St Vincent's Fleet; but his original squadron comprised only three sail of the line, being later reinforced). A fleet was, technically, a group of more sail of the line than a squadron and therefore larger than a rear-admiral's command. In practice it usually meant a dozen or more commanded by a vice-admiral or admiral. In this narrative the force will be referred to as a fleet except where otherwise described in quoted passages.

(although it is certainly the work of Spencer and Nepean, rather than the full Board) and intended to be a complete résumé for St Vincent.

The ships in the margin [see below] are intended for Sir Hyde Parker's squadron. Those marked X are ready for sea; those marked √ are nearly ready. Those marked 'G' are ordered to carry two 24-pounder guns, with their carriages, and a proper proportion of cartridges and shot, for the use of the gun brigs, which may not be able to carry them across the North Sea.

The frigates and sloops have not yet been appointed as there appears to be no reason for preferring one before another, those which happen to be in port may be ordered on the service; it will only be necessary to insure a proper number being in port before the squadron assembles. The *Harpy* should be one of the sloops, her captain having served in the Baltic.

The bombs mentioned in the margin are to go with the squadron.

The fire ships in the margin are also to attend the squadron. By the new mode of fitting fire ships, if the combustibles are carried in the magazines of large ships, any vessel may in a very short time be converted into a fire ship.

The gun brigs in the margin due to be of the squadron; and there are five others in Yarmouth Roads ready for sea; but as they are ordered on a particular service they cannot be depended on.

The cutters and luggers are not appropriated, no reason for preference existing. The *Lark* lugger should be one, her commander having been in the Baltic.

Six ships of light draught of water, intended to carry 24-pounder guns as battery ships, and to act against the enemy's gun boats, are fitting out in the river [Thames] but the time of their being ready is uncertain.

There are 21 flat boats at Deal and 16 carronades for them at Dover; the Ordnance [Board] have been desired to send more carronades to Dover [where they could be collected by larger ships] that each boat may have one.

Sir Hyde Parker to hoist his flag when the *London* arrives at Spithead – Lord Nelson to be ordered to join him, and all the ships to be put under his orders. Everything should be prepared, but the squadron should not assemble, nor should any display of preparations be made until a very short time before it is to sail, that the expectation of it may not render the enemy more active in their preparations.

The ships listed in the margin (the number of guns they carried are inserted in brackets) were:

London (98) At sea	*Raisonable* (64) Yarmouth X
St George (98) Torbay X	*Polyphemus* (64) Yarmouth X
Warrior (74) Portsmouth X G	*Agamemnon* (64) Sheerness X
Saturn (74) Portsmouth √ G	*Ruby* (64) Chatham, doubtful
Bellona (74) Portsmouth √ 22 Feb. G	*Glatton* (54) Yarmouth X
Defence (74) Portsmouth X G	*Monmouth* (64) Yarmouth X
Edgar (74) Plymouth √ 20th	*Isis* (50) Portsmouth X

Veteran (64) Yarmouth ✗
Monarch (74) Sheerness ✗   *Powerful* (74) Chatham, doubtful
Defiance (74) at sea   *Asia* (64) Chatham, doubtful

The bomb ketches:
Terror, Sheerness ✗   *Hecla*, Sheerness ✗
Explosion, Sheerness   *Volcano*, Sheerness ✗
Sulphur, Sheerness ✗   *Discovery*, Portsmouth ✗
Zebra, Sheerness ✗

The fire ships:
Otter, Portsmouth ✗   *Trimmer*, Sheerness
Alecto, Portsmouth ✗   *Victoire* [sic: *Victorieuse*], Sheerness
Zephyr, Woolwich ✓

The brigs:
Pelter, Portsmouth ✗   *Bouncer*, Portsmouth ✗
Force, Portsmouth ✗   *Sparkler*, Portsmouth ✗
Teazer, Portsmouth ✗

When Lord St Vincent attended his first Board meeting as First Lord on Friday, all the new members except Troubridge were present. The only matter of importance noted in the minutes was, ironically (for St Vincent had not yet been replaced as Commander-in-Chief of the Channel Fleet): 'Admiral the Earl of St Vincent not to consider Admiral Lord Nelson as any longer under his command.' This was, of course, a routine order noting officially that Nelson was no longer serving in the Channel Fleet and most likely an omission which St Vincent's keen administrative eye had noted.

One of the first letters written in his new role was characteristic of St Vincent. Dated 21 February, it told Admiral Lord Keith in the Mediterranean simply:

Your friends will have told you how I came here. What sort of figure I shall make will be seen. I have known many a good admiral make a wretched First Lord of the Admiralty. I will, however, support Commanders-in-Chief upon all occasions, and prohibit any intrigue against them in this office. Health and success to you. – St Vincent.

But the new Lords Commissioners had more than the gathering of fleets to bother them. The King's Messenger William Ross had been very late reaching London with the despatch of 29 January (see page 141) in which Drummond reported 'This Court now positively refuses to decide what part it will take in case of an open rupture between Great Britain and Russia.' It now transpired that much of the delay had been caused by the Royal Navy.

'I herewith transmit to you by Lord Hawkesbury's direction,'

Dundas wrote to the Admiralty, 'the complaint of Mr William Ross, one of the King's Messengers, against Lieutenant Balfour commanding His Majesty's hired armed cutter *Fox*, for detaining Mr Ross unnecessarily in his passage to and from Copenhagen, when charged with despatches on His Majesty's Service. . . .' The letter was brought up at a Board Meeting and annotated 'Send to Admiral Dickson directing him to call upon Lt Balfour to state what he has to offer in justification of his conduct on the charge exhibited against him. . . .'

Nor was that the only complaint against naval officers: the second was from the Danish Minister in London, Count de Wedel Jarlsberg, addressed to Lord Hawkesbury, and backed up by attested statements. Dundas sent the Admiralty a copy of a letter from the Count and enclosures 'complaining of the conduct of the officers and crew of H.M.'s sloop *Driver*, after they had captured and boarded the Norwegian vessel *Providentia*', and requesting an inquiry and report. A postscript emphasized 'Lord Hawkesbury particularly requests Mr Nepean's immediate attention to this business'.

The Danish Minister's letter complained that the *Providentia*, under Captain Gabriel Faye, bound for Falmouth from a Norwegian port with a cargo of spruce, was detained by the British sloop *Driver* and ordered into Leith by her commanding officer, Captain Dunbar, who put a lieutenant and a prize crew on board.

'The English crew sent on board behaved like pirates,' the Count wrote, and Lord Hawkesbury must have been incensed at an incident which allowed the Danish Minister to conclude his Note with: '. . . a conduct against the rules observed by civilised nations, and contrary to the intention and declarations of the British Government which merits, my Lord, your serious attention.'

With the letter was a regular marine 'protest' by Captain Faye, drawn up in Leith in the presence of Captain Dunbar, and witnessed and attested by 'William Smith, Notary Public by Royal Authority' at Leith. The protest had a good point: Captain Faye began by describing how the *Driver*'s boats had boarded the *Providentia* and captured her under the recent British order. 'But the order is simply to seize and detain, and gives no authority to plunder such vessels or the crews. . . .' However, no sooner were the British seamen in possession of the *Providentia*, Faye claimed, than they broke open locks and took various items from his own cabin, including wine, brandy and provisions. They also broke open seamen's chests and stole clothing, 'while the Lieutenant immediately on making the capture took away with him a half anker [five gallons] of French brandy, salt fish, a pot of mustard and a speaking-trumpet.

'Therefore the said Gabriel Faye protested and hereby protests that as the said Captain Dunbar or at least his officers and men for whose conduct he was answerable,' had acted in a manner totally inconsistent with the British Order in Council, damages were claimed by Captain Faye, the crew, and the *Providentia*'s owners.

The notary attested that Faye's sworn protest had, in the notary's presence, been 'delivered into the hands of the said Captain Dunbar, who received the same and read it over audibly in our hearing . . . with an observation which I [Smith, the notary] decline inserting in this instrument. . . .'

The Admiralty lost no time in getting to the bottom of the affair: across the corner of Dundas's letter is the note: 'What report has been made of this? Send to Sir Hyde Parker with directions to him to call upon the Captain of the *Driver* accordingly.'

A few days earlier the Admiralty had written to Lord Hawkesbury about a number of Russian officers serving in ships of the Royal Navy, under training. Hawkesbury's reply, dated 27 February, also indicates the problems the new Administration was having because of the King's illness, which had by then lasted nearly two weeks. Acknowledging the Board's letter he explained, 'I have not yet had an opportunity of laying it before the King, on account of His Majesty's indisposition: I am however of opinion that these officers should not be any longer allowed to serve on board H.M.'s ships of war, but that they may be permitted to come to London on their parole.'

While Lord St Vincent at the Admiralty and the members of the Navy Board did all they could to get the Baltic Fleet ships ready, the Secretary of State for the Home Department suddenly received information which led him to warn the First Lord that delegates from all the Royal dockyards had arrived in London and were holding secret meetings to decide on the terms of pay claims they intended presenting to the Admiralty.

St Vincent, under no illusion about the short time available to get the Fleet to the Baltic before the ice melted, promptly had the matter raised at a Cabinet meeting. As First Lord he was not a member, but was invited to attend.

The ministers, equally anxious to get the Fleet to sea, were almost unanimous in advocating conciliatory measures. St Vincent, with fifty years, experience of enforcing discipline and very fully informed on the inefficiency and corruption in the dockyards, was most decidedly not, predicting the 'worse than uselessness of such milk and water physic'. He agreed to meet the delegates for 'one short trial', according to his secretary, on condition that 'nothing should be attempted which he might think would indicate fear or compromise authority'.

The shipwrights based their claim on the increased price of bread. When the Navy Board pay-books were checked it was found their average yearly earnings were £91 – high wages for the times.[1] The shipwrights were offered an increase related to the extra cost of scarce food and in proportion to the number of people in each man's family, with the proviso the increase would be paid only as long as there was a food scarcity. It was already known that the shipwrights had collected money to pay the delegates' expenses for their trip to London, and at the Admiralty the delegates referred to their 'constituents'.

When the delegates reported the offer back to the dockyards, the shipwrights promptly rejected it. With a dozen sail of the line, a dozen bomb ketches and fire ships, five brigs and a number of frigates for the Baltic Fleet either being worked on or waiting for berths in the yards, the men thought they were in a strong position to dictate their terms – the newspapers left them in no doubt the ships were needed urgently for the Baltic. The delegates in London therefore returned to the Admiralty with the shipwrights' new demands: their pay must be doubled, and the increase was to be permanent.

They were told to return later for the Board's answer. To emphasize the claims there were disorders and demonstrations at the Plymouth yard which became so violent that troops were called out, and the artillery had their loaded guns in the roads leading to the dockyard, trained on the gates.

St Vincent appeared to be in an unenviable position. On the one hand the new Government's Cabinet Ministers were more than anxious to get the Baltic Fleet to sea and at the same time avoid civil disturbances at home which might topple them from office.

On the other, the shipwrights' action had, in St Vincent's view, passed the point where free men were freely negotiating the price oi their labour: at a critical stage of a critical war he saw their activities as sedition and open defiance of the Admiralty with an unjustified wage claim which was little more than blackmail. (It should be borne in mind that their claim was now for double pay, bringing it to nearly twice that of a naval lieutenant.)

St Vincent, having decided the shipwrights' behaviour was insubordination, did not waste time talking polemics with his fellow ministers

[1] Compared with, for instance, the gunner, boatswain, and purser of a first rate at £83 12s. a year (less £5 0s. 6d. income tax); carpenter of a sloop at £48 13s. 6d., and of a first rate £96 9s. 6d.; master of a sloop £91 10s., lieutenant £72 16s., and the captain of a sixth rate £284 7s. 9d.

because he was only too aware that their opinions were influenced by political expediency, not by any knowledge whatsoever of ships, war, men and the sea. But it was St Vincent's task to get Sir Hyde's fleet ready for sea. So, according to Tucker, he first decided the men should be punished, then told the Cabinet he 'had determined on measures of vigour'.

When the delegates returned to the Admiralty to receive the Board's reply, they received a triple shock: they were immediately told that the Board had ordered them to be turned out of the Admiralty into the street; every one of the delegates was discharged from the service; and every man in every dockyard who had acted as a committeeman or who had been active in collecting money 'to support the combination' would also be dismissed.[1]

St Vincent was not making idle threats: instructions were given to the Navy Board who sent a committee to every dockyard to investigate and report the names of the men involved. With the dissident men dismissed, work soon began again.

The episode led to an interesting comment by St Vincent which is recorded by Tucker:

And the Baltic Fleet having been thus equipped, when the sailing orders were despatched to it from the Admiralty, Lord St Vincent appeared to be under some anxiety as to its success.

Upon his secretary's remarking that the squadron was in excellent order, well fitted, well manned, well officered and well commanded, Lord St Vincent replied that 'he was quite sure of Nelson', and should have been in no apprehension if he had been of [sufficient] rank to take the chief command; but that he could not feel quite so sure about Sir Hyde, as he had never been tried.

This is the first time any such doubt was expressed and – since Tucker was writing long after the event – there is no way of checking it.

Meanwhile there was much bustling at the Admiralty. *The Times* reported on 28 February that Lord St Vincent's hours of audience 'do not suit the generality of visitors. They are from 5 to 7 in the morn ng. After that hour he will receive no visitor.'

That the British action in the Baltic ought to be bold was borne out by despatches and private letters from envoys in Europe during the whole of February. The Earl of Carysfort, after writing to Lord Grenville from Berlin on 18 February that the Czar 'is so vigilant to prevent naval stores getting out [of Russia] to England that much more caution is

---

[1] 'Combination' was used at this time to describe any assembly of men planning insubordination, sedition or mutiny.

necessary for them than in the case of corn', wrote again three days later that, 'Against the Northern Courts I hope you will act with vigour. I am confident it will rather advance than retard a reconciliation with the Emperor. . . .'

It was ironical that the Russians should at this time have been more concerned to prevent Britain getting naval stores than corn because, although there were enough naval stores in the Royal dockyards, the bad harvest had caused such a desperate shortage of corn that with the price of flour rising rapidly not only shipwrights but the whole nation was complaining.

The King's illness had resulted in the curious situation where, although he had resigned, Pitt was left to present the Estimates to Parliament on 18 February. These included £15,800,000 for the Navy and £15,902,000 for the Army. The money was to be raised by increasing taxes on, among other things, sugar, malt and tobacco (£2,750,000), while income tax would yield £4,260,000. New taxes included ten per cent on all tea costing 2s. 6d. a pound, 3d. a pound on pepper, and 1s. 6d. a hundredweight on raisins. The tax on paper was, with few exceptions, doubled.

St Vincent's secretary summed up his view of the situation by saying:

. . . Nine years war . . . had fatigued and well nigh exhausted the country. Petitions for peace, especially from the northern counties, were very frequent. By no inconsiderable portion of the nation, the necessity then of war at all was denied; by many more our conduct in it was impugned, who attributed our failure at Quiberon, Ferrol and North Holland [the Helder expedition] to more than misfortune. Then the violation of the treaty of El-Arish, and the submission to repair the Danish frigate the *Freya*, were highly unpopular. . . .

16

THE FRETFUL LOVER

Nelson had no sooner become a father than once again he became a jealous lover. Within a few days of telling Emma on Sunday, 1 February, that he was chafing to get three days' leave for a visit to London that would give him his first sight of his baby daughter, his excitement over her birth turned to jealousy because on Monday the *Morning Post* reported: 'The Duke of Norfolk yesterday gave a grand dinner at his house in St James's Square to Sir William and Lady Hamilton, the Duke of Queensbury and several others.' There was a brilliant concert in the evening and, the newspaper added, the Prince of Wales was present.

The next day, before he had seen this issue of the newspaper, Nelson wrote to Emma (addressing the letter to 'Mrs Thomson'):

Your good and dear friend does not think it proper at present to write with his own hand but he hopes the time may not be far distant when he may be united for ever to the object of his wishes, his only, *only* love. He swears before Heaven that he will marry you as soon as it is possible, which he fervently prays may be soon. He charges me to say how dear you are to him, and that you must, every opportunity, kiss and bless for him his dear little girl, which he wishes to be called Emma, out of gratitude to our dear good Lady Hamilton, but in either its form Lord N. [sic] he says, or Lady H. [sic], he leaves to your judgment and choice [i.e. the choice of 'Horatia' or 'Emma']. . . .

His next letter the following day, addressed to Lady Hamilton, said:

. . . it has made my head ache stooping so much [he still suffered from ophthalmia], as I have been making memorandums for my will and, having regularly signed it, if [I] was to die this moment I believe it would hold good. . . .

I have been obliged to be more particular than I would, as a wife [i.e. Emma] can have nothing, and it might be taken from you by [Sir William's] will or the heirs of your husband. . . . I shall now go to work and save a fortune. . . .

Obviously Emma did not have the tact to know when not to mention certain subjects, and fortunately for both of them Saturday's *Morning Post* had not arrived, and Nelson continued

Sir William should say to the Prince that, situated as you are, it would be highly improper for you to admit His Royal Highness. That the Prince should wish it, I am not surprised at, and that he will attempt every means to get into your house and into any place where you may dine. Sir W^m should speak out, and if the Prince is a man of honour he will quit the pursuit of you. I know his aim is to have you for a mistress. The thought so agitates me that I cannot write. I had wrote a few lines last night, but I am in tears, I cannot bear it. . . .

However he composed himself enough to write next day to 'Mrs Thomson' that

. . . it is not unusual to [wait to] christen children till they are a month or six weeks old; and as Lord Nelson will probably be in town, as well as myself, before we go to the Baltic, he proposes then, if you approve, to christen the child, and that myself and Lady Hamilton should be two of the sponsors. It can be christened at St George's, Hanover Square; and, I believe, the parents being at the time out of the Kingdom, if it is necessary, it can be stated born at Portsmouth or at sea. It's name will be Horatia, daughter of Ioham and Morata Etnorb. It you read the surname backwards and take the letters of the other names it will make, very extraordinarily, the names of your real and affectionate friends, Lady Hamilton and myself. . . .[1]

In the meantime, before Nelson saw the earlier issue, the *Morning Post* was forced to print a retraction of Monday's report, saying 'Lady Hamilton did not dine at the Duke of Norfolk's last Sunday, as mentioned in this paper of Monday. We are concerned to find her Ladyship was indisposed.'

Writing daily to Emma, Nelson's letters alternated between almost hysterical tirades against the Prince of Wales and boyish exclamations of his affection for Emma. '*Your letters are to me gazettes*', he wrote, reminiscing of the times when 'we have almost quarrelled for a first reading' of newspapers, and trusting 'the time will soon arrive when we shall have those *amicable squabbles* again'.

Emma, of all people, wrote worrying about the jubilant father's discretion, and Nelson assured her:

You may rely I shall not open my mouth on poor Mrs Thompson's business to any creature on this earth. You and I should be very unworthy if we did any such thing, as all the secrets of those two people rest solely in our bosoms.

[1] 'Bronté' and anagrams of 'Emma' and 'Horatio'.

It might be better, he wrote

> to omit christening the child for the moment, and even privately baptising it. The clergyman *would naturally* ask for its parents' name which would put poor Mrs T. in trouble or cause suspicion.

His friend Alexander Davison, arriving on Friday, dined on board with Nelson, bringing more letters from Emma.

> He says you are grown thinner, but he thinks you look handsomer than ever. He says you told him to tell me not to send you any more advice about seeing comp^y [the Prince of Wales], for that you are determined not to allow the world to say a word ag^t you, therefore I will not say a word; I rest confident in your conduct. I was sure you would not go to Mrs Walpole's; it is no better than a bawdy house.

Soon a letter arrived containing a lock of Horatia's hair and a joyful Nelson told Emma it reminded him of the colour of his own when a child. Still writing as the friend of 'Mrs Thompson' he reported that 'he has put it in a case with [a lock of] his dear Mother's.' He sympathized with Emma for the trouble she was having with the nurse, commenting 'children bring their cares and pleasures with them'.

One of the matters Davison had to discuss with Nelson was a deed by which Sir William Hamilton assigned to Davison, in trust for Lady Hamilton, the furniture and other contents of 23 Piccadilly. The reason for this was referred to tactfully in a letter to Davison from Sir William's lawyer. 'As it is not convenient for Sir William to buy the furniture, plate, &c., necessary for them, Lady Hamilton sold her diamonds for that purpose.'

Davison acted as postman when he returned to London, allowing Nelson to write directly to Emma without the 'Mrs Thompson' subterfuge. However,

> I am not in very good spirits; and except that our Country demands all our services, and abilities to bring about an honourable peace, nothing should prevent me being the bearer of my own letter. But, my dear friend, I know you are so true and loyal an Englishwoman that you would hate those who would not stand forth in defence of our King, Laws and Religion, and all that is dear to us. It is your sex that make us go forth; and seem to tell us – 'None but the brave deserve the fair!' and, if we fall, we still live in the hearts of those females who are dear to us.

Emma must have been a puzzled woman at times because among the letters Davison brought to London was the following one written by Nelson later the same day – but after he had seen the issue of the *Morning Post* with the erroneous report that she had dined at the Duke of Norfolk's with the Prince of Wales. Gone was 'none but the brave', swept away by an uncertain lover's jealousy.

I do not think I ever was so miserable as this moment. I own I sometimes fear that you will not be so true to me as I am to you, yet I cannot, will not, believe you can be false. No, I judge you by myself; I hope to be dead before that should happen, but it will not. Forgive me, Emma, oh forgive your own dear, disinterested Nelson. . . .

I have a letter from Sir William; he speaks of the Regency [because of the King's illness] as certain, and then probably he thinks you will sell better – horrid thought. . . .

His letter next day began in an unusual style, as if in his misery he recalled boyhood memories of his father reading the measured cadence of psalms in Burnham Thorpe church. Yet the sentiments were familiar enough and ended with a lover's plea.

I may not be able to write to you tomorrow, but thou are present ever to my eyes. I see, hear, no one else. Parker sits next to me to cut my meat when I want it done. . . . I am writing in a room full of interruptions, therefore give me credit for my thoughts. You can guess them; they are, I trust, like your own.

But the passing days did not lessen a jealousy which was fast becoming corrosive. To 'Mrs Thompson' he wrote the following day that,

Your dear friend . . . is almost distracted; he wishes there was peace, or that if your uncle would die, he would instantly come and marry you, for he doats [sic] on nothing but you and his child; and, as it is my godchild, I desire you will take great care of it. He has implicit faith in your fidelity, even in conversation with those he dislikes, and that you will be faithful in greater things he has no doubt. . . .

All this stung Emma into a sharp reply over Nelson's jealousy, throwing in some of her own for good measure. Her letter startled Nelson into hurriedly reassuring her.

Well, my dear friend, I only wish you could read my heart, then, I am sure, you would not write, or even think a hard thing of me. Suppose I did say that the West Countrywomen wore black stockings, what is it more than if you was to say what puppies all the present young men are. You cannot help your eyes, and God knows I cannot see much.

Then, to make the point again, he wrote:

If you see Mrs Thompson, say her friend has been a little fretted at her nonsense, but is better, as he is sure it can only proceed from her affection for him, but he desires me beg of you to tell her never to harbour a doubt of his fidelity.

By Thursday, 12 February, he was reporting to Lord St Vincent that his flag was on board the *St George*, and the new head of the Admiralty was assured that he could rely on the fact that 'all your directions and wishes, if I can guess them, shall be complied with'.

Nelson – who had earlier written, 'I conjectured that the Earl was driving past for something good' – told Davison that the moment Lord St Vincent came from the King, having agreed to serve as First Lord, the old admiral wrote him a 'very flattering' letter seeking his support. 'So,' Nelson said, 'I will support him as a great sea officer.'

Writing to St Vincent again the following Monday, apparently in reply, he said:

I feel all your kind expressions, and in return I have only to assure you that I never will ask you for what my judgment may tell is an improper thing. My sole object . . . is to bring this long war to an honourable termination; to accomplish which, we must all pull in the collar, and as we have got such a driver who will make the lazy ones pull as much as the willing, I doubt not but we shall get safely, speedily and honourably to our journey's end. With every kind wish, both as a friend and as an Englishman, for your Ministerial prosperity. . . .

Nelson found the *St George* extremely uncomfortable; nor was his peace of mind eased in compensation for his physical discomfort when he heard that a certain Mr Hodges was in London.

I remember your story of that Mr Hodges at Naples [he told Emma] how he used to get suppers at this place and the other and pay for them on purpose for your company, but I feel confident you will never admit him to any of your parties. As for the Prince of Wales, I know his character, and my confidence is firm as a rock till you try to irritate me to say hard things, that you may have the pleasure of scolding me; but recollect it must remain four days before it can be made up, not, as before, in happy times, four minutes. . . .

I never intend, if I can help it, to set my foot outside the ship, but she is so completely uncomfortable you can have no conception how miserable she is. By Hardy's account he has been on board two days endeavouring to make my place a little decent, but it is neither wind nor watertight, but I shall religiously stay on board, as you like me to do so, and I have no other pleasures. . . . I am certainly much better for leaving off wine; I drink nothing but water at dinner, and a little wine and water after dinner. I believe it has saved me from illness.

Davison was told the same day that the ship was 'in a truly wretched state. I had rather encounter the [newly] painted cabbins[1] than her dreary dirty and leaky cabbin, the water comes in at all parts and there is not a dry place or a window that does not let in wind enough to man

[1] The smell of new paint always made him ill.

a mill.' He concluded, 'I shall take my [silver] plate with me; sink or swim it goes with me.'

The next letter from Emma chided him over an anniversary she thought he had forgotten, and late at night on 16 February he wrote: 'Ah my dear friend, I did remember well the 12th February, and also the two months afterwards I shall never forget them, and never be sorry for the consequences. . . .' He went on to mention one of them. 'I admire what you say of my godchild. If it is like its mother it will be very handsome, for I think her one, aye, the most beautiful, woman of the age. Now do not be angry at my praising the dear child's mother, for I have heard people say she is a very little like you. . . .'

Because Nelson and Emma had never been together on any 12 February from their first meeting nor for any 'two months afterwards', this reference has been a puzzle. But although it is not known exactly what Emma's letter said, if one bears in mind they feared their letters might be opened or fall into the wrong hands – hence the 'Mrs Thompson' subterfuge – there are many clues. Nelson refers to a specific date; to the two months afterwards; and 'will never be sorry for the consequences'. Almost immediately he refers (since the letter is addressed to 'Lady Hamilton', not 'Mrs Thompson') to his 'godchild'. Horatia, only a few days old, is the only significant 'consequence' of their relationship that he need assure Emma he would never be sorry for.

So there can be little doubt that he and Emma meant 12 May, changing it to February for fear of prying eyes, and were referring to the time just over nine months earlier when Horatia was conceived. On 12 May the Hamiltons were with Nelson on board the *Foudroyant* for a long cruise which began at Palermo on 22 April, included a visit to Syracuse, a stay in Malta from 3 May to 20 May, and ended at Palermo on 31 May. For most of the two months after the 12th Nelson was with Emma. So, assuming they had changed the month to deceive prying eyes, it is interesting to speculate why Emma was chiding Nelson for forgetting a particular day, for it is unlikely she could be sure that was the precise day Horatia was conceived. The 12th could, however, have been the first night they spent together as lover and mistress – much later in their relationship than most people would think; but then it was a strange relationship. . . .

Nelson's confidence in Emma's fidelity vanished once again only a few hours after writing the above letter because he received one from Sir William Hamilton saying:

Whether Emma will be able to write to you today or not is a question, as she has got one of her terrible headaches.

Among other things that vex her is that we have been drawn in to be under the absolute necessity of giving a dinner to the Prince of Wales on Sunday next [22 February]. He asked it himself, having expressed his strong desire of hearing Banti's and Emma's voices together.

I am well aware of the danger that would attend the Prince's frequenting our house, not that I fear that Emma could ever be induced to act contrary to the prudent conduct she has hitherto pursued, but the world is so ill-natured that the worst construction is put upon the most innocent actions.

As this dinner must be, we shall keep it strictly to the musical part, invite only Banti, her husband, and Taylor and as I wish to shew a civility to [Alexander] Davison I have sent him an invitation.

In short we will get rid of it as well as we can and guard against its producing more meetings of the same sort. Emma would really have gone any lengths to have avoided Sunday's dinner, but I thought it would not be prudent to break with the Prince who really has shown the greatest civility to us when we were last in England and since we returned, and she has at last acquiesced to my opinion. I have been thus explicit as I know well your Lordship's way of thinking and your very kind attachment to us and to every thing that concerns us. . . .[1]

But Nelson had already heard the news from Emma, to whom his reply was hysterical.

I am so agitated that I can write nothing. I knew it would be so, and you can't help it. Why did you not tell Sir William? Your character will be gone. Good God he will be next you, and telling you soft things. If he does, tell it out at table, and turn him out of the house. Do not sit long. If you sing a song, I know you cannot help it, do not let him sit next you, but at dinner he will hob glasses with you. . . . O, God, that I was dead! But I do not, my dearest Emma, blame you, nor do I fear your inconstancy. I tremble, and God knows how I write. Can nothing be thought of? I am gone almost mad but you cannot help it. It will be in all the newspapers with hints. Recollect what the villain said to Mr Nisbet, *how you hit his fancy*. . . .

He continued the letter next day, still hysterical:

I shall that day have no one to dinner; it shall be a fast day to me. He will put his foot near you. I pity you from my soul, as I feel confident you wish him in hell. Have plenty of people. . . . He wishes, I dare say, to have you alone. Don't let him touch you, nor yet sit next you; if he comes, get up. God strike him blind if he looks at you – that is high treason, and you may get me hanged by revealing it. . . . He will stay and sup and sit up till 4 in the morning, and the fewer that stay the better. Oh God! Why do I live? . . . I am only fit to be second, or third, or 4, or to black shoes. . . .

[1] To a sophisticated eye, this letter makes it quite clear that Sir William was aware of the relationship between Nelson and Emma, and was certainly not against it. Otherwise it is difficult to explain why Sir William felt it necessary to write to Nelson in this fashion about the unwelcome guest.

Sending that letter on shore to be posted on the night of the 18th, he had calmed down by the next morning – at least, he began his new letter quietly enough. 'Forgive my letter . . . perhaps my head was a little affected. No wonder, it was such an unexpected, such a knock-down blow, such a death. But I will not go on, for I shall get out of my senses again. . . .'

His resolution held only until the next day, when he finished the letter after receiving one from Emma.

I have just got your letter and I live again. *DO NOT* let the lyar come. I never saw him [the Prince] but once. . . . May God blast him! Be firm! Go and dine with Mrs Denis on Sunday. Do not, I beseech you, risk being at home. Does Sir William want you to be a whore to the rascal? Forgive all my letter; you will see what I feel, and have felt. I have eat not a morsel, except a little rice, since yesterday morning. . . .

I have this moment got my orders to put myself under Sir Hyde Parker's orders, and suppose I shall be ordered to Portsmouth tomorrow or next day, and then I will try and get to London for 3 days. May Heaven bless us! but do not let that fellow dine with you. Don't write here, write a note to Sir Hyde Parker, asking if the *St George* is ordered to Spithead. If so write to Portsmouth desiring my letters to be left at the Post Office till the ship's arrival. Forgive every cross word, I now live.

In the last three days before the dinner, arranged for Sunday, letters were sent to Emma by almost every post. Each one of more than half a dozen reveal how overwrought was Nelson.

I again, my dear friend, entreat both you and Sir William not to suffer the Prince to dine, or even visit. 'Tis what no real modest person would suffer, and Sir William ought to know that his views are *dishonourable* [he wrote on Thursday]. Do not let the villain into your house. Dine out on Sunday. . . .

On Friday 'Mrs Thomson' was told,

Your friend is at my elbow and enjoins me to assure you that his love for you is, if possible, greater than ever, and that he calls God to witness that he will marry you as soon as possible, and that it will be his delight to call you his own. He desires you will adhere to Lady H's good advice [Nelson wrote with a lover's cunning], and like her, keep those impertinent men at a proper distance. . . .

The next letter described how,

I feel very much for the unpleasant situation the Prince or rather Sir William, has unknowingly placed you, for if he knew as much of P's [sic: the Prince's nickname was 'Prinny'] character as the world does, he would rather let the lowest wretch that walks the streets dine at his table than that unprincipled liar. I have heard it reported that he has said he would make you his mistress. Sir William never can admit him into his house, nor can any friend advise him to it unless they are determined on your hitherto unimpeached character being ruined. No modest woman would suffer it. He is permitted to visit only houses of *notorious* ill-fame. . . .

'Mrs Thomson' received the oblique plea:

He says he feels confident of your conduct, and begs you will follow the admirable conduct of our dear Lady Hamilton, who will send the Prince to the Devil. He again begs me to be his bondsman, and that he will marry you the moment your uncle dies or it comes a peace, and he desires his blessing to his child. . . .

The next, also addressed to 'Mrs Thomson' and again referring to Sir William as 'Uncle', was dated 'Off Portland 10 o'clock, Friday,' and said her dear friend

. . . Has been very unhappy at the shocking conduct of your uncle, but your firmness and virtue has made his mind at ease, and he desires me to tell you that if you are forced to quit his house by his shameful behaviour, that then nothing should make him go to sea, even under my flag. . . .

At eight o'clock next morning, 'In a gale of wind, S.W. of the Isle of Wight', he added:

I have been unwell all night, and horrid dreams. If your uncle persists in having such bad company to dinner your friend begs . . . that you should dine out of the house . . . and after all, if the beast turns you out of his house because you will not submit to be thought a w——e, you know then what shall happen. . . .

Nor had Nelson neglected to get one of his friends to be present at 23 Piccadilly on the night of the dinner. His old friend, Captain Sir Thomas Troubridge, had to leave the Channel Fleet, travelling from Torbay to London to take his seat on the new Board of Admiralty, and he sailed with Nelson in the *St George* to Portsmouth, thus avoiding the tedious journey by road from Torbay. When he left Portsmouth for London on Sunday morning Nelson gave him a letter for Emma. 'I hope you will have seen Troubridge last night', Nelson wrote on Monday,

and he will probably tell you that he did not leave me perfectly at ease. . . . In short, when I gave [him] a letter for you it rushed into my mind in that ten hours he would see you. A flood of tears followed – it was too much for me to bear. . . . I hope very soon to get a few days leave of absence but Sir Hyde does not come down till next Monday or Tuesday.

Nelson was careful not to leave himself open to any counterattack by Emma.

I have been pressed to dine ashore by the Admiral, an old man, eighty, with an old wife dressed old ewe lamb. . . . Admiral Holloway, an acquaintance of 25 years, wanted me to dine with him . . . Sir Charles Saxton, the Commissioner, an acquaintance of near 30 years, was also very pressing . . . but I will dine nowhere without your consent, although, with my present feelings, I might be trusted with 50 virgins naked in a dark room. . . .

It is difficult to realize that the writer of these irrational and often hysterical letters was, when in battle or considering the strategic, tactical or diplomatic aspects of a situation, one of the shrewdest and coolest men not just of his day but in the history of sea warfare; but he was also experiencing real love for the first time.

Within a few hours of Troubridge's departure, the storm was over and Nelson wrote:

Poor Thompson seems to have forgot all his ill health, and all his mortifications and sorrows, in the thought that he will soon bury them all in your dear, dear bosom; he seems almost beside himself. . . . I daresay twins will again be the fruit of your and his meeting.[1] The thought is too much to bear. Have the dear thatched cottage ready to receive him, and I will answer that he would not give it up for a queen and a palace.

On the Friday that he wrote to Mrs Thomson from Torbay about the 'shocking conduct' of her 'uncle', Nelson wrote to Lord St Vincent that 'Before we go to the North, I shall have to request either public or private leave for three days, to settle some very important matters for myself.' A postscript said that if St Vincent was not taking his musicians from the *Ville de Paris* on shore, 'I shall be happy to have ten or twelve of them, and will with pleasure pay them the same as you do.'

The new First Lord of the Admiralty was later told of difficulties the Customs authorities were making about allowing the Earl's locked plate-chest to be sent to London after being landed from the *Ville de Paris*: no one had the keys to open it for their inspection – 'I offered to pass my word that you were sending up no smuggled goods; but my word would not pass current.' He was still writing when a message arrived from the Secretary of the Admiralty, sent by the telegraph,[2] telling him 'I have their Lordships' commands to acquaint you that they are pleased to grant you three days leave of absence to come to Town on your private affairs.' He added a note to St Vincent's letter – 'I shall see you tomorrow.'

---

[1] It is not known if Horatia was the survivor of twins; this reference certainly makes it appear she was, although previous ones do not express any consolation or grief.

[2] Using a system of signal towers between London and Portsmouth, and passing messages by a type of semaphore. The Plymouth telegraph, which began in July 1806, could send a message to the Admiralty and receive an answer in less than thirty minutes. A short message would receive an answer in ten minutes.

Nelson spent Monday night in a carriage taking him the seventy-two miles from Portsmouth to London, where he arrived in time for an early breakfast with the Hamiltons at 23 Piccadilly. Apart from seeing his baby daughter Horatia for the first time, there was much for him to do in anticipation of the Baltic expedition. Nor was it any comfort that 'the villain' was, at that moment, quite likely to accede to the Throne as George IV: the King, still seriously ill from the cold he caught on the Day of Fast, was now unconscious. . . .

The issue of *The Times* published on Tuesday, the day Nelson arrived in London, contained the usual mixture of correct and highly secret information mixed with wild inaccuracies that characterized Press reports of the Government's intentions.

Noting that Sir Hyde Parker had hoisted his flag on board the *London* at Portsmouth the previous day, it added Nelson had arrived from the westward in the *St George*. 'Admirals Sir Hyde Parker and Lord Nelson are expected to sail immediately for the North Sea.'

The newspaper added,

The Fleet for the Baltic is already assembling. Several vessels have sailed from Portsmouth to the eastward. As we are doomed to fight our way to peace by victory, we anticipate, with the highest satisfaction, the new laurels which are preparing for our gallant seamen; and soon shall we see Lord Nelson lead the van into the harbour of Cronstadt, and serve the Russians as he did the French at Aboukir.

Sir Hyde did not join the *London* in Portsmouth – he had not in fact left his house in London. On the Monday that Nelson set off for the capital, Henry Dundas was drawing up the detailed orders to the Admiralty for Sir Hyde, already quoted.

Every Commander-in-Chief was required by the Admiralty to keep a journal, a cross between an official diary and a ship's log, and Sir Hyde's first entry was for the middle of February.

I was then in Town, on leave [he wrote]. On 17th February received order to take the flag officers, captains, commanders and the ships and vessels herein mentioned under my command and when ready to repair to Yarmouth Roads, issued my orders on 18th for that purpose, and sent them to the different ports.

However, the days passed and Sir Hyde remained in London with his young wife, waiting for the Admiralty's orders. These, lengthy and based on Dundas's instructions, were written on the 24th, the day Nelson arrived in London.

In normal circumstances – particularly when taking over a newly-formed fleet comprising ships which had never worked together as a complete unit before – a Commander-in-Chief would be anxious to hoist his flag and start the process of making the Fleet efficient. Sir Hyde was in no such hurry, even after receiving his final orders on 24 February. He decided to leave Nelson to bring the Spithead ships to Yarmouth; but he showed no haste to go to Yarmouth himself, although other ships of his fleet were already there and his preliminary orders of the 17th told him that he was 'to repair to Yarmouth Roads' when ready.

Hyde Parker's tardiness in joining the nucleus of his fleet already at Yarmouth was only the first display of tardiness on his part. It is also unlikely that Nelson failed to conceal his impatience from his friend Troubridge, who was now attending as a member of the Board of Admiralty, because the day after Nelson arrived in London Parker wrote in his journal what was an unusual entry, since it is in the same sentence that he records the phrase 'when ready'. He noted, '. . . on 25th received orders to proceed to Yarmouth and hoist my flag on board any ship I thought proper 'till joined by the *London* and get ready for sea'.

And, travelling next day with his wife, he made a leisurely journey of it, noting: 'On the 26th I left Town and arrived at Yarmouth on the 28th. Ordered my flag to be hoisted on board the *Ardent*.' However he and his wife stayed at the Wrestler's Arms and young Lady Parker settled down to make the best of what social life that old Norfolk seaport could offer.

Meanwhile Nelson had, as he mentioned in a letter to Emma, received Parker's orders. Although they were signed by Parker, they were written by his secretary, Osborn, whose remarkable carelessness in writing letters for the admiral to sign throws an interesting sidelight on Sir Hyde. Although so fussy about detail, he rarely noticed that Osborn frequently made mistakes in rank, or spelled the same word two different ways in the same letter. The order to Nelson is one of many examples. At the bottom left-hand corner Osborn had written, following the usual formula:

'Rear Admiral Nelson,
by command of the Admiral,
B. Osborn.'

He had then crossed out the word 'Rear' and corrected it by sub-stituting 'Vice'. But it was still wrong since Nelson was a peer of the realm and failing to address him as 'Vice Admiral Lord Nelson' was unpardonable carelessness – sufficient to have a seven-line order of this importance written again – or if the error in rank was corrected but the peerage ignored, a deliberate slight. Either way it would hardly go unnoticed even by someone much less touchy than Nelson.

When Parker's carriage had finally left Cumberland Place the Admiralty wrote to Nelson that 'Admiral Sir Hyde Parker has left Town this day for North Yarmouth', and the ships under Parker's command still in Spithead were to sail for Yarmouth Roads without waiting for each other. Nelson was to follow in the *St George* 'the moment she is ready'. The ships were to pick up the flat-bottom boats at Deal and the carronades at Dover, stopping in the Downs.[1]

Sir Hyde was soon joined at Yarmouth by the Reverend Alexander John Scott. Although four years later he was to become the most famous chaplain in the Royal Navy's history because he tended the dying Nelson at Trafalgar, he was at this point thirty-two years of age and a fine scholar with a remarkable facility for learning foreign languages. This alone made him extremely useful to an admiral, since he could and did act as translator – newspapers and documents from an enemy prize were always a good source of intelligence.

Scott provides an example of 'interest' at work; but more important he is also a good example of a case where 'interest' made a talented man available to others who needed him. His father, a half-pay lieutenant in the Royal Navy, died when Alexander was four years old. He was nominated to a scholarship at Charterhouse at the age of ten, and then went on to St John's, Cambridge, where he took a BA and was ordained at the age of twenty-one.

Wanting to repay debts accumulated earlier, he joined the 74-gun *Berwick* as chaplain, serving in the Mediterranean. Among the young captains Scott met at this time was Horatio Nelson. In May, 1795, he became chaplain in Sir Hyde Parker's flagship, and when Sir Hyde went to Jamaica as Commander-in-Chief, Scott accompanied him as his secretary – and also obtained a benefice there. When Sir Hyde subsequently returned to England Scott travelled with him, having been given leave of absence from his benefice 'on account of health' but, of course, still receiving his stipend.

When Sir Hyde returned from his honeymoon, he asked Scott to be chaplain of the *London* and 'interpreter and translator of languages' to the Baltic expedition. Scott accepted and Parker gave him a warrant confirming the appointment.[2]

Of the languages he already spoke – French, German, Italian and

---

[1] The anchorage off Deal, inside and sheltered by the Goodwin Sands.

[2] Unfortunately for Scott the Admiralty subsequently considered the appointment a private arrangement so that Scott received no pay for his role as interpreter and translator.

Spanish, in addition to Latin and Greek – only French, used in diplomacy, would now be of use to him, so Scott began learning Danish and Russian. He had no trouble in buying a Danish grammar and a dictionary, but it was more difficult for Russian. Finally a friend who knew someone who had lived in Russia helped strike a blow against the Czar by providing a copy of *Elemens de la Langue Russe*, published by the Imperial Academy of Sciences in St Petersburg, which was sent to Scott at Yarmouth.[1]

As soon as it became known a fleet was assembling for the Baltic, many officers who knew the waters called at the Admiralty with plans for defeating the Danish and Russian Fleets. They were not 'the lunatic fringe' but men like Captain Nicholas Tomlinson who not only had a great deal of experience commanding a Russian sail of the line in the Baltic but had the courage of his convictions, which he proved by volunteering to serve without pay so his knowledge could be used, whether or not his plans were adopted.

The son of a naval officer, Tomlinson had considerable experience of action – including command of a gun boat in expeditions up the rivers in Virginia, and one of the advanced batteries at Yorktown (earning Lord Cornwallis's personal thanks). He joined the Imperial Russian Navy while on half-pay in peacetime but resigned his Russian commission and came home when war seemed likely between Britain and France.

When reports of a Baltic expedition began to circulate, Tomlinson drew up and sent to Nepean at the Admiralty a well-thought-out 'Plan for Destroying the Russian-Danish Fleets'. It was based on four factors, the first three of which were little known in the Admiralty: a wide knowledge of the Baltic, the Russian mentality, the condition of her ships and men, and considerable experience of handling ships of war close inshore in shoal or rocky waters. With it were some charts of the Baltic and Cattegat.

The plan showed an extremely good grasp of strategy and tactics applied to the Baltic. It began by assuming Parker's squadron could force its way into the Sound – with a fair wind this 'may always be done with great ease', he wrote – and in his opinion the Danish Fleet could be destroyed 'either in the Mole [Copenhagen Harbour], or in the Roads of Copenhagen before that of Russia or Sweden are disengaged from the ice'.

[1] With the inscription 'This book kindly lent by Dr Rogers, late of St Petersburg, to John Sewell, 32 Cornhill, for the express purpose of accommodating the Rev. – Scott, going in the present armament to the North. Sewell procured it from Dr R., with intent to have it translated into English, and printed, in which work Mr Scott can probably assist. 32, Cornhill, 4th March, 1801.'

Emphasizing that 'as the Gulf of Finland is open at Revel at least a week or ten days before it is opened at Cronstadt', the Russian squadron there 'may be destroyed by the same means, before that of Cronstadt can come to their assistance, or can even be got to the outside of the Mole heads'. In addition, because the roads of Copenhagen, Revel and Cronstadt were similar, being so open they could not be properly defended by batteries, he wrote, an example for putting his plan in execution at one place would serve for the others.

Tomlinson pointed out that the hulls of line of battle ships lying in the moles at all three ports were considerably higher than the piers, so 'they may be set on fire not only with bomb vessels but by gun boats, which should have two long guns each, with a furnace for heating shot'. As the enemy's ships lay close to each other, 'by setting only two or three of them on fire, the remainder would soon share the same fate'.

After destroying the Danish Fleet at Copenhagen, to make sure of finding the Russian ships within the Mole of Revel it would be advisable to push through the loose ice because, 'as it is rotten and spongy in the Spring of the year, there is no danger, as [there is] in the Autumn, of its hurting or cutting the ships' bows'. After Revel the Fleet 'should immediately push on for Cronstadt, where they would find the Russians still in the Mole, or at least the greater part of them'. He indicated where the bomb vessels and gun boats should anchor to avoid the enemy's fire.

If the enemy ships were 'at anchor in the roads of their principal seaports' instead of at the moles, Tomlinson said there would be little difficulty in defeating them with a smaller force of ships of the line if it was assisted by fire ships, but he cautioned that the fire ships 'should be conducted in a very different way from that at present in practice'.

He proposed using two fire ships instead of one to attack each enemy ship, but the extra one 'need not be near so large, or expensive as those now in use'. His point was that two fire ships connected together would 'be almost sure of success', but a single fire ship attempting to run alongside an enemy could be boomed off after cutting rigging which the grapnels might have hooked.[1]

In a memorandum on the Russian Fleet at Cronstadt, of which he had considerable knowledge, he began:

As the principal part of the Russian Fleet winter within the Mole at Cronstadt, such as are wanted for the service of the ensuing summer get their guns and stores on board and bend sails before the ice breaks up, when they begin to haul out of the Mole.

[1] Fire ships had grapnels hanging from the outer ends of their yards – which projected beyond their sides – to catch in the enemy ships' rigging.

This generally happened between the end of April and the middle of May, and though the van division might begin to haul out of the Mole as soon as the ice allowed, if the wind was westerly (which is very prevalent at that season), it took nearly a fortnight to get them all into their stations in the inner road of Cronstadt.

Their van (with 20 ships of the line) then extends four or five miles from the batteries on the Western Mole Head, and their rear is within a mile of them. In this situation they may be easily attacked; particularly if the wind is westerly, which would carry His Majesty's ships to their station; for the channel in which the rear division lays is so narrow, that with the wind in that direction they could not come to the assistance of their van, which may be attacked to great advantage as far down as the centre, without going within reach of the batteries. . . .

But if – as he now considered there was reason to suspect – the Russian Fleet went to the Outer Road so they had room to moor in order of battle, they would be too far out for shore batteries to protect them 'and of course lay exposed in an open Road to the attack of the British Fleet; which with the assistance of fire ships would (I have no doubt) soon defeat them; for a Russian Fleet once put in confusion cannot easily be rallied'.

The Admiralty accepted Tomlinson's offer to serve as a volunteer and the Board Secretary sent copies of Tomlinson's plan and memorandum to Sir Hyde Parker. As Tomlinson dated both 5 February it is certain Parker received them within a week.

It might seem strange that the Admiralty was grateful for navigational and operational information such as Tomlinson's; but at that time there was no such thing as a properly-organized hydrographic department and no plans division. Captains and masters of ships of war usually had to obtain their own charts, and masters had standing instructions to make charts and drawings of any unusual coasts and ports they visited. Several private firms published charts of varying accuracy, usually drawn up with the help of masters of merchantmen regularly trading in the various areas. It will be seen later that although about to take a fleet to the Baltic, even Sir Hyde Parker had trouble in finding suitable charts.

In 1801 only a rudimentary chart department existed; little more than a filing system.[1] When possible, the Admiralty chose captains who knew the waters, and in this case Lord St Vincent also recommended a man to Nelson, who knew the value of such captains – unlike Parker who, as will be shown later, ignored them. From Spithead, Nelson

[1] After the Battle, Nelson sent Nepean 'remarks made on the passage of the Belt, also drawings of the same, which I beg you will be pleased to lodge in the records of the Admiralty, that they may be referred to, in case they are wanted'.

wrote to St Vincent, 'I have not yet seen Captain Thesiger here, I shall receive him with much pleasure; if he is still in Town pray send word to him to meet me in the Downs or Yarmouth.' It was to be a fortunate meeting.

Frederick Thesiger had first gone to sea as a boy with 'John Company', but after several voyages to India he found life in the service of the Honourable East India Company too monotonous and joined the Royal Navy as a midshipman. He was Rodney's ADC at the Battle of the Saintes but, at the end of that war, became impatient with the years of peace and joined the Russian Navy, along with many other British officers (several of whom Rodney had himself recommended to the Russian Ambassador).

By 1789 he was commanding a Russian 74-gun ship and in the war with Sweden distinguished himself. In one action he forced the Swedish admiral in the *Gustavus* to surrender; a few months later in another battle, off the island of Bornholm, he was the only one of six British captains to survive – though wounded several times – and the Empress Catherine (mother of Czar Paul) presented him with a sword of honour and the insignia of the Order of St George.

A few years later, after Catherine's death, Thesiger was dissatisfied with the new Czar and resigned his commission. This angered Paul who, with his usual wilfulness, refused him a passport and his pay, so Thesiger could not leave St Petersburg. More than a year passed and, as Paul began forming the Northern Convention, Thesiger escaped and returned to England, where Lord Spencer was quick to make use of his practical knowledge of the Baltic and the Russian Fleet and the fact he spoke both Russian and Danish.

The captain of the *Edgar*, George Murray, the son of a Chichester magistrate, and at this time forty-one years old, had a good knowledge of one part of the Cattegat. The previous summer he had made a detailed survey of the Great Belt which (see chart on page 264) is to the west of Zealand, the island on which Copenhagen stands, and provides a route for approaching Copenhagen from the south by going right round the island. It will be shown later that this knowledge of a very small area was something upon which Parker placed too much reliance, and which nearly led to his undoing.

By ignoring Tomlinson, Thesiger and several other officers – who knew the Sound and the whole of the Baltic extremely well – and listening to Murray, who did not know the Sound but knew the Great Belt, Parker gives yet another interesting insight into his cautious mentality. But Murray's knowledge had been set down as soundings on a chart: for Parker it was obviously something tangible: paper with writing on it that Parker could unroll, spread out on a table and look at in the privacy of his cabin. The infinitely greater knowledge of the whole Baltic possessed by Tomlinson and Thesiger was, to Parker, intangible: he could not touch it, and to use it he had to stow his pride and ask questions and rely on the spoken answers of mere captains; men who had served under foreign flags. So he never asked any of them a single question; indeed, he even ignored Tomlinson's presence in his ship.

Nelson's three days in London were busy from the time he arrived at 23 Piccadilly, on Tuesday morning, until he arrived back on board the *St George* at Spithead on Friday. As his own house in Dover Street was closed up, he stayed at Lothian's Hotel in Albemarle Street. Emma wrote to his sister-in-law, Mrs William Nelson (her relations were good with all Nelson's family),

Your dear Brother arrived this morning by seven o'clock. He stays only 3 days. . . . I am in health *so so*, but in *spirits* today excellent. Oh, what a real pleasure Sir William and I have in seeing this our great good virtuous Nelson. His eye is better. Tom Tit [the family's nickname for Lady Nelson] does not come to Town. She offered to go down [to Portsmouth] but was refused. She only wanted to go to do mischief to all the great Jove's [Nelson's] relations. 'Tis now shown, all her ill-treatment and bad *heart*. Jove has found it out. . . .

Apart from reassuring himself about Emma's fidelity after the dining-room crisis with the Prince of Wales, Nelson was excited and anxious to have his first sight of his daughter Horatia. There were talks at the Admiralty over the forthcoming expedition; Baltic charts had to be obtained; special stores were selected and bought for himself to make the forthcoming expedition more comfortable; relations and fellow officers had to be seen.

Nelson and Sir William had several discussions about the Prince of Wales. They decided that as a last resort the talkative wife of Nelson's boring brother William could be brought to London: at dinner she could act as both depressant and chaperon.

The Admiralty was only a short distance from Lothian's Hotel, and Nelson called on Lord St Vincent the morning he arrived. No record of their conversation exists; but one can be sure Nelson expressed surprise that Sir Hyde Parker was still in Town since, as described earlier, the very next day the Admiralty gave a direct order to Parker to leave for Yarmouth. Perhaps significantly, Parker did not meet his second-in-command while Nelson was in London.

The first day in London also saw him discussing two diverse items of business with Alexander Davison. The first again concerned Sir William, who was still short of money and had told Nelson he was selling some of his collection of china and paintings – among them Romney's painting of Emma as St Cecilia. Davison was instructed to buy the painting secretly for Nelson and keep it in store. The second concerned the forthcoming Baltic campaign. Davison had already bought charts, and in his house Nelson used them to show how he would attack the Danes – if he was commanding the expedition.

Guests for dinner at 23 Piccadilly the first night of his stay in London included Troubridge and Nelson's brother Maurice, who was a clerk in the Admiralty and whose poor health was a constant worry to Nelson, who little guessed he was dining with him for the last time.[1]

Busy as he was, Nelson had time to finish a letter to his wife which he had begun writing at Portsmouth. Lady Nelson was told:

As I am sent for to Town on a very particular business for a day or two I would not on any account have you come to London but rest quiet where you are. Nor would I have you come to Portsmouth, for I never come on shore. The King is reported to be more than very ill, but I and every good subject must pray for his life. I hope Josiah may be able to get a ship now this change of ministers has taken place.

Lady Nelson's son was fortunate because his step-father was able to add to the letter when he reached London: 'Josiah is to have the *Thalia* [frigate], and I want to know from him two good lieutenants, they must be of my approval.'

Leaving London soon after midnight, Nelson's coach arrived at Portsmouth before noon on Friday, 27 February. He had time to send a brief note to Emma: 'Parting from such a friend is literally tearing one's own flesh; but the remembrance will keep up our spirits till we meet. . . .' Since arriving, he wrote, he 'had my hands full of business. Tomorrow we embark troops.'

Unfortunately he had forgotten to mention the troops when he was with Emma, and she became very alarmed. In the meantime he wrote again (at '8 o'clock in the morning') saying that she would have read the letter from his brother William 'and if you like to have Mrs Nelson up [in London], say that I will pay their lodgings, and then you can have as much of her company as you please; but Reverend Sir you will find a great bore at times, therefore he ought to amuse himself all the mornings, and not always dine with you, as Sir William may not like it'.

Then, he wrote in a second letter at noon,

[1] Nelson first saw his baby daughter on Wednesday. Horatia was being looked after by Mrs Gibson in Marylebone.

After my letter of 8 o'clock this morning went on shore, on board came Oliver, and when he was announced by Hardy, so much anxiety for your safety rushed into my mind that a pain immediately seized my heart, which kept increasing for half an hour, that, turning cold, hot, cold &c., I was obliged to send for the surgeon, who gave me something to warm me, for it was a deadly chill. . . .

Francis Oliver, Sir William's manservant and occasional secretary, had brought a tearful letter, and Nelson continued,

Why, my dear friend, do you alarm yourself? Your own Nelson will return safe as if walking London streets. The troops are only 800, and are intended for the better manning of our ships. Recollect the more force we have the less risk. You may rely we shall return in May – perhaps long before; the sooner we are off, the quicker we return, the enemy much less prepared to receive us. . . .

Since Oliver was returning to London, Nelson could write without fear of the letter being opened in the post, and in the third that day wrote:

Now, my dear wife, for such you are in my eyes and in the face of Heaven, I can give full scope to my feelings, for I daresay Oliver will faithfully deliver this letter. You know, my dearest Emma, that there is nothing in this world that I would not do for us to live together, and to have our dear little child with us.

I firmly believe that the campaign will give us peace, and then we will sett [sic] off for Bronté. In twelve hours we shall be across the water and freed from all the nonsense of his [Sir William's] friends, or rather pretended ones. Nothing but an event happening to him could prevent my going, and I am sure you will think so, for unless all matters accord it would bring 100 of tongues and slanderous reports if I separated from her (which I would do with pleasure the moment we can be united), I want to see her no more, therefore we must manage till we can quit this country or your uncle [Sir William] dies.

I love, I never did love any one else. I never had a dear pledge of love till you gave me one, and you, thank God, never gave one to any one else. I think before March is out you will either see us back, or so victorious that we shall insure a glorious issue to our toils. . . .

He assured Emma yet again,

Never, if I can help it, will I dine out of my ship, or go on shore, except duty calls me. Let Sir Hyde have any glory he can catch – I envy him not. You, my beloved Emma, and my country, are the two dearest objects of my fond heart – *a heart susceptible and true*. Only place confidence in me and you never shall be disappointed. I burn all your letters, because it is right for your sake, and I wish you would burn all mine – they can do no good, and will do us both harm if any seizure of them, or the dropping even one of them, would fill the mouths of the world sooner than we intend. My longing for you, both person and conversation, you may readily imagine. What must be my sensations at the idea of sleeping with you! It setts me on fire, even the thoughts, much more would the reality. . . .

Monday morning – Oliver is just going on shore; the time will ere long arrive when Nelson will land to fly to his Emma, to be forever with her. Let that hope keep us up under our present difficulties. Kiss and bless our dear Horatia – think of that.

When Lt-colonel Stewart arrived in Portsmouth to take command of the troops and embark them in the ships he began a diary in which he recorded everything he considered of interest. Being above all things a soldier, he began his 'Narrative of events' by listing the detachment he commanded[1] and then continued:

On the 27th Febr., in the forenoon, the troops proceeded to Southsea Common, awaiting orders to embark. Nelson arrived from London, about 10 a.m.: – He sent for me, immediately on his arrival, to Major General Whitelocke's: on first acquaintance with Lord Nelson I witnessed the activity of his character – he said that 'not a moment was to be lost in embarking the troops for he intended to sail next tide'. . . . Orders were sent for all boats, and the whole were on board of the men-of-war before midday.

Nelson had to give written orders to the captains of ten ships of the line to get ready for sea 'and paid (should any wages be due)', and then join Sir Hyde at Yarmouth, each calling at Dover to pick up two carronades for the two flat bottom boats they were to collect in the Downs.

Nelson had most of Portsmouth buzzing with activity. The Dockyard Commissioner, Sir Charles Saxton, promptly authorized the issue of bedding to the troops from the Navy stores; General Whitelocke, commanding the Army forces at Portsmouth, co-operated by signing orders for the immediate issue of canteens, haversacks and camp kettles.

Stewart gives an interesting word portrait of the admiral in a hurry.

Lord Nelson, in three hours after, left the sally port for the *St George*: this ship was commanded by his old friend Capt[n] Hardy . . . and was under considerable repairs at Spithead. No time, however, was to be lost; the caulkers and painters were detained on board, and we proceeded with them to St Helens [on the Isle of Wight], Lord Nelson observing that 'if the wind proved fair in the morning, they should be sent up the harbour, but if unfair no time would have been lost.' The wind became fair during the night, and we got under way at daylight on the 28th. . . .

---

[1] 'The 49th Reg[t] about 760 R[ank] and file, commanded by Lt Colonel Brock and a company of the Rifle Corps (now ye 95th Reg[t]) 100 R and file, commanded by Captain Sidney Beckwith.'

He then gave a description of Nelson which, since his knowledge of seamanship was nil and his criticism of the admiral's seamanship therefore of no value, still lights up another aspect of the man's personality.

Nothing particular occurred until our arrival in the Downs. The seine [fishing net] was frequently hauled by Lord Nelson's directions and the eagerness and vivacity which he showed upon the occasion, to the great delight of the seamen, early pointed out to me the natural liveliness of his character, even on trivial matters.

Another trait may be worthy of remark, as illustration of much *naiveté*: His Lordship was rather apt to interfere in the working of the ship, not always with the best success or judgment; the wind, when off Dungeness, was scanty, and the ship was to be put about. Lord N. would give the orders, and caused her to miss stays; upon this he said rather peevishly to the Master, or officer of the Watch (I forget which) 'Well now, see what we have done – well, sir, what mean you to do now?'

The officer saying, with hesitation, 'I don't exactly know my Lord, I fear she won't do,' Lord N. turned sharply towards the cabin and replied, 'Well, I am sure if you do not know what to do with her, no more do I either.' He went in leaving the officer to work the ship as he liked.

Anyone who has ever handled a ship under sail will read that passage with some amusement. The occasional wilfulness of a sailing vessel of any size with a 'scanty' wind usually provokes more surliness than Nelson displayed; and to use the episode to doubt the admiral's ability to tack a ship is to forget the years he had spent at sea.

Before leaving Spithead, Nelson had drawn up a report for the Admiralty on the condition of the ships of the line, the *Discovery* bomb vessel and, more interesting, a list which the Admiralty had requested of all the foreigners serving in each of them.

Three ships listed only the Scandinavians on board – the *St George* (one Swede), the *Bellona* (one Dane), and the *Discovery* ('Aaron Winholm . . . Sweed'). The other six ships listed all the foreigners – a total of thirteen Swedes, nine Danes, eight Americans, seven Dutchmen, seven Frenchmen, six Portuguese, five Germans, four Norwegians, three Italians, two from 'Africa', two Swiss, and one each from Curaçao, 'India', Austria and Grenada.[1]

Nelson knew that time was now as great an enemy as the Danes or Czar Paul. His brief visit to London had shown him that the Admiralty's preparations had kept pace with the swift sequence of events in the diplomatic field; but conversations with friends, apart from what he

[1] The *Russell* with a total of more than 700 men had the most cosmopolitan ship's company: Netherlands 3, Portugal 3, two each from Norway, Italy, 'Africa', France, America and Austria, and one each from Germany, Curaçao and 'India'.

knew of the man already, now raised doubts about his new Commander-in-Chief. Nelson knew better than most men the value of time – when to hasten, when to wait. He was to comment to an army officer on another occasion, 'Time, Twiss – time is everything; five minutes makes the difference between a victory and a defeat.'

Time now meant advancing spring and melting ice; a thaw in the Baltic which would release the cage into which winter always locked the Russian Fleet. The month of March was here; the Gulf of Finland would thaw in the next six or eight weeks . . . but Sir Hyde Parker seemed oblivious of any need for urgency. . . .

On the day before the *St George* left Spithead, Nelson wrote a carefully considered private letter to Lord St Vincent to emphasize his views:

Time, my dear Lord, is our best ally, and I hope we shall not give her up, as all our Allies have given us up. Our friend here [Sir Hyde] is a little nervous about dark nights and fields of ice, but we must brace up, these are not times for nervous systems. I want Peace, which is only to be had through, I trust, our still invincible Navy. . . .

Next day he added to the letter:

I am always happy when my conduct meets with your approbation and whilst I remain in the service my utmost exertions shall be called forth for although, I own, I have met with much more honours and rewards than ever my most sanguine ideas led me to expect, yet I am so circumstanced that probably this Expedition will be the last service ever performed by your obliged and affectionate friend, Nelson and Bronté.

The last sentence seems ambiguous. 'I am so circumstanced . . .' – was he referring to his poor health? Or was he referring to Emma? St Vincent was in no doubt and replied forthrightly:

Be assured, my dear Lord, that every *public* act of your life has been the subject of my admiration, which I should have sooner declared, but that I was appalled by the last sentence of your letter; for God's sake, do not suffer to be carried away by any sudden impulse. With many thanks for the spur you have given to the movement of the ships at Spithead, believe me to be yours most affectionately, St Vincent.

In London the Board of Admiralty, meeting on Sunday, 1 March, gave orders which illustrate the scope of its work. The minutes of the meeting record an order: 'Captain Flinders: *Investigator*, to receive on board the several persons apptd to make observations &c.: on the voyage of discovery, victualling them while on board in the usual manner.'[1] And four days later the minutes noted, 'Sir Charles Saxton

[1] Flinders bars, small magnets fitted to correct errors in a ship's compass, were named after him.

to order the Rat Catcher on board the *Alcmene* and destroy the rats on board her.' The *Alcmene* was under orders to join Sir Hyde's fleet as soon as she could get to sea.

On 4 March Nelson wrote his last letter to his wife. Its terms are quite clear, and read in conjunction with his 'I am so circumstanced' letter to St Vincent on 1 March it seems that his last visit to London had resulted in a final decision that his future was with Emma, at whatever cost and however long he had to wait for her to be free.

Josiah is to have another ship, and to go abroad, if the *Thalia* cannot soon be got ready [he wrote]. I have done *all* for him, and he may again, as he has often done before, wish me to break my neck, and be abetted in it by his friends, who are likewise my enemies; but I have done my duty as an honest, generous man, and I neither want or wish for anybody to care what becomes of me, whether I return, or am left in the Baltic. Living, I have done all in my power for you, and if dead, you will find I have done the same; therefore my only wish is, to be left to myself: and wishing you every happiness, believe that I am your affectionate. . . .

Lest this reference to death should seem melodramatic, it should be recalled that he had been wounded in all the major actions he had fought; indeed, as he wrote later to a friend 'Eye in Corsica, Belly off Cape St Vincent, Arm at Teneriffe, Head in Egypt. . . .'

The *St George*'s passage from the Downs to Yarmouth was far from enjoyable.

How tiresome and alone I feel at not having the pleasure of receiving your dear, kind, friendly and intelligent letters [he told Emma]. I literally feel as a fish out of water. Calms, and foul winds, have already prolonged our passage from what is often done in fourteen hours to three days, and yet no appearance of our arrival this day. It now snows and rains, and nearly calm.

All day yesterday I was employed about a very necessary thing; and I assure you it gave me pleasure instead of pain, the reflection that I was providing for a dear friend. I have given you, by will £3,000, and three diamond boxes, and the King of Naples's picture in trust, to be at your disposal, so that it is absolutely your own. By the codicil I have given you the money owing me by Sir William, likewise in trust.

Half past eight [a.m.] – Just anchored in the sea, thick as mud. I am already miserable; I look at all your pictures, at [the lock of] your dear hair, I am ready to cry, my heart is so full. Then I think you may see that fellow. I should never forgive it. It would go near to kill me; but I never will believe it till I know it for certain.

Noon – under sail, steering for Yarmouth. . . . Three o'clock – In sight of Yarmouth. With what different sensations to what I saw it before! Then I was with all I hold dear in the world [i.e. returning from Naples with the Hamiltons]; now, unless the pleasure I shall have in reading your dear, dear letters, how indifferent to the approach.

Writing again at 10 o'clock after the *St George* had anchored[1] that night he declared:

Nothing shall make me go on shore to any amusement or dinner. In the morning, if very fine, I shall go to make my bow to the Commander-in-Chief, but have asked some sailor folks to dinner. Our expedition must be very short. I don't think at most more than six weeks, probably not half so long, and if necessity should call me to England I will come directly. . . . Aye, would to God our fates had been different. I worship – nay, adore you, and if you was single and I found you under a hedge, I would instantly marry you. Sir Wm. has a treasure, and does he want to throw it away? That other chap did throw away the most precious jewel that God Almighty ever sent on this earth. . . .[2] Just going to bed with much rheumatism.

Next morning early he added:

I am just going on shore with Hardy to pay my formal visit. . . . I hope Sir Hyde will be pushed on to sail. The sooner we go the less resistance [we will meet], and, oh heavens grant it, the sooner your Nelson will return to his own dear, good, only friend. . . .

The fact Sir Hyde was staying on shore, not on board the *Ardent*, which was flying his flag until the *London* arrived, gave Nelson a fair warning that his forebodings about Sir Hyde's lack of urgency were coming true. Colonel Stewart noted that Nelson 'regretted' finding that Sir Hyde was staying at an hotel and 'reported his arrival and his intention of waiting on him the next morning'.

We breakfasted that morning, as usual, soon after six o'clock, for we were always up before daylight. We went on shore, so as to be at Sir Hyde's door by eight o'clock, Lord Nelson choosing to be amusingly exact to that hour, which he considered as a very late one for business.

So at eight o'clock precisely Vice-admiral Lord Nelson, Lt-colonel the Honourable William Stewart, MP, and Captain Thomas Masterman Hardy, were announced to Sir Hyde Parker at the Wrestler's Arms. There were many smiling faces among the staff to greet Nelson, for this was the hotel at which he and the Hamiltons stayed for the first night of their return to England.

The first official meeting between the Commander-in-Chief and his

---

[1] The first three-decker ever to anchor in the Roads, which can only be reached by narrow channels through shoals which frequently move.

[2] The 'other chap' was Charles Greville, Sir William's nephew and Emma's former lover.

second-in-command was also their first encounter for many years. It was also the first meeting between Sir Hyde and Stewart who, since he commanded the troops to be carried, anticipated either a discussion on the way his troops might be used to attack Cronborg Castle at Elsinore and the Arsenal at Copenhagen, or an appointment to do so later.

Sir Hyde was polite: he greeted Nelson and Stewart and made all the formal remarks they expected. But to the surprise of both men they were not the preliminaries to a discussion: they found Sir Hyde made his farewell and left to rejoin his wife in their suite without mentioning a word about the expedition. There had been no mention of a date for the Fleet to sail, no reference to navigational problems or comparison of the charts each admiral had, no hint of the way he was proposing to attack the Danes – no hint, indeed, that he was even going across the North Sea.

Stewart, being unfamiliar with naval procedure, did not at first realize the significance of Sir Hyde's behaviour. Nelson, apart from any personal considerations, was appalled for professional reasons: an important part of his own success in the past had been that he always made sure his own subordinates had as much information as possible about his intentions and, when possible, gave them an insight into the way he thought.

Lord Nelson's plan [Stewart wrote] would have been to have proceeded with the utmost despatch, and with such ships as were in readiness, to the mouth of Copenhagen Harbour; then and there to have insisted on amity or war, and have brought the objects of Messrs. Drummond and Vansittart's negotiations to a speedy decision.

He would have left orders for the remainder of the Fleet to have followed in succession, as they were ready, and by the rapidity of his proceedings have anticipated the formidable preparations for defence which the Danes had scarcely thought of at that early season. The delay in Yarmouth Roads did not accord with his views.

Boarding a three-decker from an open boat was no easy task for a one-armed man. In his cabin Nelson sat down to consider the visit to the Wrestler's Arms. It had yielded precisely three pieces of information, one of which had come from William Domett, the Captain of the Fleet, who had been far from happy. First, Nelson's fears that Sir Hyde would dally were confirmed; second, Nelson was himself being shut out; third, Domett's concern showed there were things concerning the Fleet worrying that extremely competent captain about which Nelson knew nothing, but the fact they worried Domett was all he needed to know.

Alone in the great cabin, the deck of which was covered in canvas painted in a chess-board pattern of black and white squares, Nelson considered what to do. The loneliness of high command never worried him. In this cabin he had sat at the desk and written hasty, ill-considered, hysterical letters to Emma; here he had railed at the Prince of Wales with all the outraged indignation of a wealthy bishop robbed by a pickpocket. In a cabin similar in many ways to this he had tried to outguess Napoleon in the long hunt the length and breadth of the Mediterranean for the French Fleet carrying the Army of Egypt.

Now he considered, decided and acted. A few hours after he had written to Emma that if she was single 'and I found you under a hedge, I would instantly marry you', he wrote to Troubridge. It was his only hope of getting to windward of the twin enemies, time and lethargy, and he knew the moment Troubridge received it he would note the instruction, probably have a quiet chuckle to himself, and promptly disobey it.

Aye, my dear Troubridge [he wrote] had you been here today you would have thought had the pilots [for the North Sea and Baltic] arrived a fortnight hence, they would have been time enough. Fame says we are to sail the 20th [in thirteen days time] and I believe it, unless you pack us off.

I was in hopes that Sir Hyde would have had a degree of confidence [in me] but no appearance of it. I know he has from Nepean the plan of the fortifications of the New Islands off Copenhagen, and the intended station of some Danish ships.

I have, be assured, no other desire of knowing anything than that I may the better execute the service; but I have no right to know; and do not say a word of it to Lord St Vincent, for he may think me very impertinent in endeavouring to dive into the plans of my C.-in-C.; but, the water being clear, I can see bottom with half an eye. I begged Domett only to use the *St George* and we would do anything.

The *Squirrel* [sloop] will be refitted in two hours tomorrow from a list of complaints on two sides of paper. The gun brigs are in wretched order, but they will get on.

Poor Domett seemed in a pack of troubles. Get rid of us, dear friend, and we shall not be tempted to lay abed till 11 o'clock. . . .[1]

Sir Hyde had found little or nothing to his liking when he arrived at Yarmouth and soon busied himself sending a stream of letters to Nepean at the Admiralty. Unfortunately, a comparison of Parker's letters and Nelson's shows his approach to be that of a meticulous clerk rather than a Commander-in-Chief. The first request in the first letter

---

[1] A note from Troubridge waiting at Yarmouth chided him for the 'I am so circumstanced' letter to St Vincent. He told Troubridge, taking little care to hide that he was hurt, 'You are right . . . in desiring me not to write such letters to the Earl. Why should I? As my own unhappiness concerns no one but myself, it shall remain fixed in my own breast.'

was a reasonable one; the second must have left Nepean wondering why the chart had not been obtained in January or February, since Lord Mulgrave's house in Harley Street was within walking distance of Sir Hyde's.

Finding you have lately struck off a new edition of Signal Books with all the corrections, I am to beg you will order a few to be sent to me, as those we already have are so interlined as to be almost useless. . . . Do not forget a copy of the chart of Lord Mulgrave's of the soundings &c. up to Copenhagen. . . .

A postscript added, 'I have none of the new Private Signals issued the first day of this month,' and once the *London* arrived in Yarmouth Nepean was to send Captain Tomlinson down.

Later that day he wrote again. He had ordered the twelve pilots who were ready at Hull to join him at Yarmouth; but only eleven of the twelve reported by Admiral Dickson (at Yarmouth) could be found and he had sent them to the Downs to join the ships coming round from Spithead.

Not having yet received any list of gun vessels to be put under my orders, you will not forget to send orders for all those intended for me to rendezvous here, and I trust they will be in better order than those at present here, otherways [sic] I am sure we shall be beat out of the battle by the flotilla of our enemies, as I understand from the officers commanding of these [vessels] that they are perfectly unmanageable with oars even in calms and smooth water. . . .

'I beg you will not, my dear friend, omit any paper that can any ways [sic] be useful to me,' he told Nepean, and in the inevitable postscript added: 'We are very ill off for want of our scanty allowance of stationary, as it is not arrived.'

On 6 March he was complaining that 'The number of gun vessels fall short of numbers very much, and I much fear from the state of those here we shall find great difficulties in getting them over [the North Sea] to the Cattigatt [sic], but that we may be as strong in that line as circumstances will admit,' he requested Nepean to mention the *Arrow*, *Dart* and *Wolverine* to Lord St Vincent 'which I understand to be three strong vessels carrying 32-pounder carronades'. These would be useful, and he requested they should be ordered to join him.

'Among the plans and charts you have sent, I cannot find the one taken by Lord Mulgrave's master and dedicated to the late Lord Mulgrave, do let it be copied and sent to me, as it appeared much more correct than the one of Mr Tomlinson's.'

Within forty-eight hours he was writing to the Board about gun brigs coming round from Portsmouth without their heavy guns and was told they were being sent from Portsmouth and Sheerness, but he wrote privately to Nepean before the Board's reply arrived:

They have committed a confounded mistake in sending the gun brigs from Portsmouth without taking in the heavy guns, this adds to many other difficulties as we have not even guns for those vessels that are already here, [he wrote] and from Col. Whitworth's account we are likely to meet a very formidable force of that class at Copenhagen of the Dane's own, independent of what the Swedes may assist them with. I dare say we shall at least count [i.e. need] forty 24-pounders, with shott, cartridges, spunges, rammers. . . . Have the goodness to order Mr Lally, gunner of the *Cormorant*, at Woolwich, to join me here, I forgot to speak upon this subject before I left Town.

The delay of the office of stationary distress's us much. . . . I found myself under the necessity of sending an Express yesterday to the Navy Board.

In the course of a few days the threat of the Danish gun boats had grown in his mind. Not one letter was concerned with his big ships and frigates; instead he could see only gun boats rowing out in a calm to rake the helpless sail of the line, and his clerks running out of stationery.

There was indeed plenty of routine paperwork to keep his staff busy, despite the lack of stationery. An example is a petition sent to the Admiralty from Portsmouth on 25 February and forwarded to Yarmouth:

The humble petition of John Ramsay sheweth that petitioner has a son-in-law on board His Majesty's ship *London*, of the name of Wm. Twisell, who has lately been left a freehold property in the town of Sunderland. Your petitioner is willing to find two able men as substitutes for the said Wm. Twisell, should Your Lordships humanely grant him his discharge. If not, to give orders for his removal into the *Royal William*, as the *London* is under sailing orders.

Sir Hyde forwarded the reply of the *London*'s captain to the Admiralty without comment: it acknowledged the letter 'and inform you that he deserted from His Majesty's ship *London* under my command on the 27th February last in Portsmouth Harbour'.

17

'BY A SIDE WIND...'

In London *The Times*, among other newspapers, had been keeping everyone informed about the new First Lord of the Admiralty and the Baltic expedition. An early report said that Lord St Vincent 'follows closely the footsteps of his noble predecessor in regard to early rising and the dispatch of business. His Lordship gives audiences at 7 in the morning; and he has declared that such clerks as are not in their offices at 9 in the morning will not suit him.'

On 4 March it noted that 'The workmen at the dockyards work by candlelight morning and evening' to get the ships of the Baltic Fleet ready for sea. In addition, 'Orders are issued to detail all Russians, Danes and Swedes now serving on board any of H.M. ships of war.' (This followed the Admiralty's request to the ships to send in lists of foreigners on board.)

On Saturday, 7 March, the day Nelson wrote his 'pack us off' letter to Troubridge, *The Times* by a remarkable coincidence, in a report saying the ships were collecting in the eastern ports of England, announced that 'In consequence of the open weather and mild season [in the Baltic], the Fleet to which our cause is confided will sail tomorrow from Yarmouth if the wind permits. The van will be led by the CONQUEROR OF ABOUKIR, to whose immortal name every epithet is distraction.'

Troubridge received Nelson's letter next day, as if to emphasize that it was hardly the fault of *The Times* that its report was wrong; but it is unlikely he would have noticed that when any newspaper referred to the Baltic expedition, it was always Nelson's name that was mentioned; rarely was Sir Hyde Parker included. As this had been going on since long before Sir Hyde left London, it was probably one of the causes of Sir Hyde's present mood, which Nelson described in a letter to Davison.

'Sir Hyde is on board sulky. Stewart tells me his treatment of me is now noticed. Dickson [commanding a squadron blockading the Dutch and based on Yarmouth] came on board today to say all were scandalized at his gross neglect. ...'

Whether Troubridge passed a discreet word or not, two days after he received Nelson's letter *The Times* reported from Yarmouth: 'Since the arrival of His Lordship here we have been in one continual bustle. People are coming in from all parts of the country round, to see the hero of the Nile.'

If Nelson was impatient to get under way, so were most of the men in the ships now anchored off Yarmouth. Among them was a young, round-faced and round-headed, earnest yet animated midshipman in the *Polyphemus*, John Franklin. Although later to achieve great fame as a Polar explorer, he had just joined the ship. A friend, writing to his father, said:

I have just seen your delightful boy off in the Yarmouth coach, inside; paid all for him and gave him ten pounds in his pocket. This I thought necessary as he has his bedding &c. to buy at Yarmouth, and if he is admitted to a mess with the officers he will have to subscribe to it.

On 11 March a proud young John wrote:

Dear Parents. . . . We were yesterday put under sailing orders for th Baltic, and it is expected that we shall certainly sail this week. It is though we are going to Elsineur to attempt to take the Castle, but some think we cannot succeed. I think they will turn their tale when they consider we have thirty-five sail of the line, exclusive of bombs, frigates and sloops, and on a moderate consideration there will be one thousand double-shotted guns to be fired as a salute to poor Elsineur Castle at first sight.

I am afraid I shall not have the felicity of going out with Captain Flinders[1] for which I am truly sorry, as we in all probability will be out above four months; but if we do return before the *Investigator* sails I will thank you to use your interest for me to go.

He asked them to write to friends and relations 'of our expedition up the Baltic, by which time some of us will "lose a fin" or "the number of our mess", which are sailors terms'.[2] He concluded confidently, 'I think we shall play pretty well among the Russians and Danes if they go to war with us.'

Over in the *St George* Nelson's mood was black. Still studiously ignored by Sir Hyde, he was jealous of what Emma might be doing, irritated at the thought that his brother William and a cousin were both coming to stay on board, and missing the company of Alexander Davison, the one man in whom he confided completely.

He wrote distractedly to Emma on Sunday night, 8 March,

[1] He was preparing the *Investigator* for a survey of the Australian coast.
[2] 'Fin' – arm. Six or eight men usually made up a mess, and plates, mugs etc. were numbered to identify both men and mess. Death, desertion or transfer to another ship were the only ways of 'losing the number' of one's mess.

Your letters today have made me miserable; there is a turn in them that I have noticed, it almost appeared that you like to dwell on the theme that that fellow [Hodges, see page 165] wished, and what he would give, to enjoy your person; but never, no never, will I credit that you will ever admit him into your presence, much less the other. The first drives me for ever from you, and probably out of the world.

My senses are almost gone tonight; I feel as I never felt before. My head! My head! but I will lay down and try to compose my spirits, miserable wretch that I am. Good night; all [your letters] are burnt. Surely you would not go to meet Mr Hodges after his messages to you. No, I will never believe anything against my friend's honour and faith to me. Good night, I am more dead than alive, but all your's till death – no, the thought of Horatia cheers me up. We will be yet happy. My God! my God! look down and bless us; we will pray to thee for help and comfort, and to make our situation more happy. . . .

On Tuesday he wrote,

The Commander-in-Chief has his orders, but I dare say it will be two or three days before he is off. I long to go that I may the sooner return. . . .

What can Sir William mean by wanting you to launch out into expense and extravagance? He that used to think that a little candlelight and iced water would ruin him, to want to set off at £10,000 a year, for a less sum would not afford concerts and the style of living equal to it. Suppose you had set off in this way, what would he not have said? But you are at auction, or rather to be sold by private contract. Good God! my blood boils; to you that everything used *to be refused*. I cannot bear it. Aye, how different I feel! A cottage, a plain joint of meat, and happiness, doing good to the poor, and setting an example of virtue and godliness, worthy of imitation even to kings and princes.

My brother and Mr Rolfe, a cousin of mine, are on board – the former is prying, and a little of a bore. . . .

After another night's brooding he declared:

I see clearly, my dearest friend, you are on SALE.[1] I am almost mad to think of the iniquity of wanting you to associate with a set of whores, bawds and unprincipled lyars. Can this be the great Sir William Hamilton? I blush for him. . . . My brother is gone on shore, and if the weather is moderate we are off at daylight.

Sir Hyde Parker's intended flagship, the *London*, arrived at Yarmouth on Monday, 9 March. By that date he had received several orders

---

[1] With Sir William anxious to get his pension granted and, so far, unsuccessful in obtaining compensation for his expenses and losses in Naples, Nelson was sure Sir William intended using the Prince of Wales's influence. Emma was the obvious bait but in any case Sir William was in an unenviable position because offending the Prince could blast any hope of pension or compensation.

concerning sailing, and his full Admiralty orders (written from Dundas's instructions) sent to him on 23 February made it more than clear he was to sail as soon as he could and gave him all the reasons. Despite that, the Admiralty had to take the unusual step of actually sending him written orders on 25 February to leave London and go to Yarmouth. Finally, on 9 March, it had to take the even more unusual step of sending him a direct order to sail.

Was Sir Hyde slow of wit, lethargic, nervous or so completely absorbed in the minutiae of gathering his fleet around him, complete to the last little cutter and ream of stationery – despite orders which said ships not ready should be told to follow – that he never really understood that to the north-east of him the ice was thawing and Drummond and Vansittart were negotiating?

The direct order to leave London was given within a few hours of Nelson arriving there on leave; the direct order to sail from Yarmouth was given within a few hours of Nelson's 'pack us off' letter reaching Troubridge. It would have been enough, one might think, to get the Fleet to sea; but it was not.

On the 9th in the evening the *London* anchored in the Roads. On the 10th at 8 a.m. shifted my flag to that ship, received orders to proceed to sea the moment the wind will admit with the ships I have with me, without waiting for those ordered to join me, made the signal for all officers to repair on board their ships with the signal for sailing. . . .

Thus Sir Hyde wrote in his journal. But he remained at the Wrestler's Arms.

The orders, written on Monday, had arrived by a special messenger who rode through the night to ensure they reached Parker on Tuesday morning. He kept the messenger while he wrote his reply and sent him back to London with it. Dated '½ past noon' and addressed to Nepean, it acknowledged the orders and 'in answer thereto, desire you will be pleased to acquaint their Lordships that the wind is at present in the S.E. but the moment it is fair, I shall put their orders into execution'.

Lord St Vincent read the letter. Very well, the wind was south-east; but it never blew very long from that direction before veering to the west. Sir Hyde's reply still showed quite clearly he had no realization of the urgency required.

More important, St Vincent knew – not through Nelson, incidentally: obviously several other officers were writing to London – that Lady Parker had arranged an elaborate ball for the following Friday. He probably guessed this meant it would be Saturday before what Sir Hyde would regard as a fair wind blew in Yarmouth Roads. So at

2.30 p.m., within an hour of Parker's reply arriving at the Admiralty, St Vincent wrote him a private letter. Nelson had fought a good fight at the Nile and *then* dallied at Naples – mistakenly, but there had been no prospect of action to speed him on his way. Parker was dallying with the prospect of battle just over the horizon.

I have heard by a side wind [St Vincent wrote] that you have an intention of continuing at Yarmouth until Friday, on account of some trifling circumstance. I really know not what they are, nor did I give myself the trouble of inquiring into them, supposing it impossible, after what you have written in your [last] letter to Mr Nepean that there could be the smallest foundation of this report.

I have, however, upon consideration of the effect of your continuance at Yarmouth an hour after the wind would admit of your sailing would produce, sent down a messenger purposely to convey to you my opinion, as a private friend, that any delay in your sailing would do you irreparable injury. . . .

You will, I am sure, on considering this subject fairly, think that I could not give you a stronger proof of my friendship than by conveying this opinion to you in the way I have done.

As soon as Sir Hyde received it, the ball was cancelled, Lady Parker's bags were packed and she was sent off in Sir Hyde's carriage rattling along the London road bound for Cumberland Place. Sir Hyde's gear, too, was packed, carried down to the jetty in the rain and taken out to the *London*. Sir Hyde, wrapped in his boat cloak, followed. The whole episode was recorded in the next sentence of his journal when he wrote briefly: 'On Wednesday, 11th, embarked and issued several orders. . . .'

On board the *St George* Nelson watched the Commander-in-Chief go out through the rain squalls to board the flagship with some satisfaction. The meanings of the various hoists of signal flags which were soon being run up in the *London* were passed to him, and he sat down and wrote to Troubridge.

The signal is made to prepare to unmoor at 12 o'clock [midnight], but I think the wind being at S.S.E. and very dirty, that our chief may defer it. If it rains a little harder the wind will fly to the westward.

Now we can have no desire for staying, for her Ladyship is gone, and the ball for Friday night knocked up by you and the Earl's unpoliteness to send gentlemen to sea instead of dancing with nice white gloves.

I will only say as yet I know not that we are even going to Baltic except from newspapers, and at sea I cannot go out of my ship but with serious inconvenience. I could say much, but patience. I shall knock down my bulkheads throughout the ship [done when clearing for action], then let what will happen, the *St George* – she has only to trust to herself – will be prepared. . . .

Although Parker had been in Yarmouth for eleven days and had known since 17 February the names of all of the ships of the line he would be commanding, the sudden order to sail caught him completely unawares. For all his requests for stationery he had not prepared the most important lists of all – the Order of Battle and the Order of Sailing. Usually they were the same and, as their titles indicate, showed each ship's position in the Fleet, which was divided into three divisions. With more than twenty sail of the line, there would be chaos if they sailed from the anchorage without knowing the Order of Sailing: they would be like a flock of sheep trying to get through a hole in a hedge.

At this time and for many more years, admirals did not have the host of well-trained staff officers who are a commonplace of modern navies. Instead, a Commander-in-Chief had, in addition to the captain of his flagship, a much senior captain whose title was 'first captain', or 'captain of the fleet'. He was in effect the Commander-in-Chief's chief of staff. It was a much-prized appointment because, apart from the experience to be gained, whoever held it was free to make suggestions, put forward plans, and generally offer advice to the admiral. Apart from him, the Commander-in-Chief had his own secretary (Osborn, in Sir Hyde's case), and several clerks who were little more than writers employed making the required number of copies when similar orders were sent to several captains.

Domett, as Captain of the Fleet, knew how important it was that the Order of Battle and Order of Sailing should be ready with copies for every captain, and he certainly would have been trying to get Sir Hyde to approve the drafts he had drawn up. His knowledge that Sir Hyde had done nothing about them probably accounted for Nelson's comment to Troubridge a few days earlier that he 'seemed in a pack of troubles'. Since ships were joining as soon as they could get round to Yarmouth it was by no means certain how many ships would comprise the Fleet on the day it sailed – although any remaining would catch up independently – and for this reason the Order of Battle and Order of Sailing should have been prepared and amended as necessary.

Drawing up the Order of Battle was more difficult than it would seem, particularly with a fleet ranging in size from the 98-gun *London* and *St George* to ships of 74, 64, 54 and 50 guns. By this time a 74-gun ship was regarded as the smallest really suitable to stand in the line of battle; but shortages or special requirements (such as shallow draft) meant that ships with fewer guns had to be used. A vital factor in drawing up the Order of Battle was that each division should have enough large ships to balance the smaller. The personalities and abilities of individual captains had to be considered, while certain positions were places of importance and honour – the leading ship of the van, for instance, in fact led the Fleet and the position of next ahead or next astern of the admiral in each division was a proud one.

Sir Hyde issued his Order of Battle and of Sailing late in the afternoon after receiving the Admiralty order to sail. He had divided his twenty-two sail of the line into the usual three divisions – a starboard division of eight commanded by Nelson, the centre of seven which he commanded and which would include his third-in-command, Rear-admiral Graves, and a larboard division of seven ships under Rear-admiral Totty. Neither Graves nor Totty had joined the Fleet yet.

The way he finally allocated the ships was either slapdash or stupid: Nelson's division, for instance, which would lead in battle, included three of the five weakest sail of the line in the Fleet. But the Order of Battle he issued to the ships was not the one originally drawn up by Domett; nor was it one which found much favour with Nelson.

'When I received a message from Domett both by Hardy and Murray [commanding the *Edgar* and leading Nelson's division],' Nelson wrote to Troubridge, 'there can be no reason why I may not tell it.' Domett had said, 'Tell Lord Nelson that the present composition of the van is not my arrangement. I had placed Foley [*Elephant*, 74 guns] and Fremantle [*Ganges*, 74] instead of a 64 and 50, but Sir H run his pen through them and placed them as they stand; that when I said, "Sir H, will two 64s and a 50 do well together?" his answer was, "Well, put the *Zealous* between them".'

Nelson wrote angrily,

You may make your own comments, I feel mine. It was never my desire to serve under this man. He approved and seemed more desirous of it than myself, but I saw it the first moment and all the Fleet see it. George Murray, I have no doubt, will support me, and the *St George* shall do her duty. To tell me to serve on in this way is to laugh at me, and to think me a greater fool than I am. If this goes on, I hope to be allowed to return the moment the fighting business is over.

Sir Hyde's sudden order for the Fleet to prepare to sail at midnight caused turmoil at Yarmouth: everyone knew of Lady Parker's intended Friday evening ball and had seen the leisurely pace of Sir Hyde's preparations. Not unreasonably, the captains and officers assumed the squadron would not sail before Saturday at the earliest.

Midshipman W. S. Millard, serving on board the *Monarch*, wrote revealingly that from the moment the signal was hoisted in the afternoon

. . . all was hurry and apparent confusion; the officers [had been] ignorant

14 Count Bernstorff: caught between Russia and Britain, his determination to remain neutral led Denmark into a war.

15 Captain Hans Lindholm, the naval adjutant to the Crown Prince, who proved to be a skilled negotiator and became a good friend of Nelson's.

On the opposite side of Cronenberg Castle 7 Bomb with 2 Mortars in Each, which plaid on it during the time the Fleet were passing the Ships fired in Succession as they came up. The Smaller Vessels left on the Swedish Side of them —

Town of Elsineur

Cronenburgh Castle
or Cronberg.

The British passing Cronenburgh Castle

17 The entrance to the Sound, looking north. This picture shows Cronborg Castle within a few years of the Battle, with the Swedish coast in the distance and, just below the tip of the nearest ship's ensign, the Swedish port of Hälsingborg. Cronborg's guns were mounted in emplacements in front of the Castle, on each side of the flagpole.

...er of the Castle of Cronenburg is the Danish Telegraph Sketch in the margin is a representation when at look Consist of a number of square boards (suspended to a pole) which & hoisted at pleasure, by means of hinges slung as is usual to the pole B is let down or folded up.

16 Sir Hyde's days of indecision are temporarily over: the *Monarch* leads the British Fleet through the Sound, under fire from Cronborg Castle while the guns on the Swedish side remain silent. In this picture – by Robinson Kittoe, secretary to Nelson's second-in-command – the town and harbour of Elsinore are shown on the left while Cronborg Castle is half-hidden by the smoke of its own guns and the shells of the British bomb vessels anchored beyond. (The semaphore mast mounted on the left-hand tower is shown in detail top right.) Of the ships Kittoe named in this drawing his own *Defiance* is on the left, with the *Monarch* to the right, and then Nelson's temporary flagship, the *Elephant*, and the *Bellona*. The Swedish castle and port of Hälsingborg is on the extreme right.

18 Safely through the Sound and with Cronborg Castle well astern, the British Fleet sails down under topsails to anchor north of Copenhagen, just abreast Taarbaek and in full view of the country mansion of Denmark's Foreign Minister, Count Bernstorff. Robinson Kittoe's drawing shows how, once past Cronborg, the Fleet has formed into two divisions.

19 Copenhagen and its defences before the Battle. This page from Kittoe's notebook shows the whole Danish Defence Line from the *Provesteenen* (*extreme left*) at the south end to the *Mars* and *Elephanten*, part of Steen Bille's division, on the right. The notes written perpendicular to the horizon describe the defences. For the thirteenth and fourteenth from the left he notes, '2 floating batteries, they are square with a breast-work thro' which ports are cut but their gunwales do not appear to be man high, they are moor'd head & stern.' The note for the *Mars*, *Elephanten*, *Sarpen* and *Nidelven* (the four ships above which is the word 'windmills') says, 'These two ships and brigs lay on the North Shoal to defend the entrance to the harbour.'

of the day, or even the week, that we were to sail, and had laid in no stock of provisions for the voyage.[1]

As proof of their want of intelligence [i.e. information] the commanding officer gave me leave to go on shore but half an hour before the signal; and I had just cleared the ship in time to avoid a recall. . . .

The scene upon Yarmouth jetty this evening was highly interesting, and in the hand of Hogarth might have made a good companion to [the painting] 'The March to Finchley', but that the importance of the event left no room in mind for levity or ridicule.

Besides the provisions of all sorts which hurried down to the boats, a considerable body of troops . . . were embarking with their baggage and stores. . . .

When it is considered that each vessel, of about fifty, stood in need of these preparations, that they were all to be furnished from this pier, and in the space of a very few hours, any one may fairly conclude that the picture need not want of life. I never witnessed such a complete buzz. Many officers were, like myself, on shore upon liberty, and were hastening to secure their passage; I do not know that any were left from their own negligence.

Midshipman Millard could hardly be blamed for thinking all the soldiers he saw were embarking. In fact some were being redistributed among the ships, while the others were men of the Royal Artillery.[2] Colonel Stewart had already reported to Colonel Calvert, the Adjutant General at the Horseguards in London, that all the infantry had embarked, adding 'The whole are discumbered of heavy baggage and women'.

A small part of the rush which Millard felt the brush of Hogarth should have portrayed was caused by the loading of Army stores which had to be kept perfectly dry – no easy task when they had to be carried out to the ships in open boats with a choppy sea. Within a few hours of arriving in Yarmouth Colonel Stewart had written to Mr David Jones, the Ordnance Storekeeper, asking him to issue 'Musquet ball-cartridges, 99,000; musquet flints, 4,000; carbine ball-cartridges, 10,000, cartridge paper for carbine ammunition, 6 reams; thread for cartridges, 10 lbs.' A number of spikes for spiking guns, and entrenching tools for 100 men, were also sent from the Ordnance Store, but Mr Jones, like everyone else, thought the Fleet would sail later.

When Colonel Stewart had gone with Nelson to make the first

---

[1] The purchase of eggs, vegetables, fresh meat etc. was always left until just before sailing so they would keep as long as possible. Knowing this, an admiral was always careful to give his captains sufficient warning – as Sir Hyde would normally have done had the Admiralty order not arrived.

[2] The detachment of the 49th in the *London* was removed to the *Monarch*: those troops in the *Agincourt* were distributed in seven other ships to form eight divisions. A platoon of Captain Beckwith's riflemen went to the *London*.

official call on Sir Hyde, two of the things he intended to discuss with the Commander-in-Chief were the provisioning of his troops and the division of prize money. However, when he and Nelson found the interview terminated by Sir Hyde with little more than formal introductions he had gone back to the *St George* and written a formal letter – probably, judging from the wording, with Nelson's help. In it he suggested the troops be 'placed on a footing similar to Marines as to the issue of all provisions. They will thereby become subject to all Marine duty, prove possibly of more essential use on board of the several ships . . .' and 'begged to submit the expedience of one general resolution being come to . . . upon the subject of the distribution of any such prize money as may be made under your orders'.

The days passed without any reply, and the Fleet was actually at sea before Sir Hyde answered that he had written to Lord St Vincent, and 'Orders are given to victual the soldiers &c., at the whole allowance of all species as the ships' companies' and, as far as prize money was concerned, 'all those who may be on board the Fleet . . . at the time of any capture, will share in such capture or captures as supernumaries'.

As Nelson had predicted – indeed, as any competent seaman could have guessed – the wind did veer to the south-west on Wednesday night and at half past midnight light signals were hoisted in the *London* ordering the Fleet to unmoor. In an open roadstead like Yarmouth, where there was little room to swing, the big ships moored, putting down two anchors; so a preliminary to the order to sail was to unmoor, getting in one of the anchors and lying at a single anchor. This in itself was a lengthy process – the cable, which was at least ten inches in circumference, and the anchor weighing more than three tons for a 74-gun ship, had to be raised by men heaving at the capstans.

Yarmouth Roads, in which the Fleet was anchored, is just north of the town off a coast which runs north and south and is protected to seaward by large sandbanks whose positions frequently changed. At this time there were four main shoals, three of which were roughly parallel with the coast.

With a fresh breeze blowing offshore, the signal to weigh was made at daylight and the capstans of the ships began clanking round as dozens of men, heaving hard against the capstan bars sticking out horizontally, chest high, from the capstan barrels like spokes from wheels, hauled in the anchor cables. Finally, the anchors aweigh and topsails set, they steered one after the other for the buoys marking the St Nicholas Gat, captains and masters anxiously watching the pilots, who gave the courses to steer. In each ship the monotonous chanting from the leadsman standing in the forechains gave the depth he was finding with each heave of the lead.

One by one the great ships of the line sailed through the channel and out into open water; one by one the frigates, bombs, gun brigs, cutters, luggers and fire ships followed. The *London* steered away to the east-north-east under easy sail and at half past seven, with Yarmouth church just in sight twelve miles away to the west-north-west, Sir Hyde 'made the signal to close round the Commander-in-Chief'. Now, with plenty of sea room, the Fleet was to form into the Order of Sailing.

Sir Hyde recorded in his journal that he had left orders behind at Lowestoft for his two other Rear-admirals, Totty and Graves, who had not yet arrived, 'to join me off the Skaw with the *Invincible*, *Defiance*, *Elephant* and *Edgar*, [and if] not meeting [me there] off the Knoll Point, and if not there to proceed up the Sound'. In fact the *Edgar* joined the Fleet at 10.00 a.m., and 'at 53 minutes past eleven', Sir Hyde noted, 'made the signal to make more sail and at noon Lowestoft SW 17 miles.'

The two elements of a tragedy – small in terms of the whole Fleet, but large in the cost of human lives since it caused the death of more British seamen than the forthcoming battle – were now present. The first was the fact there were two channels leading from Yarmouth Roads; the second was that Sir Hyde Parker left his orders for Admirals Totty and Graves at Yarmouth.

Since both admirals and the ships to complete the squadron were coming up from the south and would have to pick up local pilots at the Downs or Sheerness in order to call at Yarmouth, it would have saved at least one day, perhaps two or more with the chances of missing tides, if Parker had sent copies of the orders to the Downs and Sheerness, so that neither admiral need call at Yarmouth: instead each could have made his departure for the Naze of Norway direct from the Thames Estuary or the Downs.

But unfortunately Sir Hyde, still showing no sense of the urgency of his mission, did not take these elementary steps, with the tragic results that will be described later.

As Nelson filled in his journal that day he made a curious mistake, in view of the significance of the sentence, by repeating himself: 'At $\frac{1}{2}$ past five weighed as did the whole fleet as did the whole fleet. . . .' And Midshipman Millard, describing how the Fleet formed into the Order of Sailing, noted: 'Even at this time we did not know the place of our destination: the course given out by signal was NE by N, this being a due course for the Naze of Norway; and this was the first assurance we had of being bound towards the Baltic.'

Fortunately there had been no delays in the West Indies. Four days after Parker's fleet sailed from Yarmouth, Rear-admiral Duckworth, whose orders had to be sent across the Atlantic, sailed from Martinique with a squadron to capture the Danish and Swedish islands to the north-west, escorting transports carrying 1,500 troops under Lt-general Trigge.

The squadron arrived at St Bartholomews on 20 March, and Brig-general Fuller, and Captain King of the *Leviathan* delivered a summons to the Governor, requiring him to surrender. He agreed. The squadron then went on to St Martins, whose Governor was made of sterner stuff and refused, so troops and seamen were landed on the small island and by midnight it was in British hands. The squadron then sailed on to the Virgin Islands, taking the surrender of St Thomas[1] and St John on 28 March and St Croix on the 31st, without a shot being fired.

With Sir Hyde at last at sea with his Fleet it is worth going through the stages which led to his appointment. As early as 7 December the previous year, St Vincent had written to Spencer, 'Should the Northern Powers continue their menacing posture, Sir Hyde Parker is the only man you have to face them. He is in possession of all the information obtained during the Russian armament, more important that which relates to the navigation of the Great Belt.' (The information Parker possessed was not of course gained first-hand.)

On the authority of his secretary, St Vincent changed his mind later, but it is not possible to place much credence in Tucker's recollections because they were published more than forty years after the event, and contradict the fact that only a few days before taking over as First Lord, St Vincent wrote to Spencer who replied that he was 'glad to find that our arrangements here respecting the Baltic Fleet have as far as they have gone met with your approbation. . . .' And just before telling Spencer that Parker was 'the only man you have' for the Baltic, St Vincent had written a particularly harsh judgment of Nelson in a letter to Nepean saying that Nelson was unfit to command a fleet (see page 40). For these reasons one cannot agree with Admiral Mahan that 'the old seaman [St Vincent] would much preferred to see Nelson at the helm'.

This, based on Tucker's reference, hardly agrees with denigrating Nelson in November, recommending Parker as 'the only man' in December, approving Spencer's appointments and dispositions at the beginning of February, and making no changes when becoming First

---

[1] Despite its having one of the largest and best-defended harbours in the Caribbean east of San Juan, Puerto Rico.

Lord a few days later. And, perhaps more significantly, before the news of the victory at Copenhagen arrived in London St Vincent did not write a line expressing any doubts about Parker or preference for Nelson. For that reason the single unsubstantiated recollection of Tucker forty years later must be regarded as flatly contradicted by written contemporary evidence.

Lady Malmesbury, writing after the Battle, summed it up quite fairly: 'I feel sorry for Sir Hyde, but no wise man would ever have gone with Nelson, or over him, as he was sure to be in the background in every case.'

Addington did nothing to change the command when he became Prime Minister, but had he come to power in time to initiate the expedition there is little doubt he would have selected Nelson. The two men were good friends and Nelson had written to him on 2 February, when he was still Speaker and there was no hint the Government was going to resign, about the fortifications at Copenhagen.

Fortunately we have Addington's views on the subject, expressed after the Fleet had sailed from Yarmouth but *before* news arrived of the Battle. George Rose, a man of varied experience – a clergyman's son who had served in the Navy as a midshipman, taken up politics to become Secretary to the Treasury, a friend of Pitt's and owner of a large country house where guests included the King – called on Addington at Downing Street on 6 April.

In speaking of the Danish business [Rose wrote in his diary] he expressed himself sanguinely; I answered I was sure that what could be done by man would be executed by the two admirals who commanded; he observed that Lord Nelson was the most likely to strike a great blow, though both were good, on which I reminded him of the distinguished courage and still more remarkable presence of mind of Sir Hyde Parker when he faced the passage of the North River, above New York, early in the American War, under circumstances as trying to an officer as ever happened in a hazardous enterprise.

Mr Addington said [Parker] was then almost thirty years younger; that he should prefer him to command the great fleet in the Channel; but that for such a service as that at Copenhagen he should prefer Lord Nelson; from whence I infer that Sir Hyde has stated to the Ministers some greater difficulties in the way of destroying the Danish Fleet than were expected. . . .

Rose was almost right: Sir Hyde had not discovered greater difficulties than anyone else might have expected to meet; but he had made it abundantly clear in his correspondence that to him the difficulties seemed enormous. He was not the man with enough buoyancy to rise to a big problem; on the contrary, it swamped him.

18
DIVIDED COMMAND

In Copenhagen the Danes were making good use of time, the unexpected ally that Sir Hyde had given them. They began to speed up their defence preparations while in the Cabinet certain ministers vied with each other in attempts to sway the Crown Prince.

Vansittart had not yet arrived, and the Crown Prince's policy was still tending to be moderate; to wait and see. To men like him and Count Bernstorff, the long and close friendship with Britain, based on personal inclination and trade, had become such a part of the normal way of life that any break seemed almost unthinkable: as unthinkable as a childish argument between a happily-married couple leading to a divorce.

But within the Cabinet some ministers had come or were coming under other influences, most of them resulting from the fear of Russia or the fear of France, or both. It was not so much the ministers or the Danish people becoming anti-British; rather that in the face of apparently more powerful threats it was not the time to be anti-Russian or anti-French. A minority, of course, hoped to gain something from Napoleon and were careful to make their sympathies known.

The effect of these fears was that through such ministers the interests of Russia and France were more than adequately represented in the councils of the Danish Government, and, being so frequently expressed at a time when Britain's reaction to the Convention was proving so unexpectedly strong and potentially threatening, began to gain ground.

At the beginning of February the defence preparations were little more than the normal fitting out of warships as Spring approached. Then, on 13 February, in the first move to strengthen Cronborg[1] Castle, the War Office ordered the Sælland Infantry Regiment to march to

---

[1] The Danish spelling of 1801 is used here, although now written Kronborg. Likewise Castellet and Sælland are used although the modern spellings are Kastellet and Sjælland. Where possible other old spellings are retained.

Elsinore and strengthen the garrison, while the 2nd Artillery were told to send a captain, two lieutenants and as many gunners as were required to bring the number there to one hundred.

From the earliest times the narrow Sound between Denmark and Sweden had been regarded as the door to the Baltic; for almost as long Cronborg was considered both lock and key. And so many years of peace, with no one challenging it, had led to it being accepted as a major factor in Copenhagen's defence: an attacker from the North Sea would first have to pass the guns of Cronborg, and it was unthinkable any ship could survive such a hail of fire.

Cronborg's reputation as defender of the Sound was as legendary as its setting for Hamlet; but for many years it had about as much basis in fact. The explanation for this goes back to the time when 'Trekroner', or 'Three Crowns', referred to the fact that Denmark, Sweden and Norway were one kingdom. In other words the Danish side of Cronborg and the Swedish side at Hälsingborg, were under the same rule or so closely allied they would always work together. It was assumed no foreign fleet could pass through in safety by going close along the Swedish shore, out of range of Cronborg's guns: there were batteries on the heights above Hälsingborg to stop that.

When Sweden became an independent nation, a combination of Cronborg's reputation and the assumption that Sweden's policy would be the same as Denmark's still did not lead anyone to take a chart of the Sound and draw in the arcs of fire of Cronborg's guns. The legend made up for their lack of range, should the Swedish batteries stay silent, and the legend was strong in the minds of the Danish people – and Sir Hyde Parker.

As the work of commissioning the ships of war neared completion, so officers were appointed to them. The Crown Prince summoned the Defence Commission to a meeting on 16 February and among the appointments made were Captain Braun to command the 60-gun *Dannebroge*,[1] Captain Egede to command the cavalry transport *Rendsborg* and Captain C. A. Rothe to command the *Nyeborg*, also a cavalry transport. Lt Holsten was given command of the *Elven* frigate and told to prepare her for sea.

Then, on Friday, 20 February, the people of Denmark were startled by a Royal proclamation which was read out in the cities, towns and villages of the nation and pasted up on walls. The result of the latest diplomatic exchanges between Copenhagen and London, it was made

---

[1] Her previous captain 'fainted' and fell into the ship's gig and, a discreet report told the Danish Admiralty, 'had to leave. As he will not recover for a long time, he must be relieved of his command.'

in the name of 'We, Christian the Seventh, in God's name King of Denmark and Norway . . .' and asked all

. . . Danish and Norwegian seamen doing duty in foreign ships to come home to the Fatherland, where they should immediately report to the recruiting officer responsible for the district in which they land.

His Majesty is certain that every honourable man of any rank will not fail to answer this appeal . . . [and if] without documents, permission or passport have gone on board foreign ships you will be free of any possible punishment for which you might be liable, and you will have all the rights and privileges which follow the normal enrollment of Danish seafaring folk.

On the other hand [the proclamation concluded] if you ignore this appeal you will be looked upon as unpatriotic and a traitor and unworthy of your King and Country.

On 23 February, the day Bernstorff wrote the Note warning Britain she should raise the embargo on Danish ships or Denmark 'must act', the Defence Commission decided to strengthen Copenhagen's defences by adding two ships which would shortly be ready. A letter was sent to the Commander-in-Chief of the Defence of Copenhagen Roads, Captain Olfert Fischer, telling him that the 74-gun *Sælland* and the 60-gun *Holsteen* were being put under his command. As usual the letter was signed by the Crown Prince and Admiral Friderich Kaas. However, the Crown Prince also made his own appointments with the result that on one occasion the Defence Commission would give the order and on another the Crown Prince.[1]

At the same time, of course, the Crown Prince was conducting Army and State business. There was correspondence with Colonel Stricker, the commandant at Cronborg Castle; long discussions with Count Bernstorff about relations between Russia and Britain; reports from Paris and Stockholm to be studied, and replies and instructions drafted.

Everything, in other words, was in the hands of the Crown Prince, whether concerning the armed forces, Government, or foreign policy. In Britain almost everything was done in the King's name, and although this was partly a formality, in general he simply approved policy and decisions made by his ministers. In Denmark the Crown Prince to a far greater extent made his own policy and decisions, using his ministers more as advisers. Considering the detail into which he went it was impossible to avoid mistakes. It was one thing to decide broad naval operations as part of foreign policy, for example, and leave the Admir-

---

[1] The Defence Commission comprised (under the Crown Prince) members of the Admiralty Department: Admiral F. C. Kaas, Vice-admiral Johan Peter Wleugal, Chamberlain Friderich von Knuth, and *Generalauditor* Laurits Nørregaard (in effect the Judge Advocate General).

alty to carry them out; it was another to concern himself with the appointment of lieutenants, as he did. The result was the Prince, carrying an enormous burden, had neither the time nor the opportunity to retain any sort of detachment – the very thing that might have led him, if not Bernstorff, to realize how Britain would have to react to the Convention or, failing that, to detect much earlier that her attitude was hardening.

Apart from this diplomatic failure, for which Bernstorff shares much of the blame, there was one step the Crown Prince should have taken concerning the Navy. As it stood, there was the Defence Commission, which acted in effect as a committee under his chairmanship. Then there was Olfert Fischer, who commanded the squadron of ships defending the Roads – the stretch of water off the city of Copenhagen – and later Steen Bille would be put in command of a separate squadron of ships covering the actual entrance to the harbour. Neither man could give orders to the other, yet the defence of the Roads and the harbour entrance was a single task: indeed each squadron formed one side of an inverted V, and at the apex the nearest ships of the two squadrons were only 600 yards apart.

Had the Crown Prince appointed a Commander-in-Chief of the Navy to act under him (Kaas, as senior member of the Defence Commission, for instance), and put Fischer in complete control of the defence of Copenhagen (under Kaas) the result of the forthcoming battle might have been quite different. The divided command was a fatal mistake, and the Crown Prince could never control both squadrons – as he proposed doing – from the shore. The most obvious obstacle was that whichever way the wind was blowing the smoke of battle would not only prevent him from seeing what was going on but obscure signals made by and to him.

By the end of the first week in March the Danish Government was at last beginning to have grave doubts about their estimate of Britain's intentions: she was showing no signs of climbing down and her refusal to lift the embargo on Danish ships was providing plenty of ammunition for both the pro-Russian and pro-French ministers.

Then two items of news arrived from London. The first, about the King's illness, further strengthened these ministers; but the second put them in the ascendancy – Pitt had resigned as Prime Minister!

His reputation as a war leader at once led the Danes and the French to interpret his resignation as meaning he had been forced out by the anti-war element in the country. The Irish question was regarded as an excuse, and the conclusion seemed obvious: the fire had gone out of

Britain's belly. Now they could expect she would begin peace negotiations with Napoleon. And she would be negotiating from a very weak position – her new government would be only too well aware the nation wanted peace; Napoleon, knowing this, would demand a high price. It was time, the Danes saw, to apply pressure.

An invitation arrived in Copenhagen from the King of Sweden inviting the Crown Prince over for talks. The Crown Prince crossed to Hälsingborg for the meeting, to find the King proposed holding it at an inn. The talks yielded little and are best described in Drummond's despatch to London. The King appeared decorated in all his orders, and wore the Collar which he had recently received from the Czar.

It is said that very little conversation passed between the illustrious strangers. Much etiquette was observed by His Swedish Majesty, which in the little town of Elsinburg [sic] and in one of the dirtiest inns I ever saw, must have been somewhat out of place. They say here the Prince Royal was very much of that opinion, and upon his return expressed some surprise at being invited to a conference when there was no conversation.

A postscript added that Baron de Bourgoing, the French Ambassador in Copenhagen, 'says he was very well received by the King of Sweden. M. d'Oxenstierna [the Swedish Ambassador in Copenhagen] says just the reverse.'

The Crown Prince returned to Copenhagen on 14 March, and although there were some policy changes they were due to British moves, not to anything the King of Sweden had said or done. These came into effect after 17 March, but the quickening tempo of Danish defence preparations is best shown by looking at the Crown Prince's orders before 17 March and after.

The first orders in March concerning the Army were given on the 7th, when a troop of Hussars – one officer, two NCOs and twenty men – were ordered to go to Cronborg. On the 11th, Second Lt Østrup of the Sælland Rangers was ordered to serve 'until further notice' as the adjutant of the garrison at Cronborg. Three days after that Colonel Stricker was told that troops of the garrison must serve as guns' crews, and later that orders had been given to 100 artillerymen to march to Cronborg to strengthen his garrison.

The naval orders up to 17 March were little more than routine. Lt Peter Willemoes (who was within a month to become one of Denmark's heroes) was sent to the *Danmark* to help her fitting out. On the 12th Olfert Fischer was told by the Crown Prince to arrange for the two blockships *Wagrien* and *Jylland* to pass out through the boom on the 14th, ten gun boats on the 15th, the 'defence ships' *Charlotte Amalia* and *Cronborg* and the blockship *Prøvesteenen* on the 16th. All were to take on stores before they sailed, and stores were to be sent out to the Trekroner battery.

With these and more ships about to be commissioned, the Crown Prince issued an order on the 16th to Steen Bille, Fischer and all captains saying:

In view of the situation, it is of the greatest importance that the trained crews ordered to the Royal ships really report at the times fixed and carry out the work to which they are ordered. It has been found necessary to provide that any man who wilfully reports late or stays away shall be fined 24 shilling for the first hour, three marks for the second hour, and for the remaining time half the pay due to him, and that these fines should be deducted from the pay due to him and for that purpose it should be entered in his pay book. You are to announce this to your ship's company so that each man knows of the fine he risks.

This order was no doubt due to the fact that by this time Vansittart had arrived from London as a special envoy, and then within a few hours news reached Copenhagen that a British fleet had sailed from England. At once, the defensive measures speeded up, beginning with another Royal proclamation to all seamen.

After their scramble over the ice to get on shore at Cuxhaven, Nicholas Vansittart and his secretary Dr Beeke went on to Hamburgh, but no sooner had they got there than, Vansittart wrote, 'Dr Beeke was taken ill, which detained us for three days, when we proceeded to Sleswick'.

At Gottorp Castle they found Prince Charles, 'who received us most cordially, but said he feared my mission would be in vain, as the French influence, combined with the fear of the Emperor Paul, was predominant at Copenhagen'.

In another letter Vansittart said that the Prince of Hesse gave him news of the British King's 'second illness'. This was in fact a worsening of the first, which had purposely been minimized.

The Prince appeared deeply affected with the news ... I was myself greatly shocked. He appeared to value himself on his connexion with England, and to have the highest respect for the nation in general, and the character of His Majesty in particular. He described the Prince Royal [of Denmark] as actuated by the same sentiments. . . .

He appeared to think the Danes much more engaged in this dispute as a point of honour, than from any material importance in the question or neutral navigation in itself; but he seemed to think his own influence had been injured by espousing too warmly the cause of England; and therefore it is possible that some leading members of the Danish Government may entertain a different opinion.

He was persuaded (which I find is very general on the Continent) that the late change in administration was nothing more than a concerted plan to bring about a peace; and spoke with high admiration of Mr Pitt and Lord Grenville.

Once again Vansittart and Beeke packed their bags and began a miserably cold journey to Copenhagen. Arriving there on 9 March, he found that Mr James Talbot, the Secretary of the Legation and chargé d'affaires at the British Embassy in Stockholm, was staying with Drummond 'having been ordered away by the Swedish Government'.

Talks with Drummond revealed that relations were now so bad between the British and Danish Governments that Drummond had 'held no communication for some time' with the Danish Court. Even worse, news of the King's illness 'had reached Copenhagen before my arrival there, and greatly increased the influence of the [pro] French party'.

He wrote a polite note to Count Bernstorff asking to be received privately and stating his credentials. After that he could only sit back and wait in the British Embassy in Castelvej. More than a hint of what he could expect came from the fact Bernstorff kept him waiting three days, finally agreeing to receive him with Drummond on Saturday morning, 15 March.

The two men began the meeting by explaining to Bernstorff that they had requested a private conversation 'before we asked leave to present our credentials' so they could discuss without restraint the points that had to be considered 'for removing all differences between the two countries'.

The men talked for a long time; and at first it seemed that Prince Charles of Hesse's verdict was correct – the Danes were 'much more engaged in this dispute as a point of honour. . . .' Then a remark of Bernstorff's showed that Britain's idea of Denmark acting through fear of the Czar was completely wrong.

Bernstorff began by saying the private talk was perfectly agreeable to Denmark, which had always kept to her treaties 'with strict fidelity and was very desirous of an amicable arrangement it had entered into with other powers'.

Vansittart was not a lawyer nor Drummond a skilled diplomat for nothing, Vansittart recording that they said that if he was referring to the Armed Convention, he must see it was contrary to existing treaties with Britain, and that good faith required that any stipulations in the Convention contradicting an existing treaty must be annulled or modified.

Bernstorff answered that although Britain considered the Convention hostile, it was 'nothing more than avowal of principles' always held by the Northern Powers and by no means infringed any former treaty. 'It was not considered hostile by Great Britain in 1780 when the Treaty was concluded, of which this is merely a republication.'

Vansittart and Drummond said that not only did Britain regard it as hostile to her, but so did every other country in Europe. The 1780 Treaty, they pointed out, had been signed under very different circumstances: Russia was then 'in profound peace', whereas the present Convention was signed after a violent attack by Russia against Britain; and the late Count Bernstorff (father of the present minister) had claimed the 1780 Treaty was directed against Spain, not Britain.

But Bernstorff stuck to his original point that Britain chose to consider the Convention hostile, although it was not meant to be, and 'if it should become injurious to her, it would be by her own fault'.

Vansittart asked if Bernstorff doubted that France and her allies believed the Treaty to be hostile to Britain.

The belligerent nations might, the Count answered, but the neutral nations did not; furthermore the 1780 Treaty had always been considered as still in existence by the nations that signed it.

Vansittart promptly cited several examples where Sweden and Russia had contradicted it, 'and among others mentioned the order of the Emperor to seize all ships going to England'.

To this Bernstorff admitted that in his war with Russia the King of Sweden had violated the principles but 'had seen his error and corrected it'. Whatever Russia's conduct in the present war, she never had any intention of giving up her principles of maritime law. The order to seize all ships going to England, he declared, was a mere newspaper fiction, and if war had begun between Britain and Russia at the time of the conclusion of the Convention, Denmark would not be bound to interfere, nor would the treaty apply since it related merely to a state of neutrality. 'In fact, the embargo laid by the Emperor on English ships is no more a hostile proceeding' than the one laid by Britain on Danish and Swedish ships.

When the two Britons said the cases differed because the Russians had confiscated the ships and imprisoned the sailors, 'The Count positively denied the confiscation . . . and said the detention of the seamen was not to be considered as an imprisonment – that they are treated as Russian sailors usually are, and though such treatment might appear harsh to Englishmen, it was not intended to be so. . . .'[1]

---

[1] The crews of three hundred merchant ships had been marched through snow to prison camps in Siberia and the cargoes in the ships had been unloaded and sold. By comparison the captain of the Norwegian ships had made a formal protest against the captain of a Royal Navy ship (see page 156).

The Convention was concluded, although not signed, long before the Russian embargo, Bernstorff said, adding that it had been agreed after Lord Whitworth's mission (the previous year, following the *Freya* episode), as a condition of the Czar giving assistance 'for which his [Bernstorff's] Court had applied when menaced by England'.[1]

Vansittart quoted Bernstorff as saying that England, after having for a long time coaxed the Czar, had then shown 'an impolitic and precipitate degree of resentment against him', and the Czar had reason to complain of the breaking of the agreement by which he had been promised Malta – an agreement which 'though perhaps never signed might be considered as concluded'.

Vansittart told Bernstorff in no uncertain terms that he did not understand what was meant by the *conclusion* of a treaty or agreement before it was signed, and Denmark and Sweden should never have signed the Convention after the Czar's seizure of the British ships. By signing at such a time they made their own countries responsible for all the consequences. Russia derived no right to Malta from an engagement which was never signed. In any case Britain, far from resenting the Czar's behaviour, had been blamed, 'and with some appearance of reason', for too much lameness in avoiding any show of resentment.

Bernstorff then declared that 'indeed all Europe' had felt the difference between Britain's conduct towards Russia and towards Denmark and Sweden, and the British had 'purposely confounded two subjects entirely distinct' so she could attack two nations she thought she could crush.

Bernstorff was promptly told that what he had just said was itself an answer to the charge he had made against the British Government of 'rash and intemperate conduct' towards Russia. And the accusation that Britain wanted to attack Denmark, Vansittart declared, was refuted by his own 'conciliatory and amicable mission', which was the strongest proof of Britain's pacific sentiments towards Denmark.

Would Denmark, he asked Bernstorff, 'now separate the subjects she accused us of confounding'? Would Denmark now disclaim all intentions of supporting Russia in her dispute over Malta?

Vansittart's question was blunt; but both he and Drummond were obviously having difficulty in concealing their anger at Bernstorff's revelation that far from Denmark being forced into the Convention, she had joined it as the price for the Czar protecting her against Britain.

---

[1] This confirmed Drummond's first revelation (see page 108) that Denmark had asked Russia for help and is one missed by many subsequent historians, who concluded the Czar's concern for Denmark sprang only from his own reaction to Britain sending in a squadron with the Whitworth mission, not as the result of a request from the Crown Prince.

His repeated accusations that Britain wanted to attack Denmark when their very presence in Bernstorff's office was to negotiate a new treaty to ensure peace was sufficiently absurd that both men were probably trying to guess the reason for it.

Bernstorff's answer left them no wiser. After the turn affairs had taken, the Count said, he could not be expected to give such a disclaimer. He repeated what he had previously told Drummond 'in stronger terms', that Britain 'had neglected the fit opportunity for conciliating Denmark'. And he made it quite clear that from the moment the Convention was signed his Government was no longer 'at liberty to act as it might have done previous to that event'.

The two men said Britain was very unwilling to suppose Denmark would act in opposition to its treaty with Britain. They were armed with full powers to renew treaties and connect the two countries still more closely, and for that reason 'were desirous as soon as possible of presenting our credentials.'

Bernstorff's reply was simple: it was impossible that they could be received while England 'persisted in her unjust and violent proceedings against neutral powers'.

The meeting had now, as far as the two Britons were concerned, reached a critical point: it was the time to show their cards.

They told Bernstorff they were authorized to declare that the British embargo would be lifted as soon as Denmark entered into an agreement confirming her ancient treaties, and settling – with 'the most complete equality and reciprocity' – the rules of maritime law on which differences had lately arisen. Britain was willing to make the return of all Danish ships and property the first article of such a treaty, and it depended on Denmark herself how quickly the new agreement was concluded.

However, if Vansittart's credentials were not officially accepted, 'the mission became evidently fruitless and nothing remained for us to do but quit the country. . . .'

It is impossible to know for certain if the offer and the threat caught Bernstorff off his guard, but his extraordinary reply indicates this was probably the case. He told them that the points 'would have to be treated of in joint negotiations with all the powers in the Confederacy, and Berlin would be a proper place for such negotiations and the King of Prussia would act as mediator'.

Obviously Vansittart, sensing Bernstorff was playing for time, pointed out it was unusual for someone concerned to act as a mediator, and the proposal of a joint negotiation 'evidently showed the hostile nature of the Confederacy' – it was nothing less than an attempt by force of arms to make Britain acknowledge certain principles; that several powerful nations required her to submit to certain rules by threats of hostility.

If other powers should successively join, Vansittart said, Britain 'must either renounce the principles she had always held or go to war with all the world. . . .'

The three men then had a long argument over the right of search of merchant ships in convoy, Bernstorff claiming that 'the whole system of maritime law as adopted by England is contrary to that admitted by other countries, and is as absurd in its principles as it is unjust in its practice'.

Finally Vansittart 'again asked whether our credentials would be received. The Count answered that unless the ships . . . were released it was impossible'. When the Count gave 'this positive refusal' the two men told him Britain had consulted Denmark's honour by sending the present pacific mission in hope of settling all differences before the appearance of the British Fleet; and that they had informed him of the assistance Britain would give Denmark if she agreed to a treaty.

'The Count answered that the appearance of a British Fleet would make no difference in their resolution. We then expressed our regret at an answer which appeared to put an end to all amicable discussion, and required the Count to give it us in writing, which he promised to do.'

Drummond, in a despatch to Lord Hawkesbury, commented that the Danish refusal to receive British representatives who declared that their principal object was to preserve peace, 'is but too strong a proof of the spirit of hostility against England which exists in the minds of those who conduct the counsels of Denmark'.

In reporting to the Prime Minister, Vansittart wrote: 'Unfortunately, the interview . . . was but too decisive, and proved this Cabinet to be at present entirely under Russian influence. Nothing remains but to strike a speedy and severe blow; and on that subject Beeke has written our sentiments fully to you.' With this rejection of the British overtures, 'I propose to set off for England as soon as the resolution of the Danish Government has been officially notified to me.'

Dr Beeke, who wrote the official report of the meeting, said bluntly that the only remaining hope of an agreement rested on the effect of the force of the British Navy on the Northern Powers, 'and on the discontent which the previous rejection of pacific overtures would occasion amongst them'.

Bernstorff's reply (addressed to Drummond, of course, since Vansittart had no official existence) came on Monday, 16 March. It was uncompromising. After the usual preliminaries it said, 'The King will receive with great pleasure your credentials, also those of M. Vansittart, directly your Court shall have given to mine [the assurance] of the cessation of the violent measures and injuries adopted by England against the King's flag and that of his allies in hatred of the engagements contracted for the maintenance of maritime neutrality.'

The reply was even stronger than Drummond and Vansittart had expected. They told Hawkesbury in a joint despatch that they considered the language 'is so offensive and the pretension which it implies that not only the ships of Denmark but those of her allies should be released without any stipulation of a reciprocal restitution on their part' – and this a condition which had to be accepted even before a British minister would be received – is 'of so extraordinary a kind that they can leave little doubt of the hostile determination of the Danish Government'. However, there was an ambiguity in some of the expressions which made it 'desirable to have an answer more positive and explicit'.

Drummond's position as the accredited British Ambassador was, of course, completely different from that of Vansittart, and this was one of the points both men were trying to clear up. Was the Danish Note saying that, although as the British Ambassador Drummond's credentials had been accepted long ago, the fact that he and Vansittart formed a new mission meant that Drummond's original accreditation was now withdrawn? Or that although not acceptable as a member of the mission, Drummond was still acceptable as an envoy?

The point was of vital importance because withdrawing Drummond's accreditation meant that legally Denmark had severed diplomatic relations with Britain – the usual preliminary to war. To clear it up one way or the other Drummond asked Bernstorff on Monday that since his Court would not receive him 'in the role which His Majesty has assigned me for the reason explained in the attached Note, I beg you to inform me in what manner I must envisage my position in Copenhagen. . . .'

Before sending replies to the British Embassy, Bernstorff wrote letters to Dreyer, the Danish Ambassador in Paris, and to de Wedel Jarlsberg in London.

He told Dreyer, in a despatch revealing much about the Danish attitude towards France, that the British Government had sent *'Un certain Vansittart'* to negotiate a separate agreement between the two nations. 'We have not hesitated to declare to him' that until the embargo was lifted Denmark did not wish to enter into discussions with Britain which could not be made the object of a general negotiation between Britain and the United (i.e. Northern) Powers. He felt obliged to give

Dreyer these details, he added, so the envoy could correct 'any erroneous ideas which might circulate in Paris' about Vansittart's mission, and answer any questions from the French Government.

In an equally revealing phrase showing his sentiments towards Napoleon, Bernstorff said he wished Dreyer to demonstrate the firmness with which the Danish Government had rejected the British efforts 'to detach us from our allies' and rejected the British offers 'to compromise with them'. However, he pointed out, the British would not 'lose this pretext to reproach us for having repulsed the means of conciliation they have offered us, and it will serve to colour its violence in the eyes of the English nation.

'For the rest, I persist in the belief that [Britain] will become more accommodating "*vis à vis de la France*", but will stiffen its attitude towards the Northern Powers, and I like to hope that Bonaparte, instead of losing the advantage which the situation this moment offers him of carrying matters to an extremity [i.e. war] will have the skill to prevail and clear a way to a general peace which is also honourable to France.'

A cynic might say Bernstorff wanted to reassure the French that Denmark was doing nothing that could upset such a champion of liberty and guardian of the rule of law as Napoleon.

Count de Wedel Jarlsberg was told of Vansittart's visit but, Bernstorff assured the Ambassador, since from all appearances Britain was intending to detach Denmark from her allies or compromise her with them, Vansittart had been told there was no question of receiving a British minister until the embargo was lifted, and any discussions of maritime rights would have to be between Britain and the United Northern Powers.

Since this was not the reply that Vansittart expected, 'he now prepares to leave us, and it is an insight that the British Government will find in the failure of her mission a pretext for reporting that we have repulsed the means of conciliation it will boast of having offered us'.

The terms of Bernstorff's reply to Drummond and Vansittart, written the same day, were quickly reported to Hawkesbury. Since it contained 'the express declaration that our credentials would not be received except upon conditions with which we had repeatedly declared it impossible to comply', it evidently made Vansittart's continued presence in Denmark 'improper'. He had immediately applied for a passport and taken steps to get a passage to Lübeck as soon as the wind became favourable.

Drummond was staying because 'the circumstances under which he ought to leave' were already covered in Hawkesbury's instructions concerning the Fleet's arrival. But there was another reason, not covered by instructions or precedents, which had decided him. He told Hawkesbury that 'In the event of an English fleet destroying the naval arsenal of Copenhagen, the Danes might afterwards pretend that they would have treated from the moment the British Fleet arrived in the Cattegat, if any person had been on the spot with full powers for that purpose. If after what has passed they ever do abandon the Coalition it will be from necessity and only upon that plea.'

Drawing Hawkesbury's attention to the fact that 'we on all occasions avoided every expression of resentment in answer to the harsh language which was occasionally used towards us', they thought they best expressed the 'pacific and amicable sentiments of His Majesty by the most conciliating behaviour and address', and at the same time 'felt that the character and dignity of Great Britain were best supported by the mildest and most moderate assertion of its rights'.

And that, regrettably, was the mistake which both men and the British Government made, and was caused by the assumption that Denmark had been acting under the twin fears of the Czar and Napoleon. In fact if Britain was to look after her own interests the only way to sway Denmark's policy would have been by inducing a greater fear. Instead of arriving overland by carriage like a King's Messenger, so that the first the Danish Government knew of his arrival was the delivery of a Note to Bernstorff, Vansittart should have landed in Copenhagen from an admiral's barge, with a British Fleet anchored in the Roads.

Bernstorff's letter to Dreyer in Paris telling him he was to demonstrate to Napoleon how Denmark had rejected the British efforts 'to detach us from our allies' is proof enough that the Danish Government had come to regard signing the Convention not only as allying themselves to Russia but also throwing in their lot with France.

So Vansittart needed a British fleet at his back to ensure the Danes would negotiate. Unfortunately the Fleet was, as far as diplomatic negotiations were concerned, a couple of days late. The joint despatch of Drummond and Vansittart, just quoted, was written on Thursday, 19 March and sent by special messenger to London. On Friday morning, as Drummond later reported to Hawkesbury, 'several accounts reached us of the appearance of the British Fleet near the Skaw, and about eight o'clock in the evening Lieutenant McCulloch of the *Blanche* frigate arrived here with your Lordship's despatches accompanied by a letter from Sir Hyde Parker. I lost no time communicating to Count Bernstorff your Lordship's Note. . . .'

But no haste on Drummond's part could call back the time wasted by Sir Hyde. In brushing aside Vansittart's reference to the appearance of a British fleet Bernstorff thought he acted from strength, little realizing it was already within sight of the Danish North Sea coast. Had the British Fleet arrived forty-eight hours earlier, Bernstorff would have known he had no choice but to negotiate.

It is easy to see how Sir Hyde could have saved those forty-eight hours by sailing that much earlier from Yarmouth, instead of being bedevilled by shortages of stationery and her Ladyship's ball. Even after sailing he could have made up the time crossing the North Sea, but instead he backed and filled like an indecisive suitor.

19

'THE FIRE OF ENGLAND'

On Monday, 16 March, the day Bernstorff wrote to Vansittart and Drummond refusing to accept the credentials of their mission, Sir Hyde's fleet was four days out of Yarmouth with a fresh gale blowing from the west-south-west and bringing snow with it. Ropes which the men had to handle were frozen stiff; the upper decks of all the ships were slippery with ice. And by an ironic coincidence Nelson wrote a letter which could not have been more relevant to the situation had some sixth sense told him what was happening in the Danish capital.

Soon after midnight Sir Hyde had made the signal for the Fleet to shorten sail, then the wind and sea increased until, firing guns every hour to help the other ships keep in position, the *London* had to strike her topgallant yards, close reef the topsails and bend on storm staysails. It was miserable sailing but the wind was blowing them directly towards their destination.

At daylight Sir Hyde surveyed the grey horizon and was thankful to note all the ships of the line were in position – a credit to sharp-eyed lookouts. At 7 o'clock the deep sea lead was got out and, as the *London* backed her maintopsail, let go from the jibboom end. Thirty-eight fathoms, and the sea bottom was fine sand.

Soon after the flagship got under way again the *Alecto* fire ship signalled that she had sprung a leak and the men on watch in the *London* cursed as they hauled once more on frozen sheets and braces to back the maintopsail. A boat was hoisted out and the carpenter was sent across to make a report. It was not the sort of weather to be rowing around in the North Sea in an open boat – even lowering it needed fine seamanship and good timing, while getting the carpenter on board the *Alecto* would be like jumping from the back of one run-amok camel to another. When the carpenter returned to make his report Sir Hyde ordered the *Alecto* to the nearest port, Leith, 'to stop her leaks etc.', and the *Rover*

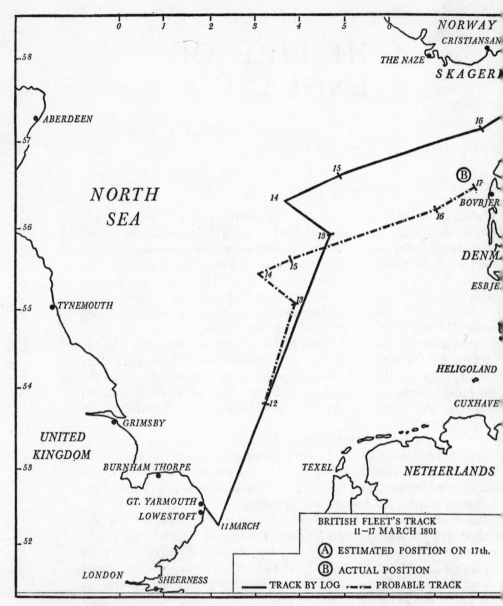

Copyright © 1972 by The Ramage Company

The track of Sir Hyde Parker's Fleet from Lowestoft to the entrance of the Skagerrak, showing
noon positions (civil time) recorded in Sir Hyde's journal (solid line) and how it was in fact set
southward (broken line). The position marked (A) is where Sir Hyde estimated the Fleet was at
noon on 17 March while (B) shows the actual position an hour later after a frigate sighted Bovb

lugger was told 'to attend and see her in safely, and both to join me as soon as possible'.

Sir Hyde's log for the next few hours reflects the problem of keeping a fleet in some sort of order in heavy weather – at 1.30 p.m. signal number 107 was hoisted (*'Close round the Admiral, as near as the state of weather and other circumstances will permit'*); two hours later the *London* made number 89 (*'Ships astern, or in the rear of the fleet, make more sail'*); then at 4.00 p.m. – in good time so that the manoeuvre would be over and the Fleet in good order before darkness fell – number 106 (*'Wear, the sternmost and leewardmost first; and come to the wind on the other tack'*).

Meanwhile, as the gale eased a little and the larger ships swayed up topgallant masts and let out the second reefs in their topsails, Nelson, who had been brooding about Sir Hyde and thinking of the Danes, wrote a long letter to Troubridge which was a good blend of injured indignation and excellent tactics.

I am yet all in the dark, and am not sure we are bound up the Baltic. Reports say (and I only make my remarks from reports) that we are to anchor this side of Cronborg to give time to negotiate.

I earnestly hope this is not true, for I wish for peace with Denmark, and therefore am clearly of opinion that to show our Fleet off Copenhagen would, if [the Danes were] in the least wavering, almost ensure it, for I think the Danish minister would be a hardy man to put his name to a paper which in a few minutes would, I trust, involve his master's navy, and I hope his capital, in flames.

But as I am not in the *secret*, and feel I have a right to speak out, not in the Fleet certainly, but in England and to England.

My ideas are to get up the Cattegat as soon as possible (we are now standing on a wind at WSW, moderate weather off the Naze), to send a flag of truce, if such is necessary, to Cronborg to say that I should pass the Castle, and that if they did not fire at me I should not at them. The despatches, if any, for our Minister at Copenhagen at the same time to be sent.

I should certainly pass the Castle whether they fire or not, and send the same message to Copenhagen until negotiation was over. Being off that city, I could prevent all additional preparations from being carried on or any more gun boats &c. placed outside, whilst I should prepare everything, and the moment the Danish minister said war, he should have enough of it, but he would say peace, and save his honour with his new friends. . . .

Thus we should have peace with Denmark to a certainty either by fair or foul means, but I may be all wrong, and the measures [Sir Hyde is] pursuing much better. I wish they may but I doubt. Bold measures from ministers and speedily executed meet my ideas. If you were here just to look at us! I had heard of manoeuvres off Ushant, but ours beat all ever seen. Would it were over, I am really sick of it! . . .

He wrote trenchantly to Emma:

Reports say we are to anchor before we get to Cronenburg [sic] Castle, that our minister in Copenhagen may negotiate. What nonsense! How much better could we negotiate was our fleet off Copenhagen, and the Danish minister would seriously reflect how he brought the fire of England on his Master's fleet and capital; but to keep us out of sight is to seduce Denmark into a war.

If they are the plans of Ministers, they are weak in the extreme, and very different to what I understood from Mr Pitt. If they originate with Sir Hyde, it makes him, in my mind, as – but never mind, your Nelson's plans are bold and decisive, all on the great scale. I hate your pen and ink men; a fleet of British ships of war are the best negotiators in Europe.

It was fortunate Nelson did not then know that Sir Hyde at no time had any plans for what he would do once his Fleet sailed from Yarmouth, and his orders said only that if diplomacy failed he was to attack. They did not specify how he was to attack – nor, indeed, should there have been any necessity.

Nelson had already shown he understood not only the need for haste but the advantage of negotiating with a powerful squadron at one's back. Even allowing for pique at having been completely ignored by Sir Hyde, his letter to Troubridge (which repeats sentiments expressed in previous correspondence weeks earlier) contains the correct plan. It was correct on the day he wrote it in March; more than one and a half centuries later, with a full knowledge of all the British and Danish plans, aims and preparations, and which are given in this narrative, it is still beyond question that Nelson's plan was the only correct one for the British, and one which might have led to a settlement without bloodshed.

As darkness came down that night and Drummond and Vansittart in Copenhagen read and re-read Bernstorff's reply, seeking anything that would give a deeper insight into the Danish intentions, the gale battering Sir Hyde's ships slowly began to ease, apart from an hour's squall which led to mizen topsails being hurriedly handed. By now Sir Hyde was beginning to worry about the navigation, anxious in case a current sent him down to the south, running the Fleet ashore on the low-lying coast of northern Denmark.

Since the ships and the men of the Fleet were having a hard time of it in such bitterly cold weather, as though Nature wanted to give them battle before the Danes opened fire, this is a good time to look at the Fleet that Sir Hyde commanded.

There has been a good deal of nonsense written about the number of foreigners serving in the Royal Navy during this war, and it is based on two misconceptions. The first thing to understand is that until modern times – until, in fact, trade unions secured better pay and conditions for the men of the world's mercantile fleet, but at the same time imposing rules which put a stop to it – seafaring was an international calling. Men born to the sea served in whichever ships offered the best pay or, in bad times, even employment. Since many of the world's great seaports, particularly in the Mediterranean, did not have large merchant fleets to employ the seamen available, the men signed on in foreign ships and often spent a lifetime serving under foreign flags.

In wartime most men, whatever their nationality, tried to remain in merchant ships because the pay was higher though – and this is not generally realized – conditions were often no better than in warships. And it was quite common for the men to have trouble getting their pay from the masters. Unlike the Royal Navy, where conditions were governed by regulations, in the mercantile marine there was no set scale of food and allowances; all too often men had to go on short rations for the last part of a long voyage because the master skimped on buying provisions. And discipline was what the master cared to make it. Like other belligerents, Britain wanted seamen for her fleets. Captured enemy merchantmen and warships meant prize money but rarely a lot of prisoners because, when offered the chance of serving their captors for pay and regular meals as an alternative to being kept prisoner, the men frequently accepted. In the case of French merchant ships this was not due to any traitorous instinct; to them the Revolution had changed their established world, and many of them came from areas where the Directory's – and later Napoleon's – ideas were not popular; from the ports near the Gironde and from Brest, for example. In any case, the men serving in French and Spanish ships were rarely all of the same nationality: many Irishmen served in Spanish ships – and an Irishman designed the best of them.

Equally important, except in France where the Revolution had changed many accepted methods, in most other countries war was regarded as a matter for regular armies and regular navies. No young man was regarded as unpatriotic if he did not volunteer to serve, although when Britain appeared to face invasion wealthy young men delighted in forming local regiments whose uniforms they designed and paid for, along with arms and ammunition. But apart from that, war was for the professionals, modified by the Irishman's query – 'Is this a private fight, or can a gentleman lend a hand?'

Enough has been said elsewhere of the British system of impressment to make it unnecessary to describe it here, other than to point out that any foreigner, particularly an American with a 'Protection' – a document issued by US Customs collectors and notarized – could not under British regulations be forced to serve in a British ship; but should some wayward captain loath to lose a man refuse to release him, if the man could pass the word to his consul he was released by Admiralty order. In the case of Americans, for example, in the archives there are hundreds of letters forwarded to the Admiralty by Mr Samuel Williams, the American Consul in London at this time, which secured the release of such men.

The problem was that blank or forged Protections were easy to get, and so were genuine ones, properly sworn as required before an American notary or Customs officer. The Protections meant little because the Admiralty was well aware of what every seaman knew – no proof was required that the man applying for the Protection was an American citizen, and there was no way of proving the man possessing a Protection was the person to whom it was issued.

A Royal Navy lieutenant leading a party searching a neutral merchant ship on the high seas, looking for British seamen whom he could legally impress into the King's service, therefore often viewed Protections with a certain cynicism. And in 1801 it was difficult to distinguish an American. His accent, for instance, was no guide. In 1801 no man over the age of twenty-five was born an American citizen, since the Declaration of Independence was made in 1776, and the thirteen states' independence was finally recognized by Britain in 1782. It was almost impossible for an American to have any legal proof of citizenship; indeed, to obtain his Protection, signed by the Collector of Customs, a seaman was required only to swear that he was American, and perjuring himself was regarded by a British seaman as a small price to pay if it equipped him with a Protection 'proving' him to be an American citizen and keeping him out of the hands of the Royal Navy.[1]

Of the sail of the line in Sir Hyde's Fleet, the 74-gun *Elephant* (which was to have Nelson on board during the forthcoming battle), the 74-gun *Ganges*, commanded by the amiable Captain Thomas Fremantle, and the *Monarch*, in which Midshipman Millard served, are good random examples whose muster books reveal the various nationalities, ages and home towns of their ship's companies and which have been chosen since they figure most prominently in the narrative.

The *Ganges* had the most foreigners on board. Her total complement

---

[1] Before and after the worst single-ship mutiny in the Royal Navy several British subjects, among them leaders of the mutiny, had Protections which they had obtained by various means. For details of this and the question of Protections, see the author's *The Black Ship* (London 1963, Philadelphia 1964), pp. 282–3.

was well under the seven hundred established for her by the Navy Board, but few ships ever managed to have a full complement. Four Danes, two Swedes and a Norwegian had already been transferred before she sailed to ships not intended for the Baltic, leaving twenty-seven non-British seamen on board. By far the largest number of them were Americans – a total of fifteen.[1]

Of the rest, two men were Dutch, one Portuguese, and one each from Hamburgh, Hanover, and Prussia. Two came from India – Lewis Mayby, an ordinary seaman from Calcutta, and William Walker, aged twenty-seven, an ordinary seaman from Bengal (their English names were probably the nearest the clerk could approximate to the originals, and no doubt both first went to sea in East India Company ships). Two men were listed as from Goree, and with a West Indian from Martinique was one man noted as from 'Africa'.

The Britons naturally came from the far corners of the nation. Three midshipmen came from London – Francis Molesworthy and William Agar were both aged thirteen, and John Green was seventeen. A fourth midshipman, Charles Crowdy, was sixteen and from Highworth, in Wiltshire, and a fifth, George Allcot, who was sixteen and came from Portsea, was related to the *Ganges'* purser, John Allcot.

Among the ordinary seamen were John Shaw from the Isle of Skye, Isaac Robinson from the tiny fishing village of Beer, nestling among the Devon cliffs, and James Spence, a forty-one-year-old Scot from Dundee. The able seamen ranged from Thomas Delaney, thirty-two, of Waterford in Ireland, to Henry Tregowing, a sixty-five-year-old Cornishman of Gwennap and William Thomas, aged thirty-six, of Appledore, the West Country home of a great fleet of trading ships. Among the landsmen were Richard Leigh, nineteen, from Cranbrook in Kent and Edward Furber, aged twenty-eight, from Stratton in Dorset. John Fordham, a bosun's mate and thirty years old, came from Ware, in Hertfordshire, while Peter Christy, aged twenty-eight, until recently an able seaman but just made a clerk, came from Belfast.

There were fewer foreigners in the *Elephant* – only fourteen men were non-British. Exactly half were Americans. Thomas Joyce, aged thirty-five and from New York, was one of the senior petty officers since he

---

[1] Of these, three were New Yorkers – Robert Barras, who was 26 years old and an able seaman, John Bocker, aged 52 and John Wood, aged 20, both of whom were ordinary seamen. Hugh Tiernan, aged 27 from Albany, John Hassell, aged 25 from Marblehead, William Lane aged 44 from Philadelphia, and John Newton, from Wilmington, 'South Carolina', were all ordinary seamen, while other able seamen included George Read, aged 23 of Rhode Island, William Hermitage, aged 38, from Baltimore, and James Harris, aged 22, from Virginia, while William Edwards of Newhaven, Connecticut, aged 27, was a landsman. The remaining Americans were all ordinary or able seamen.

was a quartermaster, while one of the bosun's mates (whose task included handling the cat o' nine tails if anyone was to be flogged) was John Hoy, a forty-seven-year-old Virginian. Among the able seamen were Richard Call, thirty, from Boston; Christian Hollenway, twenty-five, of New York, and James Thomas, twenty-three, of Portland.

No doubt the Czar would regard John Bell, an ordinary seaman, as a traitor since he came from Malta. A young ordinary seaman from Leghorn (in the Kingdom of Tuscany) was Guitano Dano, who was also listed as a trumpeter. John Wise was an able seaman from Prussia, while a fellow countryman, Francis Rainbott, was an ordinary seaman. The only Portuguese on board was Peter Fernandreno, an ordinary seaman. A Corsican born at Ajaccio (Napoleon's birthplace) was rated a landsman. Once again, the spelling of the names was the nearest the clerks could get to the originals.

The Britons on board, like those in the *Ganges*, ranged from all over the nation. The boatswain, Hugh Mitchell, was obviously a very fine seaman since he held the position despite the fact he could not read. James Page was an ordinary seaman born in Gibraltar while William Johnson was an able seaman from Jamaica. The ship's corporal – in effect a policeman – was an Irishman, Robert Higgins, from Tyrone.

The midshipmen were also from a variety of places – William Milne, who was sixteen, came from Carron, in Scotland, where the famous carronades were cast by the Carron Company; Harrison Fryer, a year older, was born in the cloistered quiet of Wells, in Somerset. Richard Foley was fourteen and from Haverfordwest, while James Huggins, seventeen, came from the island of Nevis, in the West Indies, where his father was probably a plantation owner. Thomas Boweth, who was thirty years old and an example of the older midshipman unable to pass his examination for lieutenant, came from Alnwick in Northumberland, while Charles Oram was born eighteen years earlier at Upavon in Wiltshire. The ship's Second Master, Robert Kipping who was thirty-two, was familiar with the waters in which the Fleet had been anchored, since he came from Yarmouth.

The *Monarch*, although she had a complement of nearly seven hundred, had no foreigners on board, and several of her crew came from the east coast of England. Richard Perkins, twenty-two, a caulker, was from Whitby, Midshipman John Green, twenty-one, from Lowestoft,[1] within sight of Yarmouth, and Midshipman James McKain, twenty-one, from Bungay, only a few miles inland. However, like the *Elephant*, the *Monarch* had an Irishman as ship's corporal, Timothy Connor, who was twenty-three and from Tipperary. All Danes, Swedes and Nor-

[1] Noted in the *Monarch*'s muster book by its old spelling of 'Lowestoffe'.

wegians had, by an Admiralty order, been transferred before the ships left Yarmouth.

Like the crews, the ships and their captains were a fair cross-section of the Navy. The 74-gun *Edgar*, leading the starboard column, was commanded by Captain George Murray. Built on the Thames at Woolwich in 1779, she was 168 feet long on the gun deck and of 1610 tons. George Murray was the man who had not only made a detailed survey of the Great Belt in the previous summer, but was believed to be the only officer in the whole squadron who had sailed through it. The son of a magistrate, Murray was thirty-two years old and had gone to sea when he was thirteen. Soon after being promoted lieutenant he was in the *Arethusa* frigate when she struck a reef off the Breton coast while chasing a French frigate, a mishap which resulted in Murray spending two years as a prisoner of war. After his release he served in the East Indies in several actions against de Suffren, being wounded in the fourth one. He commanded the *Colossus* at the Battle of Cape St Vincent and in 1798, having joined Nelson at Naples and receiving orders to return home, took on board much of Sir William Hamilton's valuable collection of china and pottery. The *Colossus* was almost home when she struck a reef off the Scilly Isles and sank. Murray was acquitted of any negligence and given another command.

The *St George*, Nelson's flagship, was next in the column. Carrying 98 guns and built at Portsmouth in 1785, she was by Nelson's special request commanded by Captain Thomas Masterman Hardy, the tall and burly Dorset man already a close friend of the admiral's.[1]

The *St George*'s next astern in the starboard division should have been the *Warrior*, which was to join the Fleet later. She had been commanded for the last twenty-two months by Captain Charles Tyler – who knew Nelson well, having previously served with him at Calvi (and was to command the *Tonnant* with great distinction at Trafalgar, where he was wounded). Tyler was forty-one, the third son of an Army officer who fought at Bunkers Hill in the 52nd Regiment. Now, thanks to Nelson's influence, his son Charles was serving in the Fleet as a lieutenant in the *Alcmene*.[2]

[1] By coincidence the *St George* was, on 16 March, within a short distance of what was to be her last resting place. In 1811, escorting the last of the season's convoys from the Baltic to England, she was delayed by weather and eventually anchored in a gale off Nysted (Laaland) on 15 November. Many of the convoy were sunk or driven ashore and the *St George*, fouled by a merchantman, also drove ashore, losing her masts and rudder. She was refloated, jury rigged and sailed for England with other ships escorting her. She cleared the Skaw but, on 23 December, ran into bad weather, did not allow enough for the southerly current, and went up on the Jutland coast, near Holmen. Only twelve men survived.

[2] But bolted from the Service in 1805.

The *Warrior* was built at Portsmouth in 1781 and would be followed in the line by the *Raisonable*, an old ship of 64 guns, built – despite her name – at Chatham in 1768, and commanded by Captain John Dilkes.

In the *Warrior*'s place was the *Polyphemus*, commanded by Captain John Lawford, and another old 64 built at Sheerness in 1782. Apart from being at Trafalgar herself, she was acting as a good training ship for that battle. Among her midshipmen was John Franklin (who, already referred to, was to become the great Arctic explorer) while another was Lewis Hole, a parson's son from Kuscott Hill, Barnstaple. Hole, who died an admiral and would be First Lieutenant of the *Revenge* at Trafalgar, had passed his examination for lieutenant at the age of seventeen and was serving in the *Polyphemus* as a volunteer while waiting for his twentieth birthday (the earliest he could serve as a lieutenant).

Also in the midshipmen's berth was John Mawbey, aged nineteen and born at Portsmouth, who would be at Trafalgar, as a midshipman in the *Spartiate*. Yet another of the *Polyphemus*'s midshipmen, Robert Mayne, was still serving in her – as a lieutenant – at Trafalgar.

The *Zealous* was to have been the next in line but never joined the squadron, and the last ship in the division was the *Glatton*, a strange ship with a strange captain. The *Glatton* was originally a 'John Company' ship, a beamy and slow-sailing merchantman belonging to the Honourable East India Company. She was bought by the Navy in 1795 as an experiment and converted to a warship at Sheerness with unique armament.

The Admiralty wanted to experiment with the new types of carronade – the Carron Company were successfully casting 68-pounders – to see if it was possible to design a large ship intended solely for close-range fighting. The quickest and most economical way of making the experiment was to convert a merchantman, so the *Glatton* was bought and taken to Sheerness, where twenty-eight 68-pounders were fitted on her lower deck, and twenty-eight 48-pounders on her upper deck. This gave her a crushing broadside at close range – a 68-pounder's maximum effective range was 600 yards.

The *Glatton* was an ideal large ship in which to mount all carronades as an experiment, and her first captain was sufficiently confident to attack a French squadron comprising a 50-gun ship (which theoretically was the equal of the *Glatton*), five frigates, a brig and a cutter in the Channel and drive them all into Flushing.

However, although she was a formidable floating battery the *Glatton* had been designed as a merchantman, which meant that speed and ability to get to windward had been sacrificed to gain cargo-carrying capacity. That she and the *Ardent* found little favour with Nelson had nothing to do with her carronades: as he later told the Admiralty, 'they sail so very heavy that no rapid movement could be made with them in the Line or Order of Sailing'.

The man commanding the *Glatton* was Captain William Bligh, one of the Navy's foremost navigators, a fine seaman and a brave fighter. But he was completely lacking in natural leadership, for which he substituted the character of a martinet with a violent temper, a strong belief in the efficacy of flogging, and a sneering manner which antagonized his officers. His lack of leadership which resulted in a mutiny on board the *Bounty,* and his subsequent epic voyage of more than 3,000 miles across the Timor Sea in an open boat, are the best indication of both his shortcomings and abilities.

Intended to lead the centre division was the 74-gun *Elephant,* built at Bursledon in 1786. Although she had not joined the Fleet, she was to be the ship from whose deck Nelson fought the forthcoming battle, and her Master, Thomas Atkinson, was one of Nelson's favourites – in fact Nelson was godfather to Horatio Nelson Atkinson, the Master's infant son (who was later to become a lieutenant in the Navy). Atkinson had served with Nelson at Teneriffe and the Nile, commanded a boat at the Siege of Acre, and was to be with Nelson at Trafalgar as the Master of the *Victory.*

Commanding the *Elephant* was Captain Thomas Foley, who came from Pembrokeshire and was a lieutenant in the 98-gun *Prince George* when one of the midshipmen was the Duke of Clarence, the future King William IV. He had considerable experience of fleet actions, having commanded the *Britannia* at Cape St Vincent and, commanding the *Goliath,* leading Nelson's squadron into action at the Nile.[1]

The 74-gun *Saturn,* commanded by Captain Robert S. Lambert, came next but neither ship nor captain have any interest in this narrative. The *London,* with Sir Hyde's flag was third in the centre division, and had William Domett on board as Captain of the Fleet. A Devonian and forty-one years old, Domett was one of the most experienced officers in the Fleet and had been in action many times – with Keppel off Ushant in July, 1778; off the Chesapeake against Ternay's squadron in 1779; in Admiral Graves's disastrous Battle of the Chesapeake off the Virginia Capes; and with Rodney against de Grasse off Martinique in 1782. In the next war he commanded the *Royal George* at the Glorious First of

---

[1] When he died in 1833, as Admiral Sir Thomas Foley, Commander-in-Chief at Portsmouth, he was buried in a coffin made from some of the *Elephant*'s quarterdeck planking, at the Garrison Chapel at Portsmouth.

June and stayed with the ship for the next seven and a half years, until St Vincent took over command of the Channel Fleet and appointed Domett to be his Captain of the Fleet.

Sir Hyde appointed him Captain of the Fleet in the *London*, which was commanded by Robert Waller Otway who, as described earlier, was already a wealthy young man through prize money, and one of Hyde Parker's favourite captains.

The 74-gun *Ganges*, built on the River Thames in 1782 and commanded by Captain Thomas Fremantle, was next astern of the *London*. Fremantle had been one of Nelson's young captains in the Mediterranean, and commanding the *Inconstant* in June 1796 when ordered to Leghorn to take on board British refugees likely to be captured by advancing French troops. Among the refugees were Mr Richard Wynne and his family, which included a daughter, Betsey.

Fortunately for posterity this eighteen-year-old girl kept a diary. She confided in it the first day she saw him:

How kind and amiable Captain Fremantle is. He pleases me more than any man I have yet seen. Not handsome, but there is something pleasing in his countenance and his fiery black eyes are quite captivating. He is good natured, kind and amiable, gay and lively in short he seems to possess all the good and amiable qualities that are required to win everybodies heart the first one sees him.

By the time the Wynnes left the ship on 13 July, Betsey was recording that Fremantle professionally 'has reason to flatter himself that he will reach to the highest . . . but as he says an imprudent match at present would be his ruin and make him lose the fruits of eighteen years service and pain'. On the very same day Fremantle noted in the spasmodic diary he kept: 'Serious thoughts about Betsey. If I was not such a poor wretch.'

Six months later they were married in Naples, Lady Hamilton and Nelson helping to squeeze an £8,000 dowry out of Mr Wynne, and her ladyship arranging for the ceremony and reception to be at the Palazzo Sesso. Eugenia also kept a diary, written with a sharper pen than her sister's, and of Lady Hamilton she wrote, 'a beautiful and amiable woman', while Betsey thought she was 'a charming woman, beautiful and exceedingly good humoured and amiable'. These were significant verdicts, coming from two critical young ladies aged seventeen and nineteen respectively.

Betsey stayed on board when Fremantle sailed in Nelson's unsuccessful expedition to Santa Cruz, Teneriffe and after one wild night, when the British landed and were driven off again, found herself nursing a husband who had a bullet through his arm. He was luckier than Nelson, who lost an arm.

Nelson, was rowed out in heavy seas to the *Theseus* when his stepson, Josiah – who was at an oar – saw a frigate much closer in the darkness and made for her. Nelson, although faint from loss of blood, realized she was Fremantle's *Seahorse* and ordered Josiah not to go alongside. Warned further delay in getting medical aid might be fatal, Nelson replied, 'Then I will die; for I'd rather suffer death than alarm Mrs Fremantle by her seeing me in this state, when I can give her no tidings whatsoever of her husband'.

Fremantle was no stranger to battle: he had been at the siege of Toulon, with Nelson at the siege of Calvi, and in Hotham's dithering action off Genoa.

The *Ganges* was followed by the 64-gun *Ardent*, built in 1796 at Pitcher's Yard, Northfleet to replace a previous *Ardent* of 64 guns which had blown up in 1794 with the loss of all her crew. To build a 64-gun ship as late as 1796 was unusual and Nelson's views on her sailing abilities have already been quoted. Her present captain, Thomas Bertie, had commanded her for the past three and a half years.

Bertie, forty-three years old, had been born Thomas Hoar and changed his name to his wife's family name on marrying in 1788. He first went to sea in the frigate *Seahorse* in 1773 – and among his messmates were the young Horatio Nelson and Thomas Troubridge. Bertie, then still Lieutenant Thomas Hoar, is credited with having invented the lifebuoy while serving in the *Monarch* in 1778. After experiments at Spithead it was adopted by the Channel Fleet.

The *Ardent* was followed by the *Defence*, commanded by Lord Harry Paulet, son of the Marquis of Winchester and one of the Navy's more eccentric and colourful captains.[1] However, his ship took no active part in the battle. Last in the centre column was the 74-gun *Bellona*, destined to suffer many casualties in the forthcoming battle. Built in Chatham in 1760, she was commanded by Captain Sir Thomas Boulden Thompson, one of the select band of captains who had received a knighthood for gallantry. Born at Barham, in Kent, he had celebrated his thirty-first birthday a few days before the squadron sailed. While commanding the *Leander*, he was with Nelson and Fremantle at the attack on Teneriffe; the following year he was with Nelson at the Nile

---

[1] At Portsmouth, refused leave to go to London by his admiral but told he could go as far as his barge would take him, he loaded the barge on a carriage and set off for Town. On another occasion, irritated like most officers at the Navy Board's meagre allowance of paint, wrote to the Board requesting to know which side of his ship he should paint with it.

and, although the *Leander* was only a 50-gun ship, engaged several French 80-gun ships.

Chosen by Nelson to carry Captain Edward Berry home with the despatches announcing the victory – an honour for both men – the *Leander* was caught by the 78-gun *le Généreux*, which had managed to escape from the Battle of the Nile. Unable to get away in light winds, Thompson boldly turned back to engage and fought her for one and a half hours during the morning, beating off one attempt to board and managing to get clear in a sudden breeze (raking *le Généreux* in the process). But the battle continued until late afternoon, by which time the *Leander* was a shambles: all three masts had gone, the wreckage putting nearly all the starboard side guns out of action. With thirty-five men killed and fifty-seven wounded – among them Thompson – he surrendered the ship, with Berry's agreement.

The French plundered her, even seizing the surgeon's instruments, with the result that Thompson nearly died of his wounds. The subsequent court martial – always held when a ship was lost – declared that Thompson's 'gallant and almost unprecedented defence of the *Leander* against so superior a force . . . was deserving of every praise his country and the assembled court could give.' Thompson later received a knighthood and a pension of £200 a year.

One of the *Bellona*'s midshipmen, John Felton, was a Londoner who would serve with Nelson in the *Victory* at Trafalgar, while another Londoner, William Anderson, whose home was in Bell Street, Paddington, wrote a graphic description of the forthcoming battle in a letter to his parents which will be quoted later.

The larboard division was led by the 74-gun *Monarch*, which suffered the worst casualties in the battle – nearly a quarter of the total killed, among them her captain, Robert Mosse. Built at Deptford in 1765, the *Monarch* had led the van division in Keppel's action off Ushant in July 1778; was Admiral Elphinstone's flagship at Saldanha Bay; and Vice-admiral Onslow's at the Battle of Camperdown in October 1797.

The *Defiance* would follow the *Monarch* when she joined the Fleet with Parker's third-in-command, Rear-admiral Thomas Graves. Built at Randall's Yard on the Thames in 1783 to one of Sir Thomas Slade's designs, she had been badly affected in the Spithead Mutiny of 1797. Her present captain was Robert Retalick.

Admiral Graves, who was fifty-four and the son of a parson, had two brothers in the Navy. He had served on the American coast for much of his early service at sea. In 1774 he was in an operation which was almost a family affair. While in a ship commanded by his uncle, he was given command of a small schooner, and on 27 May 1775 he was patrolling in the Charles River at night when the wind dropped and the ebb tide put the schooner aground. She immediately came under fire from colonial forces and the ship sent in boats to help, one of them commanded by his brother John. The colonial forces managed to set fire to the schooner and both brothers sustained burns.

By 1781, commanding the *Bedford*, he was at the Battle of Chesapeake Bay, Hood's action against de Grasse off Nevis in January 1782, and Rodney's off Martinique in April of that year.

The *Defiance*'s next astern was the 74-gun *Ramillies* but she took no part in the battle. The next ship listed in the Order of Sailing, the *Powerful*, never joined the Fleet and her place was taken by the 64-gun *Veteran*, which also took no part in the battle. The sixth in the division was the 74-gun *Russell*, another ship built on the Thames and one with a distinguished record. She was now commanded by Captain William Cuming.

The last ship in the division was the 64-gun *Agamemnon*, one of the ships built by the master shipwright Henry Adams at Buckler's Hard in 1781. The young captain appointed to command her in February 1793 – after he had been unemployed for five years – and she was his first ship of the line – wrote to his brother, a parson, 'My ship is, without exception, the finest sixty-four in the Service, and has the character of sailing most remarkably well.' As the *Agamemnon*, now commanded by Captain R. D. Fancourt, kept her position in the Order of Sailing, it is interesting to speculate whether that man, as he looked across the Fleet, ever recalled his excitement when he first boarded her that February day eight years earlier – for he was Horatio Nelson, then merely one of many scores of captains named in the Navy List.

The *Isis*, a late arrival and commanded by Captain James Walker, was another ship built on the Medway and launched in 1774. Although only a 50-gun ship and by this time regarded as lacking the fire power to stand in the line of battle, she had already fought at Camperdown and was to do so again at Copenhagen, receiving heavy damage and many casualties.

Of the smaller ships, we are concerned only with those that played an effective role in the battle. The first among them is the 38-gun frigate *Amazon*, which was to suffer more casualties than several of the line of battle ships. Built only recently in the King's Yard at Woolwich, she was commanded by Captain Edward Riou, whose behaviour in the next three weeks was to immortalize him as 'the gallant good Riou' of Campbell's ballad, 'The Battle of Copenhagen'.

Joining the Navy without influence to back him and coming from a poor family, Riou proved a fine seaman. One example, unusual inasmuch as it does not concern war, is sufficient. Late in 1789 Riou sailed in command of the *Guardian*, formerly a 44-gun frigate, bound for Botany Bay with convicts and £70,000 of stores, livestock and seeds for the new colony of New South Wales.

Twelve days after leaving the Cape of Good Hope,[1] he sighted a huge iceberg and decided – because he had so many extra men and animals on board – to send over the boats to fill casks with fresh water. As soon as this was done – just before night fell – the *Guardian* got under way again, and ran into fog.

Although she had been steering away from the iceberg, she suddenly struck a submerged part of it (or another one) and, although Riou managed to get her off, she appeared to be sinking and by midnight, with a gale starting, had six feet of water in her.

Everyone, convict and seaman, took his turn at the pumps for the rest of the night and next day, which was Christmas Eve. By the morning of Christmas Day it seemed certain the ship would sink, and Riou decided the only chance of saving some lives was to let the five boats, with as many of the 300 men on board who wished to go, try to reach the Cape of Good Hope, 1,200 miles away. The first boat launched was swamped and the men drowned; the other four boats got away safely.

Riou was, of course, a true leader; a man others wished to follow, not because the alternative was punishment contained in the Articles of War. Bligh, with whom he had talked only a fortnight earlier, was cast adrift by his crew. By comparison Riou, with all the ships' boats leaving in an attempt to reach the Cape, was not left alone in the listing and sinking *Guardian*; three midshipmen, the boatswain, carpenter and twenty seamen refused to leave him.[2]

The four surviving boats headed for the Cape in very bad weather. One was picked up after fourteen days by a French merchantman; the rest were never seen again. And nine weeks later, long since given up as lost, the *Guardian* sailed into Table Bay. As the boatswain wrote later, 'After the boats left us we had two chances, either to pump or sink.'

---

[1] Meeting, before he sailed, Captain Bligh, who was on his way back to England with news of a mutiny on board his ship, H.M.S. *Bounty*, and having just completed a 3,618-mile voyage in an open boat across the Timor Sea.

[2] Since it is dangerous to *judge*, as opposed to describe, a man's behaviour by any other standards than those of his own people in his own day, this chance meeting of Bligh and Riou at this particular time provides what is probably the fairest judgment of Bligh. Riou kept complete control in a sinking ship with more than two hundred convicts on board who, far from panicking or seizing the opportunity of breaking into the spirit room and getting drunk, stood their turn at the pumps, while many of his men, far from casting him adrift, refused to leave him. Nor, as the rest of the episode shows, was that the end of their response to Riou's leadership.

They pumped and began to repair the ship. 'Sometimes our upper deck scuppers was under water outside, and the ship lying like a log in the water. . . . Sixteen feet of water was the common run for the nine weeks in the hold.' After arriving in Table Bay the ship, which had survived so much, was at anchor when another storm blew up, and she sank.

One of the three midshipmen who had stayed on board with Riou was a Pitt, nephew of the great Lord Chatham and son of Lord Camelford. Having been originally reported dead, the fact he was still alive due to Riou's seamanship ensured the young captain was quickly rewarded with promotion.[1]

One of the *Amazon*'s lieutenants was John Quilliam, who had received £5,000 as his share of the prize money when the *Ethalion*, of which he was third lieutenant, captured the treasure ship *Thetis*. Serving in the *Victory* at Trafalgar it was he who, responsible for signals in the battle, suggested to Nelson that because it would not have to be spelled out, 'expects' was perhaps a better word than 'confides' in the signal Nelson wished to make – 'England confides that every man will do his duty'. Nelson agreed and, thus amended, the most famous signal ever made in a ship of the Royal Navy was hoisted.

The *Blanche*, a 36-gun frigate, was the newest vessel in the Fleet, having been completed at Deptford just in time for Captain Graham Hamond to commission her in February. Hamond was also the youngest captain in the Fleet. Twenty-two years old, he was the only son of Sir Andrew Snape Hamond, Comptroller of the Navy. (In October 1804, while commanding a frigate, he captured three Spanish frigates carrying treasure and, later in the year, captured yet another treasure ship. His share of the prize money for the four ships was estimated at more than £100,000.)

Another frigate, the 32-gun *Alcmene*, which was to suffer more than a score of casualties, was built in Chatham in 1794. Her presence in the Fleet is explained in a letter of 24 February from Lord St Vincent to Admiral Cornwallis: 'Captain Sutton, late of the *Prince George* now of the *Alcmene*, was removed into the latter ship for the express purpose of accompanying Sir Hyde Parker on the Baltic Expedition, where he has much local knowledge. . . .'

The other frigate which went into action was the 36-gun *Désirée*, commanded by Captain Inman. She was a beautiful ship, captured from the French by Inman himself, cutting her out of a bay while

---

[1] The midshipman, who succeeded to the title of Lord Camelford, proved no credit to his family or Riou, being a poor sailor (despite a passion for the sea) and an ardent duellist: a fact which led to his death in the West Indies from the pistol shot of an opponent.

commanding the *Andromeda*. He earlier applied to the First Lord to be transferred to another ship but Lord St Vincent replied on 10 February: 'I am very well disposed to contribute to your aggrandisement by every means in my power, for I know you, by reputation, to be an officer of great merit, but I should injure your fair name if I took you from under the command of Sir Hyde Parker when going upon the most important service'.

One of the *Désirée*'s lieutenants was Andrew King, of Southampton, who had been a midshipman in the *Bellerophon* at Howe's victory of 1794, and was to be fourth lieutenant of the *Victory* at Trafalgar.

The two remaining ships of interest apart from the brigs, bombs and fireships were the *Arrow* and the *Dart*, each of 30 guns and designed by one of the most advanced and inventive naval constructors the Admiralty has ever had the fortune to employ, Samuel Bentham.

In 1796, Bentham designed two advice schooners, the *Redbridge* and the *Eling*, whose hulls underwater were cut away, making them much sharper than usual. More important, they were among the first sailing vessels with outside ballast: four-foot lengths of cast iron were bolted on along the bottom of the keel.

Bentham designed the *Dart* and the *Arrow* the same year. They were 128 feet long on deck, but whereas ships of war had bluff, apple-cheek bows and broad quarters, these two had sharply raking bows and the pointed sterns usually seen only on whalers. Whereas a cross-section of a normal ship of war was almost rectangular, with the lower corners (the bilges) rounded, the *Dart*'s and the *Arrow*'s bow were V-shaped, gradually becoming U-shaped amidships and V-shaped again towards the stern.

But the revolutionary hull shape was only part of the story. Rounded bluff hulls did not go well to windward; the hull, with little keel to 'bite' into the water, did not stop the ship making leeway. To lessen this and give a 'bite' when going to windward, Bentham fitted each ship with three drop keels, basically similar to the single ones fitted in some modern sailing boats.[1]

Captain James Brisbane, commanding the *Cruizer*, one of the two sloops in the squadron, was the fifth son of an admiral and had been Lord Howe's signal midshipman in the *Queen Charlotte* at the Glorious First of June. As a lieutenant he was at the capture of the Cape of Good Hope.

[1] The centreboard with a pivot is believed to have been invented by a British naval officer, Lieutenant Molyneux Shuldham, in 1809 while held a prisoner by the French at Verdun. At this moment Shuldham was serving in the *Edgar*, the second ship in the starboard division. The first effective drop keel is believed to have been invented by Captain Schank, a British naval officer, in 1774.

Of the small vessels, the *Harpy* sloop and the *Lark* lugger had been chosen by the Admiralty because their commanding officers had served in the Baltic. Among the bomb vessels, the *Discovery* was commanded by John Conn, an Irishman from Waterford and a cousin by marriage of Nelson. Conn was yet another man in Parker's fleet who would be at Trafalgar, where he commanded the *Dreadnought*. As part of their normal complement the bomb vessels carried men of the Royal Artillery.

One of the 28-gun *Jamaica*'s lieutenants was Henry le Vesconte, son of a Navy purser. His own son, also named Henry, was to serve in the Navy and lose his life in the Arctic with Sir John Franklin, who was of course at this time a midshipman in the *Polyphemus*.

This survey of the ships and men of Parker's fleet shows how closely knit was the Navy; how many captains had served together as midshipmen and how men like Fremantle and Nelson had been wounded while storming the same beach. All this created a unity and was the very bricks and mortar of the Navy's tradition. There was the occasional Bligh; but Riou was to windward of him in the *Amazon*.

Fremantle, Foley, Hardy, Thompson, Bertie, – all these captains, and many more of the officers, had served before with Nelson and knew him well. Likewise he knew them; their abilities and their shortcomings. In planning and fighting a battle, this knowledge was worth many broadsides.

The rest of Monday night, 16 March, was a tiring mixture of strong squalls and moderate breezes, with seamen frequently scrambling aloft and out along yards covered with ice and snow. In the *London* the second reefs had been let out of the topsails soon after dark; the ship had hove-to for soundings at 11.00 p.m.; by 2.00 a.m. heavy squalls sent the topmen aloft again to take in the mizen topsail. The bitterly cold weather combined with the fact that their hands were rarely dry started cracks in the skin so that many of the men were soon suffering from salt-water boils.

But Sir Hyde was becoming even more nervous about the Fleet's position. With the Naze still reckoned to be more than fifty miles away, from midnight on the *London* hove-to every hour to heave the deep sea lead.

North Sea fishermen and pilots relied mostly on charts which, often handed down from father to son, gave detailed pictures of the bottom of the sea, which varied from fine sand to coarse and smelly mud. With current then not predicted, the tidal stream affected by weather, and the sky often overcast for days, preventing anyone taking a sun or star sight, dead reckoning and 'a cast o' the lead' was the usual way of being sure of one's position.

The lead, like the weight of a grandfather clock, had a cavity at the bottom in which was smeared a handful of tallow – 'arming the lead', as it was called. A cast of the lead gave not only the depth but brought up a sample of the bottom and an experienced pilot or fisherman could usually by sight and smell (and often taste) use the information, with courses steered, wind direction and experience, to confirm his position on the chart.

By noon on Tuesday the Fleet was approaching the entrance to the Skagerrak with a west wind bringing fog and misty rain. At 1.00 p.m. the *Cruizer*, which had been sent off to reconnoitre, returned to report that 'Borenbergen' was twelve or fifteen miles to the south-east. This was Bovbjerg, and put the Fleet sixty miles too far south for the entrance to the Skagerrak (and less than thirty miles from where the *St George* was to be wrecked in 1811).

Sir Hyde promptly tacked the Fleet to the north-west, sounding as he went, and by something approaching a miracle the *Defiance* hove in sight with Rear-admiral Graves on board and saluted the flagship. But with the entrance of the Skagerrak to the north-east of him and night coming on, Sir Hyde's nerve failed and, as Colonel Stewart noted in his diary, 'Fleet stood to sea. Weather and wind favourable, hard N.W. Lay off and on off the Cattegat [sic], to enter it at daylight.'

That the *Defiance* found them on 17 March was a coincidence because Sir Hyde's handling of the Fleet since leaving Yarmouth on 12 March was lamentable. Nelson's reference in his letter to Troubridge about the manoeuvres off Ushant, 'but ours beat all ever seen', was no exaggeration; and apart from a one-day gale giving Sir Hyde head winds, his whole progress was as slow and as cautious as that of a captain on a voyage of discovery approaching an uncharted coast.

From Yarmouth his course for the Holmen (Hanstholm, the north-west tip of Denmark) was north-east (see chart on page 218) with the Skaw farther into the Skagerrak and forming the north-eastern tip of Denmark. The entrance to the Skagerrak, between the Naze of Norway to the north and the Holmen of Denmark to the south is sixty miles. Any gale between north and south by way of west would allow the whole Fleet to pass through.

From the Fleet's noon position the day it sailed from Yarmouth until noon the next day, 13 March, Sir Hyde steered for the Naze, recording it as 277 miles away. He then, for no clear reason unless it was nervousness of the Danish coast, altered course more to the north and hove-to five times in the next twenty-four hours to sound.

By noon on 14 March with strong breezes from the WNW – an ideal direction – he was more than halfway to the Naze and quite far enough north to turn and steer directly for the entrance to the Skaggerak. In his journal he noted the Naze was 147 miles away, bearing north 34 degrees east.

Later in the day the wind went light, then it blew a gale from between north and east, the first head winds. Still apparently haunted by the idea of Denmark to the east of him he tacked the Fleet to the north and his noon position next day, 15 March, showed he had been steering a course towards Scotland, 90 degrees to the west of the course for the Holmen. Whereas the Naze had been 147 miles away the previous noon, it was now 131 miles. In twenty-four hours he had made sixteen miles in the vital direction of north-east. Yet with this wind the other tack was by far the most favourable one and perfectly safe.

For the next twenty-four hours, with a fresh gale from the WSW – again an ideal direction – which blew itself out within a few hours, leaving a fresh breeze – the Fleet actually steered for the entrance to the Skaggerak but made pathetically little progress, so that by noon on Monday, 16 March, the Naze was 106 miles away to the north-east and Sir Hyde was repeatedly signalling to the frigates out ahead to keep a close lookout. Since noon the previous day the Fleet was twenty-five miles nearer the Naze.

Finally, between noon Monday and noon Tuesday, with a fair wind, he made good progress but, as we have seen, as soon as the *Cruizer* reported, Sir Hyde promptly took the Fleet away to the north-west.

At 10.45 next morning Parker noted in his journal, 'Saw land bearing from NNE to NE.' This was the Danish side of the Skaggerak, and he must have felt safe at last. The wind was west, fresh and squally with showers of sleet, and the course to take the Fleet through was east so it was 'a soldier's wind'.

The *Elephant* joined the Fleet just after noon and Captain Foley could be forgiven for thinking he had joined a circus. Sir Hyde knew exactly where the Fleet was – his journal notes the Skaw as thirteen miles away, and two other places each twenty-four miles.

But instead of heading east he signalled the Fleet at 3.00 p.m. to head up to the north-east. This was followed at 3.50 by orders that every ship was to carry a light during the night, and repeat his signals by showing signal lights and burning false fires (flares). At 4.45 he made the signal for the Fleet to steer south-east, and at 5.50 p.m. ordered it to wear again, heading back once more to the north-east. While this zig-zagging went on, the *London* was taking soundings every hour and eventually at 1.00 a.m. the signal was made to steer east.

Finally at daylight on Thursday, 19 March, Sir Hyde wrote, 'Moderate and clear, land bearing south.' Nelson noted more explicitly in his journal, 'Very fine weather. Saw the Skaw ESE. . . .' Topgallant sails were set, reefs shaken out of topsails, and Sir Hyde recorded: 'At 9 passed the Skaw at 10 miles distance.'

Sir Hyde had taken exactly seven days, almost to the hour, to cover the 400 miles between Yarmouth and the Skaw. Except for one day, he had fair winds, ranging in strength from moderate to gale force. Walking at four and a half miles an hour, he could cover 108 miles in twenty-four hours. His Fleet had averaged fifty-seven miles for every twenty-four hours so far, the speed of a child dawdling to school, and still had another 175 miles to cover before reaching Copenhagen. Nor did he have the excuse that the gun brigs were slow – they were towed by the sail of the line.

The *Elephant* had brought terrible news for the Fleet. The *Invincible*, commanded by Captain John Rennie and with Rear-admiral Totty on board, had hit a sandbank and sunk, drowning more than 400 men, including Captain Rennie. And by a tragic coincidence she had foundered very near to where the previous *Invincible* had sunk some forty years earlier.

On sailing from Sheerness the *Invincible* had taken on a pilot at Harwich and sailed to Yarmouth Roads, where she anchored while Sir Hyde's orders – which should have been sent to Sheerness to save time – were collected from Admiral Dickson. When she weighed, the pilot, instead of going out through the main channel which led out to the south-east, took the ship out to the north-east, through the narrow Cockle Gatway, despite objections by the ship's officers that there was a sandbank, Hammond's Knoll, in the Gatway.

There was a strong wind and a heavy sea, and soon after 2.00 p.m. the *Invincible* hit Hammond's Knoll, ran right up on it, and for the next three hours pounded heavily. The mizen mast went over the side, and to lighten the ship the mainmast was cut away. Distress signals were seen in Yarmouth and a fishing smack put out. Then the *Invincible* was driven over the sandbank into deeper water but her rudder was wrenched off, making her unmanageable, and she drove on to another bank.

By this time the fishing smack was near by and the *Invincible* launched two boats, one of which carried Admiral Totty, the purser, four midshipmen and ten men. Both boats reached the smack safely, put their quota of men on board and returned to the stricken ship to take on more. A passing collier sailed down to help, and as the two boats returned to the smack heavy seas forced one of them away and it would have capsized on a sandbank but for the collier, which managed to save the men.

As darkness fell, with increasing wind and sea, the fishing smack was unable to get near the *Invincible*, and anchored for the night. At daylight the skipper of the smack refused to weigh, saying the seas were too heavy, so Admiral Totty ordered his men to cut the cable, and the smack worked her way up to the wreck, but Admiral Totty was unable to get close enough to help. To the horror of all the men in the smack the *Invincible* was then gradually driven off the sandbank into deep water and slowly began to sink. Immediately Captain Rennie gave the order to hoist out the launch, which managed to get clear just as the ship sank, with more than 400 men still on board. Rennie himself swam to within a few feet of the launch before becoming exhausted, and the men saw him put his hands over his face and sink. All the other officers, except two lieutenants, were drowned.

The smack saved more than seventy men from the launch and then went back to Yarmouth. Several days later five seamen reported to the Admiralty in Whitehall – they had clung to a piece of wreckage, the foremast and foretopsail yards, for two days and nights before being spotted by the brig *Briton*, of Sunderland, who picked them up and took them to London. While they were clinging to the wreckage the men had nothing to eat, but chewed some tobacco which one of the men had in his pocket.

Had Sir Hyde enclosed Totty's orders in one of his letters to Nepean requesting stationery, with instructions for them to be forwarded to Sheerness, the loss of a sail of the line and 400 men – more than the entire British losses at the Battle – would have been avoided. . . .

Later that Thursday morning Sir Hyde wrote in his journal:

Wrote to Mr Drummond, chargé d'affaires at Copenhagen, with a list of the ships &c. under my command and desiring him to let me know the determination of the Court of Denmark with respect to His Majesty's most gracious offer for negotiation which if not acceded to in 48 hours he is to give immediate notice thereof to Captain Hamond of the *Blanche*, who will receive him, his suite &c., together with such British merchants as may be willing to quit the country, and I shall commence hostilities.

The *Blanche* left the Fleet at 2.00 p.m., and with her departure Sir Hyde seemed to have decided he had gone far enough for the time being. There was a strong and expected current setting to the north and Vingå Sound – better known to the Navy at this time as 'Wingoe', and an often-used anchorage over on the Swedish side – was only eight miles to the east, so Sir Hyde altered course for it.

In the time Sir Hyde had been at sea Vansittart had, of course, seen Bernstorff the previous Saturday and by Monday decided to return to England by way of Lübeck. On the same Monday the British expedition sailed from Martinique to capture the Danish and Swedish Islands.

Sir Hyde's secretary, the Reverend A. J. Scott, wrote to his uncle, Rear-admiral Scott, the day before that, 'It is impossible for me to impress upon your mind more strongly than you feel, the importance and risk of our present expedition. . . . We are all made up of anxiety and determination to do something. . . .'

After Sir Hyde had written to Drummond, but before the *Blanche* sailed, Nelson for the first time 'went on board the Commander-in-Chief to say my compliments. At 11 returned to my ship, found the *Blanche* dispatched to Copenhagen.'

He described the meeting in a letter to Troubridge.

It being moderate I got on board the *London* yesterday for an hour, for whatever inattentions may be shown to me, nothing of respect shall be wanting on mine. I was glad to find that he was determined to pass Cronborg and to go off Copenhagen in order to give weight to our negotiator, and I believe this conduct will give us peace with Denmark. Sir Hyde told me, on my anxiety for going forward with all expedition, that we were going to go no further without fresh orders. I hope this is all right, but I am sorry, as I wish to get to Revel before the departure of the [Russian] Fleet. We should recollect it is only twenty hours' sail from Cronstadt, and the day the ice is open they sail. . . .

I suppose we shall anchor this evening about 8 o'clock, between the Koll and Cronborg, not only to prepare for battle, for no signal is yet made, although I believe several [other ships] have followed my example. I have not had a bulkhead in the ship since last Saturday. It is not so much their being in the way, as to prepare people's minds that we are going at it, and that they should have no other thought but how they may best annoy their enemies.

Two references in this letter are particularly important. The first is Sir Hyde's declaration that he was 'going no further without fresh orders'. Nelson might well 'hope this is all right' because he must have guessed what was indeed the case: the Admiralty orders already given to Sir Hyde were detailed and more than covered the situation. Dundas's instructions said specifically that 'the commanding officer . . . should on his arrival be instructed to make such a disposition of the ships under his command as in his judgement may appear most likely to ensure the success of the attempt it will be his duty to make (should all proposals for conciliation fail) to destroy the Arsenal . . . with the whole of the shipping in that port'.

Furthermore, the note being sent to Drummond gave the Danes forty-eight hours to reply, and Parker was given strict orders that if he heard nothing from Drummond within forty-eight hours he was 'immediately [to] proceed to vigorous hostilities'.

Despite this, Parker had sent the *Blanche* ahead from off the Skaw and anchored one hundred miles from Copenhagen so that the physical presence of the Fleet had no effect at all. The day before going on board the *London* Nelson, in a letter to Davison, had repeated the remark he made to Troubridge about the advantages of the Fleet being off Copenhagen to give weight to negotiations with Bernstorff, adding '*but out of sight is out of mind* is an old saying, the fellow should see our flags waving every moment he lifted his head.'

The second important reference in Nelson's description of his visit to Sir Hyde, was to the urgent need to get to Revel to deal with the Russians, a matter which was also causing concern in London. By chance Lord Hawkesbury had written a day earlier to his predecessor, Lord Grenville, his views of the over-all situation.

It is impossible to judge what will be the issue of our contest with the Northern Powers [he wrote]. France and Vienna are drawing together. Prussia is alarmed to the greatest degree; but is so pressed by Russia on one side, and France on the other, that she pretends to have no will of her own. Unless the appearance of our Fleet in the Baltic makes a sudden change in the policies of Russia, the Electorate of Hanover will, I am convinced, be sacrificed.

And Hanover, whence came the present Royal Family, had a great significance.

Nelson was a few minutes but many miles out in his guess that Sir Hyde would anchor for the night at 8 o'clock. 'At half past 7 shorten'd sail and came to with best bower in 33 fms,' Sir Hyde's journal noted. 'Wingoe beacon ENE 7 or 8 miles.'

But he did not get an undisturbed night: at 11.00 p.m. a west-south-westerly breeze set in, quickly strengthening to gale force, and putting the whole Fleet on a lee shore. In the darkness several ships had to get under way and claw off to get sea room. The *Monarch* was one that stayed – Midshipman Millard recording they had to strike topgallant masts and veer away two cables 'in consequence of heavy sea'.

Colonel Stewart, who was on board the *London*, filled in an omission from Sir Hyde's journal for that night, '*London* nearly on the shoal off

Warberg [Varberg] Castle. Fleet obliged to tack off it.' (And Mr Scott told his uncle about it in a letter next day – 'The *London* was nearly lost yesterday on a shoal with only 19 feet water on it. It is called "New Danger" on the charts, a place lately discovered').

The *London* bore up under topsails which by 3.00 a.m. had to be double-reefed. At 5.00 a.m. Nedding Lights were sighted six or seven miles away, much to Sir Hyde's relief. But daylight brought no cheer, as Nelson's next letter to Troubridge on 21 March recounted:

We anchored last night. It blew fresh all night, and this morning only 38 sail out of 58 were with us. *Bellona* and *Russell* missing. . . . Much snow and ice about our rigging. I find it very sharp. I suppose we shall anchor in the passage, [and] in the night collect our ships.

By next day, the wind still west, the squadron managed to get down to within a dozen miles of the Koll (Kullen, the northern end of the spur forming the Swedish side of the Sound) when a south-westerly gale sprang up and Sir Hyde took the fleet inside Skälderviken, the great bay formed by the spur, and at 8.30 p.m. anchored in the lee of the Koll. By 4.00 a.m. next morning, Saturday, 21 March, there were 'Very strong gales, rain and sleet' and the *London* 'veer'd away to a cable and two thirds. Struck topgallant masts. At 6 [a.m.] struck lower yards.' In the meantime the *Kite* reported her bowsprit damaged, and the *London* sent over carpenters to repair it.

Soon after noon the wind eased enough for the *London*'s lower yards to be got up, and scores of men at the capstans hove in to one cable. Sir Hyde hoped to get the Fleet under way, but the wind, still from the south-west, increased again as darkness fell and by 2.00 a.m. on Sunday, the *London*'s lower yards were being sent down once more and the two thirds of cable the men had painfully got in earlier was veered again.

By 7.00 a.m. Sunday morning Sir Hyde was finally able to signal the remains of the Fleet to prepare to weigh, and by half past eight the ships were beating out of Skälderviken to round the Koll and head down towards the Sound. By noon the gale had eased down to a fresh breeze, but it was a miserable sail: 'At half past 1 p.m. tack'd, at 2, tack'd, at ¾ past 3 tack'd. . . .' Sir Hyde's journal recorded.

Then at 6.00 p.m., the *Blanche* was sighted coming northward through the Sound. What news did she bring? Was it peace or war?

20

THE HORSE-DRAWN
ULTIMATUM

Nelson had little doubt what news the *Blanche* would bring, and soon
after the Fleet left Yarmouth he had written to Alexander Davison
asking, 'Will you have the goodness to take care of my will'. He had
already written the will on the passage from the Downs to Yarmouth
on four folio pages, and it had been witnessed by Captains Hardy and
Thesiger.

The provision he had made for Emma has already been described;
for himself, he drew up a codicil on a single quarto sheet on 16 March,
the day the Fleet ran into a gale in the North Sea, in which he wrote:

My body, if my Country choose not to pay the carcase [sic] of him who,
when alive, devoted it to its service, any honours, I desire, if its in England,
that it may be buried at Burnham Thorpe, near where my Mother is and my
Father is to be buried, without any funeral pomp, and that what the custom
of the world would allow to a person of my rank, I desire it may be given to
the poor of those parishes where my father is rector. . . .

The codicil also left to Emma the sable pelisse, which was one of
many gifts from the Sultan of Turkey after the Nile, while to Hardy, 'my
worthy captain', he left all his furniture on board the *St George* ('except
my plate and table linen'), with 'my spying glasses, wine china and
glassware'. His servant Thomas Allen was to receive £50 and all
Nelson's clothes.

In England the King was making a good recovery from his illness and
had been able to take a walk in the gardens of the Queen's Palace and
later spent some time reading despatches.[1] He had been well enough
for the new Administration to take office on 14 March, two days after
the Fleet sailed from Yarmouth.

[1] Reporting this, a newspaper added a note about the cure used to abate the King's fever:
'Several opiates having been tried without the desired effect, hops were placed under His
Majesty's head, which, acting as a soporific, produced complete success'.

When Lt McCulloch of the *Blanche* arrived at the British Embassy in Copenhagen at 8 o'clock on Friday night, 20 March, with despatches for Drummond, the British Minister at first assumed the frigate was anchored in Copenhagen Roads. He was too busy to question the young lieutenant until after he had read his instructions and discussed them with Vansittart. Then he discovered the *Blanche* was at Elsinore, and McCulloch had covered the last twenty-five miles to the capital by carriage.

Once again Britain's threats and offers had arrived behind a pair of horses. This time the responsibility was Sir Hyde's: his orders to Captain Hamond before the *Blanche* left the Fleet were that he should 'proceed to Cronenberg with a flag of truce and acquaint him [Colonel Stricker, the Governor] that he has despatches for Mr Drummond'.

The *Blanche* had arrived off Cronborg Castle and anchored in Elsinore Roads at 10.30 in the morning. With the fresh west wind that was blowing she could have been anchored in Copenhagen Roads by 1.30 p.m., in full view of the Danes. But instead, all the formalities had to be gone through at Elsinore: a 15-gun salute fired, to which Cronborg returned fifteen; then the call on Colonel Stricker, and finally the hiring of a carriage for McCulloch, with the result that he arrived at the Embassy more than six hours later than necessary. Thanks to the telegraph on one of Cronborg's towers, the rumours of the British Fleet's approach and news of the arrival of the *Blanche* reached Copenhagen long before McCulloch. That hours counted is shown by the fact that the special messenger sent to London with the joint despatch of Vansittart and Drummond, reporting the failure of the mission, had left Copenhagen while the *Blanche* was in sight of Cronborg. Had the *Blanche* come to Copenhagen the thunder of her salute would have made something of an impression; instead, carriage wheels clattered along Castelvej in the dark and came to a stop at the Embassy door.

The instructions delivered by Lt McCulloch to Drummond and Vansittart had been drawn up very carefully. Hawkesbury had written to his predecessor, Grenville,

I send you a note I received on Monday from the Danish Minister, and the answer which it is proposed to return to it through Sir Hyde Parker. In case it should be necessary to have recourse to hostilities it is intended as a kind of manifesto. I should be particularly obliged to you if you would criticise it without mercy, and make any alterations in it you may think proper.

The answer was preceded by a paragraph Drummond was to sign and which said: 'The undersigned, His Britannic Majesty's Chargé des

Affaires, has been instructed by his Court to deliver to Count Bernstorff, the enclosed answer to the Ministerial Note, dated 23rd February, 1801, which Count Wedel Jarlsberg delivered upon that day by order of his Court, to Lord Hawkesbury. . . .'

The Note itself, signed by Hawkesbury, made some telling points which Grenville had never mentioned. Saying His Majesty had earlier seen Denmark show 'the most marked partiality to the cause of His Enemies', he pointed out that in 1797 the French Directory, in violation of both law and justice, ordered that all vessels in which British manufactures were found (whether the property of enemies or neutrals) should be condemned [as prizes to France].

In 1798, when France 'determined on the invasion of Egypt, they seized more than a hundred neutral vessels at that time in the ports of France, by which they were materially assisted in transporting thither the French forces; and His Majesty is yet to learn that any disposition was manifested by the neutral Powers to resent this flagrant outrage of their rights'.

Without emphasizing the contrast, Hawkesbury referred to the *Freya* episode, and he continued: 'With the utmost surprise that after having given this striking proof of moderation,' His Majesty then learned of Danish negotiations and that Denmark 'had even taken steps for entering into engagements with his Enemies, in support of this Confederacy'.

All this was aggravated, Hawkesbury declared, by the fact 'this pretended treaty of neutrality has been concluded under the influence and at the instigation of a Power' which was at the very same time actually committing the most unprovoked hostilities against Britain.

After such conduct, the King might be fully justified in refusing any further negotiations; however, he still had 'the most earnest desire to prevent those fatal Extremities which would be so repugnant to the real interests of both countries; and whilst it is inconsistent with his duty, after the experience which he has already had, again to commit to doubtful negotiation and procrastination the deep and important interests of his Dominions, he has taken the only effectual step which remained to him of bringing the existing differences to an immediate and final adjustment'.

If his latest propositions were accepted by Denmark, 'they will not only avert the Evils of War, but cement and strengthen the connection which has so long subsisted between the two countries'. If they were rejected, 'it will only remain for him to avail himself of those means which Providence has entrusted to him, to assert the Dignity of his Crown, and to maintain the Rights and Interests of his people'.

Drummond did not waste a moment: he had a copy made of the last part of the instructions, intending to give it to Bernstorff so there should be no misunderstanding. He also drafted a private note to the Count saying that as the Danish Court did not now recognize him officially, he wrote 'in the quality of a simple individual who has always desired and who still desires ardently to see the most perfect union re-established between Great Britain and Denmark'.

This private note was in French, the language in which all diplomatic exchanges were made; but his instructions from London concerning the Notes were explicit: 'The first Note should be signed by you, and delivered, together with my answer to the Note of Count Wedel Jarlsberg, to the Danish Government.'

Hawkesbury must have known both should have been in French; but in sending them already written in English and instructing Drummond simply to add his signature to one of them, he left the envoy no alternative but to obey – and invite a severe snub from Bernstorff.

Drummond did what he could to conform to the quaint procedures so beloved by diplomats. In times of peace these keep them gainfully employed searching the French language for appropriate clichés and those vague but elegant phrases which allow them to consider their rather sloppy marching to be a graceful quadrille. But a study of the diplomatic exchanges preceding all the major European wars in the last two centuries makes it tragically clear the procedures break down in times of emergency, often forcing a nation into a course of action because the procedures are not flexible or fast enough to allow itself a way out of a dangerous situation. This, coupled with the usual inability of men in power to understand the enormous difference between false pride and true honour, has so often resulted in a nation going to war and losing thousands of its own people's lives because it was afraid it might lose face. In this respect politicians have never learned that a true man of honour is never afraid to admit he is wrong.

As a diplomat Drummond fortunately was one of the exceptions: in addition to his private letter he sent a formal Note in French to accompany the official Notes in English, so phrasing it that Bernstorff should be able to read between the lines and see why they were in English – 'The undersigned has been charged by his Court to remit to Count Bernstorff the reply enclosed. . . .'

The letter and two Notes were sealed and sent round to Bernstorff late that night. The reply arrived early next morning, and in reporting to Hawkesbury the same day, Drummond described how 'in order to furnish a further opening and which the Cabinet of Denmark might avail itself to prevent matters from being carried to an extremity I accompanied it with the private note subjoined'. But Bernstorff's reply was not only prompt; it was uncompromising: it came 'together with the passports required, whereupon we immediately came to the resolution of retiring on board His Majesty's Fleet'.

A letter Bernstorff wrote to the Danish Ambassador in Paris the same day (sending a copy to de Wedel Jarlsberg in London) is even more illuminating. Written in French, it said Drummond had just delivered the British answer to Denmark's representations for lifting the embargo, and it recapitulated all the British grievances against Denmark. The British Government, Bernstorff wrote, believed it necessary to take the only effective step which remained to them to make 'an immediate and definitive settlement' of their differences.

'The future will without doubt explain the sense of this declaration,' Bernstorff told Dreyer. 'But Lord Hawkesbury's note being worded in the English language, I have just been authorized to send it back' and tell him he could not accept a document which was such a departure from 'the general custom of the courts of Europe'.

'We have no illusions of the danger of our position,' Bernstorff assured Dreyer, 'but the British Government is mistaken in thinking we would be intimidated to the point of betraying our engagements [to other countries] or sacrifice our honour.'

The despatch, making no reference to the British offer of a fleet of twenty sail of the line, was obviously written with an eye to its contents being read by Napoleon – the story of the British Note being returned because it was not written in French would have an added piquancy when told in Paris.

The reply Bernstorff had sent to Drummond said briefly that 'The Count Bernstorff, having received with surprise' the British Note, thought Drummond might like to repair 'this deviation from the customs accepted among the Courts of Europe' and 'to allow Mr Drummond the means of repairing it he has the honour to return to him a document which did not conform to those customs'.

Bernstorff added: 'It is with much regret that the passport Mr Drummond had requested is enclosed.'

There was nothing more for Drummond to do now in the diplomatic field. A messenger was sent to Elsinore to tell Fenwick, the British Consul there, what had happened and instructing him to inform all British families at Elsinore that the *Blanche* would take them. He warned the Britons in Copenhagen, and began sorting out the Embassy archives, packing important documents and destroying the rest. At Elsinore, Captain Hamond was warned that the British diplomatic mission would soon be arriving, and he could expect British families as well.

Hamond had been keeping his ship's company busy while at anchor in Elsinore Roads. Saturday was spent setting up the rigging – which had stretched after the strains of the recent bad weather – and doing minor repairs. On Sunday morning he had them mustered aft, 'in fresh breezes and showers of rain' and read aloud the Articles of War, as he was required to do at least once a month.

While this was going on a convoy of carriages, led by one containing Lt McCulloch rattled along the coastal road from Copenhagen to Elsinore, bringing Vansittart and Dr Beeke and several British business men and their families. Two hours later Drummond followed with Talbot.

In happier times it was a beautiful journey, because for the entire distance the road rarely leaves the coast, skirting gently rolling country-side and winding through rich forests, meeting small fishing hamlets every few miles with boats hauled up on the beach and nets hanging on racks to dry or be repaired.

Three miles after passing out through the city gates the carriages reached the village of Ordrup where, built in a three-sided valley, was Count Bernstorff's mansion, described as 'certainly the most magnificent country residence in the island'. The valley opens on to the Sound, giving the Count a splendid view of the passing ships and the distant Swedish shore.

A mile or two beyond they passed 'The Weeping Eye', where another member of the Danish cabinet, Count Schimmelmann, the Finance Minister, had his country mansion on a hill overlooking the Sound. At the foot of the hill was a spring where the Count had built a monument to the memory of his wife, and his grief was symbolized by the spring water running from an eye, giving the mansion its nickname. And the Count had arranged that a peasant girl was always there to hand a cup of spring water to any thirsty traveller.

By then the carriages were skirting Jægersborg, the great deer park, where from the Hermitage, the Royal hunting lodge, one could see Landskrona on the Swedish coast and the island of Hven in the middle of the Sound. Near by, with several hundred deer grazing round it, was a newly-built telegraph tower, one in the chain linking Elsinore and Copenhagen.

As they travelled north so the Sound narrowed, like the neck of a bottle. From being ten miles wide opposite Count Bernstorff's house, it was down to four as the road gently curved round for the last two miles before Elsinore itself.

The second largest town on the island, Elsinore was well described by a Dane a year later.

It needs little penetration to discover to whom this town owes its prosperity. Everything tells you, and if it were not for the flag on the castle which informs you it is Denmark, you would fancy yourself in England. This resemblance in the exterior is verified with still greater exactness in the interior. Many of the inhabitants are Britons born, they naturally retain the manners and customs of their country, and those who are not, take peculiar delight in wishing to appear like Englishmen.

The Consul, Fenwick, and his family, were waiting for Drummond, having locked up their home in Strandgade. Because he not only lived in Elsinore but had been free to walk round and observe the Danish preparations, he knew better than anyone else in the party the strength and weakness of Cronborg.

By 1.00 p.m. the *Blanche*'s boats were at the bridge which formed the bustling centre of the town; within half an hour all the Britons were on board the frigate. Hamond had already given orders to heave in to half a cable and David Spence, the Master, noted in his log: 'At 2 weighed and made sail to ye NE. At 6 join'd the Fleet.'

In the Danish capital the small cloud on the horizon had been growing rapidly from the time Vansittart arrived and, a couple of days later, the Crown Prince received the news that a British fleet had sailed. By 20 March, when reports came in that it had not only sailed but was actually in the Skagerrak, it was suddenly realized the cloud heralded not a squall but a hurricane. And equally suddenly it was realized the nation was desperately short of seamen to man the ships being fitted out along the quays of the Navy Yard, on the other side of the inner harbour from the Crown Prince's palace.

As soon as Count Bernstorff read Drummond's Notes late on Friday night he warned the Crown Prince. Early on Saturday printers hurriedly set up the type and printed hundreds of copies of a new Royal proclamation, while at the British Embassy in Castelvej Drummond had received Bernstorff's reply and his passport and had begun packing.

On Sunday, while the carriages carrying Drummond and Vansittart journeyed northward to Elsinore, the posters were being pasted up in the city and messengers were sent out delivering copies the length and breadth of the kingdom.

The proclamation told the people of Denmark in the King's name that 'the circumstances now demand we must use and secure means for the defence of the State, and we therefore order our dear and true

Danish landsmen immediately to prepare themselves to arms in readiness to report at the times and places that councillors will make known'. The proclamation added that 'we will ensure that you will be given the necessary arms and equipment which, with your courage, will be necessary to defend the Fatherland'.

It added that all seamen called in under the previous proclamation would be used to serve in the Navy.

His Majesty also needed a great number of able-bodied, as well as more untrained men, for various defences and 'calls upon the mayors of small towns in the King's name to order that all able-bodied men who have not already reported for duty should by law report to the said mayors within four days'.

In Copenhagen the men were to report to the police stations, and elsewhere at town halls, 'and where there are no town halls, to the local magistrate or town councillor'. Every man would get 'free board and lodging, pay and gratuity of 15 Rixdollars, and in case of sickness have free medical treatment as the King sees fit'.

A few days earlier, on the 18th, the shortage of men for the ships was highlighted in a bizarre manner by an order from the Crown Prince to Steen Bille, commanding the *Danmark*: he was told to make up his crew from soldiers of the 1st Jutland Regiment – four NCOs, one piper, one drummer and one private soldier, who were to go on board next day.

On the 20th, when word came the British Fleet was approaching, Fischer had received several letters and orders from the Crown Prince. One, referring to the proclamation to be published next day, said that as the recruits ought to be used in the ships of war now in the Roads, they would be received at the recruiting office in Gammelholm [the Navy Yard] by the deputy there, Secretary Aadsen, 'who will issue them with pay books and the pay due at the normal rate, and whereupon they are to be taken on board the ships of the defence'. Fischer was also told to arrange that one of his officers called on Secretary Aadsen each day to collect a list of names of the new recruits.

In a second letter the Crown Prince told Fischer: 'If and when British men of war arrive you are to demand from [their] Commander his destination and the intentions . . . and your action will depend upon the answer.' In the same letter Fischer was also told that the boys serving in his ships who could not be used to serve at the guns should be sent to Holmen; and finally, 'when two flags are shown with one gun fired from the blockship *Dannebroge*, more seamen may be expected for your ships and will be sent out in the boats of the Town'.

In the meantime some of the ships to defend Copenhagen had been taking on stores and preparing to be towed or sailed out through the boom which closed off the Inner Harbour. The blockships *Wagrien*, *Jylland* and *Prøvesteenen* were already at anchor in the Roads, with the 'defence ships' (as they were described in the Crown Prince's correspondence) *Charlotte Amalia* and *Cronborg*, and ten gun boats. The *Elven* and the gun boat *Viborg* were due to pass through the boom on Sunday. The date had been arranged nearly a week earlier; but by chance it was also the day before Drummond left Copenhagen for Elsinore.

Young Lt Peter Willemoes, previously ordered to help fit out the *Danmark*, was on the same day ordered by the Crown Prince to command *Floating Battery No. 1* (illustration number 26). The floating batteries were in effect large rectangular rafts with low bulwarks, equipped with a capstan at either end and a dozen 18-pounders along each side. They were towed or warped into position.

The next day was Sunday, and no orders were issued; but on Monday, the day that Drummond went on board the *London* and was telling Sir Hyde about the strength of Copenhagen's defences and the 'great preparations being made', saw the Crown Prince at work again. Captain L. F. Lassen was ordered to take command of the *Prøvesteenen*, an old three-decker now cut down to two decks, Captain Risbrich was given command of the *Wagrien* and Captain Ferdinand Braun the blockship *Dannebroge*.

On this day the *Elven* went through the boom, two days later than intended, and her log contains the cryptic entry: 'Ordered to go out to the Roads, and the Crown Prince says he [the lieutenant in command] will not be held responsible for shortages on board as he was interrupted while provisioning.'

Apart from receiving letters and orders, Olfert Fischer was, of course, sending reports to the Admiralty, and it is worth citing one he wrote on Monday, 23 March, as an illustration of the dozens of varied problems he was facing in preparing Copenhagen's defences.

Many of the boys serving in the Navy were the sons of sailors, and their pay consisted of a daily ration of rye, hence their description, 'rye boys' (*Rugdrenge*). Many of the boys' homes were in Nyboder, the seamen's houses built in long terraces near Castellet, the streets then being named after flowers, ships and large fish.[1]

Captain Fischer reported to the Admiralty on 23 March, 'The blockship *Dannebroge* [has been sent] ten or twelve partly-trained rye boys who are of more trouble than use. It would be better for these children

---

[1] The single-storey houses, built by Christian IV, still stand, looking much as they did in 1801, although many of the original street names have changed. Originally there was one oven for each two apartments, and legend has it that when neighbouring wives quarrelled, one was not above quietly dropping a handful of salt into the other's cooking pots.

if they were sent off the ship as they might become cripples without having been any use. As I fear that this is also the case with most ships, I report the matter hoping that the Admiralty will approve their leaving the ship.'

Fischer went on to complain that the crew of his ship were very occupied with boats coming out from the city – taking men on leave, bringing out volunteers (who apparently came out direct without calling on Secretary Aadsen at the recruiting office), provisions, and 'innumerable necessities' for the ship. He asked that Captain Kierulf, the Harbourmaster of Copenhagen, should be requested to control the boats.

But that was almost the least of Fischer's complaints that Monday. Far from underestimating the enemy (a major fault of the British) he considered the positions of the ships under his command – upon which the fate not only of Copenhagen but Denmark, Norway and probably Sweden, depended – and reported to the Admiralty:

Most of the defence ships have only two sea officers, and the crews are poorly exercised, and on the last ship sent out [*Elven*] hardly exercised at all. I am only praying for good weather so that I can moor them up and get the ships properly manned and exercised. With a small medicine chest we [the *Dannebroge*] have been sent five roll bandages and an old sheet, two pounds of lint, and three simple tourniquets. As this is all the linen for bandages and for staunching bleeding we have in the ship, I fear the other ships are as poorly equipped, and report accordingly.

On this same day the people of Copenhagen were reading in the *Berlingske Tidende* a despatch from Hamburgh that a cutter had arrived bringing the courier from London to Berlin, and it was reported that 'A fleet of about 20 British ships of war under the command of Admiral Nelson have sailed towards the Sound.'

In the same issue was a report from Copenhagen urging that 'The equipping of the ships ought to continue with great energy, and Parliament should do its best to defend the country and keep its independence. Everyone according to his conscience should try to defend his land, and every day,' it added, 'large numbers of volunteers are reporting for duty.'

Another report the same day said that 'A watch is being kept on the Sound [for the British Fleet] from Hornbæk, from the towers of Cronborg and the tower of the church at Elsinore. There is gossip in the streets and public places, which are full of excitement.'

On Tuesday, 24 March, one of the most important letters the Crown Prince received was a report from Adjutant-general Bulow, who had been sent up to inspect Cronborg Castle and discuss matters with its commandant, Colonel Stricker. Bulow's report gave in detail the Castle's present situation and outlined what more was necessary to prevent a surprise attack.

Definite news of the British Fleet's position reached the Crown Prince on Wednesday: Major-general Waltersdorff, who was at Odense, sent a message that the British were two miles north west of Hornbæk, confirming news just received from Stricker by the new telegraph at Cronborg.[1] Stricker's telegraphed report said the British Fleet comprised fifty ships and was now at anchor.

So at last the speculation was over. The Crown Prince knew the whole nation was behind him. The problem was how best to mobilize it in the time left – the British could be bombarding Copenhagen less than eight hours after weighing anchor at Hornbæk. . . .

In the meantime the despatches continued to arrive at his headquarters. Among the first reports the Crown Prince received next day, Thursday, was one telegraphed from Stricker: the British Fleet, totalling fifty-two ships, was now at anchor half a mile from Nakkehoved (the northernmost point of the island, just east of Gilelleje and twelve miles from Cronborg).

At the morning parade of senior officers – in effect a briefing – the Crown Prince's orders concerned not just the safety of Denmark but of Copenhagen itself: instructions were given how the regiments were to man Christianshavn Gate – one of the entrances to the city – and the batteries at Lynetten, Langebro and Quintus. (See illustration number 9.)

At the day's Defence Commission meeting it was decided that the gun boats hitherto under Olfert Fischer's command should be transferred to Steen Bille, who was to man and provision them from the ships already under his command. Since the gun boats were to anchor along the coast parallel to and close inshore from Fischer's defence line, which they could hail, this was a bad arrangement because Steen Bille's flagship would be a mile away.

The shortage of men, let alone trained men, was now really making itself felt in the ships. Captain Risbrich, who had taken command of the *Dannebroge* on Monday, wrote to Fischer almost at once reporting that six men could handle the carriages of heavy guns 'only with difficulty', and 'in my opinion, in the present circumstances where an action may

---

[1] Illustration number 16: it was a type of semaphore telegraph similar to that between the Admiralty in London and Portsmouth, and ran from Cronborg Castle to Copenhagen, and later to Altona (Hamburgh). Cronborg was also linked to Gilleleje to the west (almost the northernmost point of the island) and across the Sound to Sweden. At Cronborg the telegraph was fitted on one of the towers and on the Swedish side the telegraph mast was at the Signal Battery. The Cronborg–Gilleleje telegraph's existence was first reported in London by *The Times* on 28 January.

be expected with an enemy who is quick and well equipped, these are too few to handle the guns with any speed. The numbers should, therefore, be increased by three men per gun. . . .' Fischer agreed, and in a covering note to the Admiralty 'hoped that this would be the rule for all the ships with these guns'.

Next day, Friday, was much the same: Colonel Stricker reported from Cronborg that the British Fleet, now fifty-four ships, had weighed anchor and set sail towards Hornbæk (i.e. towards the Sound) and that the Sælland Infantry Regiment (ordered on 18 February to march)had arrived to join the Cronborg garrison.

The *Berlingske Tidende*'s correspondent at Elsinore reported that 'After all the conflicting rumours, we can now see the British Fleet of about 50 sail from time to time. Today you can see them at anchor between Kullen [Sweden] and Gilleleje. Some of the British seamen came ashore for water without committing any excesses'.[1]

The same issue of the newspaper reported that in the two previous days a floating battery and the *Sværdfisken* and *Søhesten* had passed out through the boom into the Roads. The British frigate *Blanche*'s visit to Elsinore was also recorded.

On Saturday, 28 March, the Crown Prince again received a stream of reports and sent out many orders. Fischer was told that three more men would be allowed for each of the heavy guns on one side of the ships under his command, and the men would be sent out from the Navy Yard. Major-general Waltersdorff wrote from Odense, on the nation's third largest island, that Major Ely's and Major Beckker's battalions were short of cartridge powder.

Among the letters forwarded to the Crown Prince on Saturday was one which had been sent to the War Office and which was recorded in the Crown Prince's files as follows:

A priest named Faber at Stavreby, near Præstø, says that he has taken various measures to defend the coast of that place, and that the Admiralty had answered [a request from him with the result] that 'I cannot get any arms for the church. I was promised some guns, but as I have no powder for them I now request a small barrel of powder, either from Copenhagen or from Næstvet, and any small quantity of equipment which can be spared. I further request to be appointed to the local militia, where I could take care of the defence of the coast. I further recommend that certain local people at Stavreby be appointed as officers. . . .'

The martial priest also requested that the singer in his church should have an appointment in the telegraph service.

[1] This appears to be the only reference to British boats taking casks in to water: none of the ships' logs mention it.

When the *Berlingske Tidende* at the beginning of the week published the report already quoted that 'Everyone according to his conscience ought to try to defend his land, and every day large numbers of volunteers are reporting for duty', it was not exaggerating; and from the men who were to be killed or wounded one can see how representative of the nation were those who volunteered or were conscripted into the King's service by the proclamations.

Peder Schultz, a journeyman dyer, lived in Copenhagen at Store Kongensgade 222 with his wife, Anna-Marie, who was thirty-five and the daughter of a master shoemaker in Odense. Schultz had four children. The eldest, Anne-Dorothea, was six, and the youngest a year. He decided to volunteer for the Navy and it was only a brief walk of a few hundred yards from his home past the Royal Theatre in Kongens Nytorv, along Østergade and down to Secretary Aadsen's Recruiting Office. There he was issued with his pay book, given 15 Rixdollars advance, and sent to the *Holsteen*.

Pierre Felgin, a Frenchman by birth, lived at Løngangstræde 271 with his wife, also called Anna-Maria, and sold umbrellas for a living. He too reported to Secretary Aadsen and was sent off to the *Wagrien*. Emanuel Carlsen lived with his wife and child – his wife was expecting their second – in the shadow of the Karlsbod Bastion protecting the city on the south-east side. His home was a corner house in Torvegade, a few yards from the Naval Hospital[1] and only a short distance from Secretary Aadsen's office. He was sent off to the *Prøvesteenen*.

Two men working at Selbye's sugar warehouse beside the quay in Christianshavn, very near Carlsen's home and almost next to the Navy Yard, volunteered together. One, Hans Ibsen, came from the island of Bornholm and at forty was still a bachelor, lodging at the warehouse. Jens Christensen, from Aarhus and three years younger than Ibsen, was married. Both men were labourers, and when they reported at Holmen each was paid 15 Rixdollars and sent to the *Sælland*.

Hans Christensen, a bachelor and forty-eight, but no relation to Jens, worked for a brewer named Svane and lodged in the basement of a gin distillery in Ulfeldt's Plads (now Graabrødretorv). He volunteered first thing on Monday morning and was sent to the *Charlotte Amalia*. Søren Wingaard, a tobacco spinner, living at Vesterbro 236, in Copenhagen, volunteered and was sent to the *Prøvesteenen*, leaving his wife Dorothea-Elisabet who, like several other wives of volunteers, was expecting a baby.

A journeyman mason and well into middle age, Niels Lindgreen

---

[1] In Over Garden neden Vandet. The building, No. 60, is outwardly unchanged, and today houses the Naval Library.

lived at Lavendelstræde 103, and he left his wife Sophie, who was sixty-four, to look after the rest of the family while he went off to serve in the *Prøvesteenen.*

One of the men conscripted under the King's proclamation was a journeyman glovemaker, Søren Kaas, working at Kioge, south of Copenhagen. His father, David Kaas, was a glovemaker at Nakskov, a small town at the head of a fiord on the island of Lolland. Søren was sent to the *Sværdfisken* with his 15 Rixdollars advance pay. He wrote to his parents that he had given most of this (either 11 or 13 dollars: his writing was not very clear) to the ship's surgeon for safekeeping, and subsequently they tried to get it back.

Another conscript was Martin Rollof, from Møgeltonder, in south Jutland. He was sent to Copenhagen, leaving behind his wife Kirsten, who was forty-five and suffering from cancer of the liver, and five children. The eldest, a girl, would be twenty-two on 12 April; the youngest, also a girl, was only two.

Two men from Holbæk, a town on the banks of Isefjord and west of Roskilde, volunteered for the Navy. One, Christen Hugger, had to leave his wife to look after their three children (the youngest of whom was two and the oldest six) although she was expecting their fourth child almost any day when he joined the *Søhesten.* The second man was a master mason, Christopher Jensen, who had married a widow, Bodil. They had two daughters, Helene, who was twelve, and Bodil-Marie, who was four.

Lt Willemoes, who was now commanding *Floating Battery No. 1,* came from Assens, on the island of Fyn and overlooking the Little Belt. In the same town lived Rasmus Larsen, nicknamed '*Nifinger*' ('Nine Fingers'), and he volunteered for the Navy, leaving his wife to look after their five children. Mrs Bodil Christiensen was the widow of a crofter, and she lived at Wedlebye, near Roskilde. Sixty years old, she had four sons, three of whom now volunteered for the Navy and one of whom, Øle, was to be killed while serving in the *Charlotte Amalia.*

Andreas Halberg was a tailor of Asminderød, near Fredensborg, and he had five sons. The eldest, already in the Navy, was a carpenter in the *Freya* frigate – the same ship that had defended the convoy; the next two were in the Army; the fourth, Sven, a cook's boy, was now conscripted into the Army under the Royal proclamation; and the youngest, Jacop – who, the father later claimed, was to be his 'help and support in his old age' – was conscripted into the Navy and sent to the *Jylland.*

Since Norway was part of Denmark there were a number of Norwegians in the battle, but because of the time and distance involved they were men who were already serving in the Navy or Army. Two such men came from Porsgrund – Halvor Jensen, who had a wife and three-year-old daughter, was an able seaman in the *Rendsborg*; and Christen Madsen, an ordinary seaman in the *Elven*. He was a bachelor whose pay supported poor parents.

Wilhelm Sacariasen was a seaman in the *Aggershuus* and engaged to Anne-Margrethe Bøhrn, of Hammersburg, near Christiana (now Oslo). Anne-Margrethe was later to claim that when he last returned to the ship from leave he not only had no money but owed 20 dollars, a debt which she paid when she heard he had been killed.

Not all those people volunteering or conscripted reported directly to the recruiting officers or town halls, nor were they all Danish. Sinnia Naiker, who lived in Copenhagen at Madstræde 37, within a stone's throw of Christiansborg Castle in the centre of the city, was an Indian who sent the Crown Prince 'a humble petition'. He wrote that all normal work at the Department of Commerce had stopped and both the Department and the Crown Prince 'know me well'. He said that 'As a war is now a matter of earnest, I petition you to appoint me to the naval vessel *Trekroner* under the command of Captain Riegelson to serve as a naval officer, or in any other suitable way, as I shall fight for Denmark with all my power.'

He pointed out that 'His Royal Highness also knows of my Indian education, combined with an overseas one, and as I am a Naiker I must have a respectable appointment, because any duties other than those of an officer I cannot accept. . . . I shall do all this in the name of Mohammed.' For good measure he enclosed a personal reference from the Department of Commerce.

But not all the volunteers were happy with what they found. A young surgeon, Dr C. A. Hansen, wrote of his experiences to the Crown Prince, who received the letter on the eve of battle.

I volunteered at the Admiralty to be employed as a second surgeon with the Navy, and it pleased Doctor Falkenthal [of the Admiralty] on 27 March to allow me to be employed as the surgeon on board *Floating Battery No. 1* under the command of Lt Willemoes. On Monday, 30 March I went off to the *Floating Battery* and spent the whole morning with water over my ankles and as a result, apart from the fact I have a weak constitution, I was affected by a sudden fever together with cramp in my stomach, so that Lt Willemoes, who that evening could not send a boat on shore from the battery, had to transfer me to the *Sælland*, where I spent an extremely uncomfortable night, which 1st Surgeon Schmidt of that ship can verify, until mid-day on Tuesday, when I departed at once from the *Sælland* and landed. Immediately on arriving on shore I reported my sickness in writing to Dr Falkenthal.

In my father's house I hope I shall be well looked after and thereby prevent any recurrence of my sickness. In spite of the abovementioned discomforts I have been [reflecting] just how impossible it would have been for me on board the *Floating Battery* under the open heaven and in a foot's depth of water in a small room on the deck alone to look after anyone who was ill and do my duty as a surgeon.

Not to further consume my strength without reason, I beg Your Royal Highness to accept my resignation. I will in return pay back my advance pay of 24 Rixdollars.

He added that he thought this was very reasonable of him because as soon as he was well enough to serve the Crown Prince again he would 'join the corps which had been started by students and named "The Crown Prince's Lifeguards".'

In the Admiralty file were two notations, the first saying Hansen wished to be released in return for refunding his advance pay, the other saying cryptically: 'Tell one of the reserve members to take his place.'

21

BY THE SOUND OR
THE BELT?

The *Blanche* reached the Fleet as it was tacking south against a strong
north-going current, and with darkness coming on Sir Hyde would
obviously anchor within an hour. The Fleet was now six miles west of
the Koll, which overhangs the northern end of the island of Sælland so
that Cronborg and the entrance to the Sound are more than fifteen
miles to the south-east.

However, Drummond and Vansittart were anxious that Sir Hyde
should know at once what had passed in Copenhagen and receive his
instructions from Vansittart, who had already written a letter telling
him officially. Captain Hamond had a boat lowered so that Dr Beeke
could deliver it to the *London* and, Vansittart wrote, 'communicate such
observations as we were able to make at Copenhagen'.

I have to inform you [Sir Hyde read] that Mr Drummond this morning
received from Count Bernstorff a note enclosing a passport for him. This
proceeding accompanied by the repeated refusal of the Court of Copenhagen
to acknowledge the character with which His Majesty has been pleased to
trust us, may be considered as equivalent to a declaration of war.

You will therefore consider all negotiations as at an end, and proceed to
execute such Instructions as you have received.

This letter was written and signed by Vansittart because, whether or
not the Danes had accepted his credentials, he had been appointed head
of the mission and was the person who, on behalf of the Government,
gave instructions to Parker.

At half past six, twenty minutes after sunset, Sir Hyde signalled to the
Fleet to tack in towards the Swedish coast and at seven, with the lead
showing sixteen fathoms and a muddy bottom, made the signal to
anchor.

This was the point where a minor decision was to have an effect out of

259

all proportion to its apparent importance. Sir Hyde had received his instructions from Vansittart; there remained only to tell him what more they knew of the Danish defences in Copenhagen than Dr Beeke had mentioned. It was decided that Drummond should do this since he had been in Copenhagen all the time, and late at night he was rowed over to the *London*, where he described them to Sir Hyde.

Unfortunately, although the information Dr Beeke and Drummond gave was from laymen, Sir Hyde treated it as coming from experts. And he found the information alarming. After Drummond departed, Sir Hyde recorded in his journal that the diplomat 'informed me of the great preparations made by the Danes, both at Cronenbourg Castle and in their line of defence &c. &c., at Copenhagen'.

Then the Commander-in-Chief spent a troubled night. Next morning he wrote to the Admiralty describing 'my proceedings to this day, with the treatment of Messrs. Vansittart and Drummond met with at Copenhagen, and that the moment the wind was fair I should enter the Sound and put their [the Admiralty's] orders into execution'.

The important point in this entry is that before 9.00 a.m. on Tuesday, 24 March, Sir Hyde intended to enter the Sound. He did not specifically say this in his despatch, but the entry just quoted from his journal makes it quite clear.

The despatch – written without any discussion with Nelson or Graves, who were still unaware of the news the *Blanche* had brought – was not one calculated to convince their Lordships that Sir Hyde's sword was either sharp or swift. After the usual formal beginning he wrote: 'I arrived off the Scaw the 19th with only three or four of the gun boats and bomb tenders missing. On the 20th at night it came on to blow from the south to the southwest, and has continued, in consequence the *Russell*, *Hyena* and about 12 of the small vessels are missing.'

He had duly sent off the *Blanche* and she had returned with Drummond and Vansittart, they 'having been dismissed from the Court of Denmark without the smallest communication with the Ministers, but on the contrary, with particular haughtiness'.

From the rough sketch these gentlemen have been enable to furnish me with of the mode of defence the Danes have adopted for the preservation of the Arsenal, it appears to be a very strong one, and from the shoalness of the water, it will be very difficult for us to dislodge them without vessels of force, of a less draught of water than the ships of the line.

It now blows hard at SSW. As soon as the wind shifts to the northwards I shall proceed to put the remainder of my instructions into execution, in doing which their Lordships may depend upon every exertion in my power

20 A rough sketch by Robinson Kittoe during the Battle shows how he visualized the
Danish view from the shore to the north of Castellet. Steen Bille's flagship, the
Danmark, is shown (out of position) in the foreground with the Trekroner Fort beyond,
the *Mars* and *Elephanten* to the left, and the ship *Trekroner* and *Iris* frigate to the right.
Beyond are the ships of Fischer's Defence Line and Nelson's division. Immediately
above the *Danmark*'s mainmast is the *Hiaelperen* at the north end of Fischer's line.

21 The Battle, looking northwards across Nyeholm. From the left, the picture shows
Steen Bille's ships above the roof of the building, with the Trekroner Fort in line with
the third ship's masts and Lynetten to the right. The mast crane – a rectangular
tower with the crane built into the roof – still stands, and next to it are the building
slipways. To the right, beyond the third building, is the Sixtus Battery with the
semaphore mast standing out against the smoke of its guns. The buildings in the

centre of the picture house the sail lofts, ropewalks and workshops for the Navy yard, with the city walls beyond and extending to the right. Horses drawing covered carts are carrying away the wounded while in the foreground, in front of the nearest building, men are hauling a fire engine. The nearest ship on the right with a single mast is the *Provesteenen* under attack by the *Polyphemus*, while at the other end of the line, beyond Lynetten, Captain Riou's frigates are in action.

22 In a drawing of the Danish defences from another angle, Robinson Kittoe shows the gun boats anchored between Olfert Fischer's line and the shore and more detail of the city of Copenhagen. Above the *Provesteenen* is Stricker's Battery, which Kittoe marks with a single seagull, while the masts of shipping in the harbour are shown by two seagulls, and the Arsenal by three (with the mast crane just to the left). The four seagulls just above and to the left of the tall spire mark the famous Round Tower 'to the top of which,' he noted, 'carriages may ascend by means of a spiral road.'

23 Kittoe's rough plan of the positions of Fischer's and Nelson's ships in the Battle. A is the *Provesteenen*, D the *Jylland*, H the *Dannebroge*, I the *Hayen*, M the *Sjaelland*, P the *Holsten*, Q the *Indfødsretten* and the *Hiaelperen* on the extreme right. The lozenge shapes represent the Trekroner Fort (*right*) and Lynetten. Although the relative positions of the *Agamemnon*, *Russell* and *Bellona* are correctly shown, the Middle Ground Shoal extended much further to the left between the *Agamemnon* and the two other grounded ships. The notes for this drawing are given in illustrations 24 and 25.

that the force under my command will admit of, in the peculiar navigation in which we are to be engaged. . . .

Although he referred to 'these gentlemen' he had in fact only seen Drummond and Beeke at this point. He then 'Ordered Captain Digby of the *Kite* to receive the above gentlemen with their suite and such British subjects as were on board the *Blanche* and proceed with them and my despatches to the first port he can reach in England'.

At last, one would think, Sir Hyde was in a position where everything was clear cut; there was no further room or need for indecision. His orders completely covered the point; Britain was now, by the explicit wording of those orders, at war with Denmark from the moment Sir Hyde chose to fire the first shot.

But Drummond, excellent a diplomat as he had proved to be, was no expert on guns, gunnery, ships of war, fortifications or the effectiveness of shore defences. To him a cannon was a cannon; he had not the knowledge needed to note that it was an iron gun clearly a hundred years old, that its wooden carriage was rotting, with vital nuts and bolts rusted through, its bore as pitted by rust as an old drain pipe, the shot enlarged by flaking rust so it would not fit the gun. He did not know when they were last fired; how often the guns' crews were exercised. Nor did he know whether the Danish ships were well or badly manned.

Yet Sir Hyde had listened to his descriptions without question; this is clear from the fact that Drummond was wrong in precisely the way a layman would be wrong. Even worse, twice within a few lines Sir Hyde referred in his journal to the Danish defences in a style that makes it clear the muzzles of the guns grew larger, more numerous and more menacing the more he thought of them. But since all the Danish preparations made so far have already been described in this narrative, the value of Drummond's report – to the British, anyway – is only too obvious.

After writing the despatch Parker had no discussion with Nelson, Graves or his First Captain, Domett, although this would have been usual in the circumstances. Instead, after sending Captain Digby's orders over to the *Kite* he maintained a gloomy aloofness (Nelson saw it as haughtiness), his gloom spreading through the *London* as the word was passed about the Danish preparations, the size and number of their guns growing in the telling.

The only people Sir Hyde spoke to were the pilots specially embarked in the *London* because of their knowledge of the Cattegat and the Baltic. They were, of course, normally employed in merchant ships and were not naval personnel. They had little heart for the business in hand – the more so, having now heard of the Danish preparations – and passed on their misgivings to Sir Hyde.

The atmosphere was strained enough for his chaplain, Scott, to write to his uncle the rear-admiral that morning: 'I fear there is a great deal of Quixotism in this business; there is no getting any positive information of their strength'. It seems clear that this worthy cleric, if not his Commander-in-Chief, was dubious of the significance, if not the actual facts, of Drummond's report on the Danish defences.

In the meantime Nelson on board the *St George* was writing once again to Troubridge – a letter interrupted by a signal from the flagship.

As I hear the Danes will listen to no terms, I have only to regret our loss of time. Till our arrival here we have had only one day's foul wind. Our small craft are behind – there is no activity. Now we have only to fight. . . . We anchored off the Koll the 20th, 1801. Since then, the wind has been foul. The Commander-in-Chief has just sent for me, and shall have my firm support, and my honest opinion, if he condescends to ask it. The wind will be at west or NW tomorrow.

Sir Hyde had also asked Vansittart to visit him. Nelson's boat arrived alongside the flagship with Lt Layman commanding it, enabling Layman to provide the material for a subsequent description of this day.

'On board the *London*,' he recorded, after Nelson had been hoisted on board (it was next to impossible for the one-armed man to get on board any other way) they found 'the heads appeared very gloomy. Mr Vansittart, who arrived [from the *Blanche*] at the same moment Nelson did, said that if the Fleet proceeded to attack, it would be beaten, and the attempt was in danger of being relinquished.' Layman's account was written long after the event, although his description of the atmosphere is likely to be correct.

Nelson went to the great cabin, where he met Sir Hyde and Vansittart. They were the only people present at this first conference. Captain Domett was not included and resented it, although it was much more surprising that Rear-admiral Graves, the third-in-command, was not present.

However, Layman continues (in the third person),

The Captain of the Fleet [Domett] said to Layman that the Danes were too strong to attack, and a torpor verging to [sic] despondency prevailed in the councils [i.e. between Parker, Drummond and Vansittart].

While others were dismayed, however, Lord Nelson questioned those just arrived from Copenhagen, not only as to the force, but as to the position of the enemy. Such interrogatories he called 'bringing people to the post'.

Having learned that the great strength of the enemy was at the head of the line, supported by the Crown [Trekroner] Battery, his Lordship emphatically observed that to begin the attack there would be like taking the bull by the horns, and he therefore suggested the attempt by the tail.[1]

Nelson used the phrase 'taking the bull by the horns' in a letter written next day but with a different meaning, and Layman's memory is probably at fault though the sense is clear enough.

There were two ways of approaching Copenhagen (see chart on page 264): directly from the North through the Sound with the city twenty miles beyond and at the most five hours' sailing with a fair wind; or by sailing 200 miles right round the island of Sælland through the Great Belt, approaching finally from the south. If Copenhagen was 12 on the dial of a clock, going by the Sound was sailing clockwise from 11 to 12; if by the Great Belt, it was sailing counter-clockwise from 11 to 12, which in turn meant waiting for wind shifts and could take the Fleet up to two weeks.

As the *London* swung at anchor in a fresh south-west wind, the long peninsula of the Koll in Sweden, rising from flat land to hills at its point and better known today as Kullen, was on the larboard quarter; Cronborg Castle was on the beam nearly twenty-five miles to the south-east; and fine on the bow, nearly twelve miles to the south, was Gilleleje. By a curious coincidence of wind and current, the flagship was lying as if undecided whether to make for the entrance of the Sound or the entrance to the Great Belt.

The conference in the *London*'s great cabin between the two young men, one a vice-admiral, the other a politician, and the elderly and cautious Commander-in-Chief, was one of the most interesting and critical episodes in Nelson's whole naval career. Before, he had faced death many times; in the Mediterranean, while chasing Napoleon and his fleet, the fate of Egypt hung on his decisions. Now by comparison the stakes were enormous, both for the future of Britain and for his own career. Fortunately for him, never before, and never again, did he have to try to persuade a reluctant senior to adopt a particular course of action upon which so much depended. Such are the quirks of history

---

[1] A story, originated by Layman, was how several years later he told Nelson: 'I well recollect your great desire to catch a turbot, and your astonishing many, by insisting upon its being immediately sent to Sir Hyde, who condescended to return a civil note; without which opening your Lordship would not have been consulted in the Cattegat, and without such intercourse your Lordship would not have got the detached squadron; without which there would not have been any engagement, and consequently no victory.' The story was printed in *The Naval Chronicle* after Nelson's death and although a good tale, is unfortunately not true. None of the logs of the *St George* or the *London* refer to a boat being launched or received alongside – which they would do, if it happened; and Nelson's letter to Troubridge, written as he left for the conference on board the *London* and described by Layman, shows no 'opening' had yet been established – far from it.

The approach from the North Sea to Copenhagen and the Baltic, showing (inset) the direct route
Elsinore, and the alternative, through the Great Belt.

that no minutes were taken of the meeting. It was not a council of war, and at the time there probably seemed no need for them.[1]

Nevertheless much of what was said and decided can be reconstructed from letters and reports, and only those written at the time will be considered. Four are important: the letter Sir Hyde wrote to the Admiralty immediately after the conference; the letter Vansittart wrote to Nelson upon arriving in London; a letter from Nelson to Sir Hyde written the next day; and an entry in Colonel Stewart's diary describing the Danish defences as reported by Vansittart and Drummond, written the day of the conference.

Colonel Stewart's description sets the scene. He was a man of considerable perception, and as he was the only man on board apart from Sir Hyde who knew the details given by Drummond, he was presumably present at the meeting the night before. The entry in his diary for 23 March says:

Mr Vansittart repaired on board the *London* this morning. A consultation took place between the Commander-in-Chief, Lord Nelson and this minister, relative to the measures to be pursued; which, from the nature of the defences prepared by the Danes in front of Copenhagen, became considerably changed from those which were expected to be called for by the Government.

It should appear that, whilst [sic: when] the present Fleet was despatched off the ports of Denmark, with a menacing aspect, hopes were entertained that terms of accommodation might still be offered with some success at Copenhagen.

He noted the terms had been rejected, and the general outline of the defences as reported by Drummond and by Vansittart was, Stewart wrote, as follows:

At Elsinore, Cronborg Castle and the seaward batteries defending the west coast of the Sound: not less than 200 cannon reported mounted towards the sea; the landward side without much defence; the garrison numbering about 3,000 men.

Down the Sound: no defence appeared to have been mounted on the island of Hven.

At the entrance of the Channel into Copenhagen (the King's Deep): on the north side two floating batteries, several gun boats and hulks (cut-down line of battle ships) lined the Shoal (see chart on page 310). Two line of battle ships – 'in service order', as Stewart noted – and two frigates were moored in the Channel itself.

---

[1] That they were not taken is shown by the fact neither Parker nor Nelson ever referred to any – when their existence would have been very useful – and Vansittart would certainly have taken a copy with him to London. Instead, as will be seen later, he delivered a verbal report.

Two islands, formed by piles (the Trekroner and Lynetten forts) and strongly fortified, were on either side of the harbour entrance and 'presented 100 pieces of ordinance'. Two more line of battle ships, three floating batteries and hulks and several gun boats were anchored along the shoal on the southern side. 'The whole were hauled into the shallowest water, being lightened accordingly, and were within complete command of the Citadel and batteries on shore' (i.e. were covered by the batteries.) The remainder of the other vessels 'both Government and trade' were still inside the harbour.

This chain of defence was protected by the Middle Ground shoals which Stewart wrote, 'do not have above 21 feet [of water] on them in general'.

The Swedes, he continued, 'were said to have made many promises to send gun vessels etc.' to help the Danes, and of having 'eight sail of the line ready for sea as soon as possible (two months at the soonest) at Carlskrona', but they were 'not very heavy in the cause, having as yet done nothing towards the general cause'. The Russians, on the other hand, were reported to be making every exertion to get their Fleet to sea, and even to be cutting through the ice at Revel.

The situation Nelson found when he entered the great cabin of the *London* was that Sir Hyde was in a state of agitated indecision because the pilots were extremely nervous about the Fleet passing through the Sound, and insistent that in any case the Fleet would have to keep over to the Swedish side because of the guns of Cronborg. They were equally nervous of the Great Belt, which none of them knew. The result was Sir Hyde, fearful of either passage, was proposing to stay where he was.

For Nelson's impressions when he went on board there is his own description.

The difficulty was to get our Commander-in-Chief either to go past Cronenburg or through the Belt, because, what Sir Hyde thought best, and what I believe was settled [i.e. decided by Sir Hyde] before I came on board the *London* was to stay in the Cattegat, and there wait the time when the whole naval force of the Baltic might choose to come out and fight – a measure, in my opinion, disgraceful to our Country.

I wanted to get at an enemy as soon as possible and strike a *home* stroke, and Paul was the enemy most vulnerable, and of the greatest consequence for us to humble.

From this it is possible to see what had happened before Nelson was called on board and Vansittart arrived. After having been told by Drummond that the Danish capital was strongly defended, Sir Hyde spent the night worrying about it, but nevertheless his orders gave him no choice and he wrote his despatch to the Admiralty, emphasizing the defences, and indicating he would take the Fleet down the Sound to attack Copenhagen. But, having sent the despatch to the *Kite* with Digby's orders he then went on deck and talked not with Domett but only with the pilots.

Their despondent and alarming opinions may not have broken his nerve; but as a result of what they said he decided to stay up in the open Cattegat, where he had plenty of room to manoeuvre in comparatively deep water and wait for the Danish Fleet to come up and meet him in a standard action.

Was the fear of shallow water and mud banks sufficient to make him ignore categorical orders from the Admiralty to attack Copenhagen? This will never be known; but certainly it was enough to make him consciously or subconsciously seek a reason why he should not obey them.

It is possible to deduce the time he changed his mind. His despatch and Digby's orders were written and on their way to the *Kite* before 9.00 a.m. He talked with the pilots, then at 10.00 a.m. gave orders for the *London* to clear for action (Nelson had the *St George*'s bulkheads down since before leaving Yarmouth) and at the same time made the signal for all captains. Then at 10.30 he called Nelson to the flagship. Before 9.00 a.m., as his journal and despatch shows, he was going down the Sound; soon after 10.30 Nelson found him anxious to stay where he was.

From his subsequent attitude and activities, it seems unlikely that Vansittart was as alarmist as Drummond had been; in fact it seems more probable he was surprised at the effect of Drummond's visit the previous night. He recorded 'a long conference' with the two admirals and 'a very interesting conversation with [Nelson]' in the stern.

With Nelson and Vansittart sitting in the *London*'s great cabin, Sir Hyde first described his intentions, then sat and listened while Nelson questioned Vansittart, extracting from him more information about the defences of Copenhagen and Elsinore than he realized he possessed.

At the end of it, Nelson must have dumbfounded Sir Hyde, and probably Vansittart as well by then giving his opinion on the whole strategic situation facing them, as distinct from the tactical one. The Commander-in-Chief was told his most dangerous enemy, at whom they should strike at once, was the Russian Fleet.

With Sir Hyde so obsessed by Copenhagen and Cronborg and thinking so little about the Russian Fleet lying beyond that he had not even mentioned the word 'Russia' in the despatch written to the Admiralty an hour or so earlier, his bewilderment at this statement by his second-in-command can be imagined.

Vansittart was quick to realize how right was Nelson. More important, it is clear from letters to be quoted later that at this point Sir Hyde gradually began to realize Nelson had a remarkable ability to pick the significant point from a welter of bewildering facts – or, as in this case, realize its omission. It was not a sudden change of heart on Sir Hyde's part; simply the beginning of a partial awakening.

Nelson's first written reference to the conference (other than a letter to Parker) was in a note to Troubridge. In this he blamed Domett for influencing Sir Hyde; but if a subsequent letter from Domett to Lord Bridport is to be believed, this was far from being the case since Domett was not consulted. When Nelson wrote the letter it is doubtful if he fully realized Sir Hyde's fear of responsibility, since it was only the third time he had spoken to him – the first time being at Yarmouth.

You will, no doubt [Nelson told Troubridge] be very much surprised by the account [of the conference] given by Mr Vansittart, and I hope he has fully stated the conversation and language I held to Sir Hyde Parker, which I believe – for I do not know the contents of Sir Hyde's letters, except the last [the second, quoted below] – completely altered his opinion, or rather the opinion of Captain Domett; for let me do justice, and if I speak of such a delicate subject, that it may be as clear as it is true.

That being the case, I do say that from all I have heard, that Sir Hyde would never have thought of not passing [through] the Sound if Domett had not seen great difficulty and danger in the passage, and no possible good. Far, very far be it from me to detract from the very high character of Captain Domett: his bravery, his abilities in the conduct of a fleet are, I hear (for I never served with him), of the very highest class; but perhaps they are calculated for the fleet off Ushant; not, clearly in my judgment, for a situation such as Sir Hyde Parker's, where the spur of the moment must call forth the clearest decision and the most active conduct.[1]

On occasions we must sometimes have a regular confusion, and that apparent confusion must be the most regular method which could be pursued on the occasion. To this service (with all respect for Domett) I cannot yet think Domett is equal, and so much was working on my mind that I would not trust myself, after I had seen Sir Hyde the day Mr Vansittart [left], to write the scrape of a pen. My last line to you before I left the *St George* [when called to the *London*] was, if you recollect, 'Now we are going to fight, I suppose I am to be consulted'.

Little did I think it was to converse on not fighting. I feel happy I had so much command of myself, for I should have let out what you might have

[1] By this he meant that when blockading the French at Brest the Fleet would usually have several hours' warning – if not a day or two – that the French were preparing to sail, since yards would be hoisted etc. It should be remembered, too, that Parker had in the preceding years been handling ships in the very clear waters of the Caribbean, where in daylight reefs can be seen clearly and the bottom is usually visible at depths of thirty feet or more, compared with the North Sea and Baltic, where it is rarely visible at three feet.

been sorry to see, especially fancying I had been, to say no worse, very unkindly treated by Sir Hyde; that is, with a degree of haughtiness which my spirit could not bear.

However, I have now every reason to believe that Sir H has found it not necessary to be high to me, and that I have his real honour at heart, and in having that I have the honour of my country. His conduct is certainly the very reverse of what it was. God knows, [he concluded] I wish Sir Hyde could perform such services that he might receive more honours and awards than any admiral.

From all this it is clear that Nelson was successful in changing Sir Hyde's decision to wait for the Danes to come out to meet him, and that the Commander-in-Chief had failed to realize that because of the lateness of the season, the ice thaw would soon – if it had not done so already – release the Russian Fleet. Combined with the Danes and probably the Swedes it became a considerable threat but at the time Sir Hyde's orders were drawn up in London in late January, it was expected still to be frozen in when the British Fleet arrived off Copenhagen.

But although the conference did not end until late – Nelson returned to the *St George* at 4.30 p.m. – Sir Hyde was adamant about not going through the Sound. He accepted Nelson's argument that the Russian Fleet was the main menace; he accepted that the Danes ought to be attacked. But he refused to go down the Sound to attack Copenhagen; nor would he agree to give Nelson a small squadron to go on and attack the Russians while he dealt with Copenhagen.

Having persuaded Sir Hyde to accept that much, Nelson's next problem was how to get at the enemy without wasting more time. With Sir Hyde refusing to go down the Sound – by far the shortest route – it left only the Great Belt, a route which would waste many days but would at least eventually get the British Fleet into action. Nelson found Sir Hyde was more receptive to the idea of passing through the Belt. Then Sir Hyde decided: if when the Fleet got to the south of Sælland the wind was fair, he would sail on to attack the Russians; if foul for the Baltic but fair for Copenhagen, he would go on to attack the Danes. He regarded it as an excellent compromise. It was in fact as useless as any compromise and revealed only the lengths to which he would go because he was scared of passing Cronborg to go into the Sound.

In his diary Colonel Stewart wrote a summary of events up to the conference which showed his remarkable grasp of the whole situation since, in naval matters, he was a layman. (The present author's comments are given in italics.)

. . . Affairs this day took a new turn – a turn which remains to be proved as to its merits by ulterior events, but which is certainly contrary to the expectations formed by Government. The matter seems to me to be this. The instructions of Government have been to proceed with the utmost expedition with the formidable fleet confided to Sir Hyde Parker off the Sound, and upon a rejection of those terms which were *falsely* expected to have been attended to by the Danes, to force a passage of the Sound and do all such damage, off the port of Copenhagen to either its fleet, which it was supposed would be found out of dock, or to its arsenals, &c., by bombs, fire vessels, or otherwise, as opportunity or means might offer.

Since Hyde Parker did not show Nelson his orders, it is unlikely Stewart saw them. He is wrong in assuming the British Government expected the Danes to accept the terms. For obvious reasons it was hoped they would; but, as shown earlier in this narrative, the British Government, the Admiralty, Nelson and most people whose opinions mattered assumed there would be a battle. Most probably Sir Hyde had conveyed the impression to Stewart. In any case Parker had a powerful enough fleet to carry out his clear-cut orders – powerful enough that Nelson proposed detaching ships from it for a separate attack on Revel.

In the event of that success which is always counted upon too rapidly, and with too much assurance by our Government, measures of destruction were to be adopted against Revel, or Cronstadt, or other such ports of the Russians in the Baltic as were open to molestation, or the fleet of the [Northern] allies in that sea at least counter-acted, and all junctions prevented. . . .

This gives an impression Stewart probably did not intend. If the orders to attack Copenhagen were successfully carried out with the speed urged on Parker but which he had in fact not shown, there would still be plenty of time for a squadron – if not the whole Fleet, since some ships would have had battle damage – to carry on to Revel and Cronstadt. Neither the Government nor the Admiralty can be blamed because Sir Hyde's own tardiness caused the Fleet to arrive later than expected. More important, it could hardly be anticipated Sir Hyde would baulk at passing Cronborg – which by the terms of his orders was also to be attacked – and decide to go round by the Belt on the information supplied by laymen and the fears of pilots.

The new line of measures resolved upon *finally this day* by Lord Nelson and Sir Hyde Parker (in consequence of the preceding day's conference with Mr Vansittart) is, the attack of Copenhagen on the Baltic side, by the passage of the whole Fleet through the Belt, and that it should arrive with as much expedition as possible at the new point of attack. . . .

On the side of the former plan, the chance of [ships] being injured in passing Elsinore in the first instance, and of finding the defence of Copenhagen not only too formidable to overcome, but also too much for the security of this fleet (which is of too important and scarce a nature at this period of the war to expend on slight grounds) seem the only justifiable grounds on which the dereliction of the instructions of Government can be founded.

Here Stewart has put the Sound question in a nutshell: disobeying the orders to attack Copenhagen directly could only be justified if the destruction of a major part of the Fleet would result. In a narrative he wrote later he said that Vansittart's reports and those of pilots which the Fleet had brought from England 'induced the Commander-in-Chief to prefer the circuitous passage by the Great Belt. Lord Nelson, who was impatient for action, was not much deterred by these alarming representations. . . .' Apart from the fact Nelson had been trying to persuade Parker to go through the Sound, however strongly Cronborg had been reinforced, the risk from the guns was a matter of ballistics. The extreme effective range of a 36-pounder – the largest used by the Danes at Cronborg – was one and a half miles; the Sound was two and a half miles wide; and even allowing that care had to be taken in case the Swedish batteries opened fire, no British ships need pass within range of the Cronborg guns. The Swedish batteries were known to be weak, mounting only a few guns. More important, every captain knew that it required extremely good gunnery and constant practice to hit a passing ship. Denmark had been at peace for more than four score years.

On the other hand [Stewart wrote] the plan proposed is expected, by taking the enemy in the rear, to meet them in a defenceless point, and, by an attack in rear as well as in front of the island of Amak [Amager], to gain advantages not to be attained on the other side [i.e. attacking from the Sound]. . . .

In the first place, the circuitous passage of the Belt may take us ten days or a fortnight to arrive at our place of destination. We shall be every one of those days in complete view of the enemy; and the object of our new attack will be foreseen or provided against.

In the second place, the principal object intended by Government, and with the greatest justice, *surprise and impression,* is at once lost and done away; for even slowly as we have advanced to the point of attack (in consequence of a long voyage, and *perhaps* a want of energy in the mode of pushing the Fleet forwards, of which, however, I am not a competent judge), we are nearly a month sooner off the Sound, by Mr Vansittart's account, than was by the Danes expected.

Copenhagen could be attacked from the southern end even if the Fleet went down the Sound, of course. The passage of the Belt, 230 miles, would take the Fleet at least a week under the most favourable conditions, with the ships being given the utmost freedom to manoeuvre. But if Sir Hyde attempted to take the Fleet through in the order of sailing, with him giving the orders to tack and wear etc., it would take much longer even with fair winds.[1]

---

[1] The present author has, in his own yacht, sailed over the whole of the route several times, meeting with head winds all the way on two occasions, once going northabout from Copenhagen, and once southabout.

Stewart could hardly know how right he was about being in view of the enemy who could foresee the object and plan against it. More important, since Fischer had by no means finished placing the ships for his defence line, he could have easily covered an attack from the south by shifting ships, but he would need a few days in which to do it. Nevertheless he was – as Nelson had been quick to spot – open to an attack from the south; but it had to be a surprise attack.

That the Fleet arrived a month earlier than the Danes expected is partly true but the implication is not. As we have seen from the Danish documents, Bernstorff and the Crown Prince had not reckoned on Britain reacting so strongly. In other words, they never anticipated battle and therefore never expected the Fleet.

In the third place, our heavy ships cannot get opposite to Copenhagen on the Baltic side, the east wind always diminishing the water on the Grounds, even to 19 ft occasionally.

In the fourth place the passage of the Belt is intricate, although a good one to those to whom it is known, and will require a number of various winds.

If we do not, moreover, leave a force to secure its being free in our rear, or for our return, the greatest possibility exists of the enemy's blocking up the passage, in various parts, by the erection of batteries and by sinking of ships.

The possible junction of the Dutch with the Danish Fleet, during [the] absence of all our forces from the Cattegat, unless the vigilance of Admiral Dickson's squadron [blockading the Dutch] should prevent it, may form a sixth and not unimportant point of consideration. . . .

The chances of the Dutch Fleet joining the Danes was remote; but if it did manage to escape, Dickson would probably have had some knowledge of the direction in which it sailed and would, as a matter of routine, send a frigate to tell Parker. The frigate would certainly reach Parker in time to give him fair warning since a single frigate can almost always outpace a fleet unless the fleet has a strong fair wind all the way to its destination – a remote chance. And a British squadron would be following the Dutch.

Obviously the possibility of the Danes sinking ships to block the Belt behind Parker's fleet must have been discussed on board the London *for it to have been seriously considered by Stewart; but it would require several large ships which would need to be 'disposable' and therefore surplus to Denmark's needs. But the Danes would be unlikely to shut the back door of the Belt while leaving the front door of the Sound open. Since they never considered an enemy fleet would go by the Belt, if the Danes ever thought of using blockships it would have been to block the King's Deep off Copenhagen itself.*

After the conference with Nelson and Vansittart, Sir Hyde wrote a second despatch to the Admiralty – 'the last one' Nelson referred to in his letter to Troubridge. It is, in some respects, a despicable document, because Sir Hyde tried to cover himself, in the event of blame, by involving Vansittart in the decision not to go by the Sound; Nelson in going by the Great Belt;[1] and both in disregarding his orders from the Admiralty. Making sure blame is shared in the event of failure is not admirable in a man who should be a leader, although not uncommon; but it carries the corollary that in the event of success he should ensure the praise and the glory is also shared.

Since writing my letter of this morning's date [Parker told their Lordships in a despatch even more disjointed and ungrammatical than usual] I have had recourse to a consultation with Vice Admiral Lord Nelson and Mr Vansittart on the very formidable defence the Danes have made . . . not only by many additional batteries to Cronenburg Castle but also the number of hulks and batteries which have lately been placed and erected for the defence of the Arsenal at Copenhagen, and renders the attack so hazardous, join'd to the difficulty of the navigation of the passage of the Sound [h]as led us to agree in opinion that it will be more beneficial for His Majesty's service to attempt the passage of the Great Belt which having passed and [then if I find] the wind favourable for going up the Baltic is, to attempt the destruction of the Russian ships at Revel which are expected as soon as the season will permit their coming down the Baltic to cooperate with the Danes, but in the event of the wind being contrary for getting up the Baltic, after having passed the Belt in this case to attempt destroying Copenhagen by coming down the passage from the Baltic.

This measure will be attacking them in the rear, which [sic: where] it is evident they do not expect an attack, nor is it in their power to render it so defensible as by the other [the northern] channel.[2]

My intention is, [Sir Hyde continued] should I be so fortunate as either to meet the Russian Squadron on their passage down or at Revel, the moment either service is performed, to return immediately to the object of Copenhagen; and I must, great as the responsibility I take on myself, [hope their] Lordships will do me justice to believe that I could only be activated by what appears to be for the great object my country has in views [sic] consistent with the peculiar situation I find myself in by the formidable disposition of Copenhagen, and which cannot be known to their Lordships. I therefore rely with confidence on their approbation. . . .

One hardly has to bother reading between the lines to see that, although Sir Hyde referred to attacking Copenhagen from the south if he found a fair wind, it was a cover, and his heart was not in the idea. The proof of this is that after passing the Great Belt almost any wind

[1] Leading Admiral Mahan to give the impression Nelson wanted to go by the Great Belt to attack the Russians, whereas he wanted to go by the Sound. However, knowing Parker would not agree to that but might take the bait if it meant going by the Belt, Nelson put forward the alternative idea on a 'better than waiting' basis.

[2] This reasoning would have been remarkable in its fallaciousness even if advanced by a befuddled potman, and Colonel Stewart's comments on it are given later.

that was fair for the Baltic was also fair for Copenhagen, which he had been ordered to attack. When Nelson, anxious to get into action, had seen Sir Hyde's reluctance to attack Copenhagen and had pointed out the thaw now made Russia a threat, his intention was not to provide Sir Hyde with an excuse for not tackling Copenhagen; merely to get the Commander-in-Chief moving instead of wasting time. Sir Hyde's enthusiasm for the Russians and the open water of the Baltic is in fact a measure of his fears of Denmark and the shallows of the Cattegat.

However, the most important factor in the whole operation was that Sir Hyde was basing *all* his decisions and plans on one man's information on the amount by which the Danes had increased the defences of Copenhagen and Elsinore. Drummond was no expert, yet, vital as this information was in making his decisions and plans, Sir Hyde did not bother to check it.[1]

One can understand a defect in leadership which makes a man nervous of shoals and powerful defences; but when a Commander-in-Chief completely neglects routine checks, he must expect to be blamed – particularly since Drummond was in fact far from being his only source of information. Two of his own officers were better informed. . . .

Drummond and Vansittart spent no more than an hour in Elsinore. The *Blanche* was at anchor a short distance from Cronborg Castle from 10.30 a.m. on Friday until 2.00 p.m. on Sunday. Captain Hamond had fired a fifteen-gun salute which the Castle returned; he went on shore and into the Castle to call on Colonel Stricker at his office on the north side of the ground floor. Cronborg is so constructed that anyone making that visit can get an excellent view of the Castle's defences, quite apart from an inspection of the batteries by telescope from where the *Blanche* was anchored.

The same applies to Copenhagen: Lt McCulloch twice made the journey along the coast road from Elsinore to Copenhagen; he saw the positions of the Danish ships anchored in the Roads and, more important, the ships still fitting out in the Inner Harbour. He could see all the batteries defending the city quite as well as Drummond; more important, he could determine their efficiency with a skilled eye.

But Sir Hyde did not ask Captain Hamond or Lt Thomas McCulloch; instead he took Drummond's word for it. It almost goes without saying that had he sent the *Blanche* to Copenhagen with the despatches for

---

[1] It is doubtful if Drummond painted as gloomy a picture as Sir Hyde indicates. Drummond had in fact reported to Lord Hawkesbury on 24 February: 'The batteries round Copenhagen are planted with pieces of artillery drawn from all the arsenals in Denmark, many of which have not probably been used for a century. The Danes seem to think, however, that these antiques make a very formidable appearance.' In this, of course, the Danes were correct; but Drummond may have been the man who was fooled by them.

Drummond and Vansittart in the first place *instead* of Elsinore, Captain Hamond could have returned with the exact positions of the Danish ships in the Roads plotted on a chart, a complete list of the state of the remaining vessels being fitted out in the Inner Harbour, and an exact count of the number and size of guns in the Trekroner, Lynetten and Quintus batteries and at Castellet.

Luckily for Parker, the subsequent relief in London that Nelson had persuaded Parker to do something was sufficient for the *Blanche* episode to have been ignored. This is shown in a letter to Nelson from Vansittart.

Nelson had spoken in private to Vansittart after the conference in the *London*. Vansittart was due to sail for England that afternoon in the *Kite*, and Nelson asked him to relate to the First Lord of the Admiralty what had passed at the conference. As second-in-command Nelson could not himself write officially to St Vincent and anyway there was neither time nor opportunity. Nevertheless he wanted there to be no misunderstanding.

Vansittart later wrote from London:

The solicitude you expressed that I should undertake the explanation of the reasons which induced you to propose a deviation from the original plan of operation designed for the Fleet would have been a motive with me of the strongest kind to enter into as early and complete a vindication of them as possible [even] if I had been in no respect personally interested in the question.

But as your wish at parting with me, that I should meet with a foul wind, was completely gratified, it was not until last Wednesday [1 April] that we were able to get ashore at Leith.[1]

I got to Town on Saturday and went immediately to the Admiralty, but not finding Lord St Vincent in Town I called on Mr Addington, to whom I gave a full account of what had passed in Sir Hyde Parker's cabin on the 23rd ulto.

I have the pleasure to assure you that he was fully satisfied with the propriety of your advice, and of Sir Hyde Parker's ultimate resolution, and that he considers your readiness to take on yourself the responsibility attaching on a deviation from your instructions as not the least eminent among the services which you have rendered your country in so many years of glory.

Mr Addington has since communicated the whole affair to Lord St Vincent, who equally acquiesces in the propriety of the determination, so that whatever may be the event of the plan (which Providence must decide) you will have the satisfaction of meeting with the approbation of those who have the best right to judge of it; and I need not say may depend on the confidence of the public. . . .

[1] Nelson said he hoped a foul wind would delay Vansittart so that the whole affair would have been decided one way or the other before he arrived in London – presumably on the basis that in victory, vindication; in defeat, disgrace.

With Vansittart on his way to London in the *Kite*, before nightfall, the last part of Colonel Stewart's diary entry for 23 March is a suitable recapitulation of the situation as most people *thought* it had been decided by Sir Hyde at the conference. After considering the report on the Danish defences, he said:

... the opinions of the two admirals in command were compared, and the result despatched to England. ... The intentions were now directed to a new plan of campaign – to the passage of the Belt, and direct to Revel, in lieu of an attempt on Copenhagen. The wind, however, continuing contrary, the Fleet remained at anchor. Three or four absent ships appeared and rejoined this afternoon.

Next, there is Sir Hyde's recorded version of the day's happenings in his journal and, considering the sober phrases normally used, the entry is significant in showing his frame of mind:

Mr Vansittart came on board when on considering the immense preparations of defence against an attack made by the Danes both at Cronenberg Castle [and] at Copenhagen and also the difficulty of the passage of the Sound, I had consultation with Mr V [sic] and Lord Nelson on the propriety of proceeding into the Baltic, by the passage of the Belt, which being approved determined accordingly [and] acquainted the Admiralty. ...

Certainly this version differed from those of Nelson and Vansittart; but the situation seems, from another version of the day's events, beyond Sir Hyde. Captain Nicholas Thomlinson, who submitted to the Admiralty his suggested plan for an attack on Denmark and Russia and was now on board the *London* (see page 174). He subsequently wrote an account for the Admiralty which confirms both the role and the attitude of the pilots.

The wind blew fresh from the west and west-north-west, and it was then the opinion of such of the pilots as were consulted [by Sir Hyde] that the Fleet should not attempt the passage of the Sound unless the wind came so far to the northward as NW although they admitted that the highest course they had to steer in passing Cronberg Castle ... was south by west, in which case (as I observed at the time) they would have the wind a point abaft the beam; but about 2 o'clock in the afternoon, it came to NW and afterwards to north, and I believe it was expected by the whole Fleet that while the wind was at NW and sufficiently moderate that the signal would have been made to weigh, as the *same* pilots (who were again consulted) then (about 2 p.m.) gave it as their unanimous opinion that the wind would answer and that there was time enough for the Fleet to pass through the Sound before it became dark.

There was still remaining five hours good daylight and as the whole Fleet could have run at least six knots it would have been at anchor two or three leagues within the Sound before sunset as at that time the Fleet was not more than three or four leagues from Cronberg Castle.

While Nelson was away in the *London* for six hours, on board the *St George* the normal life went on. With a complement of several hundreds, the seamen's natural liking for rum was heightened by the cold weather, and the entry Thomas Atkinson, the Master, made in his log reflects this: 'Punished Daniel Kelly, Nicholas Donnelly, and James Ryan, seaman, with 12 lashes for neglect of duty; and John Smith, seaman, with 36 lashes for drunken behaviour and insolence; Thomas Lyster, seaman with 24 for drunkeness, James Burke and William Robinson, 12 for drunkeness, and Nicholas Power 12 for neglect of duty.'

When Nelson returned on board the *St George* at 4.30 p.m. he was considerably disturbed by his brief private talk with Vansittart and sat down to write a letter to Sir Hyde. It was a brilliant document which Nelson intended to send across to the *London* next morning.

However, during the night the wind eased and at 4.00 a.m. Sir Hyde ordered the Fleet to weigh anchor. The wind was strong enough for the *London*'s topsails to be single-reefed, and most of the smaller ships in the Fleet had trouble weighing their anchors. It was 7.00 a.m. before the *London* set her foresail and Sir Hyde could note, 'Fleet in company'. Then he gave the order to tack to the westward. This was the course for the entrance of the Great Belt, and the Fleet was led by the man who had recently made a detailed survey of it, Captain George Murray. But this was simply a coincidence: the *Edgar*'s position in the order of sailing was leading the van. Murray had no idea Sir Hyde now intended to sail right round Sælland through the Great Belt.

On board the *London* even Sir Hyde's Captain of the Fleet, Domett, and the flagship's captain, Otway, did not know either; in fact the only men who did were Sir Hyde himself, and Nelson. But when the order to tack was given, the new course was so obviously not one to put the Fleet in a position to tack again to go through the Sound that Domett became worried.

In a letter to Lord Bridport he said that

This measure [going by the Belt] was contrary to Sir Hyde's orders. . . . Whilst we were running for the passage in a conversation with the Admiral I found their plan, after getting into the Baltic, was to anchor [in Kioge Bay], hardly within sight of the steeples of Copenhagen [it is twenty-seven miles south] which was to be attacked by sending the 64-gun ships, frigates, bombs, gun vessels &c., over the Grounds from [the south] side.

I told him I could not agree with him that it was a proper way of attacking the place, that I feared the ships that could be got over the Grounds from the

Baltic would not be force enough as they must have a fair [southerly] wind, which by every information I could collect reduced the depth of water near two feet,[1] which would make it difficult for even 64-gun ships to pass; that he would lose the imposing appearance of his three-deckers, and heavy ships, which would not be in sight of the city; that the wind which carried the attacking ships down would prevent their returning to us, and in the event of them getting aground, being crippled or, what was possible, repulsed by the enemy, it would be impossible we could go to their assistance [because of] the shoal water between us, and that the Fleet would be quite divided, all of which the Danes would be sensible of, and which would induce them to defend themselves possibly better than they would were we all present.

Added to this I begged he would recollect that in going into the Sound *from* the Baltic, it was necessary to pass a point of land called Draco[2] (which might also be fortified for what we know) as near, nearer indeed, than you pass Cronenburg Castle in entering the Sound *from the* Cattegat. . . .

This and some other arguments that were used induced the Admiral to change his plan altogether, recall Captain Murray that was ahead, stood back to the entrance of the Sound, and made up his mind to pass the Castle the moment the wind would permit.

Unfortunately Domett's account is not by any means the whole story. His letter, written on 4 May, tells the truth, but only part of it; likewise Sir Hyde had told him the truth about attacking Copenhagen – but only half of it, since the Russians were not mentioned.

But if the Captain of the Fleet claimed credit for making Sir Hyde turn again, so did the captain of the *London*, Robert Waller Otway. A privately published memoir claims that when Otway heard they were going to pass through the Great Belt, not the Sound, he

saw that if such measures were persevered in, the object of the expedition would be defeated. The sailing round to Copenhagen by the tedious passage of the Belt would be attended with difficulties which would never be sur-mounted even by the energies of British seamen, as the whole of the guns and heavy stores belonging to the line of battle ships must have been taken out to enable them to pass the Grounds in going to Copenhagen by that route.

Otway's position, the memoir says, was difficult since he was not at the previous day's conference, but he knew Sir Hyde well and 'determined on laying his opinion before the Commander-in-Chief'. Parker was not, it adds, 'a man to persevere in an error when pointed out'.

---

[1] Gales between south and east can reduce the level by as much as three feet.

[2] 'Draco' is Dragør, the eastern tip of the island of Amager, which in effect forms part of Copenhagen. The nearest part of Saltholm is three miles away, and the Fleet would have to pass within a couple of miles of Dragør.

It continues:

The interview almost instantly took place; and Sir Hyde as soon became convinced that he was not taking the shortest route to victory, which was as speedily acknowledged by Domett. The Fleet was brought to, and Captain Otway was sent to apprise Lord Nelson of the reasons.

On going on board the *St George* he was immediately introduced to Lord Nelson; and on explaining to his Lordship the alteration that had been made in the route, he [Nelson] exclaimed, 'I don't give a damn by which passage we go, so that we fight them.'

Nelson sent Otway on ahead to collect Captain Murray from the *Edgar* and went across to the *London*, taking with him the rough draft of the letter he had prepared the previous evening for Sir Hyde. The wind was by then blowing so fresh he was hoisted out in one of the *St George*'s boats.

Thus both captains on board the *London* claim credit – and of the two the best argument was Domett's – that the channel between Dragør, which might be fortified, and Saltholm, was less than the distance at which the Fleet needed to pass Cronborg.

However, the credit is not due to either man alone, and both recollected the episode incorrectly. Parker's journal shows the *London* hove-to at 10.15 a.m. for Otway to leave for the *St George*, and got under way again with the Fleet at 10.45 a.m., by which time Nelson was on board, and *still steered westward*, towards the Belt. A 11 o'clock one of the bomb ketches ran aground on a shoal, Sællands Rev. And it was not until 11.15 a.m., half an hour after Nelson had boarded the *London* and fifteen minutes after the bomb had run on the shoal – which could also have claimed several of the ships, since it is hard to see – that the Fleet turned back towards the entrance to the Sound and anchored.

The times show Otway's biographers were wrong because apart from another major factor described below, the Fleet continued steering west for an hour after Otway was sent to tell Nelson that he had convinced Sir Hyde 'he was not taking the shortest route to victory'.

Nelson's journal and Colonel Stewart's diary both tell a different story and when compared with Domett's (written a month later) and Otway's (published thirty-nine years later) must be given priority.

Being on board the *London*, Stewart would almost certainly have heard something of Otway's and Domett's conversations with Sir Hyde, but his diary makes no reference to them having any part in changing Sir Hyde's mind. Stewart simply records that Nelson and Murray 'held a conference on board this ship with Sir Hyde Parker, the result of which was that at 11 the Fleet put about, and before night resumed their former anchorage, two leagues nearer the Sound, the former plan of

operations, as instructed by Government, being again resolved
upon. . . .'

'At 10 Captain Otway came on board to desire my attendance on
board the Admiral,' Nelson briefly noted in his journal. 'Sir Hyde told
me he was uneasy about going by the Belt in case of accidents and therefore he thought of going by Cronenburg, and which I cordially assented,
and the Fleet was tacked. . . .'[1]

The entry was tactfully written (the journal eventually had to be sent
to the Admiralty) and in fact as soon as he reached Sir Hyde's cabin,
and the Commander-in-Chief began the discussion – with the Fleet
still steering for the Belt – Nelson read him the rough draft of the letter
which he had intended sending over as soon as a fair copy was made.

Fortunately another letter from Nelson to Parker describes the episode. Many weeks after the battle, when Parker was being attacked in
the Press, Parliament, pamphlets and drawing rooms, Nelson wrote
'. . . I cannot but feel an interest that no act of yours should bring
forward that paper war which you must expect from unknown persons.
Reflect . . . before you place yourself in a situation to have your actions
criticized by any hidden enemy.'

He went on to give Parker sound and friendly advice and concluded
with a postscript saying that since

> . . . I have heard a great deal of blame has been attributed to you for not
> instantly determining to pass the Sound, as a very serious conversation
> doubtless passed with Mr Vansittart before I saw him, and the result of ours
> with Mr Vansittart being a determination to pass the Belt, in consequence of
> which I took the liberty of writing you a letter of the 24th [March], the
> rough copy of which I read to you [i.e. when called on board the *London*] but
> as circumstances took a turn which removed the necessity of copying it [the
> Fleet turning back to the Sound], I did not give it to you, but now under all
> circumstances, I think it right to send it to you, as it brings forward all which
> passed on that occasion.

Writing to Parker at a time when the old admiral was being savagely
attacked and stating flatly he was also in part responsible for the final
decision to go by the Belt, and enclosing the 24 March letter, shows
something of Nelson's greatness. Had he kept the letter and remained
silent, he could have left Parker to the critics and been absolved of any
blame for sharing in the decision. That his reason for finally agreeing
to the Belt was because he wanted to get Parker into action and, at the

---

[1] Nelson kept his journal using civil time (the new day beginning at midnight) while
Parker kept his by nautical time, beginning the new day at noon. This has caused several
historians to confuse dates. There is a discrepancy, though, between the two journals over the
time Otway left the *London*.

same time, saw the Russian Fleet was the great enemy, is of no consequence since he did not elaborate on it. Left to his own devices, Nelson
would have gone through the Sound, attacked the Danes and gone on
to deal with the Russians: this is what he originally thought Parker was
going to do anyway.

So, in the *London*'s great cabin, Nelson read the draft letter in his high-
pitched, nasal voice.

The conversation we had yesterday has naturally from its importance been
the subject of my thoughts [he said] and the more I have reflected, the more
I am confirmed in opinion, that not a moment should be lost in attacking the
enemy; they will every day and hour be stronger, we shall never be so good
a match for them as at this moment. The only consideration in my mind is
how to get at them with the least risk to our ships.

By Mr Vansittart's account the Danes have taken every means in their
power to prevent our getting to attack Copenhagen by the passage of the
Sound, Cronenburg has been strengthened, the Crown Islands [Trekroner,
etc.] fortify'd (on the outermost of which are 20 guns pointing mostly
downwards) and only 800 yards from very formidable batteries placed under
the Citadel [and] supported by five sail of the line, seven floating batteries
of 50 guns each, besides small craft, gun boats &c. &c., also that the Revel
squadron of 12 or 14 sail of the line are soon expected, as also 5 sail of Swedes.

It would appear by what you have told me of your Instructions that
Government took for granted that you would find no difficulty in getting off
Copenhagen, and that in the event of a failure of negotiation that you might
instantly attack, and that there would be scarcely a doubt but the Danish
Fleet would be destroy'd, and the capital made so hot that Denmark would
listen to reason and its true interest.

By Mr Vansittart's account their state of preparations exceeds what he
conceives our Government thought possible, and that the Danish Government is hostile to us, in the greatest possible degree; therefore here you are,
with almost the safety, certainly the honour of England more entrusted to
you than ever yet fell the lot of any British officer. On your decision depends
whether our country shall be degraded in the eyes of Europe or whether she
shall rear her head higher than ever.

Again do I repeat, never did our country depend so much on the success
of a fleet as on this. How best to honour our country and abate the pride of
her enemies by defeating their schemes must be the subject of your deepest
consideration as Commander-in-Chief, and if what I have to offer can be the
least useful in forming your decision you are most heartily welcome.

In considering the letter thus far, it is worth remembering that Nelson
had already spent some five hours in conference with Parker and
Vansittart the previous day; and even allowing that a high percentage
of the time was spent questioning Vansittart, it is remarkable that Nelson
had to start his letter with a very clear exposition of 'first principles' –

for that is what he has so far written. But the hours spent with Parker the day before had obviously given him a clear insight into the Commander-in-Chief's limited capacity and he knew it was a necessary preliminary.

I shall begin by supposing [Nelson continued] that you are determined to enter by the passage of the Sound, as there are those who think if you leave that passage open [by going through the Belt] that the Danish Fleet may leave Copenhagen and join the Dutch or French. I own I have no fear on that subject, for it is not likely that whilst the capital is menaced with an attack that 9,000 of her best men should be sent out of the Kingdom.

Suppose that [if we pass through the Sound] some damage may arise amongst our masts and yards [from the Cronborg batteries] but perhaps not one but can be made serviceable again.

You are now above Cronenburg. If the wind is fair and you determine to attack the ships and Crown Islands, you must expect the natural issue of such a battle: ships crippled, perhaps one or two lost, for the wind which carries you in will most probably not bring out a crippled ship. This mode I shall call taking the Bull by the Horns.

This will not prevent the Revel ships or Swedes from joining the Danes, and to prevent that from taking effect is in my humble opinion a measure absolutely necessary, and still to attack Copenhagen two modes are in my view. [The first one is] to pass Cronenburg, taking the risk of damage, and to pass up [southward] the Channel deepest and straightest above the Middle Grounds to come down [northward] the Garbar or King's Channel to attack their floating batteries, &c. &c., as we find it convenient, and it must have the effect of preventing a junction between the Russians, Swedes and Danes, and may give us an opportunity of bombarding Copenhagen.[1]

A passage also, I am pretty certain, could be found to the northward of Saltholm for all our ships. Perhaps it might be necessary to warp a short distance in the very narrow part.

Should this mode of attack be ineligible, the passage of the Belt, I have no doubt, would be accomplished in four or five days: then the attack by Draco [Dragør] could be carried into effect, the junction of the Russians prevented, and every probability of success against the Danish floating batteries.

What effect a bombardment might have I am not called upon to give an opinion, but I think the way would be clear for the trial. Supposing us through the Belt with the wind fresh westerly, would it not be feasible to either go with the Fleet or detach 10 ships of three or two decks with one bomb and two fire ships to Revel to destroy the Russian squadron at that place?

I do not see the great risk of such a detachment, and with the remainder to attempt the business of Copenhagen. The measure may be thought bold,

[1] 'Up' and 'down' are used in relation to the Baltic; thus 'up' to the Baltic means going southward past Copenhagen before turning northward towards Revel, while 'down', leaving the Baltic, means sailing northwards past Copenhagen.

but I am of opinion the boldest measures are the safest, and our country demands a most vigorous exertion of her force directed with judgment.

In supporting you through the arduous and important task you have undertaken, no exertion of head or heart shall be wanting, my dear Sir Hyde, from your obedient and faithful servant. . . .

Sir Hyde agreed to pass Cronborg, but he refused to consider detaching ten ships to go on to attack the Russians. But in agreeing to go by the Sound he also agreed to Nelson's plans for tackling the Danes – by attacking from the south – 'to come down the Garbar or King's Channel. . . .' With that Nelson returned to the *St George*, the Fleet turned back and later anchored off Gilleleje.

22

SQUANDERING VICTORIES

The events in Britain and Russia during the week ending the night of 24 March – when Nelson drafted his letter to Sir Hyde – were as bizarre as any seven days in history. Although the climax which came in the darkness in the Winter Palace at St Petersburg could have been taken from the pages of some improbable novel, the activities in London were more suited to a farce written and staged by a whimsical March Hare.

In Downing Street the situation was ridiculous, even if making full allowances for the fact that most politicians play party politics, using all the short-sighted and naive stratagems that gain them a brief popularity. Not only was the new Addington Government no exception, it was one of the most blatant examples.

On the very day that Nelson was doing his best to get Sir Hyde to the starting post, the Foreign Secretary, Hawkesbury, sent a letter to Carysfort in Berlin which, considering the Government had just sent a strong fleet to the Baltic, is almost beyond belief.

I send your Lordship by a messenger the full powers which are necessary for authorising you to conclude a treaty with the Russian Government conformable with the instructions you have already received.

You will endeavour, in the first instance, to negotiate a treaty, or maritime law, similar to that which Mr Vansittart is instructed to negotiate with the Government of Copenhagen, but if you should find the Russian Government unwilling . . . His Majesty will be satisfied with a formal renunciation of the Convention . . . and will, on this consideration, and on that of the embargo [on the British ships] being immediately taken off, consent to the terms which have been proposed [by the Russians] respecting Malta. . . .

Carysfort would have been justified in assuming Hawkesbury had written from a madhouse which also contained the rest of the Cabinet since under the present circumstances no sane and sober man would think of surrendering Malta or even implying that the question was negotiable, let alone linking it with the embargo.

If Carysfort had turned to his files to see if past despatches had shown any symptoms of the onset of insanity he would have found none: a week earlier Hawkesbury had written: 'The Fleet sailed from Yarmouth Road with a very fair wind . . . and there is every reason to believe that it is at this time in Copenhagen. . . .'

As far as Addington and Hawkesbury knew, Sir Hyde was within a few days of attacking Copenhagen, and long before Carysfort could reach St Petersburg might have gone on to attack the Russian Fleet at Revel and Cronstadt, both of which were almost within sight and sound of the Winter Palace. The Czar, having had a few broadsides fired into one cheek by Parker, was hardly the man to turn the other to have it kissed by Carysfort.

In any case it must have been obvious to the most veritable dabbler in foreign affairs that whatever permutation of circumstances had happened in the North, the Czar would not negotiate. If the Danes had accepted the British terms, it would mean he had been outmanoeuvred and lost one of his allies in the Northern Confederation; if the British terms had been rejected there would have been a battle.

The offer of Malta in exchange for the release of the British ships and seamen is almost beyond comprehension. To accept the Czar's demands for Malta, which were not based on any geographical, moral or historical grounds, nor on any legal claims that were still valid, was to let Napoleon win his astute move made just before the French garrison surrendered. But Hawkesbury's most startling piece of information was yet to come. His letter to Carysfort ended in what seems to have been an afterthought:

I think it right to apprize your Lordship in confidence that a proposition has been made on the part of His Majesty to the French Government to open a negotiation for peace. The answer has not yet been received, but may be expected in the course of 3 or 4 days. . . .

By twentieth-century standards, this behaviour of Addington and Hawkesbury would, of course, have qualified them both for immediate earldoms, and in case this seems a superficial judgment, it is worth looking at Britain's position on this same Tuesday, 24 March, as it was known to Addington.

A powerful fleet was in the Baltic with orders to attack Denmark if Vansittart's negotiations failed, so Denmark would be separated from the Northern Convention, one way or the other. Whether this fleet negotiated or fought, it would probably go on to attack and destroy the Russian Fleet.

Duckworth and Trigge had already been sent from Martinique to capture the Danish and Swedish islands in the West Indies and there was no doubt they would succeed.

A British army of 16,000 men under General Ralph Abercromby had sailed from Turkey in Admiral Keith's ships on 22 February and, as far as Addington knew, had already landed in Egypt to destroy the French army which had remained there since Nelson's victory at the Nile. There was no reason to anticipate Abercromby would fail.

Finally, Britain's naval supremacy throughout the world was unchallenged.

So, with three British naval forces despatched on offensive operations against Denmark, Russia and France, and all reasonably certain of success, Addington decided the time was ripe to go cap in hand to Napoleon and the Czar, begging peace from the former and offering Malta to the latter.

It can be argued that the British people were at this time sick of war and with a food shortage there were signs of unrest in the country. This was true; it is also true that almost any nation is always sick of war, however long it has been fighting, and whether it is winning or losing, since few people are by nature warlike.

But it is even more true that firstly, if even one of the expeditions was successful the spirit of the British nation would rise enormously (as indeed happened in each case) and secondly, the majority of the people of Britain could see clearly enough there would be no real peace for anyone while Napoleon ruled France. Although people like Charles James Fox might profess a liberal sympathy for the French Revolution, the more pragmatic majority of Britons would sooner see the price of bread go up ten times than have Britain become another of Napoleon's puppet republics. In the last two decades, a number of specialists in everything but human nature have provided statistics and reasons to explain how and why Britain kept on fighting after Dunkirk in 1940. Most of them ignore the fact that if the British people had lacked the determination, the nation would have collapsed without the need for Hitler to attempt an invasion.

Bearing in mind that Addington took office on 10 February, that the actual proposal for peace had been made to Napoleon on 17 March, and Hawkesbury had referred to it a week later in his letter to Carysfort, the actual naval and military events of that week take on a particular interest.

On 18 March, a few days after getting his army on shore in one of the most daring amphibious landings ever made up to then (at the north end of Aboukir Bay, where the French squadron had been destroyed by Nelson three years earlier), Abercromby attacked Aboukir Castle. By the time the battle ended on 21 March with a British victory, a thousand French dead were left on the sands of Aboukir.

Far more important, the legend of the invincibility of the new French armies had been destroyed. Although Abercromby died of wounds that day, his senior officers learned valuable lessons which they were to use on future battlefields. Among them were Moore, to win fame and die at La Coruña; Paget, who was to be Moore's right-hand man; Coote and Stuart. Baird and Arthur Wellesley (who was to become the Duke of Wellington) arrived with reinforcements, and by the end of June the 26,000 men of the French army in Egypt were either dead or had surrendered.

Thus Nelson and Abercromby had ended for all time Napoleon's dreams of an Eastern Empire.

In the West Indies, Duckworth's squadron captured St Bartholomew's on the 20th, St Martin's on the 24th, St Thomas and St John on the 28th, and St Croix on 31 March.

Two of the three expeditions had in fact been a complete success; only the third, led by Sir Hyde, was yet to be decided.

It requires no hindsight to condemn Addington and his Cabinet. They were confident the Baltic expedition would succeed, whether there was negotiation or battle; the West Indian expedition was certain of success even when the orders for it were written in Whitehall. Though the Egyptian expedition was by no means a foregone conclusion, there was no reason to expect failure. In other words, however much Addington's administration wanted peace, it had nothing to lose by waiting a few weeks, and everything to lose by rushing. It rushed, as if possessed of a lemming-like urge to turn victories into defeats, to negotiate from weakness, not strength.

On the night of 24 March no doubt Addington and Hawkesbury fell asleep with dreams of friendship with the Czar as a result of the day's instructions to Carysfort, and peace with Napoleon as a result of negotiations begun a week earlier.

In St Petersburg, the city built on nineteen islands, Paul Petrowitz Romanov, Emperor and Autocrat of all the Russias, went to bed in the Winter Palace on the left bank of the Neva. He was guarded by several scores of Cossack Life Guards, who were on sentry duty throughout the Palace, which contains more than 2,500 rooms, with fifteen miles of corridors.

There was, apart from the Czar's life, much for them to guard. His Mother, Catherine the Great, who had completed and furnished it, had created the most splendid palace in the world. Some of the galleries alone were as big as the inside of large churches; the finest Italian marble from Carrara, and Russian from the Caucasus, were used for the columns supporting elaborate ceilings from which hung enormous gold chandeliers flashing with crystal. Walls were lined with green malachite inlaid with gold and hung with rare paintings; staircases were master-pieces of porphyry and gold. The paintings in the Palace were num-bered by the thousands; a fantastic collection where Rembrandt, Raphael, Botticelli and Velasquez, Rubens and Titian, Franz Hals and Van Dyck were commonplace. Even the floors were intricate mosaics of rare woods.

The Palace was on the same scale as the woman who supervised its completion: Catherine the Great had been an unimportant German princess until the present Czar's father married her. But he was a man of little intelligence and crude tastes. When he was assassinated his widow knew the identity of the murderers; but they went unpunished.

The Palace is vast; from a distance it seems menacing. It was at this time the centre of the kind of intrigue inevitable where gaining the Czar's favour was the only road to success – and where losing it was a sure road to Siberia or the gibbet. Like St Petersburg itself, it was a contradiction. Beyond the jasper and porphyry, the gold and the malachite, the art treasures and the great public rooms and luxurious private suites, 2,000 servants lived in squalor and added to it by keeping livestock in some of the ground-floor rooms. Pigs and ducks, hens and goats lived in part of one wing, the floors covered in straw, while princes lived in another, treading on the rarest carpets that could be obtained.[1]

So, amid the usual ceremony, the Czar retired for the night; the Cossacks settled down to their vigil. But a small group of men stayed awake; only they knew that within a very few hours the whole situation would change so rapidly and radically that every country in Europe would be affected; that two hands would achieve more than a series of great battles on land and sea.

At four o'clock in the morning the Czar awoke to find an assassin's hands round his throat as a palace revolution overthrew the world's most brutal and despotic monarch. But news of the death of the man

[1] When a small fire broke out on the second floor in 1827 it spread to the piles of straw and hay stored in some of the ground-floor rooms. Much of the Winter Palace was destroyed as fire raged through it for five days. It was rebuilt by Nicholas I, great-grandfather of the last Czar, who was murdered during the Russian Revolution in 1918.

who had ruled a sixth of the world travelled slowly; and a week later a great sea battle – of which he was the direct cause – was fought before the one thing that would have averted it, the news of his death, reached Copenhagen.

The messenger taking Lord Carysfort's new instructions had not reached Dover by the time the assassin had finished his work. . . .

23

THE SIGHT OF THE SOUND

The events on board the *London* on the 24th and 25th of March completed the change in Sir Hyde Parker's attitude towards Nelson. At last he realized that Nelson's burning ambition was to fight and beat the enemy, not undermine, disobey and humiliate his Commander-in-Chief. He had seen the sheer brilliance of his second-in-command's grasp of both the strategic and tactical situation facing the British Fleet, his remarkable ability to pinpoint their own and the enemy's advantages and disadvantages, and his instinctive knowledge of when to accept and when to reject a great gamble.

It was probably the first time a man as cautious as Sir Hyde had ever seen a brain at work on what could be called precision gambling.

Perhaps more important, Sir Hyde at last realized that Nelson's reputation for brilliant but highly unorthodox tactics which often led him to pay scant attention to his orders was certainly deserved – but it produced victories. And, as far as the officers and men of the Fleet were concerned, Nelson's was a name to conjure with.

The result was that from now on Nelson had much less trouble in getting Sir Hyde to accept most of his ideas, having a facility for letting the Commander-in-Chief think they were his own. This began – even before the Fleet had anchored after turning back from the Belt – with Nelson explaining how best, in his view, the Fleet should pass Cronborg, and ended with a brief outline of his grand plan for attacking Copenhagen.

The immediate task, passing Cronborg and entering the Sound, had never worried Nelson from the beginning. He had ignored the legend of the 'Guardian of the Sound' and gone to two more trustworthy sources of information: a chart and a pair of dividers.

The distance between the batteries at Cronborg and the batteries on the Swedish side is two miles eight hundred yards, with water deep enough for sail of the line close in to either coast.

The maximum effective range for a 32-pounder (firing a shot a fraction over six inches in diameter), or the 36-pounders used by the Danes, was one and a half miles, and about the same for a 24-pounder (with a shot just over five and a half inches in diameter) and under a mile for a 12-pounder. In practice, if any of the ships were hit at the range of a mile it would be good fortune rather than good gunnery; blazing away hopefully into the midst of a distant covey. And since the Fleet would wait for a wind from the northern quadrant, any ship whose masts or spars were damaged could easily be taken in tow.

These ranges show that, effective shooting apart, the guns of Cronborg alone could not prevent a fleet passing through, providing it kept two-thirds of the way over towards the Swedish coast.

The Swedish batteries were small and compared with Cronborg a comparatively minor threat. The direction of the current – there are no tides or tidal stream – depends on the wind: a strong southerly blowing for several days brings a fast north-going current which continues flowing for some time even if the wind suddenly veers to the north. This north-going current, which is predominant in the Sound, was the main reason why the Fleet needed a wind between west-north-west and east-north-east: beating through against foul wind and current would sweep them to leeward so they would gain little or nothing on each tack.

In addition, almost midway between the Danish and Swedish coasts, and beginning a mile south of a line joining Elsinore and Hälsingborg, the narrow Disken shoal runs north and south. There was in fact enough water over it for the sail of the line; but the pilots were sufficiently nervous not to want to cross it.

The worst situation Parker could meet would be a light north wind to take his ships through against a strong foul current, and the Swedish batteries firing as well as those at Cronborg. If he kept in the middle of the Sound there was a distance of one and three quarter miles where his ships would be under fire from both sides at a range of one mile and four hundred yards. Assuming a two knot current against them, if they were making eight knots they would be travelling at six knots 'over the ground' and would be under fire for about seventeen minutes. At five knots it would be twenty minutes and at four knots twenty-five minutes.

Even these figures certainly do not tell the whole story. Denmark had been at peace for years; many of the guns were old. The shot kept outside, even though painted, would probably have rust flakes beneath the paint and these flakes, however thin, meant the shot would not be absolutely spherical and would not fly true; even more important the diameter would be slightly greater – often enough to make the shot jam in the barrel, or make it necessary to ram it home with brute force, slowing the rate of fire. And the gunners had no practice in firing at moving ships. Shore batteries were generally a menace to ships only at close range.

Thursday, 26 March, brought a moderate breeze from the south-south-west which was foul for the Sound, but both Sir Hyde and Nelson made good use of the time, keeping their clerks busy drawing up orders and lists. Stewart had already noted that a new plan had now been made for 'a general attack', and all the troops were put under Nelson. 'The plan, as hitherto laid,' he commented, 'seems spirited and such as, it is only to be lamented, was not adopted on the 23rd. . . .'

Nelson's advice to Sir Hyde for passing the Sound was that if the Fleet kept two thirds of the way over to the Swedish shore there was little danger; but he suggested that Captain Murray in the *Edgar* with the bomb vessels should anchor close under Cronborg, to the north-west and out of the arcs of fire of the Castle's guns. As the Fleet passed through, the bomb vessels could lob mortar shells on to the batteries to distract the Danish gunners, while the *Edgar*'s own guns could help to rattle the bars.

The most important order made on Thursday was a formal one to Nelson covering what had been decided in conference with Sir Hyde, who had adopted Nelson's proposal. Nelson noted it in his journal as, 'Received directions from Sir Hyde Parker to take under my directions ten sail of the line, four frigates, four sloops, seven bombs, two fireships and twelve gun brigs which have to be employed on a particular service. . . .' At the same time, since the *St George*, a three-decker, drew too much water to be useful in the attack on Copenhagen, Nelson received orders to shift his flag to the *Elephant*, a two-decker commanded by Foley.

This left Parker's division comprising two three-deckers (the *London* and *St George*), and the *Warrior, Defence, Saturn, Ramillies* (all 74s), *Raisonable*, and *Veteran* (both 64s).

Nelson promptly prepared a memorandum for all his captains. Intended for the attack on Copenhagen, it shows that without having seen either the port or the Danish defences he had already decided on his tactics.

The memorandum began by saying, 'The ships and vessels placed under my directions are to get their sheet and spare anchors over the side, ready for letting go at the shortest notice.' He wanted to have the ships anchor by the stern, instead of by the bow, and the memorandum said that when he hoisted signal number 14, a cable was to be led aft out of a stern port and then forward again and bent on to an anchor, 'taking care to have that anchor hanging by the stopper only, as great

precision is necessary in placing the ships. As much warping [manoeuv-
ring the ships by hauling on the cable, or laying out anchors with boats
and hauling in the cables] may be necessary it is also strongly recommended that the foremost capstan should be got up and ready for
service.'

He had all the captains come on board the *St George* to explain his
plans, both for passing Cronborg (his division was to lead the Fleet)
and for the attack on Copenhagen. To his surprise he found some of
them less keen than he had expected: his journal that day notes briefly
(in the only critical reference to anything in the whole period it covers
from 12 March to 13 May): '. . . All day employed in arguing and convincing to [sic] the different officers the intended mode of attack.'

Captain Thomas Fremantle probably summed up the mood of many
of the senior captains in a letter to his wife Betsey:

You find us almost in the same situation as we were when last I wrote you,
except that we are a few miles nearer the Castle. . . . I confess myself to
think if we had had the good fortune to have undertaken this business a
week ago, we should have more probability of succeeding; however, to it we
shall go whenever the wind shifts to the northward. If I were to give an
opinion on this business, I should say the Danes are exceedingly alarmed;
but delay gives them courage, and they will by degrees make Copenhagen
so strong that it may resist the attack of our Fleet. The whole coast is lined
with guns and mortars, but yet I think if we pass the Castle in a day or two,
we may succeed.

Lord Nelson is quite sanguine, but as you may well imagine there is a
great diversity of opinion. In the mode of attack intended to be adopted and
which is planned by Lord Nelson there seems but *one*. Generally speaking
most people are anxious to try how these Danes will receive us.

He reminded Betsey, who knew more of the sea life than most naval
wives after her experiences in the Mediterranean and at Santa Cruz,

. . . that we are now not contending with Frenchmen, or Russians, but
with people who have not been at war for seventy or eighty years, and,
consequently can never have seen a shot fired.

He went on to describe his own role and one can sense disappoint-
ment in the first few words:

I do not belong to the van division of the Fleet but am appointed to
command all the flat-bottomed boats, with each a 24-pounder in them. They
carry each of them from fifty to sixty men, and my detachment will consist
of about 1300 men. I am under the orders of Nelson, who is just the same
man I ever knew him, and shews me every attention and kindness possible.

My ship is in high order and at this moment I have only five men sick with colds. The sudden change from Ushant here has been the cause of our losing four men, who were very old and infirm. . . .

On board the *Elephant*, the Master, George Andrews, began a new 'Journal of the Proceedings on board H.M. ship *Elephant*, Thomas Foley Esqr commander . . .' on the 26th, dated it the 27th as the nautical day began at noon, and noted 'Ans^d the signal for a lieut. on board the *London*.' The lieutenant returned with orders from Sir Hyde which led to Captain Foley hastily vacating his cabin and Andrews noting: 'At 8.00 p.m. Vice-admiral Lord Nelson shifted his flag from the *St George* to this ship.' The reason for the late transfer was the lengthy 'arguing and convincing' that Nelson referred to in his journal.

For Foley it was an unexpected honour. The nephew of a naval officer who had been round the world with Anson in the *Centurion*, Foley was more than six feet tall, with blue eyes and brown hair, and had the full confidence of Nelson – who probably suggested to Sir Hyde that he would like the *Elephant* as his flagship. Lord St Vincent had written to the Secretary of the Board, Nepean, earlier in the year saying: 'When you are better acquainted with Captain Foley you will esteem him as we all do; for, under a heavy look, lies a sound and excellent understanding; great [i.e. good] temper, and a pleasant wit. . . .'

Friday saw a complete change in the Fleet. In contrast to the indecision and waiting of the past days, a stream of signals were hoisted in the *Elephant* and *London*; captains and lieutenants were rowed back and forth, the former for conferences, the latter to carry orders. Nelson was at last able to make his presence felt.

The *Elephant*'s master's log says revealingly:

Moderate and fair, washed ship, emp^d variously. Made the signal for several capt^s, the general signal for lieuts &c. – the signal to exercise great guns and small arms. . . .

Sir Hyde sent orders, obviously at Nelson's request, to all captains:

The ships having flat boats are to hoist them out immediately, to fit them completely with carronades, to man them, then to row them round the *Elephant*, reporting to that ship which ship they belong to.

And from Nelson there was yet another order about boats:

The launches of the [van] line of battle ships to have each a hawse coiled in them and their carronades mounted with six Marines in each launch, their barge and pinnace each having four Marines with muskets and the seamen armed only with cutlashes [sic], poleaxes and pikes, with a broadaxe. A barge and pinnace with four Marines in each belonging to the [van division] frigates are to be armed in the same [manner] as those belonging to the ships of the line. A lieutenant is to be in each launch.

All this provided much excitement for the young midshipmen. 'We . . . prepared for action and exercised the men in the use of the great guns and small arms,' Midshipman Millard wrote to his parents. 'We hoisted out the flat-bottomed boat and the launch and practised them with a carronade and a party of soldiers in each.'

By 9.00 a.m. Sir Hyde had left the *London* to visit Nelson on board the *Elephant* – a significant visit showing how much his attitude had changed – and while he was there fifteen merchant ships came northward through the Sound from Hamburgh and Lübeck. 'Made the signal for the *Cruizer* to examine [them],' Parker noted in his journal, while Nelson, who probably prompted the signal, was more explicit: the ships, he wrote, 'report the consternation and confusion at Copenhagen. . . .'

For all the preparation, even though Parker had decided to pass Cronborg he still seemed to be unsure of himself, and as he recorded in his log:

Sent a message by Captain Brisbane of the *Cruizer* to the Govr of Cronenberg Castle to know the determination of the Court of Denmark and whether orders are given to oppose my entering the Sound, as I shall consider the first gun fired from the Castle as a declaration of war.

Since the Fleet would be passing the Sound to attack Copenhagen the message was irrelevant and, more important, revealed to the Danes, had they paused to think, the indecision of the British Commander-in-Chief.

Addressed to Colonel Ezechias Henrik Stricker, the Governor of Cronborg, the letter said:

From the hostile transaction, by the Court of Denmark, of sending away His Britannic Majesty's Chargé d'Affaires the Commander-in-Chief of His Majesty's Fleet is anxious to know what the determination of the Danish Court is, and whether the commanding officer of Cronenburg Castle has received orders to fire on the British Fleet as they pass into the Sound as he must deem the firing of the first gun a Declaration of War on the part of Denmark.

Nelson took the opportunity of sending the *Blanche* and two bomb vessels with the *Cruizer* to anchor in a position 'to be ready to throw shells into the Castle of Cronenburg if the Danes fire at us'. Nelson did not view Parker's letter to the Danes with much enthusiasm; indeed, he made only a passing reference to it in his journal the next day.

Colonel Stewart, on the other hand, who was still on board the *London* with Sir Hyde, expressed his views strongly. After noting the despatch of the letter he wrote:

The delay of these two days [since Parker turned back from the Great Belt], and of every day since the 24th [the day of the conference with Vansittart] must cause the greatest regret to every man's mind who is alive to the political state of things. . . . The loss of 48 hours, and the dispatching of the *Blanche*[1] as an *avant courier*, was a weak manoeuvre. . . . The diffidence of our Commander, the hesitation of action on the 24th, completed the mischief. . . .

For two days the wind had been from the south-south-west and light, but on Saturday, 28 March, it came from the west – 'light airs and pleasant weather', as Sir Hyde noted in the most cheerful phrase in the whole of his journal. He saw it as a good opportunity to move the Fleet closer to Elsinore while awaiting the Danish reply.

At 9.00 a.m. (according to Parker's journal: Nelson recorded it at 10.00 a.m.) Sir Hyde ordered the Fleet to weigh but 'found the ships would not steer owing to a counter current'.

Although the general action of the current in and near the Sound has already been described, it can often be erratic. Generally winds from north-east through south to west produce a north-going current, the direction sometimes being changed by different weather in the North Sea or the Baltic. This produces currents going in a different direction from the wind and often setting across reefs and shoals. To navigators accustomed to tidal streams or the more regular currents of the Caribbean, it was bewildering because at this time the causes were little understood and it could not be predicted.

With his fleet being swept northward, Sir Hyde finally gave the order to anchor, with Cronborg in sight to the south-east about eight miles away and the little fishing and boatbuilding village of Hornbæk four miles to the south. Shortly after that the *Cruizer*, having been delayed by the light wind, returned from Cronborg with a reply in Danish from Colonel Stricker which was translated by Dr Scott. It told Sir Hyde:

In answer to the Admiral's honour'd letter, I have to inform you that no orders are given to fire on the English Fleet. An express has gone to Copenhagen and should any orders be sent, I shall immediately send an officer to inform the Admiral.

It was left to Midshipman Millard of the *Monarch* to write the

[1] Stewart, seeing the *Blanche* and *Cruizer* leaving together, assumed the former was carrying the letter to the Danes.

appropriate comment: 'The Governor, probably to gain time, pretends to wait for an answer from his Court at Copenhagen, a distance of twenty or thirty miles; but as they had a telegraphic communication one might suppose a few minutes could have decided the question. . . .'

However, something was gained by sending in the *Cruizer* because Captain Brisbane kept his eyes open and was able to report that the new batteries at the Castle contained about fifty guns and were of a 'low and weak construction' – a direct although unwitting contradiction of Vansittart's and Drummond's reports. He told Colonel Stewart that 'the upper and old batteries he was not permitted to see. Great politeness was shown him; and the enemy appeared to be evidently under considerable alarm, although they held high language.'

While awaiting the Danish Government's reply, Parker ordered Murray of the *Edgar* to take the bomb vessels 'under his protection' and 'anchor off within a distance of Cronenberg and Elsineur Castle, prepare for bombardment, but not to fire or bombard those places unless attacked, but wait for my [the Fleet's] coming up'.

Nelson was busy putting the finishing touches to the details of his attack on Copenhagen itself, but was not too busy to write some personal notes. After the Fleet passed through, the *Edgar* would have to follow, shepherding and giving as much protection as possible to the slow and unwieldy bomb vessels while possibly under heavy fire – they would have to sail over towards the Swedish coast before turning south, to avoid passing too close to the batteries.

He told Murray that 'I was glad to see you placed where you are, for it is a post of great consequence. I take it for granted you will follow the last ship; and I hope the guns of Cronenburg will be lessened, and the heads too, by that time. God will prosper us if we conduct ourselves well.'

He had already written a reassuring note to Captain Bertie, whose ship, the *Ardent*, was very slow and unwieldy. Bertie was worried about the *Ardent*'s sailing ability, and his pilot had freely expressed fears. Nelson assured him: 'I will talk to your pilot; but I do not much mind what they say. Our ships will ride anywhere, and the wind which makes a sea will send us to our destination. Last night the Governor of Cronenburg had *no* orders to fire on us; but the Devil trust them – I will not.'

The Danish reply was received on board the *London* at midnight: the *Cruizer* brought out a Danish officer who handed Sir Hyde a letter from Stricker which said:

In answer to your Excellency's letter, which I did not receive until the day following, at half past eight, I have the honour to inform you that His

Majesty the King of Denmark did not send away the Chargé d'Affaires, but that at his own request obtained a passport.

As a soldier I cannot meddle with politics, but am not at liberty to suffer a Fleet, whose intention is not yet known, to approach the guns of the Castle which I have the honour to command.

In case your Excellency should think proper to make any proposals to His Majesty the King of Denmark, I wish to be informed thereof before the Fleet approaches nearer the Castle. An explicit answer is desired.[1]

This reply was in fact from the Crown Prince himself – the Danish records note it was made 'at the order of His Royal Highness', to whom Stricker reported with an optimism later to prove embarrassing that he 'has taken the necessary measures to prevent the passage of the Fleet'.

The last paragraph of the reply reveals a complete change in Danish policy, which will be described later. With the British Fleet in sight of the Sound, and because of new information from Russia, the Danish Government was now not only prepared to negotiate but was asking Parker for proposals. And, since Parker had said bluntly that he 'must deem the firing of the first gun a declaration of war on the part of Denmark', the Crown Prince had been careful to request that a warning should be given if the Fleet approached nearer, thus ensuring that if Parker did have any proposals, war should not start accidentally by Stricker firing on the Fleet.

Parker completely missed the full significance of the Danish reply. It was a perfect opportunity for him to present once again the proposals already put forward by Vansittart (of which he had a copy). Had he seized it, he would have been doing what the British Government originally intended, and people like Nelson had wanted: negotiating from strength. The proposals would, at long last, be following a large fleet, not a pair of horses.

But Sir Hyde decided what he would do, without showing the Danish reply to Nelson – who would certainly have been quick to spot the change in the Danish attitude and seen it as a chance to deal with the Danish Fleet quickly by diplomatic means while leaving the British Fleet undamaged to go straight on to deal with the Russians without a moment's delay.

While the Danish officer brought out by the *Cruizer* waited (with less hauteur than on his previous visit because he had just discovered for certain that Lord Nelson was indeed with the Fleet) Sir Hyde dated his reply 'On board the *London*, 29th March at 2 a.m.' and wrote:

[1] The original was written in Danish. The translation by Scott which Parker sent to the Admiralty is poor and the last sentence put a stronger emphasis than was intended – Scott translated it as 'A determined answer . . . is desired.' The version given here is retranslated from the Danish original.

Sir, In answer to your Excellency's Note, just now received, the under-signed has only to reply that, finding the intentions of the Court of Denmark to be hostile against His Britannic Majesty, he regards the answer as a Declaration of War, and therefore agreeable to his Instructions, can no longer refrain from Hostilities, however reluctant as may be to his feelings.

But, at the same time will be ready to attend to any proposals of the Court of Denmark for restoring the former amity and friendship which has for so many years subsisted between the two Courts.

Once having spurred himself to act and sending his reply off to Colonel Stricker, Sir Hyde found the wind did not serve, blowing hard from the south-south-west. However, the Fleet could move closer to Cronborg and at 2.00 p.m. the signal was made to weigh, the big ships with double-reefed topsails, and by 4.15 p.m. the *London* had anchored again about four miles north-west of Cronborg, just short of the entrance to the Sound, with a fine view of the beaches and heavily wooded land running along the north shore from Elsinore to Hellebæk, and along to Hornbæk (whose church made a useful landmark from which the ships of the Fleet could take bearings).

The Swedish coast to the eastward was as near as Cronborg; the town of Hälsingborg, with its gun batteries, was clearly in view. And, as if to emphasize its role, Nature played tricks, giving the Fleet a glorious sunset – and strong south-westerly winds when it prayed for northerlies. Midshipman Millard in the *Monarch* – the ship that was to lead the Fleet through the Sound – was lyrical and wrote:

We came-to about sunset; the sun retiring behind the Castle illuminated all that part of the horizon which was a bright crimson; the Castle itself, and neighbouring shores, being in shade and opposed to the brightness behind, were a fine purple: the picture could not be seen to better advantage.

The neck of land upon which the Castle stands is very low for some way, and then rising suddenly forms a ridge of hills at the back of Elsinore along the coast to the northward, so that the Castle appears from a distance to stand in the water between two shores.

The crimson sunset and purple shadows gave way to a strong wind which forced most ships to veer more cable to prevent anchors dragging, and the line of battle ships sent down their topgallant yards to reduce windage. All that remained to do now was to wait for the wind to veer to the north.

The sun set at 6.22 p.m. on Sunday night, when several officers, including Captain Fremantle, dined with Sir Hyde, and the moon rose at 2.15 a.m. on Monday morning, followed by a partial eclipse visible from the Fleet. The *Elephant*'s log recorded, 'At 8 [p.m.] the *London* made our signal for a midshipman and at ½ past 11 the general signal for lieutenants'. Lieutenants were always called to a flagship to collect important written orders for their captains. That night anxious eyes watched the barometer.

The strong winds of the previous evening slowly dropped to light airs and equally slowly veered – 'west-south-west, west by south, north-west' noted the *Monarch*'s log. Then, just before sunrise at 5.36, the *London* made the signal for the Fleet to prepare to weigh.

In Copenhagen Count Bernstorff read Sir Hyde's first letter and the same day wrote his reply to Lord Hawkesbury, complaining that the British Note delivered by Drummond was not written in French. The cool tone he used to Hawkesbury belied the excited circular despatch which he had sent three days earlier to the Danish representatives at The Hague, Lisbon, Vienna, Dresden and Ratisbon, who were told:
'English squadron from Yarmouth believed composed of 30 to 40 sail at entrance to Sound. We shall not dally to learn their intentions; we shall prepare ourselves and meet force with force. The outcome of our efforts depends on Providence; but she is sensible to our cause and will not lead us to sacrifice our honour in the faith of our engagement.'

On the same day, writing to de Wedel Jarlsberg in London that the British Fleet had arrived, he commented, 'The conciliatory propositions of which [the British Government] has spoken to your Excellency do not succeed with us. If the British Government judges it to be in their interest to attack us, we shall defend ourselves with the means at our disposal, and if Providence allows us to succumb, Europe shall not reproach us that we have degraded our honour or have betrayed our duties to our allies.'

The letter was curious and contradictory, completely ignoring the fact that by a much older treaty Denmark was an ally of Britain, and it was because of her new alliances with Russia that the present situation had arisen. And a pragmatist might have pointed out that Bernstorff was displaying an optimism usually reserved for young lovers since the alliance with Russia – and by association, with France – was precious little help since neither country could do anything at the moment when a British fleet was only a few miles from the nation's capital.

The day before, in a letter to Dreyer in Paris, he had given instructions for the French Government to be told that Denmark was persuaded that the First Consul and his allies would do their best to prevent Denmark becoming 'a victim of unjust and heinous vengeance' and of Denmark's good faith in Napoleon's attachment to the Danish cause.

Two days before Sir Hyde sent his first letter, Bernstorff wrote to the Danish Minister in Stockholm that the Swedish King, informed of the approach of the British Fleet, had sent an admiral to Copenhagen 'entrusted with a letter for the Crown Prince. His Majesty offers very amicably all help, and that they may depend upon Sweden and intended to send an order to Carlskrona to speed up the departure of the squadron as far as possible.'

But in spite of all this, on the day the reply was sent to Sir Hyde Parker, the Count wrote again to de Wedel Jarlsberg saying, in violent contrast to the letter of the previous day,

The sign of an appeasement in the dispositions of the Czar towards England which begins to manifest itself, and which appears to have been reinforced through the new change of the *opére* Ministry, offers us the hope of seeing the Northern affairs arranging themselves in friendliness, if the provocative measure of sending a fleet to the Sound has not stifled all feelings of moderation. . . .

It seems to me more likely that the eagerness of Bonaparte to conclude with the Russian Court the Peace of Luneville, the stipulations of which have not yet met with the Czar's approval, has already served to disgust this monarch with the project of forming some liaison with the French Government, and [he added] if the London Court is able to sacrifice its passions and most palpable interests, it would be quite possible the Czar will start drawing towards them.

On the same day, 28 March, yet another circular letter to Danish envoys abroad told them the British Fleet numbered more than sixty, of which nineteen or twenty were ships of the line. The 'resolution to defend our capital and port to the last extremity against an atrocious attack is universally approved and shared in'. The great qualities of the Crown Prince 'appear in their most perfect light. . . . Nothing is equal to his ability, his firmness and his devotion to the people.'

Then on Sunday, 29 March, as Parker received the Danish reply through Colonel Stricker and answered that he regarded it as a declaration of war, Bernstorff wrote once more to de Wedel Jarlsberg giving him important new instructions: 'The measures the London Court pursues towards us take on a more hostile character every day.' He was therefore to declare to the British Government 'that because of their persistence in their injustices towards us, [your] presence at the Court of His Britannic Majesty is becoming absolutely useless and . . . you are to regard your mission suspended and demand passports to leave England with the Secretary attached to your Legation'.

At the same time Bernstorff wrote to Dreyer in Paris saying that the British Fleet had delivered an ultimatum and he was to explain the position to Napoleon, adding 'We are well persuaded that he will take interest and render justice to the sentiments that guide us. . . .' Dreyer was also told to find a prompt means of telling the Danish ships of war in the Mediterranean of 'the danger that menaces them' and also to warn those returning to Denmark 'that the beacons in the Cattegat have been extinguished'.[1]

While Bernstorff wrote his despatches, the Crown Prince worked hard with the Defence Commission, Olfert Fischer and Steen Bille to complete the capital defences – and hope against hope the Swedish Fleet would sail to their help.

The *Berlingske Tidende* continued keeping the Danish people well informed of what was happening: in each issue the various reports were printed one beneath the other as they were received, giving an almost hour-by-hour account of events at, for example, Cronborg.

It reported that the magistrate of Elsinore had been allowed to reveal to the people there the contents of Parker's first letter. Then the letter itself, Stricker's reply and 'Parker's warlike answer' were printed, the newspaper reporting on the 30th that 'everything at the Castle was in readiness to forbid him to enter the Sound'.

More reports followed fast – 'The wind went to the west and the English weighed anchor and started to sail in towards the Castle. . . . The wind died and they were forced to anchor.' The next account described how the Fleet had formed into three divisions and headed towards the entrance to the Sound.

Then, on 30 March,

At this moment, at 6.30 a.m., the entire British Fleet have weighed anchor and will go through the Sound. At 6.45 they have begun a very heavy cannonade. The castle of Cronborg keeps up a continuous and heavy fire and the ships that have already passed are badly damaged. Of the bombs [from the British bomb vessels] that fell in the town, none started any fires. The first bomb to fall landed on the British Consul's house.[2]

---

[1] The principal ones being a single beacon at Cronborg and two at Nakkehoved, to the westward. The lights on the Swedish coast were not affected.

[2] Fenwick's house was in Strandgade and the round shot (not a bomb) is still embedded in a roof beam. Another hit the St Olai Church and is still there.

24

'...IN COPENHAGEN ROADS'

Along with El Morro guarding San Juan in Puerto Rico, Dover Castle towering over the English Channel, Roumali Hissar on the Bosporus near Istanbul, and San Felipe at Cartagena on the Spanish Main, Cronborg is one of the most impressive of coastal fortresses. Built out at the end of a narrow wedge of low land, it has none of the four-square, massive stone appearance of the others: instead, with bright green copper roofs, red brick walls, slender towers topped by almost Moorish cupolas which are also coppered, it looks more like an enormous yet elegant château, an impression heightened by the grass-covered earthworks surrounding it and stretching down to the water's edge.

The original castle, called Krogen, was built in 1425 by Erik of Pomerania to enforce his new law introducing the payment of dues by every ship passing the Sound. Its name was changed to Cronborg in 1577, when the King ordered that anyone using the old name should be fined 'a good bullock'.

Its strength lay not in its ability to withstand a siege by land – although it was moated – but in the ramparts, all four corners of which are strong bastions, with casemates under them. The batteries cover some 265 degrees – the harbour on the north side and the seaward approach from Hornbæk along the west coast right round to Humlebæk, inside the Sound on the shore stretching southward to Copenhagen. But none of the Danish artillerymen serving the guns had ever heard them fire in anger; none had ever practised firing at a moving ship target.

Sentries at the batteries who had been keeping a close watch on the British ships, raised the alarm at first sign of the Fleet weighing anchor.

All hands were in motion early in the morning [Midshipman Millard wrote]. We got under way about half past four, and hove-to for the rest of

303

the Fleet; soon afterwards the signal was made to sail. So alert were the men that before the answering pendant was hauled down the jib was up and all filled. We ran along under the three topsails and foresail, with a pleasant breeze on the starboard quarter.

The *London* hoisted the signal to form the line of battle, and one after another the ships backed and filled sails to get into their correct positions astern of the *Monarch* which, with the *Edgar* standing by the bomb vessels, now had the honour of leading the Fleet.

About six, being abreast the Castle [Midshipman Millard wrote] the Captain ordered the colours to be hoisted. This appears to have been the signal they were waiting for; before the ensign was halfway to the peak, a shot was fired from the Castle, and with such precision as to drive water into the lower deck ports, though it fell short of the ship. We immediately commenced firing. . . .[1]

Sir Hyde, formally noting in his journal that the Castle had opened fire on the Fleet, 'made *Edgar*'s signal to engage, when the bombs began to bombard'.

The *Monarch*, in her eagerness to lead the Fleet, was soon well ahead, turning to keep roughly midway between Cronborg and Hälsingborg on the Swedish coast. Abreast of Cronborg she set her topgallants above her topsails, and as the bomb vessels began firing at the Castle, she opened fire with her starboard broadside. Her captain waited for the Swedish batteries to come into action, but not one puff of smoke could be seen along the eastern shore.

The *Monarch* looked a magnificent sight, the smoke of her broadside streaming from her gun ports and drifting ahead of her in the wind. (See illustration number 16.) Midshipman Millard noted that considering Cronborg's reputation people

. . . will be somewhat surprised to hear that not one of their shot reached us; such however was the fact. We expected to be 'saluted' from both shores, and were prepared accordingly; but when the succeeding ships found that the batteries on the Swedish side were silent, they hauled over to that shore; and many of them, finding that the [Danish] shot fell short, would not condescend to fire at all.

We did not, however, entirely escape damage. The Captain of the Marines, observing from the poop that none of our shot reached the shore, came down to my quarters in the cabin and took the bed of the gun entirely out, that he might see the effect.[2]

[1] In heading for the point where she would turn south to make the passage through the Sound the *Monarch* passed well within range of the guns on the north side of Cronborg but was soon outside their arcs of fire.

[2] 'The Cabin' always meant the captain's accommodation, which had gun ports. The bed of the gun (also known as the quoin, or coin) was a wooden wedge under the breech which, slid in or out, lowered or raised the breech to increase or decrease the range.

Not being much used to the great guns he kept the lanyard [to the trigger of the flintlock] in his hand while the gun was run out, which pulled the lock before the muzzle was out at the port [and fired it].

The man [a seaman] being priming at the time, the fire communicated with the contents in the powderhorn, and it burst in the man's hand, carrying away the tips of his fingers. One man, being green, contrived to have his leg in the way of the tackle when the gun recoiled, by which means the leg was broken.

Ironically these were the only two casualties in the whole Fleet while passing the Sound. . . .

Considering all the nervous talk by people ranging from Vansittart to the pilots, and knowing that of all people he had the most responsibility for finally getting Sir Hyde to take the Fleet past Cronborg, one would assume Nelson was on the *Elephant*'s quarterdeck as the Fleet began the belated passage. But anyone imagining that tiny figure – one empty sleeve pinned to his coat, an eye shade fitted to his hat to protect his blind eye (not the eye patch of popular legend) – pacing back and forth on the landward side, anxiously watching the *Monarch* leading the van division which he commanded, and glancing over to Cronborg's batteries for the first puffs of smoke heralding their tremendous barrage, would have been completely wrong: he was in his cabin writing letters – and making a weak pun.

We are now standing for Cronborg [he wrote to Troubridge]. The van is formed in a compact line, and old Stricker, for that is the Governor's name, had better take care we do not strike his head off. I hope we shall mend on board the *London*, but I now pity both Sir Hyde and Domett; they both, I fancy, wish themselves elsewhere. You may depend on every exertion of mine to keep up harmony. For the rest, the spirit of this Fleet will make all difficulty from enemies appear as nothing. I do not think I ever saw more zeal and desire to distinguish themselves in my life.

At 7.45 a.m., as the last British ships were passing through the Sound, Sir Hyde signalled the *Edgar*, *Blanche* and the bomb vessels to weigh and rejoin the Fleet.

Nelson recorded that Cronborg, after opening fire, 'continued it without intermission till our Fleet and bombs etc. were past, which was about ½ past 8. Not one shot reached the Fleet nor was a single shot fired from the Swedish shore.' As far as the British hits on Cronborg were concerned, 'I hear from the officers of the bomb vessels that their shells fell into the fort, but I could not perceive their effect.'

And later he added a sentence which at times he must have despaired of ever writing: 'The van division anchored in Copenhagen Roads in line of battle. . . .'

The date was 30 March. Parker sailed from Yarmouth on the 12th, arriving in sight of Cronborg on the 24th.

'Found the Danish force drawn up as follows,' Nelson wrote in his journal, describing the defences of Copenhagen. He listed the ships and noted the Crown [Trekroner] batteries mounted between 50 and 100 guns, 'making 22 ships of force and two brigs besides some schooner gun vessels. . . . The Crown Islands and the point of the Island of Amak [Amager] seems strongly fortified. There are additional means of defence besides batteries and etc. added under the Citadel, and guns of course mounted on all the works. . . .'

The French Ambassador in Copenhagen took the opportunity offered by the Batavian Minister of sending a despatch to Talleyrand, the French Foreign Minister, via The Hague. Dated '9 Germinal' (30 March) it said: 'The war between England and Denmark has broken out.' He then went on to describe Parker's letter to Colonel Stricker ('an old, brave officer who has served in Russia'). The Ambassador, Baron de Bourgoing, gave the wording of the correspondence between Parker and Stricker and said the British Fleet finally weighed anchor to pass the Sound. 'The Castle fired first, the English replied; the Governor, at the first shot, sent a messenger to the Crown Prince, and in a second despatch during the little battle . . . reported that he had one man killed and ten wounded.'

From the city of Copenhagen, the Baron wrote, 'one sees distinctly the blue colours on board the ship of Admiral Parker and those on board Nelson's ship, also the white colours of the Major Général of the squadron.[1]

'For some two hours we saw all these ships at anchor and then, towards evening, two frigates and a lugger seemed to cruise between the large battery [Trekroner] which protects the City from the English Fleet.' One of the frigates was fired on by the guns of Trekroner, a Danish frigate, and a blockship. Bourgoing described how he watched the firing, which lasted about three minutes and to which the British did not reply, although 'the indiscreet frigate sheered off'.

And that, Citizen Minister [he wrote] is how things stand at this moment, six o'clock in the evening. One knows only too well what the Danes wish the English. I expect the bombardment to start any moment, although the resistance they will meet will make the attempt fruitless. [He conjectured the British would then force their way past into the Baltic.]

[1] Parker, an Admiral of the Blue, flew a Blue Ensign; Nelson was a Vice-admiral of the White and Graves a Rear-admiral of the White. The 'Major Général' was probably Neslon who had, of course, shifted his flag to a smaller ship.

The Crown Prince, meanwhile, had received Colonel Stricker's reports. The first said:

The English Fleet set sail this morning, 30 March, and entered the entrance of the Sound at seven o'clock. The firing soon began and was continued reciprocally without interruption and with great vigour. . . . I have every reason to think that the fire from the Castle has done the Fleet considerable damage, though this cannot be ascertained because of the great distance of the enemy, who passed as close as possible to the Swedish coast. Some of his shells fell in the Castle, but did no damage. The Castle walls were lightly hurt in some places. Two men of the garrison were killed and two wounded, but the town has not suffered the least from all the shells that were thrown upon it.

The Crown Prince ordered that the garrison of Cronborg should have a double bread ration, which resulted in Stricker's next message asking, 'Could two journeymen bakers be sent up from Copenhagen?' He also reported that the King of Sweden had sent an ADC to Cronborg to compliment Stricker 'on the vigour he had shown and to congratulate the Crown Prince'. No doubt the Crown Prince, on reading that, asked himself why the Swedish batteries had not fired and wondered if he would ever see the Swedish Fleet coming to his assistance. He knew the Swedish King – who was staying near by – was probably watching the Fleet from Karnan, a high point at Hälsingborg, and yet Karnan's batteries did not fire. . . .

But even with the British Fleet at last anchored in Copenhagen Roads both the Crown Prince and his senior officers were bedevilled with bureaucracy. Typical was an instruction from the Prince to Olfert Fischer, who was doing his best to prepare his ships to receive the British attack, enclosing a memorandum from the Chief Constable of Copenhagen listing twenty-eight men. Fischer was to find out which ships they were serving in and send them on shore to Gammelholm, where they were to report to Secretary Aadsen, who was to be sent the memorandum so he could check the men against the names.

More significant was another letter the Crown Prince sent to Fischer and the captains of the ships: if it became necessary, it was permissible for their guns to fire shorewards.

Copenhagen is one of the most beautiful of all capitals built next to the sea. In 1801, as now, it combined the elegance of Paris, the neat rows of houses seen in many old Dutch towns, the narrow-street intimacy of the City of London, the canals that blend Venice and Bruges, and the quays reminiscent of Breton fishing ports.

Even its Danish name of København – Merchant's Harbour – gives little idea how much the city is built on the sea. In 1801, as now, the Royal palace of Amalienborg was less than a hundred yards from the quays; ships' masts seemed to rise from the roofs of houses.

The city that waited for Nelson's attack was small, almost circular and surrounded by defensive walls and a moat; but while more than half was built on the mainland (the large island of Sælland) the rest spread over on to the tiny island of Amagar, none of which is more than twenty feet high and from which it is divided by a wide channel nearly four miles long. In effect a wide canal, this forms the harbour and allows small ships to reach the middle of the city.

At the northern end of the city, where the walls meet the sea, is the Castellet (see illustration number 9), covering the seaward approach to the harbour entrance – which is, of course, the canal. Less than 500 yards from the ramparts of Castellet and only a short distance back from the quays, is Amalienborg Palace while on the opposite side of the canal, on the north end of Amager island, was the Sixtus battery with, on the eastern and seaward side and farther south, the Quintus battery.

Along the edge of the canal (which is wide and divided by names into various harbours) and standing back only a few yards are the buildings whose bright green copper roofs and towers make Copenhagen appear from seaward a city of slender spires – among them the Børsen, its slender spire formed of four dragons' tails twisted upwards like a rope, and Our Saviour's Church, whose elongated, cone-shaped steeple has an open-air staircase spiralling round it.

In addition to guns at the Castellet on the west side of the canal and at Sixtus and Quintus to the east, there were two artificial 'islands' out to sea: Trekroner ('Three Crowns', usually referred to by the British as the Crown Battery), which was nearly a mile out, built beside the channel to the harbour, and Lynetten, midway between it and Sixtus on Amager. The naval establishment and dockyard, Gammelholm, was on the canal side of Amager and inside the city ramparts.[1] Lining Gammelholm and several other parts of the harbour were large slipways where ships were built, and towering over them was the big mast crane (which still stands today). The docks and quays were the heart of the city; the reason for its very existence.

Farther offshore from Amager and to the south is another low and much smaller island, Saltholm, and between the two is the deep channel linking the Sound with the Baltic (see chart on page 310). In the middle of the northern end of this channel is a large shoal, the Middle Ground. Ships bound for the Baltic can pass down the eastern side, through the

[1] Owing to large-scale land reclamation, the Amager side is now considerably changed: there are huge shipyards, for instance, between Sixtus and Lynetten.

Holland Deep, or the western side, through the King's Deep. At this time those bound for Copenhagen itself from the north turned before reaching the Middle Ground to enter the main channel leading to the harbour entrance, passing Trekroner and Lynetten. Those from the south came up the King's Deep and turned into the main channel at Trekroner.

Outside these main channels the water is very shallow. Although Saltholm is more than two miles from Amager, the navigable channel for big ships was then less than three quarters of a mile wide, while shoals extend all the way round Saltholm for more than a mile. The King's Deep and the Holland Deep on either side of the Middle Ground were a scant three quarters of a mile wide, while the Middle Ground itself, an oval lying north and south, was a mile wide and two miles long.

By the time the British Fleet arrived, not a buoy marked the main channel to Copenhagen, the King's Deep, the Holland Deep, the Middle Ground, or the Saltholm Flats; nothing indicated where either channel lay. The buoys had all been lifted and were now up on the quays in Gammelholm. The only charts available to the British Fleet were rudimentary enough to be almost useless without buoys, and the lack of buoys meant that now few if any of the pilots agreed on any single fact about the area. This was the Copenhagen that awaited the British Fleet; a city which mingled fear and defiance.

Sir Hyde Parker, with Nelson, Rear-admiral Graves, Colonel Stewart, and Captains Foley and Fremantle went on board the frigate *Amazon* and, in Sir Hyde's words, 'reconnoitred the Enemy's line'. Before the *Amazon* weighed, the *Cruizer* and a lugger were signalled to pass within hailing distance and ordered to accompany the *Amazon*.

The frigate was commanded by Captain Riou, the man who had saved his ship after hitting an iceberg and whom Nelson knew only by reputation but, within an hour of meeting him, was considerably impressed by his personality and ability. With a light north-west wind the *Amazon* steered in towards the city – 'the enemy fired a number of shot at the ship but without effect', her log noted. The French Ambassador, Baron de Bourgoing, who was of course watching, little dreamed as he described the episode in his despatch to Talleyrand that evening what a valuable target the frigate presented.

As the *Amazon* tacked to rejoin the Fleet the *Cruizer*, watching to the south, 'observed the beacons on Draco to fall'. This was the last step the Danes had to take in removing all the navigational aids near Copenhagen: they were posts at Dragør, on the south-eastern corner of Amager, marking the west side of the entrance to the channel.

COPENHAGEN ROADS

STUBBEN

HOLLAND DEEP

MIDDLE
GROUND

N
NW   NE
W   E
SW   SE
S

RANGE
2000

STEEN
BILLE'S
LINE

TREKRONER

LYNETTEN

OLFERT FISCHER'S LINE

CASTELLET

BOOM   SIXTUS

QUINTUS

NYHOLM

ARSENAL

STRICKER'S
BATTERY

KING'S
DEEP

NELSON'S
ANCHORAGE

AMAGER

0   500   1000   1500   2000
YARDS

COPYRIGHT © 1972 BY THE RAMAGE COMPANY

Copenhagen Roads, showing the positions of the Danish ships and Nelson's course (broken line)
southward down the Holland Deep to the night anchorage south of the Middle Ground. Depths
shown in feet and ranges are in yards. The precise positions of the shoals will never be known for
certain. The standard drawing of the Battle (by Bundesen in 1901) was based on a chart of 1840
documentary evidence and a chart from a survey made a few months after the Battle (and not se
by Bundesen) shows it to be wrong in certain respects. The above chart, by the author, relies mo
Danish and British battle reports giving ranges, bearings and arcs of fire, which allows considera
cross-checking. Although drawn independently and before the existence of the 1801 chart was kn
it subsequently proved to be nearer the 1801 chart in showing the position of shoals than the pre
charts – by Andreas Lous in 1763 and 1775 – which were probably in use at the time of the Battl
The experience gained in the Battle and in replacing the buoys probably led to the new survey i
1801 – it was begun in August and completed in November.

Even before the *Amazon* had returned to the *Elephant* Nelson was preparing his final plan for the attack on the Danish line. The *Amazon* anchored at 1.30 p.m., Nelson was on board the *Elephant* by 2.00 p.m., and at the same time the *Cruizer*'s log noted: 'Answered our signal for a lieutenant. The Captain and Master went on board the *Elephant*.' The captain was Brisbane; the Master was William Fothergill.

Nor had any time been wasted on board Nelson's flagship while he had been away in the *Amazon*: one end of the enormously thick cable for the sheet anchor had been hauled aft and passed out through the larboard sternport, taken forward again along the larboard side outside all the rigging and bent on to the anchor, ready for the *Elephant* to anchor by the stern.

Nelson immediately gave instructions to Captain Foley for the construction of four buoys to be used to mark a safe channel through the Holland Deep, past the Middle Ground. Some of the *Elephant*'s seamen were soon at work with four breakers (wooden water barrels) which would serve as buoys, each with three double-headed shot secured together as an anchor. And Mr George Andrews, the *Elephant*'s master, knowing he would later have to account for every item to the Navy Board clerks, made a formal entry in his log – 'Expended four brakers, 12 double-headed shot and a quantity of small rope to buoy the Middle Ground.'

Orders were given to Captain Brisbane and Fothergill; two pilots chosen by Nelson were also given their instructions, and all of them, with the four buoys, were sent off in a boat belonging to the *Cruizer*, whose log noted laconically: 'Sent the Master to buoy the Middle Passage.' Fortunately for Mr Fothergill his preliminary survey, made with the pilots, was to mark the channel with small dan buoys: the larger buoys were to be laid that night by the *Cruizer* and *Amazon*.

Nelson then joined Sir Hyde and Rear-admiral Graves on board the *London*, and various other officers were present. The discussion that followed was not a council of war – that was to be held next day.[1] Before describing what passed at the meeting it is significant how three men, Parker, Nelson and Stewart, regarded the defences of Copenhagen which they had inspected from the *Amazon* a couple of hours earlier.

Parker recorded in his journal that the enemy's line 'was found to be far more formidable than we had reason to expect'. Reporting later to the Admiralty he wrote of 'the formidable line of ships, rideaus, pontoons, galleys, fireships and gunboats flanked and supported by two

---

[1] Some accounts have confused the discussions of 30 and 31 March on board the *London* because the dates in Nelson's and Parker's journals do not coincide, one using civil and the other nautical time, but the ships' logs and other reports make it clear.

extensive batteries on the two islands called the Crownes [sic], the largest of which was mounted with from 50 to 70 pieces of cannon – these were again commanded by two ships of 70 guns and a large frigate in the Inner Roads to Copenhagen, and two 64-gun ships without masts, were moored upon the Fleet on the starboard side of the entrance into the Arsenal. . . .'

Nelson's journal simply listed the defences without comment. However, at 9.00 p.m. that night he wrote to Emma describing the day and giving his views:

We this morning passed the fancied tremendous fortress of Cronenburg, mounted with 270 pieces of cannon. More powder and shot, I believe, never were thrown away, for not one shot struck a single ship of the British Fleet. Some of our ships fired; but the *Elephant* did not return a single shot. I hope to reserve them for a better occasion.

I have just been reconnoitring the Danish line of defence. It looks formidable to those who are children at war, but to my judgment, with ten sail of the line I think I can annihilate them; at all events, I hope to be allowed to try. I am not very well and tired, but Foley [commanding the *Elephant*] is very good to me. I have much to do here, exactly what you said in London. . . .

Colonel Stewart observed:

We soon perceived that our delay had been of important advantage to the enemy, who had lined the northern edge of the shoals near the Crown Batteries, and the front of the harbour and arsenal [the King's Deep] with a formidable flotilla.

At the meeting on board the *London* Nelson simply offered his services saying that for his attack on the Danes from the south he would need ten sail of the line (his van division comprised ten such ships) and all the smaller craft. Both Parker and Graves were gloomy, and Parker at least was worried about the guns of the batteries, particularly those covering the Arsenal: he was afraid they might prevent troops being landed. It was decided to make another reconnaissance next morning, taking the artillery officers to get their opinion.

As soon as Nelson, Graves and the rest returned to their ships Sir Hyde began dictating orders for various officers, beginning with Nelson, who was to have the ten ships he requested (two more were added later, after the next day's council of war). Sir Hyde's secretary, Osborn, then set the clerks to work making fair copies for the Admiral to sign, while signals for lieutenants were made to the various ships concerned for them to be collected.

The most important order was the one Parker noted first in his journal: 'Ordered V. A. Lord Nelson to take the ships, frigates, bomb vessels, fireships and guns therein mentioned under his command for the purpose of attacking the enemy's line, &c. &c.'

Captain Rose, commanding the *Jamaica*, was put in command of the gun brigs. That left the flat boats which would carry the soldiers to the ships or fortresses they were to attack. Parker divided the boats into two divisions, putting one of his favourite young officers in the *London*, Lt Hancock, in command of one, and possibly because of a suggestion from Nelson, a lieutenant from the *St George*, whom he did not bother to name, in charge of the other.

The two divisions of flat boats were to be commanded by Captain Fremantle – news which did nothing to cheer him up as he was already depressed that the *Ganges* was not part of Nelson's van division and, from what he could see of the future plans, it would be the van that did the fighting while the *Ganges* was part of Sir Hyde's division watching from a distance.

With the signing of these orders Sir Hyde's role had, for all intents and purposes, come to an end – with the exception of a single and disastrous order signalled during the Battle.

Sir Hyde's clerks were busy copying out the orders when the *Cruizer*'s master, William Fothergill, went off in a boat to start soundings and marking the Holland Deep. He was also one of the several – including Captains Hardy and Riou, and masters of ships – who went out again that night, rowing among floating ice, with seamen busy with leadlines quietly passing back the depths they found. These were noted and bearings taken, using boat compasses lit by guttering candles and shielded with strips of canvas. Oars were muffled because any moment they expected to meet Danish guard boats rowing through the channels to prevent them carrying out just this sort of survey.

All the officers had been given the night's parole: Parker had issued Nelson with a numbered list of twenty words: – 'the parole or watchword for the officers to know each other when employ'd in boats in the night'. The list was a weird mixture of county and town names, admirals, rivers and places – the first two, challenge and answer, were 'Northumberland' and 'Westmoreland' (which could easily be confused), the eighth 'Spencer', ninth 'Jervis' and tenth 'Portsmouth', while the sixteenth, seventeenth and eighteenth were 'Tweed', 'Ireland' and, probably by an association of ideas, 'Union'.

It was bitterly cold work and the leadsmen were soon soaking wet. But slowly the soundings began to form a pattern; slowly the position of the Holland Deep began to emerge, the captains and masters being like men groping in the darkness to find and plot their way through a

maze. They worked through the night, and as dawn broke the men in
the rest of the ships of the Fleet were startled to see that what had
previously been a featureless expanse of water off the city – broken only
by floating pieces of ice and logs and branches of trees – was now buoyed,
the line showing clearly the Swedish side of the Holland Deep running
north and south.

The morning of Tuesday, 31 March, brought light south-westerly
winds. Once again the *Amazon* was called to the *London*, along with the
Cruizer, *Harpy* brig, *Lark* lugger and *Fox* cutter. Nelson was rowed over
from the *Elephant* and Graves from the *Defiance*. Sir Hyde had also
ordered the 'artillery officers' – those in the bomb ketches – to join
them and they all boarded the *Amazon*, along with Stewart, Domett and
Otway, for another reconnaissance.

Sir Hyde had asked the artillery officers a single question: if in their
opinion they could shell the Arsenal and Dockyard if the Danish line of
defence – Olfert Fischer's ships and batteries anchored in a long line in
front of the city – was in part or wholly removed. Meanwhile the
artillery men were using their telescopes to count those guns which were
visible. On Trekroner they reckoned nearly seventy, with only six or
seven on Lynetten, but behind the line of ships there were several
batteries on Amager whose guns they could not count but all of which
were in range of the King's Deep, which was the channel the bomb
ketches would have to use to get within range of their target.

The *Amazon* then tacked back and forth and Captain Riou and Pike
Channell, her master, took as many soundings as possible, plotting
them on a chart for use that night when the next set of buoys – those on
the Copenhagen side of the Holland Deep, along the east side of the
Middle Ground – had to be laid. Finally, the *Amazon* returned to the
Fleet and, as Mr Scott noted in his diary, 'The Admirals are employed
in arranging the mode of attack on board the *Elephant*.' The parson was
not quite accurate: Sir Hyde was holding a council of war with Nelson,
Graves, Domett, Fremantle, Foley, Murray, Riou and Stewart.

The discussion was wide-ranging and Col. Stewart gives a good description.[1]

The energy of Lord Nelson's character was remarked: certain difficulties
had been started by some of the members [of the council of war] relative to
each of the three Powers we should either have to engage, in succession or

[1] But his narrative, printed in *Despatches and Letters of Lord Nelson*, was written several years
later. Although this version has been used by most authorities, several sentences and even
paragraphs have been omitted, including an important question Parker asked, requiring the
answers in writing – a significant action at a council of war. The question is covered by Domett
later in this narrative. Stewart's Diary, quoted several times in this book, is not used in
Despatches and Letters although it was clearly the basis of Stewart's later narrative.

united, in those seas. The number of the Russians was, in particular, represented as formidable. Lord Nelson kept pacing the cabin, mortified at everything which savoured either of alarm or irresolution.

When the above remark was applied to the Swedes, he sharply observed, 'The more numerous the better,' and when to the Russians he repeatedly said, 'So much the better; I wish they were twice as many, the easier the victory, depend on it.'

He alluded, as he afterwards explained in private, to the total want of *tactique* among the Northern Fleets; and to his intention, whenever he should bring either the Swedes or the Russians to action, of attacking the head of their line, and confusing their movements as much as possible. He used to say, 'Close with a Frenchman, but outmanoeuvre a Russian.'

Stewart began his account of this council of war with the remark:

Lord Nelson offered his services, requiring ten line of battle ships, and the whole of the smaller craft. The Commander-in-Chief, with sound discretion, and in a handsome manner, not only left everything to Nelson for this detached service, but gave [him] two more line of battle ships than he demanded.

Sir Hyde received the opinions of the artillery officers, Stewart noted: 'Captains Lawson and Fyers and five lieutenants of artillery, gave it as their opinion that, "If the outer line of the enemy's defences afloat – that is, all the vessels to the southward of the two Crown Islands [Trekroner and Lynetten] – were removed, a bombardment would be attended with the best probable success; but that until that was done the attempt could be attended with none." '

However, Domett, in his letter to Lord Bridport a month after the Battle, throws more light on what happened at the council. While complaining that his own role had not been publicly acknowledged by Parker, he told Lord Bridport that:

On his arrival before Copenhagen he tells the public that he called Lord Nelson and Lord Graves[1] to his assistance, reconnoitred the position of the enemy's line of defence, and on a consultation with *them*, came to a determination to make an attack, without doing me the honour to mention my name, though he had also called upon me to attend him on this reconnoitring service, as well as to give my opinion in writing with respect to the propriety of attacking the enemy, and as my vote was for the attack, which terminated so successfully . . . and that of Admiral Graves decidedly against it, I am astonished, as well as Lord Nelson and all the captains in the Fleet, that the Commander-in-Chief should not have thought proper to name me as well as the Rear Admiral, for he was very particular and got our opinions in writing, calling on me first as the youngest officer.

[1] A slip of Domett's pen: he meant Rear-admiral Graves, who received a knighthood after the battle.

Domett was an angry man. Since he was writing within a month to one of the Navy's most senior, and certainly one of its most respected admirals, he would not have distorted actual facts, because Bridport could check them, and he was seeking to have his complaint remedied. It is obvious, therefore, that this was far from being a routine council of war which simply agreed to everything Nelson proposed – a hitherto common and popular view. It was something quite different, recalling the wretched council of war called by another indecisive admiral whose courage was never questioned but whose capability was – Admiral the Hon. John Byng.[1]

Far from Parker 'with sound discretion and in a handsome manner' not only leaving everything to Nelson but giving him two more sail of the line than he asked, we see Parker still so uncertain of what to do that, with his Fleet anchored off the Danish capital, he required Nelson, Graves, and Domett, to give their view in writing on 'The propriety of attacking the enemy'.

He was, quite simply, asking 'Shall I attack or not?' Had his admirals said no, in writing, Parker would have used these answers as a sufficient reason for not attacking. As it was, the fact that Graves voted against it was outweighed by Nelson and Domett being decidedly for it.

In every navy's history a council of war has proved to be a way out for a weak admiral; a timid man's testimony to what might have been – if. . . . No decisive, competent admiral ever held one. Discussions with his junior officers, yes; a council, no – particularly with the example of the Byng case only forty-five years behind.

Even more surprising is that Parker's third-in-command, Rear-admiral Graves, was against the attack. It will be recalled that Graves was also (on Domett's authority) against the Fleet passing Cronborg. (However, to be fair to Graves, Nelson had no doubts about him and his ship, the *Defiance*, fought bravely in the Battle, Graves behaving magnificently.)

Fremantle, finding that he was to command the flat boats, had been fairly satisfied since, with the *Ganges* in Parker's division, it would be his only chance of getting into action. But after Parker offered Nelson two extra sail of the line, Fremantle saw his chance. 'When I found a larger force was to go against the batteries,' he wrote to Betsey, 'I begged Sir Hyde to allow the *Ganges* to go.'

Sir Hyde agreed – no doubt Nelson gave his approval and may well have pressed Fremantle's claim, since they had fought together on many occasions. Nelson probably pressed the claim of the second ship

---

[1] For a detailed study of Byng's action, trial and execution see the author's *At 12 Mr Byng Was Shot* (London and Philadelphia, 1962).

chosen, the *Edgar*, because although Captain Murray had led the van both when the Fleet sailed for the Belt and later passed Cronborg, his ship had not in fact been under Nelson's orders as part of the van division.

So this curious council of war ended, with Parker having made no decisions – except in the negative sense that he did not decide to call off the attack. He made no reference in his journal that the *Ganges* and the *Edgar* were now part of Nelson's division; in fact the only orders he recorded for the rest of the day were those of the *Ramillies* and the *Defence* and the 64-gun *Veteran*, telling them that, when Lord Nelson's division weighed anchor to attack the southern end of the Danish line, they were also to get under way and 'menace the northern part of the enemy's line, [i.e. close to Trekroner] as well as to be ready to assist disabled ships coming out of action'.

From now on, everything was up to Nelson, who contented himself with two orders to his captains that day – the numbers of the flat bottom boats were to be painted on their sterns, and when a red pendant under a Union Jack [sic] was hoisted on board the *Elephant*, 'artillery officers are to repair on board the Admiral'.

Orders such as these show the limitations of signalling at this period. If the order was not listed in the signal book (with the flag signal that represented it) then the intention or order could not be signalled without being spelled out letter by letter. For this reason the signal book had many blank spaces next to various signal numbers so that an admiral could write in his own extra signals to cover specific situations.[1]

There was still more work to be done on marking the channels that night. Riou and Brisbane, helped by the lugger and cutters, needed several more hours to complete sounding and marking the Holland Deep.

Nelson, who had of course proposed attacking from the south even before the Fleet had passed Cronborg, wanted to move his division down to the other end of the Holland Deep and anchor off the south end of the Middle Ground shoal, so that he could attack the moment the wind went south. And the beauty of the plan was that the southerly wind taking his ships in to attack the Danish line would also carry any disabled out of danger and up towards Parker's division, which would stay north of the Middle Ground and north-east of Copenhagen.

Once again the boats, oars muffled, rowed out from their ships in the darkness, found the buoys they had already laid, and carried on

---

[1] The code where numbers meant specific words or complete phrases, so that sentences could be formed (the most famous being, of course, Nelson's signal at Trafalgar), had yet to be adopted.

sounding and marking the channel beyond. There were too few buoys, so empty boats were left anchored, the men transferring to others.

A few moments after 5.30 the sun rose over the Swedish coast, bringing a south-west wind – 'moderate breezes and fair weather' as the *Elephant*'s log noted. But even before sunrise the seamen of the British Fleet were at work at the dozens of jobs done daily, in war or peace, sunshine or rain, to keep each one of the King's ships seaworthy and smart.

On board the 32-gun frigate *Alcmene*, men were busy scraping down one of the topmasts before sunrise while others worked under the supervision of John Custance, the acting master, and the bosun, setting up the fore-rigging. The ship's master-at-arms was keeping an eye on two prisoners-at-large, John Buchanan and Joseph Kitchener. A bosun's mate was busy making two cat-o'-nine tails, neatly sewing red baize round the handles. Even though the Fleet was on the eve of battle, discipline had to be maintained, and within a few hours the two men would be flogged.

On board the *Elephant* Nelson, by now very tired and feeling ill – excitement, on which he thrived, always brought with it what appears to have been a form of nervous dyspepsia – was up before dawn. At 5.50 a.m. the *Elephant* made the signal to the van division ships for all masters and pilots to come on board the flagship.

In the meantime Captain Foley was supervising the shifting of the stern cable – by which the *Elephant* would anchor in the battle – so that instead of it leading out of a stern port on the larboard side it was taken out the other side and led forward to starboard, where it was bent on to an anchor. This would ensure that with a south or south-east wind the *Elephant* would lie to a stern anchor more in line with the Danish ships. Yet the wind that day was from the south-west, the prevailing direction, and if it was south-west on the day of the battle the ship would lie better with the cable from the larboard side. . . . However Foley was obviously acting under Nelson's orders; and in the event Nelson's guess about the direction of the wind was right.

While the masters and pilots were being rowed to the flagship, signals were made for the *Amazon*, *Cruizer*, the *Harpy* brig, *Lark* lugger and *Fox* cutter. By the time they had closed with the *Elephant* the masters and pilots had received their instructions from Nelson, who boarded the *Amazon*, taking some of the masters and pilots with him while the rest went on board the *Cruizer*.

Led by the *Amazon*, the little flotilla then beat up to the new buoy at the north end of the Middle Ground, marking the beginning of the Holland Deep – and which, not so many hours earlier, had been one of the *Elephant*'s water breakers – in a light south-westerly wind to begin the morning's work: to make a final survey of the channel down the outside of the Middle Ground. The *Cruizer* anchored by the north buoy and the masters and pilots went off in boats to continue surveying while the *Amazon* tacked up the channel, sounding as she went. By noon the masters and pilots were satisfied they knew the way, and under Nelson's instructions the *Cruizer* remained by the north buoy while the *Harpy*, *Fox* and *Lark* anchored one beyond the other to the southward, marking the edge of the shoal.

With the wind veering to the west and the sky clouding over, the Danish shore batteries opened a desultory fire on the line of anchored vessels but caused no damage. The *Amazon* did not even bother to note the fact in her log; the *Cruizer* made only a passing reference. The anchored vessels hoisted signals indicating they should be left to starboard; then the *Amazon* tacked and, the wind having continued to veer to the north-west, had to beat back up the channel to the Fleet.

This time she went close to the *London* and anchored. Nelson had waited a long time for this moment, and he recorded it in his journal with a brevity which hid his true feelings but revealed his admiration of Captain Riou, the entry beginning: 'The *Amazon* explored the channel in the most satisfactory manner. At $\frac{1}{2}$ past 1 I returned on board the Commander-in-Chief. . . .'

Nelson had also waited too long to waste a moment: on leaving the *London* he had his boat pass close to as many of the van division ships as possible to hail them to prepare to weigh.

In the *Monarch*, Midshipman Millard

observed a light gig pulling towards us, though at a great distance. On directing my spying-glass towards her, I observed several officers in her, but at the end of the boat was a cocked hat put on square, with a peculiar *slouch*, so as to be at right angles with the boat's keel.[1] I immediately ran to the officer of the watch and assured him Lord Nelson was coming on board, for I had seen his hat.

My information did not receive much credit, until in the process of time the old checked surtout was discovered; and soon after a squeaking little voice hailed the *Monarch* and desired us, in true Norfolk drawl, to prepare to weigh.

Just as the ships were getting ready a Prussian brig came in sight, passing northward through the Sound laden with cargo. Her captain had no choice but to sail through the anchored British Fleet, no doubt alarmed that he might be detained.

---

[1] The cocked hat was, at this time, more usually worn 'fore and aft' than 'athwartships' (i.e. more like a helmet).

In the meantime, with the *Elephant* hoisting the van squadron's signal to prepare to weigh, the *Alcmene* hove short on her anchor cable and, while waiting for the next order, John Buchanan and Joseph Kitchener were each given a dozen lashes 'for rioting and disobedience to orders'.

Finally the van weighed. 'At 4 [p.m.] bore up and made sail ahead of the van division' the *Amazon*'s log recorded, 'and ran thro' the Outer [Holland] Deep'.

Colonel Stewart, who had transferred to the *Elephant*, noted that having checked over and marked the channel by 11.00 a.m., rejoined the Fleet, received his orders from Sir Hyde, and made the signal for his division to weigh, Nelson had the van division under sail 'with astonishing alacrity, and anchored them all without damage before dark, in the new roadstead. The whole thing was done with a correctness and at the same time with a rapidity which could never have been exceeded....'

Captain Riou showed the greatest ability in ascertaining the course of the channel this forenoon, and worked his frigate through it in a most masterly style. She, on one occasion, touched the rocky shore on the island of Saltholm side, and by his presence of mind, and rapidity of giving her a press of sail fairly pushed her over a shoal. ... Lord Nelson was in raptures with this able officer.

In another account Stewart wrote that on returning to the *Elephant* from the *London* Nelson 'threw out the wished for signal to weigh. The shout with which it was received throughout the Division was heard to a considerable distance.'

Although the channel was very narrow – so much so the ships had to sail in line ahead – Nelson did not find it necessary to make a lot of signals to keep his thirty-three ships in position.

The first, to the whole van division, was number 66 and hoisted at 3 p.m. – '*Weigh, the outer or leeward ships first.*' This was followed by one from the *Amazon* to the *Glatton*, 103, '*Keep in the Admiral's wake*'. This must have been a galling signal for Captain Bligh, a fine seaman but highly sensitive to the views of his superiors. Nelson knew the *Glatton* was a difficult ship to handle, and five minutes later the *Elephant* made the same signal to the whole Division. (However, ten minutes later, at 3.45, the *Elephant* was making the same signal again, this time with the *Glatton*'s pendant.)

The flagship made no more signals until 4.35 p.m., as the ships reached the end of the channel, when she hoisted 63, '*Anchor as soon as convenient*'. At 5.25 number 196 with the *Ardent*'s and *Agamemnon*'s pendants was hoisted, '*Take the guard for the next twenty-four hours*'. A Spanish Jack with the number five told the van division that the 'parole or watchword' for the night was the fifth in the list of twenty – 'Winchester'.

The entry in Nelson's journal ended with '... and having received his directions 12 sail of the line, frigates, bombs, gun vessels &c. &c., [passed down the Holland Deep and] were safely anchored to the southward of the Middle Ground'.

Stewart added:

About dark the whole Fleet was at its anchorage off Draco Point; the headmost [southernmost] of the enemy's line not more than two miles distant. The small extent of the anchoring ground ... caused the ships to be so much crowded, which the calmness of the evening increased, that had the enemy but taken due advantage of it by shells from mortar boats, or from Amak Island, the greatest mischief might have ensued.

They threw two or three about eight p.m., which served to show that we were within range. The Danes were, however, too much occupied during this night in manning their ships, and strengthening their line; not from immediate expectation, as we learned afterwards of our attack – conceiving the Channel [the King's Deep] impracticable to so large a fleet, but as a precaution against our nearer approach.

There must have been some rivalry between the *Cruizer* and the *Amazon* since the master of each ship claims the honour of having led the van through the Holland Deep. The most probable explanation is that both led, but at different times: the *Cruizer* had been left at anchor at the north end of the Middle Ground when the *Amazon* took Nelson back to the Fleet, so when the van got under way the *Amazon* led it down to the Middle Ground, where the *Cruizer* weighed and went ahead.[1]

With his fighting ships now anchored to the south of the Middle Ground, Nelson's view of Copenhagen was, of course, reversed: now, as he faced north – where lay Sir Hyde's ships – the island of Amager and Copenhagen were on his left with the King's Deep in front of him between Amager and the Middle Ground, and the Holland Deep, between the Middle Ground and Saltholm Island on his right.

All along the Amager and Copenhagen shore, flanking the King's Deep, were Olfert Fischer's ships moored bow to stern, seeming – from the angle at which Nelson viewed them – a continuous line of guns' muzzles protruding through gun ports, while on the Middle Ground side of the channel was shoal water: indistinguishable shallows which could keep a sail of the line aground and out of the battle more effectively than action damage.

More important, there was nothing to show the channel through the

---

[1] Several accounts say that Riou hit the rock off Saltholm while leading the van; but this is due to misreading Stewart's account. She hit the rock in the morning with Nelson on board while beating through on the reconnaissance.

King's Deep. The Holland Deep had been well buoyed, thanks to all the previous work; but the King's Deep, up which Nelson's twelve sail of the line had to pass to attack, was an unknown quantity. One small shoal could strand every one of his ships before they could get into action. . . .

From the quarterdeck of the *Elephant* the King's Deep now appeared a smooth expanse of brownish green water; there was no way of knowing whether there was four or forty feet of water at any point. Nelson's greatest danger for the moment was mud, sand or rock hidden beneath the water and which was – for the moment – the Danes' greatest ally, but, like the King of Sweden and the late Czar, a fickle one.

Dinner was normally taken by officers on board ships of war in the early afternoon and had been delayed on board Nelson's flagship. As soon as the *Elephant* had anchored Nelson invited his second-in-command, Rear-admiral Graves, and some of his old friends to join him. They were men he had, in many cases, fought alongside in several battles – like Thomas Foley, who had commanded a ship at Cape St Vincent; Thomas Fremantle, who had been with Nelson at Santa Cruz and the siege of Bastia; and Thomas Hardy, who had commanded the *Mutine* at the Nile.

Some years earlier Hardy had led to one of Nelson's more famous expressions: the *Minerve* frigate, being chased and overhauled on leaving Gibraltar by two Spanish sail of the line and a frigate, had one of her seamen fall over the side. A boat was lowered and Lieutenant Hardy went away in it looking for the man. With the leading Spanish ships closing rapidly Hardy signalled that the man could not be found, and his boat's crew pulled for the *Minerve* but could not catch up.

Very soon the nearest Spanish ship of the line was almost within range but Nelson exclaimed, 'By God! I'll not lose Hardy! Back the mizen-topsail!' While every man on board, with few exceptions, anticipated being made a prisoner in a matter of minutes as the frigate stopped, to their surprise the great Spanish ship shortened sail to let the other ship of the line catch up – apparently fearing a trap – and giving Nelson time to run the *Minerve* down to Hardy's boat and get him on board.

The other guests included Colonel Stewart, Lt-colonel Hutchinson (who commanded a detachment of the 49th Regiment), Captains Inman (commanding the *Désirée*) and Riou, the only naval officer present not previously known to Nelson. He was invited because Nelson was quick to appreciate his agile mind and superb seamanship, and before the night was out he was to prove the quality of his brain.

It was a night Colonel Stewart described as 'an important one. As soon as the Fleet was at anchor the gallant Nelson sat down to table with a large party of his comrades in arms. He was in the highest spirits, and drank to a leading wind, and to the success of the ensuing day.' Since his division had not left Sir Hyde more than six hours earlier this was an indication of his determination to lose no time – and that he was sure the wind would change. At the end of dinner, 'every man separated with feelings of admiration for their great leader, and with anxious impatience to follow him to the approaching battle'.

Nelson said his farewells to Rear-admiral Graves and the other captains; but Riou and Hardy were told to remain on board the *Elephant*. As night fell there was a lot of bustle round the flagship. 'When I went on board the *Elephant* at night,' wrote Midshipman Millard, who brought a boat from the *Monarch* to fetch Colonel Hutchinson, 'I found the quarter deck full of officers, and heard Lord Nelson giving his orders to a party which was going to take soundings along the enemy's line.' (Unknown to Millard the party was headed by Captain Hardy, who was going to sound as close to the Danish line as possible.)

'Are your oars muffled?'
'Yes, my Lord.'
'Very well, should the Danish guard boat discover you, you must pull like devils, and get out of his way as fast as you can.'
On our way to the *Monarch*, Colonel Hutchinson informed me that Lord Nelson intended to attack the enemy in the morning; and that he [Hutchinson] was himself to storm the Crown Batteries at the head of a division of the 49th Regiment, providing the men of war could succeed in capturing the shipping, and act with any effect against the batteries previous to the assault.
As soon as we came on board I hastened to communicate the intelligence to the two midshipmen's berths, where it was received with three cheers, and the bearer rewarded with grog he would gladly have refused, being already kept up beyond his usual time, and having to turn out again at midnight to walk the deck till four in the morning. The joy expressed on this occasion was unfeigned, which may be easily believed when it is remembered that we had been in sight of our opponents three days, and knew that sooner or later the bloody day must come.

While Nelson, Foley and Riou were working in the *Elephant*'s great cabin on the final details of the plan of attack, Hardy was out in the boat trying to find the southern end of the Middle Ground shoal and get its bearings from the flagship. After that, he intended finding the King's Deep channel. This was more difficult than it sounded, for it was as important to know where the Middle Ground shoal lay to the eastward as it was the depths on the Copenhagen side up to the Danish line. Many of the British ships would have to pass others already in action alongside their chosen opponents, so it was very necessary to know whether the channel was wide enough for three ships – for one sail of the line to pass another at anchor alongside an enemy.

By mid-evening Nelson was completely exhausted, yet the whole plan of attack had to be drawn up in writing and copies made for all the captains. Apart from the selected few who had dined with him, none of the others knew anything more than his own instinct could tell him – that the light northerly wind that had been just enough to bring them down through the Holland Deep would probably veer during the night, becoming the southerly wind in the morning needed to carry them the short distance up the King's Deep to attack the Danish line.

With Nelson, Foley and Riou in the great cabin was Colonel Stewart, not because he had anything to contribute, but he was good company and had a nice sense of judgment, apart from being in over-all command of the troops. The other person who was busy in the cabin was Nelson's servant, Tom Allen, who was no taller than his master and treated the admiral with that curious mixture of deference, impertinence and respect that is common among good servants. Allen could neither read nor write but had an almost proprietary interest in Nelson's welfare and health, but in this case the relationship was closer than usual because he had been born in the same village, Burnham Thorpe, where the admiral's father was the rector. When the Reverend Edmund Nelson christened Allen, the baby gave no indication that he would grow into a pug-faced, black-haired youth, fully endowed with all the dogmatic self-righteousness of the truly ignorant; nor could anyone dream the youth would eventually serve the rector's son long before the son had become the most famous fighting admiral of any navy. Allen was also something of a 'Dutch uncle' to Nelson: knowing the Admiral's delicate health, bouts of depression, and the trouble he suffered with his eyes, Allen was not above successfully bullying Nelson into doing what Allen thought was best for him.

This night was no exception: Nelson began by sitting in a chair and dictating to Foley and Riou; but as each part of the plan was completed Nelson's weariness began to worry them. They suggested his cot should be brought in and slung from the deckhead, so that he could lie down and dictate, but Nelson would not agree. Allen, without any more ado, brought the cot in and placed it on the deck. Nelson finally agreed to lie down in it, resting back on several cushions and continuing to dictate while Allen brought him hot drinks – like the previous nights, it was bitterly cold: chunks of ice floated past the ship – part of the mass of ice melting up the Baltic and slowly freeing the Russian Fleet.

The orders were succinct, containing just as much detail as was

British Ships № 1.

Agamemnon — As in Sketch № 1. was not aground but had her Sails loose, & at an Anchor in consequence of not being able to weather the Shoal dotted. She is painted with a yellow stripe two black mouldings one above & one under her main deck ports.

Russell & Bellona — are aground, with the Russells Gib boom over the Bellonas Tafferail., their Sails loose

Isis — a yellow side with a black Strake thro. the upper part of her main deck ports

Edgar — a yellow sides

Ardent — An Iventhen Ship. with a black Strake between her main & lower deck ports, the side yellow to the upper part of the bends

Glatton — the Same. The Glattons fore topmast is gone just under the hounses the top gallantmast & yard hanging

Elephant — 74 — the Same — had Lord Nelsons Flag flying (blue at the fore)

Ganges — 74 — a Broad yellow side

Monarch 74 — The Same as the Glatton & Elephant

Defiance 74 — Black from the Water to the upper part of Lower decks ports the yellow goes just above the main deck ports She had Rear Adm: Graves's flag. which at the Mizen

The Frigates — have a yellow Strake. all of them, Every Ship is brought up by the Stern Shewn their Topsails & Stay Sails lower'd down, All keeping up a heavy Sea a fresh of Wind from the Southward

Λ Λ Λ — On this Line about 5 miles to Leeward. is Sir Hyde Parker with 8 Sail, Under a press of Sail. top gallant Sails set but not able to fetch. № 2

The Water Smooth, every Ship has the Signal № 10 flying

The Seven bombs, some of them are firing

2. Shou'd not the View be taken. somewhere at + or on a line extended from it. these Strokes shew from whence they fired The Enemys Ships were about 4 Cables length. from the Shore & about a Cables length from each other. & the British Ships about three Cables Length from them —

24 A page from Kittoe's notebook describing the British ships, particularly the colours of their hulls, and reporting 'The water smooth, every ship has the Signal No. 10 [sic: No. 16, for Close Action] flying. . . . The enemys ships were about 4 cables length [800 yards] from the shore and about a cables length [200 yards] from each other & the British ships about three cables length from them.'

Enemies Ships

The line Alphabetically arranged is the Enemies line

A a three decker cut down. B a 74 with stump mast

C a very long low vessell no head, & her masts very small & low

D is a two deck'd Ship, the upper tier of guns pointed through
white Cloths & appears like hammock Cloths, she has neither
Quarter decks nor forecastle, E is a very long low vessell
painted with a narrow yellow Streak below her guns
which are pointed thro black Canvas bulwarks,

F the same as C, mounting 20. 112 pounders

G is a frigate without Quarter deck or foucastle, the
Ornaments of her Stern taken off, H is a 74 with her ——
with her Quarter deck & foucastle complete & guns pointed
thro them, she has a Stump mast as in the Sketch & a broad
pendant flying I is a vessell of the same description as F
they have no mast & are more like a chest than a vessell
their heighth altogether from the Water ab:t 7 feet they draw
only 3 feet water K a very long low vessell like G & pointed
the same way L the same as F & I but longer, she mounted
24. 24 pounders M a 74 complete her jib boom in & top
masts struck, low yards & Mizen Yard down the Topsail yards
laying in the Top. N The same as I E & O. the same but
shorter P a 74 complete laying in the same manner as
M. Q a 74 hulk with a Stump mast. R a very long low
vessell not above 3 feet from the Water, she had a high Quarter
& foucastle, her masts very low & small in Proportion to her
Length she had a Yellow Streak under her Guns close
to the Water Line, they were generally painted as our
ships are their Sides were dark & dirty they
were all moor'd head & Stern.

The figures 1 2 3 4 5 6 7 8 9 are meant to shew where small
Schooner gun boats lay, they also kept up a fire

25 Kittoe's notes for the Danish line, describing each of the ships he has marked with
a letter of the alphabet and estimating her armament. The figures, he notes, 'are
meant to shew where small schooner gun boats lay, they also kept up a fire'.

26 On board *Floating Battery No.* 1 at the height of the Battle: Lieutenant Willemoes (beside the mast) encourages his men. On the extreme left a wounded man leans back against net bags containing round shot, with a tub of water used for wetting the sponges in front of him. The small cylinder on deck by the dismounted gun is a case in which the powder charge is carried from the magazine to the gun. Men in the centre of the picture are using handspikes to train the gun. The ship partly hidden by smoke on the left is Nelson's flagship, the *Elephant*, with the masts of the *Glatton* and *Ardent* beyond. Boarding pikes are kept in a rack round the foot of the *Battery*'s mast, and in line beyond is Olfert Fischer's flagship, the *Dannebroge*. Although the artist has not shown it, the *Battery*'s deck was under several inches of water.

27 A British shot embedded in a piece of an oak beam from the Danish *Indfødsretten*. Flying splinters usually killed or wounded more men than actual shot.

28 The pocket telescope traditionally reputed to have been the one Nelson put to his blind eye to avoid seeing Sir Hyde's signal to discontinue the battle.

required and no more. Much would depend on each captain knowing what Nelson would want him to do should he meet with a situation not covered by his orders. Imparting this to the captains was, indeed, Nelson's greatness; he planned to do it next morning. Even meeting a captain for the first time – for several of those in the van division were comparative strangers – he could, with the curious vivacity that his high-pitched, nasal voice emphasized, somehow infuse such men with his own attitude. It was attitude rather than method; the attitude that while even one enemy ship remained afloat or not captured, the job was not done. This was, of course, not an attitude which had been wide-spread in any navy up to that day, as shown by the losses and captures in battles preceding the Nile.

While Nelson dictated, and anxious that Hardy should complete his survey without being captured, he could only speculate how well manned the Danish ships were and hope there were no shoal patches in the King's Deep. He had taken an enormous responsibility upon himself; this was his great gamble.

Elsewhere on Wednesday, 1 April, with Good Friday two days off, diplomats went about their business. One at least had an indication that something had happened in St Petersburg, though never in his wildest dreams thinking how near his speculation was to the truth. Lord Carysfort wrote a private note from Berlin to Lord Grenville on this day saying, of Prussia's attitude,

. . . there is some juggle about the business which has been managed through Lutzow [representing Mecklenberg-Swerin in Berlin] that I am not able to understand; but it should seem either that the communication to the Emperor [the Czar] has been suspended, or that they wait to declare his sentiments till the result of the operations of Sir Hyde Parker's fleet is known.

In London on the same day Count de Wedel Jarlsberg was at his desk in Wimpole Street, abandoning diplomatic channels and writing a letter not to the Foreign Secretary but to the Prime Minister, Addington.

The present critical moment will, I hope, excuse intruding myself on your Excellency's time. Our countries are exposed to serious calamities which both nations regret as contrary to their wishes and also to their dearest interests. Your personal sentiments upon this subject are not doubtful to me; and I trust, Sir, that after eleven years' residence in this country I shall not in vain call on your Excellency's confidence. Under this persuasion I desire a conference at your most convenient hour. . . .

Two days after the conference he wrote again to Addington, sending him a copy of Bernstorff's 'we shall defend ourselves' letter (see page 301) and adding:

Such Sir, is the lamentable situation of Great Britain's old ally and friend; – such are the sentiments of a court who never in the hour of danger will forsake her duty – never sacrifice her honour, dearer than her existence. It was perhaps decreed by Providence that Denmark should be put to such a trial, for to awake the attention of a nation which always did justice to firmness and virtue. But, being in the power of a man to stop the extent of calamities, and to prevent the spilling of innocent blood, I trust to God it may be done! My hopes are fixed, Sir, on your valuable sentiments. Since many years my respect for your person was unbounded; but the conversation which this critical moment has procured me with your Excellency has left an impression on my heart and feelings which always will remain.

Be, Sir, the instrument which God has chosen for the restoration of peace, and posterity will, in future ages, bless your memory.

You will excuse, Sir, the frankness of my style in favour of the confidence you have inspired me. . . .

Count Bernstorff's orders to de Wedel Jarlsberg telling him to close the Embassy had been sent three days earlier and would be received on 9 April. In the meantime the new Czar and Autocrat of All the Russias, Alexander, had been on the throne for a week.

25

THE EVE OF BATTLE

Although the Crown Prince and Bernstorff had made a major strategic mistake in underestimating Britain's reaction to the Northern Confederation and been slow in heeding the warning signs that Britain would act positively and strongly, once the British Fleet appeared off Elsinore the Crown Prince and Olfert Fischer made the best possible use of the extra time provided by Sir Hyde Parker's indecisiveness.

For the defence of the city itself, the guns of Castellet were out of range of the enemy unless they reached the channel to the harbour itself. The Sixtus battery at the northern corner of Gammelholm, however, now mounted forty-four guns (five 24-pounders and thirty-nine 18-pounders) and two mortars. Nineteen of these guns on the north wall covered the entrance to the harbour while the remaining twenty-five on the east wall covered the gun boats and part of Fischer's Defence Line beyond.

Quintus, the next battery a few score yards southward along the city wall, had twenty-six guns, all facing east towards the Defence Line, and five mortars. The nearest Danish gun boats – which stretched in a line in front of the battery – were 1,000 yards away while the range to the nearest of the Defence Line ships was 1,500 yards.

South of Quintus the city walls curve away inland while the shoreline trends south-east. Nearly 2,000 yards from Quintus, in open country beyond the city walls, was a battery up to then referred to simply as the 'Amager Battery', which had been hurriedly refurbished and armed with eight 36-pounders and two mortars. It had been put under the command of Lt Stricker of the Nordenfjelske Regiment, and his appointment to command this battery – the one that fired a few mortar shells at Nelson's division soon after it anchored – was to give the young man's name a place in Denmark's history because, although the guns played only a very small part in the battle, it was subsequently called 'Stricker's Battery'.

The Danes expected the British attack to come from the north, and this had been confirmed by the position in which Sir Hyde had first anchored the Fleet. The assumption was very logical: they assumed, quite correctly, that the British objectives would be the Arsenal and Navy Yard, both of which were inside the city walls at the north end of Amager. The channel leading to the harbour was deep and the Trekroner Fort, apart from being a formidable guardian, also acted as a good leading mark – particularly for the pilots the British would obviously have on board.

The British could be expected to attack as soon as the wind had any north in it. But the city's position was such that bomb vessels and even ships of the line could bombard from the King's Deep. So with the main attack coming from the harbour channel, a secondary attack could be expected from the King's Deep.

The Danish defences were prepared on these two assumptions, and in each case hinged on Trekroner, which was on a shoal south of where the harbour and the King's Deep channels diverged, and the smaller fort of Lynetten.

Trekroner and Lynetten should have been part of a larger line of defences which included two more sea forts, but years of peaceful neutrality had charged the nation a price in preparedness. The original plan submitted to the King in 1784 (illustration number 10) called for three powerful sea forts – Trekroner, Stubben (to the north-west of Trekroner) and Prøvesteen (well to the south, off Stricker's Battery), in addition to Lynetten, which was smaller and old. The plan was approved on 27 October 1784, and work began on Trekroner in 1787. Lynetten meanwhile was falling into disrepair, but some work was done on Prøvesteen.

By the time the British Fleet anchored off the city, Trekroner was the only one anywhere near completed. It was built with an open section forming a small, well-sheltered harbour. All the forts were to have wooden bulwarks. Trekroner's had been built up ten feet above sea level, with thick earthworks behind forming breastworks on which the guns were mounted (see illustration number 11). No proper accommodation had yet been built for the garrison, who were living in tents, but for the 572 men stationed there by 28 March there were fifty-six 24-pounder guns, eight 36-pounders, and a 94-pounder carronade. Three furnaces and plenty of firewood were ready to heat shot. Since a 74-gun ship can, of course, fire only half her guns at one time in a broadside, Trekroner represented a formidable and unsinkable opponent since two thirds of its guns could fire at most targets (see illustration number 10). The only way it could be disabled was for the garrison to be killed or the guns smashed off their carriages, and since it was built in shallow water it could not be attacked from the rear, except by small vessels.

We have seen that the sea defences were in two parts – Steen Bille's division, and Olfert Fischer's Defence Line. Steen Bille's division had the task of guarding approaches to the harbour entrance and his ships were moored the length of the channel. The 74-gun *Elephanten* was the farthest out, just north of Trekroner and at the entrance of the channel. The 64-gun *Mars* was 300 yards nearer the city, with the *Sarpen*, an 18-gun brig, south of her and the brig *Nidelven* beyond and due west of Trekroner. Any British ships which managed to pass between Trekroner on one side and these ships on the other would then be met by Steen Bille's flagship, the 74-gun *Danmark*, the 74-gun *Trekroner* (which was abreast Lynetten) and finally the 40-gun frigate *Iris*, which was at the entrance itself and less than a quarter of a mile from the guns on Castellet and the Sixtus battery.

In planning his Defence Line, Olfert Fischer knew what an ally Copenhagen had in the Middle Ground shoal and had so far made good use of it. But with his ships sent out of the harbour before they were properly manned, he appears to have been too busy preparing them to realize the significance of what the British were now doing.

When he saw them surveying and buoying the Holland Deep one can only conclude, since he made no comment in writing, that he thought it was being done to allow some small ships – probably the bomb ketches and frigates – to pass through and anchor south of the Middle Ground, and that this division would be the one that would make a secondary attack along the King's Deep while the main British force came in from the north. Alternatively, he may have thought this was preparing for the British force to pass into the Baltic to attack the Russians.

He certainly could never have considered that the main, indeed the only, attack would be from that direction: he made no attempt to send out frigates whose captains knew the waters well to drive off the *Amazon* and sink the *Cruizer*, *Lark* and *Fox* when they anchored as markers; nor did he send out boats to cut the buoys adrift in the darkness and attack the surveying parties.

This was the first part of a grave mistake on the eve of the battle and equal only to one that Nelson was himself making and which will be described later. Even when Fischer saw Nelson's division move down and anchor south of the Middle Ground, a clear indication that a dozen sail of the line would be attacking up the King's Deep, the second part of his mistake was that either he did not realize or he ignored the fact that the Middle Ground was still his greatest ally – providing the British could not survey it.

While the King's Deep was to the British a featureless stretch of water, Fischer's own charts showed him there were some bulges in the Middle Ground which might strand some of their ships and keep them out of action. But instead of sending out boatloads of armed seamen and soldiers to destroy any British craft trying to make a survey in the darkness, he did nothing. Perhaps the sight of the rest of Parker's ships – the largest in the Fleet – still at anchor at the other end of the Middle Ground convinced him the main attack would come from the north, and this southward move by the smaller British sail of the line was a feint, or the prelude to a diversionary attack.

But for all that, the defences that Fischer had managed to prepare in the time available were little short of miraculous. All the ships and batteries were moored, some to four anchors and the rest to two. The southern end of his Defence Line, as the chart on page 415 shows, started just north of the Trekroner Fort and stretched almost as far as Stricker's Battery. Last-minute concern that no shore guns covered the southern ships led to Stricker's Battery being hurriedly reinforced with some guns, and two mortars, which were ready by nightfall after Nelson's division anchored and fired a few shells.

Fischer originally had his line slightly staggered, with the heavier ships farthest out in the channel and the smaller a little closer inshore; but when he saw how many ships were likely to oppose him, he ordered the inner ones to move out slightly to form a more continuous line. This was still going on during the night as Nelson drew up his plan of attack and Hardy quietly sounded the channel.

The southernmost Danish ship, heading south and moored with an anchor from each bow and quarter, was the *Prøvesteenen*, not to be confused with the battery. She had been built thirty-four years earlier at Nyholm, on a slipway just inside the Navy Yard and a few hundred yards from the Sixtus Battery. She was now an old three-decker which, cut down to two decks, served as a blockship armed with fifty-eight guns (thirty 36-pounders and twenty-eight 24-pounders). Commanded by Captain L. F. Lassen, she was the best-manned of all the ships, having 529 officers and men on board – 147 more than her 'establishment' of 382 men. She also had a far higher proportion of volunteers and pressed men – nearly all untrained – than the other ships. She carried nine officers, seven 'officials' (*'Betjente'* – paymasters, pursers, clerks etc.), 172 naval warrant and petty officers and seamen, 110 NCOs and soldiers, and 231 volunteers and pressed men. The *Prøvesteenen* was 1,350 yards from the nearest land – which was part of the city wall, one bastion south of Quintus.

There was a difference between Danish and British guns. The Danish 36-pounder shot was 39 lbs 11½ ozs by British measures. (The Danish

24-pounder was 26 lbs 7¾ ozs; the 18-pounder 19 lbs 13¼ ozs; the 12-pounder 13 lbs 3¼ ozs, and the 8-pounder 8 lbs 13¼ ozs.) Whereas the Danes used 36-pounder guns as the main armament of their line of battle ships, the British used the 32-pounder: there was no 36-pounder gun cast for the Royal Navy.

The differences are only noted here. To compare the total weight of a broadside from the 36-pounders of a Danish 74-gun ship and the 32-pounders of a British and claim advantages and disadvantages is an exercise in futility best left to hard-pressed apologists for one side or the other. The reason for this is that most casualties were caused not by the shot but by the wood splinters it threw up. (An 18-pounder shot at thirty yards' range could penetrate nearly four feet of well-seasoned oak planks.)

At the ranges the battle was to be fought, the rate of fire was considerably more important than a few pounds' weight of shot at the sizes involved, 36 pounders and 32 pounders.

The next ship to the north of the *Prøvesteenen* was another blockship, the *Wagrien*, an old two-decker without masts, built in 1773 in the same yard as the *Prøvesteenen*. Captain F. C. Risbrich, with 261 men on board, was a few short of his official complement, but his fifty-two guns were all 24-pounders, which needed fewer men to handle them.

Astern of the *Wagrien* and anchored only by the bow was a curious vessel to find in a line of battle – the *Rendsborg*, 504 tons, 128 feet long on the gun deck and drawing less than seven feet. She had her masts stepped, yards across and sails bent on. Her normal task was carrying cavalry. Captain-Lt Egede[1] had 211 men to fight his twenty-two 24-pounders, and was lucky since among them were more than one hundred trained seamen.

Where these three ships were moored, one astern of the other and as close to the shore as possible, the navigable channel of the King's Deep was at its narrowest – 1,050 yards from the *Prøvesteenen* to shoal water for a line of battle ship on the Middle Ground.

Closer inshore and making a kink in the line, the *Rendsborg*'s sister ship, the *Nyeborg*, was also rigged with masts and sails. Both ships were built in 1786 to the designs of Henrik Gerner at Bodenhoffs Plads, alongside the Arsenal. Both had nearly the same numbers on board; both were to suffer heavily with an almost identical number of casualties. And both were to have their anchor cables cut by enemy shot.

[1] The Danish system of ranks differed slightly from the British. Commander-captain was in effect a senior captain (like Fischer and Steen Bille); captains commanded ships of the line; captain-lieutenants commanded smaller vessels of about 20 guns, as did some first-lieutenants. Below them were second-lieutenants. There were also many reserve lieutenants (*Maaned-sløjtnant*), usually mercantile marine officers, serving in the Battle.

The *Jylland*, farther out and continuing the line of the first three ships, was an old two-decker built at Nyholm in 1760, sold to the Asiatic Company in 1800, and taken back a few weeks before Parker's fleet arrived for use as a blockship. Without masts, her poop removed, she was little more than a hulk; but she was an effective gun platform and carried 54 guns, most of them 24-pounders, with 425 men (54 more than her original establishment).

Astern of her and moored with four anchors was the *Sværdfisken*, an odd sight to British eyes for she was a floating battery. With no masts she was in effect a rectangular box, ninety-two feet long with a beam of twenty-five feet, and drawing only four feet. But with 176 men on board and eighteen 24-pounder guns she was, despite her age (she was built at the Navy Yard in 1764), a formidable opponent since at close range a ship of the line could barely depress her guns enough to fire into her.

Next, and still preserving the line, was the cut-down frigate *Cronborg*. She had no masts stepped, was commanded by Lt J. E. Hauch, and had 192 men to serve her twenty-two 24-pounder guns.

Astern, still in line, the *Hayen* was a considerably more modern version of the *Sværdfisken*, a floating battery built in Copenhagen only eight years earlier, but she had less fire power, mounting only twenty 18-pounders, and was commanded by Lt J. N. Müller.

Inshore of the *Hayen*, making yet another kink, the *Elven* corvette was the newest ship in the Danish Fleet – she had been built in the Navy Yard the previous year, and her commanding officer, Captain-Lt Baron Holsten had just completely changed her armament: instead of the ten 24-pounders for which she was designed, she now carried six 36-pounders: a change in weights which would have had to be authorized by her designer, Frans Hohlenberg.

The *Dannebroge* came next, Fischer's flagship and the tenth ship in his motley Defence Line. Formerly a two-decker built at Nyholm in 1772, she was now a blockship of 60 guns (twenty-four 24-pounders, the same number of 12-pounders, and twelve 8-pounders). Once a fine-looking ship she now seemed, with only a single stump mast, a hulk. The *Dannebroge* was exactly 1500 yards from the Trekroner Fort, which was to the north-west, and was the first of the line with her bow to the north.

Inshore of the *Dannebroge* and broad on her bow was the *Aggershuus*, another cavalry transport and sister ship to the *Rendsborg* and *Nyeborg*: all three were built to the same designs and in the same yard in 1786. She had her masts stepped, yards across and sails bent on.

Farther out in the channel and continuing the line was yet another curious craft, *Floating Battery No. 1*, also known as 'Gerner's Floating Battery', after her designer. She was larger than the *Sværdfisken* and the *Hayen*, being 146 feet long with a forty-one-foot beam. With a draft of three feet three inches, and no masts, she too was little more than a large raft fitted with bulwarks. And as shown earlier by the young doctor's comments (see page 257), she leaked badly. She was armed with twenty-four 24-pounders.

Next in line to her, bow to the south, was the *Sælland*, a two-decker designed by Gerner and, like so many of the ships, built at Nyholm. She was second only in size to the *Prøvesteenen* and mounted 74 guns (thirty 24-pounders, thirty 18-pounders and fourteen 8-pounders). She had a ship's company of 553.

The *Charlotte Amalia* was the next ship, fourteenth in the line and moored bow to the north. Formerly an East Indiaman and built in 1765, she had been converted into a blockship in 1798. She had 241 men on board and mounted twenty-six 24-pounder guns.

The *Søhesten*, a floating battery similar to the *Sværdfisken* and *Hayen*, but drawing even less, two feet seven inches, was fifteenth in the line and mounted twenty 24-pounders. The sixteenth, moored level with Trekroner and only 750 yards away, masking its fire to some extent, was a two-decker, the *Holsteen*. Newly repaired, she mounted 60 guns (twenty-four 24-pounders, the same number of 12-pounders and a dozen 8-pounders) and was a sister ship to Fischer's flagship, having been built at the same yard and at the same time.

The last two ships in Fischer's line were the *Indfødsretten*, which was moored directly in front of the Trekroner Fort, 850 yards away, and the *Hiælperen*, which was almost up to the main channel forming the fairway into Copenhagen harbour.

The 64-gun *Indfødsretten* was another old two-decker fitted out as a blockship without masts. Designed by Gerner and built at Nyholm[1] in 1776, she had 394 men on board. The *Hiælperen* was a frigate, rigged and in good condition. With 269 men on board she had, like the *Elven*, been specially fitted out with an unusual armament for a frigate, although one well-suited to her present role: sixteen 36-pounders (usually carried only by line of battle ships, and even then on their lowest gun deck,

---

[1] None of the ships built at the Nyholm yard was now more than a mile from where she had first been launched; and at that moment two incomplete hulls were still on the slipways. Those in Fischer's and Steen Bille's division built at Nyholm were the *Prøvesteenen*, *Wagrien*, *Jylland*, *Cronborg*, *Dannebroge*, *Sælland*, *Holsteen*, *Indfødsretten*, *Elephanten*, *Danmark*, and *Trekroner*. Built in the Gammelholm yard on the other side of the canal, almost opposite the Børsen, were the *Elven*, *Sværdfisken* and *Iris*. Bodenhoffs Plads, where the *Søhesten*, *Rendsborg*, *Nyeborg* and *Hiælperen* were built, was only a few hundred yards from Nyholm, close to the Arsenal.

because of their great weight), two 12-pounders and four 150-pounder mortars. No doubt her designer, Ernest Stibolt (she was built at Boden-hoffs Plads in 1787), would have been alarmed over her stability, with so much weight high up.

The remaining ships were behind Fischer's Defence Line but had just been transferred to Steen Bille's command: the eleven gun boats, again of an unusual design. The hulls were more like the galleys of the Mediterranean, and the rig being similar to the lateen sail familiar to old Mediterranean hands who would have likened them to xebecs. The gun boats, which also had oars, each mounted two 18-pounder guns firing over the bow and two 12-pounder mortars. They had a large crew for their size and armament – between sixty and seventy – because of course they were needed to man the oars. The 18-pounders were effective since they permitted a head-on attack – allowing them to tackle large ships from ahead or astern, out of the arcs of broadsides – but had a distressing tendency to set fire to their own headsails, which had to be kept doused with water because of the flash from the powder and the burning fragments from the wad. (In the event nine of the eleven gun boats had their jibs destroyed.)

The gun boats, all named after various ports in Denmark and Norway,[1] were anchored in a line parallel with, but inshore of, the Defence Line.

The *Elephanten*, leading Steen Bille's division, was an old two-decker which had recently undergone major repairs to convert her into a blockship. Now without masts, she carried 74 guns. The next ship, the *Mars*, was also a two-decker without masts, mounted 60 guns and had 346 men on board. Next came the *Sarpen* brig, a comparatively new ship built at Tonsberg in 1791 and armed with eighteen 18-pounders. Her complement was eighty-five, one less than her sister ship, the *Nidelven*, which was fourth in the division and built a year later. (Although he gave no explanation, presumably Steen Bille had the two small brigs as the third and fourth in his line because they were almost opposite Trekroner and only 400 yards away, and the Fort's guns could back them up.)

Steen Bille's flagship, the *Danmark*, was fifth in the line and one of the most powerful. Only seven years old, she had been built at Nyholm to the plans of Stibolt, who had also designed the two brigs. Although built as a seventy-four she now mounted only seventy guns. Steen Bille had done well as far as men were concerned: 600 to handle seventy guns, compared with the *Elephanten*'s 364 for seventy-four and the

[1] *Aalborg, Arendel, Christiansund, Flensborg, Langesund, Naskou* (now Nakskov), *Nykøbing, Odense, Staværn, Stege* and *Viborg. (See Appendix II).*

Wagrien's 261 for fifty-two. (However, twenty-eight of them were 36-pounders and, if the main attack was from the north, she and Trekroner might well bear the brunt of the fighting.)

The last two ships were the *Trekroner*, not to be confused with the fort, which was 1,000 yards from where the *Dannebroge* was moored, and the *Iris*. The *Trekroner*, a 74-gun ship, was yet another launched at Nyholm in 1789. The *Iris*, a large and modern frigate built at Gammel-holm, a quarter of a mile from where she was at present anchored, was launched in 1795.[1] These, then, were the ships with which Denmark was to defend herself.

Steen Bille had not positioned his ships very wisely: as the chart on page 415 shows, the first five were all moored in the channel and thus formed a half circle round the Trekroner Fort, which was less than 600 yards away. Not only was there a great risk of firing into each other, but because the *Elephanten* and *Danmark* were anchored in the middle of the Channel, British ships could pass on the landward side of them, using them to mask the Trekroner Fort's fire.

Apart from that it is difficult to understand, since Steen Bille's division had only one task – to protect the actual entrance to the harbour – why his seven ships were moored parallel with the channel along a distance of 2,000 yards, which restricted them to firing at British ships only as they passed, not as they approached.

The navigable channel was about 400 yards wide abreast of Trekroner. Had he moored his ships from abreast of Trekroner westward towards the shore, all seven of his ships would have had all their broadside guns raking any British ships trying to get along the channel; more important, since they would be heading for Steen Bille's ships, the British would have been unable to fire back, and for the whole of the approach would also have been under fire from Trekroner.

Nelson had already shown at the Nile that anchoring ships in line ahead when the enemy could attack along the line meant that no ship could help its next ahead or next astern. It was vital when possible to

---

[1] The *Iris*, later captured in the British attack on Copenhagen in 1807, was kept as a prize. British Admiralty records show major repairs were made at Deptford in 1815 and she was sold for £2,850 on 31 July 1816 – a few months after the end of the war. During repairs in 1809 a note in the Admiralty records says 'Oak timber from Holstein was used in repairs of this ship,' a tribute, it would appear, to her original construction.

The *Danmark*, also taken as a prize in 1807, was added to the Royal Navy as a 74-gun ship. In April 1815 she was sold to a Mr J. Cristall, of Rotherhithe (on the Thames) for £2,400. Mr Cristall was probably a ship breaker as he bought several other ships, including the *Princess Caroline* (74) for £3,130, *Rota* (28) for £3,660 and *Odin* for £3,000, all prizes from the 1807 expedition. The *Elven*, also a prize from 1807 and which took part in the 1801 battle, was commissioned in the Royal Navy under the same name and served until 1814, when she was sold for £660.

anchor them at right angles to the approaching enemy so they had to sail towards massed broadsides.

The shortcoming of the Danish defences against the actual method of attack that Nelson was going to use – and one he had decided on long before passing the Sound – is less of a reflection on the Danes than an example of Nelson's tactical ability. Speculation on how Sir Hyde would have planned an attack is pointless apart from noting that he certainly would not have attacked from the south. Since this leaves only an attack from the north, the Danes can hardly be blamed for preparing against just such an attack.

It was the obvious way; navigationally it was by far the least risky. But Nelson knew instinctively what was not generally recognized at the time, that surprise – by which is meant doing the unexpected – is an almost essential ingredient for victory. This is beyond argument: he did the unexpected as a commodore at Cape St Vincent, and when in complete command at the Nile. He was doing it again here at Copenhagen; he was to do it again at Trafalgar. They were the only fleet actions of any note where he had the opportunity (at St Vincent) or the authority (Copenhagen and Trafalgar). It might be asked how one can surprise an enemy when in sight of him for several days. In fact Nelson was doing just that: there was no time for Fischer to make any counter-move even if he had guessed every detail of his plan. Surprise had thus been achieved.

Fischer's Defence Line was badly conceived, even allowing for haste and the fact he did not know exactly how many ships would be ready to meet the British attack. Whatever his intention, its major defect was that it was badly positioned to defend the city against an attack from the north or the south or both. He was obviously concerned that bomb ketches – of which the British had several – should not anchor in the King's Deep.[1]

Although the southern entrance to it was only 1500 yards wide, as far as the depth of water for a bomb ketch was concerned, and about 2,200 yards abreast the city, he made no attempt to seal off either end by placing ships across the channel to use their full broadsides against an enemy who had to make a head-on approach.

If Fischer expected the main attack from the north, he had moored his Defence Line so that it could deal only with an attack from the south. Only two of the northernmost of his eighteen ships could open fire on a force steering for the harbour channel, and only one of them, the 16-gun *Hiælperen*, could fire effectively.

[1] Experiments made in England in 1797 showed 10-inch mortars in the *Vesuvius* had ranges of from 2,200 to 2,500 yards. A 10-inch shell filled with explosive weighed 91 lb.

Yet if he expected an attack from the south he had, by mooring his ships in a line along one side of the King's Deep, given away much of his strength: he, like Steen Bille, had not seen the lessons to be learned from the Nile: not one of his ships could fire on an approaching enemy until it was within the arc of fire of the broadside guns – almost abreast, in other words. By having his ships along one side of the channel he also revealed where the western edge was (he was lucky the pilots in Nelson's division were too nervous to take advantage of this). And few of his ships could give covering fire to their consorts.

He had two practical alternatives. The first was to moor part of his division right across the northern entrance of the King's Deep and part across the southern, between the Middle Ground and the coast. Whichever way the British came they would then be approaching head-on, unable to use their guns, and under raking fire from massed broadsides. The smaller ships and gunboats could take care of any that might break through. The second was to moor his ships in two close parallel lines right across the King's Deep, east of the Sixtus battery – approximately where he had moored his flagship, the *Dannebroge*. The broadside guns of the line on the north side would cover targets to well beyond the level of Trekroner – as far, in fact, as the northernmost ship in his *actual* Defence Line – while the guns of the south line would reach well beyond where the *Prøvesteenen* was moored.

If one arbitrarily takes the nine southern ships of his actual line and the nine northern, then British ships approaching from the south, pinned in by the Middle Ground to the east and the shore to the west, would have faced 137 guns, and if approaching down the King's Deep from the north, 185.

However, the Defence Line was moored along the coastal side of the channel; it was moored in a similar way to the French squadron in Aboukir Bay, which also relied on shallow water inshore to give it some protection.

In outlining the alternatives available to Fischer it is not being argued they would necessarily have been more effective; the important point is that there *were* alternatives to a system whose defects and weaknesses Nelson had already demonstrated at the Nile. It will always be a matter of conjecture, since neither Fischer nor Bille left any written descriptions of the reason behind their actions, why there is not the slightest hint that the Danish Admiralty had learned anything from the Nile. Yet of all the maritime nations Denmark was the one for whom that battle, a very rare action where a squadron was attacked at anchor, had the greatest tactical significance.

Quite apart from whether the British would attack from the north or

337

from the south, as far as their objective was concerned they had two options. First, they could attempt to destroy the Danish Fleet and, having done that, with the city then at their mercy, force the Government to surrender; or second, they could avoid engaging the Danish Fleet as much as possible and concentrate on bombarding the Arsenal and Dockyard – and, indeed, the whole city. A bombardment was something the people of Copenhagen could imagine only too well – less than six years earlier the great fire in the city which burned down Christiansborg Palace also destroyed nearly a thousand homes, and the blackened ruins had not yet been completely cleared away.

Had the British chosen the second option, it would have been a comparatively simple operation: Nelson could have used his twelve ships to destroy the first two or three at the south end of Fischer's line – the *Prøvesteenen*, *Wagrien* and perhaps the *Rendsborg* – and, with none of the rest of the Danish ships able to get down to him, placed his bomb ketches less than 1,500 yards from the whole Navy Yard and the Arsenal. The only opposition after the destruction of the three Danish ships would come from the Quintus battery, which would not have been able to hold out against the concentrated fire of so many ships, apart from the bomb vessels. Taking 2,500 yards as an effective range for their shells, the bombs could have bombarded every target they wished on the Amager side, as well as reaching as far north as Castellet and, more important, shelling the Trekroner Fort from well outside the range of guns.[1]

The night of 1 April, the eve of Maundy Thursday, was for Copenhagen a night of tension, of men carrying shot and powder to the batteries until they were almost dropping with fatigue, of weary boatmen rowing to the ships and back, ferrying men, powder, shot, provisions and medical supplies. Stretchers (oblong boxes the length of a man's body, with two handles at each end) were being hurriedly prepared; four-wheeled covered wagons drawn by one or three horses were carrying supplies down to the boats at the jetties and would later act as ambulances. Fire engines – metal water tanks on wheels with the pump handles on top worked like see-saws – were being filled and wheeled into position at the Navy Yard and Arsenal.

At the King Frederick's Hospital, between Bredgade and Amalie-

---

[1] It is relevant at this point to mention, in view of the allegations to be made later against Nelson over the flag of truce, that at no time did he (or, for that matter, Parker or the British Government) ever contemplate the deliberate destruction of the capital. He wanted to destroy the Danish Fleet because he knew that was the root, with that gone, the tree could be toppled – or left.

gade,[1] and the maternity hospital next door, Inspector of Hospitals Benz was preparing for the flood of casualties expected within an hour of the sound of gunfire. The bas-relief of the Good Samaritan over the hospital entrance on Bredgade was soon to witness some harrowing sights.

For men like the Crown Prince, Bernstorff, the Defence Commission and Fischer, it was obviously a time of great tension, but they were leaders in possession of all the facts. For a great many Danes, particularly those living in the city, it was a time of great fear, because few families did not have a husband, father or son on board one of the ships or at the batteries now waiting to defend them all against the British.

Since Copenhagen, unlike almost any other, is a city where the sea is metaphorically at everyone's front door, the Crown Prince had to walk only a few yards from his apartments at Amalienborg Palace to stand on the quay and look across the canal to see the ships in Nyholm. His poorest subject in the city need walk only half a mile to stand on the ramparts and see both the Danish and the British ships. Indeed the wives living in Nyboder, the neat rows of homes which housed some of the Danish Navy's sailors, were under the shadow of Castellet, and a walk of less than 500 yards brought them to Toldboden, the Customs House jetty, beside the boom at the harbour entrance and the Sixtus battery opposite.

From the addresses of some of the men who had volunteered or been pressed into service, given earlier (see pages 255–7), it will be seen that there was hardly a street where a family was not affected. The city was, at this time, entirely within the walls.[2]

If one has not visited Copenhagen it is difficult to visualize just how close the forthcoming battle would obviously be. The comparison illustrating the distance between the Crown Prince's apartments and the Danish line would be if one stood in Piccadilly Circus, London, the ships would be anchored in a line beside Big Ben; if in the Forum in Rome, then along the Tiber in front of Castle Sant' Angelo; and if at the Rockefeller Center in New York, then by the Lincoln Statue in Union Square.

Although still very short of trained men, the Defence Commission had been able to send about 5,230 officers and men to the ships. Of these nearly half were trained warrant and petty officers and seamen; 950

---

[1] Now the Museum of Modern Art.

[2] Bounded today by the walls on Amager and then by Vester Voldgade, Nørre Voldgad and Øster Voldgade to Castellet. From Vesterport to Frederiksberg Palace there were fields, with a few scattered houses along Vesterbrogade, a country road. Valdby, Rolighed, Blegdammene and Classens Hange were small hamlets. There was marshland where Tivoli now stands.

were Army NCOs and soldiers; and 1350 were untrained volunteers and pressed men. In other words, a quarter of the men in the ships were, a few days earlier, pursuing their normal work as farm labourers and weavers, butchers and bootmakers, tobacco spinners and flax weavers and tailors.

Without detracting in any way from the enormous problems the Defence Commission faced, it must be noted that at this stage of the war almost any newly-commissioned British warship sailed with at least a quarter of its ship's company made up of untrained volunteers and pressed men. These were ships that within hours of leaving port for the first time could be fighting a winter's gale or any enemy fleet, so the landsmen had to learn quickly.

The plan that Nelson was dictating on board the *Elephant* this night was a fine combination of a knowledge of tactics and of human nature. He knew instinctively what risks he and the enemy could or could not take. When one man combines this instinct with an unhesitating trust in his own judgment and takes full responsibility for success or failure, the result is unique. It was fortunate for Britain in her war against Revolutionary and Napoleonic France that he was British.

Although Sir Hyde Parker was not only his Commander-in-Chief but enormously superior to him on the list of admirals, Nelson had emerged as the leader after only a couple of meetings with Sir Hyde: not by bullying or toadying but because Sir Hyde finally acknowledged it, obviously much against his preconceived notions of Nelson, and dangerously late in the day. The reason was simply that Nelson produced the ideas and plans; reduced apparently complex problems to their bare essentials by his grasp of the strategic and tactical situation; and, perhaps even more clearly than the Admiralty, had seen the need for urgency. It was his prodding from Great Yarmouth that led to St Vincent stirring Parker into sailing; neither St Vincent nor Troubridge had previously hurried the tardy knight, although they reacted quickly enough when Nelson urged haste.

At this point in his career, Nelson was the most famous fighting admiral in the world. His was a name to conjure with, whether among a boisterous crowd of Londoners taking the horses from his carriage for the privilege of pulling it themselves, or Danish officers sent by Colonel Stricker with a letter for Sir Hyde Parker.

In fairness to the Danes it should be borne in mind that Nelson and his captains, like most of the ships and all the men of the Royal Navy, had been at sea in all weather in winter and summer almost continually since the war began eight years earlier. For them their ships were their homes and the sea their province. And Nelson was, to these war-toughened men, a hero because he produced victories.

So night came to Copenhagen and, among the neat rows of sailors' homes in Nyboder, wives and mothers gathered and shared their anxieties. Typical were three adjoining houses in Svanegaden, one of the shortest streets in Nyboder and one of the nearest to Castellet, whose moat was only a few yards away. From number 21, Reinert Adriansen had gone to serve in a ship; at number 22 the family of Jens Andersen Holm waited for his return; from number 23 had gone Jochum Jorgensen. (All three men were to be brought back wounded.) Two streets away in Delphingaden (now Delfingade) Mrs Anne-Pernille Valentin had put her daughter Bodil, who was fifteen, and Peder and Marensara, twins and nine years old, to bed at number 15. Peder was a weakly child, unlike his father, Jens Peder, who was the bosun of the *Jylland*.

A few houses away in the same street, Mrs Bodil Gundersen at number 46 had also put her year-old son Ole and his sister to bed, not sure in which blockship her sailor husband Niels was serving. In Tulipangade (later renamed) the wife of Niels Jorgensen, a gunner, was at number 15; the wife and child of Johan Vigant waited at number 13. Both men were to be wounded. At Hjertensfrydsgade, Jacob Hofman, a gunner's mate, had left his family at number 2; Jørgen Larsen's wife and child waited at number 28, Elephantgade (also renamed later).

The story was repeated all over Copenhagen and examples of the volunteers and conscripts have been given earlier. While Mrs Sophie Lindgreen waited at Lavendelstræde 103 her husband Niels, a journeyman mason, was being hurriedly trained with 231 other volunteers and pressed men on board the *Prøvesteenen*. Within a few hours Mrs Lindgreen and Mrs Carlsen, who lived at Christiansholm, on the corner of Torvegade, on the Amager side of the city and whose husband was now in the *Prøvesteenen*, would be widows. Mrs Anne-Marie Schultz at Storekongensgade 222, would lose her husband Peder in the *Wagrien*, and Mrs Dorothea Wingaard, at Vesterbro 236, would hear her husband Søren had been killed in the *Prøvesteenen*. Not all the men were serving in the ships: a mother now seventy years old waited at Bjornegaden 28, worrying for her son Haagen Jansen Mandahl, the breadwinner of the family and now one of the crew of a boat ferrying supplies to the ships from the dockyard. In a sense the story was repeated all over Denmark, except that only those in or near Copenhagen knew how imminent was the battle.

On board the ships, the captains had few illusions about the forthcoming battle. Captain Friderich Risbrich, commanding the *Wagrien* blockship, had resigned his commission when a lieutenant to serve in the British Navy for five years under such famous admirals as Hood and Rodney. After another four years in merchant ships he had returned to serve in the Danish Navy. He was now forty-six years old and his brother Christian, now in the *Jylland*, had also spent five years in the British Navy.

Lt Peter Carl Lillienskjold, commanding the *Hiælperen* in Fischer's line, was thirty-three and born in Vordingborg, the son of a naval officer. He had been awarded a sword of honour for his behaviour in the West Indies when commanding the schooner *Iresina* when she was attacked by a large British privateer.

Lt Bernhart Middelboe, now commanding the *Søhesten*, had a similar experience when commanding the *Den Aarvaagne* schooner in the West Indies – privateers paid little respect to ships of their own country's navies and none to those of others. Born in Aarhus and the son of a bishop, Middelboe was thirty-two years old.

Commanding the *Mars* in Steen Bille's division, Captain Niels Gyldenfeldt was the son of a colonel and by the time he was twenty had made three voyages to China. Lt Carl Rothe, commanding the *Nyeborg*, fourth in Fischer's line, had at the age of twenty been on a two-year expedition to find a passage to the west by way of Greenland – and one of the other young officers with him was Lt Christian Egede, now commanding the *Rendsborg*. Captain Peter Brown, commanding the *Iris* in Steen Bille's division, had commanded the *Freya* frigate in the West Indies between 1798 and 1799, while Lt Johan Gether, now commanding the *Nidelven* brig, had been his second-in-command.

These few examples show that Fischer's and Steen Bille's captains were men born to the sea; and although Denmark had been neutral for so many years several of them had been in action.

The activities of the *Elven* in the previous few days are typical of the Danish defence preparations. On 16 February orders had been given for Lt Baron Hans Holsten to take command. Thirty-two years old, Holsten had served in the West Indies in the *Wagrien* with Vice-admiral F. C. Kaas whose daughter Holsten had married.

On 20 March he was ordered to take the *Elven* outside the boom next day, and then received further orders to take her out into the Roads, the Crown Prince assuring Holsten he would not be held responsible for any shortages on board as 'he was interrupted while provisioning'.

His position was ninth in Fischer's line, just inshore of the floating battery *Hayen* and Fischer's flagship *Dannebroge*. The log for 1 April – when Nelson's division moved south – gives a brief outline of the *Elven*'s day – '5 a.m. Crew roused. 6.30 Signal to haul round broadside to enemy. 8.30 Transport arrives with bread and firewood. 11.00 Transport left. 3 p.m. Signal to exercise action stations. ... 7.00 Examined draft fore and aft. 9.00 Guard mustered. 11.00 Lt Grodtschilling inspected fire guards.'

The *Hayen*'s story was quite different. Lt Jochum Müller, born in Trondheim, in Norway and who was just past his twenty-sixth birthday, was serving in a frigate when on Monday evening, 30 March, he was given orders to take command of the floating battery *Hayen*, which was at Holmen. He arrived to find an almost empty vessel: she had no guns, powder, shot or provisions on board; no officers and few men. He worked all night with the men he had, getting eighteen 24-pounders and most of the shot and provisions on board.

On Tuesday morning Reserve Lt Lind reported for duty, followed by other officers, two Army officers, twenty private soldiers and one hundred volunteer workmen from Holmen. By noon Müller had the *Hayen*, which was 99 feet long with a beam of 32 feet and a draft of four feet, under way and passing through the boom. He had a Holmen pilot on board but despite or because of that went aground south of Lynetten. This irritated Müller considerably, particularly since the floating battery had such a shallow draft, and with her flat bottom the suction effect made it difficult to get her off the mud. 'After extremely strenuous efforts during the night', he wrote, they managed to get her off next morning, 1 April, just before Nelson's division moved southwards.

Müller recorded that they had no medical staff on board, the Admiralty saying it was not necessary, and they were issued with some linen and two towels to serve as bandages. Müller had the *Hayen* moored in position with four anchors by the afternoon and went on board the flagship *Dannebroge* to report the fact. Müller wrote later that on leaving the flagship a friend of his, Lt Rasmus Wulff, said to him, 'Goodnight, by this time tomorrow I shall be either a captain or an angel.'

Back on board the *Hayen* Müller thought about putting a warp on shore to hold her in case her anchor cables were cut, but decided against it 'because of the danger to morale'.

The food on board the Danish ships was comparable to that eaten by the British sailors and, in the case of fresh meat, much better. The 'Provision Account Book' for the gun boat *Altona*, one of the eleven inshore of the line shows that the food issued for the week 2–8 April was: salt meat – Sunday and Tuesday; fresh meat – Thursday; butter – daily; rice and crushed barley – daily, but double ration on no-meat days; pease – Saturday, Sunday and Tuesday; soft bread – none; smoked pork and bacon – none; hard bread – thrice daily; beer – thrice daily except for Friday, Saturday, Monday and Wednesday, when it was not issued for breakfast; brandy or gin – daily for breakfast; salt – daily for noon meal and supper; vinegar – none.

The intended issue for 2 April was: butter for breakfast; fresh meat for noon meal; rice and crushed barley for supper (to make barley porrage); hard bread and beer for all three meals; gin for breakfast, salt for noon meal and supper; candle to each mess at every meal; firewood to each mess for lunch and evening meal. (The firewood would be handed over to the ship's cook for heating and cooking coppers.)

26
MAUNDY THURSDAY

When Captain Hardy left the *Elephant* in the open boat to start his survey of the King's Deep he was by no means sure that all the British ships were anchored clear of the southern end of the Middle Ground. If any were to the south-east of it, they could easily run up on the southern tip as they headed for the Danish line.

It was completely dark and bitterly cold, the boat's oars were muffled, and Hardy's first task was to find the bearing of the south end. From there he worked along the edge of the shoal, then across the channel and along the inshore side. The soundings surprised him. It is an old rule of thumb that low-lying land means shallow water well offshore (good examples being off East Anglia and the Dutch coast) while high land means deep water close in.

In the King's Deep, the pilots had led Hardy to expect the deep channel to be close to the edge of the Middle Ground, with the water getting shallower the closer he got to the shore. But he found that in fact the nearer he got to the shore – and also to the first ship of the Danish line – the more the opposite was true: the deeper channel was on the inshore side.

The chart on page 310 gives a clue: the current runs mostly northward and the King's Deep has a slight curve bending in towards Trekroner and then out again. The current would tend to scour and deepen the channel on the inshore side.

Gradually Hardy worked the boat up towards the Danish line and as he approached the *Prøvesteenen*, afraid the splash of the lead dropping into the water would be heard by the Danes, used a long pole to get the depths.

Midshipman Millard noted that one of the *Bellona*'s pilots who went with Hardy 'told us that they had pulled so near the enemy's ships as to hear the sentinels conversing, but returned without being discovered'.

After noting all the depths and bearings he could in the time available Hardy returned to the *Elephant* and reported to Nelson. The rest of the

345

pilots were called to listen and the majority of them did not agree with his report, which was that the deep channel ran close to the Danish line. This had to be a supposition based on the soundings up to the *Prøvesteenen*. Riou apparently considered Hardy was right; but most of the pilots claimed the water rapidly became shallower on the shore side of the channel, and that the division should therefore keep over on the Middle Ground side when it went up to attack. Hardy pointed out that the *Prøvesteenen* was moored in more than thirty feet of water, while the channel shoaled on the Middle Ground side, but they would not budge, claiming the deep channel was on the Middle Ground side.

In fact Hardy was correct; in addition, the whole of Nelson's division was not anchored south of the Middle Ground – there being so many ships, each requiring swinging room, that several were south-east of the end of it. And unknown to anyone, since Hardy had not been able to survey that far up, a short spur stuck out from the shoal to the south-west, while farther up there was a small bulge into the main channel.

Parker's division was still anchored several miles north-north-east of the northern end of the Middle Ground, almost abreast the village of Taarbæk and, by an ironic coincidence, in full view of the country homes of Count Bernstorff at Ordrup and the Finance Minister, Count Schimmelmann, at Klampenborg. The city of Copenhagen was in line with the Trekroner Fort, some eight miles to the south-west.

Sir Hyde intended his division should weigh anchor at the same time as Nelson's got under way to begin the attack: this had been agreed between the two admirals. In addition, Sir Hyde had ordered three of his ships, *Defence*, *Ramillies* and *Veteran*, to get under way the moment Nelson sailed 'and menace the northern part of the enemy's line. . . .' These three ships would work their way up independently.

There was one enormous flaw in this plan. Parker's ships were a few yards short of eight miles from the nearest Danish ships – the *Hiælperen* at the end of Fischer's line and the *Elephanten* at the beginning of Steen Bille's, with the Trekroner Fort just beyond. But Nelson's ships had to cover only a mile before meeting the *Prøvesteenen*; Trekroner was less than three miles. Nelson would attack as soon as the wind went south, and from his present anchorage it would take any of his sail of the line little more than ten minutes to get abreast the *Prøvesteenen*, with a fair wind and current.

But what were a fair wind and current for Nelson would be foul for Sir Hyde. The point is best made by seeing the distances over which Parker's three ships had to tack with various winds. With it south-west, and assuming they could sail as close as six points off the wind, they had to cover twenty-three miles to get to Trekroner; if south, eighteen miles. A south-east wind would let them just lay Trekroner without tacking, a distance of eight miles.[1] Since a strong wind would increase the speed of the current sweeping them to leeward, five knots would be the best figure Sir Hyde could work on for the three detached ships, so they would take from two to five hours. His division as a whole would take much longer since it would be tacking by signal from the flagship and having to keep in position.

Obviously Nelson realized all this because his entire plan of battle did not depend on even the distant threat of Parker's presence, let alone the participation of his ships. Equally obviously, Parker did not realize it, otherwise he would have anchored his division close off the north end of the Middle Ground – there were six fathoms right up to it, and he could have been a couple of miles due east of Trekroner, out of the range of its guns, and with the last three of Fischer's ships only a mile and a half away. Much more important, from that position the southerly wind that allowed Nelson to attack would be excellent for Parker, so that even the most unhandy of his ships could get into action. With a south or south-east wind each could sail the distance direct; with it south-west they would have to tack only twice, covering three and a half miles, to get right alongside Trekroner, but would be engaging ships long before that.

However, as far as Nelson was concerned it did not matter what Parker did: by the time the *Defence*, *Ramillies* and *Veteran* could beat up to Trekroner the battle should have been decided one way or another. They might, by rattling the bars in the distance, have a psychological effect on the enemy; but long before they could be within range the Danes would know that Nelson's was the main attack.

When Hardy returned to the *Elephant* to make his report, he had found Nelson still lying in his cot dictating orders, fretful and querulous at the time it was taking because he was sure the wind would go south in a few hours.

From the *Elephant*'s position it was hard to distinguish the precise types of several of the Danish ships as one overlapped another, and because of the acute angle Steen Bille's line made with the Defence Line, some of his ships appeared to form part of it. It seemed that there were twenty Danish ships which Nelson had to attack with his twelve. The problem was to arrange the best permutation, since Danish floating batteries were scattered among the blockships, and Nelson did

[1] These figures assume no north-going current and that the ships tacked when the water shoaled to five fathoms, although in fact they would tack sooner and have farther to sail.

not make the mistake of underestimating their fire power or the difficulty of dealing with them because of their low profile.

Hardy's report did nothing to reassure Nelson: he had already lost
most of what little faith he had in the pilots; the charts he had were
useless for his purpose. But working with Foley and Riou, with Colonel
Stewart listening, Nelson finally drew up his Line of Battle and individual orders for the other ships. Tom Allen brought them hot drinks
from time to time, and Nelson finished dictating by 1.00 a.m., having
interrupted himself with frequent demands to know how stood the wind.

The orders were then given to six clerks, who had been waiting in the
forward cabin with quills, ink, paper, sand boxes to blot the ink, and
knives to keep the quills sharp. Copies of the complete orders were
needed for each of the captains, with supplementary orders for certain
ships. (Since the clerks had only one much-altered copy to work from,
the result was that some of the orders varied slightly in their wording.)

The 'Orders for the Attack' were the most detailed Nelson ever wrote
for any of his three great victories: never before or later was he able to
give such precise instructions. This attack was unique in his experience
because he could see where the major units of the enemy defence were
and knew they could not move. At the Nile he and his Fleet had sailed
along the coast, sighted the French, and attacked almost at once; at
Trafalgar, four years after the present battle, although he guessed how
he would meet the combined Fleets of France and Spain, his orders had
to be in general terms, because the enemy would be under way.

Now, having been in sight of the moored Danish ships for a couple of
days, his orders could be precise. Even so they were brief, telling each
ship her position in the line and her opponent. (Material enclosed in
square brackets are interpolations by the present author intended to
identify ships by name or indicate correct figures which had to be
guesses on Nelson's part.)[1]

Headed 'General Orders H.M.S. *Elephant*, Copenhagen Roads, 2
April, 6 a.m.,' they began:

The arrangement for the attack is as follows but as Vice-Admiral Lord
Nelson cannot with precision mark the situation of the different descriptions
of the Enemy's Floating Batteries and smaller vessels lying between their
two-decked ships and Hulks, the Ships which are to be opposed to the
Floating Batteries will find their stations by observing the stations of the
Ships to be opposed to the two-decked Ships and Hulks:

[1] The wording of the orders is usually taken from *The Despatches and Letters of Lord Nelson*,
published in 1845. The editor, Sir Nicholas Harris Nicolas, unfortunately reprinted the version
given in the *Naval Chronicle*, which is not accurate. The version given here is from Nelson's
Order Book with some additions from a copy in the Cumloden Papers.

LINE OF BATTLE

These ships are to fire in passing on to their stations	*Edgar* *Ardent* *Glatton* *Isis* *Agamemnon*	Are to lead in succession.

The *Edgar* will anchor abreast of No. 5, (a sixty-four gun ship or hulk). [*Jylland*]

The *Ardent* to pass the *Edgar*, and anchor abreast of Nos. 6 and 7. [*Sværdfisken* and *Cronborg*.]

The *Glatton* to pass the *Ardent*, and to anchor abreast of No. 9, (a sixty-four gun Ship Hulk). [The *Dannebroge*, actually tenth in the line but preceded by floating batteries.]

The *Isis* is to anchor abreast of No. 2 (a sixty-four gun Ship Hulk) [*Wagrien*], and the *Agamemnon* to anchor abreast of No. 1 [*Prøvesteenen*].

Bellona *Elephant* *Ganges* *Monarch* *Defiance* *Russell* *Polyphemus*	To take their stations and anchor as prescribed by the following arrangement.

N.B. The enemy's ships are to be understood to be numbered: No. 1 beginning with their first Ship to the southward.

No.	Rate	Supposed number of guns mounted on one side	Station of the line as they are to anchor and engage
1	74 [*Prøvesteenen*]	28	*Agamemnon*. The *Désirée* [frigate, 40] is to follow *Agamemnon* and rake No. 1.
2	64 [*Wagrien*, 52]	26	*Isis*
3	Low floating batteries ship-rigged, rather lay	10	It is hoped the *Désirée*'s fire will not only rake No. 1,
4	within the line [*Rendsborg* and *Nyeborg*, 20]	10	but will also rake these two floating batteries. Captain Rose [*Jamaica*] is to place the gun brigs so as to rake them also, with the *Jamaica*.
5	64 [*Jylland*, 54]	27	*Edgar*
6	Pontoon [*Sværdfisken*, 18]	10	*Ardent*
7	Frigate Hulk [*Cronborg*, 22]	12	
8	Small, no guns visible [*Hayen*, 18]	—	*Glatton*

No.	Rate	Supposed number of guns mounted on one side	Station of the line as they are to anchor and engage
9	64 [*Dannebroge*, 60]	30	
10	Ship gun-boat of 22 guns [*Elven*, 6]	11	
11	Pontoons or floating batteries [*Aggershuus*, 20]	12	*Bellona* and to pay her attention to *Glatton*.
12	Batteries [*Floating Battery No. 1, 24*]	9	
13	74 [*Sælland*]	36	*Elephant*
14	Pontoon [*Charlotte Amalia*, 26]	12	
15	or low floating batteries [*Søhesten*, 18]		*Ganges*
16	64 [*Holsteen*, 60]	30	*Monarch*
17	64 [*Indfødsretten*, 64]	30	*Defiance*
18	64 [*Elephanten*, 74, in Steen Bille's division]	30	*Russell*
19	64 [*Mars*, also in Steen Bille's division]		*Polyphemus*
20	A small float supposed a bomb [probably the *Hiælperen*, 18]		

[The actual order of the Danish line was not quite as Nelson listed it: the correct sequences, using Nelson's numbering, were 8, 10, 9, 11, 12, and then 17, 20, with 18 and 19 in Steen Bille's division. But from certain angles this division could appear as a continuation of Fischer's.]

The six gun brigs Captain Rose is to place with the *Jamaica* to make a raking fire upon No. 1 [*Prøvesteenen*]. The gun brigs, it is presumed, may get far enough inshore of No. 1, to rake Nos. 3 and 4 [*Rendsborg* and *Nyeborg*]; and Captain Rose is to advance with the Ship and Vessels under his orders to the Northward as he may perceive the British fire to cease, where he is first stationed.

Nos. 1, 2, 3 and 4, being subdued, which is expected to happen at an early period, the *Isis* and *Agamemnon* are to cut their cables and immediately make sail and take their station ahead of the *Polyphemus* [attacking the *Mars* in Steen Bille's division], in order to support that part of the line.

One Flat Boat manned and armed, is to remain upon the off side of each Line of Battle Ship.

The remaining Flat bottom Boats, with the Boats for boarding, which will be sent by Admiral Sir Hyde Parker under the command of the First Lieutenant of the *London*, are to keep as near as possible to the *Elephant*, but out of the line of fire, and to be ready to receive the directions of Lord Nelson.

The four Launches, with anchors and cables, which will be sent by Admiral Sir Hyde Parker under the command of a Lieutenant of the *London*, to be as near the *Elephant* as possible, out of the line of fire, ready to receive orders from Vice-Admiral Lord Nelson.

The *Alcmene, Blanche, Arrow, Dart* [and the] *Zephyr* and *Otter* fireships, are to proceed under the orders of Captain Riou, with the *Amazon*, to perform such services as he is directed by the Vice Admiral.

Nelson and Bronté.

The plan was simple and designed to ensure the southern section of the Danish line would be overwhelmed very early on, allowing the British ships to work their way north. It must be remembered Nelson had twelve sail of the line with which to destroy what he thought were twenty enemy ships and were in fact twenty-five, omitting gun boats and brigs.

There were a few separate orders. The captains of the *Sulphur* and the *Hecla*, two of the 10-gun bomb vessels, were 'to get to the northward, to throw shells at the Crown Islands [Trekroner] and vessels within them'.

The other five bombs, *Discovery, Terror, Zebra, Explosion* and *Volcano* were 'to take their stations abreast of the *Elephant* and throw shells at the Arsenal.'

Having seen the Danish and British dispositions, and Nelson's plan of attack, it remains to comment on only one point: why Nelson did not repeat the tactics which had proved so successful at the Nile – doubling on the enemy ships. This entailed two ships attacking one enemy – one on each side. It would have been particularly effective against the Defence Line because the Danes were very short of trained men. If attacked on only one side they need man only half the guns, making the best use of the trained seamen; but if they had to fight both sides their situation would be desperate. The argument for it was similar to the one for the Nile: if there was water deep enough for an enemy ship to be moored, it was fairly certain there would be enough water inshore of her for a British ship to get alongside.

Nelson may have given the Danes too much credit in deciding against this type of attack: they had had – as far as he knew – plenty of time to moor their ships. Had the Danes, knowing what he had done at the Nile, carefully moored them right along the edge of the shoal (even letting the blockships sit on the bottom) so there was not enough water for the British ships? Had they set a trap for him? We do not know why he rejected doubling; we do know the Danes did not set such a trap – there was in fact sufficiently deep water. Apart from the fear of a trap, the most probable explanation is that he had only twelve ships against a line which appeared to comprise twenty ships and floating batteries, and doubling meant engaging only six at a time. With each British ship having to anchor to engage and cutting the cable before going on to attack the next ship, there was obviously a limit to how often this could be done because of the time needed to rouse out new cables and the number of anchors carried.

Nelson's greatest mistake, comparable to Fischer's mistaking the direction of the British attack, was that he completely underestimated the Danish gunnery and the tenacity of the men serving the guns. He also underestimated the fire power of the floating batteries because – as his orders make clear – their guns could not be counted. In addition, although he did not underrate the bravery and seamanship of the Danes, he undoubtedly assumed that more than half a century of peace would have materially reduced the efficiency of their gunnery. Up to now the British Navy firmly believed that one British sailor equalled three French or Spanish and, where Nelson had been concerned, at Cape St Vincent and the Nile a comparison of casualties shows there was little to prove it much of an exaggeration. But, more important, he had miscalculated the very nature of this particular battle for a brave and tenacious seafaring people like the Danes.

This battle was different because the Danes were not in a fleet of ships on some remote ocean, where victory or defeat would be counted *only* in terms of ships lost or captured. Instead, they were in a fleet of ships anchored a few hundred yards from their very capital; many would be fighting within sight and sound of their homes and families. If their ships sank under them they would and could swim to the shore and be taken out by boats to other ships; and when there were no more ships they would man the shore batteries. They were as desperate as men can only be when fighting for the direct safety of their families and homes. Victory would save them; defeat might destroy them completely. This, and this alone, can turn peaceful mercers, masons, wainwrights or farm labourers into fighters overnight.

In the twentieth century, Hitler did not realize this: in Britain every night for many long and lonely months after Dunkirk, farmers and schoolboys patrolled fields and towns armed only with their own shotguns and cartridges awaiting a German invasion. Unbeknown to them the man who by his leadership – with the armouries empty he had little else to offer – was responsible for what was to be known as Britain's 'finest hour', had a slogan ready if the invasion began – 'You can always take one with you'. Unfortunately the succession of nondescript premiers in the subsequent period of peace has dulled, though probably not destroyed, that hidden strength the people of Britain then showed.

It was an apt slogan for Britain for the year and a half between

Dunkirk and Pearl Harbor; it would have been an apt one for Denmark, and particularly Copenhagen, during the Easter of 1801. And because Nelson, who was the first to recognize bravery where other men might see only bravado, did not take sufficiently into account this transfusion of desperation into men normally brave, he had to fight the hardest and hottest fleet action of his career.

When the sun rose at 5.30 on Maundy Thursday, 2 April, the six clerks on board the *Elephant* still had not completed their task. Nor had Nelson slept: although he finished dictating at 1.00 a.m., every half an hour or so he had called from his cot to know what the wind was doing, and on being told it was coming fair, repeatedly urged the clerks to hurry.

The perfect wind would be from the south-east.... The acting master of the *Alcmene*, John Custance, described in his log (one of the few to do so) the wind making its fateful change. Noting that at midnight it was 'calm and fine' he continued: '1.30 sprang up a breeze from the SE quarter, veered away 15 fathom of cable. 4 a.m. wind SE – moderate breezes and cloudy weather.' Ironically the master of the *Elephant*, one of the men who spent much of the night keeping the Vice-admiral informed, failed to note the direction in his log: George Andrews merely recorded: 'A.M. fresh breezes and cloudy....'

But when every man in the van division was roused out to the shrilling of bosuns, calls that morning and saw the wind was south-east he knew that the day of the battle had arrived. The preliminary British moves are best described by the signals made. (It is noteworthy that once his ships were in action Nelson made only half a dozen signals.)

The first signals from the *Elephant*, five minutes after sunrise and almost as soon as the colours of the flags could be distinguished, called for lieutenants from the *Isis* and *Ganges*; then Captain Brisbane of the *Cruizer* was called on board the flagship.

There Brisbane was given his instructions for a task similar to the one he had performed before: the *Cruizer* – as the Master noted in the log – was 'to lay on the south end of the Middle [Ground] for the direction of the Fleet'. Brisbane returned on board his ship to find there was not yet wind enough to beat into position, so he had to order her to be warped, the ship's boats carrying out an anchor and cable, dropping it, and when the *Cruizer*'s capstan had pulled her up to it, taking a second anchor farther ahead and repeating the process until the ship had moved 400 yards, where she anchored to act as marker, to be left to starboard by the ships going up to attack.

This was wearying work for men who were already weary: the *Cruizer*'s boats had been out from midnight until 5.00 a.m. with some from the *Ardent* helping the *Blanche*, which began drifting at midnight in the current and had to be towed clear of the Middle Ground by boats and re-anchored.

A considerable amount of work had already been done in the van division before daylight. The *Zephyr* fire ship, for instance, began 'getting the guns and powder out, and sending them on board the *Bellona* and *Ganges*' at 4.00 a.m. With that done the fire ship was 'primed for immediate use'.

On board the *Monarch* hammocks were piped up at 6 o'clock. Midshipman Millard, however, 'having had the middle watch I indulged myself with another nap, from which I was roused by the drum beating to quarters. I bustled on deck, examined the guns under my directions, saw them provided with handspikes, spare breechings, tackles &c., and reported accordingly.' His report was made to the First Lieutenant, John Yelland, who 'had taken care to have the decks swept and everything clean and nice before we went into action.'

Yelland, like most of the officers in the Fleet, 'had dressed himself in full uniform, with his cocked hat set on square, his shirt-frill stiff-starched, and his cravat tied tight under his chin as usual'.

Millard described how, when he and his fellow midshipmen left their berth,

. . . we had to pass all the dreadful preparations of the surgeons. One table was covered with instruments of all shapes and sizes; another, of more than usual strength, was placed in the middle of the cockpit: as I had never seen this produced before, I could not help asking the use of it, and received for answer 'that it was to cut off legs and wings [arms] upon'. One of the surgeon's men, called loblolly boys, was spreading yards and yards of bandages about six inches wide, which he told me was to clap on my back.

Millard noted that people would probably be shocked by the dialogues between the surgeon's mate and the midshipmen as they passed.

'Damn you, doctor,' said one, 'if you don't handle me tenderly, I will never forgive you,' to which the mate answered, 'By George, sir, you had better keep out of my clutches, or depend on it, I will pay you off old scores.' Some such compliments as these were passed with almost everyone.

As soon as the *Monarch* was reported cleared for action the men were ordered to breakfast – a routine carried out in every ship – and, Millard wrote, 'our repast, it may fairly be supposed, under these circumstances, was a slight one'.

Apart from the fact that all the bulkheads – made of light wood, or wooden frames across which canvas was stretched – had been taken down and stowed below or swung up horizontally on hinges so that shot would not smash them into lethal splinters, and the seamen's tables and forms had been stowed below out of the way, the galley fire was always doused when the drum beat to quarters, so there were no hot drinks or hot food. Hammocks had been rolled into long cylinders, tied with the regulation number of turns of line, and stowed in the hammock nettings – racks fitted along the top of the bulwarks and covered with long strips of canvas. There they helped, in battle, to form a barricade against small-arms fire.

By 7 o'clock the ships were hoisting out their flat-bottomed boats and the troops were being inspected by their officers. Lt-colonel William Hutchinson in the *Monarch* had drawn up the orders for his detachment of men of the 49th Regiment:

The troops when about to disembark, shall be drawn up on the quarter-deck, with 60 rounds of powder, canteens and haversacks, one good flint well fixed in each firelock, three others carefully deposited in each pouch. The men are to get into the boats by single files, handing their musquets to a man stationed at the ship's side to receive them. When the soldier is in the boat the firelock is then to be delivered to him, and he is to take his seat as quickly as possible when ordered by the Naval Officer appointed to conduct the boats.
Silence is to be most particularly observed. Arms not to be loaded, as no firing can take place from the boats. When the flat-bottomed boats touch ground those in front are to leap out, all in regular succession (without jostling or confusion) following, and instantly to form in front of the enemy. Load by such divisions as may have landed and formed.

Soon after 7 o'clock the *Elephant* hoisted signal number 213 addressed to all the ships: '*The Captains of the Fleet are to come to the Admiral.*'[1]

Despite a sleepless night and the strain of having the entire responsibility for planning the attack, when the captains came on board the *Elephant* they found Nelson in good spirits. Once again the prospect of battle had wrought a miraculous cure of all his ailments. Each captain was given a copy of the 'Orders for the Attack'. According to one source they were written on cards and at least one captain, Mosse of the *Monarch*, went into action holding the card in his left hand and a speaking trumpet in his right.

Nelson did not make any stirring speech, and certainly no exhortation was needed. Colonel Stewart referred only to the instructions being

---

[1] This signal indicates the difficulty of being precise about times: the *Elephant* logged it as made at 7.15, *Bellona* 7.30, the *Polyphemus* 7.37, the *Glatton* 7.40 (although her captain, William Bligh kept one of the best logs of the battle) and, worst of all, the *Russell* 9 o'clock, an hour after logging the signal to prepare for battle, which was made at 7.45 according to the *Elephant* (the *Glatton* also records it as 7.45 while the *Polyphemus* recorded it as 8 o'clock).

delivered to each captain, but mentions that 'a special command was given to Captain Riou to act as circumstances might require'. Riou had the *Alcmene*, *Blanche*, *Arrow*, *Dart*, *Zephyr* and *Otter* under his command in addition to his own *Amazon*, and the impression he had made on Nelson must have been considerable for him to be given orders of such latitude.

With the plan for the Battle understood, the captains returned to their ships and Nelson saw the masters and pilots of all the ships, who had come on board to receive their instructions and for Nelson to hear their views on the channel up the King's Deep.

Having just said goodbye to a cheerful crowd of his captains, Nelson was appalled to find the pilots gloomy, full of doubt and foreboding. Colonel Stewart wrote:

The pilots, who were, in general, mates of trading vessels from the ports of Scotland and north of England to the Baltic, and several masters of the Navy, were ordered on board the *Elephant*. . . . A most unpleasant degree of hesitation prevailed among them all, when they came to the point about . . . the exact line of deep water in the King's Channel.

Not a moment was to be lost; the wind was fair, and the signal made for action. Lord Nelson urged them to be steady, to be resolute, and to decide.

All this became too much for the master of the *Bellona*, Alexander Briarly, who had served at the Nile as master of the *Audacious*. Stewart wrote that Briarly 'declared himself prepared to lead the Fleet; his example was quickly followed by the rest [and] they repaired on board their respective ships.'

Briarly returned to the *Bellona*, told Sir Thomas Boulden Thompson what had happened and that he would have to transfer to the *Edgar*, and asked to be allowed to have a boat to make some soundings to lay a buoy.

This Briarly modestly recorded in the master's log of the *Bellona* as though referring to someone else: 'Sent the Master to sound inshore and place a buoy by which the fleet were to avoid the south [end of] Middle Grounds. 9.30 The Master returned.' Briarly was then taken over to the *Edgar*. (Southey in his life of Nelson says to the *Agamemnon*, a surprising mistake since Southey's brother Thomas was a lieutenant in the *Bellona*.)

Although Nelson's feelings as he faced the nervous pilots can be imagined, he described them later in a letter to Lord St Vincent, saying that he

. . . experienced in the Sound the misery of having the honour of our country intrusted to pilots, who have no other thought than to keep the ship clear of danger, and their own silly heads clear of shot.

356

At eight in the morning . . . not one pilot would take charge of a ship. Briarly, who was Davidge Gould's Master in the *Audacious*, placed boats for me, and fixed my order, saying, 'My Lord, if you will command each ship to steer with the small red house open with a mill, until such a church is on [i.e. in line with] a wood, the King's Channel will be open.'

Everybody knows what I must have suffered; and if any merit attaches itself to me, it was in combating the dangers of the shallows in defiance of the pilots.[1]

At 8 o'clock the *Elephant* had hoisted signal number 14 – '*Prepare for Battle, and for anchoring, with springs on the anchors, and the end of the sheet cable taken in at the stern port.*' Several ships already had the cables led in the stern port. By taking a spring – another heavy rope – from the bow and securing it to the cable, it meant that when the anchor was let go to hold the ship by the stern, the ship could be turned by hauling on the spring, pulling the bow round and allowing the broadside guns to be aimed further aft. (Otherwise the ships, lying in line with the wind, would have their arcs of fire limited to the amount the gun carriages could be trained – which was only a few degrees because of the narrowness of the gun ports.)

In fact the wind was now blowing right down the length of the Danish line, which if it held meant that as each of Nelson's ships anchored abreast her opponents she would be able to open fire immediately: the guns could be trained one way or the other sufficiently without turning the ship on the spring.

While the flat-bottomed boats were being prepared ready to tow behind each ship, Nelson signalled to Parker annulling the sending of the launches, which had been arranged the day before and included in Nelson's orders written a few hours earlier. Parker was several miles to leeward and no doubt Nelson saw the boats could not reach him in time.

As each man in the division waited for the *Elephant* to hoist the signal to weigh anchor, he was alone with his thoughts. Colonel Stewart, a veteran of many land battles, waited with curiosity for his first sea battle; Alexander Briarly, now in the *Edgar*, knew that once past the *Prøvesteenen* – the limit of Captain Hardy's survey – it was upon his instinctive knowledge of where the deep water channel lay in the King's

---

[1] That eminently fair historian Admiral Mahan comments: 'There is in these words scarcely fair allowance for the men's ignorance.' But he misses the point that they were employed to act as pilots *in just this situation*. No ship of war required a pilot to get from Yarmouth to Copenhagen: it was the narrow channels off the city where pilots were needed and why they were carried. That their nerve failed at the only moment they were really needed, having been prophets of doom since before reaching the Sound, would have resulted in courts martial if they had been serving in the Royal Navy.

Deep that the whole battle depended: he alone could put Nelson's ships of the line helplessly aground. And it would probably be aground on shoals to leeward, with wind and current pushing them on harder. . . . But since he knew that when he volunteered, it is unlikely the responsibility worried him.

Few of the men in the 64-gun *Ardent*, which was to be second in the line, had any illusions that all of them would see this day's sun set. She had fought at Camperdown and the majority of the ship's company were the survivors of those who went into that bitter battle, when at one point she was fighting five Dutch ships at the same time.

Midshipman Millard's ship, the *Monarch*, had also been at Camperdown, losing thirty-six killed and ninety wounded in one of the hardest fights of the ship's thirty-six years. The *Isis*, with only fifty guns, was also put in the line at Camperdown but escaped comparatively lightly. Commanding the *Isis* now was the man who had commanded the *Monmouth* at Camperdown, Captain James Walker. The *Russell* had also been at Camperdown – one of many battles in her thirty-seven years. The *Glatton* had not been at Camperdown, but her present captain, William Bligh, had commanded the *Director* in the battle. Although Bligh lacked humanity, he had enough courage and seamanship for two men.

The drums beating to quarters in each of the sail of the line, punctuated by bosun's mates bellowing 'All hands to quarters' sent scores of men running. Lieutenants went to the decks for which they were responsible (there were usually two per deck, one forward and one aft); midshipmen to the groups of guns they would supervise. The gunners began issuing flintlocks, trigger lines, powderhorns and priming wires to the gun captains who ran back to their guns to fit the locks, snapping them to make sure the flints were giving good sparks. Powder horns – containing fine powder for priming – were hung on hooks overhead; priming wires were tucked into belts.

Powder monkeys – usually ships' boys – ran to the magazine scuttles to collect the cartridges, cylindrical bags of powder which they carried in special boxes, and then went up to squat on the centre line behind the guns they served.

Marine sentries went to the hatches. Their standing orders were that once the ship went into action no one could go up or down the ladders unless he was an officer, midshipman or powder monkey. At the guns the crews assembled and checked over the rammers, wormers and sponges, cast off the lashings securing the guns, and overhauled the tackles.

In the galley the cook had doused the fire; some men with buckets and pumps were wetting all the decks while others were sprinkling sand on them – a double precaution which prevented men slipping and avoided loose grains of gun powder being ignited.

The port lids, covering the gun ports, were triced up and, painted red on the inside, as soon as they hinged open like vertical trap doors, they gave a chequer-board effect to the ship's side. The lieutenants and midshipmen checked each gun to make sure the tompion sealing the barrel at the muzzle was removed; gun captains uncoiled the trigger lines which were exactly the right length so that when pulled to fire the gun the captain would be just beyond the point to which the gun recoiled.

Round the magazine, fire screens – like large blankets – had been unrolled to hang down in heavy curtains and soaked with water to prevent any flash reaching the powder stowed inside. The magazine men were wearing slippers of felt and the whole of the magazine was lined with lead, so that no metal could cause a fatal spark.

Fighting lanterns were hung up in dark places, each guarded by a Marine sentry; fire engines were rigged and the tanks filled with water. Near the tubs of water between the guns for the sponges, other tubs were placed. These, half-filled with water, were smaller and had notches cut round the top edges. Slow matches – in effect slow-burning fuses – were brought to each tub and jammed in the notches, the burning end hanging inside the tubs. If the lock of a gun jammed or the flint failed to make a spark, the slow match could be used to ignite the priming powder and fire the gun.

The weather was cold but the men would soon be hot; many of them tied strips of cloth round their heads to stop perspiration running into their eyes. All were barefooted; all waited until the lieutenants were satisfied every gun was ready. Then came the order on each deck, shouted through speaking trumpets: 'Load!'

A well-trained gun's crew worked like a machine: the powder monkey pulled up the lid of his case and slipped out the bulky cartridge, handing it to the assistant loader. Two paces and it was transferred to the loader who slid it into the barrel of the gun and jumped back out of the way. The sponger, rammer in hand, pushed the cartridge down the bore until it reached the end and gave it a couple of heavy blows to make sure it was all the way home.

By this time the loader was waiting with a shot. For the first round a wad was put between the cartridge and shot; after that none would be used. The loader tipped the shot into the barrel; the sponger gave it a jab with the rammer, then both men rammed it home, and leapt back to stand by the gun, since in most ships there was keen competition to be the first gun ready, and the lieutenants were watching closely.

With all the guns loaded, the lieutenants then ordered: 'Run out!'

Men seized the gun-tackle falls, each in a pre-arranged sequence, and hauled. The gun rumbled out until the carriage thudded against the ship's side, its muzzle poking out clear of the port.

At the order 'Prime!' each gun captain jammed his priming wire into the vent, making sure it penetrated the flannel of the cartridge, then slid a thin tube – a quill packed with powder – into the vent. He shook a small amount of powder from his powder horn into the pan so that it covered the end of the tube. The hammer of the lock was flicked down to cover the pan, and the gun was ready to fire.

Once the ship was in action, each gun would be fired and reloaded as fast as its crew could manage: there would be too much noise for orders; too much smoke everywhere for anyone to see more than a few feet. Wounded men would be pushed to one side; all that mattered would be that powder monkeys were ready with fresh cartridges, and shot – stowed in cup-shaped cavities round hatch coamings, and lodged in garlands (rope rings) on deck – were available.

With all the guns loaded and run out on their decks the lieutenants reported to the first lieutenant who in turn, and usually with a flourish on an occasion such as this, reported to the captain that the ship was ready for action.

27

INTO BATTLE

Officers and midshipmen on board every one of the ships in Nelson's division were watching the *Elephant* as closely as they might an enemy fire ship. Nelson's Blue Ensign was flying at the foremast. With her hull painted yellow she looked distinctive and the broad black line running the length of the ship between the main and lower deck gun ports was now chequered with red squares because the lids of the gun ports were open. Suddenly, as a tight bundle of cloth soared up on a signal halyard, telescopes swung to watch. It reached the block and as the seaman tugged the halyard to release the hitch a flag divided horizontally into blue and white stripes streamed out in the wind.

As midshipmen reported '*Preparative*' to the officers of the watch, more bundles went up on another halyard: number 68. No one had to look up the meaning in the signal book, since they were all anticipating it – '*Weigh, the outer or leeward ships first.*' The order would not be obeyed until the '*Preparative*' was hauled down.[1]

Because the ships were anchored in different positions in relation to the end of the Middle Ground and some were less weatherly than others – particularly the *Ardent, Glatton* and *Isis,* which were to be the second, third and fourth ships in the line – Nelson ordered these three ships to weigh first, and as soon as this was done made the same signal to the rest of the division.

This was followed by '*To make more sail, the leading ships first*'. The first Danish ship was a bare 3,000 yards away: less than fifteen minutes sailing time, even with the light wind that was ruffling a smooth sea, but helped by the current.

The little *Discovery,* which earlier had to carry out her stream anchor ahead to heave clear of the Middle Ground, suddenly found the yellow and black striped *Agamemnon* bearing down on her and hurriedly veered more cable to drop astern with the wind and current and let her pass ahead.

[1] Nelson noted in his journal that 'at half past nine made the signal to weigh and engage the Danish line'. The *Elephant*'s master's log says it was made at 10.

The *Agamemnon* had set double-reefed topsails, and following the *Elephant*'s signal to make more sail Captain Fancourt had just given the order to set topgallants. But from the *Elephant* it was clear to Nelson and Foley that the *Agamemnon* would not pass clear of the south end of the Middle Ground: she was making too much leeway, was being pushed down by the current and, being to the north-eastward of the end of the shoal, obviously could not point high enough.

The *Elephant* promptly hoisted the *Agamemnon*'s pendant and signal number 333 – '*The particular ships pointed out ... are standing towards danger.*'

As the *Agamemnon* moved slowly crabwise, Nelson's feelings must have been mixed because she had a special place in his heart: she was the first ship of the line he ever commanded and, he wrote during that time, 'the finest ship I ever sailed in.'

According to Fancourt they were in the act of setting the topgallants when 'the Admiral made our signal for standing into danger. [As we] found we could not weather the shoal [we] let go the small bower anchor in six fathoms, veered to one third of a cable, clewed up the sails and handed them.' In the process she passed close to the *Volcano* which, like the *Discovery*, promptly veered more cable to keep clear of her.

Fortunately the *Agamemnon* had been towing both the launch and the flat-bottomed boat – a ship going into battle usually hoisted out and towed all her boats to avoid them being damaged by shot – and now they were hauled forward. The anchors and cables were lowered into them and both boats were rowed into deeper water and the anchors let go.

Immediately the Agamemnons began straining at the capstan to haul the ship off the mud and up to the anchors – more than a hundred men straining at the bars of two capstans linked to each other. As the sound of the first Danish guns rumbled across the King's Deep the *Agamemnon* had hauled herself up to the small bower anchor but then, despite all their efforts, Fancourt wrote, 'owing to the strength of the current and hardness of the ground made very little progress'.

This was the kind of emergency which showed Nelson at his best: in a few seconds he had lost one of his twelve sail of the line. This was not so important as the fact that although fifth in the line of battle in the approach, the *Agamemnon* was to anchor alongside and engage the first ship in the Danish line, the 58-gun *Prøvesteenen*.

Captain Murray already had the *Edgar* in position and Alexander Briarly was piloting her into the King's Deep, with the *Ardent, Glatton* and *Isis* manoeuvring to get into her wake. These three were such slow sailers that the yellow-hulled *Edgar* began to draw ahead. Nelson spotted this and, knowing neither Murray nor any other captain in his position would voluntarily slow down in such a situation, made signal number 92 to the *Edgar* – '*Shorten Sail and carry as little as can be carried without breaking the order of the Fleet.*'

With less than a mile for the ships to sail before firing their first broadsides, Nelson had only moments to alter his plan to make up for the loss of the *Agamemnon*: with several ships still backing and filling ready to get into position, any change must not risk causing confusion. And whatever he did could not alter the fact his line would be shorter by one ship, and his plan had allowed twelve to straddle the twenty he planned to attack. . . .

The only piece of good fortune was that the *Agamemnon*'s opponent was the first ship in the Danish line; and although Nelson's solution seems obvious in retrospect, it was arrived at swiftly amid the noise and bustle of the *Elephant* preparing for battle and while he kept a sharp eye on all his ships – whether sail of the line, frigates, brigs or bombs – and those of the enemy; a task comparable to a landscape artist working in the driver's compartment of an express train.

The *Polyphemus* was to be the last in the British line and would pass all the rest – after they had anchored abreast their opponents – to attack the twentieth Danish ship. Nelson decided that instead she should take the *Agamemnon*'s place: in that way no other ship would have to change opponents, and only the twentieth Danish ship would not be attacked.

Yet the Fleet had to be handled as well, and in quick succession the *Elephant* signalled the ships astern to make more sail – to catch up with the *Edgar* – then for them to form the line of battle in close order, each one and a half cables (300 yards) astern of her next ahead.

Then came the sequence of signals which would put the *Polyphemus* in the fifth place in the line, the position left vacant by the *Agamemnon*. Owing to the rudimentary form of signalling used, Nelson could not make a single signal that would make his intention clear.

First the *Elephant* had to hoist number 269 addressed to the *Polyphemus*: '*Take a station astern of the ship whose distinguishing signal will be shown after this signal has been answered.*' (And Nelson could only hope the *Isis* and *Désirée* saw the signals and took heed of the note against this signal in the Signal Book – 'The [other] ships are to act as circumstances may require, to make room for the ship to take up the station pointed out for her'.

As soon as the *Polyphemus* answered, the *Isis*'s pendant was hoisted, and at once Captain Lawford steered the 64-gun *Polyphemus* to get into position ahead of the *Désirée*, which had a black hull with a yellow strake, and in the wake of the *Isis*, whose yellow hull had a black strake along the main deck gun ports.

By now the *Edgar* was almost up to the *Prøvesteenen* and coming under heavy fire, and the rest of the British ships were either in her wake – although some distance astern – or converging on it, like an excited crowd heading for the entrance to a narrow corridor; and the *Amazon* had hoisted Captain Riou's signal for the *Alcmene, Blanche* and the rest of his little squadron to join him.

Once again Midshipman Millard gives the best description of this period.

The *Monarch* being last but two or three in the line, we had a good opportunity of seeing the other ships approach the enemy to commence the action. A more beautiful and solemn spectacle I never witnessed.

The *Edgar* led the van, and on her approach the battery on the island of Amak [Lt Stricker's battery on Amager] and three or four of the southern-most vessels opened their fire upon her.

A man of war under sail is at all times a beautiful object, but at such a time the scene is heightened beyond the powers of description. We saw her pressing on through the enemy's fire and manoeuvring in the midst of it to gain her station; our minds were deeply impressed with awe, and not a word was spoken throughout the ship but by the pilot and helmsman; and their communications being chanted very much in the same manner as the responses in our [Edinburgh] cathedral service, and repeated at intervals, added very much to the solemnity.

The *Edgar* was followed by the *Isis* and *Russell*, accompanied by the *Désirée* frigate. As our line [sailed on] to the northward, more of the enemy's ships opened their fire; and so on down their line till lastly the [Trekroner] batteries got to work, and the action became general along the whole line.

In the *Edgar* Captain Murray had ordered that no guns were to be fired until she was abreast of her opponent. Although it would have helped the ships astern, Murray knew the value of the first broadside: it would be well aimed and the men would be calm. The moment the guns first thundered back in recoil the ship would fill with smoke, and in the excitement and haste all subsequent rounds would almost certainly be fired with less accuracy, and the danger of a gun being accidentally loaded with two charges – which would probably blow it up – was much greater, as the *Bellona* would soon discover.

Murray had picked out his appointed opponent, the 54-gun *Jylland*, fifth in the line, and some 700 yards beyond the *Prøvesteenen*. Her upper tier of guns seemed to be pointing through white hammock cloths hanging down like curtains. From the wind and current the *Edgar* was making about five knots: it would be a little under four minutes after passing the *Prøvesteenen* – and after his ship had also been fired at by the *Wagrien*, *Rendsborg* and *Nyeborg* – before Captain Murray gave the order to cut the anchor away.

Such anchoring needed perfect timing and judgment of distance: cutting too soon, so that a lot of cable had to run out through the stern port to bring the *Edgar* level with the *Jylland*, would waste time: time when the *Edgar* was vulnerable and which the *Jylland* could use to advantage by hauling and veering anchor cables to turn herself and get a couple of broadsides into the *Edgar* before she could fire back. Letting the anchor go too late would be even worse: there was a minimum amount of cable that would ensure the anchor holding, and hauling the ship astern against wind and current to get into a firing position meant using the capstan and would be a long and tedious job. So Murray held his fire and listened to Mr Briarly and to the men forward heaving lead lines and chanting the depths.

On shore the crowds had been gathering since daylight. They represented all walks of Copenhagen life. Johan George Rist, private secretary to Count Schimmelmann, the Minister of Finance, records that he was alarmed by the sound of gunfire. 'I hurried immediately with Count Schimmelmann to the balcony of the West India warehouse building,[1] where already a small number of onlookers had gathered. The crowd grew and grew in number and consisted mainly of workmen for whom there were no jobs.'

A young student, later to become a vicar, was near by at Toldboden, the Custom's House Quay (where today the King of Denmark welcomes distinguished visitors). 'At the Custom's House building all types and classes were represented, all ages and all sexes. And they stood around in great crowds.'

But, as the Battle began, the wind brought the smoke from the guns and burning ships to the shore.

In fact none of the ships out there could properly be seen, [and there was] only the impression of the enemy guns and cannon balls which were skimming across the water towards the Custom's House. All that the crowd could see was smoke and the occasional flashes of the guns. They stood there without a thought of going home for food or water for five or six hours. They all wanted to experience the mood of this unforgivable attack and bloody butchery.

A twelve-year-old boy who was later to become a prominent Copenhagen businessman wrote:

[1] The West India Company warehouse was in Nordre Tolbod, near the Custom's House quay and opposite the mast crane (which still stands).

I went down to Quæsthuusgade [now Kvæsthusgade] where there was an old high crane. [The street opens on to a quay running along the inner harbour, almost opposite the Arsenal and the Dockyard.] As a result of my good practise in climbing I was immediately halfway up the crane, and I could look over the buildings at Nyholm and see most of the battle.

Higher up the crane above me sat an old sailor, and he reported to me because he could better see what was going on, and then I repeated everything down the crane to the masses of people below. He referred among other things to the terrible damage that the floating batteries had done to the enemy.

The Crown Prince with his staff had gone from Amalienborg the few yards to the boom, across the canal to the Dockyard and over to the Quintus battery on the north-east corner of the city walls: from there he had a good view of Fischer's line and Steen Bille's ships, Nelson's division and Parker's; from there he could see what happened when diplomacy failed.

From the *Dannebroge* flew Fischer's broad pendant, while Steen Bille's flew from the *Danmark*. Close beside the Crown Prince was the telegraph tower by which messages could be passed to Cronborg in the north and Hamburgh in the south. Next to it was the flagpole being used to signal to the Fleet, and nearby, incongruous in such a setting, a windmill, with several more in the background to the north and south of the city.

Within the next hour or two the Crown Prince's one failure would become very apparent. He had kept his head and done great work in preparing the nation. Unfortunately he had not delegated authority. He was acting as the Commander-in-Chief of both the Army and Navy; as late as 26 March he had relieved General Baron Gersdorff as Governor of the Castellet and taken command himself – an unnecessary move.

Far worse, there was no one, apart from himself, in command of the naval defences: neither Fischer nor Steen Bille were in over-all command; each led his division, with the Crown Prince on shore as Commander-in-Chief. However, the Crown Prince had no knowledge of naval matters which meant that, for example, if Fischer wanted Steen Bille's division or even one of his ships to come to his assistance, or attack Parker's division, he could give no orders: he could only suggest it to the Crown Prince – sending an officer on shore by boat with a message. The Crown Prince did not have a regular headquarters during the Battle, so finding him to pass messages and receive replies would and did waste valuable time. Nor, and this was more important, had any plans been made to meet some of the more obvious contingencies – for instance, that part of Fischer's line would be overwhelmed while another part remained undamaged.

Because several of the ships were not rigged they could only be towed by boats, but no attempt was made to group the ships that were rigged and could sail at the southern and northern ends of the line so they could reinforce any part of the line by sailing to leeward, depending on the direction of the wind and the British attack.

We have already seen that nearly all Army and Navy orders, even for lowly lieutenants, went out under the Crown Prince's actual signature. He had allowed himself to become involved in the minutiae; a fatal mistake for any commander.

As Midshipman Millard noted, the first Danish guns to fire in the Battle were those in the battery on Amager, commanded by Lt Stricker. But what has become one of the standard Danish accounts of the action also illustrates the lack of detachment in the way some aspects of it have been recorded. The battery had been built to strengthen the southern end, one account says.

From this they threw a few shells between the ships of Nelson as they approached [the previous afternoon to anchor]. And the enemy agrees that if we had continued the Fleet would have suffered greatly, it laying very close and the weather calm, so that it could not withdraw. [This was true, as Colonel Stewart has recorded.] But circumstances hindering [the Danes] from employing this previous night to enlarge the battery it could not, on the following day, perform the hoped-for service with its six 36-pounders and two mortars, being also too far behind the line.

The last seven words contradict all the rest. The Danish charts illustrating the Battle bear out the contradiction: as the sail of the line entered the King's Deep to attack the Danish line, every one of them passed within two thousand yards of the battery, well inside mortar range but at the limit of the effective range of the 36-pounders. So even if a thousand men had spent the night placing a hundred guns there, the battery would have achieved very little, apart from adding to the noise and the clouds of smoke drifting over the city. More mortars might have made a difference, but they were notoriously difficult to use against a moving target. More important, no British ship was hit by a shot or mortar shell from Stricker's battery or, apart from Midshipman Millard's brief reference, even referred to its fire.

While the *Edgar* bore down on the *Prøvesteenen*, with a few ships in her wake, because of the short distance to the Danish line the last of the British ships had to wait some time to get into position for making their approach. To the waiting Danes the *Edgar*, *Ardent*, *Glatton* and *Isis* must have seemed like the first part of a coiled snake unwinding itself to strike.

Soon after Stricker's battery fired the first shots in the battle, the *Edgar* came abreast of the *Prøvesteenen* and Captain Lassen ordered his guns to fire as they bore.

The smoke blew back into the ports, filling the *Prøvesteenen*; but the *Edgar* passed less than four hundred yards away without firing a shot and without receiving any damage that Captain Murray considered worth noting.

Some two hundred yards astern of her came the *Ardent*, her hull also painted yellow with a black strake between the two rows of gun ports, and the *Prøvesteenen*'s guns were reloaded by the time she came abeam. Almost simultaneously both ships fired their full broadsides. In the *Prøvesteenen* several of the upper deck guns were smashed from their carriages, but the effect of the Danish fire on the *Ardent* was not noted. The *Prøvesteenen*'s second-in-command, Lt Michael Bille, reported the damage to Captain Lassen as the *Ardent* passed, following the *Edgar* and going towards the ship in which his brother Søren Bille was also the second-in-command.

The ugly and unwieldy *Glatton* followed, yet another yellow hull with a black strake, and there is little doubt her fire did a great deal of damage to the *Prøvesteenen*: at such close range her massive carronades could do far greater destruction than the 32-pounders carried in the sail of the line.

More important, they could be reloaded very quickly, to fire another broadside into the *Wagrien*. Captain Risbrich, noting the leading British ships were firing fast at the southern ships, wrote: 'Several sail of the line were following and they also gave us everything they could. As they passed us going north we fired back as fast as we could as they came level with us and our guns would bear.' For Risbrich the sight of the British ships approaching and firing at him must have brought back memories of when he had served in the British Navy under Hood and Rodney.

But the *Edgar*, *Ardent* and *Glatton* passed on without anchoring, leaving the *Wagrien* enveloped in smoke. The *Edgar* was the first to come under heavy fire from the *Rendsborg* and then the *Nyeborg*; then she reached her chosen opponent, number five, the 54-gun *Jylland*, commanded by Captain Brandt.

The *Edgar*'s log records baldly: 'Came to anchor in seven fathoms water and opened our fire on the enemy.'

Her first broadside of the battle, fired unhurriedly and well-aimed, did a great deal of damage to the *Jylland*. Captain Brandt had only one regular navy lieutenant; his other five lieutenants were all reserve officers, and he had two Army lieutenants as well. Very soon Reserve Lt

Johansen, commanding several upper deck guns, was killed, leaving Lt Wleugel to carry on encouraging the men, which he did so well that his conduct was later reported to the Crown Prince.

Astern of the *Edgar*, the *Ardent* appeared out of the smoke, 'Ran between the *Edgar* and the Danish batteries and brought up with the stream anchor. Engaged with five of the enemy's floating batteries,' her log noted. Her selected opponents were numbers six and seven, the *Sværdfisken* floating battery and the cut-down *Cronborg* frigate.

The *Ardent*'s first broadside killed Reserve Lt Bohne on board the *Cronborg* and a few minutes later the second-in-command, Lt Søren Bille, was badly wounded and carried down to the cockpit. This left Lt Hauch, who was commanding the *Cronborg*, with only one officer left, Reserve Lt Helt. Hauch and Helt divided the eleven 24-pounders on the engaged side between them.

The *Glatton*, following the *Ardent* until the latter anchored abreast her opponents, fired a broadside from her carronades into each of the Danish ships as she passed. Then, with the *Ardent* anchoring beyond the *Edgar*, Captain Bligh could see his opponent, Fischer's flagship the *Dannebroge*, a broad pendant flying from her stump mast.

'After engaging from the south end of the line we anchored precisely in our station abreast of the Danish Commodore. At 10.26 the action began,' Bligh noted in his log.

Beyond him were the *Bellona*'s intended opponents – the *Elven* and the *Aggershuus*, lying further inshore, and *Floating Battery No. 1*. And beyond the *Battery* was the *Sælland*, the most powerful ship in Fischer's line and the opponent Nelson had picked for his own ship.

Meanwhile Captain James Walker had brought the *Isis* into position to attack her chosen opponent, the *Wagrien*, second in the Danish line. On his own initiative, seeing the *Agamemnon* was aground and knowing she was supposed to attack No. 1, Captain Walker decided to deal with the *Prøvesteenen* as well. Since the *Isis* was a 64-gun ship, the *Wagrien* a 52 and the *Prøvesteenen* a 58, this indicated considerable courage on Walker's part because he had almost certainly decided what he was going to do before Nelson completed his signals to the *Polyphemus*.

'At 10,' the *Isis*'s log reports, 'observing the *Agamemnon* had previously anchored, took our station and anchored exactly between the enemy's ships Nos. 1 and 2 . . . and opened our fire.'

The *Polyphemus*, taking the *Agamemnon*'s place, followed the *Isis*. Midshipman Alexander Nairn, who came from Edinburgh, wrote to his brother that:

I was on the quarterdeck and aidecamp [sic: ADC to Captain Lawford] and during the action was in different parts of the ship. There was besides me five other gentlemen [midshipmen], each having one gun to command, and I being the oldest officer amongst them had the first gun. . . .

The only midshipman that was killed on board was a messmate of mine [James Bell] and a particular friend. We had about half an hour before the action been playing the flute together.

I was running along the main deck with some orders to deliver [when] what should I hear but poor Bell was killed. Never did anything affect me so much since I was born, but upon going a little further [I realized it] was no use to lament for him alone as there was [sic] so many who was wounded most cruelly without it ever being probable they would recover.

The *Désirée* followed the *Agamemnon*, under orders to rake the *Prøvesteenen*. Midshipman Millard wrote:

This service was performed by Captain Inman in a masterly style at the instant we were passing; he ran down under his three topsails, came to the wind on the larboard tack about half a cable's length ahead of her, hove all a'back, gave her his broadside, filled and made sail, then tacked and ran down to his station.

(Millard was mistaken on this point: the *Désirée* stayed at the southern end of the line.)

The *Bellona* was the next in the British line. The *Edgar*, *Ardent* and *Isis* were already in action by the time the *Bellona* was under way, such was the short distance involved. With Alexander Briarly on board the *Edgar*, the *Bellona*'s captain, Sir Thomas B. Thompson, had to conn the ship and now try to follow the *Isis*, which was so far ahead and frequently hidden by the drifting smoke that Thompson could not see the exact course she had steered.

By the time the *Bellona* came within range of the *Prøvesteenen*'s guns the *Isis* had just anchored by the stern abreast of the *Wagrien*, and Thompson began passing between her and the Middle Ground, as laid down in his orders. Unknown to anyone in Nelson's ships there was a spur jutting out of the natural curve of the Middle Ground almost abreast of the *Prøvesteenen*: it protruded roughly one hundred yards into the channel and was about seven hundred yards long, with an even smaller spur sticking out a few score yards farther north. A ship coming up from the British anchorage but too close to the Middle Ground would run a mile – to abreast the *Prøvesteenen* and *Wagrien* – before reaching the main spur and until the last moment would be finding at least seven fathoms with the leadline, which was more than enough.

And the *Bellona* did just that: she ran past the *Prøvesteenen* along the edge of the shoal and then touched on the spur. Sir Thomas had been standing up on the fourth quarter deck gun on the larboard side to see the Danish line better. His intended opponents were the tenth, eleventh and twelfth Danish ships, which meant he had to pass in turn the *Isis*, *Edgar*, *Ardent* and *Glatton*, anchoring ahead of Captain Bligh's ship.

Although the first ten ships were already being engaged by the first four British ships there were several gaps through which the *Bellona* would be able to fire broadsides without endangering them; and with the *Prøvesteenen* and *Wagrien* (straddled by the *Isis*) coming abeam Sir Thomas gave the order for the lower deck guns on the larboard side 'to be well pointed and fired'.

Suddenly Thompson realized the Danish ships were no longer drawing astern: the bearings of the *Prøvesteenen* and *Wagrien* remained the same. . . . The *Bellona* was aground. There was no shock or thump: she had slid imperceptibly on to soft sand. The leadsman on the Middle Ground side was now reporting three fathoms – eighteen feet. The *Bellona* drew a little over twenty feet forward.

The *Wagrien* was almost bows on, about eight hundred yards away, in a perfect position for the *Bellona*'s guns to rake her, and from the angle the British ship was lying the *Prøvesteenen* was almost abeam At once the *Bellona*'s guns fired.

The *Bellona*'s grounding was a mortifying experience for Thompson: thirty-five years old, he was one of Nelson's most trusted captains who, for the attack on the Danes, had been given a coveted position in the line: the *Bellona* was Nelson's 'second-ahead'.

From the *Elephant*, which was astern of the *Bellona* but with ships between them, Nelson could see only that the *Bellona* had stopped and was engaging the enemy. It was difficult, with all the smoke, to estimate how far she was along the line. But one thing was clear to Nelson – she was too far away.

At once the *Elephant* hoisted the *Bellona*'s pendant and signal number 16 – '*Engage the enemy more closely.*' Soon after that the same signal was made to the whole division – probably to make sure that the ships still sailing up towards the line did not anchor as far away as the *Bellona*, since the four already anchored were close enough to their Danish opponents.

Before Thompson could do anything – apart from ordering the signal to be acknowledged – he toppled from the gun on which he was standing: a shot had cut off his left leg. As he was carried below to the surgeon waiting amid his pile of instruments in the cockpit, Thompson ordered his First Lieutenant, Delafons, to take command.

Delafons ordered signal number 344, '*The ship has struck on a shoal*', to be hoisted.

The *Russell*, which should have been the last ship in the line, astern of Rear-admiral Graves in the *Defiance*, had obeyed the *Elephant*'s earlier signal to make more sail, and most probably Captain Cuming, sharing the other captains' anxiety to get into action, saw the signal as both an opportunity and an excuse – if anyone later asked questions – for moving up a few places in the line.

Whatever the reason, the *Russell* had been following some distance astern of the *Bellona* but still well ahead of her intended position in the line, and was approaching the *Prøvesteenen* and *Wagrien* as the *Bellona* opened fire on them. The thick, oily smoke from her broadsides drifted across the whole channel ahead of the *Russell*, whose log describes what happened next. Losing sight of the *Bellona*, the *Edgar*, and most of the other ships in the smoke, Captain Cuming and Peter Burn, the Master, then saw a ship's masthead dead ahead and assumed it was the ship they were following and that she must have anchored in her assigned position. The *Russell*'s topsails were hurriedly lowered on the cap – the quickest way for the ship to reduce speed and avoid a collision – but of course the ship continued firing, adding her own quota of smoke.

A few minutes later, she

. . . ceased firing, one of our own ships passing us, and when the smoke cleared away found ourselves in the *Bellona*'s wake and close on board her, both ships being aground.

Made the signal for assistance and got our stream and kedge anchors out . . . to heave the ship off, there being deep water (six and seven fathoms) close to on our larboard side.

Fired guns at the enemy when we thought they could do execution, and at $\frac{1}{2}$ past 11 (there being no chance of getting the ship off without further assistance), commenced action again with every gun that we could get to bear on the enemy without injuring our own ships.

Got our after guns to bear on the two southernmost floating batteries [*Prøvesteenen* and *Wagrien*] and the bow ones on numbers 3, 4 and 5 ahead of the *Isis* [*Rendsborg, Nyeborg* and *Jylland*] so that every one did execution except three on the lower deck and the same number on the main deck, which could not be fired for some time on account of the *Isis* being in the way, although they were afterwards angled so as to do execution. . . .

By the time the *Russell* struck the shoal, her jib-boom almost over the *Bellona*'s taffrail, the *Elephant* was nearly up to her. Nelson now had only nine sail of the line to carry out his plan – but he could see both the *Bellona* and *Russell*, although aground, were fortunately well placed to engage the southern ships.

However there was no ship to tackle the *Bellona*'s appointed opponents (the *Elven, Aggershuus*, and *Floating Battery No. 1*) nor the *Russell*'s (the *Elephanten*). And the *Jamaica* and her gun brigs, which were to stay farther inshore and rake the *Prøvesteenen* and gradually work their way north, were making no progress: although in the middle of the King's Deep the current was running north, closer inshore – where it was much shallower – Captain Rose had unexpectedly run into a south-going eddy current strong enough to stop the gun brigs making much headway in the light wind, and had to signal the fact to Nelson.

A mind less invincible than Nelson's [wrote the *Elephant*'s surgeon, Dr Ferguson] might have been discouraged: though the Battle [proper] had not yet commenced, yet he had approached the enemy; he felt that he could not retreat to wait for reinforcements without compromising the glory of his country.

The signal to bear down was still kept flying. His agitation during these moments was extreme: I shall never forget the impression it made on me. It was not, however, the agitation of indecision, but of ardent, animated patriotism panting for glory, which had appeared within his reach, and was vanishing from his grasp.

Although we now know that both the *Bellona* and the *Russell* had struck on a spur at the western edge of the Middle Ground, there was no certainty for anyone in the *Elephant*: both ships could have hit an isolated shoal in the middle of the Channel. Should the *Elephant* pass inshore of them, on the Danish side – but with the pilots all unanimous that the water shallowed inshore? Or pass on the Middle Ground side, which the pilots swore was where the deep water lay? Whatever the *Elephant* did, she would be followed by the rest of the British ships. . . .

In a decision which saved him from defeat, Nelson ignored the *Elephant*'s master and the pilots, deciding the deep water lay on the inshore side, and ordered Foley to pass the *Bellona* and the *Russell* to starboard. And as the flagship went by, the men in both ships cheered her.

As the *Elephant* came abreast the *Isis*, Nelson could see first the *Ardent* and then the *Glatton* engaging Commodore Fischer's flagship. But between her and the *Sælland*, which Nelson intended to attack, were the *Elven*, *Aggershuus* and *Floating Battery No. 1*, the *Bellona*'s opponents. . . .

There was no time to signal to the ships astern to make further changes, and anyway they might not be seen in the smoke. Nelson promptly decided to use the *Elephant* to fill the gap left by the *Bellona*; he could then hail the rest of his ships coming up astern as they passed the *Elephant* and order them to attack one opponent earlier.

But these were not his only considerations: as he quickly amended his plan for the whole division, he and Foley were still having trouble with the Master, George Andrews, and the pilots on board the *Elephant*. Finally the ship reached the position which should have been occupied by the *Bellona*. Colonel Stewart, watching from the quarter deck, wrote:

Our distance was nearly a cable's length [two hundred yards], and this was the average distance at which the action was fought; its being so great caused the long duration of it.

Lord Nelson was most anxious to get nearer; but [he added] the same error which had put the *Bellona* and *Russell* on the Middle Ground, induced our Master and pilots to dread shoaling their water on the larboard (Danish) shore; they, therefore, when the lead was a quarter less five [twenty-eight feet], refused to approach nearer, and insisted on the anchor being let go.

We afterwards found that had we but approached the enemy's line, we should have deepened our water up to their very side, and closed with them: as it was the *Elephant* engaged in little more than four fathoms [twenty-four feet].

The pilots, in their anxiety to avoid running aground on the landward side of the channel had in fact nearly put the *Elephant* on the Middle Ground. It is hard to understand why the pilots should think that where the *Dannebroge* and *Sælland* were anchored – for they were the same size as the *Elephant* – there was not enough water for the *Elephant*. It is equally hard to understand why Nelson did not overrule them on this point as he had just done on passing the *Russell*.[1]

However, it was caution, not cowardice, that led to the *Elephant* being too far off.

The lead was in many ships confided to the Master alone [Stewart noted] and the contest that arose on board the *Elephant* which of the two officers who attended the heaving of it should stand in the larboard chains [the engaged side] was a noble competition, and greatly pleased the heart of Nelson as he paced the quarter deck.

With the *Elephant* anchored Nelson waited for the next British ship to pass. It proved to be the *Ganges*, in her correct position in the line, and Captain Fremantle wrote to his wife,

We followed the *Elephant*, and I dropt my anchor on the spot Lord Nelson desired me from the gangway of the *Elephant*.
In passing the line, my master [Robert Stewart] was killed and my pilot [Isaac Davis] had his arm shot off, so that I was obliged to carry the ship in myself, and I had full employment on my hands.

The *Ganges* and the *Sælland* were possibly the two most equally matched ships in the battle. Both mounted 74 guns; both had good captains. Captain Frederik Ludwig Harboe was forty-two and born in Hamburgh, the son of a judge. He had been in the Danish Navy since the age of thirteen and had served in the Mediterranean and the West Indies.

[1] The *Dannebroge*, without masts and yards, drew 19 ft. 3 ins. aft and the *Sælland* 20 feet. The British 74s varied between 20 and 25 feet.

Harboe had five naval and two Marine officers on board the *Sælland*. His second-in-command, Lt Philip Schultz, was thirty-eight and had been in the Navy for twenty-three years. Lt Johan Hoppe, the only other regular officer, was to the day a month short of his twenty-eighth birthday, and had been serving since he was twelve. The son of a member of the Supreme Court and born in Copenhagen, he was a very competent young officer. Lt Gabriel Dietrichson, three weeks short of his twenty-fourth birthday, was the son of a major-general and had been serving nine years. The senior Marine officer was Captain Westerholt. Within an hour of the *Ganges* anchoring and opening fire, two of these officers were to distinguish and two to disgrace themselves.

The *Monarch* followed the *Ganges*, and her opponent was to have been the sixteenth ship in the Danish line, the 60-gun *Holsteen*. However, with the *Ganges* ordered by Nelson to attack the *Sælland*, the *Monarch* anchored to attack the *Ganges'* original opponents – the *Søhesten* floating battery and the *Charlotte Amalia* blockship.

There remained only the *Defiance* to get into action. Rear-admiral Graves took his ship through the smoke almost the length of the Danish line until he found the last British ship, the *Monarch*, anchored abreast the *Søhesten* and the *Charlotte Amalia*. The *Defiance*'s intended opponent had been the *Indfødsretten*, seventeenth in the Danish line and anchored with the *Hjælperen* abreast of and 750 yards from the Trekroner Fort, but Nelson hailed Graves to take the *Holsteen*, the sixteenth and previously intended for the *Monarch*. Graves anchored the *Defiance* to cover the *Holsteen* and, because of the outward curve in the Danish line, a little short of abreast the *Indfødsretten*, leaving his ship exposed to the Fort. Almost as he anchored, Trekroner fired its first salvoes.

With all the British sail of the line except the *Agamemnon* anchored (or, in the case of the *Bellona* and *Russell*, aground) and engaging the enemy, the action was now reduced to many individual battles of broadsides.

Several British ships suffered badly because, being outnumbered, they were being raked by enemy ships on their bows and quarters, beyond the arcs of their guns which in any case were fully occupied with their opponents abeam.

Almost at once the floating batteries proved their worth. Low in the water, and a type of vessel the British gunners were unused to aiming at, with no masts or rigging, the Danes found in many case the British shot were passing over them – particularly the carronade shot of the *Glatton*.

In the *Defiance* there was one man who had very little work to do – Rear-admiral Graves's private secretary, Robinson Kittoe, whose hobby was making pencil sketches and painting with water colours. He had already made a good drawing of the whole Fleet passing Cronborg

Castle (see illustration number 16) and as soon as Nelson's division had anchored south of the Middle Ground the previous day he began drawing the skyline of Copenhagen seen from seaward and making notes of the Danish ships for use with other drawings.

Now, while the Battle was being fought round him, he drew plans showing the positions of all the Danish and British ships. These were the only ones known to have been made during the Battle (although Bligh made some subsequently) and, combined with the panoramic water colour drawings he did a few hours later (see illustration number 32), provide the most graphic contemporary descriptions known to exist.[1]

Kittoe's notes on the Danish ships show how strange some of them appeared to British eyes. The *Rendsborg* cavalry transport, for instance, was 'a very low, long vessel, no head and her masts very small and low'. He noted the white hammock clothes through which the *Jylland*'s upper deck guns were pointed, while the *Nyeborg* had a yellow band painted below the line of her guns, which were 'pointed through black canvas bulwarks'. The *Elven* frigate had the ornamentation removed from her stem, and 'the upper bulwark seems to be built up with sand bags', while *Floating Battery No. 1* and the *Sværdfisken* 'have no mast and are more like a chest than a vessel'. Their gunwhales 'do not appear to be man high'. The *Hiælperen* had a yellow band along her hull, close to the waterline. Kittoe noted that the Danish vessels 'were generally painted like our ships are only their sides were dark and dirty'.

Sir Hyde Parker's division was by now engaged in the long, slow beat against wind and current towards the city of Copenhagen. Sir Hyde's journal recorded: 'At noon the van division engaging the batteries, the centre [i.e. Parker's] working up to join them.'

Sir Hyde had in fact signalled the *Ramillies*, *Veteran* and *Defence* at 10.30, '*Make sail after lying by, leading ship first,*' sending them off ahead, as arranged with Nelson, to rattle the bars. The rest of the division had followed ten minutes later.

The next reference in Parker's journal is important because it precedes the hoisting of signal number 39, one of the most controversial signals ever made in the history of naval warfare. It said: 'Moderate breezes and hazy. At 1 p.m. turning up to Copenhagen. . . .'

Parker's division was closing with Copenhagen at less than one knot. The division was, of course, sailing faster than that; but it was tacking

---

[1] Their existence was unknown to historians for nearly one and three quarter centuries. But when the positions in which he shows the ships are compared with the written reports of Danish and British captains and officers, they are shown to be very accurate; certainly considerably more accurate than the demonstrably incorrect charted positions hitherto accepted, all of which show the Middle Ground extending much too far south.

and being set to the north, away from the city, by the foul current.[1]

Captain Riou had taken the *Amazon* and his little squadron, the *Alcmene*, *Blanche*, *Arrow* and *Dart* (the *Zephyr* and *Otter* fire ships being removed and the *Cruizer* added at the last moment) up to the northern end of the line. Going between the *Isis* and the two grounded sail of the line, the *Amazon* led up past the last British ship, the *Defiance*, which was engaging the *Holsteen*, the 64-gun *Indfødsretten* and the *Hiælperen* floating battery. Inshore there were the Trekroner battery and, beyond, Steen Bille's ships.

Riou anchored the *Amazon* by the stern just ahead of the *Defiance* in a position where the ship formed the apex of a triangle of which the *Indfødsretten* and *Hiælperen* were the base and both under 750 yards away. The Trekroner Fort, 1,150 yards away, had a clear field of fire. All the *Elephanten*'s broadside guns could be trained on the British frigate at under 1,250 yards, as could those of the *Mars* at 1,450 yards.

The *Alcmene* frigate, following the *Amazon*, anchored by the stern well forward of the frigate's beam, where she had a clear field of fire. The *Blanche*, 36 guns, then came down in the smoke, having been firing at enemy ships as she passed, and anchored by the stern between the *Amazon* and the *Alcmene* – not, apparently, where Riou wanted her, for he immediately signalled her to 'take up appointed station'.

The *Dart* came next, anchoring by the bow and stern, lying almost diagonally across the end of the Danish line, with Trekroner abeam and the *Elephanten* and the *Mars* beyond. The *Arrow* anchored by the stern, and Captain Brisbane arrived a few minutes later in the *Cruizer*, having had to weigh after acting as the marker at the end of the Middle Ground. 'At noon passed the *Bellona* and *Russell* aground on the Middle under a heavy fire from the enemy,' William Fothergill noted in his log. 'Received a shot through the head of our foremast.'

The *Otter* and the *Zephyr* fire ships could contribute little. George M'Kinley, commanding the *Otter*, wrote in his journal after sending all the powder over to the *Amazon*, 'primed the ship'. She was now ready to fulfil her role as a fire ship by lighting various fuses. As soon as the *Edgar* opened the battle, the *Otter* 'bore up for the Roads; hove-to, sent the ship's company on board the *Dart*, except the Lieutenant [M' Kinley], one midshipman and eight men'. These were all the men needed to sail the ship, and after lighting the fuses and directing the vessel at her target they would hurriedly escape in a boat. In the event,

[1] The speed of approach can be determined almost exactly: the *London*, anchored eight miles from Copenhagen, weighed at 10.30 a.m.; at 3 p.m. Trekroner was, according to Sir Hyde's log, bearing S.W. by W., 3 miles. Trekroner was 1,500 yards from the Castellet, the nearest part of the city, so the city was in fact nearly 4 miles from the *London*. Sir Hyde's division had thus taken 4½ hours to cover about three miles.

of course, the fire ships were not used: in a close action such as this a burning ship, let alone a fire ship, was a menace to both sides. 'Ran down inside of the *Ardent* and *Bellona*, which appeared very much cut up about the rigging, sails &c.; half past 11, anchored a little to the westward of the *Elephant*', M'Kinley added.

The *Zephyr* did much the same: her guns and powder had earlier been sent over to the *Bellona* and *Ganges*, and after weighing – for which she, like the *Otter*, required all her crew – she hove to and sent thirty-five men over to the *Amazon*. James Elsworth, commanding her, noted that after the action became general, the Danish fire was being 'returned by our fleet with two guns for one'. The *Zephyr* anchored to the westward of the *Elephant*.

The frigate *Désirée*, which had so impressed Midshipman Millard by the way she raked the *Prøvesteenen* had not, as he thought, gone on to engage the rest of the line: Captain Inman's orders had been to rake the *Prøvesteenen*. But sailing inshore to fire one broadside, then tacking out and firing the other broadside – zig-zagging across the enemy's bow – decreased the number of broadsides that could be fired, so Inman anchored ahead of the *Prøvesteenen*, hauling the ship round with a spring so that his bow pointed towards the shore with the Danish ship on his starboard beam.

Since the *Désirée* was south of the *Prøvesteenen* and closer inshore she was within range of Lt Stricker's battery, and the Danish gunners, delighted at getting a target – and a stationary one at that – wasted no time in engaging. 'A battery on shore annoying us very much,' the *Désirée*'s log noted. Captain Inman soon found he could also rake the *Wagrien* and kept up a hot fire on her as well.

Captain Rose, in the *Jamaica*, was still trying to lead five of his bomb vessels against the counter current to a position abreast the *Elephant*. (This, a deviation from the original battle plan, was the result of last-minute instructions which the captains of the gun brigs received when on board the *Elephant*.) Some, including the *Jamaica*, failed to get into position but the *Explosion* was one that succeeded, and her log records that she anchored abreast of the *Elephant* 'and opened our fire with the mortars on the enemy. . . .'

The *Discovery* was also successful – 'at 12.10 opened our fire from the mortars in passing the line. . . . At 12.50 Lieutenant Hill lost his right arm and two men wounded. At 1.10 came to on the Admiral's starboard quarter; kept up a constant fire [with the mortars] upon the town and dockyard.'

The *Volcano* did not anchor so far north, but her master, Thomas Brightman, kept an excellent log – one of the best in the division – in which he carefully listed the opening of the battle, continuing '. . . Lord Nelson began to engage the enemy with the signal to engage closer, which was kept flying during the whole of the action. . . .'

By chance, one of the seamen on board the *Volcano* was at this time occupying the attention of his Government and the British Admiralty. Mr Fridag, the Prussian Consul, had 'applied to My Lords Commissioners of the Admiralty,' – as the Board Secretary was to write to Sir Hyde Parker – that Johan Christopher, 'said to be a subject of Prussia', was 'detained on board the *Volcano*,' and that Sir Hyde was 'to report this man's case' and discharge him if he was a Prussian.

Thus all Nelson's ships, except the *Agamemnon*, the *Jamaica* and some of the gun brigs, were in action, even though the *Bellona* and the *Russell* were well out of position, and as the chart on page 415 shows, every ship in Fischer's line and some in Steen Bille's division, were under attack.

The most desperate fighting in the early part of the battle was at the southern end. The 50-gun *Isis* suffered severely from the *Prøvesteenen*'s guns and Colonel Stewart – who was unaware of the damage to the *Prøvesteenen* – noted that the weight of the Danish ship's fire would have destroyed her but for 'the judicious diversion of it' by the *Désirée* and the *Polyphemus*. In fact the *Bellona*'s fire helped, but this came later.

The *Bellona*'s First Lieutenant, having taken over command from the wounded Thompson,

broke off part of the people from the guns to lay the stream anchor out on the larboard bow, which we effected. Manned the capstan and hove; but finding the anchor came home [dragged], held fast and went [back] to the guns. At this time engaging two of the enemy's floating batteries.

The *Prøvesteenen* was suffering badly. Her ensign halyard was shot away twice, and each time replaced. Lt Bille wrote, 'Various carriages had been shot to pieces and half the guns almost shot away when I ordered the crews of the guns on the upper deck to be distributed among the guns on the lower deck so we could keep up a more effective fire for a longer time'. The upper deck was being swept with shot, and almost unknown sailors, volunteers and pressed men were emerging as heroes. Bille describes one soldier named Govel who, with linstock in one hand, wounded in one eye, was looking after four guns, supervising their aim 'and giving fire when they would bear'.

The ship had five surgeons, all of whom were working as fast as men could be brought down to the cockpit, put on the table, and carried away again. Among them were Niels Lindgreen, the journeyman mason of Lavendelstræde 103, Copenhagen, who had left his wife Sophie and children and volunteered for service. Badly wounded, he died later in hospital. Emanuel Carlsen, another volunteer whose pregnant wife and small child waited less than a mile away in their home at Christiansholm, on the corner of Torvegade, was blown over the side into the sea. (Although first reported missing he came back later, having been picked up by a British ship, but died of his wounds.)

Søren Wingaard, the tobacco spinner who volunteered and left his wife Dorothea – also expecting a baby – at their home in Vesterbro 236, was carried below to the surgeon with his right arm shot off; Rasmus Larsen, known by his nickname of '*Nifinger*' (Nine Fingers') was killed outright, and at Assens his thirty-five-year-old widow was left with five children.

Nor was enemy shot the only hazard the *Prøvesteenen*'s crew faced: the ship caught fire and no sooner had men left the guns to douse the flames with fire buckets than a second blaze began. This was put out and was followed by a third, which they also successfully extinguished.

'Eventually,' Captain Lassen wrote, 'we could use only two guns on the lower battery, whereupon we eventually ceased fire as there was nothing else we could do. . . . None of the standing rigging was left. . . .' Danish figures show that of the nine naval officers on board, one had been killed and one wounded; of 172 warrant and petty officers, seventeen were killed and four wounded; of 110 Army NCOs and soldiers, six were dead and nine wounded; of 231 pressed men and volunteers, sixteen had been killed and twenty-one wounded. In all forty had been killed and thirty-five wounded out of a total of 529.

By comparison the *Isis* had the Master, a Marine lieutenant, two midshipmen, an Army lieutenant, twenty-two seamen, four Marines and two soldiers killed, and one lieutenant, three midshipmen, sixty-nine seamen, thirteen Marines and two soldiers wounded: a total of thirty-three killed and eighty-eight wounded (she was under fire from the *Wagrien* as well as the *Prøvesteenen*). The *Désirée* escaped with one officer and three seamen wounded.

The *Polyphemus*, the *Prøvesteenen*'s other opponent, 'came off well by what some of them did,' Midshipman Nairn wrote, 'owing I believe to keeping up a smart fire'. Nairn was sent off in a boat to help the *Bellona*, and when he returned on board late that night 'found all our place in the cockpit was taken up with wounded, and as we expected to be at some of the batteries in the morning we did not get our hammocks down that night and I slept upon the bare deck, and never in my life did I sleep so sound. . . .'

The *Polyphemus*'s log said more prosaically,

The firing continued between us and the enemy [*Prøvesteenen* and *Wagrien*] without intermission until ¾ past 2 when the two hulks ceased fire. Our fire was kept up for ¼ hour longer, [we] not perceiving they had struck until we saw the Danes quitting them in their boats. 10 minutes past three our boats and the *Ramillies*' [sic] boarded and we took possession of the prizes.

Captain Lassen, reporting this, wrote:

When I finished firing the British stopped a little afterwards. I saw two armed boats bearing down upon us, and ready to board. As I could not prevent them from doing this I ordered that those [of my ship's company] who could, were permitted to leave in our boats to avoid being taken prisoner. Lieutenant Rafen left the ship with some of the crew in a small boat [on the starboard side] as the British boarded us on the larboard side.

Lt Bille's report said that a British officer, Lt Grover, came on board 'and gave a receipt for eighty-six prisoners'.

The *Wagrien* had fought no less bravely than the *Prøvesteenen* and had suffered as much. The battle had begun in earnest for the *Wagrien* when, according to an account written from Captain Risbrich's journal,

As the smoke cleared up a little we saw that a line of battle ship with sails set had anchored by the stern alongside the *Wagrien*, so near that its bow was nearly touching our anchor buoy, and another sail of the line a little further away lay right across our bow. The nearest was the *Isis* with 64 guns [actually 50] and the other was the *Bellona*. The latter was aground on the Middle Ground, but not incapacitated, with an anchor out, and she fired full broadsides at us.

The *Wagrien* was at this time firing with all her strength, the officers and men working with courage and a great sense of duty. They defended themselves well against a stronger enemy who continued a heavy fire with double-shotted guns.

[Although] I realized that against this great opponent [presumably both ships] that I had no other choice than to try to find a way of destroying their guns to stop them firing, I did not allow my crew to fire double-shotted broadsides because I did not want them to weaken their guns.

Risbrich was wise in doing this, as will be seen from the experiences of the *Bellona*. Loading a gun with two shot put an enormous strain on the barrel, which should be more than strong enough to stand it – providing the gunfounder had cast it properly, with no tiny air bubbles that, when the metal cooled, left a section here and there like a honeycomb (which it was difficult to detect), and providing the gun was not old and damaged by years of rust pitting the bore.

About midday, when the *Rendsborg*, which was in position north of the *Wagrien* and was badly prepared, and had her holds full of water, drove inshore, the British ship which had been engaging her [the *Edgar*] hauled in on her spring and gave the *Wagrien* her whole larboard broadside, to which we were unable to reply, so we continued to give our attention to the ships alongside us.

The frigate *Désirée* with 44 guns had anchored right between the *Prøvesteenen* and *Wagrien* [in a position to rake both ships from ahead] and her fire dismounted two of our guns. Some smaller ships and gunboats at 1 p.m. had taken position on the south flank in such a way they could fire at us [Brisbane's brigs trying to pass on their way northwards].

At this time I believe I felt the enemy was firing at us with incendiary shot. The way fires started made me think this. I gave the gunner orders to use the fire grenades we had brought with us. I myself laid [aimed] the lower battery gun from which it was fired.

Some time afterwards I observed that this had worked and I saw a fantastic amount of smoke from the *Isis* which very soon dispersed. The guns continued to fire heavily from the enemy's line.

The *Isis* had not in fact been using incendiary shot (carcasses); and from the frequency with which Danish ships were catching fire in the battle – they will be detailed later – it seems likely that the strict anti-fire drill observed in British ships was not being carried out in the Danish ships – which, with so many untrained men on board, would hardly be surprising.

In this position, completely surrounded by the enemy, we continued to defend ourselves until 2.30, by which time further defence was hopeless. All but three of our guns lay around, completely broken and unusable. The ship's side was riddled, nearly half the crew were dead or wounded, and those left so exhausted they could not speak.

[I then saw] some armed boats coming from the enemy ships and I feared they would board us because we had no means of stopping them. I made up my mind to leave the ship with as many of the officers and crew as the boats could carry to avoid them being taken prisoner, which was otherwise unavoidable.

I allowed the gun captains to dismount the remaining guns on the upper deck, and gave permission for the surgeon to remain on board to look after the wounded, as best his equipment would allow him.

The *Wagrien* was fitted out so hurriedly, amid shortages of equipment, that only her larboard side guns had been mounted. The starboard guns (which would face inshore) were on board but she had to leave the harbour before the carriages for them arrived. Risbrich could do nothing about them, but

I had all the cartridges thrown over the side so that the enemy could not use them. When I had done everything within my power I left in the jolly boat and Lt Henne [the second-in-command] in the launch, taking as many of the crew as they could hold.

The British continued to fire at the ships [*Wagrien* and *Prøvesteenen*] as we rowed for the shore. When I left the ship the ensign and [my] pendant were shot away and the *Wagrien* had, towards the end of the battle, been without flags.

Fortunately both boats arrived safely at Quintus. I had the boats hauled up on the shore and went to report to the Crown Prince. I found him at Castelboden where he received me and I reported my actions and experiences during the attack.

Out of a ship's company of 261 men, the *Wagrien* had lost twenty-one killed, thirty-five wounded, and seven more died of wounds: a total of sixty-three. Among those wounded was the French-born Pierre Felgin, the umbrella-seller of Løngangstræde 271 and Johan Capracanniche of Larsleistræde 255, an eighteen-year-old apprentice in a flax factory owned by Alexander Watt. Among the killed was a regular sailor, Niels Gundersen, whose wife Bodil, their year-old son Ole, and daughter, lived in Nyboder, at Delphingaden 46.

The third ship in Fischer's line, the *Rendsborg* cavalry transport, was one of the four ships under fire from the *Edgar*. Her captain, Christian Egede, son of a bishop, had his ship moored heading to the south.

His report shows that the very first enemy broadside – probably from the *Edgar* – put the *Rendsborg* out of the battle as an effective fighting ship: one shot hit forward and penetrated just below the waterline, so that she began leaking badly; another cut one of the anchor cables so that 'we turned with our stern towards the enemy'. This at once exposed the ship's most vulnerable part, her transom, and she was subsequently raked, receiving 'a great many hits' which caused 'considerable damage'.

Egede had the other cable cut 'in order to be able to turn broadside to the enemy again' and then by setting a jib and staysail managed to head the ship inshore and run her towards the shallows between the line and the shore. She grounded abreast the *Jylland* and *Sværdfisken*, fifth and sixth in the line, and roughly parallel to them, 'so that I could use the guns'. And use them once again he did: by the time the battle was over, her ten-gun broadside had fired 551 rounds. Fifteen of her crew of 211 had been killed; seven of the forty-three wounded died later.

The *Rendsborg* had several men from Norway on board: among them was Halvor Jensen, a regular sailor from Porsgrund, in the Bragnæs district. He had both arms shot off and was one of the men who died, leaving a widow, Anna-Dorothea, and a three-year-old daughter. Another Norwegian, Søren Christiensen, an able seaman, was killed, leaving a son of seven and a daughter of three and a half to be brought up by his widow, Pernille.

The fourth ship in the Danish line, the *Nyeborg*, a sister ship to the *Rendsborg*, was commanded by Lt Carl Rothe, who had two reserve lieutenants on board and a crew of 221 (including sixty-four volunteers and pressed men, and thirty soldiers). She was under heavy fire from the *Edgar* and occasionally the *Bellona*, and had suffered badly in the early stages from the broadsides of passing ships.

With the *Rendsborg* drifting away so early in the action the *Nyeborg* then received more than her share of the *Edgar*'s attention. Finally, with twenty-three killed and thirty-five wounded – five fatally – a shot cut her cables and she drifted out of the battle, being carried by wind and current across the shallows until she was near the 74-gun *Trekroner*, which sent a long boat full of men to help her.

The *Bellona* by this time had been very badly damaged, mostly by the bursting of her own guns. Firing at the *Rendsborg* and *Nyeborg* ahead and beyond the *Isis* with her forward guns, and the *Wagrien* and *Prøvesteenen* astern of the *Isis* with her after guns, she often had to cease firing in the early stages while other British ships passed to reach their assigned positions.

While Sir Thomas Thompson lay in his cabin, in great pain from the stump of his leg, helpless while his ship was not only aground but in action, and convinced, as he wrote later, that he was 'now totally disabled and my career is run through, only at the age of thirty-five', his First Lieutenant kept the *Bellona*'s guns firing.

Suddenly there was a tremendous explosion at the forward end of the lower deck which blasted upwards, tearing a hole in the main deck, ripping away a section of the gangway and breaking one of the massive beams. Smoke poured out of the hole and filled the entire lower deck. From the midst of it came the agonized screams of badly wounded men.

Slowly the smoke cleared to reveal that the fourth 32-pounder gun on the larboard side had burst. Several men lay dead and many more wounded, among them Lt Thomas Southey (whose brother Robert was later to write a popular life of Nelson), Lt Thomas Wilks, and two midshipmen – the young Scotsman William Anderson, and Edward Daubeny. Anderson was temporarily blinded and had to walk with crutches for three months because a piece of the exploding gun hit his left knee. Daubeny, the parson's son from Stratton, in Gloucestershire, was burned and hit on the cheek by a splinter 'which had swelled it a great deal', Sir Thomas later wrote to the Rev James Daubeny, 'but from which no serious apprehensions were, in the smallest degree, entertained'.

The force of the explosion going upwards had saved the third and fifth of the lower deck guns from damage but had smashed the carriages of guns on the main deck above and flung the guns across the ship. There were no survivors from the 32-pounder's crew to reveal what had happened, but most probably in the excitement, with smoke cutting down visibility, the gun had either been accidentally loaded with two charges of powder or, if being fired double-shotted, a third shot had been rammed home by mistake.

The wounded were carried below to the cockpit, the dead dragged away, and the ship was back in action. An hour later another terrible explosion almost amidships tore away a good deal more of the main deck and flung three 24-pounders into the air as if they were toys. Again the smoke cleared to reveal that another 32-pounder had blown up, this time the fourteenth gun, and many more men had been killed or wounded. The big launch, which had been towing astern until the *Bellona* grounded and now lay almost alongside, began slowly filling with water – a piece of an exploding gun had landed in it and sprung some planks. These two guns exploding accounted for most of the *Bellona's* eighty-three killed and wounded.

The *Russell*, aground just astern of the *Bellona*, had continued firing at the *Prøvesteenen* and the *Wagrien* with her after guns, and at the *Rendsborg*, *Nyeborg* and *Jylland* with the forward ones, until the *Rendsborg* drifted out of the battle, when they concentrated on the *Nyeborg* and the *Jylland*. Finally, when the *Nyeborg* followed the *Rendsborg*, all the forward guns concentrated on the *Jylland*.

But no one on board the *Russell* had any illusions about the way the Danes were fighting. 'At 1.20 observed one of the ships that we were engaged with to have her colours and mast shot away,' Mr Peter Burn, the Master noted, 'but still firing.' Some of the shot smashed into the *Russell's* hull, others tore sails and cut rigging, and by the time the *Prøvesteenen* and the *Wagrien* gave up the fight the *Russell* had five seamen and a Marine wounded.

Farther along the line the *Edgar* and the *Jylland* were fighting a fierce and bitter battle. When the First Lieutenant, Edmund Johnson, was killed, Lt Joshua Johnson (no relation) took his place, helping Captain Murray until his left arm was shot off. ('He refused the idea of being sent to England,' Nelson later wrote to Lord St Vincent, 'and hoped Captain Murray would be content by a First Lieutenant's duty being done by a one-armed officer.')

The midshipmen were unlucky: five of them – including the son of Captain Domett, Sir Hyde's Captain of the Fleet – were wounded. Descriptions of the *Edgar's* role are meagre, the First Lieutenant's journal and the Master's logs being among the briefest of all the ships. The Master, George Morrison, recorded:

Our mizen sails suffered much. . . . Found two of our lower deck guns rendered useless. . . . Our running rigging shot to pieces, the masts and spars very much wounded, the sails shot through in various places and rendered unserviceable, but repairable with many yards of canvas. . . .

Lt Molyneux Shuldham, the Third Lieutenant, contented himself with copying Morrison's log as his journal entry for the day. Neither indicated the *Edgar*'s casualties – 31 killed and 111 wounded, about a fifth of the ship's company, and a fifth of the entire British casualties in the Battle.

The man who would soon be reading the burial service over so many dead was the Reverend John Rundall. Two years earlier, at the age of forty-five, he had quit his vicarage at Crediton, in Devon, leaving a curate to look after his flock, to serve as a chaplain in the Navy for seven years. (His next great battle was to be Trafalgar, a year after which he returned to the quiet of Crediton.)

On board the *Jylland* the losses were less severe, she being only one of the ships the *Edgar* had been engaging and, because the *Edgar* had been the first to anchor, the following British ships had been unable to fire into the Danish 54-gun blockship as they passed.

Captain Erich Brandt, who had just celebrated his forty-fifth birthday, was the son of a landowner at Sandvær, and he must have viewed the *Jylland* with mixed feelings: she was ugly, even when compared with the other blockships, with no poop and no masts.

Brandt's one regular navy lieutenant was Peter Wleugel, the son of an admiral and one of the Navy's finest young navigators. Among the reserve lieutenants was Christian Risbrich, a forty-six-year-old bachelor whose brother was commanding the *Wagrien*. Serving in one of the Danish East India Company ships, he was by chance in Copenhagen when the present emergency began.

Brandt had put Wleugel in charge of the upper deck guns, and Risbrich commanded those on the lower deck. His written report to the Crown Prince praised both for the way they encouraged the men at the guns, as well as Lt Johansen who spent more than an hour spurring on the men before he was killed.

When a British shot cut away the ship's ensign, the Bosun, Jens Peter Valentin, found another, bent it on to a halyard and hoisted it. A moment later he was killed by a shot. His home was in Nyboder and his wife Anne-Pernille had three children.

Peter Lindquist was a seaman and captain of a gun on the upper deck which was destroyed. He immediately took over another gun whose captain had been killed. Finally that gun was destroyed and Lindquist took over a third which he kept firing until the ship surrendered. His bravery was later reported to the Crown Prince.

The casualty list was the usual story of private tragedies: among the killed was Jacop Halberg, the nineteen-year-old tailor from Asminderød, near Fredensborg, the youngest of five sons and intended to be his father's 'help and support' in his old age.

Peder Larsen was twenty-two, a regular seaman from Yderby, the long peninsula sticking out from the north-west corner of Sælland, had his right hand crushed and lost two fingers. (His pension was to be two dollars a month.) Friderich Bøhn, of Præstø, who was killed, left a wife and three children, one of whom was paralysed, and the youngest only a year old.

The *Jylland* fought on until, almost shot to pieces, she stopped firing with twenty-eight killed and forty-three wounded (seven fatally). She had suffered the fifth highest casualties – but there was little difference between the third highest (the *Prøvesteenen* with seventy-five) and the tenth (the *Rendsborg* with fifty).

The next group of Danish ships were being engaged by the *Ardent* and, ahead of her, the *Glatton*. There was an overlapping because some of the *Ardent*'s forward guns could fire at targets almost abreast the *Glatton*, whose main target was Fischer's flagship, the *Dannebroge*.

The group comprised, northward from the *Jylland*, the *Sværdfisken* floating battery, the *Cronborg* blockship, the *Hayen* floating battery with the *Elven* frigate almost abreast of her but farther inshore, then the *Dannebroge*. The *Ardent*'s opponents were the sixth and seventh in the line (the *Sværdfisken* and the *Cronborg*) and she had anchored abreast the *Cronborg* so that her after guns could engage them and her forward the *Hayen* and the *Elven*, while a few could be trained far enough round to fire on the *Dannebroge*.

The floating battery *Sværdfisken* was commanded by Lt Søren Sommerfeldt,[1] with a reserve lieutenant as the only other officer. His crew of 176 included seventy-seven pressed men and volunteers, twenty-eight soldiers and sixty-five regular seamen. By the end of the Battle eighteen had been killed and nineteen wounded, four of whom died later.

Among the casualties were Søren Kaas, the journeyman glovemaker from Nakskov, who had been pressed. His father later complained that his son had given '11 or 13 dollars' to the *Sværdfisken*'s surgeon before he died, and that they had never received it. A man who survived but was left in 'a pitiable state', was Jacob Andersen, of Vordingborg, twenty-five years old and a journeyman shoemaker who had volunteered. Andersen was wounded in both legs, and after four months in hospital

---

[1] Born at Randers, in Jutland, the son of a vicar, and two weeks short of his thirtieth birthday. Unfortunately he was accused, several years later, of taking certain 'perquisites'. When found guilty and his commission cancelled, he committed suicide.

was discharged with a pension of twenty-four marks a year, half what he had claimed.

The *Cronborg*, commanded by Lt Jens Hauch, had more regular seamen than most of the ships – 105 out of the total of 223. Her First Lieutenant was Søren Bille, brother of Michael Bille, of the *Prøvesteenen*; the other two were reserve lieutenants, Helt and Bohne.

The first British broadside, believed to be from the *Glatton*, killed Bohne, who was commanding the forward guns, and Lt Bille took his place. Then the *Ardent* anchored and turned the majority of her guns on the *Cronborg*. Once again there was a straightforward battle of broadsides.

Captain Bertie, commanding the *Ardent* as Danish shot ripped into his ship and seeing his own broadsides pounding the *Cronborg*, might have reflected on the reply he had received from Lord St Vincent a month short of a day earlier – 'I conclude your wish is not to be removed from the *Ardent* until the important and critical service Sir Hyde Parker has been so judiciously called upon to carry into execution is performed. . . .'[1]

The *Ardent* was in action against five of the enemy, and the log of her master, Garde, is about as informative as all the others: 'At noon warmly engaged with the enemy. Our masts, yards and rigging very much wounded. At 30 past 1 one of them struck and in 10 minutes after [sic] 2 more hauled down their colours. At ½ past 2 ceased firing having silenced the enemy. . . .'

The only wonder was that the *Ardent* herself had not been silenced: twenty-nine men and a midshipman had been killed and sixty-four wounded: not as many as at Camperdown (forty killed, ninety-six wounded), but by the time the last gun was fired this Maundy Thursday, the fourth highest among the British ships. Most of the ship's quarterdeck guns had been smashed from their carriages and two-thirds of the guns on the maindeck were useless. (But by the end of the Battle her guns had used 2,464 cartridges and fired 2,693 shot – showing, incidentally, how few times her guns were double-shotted.)

Seventy-eight Danish shot had hit the ship well above the waterline – some going right through the ship and out the starboard side, smashing deck beams, lodging and hanging knees (many of them iron) and deck pillars. Sixteen more shot were low down ' 'twixt wind and water'; at least one had hit below the waterline – as the ship gave a roll to

---

[1] Bertie is credited with having invented the lifebuoy in 1778. Soon after taking command of the *Ardent* he saw that the carriages of the new 42-pounder carronades sloped inboard. He saw if they sloped outboard the carronades would need fewer men to run them out – the weight would be tending to run down a slope – and the recoil would be absorbed better since the guns would then be going up a slope. The Board of Ordnance finally agreed and the idea was adopted in all ships.

Lord Nelson has directions to spare Denmark when no longer resisting but if the firing is continued on the part of Denmark Lord Nelson will be obliged to set on fire all the floating batteries he has taken, without having the power of saving the brave Danes who have defended them. Dated on board his Britannic Majesty's Ship Elephant Copenhagen Roads April 2nd 1801

Nelson & Bronte Vice admiral under the command of admiral Sir Hyde Parker

To the Brothers of Englishmen the Danes.

29 Nelson's letter to the Danish Crown Prince proposing a truce, written in the heat of battle.

30 Although the ship was under fire, Nelson insisted on using this seal, bearing his coat of arms, for the letter offering the Danes a truce.

32 Robinson Kittoe drew this panorama within a few hours of the Truce from
sketches and plans made during the Battle. From the left, A is the *Provesteenen*, with
Stricker's Battery above her on the skyline (he has accidentally omitted the *Polyphemus*,
which was engaging the *Provesteenen*). H represents Olfert Fischer's flagship, the
Dannebroge. The mast crane in the Dockyard is just above K (the *Aggershuus*). The
Saelland's position was at M, while the Danish frigate *Iris* – the nearest to the harbour

31 Captain Thesiger brings Nelson's truce letter to the Crown Prince. This painting, completed a few weeks after the Battle, shows the *Elephant*'s boat at the jetty with a flag of truce in the bow, and Thesiger, handing the letter to one of the Crown Prince's ADCs. The Crown Prince is standing at the centre of the group on the left (in line with the second tree). The sentry box above the group on the left forms part of Castellet. The Trekroner fort is in line with the end of the jetty, with the *Nidelven*, *Sarpen* and *Mars* to the left (the *Elephanten* is hidden by smoke) and the *Danmark*, 74-gun *Trekroner* and the frigate *Iris* to the right. The Lynetten fort can be seen clearly between the *Danmark* and the ship *Trekroner*, and the line of ships under way on the horizon above Lynetton are Sir Hyde Parker's division.

entrance – is above the *Ganges* with the Lynetten Fort to the right and the ship *Trekroner* and Steen Bille's flagship, *Danmark*, between Lynetten and Trekroner Fort. P represents the *Holsten*, Q the *Indfødsretton* and R the *Hiaelperen*. On the right of Trekroner are the *Nidelven* and *Sarpen* drawn in with the blockships *Mars* and *Elephanten* (extreme right, with stump masts).

[Handwritten letter in Nelson's hand — transcribed below in the printed caption]

33 A few days after the Battle, Nelson visited the Naval Academy in Copenhagen,
where the Commandant, Captain Hans Sneedorff showed him round and later
received this letter and the two medals. The letter (spelling Sneedorff's name
wrongly) reads: 'Lord Nelson's compliments to Captain Schneder and begs leave to
present to the academy under his able direction two medals, one struck in commemoration of the Battle of the Nile[,] the other on that of my reconquest of the city
of Naples & of the kingdom[.] I cannot find the discription of the latter medal but
the Rising Sun is meant to mark the return of the proper Government, the *Foudroyant*
my ship bringing the King and the Cardinal meeting over the Punta Madelena. I
send you also a short account of my life it cannot do harm to youth and may do good,
as it will show that Perseverence and good conduct will raise a person to the very
highest honours and rewards. That it may be useful in that way to those entrusted to
your care is the fervent wish of your most obt. Servt. Nelson and Bronte.' Unless
Sneedorff was familiar with Neapolitan politics, the significance of the King's meeting
with Cardinal Ruffo must have been hard to understand.

starboard – and gone through to tear up planking on the orlop deck, the lowest deck of all.

Aloft several shot had gone right through the foremast, others had gouged out great pieces of wood; the same thing had happened to the mainmast, while several more had gone through the mizenmast. The bowsprit was badly damaged; the jib-boom – in effect an extension of it – had been shot away altogether. Nor was the damage confined to the lower masts: the foretopgallant mast had been shot away; both arms of the enormous fore yard had been smashed off by shot, leaving only the centre section; the larboard part of the foretopsail yard had suffered the same fate.

The standing rigging was hanging in shreds: every one of the main shrouds, except one on the larboard side, had been cut through – and without these (which were in effect guys) only the inherent strength of the spar stopped the mast falling over the side. Most of the shrouds on the foremast were also cut and almost all the running rigging had gone.

The *Ardent*'s foresail, a rectangle roughly fifty feet by seventy feet, had 138 shot holes in it; the foretopsail, a little smaller, had sixty-seven. The maintopsail, roughly sixty feet by ninety feet, was so cut to pieces it was impossible to count the shot holes.

One anchor had gone overboard with a splash when a shot cut through its cable. But amidst all this damage, Captain Bertie was sending off boats with boarding parties to take possession of the Danish ships which had surrendered: by nightfall he had on board the swords of the commanders of four Danish ships.[1]

On board the *Cronborg* the men had fought to the limit of endurance and some had passed beyond it; only her commander, Lt Hauch, and Lt Helt were left on their feet. Helt later reported to the Danish Admiralty:

Lt Hauch came to me and reported that we were the last two [officers] left, and we had to stand by each other. . . . As he said that a piece of langridge cut off one of Haunch's arms and damaged the sight of an eye. He fell into my arms and I carried him amidships.

I then took command forward and ordered Mate Møhl to take command aft. He made objections and said that the Commander-in-Chief [Fischer] had struck and that we should, and that the battle had already lasted so long the crew could not stand it any longer.

I refused to surrender and ordered the firing to restart [and continue] as

[1] Two days later, Bertie took with him the swords, one of the Danish captains and three lieutenants (representing their captains who had been killed or wounded) to the *London*, with the request that because of the bravery of their late owners, he be allowed to return the swords. Sir Hyde agreed and the swords were restored, Bertie 'expressing his admiration for the able and gallant manner in which they had been used'.

long as we had men to handle the guns. The ensign was at that moment shot down and I ordered it to be rehoisted but received no assistance from Møhl, who went from where I was standing amidships and shouted to the crew that the ship was sinking and that they should report to the boats, to which he went himself.

All the crew then left the ship, except four faithful men – the master-at-arms and three volunteers, who remained at their posts. I then made an inspection of the ship and sounded the well.

Helt found three more men hiding in the hold and sent them up on deck. There he had no choice but to wait for the British boarding party, alone in the ship except for the seven men and the wounded, and surrender.

So far the first seven ships in the Danish line and four in the British, plus the two grounded ships, have been described. The next four Danish ships appeared to be at each corner of a square because two of them, the *Elven* frigate and the *Aggershuus* cavalry transport were anchored inshore, with the *Hayen* floating battery, and Fischer's flag-ship, the *Dannebroge*, on the seaward side.

The way Captain Bligh's *Glatton* had anchored slightly abaft the *Dannebroge*'s beam so she could also engage the *Hayen* and *Elven* – which were also being fired at by the *Ardent* – has already been described. The *Dannebroge* had Captain Ferdinand Braun commanding the ship as Fischer's flag captain, with eight other regular lieutenants (including Fischer's flag lieutenant, or adjutant, Lt Uldall) and two Army officers. Of a total ship's company of 357, 224 were trained seamen and 112 soldiers. She had no volunteers or pressed men on board.

Her armament of sixty guns comprised twenty-four 24-pounders, the same number of 12-pounders and twelve 8-pounders, while her main opponent, the *Glatton*, had fifty-six carronades. No comparison is possible between the armament of the two ships: at close range the *Glatton* had a great advantage because of her carronades; at a longer range the *Dannebroge*'s guns were more effective.

The beginning of this part of the Battle is described by Lieutenant Müller, the young lieutenant given command of the *Hayen* the previous Monday evening and who, as described on page 343, had so little time to get his floating battery ready with enough powder and shot for his twenty 18-pounder guns.

The first hour of the battle was, Müller wrote, just 'fencing', and the *Hayen* had only four casualties in this period. Müller attributed this to two things – the box-like *Hayen* had low bulwarks, so enemy shot did not cause so many splinters and the fact the *Glatton*'s guns were firing too high.

After an hour the picture changed. As had happened nearer the head of the line, the British were finding that the floating batteries, although weird-looking, were formidable opponents. With more space for the men to work the guns, no deckhead forcing them to crouch (in the sail of the line the headroom was often less than five feet), and a clear view all round instead of a glimpse through a narrow gunport, they were a highly effective way of concentrating fire power. For that reason the *Glatton* soon turned more of her carronades on to the *Hayen*, to sweep her with grapeshot; the *Ardent*'s forward guns were brought to bear on her; and some of the *Elephant*'s after guns joined in. The *Hayen*'s gun captains, Müller wrote, 'were nearly demented' because no sooner had fresh men taken the place of the wounded than they were shot down.

But the unwounded kept firing at whatever targets they could train their guns on. Müller handed round drinks 'to cheer up and to help the men, many of whom were completely exhausted', and very soon the battery ran out of powder. A signal was made to the shore and boats rowed out with more.

During the whole battle, boats were coming out from the harbour amid heavy fire – not aimed at them, but ricochets and shots that had missed or gone over their targets – bringing out extra men, powder and shot. (Although it was impossible to keep a check on total figures, at least 171 extra men are known to have been taken out to the Danish ships during the Battle, and of these thirty-three were subsequently killed or wounded.)

One of the worst problems was that the enemy's fire was wrenching the *Hayen*'s guns from their carriages. Müller, completely disregarding his own safety, led his men in the task of remounting as many as possible. Often it meant finding a relatively undamaged carriage and hauling it over to an undamaged but dismounted gun. Train tackles – used to haul the carriages round to train the guns on their targets, and breechings, the heavy ropes which took up the recoil – had to be fitted, gun captains appointed, and unwounded men found to load and fire. And always there was the danger of fire and explosion. In this respect a defect of the floating batteries meant they had less to fear than most ships: they leaked, and the problem was more of keeping the powder dry than keeping the decks wetted. Müller, whose account is both clear and fair, says that had the *Glatton*'s guns not been firing too high, she would have killed every man on board the *Hayen* and sunk her. Eventually, however, the time came when the *Hayen*'s fight was over and British boarding parties captured her. Müller was taken to the *Elephant* where, before the battle was over, he had a conversation with Nelson, which he recorded.

391

The *Elven* frigate, closer inshore than the *Hayen*, had been under fire mostly from the *Glatton* but also from the *Ardent* and the *Elephant*. Lt Baron Holsten also attributed his low casualty rate (nine dead, five seriously and two slightly wounded) to the fact the *Elven* 'lies low in the water', a fact noted by Robinson Kittoe in the *Defiance*.

By 1.00 p.m. twelve shot had hit her hull, five penetrating completely, and all her masts, mainyard and cro'jack yard had been shot through, as well as much standing and running rigging. Then, shortly after the *Dannebroge* had surrendered, the *Elven* received first one and then a second shot below the waterline; hits that occurred as she rolled. At once Holsten realized he could not hope to keep the ship afloat without many men at the pumps – men who were needed at the guns if he was to continue fighting. He ordered the anchor cables to be cut and ran the *Elven* down to the shallower water, closer to the harbour and under the protection of the Trekroner battery, where he anchored her.

One of the *Elven*'s wounded, Christen Madsen, a regular seaman from Bragnæs, Norway, had already watched the *Rendsborg*, in which was serving Halvor Jensen, who came from the same district, drift out of action; now his ship had to do the same.

Fischer's flagship had fought bravely and, towards the end, desperately. Captain Ferdinand Braun was an experienced officer and unlucky enough to have his right hand shot off early in the Battle. Just before that Lt Rasmus Wulff, the young officer who had joked with Müller of the *Hayen* the evening before that 'By this time tomorrow I shall be either a captain or an angel' was killed at Braun's side.

The fire of the *Dannebroge* and *Hayen* had done considerable damage to the *Glatton*; after the *Hayen* was silenced, a shot from the *Dannebroge* cutting into the *Glatton*'s foretopmast brought it crashing down, and seven of her upper-deck carronades were put out of action, either by the carriages being smashed to pieces or the carronades themselves being torn off.

However, the *Glatton* soon began firing carcasses at the *Dannebroge*. These were hollow iron shells filled with a mixture of resin, tallow, turpentine, saltpetre, sulphur and antimony, producing a fire which, in a wooden ship, was difficult if not impossible to put out. (They were rarely employed because, without extreme care, they were more dangerous to the user than the intended victim.)

The few carcasses the *Glatton* fired were well aimed: the range was two hundred yards, and soon the *Dannebroge* caught fire. By then the *Glatton* had been further damaged – two lower-deck carronades were destroyed, all three lower masts were badly cut about with shot, the lower yards had been hit several times, and of the 309 officers and men on board, eighteen would be killed and thirty-seven wounded before the Battle was over.

Captain Bligh was more concerned with the damage above deck level than below: 'Rigging and sails shot to pieces. . . . If there had been a fresh breeze we must have been a mere wreck,' he noted in his log, conscious that a rough sea would put such a strain on the remaining rigging and damaged masts that the ship would roll her masts out.

The *Elephant* had meanwhile also been hammering the *Dannebroge* and was being heavily engaged by her in return. She was also receiving the fire of the *Floating Battery No. 1*, almost under her stern and in a position to rake her, but almost out of the arcs of fire of the flagship's guns – and the *Aggershuus*, another battery.

Commodore Olfert Fischer, in a report to the Crown Prince, wrote that 'At half past eleven the *Dannebroge* . . . was set on fire. I repaired with my flag on board the *Holsteen*. . . . But the *Dannebroge* long kept her flag flying in spite of this disaster.' The *Holsteen*, at the northern end of the line, was not at this time engaged.

At this point the Danish flagship had been under fire from the *Elephant* and some of the *Glatton*'s guns for about half an hour. Fischer's own pendant being hauled down led the *Glatton* to think at first she had surrendered – 'Our opponent, the Danish Commodore, struck to us, but his seconds ahead [presumably the *Cronborg* but possibly the *Hayen*] and astern [presumably the *Sælland*, but *Floating Battery No. 1* was in between] still keep up a strong fire,' Bligh noted. However, the Danish ensign remained flying on board the *Dannebroge*, which was of course heading north.

So far this narrative has dealt with groups of ships beginning at the southern end, and the point when Fischer was forced to quit the *Dannebroge* and hoist his flag on board the *Holsteen* at the north end of the line is a good time to review the Battle so far.

The *Prøvesteenen* and the *Wagrien* were being heavily engaged by the *Polyphemus* and the *Isis*, with the grounded *Bellona* and *Russell* also firing at them and the *Jylland*. The *Rendsborg* had long since left the line and the *Nyeborg* would soon follow. The *Prøvesteenen* and the *Wagrien* surrendered at 2.00 p.m. according to the *Isis*, (2.30 according to the *Désirée* and the *Volcano*, 2.45 by the *Polyphemus*'s log, 3.00 p.m. *Otter*, 3.15 *Russell* and *Bellona*). The fifth in the Danish line, the *Jylland*, fought until 3.00 p.m., almost the end of the Battle; the sixth, the *Sværdfisken*, fought nearly as long but by noon had only a few guns left in action. The seventh was the *Cronborg*, and she too had only a few guns left by noon. The eighth and ninth were the *Hayen* and *Elven*, which were out of the fight, the tenth the *Dannebroge*.

Because the central part of the Battle is finally focused on the *Elephant* and the *Dannebroge*, it will be clearer if we return to those ships after seeing how the rest of the Danish and British ships were fairing.

Ahead of the *Elephant* the *Ganges* was engaging the *Sælland* (with *Floating Battery No. 1* firing at her). Ship for ship they were well matched, both being seventy-fours. As described earlier, Captain Fremantle had his master killed and the pilot wounded even before the *Ganges* had anchored abreast the *Sælland*.

'The fatigue of firing so long was great,' Fremantle wrote to the Marquis of Buckingham, 'but our unexampled good fortune in the *Ganges* is surprising.' Nor did he exaggerate: apart from the Master, only six seamen were killed, and the pilot, Mr Isaac Davis, wounded. 'Our masts and rigging were cut to pieces, but I think in a few days I shall be as effective as the day I left Yarmouth.'

He added: 'I have to attribute our good fortune in losing so few men to the bad gunnery of our opponents, and beating them most completely in less than an hour.' Later, having been on board some of them, he reported, 'The carnage on board the Danish vessels taken exceeds anything I ever heard of; the *Ca Ira* or Nile ships are not to be compared to the massacre on board them. The people generally were carpenters, labourers and some Norwegian seamen.'

Fremantle's reference to 'beating them most completely in less than an hour', and the *Sælland*'s bad gunnery, are borne out by the casualties: those in the *Ganges* were among the lowest of the British ships; those in the *Sælland* were by far the highest of any of the Danish – a third of her ship's company. Out of a total of 533 officers and men she had thirty-nine killed and 125 wounded (of whom seventeen died later). The *Ganges*' first few broadsides must have been devastating.

Fremantle's description of the *Sælland*'s motley ship's company was, of course, true but no more so than of any of the Danish ships. Ole Hansen, of Aarby near Kalundborg, was a regular soldier in a Norwegian regiment, and his wife and year-old daughter lived at the rectory at Aarby while Hansen did his service. He was one of the men killed in the Battle.

Hans Ibsen, from the island of Bornholm, was a bachelor working at Selbye's sugar warehouse in Copenhagen. With the call for volunteers, Ibsen offered his services, received fifteen dollars advance pay, and was sent to the *Sælland*. He was one of the wounded, receiving a crushed left knee which left him badly lamed. Jens Christensen, from Aarhus, who was married and worked at Selbye's sugar warehouse with Ibsen, went with him to Holmen to volunteer and was also sent off to the *Sælland*. By a curious coincidence, he too was wounded in the leg.

Unfortunately, soon after the *Dannebroge* caught fire, by which time the *Sælland* had been badly damaged by the *Ganges*' gunnery, the nerve of Captain Harboe's second-in-command, Lt Philip Schultz, and the Marine captain, Westerholt, failed. Schultz later claimed at his trial that he was frightened because he heard that the ship had been hit below the waterline and he saw fire close by on board the *Dannebroge* which, he said, was drifting towards the *Sælland*. Then he heard that Captain Harboe had been killed (which would, if true, have left him in command).

He went to the captain's barge, which was on the shoreward side of the ship, intending to leave the ship in it. The captain's coxswain refused to let him take it – in itself a brave act since Schultz was certainly second-in-command and, on his own account, in full command. Schultz then decided to take the gig, which was also alongside, and with Captain Westerholt and some wounded he left the ship and was rowed to the Lynetten fort. His departure was seen by three witnesses.[1]

Schultz's cowardice serves only to highlight that he, Westerholt and the master's mate Møhl in the *Cronborg*, were the only ones among more than five thousand who disgraced themselves. Indeed, Captain Harboe reported to the Crown Prince that two of his lieutenants, Hoppe and Dietrichsen, 'bravely distinguished themselves'. Soon after Schultz left the ship, the *Sælland*'s cable was cut by a shot and she drifted out of the Battle.

Beyond the *Ganges*, the *Monarch* was in action against the *Charlotte Amalia* and the *Søhesten* floating battery, and under heavy fire from the Trekroner Fort. It is fortunate that the best description of the Battle was written by someone on board the ship that suffered the heaviest casualties on either side: the *Monarch* had 220 casualties (fifty-seven dead and 163 wounded) compared with the *Sælland*'s 164.

Midshipman Millard's account describes the whole action. When the *Monarch* came to,

> I was on the quarter deck and saw Captain Mosse on the poop. His card of instructions was in his left hand, and his right was raised to his mouth with the speaking trumpet, through which he gave the word, 'Cut away the anchor'.
> I returned to my station at the aftermost guns; and in a few minutes the Captain was brought aft perfectly dead.

[1] The Judge Advocate, in a letter of 8 April to Fischer recommending Schultz's arrest and that he 'be carefully guarded at the Guard Room of Gammelholm', also requested that, in case of a new battle or bombardment, Schultz and the witnesses should 'not be exposed to the danger of their lives until their statements have been taken on oath. . . .' Schultz was found guilty and sentenced to be shot. Later reprieved, he was sent to a prison at Munkholm, Trondheim and eventually freed on expulsion from the country. He went to North America where he worked as a shipbuilder.

Colonel Hutchinson was with me, and was asked if he thought it right that the Captain should be carried below; he answered that he saw no signs of life, and it might only damp the spirits of the men. He was then laid in the stern walk, and a flag thrown over him. Colonel Hutchinson turned round and exclaimed with tears in his eyes, 'Poor man! He has left a wife and family to lament him.'

I did not see the Captain fall, but I understood afterwards from the quartermaster at the gun, Edward Kilgore, that he had left the poop and fell on the quarter deck on the very spot where I stood when the anchor was cut away.

I was conscious that employment was the surest mode to escape those unpleasant sensations which must arise in everyone's breast that has time for reflection in such a situation. I therefore pulled off my coat, helped to run out the gun, handed the powder, and literally worked as hard as any dray horse.

Every gun is supplied at first with a portion of shot, wadding &c., close by it [Millard explained] but when these were expended we applied to a reserve placed by the main mast. It immediately occurred to me that I could not be more usefully employed than in conveying this supply, which would enable the stronger ones to remain at the guns, for the men wanted no stimulus to keep them to their duty, nor any directions how to perform it.

The only cautions I remember to have given were hinted to me by the gunner before the action, viz to worm the guns frequently, that no fire remain from an old cartridge,[1] to fire two round shot in each gun, and to use nothing else while round shot could be had.

The *Monarch*'s gunner was obviously an experienced man: he knew at the present range, about two hundred yards, round shot would do much more damage than grape or canister.

The men remained at the wheel for a very considerable time after the ship was anchored in order to steady her, for the shock of bringing up [anchoring] suddenly occasioned a very considerable 'oscillation' (if I may apply that term).

As I was returning from the main mast and was abreast of the little binnacle, a shot came in at the port under the poop ladder and carried away the wheel; and three out of the four men stationed at it were either killed or wounded, besides one or two at the gun.

Lt Dennis[2] of the 49th Grenadiers had just come up the companion-ladder, and was going aft; the splinters shattered his sword, which was in the sheath, into three pieces, and tore off the finger ends of his left hand.

[1] Burning ends of cartridge bags left in the breech could prematurely explode a fresh cartridge. A wormer, like an enormous corkscrew, was used to pull out any pieces that might have been packed hard. A sponge, on a long handle, was soaked in water, and pushed down the bore between each shot to extinguish any burning debris.

[2] Later Major-general Sir James B. Dennis.

This, however, he scarcely seemed aware of, for lifting up the sheath with his bloody fingers, he called out, 'Look here, Colonel!'

On being reminded by Colonel Hutchinson of his wounded hand, he twisted his handkerchief round it and set up a huzza, which was soon repeated throughout the ship.

This brave officer had, strictly speaking, no particular duty to do; those soldiers who were intended to assist in the projected assault were dressed in uniform and stationed upon the poop and on the gangway, where they kept up a fire of musketry, till they were mowed down so fast that they were ordered below to await further orders. The remainder, in their working jackets without accoutrements, were attached to the great guns; so that some of the officers, being unacquainted with ship's duty, thought it prudent to retire.

Dennis, though he could not act against the enemy, found means to make himself useful; he flew through every part of the ship, and when he found any of his men wounded carried him in his arms down to the cockpit.

When the carnage was greatest he encouraged his men by applauding their conduct, and frequently began a huzza, which is more important than might generally be imagined; for the men have no other communication throughout the ship; but when a shout is set up, it runs from deck to deck, and they know that their comrades are, some of them, alive and in good spirits.

Lieutenant Colonel Hutchinson, being commanding officer of this detachment, did not leave the quarter deck, but walked backward and forward with coolness and composure; till at length, seeing the improbability of being ordered away [in the flat boats to attack the Trekroner Fort], he begged I would employ him if I thought he could do any good.

In case it should seem an odd request to a midshipman, it must be remembered that with Captain Mosse dead, Lieutenant Yelland had succeeded to the command, and all the other lieutenants were in charge of divisions of guns on various sections of the decks. Millard continued:

I was at this time seated on the deck, cutting the wads asunder for the guns; and the Colonel, notwithstanding the danger attending his uniform breeches, sat himself down and went to work very busily.

Indeed, afterwards, I was often obliged to leave the charge of my guns to the Colonel, for I was now the only midshipman left on the quarter deck, and was therefore employed by Lieutenant Yelland, the commanding officer, as his aide-de-camp, and dispatched occasionally into all parts of the ship. On my return, the Colonel made his report of what had passed in my absence.

Our signal midshipman (the Hon. William Bowes) was bruised from head to foot in such a manner as compelled him to leave the deck; Mr Levescombe, another midshipman, who was my companion on the quarter deck, and who was as cool and apparently unconcerned as usual, shared the same fate. I attended him to the deck, but could not prevail upon myself to set foot on the cockpit ladder; so there I left him to make the best of his way.

As the splinters were so plentiful, it may be wondered how I escaped. The fact is I did not escape entirely. When the wheel was shot away, I was in a cloud [of them] but being some little distance [forward of] the wheel I did not receive any of the larger pieces.

When I passed backwards and forwards between my quarters and the mainmast, I went on the opposite side to that which was engaged, and by that means probably escaped a severe wound; for as I was returning with two shot in one hand and a cheese (or packet) of wads in the other, I received a pretty smart blow on my right cheek. I dropped my shot, just as a monkey does a hot potato, and clapped my hand to the place, which I found rather bloody, and immediately ran aft to get my handkerchief out of the coat pocket.

My friend Colonel Hutchinson came to me immediately to return the compliment I paid him when passing the Castle and seemed really afraid lest my jaw was broken; however, after having felt it and found all right [sic], he let me return for my burthen.

Towards the close of the action the Colonel reported to me that the guns wanted quill or tin tubes (which are used as more safer and expeditious than loose priming) and wanted me to send someone, adding 'his own men were too ignorant of the ship, or he would have sent one before my return'.

I told him 'I knew no one that could so well be spared as myself'. He, however, objected to my going, and as I was aware of the dreadful slaughter which had taken place in the centre of the ship, I was not very fond of the jaunt; but my conscience would not let me send another on an errand I was afraid to undertake myself, and away I posted towards the fore magazine.

When I arrived on the maindeck, along which I had to pass, there was not a single man standing the whole way from the main mast forward, a district containing eight guns [on each side: there would normally be seventy or eighty men to serve them], some of which were run out ready for firing; others lay dismounted; and others remained as they were after recoiling.

In this dreary scene I shall be excused for shuddering as I walked across the body of a dead soldier. I hastened down the fore ladder to the lower deck and felt really relieved to find someone alive. From thence I reached the fore cockpit, where I was obliged to wait a few minutes for my cargo; and after this pause I own I felt something like regret, if not fear, as I remounted the ladder on my return.

This however, entirely subsided when I saw the sun shining and the blue old ensign flying as lofty as ever. I never felt the sense of glory so completely as at that moment; and if I had seen anyone attempt to haul that ensign down, I could have run aft and shot him dead in as determined manner as the celebrated Paul Jones.

I took off my hat by an involuntary motion and gave three cheers as I jumped on to the quarter deck. Colonel Hutchinson welcomed me at the quarter deck as if I had been on a hazardous enterprise and had returned in triumph; Mr Yelland also expressed great satisfaction at seeing me in such high spirits and so active.

Millard then described how Yelland was dressed in full uniform, his cocked hat set on square, his shirt frill starched, and his cravat tied tight under his chin.

After the fall of our captain, he sent me down to desire the lieutenants from the different quarters to come on deck, when he informed them of the Captain's death, and appointed himself of course, commanding officer; the remaining officers having, as it were, sworn fealty to him, returned to their different stations.

How he escaped unhurt seems wonderful; several times I lost sight of him in a cloud of splinters; as they subsided I saw first his cocked hat emerging, then by degrees the rest of his person, his face smiling, so that altogether one might imagine him dressed for his wedding day.[1]

Soon after my return from the magazine, Mr Ponsonby (Midshipman), who had been quartered on the fo'c'sle, came on to the quarterdeck, his face and the collar of his coat covered with a coagulated compost of human blood and brains.

He presented himself and three of his men to Mr Yelland as all that were left [of the fo'c'sle guns' crews], and requested that he would apply them where he thought proper, as they were no longer of service by themselves.

There were [originally] two other officers quartered on the fo'c'sle, the boatswain [William Joy] who was very dangerously wounded on the body, and Mr [George] Morgan, midshipman, who had both feet shot off, and I suppose twenty men, of whom only three remained with poor Ponsonby.

Mr Yelland shook his head at Ponsonby's [account] and begged, as he had fought so gallantly, that he would attach himself and men to whatever quarters he thought proper; so they remained where they were on the quarterdeck.

So the Battle continued. Eventually, Millard wrote,

. . . most of the enemy's vessels had struck their colours, in consequence of which I was desired to send Mr Home (a lieutenant) who commanded the flat-bottomed boat and launch, which were both manned and armed alongside, to board the prizes opposed to us.

He accordingly set off for that purpose. When almost halfway he saw a boat which was probably sent on the same errand knocked to pieces, the crew of which he picked up; but as the other ships and batteries continued firing he thought it in vain to attempt boarding the prizes, which were moreover prepared to resist, notwithstanding they had struck their colours.[2]

[1] Millard's description of the clouds of splinters seems an exaggeration because he omits mention of the the extraordinary quantity of dust accompanying the splinters. He actually saw Lt Yelland emerging from the dust: the splinters were flung up almost faster than the eye could see.

[2] This was a frequent complaint among British ships but was mostly due to the Danish flags being shot away. The blockships had only stump masts.

Mr Home then pulled to the *Elephant* to know if Lord Nelson would cease firing. His Lordship desired him not to think of the prizes, but return to his own ship, and keep a look-out on the Rear-admiral [Graves in the *Defiance*] ahead of us, for that he had sent in a flag of truce, and if it was accepted, he should remove from the scene of action as soon as possible.

Obviously the British ships would leave the scene of the battle by making sail and cutting the cables of their anchors. The *Monarch* nearly did this by accident, and Millard suddenly 'saw Mr Yelland storming and raving, stamping and swearing, as if he had been in a high state of delerium'. Colonel Hutchinson, Lt Bateman, the Master, Grey, and a couple of midshipmen were trying to quieten him.

I could not conceive what all this meant [Millard wrote] until at length, when the storm subsided, Colonel Hutchinson told me that Mr Bateman, who was quartered in the aft part of the lower deck, had discovered a man with an axe just about to cut the cable by which the ship rode.

The man declared that he had been called to from above to do it; but Mr Bateman chose to have better authority upon so serious a point, and for this purpose came on deck with the Master . . . to inquire of Mr Yelland.

The very mention of it nearly upset the old gentleman; for some time he could only say, 'Where is the rascal? Who is the rascal?' &c., and had he fallen in with the poor man he would most certainly have run him through the body without much further inquiry.

When they had quieted him a little, they had some trouble to convince him that the mischief was not actually done. 'Are you sure, Mr Bateman, you stopped the villain in time? Mr Grey, go down yourself and see all fast.' 'Sir, I come from thence.' 'Go again, sir.'

The origin of all this confusion was this. The small bower anchor was shot from the bows, and the spring hawser which was fixed to it prevented the ship's head from being sheered off from the Crown batteries, upon which they wanted the guns to bear.

When this was discovered, someone called out 'Cut it away.' This being repeated from one to the other reached the poor fellow, who had caused all this uproar by mistaking the cable for the hawser.

The first of the group of ships opposed to the *Monarch*, the 26-gun *Charlotte Amalia*, formerly an East Indiaman and now a 26-gun block-ship, was commanded by Captain Hans Koefoed, who left no report on the Battle, apart from commending the bravery of his second-in-command, Lt Johan Bardenfleth, the son of a general and who, as a fourteen-year-old cadet, had taken part in the Greenland expedition of 1786 seeking a Western passage. Also commended was the ship's surgeon, Dørn, for his bravery in attending the wounded. Among those Dørn treated was Ole Larsen, a conscript aged twenty-six from the village of Svendstrup. The son of an eighty-year-old farm labourer,

Larsen lost his right arm and died of haemorrhage despite Dørn's efforts. One of those killed in the *Charlotte Amalia* was a volunteer named Ole Christiensen, who had two brothers serving in other ships in the Battle. They were the sons of Mrs Bodil Christiensen, a crofter's widow of Wedlebye, near Roskilde. One of the first men to volunteer at Holmen was Hans Christensen, forty-eight and a bachelor, who worked for a brewer and lived in lodgings at a gin distiller's basement in Ulfeldt's Plads (now Graabrødretorv), Copenhagen. He was badly wounded in the head and face and blinded in his right eye.

The second in the group engaging the *Monarch* was the *Søhesten* floating battery. Her captain was Lt B. U. Middelboe, who eventually had to surrender the *Søhesten* with twelve men killed and twenty-one wounded, seven fatally. Among the men killed was Christen Sørensen Hugger, of Holbæk, who had left his wife and their three children (the youngest two-years-old) and volunteered for service.

The third of the *Monarch*'s opponents was the *Holsteen*, although it seems certain that it was the guns of the Trekroner Fort that did her most damage. The 60-gun *Holsteen*, similar to the *Dannebroge*, was commanded by Captain Jacob Arenfeldt, son of a rear-admiral, and who had spent a year in command of the King's yacht *Søormen*, a prestige appointment usually given only to the most promising young captains. His second-in-command was Lt Niels Andresen who – if he survived the Battle – would celebrate his fortieth birthday in three days' time, on Easter Sunday.

At 11.30 Olfert Fischer reached the *Holsteen* in an open boat from the *Dannebroge* and hoisted his flag. For the next two hours he watched as one after another of the ships of his line were forced to surrender or drifted helplessly to leeward. By 1.30 p.m. the *Holsteen*'s upper deck was almost bare of living men; guns had been knocked from their carriages, and carriages had been smashed from under the guns. On the lower deck conditions were little better. Altogether the ship suffered fifty-three wounded (of whom four died later) and twelve killed.

Among those killed was Peder Schultz, the journeyman dyer, who had left his family of five at number 222 Storekongensgade, and volunteered. The shock of his death left his widow 'not quite right in her senses', according to a report to the Admiralty, and by then she had no permanent address: the Commissioners for the Poor were paying a family to act as fosterparents for two of the children; the third was with its grandparents in Odense; the youngest had been left at the hospital in Copenhagen.

Eventually the position in the *Holsteen* was such that 'The Commander-in-Chief was obliged to leave the ship,' Arenfeldt reported, 'and wanted to go northward to the other ones, but a little later he saw the *Indfødsretten* strike. . . .' At 1.30 p.m. Fischer 'left the *Holsteen* and went to the Trekroner Fort. This was the last possible place and would have to be taken with sword in hand.'

The 64-gun *Indfødsretten* blockship was moored with her bow to the north in continuation of the Danish line, with the completely rigged *Hiælperen* frigate, the last of Fischer's ships, moored closer inshore. Both these ships were right in front of the Trekroner Fort.

The *Defiance*, Rear-admiral Graves's flagship, had been engaging the *Indfødsretten* with some of her guns, although her main target was the *Holsteen*. The brunt of the task of dealing with both the *Indfødsretten* and the *Hiælperen* had fallen on Captain Riou in the *Amazon* frigate, with his little force of the *Blanche*, *Alcmene*, *Dart* and *Arrow*, all of which were anchored beyond the *Defiance*, abreast the two Danish ships and between 750 and 1000 yards from Trekroner.

All were in range – within 1000 yards – of the first two of Steen Bille's ships anchored in the channel leading to the harbour, the *Elephanten* and the *Mars*.

Captain Albert de Thura, commanding the *Indfødsretten*, was killed by one of the first broadsides fired at his ship. The shot that killed Thura then hit a volunteer seaman, Jens Hansen Bønsvig, and knocked him over the side. Bønsvig, a bachelor who had been living with his mother at 33 Vordingbordampt, in Copenhagen, was never seen again.

Command of the ship then fell to Lt Jesper Cortsen, a reserve officer, who was in turn killed. (His widow received a pension of 200 dollars a year, and 120 dollars for his lost clothes.) Lt Heich Meinertz, another reserve officer, then took command.

The *Indfødsretten*'s casualties totalled twenty-one killed and forty-one wounded (six fatally) out of a ship's company of 394. Like the *Holsteen*, she had a high proportion of regular seamen on board, among whom was Johan Christian Schou, carpenter second class. Schou was wounded in the chest and spent many months in hospital, constantly visited by his wife Inger, his seven-year-old son Knud – who was in the Crown Prince's service as a coachman's boy – and Georg, who was three and a half. But the efforts of the surgeons were in vain and Schou died on 3 August.

The *Hiælperen* frigate was commanded by Lt Peter Carl Lillienskjold, and, as described earlier, had an unusual armament, including sixteen 36-pounders. However, Lillienskjold did not fight his ship as hard as some of his fellow captains. His report to the Admiralty said the *Hiælperen* was attacked by two 74-gun ships (the *Defiance* and the *Monarch*, although he neglected to mention they were also engaging the

Indfødsretten, Holsteen, Søhesten and *Charlotte Amalia*) and because his ship 'could not affect the issue,' after having 'fought for two hours I saw that the [Defence line] had been destroyed, and I surrendered', cutting both anchor cables.

His report said that the *Hiælperen* fired two hundred rounds – less than ten broadsides – and the number of casualties suffered hardly substantiated Lillienskjold's claim to have fought two 74-gun ships for two hours: of the ship's company of 269, no one was killed and six were wounded.

SIGNAL NUMBER 39

When Olfert Fischer was forced to haul down his flag on board the *Holsteen* at 1.30 p.m. and go to the Trekroner Fort, it must have been only too obvious to him that his Defence Line was shattered, although several of the ships were still in action. But his only real knowledge of the situation was what he could see through the smoke: as ships surrendered their captains or surviving officers were reporting directly to the Crown Prince on shore.

On his left, as he looked seaward, Sir Hyde Parker's division slowly but inexorably tacked up towards the northern fairway, and although hidden from time to time by great banks of smoke drifting northwards like fog, there was no disguising the fact that eight more British sail of the line would be joining Nelson's division. Even if they arrived too late to get into action before darkness fell, they would be ready to attack next morning – by which time Nelson's three sail of the line stranded on the Middle Ground would have been refloated.

Directly in front of Fischer the *Hiælperen* and the *Indfødsretten* had surrendered and the *Holsteen* was almost out of the fight. Farther south the *Søhesten* and *Charlotte Amalia* were obviously almost at the end of their tether; the *Sælland* and *Floating Battery No. 1* were still in action; the *Aggershuus* had left the line, towing the helpless and sinking *Nyeborg*; the *Dannebroge* was on fire and almost out of the action; the *Elven* was trying to get into the harbour before she sank; the *Hayen* floating battery was still in action; the *Cronborg* was on the verge of surrender; the *Rendsborg* had drifted out of the Battle very early on, her cable cut. The *Jylland* was still in action, as was the *Sværdfisken* floating battery. The *Wagrien* and the *Prøvesteenen* were still spasmodically firing a few guns, but were on the verge of being boarded and captured.

The southern and centre sections of the Defence Line had, for all practical purposes, been crushed; the main weight of the British attack was now on the northern end, and although there was still bitter fighting to come – Trekroner itself was shaking every few moments as its guns fired – it was obviously going to be overwhelmed, particularly if the British ships to the south, whose opponents had either surrendered or were now capable of little resistance, came north to reinforce the others. Fischer had no way of telling how badly damaged they were.

Yet behind where Fischer stood on the Trekroner Fort were the 74-gun *Elephanten*, 60-gun *Mars*, 70-gun *Danmark*, 74-gun *Trekroner*, the 40-gun *Iris* frigate, and the two 18-gun brigs *Sarpen* and *Nidelven*, all fresh and all undamaged. These ships, Steen Bille's division charged with guarding the harbour entrance, came under the direct command of the Crown Prince, who was watching the battle from the Quintus battery, by the harbour entrance.

The first two had no masts; but if the rest of Steen Bille's division weighed anchor it could, with the wind as it was, have come to the help of the northern end of Fischer's line. Even allowing a strong current and the limitations imposed by the Middle Ground, the *Danmark* and the *Trekroner* could have attacked the *Defiance* and the *Monarch* at the north end of Nelson's line, 'doubling' on them by attacking from the Middle Ground side, so they were also under fire from the Trekroner Fort as well as from seaward. The *Iris* and the two brigs could deal with the *Amazon* and her little flotilla, while the *Elephanten* and the *Mars* stayed in the fairway, guarding it with the help of Trekroner.

But Olfert Fischer never asked the Crown Prince for the assistance of Steen Bille's ships; Steen Bille never proposed it to the Crown Prince; and there is no record that the Crown Prince or the members of the Defence Commission ever considered it.

So Steen Bille's division remained in the northern fairway, anchored in tactically the worst position for defending it against a possible attack from Parker's division. It was an attack now unlikely to happen because it would not be necessary: Nelson's ships had already captured or silenced enough ships at the southern end of the Defence Line to enable them to anchor bomb ketches in a position to bombard the city.

Clearly Olfert Fischer should have been given complete command of all the ships, not just the Defence Line, although it can be only a matter of speculation what the effect would have been. Had he originally used them to reinforce the work and extend his Defence Line southwards, the result of the Battle might well have been different on this day, though the British would have been able to attack again the next. Yet the fact remains that although forced to quit the *Dannebroge* at 11.30 a.m. and the *Holsteen* at 1.30 p.m., Fischer did not appeal to the Crown Prince for more ships.

From this it is reasonable to conclude that had he commanded all the ships and placed Steen Bille's division in the fairway, he would not have ordered it into action. It may well be that he considered it necessary to keep that division intact to defend the harbour, against an attack by Parker, although it would have been a case of keeping the stable door shut long after the stable itself had collapsed because of the bomb ketches.

Quite apart from all this, there remain two vital factors which have often for other reasons (primarily Nelson's truce offer) been glossed over or ignored in Danish accounts of the Battle: first, every one of Nelson's nine British sail of the line was still in action and some, such as the *Ganges*, had not suffered a great deal of damage. Secondly, and far more important, time was on Nelson's side, although he did not realize it in the noise and heat of the action.

The circumstances surrounding the truce offer, which will be described later, have been so distorted that it is claimed Nelson was running out of time. As far as the *Defiance* and *Monarch* at the north end of the line were concerned, their position was dangerous; but Nelson still had the *Agamemnon*, which was completely fresh, and Sir Hyde's division was approaching Copenhagen – two 98-gun ships, four 74s and two 64s. Nelson would thus have nine sail of the line fresh and undamaged to resume the Battle next day. Nine ships – as many as he had to make his first attack, plus the less damaged ships of his own division which were already in action.

We can now return briefly to the *Elephant*, which was engaging the *Dannebroge*, *Floating Battery No. 1*, and the *Sælland*. Colonel Stewart notes that (half an hour before Fischer quit the *Holsteen*), 'The contest, in general, although from the relaxed [i.e. reduced] state of the enemy's fire, it might not have given much room for apprehension as to the result, had certainly, at one p.m., not declared itself in favour of either side. About this juncture, and in this posture of affairs,' Stewart added, the *London* made a signal.

It was to become the most controversial signal in the history of sea warfare: controversial as to what it was intended to mean, and controversial over Sir Hyde's motives in making it. The controversy arose *after* the Battle, partly through ignorance and partly because apologists for Parker deliberately distorted matters. (The way in which it was interpreted by various people is given in Appendix I.)

According to Sir Hyde's journal the signal was made at 1.15, while his flagship's log gives 1.30 p.m. which was the time Olfert Fischer hauled down his flag and left the *Holsteen* for the Trekroner Fort. At 1.30 p.m. the *London* was almost exactly four miles from Nelson's flagship: his division, tacking up to Copenhagen, was approaching the city at the rate of a little over one mile an hour.

Sir Hyde never explained, beyond the bare words of his journal, the reasons for his action. The journal says, '[noon] Moderate breezes and hazy, at 1 p.m. turning up to Copenhagen [,] ¼ past made signal 39 and sent Captain Otway on board the *Elephant*[,] the van division still in action. . . .'

The Signal Book devotes three words to the 'Signification' of that signal: '*Discontinue the action.*'

The most important point about the signal has never been fully appreciated: it was made '*General*', with two guns. This meant, of course, that Parker was giving a *direct* order to every ship in Nelson's division (and in his own, if any had been in action); not signalling an order to Nelson, who would in turn make it to the ships of his division.[1]

Every ship in Nelson's division, seeing the Commander-in-Chief's signal, was duty bound to repeat it and to obey it, disregarding any signal which Nelson, as second-in-command, might make. Those that saw and repeated it were the following, their names followed by the references in their logs, most of which indicate how the signal was interpreted:

The *Dart*: 'At ½ past 1, the Commander-in-Chief made the signal to cease the action, Lord Nelson still [had] the signal flying to close the enemy . . . at ½ past 2, cut our best bower and stream cables to obey the signals made by the Commander-in-Chief. . . .'

The *Cruizer*: 'Observed the *London* to have made signal number 39. Repeated ditto. At ½ past 2 anchored [i.e. near Parker's division, having obeyed the signal].'

The *Volcano*: 'At 10 past 1, Admiral Parker in the offing made the signal to discontinue the action, which was repeated by the *Désirée* and *Agamemnon*.'

The *Amazon*: 'The *Alcmene* . . . made the signal number 39, cut her cable and stood off; she was soon followed by the *Blanche*. Observed the same signal flying on board the *London*, but we continued our fire until 1.15, when the signal being repeated by the Rear-admiral [Graves in the *Defiance*], cut the cable and stood off.'[2]

The *Blanche*: 'At 1.15 the Admiral [Parker] made the signal to discontinue the engagement.'

The *Otter*: '. . . Sir Hyde Parker made the signal 39. Lord Nelson still flying No. 16 [*Engage the enemy more closely*].'

[1] This has been overlooked in almost every argument concerning the signal because it has been wrongly assumed the signal was made to the *Elephant* alone. The *St George*'s log makes it quite clear this was not the case. This alone destroys any argument that it was for Nelson and 'permissive'.

[2] The *Alcmene* did not refer to the signal in her log. Rear-admiral Graves had ordered the signal to be hoisted in the *Defiance* in a position where it could not be seen from the *Elephant*.

The *Bellona*'s Master noted, after recording the bursting of several guns: 'Prior to these accidents the Commander-in-Chief made the signal to discontinue the action, which was not obeyed by our squadron, several of them being aground at the time.' (The reference to being aground referred only to the *Bellona* herself, the *Russell* and *Agamemnon*.)

The *Polyphemus*'s signal log noted the signal at 1.15 p.m. as made by the *Désirée* to the *Agamemnon*, and she did not repeat it.

Finally, the signal as recorded in the Master's log of one of the ships in Sir Hyde's own division – a ship whose captain and master would be very careful to see the signal was correctly noted. The ship was the *St George*, Nelson's flagship until he transferred to the *Elephant* for the Battle; the captain was Thomas Hardy, who was to kneel by the dying Nelson on board the *Victory* at Trafalgar; and the Master was Thomas Atkinson, who was to be master of the *Victory* at Trafalgar. Both men would immediately see the significance of the signal and ensure it was properly logged.

In a list of signals including Nelson's number sixteen, which it notes as 'General to van division', Atkinson's log records it in tabular form. The entry reads:

TIME	FROM	SIGNAL	TO
12.30	*London*	39	General with two guns

Having seen what the signal meant and how it was received, we can now try to understand why it was made. The biographers of Captain Otway in a brief account published thirty-nine years after the Battle quote Southey, but significantly not Otway, for the following description:

When Sir Hyde saw the critical situation of the squadron under Nelson, it became a question between him and the Captain of the Fleet [Domett], whether he should make the signal to leave off action; but as that measure was strongly opposed by Captain Otway, it was determined that the Captain of the Fleet should proceed to Lord Nelson to ascertain the situation of affairs; he went below to adjust some part of his dress; but while he was so doing, Captain Otway solicited and obtained leave from Sir Hyde Parker to execute the intended mission.

At this moment a boat was passing the *London*; she was instantly hailed and Captain Otway pushed off in her. The boat had on board a ship's hawser coiled up; but Captain Otway would not wait to have it discharged; and in that dangerous vehicle passed through the enemy's fire to the *Elephant*. Had a shot struck her she must have sunk like a stone, but Captain Otway fortunately reached his destination in safety; but before he got on board the signal to leave off action was made.

This account alone is reason enough for throwing out the idea, which became popular, that Otway carried verbal permission for Nelson to disregard this vital order if he saw fit: obviously, if it was true, Sir Hyde would not have made the signal *until after* he saw Otway's boat had arrived at the *Elephant*. (No one in the *Elephant* even noted his arrival – a significant indication of its importance – or referred to him being on board.)

It will be recalled that Captain Nicholas Tomlinson was on board the *London* as a volunteer. He was later directed by Lord St Vincent to write an account of the Battle, which he sent to the Secretary of the Board of Admiralty. This has been overlooked, yet is extremely valuable evidence.[1] At the end of a description of how Sir Hyde had from the beginning been anchored too far away to help Nelson, he comments: 'The events of the Battle and the consequences that would have resulted from an obedience to the Signal to discontinue the Action which was made from the *London*, and repeated with guns, are too well known to require any comment.'

Even more significant is the fact that Parker's third-in-command, Graves, whose *Defiance* was in action only a few score yards from Nelson's flagship, ignored the signal for as long as possible and finally – as he was duty bound to do – repeated it. But he had it hoisted in a position where it could not be seen from the *Elephant*.

Colonel Stewart records how the signal was received on board the *Elephant*.

Lord Nelson was at this time, as he had been during the whole action, walking the starboard side of the quarter deck; sometimes much animated, and at others heroically fine in his observations.

A shot through the mainmast knocked a few splinters about us. He observed to me, with a smile, 'It is warm work, and this day may be the last to any of us at any moment,' and then stopping short at the gangway, he used an expression never to be erased from my memory, and said with emotion, 'but mark you, I would not be elsewhere for thousands.'

When signal No. 39 was made, the signal[2] lieutenant reported it to him.

He continued his walk, and did not appear to take notice of it. The lieutenant meeting his Lordship at the next turn asked 'Whether he should repeat it?'

Lord Nelson answered, 'No, acknowledge it.' On the officer returning to the poop his Lordship called after him, 'Is No. 16 [*Engage the enemy more*

---

[1] The covering letter says significantly, 'I am ignorant whether this paper is to be considered a private or public communication; but if the latter I may probably be called upon to verify it upon oath; therefore his Lordship will be persuaded that I did not write it without having first most seriously weighed its importance.'

[2] There was no rank as such: usually a junior lieutenant in a flagship was put in charge of signals in battle.

closely] still hoisted?' The lieutenant answering in the affirmative, Lord Nelson said, 'Mind you keep it so.'

Stewart could not know what was going through Nelson's mind, nor did Nelson ever describe it; but it is not hard to guess. Nelson would have known instinctively that, bloody as the fighting still was, the tide of battle had turned in his favour: another hour and victory would be his. But to obey this direct order would be suicide. As Rear-admiral Graves later wrote to his brother, 'If we had discontinued the action before the enemy struck, we should have all got aground and have been destroyed.'

Graves could see, as could Nelson, the confusion resulting from damaged ships leaving through the northern end of the narrow King's Deep, and the risk of going aground well within range of the guns of the Trekroner Fort (which were effectively engaging the *Monarch* and the *Defiance*). It would have been the same as a platoon of soldiers who had been keeping the enemy pinned down by their heavy fire suddenly standing up, turning their backs to the enemy, and walking away.

Certainly the signal came as a complete surprise to Nelson. Some people have subsequently claimed there was an earlier agreement between Sir Hyde and Nelson that if the position became desperate the signal would be made, thus giving Nelson official sanction to retreat, if he felt it necessary. This claim is hardly worth discussing: if there had ever been such an agreement, obviously Nelson would have informed his second-in-command, Graves, and almost certainly warned his captains, and Parker would have made the signal to the *Elephant* only, not 'General', to avoid the very situation that arose, where some ships obeyed the Commander-in-Chief and the majority ignored him.

It is ridiculous to think that Nelson would have left his captains in ignorance of the fact that a 'General' signal from the Commander-in-Chief to discontinue the action was in fact intended only to give Nelson discretionary power to withdraw. And if there was prior agreement, why did the question of sending Domett or Otway arise?

Stewart's description makes it beyond argument that the signal was completely unexpected. Nelson, the colonel wrote,

. . . Now walked the deck considerably agitated, which was always known by his moving the stump of his right arm.

After a turn or two he said to me, in a quick manner, 'Do you know what's shown on board of the Commander-in-Chief, No. 39?'

On asking him what that meant he answered, 'Why, to leave off action. Leave off action!' he repeated, and then added, with a shrug, 'Now damn me if I do!'

Then, turning to Captain Foley, a massive man and who was a foot taller, he said, according to Southey, 'You know, Foley, I have only one eye – and I have a right to be blind sometimes,' and putting his small telescope to his blind eye, he exclaimed, 'I really do not see the signal!' A few moments later he was reported as saying bitterly, to no one in particular, 'Damn the signal. Keep mine for closer battle flying. That's the way I answer such signals! Nail mine to the mast!'[1]

The consequence of this was that in simply acknowledging No. 39 and keeping his own for closer action still flying, Nelson was flatly disobeying Sir Hyde. By not repeating it to his own division he could only hope his captains would obey him and not Sir Hyde. It put them in a terrible quandary, since Sir Hyde's order was mandatory, and Nelson was relying on them looking to the *Elephant* for confirmation and, not finding it, remaining in action.

Fortunately most captains did; but in some cases the damage was already beyond repair or recall. On board the *Amazon*, Captain Riou's concern typified the position in which the captains of the smaller ships found themselves.

Already wounded, Riou had not only successfully kept his frigate's guns hard at it against the 36-pounders of the *Indfødsretten* and the *Hiælperen*, and the guns of Trekroner Fort (also coming under fire from the *Elephanten* and the *Mars*) but made sure his little squadron was precisely placed to bring the maximum number of guns to bear.

Then one of his officers drew Riou's attention to the *Alcmene*: she had hoisted signal number 39, obviously repeating it. The *Amazon*'s First Lieutenant, John Quilliam, noted that the *Alcmene* then 'cut her cable and stood off; she was soon followed by the *Blanche*'.[2] His log continues 'Observed the same signal flying on board the *London*, but we continued our fire till 1.15. . . .'

It was at that moment (the *Amazon*'s times are wrong) that Rear-admiral Graves, duty bound to repeat Sir Hyde's signal, eventually hoisted it at the starboard maintopsail yardarm, where it could not be seen from the *Elephant*, and kept Nelson's No. 16 flying at the mainmast head. Graves had delayed repeating it for about a quarter of an hour, and the Master's log of the *Defiance* makes no mention of it.

---

[1] Southey's account is of more than doubtful accuracy because he credits the remarks made to Stewart as being made to Ferguson, the *Elephant*'s surgeon, who was the last person likely to be on deck at that moment: he would have been down below in the cockpit attending the wounded. Also Nelson would have used the phrase 'for closer action', not 'for closer battle'.

[2] The *Blanche*'s log says: 'At ½ past 1, the *Amazon* made our signal to discontinue the engagement.' This was completely untrue and is as puzzling as the alacrity with which Captain Sutton obeyed Sir Hyde's signal, since with the exception of the *Alcmene*, the captains of all the smaller ships showed some hesitation.

Riou was obviously puzzled to know what to do: Nelson's *Elephant* and the *Defiance* were still in action; but the *Alcmene* (with twenty-four killed and wounded) and the *Blanche* (sixteen killed and wounded) had obeyed Sir Hyde, and Rear-admiral Graves had just repeated the order. Although the signal flags could not be seen from the *Elephant*, they were only too obvious to the *Amazon* which was anchored ahead and to starboard of the *Defiance*.

The *Amazon*'s log reflects Riou's predicament: Captain Bolton of the *Arrow* and Captain Devonshire of the *Dart* were still close by, at anchor and in action. The *Dart*, anchored by the bow and stern, was held across both wind and current to train her guns far enough round. Her master noted that she was 'close to two of the enemy's line of battle ships abreast Crown Island who kept up a very heavy fire from the ships and batteries. . . . During the action the ship's log book was cut in two and torn to pieces by a shot.'

The *Defiance* repeating the signal seemed to have convinced Riou – who of course commanded this little squadron – that he had no option but to obey. With more than a dozen men killed and a couple of dozen wounded, he gave the order for the anchor cable to be cut and topsails let fall.

Up to then the *Amazon*, like several of the other ships, had frequently been hidden from the Danish gunners by the smoke of her own guns. The moment she stopped firing her outline became clear and, much more dangerous, bearing up to join Sir Hyde meant turning away from the guns of Trekroner, exposing the *Amazon*'s stern to their raking fire.

Far worse for Riou was the realization that it meant defeat for Nelson, the man he had met only a few days earlier, who had given him a major part in the planning of the Battle, and put a little squadron under his command. Now, for Riou, it was all over: not because of the Danish fire but because of a signal hoisted by Sir Hyde Parker. Like Nelson, Riou must have known the tide had already turned in favour of the British; unlike Nelson, he could not disobey the signal now that Graves had repeated it – he least of all, since the *Amazon* was one of the nearest ships to Parker's division. Because the *Elephant* was hidden from him he had no hint that Nelson was ignoring it. Had he seen that the *Elephant* merely acknowledged but kept Number 16 flying, he would have guessed.

So he had given the order to cut the cable, and as the *Amazon* got under way and turned to the north-east, towards Parker's division and out of the Battle, Riou was feeling faint from his wound, and weary, and probably defeated.

'What will Nelson think of us,' he said bitterly.

A moment later the *Amazon* was raked by several Danish guns and Riou collapsed to the deck, his body almost cut in half by a shot. Lt John Quilliam, who was to be the officer in charge of signals in the *Victory* at Trafalgar and responsible for hoisting the famous 'England Expects' signal, took over and sailed the *Amazon*, with thirty-seven killed and wounded on board, to join Parker, and that night 'committed the body of Captain Riou to the deep'.

Fortunately for Nelson the frigates and some smaller vessels were the only ones to obey Sir Hyde: the sail of the line continued in action. In the meantime most of the bomb vessels had finally managed in the light wind to get into position between the British line and the Middle Ground, anchoring in a rough line abreast the ships between the *Monarch* and the *Glatton*.

Some of the bomb vessels and fire ships had a difficult time. The *Otter* fire ship, for instance, which had anchored near the *Elephant* and was of course full of highly inflammable materials, was in the unenviable position of being under heavy fire – mostly from shot aimed at the flagship – and unable to fire back. Her log noted:

. . . Received a very heavy shot in the boatswain's store-room, several grapeshot in different parts of the hull. Hoisted signal No. 16 as repeated from the *Elephant*, which was shot away. . . . A shot carried away the ensigns, halliards &c. . . . Sir Hyde Parker made the signal 39. Lord Nelson still flying No. 16. Received a very heavy fire from the Crown Island. . . .

The *Explosion* bomb had the same trouble experienced by many of the Danish gun boats: damage caused by her own guns. Anchored just to the east of the *Elephant* and firing at the enemy with her mortars, the *Explosion* noted: 'The booms caught fire from the mortars, cut the lashings and hove the sweeps [large oars], royal yards, and several other spars overboard.'

On board the *Elephant*, as Sir Hyde made his signal and Olfert Fischer went to Trekroner, it was hard for anyone to know what was happening in individual Danish ships. The narrative so far has used the reports written subsequently by Danish officers, but for the British the main problem was ensigns, since many of the Danish ships had either stump masts or their ensigns were hoisted on ensign staffs.

This led to a lot of confusion for the British. To them, Danish ships which had apparently struck in surrender were still firing, against all accepted rules of war (but in most cases because the flags had been shot away, not struck); on the other hand some ships which had stopped firing still had their ensigns flying (all too often the surviving officers were hurriedly getting guns repaired and new crews assembled).

Far more of a problem for the British was dealing with the batteries, both Trekroner and those on shore, particularly Quintus and Sixtus. The situation arose now because, seen from Trekroner, Sixtus and Quintus, many of the British ships were behind the Danish, since they had anchored abreast their various opponents, and could not be fired on by the Danes for fear of hitting their own ships, most of which were now out of action and all crowded with wounded men. (This is made clear in Robinson Kittoe's sketch, illustration number 20.)

However, as soon as the British started sending boats to take possession of their prizes, the batteries opened fire on them. But the combination of long range, poor visibility because of the smoke, unskilled gunnery and poor aiming meant that many of the Danish shot were in fact hitting or ricocheting into their own ships.

In turn the British were finding it difficult to silence the batteries because the trajectories meant there was a risk their shot would hit Danish ships which had definitely surrendered and were known to be full of wounded. With the batteries still firing, they could not take possession of their prizes; without taking possession of their prizes the Battle would be unfinished. And not silencing the batteries also left the British ships at the northern end of the line in danger.

This was the point where one of Nelson's finest gestures has been distorted in some accounts. This distortion can be removed once and for all by examining the position of both sides at 2.00 p.m. Using mostly Danish and some British reports and taking the times given by the majority, it was as follows.

All the nine British sail of the line which had anchored in their proper stations were still in action with the majority of their guns still firing, and two of the three grounded ships, the *Bellona* and *Russell*, were also able to keep up a steady fire. The damage to the British ships has already been described.

The position on board ships of the Danish line, beginning from the south was:

Prøvesteenen (58 guns): badly damaged, a few guns still in action, abandoned soon after 2.00 p.m. and boarded by boats from the *Polyphemus* and the *Isis*.

Wagrien (52): same position as the *Prøvesteenen*; boarded at the same time.

Rendsborg (22): cable cut and drifted out of the action by noon.

Nyeborg (22): drifted out of the action shortly after the *Rendsborg*.

Jylland (54): still in action despite heavy casualties (seventy-one killed and wounded by the time she was boarded) and continued firing until the flag of truce was hoisted by the *Elephant* at 3.15 p.m.

Sværdfisken (18): very few guns left firing by noon, and completely silenced by the *Ardent* at 2.00 p.m.

STUBBEN

MARS
ELEPHANTEN
SARPEN
NIDELVEN
DANMARK
TREKRONER

TREKRONER
FORT

HJÆLPEREN
INDFØDSRETTEN

LYNETTEN

IRIS

STILLET

18 30 30 18 9

DBODEN

WARSHIP
HARBOUR

NYEHOLM

SIXTUS

QUINTUS

1500 YARDS

HOLSTEEN
SØHESTEN
CHARL. AMALIA
SÆLLAND
F. BATTERY NO.1
AGGERSHUUS
DANNEBROGE
ELVEN
HAYEN
CRONBORG
SVÆRDFISKEN
JYLLAND
NYEBORG
RENDSBORG
WAGRIEN
PROVESTEENEN

DART
ARROW
ALCMENE
BLANCHE
AMAZON

DEFIANCE

MONARCH
GANGES
ELEPHANT
GLATTON

ARDENT

EDGAR

BELLONA
RUSSELL

ISIS
POLYPHEMUS

DÉSIRÉE

BOMB
VESSELS
AND FIRE
SHIPS

MIDDLE
GROUND
42

18 30

1000
800
600

WIND

W
E

200

YARDS

STRICKER'S
BATTERY

2000 YARDS

9 18 30

18
30 42
1500 YARDS
1000 YARDS

HT © 1972 BY THE RAMAGE COMPANY

osition of the Danish and British ships during the Battle. This chart by the author is based
y on the reports of Danish and British officers and the logs of their ships, which agreed with each
to a remarkable degree. They allowed the positions of *Russell* and *Bellona*, for example, to be
shed with some precision, and this in turn located the edge of the Middle Ground shoal. Depths
feet and ranges in yards.

Cronborg (22): so badly damaged by noon that all but one officer, the master at arms and three seamen quit the ship.

Hayen (20): out of action by 1.30 p.m. and her commanding officer, Lieutenant Müller, a prisoner on board the *Elephant* before 2.00 p.m.

Elven (frigate): cable cut and out of the battle by noon; after helping the *Aggershuus* she went into the harbour at 1.45 badly damaged and in a sinking condition.

Dannebroge (60): so badly damaged and on fire that Commodore Fischer had to leave her at 11.30 a.m.; by 1.00 p.m. had several bad fires but stayed in action with only three guns until about 2.30 p.m.

Aggershuus (20): cable cut and ship sinking before noon; went aground on the Stubben Shoal north of the harbour entrance.

Floating Battery No. 1 (24): still in action by 2.00 p.m.: twelve killed and twenty-eight wounded. Five gun carriages destroyed, a sixth gun burst, seventh out of action with damaged trunnion, some others slightly damaged.

Sælland (74): Soon after the *Dannebroge* caught fire the ship was badly damaged by the *Ganges'* broadsides; in less than an hour, with the heaviest casualties sustained by any Danish ship, a shot cut her cable and she drifted out of the line.

Charlotte Amalia (26): badly damaged by the *Ganges*; abandoned by noon with thirty-nine killed and wounded.

Søhesten (20): Surrendered before 2.00 p.m.

Holsteen (60): by 1.30 p.m. was so badly damaged that Commodore Fischer hauled down his flag and went to Trekroner; a few guns still firing at 2.00 p.m.; surrendered at 2.15 p.m.

Indfødsretten (64): her captain killed by the *Ganges'* first broadside; surrendered just before 1.30 p.m. when Fischer – who was going to transfer to her from the *Holsteen* – saw her strike and decided to go to Trekroner.

Hjælperen (22): surrendered about 1.00 p.m.

The eleven gun boats which had been stationed inshore of the Danish line contributed little and were out of the action within an hour of the Battle starting. (See Appendix 2.)

Although that was the actual state of the Battle, Nelson (like everyone else, from Fischer on Trekroner and the Crown Prince at Quintus to the little *Volcano*, whose master was keeping a meticulous log) could see none of this in detail because of the smoke of battle. However, from the quarterdeck of the *Elephant* Nelson could see enough.

He wrote later that Trekroner and the batteries on Amager and by the Dockyard

were firing at us, one half their shots necessarily striking the [Danish] ships that had surrendered, and our fire did the same, and worse, for the surrendered ships had four of them got close together, and it was a massacre.

It was a sight [he added] which no real man could have enjoyed. I felt when the Danes became my prisoners, I became their protector; and if that had not been a sufficient reason, the moment of a complete victory was surely the proper time to make an opening [for a truce] with the Nation we had been fighting with.

The truce which, at 2.00 p.m., Nelson was about to propose has been deliberately misinterpreted by some historians for reasons which are based on extreme nationalism and therefore understandable but still hardly commendable.

Nelson did not exaggerate: his victory was complete. The list given above, where the events in sixteen out of nineteen ships come entirely from Danish official reports written at the time, show that at 2.00 p.m. five of the eight blockships had surrendered or were out of action, leaving two still in action with a few guns and one with only three guns; three of the four floating batteries were out of action; all three cavalry transports had been driven out of the line; all three frigates were out of action as were all eleven gun boats.

By comparison, although the *Monarch* had suffered severe casualties, every one of the eleven British line of battle ships was still in action.

Of the Danish ships at the northern end of the line and endangered by the fire of the British ships, Trekroner and the shore batteries, the *Indfødsretten* had forty-one wounded, the *Holsteen* fifty-three, the *Søhesten* twenty-one, the *Charlotte Amalia* twenty and the *Sælland* 125. In addition, the *Dannebroge* was in danger of blowing up with a ship's company of 357 on board. The total of 260 wounded in the five ships was by no means the total of all they had on board because, in addition to their own ships' companies, the wounded from several of the smaller ships and floating batteries to the south had been transferred to the blockships.

Although the exact figures were not known for months, out of the total of 5,234 Danes in the ships nearly a fifth were casualties: 370 had been killed and 665 wounded, 106 of whom died later.

For once Colonel Stewart's description of the events leading up to the sending of a message to the Crown Prince under a flag of truce is inaccurate, and to be fair to him he made it clear he was writing from memory. He says that the Danish ships to the north (*Hiælperen, Indfødsretten* and *Holsteen*) were still in action, which by both British and Danish official reports is wrong. Unfortunately the colonel's faulty memory provided more erroneous material for those wishing to distort Nelson's motives.

Ironically one of the best descriptions of Nelson writing the letter to the Crown Prince proposing a truce comes from a Danish officer – Lt Müller, who had commanded the *Hayen* until forced to surrender and been taken back to the *Elephant* by the British boarding party with Lt Friderich Lind, a young reserve officer. Müller says that on boarding the *Elephant* he met various other Danish lieutenants who had also been taken prisoner, and heard some of them saying that they had done their duty 'and now I believe I'll be made captain'.

Although the ship was still in action, Müller was allowed to go where he pleased and soon saw Nelson, whom he described as 'small, thin and very straight, dressed in a green Kalmuk's overcoat and a little three-cornered hat which he wore in the same way as Napoleon wore his.'[1]

Some of the time Nelson stood opposite Müller, but mostly he walked to and fro in front of him. Although Müller did not realize it, this was the time Nelson was deciding about the truce; and when he reached his decision and the time came to write it, Müller saw that 'a rather handsome great man [Captain Foley], completely covered in orders [of chivalry] stood at his left side and a junior officer [the purser, Thomas Wallis] stood at his right side and wrote'.

Müller did not realize that Nelson was writing the actual letter. Wallis himself noted later: 'Lord Nelson wrote the note at the casing of the rudderhead, and as he wrote I took a copy, both of us standing.'

On one side of a sheet of note paper which had been folded in half, and then folded again, Nelson wrote with his left hand very clearly (although the nib of his pen gave the appearance of needing wiping), the writing sloping backwards slightly. The letter, (illustration number 29) gave no indication of having been written while standing up using the rudderhead as a desk: indeed, it is clearer than almost any letter Nelson wrote after losing his right arm, though he was sparing with punctuation.[2]

Lord Nelson [the letter began, the pen spluttering a small blot on the 'd' and blurring part of the 'N'] has directions to spare Denmark when no longer resisting but if the firing is continued on the part of Denmark Lord Nelson will be obliged to set on fire all the floating batteries he has taken, without having the power of saving the brave Danes who have defended them,

Dated on board His
Britannick [*sic*] Majestys Ship Elephant
Copenhagen Roads April 2nd: 1801
Nelson and Bronte Vice
admiral under the Command of
admiral Sir Hyde Parker

To the Brothers of Englishmen
    The Danes.

[1] Kalmuks were worn by a Mongolian tribe and made of sheepskin and astrakhan. Nelson wore his hat 'athwartships' at a time when many officers wore it 'fore and aft'.

[2] Most of the printed versions of this letter insert extra punctuation, including *Despatches and Letters*. The version here is taken from the original which is in the State Archives in Copenhagen.

After signing he accidentally made a large blot which almost completely covered the 'B' of 'Bronté', but there was no time to rewrite it. Wallis had an envelope ready (a sheet of paper which was folded, as was the custom) and was about to stick it down with a wafer – a circular red piece of paper gummed on one side so that when wetted it became adhesive.

Nelson immediately stopped him, insisting that wax was used, with his own seal, telling Wallis that 'it must be sealed, or the enemy will think it has been written and sent in a hurry'.

Wax, Nelson's seal, and a candle to melt the wax were needed. A man was sent below to fetch them and Nelson waited impatiently. The man never returned, having been killed on the way, and another was sent. Finally the second man returned, the wax was heated, and Nelson's seal – silver-mounted on an ivory handle – was applied.

Captain Sir Frederick Thesiger, who had come on board the *Elephant* during the Battle from one of the other ships, now volunteered to take the letter into the city. This was an act of some bravery because the shot landing between the *Elephant* and the harbour entrance made the sea look like a pond which small boys were showering with dozens of pebbles.

Nelson immediately accepted, since Thesiger spoke Danish and Russian. The *Elephant*'s gig was prepared, a large white flag was rigged on an oar which a seaman held up in the bow, and a Blue Ensign was hoisted at the stern, and with Thesiger in the sternsheets the boat shoved off.

The safest route to the harbour was to go north, clear of the *Ganges*, *Monarch* and *Defiance*, and then skirt the Trekroner Fort in a half circle and approach the harbour along the fairway – a total distance of more than three miles: nearly an hour's rowing. Thesiger, however, knowing the urgency of his mission, directed the coxswain to steer straight for the first Danish ship in the fairway – the *Elephanten*. This took the gig close to the *Charlotte Amalia*, across the position in which the *Sælland* had been anchored, and between Trekroner and the *Søhesten*, *Holsteen*, *Indfødsretten* and *Hiælperen*.

As soon as the gunners saw the boat carrying a flag of truce, the Trekroner Fort guns did not fire at it; but shot was falling all round from the shore batteries, whose gunners could not see it. Finally Thesiger reached the *Elephanten* and went alongside.

The Danish ship's log noted:

'2.30 p.m. Came on board the *Elephanten* flag of truce from the British Fleet with orders which were to be sent on shore. Lieutenant [Carl] Lundbye left to pilot the gig.'

Thus it fell to a twenty-six-year-old Danish reserve lieutenant to pilot into the harbour of the city in which he had been born a British boat which, although he did not know it, carried a letter which could bring peace to his country and save the lives of the scores of Danish wounded in the Defence Line ships.

The Crown Prince had watched the early part of the Battle from the Quintus battery; but as the Battle moved north he had walked round the bastion and crossed over the boom gate from the island of Amager to Nordre Toldbod, in front of the Castellet.

From here he had a good view: Trekroner was almost in line with the *Hiælperen* at the north end of the line; Nelson's flagship, although hidden by smoke and the hulk of the burning *Dannebroge*, was in front of him. To his left, well beyond Trekroner, he could see Sir Hyde Parker's division slowly approaching, the *Defence*, *Ramillies* and *Veteran* well ahead of the rest.

Behind him were the earthworks surrounding the Castellet and a few bare trees – spring had not yet arrived to bring out the leaves – and just in front was a small wooden jetty normally used by fishermen.[1] He, like every one of his subjects in the capital, had not only his nation, but also his home in peril: his palace of Amalienborg was five minutes' walk from where he stood at Nordre Toldbod.

The Prince, on foot and surrounded by his staff and guard, wore a uniform red jacket with high collar and lapels of blue, white breeches and a gold cummerbund, and a black hat edged with grey lace and topped with a grey plume. At his left side he wore a curved cavalry sabre; in his right hand he held a walking stick.

With the Prince was his aide-de-camp, Captain Hans Lindholm, who was a naval officer, and members of the Defence Commission – Admiral Kaas, Rear-admiral Wleugel, Chamberlain von Knuth and General-auditør Lauritz Nørregaard. Watching a battle in which he could take no part must have been a bitter experience for Kaas: years earlier he had commanded the *Mars*, now one of Steen Bille's squadron, and the *Jylland*. Rear-admiral Wleugel had a personal anxiety as he watched: his son, Peter Johan, thirty-five, was second-in-command of the *Jylland*, one of the few ships still firing despite very heavy casualties. (Although the admiral did not know at that moment whether his son was dead or alive, in fact Peter Johan had distinguished himself commanding the upper-deck guns, and was one of five people Captain Brandt commended for bravery.)

For more than an hour the Crown Prince and his staff had stood at

[1] Very close to where the Gefion fountain stands today and a hundred yards or so south of the 'Little Mermaid' statue.

Nordre Toldbod watching the dense smoke billowing up from ship after ship, from broadsides and from fires, and drift northward along the line. Boat after boat had been rowed into the harbour with casualties, each with a long swallow-tailed pendant flying from an oar lashed upright in the bow, the men at the oars hampered as they rowed by the wounded lying or sitting huddled on the thwarts. No sooner had each boat unloaded its wounded than it turned and headed out towards the shattered ships, often carrying fresh men.

Suddenly a boat was spotted coming from the direction of the *Elephanten*: to a trained eye it was not Danish – unlike the bluff, apple-cheeked local boats it had a sharp bow, and flying from the bow was a white flag of truce and aft a Blue Ensign.

Within a few minutes Thesiger had landed at the jetty with Lt Lundbye and was taken to the Crown Prince, to whom he delivered Nelson's letter. (See illustration number 31.)

As the Crown Prince read the letter he could see that the *Defence*, *Ramillies* and *Veteran* ahead of Parker's division would soon be in a position to join the Battle; beyond them were two great three-deckers, 98-gun ships, two more 74s and two 64s. And apart from the boatloads of wounded passing him, one after another of his captains had come to report they had fought on until their ships and men could fight no more: captains like Risbrich of the *Wagrien*, who wrote later, 'He received me reasonably, and to him I reported my action and experiences during the attack.'

Within a short while the entire defence of the city of Copenhagen, particularly the Dockyard and Arsenal, would rest on the guns of the Trekroner Fort, Lynetten, and the batteries along the seaward side of the city walls. Steen Bille's squadron could stop any British ships trying to enter the fairway to the harbour; but soon the British ships would also be able to stop Steen Bille's division getting out, so nothing, least of all Trekroner – could prevent the seven British bomb vessels closing in, anchoring to the east and south-east of the city, out of range of Trekroner, and hurling shells into the city. Most of them were already anchored near the *Elephant*. It would be only a matter of time before the shells destroyed the Dockyard, and after that they could slowly smash the city.

But what precisely was Nelson offering? The Crown Prince had a brief discussion with the Defence Commission, and then ordered Captain Lindholm (who spoke excellent English) to go out and – in the Prince's name – ask Nelson. At once the *Elephant*'s gig left the landing stage for the flagship carrying Lindholm, Thesiger, and the young Danish lieutenant, Lundbye.

In the meantime Nelson had sent for Captain Fremantle of the *Ganges* – 'he hailed and desired I would come on board,' Fremantle later told Betsey – and while waiting for him to arrive the admiral went down to his cabin with Foley to talk to some of the Danish officer prisoners.

Lt Müller described part of the conversation. According to him Nelson said, 'What has happened today hurts me, and to prove it I have suggested a truce. But in the meantime if this is refused I shall be forced to take the Trekroner Battery and burn the Arsenal.'

According to Müller he told Nelson that 'There are some circumstances about the Trekroner Battery which I am sure you know, and I am sure you will understand that the Battery is not going to be easy to take. As you possibly understand, as far as the Arsenal is concerned, my countrymen are not such idiots as to leave anything in there when they see it is going to be shelled to burn it.'

Müller wrote that Captain Foley, who was standing with Nelson, remarked that the British had never had as hot a day as this, even against the Dutch, French or Spanish. Nelson said that he 'hoped that my stay on board would not be long', and that 'I would be as comfortable as possible and that I did not lose any of my clothing' on board the *Hayen*. After that 'he said goodbye'.

Captain Fremantle, arriving on board just as Nelson was ending the conversation, wrote that Nelson 'was in his cabin talking to some Danish officers out of one of the ships captured, and saying how anxious he was to meet the Russians, and wished it had been them and not the Danes we had engaged.

'At this time,' Fremantle wrote to the Marquis of Buckingham, 'he put into my hand a letter which he meant to send immediately to the prince in a flag of truce.'

Fremantle apparently did not know that it was in fact the copy made by Wallis,[1] but he added: 'At this time he was aware that our ships were cut to pieces, and it would be difficult to get them out.' It is interesting to note that even at this stage Nelson, Foley and Fremantle never considered the very powerful force represented by Sir Hyde's division.

Colonel Stewart says that before Thesiger returned,

Lord Nelson had taken the opinion of his valuable friends, Fremantle and Foley . . . as to the practicability of advancing the ships which were least damaged upon that part of the Danish Line of Defence yet uninjured. [Trekroner Fort and Steen Bille's squadron.] Their opinions were averse from it; and, on the other hand, decided in favour of removing our Fleet

[1] He gave the wording of this first letter to the Crown Prince and the second as though they were all one.

whilst the wind yet held fair from their present intricate channel. Lord Nelson was now prepared to act when [Captain] Lindholm came on board. . . .

In no way was Nelson holding a council of war – he regarded them as a weakness. He was simply discussing the situation with two of his captains who were old friends. Stewart's reference is open to misinterpretation unless it is realized that Thesiger had already gone on shore with the letter of truce before Fremantle was hailed: in other words, Nelson had long since decided what he was going to do concerning the truce, but had in mind the Danes might refuse it.

When Thesiger arrived back on board he immediately took Captain Lindholm to Nelson, and the Danish officer delivered his verbal message from the Crown Prince. Nelson was impressed by Lindholm's manner, and asked him to put the message in writing, which Lindholm did, in English:

His Royal Highness the Prince Royal of Denmark has sent me, his General ADC Lindholm, on board his British Majesty's Vice-admiral the Right Honourable Lord Nelson, to ask him what his intentions were by sending the flag of truce.

Nelson wasted no time in giving Lindholm a written explanation for the Crown Prince, Wallis again copying as Nelson wrote:

Lord Nelson's object in sending on shore a Flag of Truce is humanity: he therefore consents that hostilities shall cease till Lord Nelson can taken his prisoners out of the Prizes, and he consents to land all the wounded Danes, and to burn or remove his prizes.

Lord Nelson, with humble duty to His Royal Highness, begs leave to say that he will ever esteem it the greatest victory he ever gained if this Flag of Truce may be the happy forerunner of a lasting and happy union between my most gracious Sovereign and his Majesty the King of Denmark.

At once the gig took Thesiger and Lindholm on shore again with the reply. The boat trip out to the *Elephant* and back to Nordre Toldboden gave Lindholm a good opportunity to see the situation of both the British and Danish ships, and since he was a naval officer his report would be the best information the Crown Prince could obtain. Soon after, firing from most of the Danish batteries ceased – an indication the terms were accepted – and the *Elephant* immediately hoisted a flag of truce. Sir Hyde noted in his journal that at 3.15 p.m. 'observed the *Elephant* to hoist a flag of truce'. At that time the *London* was three miles from Trekroner.

The Master's log of Nelson's flagship recorded: 'About 2 p.m. they being mostly subdued, Vice-admiral Lord Nelson sent a flag of truce to the Danish Government to arrange the landing of the wounded prisoners; his Lordship's terms were accepted and all firing ceased.'

The *Elephanten*'s log, which recorded Thesiger's arrival alongside in the gig, when Lt Lundbye was given him as a pilot, later noted: '5 p.m. Orders came from Captain Fischer to stop firing.'

In the city, a student wrote:

At last it went around among the crowd that an English boat with a white peace flag had tied up at Quintus [sic]. But still the cannons went on roaring, but it was not very long because suddenly everything became very peaceful and all the ships, the English as well as the Danish, suddenly appeared rather like a foggy picture in the clearest sunlight. . . .

A newspaper reported that during and after the Battle the Customs Jetty was 'a scene of awful suffering which continued for several days', and the people were worried in case there should be another attack. 'There were terrible sights of badly wounded men, many with limbs missing and nearly all angry.' Before the truce, 'on the stretchers with wild movements, they cried that they wanted to return to the battle, but shouts of "Long Live the King" drowned their cries'.

This was followed by bringing the dead on shore from the ships and floating batteries. . . . Bodies without heads and arms, and legs and arms alone, were put on carts to be taken away to be buried.

The column of dead and wounded being carried to hospitals and mortuaries were met [before the Truce] by columns of reinforcements led by drummers going out to the ships. The reinforcements were wearing smocks which the soldiers called 'dead shirts' [i.e. shrouds].

The column of dead and wounded was followed by crying women asking about their husbands and sons, and from time to time the women left the column after finding out their husbands were dead.

Even more touching was the silence and grief reflected like a mirror in the faces of those watching and who had not taken part in the battle. It was as though every hope of victory was going with the bodies of those being taken to the graves. Many wished themselves dead; others blamed the high command.

At the same time one both hoped and feared another attack was completely past. The most fantastic rumours went around, each one contradicting the other. With these contradictions many hearts were torn.

The rest of the day was like a drunken nightmare. . . . Everybody stayed away from their friends, knowing there was nothing to say to each other. . . .

Sir Hyde's division had anchored three miles from Trekroner before the flag of truce was hoisted and the frigates *Amazon*, *Blanche* and *Alcmene* had anchored near by, followed by the other ships of Riou's little flotilla. At once the men in each ship began making repairs: to the main and mizenmasts and bowsprit of the *Amazon*, to the masts of the *Cruizer* and *Alcmene*, stopping up two shot holes between wind and water in the *Dart*, knotting damaged standing and splicing running rigging in all of them, and replacing the *Blanche*'s main topsail with a spare one.

With the terms of his truce accepted, Nelson began to get his sail of the line out of the King's Deep. Even before the firing had stopped, Nelson had sent for Rear-admiral Graves to come on board the *Elephant* so that he could explain the position. 'It was beautiful to see how the shot beat the water all round us in the boat,' Graves wrote to his brother. Nelson told him that he was to lead the division out.

Foley gave the order to cut the *Elephant*'s cable and spring and make sail for the main channel. The *Defiance*, *Monarch* and *Ganges*, ahead of the flagship, all cut their cables at the same time.

Once again, Nelson was unlucky with the Middle Ground shoal: although roughly oval-shaped, lying north and south, a narrow tongue stuck out on the west side, pointing north. It ran about a thousand yards, from abreast the *Elephant* to some three hundred yards beyond the *Defiance* at the head of the British line. But for this tongue, all four ships could have weighed and steered direct for Parker's division, clearing the shoal with plenty to spare.

The *Defiance*, the first to get under way, was difficult to handle because of torn rigging, and she ran aground. 'Ran out the stream anchor and cable, which we hove home', the log noted. The bottom round the Middle Ground was too soft to hold it.

The *Defiance*'s next astern was the *Monarch*, with the *Ganges* astern of her and then the *Elephant*.

Midshipman Millard describes what happened next:

The *Ganges* which . . . had received but little damage, having but six men killed and wounded, was under way before we could well look about us. Our decks were choked with disabled guns; near half our complement were either killed or wounded; and there was not fore and aft one single brace [which trimmed the yards] or bowline that was not shot away, so that the sails could not possibly be directed one way or the other, but hung on the caps as when we first anchored.

The consequence was that the *Ganges* came directly on board us, upon the larboard quarter, her jib-boom passing over our quarter deck and her spritsail yard grappling with our main and mizen rigging. Both ships were now alike ungovernable, and both were drifting fast towards the Crown Islands. To their perpetual shame be it spoken, they [the Danes] took advantage of our distress, and opened their fire again upon us.

While we were busy in cutting away such parts of the rigging as held the two ships together, the *Ganges* let fall another anchor, and we drifted clear of her, leaving one of our mizentopmen named John Town upon her bowsprit; the lad had leaped on to it to assist more effectually in clearing away. When he found himself left on board the *Ganges* he began to swear most unmercifully; and at length came down into the head [bow] and plunged from the bumpkin into the water.

The *Monarch* was still perfectly ungovernable, and we continued to drift towards the Crown Islands. Mr Yelland desired me to fetch the Signal Book and make the signal for boats to tow.

Recollecting that the Book had been deposited on the stern walk, I ran thither for it; and as I skipped along over the rubbish that lay about I set my foot directly on the body of our dead captain which . . . was covered with a flag. When I discovered it, I felt a sensation of horror which chilled my blood. . . . Fortunately I had not much time to pause and reflect but hastened out at the other end of the gallery and ran on to the poop to make the signal.

When I got there I was obliged to call for some help, for not a man was left on the poop. The signal midshipman . . . was wounded, his assistant, a fine young man about twenty or twenty-one years old, had his leg shot off and went down without assistance into the cockpit where, from the number of persons the surgeon had to attend, he actually bled to death. . . .

I found a musket, the barrel of which was bent into a semi-circle; this I apprehended, must have been struck on the muzzle the very instant the man was presenting it [to fire]; it could not otherwise have been driven into that form. There was a barrel of water placed on the poop which was knocked to pieces, and a basket, or skep, of pistols were scattered about.

While I was making the signal I discovered [the mizentopman, John Town] swimming in the water. When some of the boats [answering the signal] approached the ship I hailed them to go and pick him up; but he had swum to a big bit of wreck that was floating by, and desired them to go and tow the ship without minding him. He was, however, brought on board.

When the boats had succeeded in pulling the ship's head round, we steered her out by hand, having no wheel.[1]

The *Ganges* had less trouble getting out, the journal of Lt R. Loud not even mentioning the ship running aboard the *Monarch*. 'Set the mainsail and cut the stern cable, and stood out in the best manner possible, the mast, yards, sails &c. being very much cut.'

The *Elephant* was less fortunate, and in her Master's words:

About 4, cut the cable and spring and made sail for the outer road; 10 past we hung on the Middle Ground, run [sic] an anchor out astern, hove a strain and the anchor came home; run several of the guns forward [to lessen the draught aft], started 25 butts of water [i.e emptied them and pumped the water over the side] and sent part of the bread on board a brig and a schooner. About 6 a gun-brig [the *Discovery*] brought us an anchor and cable,

[1] Using tackles rigged to the tiller, orders being shouted down the hatch to haul on one and slacken the other as required.

which we laid out on the larboard bow, and about ½ past 9 [p.m.] we hove, off. At 10, we made sail, and at 11 anchored in the Road in 6½ fathoms.

Shortly after the truce had been accepted, and a matter of minutes after the *Defiance*, *Monarch*, *Ganges* and *Elephant* cut their cables, the *Dannebroge*'s fires increased, and it was obvious she could not last long.

Captain Bertie, commanding the *Ardent*, sent his launch over to her, with orders to the officer in charge to save as many of the Danish crew as possible but not to go alongside in case the boat should be swamped.

As soon as the launch was within a few yards of the *Dannebroge* and picking up men who began jumping overboard, her commanding officer, Captain Braun – who had, of course, been wounded – hailed the lieutenant and asked the name of the captain of the ship who had sent the boat. He paid a compliment to Captain Bertie and said he would make a point of telling the Crown Prince of Bertie's 'generous attention and humanity'.

The launch returned to the *Ardent* with twenty-three of the *Dannebroge*'s crew, while other boats, including those from the *Glatton*, picked up more men. Once again, Midshipman Millard gives a vivid description of what happened next.

Having now time to stand still, I found those powerful sensations arising from too long abstinence no longer to be resisted. I had but little appetite for breakfast at seven o'clock . . . and I had been during the interval very hard at work. Accordingly down I sallied to the gun-room, and without much ceremony broke open the gunner's locker, where I found half a cheese and some cold potatoes; but, what was most valuable, a can of fresh water.

Having well drenched my inside with repeated draughts, I had so much thought about me as to send it to poor Mr Yelland, who I know could not leave the deck. The remainder I served indiscriminately among the seamen; and having on further examination discovered a bag of biscuits, I was enabled to serve bread and cheese to several, as far as it would go. . . .

While I was thus employed, I heard a most tremendous explosion, and looking out at the port saw an immense mass of black smoke in the air, with sparks of fire and rafters scarce discernible from the thickness of the cloud. This proved to be the ship of the Danish Commodore. . . .

It is not known exactly how many men perished when the *Dannebroge* exploded: her casualties totalled fifty-three killed and fifty-one wounded, three of whom died later. Eighty-six more, in addition to many wounded, were rescued by British ships and 148 reached the shore in Danish boats.

The fire ships *Otter* and *Zephyr* were ordered to board prizes and get the wounded to the shore. Then, as darkness fell, the seven bomb vessels, whose boats had also been busy securing prizes, taking the wounded to the shore and collecting prisoners were ordered to move closer in to the shore. . . .

'Got under way and shifted our berth more to the southward and westward,' the *Explosion*'s log noted, while the *Volcano*'s said: 'Captain Sutton of the *Alcmene* came on board with orders for us to shift our berth nearer to Crown Island. . . . Cut the cable. Employed warping into station. Crown Island NW $\frac{1}{2}$ N, two or three miles.' By midnight the bombs had the Arsenal and Dockyard – indeed, the whole city – well within range of their mortars.

Sir Hyde Parker had, once Nelson's flag of truce was hoisted, done his best: 'Sent all the boats to assist disabled ships and remove prisoners. . . .' The *Elephant* was off the shoal and anchored in the Roads by 11.00 p.m.; the *Bellona* was refloated at 8.00 p.m., the *Russell* about midnight, followed by the *Defiance* at 8.00 a.m. next day and the *Agamemnon* four hours later.

At sunset, about 6.30 p.m., a boat with a flag of truce came out from Copenhagen and went to the *London*: since Sir Hyde was the Commander-in-Chief it was now up to him to arrange the terms of whatever arrangement followed the truce. Captain Lindholm went on board, representing the Crown Prince, and was given Parker's terms in the form of a letter addressed to the Danish Government. They were in fact basically the terms offered before the Battle.

'If the Government of Copenhagen [sic] should acquiesce in the proposal of a Defensive Alliance, His [Britannic] Majesty is disposed to afford them every protection by entering into engagements (if they should desire it) for providing a contingent naval force for the defence of Denmark,' the letter began. The British would keep at least twenty sail of the line in the Baltic as long as the season allowed, providing Denmark would keep at least ten in the same area. The letter continued, 'If the Danish Government should consent to a convention founded on the above-mentioned principles, &c., a Defensive Alliance (if they should adopt that alternative) you are to require them to ratify it without delay, and to deliver to you a ratified copy, for the purpose of being exchanged in London against His Majesty's ratification thereof.'

The last paragraph reads oddly because Sir Hyde was, with his usual ineptitude, copying it almost verbatim from Hawkesbury's letter of 23 February to Drummond in Copenhagen – the 'further instructions' which Parker himself brought from England.[1]

---

[1] The letter is in the Danish archives and annotated, 'Extract from a letter from Lord Hawesbury [sic] to Mr Drummond as to the terms offered to the Court of Denmark and made by Sir Hyde Parker, Commander-in-Chief, British Fleet, before Copenhagen.'

Nelson arrived on board the *London* soon after Lindholm and joined Sir Hyde in the preliminary negotiations. He had left the *Elephant* still aground, and, Colonel Stewart noted, 'was low in spirits at the surrounding scene of devastation, and particularly felt for the blowing up of the *Dannebroge*. "Well!" he exclaimed, "I have fought contrary to orders, and I shall perhaps be hanged: never mind, let them" .' The orders were, of course, signal number 39.

Unfortunately no description exists of this first meeting between Sir Hyde and Nelson after the Battle. Little did Lindholm realize, as he discussed the terms of an Armistice with the Commander-in-Chief and his second-in-command, that it was Nelson's disobedience over signal No. 39 that ensured the final victory for which Parker was now dictating the British terms.

Lindholm then returned to the city, his boat passing in the darkness those of the British Fleet taking the wounded out of the prizes.

With this stage of the negotiations completed, Nelson left the *London* and went to his former flagship, the *St George*: there would be little chance of a rest in the *Elephant* that night, and with the fighting over there was no reason for Nelson to stay on board.

In his cabin on board the *St George*, after talking with Hardy, he wrote up his journal, making no reference to signal No. 39. The entire day's entry read as follows:

Moderate breeze southerly at ½ past nine made the signal to weigh and to engage the Danish line. The action began at 5 minutes past ten and lasted about four hours, when 17 out of 18 of the Danish line were taken burnt or sunk. Our ships suffered a good deal. At night went on board the *St George*, very unwell.

Then Nelson wrote to Emma: it was a brief note dated on board the *St George* 'at 9 o'clock at night very tired after a hard fought Battle'. He wrote, in a letter that would travel to England in the same ship that carried his despatch describing the Battle, 'Of eighteen sail, large and small, some are taken, some sunk, some burnt in the good old way.'

Meanwhile in all the British ships that had been in action, men were busy making repairs: carpenters and their mates made and fitted 'fishes' – in effect wooden splints – for damaged masts, yards, bowsprits and jib-booms; torn rigging was repaired – where it could not be replaced the running rigging was spliced, the standing rigging knotted. Down in the cockpits, working in the dim light of candles in lanthorns, the surgeons worked and fought against fatigue to treat the wounded.

'We are all fitting out as if we were at Spithead, though within five miles of Copenhagen,' Fremantle wrote to the Marquis of Buckingham.

He added that, 'Our masts and rigging are cut to pieces, but I think in a few days I shall be as the day I left Yarmouth.'

To Betsey he wrote, 'I hope the children continue well, and you may now rest satisfied that whenever we do return to port, I shall have an opportunity of seeing you as we want a new fore mast, a new mainmast and bowsprit.'

29

ANOTHER BATTLE?

Nelson had not been asleep long on board the *St George* before he was wakened with a report that one of the Danish sail of the line had fired on a boarding party, claiming that it had not surrendered. This was a clear breach of the truce and Nelson at once sent a note to Sir Hyde. Headed, '*St George*, 3 a.m.' it said:

One of the ships which struck during yesterday's Battle was by some oversight not taken possession of. I directed Lord Henry Paulet [commanding the *Defence*], late last night, to do so. His boats, I find, were fired at, and not allowed to come alongside, [the Danes] saying they had not surrendered, as their pendant was still flying.

This is a most disgraceful subterfuge, as this ship had ceased firing on hauling down her Colours. I think you had better demand her in a peremptory manner; and I recommend your sending Otway for that purpose. In much haste. . . .

Of all Nelson's correspondence relating to the expedition to Copenhagen, this hurried note written in the middle of a bitterly cold night is one of the most revealing of the new relationship between the two admirals. Nelson is punctilious – a breach of the truce is a matter for the Commander-in-Chief – hence the letter. But if the affair was badly handled it could lead to more bloodshed – so far the Danes had fired only muskets. He knew Lord Harry Paulet was notoriously a very brave but equally impetuous and hot-tempered officer and he clearly was not the man to deal with this situation. Nelson knew Otway only from recent meetings but he saw he was a young man of considerable ingenuity and tact, brave and a fine seaman, and just the man to handle the task. So, with polite and qualifying phrases like 'I think' and 'I recommend' he made sure Sir Hyde acted correctly.

That Sir Hyde was far from resenting such a letter is shown by the fact that Otway recorded later that Sir Hyde gave him the letter with 'directions to act upon it according to my judgment'.

The identity of the ship is not absolutely certain although it was most likely the *Sælland*. Colonel Stewart's account of it, written many years later from memory, is so obviously wrong in many other respects, that although the name he gives, 'Zealand', is the Anglicized version, it is of little consequence.

It has often been thought it was the *Holsteen*, but the report of her commanding officer, Captain Arenfeldt, to the Crown Prince says the *Holsteen* struck at 2.15 p.m., and 'I sent a lieutenant on shore and immediately after a boarding party came on board and took possession. I and ... various others were taken on board the *London*.' Arenfeldt's report is dated the day after the Battle.

The identity of the ship is less important than the interesting way that Otway secured her. In material he supplied years later, Otway refers to her as the *Holsteen*, which was probably a slip of the memory, and describes how he selected the schooner *Eling*, hoisted a flag of truce, and ordered her commanding officer to get under way. This is confirmed by Sir Hyde's journal – 'Sent Captain Otway to Copenhagen with a flag of truce'.

He had the *Eling* anchor off the bow of the Danish ship,

... which was at anchor within pistol shot of one of the Crown Batteries. Her pendant was still flying, though her colours were down, and she was preparing to warp into the Arsenal.

Seeing there was not a moment to be lost, Captain Otway immediately pushed alongside of her in the *Eling*'s boat, having ordered the coxswain (a bold and determined character) to take the opportunity, while he [Otway] was claiming the ship from the surviving officers,[1] to proceed, unperceived if possible, through the main chains into the maintop, haul down the pendant, and carry it into the boat.

It was accomplished to the very letter, the attention of the whole crew being directed towards Captain Otway, who was standing on the quarter deck demanding possession of the ship which they still refused to give up, but referred him to their Commodore [Fischer] who was on board a two-decker close by in the Arsenal, making use of their former plea that their pendant was still flying.

Thus far successful in his object, and his situation being such as, in the event of a discovery, would not have been a pleasant one, Captain Otway gladly embraced the offer of a reference to the Commodore.

He accordingly proceeded to [Fischer's] ship in one of the Danish boats and accompanied by a Danish officer, having ordered the *Eling*'s boat, containing the pendant, to return to the schooner.

Finding on his arrival that the Commodore spoke English very fluently, Captain Otway immediately ... demanded that the ship should be given up.

He was met with the old objection that her colours had been shot away in

[1] The only Danish captains killed commanded the *Indfødsretten* and the *Cronborg*.

the action and that she had not surrendered; as a proof of which, [Fischer] said, her pendant still remained flying.

But this argument had been effectually removed, and Captain Otway replied, 'I believe sir, you are mistaken on that point.' With the utmost confidence the Commodore requested him to walk to the stern gallery (as they could not see the *Holsteen* [sic] from the quarterdeck) saying 'I will soon convince you that it is you who are mistaken, not I.'

However, on arriving in the stern gallery and seeing that the pendant was actually down, he expressed the utmost astonishment, but was constrained to acknowledge that she was a lawful prize, and sent an order, by the Danish officer who had accompanied Captain Otway, for her delivery.

Captain Otway then hailed the *Eling* schooner, and desired Lieutenant Peek [her captain] to take possession of the *Holsteen*, to cut her cable (the wind being off the land) and make the signal to the Fleet for immediate assistance. The *Harpy* brig instantly slipped her cable and towed the prize up to the British Fleet.

The *Harpy*'s Master's log says: 'At 9 answered the signal to take a ship in tow who had struck. $\frac{1}{2}$ past anchored ahead of her. Sent a hawser on board. Slipped our cable and made sail with tow. Anchored her astern of the Commander-in-Chief.' Unfortunately the *Harpy*'s log does not mention the ship's name and Parker's Journal makes no reference to the episode.

Lord Nelson, in the meantime, had got up early on board the *St George* to find dawn had brought a bitterly cold northwest wind. He ordered his gig ('his usual conveyance', Stewart noted) and was rowed over to the *Elephant*, thinking she was still aground.

The fatigue and cold of a long row in a northern sea, and at that early hour, and after the most severe exertions of both body and mind for several successive days [wrote Stewart] had no effect in causing this uncommon man either to indulge in rest or for an instant forget those whose fate he valued.

His delight and praises in finding us afloat were unbounded and recompensed all our misfortunes. He took a hasty breakfast and then rowed to such of the prizes as were not yet removed from the Danish shore. . . .

At this point Stewart's account, obviously describing events he heard second hand and was recalling much later, becomes inaccurate, and Otway's account can be checked.

While the *Harpy* was preparing to tow the prize,

Lord Nelson, who was rowing round the prizes, accompanied by Captain Hardy, learned that Captain Otway was on board the Danish Commodore's ship, and seized the opportunity of following him in the event of a renewal of hostilities.

The arrival of a flag of truce [Nelson's boat] was reported to the Commodore whilst himself and Captain Otway were taking some refreshment (the latter not having had any since the preceding day), and Captain Otway was informed that the officer in the boat wished to speak to him.

On going on deck he was equally pleased and surprised to find that the officer was Lord Nelson: he was immediately invited on board, when both chiefs recognised each other, having both commanded frigates in the West Indies at the same time.[1]

Nelson returned to the *St George* and sat down to write his report on the Battle, which Captain Fremantle was able to tell the Marquis of Buckingham, 'in confidence, he dictated to me ... while I wrote it'. The report, addressed to Sir Hyde Parker, began in a time-honoured way – 'In obedience to your directions to report the proceedings of the Squadron ... you did me the honour to place under my command,' and went on first to praise 'that able officer, Captain Riou', and the 'unremitting exertions of Captain Brisbane and the Masters of the *Amazon* and *Cruizer*' in buoying the Outer Deep and the Middle Ground so the division could anchor to the south of the Middle Ground.

Nelson then listed the Danish forces – Fischer's ships, Trekroner, shore batteries and Steen Bille's squadron – and the succeeding paragraph said simply: 'The bomb ship and schooner gun vessels made their escape. The other seventeen sail are sunk, burnt or taken, being the whole of the Danish line to the southward of the Crown Islands, after a battle of four hours.'

He continued that 'from the very intricate navigation' the *Bellona* and the *Russell* grounded, 'but although not in the situation assigned them, yet so placed as to be of great service.' The *Agamemnon* grounded, 'but not the smallest blame can be attached to Captain Fancourt: it was an event to which all the ships were liable'.

He wrote that 'these accidents prevented the extension of our line' by those three ships, 'who would, I am confident, have silenced the Crown Islands and prevented the heavy loss in the *Defiance* and *Monarch*; and which unhappily threw the gallant and good Captain Riou (to whom I had given command of the frigates and sloops ...) under very heavy fire. The consequence has been the death of Captain Riou, and many brave officers and men in the frigates and sloops.'

Nelson made no reference to signal No. 39; however, Sir Hyde and

[1] Nelson commanded the *Boreas* in the West Indies from 1784 to 1787 and visited the Danish Virgin Islands in 1786 and 1787, while Fischer commanded the frigate *Bornholm* 1784–9. Some accounts have reported the 'Commodore' as being Steen Bille, but 'the Commodore' could only mean Fischer who held the rank (a permanent one in the Danish Navy) and to which Bille was not appointed until 1804; likewise Bille did not serve in the West Indies at the same time as Nelson.

the captains in the Fleet would be in no doubt of the real significance of the phrase 'The consequence has been. . . .'

The rest of the letter outlined the role of the bomb ketches and other vessels, and praised individual officers. Murray of the *Edgar*, leading the van, 'set a noble example of intrepidity, which was as well followed up by every captain, officer and man in the squadron'. There was praise for his second-in-command, Graves; for the captain of his temporary flagship, Foley; Colonel Stewart . . . and finally the loss of Captain Mosse and the wounding of the captain of the *Bellona*.

With his report completed, Nelson went over to the *London*, where he found the Crown Prince's Adjutant-General, Captain Lindholm, had been on board, accompanied by Captain Steen Bille. The Danish Government's reply had not been put in writing: instead Lindholm told Parker, (according to Danish sources: Sir Hyde did not record it) that Denmark offered to mediate between Britain and the 'Eastern Sea Power' if Britain lifted her embargo, but the Danish Parliament would not leave the Armed Neutrality 'because it was not aimed at England'.

It was clear to Parker that all this meant the Danes were still clinging to the same policy that led to the Battle. Since they were defeated and Copenhagen was at his mercy, they were in no position to dictate terms and their reply was obviously not one that Parker could possibly accept. But with the time limit on the Truce fast running out, it was difficult for him to know whether the Danes were being stupid, obstinate, defiant, proud, or merely making the first move in a complicated diplomatic dance which, providing everyone listened to the music and kept in step, would end in agreement. And Parker was sensible enough to know he was no dancer: he told Lindholm that Lord Nelson would come on shore to negotiate with the Crown Prince – which is quite probably what the Danes expected, and Lindholm gave an invitation from the Crown Prince for Nelson to dine at the Palace.

So as soon as he boarded the *London*, Nelson was told of the Danish visit and terms. 'Sir Hyde Parker thought that probably some good might arise if I went on shore to converse with His Royal Highness,' Nelson wrote next day to the Prime Minister, Henry Addington. He returned to the *St George* to prepare for the visit, deciding to take Thesiger with him to act as interpreter, and Captain Hardy.[1]

Quite apart from the task before him, it required a courageous man to land in Copenhagen less than twenty-four hours after wreaking such havoc: many boats, Danish and British, were still bringing wounded

---

[1] Some British and Danish accounts include Fremantle, but he did not go on this occasion and wrote in two letters written on 4 April how Nelson had described to him the visit at breakfast that morning.

Danes on shore from the ships, and the feelings of the relatives waiting on the shore to see if their menfolk were alive, wounded or dead can be imagined.

Nelson landed from his barge at the South Customs House Quay, opposite the Sixtus battery and the great mast crane on Amager. A few yards away the shattered *Nyeborg*, with all but one of her guns dismounted and only the stump of her foremast remaining, had sunk alongside the quay, leaving only her gunwales awash – a tribute to Rothe's skill and determination in getting her in. (One of the day's newspapers exhorted – 'Countrymen! repair to the Customs House, view the *Nyeborg*, and be convinced how a Danish ship must be disabled before a Danish seaman can persuade himself to retire from action!')

The description of the reception Nelson received varies with the viewer.

Captain Hardy wrote to his brother-in-law that, 'extraordinary to be told, he was received with as much acclamation as when we went to *Lord Mare's Show* [sic], and I really believe it would not have been a very hard business to have brought on a revolution in Denmark'.

A Danish eyewitness wrote:

He was received by the people neither with cheers nor murmurs; they did not degrade themselves with the former, nor disgrace themselves with the latter. The Admiral was received as one brave enemy ought ever to receive another – he was received with respect.

A carriage was provided for his Lordship, which he however declined and walked, amidst an immense crowd of people who were anxious to catch a glimpse of the British hero, to the Palace of the Crown Prince.

The *Berlingske Tidende* reported soberly:

Admiral Nelson is at this moment on land to discuss terms. His suggestions are not yet known, but every Dane is certain that our Crown Prince, with whom he has audience, will never accept any offer which could do the nation harm. This is an important and decisive moment and even more blood will run in the next attack if these negotiations fail to give results. Everyone is prepared to meet the worst and stand or fall like a man.

Nelson gave his version in a letter to Troubridge next day: 'My reception was too flattering, and landing at Portsmouth or Yarmouth could not have exceeded the blessings of the people; even the Palace and stairs were crowded, and huzzas, which could not have been very grateful to Royal ears.'

As Fremantle heard it from Nelson at breakfast next morning, with Hardy present, 'He was hailed with cheers by the multitude, who came to receive him at the waterside and "Viva Nelson" resounded until he got to the Palace, much to the annoyance, I believe, of His Royal Highness and his ministers.'

Nelson, with Thesiger and the burly Hardy, walked inland a few yards along Toldbodvej until they came to Amaliegade, a straight road on their left which ran directly to Amalienborg Palace.

Halfway down, on their right-hand side, they passed Frederiks Hospital (today the Museum of Applied Art), an impressive grey building with a black tiled roof and built round a quadrangle and which was full of wounded. Inspector of Hospitals Benz had already filled Fødsels Stiftelsen, the maternity hospital next door which he had requisitioned, while dozens more were being treated in buildings across the inner harbour on Amager.

In beds in Frederiks Hospital as Nelson passed were several Danish officers, among them Captain Braun of the *Dannebroge*, who had lost his right hand, Lt Hans Bang of the *Sælland*, who had several wounds, Lt Peter Justesen, whose left foot had been crushed on board the *Aggershuus*, and Lt Christian Müller of the *Hiælperen*, who had lost a leg and was dying.[1]

Amaliegade is a wide and gracious street: a visitor walking along it today will see it much as Nelson did on that Good Friday; the only difference, apart from the traffic, is that many of the great houses on each side, then noblemen's mansions, are now the offices of shipping companies, shipping agents and foreign legations.

Finally the great crowd, with Nelson at its centre – and soldiers of the Royal Guard trying to fulfil their orders to guard the British admiral, but acting on orders drawn up on the assumption he would be in a carriage – arrived at the square of Amalienborg.

The Palace comprises four separate and almost identical rococo buildings, one in each corner of the square, formerly the palaces of four Danish noblemen. The Crown Prince had bought it seven years earlier as the Royal residence when Christiansborg Palace was burnt down. A wooden colonnade joined the two buildings on the northern side, and Nelson passed under this to enter the building in the north-east corner, which contained the state rooms, and the Crown Prince's apartments.

Nelson arrived there at noon, and his description of the visit, written next day to the Prime Minister, is both colourful and revealing. After describing how he dined at the Palace, Nelson told Addington that he then 'had a conversation of two hours alone with the Prince (that is, no minister was present) only his Adjutant-General, Lindholm, was in the room'.

---

[1] Next day Benz complained to the Admiralty that 'no one has come to collect the body' although the hospital could arrange it 'when I am informed about the proper ceremony and economy to be used'.

Before that,

I saw Count Bernstorff for a moment, and could not help saying he had acted a very wrong part in my opinion, in involving the two countries in their present melancholy situation, for that our countries ought never to quarrel. I had not time to say more, as the Prince sent for me, and Count Bernstorff was called [to the Prince] the moment I came out of the room.

No doubt Nelson's description of his blunt conversation with both the Crown Prince and Bernstorff made a colourless politician like Addington shudder, while the sailor's directness no doubt alarmed Hawkesbury. But at the end of two hours Britain, represented by Nelson, and Denmark, represented by the Crown Prince, both knew each other's views, problems and position. In direct contrast, it is a sad commentary that by the latter half of the twentieth century many professional diplomats have become little more than professional caterers, experts at serving cocktails and canapés to other foreign diplomats but lamentably out of touch with the men forming policy in the countries to which they are accredited.

However, Nelson (who was the first to admit in a letter to St Vincent that 'A negotiator is certainly out of my line, but being thrown into it, I have endeavoured to acquit myself as well as I was able') was in a position few diplomats ever experience – he knew better than his own Prime Minister the entire strategic problem. He had just achieved a tactical victory in the previous day's battle; but the strategic problem remained – Russia.

His Royal Highness [he told Addington] began the conversation by saying how happy he was to see me, and thanked me for my humanity to the wounded Danes. I then said it was to me, and would be the greatest affliction to every man in England, from the King to the lowest person, to think that Denmark had fired on the British flag, and become leagued with her enemies.

The Crown Prince interrupted Nelson by saying that Admiral Parker had declared war against Denmark.

This I denied and requested His Royal Highness to send for the papers, and he would find the direct contrary, and that it was the furthest from the thoughts of the British Admiral.

I then asked if his Royal Highness would permit me to speak my mind freely on the present situation of Denmark, to which he having acquiesced, I stated to him the sensation which was caused in England by such an unnatural alliance with, at the present moment, the furious enemy of England.

His answer was that when he made the alliance it was for the protection of their trade, and that Denmark would never be the enemy of England, and that the Emperor of Russia was not the enemy of England when this treaty was formed; that he would never join Russia against England, and his declaration to that effect was the cause of the Emperor (I think he said) sending away his Minister;[1] that Denmark was a trading nation, and had only to look to the protection of its lawful commerce.

His Royal Highness then enlarged on the impossibility of Danish ships under convoy, having on board any contraband trade; but to be subjected to be stopped – even a Danish fleet by a pitiful privateer, and that she should search all the ships, and take out of the Fleet any vessels she might please – was what Denmark would not permit.

To this my answer was simply 'What occasion to convoy fair [i.e. non-contraband] trade?'

To which he answered, 'Did you find anything in the convoy of the *Freya*?' and that no [naval] commander could tell what contraband goods might be in his convoy, &c., &c.; and as to merchants, they would always sell what was most saleable; that as to swearing to ownership of property, I would get anything sworn to which I pleased [i.e. in a prize court].

I then said, 'Suppose that England – which she never will – was to consent to this freedom and nonsense of navigation, I will tell your Royal Highness what the result would be – ruination to Denmark, for the present commerce of Denmark with the warring powers was half the neutral carrying trade, and any merchant in Copenhagen would tell you the same.

'If all this freedom was allowed, Denmark would not have more than the sixth part; for the State of Hamburg was as good as the State of Denmark in that case; and it would soon be said, "We will not be stopped [by Denmark] in the Sound – our flag is our protection", and Denmark would lose a great source of her present revenue [i.e. Sound dues], and that the Baltic would soon change its name to the Russia Sea.'

He said this was a delicate subject; to which I replied that his Royal Highness had permitted me to speak out.

He then said, 'Pray answer me a question: for what is the British Fleet come to the Baltic?'

My answer – 'To crush a most formidable and unprovoked Coalition against Great Britain.'

He then went on to say his uncle [George III] had been deceived; that it was a misunderstanding, and that nothing should ever make him take a part against Great Britain; for that it would not be in his interest to see us crushed nor, he trusted, ours to see him; to which I acquiesced.

I then said there could not be a doubt of the hostility of Denmark; for if her Fleet had been joined with Russia and Sweden, they would assuredly have gone into the North Sea, menaced the coast of England, and probably have joined the French, if they had been able.

His Royal Highness said his ships never should join any power against

---

[1] This was the first Britain learned of the real reason for de Rosencrantz's dismissal, which Drummond had reported earlier in the year. Neither Nelson nor the Crown Prince knew, as they talked, that Czar Paul had been assassinated several days earlier.

England; but it required not much argument to satisfy him that he could not help it.

In speaking of the pretended union of the Northern Powers, I could not help saying that his Royal Highness must be sensible that it was nonsense to talk of a mutual protection of trade with a power that had none, and that he must be sensible that the Emperor of Russia would never have thought of offering to protect the trade of Denmark if he had not had hostility against Great Britain.

These last seventy-two words were, of course, the crux of the whole affair. For all Lord Grenville's skill in diplomacy, he had never managed to penetrate, let alone define, the Czar's basic attitude.

Since the Crown Prince had no answer to this he wisely changed the subject.

He said repeatedly [Nelson told Addington] 'I have offered today, and do offer my mediation between Great Britain and Russia.'

My answer was, 'A mediator must be at peace with both parties. You must settle your matter with Great Britain. At present you are leagued with our enemies, and are considered naturally as part of the effective force to fight us.'

Talking much of this subject, his Royal Highness said, 'What must I do to make myself equal?'

'Sign an alliance with Great Britain and join your Fleet to ours.'

'Then Russia will go to war with us; and my desire as a commercial nation is to be at peace with all the world.'

I told him he knew the offer of Great Britain, either to join us or disarm.

'I pray, Lord Nelson, what do you call disarming?'

'I am not authorised to give an opinion on the subject, but I consider it as not having on foot any force beyond the customary establishment.'

'Do you consider the guard ships in the Sound as beyond that common establishment?'

'I do not know.'

'We have always had five sail of the line in the Cattegat and coast of Norway.'

'I am not authorised to define what is exactly disarming [Nelson replied] but I do not think such a force would be allowed.'

'When all Europe is in such a dreadful state of confusion, it is absolutely necessary that states should be on their guard.'

'Your Royal Highness knows the offers of England to keep twenty sail of the line in the Baltic.'

'I am sure my intentions are very much misunderstood,' said the Crown Prince, and Nelson replied that Sir Hyde had authorized him to say that upon certain conditions His Royal Highness might have an opportunity of explaining his sentiments at the Court of London, adding 'I am not authorized to say on what conditions exactly.'

'But what do you think?'

'First, a free entry of the British Fleet into Copenhagen, and the free use of everything we may want from it.'

Before I could get on [Nelson wrote] he replied quick, 'That you shall have with pleasure.'

'The next is,' [continued Nelson] 'whilst this explanation [i.e. negotiation] is going on, a total suspension of your treaties with Russia. These, I believe, are the foundation on which Sir Hyde Parker only can build other articles for his justification in suspending his orders, which are plain and positive.[1]

The Crown Prince then asked Nelson to repeat what he had just said, and when that was done

He thanked me for my open conversation; and I having made an apology if I had said anything which he might think too strong, his Royal Highness very handsomely did the same, and we parted, he saying that he hoped we would cease hostilities tomorrow, as on such an important occasion he must call a Council.

'My reception,' he told Addington, 'was such as I have always found it – far beyond my deserts.' Then the King's brother and son 'desired I might be presented to them, which I was, and then returned on board'.

The Crown Prince's remark, '. . . my desire as a commercial nation is to be at peace with all the world' was an age-old lament even when he made it; in the following century and a half it has been echoed by so many neutral nations as war enveloped them that it gives tragic proof of the truth of the ancient phrase, 'History teaches that no one ever learns anything from history'. Quite apart from the First World War, a simple substitution of the Führer for the Czar saw Denmark, Norway, Holland and Belgium – all commercial nations desiring to be at peace with all the world – end up under a vicious occupation, while the United States pursued the same policy more profitably until Pearl Harbor forced a change.

The events leading up to Nelson's conversation with the Crown Prince on Good Friday, 1801, illustrates one simple but basic and always forgotten strategic factor which was as true in the day of the bow and arrow as it is in the day of the computer-guided multi-headed nuclear missiles: if only one nation in the whole world acts aggressively – either

---

[1] Dundas's original order to the Admiralty said that it would probably be impossible to destroy the Arsenal and shipping in Copenhagen 'without exposing that city to great damage, if not to entire destruction,' which the British Government was anxious to avoid, and Parker was to say that no damage would be done if all the shipping and naval supplies in the Arsenal were handed over to the British Fleet. If this was refused, Parker was to continue operations 'without regard to the preservation of the Town' to destroy the Arsenal and shipping or compel the surrender of the shipping.

by diplomacy or threat of war – then every other nation, however peaceful it may wish to be, must be ready to defend itself if it values its freedom. To an aggressor, a neutral nation is a bonus.

For all the amiable reception he had received at Amalienborg and for all the frank talking with the Crown Prince, Nelson went back on board fairly certain that the Danes would not accept the British terms.

In a letter which began

The job is done, and the state of Denmark is convinced we can fight a little; more distinguished bravery never was shown [Nelson told Troubridge that the Crown Prince] allowed me to speak my mind freely, and I believe I told him such truths as seldom reach the ears of Princes. HRH seemed much affected, and I am satisfied it is only fear of Russia and other powers that prevents the renunciation of his alliance with Russia and Sweden. However, he is to send off some proposition to Sir Hyde Parker, but I have not much hopes.

Meanwhile among the ships there was still a great deal to be done; a great many funeral services to be held. Because of its simplicity a funeral on board a ship of war had a great dignity. Each body was sewn up in a canvas bag – usually the dead man's hammock – with a couple of shot at the feet. A wide plank was fitted on the bulwark, just over the standing part of the fore sheet, so that it could tilt, like a see-saw. The body was placed on the plank and usually covered with a Union Flag, and at the end of the funeral service the plank was tilted outboard so that the body, weighed by the shot, slid from under the flag and over the side.[1]

On board the *Monarch* Lt-colonel Hutchinson asked if he could read the service over the body of Captain Mosse as a mark of respect to his memory: then Lt Yelland read the same service over Midshipman George Morgan, who had died of his wounds during the night while the surgeon was amputating his legs. In other ships the same service was being read over the bodies of both sailors and soldiers; on board the *Elephant* the Rev. Joseph Davies read it for Captain James Bawden of the Cornish Miners, serving as a volunteer in the Rifle Corps, and over Henry Youlden, a twenty-four-year-old master's mate from Brixham; in the *Amazon* Lt John Quilliam read it over Captain Riou, Midshipman the Hon. John Tuchet, and the Captain's clerk, Joseph Rose. In the *Isis* there was the Master, a lieutenant of Marines, a lieutenant in the Rifle Corps, and two midshipmen to be buried.

As Sir Hyde Parker noted in his journal, 'It appears in a general

---

[1] In contemporary naval slang, 'going over the standing part of the fore sheet' meant to die, or be killed.

return of the killed and wounded that the whole number amount to 943. . . . Made promotions accordingly.'

So far in this expedition Sir Hyde had often been slow and indecisive, and he had made many mistakes. But in making the promotions to fill the gaps in the ships of Nelson's division he behaved swiftly, decisively and despicably, even by the standards of the day.

It was customary wherever possible to promote officers who had distinguished themselves. For many men without influence, like Lt Yelland, who had commanded the *Monarch* with distinction for the whole battle after Captain Mosse's death, it represented almost the only chance of making the jump from lieutenant to captain.

Parker was bound only by honour to discuss promotions with Nelson since the vacancies were all in ships of Nelson's van division; but he did not. As far as he was concerned the casualty list in Nelson's division was quite simply a golden opportunity to promote his own favourites. And apart from replacing the captains and lieutenants killed, officers would be needed for the prizes to be sent back to England, resulting in more promotions. To be the bearer of a victorious admiral's despatches was an honour for a captain, who was usually chosen because he had distinguished himself. Sir Hyde had already chosen not Murray, whose *Edgar* had 142 killed and wounded, or Walker of the *Isis* (121) or Bertie of the *Ardent* (94), but one of his favourites, a man who had been rowed over from the *London* towards the end of the battle – Robert Waller Otway. . . .

Lt John Fordyce Maples, one of the *London*'s lieutenants, was the most deserving of Sir Hyde's favourites – but he had not been in the battle and his services most certainly could not be compared to almost any lieutenant in Nelson's division. However, he had served in the West Indies with Parker, so he was appointed to command the *Otter*.

Lt Charles Boys, who had lost a leg in Howe's action of the Glorious First of June, was another of the *London*'s officers: he was given command of the *Harpy*, while another lieutenant of the *London*, who had also watched the distant battle from the flagship, received his commission as captain signed by Sir Hyde, who gave him command of the *Cruizer*.

Although in any case Lt Yelland deserved immediate promotion for the way he had taken command of the *Monarch*, his application to Sir Hyde was backed up by Nelson. But it was refused; instead, as Midshipman Millard put it, 'a stranger was sent on board us, who had "borne none of the burthen and heat of the day", and Mr Yelland was told he might take the place of [the *London*'s] first lieutenant, who was promoted, and await another opportunity. He very properly considered this an insult, and preferred being first lieutenant in the ship he had fought. . . .' (Captain Bligh was later given command of the *Monarch* to take her back to England.)[1]

Thus four vacant commands went to four lieutenants from the *London*. . . .

However, Captain Bertie of the *Ardent* (64) was given command of the *Bellona* (74); Captain Sutton of the *Alcmene* (32) went to the *Amazon* (38); Captain Devonshire of the *Dart* (30) to the *Alcmene*; and Captain George M'Kinley of the *Otter* fire ship was given the *Dart*, a 30-gun frigate and substantial promotion.

Not only did Sir Hyde upset the officers by his promotions, but his wholesale burning of the Danish prizes, in many cases quite unjustified, was robbing them of hard-won prize money.

Nelson was sufficiently angered to write about this to Lord St Vincent at the Admiralty:

Whether Sir Hyde Parker may mention the subject to you, I know not, for he is rich, and does not want it. Nor is it, you will believe me, from any desire I possess to get a few hundred pounds that actuates me to address this letter to you; but, my dear Lord, justice to the brave officers and men who fought on that day.

It is true our opponents were in hulks and floats only adapted for the position they were placed in; but that made our battle so much the harder, and victory so much more difficult to obtain.

Believe me, I have weighed all the circumstances, and in my conscience I think that the King should send a gracious Message to the House of Commons for a gift to this Fleet; for what must be the natural feelings of the officers and men belonging to it to see their rich Commander-in-Chief burn all the fruits of their victory which, if fitted up and sent to England, as many might have been by dismantling part of our Fleet, would have sold for a good round sum?

Nor was Nelson exaggerating: the *Holsteen* was the only prize sent back by Sir Hyde.

To avoid anything that 'could give offence', Nelson had suggested that Sir Hyde's secretary, Osborn, should be the agent for prizes (for which he would receive a handsome commission); but he did nothing for two weeks, when both Sir Hyde and Admiral Graves agreed to Alexander Davison being appointed agent. Nelson later wrote to Davison that he was collecting lists of prizes and stores taken,

and as the *Holsteen* is in England, you must manage about having her and her stores valued.

The *Zealand* [*Sælland*], 74, as large and full and fine a ship as the *Sanspareil*

[1] There is a postscript to Parker's despatch on the Battle, dated 6 April, which was probably written because of Nelson's protest: 'The Captain of the *Monarch* being killed early in the action, Lieutenant Yelland continued it with the greatest spirit. I therefore cannot avoid, in justice to his merits, particularly recommending him to Their Lordship's favour and attention.' (He was made a commander by the Admiralty but, with no recommendation, was unemployed for a long time.)

[captured in 1794], because she was a little cut with shot, was by the rascals of carpenters condemned – the carpenter of the *London* at the head of them. They had the impudence to report her an old ship, when she was only seven years from the stocks [she was launched in 1787: see Appendix 2]. The *Indfødsretten* of 64 guns, never was at sea, and was desired to be sunk, which as soon was, as no person stopped her shot holes.

In short the wanton waste which has been made of our prizes which, God knows, we fought hard to get, has been hard upon the captors. Admirals &c. may be rewarded, but if you destroy the Prizes, what have poor lieutenants, warrant officers and the inferior officers and men to look to? Nothing! What their gracious King gives them, a Commander-in-Chief may take from them.

I by no means wish to prevent Commanders-in-Chief from destroying all prizes; but in certain cases, I think, the Country is bound in honour to make it up to the brave fellows who have fought for her; and if ever a case called for the consideration of the country, surely this is the most prominent.

Nelson enclosed a list written and signed by Captain Thesiger of the ships which were still in the Roads after the Battle, and eleven of which Thesiger boarded. (Two he did not board were the *Dannebroge*, which had blown up, and the *Sælland*.)

In Copenhagen the Crown Prince called his ministers and described the British terms. No record of this meeting exists, but previous policy and subsequent actions leave little doubt of the trend of the discussion. Expressed simply, some pointed out that any friendly move towards the British would bring the wrath of the mad Czar down on their heads; others noted that nevertheless Copenhagen was defenceless against destruction. The row of British bomb vessels showed the British could destroy the Arsenal, Dockyard and Castellet at their leisure, and follow that with a wholesale bombardment of the city. The city's only defence was the Trekroner Fort. By its very construction it was extremely vulnerable to the plunging fire of the mortars in the British bomb vessels, which were out of range of its guns.

Yet no one really considered just what the Russians *could* do if the Czar decided on reprisals against Denmark. Yet it was a vitally important point, since it was this fear which governed Denmark's actions.

The Czar could try to use his Fleet against Denmark – but the British Fleet now anchored off Copenhagen was ready to destroy every one of his ships. Nor was there any doubt they could do it, since the condition of the Russian ships of war was only too well known. So any move made by the Czar against Denmark by sea would fail.

This left a Russian move against Denmark only by land – and, with no Navy to convoy the troops this would mean a long march through east and west Prussia and Pomerania, passing Danzig, Stettin, Rostock and then into Mecklenburg and through Lübeck. While the Czar was on friendly terms with Napoleon, would the French allow Russia to have a powerful army along their whole northern frontier from the Russian border to Holland? And, more important, obtain ice-free ports on the North Sea? Prussia would certainly seek French help.

The only realistic answer is that Napoleon could not permit it. He knew that Russia was the only nation in Continental Europe that would always menace France: the Czar had enormous resources of men and needed only competent generals with whom he did not interfere. Bonaparte was, above all things, a realist: a year or two earlier the Czar was his enemy and Britain's ally. An insane quirk, spurred by British gold subsidies, might well make him change sides again – by which time he would have occupied Denmark and Norway (neutralizing Sweden), and Prussia, with its large and busy ports, would be a Russian highway.

The Russian threat to Denmark – providing the British now went on to destroy the Czar's fleet, or kept a squadron in the Baltic large enough to destroy or blockade it – therefore did not exist in fact; but it did in men's imaginations at this Council meeting at the Amalienborg Palace.

While the Crown Prince and his advisers talked, the people of Copenhagen slowly emerged from the shock of the great battle; and although the thunder of the guns no longer shook their houses and reverberated across the city, smoke still billowed up and drifted over the Roads as the British burned their prizes one by one.

There were more than 350 dead whose funerals had to be arranged; a hundred more in the hospitals were dying of their wounds despite the efforts of every available doctor; more than 550 wounded had to be treated. The fate of nearly 1800 men was not yet known – many were on board British ships as prisoners, but how many of them had been killed in the battle, their bodies pushed over the side by their shipmates to make room to work the guns? Of more than 5,000 men serving in the ships, only about 2,200 had so far come on shore unhurt. . . .

Whole areas, like the streets forming Nyboder, were full of women who could only wait or go from hospital to hospital, and ask every sailor they could find in the streets, for news of husbands and sons. In just one of Nyboder's streets, Svanegaden, which is its second shortest, Reinert Adriansen of number 21, Jens Andersen Holm of number 22, and Jochum Jorgensen of number 23 had all been wounded and were in various hospitals.

In Delphingaden, two streets nearer to St Paul's church, Niels Gundersen's wife, Bodil, at number 46, did not yet know that she was a widow; but near by at number 15 Anne-Pernille, with her daughter Bodil and the twins Peder and Marensara, had already heard their husband and father, Jens Valentin, the bosun of the *Jylland*, had been killed. One street away, at number 2, Hjertensfryds, the wife of Jacob Hofman, had yet to hear he had survived but had been wounded. For Nyboder the list was long. It would take many days for news to reach the rest of Denmark and Norway: to Odense that Andreas Wikkelsøe had been wounded in the *Sælland*; to Porsgrund, in Norway, that Halvor Jensen had died of wounds in the *Rendsborg*; to Vordingborg that Jacob Andersen had been badly wounded in both legs; to Kalundborg that Johannes Febret, a journeyman shoemaker like Andersen, had been killed in the *Søhesten*, leaving a wife and a son, who was an apprentice shoemaker with three years left of his indentures. To West Jutland the news would go to Møgeltonder that Martin Rollof was dead, leaving a wife with cancer of the liver and five children (the rector of Møgeltonder would soon be writing to the Crown Prince that the widow had 'neither house nor means'); to Assens that Rasmus Larsen, nicknamed '*Nifinger*', had been killed. . . .

On board the British ships the survivors were doing what they could to inform the next of kin of their dead shipmates: letters would go to aristocratic families telling them their sons, serving as midshipmen, had perished; they would go to the homes of fishermen and farm labourers. And, because of the various nationalities that served in the British Navy, there would be many who would never know why a husband or son did not return home.

The casualties on both sides were nearly the same. The returns to Sir Hyde showed 254 killed (20 officers, 234 seamen, Marines and soldiers) and 689 wounded (48 officers, 641 seamen, Marines and soldiers). The British had lost nearly twice as many dead in the wrecking of the *Invincible* off Yarmouth. . . .

In fact the British returns were not entirely accurate, although they are the only figures available, because a considerable number of slightly wounded officers and men – those treated and who later returned to duty – were not included, and the returns were sent in within hours of the end of the Battle and several listed as wounded in fact died later. Midshipman William Morgan of the *Monarch*, for instance, was listed as wounded but died the night after the Battle; Midshipman Thomas Harlow, listed as wounded, also died; while a third, Midshipman John Green, of the same ship, who was twenty-one years old and came from Lowestoft, lost an arm and an eye, but was not listed. The figures for the officers in just one ship is thus increased by two killed and one wounded.

A straight comparison between the 943 killed and wounded in the

British report and the 1035 Danish killed and wounded is misleading because, apart from the soldiers, the British casualties were among trained men, whereas a fifth of the Danish were untrained volunteers and pressed men. Likewise the British lost at least 20 officers killed and 48 wounded, a total of 68, whereas the Danish lost 11 dead and 13 wounded, a total of 24, several of them reserve officers. The reason for the disparity is that there were fewer officers in the Danish ships.

Late that evening a boat with a flag of truce came out from the city to the *St George* with a packet for Nelson. The Admiral found it came from Captain Lindholm and included a brief note which led Nelson to include in his letter to Addington a reference that it gave him 'a hope that what I had said to the Prince would make peace'. The purpose of the packet was to send Nelson copies of the latest London newspapers, which had just arrived in Copenhagen. The last issues were dated 24 March – less than a couple of weeks after the British Fleet had sailed from Yarmouth.

There was little news of interest apart from full reports of the loss of the *Invincible*. The prices of foods were rising sharply – in one month wheat had gone up from 136s. 10d. a quarter to 156s. 2d. Flour had doubled, although sugar had dropped 7s. 6d. a cwt – obviously the first of the West Indies convoys had arrived after the hurricane season.

Even a brief glance through the newspapers emphasized that Britain was fighting alone: Nelson read that the peace treaty between France and Austria had finally been accepted by the Diet of Ratisbon and the ratifications were reported to have been exchanged in Paris. The most hurtful news for Nelson was that the King of Naples had finally concluded an armistice with France – through the mediation of Russia – and all British and Turkish ships were excluded from her ports.

It was reported, too, that the Czar had given indications that he was intending to march his troops against European Turkey, and his threats had so overawed the Ottoman Court 'that it is very doubtful whether the Turkish Army will dare either entertain their British auxiliaries or even lift a hand against French invaders. . . .' Spain and Portugal were at war (giving Britain one ally, although Portugal had for years been a good friend), Spain alleging among other things that Portugal supplied the British Fleet with seamen and provisions. . . .In Britain, the King had recovered from his illness, and the new ministers had finally received their seals of office.

The news was dreary enough, Nelson knew only too well, for the arrival in London of the despatches announcing the victory off Copenhagen to set church bells ringing all over Britain.

448

30

THE TRUCE EXPIRES

Saturday, 4 April, brought a fine day, a north-west wind still blowing, but moderate with a haze which softened the outlines of the Danish and Swedish coastlines. Nelson breakfasted early and had Fremantle as a guest, giving him an account of the meeting with the Crown Prince at Amalienborg the previous day. As soon as the meal was finished Nelson went over to the *Bellona*, taking Fremantle with him, to visit the wounded Sir Thomas Thompson, and found him, in Fremantle's words, 'doing as well as can be expected'.

With so many wounded to be attended, Sir Hyde decided to turn one of the prizes into a hospital ship. He chose the *Holsteen* 'and commissioned her accordingly'. Every spare man in the Fleet was sent over to get her ready, while preparations were made to transfer the wounded.

In Copenhagen, Commodore Fischer was drawing up his report to the Crown Prince on the battle. It was a curious document which caused embarrassment to people like the Crown Prince's ADC, Captain Lindholm, and certainly failed to do justice to Fischer himself, who was a most distinguished officer who had done the best with what forces he had. (The inaccuracies and contradictions in this report are noted in square brackets.)

After outlining the preliminary moves in which the first British ships came into action, he wrote:

By degrees the rest of the ships came up, and as they sailed past on both sides of the ships already at anchor [they passed only on the eastern side], they formed a thick line which, as it stretched northwards to the *Sælland*, engaged not more than two thirds of the Defence Line under my command; while the Trekroner Fort and the blockships *Elephanten* and *Mars* and the frigate *Hiælperen* did not come into the action. In half an hour the battle was general. Ten ships of the line, among them one of 80 guns, the rest chiefly 74s, and from six to eight frigates, on the one side.

The *Hiælperen* not only came into the action but her captain's report to the Danish Admiralty says he was attacked by two 74s and because

449

he 'could not affect the issue' he surrendered. The reference to the *Elephanten* and the Trekroner Battery not coming into action is inexplicable. The *Elephanten*'s log notes that Fischer ordered her to stop firing at 5.00 p.m. As for the British ships, there were only nine anchored in position; of these none was an 80-gun ship: there were five 74s in position (and two more aground), two 64s, one 56 (*Glatton*) and one 50 (*Isis*).

Fischer continued that on the Danish side there were 'seven blockships, only one of which had 74 guns; the rest 64s and under, two frigates and six small vessels. This was the respective strength of the two antagonists.'

Fischer refers to fifteen ships, including six small vessels. But his Defence Line comprised eighteen ships, not fifteen, plus Trekroner. The Danish records show he had eight blockships, not seven, plus four floating batteries, three cavalry transports, two frigates and one corvette. Added to these were the sixty-six big guns of the Trekroner battery, and the forty-four guns of the eleven gun boats inshore of the Line.

Although Fischer and Nelson argued over the total number of guns each side had, the actual figures were: Danish Defence Line, including gun boats and the Trekroner battery but excluding Steen Bille's division – 754; including the two ships of Bille's division which joined the action – 888. Nelson's division, including the frigates but excluding the *Bellona*, *Russell* and *Agamemnon* – 806; including the *Bellona* and *Russell* – 954. It is fair to include the *Elephanten* and *Mars* if one includes the *Bellona* and *Russell* and all the British frigates, which came late into the action; thus 888 Danish guns (plus the Sixtus and other shore batteries) were opposed to 954 British.

The figures are given not for serious students of the battle, who know only too well that adding up guns of different calibres in a battle and giving grand totals for each belligerent proves nothing, but simply because much has been written incorrectly about totals; sufficient to justify giving the correct figures taken from original Danish and original British official documents.

Fischer continued:

The enemy had on the whole two ships to one, and the blockship *Prøvesteenen* had besides a ship of the line and the Rear-admiral, two frigates against her, by which she was raked the whole time, without being able to return a shot.

'Two ships to one' was obviously wrong, since Nelson had only eleven sail of the line, including the two which stranded. There were seventeen if one includes the smaller vessels against the eighteen ships of the Defence Line and the Trekroner Battery. The *Prøvesteenen* was not engaged by Rear-admiral Graves, and was raked by only one frigate, the *Désirée*.

If I only recapitulate historically what your Highness, and with you a great proportion of the people of Denmark and Europe have seen [Fischer continued] I may venture to call that an unequal battle which was maintained and supported for four and a half hours with unexampled courage and effect, in which the fire of the superior force was so much weakened for an hour before the end of the battle that several English ships, and particularly Lord Nelson's, were obliged to fire only single shots; that this Hero himself, in the middle and very heat of the battle, sent a flag of Truce on shore to propose a cessation of hostilities; if I add that it was announced to me that two British ships of the line had surrendered, but being again supported by the assistance of fresh ships, again hoisted their flags, I may in such circumstances be permitted to say – and I believe I may appeal to the enemy's own confession [sic] – that in this engagement Denmark's ancient naval reputation blazed forth with such incredible splendour that I thank Heaven all Europe are the witnesses of it.

Apart from the last twenty-four words, with which Nelson and his officers were the first to agree, the major part of this section was totally unworthy of Fischer. Having earlier wrongly reported that the Trekroner Battery, the *Elephanten, Mars* and *Hiælperen* 'did not come at all into the action', he claims an 'unequal combat'. No British ship struck and none of Fischer's captains ever claimed they did; but, like so many Danish ships, some had their ensign halyards shot away and fresh ensigns had to be hoisted. And they certainly were not 'supported by the assistance of fresh ships' since no 'fresh ships' joined Nelson's division. His reference to the circumstances of the flag of truce requires no further comment since the situation of the Defence Line at that time has already been given fully from Danish records, and the views of the Crown Prince and Lindholm are given below.

The report continued that at 11.30 the *Dannebroge* was set on fire and

. . . I repaired with my flag on board the *Holsteen* . . . at half past two the *Holsteen* was so shattered . . . that I caused the Pendant to be hoisted, instead of my flag, and I went to the Trekroner Battery, from which I commanded the North Wing, which was slightly engaged with the Division of Admiral Parker, till about four o'clock, when I received orders from your Royal Highness to put an end to the engagement.

The time Fischer gave for leaving the *Holsteen* is one hour late because Captain Arenfeldt, who commanded her, says Fischer found it impossible to go to the *Indfødsretten* and left the *Holsteen* at 1.30, not 2.30, and this is confirmed by many other reports. He goes a good deal further, writing that 'about ¼ past two struck . . . and immediately after a boarding party came on board and took possession.' Both of Arenfeldt's reports were written the day after the battle. It is not easy to understand Fischer's reference to the North Wing being 'slightly engaged' by Parker's division when the only two ships north of the *Holsteen*, the *Indfødsretten* and *Hiælperen*, had surrendered before he had even left the *Holsteen*, despite his claim that the *Hiælperen* 'did not come into the action'.

The rest of the report listed the fate of individual Danish ships and, with no reports available to calculate Danish casualties, estimated them at from 1600 to 1800 – fortunately an overestimate.

The report infuriated Nelson, and although the exchange of letters is referred to later, some of Nelson's comments are best given here – they were made later in a letter to Captain Lindholm.

Commodore Fischer having written a report in which he called upon the Crown Prince 'as a witness to the truth of it', Nelson wrote, 'I therefore think it right to address myself to you, for the information of His Royal Highness as, I assure you, had this officer confined himself to his own veracity, I should have treated his official letter with the contempt it deserved and allowed the world to appreciate the merits of the two contending officers.'

Nelson said he would make 'only a few, and very few observations'. They were:

He asserts the superiority of numbers on the part of the British; it will turn out, if that is of any consequence, that the Danish Line of Defence to the southward of the Crown Islands was much stronger and more numerous than the British. . . . [He went on to list the ships.]

I am ready to admit that many of the Danish officers and men behaved as well as men could do, and deserved not to be abandoned by their Commander. I am justified in saying this, from Commodore Fischer's own declaration. In his letter he states that after he quitted the *Dannebroge* she long contested the battle. If so, more shame for him to quit so many brave fellows. *Here* was no manoeuvring: *it was* downright fighting, and it was his duty to have shown an example of firmness becoming the high trust reposed in him. He went in such a hurry, if he went before she struck, which but for his own declaration I can hardly believe, that he forgot to take his Broad Pendant with him; for both Pendant and Ensign were struck together, and it was from this circumstance that I claimed the Commodore as a prisoner of war. . . .

As to his nonsense about victory, His Royal Highness will not much credit him. I sunk, burnt, captured or drove into the harbour the whole Line of Defence to the southward of the Crown Islands.

He says he is told two British ships struck. Why did he not take possession of them? I took possession of his as fast as they struck. The reason is clear –

he did not believe it. He must have known the falsity of the report, and that no fresh British ships did come near the ships engaged.

He states that the ship in which I had the honour to hoist my Flag fired latterly only single guns. It is true; for steady and cool were my brave fellows and did not wish to throw away a single shot.

He seems to exult that I sent on the shore a Flag of Truce. Men of his description, if they ever are victorious, know not the feeling of humanity. You know, and his Royal Highness knows, that the guns fired from the shore could only fire through the Danish ships, which had surrendered, and that if I fired at the shore, it could only be in the same manner. God forbid I should destroy a non-resisting Dane! When they became my prisoners, I became their protector. Humanity alone could have been my object, but Mr Fischer's carcass is safe, and he regarded not the sacred call of humanity. His Royal Highness thought as I did. It has brought about an Armistice, which I pray the Almighty may bring about a happy reconciliation between the two Kingdoms.

Only two points need to be made about Nelson's letter. The first is that his obvious contempt for Fischer was based on the fact Fischer left two ships and finally went to Trekroner but, as Nelson pointed out, '*Here* was no manoeuvring: *it was* downright fighting'. He meant that although it was usual for the over-all commander to leave a shattered ship when two fleets were in battle on the open sea so that he could continue to give orders for the manoeuvring of his ships, it was not the case here, where the ships fought at anchor, and although Fischer refers to 'commanding the North Wing' from Trekroner, he issued no orders to the Defence Line from before he left the *Dannebroge* until the Crown Prince ordered a cease-fire.

The second point concerns the flag of truce. Much of the nonsense written about it has been based on the ill-considered reference in Fischer's letter. No regard has been paid to the fact that the Crown Prince had as good a view of the closing stages of the battle as Fischer, combined with the breadth of vision of a ruler, and neither he nor Lindholm – nor anyone in authority at the time – ever questioned Nelson's motives; on the contrary, as Lindholm's letter, quoted below, proves beyond dispute.

Lindholm's reply, referred to later, was very fair. Referring to Fischer leaving the ships, he does not mention the lack of manoeuvring, but made the point 'He would, in my humble opinion, have been justified, from the wound he received on his head, to quit the command altogether, when he left the *Dannebroge*, and no blame can ever have attached for it to his character as a soldier [sic].'

Lindholm disputed the reference to Fischer's Broad Pendant and the Danish Ensign coming down together:

The man who had taken down the Broad Pendant, and hoisted the Captain's Pendant, was killed when coming down the shrouds, and fell upon deck with the Commodore's Pendant in his hand.

I do not conceive that Commodore Fischer had the least idea of claiming as a victory what, to every intent and purpose, was a defeat. He has only thought that this defeat was not an inglorious one, and that our officers and men displayed much bravery and firmness against force so superior in every respect. Your Lordship's Report, and your letter to me prove it. . . .

Since Nelson's letter was written to Lindholm for the Crown Prince's information, obviously Lindholm's reply was seen and approved by the Crown Prince. Quite apart from that, the last part of Lindholm's letter alone should have been enough to prevent the ugly stories concerning the truce which gained circulation years later:

As to your Lordship's motives for sending a Flag of Truce to our Government [Lindholm wrote] it can never be misconstrued, and your subsequent conduct has sufficiently shown that humanity is always the companion of true valour. You have done more: you have shown yourself a friend of the re-establishment of peace and good harmony between this country and Great Britain. It is therefore with the sincerest esteem I shall always feel myself attached to your Lordship. . . .

Lindholm was close to the Crown Prince; he played a leading role in all the Truce negotiations. If this was his view, and that of the Crown Prince, then any subsequent judgments have little importance. The significant phrase was that Nelson's motives 'can never be misconstrued. . . .'

Although this narrative has shown from original Danish documents as well as British that Nelson had achieved his purpose of destroying the Danish Fleet as a fighting force before he sent in the Flag of Truce, if further proof be required, it is contained in the answer to this question: if the ships that grounded on cutting their cables after the cease-fire – the *Defiance*, *Monarch* (only briefly) and *Elephant* – had been destroyed by the Trekroner battery, would it have had any effect on the *final* outcome of the British Fleet's attack?

The answer is no: the Danish Defence Line was for all practical purposes already destroyed, and the remaining ships of Nelson's division – eight sail of the line – were out of range of any Danish guns. The wind went north-west next day and they could have sailed back to the original anchorage. Parker still had more than enough ships – his own division of eight, plus the remaining eight of Nelson's division after repairs – to have removed the Danish prizes and gone on to destroy the Russian Fleet – and the Swedish, if necessary.

With a ship sure to leave for England in a day or so to take Otway with
Sir Hyde's despatches, everyone in the British Fleet who had the time
hurriedly wrote letters – Fremantle to his wife Betsey and his patron the
Marquis of Buckingham; Hardy to his brother-in-law, hiding his dis-
appointment that the *St George* had been unable to be Nelson's flagship
in the battle because of her deep draught, but assuring his brother-in-
law that on this occasion Nelson's 'political management *was, if possible*,
greater than his bravery'.

Nelson wrote to Troubridge about Sir Hyde's ruthless promotion of
his own protégés at the expense of those who had fought.

I am, my dear Troubridge, very awkwardly placed respecting the promotion. My duty pointed out the promotion of the First Lieutenant of the
Elephant, and all my own children are neglected.

I should hope that the Admiralty, if they promote the first lieutenants of
the ships engaged, will consider that Lord Nelson's recommendation may
have some little weight. . . .

In the almost inevitable depression he always suffered after a period
of exhilaration – for it was as much mental as physical – he told
Troubridge: 'I only hope that I may have provisional leave to return
home, for neither my health or spirits can stand the hard fag of body
and mind I have endured since the 24th of last month [the day he read
his letter to Parker urging an immediate attack].' A postscript said,
'*No* black sheep, thank God,' and praised Thesiger's activities, asking
'Will he be made post?' Thesiger was, of course, serving as a volunteer
and his rank in the Royal Navy was only a commander.

The weather on Easter Sunday gave little cheer to an already sombre
day: a south-westerly gale brought snow. Sir Hyde on board the
London began very early by writing one of his clumsily-phrased letters
to Count Bernstorff – the truce was due to expire at noon, and he was
presenting his terms for its prolongation.

Sir Hyde kept the letter ready for the expected visit of Danish
negotiators. Meanwhile the usual Sunday morning services were held
in the British ships. On board the *London* it was conducted by Mr Scott,
who yet had to make use of the Danish he had been busy learning in the
past weeks. On board the *St George* young Captain Graham Hamond
held the prayer book while the one-armed Nelson read the service to
the ship's company.

The Danish negotiators were expected on board the *London* in the
early afternoon after the funeral of the Danish men who had been
killed. A few hundred yards west of Castellet and about 500 yards from

Nyboder is Holmens Kirkegaard, the naval (and oldest) cemetery in Copenhagen. At this time it was outside the city walls, on the west side of Osterbrogade just beyond the west gate, with the garrison cemetery on the other side of the road. (Holmen's Church – the Navy Church – is down by the inner harbour near the canal. Originally an anchor forge, it was altered to a church in 1619 and subsequently rebuilt.)

Holmens Kirkegaard is one of the most fitting cemeteries in the world for seamen, and a visitor in the late twentieth century requires little imagination to picture the funeral as it took place there on Easter Sunday 1801 round a large circular grave which had been dug in the shade of an enormous elm tree.

Down at the New Harbour, beside the Søkvaesthus, a large warehouse, scores of hearses – carts which in happier days delivered bread and potatoes, carried livestock to market or beer barrels from the breweries – were drawn up. It was a fitting starting-place for the last journey of so many sailors: across the stretch of water that formed the New Harbour was the Dockyard; the Sixtus battery stood beside the entrance; the mast crane jutted out at a sharp angle from the building on which it was erected; near by were ship-building slipways and the shattered *Nyeborg* was secured alongside the quay. Amalienborg Palace was a few moments' walk away; and all round were the unmistakable signs that this part of the city was for seamen: taverns stood next to ship's chandlers; here a sailor could drink a pint of ale, while a shipmaster bought ropes and blocks, and a fisherman the line he needed to repair his nets. A young sailor could visit a tattooist; an old sailor could leave his seabag at one of the hostels and drink until dawn.

Beside the carts, each drawn by from one to three horses, were some of the families of many of the dead men; behind the procession were the people of Copenhagen, waiting to pay their last tribute to those who had fallen while defending them. Many of the hearses were still empty – the procession would halt at the hospital in Amaliegade.

Led by the Crown Prince and the senior surviving officers, including Fischer and Steen Bille, the procession began moving at 11.00 a.m., passing slowly up Amaliegade until it reached the hospital. Into the empty hearses were placed the coffins of Captain Thura, who had commanded the *Indfødsretten*; Lt Hauch who had commanded the *Cronborg*, and one of his officers, Lt Bohne; Lt Rasmus Wulff of the *Dannebroge*, and many others.

For many of the mourners it had been but a tragically short walk from their homes to the New Harbour: a few hundred yards, for example, for Anne-Marie Schultz from Store Kongensgade to follow the coffin of her husband Peder, killed in the *Holsteen*.

Then the procession made its way through the main streets of the city which were being swept by a bitter wind bringing flurries of snow and sleet. Finally it passed up Store Kongensgade, into Østerbrogade and out through the West Gate to the cemetery.

There, as the funeral service was read, the coffins were lowered into the enormous grave; then five young girls dressed in white threw spring flowers over them, and the crowd sang a hymn which had been specially written for the service.

Later the grave was covered. Today it is a large mound, and where flowers were originally planted there are now trees. Only the roots and part of the trunk of the great elm remain – it had to be cut down when it was 152 years old. The circular grave is studded with rocks on which there are brief inscriptions such as these – 'Thura paa Indfødsretten', 'Hauch paa Cronborg', Bohne paa Cronborg', 'Ebel paa Dannebroge'. There was no distinction between sailor, soldier or civilian: Ebel, for instance, was a young Army officer.

Captain Lindholm went out to the *London* under a flag of truce, taking with him Major-gen. Ernst Waltersdorff. They arrived on board at 1.30 p.m., the only fact Sir Hyde bothered to note in his journal. Lindholm told Parker that the Danish Government refused to accept the terms, and for more than two hours the two sides argued their own points of view. At the end of it the British terms were the same, and the Danes stuck to their refusal.

Parker went to his cabin and then produced a letter, which said:

Should the Count Bernstorff think himself at liberty to declare to Admiral Sir Hyde Parker, in writing, that no engagements exist between the Court of Denmark and that of Russia, for Denmark to furnish a certain quota of ships for the Combined Fleets of Russia and Sweden – but that Denmark is in a situation to declare for a perfect neutrality with respect to Great Britain.

And that the present Fleet under the command of Admiral Sir Hyde Parker is received into the port of Copenhagen, and is furnished with all supplies they may stand in need of.

These are two fundamental articles on which Admiral Sir Hyde Parker can admit of any further Truce between the Fleet of Great Britain and the town [sic] of Copenhagen.

Admiral Sir Hyde Parker will suspend further hostilities till 12 o'clock tomorrow noon, by which time he expects an explicit answer.

Waltersdorff and Lindholm agreed to deliver the letter and left the *London* at 4.00 p.m. to report to the Crown Prince. As the *Berlingske Tidende* told the people: 'Negotiations stopped that day in an excited manner, and the horizons darkened again with storm clouds.'

Thus by the evening of the day on which Denmark had buried more than four hundred of her dead, there seemed to the Government a good chance the British would attack again the following day when the noon time limit expired – because that evening Count Bernstorff was against giving an undertaking of any description to the British. This was not surprising since the *Slaget paa Reden*, the Battle of the Roads, as it was now being called, had been the final outcome of the policy he had pursued as Denmark's Foreign Minister.

The problem facing the Crown Prince on that Easter Sunday night can be simply stated: Who should Denmark defy – the British, who had just destroyed much of the Fleet and even now had their bomb vessels anchored ready to bombard Copenhagen, or the Czar and Autocrat of all the Russias?

Unfortunately there is no way of knowing who gave what advice to the Prince that night; nor do we know if anyone asked the two vital questions whose answers would have decided the problem: If we defy the British, what will they do, and what can the Czar do to assist us? If we defy the Czar, what can he do, and what can the British do to assist us?

The answers show that in fact Denmark had no real choice. Within a couple of hours of the Truce expiring, the British could leave the city in flames and the Czar would be able to do nothing to help – either immediately or in the long term, since the British would then continue into the Baltic to destroy the Russian Fleet, and there was no doubt of their ability to do that.

On the other hand, while defying the Czar might lead to an attempted Russian occupation of Denmark by land – the reason why it could not be by sea has already been discussed – there was the possibility, although the Danish Government apparently did not consider it, that France would almost certainly force a *status quo* on the Czar. And the British had already undertaken to leave twenty sail of the line in the Baltic all the time it was navigable. . . .

That night the Danish Government took the only precautions possible while it tried to reach a decision: it made sure the city's garrison was alert and the Trekroner Fort and Lynetten were ready, and attempted to get the only available warship ready for action. This was *Floating Battery No. 1*, which was in the harbour with no British prize crew on board.

An order was drawn up in the Crown Prince's name for Lt Peter Willemoes, who had commanded the battery so gallantly in the Battle, and it was dated 5 April.

By virtue of this order you are at once to report to Captain Kierulff, the King's Harbourmaster, in order to take command of *Floating Battery No. 1* once again and put it in position with Lynetten as soon as it is ready for service, and at the same time report to Captain Steen Bille, whose orders you are to carry out.

The defences of the Trekroner battery had in fact been strengthened immediately after the Battle: the East India Company gave the Government a large number of cotton bags, while Selbye's warehouse provided sugar bags, which were hurriedly filled with sand and used to strengthen and raise the battery's bulwarks.

The bitterly cold weather and the south-westerly gale continued next morning. The British ships snubbed at their anchor cables; the boats carrying men and materials between the ships had a hard fight in the short, sharp seas.

Nelson, writing to Emma soon after breakfast, had found some verses written by Miss Knight – their fickle companion on the journey from Naples to England the previous autumn – and enclosed them in the letter with the comment, 'the latter part is a little applicable to my present situation'.

This verse (in Lady Hamilton's writing, with only its relevance to commend it) reads:

> And doubly blest the hour
> When love resumes his power,
> And when the northern wind,
> To long-lorn Emma kind;
> Shall change to joy her soul's alarms
> And give back Henry to her arms.

'Henry' was one of Emma's pet names for Nelson, whose letter continued,

It is dreadfully cold. I am sure, from our communication with the shore yesterday, that it is only fear of Russia that prevents our disputes being settled. These people must sooner or later submit, and I long to get to Revel before the Russian Fleet [there] can join that of Cronstadt; but, [he added] we Mediterranean people are not used to it. Some farther propositions are to come off today, but I fear [the wind] blows too hard. . . .

With Sir Hyde's twenty-four-hour extension of the truce expiring at noon, Nelson did not seem overly worried, and while two more prizes, both floating batteries, were set on fire at 10.00 a.m. on Sir Hyde's instructions, Nelson went on board the *Ganges*.

There Captain Fremantle was less cheerful, and while Nelson waited to be summoned to the *London*, Fremantle finished a hurried letter to the Marquis of Buckingham, having just learned that Otway was sailing for England with despatches.

We shall know in an hour or two whether we are to commence hostilities or not; at all events, Otway will go in an hour. I do not presume to judge the propriety of our terms to the Danes; but I know and feel as a seaman that great sacrifices in our present situation should be made, sooner than to declare openly against them again. We are now with above 100 prisoners each, eating and drinking us out [he added] and the ships could not have been fitted out if we had not found a great quantity of stores on board the ships captured,[1] all of which ships are to be burnt, except one, which Sir Hyde has commissioned as a hospital ship. They are very fine ships, particularly one of the 74s, which is much larger than the *Ganges*.

The two floating batteries were burning when, as Sir Hyde noted in his journal, 'At 11 a.m. a Flag of Truce came on board as before with the Adjutant General Lindholm and Maj[r] Gen[l] [Waltersdorff].' Neither the journal nor subsequent letters to the Admiralty described what passed at the meeting. Colonel Stewart is silent; Scott confused the issue by getting the dates wrong in his diary and recording that on this day Nelson went on shore to see the Crown Prince.

However, there is one Danish account. This says that Lindholm and Waltersdorff took Count Bernstorff's reply 'in which he continued to keep to his earlier terms'.

The account continues:

Nelson appeared sympathetic and one even hoped for his understanding. But suddenly the entire thing was turned around. Sir Hyde Parker, who during the last part of these negotiations had, in another cabin, gone through his Minister's orders, now sent for Lord Nelson. They both stayed away for quite a long time.

When the admirals at last returned they were 'playing another tune on their trumpets'. Parker would not continue the Truce, but talked only of an armistice. He then delivered to Waltersdorff a note to Bernstorff in which the armistice terms were set out.

Waltersdorff in putting the note away said he hoped Sir Hyde would not take affront at him not reading the note, which was on matters about which he could not officially negotiate.

Nelson then remarked that it demanded a defensive alliance between Britain and Denmark, and Lindholm answered feelingly that 'Never will Denmark and the Prince dishonour themselves by conducting affairs in such a way that they would risk making a new enemy: they would rather keep the enemy they already had.'

---

[1] '. . . as to rope, those [captains] who have been industrious have more rope than when the Fleet sailed from England; for the greatest quantity of rope has been made from the wounded cables of the prizes, which were all new,' Nelson wrote to the Admiralty on 23 May.

Nelson said that, in such a case, Denmark had to disarm practically unarmed ships and Britain would defend Denmark against a Russian attack.

The [Danish] answer was, 'We do not ask for defence. We will look after ourselves. Those that carry the sword are not obliged to use it for their own defence and at the same time have another defender. If England fears our unarmed ships, they can paralyse them by accepting a truce, and the result will be that our equipping will remain in *status quo* while there is a truce.

'But if nothing else but a peace treaty can stop the existing hostility, then we must point out that it could be stopped in London with greater advantage for both nations than here. The consequences of making a hasty peace could be as dangerous as having hostilities.'

Lindholm repeated his offer to make a truce, according to the Danish account, but when Nelson kept to Parker's demands and also said that only acceptance of these could stop a renewal of hostilities, Lindholm said, 'It is regretable that hostilities have ceased. The proposals sent by you [Parker] were exceedingly unfortunate for Denmark, as we have no other choice than to accept the dishonourable proposals or take on a new or greater enemy, so let us now stand or fall as one man.'

Waltersdorff then said finally, according to the Danish account, that the British demands did not correspond with the Admiral's repeated assurances that the British did not want to weaken Denmark, because Denmark would be the counterbalance against Russia.

'The Danes left the cabin. The way to peace now did not look easy.'

If this account is accepted, it shows a considerable amount of muddled thinking among the Crown Prince's ministers. The British had Copenhagen at their mercy; the terms offered the Danes so far were generous. Indeed, once the situation is looked at realistically, it will be seen the terms were the most generous any victor had yet, or would ever, offer a vanquished enemy in the whole war; considerably different from the terms Napoleon had forced on every nation he had defeated. Putting twenty British sail of the line in the Baltic meant the Danes had a far more powerful fleet to defend them than they possessed before the battle, and one already tried and tested in several years of war at sea.

The impasse was due to stupidity on both sides. Danish pride and fear of Russia prevented them from openly agreeing to Parker's demands.

But were the demands either important or relevant? Did it matter to the British whether or not the Danes accepted them? Was a Danish rejection a cause for renewing hostilities? Were the Danes being sensible in rejecting them?

The answer to each question is no: alone in his cabin early that Sunday morning Sir Hyde had produced a masterpiece of irrelevance.

His first demand was for a declaration that no agreement existed between Denmark and Russia for Denmark to supply ships for a combined fleet.

What relevance did that have? What possible use could he have for such a declaration? The point was the Danish Fleet now barely existed, and in any case he was supposed to be going on to destroy the Russian Fleet. What was the value of a declaration about a fleet that did not exist and a fleet which was about to be destroyed?

The second demand was that Denmark should declare a perfect neutrality.

What relevance did this have? What possible use could he have for such a declaration? With her fleet out of action and only a tiny army, Denmark was already neutralized by Parker's fleet, whether she wanted to be neutral or not. There was no difference between being neutralized and being neutral in this context; the declaration was as unnecessary as making a man dying of cancer affirm that he is ill.

The third demand was that British ships should be able to enter the port of Copenhagen for supplies.

Once again – what relevance did this have? What possible use could he have for such permission? He had won the battle – who could stop him? Sir Hyde appears to have forgotten the British were the victors. There is no record of Napoleon asking permission to enter Genoa, Milan, Florence, Turin, Rome, Alexandria, Malta and dozens of other countries, cities and towns. But Napoleon already had a considerable record for entering such places and carting off all the treasures which, even as Sir Hyde wrote, were still being sorted and valued in Paris.

When the Crown Prince and Bernstorff received this letter, they must have seen at once they were dealing with a weak man: so weak he asked for what he already had. And in view of their fear of Russia, Parker was playing into their hands. A refusal would give them time. The risk was that Parker would attack again. But would he? Would a man who could write such a letter be able to do it? Nor must the Crown Prince's assessment of Nelson be forgotten: the Prince knew that Nelson regarded Russia as Britain's main enemy; that he was impatient to be on his way up the Baltic to deal with the Russian Fleet.

It was reasonable to conclude Sir Hyde was holding him back, and coupled with the weak letter certainly suggested the policy that would be best for Denmark: to play for time. Given time, perhaps Nelson's counsel would prevail so that the British Fleet would leave Copenhagen in peace and go off to destroy the Russian Fleet. With that done, the British would need no declarations from Denmark about anything.

Bearing these points in mind, it seems highly probable, from the Danish account and from what is known of Nelson's views, that when Lindholm and Waltersdorff brought Bernstorff's reply to the *London*, this was the first time that Nelson learned the contents of the original letter. At first, the Danish account says, Nelson appeared sympathetic; then Sir Hyde, out of the cabin, sent for Nelson, and when they came back 'the entire thing was turned around'.

For the rest of the talks 'Nelson kept to Parker's demands' – but he had little choice; and if Waltersdorff did in fact say the British (in other words, Parker's) demands did not correspond with Nelson's repeated assurances that the British did not want to weaken Denmark, it is further proof that the two admirals' ideas did not coincide.

Nevertheless, if in fact the Danes realized Sir Hyde was a weak man, they were only partly right in regarding Nelson as a sympathetic negotiator. It is obvious from the narrative that so far he had been concerned with ending hostilities with Denmark because he genuinely regretted the need for them, and wanted to get at the Russians. However, Nelson was well aware of two additional factors: the Government in London would want some paper agreement signed now, and Sir Hyde would not agree to move without it for fear any of his small ships, passing to and from England with despatches, were intercepted.

When Waltersdorff and Lindholm returned to the Amalienborg Palace this stormy day and delivered Parker's latest letter, the Crown Prince's and Bernstorff's reactions are not recorded, but it is reasonable to suppose they realized they had been unwise in not trying to negotiate the terms of Parker's previous letter since they were mild compared with the new ones, which allowed no prevarication. It was one thing to defy the enemy from behind a closed gate; but it would be another to defy him from behind the ruins of the gate after he had smashed the wall down.

Parker's letter, once again an ill-spelled and ungrammatical missive, said:

Admiral Sir Hyde Parker having had recourse to his Instructions, finds he is authorised to conclude a Treaty with the Court of Denmark on that Court entering into a Treaty relative to Maritime Law, agreeable to Instructions given to Mr Vansittart (which the Adm¹ takes for granted has been communicated to the [Foreign] Secretary, Conte Bernstoff). This was to be accompanied by one of the alternatives, vizt,
By an engagement immediately to disarm, or in the event of the Danish Govt being adverse to that measure, by the conclusion of a Public Treaty of Difensive Alliance with G^t Britain.

Admiral Sir Hyde Parker submits this part of his instructions to the serious consideration of the Court of Denmark. Feeling as he does, it becomes his duty to put an end to all future negotiations, unless the objects of his communication is complied with within the next twenty-four hours.

Dated on board his Britannic Majesty's Ship
London, 6th day of April 1801
sg. H. Parker, Ad[1]
and C in C of his Britannick [sic] Majesty's Fleet.

Even this letter is typical of Sir Hyde. In the first place his secretary Osborn, who actually wrote the letter, achieved the difficult feat of spelling 'Britannic' two different ways in four lines, wrote 'adverse' instead of 'averse', and was defeated by the spelling of 'Defensive'. In the second place, Sir Hyde signed the letter – one of the few he ever sent to a foreign government – without noticing the errors: errors which men like the Crown Prince, Bernstorff, Lindholm and Waltersdorff, all of whom spoke very good English, would have spotted immediately.

In fairness to Parker, for all the ridiculousness of his first letter, his second seems to have finally brought home to the Danish Government that there was no choice: the British were at the gate, offering friendship and twenty sail of the line to defend Denmark. To spurn them because of a greater fear of Russia was to see the city go up in flames. At this point the Crown Prince seems to have rejected Bernstorff's advice, which was to placate Russia, because from now on Bernstorff appears to have had no role in Denmark's handling of the situation.

Instead it seems likely that the influence of Lindholm and Waltersdorff increased. This may have been due to Lindholm's greater understanding of the role of sea power which, from the very beginning of the Armed Neutrality, Bernstorff had failed to grasp. He was certainly unable to grasp just what a threat the British Fleet was to Russia – indeed, it seemed incredible though true that a tiny island like Britain could, with a few ships, remove the Russian threat to herself with a dozen or so sail of the line. In this she was fortunate. Her seamen and the English Channel have for centuries allowed Britain to survive more than her fair share of incompetent premiers and ministers.

Three more prizes were burned on Tuesday – they were set on fire at 2.00 a.m., and as they were close inshore the flames lit up the city. Before dawn all the carpenters in the Fleet and their mates were hard at work continuing to repair damaged British ships and preparing the *Holsteen* for her new role as a hospital ship.

The weather was still bad, a fresh gale blowing from the south-west. The *Cruizer*, with Otway on board carrying Sir Hyde's despatches, had sailed the previous evening and the gale gave her a fast run up to the Skaw.

The flat-bottomed boats which the Fleet had brought from England were at last proving useful, taking stores and water, stoves and the wood to burn in them, from the *Sælland* and transferring them to the *Holsteen*.

In the first move towards doing something about the Russian Fleet, Sir Hyde sent the Masters of the Fleet on board the *Fox* cutter with orders to sound the Grounds, the southern part of the Holland Deep leading past Saltholm and Amager into the Baltic. From the information given by the pilots and the scanty charts available, it seemed possible that at the far end, abreast of Dragør, there was not enough water for the two 98-gun ships, the *London* and *St George*.

With the extended truce due to expire at noon, Sir Hyde was relieved to see a boat coming out from the city at 7.00 a.m. with a flag of truce. Once again Lindholm and Waltersdorff came on board the *London*. But they had no letter to hand to Sir Hyde: instead Lindholm delivered a verbal message. The admiral recorded in his journal that they came from the Crown Prince

to express a wish that an Armistice should be enter'd into between us until that Court and Great Britain could adjust their present differences; or to give them an opportunity for doing so; and had deputed the gentlemen above mentioned on the part of His Royal Highness for that purpose – I, being actuated from principles of humanity and by the public good, and that both countries should be restored to and united in former amity and friendship... appointed Vice-admiral Lord Nelson and the Honble Lt Col Stewart.... to meet those gentlemen on shore and to enter into an armistice....

Sir Hyde gave Lindholm a note which said:

Will the Court of Denmark solemnly engage to cease from arming? That her ships of war shall remain in *status quo*? To observe the strictest neutrality with Great Britain, and suspend the operations of their Treaty with the Northern Powers *until* the present differences between the courts of Great Britain and Denmark are determined? Or till Admiral Sir Hyde Parker receives further instructions from England? [The note was unsigned, but the date, 7 April, was written at the bottom of the page.]

Sir Hyde also arranged that Nelson and Stewart should go on shore next day, Wednesday, 8 April, and arrange the Armistice terms with Lindholm and Waltersdorff, who then left. Mr Scott was sent for, and with some pride the reverend gentleman confided to his diary that he had been appointed to act as 'secretary to the Legation'.

Nelson was given formal orders for his mission.

His Royal Highness the Crown Prince of Denmark, having deputed the

Major-General Waltersdorff, and Mr [sic] Lindholm, Adjutant General of the Marine of Denmark, to make proposals to me of an Armistice for a given time. . . . I do hereby authorise you, Vice Adm¹ Lord Nelson, Knight of the Most Honourable Order of the Bath, and the Honourable Lt Col Stewart, Commander-in-Chief of His Majesty's forces embarked in the Fleet under my command, to meet the beforementioned Deputies, and to arrange such articles in writing as may appear to you necessary to accomplish the important end of this Mission, agreeable to the fundamental basis laid down in the Paper No. 1, subject to being ratified by me.

This time Osborn managed to spell 'Britannic' correctly in the preamble to the order but Sir Hyde wrote under his signature 'Commander-in-Chief of his Brittanick Majesty's Fleet'.

Nelson helped Sir Hyde draw up the Armistice terms later on Tuesday afternoon. Both men were conscious of being in the shoal water of diplomacy. Sir Hyde would have to ratify it on behalf of the British Government – who could repudiate it, a step which would mean professional ruin for Sir Hyde. However, after going over his original instructions from London, he then wisely left the rest to Nelson ('Be it good or bad, it is my own; therefore, if blamable, let me be the only person censured' Nelson later wrote to Troubridge).

A letter which Nelson wrote to the Prime Minister on the day the Armistice was ratified reveals the factors he was weighing up in his mind when drawing up the terms.

A negotiator is out of my line, but being thrown into it, I have endeavoured to acquit myself as well as I was able, and in such a manner as I hope will not entirely merit your disapprobation. If it unfortunately does, I have only to request that I may now be permitted to retire, which my state of health, and inconvenience from loss of my limb has long rendered necessary.

Having shown his usual depression after having successfully passed through a crisis – in this case a diplomatic one, instead of a sea battle – and no doubt influenced by exasperation caused by the extreme difficulty a one-armed man had in boarding a boat from a ship of the line in the gales which had been sweeping Copenhagen Roads – he reached the illuminating part of his letter, and at once the style changed: his thoughts are described crisply and clearly, and in a logical sequence.

I trust you will take into consideration all the circumstances which have presented themselves to my view.
1st, We had beat the Danes.
2nd, We wish to make them feel that we are their real friends, therefore have spared their Town, which we can always set on fire; and I do not think if we burnt Copenhagen it would have the effect of attaching them to us; on the contrary they would hate us.

466

3rd. They understand perfectly that we are at war with them for their treaty of Armed Neutrality made last year.

4th. We have made them suspend the operations of that treaty.

5th. It has given our Fleet free scope to act against Russia and Sweden; 6th, which we never should have done, although Copenhagen would have been burnt, for Sir Hyde was determined not to have Denmark hostile in his rear. Our passage over the Grounds might have been very seriously interrupted by the batteries near Draco [Dragør, at the south-eastern end of Amager island].

7th. Every reinforcement, even a cutter, can join us without molestation, and also provisions, stores &c.

8th. Great Britain is left with the stake of all the Danish property in her hands, her colonies, &c., if she refuses peace.

9th. The hands of Denmark are tied up; ours are free to act against her confederate allies.

10th. Although we might have burnt the City, I have my doubts whether we could their ships.

Nelson drew a diagram showing the position of the British bomb vessels in relation to Copenhagen harbour, explaining that 'every ship must be separately burnt, for they have plenty of room to haul any ship on fire clear of the others'.

All these considerations weighed deeply in my mind; added to which, having shown them that it was not because we feared fighting them that we negotiated, but for the cause of humanity towards Denmark, and I wish to conciliate their affections; all these matters have affected my mind, nor shall I have a moment's rest till I know, at least, that I am not thought to have done mischief.

Nelson decided to take Captain Foley with him for the visit to the Palace, and also Captain Edward Thornborough Parker, a young officer he regarded almost as a son – indeed, there must have been many times when he compared Parker (who was to be killed a few months later) with his graceless stepson Josiah Nisbet. Colonel Stewart was Nelson's fellow negotiator and Scott came as secretary.

The wind was still blowing strong from the south-west with heavy rain, and the boat taking Nelson's party on shore was swept by sheets of spray for nearly half an hour as it punched into a head sea. Despite boat cloaks and tarpaulins, all of them were half-soaked by the time they arrived at Toldboden.

A large crowd was waiting to watch Captain Lindholm greet Nelson on behalf of the Crown Prince. This time the atmosphere was different: a few days earlier, as negotiations seemed likely to break down, the newspapers had warned the people that 'the horizon darkens again with storm clouds'; now they were reporting that the chances of an Armistice were good.

Lindholm shook hands with Nelson as he stepped from the boat and was introduced to Foley and Parker, whom he had not met. Once again the Royal carriage was waiting to take the party to the Palace, and this time because of the torrential rain Nelson used it. Colonel Stewart noted that the 'immense crowd' that escorted them to Amalienborg 'showed more satisfaction on this occasion than on the preceding one'.[1] Nelson, a diminutive figure, was almost dwarfed by the massive Foley but, as is often the case with people who have a strong personality, the *Berlingske Tidende* reporter noted that 'one's attention was drawn to him the whole time'. Another Danish account referred to the crowds of people trying to get a glimpse of 'The little one-eyed man in a fine long navy blue uniform coat, the sleeve flapping where his arm should have been, and a turn-up hat', and who 'appeared very impressive'.

Many men and women in the crowd wore mourning; the King Frederik's Hospital halfway along Amaliegade was still full of wounded men. But although on a rainy day the street is gaunt and forbidding, on this occasion the cries of the crowd made up for the lack of sun. The *Berlingske Tidende* reporter echoed Colonel Stewart's thoughts when he described how Nelson was escorted to the Palace by a 'huge mass of people who were more satisfied this day than the last day he passed'.

At the Palace the Crown Prince was waiting to greet Nelson and Stewart. This first audience was brief and Captain Lindholm and General Waltersdorff then led the British party to a conference room where the negotiations would take place. The room was sparsely furnished and the Britons were far from comfortable: most of their clothing was damp, if not wet, from the boat trip and a blazing fire soon made them hot and sticky while they wriggled their toes in sodden shoes.

For the next five hours, in Scott's words, there was '*pour et contre parler*'. Although Nelson had written out headings for the various articles of the armistice, each had first to be agreed in broad terms, then the specific wording drawn up to each side's satisfaction.

Nelson's attitude is revealed by a phrase in his letter to Addington, when he commented that Count Bernstorff was 'too ill to make me a visit yesterday. I had sent him a message to leave off his ministerial duplicity, and to recollect he had now British admirals to deal with, who came with their hearts in their hands.'

---

[1] His account, written some years later and on which some later descriptions were based, incorrectly gave the date as 9 April, a day late. The phrase also shows it was Nelson's second visit; the third was made next day, the 9th, the day the Armistice was ratified.

The first article of the Armistice presented no difficulty – from the moment of signing all hostilities would cease between Sir Hyde's fleet 'and the city of Copenhagen, and all the armed ships and vessels of his Danish Majesty in the Road or harbour of that city, as likewise between the different islands and provinces of Denmark, Jutland included'.

The second article, divided into two sections, was one which kept both sides arguing for a long time. The first part was agreed – Danish warships were to remain in their 'present actual situation as to armament, equipment and hostile position'.

The second part required the Treaty of Armed Neutrality to be suspended as far as Denmark was concerned. In return, the British Fleet would not molest Copenhagen or the coasts of any Danish islands or provinces. Waltersdorff immediately argued against the suspension, and demanded specific safeguards for Copenhagen itself.

Nelson finally agreed to accept the phrase 'in order to avoid everything which might otherwise create uneasiness or jealousy, Sir Hyde Parker shall not suffer any of the ships or vessels under his command to approach within gun shot' of the Danish warships and Trekroner Fort in Copenhagen Roads, with the exception of ships 'necessarily passing or repassing' through the King's Deep.

The question of Denmark abandoning the Armed Neutrality led to a great deal of argument because fear of Russia was still dominant. Yet unknown to any of the negotiators at the table, a messenger was at that very moment within a few miles of Copenhagen bringing almost incredible news from St Petersburg. In the meantime, however, both Waltersdorff and Lindholm were conscious of the shadow of Czar Paul and it was finally agreed to refer the final Danish decision to the Crown Prince.

They agreed on the third article, which provided that the Armistice protected Denmark against any other British naval forces and the fourth, allowing Sir Hyde's fleet to provision itself at Danish ports 'with everything which it may require for the health and comfort of the crews'.

The British agreed to send all Danish prisoners on shore in the fifth article, and in return the Danes were to give a receipt for them, as well as for the wounded the British had allowed to be landed after the battle, 'in order that they may be accounted for in favour of Great Britain, in the unfortunate event of the renewal of hostilities'. Nor did the sixth present problems: Nelson agreed on Sir Hyde's behalf that all Danish merchantmen trading along the coasts covered by the armistice should not be molested by British ships.

But the seventh and last article nearly brought the negotiations to an abrupt end. The British stipulated the Armistice should remain in force for sixteen weeks from the date it was signed, and after that either nation could 'declare a cessation' and, after giving fourteen days' notice, 'recommence hostilities'.

Waltersdorff immediately demanded a shorter period, claiming it would not take sixteen weeks for envoys to go to London, complete a final treaty and return. Nelson insisted on sixteen weeks. Waltersdorff and Lindholm continued to argue for less, making it quite clear they feared what Russia might do in that time – a period during which the Armistice made no provision for Denmark's defence. Nelson said he would not agree to less, and, Stewart noted, 'assured them, with a degree of candour not quite customary in diplomacy, that his reason for requiring so long a term as sixteen weeks was that he might have time to act against the Russian Fleet, and then return to them'.

One of the Danes turned to the other and, knowing Scott spoke Danish, muttered in French of the possibility of having to renew hostilities.

'Renew hostilities!' exclaimed Nelson, who to the Dane's surprise understood what had been said, and turning to Scott declared warmly, 'Tell him that we are ready at a moment; ready to bombard this very night!'

It was no idle threat: the bomb vessels were moored; the targets, ranges, angles and trajectories for their mortars had been calculated days earlier. The Dane apologized, and at once the sudden tension eased, although neither Waltersdorff nor Lindholm would agree to sixteen weeks. It was the second point of disagreement, and the last article, and with five hours of negotiation behind them, they all decided to refer it to the Crown Prince as well as the question of the Treaty of Armed Neutrality.

It was now 2.00 p.m., and Lindholm conducted them to a *levée* in a nearby stateroom, where many people were waiting for the presentations. Among those wishing to meet the famous Admiral were the Crown Prince's brother-in-law, Prince Augustenbourg, and the Prince Wurtemborg. Foley, Parker and Scott were presented – a fact a delighted Scott recorded at greater length in his diary than the armistice negotiations.

There was no furniture in the room in which the *levée* was held; the conference room had only the minimum required. The fact that the Palace had been hurriedly stripped almost bare, most of the furniture and works of art being removed to a safe place in case of a bombardment, did not escape Nelson, who also knew the two most important items of the Armistice had yet to be agreed.

When dinner was announced the Crown Prince led the way up the staircase to the great dining room on the first floor. Nelson, leaning on Colonel Stewart's arm as he climbed the stairs at the head of the British party, whispered 'Though I have only one eye, I see all this will burn very well.' As Stewart noted later, 'He was even then thinking more about the bombardment than about the dinner.'

It was a splendid dinner with fifty guests. Nelson sat at the Crown Prince's right hand and according to Stewart, 'much cordiality prevailed'. It was the custom for people to be allowed to look into the Royal dining room, and many took the opportunity to see a famous British admiral – indeed, the most famous in the world – two captains and a parson dining with three princes, many ministers, and all the members of the Defence Commission. One person was noticeably absent – Count Bernstorff.

It is significant that the Danish Foreign Minister had taken no part in the truce or Armistice negotiations. Parker's first notes, addressed to him, were answered by other people; an Army general and a Naval officer had been appointed Commissioners to negotiate the truce. Because decisions of the Danish Government were made after discussions of which no minutes were kept, it is difficult to see from what date Bernstorff's advice was ignored and where his influence ceased. From the many other documents which are available however, and his conspicuous absence during the negotiations it seems Bernstorff was relegated to the background from the time the British Fleet was reported approaching Cronborg, and ignored altogether after Parker's ultimatum.

The Crown Prince and Nelson talked cheerfully through the dinner: neither referred to the Armistice, and it would have been impossible for a casual onlooker to guess that the fate of the city and perhaps of the nation rested on the wisdom and mutual good faith of these two men. It was on this occasion that Nelson, commenting on the bravery of a young Danish officer commanding a small ship which had engaged the *Elephant*, jokingly added that the young man should be promoted admiral. The Crown Prince replied, 'If I were to make all my heroes admirals, there would be no lieutenants or captains left!'[1]

[1] The young lieutenant has never been satisfactorily identified but is generally believed to have been Willemoes of *Floating Battery No. 1*, although it might have been Müller of the *Hayen*. Nelson's remark and the Crown Prince's reply was first printed in a Copenhagen newspaper. The historian Niebuhr's report that all the officers of Fischer's defence line had been invited to attend the dinner but Willemoes had refused because he 'would rather be on board his battery', and that Nelson insisted on seeing him, is, like much of Niebuhr's account, fabrication. Niebuhr wrote of Nelson's truce proposal during the battle, 'It was not for Nelson to suggest the shooting should stop.' However he did not specify who else he had in mind for the job.

When dinner was over the Crown Prince took Nelson to another room where, alone, they began discussing the two outstanding points of the armistice agreement. While they talked, according to Danish sources, a messenger reached the Palace with urgent despatches from St Petersburg, and Captain Lindholm walked unannounced into the room and whispered in Danish to the Prince, 'The Czar is dead'.

The Prince continued his conversation with Nelson 'without batting an eyelid' according to the same account. If he did indeed receive the news in this way and at this moment, it meant that both obstacles to the signing of the Armistice had been dramatically removed. The new Czar, Alexander, was known to be a much more reasonable man – apart from anything else he was sane – and he certainly would not press the Armed Neutrality nor had he the obsessive hatred of Britain hitherto shown by his father.

Certainly the Crown Prince continued arguing, leading Nelson to use the expression 'force' when he wrote later that night to Addington. 'After we had forced the expression of the suspension of the treaty of Armed Neutrality, a point very difficult for fear of Russia, I said to the Prince, "Now, sir, this is settled suppose we write Peace instead of Armistice?"'

The Prince, who had already persuaded Nelson to accept fourteen weeks instead of sixteen 'replied that he should be happy to have a peace, but he must bring it about slowly, so as not to make new wars'.

With the Armistice settled, the two men discussed other but relevant matters. The Prince asked whether some method could not be thought of 'to prevent the mortifications' to which warships escorting convoys were liable when stopped by belligerent warships, to which Nelson answered, 'I thought there might very easily. I did not enter further on the subject with him, although I did [later] to his Adjutant General of the Fleet, Lindholm who seems much in his confidence.'

Nelson's idea was simple and he described it to Addington:

No convoys shall be granted to any vessels bound to ports at war with us; and that if any such convoy is granted, that it shall be considered an act of hostility; and that if any vessel under convoy proceeds to an enemy of England's ports, that the owner shall lose the value of his ship and cargo, and the Master be severely punished.

Nelson added, 'On these foundations I would build a prevention against future disputes; but all these matters I leave to wiser heads....'

His suggestion was an excellent one but it had one great defect that would prevent its adoption by any nation: no politician, diplomat, civil servant or constitutional lawyer could possibly accept any proposal whose basic idea could be clearly expressed in sixty-four words – as any attempt to understand the basic idea of any maritime or other international agreement drawn up in the last 250 years will show. The more obvious proof of that is the two previous agreements with Denmark, made many years earlier and which ran into thousands of words, still left both nations arguing over their meanings up to the time Sir Hyde's fleet left Yarmouth.

Long after dark Nelson went on board the *London* to report to Sir Hyde and yet again try to persuade the Commander-in-Chief to let him take a squadron up to Revel. But he failed. He had planned, fought and won the Battle, arranged a truce, then planned and negotiated a fourteen-week Armistice. Now the last possible reason for the Commander-in-Chief not sailing for Revel and Cronstadt with the whole of his fleet was removed. (The British were not to hear of the Czar's death for several days: the Crown Prince had ordered that the news was to be kept a secret.)

Having left the amended copy of the Armistice terms with Sir Hyde and arranged to return to the *London* in the morning – Waltersdorff and Lindholm were due at 11.00 a.m. for the signing – Nelson returned to the peace of his cabin in the *St George*, wet from spray thrown up by the south-westerly gale blowing across the Roads, weary and frustrated by Sir Hyde. Earlier he had mistakenly thought the demands and frustrations of the past two weeks were over.

31

THE SWEDISH FLEET SAILS

The *Fox* cutter returned the next morning, Wednesday, 9 April, with the masters of the Fleet who had prepared a chart to get through the Grounds to the Baltic. It had not been easy work with strong winds and heavy rain, although the gale which had come up during the night gave them a fast run back to the anchorage. They reported that the 74s could pass, but the *London* and *St George* would have to be lightened.

By ten o'clock Nelson and Colonel Stewart were on board the *London* and two fair copies of the Armistice were ready for signatures and ratification. An hour later Major-General Waltersdorff and Captain Lindholm arrived.

The preamble to the Armistice said that the Danish Government and Sir Hyde, 'being equally anxious to put a stop to the further effusion of blood, and to save the city of Copenhagen from the disastrous consequences which may attend a further prosecution of hostilities against that city, have mutually agreed upon a Military Armistice, or Suspension of Arms'.

The last words of the Armistice reflected the feelings of the men who had negotiated it, although they would probably have given constitutional lawyers apoplexy: 'The conditions of this Armistice are upon all occasions to be explained in the most loyal and liberal manner, so as to remove all ground for further dispute, and to facilitate the means of bringing about the restoration of harmony and good understanding between the two Kingdoms.'

Seals were affixed and Nelson signed first, 'Nelson and Bronte', followed by 'William Stewart', 'Ernest Frederick Waltersdorff', and 'Hans Lindholm'.

After the sentence 'In pursuance of my above-mentioned authority, I ratify this document with my hand', a space was left for the Crown Prince's signature; then, beneath, 'Ratified by me,' came 'Hyde

Parker'. The second copy was then signed and Sir Hyde recorded the ratification in his journal, adding 'which being done and order given to supply us with water, refreshments &c., &c., order'd the bomb vessels before Copenhagen, with the ships that were there to cover them, to join the Squadron'. Waltersdorff and Lindholm then went on shore to arrange for Nelson to visit the Crown Prince that afternoon for his signature on the Armistice documents.

Colonel Stewart offered to take one of the signed copies to England, and Sir Hyde agreed. For the next few hours Osborn and Scott were kept very busy as Sir Hyde dictated despatches, letters and orders.

The captains of all the British ships with Danish prisoners on board were instructed to hand them over to Danish officers who would come out from the city and from whom receipts were to be obtained. General orders were given to the Fleet that following the Armistice they were 'not to molest the Danes or their trade in the Baltic or Cattegat.'

A letter was sent off to Lord Carysfort, the British Minister in Berlin, telling him of the Armistice and its terms, and the Commander-in-Chief prepared his despatch for the Admiralty. It is ironic and indicative of his scale of priorities that the phrase in Sir Hyde's journal recording this says, 'Acquainted the Adm^{ty} with the above Armistice and enclosed a counterpart thereof, forwarded it to England with my account of promotions &c. . . .'

Nelson and Stewart went on shore, and by the time they arrived at Toldboden the waiting crowd was even larger than the previous day. That night Nelson wrote to Emma (addressing it to 'Mrs Thomson') describing the visit.

Your friend was on shore with me today to receive the ratification. . . . I received as a warrior all the praises which could gratify the ambitions of the vainest man, and the thanks of the nation, from the King [sic: Crown Prince] downwards, for my humanity in saving the town from destruction. Nelson is a warrior, but will not be a butcher.

I am sure, could you have seen the adoration and respect, you would have cried for joy; there are no honours can be conferred equal to this.

Anxious to assure Emma he was being faithful and not dallying with the blonde beauties of the Danish Court, he added:

Having done my duty, not all the world should get me out of the ship. No! I owe it to my promise and not all the world shall ever make me in the smallest article break it. You are, my dearest Mrs Thomson, so good, so right in all that you do that I will take care your dear friend shall do no wrong. He has cried on account of his child. . . . He desires me to say he has never wrote [sic] to his aunt [Lady Nelson] since he sailed. . . . He does not, nor cannot, care about her; he believes she has a most unfeeling heart.

The other letters he wrote that night after his visit to the Palace show anxieties in other directions. Lord St Vincent was told he had 'just returned from getting the Armistice ratified'.

I am tired to death. No man but those who are on the spot can tell what I have gone through, and do suffer.

I make no scruple in saying that I would have been in Revel fourteen days ago; that without this Armistice the Fleet [under Sir Hyde] would never have gone but by order from the Admiralty; and with it, I dare say, we shall not go this week.

I wanted Sir Hyde to let me at least go and cruise off Carlskrona, to prevent the Revel ships from getting in [to join the Swedish Fleet]. I said, I would not go to Revel to take any of those laurels which I am sure he would reap there. Think for me, my dear lord, and if I have deserved well, let me retire; if ill, for Heaven's sake supersede me, for I cannot exist in this state.

After writing the long letter to the Prime Minister which has already been extensively quoted, it was 10.00 p.m. before he could write frankly to his old friend Troubridge.

I have only a moment to write my letters as Colonel Stewart goes off at 4 o'clock in the morning. I am in a fright, [he admitted, about what the ministers would think of the Armistice.] Be it good or bad, it is my own: therefore, if blamable, let me be the only person censured. I shall certainly give up instantly.

I believe no one can arrive from this Fleet who will not tell you that mine has not been quite a life of inactivity since the 23rd [when they arrived off Cronborg]. Foley's and Murray's ships, and indeed, all, are perfection again.

I am trying to get over the Grounds, but Sir Hyde is slow, and I am afraid the Revel fleet will slip through our fingers. Why we are not long since at Revel is past my comprehension.

A postscript assured Troubridge 'Your son was well at six o'clock' – Midshipman Edward Thomas Troubridge, the 'Tom' of several such postscripts, was Sir Thomas's only son and serving in Nelson's ship.

To his old and close friend Gilbert Elliot, now Lord Minto, he wrote, 'Before you condemn the Armistice, hear all the reasons: they are weighty and most important. Without it we should have gone no further this year, and with it not half so far as I wish. . . .'

The last letter, and one which shows the news of the Czar's death had still not reached the British late on 9 April, was to Sir Brooke Boothby – 'I am well; the Battle was, I allow, hard fought, but our success was complete. Of the eighteen vessels of all descriptions, seventeen are sunk, burnt and taken. . . . I but wish to finish Paul, and then retire for ever.'

Sir Hyde was now more of a problem for Nelson than Czar Paul. Despite all his arguments Nelson soon found it was still as impossible to get the Commander-in-Chief to move quickly, even though the Armistice was signed, as it was before passing Cronborg. And, since he knew only too well what must be done but was being prevented from doing it, Nelson unconsciously let ill-health provide the reason to get away from an impossible situation.

Colonel Stewart sailed for England before dawn on Friday, 10 April, and Nelson had no doubt that the colonel, who had been present at the conferences on the Belt-or-Sound question, at the Battle, and at the truce and Armistice negotiations, would give unbiased accounts to the Prime Minister and St Vincent.

In the meantime Sir Hyde had the 74-gun *Sælland* burnt and on Saturday sent the *Fox* cutter to lay buoys for the Fleet to mark the passage over the Grounds.

Danish boats had come out from the capital to take the former prisoners on shore early on Friday. Altogether there were 1,779 officers and men to be returned. As far as possible the Danes arranged that officers from particular ships collected their own men from the British ships.

Inevitably there were misunderstandings. When it came to release one hundred men who had been taken from the *Prøvesteenen*, Lt Michael Bille reported that only eighty-six were in fact released, the British keeping fourteen non-Danish soldiers on board. Bille signed a receipt for eighty-six and protested at the British keeping ten. His report to the *Prøvesteenen*'s former captain made no mention of the other four.

Sir Hyde's own flagship had several Danish officers on board, including Captain Arenfeldt, who had commanded the *Holsteen*, and some of his officers, among them Lt Niels Andreson, the second-in-command. They had been treated as 'prisoners at large'.

By now Lt Müller, the former captain of the *Hayen*, had spent more than a week on board the *Elephant*, writing later that during his stay the British crew 'proved very kind', and he was allowed to move freely about the ship. One of the British officers had commented to him of the *Sælland*, 'By God, a ship so cut up has never been seen.' Müller was finally freed with the other officer prisoners in the *Elephant* and landed by boat at Charlottenlund, just north of Hellerup.

Captain Bligh was involved in an unpleasant episode with two Danish officers. Lt Johan Uldall, whose twenty-fourth birthday was in nine days' time, had considerable ability and tact – he had been one of Olfert Fischer's officers in the *Dannebroge*. Now he went on board the *Glatton* to collect the officer-prisoners taken from the Danish flagship. As they were preparing to get into the boat, Lt Uldall reported later to

Fischer, 'Lt Winkler of the Marine Corps asked me to request the captain of the *Glatton* to return his sword to him'.

Uldall went to Captain Bligh's cabin with Winkler and asked him for the sword, and Bligh 'answered he was glad that I had mentioned it to him'.

Bligh said that Lt Ditler Lorentzen (a reserve officer) had sold the sword to him for £1 sterling, and it appeared this was the sword which was later said to belong to Lt Winkler.

'I replied that there must be some misunderstanding as Lt Lorentzen did not understand the English language, and that anyway it was impossible that a Danish officer would commit such an act.'

Captain Bligh 'had Lt Lorentzen summoned to the cabin' Uldall reported, 'and asked him if he had received £1 from him for a sword'.

Lt Lorentzen thereupon showed an English banknote, which I at once took out of his hand and threw on the table, saying that I still believed it was a misunderstanding.

The Captain insisted that Lt Lorentzen was to keep the money, and he [Bligh] the sword.

In order to bring this unpleasant matter to an end, I asked Lt Winkler if he would make a present of the sword to the Captain, and he at once agreed.

I then gave the sword to the Captain, stating that Lt Winkler made him a present of it, as he so much wanted to keep it. The Captain accepted it, and then began insulting Lt Lorentzen and tried to urge the money on him.

Lt Lorentzen refused to take it. I asked all the officer-prisoners to go into the boat, told the Captain that his behaviour towards Lt Lorentzen was most incorrect and then left the ship.

It was unfortunate that Bligh was the captain involved, since Lorentzen, by producing the pound note, proved he had in fact sold a brother officer's sword; but Bligh was a man with a facility for getting into situations which embarrassed other men.

The next person Bligh embarrassed was Nelson, who three days later wrote to Lord St Vincent taking little trouble to conceal his surprise at the unusual request:

Captain Bligh has desired my testimony to his good conduct, which although perfectly unnecessary, I cannot refuse: his behaviour on this occasion can reap no additional credit from my testimony. He was my second, and the moment the action ceased, I sent for him on board the *Elephant* to thank him for his support.

With the Armistice signed on Thursday and the prisoners discharged on Friday, Nelson continued chafing to get the Fleet into the Baltic. The news of the Czar's death was still a well-kept secret in Copenhagen, and with Saturday spent carrying out Sir Hyde's order to get the *Holsteen* ready to sail to England with the *Monarch* and *Isis*, by Sunday Nelson had to relieve his feelings by writing to Troubridge.

Ah, my dear Troubridge, the wind is now at the same point as it was when I carried my division [over the Middle Ground], and all our 74s and 64s ought this day to be over the Grounds, but I am fretting to death.

We had a report yesterday that the Swedish Fleet were above the Grounds [i.e. at Carlskrona], but nothing can rouse our unaccountable lethargy. I hope from my heart that my leave is coming out, and another admiral, if it is necessary, in my place for, my dear friend, I am miserable myself at being useless to our country.

In London next day the Foreign Secretary, Lord Hawkesbury, wrote to his predecessor, Lord Grenville:

I send you a letter from Lord Carysfort [in Berlin] which will, I conclude, inform you of the important intelligence of the death of the Emperor Paul on the 24th March. I have just received . . . a letter from Count Pahlen [the Russian Foreign Minister] announcing this event, and the peaceable accession of the Grand Duke Alexander.

It is written in the most conciliatory terms, and marks the strongest disposition on the part of the new Russian Government to renew their connection with this country. We have every reason to believe that our friend Worontzow [the Russian envoy in Britain] is reinstated.

Hawkesbury added, almost as an afterthought, 'Accounts have been received from Hamburgh, dated the 6th inst., which state that an action to have taken place at Copenhagen on the first [sic]. The loss is represented to have been very severe on both sides, and the result is not mentioned; so that there can be little doubt that it has been favourable to us.'

Meanwhile in Berlin on the previous day Lord Carysfort had written a private letter to Grenville.

I cannot but pray for your return into office; and, to say the truth, I cannot sleep of nights for the terror I am in lest the inexperience of our new leaders should not steer us steadily and skilfully through the most intricate and hazardous navigation in which we are at this moment engaged.

What will come of this attempt to negotiate with France? And what could lead us to it when all the advantage seemed on her side? I trust that God will give us good success in the Baltic and Egypt. Then indeed we may hold up our heads, and it is already a great point gained to be able to keep Malta without losing on that account the friendship of Russia.

George Rose, the friend of Addington who recorded the Prime Minister's views on Hyde Parker and Nelson (see page 201), noted on 14 April that the special messenger from St Petersburg bringing Count Pahlen's letter also brought letters of credence for Count Worontzow. The Count, who was ill, had been living at Southampton since he ceased to be ambassador. The letters, Rose wrote, 'were to be used as soon as a British messenger should be sent to St Petersburg.' The messenger also brought a copy of a proclamation that the new Czar 'meant to tread in the steps of his grandmother, the Empress Catherine, which probably will put an end to the Northern Confederacy.'

The *Fox* cutter returned on Monday, 13 April, after buoying a channel across the Grounds, and Sir Hyde gave Captain Bligh – who by now had been put in command of the *Monarch* – orders to take the *Holsteen* and *Isis* under his command 'and proceed to England'.

Bligh's arrival on board had brought little joy to the officers and men of the *Monarch*, who were already resentful of Sir Hyde's treatment of Lt Yelland. Midshipman Millard's verdict appears to be a fair one:

Captain Bligh was an excellent navigator, and I believe in every respect a good seaman, but his manners and disposition were not pleasant, and his appointment to the *Monarch* gave very general disgust to the officers.

Some circumstances which occurred on our passage home served to increase the general disapprobation. On the 15th April we weighed. . . . Captain Bligh having had time to turn himself round in his new ship, began to make himself known among us. Finding our pilots were not so scientific as himself, he liberally bestowed upon them the appellations of 'dolt' and 'blockhead', and pretending that the ship was not safe in their hands, he took charge of her himself. This was as unnecessary as it was unusual. These men had been accustomed to the Baltic trade the greater part of their lives, and were certainly as well able to conduct the ship from the Naze of Norway to Lowestoffe Point as Captain Bligh.

Captain Bligh had been asked by some of the lieutenants towards what port he meant to steer. To this he answered that he should consult the convenience of the officers and the accommodation of the wounded men before any private considerations. [Sir Hyde had not specified a particular port; nor would it have been usual, with a hospital ship in company, since much depended on the wind.]

This [answer] was thought almost equivalent to a promise to return to Yarmouth, where they had all of them connexions of some sort, and where a naval hospital was established.

Very great was our astonishment to hear that the wounded officers, with all the effects of the late captain, should be removed to the *Holsteen*, to be landed at Yarmouth, and the *Monarch* was to proceed to the Nore. As this was not made known until we were within sight of Yarmouth, it was generally supposed that Admiral Dickson was the 'maukin' from which Captain Bligh fled with so much precipitation; for there was reason to believe that no great cordiality subsisted between these officers.

However this might be, the *Monarch* and *Holsteen* were hove to at sunset, and the night was employed in removing the wounded officers, with some few of the men who stood most in need of immediate assistance. [The *Monarch* then made sail] without attempting to procure vegetables for the wounded men, or letters and congratulations [waiting at Yarmouth] for those that were not. So much for the humanity and politeness of Captain Bligh.

Millard's glimpse of Bligh and Bligh's unusual request to Nelson combine with a study of the *Bounty* affair to show Bligh was not the sadist of popular accounts: instead he was completely egocentric, with an equally complete lack of understanding of people or leadership. He had the obsessive attention to detail typical of such a personality: the letter, the badgering of the pilots, the lack of common humanity that led him to have wounded men transferred by open boats at night from one ship to another. But on the credit side he was a fine seaman, a brilliant navigator, and a brave man. He lacked only humanity to make him a competent ship's officer; he lacked only leadership to make him an adequate captain. But his apologists must bear in mind that good navigators, good sailors and brave men in the Navy of the day were counted by the thousands, and Bligh was merely one of them; leaders were numbered only by the score.

With the channel over the Grounds at last charted and buoyed, Sir Hyde finally began to consider a move southward, but his first thoughts were directed not towards the Russians; instead he became preoccupied with the Swedish Fleet at Carlskrona, the naval base at the entrance to the Baltic. . . .

On Tuesday, five days after the Armistice was ratified and six days after its terms had been argued, Sir Hyde noted in his journal, 'at 3 a.m. a Prussian vessel which was prest came alongside [the *London*] to receive our guns, shot and various other stores and enable her to pass over the Grounds'.

The task of lightening a ship of the *London*'s size to reduce her draft was enormous: removing twenty tons would make her float about one inch higher. Her guns weighed roughly three hundred tons, and the shot another hundred, accounting for about twenty inches of draught. Getting the guns into the Prussian vessel was the most difficult job (each of the *London*'s 32-pounders weighed nearly three tons).

While this work was going on Sir Hyde sent Captain Sutton away in the *Amazon* frigate to Carlskrona with orders to send in a boat with a flag of truce and deliver a letter to the Swedish Governor 'acquainting him with the Armistice with the Danes and desiring to know if they will do the same'.

Just before 3.00 p.m. the *London* hoisted the signal for most of the Fleet to prepare to weigh. Sir Hyde had left orders for Nelson 'to expedite the sailing of ships bound for England', and when the *St George* had got her guns and shot out – 'for which purpose a vessel is hired' – to join him in Kioge Bay, which is on the Danish coast only a few miles south of Copenhagen, beginning at the south end of Amager. The *Harpy* was to stay in Copenhagen Roads 'for the purpose of watching the motions and conduct of the Danes' and pass on the rendezvous with the Commander-in-Chief to any newly-arrived ships.

When Sir Hyde gave the signal, twelve sail of the line got under way and headed down the Holland Deep towards the Grounds. Fremantle wrote, 'I had brought the *Ganges* to draw only twenty two feet two inches, and led the Fleet the whole way. We just touched ground once, but never stopped. . . . It made me, I confess, very nervous to be running four miles in four fathoms and a half [twenty-seven feet] of water, frequently in less.'

The *London* passed the shallows off Dragør at 6.00 p.m., and 'struck the ground twice but did not stop', Sir Hyde noted. An hour later, anchored in Kioge Bay, the deep indentation in the coast south of Copenhagen, Captain Domett reported that she 'made some water, tho' little, owing to her having struck the Ground, which took off part of her false keel, gripe &c.'

At 4.00 a.m. next morning the Prussian ship was brought alongside and the work of hoisting and parbuckling the guns, shot, bags of bread, and provisions back on board was begun. In the meantime the wind had gone round to the north-north-east, so the flagship and the rest of the Fleet were anchored on a lee shore, but by noon it had backed to the north-west and later went calm. At 4.00 p.m. everything was back on board the flagship and the Prussian vessel left.

The *Eling* and *Rover* arrived from Elsinore with fresh beef for the Fleet; then the *Amazon* was sighted coming over from the Swedish coast. Captain Sutton 'told me [that] as the Swedish squadron was at sea, he judged it best not to trust them, and therefore returned with the despatches . . . to the Governor of Carlskrona'.

The unexpected news that the Swedes were at sea alarmed Sir Hyde who 'sent a letter immediately with the information thereof to Lord Nelson and requesting him to come and hoist his flag on board the

Elephant 'till the *St George* could pass the Grounds . . . which his Lord-ship did'.

The arrival of the letter, though perhaps not the request, took his Lordship by surprise. The day before the *London* left Copenhagen, Nelson had written to his old friend Davison, 'Sir Hyde tells me he shall send me to England as soon as we are over the Grounds, my health is so indifferent – for I have a fever every night from fretting all day – that if the Admiralty would send me a commission as Commander-in-Chief, I would not now accept it'.

Next day, as Parker's ships sailed, he had written to Lindholm, 'Will you have the goodness to request His Royal Highness to give me a general order for a passage through any place which may be occupied by Danish troops, as it is my intention, from the state of my health, to return to England in a very short time, and probably by Lübeck and Hamburgh'.

The news that Nelson was intending to leave for England cannot have been very welcome for the Danes because, at this stage, they knew little more about Russia's future policy than that the new Czar was a much more reasonable man than his father (while the British did not even know Paul was dead). However Lindholm enclosed a passport in his answer next day, saying:

But I hope to see your Lordship on board the *St George* before you set out. His Royal Highness has ordered me to present his compliments to your Lordship.

We hear today the interesting news from Hamburgh that the Emperor of Russia has offered to give up the English vessels and English goods detained in Russia, when England will give up the Russian, Danish and Swedish vessels in her ports. I hope that the Northern business will soon be settled.

In passing it is worth pointing out that the letter (which is so phrased that Paul's death is not revealed) was written thirteen days after the Battle and six days after the ratification of the Armistice, and had the Crown Prince – or Lindholm, who was sufficiently trusted by the Prince to be his spokesman – felt Nelson had been guilty of any impropriety over the original truce it is unlikely the letter would have been so cordial.

On the day he received the passport Nelson wrote two more letters. The first was to his brother Maurice who, unknown to Nelson, was seriously ill and was to die nine days later.

We shall see whether the new Administration treats me as ill as the old. I think very likely Lord St Vincent will either take this late business up with a high hand, or he will depress it; but how they will manage about Sir Hyde I cannot guess.

483

I am afraid much will be said about him in the public papers; but not a word shall be drawn from me, for God knows they may make him Lord Copenhagen if they please, it will not offend me. I only want justice for myself, which I have never had yet, and leave to go home for the re-establishment of my health. . . .

To Nelson's credit, no word *was* ever drawn from him in public. His reference to 'justice' was reasonable and based on the peculiar standards which were being used in awarding honours. Under the previous Administration, Pitt's system meant that the higher the rank and the fewer the prizes, the greater the reward. Jervis, an admiral, captured four sail of the line at St Vincent and received an earldom; Duncan, a vice-admiral, captured eight at Camperdown and received a viscountcy; Nelson, a rear-admiral, captured or destroyed eleven at the Nile and received a barony, the lowest rank in the peerage, for the Navy's greatest victory.

Nelson was sufficiently a man of the world to know that a barony was often granted to a minor minister who had to be removed from office for a comparatively small mistake, while a viscountcy was reserved for a senior minister who proved remarkably incompetent.

In a second letter, to Davison, written the same day, and while the *St George*'s guns were being loaded into the hired merchantmen, he said:

For once I am left behind, and without guns, and as the wind is come contrary, I do not expect we shall ever pass the Grounds; for from what I hear [i.e. from Lindholm] I think we shall have peace in the North; and be ordered home, which God grant.

You can gather from Nepean, or Troubridge, or the Earl whether my leave is coming out; for here I *neither can or will stay*. My health is ruined by fretting, and I will not kill myself to do the work of any Commander-in-Chief.

Referring to litigation with St Vincent over prize money, he added, 'I send home the Lawyer's opinion. Justice is all I want. My Commanders-in-Chief run away with all the money I fight for [Sir Hyde had of course burned the prizes]; so let them. I am content with the honour: there they cannot get a scrap. But damn me if I suffer any man to swindle me out of my property, whilst he is at ease in England.'

Nelson had just finished writing these letters when, at 6.00 p.m., Sir Hyde's letter from Kioge Bay arrived reporting the Swedish Fleet at sea and requesting Nelson to come down to the *Elephant*. Her master, Alexander Briarly, who had piloted Nelson's division into battle on board the *Edgar*, described what happened.

The moment he received the account, he ordered a boat to be manned, and without even waiting for a boat cloak (though you must suppose the weather pretty sharp here at this season of the year) and having to row about 24 miles with the wind and current against him, jumped into her and ordered me to go with him, I having been on board [the *St George*] to remain till she had got over the Grounds.

All I had ever seen or heard of him could not half so clearly prove to me the singular and unbounded zeal of this truly great man.

His anxiety in the boat for nearly six hours (lest the Fleet should have sailed before he got on board one of them, and lest we should not catch the Swedish squadron) is beyond all conception. I will quote some expressions in his own words. It was extremely cold, and I wished him to put on a great coat of mine that was in the boat: 'No, I am not cold; my anxiety for my Country will keep me warm. Do you think the Fleet has sailed?'

'I should suppose not, my Lord.'

'If they are, we shall follow them to Carlskrona by the boat, by God!'

I merely state this [wrote Briarly] to show how his thoughts must have been employed. The idea of going in a small boat, rowing six oars, without a single morsel of anything to drink, the distance of about [150 miles] must convince the world that every other earthly consideration than that of serving his country was totally banished from his thoughts.

All this, it should be noted, was within a few hours of receiving a passport from the Crown Prince to enable him to return to England because of 'the state of my health'. Parker's letter had wrought a miraculous cure: Nelson never suffered an illness that did not vanish at the prospect of battle.

Briarly concluded, 'We reached our Fleet by midnight, and went on board the *Elephant*. . . .' His speculation on what motivated Nelson makes an interesting comparison with Nelson's description, written in a letter to Troubridge after he found it was a false alarm and which was in guarded phrases because he was afraid it might be intercepted. Saying Sir Hyde sent word that the Swedish Fleet, fourteen sail of the line, was at sea, 'you will believe that I came up seven or eight leagues in a bitter cold night, and Foley was kind enough to receive me in the *Elephant* – for this I feel much obliged to Sir Hyde, for to have been left behind in the expectation of an action would have been worse than death.'

He added that he hoped the first ship from England 'will bring my leave of absence. . . . If not I shall make my application to Sir Hyde Parker, for longer I cannot stay, and if I could tell you all which is passing in my mind I am sure you and all good men would approve.' Once again he was fretful over further delays after the Swedish alarm, and he was as good as his word: four days after the first ship arrived, with no leave, he applied to Sir Hyde.

On the day that Parker sent for Nelson, 15 April, Captain Otway finally arrived in London with Sir Hyde's despatches: the first definite news to reach Britain. One of the captains was long expected and groups of people had been waiting for several days outside the gates of the courtyard in front of the Admiralty in Whitehall. The news of the arrival of Otway's coach quickly spread. Otway delivered the despatches to the Board Secretary, Evan Nepean.

With his usual infelicity, Parker used the first part of his despatch on the victory to list in detail the contrary winds and difficulties he had met between Yarmouth and Copenhagen, and was more than halfway through it before he referred to the Battle.

By the time Otway had reported to Lord St Vincent, and Sir Hyde's despatch, Nelson's report to him on the Battle, and the remaining enclosures (Sir Hyde's two letters to the Governor of Cronborg and the replies) had been read, there was a large crowd waiting at the Admiralty gates.

Among them, reported a newspaper,

... a young gentleman of the Transport Office, about 13 years of age, was very conspicuous. His engaging figure and eager deportment interested all around him, and rivetted their attention.

He hastily asked Captain Otway about the *Monarch*: 'And my Papa, sir, how is he? Is he wounded? Is he killed?'

'Who is your Papa, my dear boy?' asked Captain Otway, struck by the boy's ingenuous sensibility.

'Captain Mosse!'

'My dear . . . the *Monarch* has been very roughly handled.'

'Oh, I know your meaning,' exclaimed the mourner, 'My dear Papa is dead.'

Captain Otway was much agitated, and the youth, bursting out in an agony of grief, bewailed the loss of his parent in few but pathetic sentences. At length he raised his head and, with his eyes streaming tears, faltered out, 'I am happy, however, that Papa died fighting for us.'[1]

Next day the news was announced to both Houses of Parliament; Lord St Vincent rose to 'call the attention' of the House of Lords to 'the recent victory over the Danes'; in the Commons, Addington 'Rose to move the thanks of the House to the officers and seamen of the Northern Fleet for the distinguished zeal and gallantry they have shown in the Battle'. No action had taken place in the course of the present war, he told Members, which contributed more to sustain the character and add to the lustre of British arms.

[1] The boy, R. L. Mosse, was one of the seven 'Extra Clerks' in the Transport Office, with a salary of £90 a year.

In outlining the Battle he said that

Sir Hyde Parker had, with a degree of judgment which reflected the highest credit on his choice, appointed Lord Nelson, whose name has already been covered with splendour and renown, to the execution of the important enterprise.

Great, however, as was the courage, the skill and the success which had been formerly displayed by this illustrious Commander at [the Nile], it was not greater than that which had been exhibited in the attack upon the Fleet moored for the defence of Copenhagen.

Other speakers included Lord Hawkesbury, Pitt, Sheridan the playwright, and William Wilberforce, whose fame rests on his fight against the slave trade.

In the Lords, Grenville told his fellow peers that Lord St Vincent 'had truly described it as a victory which was not equalled by any that had ever been achieved by the Navy of Great Britain'. The Duke of Clarence complimented Nelson for his 'courage and intrepidity, which Fortune seemed to back in every enterprise in which he was engaged'.

Lady Malmesbury, who was in Brighton, wrote to Lord Minto in Vienna the same day with the news that Minto's son George was safe, and that 'Certainly Nelson is the greatest of all heroes.' She grumbled, 'We have no *Gazette* yet, and it is vexatious to be out of Town at this moment. I must also regret extremely that the news of the Emperor Paul's death (a blessed event) did not arrive in time to spare so many thousand lives.'

Lord Carysfort had written to the Foreign Secretary from Berlin on the day Otway arrived in London. Telling Hawkesbury that although he had decided to wait before visiting the Prussian Foreign Minister to see if the British victory would mean a change in policy, since a messenger was waiting to leave for London he could give some more news about the death of Czar Paul.

It is not known with certainty whether the present Emperor had any intimation of the design against his father's life, but it seems generally believed that he was not unapprized of its being in agitation to dethrone him. The Empress, who was in an adjoining apartment, is said to have come to the door of the room before the murder was accomplished, but was instantly forced away. She is said to be deeply affected.

Although Captain Otway stayed only two days in London because the Admiralty required him to take new instructions to Sir Hyde, there was time for him to visit Clementina, the eldest daughter of Admiral John Holloway, and whom he was to marry at the end of the year.

The Admiralty's secret orders to Sir Hyde, dated 17 April, said that Lord Hobart, one of the Secretaries of State, had,

in his letter of yesterday's date acquainted us that intelligence had reached this country of the death of the Emperor of Russia, and a communication had been received from the Court of St Petersburg in consequence of that event affording some reason to hope that his successor . . . will not persevere in those measures of violence and unprovoked aggression which were on the point of involving the two countries in actual hostilities.

The King, anxious to avoid such a calamity, and wishing to 're-establish the ancient relations of peace and amity with Russia', had commanded that measures should immediately be adopted 'as may appear most conducive to this desirable object and to prevent . . . any fresh obstacles being thrown in the way of accommodation'.

This was a felicitous way of expressing a pious hope since the Admiralty's last orders to Sir Hyde, dated one month earlier, were to attack the Russian Fleets at Revel and Cronstadt, and there was no way of knowing if Sir Hyde knew Czar Paul was dead. These orders, the Admiralty now told Sir Hyde, 'should, for the present, be suspended'.

Sir Hyde was to find out 'as soon as possible' – if necessary by sending a flag of truce to Revel or some other Russian port – whether the embargo on British ships had been lifted and the crews released. If this had been done 'you shall feel yourself authorized to suspend without limitation of time or other condition, all hostile proceedings against the ships or ports of Russia'.

On the other hand, if the embargo was still in force and no order for lifting it had been given by the new Emperor, and no positive assurance could be obtained that he intended to give it, Sir Hyde was to offer a suspension of hostilities, providing he was given to understand that Russia intended to begin, or had actually started, discussions with Britain 'with a view to the satisfactory adjustment of any existing differences'. This was conditional: during such a suspension and until the embargo was lifted and the British crews released, the division of the Russian Fleet now at Revel should not join that at Cronstadt, or vice versa.

Sir Hyde was also to make it clear that hostilities could be started by either party twelve hours after they had given notice in writing to that effect. This could only happen, the Admiralty order continued, if the new Czar rejected the British offer of conciliation, refused to raise the embargo, and did not release the ships' crews.

If it did happen, however, the orders for Sir Hyde were explicit: only if he received 'the most unequivocal proofs' that under the new Czar

Russia's hostility towards Britain continued, and the British proposals were totally rejected in a manner 'as leaves no doubt on this point', Sir Hyde was to consider himself at liberty to carry out the order of 15 March – to attack the Russian Fleets at Revel and Cronstadt – 'without waiting for further instructions from this country'.

Captain Otway left London with the order late on Saturday night to join the *Lynx* and sail for the Baltic. He took with him copies of the votes of thanks from Parliament, and among other letters he carried was one from Lord St Vincent to Nelson.

Written with the First Lord's usual brevity, it said:

You have greatly outstripped yourself, and all who have gone before you, in the late most glorious conflict. I will pay the utmost degree of attention in my power to all your wishes, in which I shall be well seconded by every individual of this Board.

By chance Colonel Stewart arrived in London on Sunday, only a few hours after Otway had left. He brought Parker's despatch concerning the Armistice and its terms, Nelson's letter to the Prime Minister describing the negotiations with the Danes, and his private letter to St Vincent written the day the Armistice was ratified.

More important than the letters and despatches was the fact that in Colonel Stewart the Prime Minister, Foreign Secretary and the First Lord of the Admiralty had a man all three trusted completely and who had been present at all important conferences and negotiations.

Yet quite apart from any effect that Stewart's arrival might have had, Parker's own despatches already delivered by Otway had shown the Government that he had proved weak and indecisive before battle and redundant in the subsequent negotiations: Nelson had done both the fighting and the negotiating.

Stewart's reports, reinforcing the doubts raised by Parker's first despatch, brought home to the ministers the alarming fact that the man who now had to do most to secure peace between Britain and Russia if the Czar really wanted it or, if he did not, deal him a swift and crippling blow by destroying his Fleet, was Sir Hyde: the orders Otway was taking to the Commander-in-Chief of the British Fleet in the Baltic gave him complete authority to sign a peace or start a war, and it was now frighteningly obvious he was unfit for the task.

But even worse, from the Government's point of view, was that it needed little knowledge of human nature to guess that this time Sir Hyde was unlikely to leave either fighting or negotiating to Nelson: it would be natural for him to consider Nelson had had enough of the glory and it was time for the Commander-in-Chief to gain some for himself.

The Cabinet's discussions are not recorded but for once the Government acted quickly, decisively and, because it had no choice with so much at stake, ruthlessly. On Tuesday, forty-eight hours after Stewart reached London and the day the newspapers printed Sir Hyde's and Nelson's despatches, their decision was sent to the Admiralty where four members of the Board – Lord St Vincent, Captains Troubridge and Markham, and Sir Philip Stephens – signed an elaborate document whose wording was traditional.

Addressed to Nelson, it began:

Whereas by our Commission bearing date this day, We have appointed your Lordship to succeed Adm¹ Sir Hyde Parker in the command of His Majesty's ships and vessels to be employed on a particular service; your Lordship is hereby required and directed to take under your command all such of His Majesty's ships and vessels as may be left with you by the said Admiral (together with the Flag officers, Captains and commanders employed on board them) and carry into execution all such standing and unexecuted orders as may be delivered to you. . . .

However, a letter enclosed with the Commission was to annoy Nelson: it was a copy of one to the Admiralty from Lord Hobart about the Armistice terms which Nelson had negotiated. In fact it was not intended to convey any criticism, but the usual inability of ministers or government officials to express their thoughts clearly gave it that impression.

It is instructive to compare the following letter with the wording of the Armistice terms Nelson had drawn up, any of the private or official letters he or St Vincent ever wrote, or even Captain Fremantle's letters to his wife Betsey describing the Battle. All share one thing in common: they write precisely what they mean in simple language without the slightest possibility of a misunderstanding.

Hobart told the Board that having laid before the King Sir Hyde's despatch describing the Armistice, and a copy of its terms, 'I have received His Majesty's commands to acquaint your Lordships that upon a consideration of all the circumstances, His Majesty thought fit to approve of it,' and directed 'that the several stipulations therein sustained should be punctually observed. . . .'

The next day, with no knowledge of the Board's decision but having read the published despatches, Nelson's close friend Alexander Davison wrote from his home in St James's Square a wise warning.

Fighting for the honour of another ought not to be your station, and as

Sir Hyde is battling for a peerage, in God's name let him have it and return quietly home, leaving you in command, if it is determined that you are to remain.

I hope it is not true, what I have heard, that it is the intention of the Government to offer you the dignity of Viscount. *That* you ought to have had long ago, and any additional distinction short of an Earldom, in my humble opinion, would be degrading. Your last act of Service deserves every acknowledgment which a grateful country (whatever the Ministers think) can bestow. The nation would be gratified to see the highest mark of honour confer'd on you.

32
THE CZAR'S OVERTURE

Neither Nelson nor Sir Hyde knew of the change of command until 5 May, and when Nelson joined the Fleet again in Kioge Bay at midnight on 16 April after the long row in the gig with Briarly from Copenhagen, light winds made Sir Hyde wait until 2.30 p.m. next day before ordering the Fleet to sail. It made only a few miles to the south-east before Sir Hyde ordered it to anchor off the island of Moen.

After weighing at 4.15 a.m. on Saturday, the British ships headed towards the Baltic for the first time, arriving off the north end of Born-holm next morning and bearing up for Carlskrona. A few minutes after 10 o'clock on Sunday morning one of the frigates made the signal for a strange fleet. 'Made the signal for General chase and prepared for action,' Sir Hyde recorded in his journal, but 45 minutes later, 'the strange fleet of eleven sail of Swedish men of war were observed to be at anchor in Carlskrona.'

He had the forty-four ships of his fleet tacking off Carlskrona for the whole of Sunday night and all day Monday, being joined by the *St George*, the *Agamemnon* and the *Troy* cutter at 11 o'clock that night. By midnight the Fleet was in fog, firing signal guns to avoid collisions, and luckily at daylight on Tuesday the fog cleared away.

The previous evening Nelson, back on board the *St George*, wrote to Emma that

Yesterday we saw the Swedish squadron, not at sea but shut up very snug in their harbour, inside of their batteries and, what is worse for us, their numerous rocks. Thus all our hopes of getting alongside them is at an end, and they will not trust themselves out again this summer.

We are, at least I am, anxiously waiting for news from England, and I expect we shall be ordered to abstain from hostilities against Russia.

Lord Grenville wrote to Lord Carysfort on 21 April, the day Sir Hyde was superseded, a letter of interest only because it is remarkable coming from a man who was Foreign Secretary until the fall of Pitt's Administration and responsible for the entire diplomatic negotiations with Denmark until Parker's fleet left England. Commenting on the news that an Armistice of four months had been concluded at Copenhagen, he wrote:

I know nothing of the light in which it may be considered by the Government. . . . The critics out of office think Parker has exceeded any powers that he could have; and has very much frittered away the good effect of his (or rather Lord Nelson's) victory.

I have myself, not the smallest doubt that Denmark would have acceded to any ultimatum he had thought proper to require. I cannot therefore think he has done well in frustrating our principal view in sending him, which was the separating Denmark by force and definitely from the Armed Neutrality. . . . But much less can I conceive how any English officer could think himself justified in granting an armistice to Copenhagen while Hamburgh remains occupied against us by the Danes.

Yet in all the months of Grenville's diplomatic exchanges with Count Bernstorff which led to Parker's squadron sailing, the one point Grenville never raised was the question of Hamburgh. . . . With an Armistice signed with Denmark and the British policy towards Russia now changed, the best Grenville could think of was a blow at Sweden, the one nation which, having been blackmailed into signing Paul's Convention, had been most skilful in not firing a shot at the British. His letter went on to say that if Parker 'avails himself of the interval [i.e. the Armistice] to strike a blow at Carlskrona, for Revel is, of course out of the question now, or if he lays Dantzic [*sic*], Memel and other ports under contribution, this may excuse but (I think) not justify his conduct'. An event off Carlskrona the next day was particularly relevant.

On Wednesday, 22 April, Sir Hyde's squadron was still tacking and wearing several miles off Carlskrona, his journal and ships' logs reading like a fleet exercising off Spithead. Finally, soon after 10.00 a.m., a Danish cutter was sighted heading for the Fleet.

It brought despatches for Sir Hyde from the Russian Ambassador at Copenhagen enclosing a letter from Count Pahlen, the Russian Foreign Minister, 'expressive of the Emperor Alexander's desire to be on the same friendly footing with Great Britain as formerly,' Sir Hyde recorded in his journal, 'and hoping no hostilities would be commenced by me against Russia, Sweden or Denmark'.

Sir Hyde neglected to note that the letter also gave him the first definite news of Czar Paul's death. However, Scott noted it in his diary and, referring to the 'conciliating disposition' of the new Czar, his biographers said 'it checked the course of the Fleet towards Revel, and led to communications with St Petersburg, to which place Mr Scott was very anxious to be sent. He could not, however, persuade Sir Hyde Parker to spare him; but this did not deter his ardent mind from prosecuting the study of the Russian language.'

The same Danish cutter took back Sir Hyde's reply: the Russian Ambassador was told that 'at the request of His Imperial Majesty [I] should cease from hostilities 'till I received further instructions from England'.

With that, to the relief of the Swedish admiral at Carlskrona, Sir Hyde took the Fleet back towards Kioge Bay. On 23 April, while still under way, Nelson had written to Emma:

My dearest amiable friend, this day twelve months we sailed from Palermo on our tour to Malta. Ah! those were happy times: days of ease and nights of pleasure. How different, how forlorn! Alas, no wonder I feel so severely the difference, but as we are returning to the anchorage off Copenhagen I hope a very short time will place me in London . . . stay I will not, if the Admiralty would make me Lord High Admiral of the Baltic. . . .

A letter from Lord Carysfort was waiting for Sir Hyde at Kioge Bay: this gave more news of the murder of Czar Paul. Parker sent Carysfort copies of the correspondence with the Russians and wrote despatches to the Admiralty.

The *Arrow* received the canvas bag containing the despatches, sealed and containing lead weights so it would sink quickly if the ship was in danger of being captured by the enemy, and left the Fleet at 5.00 a.m. on Sunday morning, 26 April. At 7.30 a.m. Captain Otway arrived from England in the *Lynx*, having passed the *Arrow* off Elsinore, bringing despatches for Sir Hyde – 'With the thanks of the House of Lords and Commons . . . and the approbation of His Majesty and the Lords of the Admiralty of my proceedings,' as he noted in his journal. And there were the fresh orders of 17 April concerning Russia, described on page 488.

Nelson, in anticipation of Emma's birthday on Sunday, had invited Scott to dinner, along with several captains from his Mediterranean days, and asked Scott to conduct the Service. The invitations that Nelson sent his captains were typical: 'My dear Fremantle, If you don't come here on Sunday to celebrate the Birthday of Santa Emma, damn me if I ever forgive you, so much from your affectionate friend as you behave on this occasion.' It was an event recorded in Scott's diary as 'I have given the people a sermon on board the *St George*, St Emma's day'.

Sir Hyde Parker and Rear-admiral Graves were also guests at the dinner. Parker was cheerful, having just received the despatches brought by Otway and Parliament's votes of thanks, and so was Nelson who told Emma:

I had 24 at dinner and drank at dinner in a bumper of champagne 'Santa Emma'. The fourth toast after dinner came as usual, your mortal part, without a compliment, for I scorn to say what I do not believe, that you are an angel upon earth. I am serious.

Sir Hyde said that he had seen you at the opera, and so said his parson secretary, who was at Hamburgh when we were there. I told them I was sure they were mistaken, for I did not believe you had been there! But they were positive, so you see how little fame is to be depended upon. Poor T [Thompson] is also very angry that his wife should suspect him of infidelity [apparently replying to some accusations in Emma's latest letters]. Damn me if I do not believe he would die 10,000 deaths sooner, or have even the idea; but my dear friend, there are those who love to do mischief, as they are incapable of doing good. . . .

Captain Fremantle had to leave the dinner at 6.00 p.m. to join the *Lynx* and sail for St Petersburg: Sir Hyde had entrusted to him the Admiralty's instructions to find out about the Russian embargo on the British ships, and Fremantle was ordered to take Sir Hyde's despatches to Count Pahlen 'to know his Imperial Majesty's intentions'.

Nelson's cheerfulness over 'St Emma's Day' did not last into Monday, for Otway had not brought the Admiralty's permission to leave for England. His impatience was not helped by the fact that the days were spent with the Fleet carrying out the lengthy process of watering in Kioge Bay. To add to the feeling of routine, Rear-admiral Graves was instructed to assemble a court martial to 'try the Lieutenant and Commander of the *Tygress* for constant drunkeness'.

On Wednesday, 29 April, a Swedish ship flying a flag of truce arrived soon after daylight with a letter from the naval Commander-in-Chief at Carlskrona, to which Sir Hyde replied by describing the orders he had given after receiving Count Pahlen's letter.

Later in the day Sir Hyde received an unexpected letter from Nelson: this was to 'request my leave to go to England for the recovery of my health'. Sir Hyde's journal also records his reply – 'no one could regret the necessity of making this request more than I did but [I] could not resist complying with his wishes, I therefore gave him leave to proceed to England in the *Blanche* frigate.'

The reason for Nelson's sudden request, described in a letter to Troubridge, was that 'last night's attack almost did me up, and I can hardly tell how I feel today. . . . Whatever has again brought on my old complaint I cannot tell; the two last I had was going down to Plymouth with my Brother, and a little one in Yarmouth Roads.'

So at last Nelson's wish for leave was granted. Two days earlier he had anticipated it while writing to the Duke of Clarence, explaining that 'as I think that all our fighting is over in the North, I am going to England: my health and circumstances absolutely require it'. Sir William Hamilton was told:

I know mankind well enough to be sure that there are those in England who wish me at the Devil. If they only wish me out of England they will be soon gratified, for go to Bronté I am determined, so I have wrote the King of the Two Sicilies, whose situation I most sincerely pity.

Sir Hyde had arranged that the *Blanche* should sail for England in a week's time, on 5 May. Nelson's only worry was that he would have recovered in time to sail. As late as 1 May Mr Scott, one of his constant visitors when he was ill, recorded, 'I have spent the whole day with Lord Nelson on board the *St George*.'

So while the Fleet was at anchor in Kioge Bay, Nelson fretted on board the *St George* and Sir Hyde remained in the *London*, no doubt thankful for a few days' rest with no one badgering him with problems and queries which required prompt decisions and answers and prodding him to get the Fleet under way.

On Thursday afternoon, 30 April, the weather was fine with an easterly breeze, and Captain Lindholm came down from Copenhagen to pay a social call on the Commander-in-Chief and Nelson. Sir Hyde, who noted that Lindholm 'came on board with presents for me from His Highness the Prince Royal of Denmark', took the opportunity of asking Lindholm to have the original navigational buoys relaid on the Grounds.

During Lindholm's visit to the *St George*, Nelson raised the question of Commodore Fischer's official report on the Battle, and Nelson's letter to Lindholm about it. (Both are described on page 452.) Whether or not Nelson's letter was the sole reason for Lindholm's visit to the Fleet it is now impossible to say; but there is no doubt – from the first sentence of the reply he eventually wrote – that at this stage he had not in fact shown it to the Crown Prince. It seems certain that he now wanted Nelson to withdraw it, but Nelson refused. Fischer's report had been made public and Nelson considered it was a serious distortion, so he wanted his answer to it seen by the Crown Prince.

Lindholm left the *St George* for Copenhagen having promised Nelson – who was still lying ill in his cot – that his letter would be shown to the Crown Prince and a reply sent. He was as good as his word: two days

later the reply was on its way with its revealing opening paragraph,
'Your Lordship has imposed upon me a very painful task, by desiring
me to communicate to his Royal Highness the Crown Prince the
contents of that letter . . . in which you have treated Commodore
Fischer with a severity which, as a brother officer, I cannot but think
too great indeed. . . .'

Nelson's reply, dated 3 May, shows that although Fischer's report had
hurt him he now considered the incident closed, and it was sent off to
Lindholm on Sunday. On Monday the *Blanche* was preparing her small
cabin for a sick vice-admiral. On board the *St George* Nelson's servant,
Tom Allen, was beginning to pack; throughout the Fleet officers and
men were writing letters to their families and friends which would be
taken home by the *Blanche*, which was due to sail at dawn on Tuesday,
5 May.

The *Blanche*, however, did not sail at dawn: instead at 1.00 a.m., Sir
Hyde's journal recorded, Colonel Stewart arrived on board the *London*
from England with despatches by which

> I received the King's and their Lordships' approval of the Armistice with
> the Danes; but what was my astonishment and surprise at reading the next
> paragraph of the letter, which was an order to resign the command of the
> Fleet to Lord Nelson, and shift my flag on board a frigate or a two decker and
> return to Yarmouth Roads.

Sir Hyde's secretary had already been roused by Stewart's arrival
and he was soon joined by Scott, who wrote in his diary two stark sentences: 'Got up at two o'clock. The Admiral is ordered to England.'

The Commander-in-Chief continued:

> At 9, sent Captain Otway on board the *St George* to communicate these
> orders to the Vice-admiral, who was to have sailed this day in the *Blanche*
> for England, with my leave, for the recovery of his health.

It must have crossed Sir Hyde's mind that had he let Nelson go to
England in the *Blanche* earlier – for the application had been made on
29 April – instead of fixing the sailing date as 5 May, he would have
been spared carrying out the Admiralty order to hand over his command. Or, had Stewart arrived six hours later, the *Blanche* would have
been on her way. . . .

Sympathy for Sir Hyde, faced with the Board of Admiralty's verdict
on his ability in the closing stage of a long career, must be modified by
one sobering thought, which applies to any wartime leaders sacked for
failure: hundreds of Britons and Danes were killed or maimed on 2
April because of Sir Hyde's inefficiency. Had he arrived off Copenhagen

with the Fleet more promptly the Danes might have negotiated; even if they had decided to fight many fewer lives would have been lost because the Danes would have been less prepared.

'At noon,' Sir Hyde continued, 'waited on his Lordship, and delivered up all my public and secret instructions, unexecuted orders, &c., &c. Ordered the squadron to put themselves under his Lordship's command, and follow his orders for their further proceedings.'

The next sentence once again highlights Sir Hyde's obsession with trivia. 'Left with him the remains of stationery &c.' This was the stationery he had spent so much time and effort getting from the Admiralty while the Fleet waited at Yarmouth.

Colonel Stewart, who delivered Nelson's commission as Commander-in-Chief and several letters, also brought a letter and a verbal message from the Prime Minister. Once Nelson had signed all the necessary receipts for the documents handed over by Sir Hyde, he settled to read them. Among the letters was Lord Hobart's heavy-handed reference to the Armistice being approved 'upon a consideration of all the circumstances'.

While Tom Allen unpacked his master's belongings (Nelson decided to remain in the *St George*), Sir Hyde transferred to the *Blanche* at 3.00 p.m. 'when my flag was immediately hoisted, and struck on board the *London*'. Nelson tactfully avoided making any signals for the time being. Domett agreed to serve as his First Captain and received his commission later in the day. Nelson also invited Scott to remain with the Fleet, but the loyal parson refused, saying he could not bear to leave the old admiral at the very time when he stood most in need of Scott's company.

Nelson then began dictating a series of letters which the *Blanche* would take to England. The first was to the Board Secretary, assuring Their Lordships he would endeavour to execute the high trust reposed in him 'as well as my abilities and a most wretched state of health will allow'. Alexander Davison was told, 'A Command never was, I believe, more unwelcomely received by any person than by myself. It may be at the expense of my life; and therefore for God's sake, at least for mine, try if I cannot be relieved.'

After quickly reading through the latest instructions to Sir Hyde brought out by Otway, Nelson wrote to Lord St Vincent, beginning by confessing,

I am, in truth, unable to hold the very honourable station you have conferred upon me: Admiral Graves also is ill as to keep his bed.

I know not exactly the purport of Fremantle's mission [to St Petersburg]. If Sir Hyde were gone, I would now be under sail, leave six sail of the line off Bornholm to watch the Swedes and to cover our communications, and go to

Revel, where I should at least, if not too late, prevent the junction of the two squadrons: that I shall never suffer. I will have all the English Shipping and property restored; but I will do nothing violent; neither commit my country, nor suffer Russia to mix the affairs of Denmark or Sweden with the detention of our ships. Should I meet the Revel Squadron, I shall make them stay with me until all our English [merchant] ships join; for we must not joke. As the business will be settled in a fortnight, I must entreat that some person may come out to take this command.

Nelson had been in command less than six hours when he wrote that letter to the First Lord. The *Blanche* sailed for England at 4.30 p.m. and at daylight next morning Nelson made his first signal: *The Fleet to hoist in all boats and prepare to weigh.*

This at once showed how different a system was about to be pursued [noted Colonel Stewart] it having [previously] been intended that the Fleet should await at anchor fresh instructions from England relative to the state of the Northern affairs, an account of which had but lately been despatched. [This was, of course, the letter Sir Hyde had received from Count Pahlen.]

Lord Nelson, who foresaw every bad consequence from the inactive mode of proceeding owed his bad health more to chagrin than to any other cause. The joy with which the signal was received not only manifested what are the customary feelings on those occasions, but was intended as peculiarly complimentary to the Admiral.

For all the flurry of activity on the day Stewart arrived, Nelson made sure the *Blanche* carried back to England a reply to the letter from the Prime Minister. Thanking him for 'your truly kind letter', Nelson said:

I am sorry that the Armistice is only approved under *all* considerations˙ Now I own myself of opinion that every part of the *all* was to the advantage of our King and Country. I stated [in the letter to Addington] many of my reasons for thinking it advantageous. We knew not of the death of Paul, or of a change of sentiment in the Court of Prussia, if her sentiments are changed. My object was to get at Revel before the frost broke up at Cronstadt, that the twelve sail of the line might be destroyed. . . .

The Fleet sailed from Kioge Bay on Thursday, 7 May, bound for Carlskrona and Revel, leaving several sail of the line off Bornholm. On the same day Captain Fremantle arrived at St Petersburg in the *Lynx* with Sir Hyde's letter and instructions to see if the embargo had been lifted.

I was exceedingly well received by Count Panin [Pahlen], the Court Minister, and Prince Korakin, the Vice-Chancellor [he told his wife]. With the former I dined twice, with the latter once during the four days I remained in Petersburg, I saw the whole of the Winter Palace. the Hermitage where the museum and all the fine paintings are; I likewise went to see the Palace of the late Prince Potemkin, that of Oranienbaum where Peter was prisoned, and the Palace of St Michael, where the late Paul was strangled.

To relate you all the modes he had found out to torment and tyrannise over his subjects will fill a folio volume, and I am only surprised to think he was suffered to live so long. The affair of his decease is much spoken of at Petersburg ... and the conspirators pointed out, several of whom I had conversation with.

... The Court's being in mourning did not allow me to be presented to the new Emperor, who has the character of being a mild tractable young man, but with not sufficient firmness of character to govern Russia as his grandmother [Catherine the Great] did; he has, however, a very able Counsellor in Count Panin who is a particular friend of Lord Whitworth and Mr Grenville.

The Russian Fleet are mostly laid up at Cronstadt, and have no idea of meeting us at sea. They are, however, putting the port in as defensible state as can well be imagined. The Fleet from Revel left that place and arrived at Cronstadt only a few hours before me. . . .

In my opinion we must make our peace with Russia, tho' they seem to stickle a great deal about this armed neutrality. I met Lord St Helens[1] in the *Latona* going to Petersburg.

Fremantle assumed he was going to make a treaty. But none of the British merchant ships had been released. He concluded his letter to Betsey by saying, 'The insult of the Admiralty to my friend Sir Hyde is scarcely to be named without feeling detestation to the person who occasioned his recall in such a way as *treason only* could have rendered necessary.'

Before leaving Kioge Bay, Nelson wrote to Count Bernstorff telling him that the King had approved of the Armistice and that the Admiralty, having 'directed me to strictly adhere to the terms, I have to assure you that the strictest orders are given by Sir Hyde Parker for that purpose'. Bernstorff was asked to take care that he gave similar orders, 'particularly in Holstein, as I have heard that in some parts of Holstein it was thought the Armistice did not extend to that province'.

Next day he grumbled to Lord St Vincent about some of the captains in the Fleet, saying he was 'astonished' to 'find such a deficiency of resource'. He concluded, 'I shall endeavour to do my best whilst I remain; but, my dear Lord, I shall either go to Heaven, I hope, or must rest quiet for a time. My little trip to the Gulf of Finland will be, I trust,

---

[1] To be the British Ambassador. Benjamin Garlike, Secretary of Legation at Berlin, was travelling overland to become chargé d'affaires.

of national benefit, and I shall be kind, or otherwise, as I find the folks.'
Colonel Stewart gives an interesting picture of these days.

The keeping his Fleet continually on the alert, and thus amply furnishing
it with fresh water and provisions, were the objects of his Lordship's unremitting care; and to this may in great measure be ascribed the uniform
good health and discipline which prevailed. Another point to which he gave
nearly equal attention was his economy of the resources of his Fleet in regard
to stores; their consumption was as remarkable for its smallness in the Baltic
as it was in the Fleet that was afterwards under his command in the Mediterranean.

His hour of rising was four or five o'clock, and of going to rest about ten;
breakfast was never later than six, and generally nearer to five o'clock. A
midshipman or two were always of the party; and I have known him send
during the middle watch to invite the little fellows to breakfast with him,
when relieved. At table with them, he would enter into their boyish jokes,
and be the most youthful of the party. At dinner he invariably had every
officer of his ship in their turn, and was both a polite and hospitable host.

The ordinary business of the Fleet was invariably despatched, as it had
been by Earl St Vincent, before eight o'clock. The great command of time
which Lord Nelson thus gave himself, and the alertness which this example
imparted throughout the Fleet, can only be understood by those who
witnessed it, or who knew the value of early hours.

Arriving with the Fleet off Carlskrona, Nelson found the Swedish
Fleet still in harbour and sent a letter to its admiral which was typical
in its direct approach:

The late Commander-in-Chief of the British Fleet in the Baltic having, by
request of the Emperor of Russia, allowed the Swedish trade in the Baltic to
pass unmolested, I should be sorry that any event could happen which might
disturb for a moment the returning amity (I hope) between Sweden and
Great Britain.

However, the Swedish admiral was warned:

I have no orders to abstain from hostilities should I meet the Swedish
Fleet at sea which, as it lies in your power to prevent, I am sure you must
take this communication as the most friendly proceeding on my part, and
communicate it to your august Sovereign. . . .

A letter dated 9 May was sent ahead to Count Pahlen, telling the
Russian Government

that I am happy in this opportunity of assuring your Excellency that my
orders towards Russia from England are of the most pacific and friendly
nature; and I have to request that you will assure his Imperial Majesty that
my inclination so perfectly accords with my orders that I had determined to

show myself with a squadron in the Bay of Revel (or at Cronstadt, if the Emperor would rather wish me go there) to mark the friendship which, I trust in God, will ever subsist between our two gracious Sovereigns. . . .

But Nelson made it clear there was another reason for the visit, and he phrased it perfectly, '. . . and it will likewise be of great service in assisting to navigate to England many of the English merchant vessels who have remained all winter in Russia'.

There would be neither bomb-vessel nor fire ship in the squadron, he assured Pahlen, 'in order to mark the more strongly that I wish [the visit] to be considered as a mark of the greatest personal respect to his Imperial Majesty'.

The reduced Fleet, having left a squadron off Bornholm, arrived in Revel Roads on 12 May, six days after Sir Hyde Parker left for England in the *Blanche*. Nelson was disappointed to find the Revel fleet had sailed for Cronstadt three days earlier – as soon as the ice had broken sufficiently.

When his fleet anchored, Nelson sent a polite note on shore to the Governor asking if a salute was to be fired, and assuring him he was ready to return it. The Governor sent a friendly reply and said it would be fired.

Nothing happened, and when Nelson sent an officer on shore to inquire what had transpired, the reply recorded by Colonel Stewart was that 'the delay had arisen from the misconduct of the officer commanding the artillery, who had been put under arrest in consequence, and that the salute should be given. This was accordingly done, but at so late an hour that our salute was not returned until next morning.'

Nelson told Lord St Vincent on 16 May that Count Pahlen had come to stay at Revel, 'evidently to endeavour to prevent any hostilities against the Russian Fleet here, which was, I decidedly say, at our mercy. Nothing, if it had been right to make the attack, could have saved one ship of them in two hours after entering the Bay.'

Colonel Stewart, who by now was acquiring a good knowledge of naval operations, noted that during his stay in Revel Nelson spent a lot of time

in observing, and in acquiring information of the harbour, mole and anchorage. It was decidedly his opinion that had the Russian Fleet been hostile, it might have been attacked with success by firing the wooden mole behind which it is always moored during the winter months; a position seemed also to present itself for a three decker [to moor] across the mouth of the harbour, by which ship the whole dock might have been raked from end to end.

And Stewart drew a plan of the Bay which Nelson sent to Lord St Vincent saying that Stewart 'is an excellent and indefatigable young man and, depend on it, the rising hope of our Army. As there is no other plan in existence, perhaps you will direct a copy to be lodged in the Hydrographer's Office.'

At 3.00 p.m. on 16 May, four days after the Fleet arrived at Revel, two letters were delivered to Nelson on board the St George: one from Count Pahlen, the other from the Governor. Nelson received them, wrote Stewart, 'a few minutes before dinner time; he appeared to be a good deal agitated [by Pahlen's letter], but said little and did not return an immediate reply'.

His surprise can be imagined: Pahlen was replying to Nelson's discreet letter of 9 May telling him of the reduced Fleet's proposed visit 'to mark the friendship' between the two countries, and Nelson, who could read a certain amount of French, would have been startled even by the opening words.

Nelson's letter was, Pahlen said, a great surprise. While it assured him of the friendly disposition of Great Britain, at the same time it 'announced your intention, my Lord, to come with all your Fleet to Revel Road or Cronstadt'. The Emperor did not judge such a step compatible with the desire manifested by the British King to re-establish friendly relations. . . . The Emperor, on the contrary, found it entirely opposed to the spirit of the instructions of the Court of London and in consequence the Emperor had ordered Pahlen to declare that the only guarantee acceptable of the honesty of Nelson's intentions would be the prompt removal of his Fleet, and that no negotiations could take place with Britain 'while the Fleet was in view of Russia's ports. . . .'

With Pahlen's letter was one from the Governor of Revel 'expressing a wish that the British Fleet should retire from the anchorage of Revel'.

Nelson, unversed in the absurd subterfuges and falsehoods commonly used by governments for petty advantages, was uncertain whether 'the Count has any meaning in his gross falsehoods, or has it been an entire misunderstanding of my letter? Time will show; but I do not believe he would have written such a letter if the Russian Fleet had been in Revel.'

During dinner and after reading Pahlen's letter, Stewart noted, Nelson 'left the table, and in less than a quarter of an hour sent for his secretary to peruse a letter which, in that short absence, he had composed'.

He had in fact decided to assume it was a genuine misunderstanding and began by referring Pahlen to his original letter. 'You will see that not one seventh part of the Fleet in point of numbers were coming into the Gulf of Finland; and that, as my intention was to pay a very particular respect to His Imperial Majesty, I submitted it to his pleasure which port he would wish me to come to. . . .'

Pahlen was asked to point out to the Emperor 'that I did not even enter into the outer Bay of Revel without the consent of their excellencies the Governor and Admiral. My conduct,' Nelson wrote, was so entirely different from what Pahlen expressed 'that I have only to regret that my desire to pay a marked attention to His Imperial Majesty has been so entirely misunderstood. That being the case, I shall sail immediately into the Baltic.'

With that the signal was made for the Fleet to weigh, and the reply was sent on shore.

The Fleet then called in at the Prussian port of Rostock.

Not an hour was lost in procuring fresh provisions for the Fleet [Colonel Stewart wrote]. The greatest veneration was here shown to the name of Nelson; and some distant inland towns of Mecklenburg even sent deputations with their public books of record, to have his name written in them by himself. Boats were constantly rowing round his flagship, the *St George*, with persons of respectability in them, anxious to catch a sight of this illustrious man. He did not again land while in the Baltic; his health was not good, and his mind was not at ease: with him, mind and health invariably sympathised.

Copies of the correspondence with Pahlen were sent off to the Admiralty and to Lord Carysfort in Berlin, the latter being told that Sir Hyde's letter of 26 April sent with Fremantle and asking about the release of the British ships, had not been answered. 'I hope all is right,' Nelson told Carysfort, 'but as seamen are but bad negotiators – for we put the matter to issue in five minutes what Diplomatic forms would be five months doing – I shall have frequent communication with Rostock [the most convenient Prussian port] if our stay in the Baltic is prolonged.'

Yet Nelson's visit to Revel was not without results: on 20 May the Russian frigate *Venus* joined the British Fleet. On board was Rear-admiral Tchitchagoff, who brought with him Count Pahlen's reply to Sir Hyde's letter.

The rear-admiral went on board the *St George* and he and Nelson had a long discussion. Reporting this to the Admiralty, Nelson wrote that Count Pahlen's reply ('a very civil letter') said he was directed by the Czar to send Tchitchagoff 'to hold a confidential communication with the Commander-in-Chief of the British Fleet', and that 'I might give full credit all he said on this occasion'. The rear-admiral described the

Czar's ardent desire 'from the moment he had commenced to reign', to restore the friendship with Britain, and he fully expected a similar desire on the part of Britain. He said Lord Hawkesbury's letter (to the Russian Court) said hostilities would not be carried out against Russia, and that orders to the effect had been given to Sir Hyde. But, he told Nelson, 'Sir Hyde's letter was amicable but held forth a threat that it could only remain so in case the British shipping were immediately given up; and this threat was in opposition to Lord Hawkesbury's letter.'

Nelson explained to Tchitchagoff that the Admiralty's instructions to Sir Hyde had been drawn up only forty-eight hours after the news of the death of Czar Paul reached London, and that certainly he had been instructed to learn Russia's intentions regarding the British ships 'in order that he may regulate his conduct by that of Russia'.

Sir Hyde had been very obliging in respecting the wishes of the new Czar by abstaining from all hostility against the trade of the Baltic nations. The spirit of the instructions, Nelson pointed out to Tchitch-agoff, were that

If the Emperor wishes to be sincere friends with us, that then we wished to be sincere friends with him; which Admiral Tchitchagoff having asserted in the name of the Emperor, I said – if that is the case, and you will declare it in writing, I will make your Court perfectly at ease about the disposition of my most gracious Sovereign.

After the Russian admiral made 'the strongest declaration' of the Emperor's desire for friendship, Nelson then gave him a signed declaration and on receiving it Tchitchagoff said 'he could almost assure me that his Emperor would order the immediate restitution of the British shipping'.

Two days later Lord St Helens arrived on his way to St Petersburg to take up his duties as the new Ambassador, and Nelson gave him copies of all the correspondence.

Nelson knew that with the Russian promise to release the British ships his task in the Baltic was complete. Writing to Lord St Vincent on 24 May, he said that the news of the death of his brother Maurice, received the previous day, 'has naturally affected me a good deal; and if I do not get some repose very soon, another will go. Six sons are gone, out of eight; but I hope yet to see you, and to cheer up once more.'

Nevertheless, successful negotiations with the Russians did not mean that Nelson had forgotten the Swedish Fleet: on 23 May the Swedish admiral at Carlskrona was given a brisk reminder that in the correspondence between him and Sir Hyde Parker 'I do not see, in return to his declaration that the trade of Sweden in the Cattegat and Baltic would be allowed to pass unmolested by British cruisers, any return of declarations on the part of Sweden.' The Swedish admiral was asked for 'an explicit declaration' that British trade would not be molested. 'Your Excellency's judgment,' Nelson added, 'will show the necessity of this mutual declaration.'

On 26 May a Russian lugger joined the British Fleet bringing Count Pahlen's reply to the letter Nelson had written him on leaving Revel.

The effect intended by that letter [wrote Colonel Stewart] had been fully felt at Petersburg: a more flattering communication was, perhaps, never made from a Sovereign to the subject of another power, than was conveyed in the Minister's reply. It apologised for any misconception of his Lordship's views in having entered Revel Roads, it expressed an anxious wish that peace should be restored on the most solid basis; and in a particular manner invited Lord Nelson to Petersburg, in whatever mode might be most agreeable to himself.

Count Pahlen had written, 'I am unable to give to your Excellency a more striking testimony of the confidence of the Emperor' than the effect Nelson's letter had produced on him. The Emperor had ordered the lifting of the embargo on the British ships. 'I keenly regret, my Lord, that your preceeding letter had produced a misconception,' Pahlen wrote. His Imperial Majesty had ordered him to express 'how delighted he would be to make the personal acquaintance of the Hero of the Nile, and to have Nelson visit the Court'.

Colonel Stewart noted that the Russian lugger on leaving the Fleet with Nelson's reply 'fired a salute, an act which implies much more in the Russian service than in many others. Lord Nelson observed to his secretary . . . "did you hear that little fellow salute? Well, now, there is peace with Russia, depend on it; our jaunt to Revel was not so bad, after all." '

33

STRAWBERRIES FOR NELSON

So Nelson's role in the Baltic war came to an end. He was made a viscount; Rear-admiral Graves received a knighthood. On 3 May, nineteen days after Otway arrived with the Copenhagen despatches, news had reached London of Abercromby's great victory at Alexandria in which three French generals and four British, among them Abercromby himself, were killed.

At this point, with a great British victory in the North, and Napoleon's final defeat in Egypt – the first major victories for Britain in the long war – the Addington Government continued its feeble peace negotiations with France. . . .

Nelson, although a supporter of Addington, had few illusions: to a friend he wrote at the beginning of June, just before returning to England, 'Whatever peace we may make under the present Government of France cannot be lasting.'

Meanwhile Sir Hyde Parker had arrived back in England. When the *Blanche* reached Yarmouth he wrote to the Admiralty reporting the fact, at the same time acknowledging their letter recalling him and the enclosed letter from Lord Hobart 'signifying His Majesty's approbation of the Armistice which I had entered into . . . which had afforded me particular satisfaction by His Majesty's approval of my conduct'. He continued:

At the same time I cannot forebear marking my astonishment at [your] directing me to shift my flag to a frigate . . . and that Vice-admiral Lord Nelson was to succeed me in the command of the Fleet.

Here, sir, with great submission to Their Lordships, and in justice of my own wounded feelings at the indignant [sic] manner in which I am treated, I call upon Their Lordships and request they will point [out] any part of my letters that can dictate the reason assigned for this treatment, after the mark'd honours bestowed upon me by His Majesty, two Houses of Parlia-

ment, and Their Lordships' own approbation of my conduct on 2d. April –
which are dated the 17th of that month – and, on the 21st, only four days
afterwards, recalled in consequence 'of the difficulties I am supposed to
entertain of carrying into execution Their Lordships' further instructions'.

I here again repeat, I call upon Their Lordships to point out any paragraph in my letters that can warrant the inference drawn; nor can I suppose
when Their Lordships maturely consider the whole of my conduct [from 9
April – the day Colonel Stewart left with news of the ratification of the
Armistice – until 5 May, when he received the letter of recall] that any part
thereof mark any delay or hesitation on my part in putting Their Lordships'
instructions into execution, consistent with the information I was in possession of, on which I acted, and which conduct I have the satisfaction to find
conformable to Their Lordships' instructions on the 17th April.

The Board's reply, signed by St Vincent, Troubridge and Stephens,
was brief and phrased in the usual manner: 'Whereas you have
acquainted us . . . with your arrival in Yarmouth Roads in His
Majesty's ship *Blanche*; and whereas we think fit that you shall strike
your flag and come on shore; you are hereby required and directed to
strike your flag and come on shore accordingly.'

Parker's letter is obviously the genuine and honest reaction of a
bewildered man; it is also an indictment of his capacity that he could
not see that he had havered and delayed.

To what extent was he really to blame? The answer is, very little. The
blame lies where it never fell – on the shoulders of the men who chose
him for the command: men who knew *at the time* that he was unsuited
for the task: men who covered themselves by appointing Nelson as
second-in-command.

When ministers knowingly put an unsuitable man in command of a
vitally important expedition, the question arises, among honest men, of
the ministers' responsibility when the unsuitability of their choice is
inevitably revealed. Sir Hyde ended what had been up to then a competent, plodding career as a disgraced man because he was given a job
which was obviously beyond him. He hauled down his flag; his career
was at an end. He was luckier than Admiral Byng less than fifty years
earlier: the ministers had him tried and shot as a scapegoat for their own
mismanagement.

The politicians who appointed Parker avoided even a breath of
criticism; indeed, they snatched the credit for having sent Nelson as
well. They were wise enough to know that one can safely enter a cart-
horse in the Derby – as long as one is careful not to bet on it. But they
were stupid enough to sue for peace while the church bells rang victory
peals.

By the end of May Nelson's health was in fact breaking down and this, combined with the knowledge there was little else for him to do in the Baltic, depressed him considerably.

I know you will be sorry to hear that I have been even at *Death*'s door, apparently in a consumption [he wrote to one of his former captains, Alexander Ball, now Navy Commissioner at Gibraltar]. I am now rallied a little, but the disorder in itself is so flattering that I know not whether I am really better, and no one will tell me, but all in the Fleet are so truly kind to me I should be a wretch not to *cheer up*.

Foley has put me under a regimen of milk, at four o'clock in the morning; Murray has given me lozenges, and all have proved their desire to keep my mind easy, for I hear no complaints, or other wishes than to have me with them.

Rear-admiral Totty, who had joined the Fleet, was told the next day, 'Sir Thomas Graves is still very ill; so much so that he begged I *would not* go and see him, as the pleasure he had in seeing me did him harm, when he was left.'

Fortunately both Nelson and Sir Thomas recovered sufficiently for a colourful ceremony to take place on board the *St George* on 14 June in Kioge Bay when Sir Thomas was invested as a Knight of the Most Honourable Order of the Bath. The King had instructed Nelson to invest Graves with the Order.

While Nelson was at Kioge Bay he was in frequent correspondence with Lindholm. An indication of his relationship with the Adjutant-general and the Crown Prince is shown by a letter to Nelson from Lindholm:

'The Crown Prince has ordered Captain Sneedorff to send you as a proof of his feeling 24 bottles of old Rhine wine which is never drunk at the Royal Court unless there is a solemn occasion, dated from the 16th century. Besides this we send you vegetables and strawberries from the King's garden.'[1]

On 31 May, St Vincent wrote a private letter to Nelson which accompanied an official one from Nepean informing him that he would be relieved as soon as possible and that the Board had instructed him to inform Nelson that his 'services in the Baltic have met their entire approbation'.

St Vincent said it had been 'with the deepest concern' that he had learned from Lt-colonel Hutchinson

---

[1] Captain Hans Sneedorff was head of the naval college in Copenhagen, which Nelson had visited. The ceremony of drinking the wine is called *Solenniteter*.

that your health has suffered in so material a degree as to require immediate relaxation from the service . . . to find a fit successor, your Lordship
knows, is no easy task, for I never saw a man in our profession, except yourself and Troubridge, who possessed the magic art of infusing the same spirit
into others which inspired his own actions, exclusive of other talents and
habits of business not common to naval officers.

St Vincent had undergone a considerable change of heart where
Nelson was concerned: it was barely six months earlier that he had
written to Nepean that he had heard Lord Spencer talking of putting
Nelson in a two-decked ship and commented: 'If he does, he cannot
give him a separate command, for he cannot bear confinement to any
object; he is a partisan; his ship always in the most dreadful disorder,
and never can become an officer fit to be placed where I am. . . .'

On 19 June Nelson sailed for England in the *Kite* brig, having handed
over command of the Fleet to Admiral Pole. He landed at Great
Yarmouth on 1 July, went to the naval hospital there to visit the seamen
wounded in the Battle, and was soon reunited with Emma and his
daughter Horatia. He was treated as a conquering hero; yet perhaps
the finest part of his character emerged in the way he handled Sir Hyde
Parker.

By the time Nelson reached London, the old admiral was fighting a
campaign to clear his name of what he considered a slur, but better than
most people, Nelson knew any inquiry bringing out all the details could
only harm Sir Hyde's reputation even more. Before leaving Kioge Bay
for England, Nelson had written a postscript marked 'Secret' to a letter
to his friend Davison:

They are not Sir Hyde Parker's real friends who wish for an inquiry. His
friends in the Fleet wish everything of this Fleet forgot, for we all respect and
love Sir Hyde; but the dearer his friends, the more uneasy they have been
at his *idleness*, for that is the truth – no criminality. I believe Sir Hyde to be as
good a subject as His Majesty has.

Soon after reaching London, Nelson wrote to Sir Hyde because of
rumours he had heard. Sir Hyde, who was at Cumberland Place with
his young wife, answered promptly, his letter showing his attitude
towards his former second-in-command:

Many thanks for this proof of your friendship which, be assured, will never
be forgotten by me. My intention is not to publish the official letters, only my
application to the Admiralty for a Court of Inquiry into my conduct, and
the answer [a refusal], and this only for distribution to my particular friends,
which I cannot but think incumbent upon me for my own justification.

Nelson answered the same day, 8 July.

I wished to have seen you the day before yesterday as I cannot but feel an interest that no act of yours should bring forward that paper war which you must expect from unknown persons. Reflect, my dear Sir Hyde, before you place yourself in a situation to have your actions criticised by any hidden enemy.

Allow me to speak out. I can have no further interest in the discussion than what arises from the injury the Service must receive from such a mode of informing the public of certain facts, and to say the truth I do not think that any officer, much less one of your high rank, has a right to publish the official business of a fleet under his orders, and I feel, whatever any of your friends may think, as lively an interest in your real honour and happiness as any person in this world. . . .

Whatever mode you may adopt for every consideration of your future happiness, do not publish – Sir John Orde published, he saw his error, and recalled his pamphlet. . . . The Prince of Wales told me he would take care, as you was [sic] his friend, to prevent your publication. . . .

I have heard that a great blame has been attributed to you for not instantly determining to pass the Sound. As a very serious conversation doubtless passed with Mr Vansittart before I saw him, and the result of ours with Mr Vansittart being a determination to pass the Belt, in consequence of which I took the liberty of writing you a letter of the 24th [March: see page 281] the rough copy of which I read to you, but as circumstances took a turn which removed the necessity of copying it, I did not give it to you, but now under all circumstances I think it right to send it to you as it brings forward all which passed on that occasion. . . .

In this discreet way, Nelson was able to remind Sir Hyde of the kind of facts that would have to come out at a court of inquiry but which, for the moment, were known only to very few people: the existence of the letter which Nelson had read aloud was known only to Sir Hyde, Nelson and Colonel Stewart. Nelson could only gain even more credit if the letter ever became public, yet was doing his best to keep it secret, while Sir Hyde would be even more discredited, to the point of being a laughing-stock.

Lady Malmesbury, with her usual acuteness, summed up the situation: 'I feel very sorry for Sir Hyde; but no wise man would ever have gone with Nelson or over him, as he was sure to be in the background in every case. . . .'

EPILOGUE

Even allowing for the diplomatic ineptness which led to Britain and Denmark going to war, the Battle was completely unnecessary. Had Nelson's strategy been followed, not one Briton or Dane would have lost his life. From the start Nelson had recognized that the major enemy was Russia, while Denmark was Czar Paul's unwilling ally. Nelson wanted to leave a small squadron off Copenhagen to keep the Danes in awe while the rest of the Fleet went on to attack the major enemy, Russia, and destroy her fleet. With the Russian Fleet destroyed, the fear of the Czar which led Denmark and Sweden to sign the Armed Convention would have vanished.

As it turned out, had his plan been followed, the British Fleet would have arrived at Revel or Cronstadt to find that Czar Paul had been assassinated and, under the new Czar, Russia's policy had changed. With the Armed Neutrality abandoned, the Battle of Copenhagen would have been completely unnecessary.

The important point is that the correct strategy was to attack Russia first. Worrying about the Danes intercepting despatch vessels was absurd. That Czar Paul was to be assassinated is irrelevant: had he not been assassinated, the Russian Fleet was still the major target. Any attack on Denmark was simply dealing a blow at a lesser target, and risking damage to the Fleet. The main blow should have been aimed at the major enemy. Sir Hyde's major failure, for which the Government ironically enough never blamed him, was that he never realized who the major enemy was, nor, which accounts for the Government's generosity on this point, did the Government. . . .

In the long term, as events turned out, the destruction of a considerable part of the Danish Navy was eventually to benefit Britain before the war against France ended; but this could not have been foreseen at the time, and the destruction of the Russian Fleet would have been of more use. Before Napoleon was defeated, Czar Alexander was again to ally Russia with the French; and the British were to attack the city of Copenhagen yet again. By that time Nelson had fought and won his third and last great fleet action, Trafalgar; and so doing had ensured that while Britain might not win the war, it could not lose it.

APPENDIX I

SIGNAL NUMBER 39

To understand all the circumstances concerning signal number 39 it is important to realize (1) the significance of the fact, usually over looked, that the signal was made 'General' – to the whole Fleet, in other words, not to a particular ship or Nelson; (2) Parker hoisted it *before* Otway – who was alleged to be carrying authority for Nelson to disregard it if he wished – arrived on board Nelson's flagship; (3) The Signal Book, with its explicit instructions, has been overlooked although it provides vital evidence.

Parker's journal makes it seem that Otway left the *London* at the same time as the signal was made, at 1.30 p.m.; Otway's journal says he left at noon. In either case, had Nelson obeyed the signal, his division would have been sailing out of the battle long before Otway reached the *Elephant*.

The *St George*, Nelson's flagship until he transferred to the shallower-draft *Elephant*, was commanded by Captain Hardy (who later commanded the *Victory* at Trafalgar) and the Master's log, kept by Thomas Atkinson (subsequently Master of the *Victory* at Trafalgar), is indisputable proof that the signal was made 'General'.

Concerning the signal routine, the first paragraph of the 'Explanatory Instructions' in the *Signal Book for the Ships of War* used at Copenhagen (which was the 1799 edition) says:

'1. The signals are to be complied with by all the ships of the Fleet, unless they are specially addressed to a particular ship, squadrons or divisions, signified by their proper distinguishing signals shown at the same time.'

The tenth Instruction says: 'General signals are to be repeated by all the flag officers . . .', which is, of course, why Graves repeated the signal.

But most important of all is the twelfth Instruction:

'*When the Admiral intends that the commander of a squadron or division should direct any of the ships under his orders to perform any service, he will make the signal for the intended service, and with it the signal of such squadron or division, with a red pendant OVER it.*'

Signal number 39 was 'General'; there was no signal for Nelson's division; no red pendant over it. On this point the evidence is unanimous.

There can be no disputing, therefore, that in hoisting signal number 39, '*Discontinue the Action*,' and also making it '*General*', Sir Hyde was ordering every ship under his command which was engaging the enemy to discontinue.

It has been suggested there was an arrangement between Sir Hyde and Nelson before the battle that, if the position became impossible, Sir Hyde would hoist the signal and Nelson could obey it or not, as he wished. The suggestion hardly bears examination. If such an arrangement had been made, it would have revolved round signal No. 39. Since Parker made it 'General', Nelson would have had to explain to his second-in-command and each one of his captains that if the Commander-in-Chief hoisted signal No. 39, 'General', they were not to obey it unless Nelson also made it. By Instruction No. 10 Graves had to repeat it. If Parker had intended it to be 'permissive' to Nelson, obviously Graves would have been warned. He was not.

Nelson did *not* repeat the signal, although he should have done. Instead he acknowledged it – and disobeyed it. In any case such an arrangement would obviously be so fraught with the possibility of misunderstandings and subsequent recriminations that Parker would have included a reference to it in his orders to Nelson to take command of the van division, and Nelson certainly would have noted it in his journal. And Colonel Stewart, who was present at all the conferences, and was with Nelson when Parker made the signal, would have hardly reported the reception of the signal without a reference to the 'arrangement' – if there had been one.

Now we have the reports and opinions of eyewitnesses.

Captain Nicholas Tomlinson, serving on board the *London* as a volunteer, in a report written by the direction of Lord St Vincent, the First Lord of the Admiralty, criticized Parker for anchoring too far away, so that when Nelson weighed it was impossible for Parker to render any assistance because of the distance involved.

He concluded his account of the Battle with the comment: 'The event of the Battle and the consequences that would have resulted from an obedience to the Signal to discontinue the Action which was made from the *London*, and repeated with guns, are too well known to require any comment.' A covering letter said 'his Lordship will be persuaded' that he did not write 'without having first most seriously weighed its importance'.

Colonel Stewart was with Nelson when the signal was reported to the admiral. Stewart makes it clear Nelson was surprised, regarded it as an order, deliberately disobeyed it, spoke to Captain Foley about it and went through the mime with his telescope. Describing the scene soon after the Battle ended, Stewart wrote that Nelson was in low spirits and goes on to quote him for saying (without mentioning to whom: it would appear to be Stewart himself): ' "Well! I have fought contrary to orders, and I shall perhaps be hanged: never mind, let them." '

Rear-admiral Graves, Nelson's second-in-command, whose *Defiance* was the second ship ahead of Nelson's, delayed and then eventually obeyed Instruction number ten in the Signal Book and repeated the signal but quite deliberately hoisted it where it could not be seen from the *Elephant*, and left Nelson's No. 16 (for closer action) still flying.

More important, he wrote to his brother the day after the battle,

Sir Hyde made the signal to discontinue the action before we had been at it two hours, supposing that our ships would be all destroyed. But our Little Hero gloriously said, 'I will not move till we are crowned with victory, or that the Commander-in-Chief sends an officer to order me away.' And he was right, for if we had discontinued the action before the enemy struck, we should have all got aground and have been destroyed. As it was, both Lord Nelson's ship and the *Defiance* got aground in coming off.

Neither Nelson in his report of the battle to Sir Hyde, nor Sir Hyde in his despatch to the Admiralty, referred to the signal, although Sir Hyde must have been well aware it was one of the most important ever made in the history of the Navy. Obviously both had their reasons for remaining silent.

Lt-colonel Hutchinson, in the *Monarch* noted in his diary for 2 April: 'At $\frac{1}{2}$ past 1 p.m. a discretionary signal was made by Sir H. Parker to the van squadron either to continue or discontinue the action, not answered by the *Elephant*.' The colonel was completely in error, first because no such discretionary signal existed, and the fact that No. 39 was made is not in dispute; and second, the signal was acknowledged by the *Elephant*.

Midshipman Anderson, in the *Bellona*, wrote to his parents a few days after the battle:

[I] shall now say a little on Sir Hide [sic] P——, who was a great distance off from the battle though he perceived that our shipping were much cut up, and made a signal to discontinue the action, which was not obeyed by the squadron. The meritorious Lord Nelson made the signal to engage the enemy closer. . . .

So much for recorded views of those in Nelson's squadron. The biographers of the Reverend A. J. Scott, in the *London*, say,

Mr Scott's simple version of the circumstance is, that it had been arranged between the admirals that should it appear that the ships which were engaged were suffering too severely, the signal for retreat should be made, to give Lord Nelson the option of retiring, if he thought fit.

This notion has already been shown to be wrong; and significantly Scott himself made no reference at all to it in his diary on the actual day of the battle.

The activities of Captain Otway, described in a memoir published thirty-nine years after the battle, have already been given (see page 408), and the passage concluded that the signal was 'disregarded by Nelson; and as Captain Otway had verbal authority from Sir Hyde Parker that the battle should continue if he saw there was a probability of success, the action was continued till the enemy submitted'.

The phrase contradicts itself: it was irrelevant *what* authority Otway had from Sir Hyde, since he had arrived too late to give it and Nelson had already decided to disobey the signal. In any case such authority would need to be in writing.

However, the timetable of Otway's journey is interesting: his journal says:

'Noon. Sent the barge on board the *Elephant* with the Captain (R. W. Otway Esq) a volunteer.'

So, providing his time and story is correct, Otway left the *London* at noon and the signal was made at 1.15 (Parker's Journal) or 1.30 (*London*'s log). Yet the *London*'s log says '½ past, made signal No. 39, and sent Captain Otway on board the *Elephant*', a phrase repeated word for word in Parker's journal with the time given as 1.15 p.m.

Colonel Stewart and the *Elephant*'s log ignore Otway's arrival on board the ship; in fact his arrival was not noted by anyone.

Sometimes the truth of an incident is discovered later, when men's tongues wag more freely. Whether or not this is the case, the following accounts are of interest.

On 21 May, soon after Sir Hyde arrived back in England, Admiral Sir William Young wrote to Admiral Lord Keith, who was in the Mediterranean (and was, incidentally, not favourably disposed to Nelson):

You will be grieved to hear that after a long life spent with considerable reputation in the service of his country, Sir Hyde Parker has been recalled from the command in the Baltic with strongly marked indignity. Lord Nelson is created viscount, and Admiral Graves has a red ribbon, Sir Hyde has nothing.

His recall is in consequence of his making repeated representations and complaints of the insufficiency of his force, and his showing a total want o energy and attention to his command.

He, I understand, complains of Nelson having disobeyed his signals during the action off Copenhagen; the signals were to call off the ships, which I understand could not have been obeyed without exposing the whole [of Nelson's division] to certain destruction; that it was not obeyed is a most fortunate circumstance, for if we had not conquered on that day, it would have been such a triumph for the Danes, and such a disgrace to our Navy, as we should not easily have got the better of. A drawn battle would have been a victory for Denmark.

As Sir Hyde has been some days in England, and no inquiry is ordered or asked for, the circumstances of this business will be related as everyone chooses to relate them, and will of course give rise to much party discussion, some censuring the Admiral for neglecting his duty, the other the Admiralty for depriving him of his command unjustly. What I have said on the subject you will consider as said only to you. . . .

Admiral Young's account of the signal and sacking is the most probable of all. The Mintos were old friends of Nelson. Lord Minto was the British Minister in Vienna at the time of the Battle and he wrote later to Lady Minto:

. . . Lord Nelson explained to me a little the sort of blame which has been imputed to Sir Hyde Parker for Copenhagen; in the first place, for not commanding the attack in person, and in the next place for making signals to recall the fleet during the action; and everything would have been lost if these signals had been obeyed. Lord Nelson said he would trust to nobody sooner than to Sir Hyde against an enemy in deep water, but that he is not equal to shoals and responsibilities, and is too much afraid of losing ships to make the most of them.

From the foregoing facts the following conclusions can be drawn:

1. Sir Hyde's precise reasons for making the signal will never be known.

2. Otway must have left the *London* an hour before the signal was made. Although Sir Hyde was under strong criticism in England for making the signal, he never even hinted Otway had been sent to tell Nelson it was permissive. We can thus only speculate what Otway's mission was.

The most likely explanation is that, seeing he was making such slow progress in the light head winds, Sir Hyde sent Otway at noon to see Nelson and bring back or signal a report, and that when more than an hour later Otway had not even arrived on board the *Elephant*, Parker made the signal. The fact that Otway used a passing boat carrying a heavy hawser would account for some of the delay.

3. Sir Hyde's motives in making the signal were no doubt of the highest. As Commander-in-Chief, he carried the entire responsibility for the success of the attack; he would be the man who would suffer by defeat: the damage to Nelson's ships and the casualty figures would show that Nelson had done his best. But at this point, with three of Nelson's ships aground, and only nine properly in action, Parker must have regretted not giving him the two 64s, *Raisonable* and *Veteran*, as well, and one or two of the four 74s still with his division.

His whole career shows Parker to have been an overly cautious man; a detailed study of that career shows Nelson's comment, that Parker was 'too much afraid of losing ships to make the most of them' had already been borne out in the Belt versus Sound indecision. Now, it seems equally certain, faced with losing ships Parker could think only of cutting his losses, even if it cost him victory. In other words he was motivated by caution, not cowardice.

4. Colonel Stewart, who was with Nelson most of the time, records Nelson's surprise at the signal; a few hours later he records Nelson's 'Well! I have fought contrary to orders, and I shall perhaps be hanged: never mind, let them.' It is impossible to accept there was any prior arrangement of which Stewart would, to the end of his days, remain in ignorance; likewise there is no reason why Nelson's remark 'I have fought contrary to orders' should be taken to mean anything else than that he fought contrary to orders. To attempt to distort that can only be done on the evidence of the biographers of the Reverend A. J. Scott, *not* of Scott himself. There is no other evidence that can be taken seriously; and Admiral Graves's account is both clear and significant, written at the time.

5. Given that he feared heavy losses among the British ships, Parker was completely wrong in making the signal 'General', which meant every ship in Nelson's division should, on seeing it, have obeyed it – and would have done but for the fact Nelson merely acknowledged it and kept signal No. 16, for close action, flying. This resulted in the line of battle ships ignoring Parker's signal, although they should have obeyed it – as indeed the frigates did.

6. Not only was he completely wrong in making the signal 'General', but he had a simple, suitable and much better alternative: addressing the signal to Nelson with a red pendant over, as laid out in Instruction No. 12 in the Signal Book.

This would have allowed Nelson the opportunity (since Hyde Parker obviously never expected Nelson to disobey) of choosing the best moment from the tactical point of view of giving the order to his division. Since Nelson was there and Hyde Parker four miles away, obviously Nelson would be the best judge of that. As it was, the 'General' signal, if obeyed, could have led to a mass of ships, most with damaged masts, sails and rigging and therefore difficult to handle, all trying to leave the King's Deep in a disorderly retreat.

7. There is no evidence that bears close examination that Otway carried *any* sort of authority with him. No one who was involved or an eyewitness – Otway himself, Parker, Domett, Nelson, Stewart, Foley and Graves, for example – ever said Otway took with him any verbal authority or instruction from Parker for Nelson to continue the battle 'if he saw a probability of success'. The 'permissive' story was put about much later by people who were not there. Since Otway had for years been a protégé of Parker's, he would have been the first to record the fact – had it been the case.

Otway had many opportunities, both at the time and for years after, to record the episode. All he did was to note in his journal on the day of the battle that a barge was sent to the *Elephant* at noon with him as 'a volunteer'. Had he been carrying such an enormously important verbal message, he would surely have noted it. This, coupled with the facts that no one on board the *Elephant* ever noted that Otway delivered any message, and the signal was hoisted before Otway arrived, leads inescapably to the conclusion that the message never existed, and the signal meant just what it said in the Signal Book.

Equally as important is Sir Hyde's silence on the point. Giving such an order to Nelson with authority to ignore it could only be to save Nelson from the utterly improbable accusation of cowardice, which would have to be made at a court martial. Evidence would be necessary, and written evidence vital.

Is it likely, therefore, that Parker would *send* such a verbal message? A scribbled note would have been sufficient. Is it likely he would have failed to record the second part of the most important order he made in the whole expedition (indeed, in his career) in his journal – if he ever made it? Why did Domett, in his long letter to Lord Bridport on 4 May (see page 278) describing his own role and complaining about Sir Hyde's neglect, fail to mention it, particularly since he was, by some accounts, first ordered to go to the *Elephant*? Why did Sir Hyde, under great criticism in England upon his return because of the signal, not only fail to say openly that he had sent Otway with a message making the signal permissive – which would have cleared him entirely on the question of the signal – but was actually complaining, as Admiral Young's letter makes clear, that Nelson *disobeyed* the order?

The only answer can be that Otway never carried such verbal permission.

The proof of that can be provided quite simply by reiterating that on the authority of the person who first gave the story currency, Otway arrived on board Nelson's flagship *after* the signal had been made from the *London*.

The crux of the matter can be stated quite simply: if Sir Hyde intended that Otway should tell Nelson the signal was permissive, obviously he would have made sure Otway had boarded the *Elephant* and told Nelson *before* making the signal. If flags could be seen hoisted in the various ships, there could have been no difficulty in watching Otway's boat making its way to the *Elephant*. Since Sir Hyde did not, the conclusion is obvious.

From this it follows that it is quite absurd to argue that Otway was sent to tell Nelson the signal was permissive but did not arrive in time. And Parker had the alternative covered by Instruction 12 in the Signal Book.

It is difficult to understand why the story has ever been given credit. It is even more difficult to understand why Sir Hyde subsequently criticized Nelson for disobeying the signal and impossible to understand why he did not use the Instruction 12 method if he felt he had to make such a signal.

APPENDIX II

DANISH SHIPS: FISCHER'S DIVISION

Name and Captain	Tons	Crew Actual Establishment	Casualties Killed Died of wounds Wounded Missing	Where and when built	Designer
PRØVESTEENEN Captain L. F. Lassen	3208	529 382	40 8 27	Nyholm 1767	Krabbe
WAGRIEN Captain F. C. Risbrich	2020	261 273	21 7 35	Nyholm 1773	Gerner
RENDSBORG Captain-Lt C. Egede	504	211 221	28 — 43 7	Bodenhoffs Plads 1786	Gerner
NYEBORG Captain-Lt C. A. Rothe	504	221 209	28 — 30	Bodenhoffs Plads 1786	Gerner
JYLLAND Captain E. O. Brandt	2358	371 425	28 7 36	Nyholm 1760	Krabbe
SVAERDFISKEN Junior-Lt S. S. Sommerfeldt	466	176 190	18 4 15	Gammelholm 1764	Krabbe
CRONBORG Junior-Lt J. Hauch	934	223 201	18 2 7	Nyholm 1781	Gerner
HAYEN Junior-Lt J. N. Müller	1128	175	7 — 6	Copenhagen 1793	Stibolt

Dimensions (Gun deck) Beam Maximum draft) (in ft.)	Description	Guns	Damage
182 49 21	Old 3 decker cut down and converted to blockship with two gun decks. Only stump mast.	58 (30 36-pounders; 28 24-pounders)	All but two guns dismounted; surrendered.
158 42·6 18·3	Old 2-decker converted to blockship. Stump mast.	52 (24-pounders)	Guns dismounted; surrendered.
128 33 6·7	Praam used as cavalry transport. Masts and sails.	22 (24-pounders)	Cable cut by shot, driven ashore, later burned.
128 33 6·7	Praam used as cavalry transport. Masts and sails.	22 (24-pounders)	Cable cut by shot, drifted.
166 44 20	Old 2-decker without poop, stump mast. Was sold to Asiatic Company in 1800, taken back 1801 for use as blockship.	54 (As 70-gun ship fitted 26 24-pounders; 26 18-pounders; 18 8-pounders.)	Captured.
92 25 4·4	Floating battery without masts.	18 (24-pounders)	Captured.
130·9 35 14·9	Frigate, cut down, without masts.	22 (24-pounders)	So badly damaged all but three seamen and one officer quit ship.
99 32 4	Floating battery (similar to *Sværdfisken*).	20 (18-pounders)	Captured.

Name and Captain	Tons	Crew *Actual* Establishment	Casualties Killed Died of wounds Wounded Missing	Where and when built	Designer
ELVEN Captain-Lt Baron H. Holsten	376	88 92	9 1 6	Gammelholm 1800	Hohlenberg
DANNEBROGE Captain F. Braun	2020	357 349	53 3 48	Nyholm 1772	Krabbe
AGGERSHUUS Lt T. Fasting	—	213 219	19 13 41	Bodenhoffs Plads 1786	Gerner
FLOATING BATTERY NO. 1 Junior-Lt P. Willemoes	—	120 156	12 6 28	Copenhagen 1787	Gerner
SAELLAND Captain F. C. L. Harboe	2630	553 640	39 17 108 20	Nyholm 1787	Gerner
CHARLOTTE AMALIA Captain H. H. Koefoed	—	241 228	19 2 18	— 1765	Gerner
SØHESTEN Lt B. U. Middelboe	—	126 190	12 7 14	Bodenhoffs Plads 1795	Stibolt
HOLSTEEN Captain J. Arenfeldt	2020	400 475	12 4 49	Nyholm 1772	Krabbe
INDFØDSRETTEN Captain A. Thura	2032	394 368	21 6 35	Nyholm 1776	Gerner
HIAELPEREN Lt P. C. Lillienskold	852	269 238	— 3 3	Bodenhoffs Plads 1787	Stibolt

Dimensions (Gun deck) Beam Maximum draft (in ft.)	Description	Guns	Damage
99 26 10	Corvette. Normally carried 10 24-pounders but changed just before battle.	6 (36-pounders)	Escaped. Two shot below waterline, twelve above (five of which pierced). All masts, bowsprit and three yards unfit for use.
158 42·6 19·3	Blockship. Formerly a two-decker. Fischer's flagship. Only stump mast.	60 (24 24-pounders; 24 12-pounders; 12 8-pounders.)	Caught fire, blew up.
128 33 6·7	Cavalry transport with masts and sails.	20 (24-pounders)	Cable cut, drifted.
146 41 3·3	Floating battery. No masts.	24 (24-pounders)	Several guns disabled, escaped.
172 45·6 20·3	Two decker, not rigged.	74 (30 24-pounders; 30 18-pounders; 14 8-pounders)	Cable cut, drifted and captured.
— — —	Converted to blockship 1798, formerly East Indiaman.	26 (24-pounders)	Crew abandoned.
99 32 2·7	Floating battery (similar to *Sværdfisken* and *Hayen*).	20 (24-pounders)	Captured.
158 42·6 19·3	Built to similar design at same yard and time as the *Dannebroge*. Later rigged and sailed to England as prize.	60 (24 24-pounders; 24 12-pounders; 12 8-pounders.)	Surrendered at 2.15 p.m.
— — —	Old two decker cut down as blockship, stump mast.	64 (26 24-pounders; 26 12-pounders; 12 8-pounders.)	Captured. Captain killed at beginning of battle.
148 39 8·7	Completely rigged frigate in good condition.	22 (16 36-pounders; 2 12-pounders; 4 150-pounder mortars.)	Surrendered. Attacked by two 74-gun ships.

STEEN BILLE'S DIVISION

Name and Captain	Tons	Crew Actual / Establishment	Casualties Killed / Wounded	Where and when built	Designer	Dimensions (Gun deck) Beam Maximum Draft (in ft.)	Description	Guns
ELEPHANTEN Captain P. G. von Thun	2318	364 / 419	— / —	Nyholm 1769	Krabbe	164 44·6 20·4	Big repairs 1784; old two-decker converted to blockship. Stump mast.	74 (all 24-pounders)
MARS Captain N. S. Gyldenfeldt	2032	346 / 364	— / —	Komp Plads 1784	Gerner	158 43 19·3	Old two-decker; stump mast.	60 (26 24-pounders; 26 12-pounders; 8 8-pounders)
SARPEN Captain-Lt Fabritius	338	85	—	Tonsberg 1791	Stibolt	93·6 26 11	Brig.	18 (18-pounders)
NIDELVEN Captain-Lt. J. Gether	338	84	—	Copenhagen 1792	Stibolt	93·6 26 11	Brig.	18 (18-pounders)
DANMARK Commander-captain S. Bille	2578	600	1 / 1	Nyholm 1794	Stibolt	176·9 45·6 20·3	Line of Battle ship.	70 (28 36-pounders; 28 18-pounders; 14 8-pounders)
TREKRONER Commander-captain P. Riegelson	2430	567	— / —	Nyholm 1789	Gerner	172 45·6 20·3	Line of Battle ship.	74 (28 24-pounders; 28 18-pounders; 18 8-pounders)
IRIS Captain P. C. Wessel Brown	1316	336	—	Gammelholm 1795	Stibolt	148 37·6 16·6	Frigate.	40 (18-pounders)

DANISH GUNBOATS

Name	Casualties	Commander	Guns	Damage
NYKØBING	—	Nielson	4 (2 24-pounders; 2 12-pounders)	Jib caught fire.
AALBORG	—	Wilde	4 (2 24-pounders; 2 12-pounders)	1 shot in hull, 3 oars destroyed.
CHRISTIANSUND	—	Grove	4 (2 24-pounders; 2 12-pounders)	Raked; jib destroyed.
ARENDEL	—	Lercher	4 (2 24-pounders; 2 12-pounders)	Jib on fire; hawser cut.
LANGESUND	—	Erichsen	4 (2 24-pounders; 2 12-pounders)	Jib on fire; hawser cut.
ODENSE	—	Hohlenberg	4 (2 24-pounders; 2 12-pounders)	Caught fire twice.
FLENSBORG	—	Van Deurs	4 (2 24-pounders; 2 12-pounders)	Oars destroyed.
STEGE	—	Fabritius	4 (2 24-pounders; 2 12-pounders)	Bowsprit smashed, jib damaged.
STAVAERN	1 wounded	Jule	4 (2 24-pounders; 2 12-pounders)	Jib destroyed, shrouds cut.
VIBORG	3 dead	Giødvad	4 (2 24-pounders; 2 12-pounders)	Jibboom damaged; jib set on fire by own guns; oars destroyed.
NASKAU	—	Lous	4 (2 24-pounders; 2 12-pounders)	Jib destroyed, oars lost.

(The Crown Prince's original order was for ten gunboats, but the *Viborg* joined on 19 March.)

NOTE: In 1801, the Danish foot was 313·8 millimetres, compared with the English foot of 304·8 millimetres. One *Alen* was 24·72 British inches. One *Lost* equalled two British tons. Details of Danish ships, casualties etc. are from records in the Rigsarkivet, Copenhagen, and the Danish Naval Library.

BRITISH SHIPS: NELSON'S SQUADRON

Name and Captain	Guns	Where and when built	Casualties Killed	Wounded	Damage
Polyphemus J. Lawford	64	Sheerness 1782	6	25	Slight.
Isis J. Walker	50	Medway 1774	33	88	Masts and rigging damaged; several shot holes in hull.
Edgar G. Murray	74	Woolwich 1779	31	111	Mostly confined to masts, yards, sails and rigging.
Ardent T. Bertie	64	Northfleet 1796	30	64	Confined to lower masts, yards and rigging.
Glatton W. Bligh	56 (Carronades)	Purchased in 1795 from H.E.I.C.	18	37	One mast, all rigging and sails damaged; 9 guns disabled.
Elephant T. Foley	74	Bursledon 1786	10	13	Slight: could get under way.
Ganges T. F. Fremantle	74	Thames 1782	7	1	Mostly confined to masts, yards, sails and rigging and bowsprit.
Monarch J. R. Mosse	74	Deptford 1765	57	163	Severe: hull and masts damaged, sails and rigging torn.
Defiance R. Retalick	74	Thames 1783	24	51	Mostly confined to masts, yards, sails and rigging.

Ship / Captain	Guns	Built	Killed	Wounded	Damage
Russell W. Cuming	74	Thames 1764	—	6	Slight.
Bellona Sir T. B. Thompson	74	Chatham 1760	11	72	Mostly below deck and caused by own guns exploding.
Agamemnon R. D. Fancourt	64	Buckler's Hard 1781	—	—	Not in action.
Désirée H. Inman	36	Captured from French	—	4	Slight.
Amazon E. Riou	38	Woolwich 1799	14	23	Slight: confined to two masts, bowsprit, rigging and one gun.
Blanche G. E. Hamond	36	Deptford 1801	7	9	Slight, confined to rigging.
Alcmene S. Sutton	32	Chatham 1794	5	19	Damage to masts, hull and rigging.
Arrow W. Bolton	30	Chatham 1794	—	—	None.
Dart J. F. Devonshire	30	1796	3	1	Two shot holes in hull.

Brig sloops: *Cruizer* (J. Brisbane), *Harpy* (W. Birchall), *Jamaica* (J. Rose).

Bomb vessels: *Discovery, Explosion, Hecla, Sulphur, Terror, Volcano, Zebra.*

Fire ships: *Otter, Zephyr.*

APPENDIX III

DANISH CASUALTIES

	Killed	Died of wounds	Wounded	Totals
Officers	10	1	13	24
'Officials'	3	2	3	8
Naval warrant and petty officers, seamen	208	51	269	528
Army NCOs and soldiers	104	29	141	274
Volunteers and pressed men	45	23	133	201
Total	370	106	559	1,035

BRITISH CASUALTIES

	Killed	Wounded	Totals
Officers[1]	20	48[2]	68
Seamen and Marines	220	596	816
Soldiers	16	44	60
Total	256	688	944[3]

[1] Including Marines, midshipmen, warrant officers and pilots.

[2] Those who reported their wounds. Several with slight wounds were not included in the list. Others subsequently died of wounds.

[3] The total figure was higher because those who did not report wounds are not included.

BIBLIOGRAPHY AND NOTES

The full titles of sources are listed separately on page 560. The detailed references are given below with the main title abbreviated – e.g. *The Despatches and Letters of Vice Admiral Lord Viscount Nelson*, Volume IV, page 87 is listed as *Despatches* IV, 87. Listed page by page, the first few words of a letter or document are quoted or it is given a specific description. As a rule the most readily available source is given. In the case of Nelson's letters this is usually *Despatches* rather than the original letter, although in nearly every case published letters and documents have been checked against the originals, and errors noted. The following abbreviations are used: Rigs. (Rigsarkivet, the Danish State Archives); Mar. Bibl. (Marinens Bibliotek, the Danish Navy Library); NMM (National Maritime Museum, London); HMC (Reports of the Historical Manuscripts Commission). All material prefixed 'Adm' and 'FO' is in the Public Records Office, London, and all 'Add.' in the British Museum. Where the American title of a book differs from the British edition, the American is also given in parentheses.

Chapter 1   The Fortune . . .

Page

6   'In consequence . . .' 10 April 1800, *Spencer Papers* III, 284–5.

6   Sir Hyde's £200,000: *Social History*, 319.

7   George III's comment: *West India Sketch Book* II, 70.

7   'I trust you will . . .' 11 May 1800, *Spencer Papers* II, 285–6.

9   Otway's captures: *Royal Naval History*, Brenton II, 70.

9   Captured two hundred privateers: *Memoir . . . Otway*.

13   'I cannot but perceive . . .' 21 July 1796, *Spencer Papers* III, 227.

13   'Delicate situation . . .' 22 September 1796, *ibid*, 233–4.

13   'I am well aware . . .' 2 October 1796, *ibid*, 234–6.

14   'Ill-treated intentionally . . .' 31 August 1797, *ibid*, 259.

14   'A few circumstances . . .' 11 May 1800, *ibid*, 285–6.

Chapter 2 ... And the Fame

Page
15 Navy List: *Royal Kalendar*, 125–48.
15 'During the present war . . .' Memorial sent to the King in October 1797.
19 'If my services . . .' *Narrative . . . Cape St Vincent*, Drinkwater-Bethune, 87.
23 Battle of Cape Passaro: *At 12 Mr Byng Was Shot*, Pope, 12.
25 'If you, Fanny . . .' *Nelson*, Clarke and M'Arthur I, 113.
26 'An unfavourable opinion . . .' *Despatches* I, 287.
29 'Wonderfully kind . . .' *Nelson's Letters to His Wife*, 91.

Chapter 3   Naples–and the Nile

31 'Proceed in quest . . .' *Naval History*, James I, 171.
32 'Cruel suspence . . .' *Saumarez . . . Memoirs* II, 210.
33 'Fiddlers and poets . . .' *Despatches* III, 138.
34 'Mentions your improvement . . .' 15 April 1799, *Nelson's Letters*, Naish, 519.
34 'The roughest mortal . . .' 7 June 1799, *ibid*, 528.
34 'Admiral Dickson . . .' 23 September 1799, *ibid*, 533.
34 'I long to hear . . .' 21 October 1799, *ibid*, 535.
35 'He fears the winter . . .' 13 November 1799, *ibid*, 538.
35 'Send a cap . . .' 26 December 1799, *ibid*, 543–4.
35 'Hand on my heart . . .' 29 March 1800, *ibid*, 554–5.
35 'I am quite clear . . .' *Despatches* IV, 242.
36 'The door of his house . . .' *Life . . . Minto* III, 150.
36 'A house or good lodgings . . .' 20 September 1800, *Nelson's Letters*, Naish, 496.
37 'The populace . . .' *Naval Chronicle* IV, 429.
37 'I beg you will . . .' *Despatches* IV, 267.
37 £50 for Mayor: *ibid*, 267.
37 'The Corps of Cavalry . . .' *Naval Chronicle* IV, 429.
38 'He was waited on . . .' *Ipswich Journal*, 10 November 1800.
38 Hamburgh lace: *Nelson*, Oman, 408. Some accounts say erroneously that Nelson arrived in London on Saturday (e.g. *Nelson in England*).
39 Miss Knight's song: *Courier*, 9 November 1800. For her activities, *Autobiography . . . Cornelia Knight*.
40 'It is evident . . .' *Naval Misc.* II, 329.
41 Special medals: *Nelson in England*, 141.
42 'He gave me . . .' *Memoirs . . . Collingwood*.
42 Nelson to Sir Isaac Heard: 1 November 1799, *Despatches* IV, 81.
42 'With the fief . . .' 3 January 1801, Adm. 1/4186, State Letters, Grenville to Admiralty.
43 'Having more than once . . .' *Diary of Lady Shelley*, 78–9.
44 'Sir Hyde Parker is arrived . . .' 25 September 1800, *Spencer Papers* III, 373.

Page
44 'Utmost readiness . . .' 2 October 1800, *ibid*, 376.
44 'I repeat . . .' 15 October 1800, *ibid*, 377.
44 'Will expend this month . . .' 2 November 1800, *ibid*, 378.

Chapter 5   The New Grand Master

54 'I had rather see . . .' *England . . . in the Mediterranean*, 54.
55 'It was lucky . . .' *ibid*, 129.
57 'The Russians are anxious . . .' 5 September 1799, *Despatches* IV, 4.
57 'The bear . . .' 6 September 1799, *ibid*, 5–6.
57 'I am glad . . .' 21 September 1799, *ibid*, 25.
57 'The hobbyhorse . . .' 3 October 1799, *ibid*, 41–2.
58 'We shall lose it . . .' 26 October 1799, *ibid*, 69–71.
58 'At the same time . . .' 28 October 1799, *ibid*, 72.
58 'The utmost importance . . .' 7 October 1799, *Spencer Papers* III, 103.
58 Plan of surrender, see 25 November 1799, Nelson to Troubridge, *Despatches* IV, 109.
59 'As Grand Master . . .' 31 October 1799, *ibid*, 78–9.
59 'All my anxiety . . .' 9 November 1799, *ibid*, 94–6.
63 Poems: published London 1810.
63 'The principle object . . .' Carysfort Papers, Elton Hall.
64 'Very pressing proposals . . .' FO 22/40.
64 'My private opinion . . .' 1 November 1800, HMC Fortescue 6.
64 'The moon . . .' 15 November 1800, *ibid*.
64 'There is on foot . . .' *ibid*.
64 'I cannot but . . .' *ibid*.
65 'Nothing more important . . .' Carysfort Papers, Elton Hall.

Chapter 6   The Fate of Neutrals

67 'The accuracy of which . . .' 9 December 1800, Carysfort Papers, Elton Hall.
67 The intelligence appears: this assumption is made because it does not occur in any despatches or private correspondence with Grenville. Since most normal intelligence sources relied on hearsay, the phrase 'the accuracy of which cannot be doubted' points to the Swedish or Danish Ambassador.
67 'In order that the freedom . . .' Copies of the Convention were given to Grenville by the Danish Ambassador on 31 December 1800, and by the Swedish Ambassador on 4 March 1801.
73 'A categorical demand . . .' Carysfort Papers, Elton Hall.
73 'I think the communication . . .' 16 December 1800, HMC Fortescue 6.
73 'So manifest a madman . . .' 16 December 1800, *ibid*.
73 'I am entirely . . .' 21 December 1800, *ibid*.

page

74 'The Danes pretend . . .' 30 December 1800, Adm 3/144, Intelligence/
Denmark 289.

74 'The Court of London . . .' State Papers and also printed in *New Annual
Register*.

75 Bernstorff's reply: 31 December 1800, original version in French, FO
22/40.

Chapter 7   The Lonely Fight

77 Loans of £52 million: *Revolutionary Europe*, 291.

78 To fight a land war: *British Army*, J. W. Fortescue, vol. 7. Part II, 895.

78 Lord Romney: Replying to King's Speech at opening of Parliament.
Reported in *Gentleman's Magazine*, 2 February 1801.

81 Strength of Navy: *Naval History*, James I, 53, Appendix 5, Abstract 1;
II, 423–5. Appendices 21–4, Abstract 8.

Chapter 8   The Social Whirl

86 Lady Hamilton: *Morning Herald*, 24 November 1800.

86 Nelson at House of Lords: *Journal of the House of Lords* XLII, 661.

86 'You know how . . .' 5 December 1800, *Despatches* IV, 269–70.

87 'Your son . . .' 18 November 1800, *ibid*, 268.

87 'A few comfortable . . .' *Nelson in England*, 147.

88 At Fonthill: *ibid*, 147.

88 To the Bar of the House: *Morning Post*, 5 January 1801.

89 Swedish Minister: *The Times*, 1 January 1801.

89 The King's Speech: *The Times*, 1 January 1801.

Chapter 9   The Open Secret

91 Talbot's despatches: Adm 1/4186, 13 and 16 January 1801.

92 Fischer's biographical details: see *Det Danske Søofficerskorps 1801–1919*,
Th.A. Topsøe-Jensen, Copenhagen 1919.

92 Defence Commission: Rigs. Crown Prince Frederick's Orders and
Out-letters, 1801, No. 3. The Crown Prince's files referred to here
are those in the Rigsarkivet, and include: Orders and Out-letters;
Copy Book of the Admiralty and Defence Commissioners, 1801;
Crown Prince, In-letters, Army, synopsis of letters received and
action taken, 1801; Foreign Ministry, In-letters 1801, England.

93 General fast: see *Gentleman's Magazine*, March 1801.

94 Magic lantern: *Morning Post*.

97 'Scarcely fifteen sail . . .' 9 January, FO 22/40, received on 23 January.

97 'Judging it proper . . .' 19 December 1800, Adm 2/294, Lords Letters
to Navy Board.

Page

98 'A few days later . . .' Adm 1/4186, dated Downing Street, 3 January, and marked '6 January Acq: Lord Nelson'.

98 Minute Books: the 'Rough copy' of Board Minutes is Adm 3/144; the entry in the Minute Book is Adm 3/126 f. 33.

Chapter 10 'Fools and Madmen'

99 Drummond on second meeting: FO 22/40, No. 2.

101 Grenville to Drummond: 2 January, FO 22/40, No. 3.

101 'From what the Prime Minister': 3 January 1801. *Spencer Papers* III, 288.

101 Dundas in Parliamentary debate, 25 March 1801: *Parlt Hist.* XXXVI, 1071, Debate on the State of the Nation.

102 Casualties from sickness: see *The Black Ship*, Pope, 36–7 for further details and sources.

103 Edward Willes: as Decipherer of Letters he was paid £500 a year. He wrote the words in above and below the numbers in the way it is printed here.

103 Drummond began by: 3 January 1801, FO 22/40.

104 'Learn as accurately . . .' 13 January 1801, Carysfort Papers, Elton Hall.

104 'Explained the past . . .' 13 January 1801, HMC Fortescue 6.

105 Circular letter from Duke of Portland: 14 January 1801, Adm 1/4186, State Letters.

105 Dundas to Admiralty: 15 January 1801, Adm 1/4186.

105 'There being reason . . .' 15 January 1801, FO 22/40, No. 4.

105 De Wedel Jarlsberg's messenger: information in Drummond's despatch of 27 January 1801, FO 22/40.

105 'The accompanying despatch . . .' 16 January 1801, FO 22/40, Despatch No. 5 to Wm. Drummond.

106 Dundas's orders: 14 January 1801, Adm 1/4186, to General Trigge, No. 1.

107 'Should be attacked . . .' 17 January 1801, version in State Papers, *New Annual Register*, 22, 1801.

107 'I still think . . .' 13 January 1801, HMC Fortescue 6.

107 'Even in the midst . . .' 14 January 1801, *ibid.*

Chapter 11 'The Champion of England'

109 To begin with: See Nelson to Spencer 17 January 1801, *Despatches* IV, 274–5.

110 Landing troops: *ibid.*

111 'A cheerful conversation . . .' *Despatches* VII, 392.

112 Cancelling 'tour': *Morning Post*, 12 January 1801.

112 The first break: Nelson's journey is also recorded in Oman, *Nelson*, 416; *Nelson in England*, 151–4, and newspapers .The letter beginning 'My

Page

dear Fanny . . .' 13 January 1801 in *Despatches* IV, 272, does not include the phrase 'so tell Mrs Nelson' which is in the original now at the Huntington Library, California.

112 'Would have died . . .' Hardy to his brother-in-law, John Manfield, 16 January 1801. The dates of Nelson's arrival in Plymouth and boarding the *San Josef* are misleading because Hardy dated this letter using nautical time. (It is printed in *Nelson's Hardy* 60–4.) The date Nelson received the Freedom of Exeter is given wrongly in *Nelson in England*, 154, as 21 January. It was in fact 15 January (and reported in *The Times* and *Morning Post* of 19 January) and in a letter of 17 January Nelson refers to 'a brother Freeman'.

112 Describing attacks to Troubridge: 28 April 1801, *Naval Misc.* II.

113 Nelson's next stop: newspaper reports, including *The Times* and *Morning Post*.

114 'Nelson was very low . . .' *Naval Misc.* II.

114 Parker's letter to St Vincent: described by Nelson in a letter to Spencer 17 January 1801, *Despatches* IV, 274.

115 'Clearly of opinion . . .' *ibid.*

115 Lord Keith: he had not been recalled at this time.

115 Nelson to Fanny: *Nelson's Letters*, Naish, 618; original in Huntington Library, San Marino, California.

115 'I have this day . . .' Adm 1/118, f. 42, Admirals' Despatches, Channel Fleet.

116 'The *San Josef* . . .' 17 January 1801, *Despatches* IV, 273.

116 Queen's birthday: *Gentleman's Magazine*, January 1801.

116 'May this day . . .' *Despatches* IV, 275–6.

116 'All my things . . .' 20 January 1801, *Nelson's Letters*, Naish, 618.

117 'Half my wardrobe . . .' *ibid*, 618–9.

117 'It was never . . .' 3 February 1801, *ibid*, 619.

118 'Acquaint their Lordships . . .' 17 January 1801, Adm 1/118, f. 42, Admiral's Despatches, Channel Fleet.

118 'It is this moment . . .' *Despatches* VII, ccxxix.

118 'If you believe . . .' *ibid.*

118 'Does you great credit . . .' 31 January 1801, *Spencer Papers* III, 380. Spencer refers mistakenly to Nelson's letter of '29th December'.

118 'It is by no means . . .' 21 January 1801, Morrison MSS, II, letter No. 501 (printed privately 1894).

118 'So excellent a likeness . . .': the print, showing the head in left profile, is printed in *Nelson in England*, opposite p. 220.

119 A letter from London: the time taken is clear from Nelson's letters and the dates of replies. For the West Indies in 1801, *Spencer Papers* III, shows the time taken for official correspondence. The Post Office packets (which sailed independently) took about thirty-five days from Falmouth to Jamaica direct, and forty-five days going via Barbados (see *History of the Post Office Packet Service*, A. H. Norway,

Page

London, 1895). In the last third of the twentieth century surface mail to the Windward and Leeward islands takes between forty and eighty-five days.

120 'If you'll believe me . . .' 25 January 1801, Morrison, letter No. 502.

120 'When I consider . . .' *ibid* No. 503. This leaves out sentences given fully in *Letters from Lord Nelson*, Rawson, 304–6.

121 Nelson to Admiralty, 29 January 1801: *Despatches* IV, 278.

121 'As no order . . .' *ibid*, 279.

121 'I have this . . .' *ibid*, 279.

122 One of the people: described in letter, Nelson to Addington, 2 February 1801, *Despatches* IV, 282.

122 'Nonsensical reports . . .' BM Egerton MS 2240, Letters of Lord Nelson to Alexander Davison, 1799–1805, No. 21, f. 29.

122 'The Lady of the Admiralty . . .' BM Egerton MS, No. 22, f. 41, postscript to letter of 28 January.

122 Nelson clearly: for salaries and appointments see, for example, *Royal Kalendar*, 1801, 315.

123 'I believe poor . . .' 1 February, Morrison, letter 504.

123 'Circular letter . . .' Adm 3/144, Board Minutes (Rough).

Chapter 12   The Sword and the Olive

126 'An extraordinary occurrence . . .' 20 January, FO 22/40, Drummond-Grenville No. 4.

127 Two days later: 24 January, *ibid*, No. 5.

127 'Before this . . .' Carysfort Papers, Elton Hall. For the Dan Helder Operations, see *History of the British Army*, Fortescue, Vol. 4, Part II, 700.

128 'If it was true . . .' 27 January, FO 22/40, Grenville to Drummond, No. 7.

129 'You will see . . .' 27 January, HMC Fortescue, 6.

130 'Knowing the temper . . .' 27 January, FO 22/40, Dip. Corr.

131 Despatch on de Rosencrantz: 27 January, *ibid*.

132 Carysfort-de Haugwitz: despatches of 27 January and 1 February, State Papers, *New Annual Register* 1801.

132 'Purity of their views . . .' 12 February, Haugwitz to Carysfort, *ibid*.

132 Within the week: 8 February, Carysfort to Grenville, HMC, Fortescue, 6.

132 Opening of Parliament: described in *Gentleman's Magazine*, February 1801.

Chapter 13   Changing the Helmsman

135 'You will, of course . . .' *Life and Letters . . . Minto*, 198–9.

136 Addington forming a government: this is well covered in *Life . . .*

Page

Sidmouth, I from which the quoted extracts of Addington's letters are taken.

136 'Glad to find . . .' 9 February, *Spencer Papers* III, 383–4.

137 Addington to St Vincent: *Memoirs . . . St Vincent*, 124.

137 'Set out for London . . .' 11 February, Add. 31164, Earl of St Vincent, Letter Book, November 1800–February 1801.

137 Tucker gives the account of journey in his *Memoirs . . . St Vincent*.

138 Wednesday's *levée*: *The Times*, 12 February.

139 'This is the . . .': the timing of the letter is significant. See *Life . . . Sidmouth* I.

139 'Our reliance . . .' *Memoirs . . . St Vincent*.

139 St Vincent taking office: *ibid* for Tucker's description.

140 The Board of Admiralty: Lord Barham, First Lord at the time of Trafalgar in 1805, was the first to specify in detail the particular duties of the Sea Lords, naval and civil. See *England Expects (Decision at Trafalgar)*, Pope.

140 'Markham, then aged 39 . . .' *Naval Career . . . Markham*, 15, 288.

141 'I must observe . . .' 29 January, FO 22/40, Drummond to Grenville.

141 'Being at length . . .' 7 February, *ibid*.

142 'A fruitless waste . . .' 14 February, *ibid*.

Chapter 14   An Olive Branch?

143 Nicholas Vansittart: the *Dictionary of National Biography* says, erroneously, that he was appointed Joint Secretary of the Treasury on his return from Copenhagen. The appointment was published in *The Times* on 16 February, some time before he left London.

144 'Upon a sort . . .' 17 February, HMC Fortescue 6.

144 Vansittart's instructions: FO 22/40, and on reverse side is the note: 'Draft to Mr Vansittart Feby 17th, 1801, No. 1.' Drummond's instructions are in FO 22/40 unsigned draft dated Downing Street, 23 February. The section copied by Drummond and given to the Danish Government is in Rigs., Danish Foreign Affairs, 32C, Section 3, and signed by Hawkesbury.

146 Vansittart's account is given in a letter to the Dean of Norwich: see *Life . . . Sidmouth*.

147 Travel arrangements. These included more instructions: *ibid*, with note on reverse side: 'Draft to Mr Vansittart, Febry 20th, 1801 (No. 2).'

147 'Embarked immediately . . .' *Life . . . Sidmouth*, 368, letter to the Dean of Norwich.

147 'It is a subject . . .' See despatch of 27 January, FO 22/40.

148 Hawkesbury's letter: FO 22/40, Hawkesbury to Drummond, No. 1, 23 February. Danish copy of British offer: in Rigs., Foreign Affairs (Section 3) f. 3, headed 'Extract from a letter from Lord Hawesbury

Page

[*sic*] to Mr Drummond as to the terms offered to the Court of Denmark'.

149   Dundas's orders for Admiralty and Parker: Adm 1/4186, From Secretaries of State, Dundas to Board, 23 February 1801.

151   Duke of York: for titles see *History of the Army*, Fortescue, IV, part 2, 876 note.

152   Dundas's orders to Duke of York: Adm 1/4186, 23 February, Admiralty copy.

152   'The officer appointed . . .' 23 February, *ibid*.

Chapter 15   Storm in a Mustard Pot

153   Orders for St Vincent: it is not clear why they were signed by Dundas: Hawkesbury was by this time signing instructions.

153   Flat-bottom boats: Adm 3/144, entry dated 27 January.

154   Report for St Vincent: in Minutes, Adm 3/144, entry for 12 February.

155   'Admiral the Earl . . .' Adm 3/126, Minute Book, entry for 20 February 1801.

155   'Your friends . . .' 21 February, *Memoirs . . . St Vincent*.

155   'Court positively refuses . . .' Despatch of 29 January; see note in Chapter 13.

156   Complaint by Messenger Ross: Adm 1/4186, From Secretaries of State, Dundas to Board, 27 February.

156   *Providentia* complaint: Adm 1/4186, copy of de Wedel Jarlsberg's letter to Hawkesbury forwarded to Admiralty, 24 February 1801.

156   Faye's protest and notary's complaint: Adm 1/4186, 'Instrument of Protest', dated Leith 20 February 1801, attested by William Smith, N.P.

157   Russian officers: Hawkesbury to Admiralty, 27 February, Adm 1/4186, and 28 February, *ibid*. The Board instructed that they were to be discharged on their parole and requested they should have passports allowing them 'to come and reside in London'.

157   While Lord St Vincent: the whole episode is described by Tucker in *Memoirs . . . St Vincent*; *The Times* and *Morning Post*.

159   'He was quite sure . . .' *Memoirs . . . St Vincent*.

159   'Is so vigilant . . .' 18 February, HMC Fortescue 6.

160   'Against the . . .' 21 February, *ibid*.

160   'Nine years of war . . .' *Memoirs . . . St Vincent*.

Chapter 16   The Fretful Lover

161   'Your good and dear friend . . .' Morrison, Letter No. 505.

161   'My headache . . .' *ibid*, Letter 507.

162   'It is not unusual . . .' *ibid*, Letter 508.

163   'He says you . . .' *ibid*, Letter 509.

Page

163   'He has put it in a case . . .' *ibid*, Letter 510.

163   'As it is not convenient . . .' *ibid*, 517; Louis Dutens to A. Davison, 17
        February, deed of assignment dated 4 February.

164   'I do not think . . .' *ibid*, 510, no date but written 8 February.

164   'I may not be able . . .' *ibid*, 512, no date but written 9 February.

164   'Almost distracted . . .' *ibid*, no date but presumably 10 February.

164   'Well my dear friend . . .' 11 February, *ibid*, 514.

165   'I will support him . . .' 16 February, *ibid*, 287.

165   'I remember your story . . .' 14 February, Morrison 515.

165   'Truly wretched state . . .' Add 2240, Egerton MSS, Letters of Lord
        Nelson to A. Davison, 1797–1805, No. 26, f. 45.

166   'The two months afterwards . . .' 16 February, Morrison 512.

166   'Whether Emma . . .' 19 February, NMM, MS 9960; also given in
        Nelson's Letters, Naish, 576.

167   'I am so agitated . . .' *Nelson's Letters*, Rawson 302.

168   'Forgive my letter . . .' Morrison 521.

168   'Entreat both you . . .' *ibid*, 522.

168   'At my elbow . . .' *ibid*, 523.

168   'Unpleasant situation . . .' *ibid*, 524.

169   'Confident of your conduct . . .' *ibid*, 525.

169   'In a gale of wind . . .' *ibid*, 526.

169   'Seen Troubridge . . .' *ibid*, 527.

170   'Poor Thomson . . .' *ibid*, 528.

170   'Before we go . . .' *Despatches* IV, 287–8.

170   St Vincent's plate chest: *Despatches* IV, 289.

170   Signal towers: *Naval Chronicle* XVI, 201.

170   Leave for Nelson: Add 35934, Nelson Papers, official correspondence.

171   Sir Hyde's journal: Adm 50/65.

171   The days passed: it is not clear if Nelson played any role in getting the
        orders written on that day, but it seems probable.

172   Order to go to Yarmouth: Add 34934, f. 32.

173   'Parker has left Town . . .' Add 34934, f. 32.

174   'Plan for destroying . . .' and memorandum on Russian Fleet: *Tomlin-
        son Papers*, 229–306.

176   The Admiralty accepted: Tomlinson-Nepean, 15 May 1801, *Tomlinson
        Papers* 305.

177   'Not yet seen Captain Thesiger . . .' 1 March, *Despatches* IV, 290–1.

177   Thesiger had first gone to sea: biog details in *Dictionary of National
        Biography*; *Sailors Whom Nelson Led*, Fraser.

178   'Your dear brother . . .' 24 February, Rawson 306.

179   'As I am sent for . . .' 24 February, *Nelson's Letters*, Naish, 619–20.

179   'Parting from . . .' 27 February, Morrison 529.

180   'After my letter . . .' 1 March, *ibid*, 531.

180   'Now, my dear wife . . .' *ibid*, 532, but Rawson, 307–8 gives a more
        complete version.

Page
181 Stewart's Narrative of Events: Add 34918, Nelson Papers, f. 315.
181 'The 49th Regiment . . .' 28 February, Adm 1/4 Admirals, Despatches, Baltic Fleet.
181 Issuing stores to troops: Cumloden Papers, Stewart's Journal, entry of 1 March.
182 'Nothing particular . . .' Add 34918 Nelson Papers, f. 35.
182 Foreigners in Ships: 28 February, Adm 1/40, Admirals Despatches, Baltic Fleet, Ha. 2.
182 The *Russell*: *ibid* – a complete list of named foreigners was enclosed in Nelson's report.
183 'Time, Twiss . . .' to General William Twiss, *Despatches* IV, 290.
183 'Time, my dear Lord . . .' 1 March, *Despatches* IV, 291.
183 'Be assured . . .' Clarke and M'Arthur II, 258.
183 Captain Flinders: 1 March, Adm 3/126, Board Minute Book, 1 January–31 October 1801.
184 Rat-catcher for *Alcmene*: 5 March, Adm 3/144 Board Minutes, Rough.
184 'Josiah is to have another ship . . .' 4 March, Morrison, 536.
184 'Fish out of water . . .' *ibid*, 537.
185 'Nothing shall make . . .' *ibid*, 539.
185 'We breakfasted . . .' Stewart's Journal.
186 'Nelson's plan . . .' *ibid*.
187 'Aye, my dear Troubridge . . .' 7 March, *Naval Misc.* II.
188 'Finding you have lately . . .' Adm 1/4, Admirals, Despatches, Baltic Fleet, f. Ha 8.
188 'Not having yet . . .' *ibid*, f. Ha 8a.
188 'The number of gun vessels . . .' *ibid*, f. Ha 20a.
189 Gun brigs without guns: *ibid*, f. Ha 25.
189 'They have committed . . .' *ibid*, f. Ha 26a.
189 'The humble petition . . .' *ibid*.
189 'And inform you . . .' *ibid*.

Chapter 17 'By a Side Wind'

190 'Follows closely . . .' *The Times*, 25 February.
190 'Sir Hyde is on board . . .' Add 2240, f. 60, Egerton MSS; but Mahan, *Life of Nelson* II, 61, quotes this letter wrongly.
191 'Dear parents . . .' *Life . . . Franklin*, 14–15.
192 'Your letters . . .' Morrison, 541.
192 'The Commander-in-Chief . . .' *ibid*, 542.
193 Admiralty orders to Parker: Adm 2/141, Orders and Instructions, f. 136.
193 Dundas's Instructions: Adm 1/4186.
193 'On the 9th in the evening . . .' Adm 50/65, Parker's Journal.
193 'In answer thereto . . .' 10 March, Adm 1/4.

Page

194 'I have heard by a side wind . . .' 11 March '2.30 p.m.', *Letters . . . St Vincent* I.

194 'The signal is made . . .' *Naval Misc.* II.

196 'When I received . . .' *ibid.*

196 Midshipman Millard's account: this and subsequent quotations are from the version in *Macmillan's Magazine*, June 1895.

197 'The whole are . . .' Cumloden Papers.

197 Army stores: *ibid.*

198 'Placed on a footing . . .' *ibid.*

198 'Orders are given . . .' Although Parker did not record it in his Journal, Stewart reported it in his own Journal.

199 'To join me . . .' Adm 50/65, Parker's Journal, preliminary remarks. Although the Journal began on 31 January, Sir Hyde did not begin daily entries (using nautical time, the new day beginning at noon) until 12 March.

199 'At ½ past five . . .' Nelson's Journal, 12 March–13 May 1801, NMM.

200 'Should the Northern Powers . . .' *Spencer Papers* IV, 273–9.

200 'Glad to find . . .' *ibid* II, 383.

200 'The old seaman . . .' *Life of Nelson* II, 67.

201 'I feel sorry . . .' quoted in Mahan, *Nelson* II, 67 and *Nelson in England*, 159.

201 'In speaking of . . .' *Diaries . . . Rose* I.

Chapter 18   Divided Command

202 Danish defence preparations: the British Consul at Elsinore reported on 14 February that 16 sail of the line and seven blockships were fitting out at Copenhagen (Adm 3/144, Intelligence, 306).

202 Strengthening Cronborg: Rigs, Copy Book of Admiralty and Defence Commission and War Office Out-letters, 13 February.

203 Orders for Braun, Egede, Rothe: 16 February, Rigs. Crown Prince Out-letters and orders (1801).

203 Her previous captain: Rigs. Admiralty In-letters (1801), 652.

203 Lt Holsten: Rigs. Admiralty, 754/1801, Rough (economy) log, *Elven*.

203 Royal proclamation: Mar. Bibl. taken from *Collegia Tidende* No. VIII, side 133, 21 February.

204 Letter to Fischer: 23 February, Rigs. Crown Prince, Adm. Orders and Out-letters, 257.

206 'It is said . . .' 10 March, FO 22/40.

206 Orders for Army: 7, 11, 14 and 17 March, Rigs. Crown Prince, War Office Out-letters.

206 Orders for Willemoes: 7 March, Rigs. Crown Prince, Adm Out-letters.

206 Orders to Fischer for blockships: 12 March, *ibid*. This order was signed by the Crown Prince and the Defence Commission.

207 'In view of . . .' 16 March, Rigs. Crown Prince, Orders and Out-letters.

Page
208   Vansittart sees Bernstorff: Add 38537, f. 8, 'Minutes of a Conversation between Count Bernstorff and Messrs. Drummond and Vansittart, Saturday, March 14, 1801.'

212   'Is but too strong . . .' 14 March, FO 22/40, Drummond-Hawkesbury.

212   'Unfortunately the interview . . .' Letter of 15 March, *Life . . . Sidmouth* I, 377.

212   Dr Beeke's report: 15 March, *ibid*, 376.

212   Bernstorff's reply: 19 March, FO 22/40, Enclosure No. 1 in Drummond's despatch to Hawkesbury.

213   'Is so offensive . . .' 19 March, FO 22/40, Drummond and Vansittart to Hawkesbury.

213   'In the role . . .' original in Rigs. Foreign Affairs, England, IC 1801 (Section 2); copy is enclosure No. 2 in despatch to Hawkesbury dated 19 March.

213   '*Un certain* Vansittart . . .' 17 March, Rigs. Foreign Affairs, England IC. 1801 (Section 2) to Dreyer.

214   'He now prepares . . .' 17 March, *ibid* to de Wedel Jarlsberg.

214   Joint British despatch: 19 March, FO 22/40, Drummond and Vansittart to Hawkesbury.

215   'Several accounts . . .' 21 March, *ibid*.

Chapter 19   '*The Fire of England*'

217   The *London* striking yards: Parker's Journal.

217   Heaving the lead: *ibid*.

217   *Alecto* and *Rover*: *ibid*.

219   Signals: Admiralty's *Signal Book for the Ships of War*, 1799. This edition was in use for several years, a second part being issued in 1803.

219   Shaking out reefs: Parker's Journal; individual ship's logs.

219   'I am yet all in the dark . . .' 16 March, *Naval Misc.* II.

220   'Reports say . . .' In fairness to the Government it should be made clear these were not 'the plans of ministers', as Dundas's orders for Parker have made clear. Nelson's phrase 'I hate your pen and ink men' is often quoted out of context by the less intelligent: he was to prove himself an excellent 'pen and ink man' within a couple of weeks. The point he was making to Emma was that there was a time for pens and a time for guns.

221   An Irishman designed: named Mullins, he did great work in improving construction of Spanish warships. See *England Expects* (*Decision at Trafalgar*), Pope, 67.

222   The *Ganges'* ship's company: Muster Roll, Adm 36/15392.

223   The *Elephant's* ship's company: Muster Roll, Adm 31/15342.

224   The *Monarch's* ship's company: Muster Roll, Adm 36/13743.

225   Loss of the *St George*: for a good account of the whole disaster, see *The Mariner's Mirror*, 50. No. 2, 123–34.

Page

227 'They sail so very heavy . . .' 23 May 1801, *Despatches* IV, 383–4, Nelson to Nepean.

228 'How kind and amiable . . .' *Wynne Diaries*, entry for 24 June 1796.

228 'A beautiful . . .' *ibid*, Eugenia's entry for 12 January 1797; Betsey's for 11 January 1797.

229 'Then I will die . . .' *Nelson*, Oman, 244.

229 Lifebuoy: *Royal Naval Biography*, Marshall I, 381.

232 'After the boats left us . . .' Account written by the Boatswain and preserved, Historical Records of New South Wales.

233 'Captain Sutton . . .' Add 31146, St Vincent Letter Book, November 1800–February 1801.

234 'I am very well . . .' *ibid*.

234 Lt Molyneux Shuldham: see also page 386 for his role in the Battle. For discussion of Bentham's designs, see *History of the American Sailing Navy*, Chapelle, 237.

235 Officers serving in Baltic: Adm 3/144, Board Minutes (Rough) entry for 12 February 1800.

236 'Fleet stood to sea . . .' Stewart diary, Cumloden Papers, entry for 18 March.

238 'Very fine weather . . .' Nelson Journal, entry for 19 March.

240 'It is impossible . . .' 18 March, *Life . . . Scott*.

240 'Went on board . . .' Nelson Journal, entry for 19 March.

240 'It being moderate . . .' 20 March, *Naval Misc.* II.

241 'Immediately [to] proceed . . .' 23 February, Adm 1/4186, Dundas to Admiralty.

241 'But out of sight . . .' 16 March, Egerton MSS Add 2240, Nelson letters to Davison, f. 62, No. 28.

241 'It is impossible . . .' 18 March, HMC Fortescue 6.

241 'In consequence . . .' In account given in *Macmillan's Magazine* cited earlier.

241 '*London* nearly on . . .' entry for 20 March, Cumloden Papers.

242 'The *London* was . . .' *Scott . . . Life*.

242 'We anchored . . .' 21 March, *Naval Misc.* II.

Chapter 20   The Horse-drawn Ultimatum

243 'Take care of my will . . .' 16 March, Egerton MS Add 2240, f. 62, No. 28.

243 Codicil: previous published references have been in error over the codicil and Chelengk because *Despatches*, IV, 294, giving the letter to Davison, omits the first few words referring to the copy of the will.

243 'Several opiates . . .' *Gentleman's Magazine*, 12 March.

243 The *Blanche* at Elsinore: entry for 20 March, Journal, Captain Graham Hamond, Adm 51/1360.

243 'I send you a note . . .' 26 February, HMC Fortescue 6.

Page

244 Instructions to Drummond: 25 February, *ibid*, marked 'No. 2 to Mr Drummond'.

246 'The undersigned . . .' The original is in Rigs. Foreign Affairs, England Ic 1801 (Section II) dated Copenhagen, 20 March.

247 'Together with the passports . . .' 21 March, FO 22/40, Drummond to Hawkesbury.

247 Bernstorff to Dreyer: 21 March, Rigs. Foreign Affairs, England Ic 1801 (Section II).

247 Bernstorff to Drummond: 21 March, *ibid*.

248 On Sunday morning: Adm 51/1360, Hamond Journal.

248 'Certainly the most . . .' *A Tour in Zealand in the Year 1802*' by A. A. Feldborg (who also used the pseudonym J. A. Andersen) English edition, London 1805.

249 'It needs little . . .' *ibid*, 36.

249 *Blanche* master's log: Adm 52/5766.

249 Proclamation: 21 March, *Collegial Tidende* No. 12.

250 Order to Steen Bille: 18 March, Rigs. Crown Prince, Orders and Out-letters, Copy Book of Admiralty and Defence Commission.

250 Orders for recruits: 20 March to Fischer, *ibid*.

250 'If and when . . .' 20 March, *ibid*.

251 Crown Prince to Captains: 23 March, *ibid*, to each captain.

251 The *Elven*: Rigs. Admiralty 754/1801, Economy log, *Elven*.

251 Fischer's complaint: 23 March, Rigs. Admiralty, In-letters (1801) 632.

252 'Most of the defence . . .' 23 March, *ibid*.

252 'A watch is . . .' *Berlingske Tidende*, 23 March.

252 Report from Bulow: letter of 24 March Rigs. Synopsis of letters received by Crown Prince and subsequent resolutions on them, 1801.

253 Stricker's telegraphed report: 26 March, *ibid*.

253 Meeting of Defence Commission: 26 March, *ibid*.

253 Transferring gun boats: 26 March, Rigs. Crown Prince, Orders and Out-letters, Admiralty.

253 Risbrich on guns: Rigs. Admiralty In letters, 1801, No. 664.

254 Stricker's report: 27 March, Rigs. Crown Prince, Synopsis of letters.

254 Three more men per gun: 28 March, Rigs. Crown Prince, Orders and Out-letters.

254 General Waltersdorff: 28 March, *ibid*.

254 'A priest named Faber . . .' Rigs. War Office, In-letters 1801, No. 243.

255 Peder Schultz: details of this man and subsequent volunteers and pressed men taken from Rigs. Records of Killed and Wounded: Report of Commission for Pensions for Killed and Wounded, 2 April–31 December, 1801.

257 Seaman Sacariasen: Anne-Margrethe's claim was not allowed.

257 Sinnia Naiker: 30 March; his letter is in Rigs. Admiralty, In-letters, 1801 No. 681 (1).

257 The case of Dr C. A. Hansen: Rigs. Crown Prince, In-letters, 1801,

Page

No. 186. This letter was found and translated for the author by the late Captain H. Kiaer while he was the King's Librarian and Head of the Navy Library.

Chapter 21   *By the Sound or the Belt?*

259   'I have to inform you . . .' 21 March, Vansittart to Parker, Adm 1/4, Admirals' Despatches, Baltic Fleet, 1801, f. Ha 34.

260   'Informed me . . .' Parker's Journal.

260   'I arrived off . . .' 23 March, Adm 1/4, Admirals Despatches, Baltic Fleet, f. 215–6.

262   'I fear there is . . .' letter of 23 May, *Life . . . Scott.*

262   'As I hear the Danes . . .' 23 March, *Naval Misc.* II.

262   Captain Domett omitted: referred to by Domett in letter to Lord Bridport, 4 May, Add 35201, Bridport Papers, f. 134.

263   Lt Layman's turbot: *Naval Chronicle*, vol. 37, 446.

265   Stewart's Diary: Cumloden Papers.

266   'The difficulty was . . .' Mahan, *Life of Nelson*, II, 73.

268   Domett's letter: see above.

268   'You will, no doubt . . .' 29 March, *Naval Misc.* II.

269   '. . . Affairs this day . . .' to 'And a British squadron would be following the Dutch,' Stewart Diary, entry for 24 March, Cumloden Papers.

271   'Lord Nelson was impatient for action . . .' Stewart Diary (quoted in part in *Despatches* IV, 300). Both the Diary and the Narrative given in *Despatches* have been abridged without the editor indicating where omissions were made. The complete versions from Cumloden Papers are used here.

273   Leading Admiral Mahan: Mahan, *op. cit.*, II, 12–13.

273   'Since writing my letter . . .' 23 March, Adm 1/4, Admirals' Despatches, Baltic Fleet, f. 211–12. Parker's phrase about his 'peculiar situation . . . the formidable disposition of Copenhagen . . .' should be compared with 'the particular delicate situation in which I am placed and where so much has been left to [my] discretion . . .' of July 1796 and 'I am well aware [that] great responsibility attaches to me . . .' a month later. (See page 13.)

274   'The batteries around . . .' 24 February, FO 22/40, Drummond to Hawkesbury.

275   'The solicitude . . .' 8 April, Morrison, 566, Vansittart to Nelson.

276   'The opinions . . .' Diary, Cumloden Papers.

276   'Mr. Vansittart came on board . . .' Parker, Journal.

276   Captain Tomlinson: *Tomlinson Papers*, 305–70.

277   Flogging seamen: *St George*'s master's log Adm 52/3399.

277   'This measure . . .' 4 May, Domett to Lord Bridport, Add 35201, Bridport Papers.

277   Otway's claim: *Memoir . . . Otway*, London 1840.

Page

279 The Fleet turning back: Parker's Journal says: '¼ past 10 up foresail and hove-to, at ¾ past filled and made sail, at 11 one of the bomb tenders ran on shore . . . At ¼ past wore . . .' The *Pylades* was told to cruise off the Koll to tell any ships joining the Fleet 'that I am proceeding to Copenhagen Roads'.

279 'Held a conference', Diary, Cumloden Papers.

280 'I cannot but feel . . .' 8 July 1801, Nelson to Parker, NMM Papers Relating to Copenhagen, Phillips Collection.

281 'The conversation . . .' Adm 1/4, Admirals' Despatches, Baltic Fleet, f. Ha 48a. The version quoted in Mahan, *Life of Nelson*, II, 75–7, differs from the original and the days referred to beneath it are postdated by 24 hours. Nelson's draft is sparsely punctuated and the present author has inserted only sufficient to make the meaning clear.

Chapter 22   Squandering Victories

284 'I send your Lordships . . .' 24 March, original letter in Carysfort Papers, Elton Hall.

285 'The Fleet sailed . . .' 20 February, *ibid.*

Chapter 23   The Sight of the Sound

292 'The plan, as hitherto . . .' Cumloden Papers.

292 'Received directions . . .' Nelson Journal, entry for 26 March; Parker Journal, entry for 27 March (nautical time).

292 Nelson's Memorandum: Nelson's Order Book, entry for 26 March, NMM.

293 'You find us . . .' 29 March, *Wynne Diaries*.

294 *Elephant*'s master's log: Adm 52/2968.

294 'When you are better . . .' 4 January 1801, St Vincent to Nepean, *Memoirs . . . St Vincent*, 121.

294 'The launches of the . . .' Nelson Order Book.

295 'Report the consternation . . .' Nelson, Journal.

295 'Sent a message . . .' Parker, Journal.

295 'From the hostile . . .' Adm 1/4, Admirals' Despatches, Baltic Fleet, f. 221–2, copy sent to Admiralty. The original is in Rigs. Correspondence between Denmark and England, Battle of the Roads, 1801, I. Certain published accounts contain errors.

295 'To be ready . . .' Nelson, Journal, entry for 27 March.

296 'The delay . . .' Cumloden Papers.

296 Stricker's first reply: Scott's translation is given in Adm 1/4, f. 221, No. 2.

297 Brisbane's report: Stewart's diary, Cumloden Papers.

297 Orders to Murray: Parker, Journal.

297 'I was glad to see . . .' *Despatches* IV, 298.

Page

297 'I will talk . . .' 28 March, *ibid*, 298.

297 'In answer to . . .' Scott's translation is in PRO Adm 1/4, f. 221, No. 3. Stricker's report to the Crown Prince transmitting Parker's letter is in Rigs. War Office, In-letters, 1801, No. 263.

298 This reply: Rigs. War Office, In-letters, 1801, No. 263, recording Stricker's report, says that Stricker 'at the order of His Royal Highness has answered the Admiral . . .' It also records the 'necessary measures'.

299 Parker's reply: Adm 1/4, f. 221, No. 4.

300 'English squadron . . .' 24 March, Rigs. Foreign Affairs, England Ic 1801, Sect. 2.

300 'The conciliatory . . .' 24 March, *ibid*.

300 'A victim of unjust . . .' 23 March, *ibid*.

301 Letter to King of Sweden: 25 March, *ibid*.

301 'The sign of an . . .' 28 March, *ibid*.

301 'Resolution to defend . . .' 28 March, *ibid*.

301 'The measures the London . . .' 29 March, *ibid*.

301 'We are well persuaded . . .' 29 March, *ibid*.

Chapter 24   '. . . *In Copenhagen Roads*'

305 'We are now standing . . .' 30 March, '6 o'clock in the morning,' *Naval Misc.* II.

306 'The war between . . .' 30 March, Add 41667D, Bourgoing to Talleyrand.

307 'The English Fleet . . .' Mar. Bibl., Søkrh. A IIa. 1801.

307 'Could two journeyman . . .' 30 March, Rigs. Crown Prince, War Office, In-letters, No. 8, 1801.

307 Chief Constable: 30 March, Rigs. Crown Prince, Orders and Out-letters, to Olfert Fischer.

309 'Reconnoitred the enemy's . . .' Parker, Journal. Stewart's Narrative erroneously refers to a 'schooner' instead of the *Amazon* (*Despatches* IV, 302).

309 'The enemy fired . . .' Master's log, Adm 52/4018.

309 'Observed the beacons . . .' Master's log, Adm 52/2899.

311 'Expended four . . .' Master's log, Adm 52/2968.

311 'The formidable line . . .' 6 April, Adm 1/4, f. 6, Ha 55, ff. 217–19.

312 'We this morning . . .' 30 March, Morrison, No. 551.

314 On board the *Amazon*: Stewart's Narrative (*Despatches* IV, 302) says this was the first time Nelson met Riou; but his memory was in error because the *Amazon*, not a schooner, was also used for the first reconnaissance (see above).

314 'The Admirals are . . .' 31 March, *Life . . . Scott*, Journal entry.

315 Council of war: see Cumloden Papers. The list of names is omitted in the version of Stewart's Narrative given in *Despatches* IV, 303, line 13.

Page

315 'Captains Lawson and . . .' Cumloden Papers.

315 Domett's letter: 4 May, Add 35201, f. 134, to Lord Bridport.

315 'When I found a larger . . .' 4 April, *Wynne Diaries*.

317 'Menace the northern part . . .' Parker Journal, entry for 1 April (p.m. 31 March, civil time).

319 The *Cruizer* anchored: Master's log. The north buoy was the first one laid down by the British.

319 'My information . . .' Midshipman Millard's account, *Macmillan's Magazine*.

319 The Prussian brig: Add 40730 N, letter from Midshipman Anderson to parents, written from 'minutes' kept on board the *Bellona*.

320 Flogging in the *Alcmene*: Master's log, Adm 52/2652.

320 The van weighed: *Amazon's* Master's log: Adm 52/4017.

320 'With astonishing alacrity . . .' Diary entry for 1 April, Cumloden Papers.

320 'Threw out the wished for signal . . .' Cumloden Papers, Narrative.

322 Dinner and drawing up the orders: among several descriptions are – Stewart, Cumloden Papers and Narrative in *Despatches* IV, 304; clerks writing cards, Millard's narrative; a detailed account of the evening, presumably written from material he supplied, under 'Foley' in *Royal Naval Biography*, Marshall, 367.

325 'There is some juggle . . .' 1 April, HMC Fortescue VII, Carysfort to Grenville.

325 'The present critical . . .' *Life . . . Sidmouth*, 380.

326 'Such Sir, is . . .' letter of 3 April, *ibid*.

Chapter 25   The Eve of Battle

328 No proper accommodation: 28 March, Rigs. Admiralty In-letters, No. 674, Report by Fischer to Danish Admiralty.

330 Difference in shot: *Naval History*, James I, 45. The Swedish 36-pounder was 33 lbs 11½ ozs by British measures while the French 36-pounder was 38 lbs 14 ozs.

330 Ships of the Danish line: Construction details and dimensions from Mar. Bibl. card index of ships; ships' companies from report by Fischer on each ship's establishment, actual complement on 28 March, and number of men short, in Rigs. Admiralty In-letters No. 674, 28 March; officers on board, *ibid*, In-letters, 258B, 26 March. The description of the Danish ships given in *War for the Liberty of the Seas . . . 30 March . . . 2 April*, by K. H. Seidelin, often quoted in Danish accounts, refers to the *Rendsborg*, *Nyeborg* and *Aggershuus* as 'old' ships although all were built in 1786, considerably more recent than many of the British, and his description of the rest of the ships paints the worst possible picture. He also writes: 'A great part of the enemy's ships' companies consisted of Danish sailors pressed out of

Page

English merchant ships. The English did then violate the most sacred of rights, by forcing those that trusted in them to fight against their own country.' In view of the Admiralty order and returns sent in by the British ships of Danes, Norwegians and Swedes on board, quoted earlier, this allegation is of little consequence.

335 The *Iris* and *Danmark*: Details of these and the other Danish ships captured and subsequently sold, are from Admiralty Progress Books (in Admiralty Library, London).

339 Although still short of men: figures for the Danish ships are from Danish official records and are tabulated in *Mindeskrift om Slaget Paa Reden* by P. C. Bundesen, Copenhagen 1901. Although brief, this is one of the most accurate and detached Danish accounts of the battle.

342 Careers of Danish officers: see *Det Danske Søofficerskorps*.

342 Activities of the *Elven*: Rigs. Admiralty, 954/1801, *Elven* log.

343 Müller's activities: Mar. Bibl., BOC vi/iii, account of J. N. Müller, 'from the Norwegian Collection, officially inspected and published' by Christian Lange, Christiania 1860, Vol. ii.

343 *Altona*'s provisions: Rigs. Provision Account Book, *Altona*, 4 March–24 August No. 1.

Chapter 26   Maundy Thursday

346 Parker's division: Parker's journal gives his anchorage as 56° 12' North, 12° 10' East.

346 Orders to three ships: *ibid*, entry for 1 April.

348 Nelson's General Orders: the wording in Nelson's Order Book varies slightly from the copy in the Cumloden Papers and Fremantle's copy in *Wynne Diaries*, but the differences are insignificant.

353 *Alcmene*'s acting master: log is Adm 52/2652.

353 *Elephant*'s master: log is Adm 52/2968.

353 Wearying work: Masters' logs of *Cruizer*, *Ardent* and *Blanche*.

354 *Zephyr* prepared: log of Master, James Elsworth.

354 Millard and the *Monarch*: account in *Macmillan's Magazine*.

355 Orders for 49th Regt: diary of Lt Col. (later Gen. Sir) William Hutchinson, entry for 18 March 1801, printed in *Blackwood's*, July–December 1899, p. 323.

355 Captain Mosse's card: Millard, *op. cit.*

356 Briarly's log: Adm 52/2396.

356 'Experienced in the Sound . . .' 29 September 1801, *Despatches* iv, 499–500, Nelson to St Vincent.

357 Admiral Mahan's comment: *Life . . . Nelson* ii, 87.

Chapter 27   Into Battle

361 Colour of the *Elephant*: from notes made during the battle by Robinson

Page

Kittoe, secretary to Rear-admiral Graves, for paintings (several of which are given in this book). The colours of both Danish and British ships are from Kittoe.

361 Signal for the first three ships to weigh: the signal log of the *Polyphemus*, on which much reliance has in the past been placed, lists for 10.15 a.m. the same signal addressed to the *Monarch* and *Defiance*; a signal from the *Amazon* to the *Defiance*, *Glatton* and *Arrow* 'for captain'; and from the *Elephant* the general signal to weigh. This is obviously incorrect.

361 *Discovery* veering cable: *Discovery* log.

362 Fancourt's report: extract from log, signed by Fancourt in Add 34918, f. 27, and which differs slightly from master's log.

362 *Volcano* veering cable: master's log.

363 Colours of *Isis* and *Désirée*: Kittoe notes.

365 Rist's account: Mar. Bibl. BOC AIIa 1801, from article by B. Bergsøe. The Crown Prince, contrary to popular legend, was not at the warehouse. Neither Rist nor Count Schimmelmann mentioned him.

365 'In fact none of . . .' Bergsøe's narrative.

366 Boy's description: *ibid.*

367 Strengthening battery: reported by Seidelin, *op. cit.*

368 Lt Bille's report to Captain Lassen: Rigs. Admiralty Copy Book, Conduct List 1801, Bille to Lassen, attached to Lassen's report to Admiralty.

368 'Several sail . . .' Risbrich's report, Rigs. Admiralty In-letters 1801, 757(1).

368 *Edgar* anchoring: Journal of Lt Shuldham.

369 *Ardent* anchoring: log of master, R. B. Garde.

369 Damage to *Jylland*: Rigs. Admiralty Copy Book 1801, Recommendations and criticisms of behaviour in battle: report by Brandt.

369 *Cronborg's* casualties: Rigs. Admiralty In-letters 1801, 823, report of Lt Helt.

369 *Isis* opens fire: journal of Lt James Walker.

369 Midshipman Nairn's account: letter to his brother James, at 'c/o Mrs Ferguson's, No. 1. St James's Place, Edinburgh', in NMM.

370 'The *Bellona* was . . .' log of the *Bellona*.

370 Middleground shoal: this spur is not usually indicated in charts showing the ships' positions in the Battle. However, it is shown on the chart made in 1775 by Captain Andreas Lous but is not immediately apparent because he has failed to shade this particular area, although the depth is the same as other parts of the Middleground which he has shaded.

371 Positions of *Wagrien* and *Provesteenen*: *Bellona's* log.

371 Delafons' signal: *ibid.*

372 *Russell* grounding: master's log.

372 *Russell's* jib-boom: Robinson Kittoe's notebook.

Page

373 'A mind less invincible . . .' Clarke and M'Arthur II, 266–7.

374 'We followed the . . .' 4 April, Fremantle to Betsey, *Wynne Diaries*.

376 Robinson Kittoe: from his notebook which, with his paintings, drawings and charts now belong to Mr Acton Bjørn.

377 *Alcmene* anchoring: master's log, Adm 52/2652.

377 Riou's signal to *Blanche*: *Amazon*'s log, Adm 52/4018.

377 Shot in *Cruizer*'s mast: master's log, Adm 52/2899.

377 M'Kinley's journal: Adm 51/9852.

378 *Explosion* opens fire: master's log, Adm 52/2652.

378 *Discovery* opens fire: master's log.

378 *Volcano* anchoring: master's log.

379 *Volcano*'s Prussian seaman: 4 May 1801, Add 34934, Nelson Papers, Official Correspondence, Admiralty to Parker (among unexecuted orders and correspondence handed over to Nelson on Parker's recall).

379 *Provesteenen*'s damage: Bille to Lassen, *op. cit.*

379 Seamen wounded in *Prøvesteenen*: Rigs. Records of Wounded and Killed: Commission for Wounded, Killed and Pensions, 2 April 1801–31 December 1801.

380 'Eventually we could use . . .' Lassen to Admiralty, cited above.

380 Casualties in *Prøvesteenen*: official Danish figures, see also *Slaget paa Reden*, Bundesen.

380 Casualties in *Isis* and *Désirée*: logs and Nelson's report to Parker, *Despatches* IV, 316–19.

380 Nairn: *op. cit.*

381 Captain Risbrich's journal: Account written from journal and published in *Danish Army and Navy Magazine*, 6 November 1880.

382 *Wagrien* in battle and casualties: Risbrich's report, Rigs. Adm. In-letters 1801, 727(1); Bundesen; Commission for Wounded etc.

383 *Rendsborg*: damage described in report by Egede to Olfert Fischer, Rigs. Adm. In-letters 1801, No. 848; précis of all reports to Fischer, 890a; Bundesen; wounded and killed, see Commission for Wounded.

384 *Nyeborg*: Rigs. Copy Book of the Admiralty 1801, Recommendations . . . for Conduct in Battle, Gether; précis of reports to Fischer; Rigs. Admiralty 747A, log of *Trekroner*, 8 March–28 August 1801.

384 Explosions in *Bellona*: Midshipman Anderson's account, Add 40730N; Daubeny letter, quoted in *Logs of the Great Sea Fights*, II, 108–9; *Bellona*'s logs.

385 *Russell*'s targets: ship's logs.

385 Lt Johnson: 8 May 1801, *Despatches* IV, 364, Nelson to St Vincent.

385 *Edgar*'s casualties: Nelson's report, *Despatches* IV, 316–9.

386 On board the *Jylland*: Rigs. Admiralty, Copy Book 1801; Recommendations, report by Brandt; Commission for Wounded; logs of British ships engaging her; totals of casualties, Bundesen.

387 The *Sværdfisken*: Rigs. Commission for Wounded; Bundesen; *Det Danske Søofficerskorps*; logs of British ships engaged.

Page

388 'I conclude your wish . . .' 3 March, Add 31168, St Vincent to Commissioned officers.

388 The *Ardent* in action: Garde's log is Adm 52/2702. This passage is correctly quoted in *Logs of the Great Sea Fights* II, 113–4 which, however, fails to point out a writing error. The log says 'Ran between the *Edgar* and the Danish batteries and brought up . . .' when Garde meant 'Ran beyond the *Edgar* . . .' However, the transcription erroneously gives the time of the first ship striking as 12 o'clock. Garde's log in fact says 'At 30 past 1'. Casualties in Nelson's report already cited; *The Sailors Whom Nelson led*, 193–8.

388 The *Ardent*'s damage: listed in her master's log.

389 Bertie and swords: *The Sailors Whom Nelson Led*, 193–8.

389 The *Cronborg*: report of battle and casualties by senior surviving officer Lt Helt, in Rigs. Admiralty In-letters 1801, No. 823 (Helt subsequently denied the report on Møhl saying, improbably, that he signed it without knowing its contents); Commission for Wounded; Bundesen; logs of British ships.

390 *Dannebroge*'s ship's company: official figures given in Bundesen.

390 Lt Müller's account: Mar. Bibl., BOC VI/II, from the Norwegian collection, vol. II.

392 *Elven* in action: Rigs. 754/1801, Captain's log, 21 March–7 October; same reference, master's log; Admiralty Copy Book, Fischer's recommendation concerning Holsten's bravery; Admiralty In-letters 1801, No. 756(1) gives casualties; Commission for Wounded.

392 The *Glatton*: damage reported in Captain's log and master's log; casualties in Nelson's report, *Despatches* IV, 366–9.

393 Fischer's report to the Crown Prince: a good translation is given fully in *Despatches* IV, 320–2.

393 Review of action: this is taken entirely from entries in British and Danish ships' logs and written reports by officers to their respective admiralties.

394 Fremantle to Marquis of Buckingham: letter of 4 April, *Wynne Diaries*.

394 The *Sælland*'s casualties: given in Bundesen.

394 *Sælland*'s ship's company: Rigs., Commission for Wounded.

395 Lt Schultz: Report to Fischer by Judge Advocate, Rigs. Admiralty In-letters 1801, No. 850.

395 Schultz's arrest: two reports to Fischer by Judge Advocate dated 8 April, Rigs. Adm. In-letters 1801, No. 758.

395 Harboe's two lieutenants: Rigs. Adm. In-letters, Reports and casualties, Conduct List.

395 Millard's account: *Macmillan's Magazine*, cited earlier.

400 Koefoed's commendations: Rigs. Adm. In-letters 1801, Reports and Casualties, Conduct List.

400 *Charlotte Amalia*'s casualties: Rigs. Adm. Commission for Wounded.

Page

401 Fischer in *Holsteen*, damage etc.: Captain Arenfeldt's report, Rigs. Adm. In-letters 1801, No. 757(11).

401 *Holsteen*'s casualties: Rigs. Adm. Commission for Wounded.

401 Fischer leaving *Holsteen*: Rigs. Adm. In-letters 1801, No. 890A. *Despatches* IV, 320 says erroneously that Fischer left at 2.30 p.m.

402 Thura killed: Rigs. Adm. Commission for Wounded.

402 Lt Cortsen killed: *ibid.*

402 *Indfødsretten*'s casualties: Bundesen; Rigs. Commission for Wounded; Copy Book 1801, In-letters, 1552.

402 *Hiælperen*: Lillienskjold's report, Rigs. Adm. In-letters 1801, No. 702(1).

Chapter 28   Signal Number 39

404 Fischer's view: the situation in each ship taken from logs and written reports to the Admiralty.

406 Signal No. 39: from logs. *St George*'s master's log, Adm 52/3399. (In the list of signals, Atkinson's pen slipped when writing the one made at '2.25', number 63 by the *Elephant* to the *Isis*. It comes in sequence between one at 3.10 by the *London* to the centre division and another at 3.30 by the *London* to the *Ramillies*). All logs are in the PRO and are: *Dart*, master, Nathaniel Harned; *Cruizer*, master, William Fothergill; *Volcano*, master, Thomas Brightman; *Amazon*, Journal, Lt John Quilliam; *Blanche*, master, S. J. Gunn; *Otter*, captain, Lt George M'Kinley.

408 Southey: *Life of Nelson.*

409 Covering letter: 4 June 1801, *Tomlinson Papers*, Tomlinson to Nepean.

409 'The events of the Battle . . .' *ibid.*

409 Colonel Stewart and Signal 39: Cumloden Papers, Diary and Narrative.

410 Rear-admiral Graves' letter: 3 April, to John Graves, Barley House, Exeter. See *Logs of Great Sea Fights* II, 101–3.

413 Riou's funeral: Lt Quilliam's journal.

413 *Otter*'s damage: master's log.

413 *Explosion*'s damage: master's log.

414 Batteries opening fire: Seidelin, *Liberty of the Seas*, No. 1.

414 Poor aiming: Mar. Bibl. BOC v/5, Sea Artillery log No. 54, 1801, 142/3, 7 May 1801. Lindholm sent Fischer samples of British powder, fine and coarse, saying the Danish was as good but the shot were not so good at ranges of 60 to 80 feet. He lists some comparisons obviously found by experiment. It is not clear if the deficiencies of shot were due to size – causing excessive 'windage', the gap between the shot and the bore – rust or casting, resulting in them not being completely spherical.

414 Positions at 2.00 p.m.: most of the sources have already been cited or are given later. They are: *Hiælperen* – captain's report says sur-

Page

rendered after being in action two hours; *Indfødsretten – Holsteen*'s captain's report says Fischer was going to transfer to her but saw her strike and at 1.30 p.m. went to Trekroner; *Søhesten* – consensus of several British reports; *Charlotte Amalia* – Fremantle's letters; *Sælland* – Fremantle's letters; *Floating Battery No. 1*, Willemoes' report; *Aggershuus* – Rigs. In-letters 890A; *Dannebroge* – *ibid* 890A, captain's report, *ibid* 756(2); *Elven* – captain's log and master's log; *Hayen* – Müller's account; *Cronborg* and *Sværdfisken* – *Ardent*'s log; *Jylland, Wagrien* and *Prøvesteenen* – logs of *Russell, Bellona, Isis, Polyphemus* and *Volcano*, reports of Captain Lassen and Lt Bille; *Rendsborg* – Captain's report and of Captain Risbrich; *Nyeborg*, Rigs, In-letters 890A; *Holsteen* – Captain Arenfeldt's report.

416   'It was a sight . . .' It seems at first sight that Nelson wrote this letter to Emma and to Addington. It is given fully in *Despatches* IV, 360–1, and it is clear that Morrison, No. 579, wrongly describes the letter as being sent to Emma.

418   Nelson's 'truce letter': original is in Rigs. Dept of Foreign Affairs, England Ic, 1801.

419   Thesiger on board: see Nelson to Troubridge, 4 April, *Naval Misc.* II.

419   *Elephanten*'s log: Rigs. Adm. Captains log, *Elephanten* 748/1801.

420   Admiral Wleugl's son: Rigs. Adm. In-letters, Conduct List, report of Captain Brandt.

421   Crown Prince's reception of Risbrich: Risbrich's journal, cited earlier.

422   'He hailed me . . .': 4 April, *Wynne Diaries*, Fremantle to Betsey.

422   Müller's account: source cited above.

422   Fremantle to the Marquis: letter of 4 April, *The Wynne Diaries*.

423   'Lord Nelson's object . . .' Nelson, Letter Book; quoted in *Despatches* IV, 316.

423   'About 2.00 p.m., they . . .' *Elephant*, master's log, Adm 52/2968.

424   'At last it went round . . .' Mar. Bibl. BOC AIIA, 1801.

424   'Scene of awful suffering . . .' *Folketidende*, 5 April 1801.

425   Graves to brother: letter in *Logs of Great Sea Fights* II, 101–3.

426   'Set the mainsail . . .' Loud's journal in *ibid*, 110–13.

427   *Ardent*'s launch: *The Sailors Whom Nelson Led*, 193–8.

428   Sent all the boats . . .' Parker, Journal.

428   'Parker's truce terms: Rigs., Foreign Affairs, 32C, Section C.

429   'I have fought contrary . . .' Col. Stewart's Narrative quoted in Clarke and M'Arthur II, 261–74.

429   'At 9 o'clock at night . . .' Pettigrew II, 17.

Chapter 29   Another Battle?

431   'One of the ships . . .' *Despatches* IV, 331.

432   Arenfeldt's report: Rigs. Adm. In-letters, 1801, 757(11).

432   'Seeing there was not . . .' *Memoir . . . Otway.*

Page

434 'In confidence, he . . .' Letter of 4 April, *Wynne Diaries*.

434 Nelson's report: *Despatches* IV, 313–5.

435 'If I went on shore . . .' 4 April, *Despatches* IV, 332–6, Nelson to Addington.

436 Accounts of visit: see Stewart, *Despatches* IV, 332; Bundesen, 81.

436 Hardy's letter: to Mansfield, *Letters of the English Seamen*, 236.

436 *Berlingske Tidende*: issue of 3 April.

436 Nelson to Troubridge: letter of 4 April, *Naval Misc.* II.

436 Fremantle at breakfast: 4 April, *Wynne Diaries*, to Marquis of Buckingham.

437 Benz complains: 4 April, Rigs. Adm. In-letters 1801, 703.

437 Nelson at Palace: 4 April, Nelson to Addington, *Despatches* IV, 332–6.

438 'A negotiator is . . .' 9 April, *Despatches* IV, 339.

438 Nelson and Crown Prince: 4 April, *Despatches* IV, 332–6, to Addington.

442 'The job is done . . .' 4 April, *Naval Misc.* II.

442 *Elephant*, funerals: Muster Roll, Adm 36/15342.

444 'Whether Sir Hyde . . .' Date uncertain, Clarke and M'Arthur II, 276; *Despatches* IV, 336.

444 'Could give offence . . .' 22 April, *Despatches* VII, ccvii, Nelson to Davison.

445 Thesiger's list: *ibid*, ccviii.

446 Whole areas: details of individuals in Rigs. Commission for Wounded etc.

Chapter 30   The Truce Expires

449 Sir Thomas Thompson: 4 April, *Wynne Diaries*, Fremantle to Buckingham.

449 Commissioning *Holsteen*: Parker, Journal.

450 *Hiælperen* surrendering: Rigs. Adm. In-letters 1801, 702(1).

451 Arenfeldt and Fischer: *ibid*, 890A.

452 'About ¼ past two . . .' *ibid*, 757(11).

452 Nelson to Lindholm: 22 April, *Despatches* IV, 344–6.

453 Lindholm's reply: 2 May, *ibid*, 346–7.

455 Hardy's letter: 5 April, *Nelson's Hardy*, to Manfield.

455 'I am, my dear Troubridge . . .' 4 April, *Naval Misc.* II.

457 'Should the Count . . .' Original letter in Rigs., Foreign Affairs, England IC, 1801, Section 3, f. 6.

458 Orders to Willemoes: 5 April, Rigs. Crown Prince, Orders and Out-letters, 1801.

459 Verses for Emma: 6 April, Morrison, 555.

460 One Danish account: Bundesen, *Slaget paa Reden*. He is in error in saying Nelson heard of the Czar's death on 8 April.

460 'As to rope . . .' 23 May, *Despatches* IV, 383–5, Nelson to Nepean.

463 'Admiral Sir Hyde . . .': Original in Rigs., Foreign Affairs IC, 1801, Section 3, f. 8.

Page

465   'Will the Court of Denmark . . .' *ibid*, f. 12.

465   'His Royal Highness . . .' This was given to the Crown Prince as Nelson's authority. The original is with the two letters quoted above, f. 14.

466   'Be it good or bad . . .' 9 April, *Naval Misc.* ii.

466   'I trust you will . . .' 9 April, *Despatches* iv, 339–41.

468   'Little one-eyed man . . .' O. Sütken, lecture printed in *Near and Far*, 25 January 1880.

468   'Too ill to make . . .' 9 April, *Despatches* iv, 339–41.

470   No idle threat: Stewart, Cumloden Papers; *Despatches* iv, 326.

471   Niebuhr's report: *History and Geography* (1838), 127 and 291–300.

472   'The Czar is dead . . .' *Tidsskrift for Sovæsen*, 1944, article by Cdr Bojeson, quoting report by Rist (the Finance Minister's private secretary).

472   'Replied that he . . .' 9 April, Nelson to Addington, cited above.

Chapter 31   The Swedish Fleet Sails

474   The *Fox* cutter: Parker Journal.

474   Wording of Armistice: given fully in *Despatches* iv, 337–9.

475   Sir Hyde's orders: noted in his Journal.

475   'Your friend was on shore . . .' Morrison 557.

476   'Just returned from . . .' 9 April, *Despatches* iv, 341.

476   'I have only a moment . . .' 9 April, *Naval Misc.* ii.

476   'Before you condemn . . .' 9 April, *Despatches* iv, 342.

476   'I am well . . .' 9 April, *Despatches* iv, 342.

477   'A ship so cut up . . .' Müller's account, cited above.

477   Bligh episode: Lt Uldall's report to Fischer, Rigs. Adm. In-letters, Reports to Fischer, No. 1202.

478   The next person: 14 April, *Despatches* iv, 343.

479   'Ah my dear Troubridge . . .' 12 April, *Naval Misc.* ii.

479   'I send you a . . .' 13 April, HMC Fortescue 7.

479   'I cannot but pray . . .' 12 April, *ibid.*

480   George Rose's note: *Rose . . . Diaries*, i.

480   Bligh's orders: Parker, Journal.

482   Sutton and *Amazon*: *ibid.*

482   Fleet to weigh, etc.: *ibid.*

482   Fremantle 'nervous': 22 April, to Marquis of Buckingham, *Wynne Diaries*.

482   'Sent a letter immediately . . .' Parker, Journal.

483   'Sir Hyde tells me . . .' 13 April, *Despatches* vii, ccv.

483   'Will you have the . . .' 14 April, Morrison 560.

483   Lindholm's reply: 15 April, *ibid.*

483   To Maurice Nelson: 15 April, Morrison 561.

484   To Davison: 15 April, *Despatches* vii, ccvi.

Page
484 Briarly's account: *Despatches* IV, 344, letter dated 19 April, and printed in *Naval Chronicle* V, 452.
485 'You will believe . . .' 20 April, *Naval Misc.* II.
486 Parker's despatch: 6 April, Adm 1/4, Admirals' Despatches, Baltic Fleet, 6 Ha 55, f. 217–9.
486 Mosse's son: reported in *The Porcupine*, 25 April.
486 Job as 'extra clerk': *Royal Kalendar*, 1801.
487 'We have no *Gazette* . . .' 16 April, *Life and Letters . . . Minto*.
487 'It is not known . . .' 15 April, Proby Papers, Elton Hall.
488 Parker's new orders: Add 34934, Nelson Papers, Official Correspondence, ff. 43–45B.
489 'You have greatly . . .' 17 April, Add 31168.
490 Nelson's Commission: Add 34934, Nelson Papers, Official Correspondence, f. 57.
490 Hobart's letter: *ibid*, f. 63, copy of Hobart's letter, dated Downing Street, 17 April.
490 'Fighting for the honour . . .' 22 April, Morrison 567.

Chapter 32   The Czar's Overture

492 'Yesterday we saw . . .' 20 April, Morrison 565.
493 'I know nothing . . .' 21 April, HMC Fortescue 7.
493 Scott's diary entry: *Life . . . Scott*.
494 'At the request of . . .' Parker, Journal.
494 'My dearest amiable . . .' 23 April, Morrison 569.
494 News of Czar's death: Parker, Journal.
494 *Lynx* and despatches: *ibid*.
495 'I had 24 . . .' 27 April, Morrison 570.
495 'To know His Imperial . . .' Parker, Journal.
495 *Tygress*'s captain: *ibid*.
495 Swedish ship: *ibid*.
495 'Last night's attack . . .' 28 April, *Naval Misc.* II.
496 To Duke of Clarence: 27 April, *Despatches* IV, 350.
496 To Sir William: 27 April, Morrison 571.
496 *Blanche*'s sailing date: Nelson to Lindholm, 6 May, Morrison 576.
496 Scott visiting Nelson: diary, *Life . . . Scott*.
496 Lindholm's reply: *Despatches* IV, 346–7.
497 Parker striking flag: Parker, Journal.
498 Domett's commission: *Despatches* IV, 353.
498 Nelson's letter to Board: 5 May, *ibid*, 352–3.
498 'A command never . . .' 5 May, *ibid*, 353–4.
498 'I am, in truth . . .' 5 May, *ibid*, 354–5.
499 To Addington: 5 May, *ibid*, 355.
499 Fremantle at St Petersburg: 21 May, *Wynne Diaries*.
500 'Directed me to . . .' 6 May, *Despatches* IV, 356.

Page
500 Nelson 'astonished': 7 May, *ibid*, 359.
501 Stewart's description: Cumloden Papers and *Despatches* IV, 386.
501 'The late Commander-in-Chief...' 8 May, *Despatches* IV, 363.
501 To Pahlen: 9 May, *ibid*, 365.
502 'Evidently to endeavour...' 16 May, *ibid*, 370–1.
503 'Is an excellent...' 22 May, *ibid*, 379–80.
503 Pahlen's reply: 17 May, *ibid*, 371–2.
503 'The Count has...' 17 May, *ibid*, 373.
504 'You will see that...' 16 May, *ibid*, 371–2.
504 'Not an hour...' *ibid*, 386.
504 'I hope all is right...' 19 May, *ibid*, 375.
504 Report to Admiralty: 24 May, *ibid*, 387–9. In this letter Nelson accidentally wrote 'in opposition to Lord St Helen's letter' when he meant 'Lord Hawkesbury's'.
505 'Has naturally affected...' 22 May, *ibid*, 379–80.
505 'I do not see...' 23 May, *ibid*, 385–6.
506 Pahlen's second letter: St Petersburg, 6 May, *ibid* IV, 393–4.

Chapter 33   Strawberries for Nelson

507 'Whatever peace...' 4 June, *Despatches* IV, 400, to Alexander Ball.
507 Sir Hyde to Admiralty: 13 May, Adm 1/4 Admirals' Despatches, Baltic Fleet, f. Ha 78.
508 'Whereas you have...' 14 May, Adm Letter Book, Orders and Instructions, 7 January–15 July 1801.
509 'At Death's door...' 4 June, *Despatches* IV, 400.
509 'The Crown Prince...' quoted by Cdr Bojesen in *Tidsskrift for Søvæsen*, 1944 from original in Rigs.
509 'Entire approbation...' 31 May, *Despatches* IV, 414.
509 'With the deepest...' 31 May, *Memoirs... St Vincent*.
510 'They are not Sir Hyde's...' 15 June, *Despatches* IV, 416.
510 Sir Hyde to Nelson: 8 July, NNM, Phillips Collection.
511 'I wished to have seen...' 8 July, *ibid*.
511 'I feel very sorry...' *Nelson in England*, 159.

Appendix I

515 Tomlinson: *Tomlinson Papers*, 304–12.
515 Stewart: *Despatches* IV, 312.
516 Graves: *Logs of the Great Sea Fights* II, 101–3.
516 Anderson: Add 40730 N, Letters on the Battle of Copenhagen.
517 Admiral Young: *Keith Papers* II, 373 (Navy Records Society).
518 'Lord Nelson explained...' 22 March, 1802, *Life ... Minto*.

SOURCES

Unpublished: Danish

The Danish documentary material, mostly hitherto unpublished, is from the National Archives (Rigsarkivet) at Christiansborg Palace, Copenhagen, and the King's Library. Only the main headings are listed below; the full references are given in the Notes and Bibliography. They cover Danish foreign affairs, Navy and Army.

Rigsarkivet, Foreign Affairs, England, 1c, 1801, Sections 2 and 3. (This covers all correspondence between the Danish Foreign Ministry and foreign governments and ambassadors as well as Danish ambassadors abroad.)

Rigsarkivet, Foreign Affairs, England, 1c, 1801, Synopsis of letters received by Crown Prince and subsequent resolutions made on them.

Rigsarkivet, Admiralty: Copybook of Admiralty and Defence Commission, 1801, Orders and Out-letters. (These are from the Crown Prince and from the Defence Commission to various naval officers and cover the entire naval defence preparations.)

Rigsarkivet, Crown Prince, In-letters, 1801, General. (These include many reports to the Crown Prince from civilian sources.)

Rigsarkivet, Crown Prince, 1801, Army, In-letters, and action taken on them.

Rigsarkivet, Crown Prince, 1801, Army, Out-letters.

Rigsarkivet, Admiralty, 1801, In-letters, Sections 258–875. (These include the action reports of commanding officers and lieutenants, and casualty reports.)

Rigsarkivet, Admiralty, 1801, In-letters, Recommendations for bravery.

Rigsarkivet, Admiralty, 1801, In-letters, Conduct List.

Rigsarkivet, Admiralty, 1801, In-letters, No. 674, Report by Commodore Olfert Fischer.

Rigsarkivet, Admiralty, 1801, In-letters, Reports of Casualties received at Friderichs Hospital.

Rigsarkivet, Admiralty, 1801, In-letters, Reports of the Commission for Killed, Wounded and Pensions, 2 April–31 December 1801.

Rigsarkivet, Admiralty, 1801, In-letters, Sections 632–681.

Rigsarkivet, Admiralty, 1801, 754/1801, *Elven*, captain's log 21 March–7 October; rough log; mate's log.

Rigsarkivet, Admiralty, 1801, 748/1801, *Elephanten*, captain's log.

Rigsarkivet, Admiralty, 1801, Provision Account Book, *Altona* gunboat, 4 March–24 August, 1801.

Rigsarkivet, Admiralty, 1801, 749A/1801, *Trekroner*, captain's log.

Unpublished : British

Public Record Office:

Admiralty 50/65: Journal of the Proceedings of Sir Hyde Parker . . . 31 January–13 May, 1801.

Admiralty 1/4186, State Letters. (Letters from Secretaries of State to Board of Admiralty.)

Admiralty 3/126, Board Minute Book, 1 January–31 October 1801.

Admiralty 3/144, Board Minute Book (Rough), 1 January–31 October, 1801.

Admiralty 2/141, Letter Book, Orders and Instructions, 7 January–15 July 1801.

Admiralty 2/294, Lords Letters, to Navy Board.

Admiralty 1/118, Admirals' Despatches, Channel Fleet.

Admiralty 1/4, Admirals' Despatches, Baltic Fleet.

Admiralty 52/3299, Master's log, *Polyphemus* (Alexander Parker). (This log contains the most complete list of signals made during the battle.)

Admiralty 52/2968, Master's log, *Elephant* (George Andrews).

Admiralty 52/3399, Master's log, *St George* (Thomas Atkinson).

Admiralty 52/2964, Master's log, *Edgar* (George Morrison).

Admiralty 52/3231, Master's log, *Monarch* (James George).

Admiralty 52/4018, Master's log, *Amazon* (Pike Channell).

Admiralty 52/2773, Master's log, *Blanche* (D. Spence).

Admiralty 52/2702, Master's log, *Ardent* (Robert Boles Garde).

Admiralty 52/2656, Master's log, *Alcmene* (John Custance, acting master).

Admiralty 52/2899, Master's log, *Cruizer* (William Fothergill).

Admiralty 52/2652, Master's log, *Explosion* (E. Symes).

Admiralty 36/15342, Muster Roll, *Elephant*.

Admiralty 36/13743, Muster Roll, *Monarch*.

Admiralty 36/15392, Muster Roll, *Ganges*.

Admiralty 51/1360, *Blanche*, Captain's journal (G. E. Hamond).

Foreign Office 22/40, Diplomatic Correspondence (includes letters and instructions from the Secretary of State to ambassadors; despatches; notes from foreign governments).

British Museum:

Add. 35201, Bridport Papers.

Add. 41667, D (Baron de Bourgoing).

Add. 38537, f. 8 (Vansittart minutes).

Add. 40667, f.a. 1, f.a. 6 (Correspondence relating to Rear-admiral Thomas Graves).

Add. 40730 (Midshipman William Anderson).

Add. 34918, Nelson Papers, General Correspondence.

Add. 34934, Nelson Papers, Official Correspondence.

Add. 2240, Egerton Mss, correspondence between Nelson and Alexander Davison, 1797–1805.

Add. 31164, Earl of St Vincent, Letter Book, November 1800–February 1801.

Add. 31169, Earl of St Vincent, Letters to Commanders-in-Chief, 1801–1806.

Add. 31168, Earl of St Vincent, Letters to Commissioned Officers.

Admiralty Library:

Progress Books (for details of construction, repairs of ships).

Historical Manuscripts Commission:

Fortescue 6, 7. (Report on the Mss of J. B. Fortescue, at Dropmore.)

National Maritime Museum:

Nelson's Journal, 12 March–13 May, 1801.

Phillips Collection: Papers Relating to Copenhagen.

Midshipman Alexander Nairne: Letter to brother.

Nelson's Order Book, 1801.

Published Material

Danish:

(Only volumes from which quotations have been made are listed.)

Mindeskrift om Slaget paa Reden, P. C. Bundesen, Copenhagen, 1901. (The best Danish account. Although brief it contains the best chart of the battle before the discovery of Robinson Kittoe's drawings and a detailed examination of Danish documents referred to above.)

Tidsskrift for Sovæsen (Navy Magazine):

 1901, Article by Commander J. H. Schultz on Trekroner Fort.

 1944, Article by Commander Bojesen, quoting letters of Captain Lindholm, and the report of Czar Paul's death being given to the Crown Prince.

 1950, Article by Kontreadmiral E. Briand de Crèvecoeur, 'Some Remarks about the Royal Artillery at the Battle of Copenhagen'.

Maanedslieutenanter i Søe-etaten 1801–14 by Commander J. Teisen, Copenhagen 1961. (Published as supplement to *Tidsskrift for Sovæsen*.)

Det Danske Søofficerskorps 1801–1919, by Th. A. Topsøe-Jensen, Copenhagen, 1919.

Dannebrog (weekly Danish Army and Navy magazine): 6 November, 1880, account of battle by Lt Lucomb from Captain Risbrich's journal.

Dagen, No. 26, 13 January, 1836, eyewitness account of the battle from the *Prøvesteenen*.

Nicolai Müller and Peter Villemoes: lecture by O. Sütken and printed in *Near and Far*, 25 January 1880.

Account of Battle by J. N. Müller of the *Hayen:* from the Norwegian Collection, edited and published by Christian C. A. Lange, Christiania, 1860.

Collegial Tidende, No. 8, 21 February, 1801.

War for the Liberty of the Seas . . . or events of the War Between Denmark and England by K. H. Seidelin, Copenhagen, 1801.

Berlingske Tidende, various issues of 1800 and 1801.

German:

Lebensnachrichten Über by B. G. Niebuhrs, Hamburg, 1838, pp. 275, 291–300.

British:

The Cumloden Papers, Edinburgh, 1871, printed for private circulation. (Includes Colonel Stewart's correspondence with War Office, Sir Hyde Parker, Lord Nelson etc.)

The Hamilton and Nelson Papers, vol. 2, 1798–1815, ed. A. Morrison, 1894.

Memoirs of St Vincent, J. S. Tucker, London, 1844.

The Letters of Lord St Vincent, 1801–1804, ed. D. B. Smith, Navy Records Society.

The Private Papers of George, second Earl Spencer, vols. III and IV, ed. Rear-admiral H. W. Richmond, Navy Records Society.

The Tomlinson Papers, ed. J. G. Bullocke, Navy Records Society.

The Life of Nelson, Admiral A. T. Mahan, vol. II, London, 1897.

Dispatches and Letters of Vice Admiral Lord Viscount Nelson, ed. Sir Nicholas H. Nicolas, GCMG, vols IV and VII. (The plan of the battle given at the beginning of volume IV is extremely inaccurate, quite apart from giving the date of the battle as 4 July 1804.)

Logs of the Great Sea Fights, ed. Rear-admiral T. Sturges Jackson, Vol. II, Navy Records Society. (These were transcribed from the logs now in the Public Record Office and unfortunately contain many errors due, apparently, to difficulties in reading the original handwriting. The main errors occur in the logs of the *Polyphemus, Bellona, Isis* and *Explosion*.)

Historical Memoir of Sir Robert Waller Otway, Bt, KCB, Vice-Admiral of the Red, London, 1840, published privately.

Sir Charles Tyler, GCB, Admiral of the White, by Colonel Wyndham-Quin CB, DSO, London, 1912.

The Life of Sir John Franklin, RN, by H. D. Traill, London, 1896.

Diaries and Correspondence of the Rt Hon. George Rose, ed. L. V. Harcourt, vol. 1, London, 1860.

Life and Letters of Sir Gilbert Elliot, 1st Earl of Minto, ed. the Countess of Minto, London, 1874.

The Keith Papers, Prof. C. C. Lloyd, vol. 2, Navy Records Society.

The History of the Russian Empire, H. Tyrell and Henry A. Hankeil, London, 1879.

Nelson's Hardy – His Life, Letters and Friends, Broadley and Bartelot, London, 1909.

The Court of Christian VII of Denmark, P. Nors, ed. E. Steen, London, 1928.

New Annual Register, vol. 22, 1801.

Southey's Life of Nelson, ed. Sir Geoffrey Callender, London, 1922. (On the truce question, Callender's notes should be compared with Fischer's own comments: Callender claims more for the Danes than did Fischer.)

The Wynne Diaries, 3 vols., ed. A. Fremantle, London, 1935–40.

Nelson's Letters to his Wife, ed. G. P. B. Naish, FSA, Navy Records Society.

England and France in the Mediterranean, 1660–1830, W. F. Lord, London, 1910.

Nelson in England, E. Hallam Moorhouse, London, 1913.

Letters from Lord Nelson, compiled by Geoffrey Rawson, London, 1949.

Nelson and His Captains, W. H. Fitchett, London, 1902.

The Royal Kalendar, 1801.

Nelson, Carola Oman, London, 1947.

The Mariners Mirror (Journal of the Society for Nautical Research):
Vol. 25, No. 3, July 1929, article by D. B. Smith based on the correspondence of Midshipman William Anderson.
Ibid, 'The Sandbanks of Yarmouth and Lowestoft', H. Muir Evans.
Vol. 50, No. 2, May 1964, 'The Melancholy Fate of the Baltic Ships in 1811', A. N. Ryan. (Includes references to the *St George*.)

Recollections of the Life of the Rev. A. J. Scott, DD, the Rev. A. and Mrs Gatty, London, 1842.

Blackwood's Magazine, July–December 1899, 'Nelson at Copenhagen'. (Includes orders by Lt-colonel Hutchinson to troops, 18 March 1801.)

A Tour in Zealand ... With an Historical Sketch of the Battle of Copenhagen, 'a native of Denmark', London, 1805. (The author was A. A. Feldborg, who also used the pseudonym J. A. Andersen.)

The Life and Correspondence of the Rt. Hon. Henry Addington, First Viscount Sidmouth, the Hon. George Pellow, D.D., Vol. 1.

Life and Services of Admiral Sir Thomas Foley, GCB, J. B. Herbert, Cardiff, 1884.

The Life and Services of Admiral Lord Nelson, Clarke and M'Arthur, London, 1809 (with subsequent editions).

Naval Chronicle, Vols. I, III, V, VI, VII, VIII, IX, XIV, XVII, XXXVII.

History of the 49th Regt (subsequently the Hertfordshire Regiment).

History of the 95th Regt (subsequently The Rifle Brigade).

The West India Sketch Book, T. Wentworth, Vol. II.

A Social History of the Navy, Michael Lewis, London, 1960.

A Narrative of the Battle of Cape St Vincent, Colonel Drinkwater-Bethune, London, 1840.

A Naval History of Great Britain, William James. First edition in five volumes published 1822; the later 6-volume Macmillan edition of 1902 is used in this narrative.

Memoirs and Correspondence of Admiral Lord de Saumarez, ed. Sir John Ross, London, 1838.

Autobiography of Miss Cornelia Knight, London, 1861, 2 vols.

Naval Miscellany, Vol. 2, Navy Records Society.

SOURCES

Correspondence and Memoirs of Vice-Admiral Lord Collingwood, ed. G. N. Collingwood, 1829.

Diary of Lady Shelley, London, 1812.

History of the British Army, the Hon. J. W. Fortescue.

Revolutionary Europe 1783–1815, George Rudé, Fontana edition, London, 1964.

A Naval Career during the Old War . . . A Life of Admiral John Markham, London, 1883.

Letters of Admiral of the Fleet the Earl of St Vincent, 1801–4, Vol. I, Navy Records Society, 1912.

Macmillan's Magazine, June 1895, 'The Battle of Copenhagen', Midshipman W. S. Millard (unsigned).

The Black Ship, Dudley Pope, London and Philadelphia, 1963.

England Expects (Decision at Trafalgar), Dudley Pope, London 1959 and Philadelphia 1960.

At 12 Mr Byng Was Shot, Dudley Pope, London and Philadelphia, 1962.

INDEX

Individual ships and battles are listed alphabetically under 'Ships', and 'Battles'; monarchs and members of the British royal family are listed under their own names.

Abercromby, Lt-general Sir Ralph, 286–7, 507

Aadsen, Secretary (Danish Admiralty), 250, 252, 255

Abbott, Lemuel (artist), 87

Addington, Henry (later 1st Viscount Sidmouth), succeeds Pitt; forms government, 136–41; crisis over King's illness, 143, 153, 157; orders Baltic expedition, 148; views on Parker, 201; Vansittart's report, 275; offers Malta to Czar, 284; offers France peace, 285–7; Nelson's report, 435, 437–8, 441; Mentioned, 146–7, 200, 325–6, 448, 468, 472, 486, 489, 499, 507

Alexander I, Czar of Russia, 326, 472, 479, 488, 493, 501–6, 512

Allen, Thomas (Nelson's servant), 38, 243, 324, 348, 497–8

Amager Battery: see Stricker's Battery

Amiens, Treaty of, 54

Anderson, Midshipman William, 230, 384, 516

Andreson, Lt Niels, 401, 477

Andrews, George, 294, 311, 353, 373

Arden, Charles Perceval, 1st Baron, 123

Arenfeldt, Capt (later Rear-admiral) Jacob, 401–2, 432, 452, 477, 524

Armed Neutrality: see Northern Convention

Army at Copenhagen: whole of 49th Foot; one company (Beckwith's) of Corps of Riflemen (Manningham's) [later the 95th or Rifle Regiment];
usual complement of Royal Artillery in bomb ketches: see under Stewart, Colonel W.; Hutchinson, Lt-colonel W.

Atkinson, Horatio Nelson, 227

Atkinson, Thomas, 227, 408, 514

Baker, Capt Thomas, 60–1

Balfour, Lt William, 156–7

Ball, Capt (later Rear-admiral Sir) Alexander, 57–60, 509

Bamford's Hotel, 38

Bang, Lt Hans, 437

Battles:
   Camperdown (1797), 16, 81, 149
   Cape Passaro (1718), 23
   Cape St Vincent (1797), 16, 19, 41, 81, 86, 114, 117–18, 149, 352
   Glorious First of June (1794), 16
   Hohenlinden (1800), 65
   Malta siege, 56–60
   Marengo (1800), 50, 65
   Nile (1798), 24, 31–2, 56, 77, 81, 111, 149, 286, 352
   Saintes (1782), 17
   Trafalgar (1805), 24, 70, 149

Bardenfleth, Lt (later Rear-admiral) Johan F., 400

Bawden, Capt James, 442

Barham, Admiral Francis Middleton, 1st Baron, 140

Beckford, William, 28, 85, 87–8

Beckwith, Capt Sidney, 181, 197

Beechey, Sir William, 87

Beeke, Dr, 147, 207–8, 212, 200

Bell, Midshipman James, 370

Bentham, Samuel, 234

Berlingske Tidende, 252, 254–5, 302, 436, 457, 468

Bernstorff, Count Christian, replies on Convention, 75, 99, 103–6; seeks UK view, 102; hears of embargo, 130–1; embargo reaction, 148; Vansittart mission, 208–12; reports to envoys, 213–14; returns British note, 247; warns envoys, 300–2;
Mentioned, 61, 73–5, 91–2, 128–9, 141, 149, 204–5, 217, 220, 245–6, 248–9, 326, 346, 438, 455, 457–8, 460, 462–4, 468, 471, 493, 500

Bertie (formerly Hoar), Capt (later Sir) Thomas, 229, 297, 388–9, 427, 443–4, 529

Berry, Capt (later Admiral) Sir Edward, 23, 86–7, 230

Bille, Lt (later Admiral) Michael, 368, 379, 381, 388, 477

Bille, Lt (later Capt) Søren, 368–9, 388

Bille, Capt (later Admiral) Steen A., 205, 250, 253, 302, 334–7, 365–6, 377, 379, 402, 405, 421, 434–5, 450, 456, 459, 526

Birchall, Capt William, 529

Bligh, Vice-admiral Richard R., 14

Bligh, Capt William, 227, 232, 235, 320, 369, 371, 390, 393, 444, 477–8, 480–1, 528

Bohne, Res. Lt Poul H., 369, 388, 456–7

Bolton, Capt William, 529

Bonaparte, Napoleon (later Emperor), 31–2, 46–55, 59, 62, 65–6, 68–9, 71, 77–9, 81–4, 90–1, 129, 214, 285–7, 446

Bourgoing, Baron de (French envoy, Denmark), 206, 306–7, 309

Bowes, Midshipman the Hon. William, 397

Boys, Lt (later Capt) Charles, 443

Bragge, Charles, MP, 143

Braun, Capt Ferdinand A., 203, 251, 390, 392, 427, 437, 524

Brandt, Capt Eric O., 368, 386, 420, 522

Bridport, Admiral Alexander, 1st Viscount, 315, 520

Briarly, Alexander, 356–7, 362, 365, 484–5

Brightman, Thomas, 378

Brisbane, Capt James, 234, 297, 311, 353, 382, 434, 529

Britain:
Loans by, 77; Naval strength, 80–2; Army strength, 78, 82–3; cost of living, 78, 93, 160, 448

Brock, Lt-colonel Isaac, 181

Brown, Capt (later Admiral) P. C. Wessel, 342, 526

Buckingham, George Temple, 1st Marquis of, 107–8, 394, 422, 429–30, 434, 455, 460

Bulow, Adjutant-general F. C., 252

Burn, Peter, 272, 385

Byng, Admiral Sir George, 1st Viscount Torrington, 23

Byng, Admiral the Hon. John, 316, 508

Cadogan, Mrs Mary, 29, 38

Calvert, Colonel Harry, 197

Canning, George MP, 135–6

Caroline Mathilda, Queen, 75–8

Carron Company, carronades, 97, 112, 224, 226–7

Carysfort, John Proby, Earl of (British envoy, Prussia), reports Northern League, 64; on Convention, 65, 67, 73, 107; told of Heligoland plan, 127; told of Czar offer, 284;
Mentioned, 63–4, 104, 132, 141, 159, 285–7, 289, 325, 475, 479, 487, 492, 494, 504

Castelcicala, Princess (wife, Neapolitan ambassador), 87

Channel, Pike, 314

Charles, Prince of Hesse, 144–6, 207–8

Charles v, of Spain, 53

Charlotte, Queen (wife of George III), 88, 116

Christian VII, King of Denmark, 75–6

Clarence, Duke of: see William Henry, Prince

Collingwood, Capt (later Vice-admiral) Cuthbert, 1st Baron, 42, 118

Collingwood, Mrs Sarah, 118

Conn, Cdr (later Capt) John, 235

Cortsen, Res. Lt Jesper, 402

Cornwallis, Admiral Sir William, 233

Cost of living: see Britain

Cronborg Castle, 124, 202–3, 206, 252–3, 260–1, 265–8, 270–1, 273–4, 276–8, 280–3, 290–3, 295–9, 302–7, 375
Cronborg signal telegraph, 124, 253
Crown Island: see Trekroner Fort
Crown Prince of Denmark: see Frederick, Crown Prince
Cub, The (nickname of Josiah Nisbet, q.v.)
Cuming, Capt William, 231, 372, 529
Custance, John, 318, 353

Daubeny, Midshipman Edward A., 384
Daubeny, Rev. James, 384
Davies, Rev. Joseph, 442
Davison, Alexander, 85, 121–2, 163, 165, 167, 174, 191, 241, 243, 444, 483–4, 490–1, 498, 510
Defence Commission, members, 204; and Crown Prince, 204–5; Mentioned, 253, 302, 339–40, 405, 421
Delafons, Lt John, 371
Dennis, Lt (later Maj-general Sir) James B., 396–7
Devonshire, Capt J. F., 412, 444, 529
Dietrichson, Lt (later Capt) Gabriel G., 375, 395
Digby, Capt Henry, 261
Dickson, Admiral William, 34, 156, 188
Dilkes, Capt John, 226
Dommett, Capt (later Admiral Sir) William, 44, 186, 195–6, 227–8, 261–2, 268, 277–9, 305, 314–16, 408, 410, 482, 498, 520
Dommett, Midshipman, 385
Dreyer, M., (Danish envoy, France), 213–14, 300–1
Drummond, William (British envoy, Denmark), warns Bernstorff, 99–101, 102–3; told of embargo, 105; tells Bernstorff of embargo, 130–1; told Fleet preparing, 148–9; reports Gustavus meeting, 206; Vansittart mission, 208–15; Fleet reported, 215; new orders, 244–7; receives passport, 247; joins Blanche, 247–9; sees Parker, 261; Mentioned, 64, 73–5, 91, 95, 97, 107, 119, 124, 126–8, 141–2, 145, 155, 186 193, 217, 220, 239–41

Duckworth, Rear-admiral John T., 106, 200, 244, 251, 259–60, 262, 266–7, 274–5, 286–7, 428
Duncan, Admiral Adam, 1st Viscount, 16, 18
Dundas, Henry (later 1st Viscount Melville), and Pitt, 54–5; West Indies policy, 54–5, 101; Mediterranean, 55; strategy, 101–2, 127–8; embargo on ships, 105; Heligoland plan, 127–8; Helder operation, 127–8; resigns, 143; Baltic Fleet orders, 149–52; Ross's complaint, 156; Providentia complaint, 156–7; Mentioned, 78, 193, 441

Egede, Lt (later Capt) Christian T., 203, 331, 342, 383, 524
Ehrensward, Baron von (Swedish envoy, Britain), 95, 105–7
Elgin, Thomas Bruce 7th Earl of, 58–9, 143
Eliot, Hon. William, MP, 140
Elliot, Gilbert see Minto, Earl of
Elliot, Hugh (British envoy, Saxony), 36, 73
Elsinore: see Cronborg
Elsworth, James, 378
Erskine, Lt-general Sir James, 57–8

Fabritius de Tengnagel, Lt Carl, 526
Fancourt, Capt Robert D., 231, 362, 434, 529
Fasting, Lt (later Capt) Thomas, 522
Faye, Capt Gabriel, 156–7
Featherstonhaugh, Sir Harry, 29
Felton, Midshipman John, 230
Fenwick, William (British consul, Elsinore), 100, 103–4, 247, 302, 313
Ferdinand IV, King of Naples (I of the Two Sicilies, III of Sicily), 18, 28, 42, 57–9, 98, 122
Ferguson, Dr (surgeon, Elephant), 373, 411
Fischer, Capt (later Vice-admiral) Johan Olfert, career, 92; preparing Copenhagen defences, 250–4, 327–30, 336–8; his ships, 330–4; his officers, 341–4; in Battle, 366, 369, 373; shifts flag, 393, 401–2, 404–6, 413, 416, 424; report to

Fischer, Capt—*cont.*
  Crown Prince, 449–52, 496–7; Nelson's
  criticism, 452–4;
  Mentioned, 204–5, 302, 307, 314, 321,
  339, 352, 432–4, 456
Fitzwilliam, William, Earl, 133
Flag of Truce: *see* Truce
Flinders, Capt Matthew, 188, 191
Foley, Capt (later Admiral Sir) Thomas,
  11, 23, 196, 227, 237, 294, 309, 314,
  318, 323–4, 411, 418, 422, 435, 467–8,
  470, 486, 509, 516, 520, 528
Forbes, Maj-general Gordon, 14, 110
Foreigners in HM ships, 182, 221–4
Fothergill, William, 311, 313, 377
Fouché, Joseph, 49
Fox, Hon. Charles James, MP, 286
Franklin, Benjamin, 10
Franklin, Midshipman (later Sir) John,
  191, 226, 235
Frederick, Duke of York (son of George
  III), reorganises Army, 83; Army titles
  changed, 151; receives Dundas's
  orders, 151–2; chooses Colonel Stewart
  152;
  Mentioned, 86
Frederick, Crown Prince and Regent of
  Denmark (later Frederick VI), appoints
  captains, 203; Proclamation, 203–4;
  and Defence Commission, 204–5;
  meets Gustavus, 206; second
  Proclamation, 249–50; British Fleet
  sighted, 253; priest's appeal, 254;
  Naiker's petition, 257; replies to
  Parker, 298; Copenhagen defences,
  327, 339; during Battle, 366–7, 383,
  405, 416; and Truce, 417, 420–3, 428;
  meets Nelson, 427–8; negotiates
  armistice, 438–41, 445, 458–70;
  Fischer's report, 449–52, 496–7;
  Mentioned, 91–2, 144–6, 202, 207,
  258, 301–2, 307, 342, 432, 435, 442,
  483, 485, 509
Frederick William III, King of Prussia,
  63, 142
Fremantle, Capt (later Vice-admiral Sir)
  Thomas, 12, 23, 196, 222, 228–9, 293–
  4, 299, 309, 313, 316, 322, 374, 394,
  422–3, 429–30, 434–6, 449, 455, 459,
  482, 490, 494–5, 499–500, 528

Fremantle ('Betsey', later Lady)
  Elizabeth, 222, 228–9, 293–4, 316,
  422, 430, 455, 490
Fridag, M., (Prussian consul, London),
  379
Fuller, Brig-general Francis, 200

Gambier, Vice-admiral James (later
  Admiral, 1st Baron), 123
Ganteaume, Admiral Honoré, 118–19
Garde, R. B., 398
Garlike, Benjamin (Secretary of
  Legation, Berlin), 500
Gartshore, William, MP, 141
George III, 7, 19, 42–3, 75–6, 85, 88–9,
  93–4, 98, 112, 126, 132, 243, 439, 448
  509
George, Prince of Wales (later George IV)
  29, 34, 43, 120, 161–9, 178
Gersdorff, General Baron, 346
Gerner, Henrick (naval architect), 331,
  333, 522, 524, 526
Gether, Lt (later Rear-admiral) Johan,
  342, 526
Gibraltar, strategic importance, 54–5
Gould, Capt Davidge, 357
Grasse, Admiral François, Comte de, 227
  231
Graves, Rear-admiral Thomas (later
  Admiral, 1st Baron), 196, 199, 230,
  236, 261, 306, 309, 311–12, 314–16,
  322–7, 371, 375, 402, 409–12. 425,
  435, 444, 450–1, 494–5, 498, 507, 509,
  515–16, 519
Green, Midshipman John, 447
Grenville, William Wyndham, 1st Baron,
  Armed Neutrality, 65, 67, 75;
  Denmark's role, 101, 103; receives
  Danish reply, 113–14; placing
  embargo 105–7; Heligoland plan, 127;
  resigns, 136; tells Carysfort of crisis,
  144; Hesse peace letters, 144; writes
  Vansittart's orders, 144; final offer to
  Denmark, 145–6;
  Mentioned, 63–4, 73, 85–6, 95, 98, 100,
  126–30, 135, 141–2, 159, 208, 241,
  244–5, 325, 440, 479, 489, 492–3, 500
Greville, Charles, 29, 38
Grey, Charles, MP, 133
Grey, James, 400

Grodtschilling, Lt Frederik, 343
Gustavus IV, King of Sweden, 91, 94,
  127, 131, 206, 300–1, 307
Gyldenfeldt, Capt Niels S., 342, 526

Hamilton, Emma, Lady meets Nelson,
  28–30; after Nile, 33–5; pregnant, 35,
  86; Horatia born, 123;
  Mentioned, 14, 23–4, 51, 85, 87–9,
  111–12, 161–71, 178, 181, 183–5,
  191–2, 200, 228, 429, 459, 475, 492,
  494–5
Hamilton, Sir William, 12, 28–30, 33–5,
  42–3, 51, 85–8, 111–12, 120, 161–4,
  166–71, 179–81, 185, 192, 225, 496
Hamond, Capt (later Vice-admiral Sir)
  Graham, 233, 239, 247–8, 274, 255,
  529
Hamond, Sir Andrew S., 139, 141, 233
Hancock, Lt R. T., 313
Hanson, Dr C. A., 257–8
Harboe, Capt Frederik C. L., 374–5,
  395, 524
Hardy, Capt (later Vice-admiral Sir)
  Thomas M., 23, 35, 86, 98, 112, 116–
  17, 180–1, 185, 225, 243, 313, 322–3,
  345–8, 357, 408, 429, 433, 435–7, 455,
  514
Harlow, Midshipman Thomas, 447
Haslewood, William (solicitor), 111
Hauch, Lt Jens E., 332, 369, 388–9,
  456–7, 522
Haugwitz, Count de (Foreign Minister,
  Prussia), 132
Hawkesbury, Robert Jenkinson, Lord
  (later 2nd Earl of Liverpool), succeeds
  Grenville, 143; chooses Vansittart,
  144; reacts to Danish note, 147;
  Russian officers, 157; Vansittart's
  report, 212–5; Drummond's new
  orders, 244–7; negotiating with Czar,
  284; offers Malta 284–5; peace offer
  to France, 285–7;
  Mentioned, 148, 155–6, 241, 274, 428,
  479, 487, 505
Heard, Sir Isaac, 42, 122
Helder Expedition see Dundas, and
  Grenville
Heligoland Expedition see Dundas, and
  Grenville

Helt, Res. Lt Søren H., 369, 388–9
Henne, Lt Claus H., 382
Hesse, Prince of, see Charles
Herbert, John, 25, 27
Hobart, Robert, 1st Baron, 139, 143,
  488, 490, 498, 507
Hole, Midshipman (later Admiral)
  Lewis, 226
Hohlenberg, Capt Frantz (naval
  architect), 332, 524
Holloway, Rear-admiral (later Admiral)
  John, 170, 487
Holloway, Clementina (later Lady
  Otway), 487
Holsten, Lt (later Admiral) Hans, Baron,
  203, 332, 342–3, 524
Home, Lt Alexander P., 399–400
Hood, Admiral Alexander, see Bridport,
  Lord
Hood, Admiral Samuel, 1st Viscount,
  10, 11, 29, 88, 136, 368
Hoste, Rev. Dixon, 87
Hotham, Admiral William, 1st Baron,
  11–13, 17
Hoppe, Lt (later Admiral) Johan C.,
  375, 395
Howe, Admiral Richard, Earl, 10, 11,
  16, 234
Hutchinson, Lt-colonel (later General
  Sir) William (49th Foot), 322–3, 355,
  396–400, 442, 509, 516

Inman, Capt Henry, 233–4, 322, 370,
  378, 529

Jervis, Admiral Sir John, see St Vincent,
  Earl of
Johansen, Res. Lt Lorentz, 369
Johnson, Lt Edmund, 385
Johnson, Lt Joshua, 385
Jones, David (Ordnance storekeeper),
  197
Joy, William (bosun), 399
Justesen, Lt Peter, 437

Kaas, Vice-admiral (later Admiral)
  Friderich C., 204–5, 342, 420
Keith, Admiral George Keith
  Elphinstone, 1st Baron Keith, 96, 109,
  115, 155, 286, 517

Kierulf, Capt Ole A., (harbourmaster), 252, 458
Kilgore, Edward (quartermaster), 396
King, Lt (later Capt) Andrew, 234
King, Capt Richard, 200
Kittoe, Robinson (Graves' secretary), 375–6, 392, 414
Knight (Miss) Ellis Cornelia, 38–40, 120
Knuth, Chamberlain F. von, 204, 420
Koefoed, Capt Hans H., 400, 524
Koster, S. de, 87
Krabbe, Capt Peter, 60–1
Kronborg Castle, see Cronborg Castle
Klvest, Baron de Jacobi (Prussian envoy, Britain), 95

Lambert, Capt Robert S., 227
Lassen, Capt Lorentz F., 251, 330, 368, 380–1, 522
Lawford, Capt John, 226, 263, 269, 528
Layman, Lt (later Capt) William, 262–3
Levant Company, 117
Lillienskjold, Lt Peter C., 342, 402, 524
Lind, Res. Lt Friderich, 343, 417
Lindholm, Capt (later Rear-admiral) Hans, Truce, 420–1, 423, 428–9, 435, 437, 457–8, 460–1, 463–9, 472–5, 483; Fischer's report, 452–5, 496–7; Mentioned, 448, 483, 509
Lizakewitz, Chevalier de (Russian envoy Denmark), 126–7
Locker, Capt William, 88
Lothian's Hotel, 178
Lorentzen, Res. Lt Ditler, 478
Loud, Lt Robert, 426
Lundbye, Res. Lt Carl, 419–21, 424
Lunéville, Treaty of, 138
Lutwidge, Admiral Skeffington, 61

McCulloch, Lt Thomas, 215, 244, 248, 274
M'Kinley, Lt George, 377–8, 444
Mahan, Admiral Alfred T., USN, 200, 273, 357
Maitland, Brig-general Sir Thomas, 110
Malmesbury, Countess of (wife of 1st Earl), 135–6, 201, 487, 511
Malta (see also St John, Order of), 53, 56–62, 132, 284–5
Maples, Lt (later Rear-admiral) John F., 443

Maria Carolina, Queen of the Two Sicilies, 28–9, 33–5, 51
Markham, Capt (later Admiral) John, 140–1, 490
Mawbey, Midshipman John, 226
Mayne, Midshipman (later Capt) Robert, 226
Meinertz, Res. Lt Heich, 402
Middelboe, Lt (later Capt) Bernhart U., 342, 401, 524
Millard, Midshipman W. S., 196–7, 199, 222, 241, 245–6, 299, 303–5, 319, 323, 345, 354, 358, 364, 367, 370, 378, 394–400, 425–7, 480–1
Minto, Gilbert Elliot, 1st Earl of, 35, 135, 476, 487, 518
Minto, Anna, Countess of, 35
Morgan, Midshipman George, 399, 442, 447
Morrison, George, 385, 386
Mosse, Capt James Robert, 230, 355, 395–6, 435, 442–3, 486, 528
Mosse, R. L., 486
Mulgrave, Capt Constantine Phipps, 2nd Baron, 188
Müller, Lt (later Vice-admiral) Jochum N., 332, 343, 390–1, 395, 417–18, 422, 437, 471, 477, 522
Murray, Capt (later Vice-admiral) George, 177–8, 196, 225, 297, 314, 316, 362–5, 368, 385, 435, 443, 476, 509, 528

Nairn, Midshipman Alexander, 369–70, 380
Napoleon I, Emperor, see Bonaparte
Nelson, Rev. Edmund, 27, 38, 86, 324
Nelson, Frances ('Fanny') Viscountess, 25–9, 34, 38–9, 42–3, 86–7, 111, 115–17, 120, 122, 178–9, 184, 415
Nelson, Horatia, born, 123; possible survivor of tpins, 170–9; named, 162–3; Mentioned, 35, 161, 166, 179
Nelson, Vice-admiral Horatio, Viscount, Duke of Bronté, under Hotham, 11–13; actions, 15; at Cape St Vincent, 16, 19; personality, 18–24; in West Indies, 25–6; meets Hamiltons, 28–30; Nile battle, 31–3; stays in Naples,

Nelson, Vice-admiral—*cont.*
34–5; returns to England, 35–9;
King's snub, 42; Malta siege, 56–9;
loan to Sir William, 85; to *San Josef*,
86; seat in Lords, 86; promoted Vice-
admiral, 97–8; Dukedom approved,
98; new post, 109–10; marriage
collapses, 110–11; ill in carriage, 112;
visit to St Vincent, 112–15;
'Thompson' subterfuge, 120; meets
Simcoe, 122; Horatia born, 123;
jealous of Prince of Wales, 161–4,
167–9, 191–2; making will, 161, 184;
and codicil, 243; naming Horatia,
162–3; visits London, 170–2, 178–9;
first sees Horatia, 179; 'my dear wife',
180; foreigners in his ships, 182; urges
haste, 183; last letter to Lady Nelson,
184; visits Parker, 185–6; ignored by
Parker, 186–7; warns Troubridge,
187; Parker 'sulking', 190; angry over
Order of Battle, 196; questions
Vansittart, 262–5, 267; moving
Parker 266–9; briefs Vansittart, 275;
reads 'Sound' letter, 281–3; orders for
Sound, 292–5; for Copenhagen,
292–3; passes Cronborg, 305–6; lists
Copenhagen defences, 306; prepares
for Battle, 311–12, 314–22; prepares
final orders, 323–5, 340–7; actual
orders, 348–51; pilots' fears, 356–7;
during Battle, 361–3, 369, 371–6, 379,
385, 391–400; 405–8; Signal No. 39,
409–13, 514–21; and telescope, 411;
Truce, 414, 416–25, 429; meets
Fischer, 433–4; Battle report, 434–5;
negotiator, 435–7, 460–1, 463, 465–
76; on Fischer's report, 452–4; replaces
Parker, 490; hears he is Commander-
in-Chief, 497–9; as Commander-in-
Chief, 497–507, 509–11;
Mentioned, 14, 17, 40–1, 44, 49, 51–2,
55, 60, 69, 81, 86, 95–7, 115–18, 123,
165, 173, 176–7, 181, 190, 198, 200,
229–31, 240–1, 243, 261, 270, 272–3,
277, 284–5, 290, 296, 298, 308–9, 327,
335, 352, 431, 441, 443–4, 448, 450,
455, 459, 477, 482–7, 491–6, 512–13
Nelson, Maurice, 179, 483, 505
'Nelson Touch', 17

Nelson, Rev. William (later 1st Earl),
22, 34, 112, 178–9, 191
Nelson, Mrs William (Sarah) later
Countess, 122, 178–9
Nepean, Evan, 37, 39–41, 43, 98, 114–15,
122, 139, 153, 187–9, 294, 484, 498,
509–10
Nerot's Hotel, London, 38, 43, 85
Nesbitt, Maj-general Thomas, 110
Nicholls, John, MP, 89
Nisbet, Mrs Frances, *see* Nelson, Frances,
Viscountess
Nisbet, Capt Josiah, 24, 26–9, 33–4, 179,
184, 229
Nørregaard, *Generalauditor* Laurits, 204,
420
Norfolk, Charles Howard, Duke of, 122,
161–2, 164
Northern Convention, wording of, 67–
72; British reaction. 73–5, 84, 89, 92–3
99–108, 128–9, 133;
Mentioned, 64–5, 78, 82, 95, 284–5
Nyboder, 251, 339, 341, 386, 446

Oliver, Francis (secretary), 38, 180–1
Onslow, Admiral Sir Richard, 6, 94, 138
Osborn, B. (Parker's secretary), 172, 312,
444, 464, 466, 475
Otway, Capt (later Admiral Sir)
Robert W., 9, 228, 277–80, 314, 407–9,
431–4, 443, 455, 460, 464, 486–7, 489,
494–5, 497–8, 507, 517–18, 520–1
Oxenstierna, M. de (Swedish envoy,
Denmark), 206

Pahlen, Count Peter Louis (Russian
Foreign Minister), 479–80, 493, 495,
499–506
Parker, Capt Edward T., 164, 467–8, 470
Parker, Lady Frances (née Onslow), 6,
14, 96, 125, 171–2, 193–4, 216
Parker, Admiral Sir Hyde, returns to
London, 6; prize money, 6–10; career,
10–14; chosen by ministers, 149;
receives *Providentia* complaint, 157;
stays in London, 171; begins Journal,
171; Board's orders, 171; ordered to
Yarmouth, 172; meets Nelson and
Stewart, 185–6; complaints to Nepean,
187–9; Board order to sail, 193;

Parker, Admiral—*cont.*
cancels ball, 194; Addington's opinion, 200; effect of delay, 215–16; crossing North Sea, 217–20, 235–8; in Cattegat 239–42; sends *Blanche*, 242; Vansittart's report, 259; alarmed by defences, 260–9; alternatives, 270–2; consults pilots, 261, 276; decides on Belt, 273–5; changes mind, 279–83; Sound dangers, 291–2; messages to Stricker, 295–9; passes Cronborg, 304–5; anchors off Copenhagen, 306; council of war, 314–17; Signal No 39, 406–13, 514–21; Truce, 428–9, 435, 457–67, 469, 473–5; his promotions, 443–4; new orders, 487–8; sacked, 490; gets recall, 497–9; reaches UK, 507–8;
Mentioned, 15, 22, 28, 44, 49, 52, 60, 69, 82, 94, 96, 108, 114, 119, 123, 125, 138, 149, 174, 176, 178, 180–1, 183, 195, 198–9, 202, 215–16, 222, 234, 244, 275–7, 284–5, 287, 294, 300–1, 309, 311–13, 319–21, 323, 340, 346–7, 359, 366, 376, 379, 388–9, 418, 420–4, 428, 431–4, 438, 440–2, 447, 452, 455, 476–7, 479–85, 487, 491–7, 502, 505, 510–13
Paul I, Czar of Russia, Malta policy, 56–8, 60–1; seizes British ships, 61–2, 64; Armed Neutrality, 64, 67, 70, 72, 75, 89–91, 93, 96, 284–5; Fleet frozen in port, 125; expels Danish envoy, 126–7, 131; British peace offer, 285; murdered, 288–9
Mentioned, 46, 49–51, 53, 73, 82, 141, 159–60, 182, 287, 439–40, 445–6, 448, 458, 469, 472–3, 476, 479, 483, 487–8
Paulet, Capt Lord Henry, 229, 431
Perceval, Hon. Spencer, MP, 146
Pigot, Maj-general Henry, 60
Pigot, Capt Hugh, 9
Pitt, Right Hon. William, P. C., MP, Mediterranean policy, 54; and Dundas, 54–5; Cabinet on Denmark, 104; orders embargo on ships, 105; Act of Union crisis, 126–8, 135–6; warns Russia, 132–3; resigns, 135; ministers continue, 143; presents Estimates, 160; resignation effect on Danes, French,

205–6;
Mentioned, 7, 56, 60, 64, 86, 134, 220 484, 487
Pole, Rear-admiral (later Admiral Sir) Charles M., 510
Portland, William Cavendish Bentinck, 3rd Duke of, 105, 143

Queensbury, William Douglas, 4th Duke of, 38, 112
Quilliam, Lt John, 233, 411, 413, 442

Rafen, Lt Rasmus, 381
Rastopchin, Count (Russian Chancellor) 131
Rennie, Capt John, 238–9
Retalick, Capt Robert, 230, 528
Riegelson, Capt (later Rear-admiral) Peter, 526
Riou, Capt Edward, 231–3, 309, 314, 318–20, 322–4, 351, 364, 377, 402, 411–13, 434, 442, 529
Risbrich, Lt (later Capt) Christian V., 251, 253–4, 342, 386, 421, 522
Risbrich, Capt (later Admiral) Friderich C., 331, 341, 368, 381–3
Rist, Johan G., 365
Rodney, Admiral George Brydges, 1st Baron, 17, 227, 231, 368
Romney, Charles Marsham, Baron, 78, 86
Romney, George (artist), 14, 179
Rose, Rt Hon. George, 200, 480
Rose, Capt Jonas, 349–50, 373, 378, 529
Rose, Joseph (clerk), 442
Rosencrantz, M. de (Danish envoy, Russia), 126–7, 131, 439
Ross, William (King's Messenger), 124, 155–6
Rothe, Lt (later Rear-admiral) Carl A., 203, 342, 383–4, 436, 522
Rundell, Rev. John, 386
'Ryeboys', 251

St Bartholomew's (St Bart's), capture of, *see* West Indies, Operations in
St George, Mrs Melesina, 38
St Helens, Alleyne Fitzherbert, 1st Baron (British envoy, Russia), 500, 505
St John, Order of, 53, 55–7, 59, 62
St Thomas, capture of, *see* West Indies, operations in

St Vincent, Admiral John Jervis, 1st Earl of, critical of Nelson, 40, 114; Nelson visits, 112–14; offered Admiralty, 136–8; accepts, 139; becomes First Lord, 140; forms new Board ,140–1; receives Baltic orders, 153; sees Board's plans, 154; dockyard strikes, 157–9; Parker reservations, 159; Nelson at Admiralty, 178; tells Parker to sail, 194;
Mentioned, 14, 16–17, 23–4, 31, 33, 41, 44–5, 84, 97–8, 109, 115–16, 118 122–3, 165, 170, 176, 178, 183, 190, 193, 200, 233–4, 294, 340, 356, 385, 388, 409, 438, 444, 476, 478, 483, 486–7, 489–90, 498–9, 500–2, 505, 507, 509–10

Saumarez, Vice-admiral James, 1st Baron, 32

Saxton, Sir Charles, Bt, 170, 181, 183

Schultz, Lt Philip, 395

Schimmelman, Count (Danish Finance Minister), 248, 346, 365

Scott, Rev. Alexander J. (Parker's secretary and chaplain), 173–4, 240, 242, 296, 314, 455, 460, 465, 468, 470, 475, 493–4, 496–6, 516–19

Seaforth, Francis Mackenzie, 1st Baron, 86

Selim III, see Sultan of Turkey

Semaphore: British, 170; Danish, 124, 253

Ships
Aalborg (Dan), 334, 527
Agamemnon (Br), 11–13, 22, 28, 154, 231, 320, 350, 361–3, 369–70, 375, 406–8, 428, 434, 450, 492, 528
Aggershuus (Dan), 257, 332, 350, 369, 373, 379, 396, 404, 416, 437, 524–5
Agincourt (Br), 197
Alemene (Br), 184, 225, 233, 318, 320, 351, 353, 356, 364, 377, 402, 407, 411, 424–5, 428, 444, 529
Alecto (Br), 155, 217
Altona (Dan), 343–4
Amazon (Br), 231, 309–10, 314, 318–21, 329, 351, 356, 364, 377–8, 402, 405, 407, 411–13, 424–5, 434, 444, 482, 529
Ardent (Br), 184, 229, 297, 320, 349,

354, 358, 361–2, 367–71, 373, 378, 387–9, 414, 427, 443–4, 528
Arendal (Dan), 334, 527
Arrow (Br), 234, 351, 356, 402, 492, 529
Asia (Br), 155
Audacious (Br), 156–7
Barfleur (Br), 118
Bedford (Br), 12, 231
Bellona (Br), 124, 154, 229–30, 345, 349–50, 356, 364, 369–75, 377–81, 384–5, 393, 408, 428, 434–5, 444, 449–50, 516, 529
Bellerophon (Br), 234
Blanche (Br), 145, 147, 215, 233, 239–42, 244, 254, 259, 262, 274–5, 295–6, 305, 354, 356, 364, 377, 402, 407, 411, 424–5, 495–9, 502, 507–8, 529
Boreas (Br), 25, 434
Bornholm (Dan), 434
Bouncer (Br), 155
Bounty (Br), 227, 481
Britannia (Br), 227
Briton (Br), 239
Ça Ira (Fr), 11, 12, 394
Captain (Br), 12
Censeur (Fr), 12
Charlotte Amalia (Dan), 206, 251, 255, 333, 350, 375, 395, 401–4, 416–17, 419, 524–5
Chasseur (Fr), 100
Christiansund (Dan), 334, 527
Colossus (Br), 225
Courageux (Br), 124
Cronborg (Dan), 206, 251, 332, 349, 369, 387–9, 393, 395, 404, 416, 432, 456–7, 522–3
Cruizer (Br), 234, 236, 295–8, 309–10, 314, 318–21, 329, 353–4, 377, 407, 425, 434, 443, 464, 529
Cumberland (Br), 13
Danmark (Dan), 206, 250–2, 329, 334–5, 366, 369, 405, 526
Dannebroge (Dan), 203, 250, 332, 337, 342–3, 349–50, 366, 374, 387, 390, 392–401, 404, 406, 416–17, 420, 422, 427, 429, 437, 445, 451, 453, 456–7, 477, 524–5
Dart (Br), 188, 234, 349–50, 356, 377,

Ships—*cont.*
    402, 407, 412, 425, 444, 529
    Defence (Br), 154, 229, 292, 317, 346,
       376, 420–1, 431
    Defiance (Br), 124, 155, 199, 230–1,
       236, 314, 316, 349–50, 371, 375,
       377, 392, 400, 402, 405–12, 419, 425,
       428, 434, 454, 516, 528
    Den Aarvagne (Dan), 342
    Désirée (Br), 233–4, 322, 349, 363–4,
       370, 378–80, 382, 393, 407–8, 451,
       529
    Director (Br), 358
    Discovery (Br), 155, 351, 361–2, 378,
       426, 529
    Dreadnought (Br), 235
    Driver (Br), 156–7
    Edgar (Br), 124, 154, 199, 225, 234,
       292, 297, 304–5, 317, 349, 356–7,
       362–5, 367–70, 372, 377, 381, 383–6,
       435, 443, 484, 528
    Elephant (Br), 196, 222–4, 227, 237–8,
       292, 294–5, 299–300, 305, 310–11,
       314, 317–23, 345, 347–51, 353,
       355–7, 361–3, 371–4, 378, 391–4,
       400, 406–9, 413–14, 416, 418–19,
       421, 423–8, 454–5, 471, 477, 483–5,
       514, 516–18, 520–1, 528
    Elephanten (Dan), 329, 334, 346, 350,
       372, 402, 405, 411–12, 414, 419,
       421, 424, 449–51, 526
    Eling (Br), 234, 432–3, 481
    Elven (Dan), 203, 252, 332–2, 342–3,
       350, 369, 372–3, 376, 387, 390,
       392–3, 404, 516, 524–5
    Ethalion (Br), 233
    Explosion (Br), 155, 351, 378, 413, 428,
       529
    Flensborg (Dan), 334, 523
    Floating Battery No 1 (Dan), 251, 256,
       333, 350, 369, 372–3, 376, 393–4,
       404, 406, 416, 458–9, 471, 524–5
    Force (Br), 155
    Formidable (Br), 114
    Fox (Br), 156, 314, 318–19, 329, 465,
       474, 477, 480
    Foudroyant (Br), 35, 117, 166
    Freya (Dan), 60–2, 160, 245, 256, 342,
       439
    Ganges (Br), 222–3, 228–9, 293, 313,

    316, 349–50, 353, 374–5, 378, 394–5,
       406, 416, 419, 425–7, 433, 459–60,
       482, 528
    Généreux (Fr), 230
    Glatton (Br), 154, 226–7, 320, 349–50,
       358, 361–2, 367–9, 371, 375, 387,
       390–3, 413, 450, 477–8, 528
    Goliath (Br), 227
    Guardian (Br), 232–3
    Harpy (Br), 154, 235, 314, 318–19,
       433, 453, 482, 529
    Hayen (Dan), 332–3, 342–3, 349, 387,
       390–3, 404, 416, 422, 471, 477,
       522–3
    Hecla (Br), 155, 351, 529
    Hereux, 113
    Hiælperen (Dan), 333, 336, 346, 350,
       375–7, 402, 404, 411, 416, 419, 437,
       449–52, 524–5
    Holsteen (Dan), 204, 255, 333, 350,
       375, 377, 393, 401–5, 416–17, 419,
       432–3, 444, 449, 451–2, 456, 464–5,
       477, 479–81, 524–5
    Inconstant (Br), 12, 228
    Indfødsretten (Dan), 333, 350, 375, 377,
       402–3, 404, 411, 416–17, 419, 432,
       445, 451–2, 456–7, 524–5
    Investigator (Br), 183, 191
    Invincible (Br), 199, 238–9, 447–8
    Iris (Dan), 329, 335, 342, 405, 526
    Isis (Br), 154, 350, 353, 358, 361–4,
       367, 369–73, 377, 379–80, 382, 384,
       393, 414, 443, 450, 479–80, 528
    Jamaica (Br), 235, 313, 349–50, 372,
       378–9, 529
    Jylland (Dan), 206, 251, 332, 341, 349,
       364, 368, 372, 376, 383, 385–7, 393,
       404, 414, 447, 522–3
    King George (packet), 37
    Kite (Br), 242, 261, 276, 510
    Langesund (Dan), 334, 527
    Latona (Br), 100
    Lark (Br), 154, 235, 314, 318–19, 329
    Leviathan (Br), 200
    London (Br), 124, 154, 188–9, 192,
       194–5, 197, 217, 227–8, 235, 237,
       241–2, 251, 259, 261–4, 267–8,
       275–83, 290, 294–6, 298–9, 312–14,
       319–20, 350, 377, 393, 406–7, 423
       429, 432, 443, 445, 457, 459, 463–5,

Ships—*cont.*
473–4, 481–3, 496, 515–18, 521
Lynx (Br), 489, 494–5
Majestic (Br), 113
Marengo (Fr), 100
Mars (Dan), 329, 334, 349, 377, 402, 405, 420, 449–51, 526
Minerva (Br), 322
Monmouth (Br), 154, 358
Monarch (Br), 155, 196–7, 222, 224, 229, 296, 299–300, 304–5, 319, 323, 345, 349, 358, 364, 375, 395–402, 405–6, 410, 413, 417, 419, 425–7, 434, 443–4, 454, 479–81, 486, 516, 528
Namur (Br), 98
Naskou (Dan), 334, 527
Nemesis (Br), 60–1
Nidelven (Dan), 329, 334, 342, 405, 526
Nyeborg (Dan), 203, 331–2, 349, 365, 368, 372, 376, 383–5, 393, 404, 414, 436, 522–3
Nyøbing (Dan), 334, 527
Odense (Dan), 334, 527
Odin (Dan), 335
Otter (Br), 155, 351, 356, 377–9, 393, 407, 413, 427, 443–4, 529
Pegasus (Br), 26
Pelter (Br), 155
Phoenix (Br), 10
Polyphemus (Br), 154, 191, 226, 349–50, 363, 369–70, 379–80, 393, 408, 414, 528
Powerful (Br), 155, 231
Prince George (Br), 227
Princess Charlotte (Br), 86, 335
Prøvesteenen (Dan), 206, 251, 255–6, 330–1, 333, 337–8, 341, 345–7, 349–50, 362, 364–5, 367–72, 378–82, 385, 387–8, 404, 414, 450–1, 477, 522–3
Providentia (Nor), 156–7
Queen Charlotte (Br), 234
Raisonable (Br), 154, 226, 292, 519
Redbridge (Br), 234
Rendsborg (Dan), 203, 257, 331–2, 338, 342, 349–50, 365, 368, 372, 376, 381, 383–6, 392–3, 414, 449, 522–3
Revenge (Br), 226
Rota (Dan), 335

Rover (Br), 217, 482
Royal George (Br), 44
Ruby (Br), 154
Russell (Br), 124, 182, 231, 349–50, 358, 364–75, 377, 379, 385, 393, 408, 428, 434, 450, 529
St George (Br), 11, 97, 123–5, 154, 165, 169, 173, 181, 184–5, 191, 194–5, 198–9, 225, 262, 267–9, 277–83, 292–3, 313, 408, 429, 431, 434–5, 448, 455, 465, 473–4, 483–5, 492, 494, 496–8, 503, 508, 514
San Josef (Br), 19, 23, 86, 98, 111–12, 114–17, 119, 121–3
San Nicolas (Br), 19, 23, 98
Sarpen (Dan), 334, 405, 526
Saturn (Br), 124, 154, 227, 292
Sælland (Dan), 204, 255, 333, 350, 369, 373–5, 393–5, 406, 414, 416–17, 419, 432, 437, 444–5, 447, 449, 465, 479, 524–5
Søhesten (Dan), 254, 256, 350, 375, 395, 401, 403–4, 416–17, 447, 524–5
Søormen (Dan), 401
Sparkler (Br), 155
Spartiate (Br), 226
Squirrel (Br), 187
Staværn (Dan), 334, 527
Stege (Dan), 334, 527
Sværdfisken (Dan), 254, 256, 332–3, 349, 387, 393, 404, 414, 522–3
Teazer (Br), 155
Terror (Br), 155, 351, 529
Thalia (Br), 179
Tonnant (Br), 225
Trekroner (Dan), 257, 329, 335, 405, 526
Trimmer (Br), 155
Troy (Br), 492
Tygress (Br), 495
Vanguard (Br), 32
Venus (Russian), 504
Veteran (Br), 155, 231, 292, 317, 346–7, 376, 420–1, 519
Viborg (Dan), 334, 527
Victoire (Fr), 11
Victorieuse (Br), 155
Victory (Br), 227, 230, 233–4
Ville de Paris (Br), 116, 170
Volcano (Br), 155, 351, 378–9, 393, 407,

Ships—*cont.*
    416, 428, 529
    Voltigeur (Fr), 100
    Wagrien (Dan), 206, 251, 255, 331, 335, 338, 341, 349, 365, 368–72, 378, 380–3, 385–6, 393, 404, 414, 421, 522–3
    Warrior (Br), 124, 154, 225–6
    Windsor Castle (Br), 114, 119
    Wolverine (Br), 188
    Zealous (Br), 96, 426
    Zebra (Br), 155, 351, 529
    Zephyr (Br), 155, 351, 354, 356, 377–8, 427, 529
Shuldham, Lt Molyneux, 234, 386
Sidmouth, Lord *see* Addington, Henry
Signal Book, British, 317, 407, 426, 514–16, 519–21
Signal No. 39, 406–11, 429, 434, 514–21
Simcoe, Maj-general John G., 14, 110, 115, 119, 122
Slade, Sir Thomas, 230
Smith, William MP, 156–7
Sneedorff, Capt (later Rear-admiral) Hans C., 509
Sommerfeldt, Lt (later Capt) Søren S., 387, 522
Sotheron, Capt Frank, 100
Southey, Robert (biographer), 384
Southey, Lt Thomas, 356, 384
Spencer, David, 249
Spencer, George, 2nd Earl, Nelson to *San Josef*, 86; new job for Nelson, 109–10; considered Parker for Baltic, 110; resigns, tells St Vincent, 136; Mentioned, 7, 13–14, 35, 40–1, 43, 45, 47–8, 94, 98, 114–15, 118, 121, 123–4, 153, 177, 200, 510
Spencer, Georgiana, Countess, 42–3, 85, 122–3
Stephens, Sir Philip, Bt, MP, 140, 490
Stewart, Lt-colonel (later Lt-general the Hon. Sir) William, chosen by Duke of York, 152; troops embark, 181; describes Nelson, 181–2; visits Parker, 185–6; Nelson's plan, 186; describes Danish defences, 265–6; summarises problem, 269–92; Signal No. 39, 409–11, 515–17, 519; Truce, 417, 422–3, 429, 460, 466–8, 470, 474–5;

Mentioned, 190, 197–8, 241, 279, 296, 309, 311–12, 314–15, 320–3, 355–6, 367, 373–4, 379, 406, 432–3, 435, 477, 497, 499, 501–4, 506
Stibolt, Capt Jens P. (naval architect), 334, 522, 524, 526
Stricker's Battery, 327–8, 330, 364, 367–8
Stricker, Maj-general Ezechias Henrik, 204, 244, 252–4, 274, 295–9, 301–2, 305–7, 340
Stricker, Lt, 327–8, 330, 364, 367–8, 378
Struensee, Dr Johann, 76
Suffren de Tropez, Admiral Pierre de, 225
Sultan of Turkey (Selim III), 77, 134, 243
Sutton, Capt (later Rear-admiral) Samuel, 411, 444, 482, 529
Sweden, King of, *see* Gustavus IV

Talbot, James (British *charge d'affaires*, Sweden), 91–2, 208
Talleyrand-Perigord, Charles Maurice de, Prince of Benevento, 306
Tchitchagoff, Rear-admiral (Russian), 504–5
Telegraphs: London to Plymouth and Portsmouth, 170; Elsinore to Copenhagen, 124
Thesiger, Commander (later Capt Sir) Frederick, 177, 419, 421–4, 435, 437, 445
Thompson, Thomsom, pseudonyms, *see* Nelson
Thompson, Capt (later Vice-admiral) Sir Thomas B., 356, 370–1, 384, 449, 529
Thun, Capt Philip G. von, 526
Thura, Capt Albert de, 402, 456–7, 524
Tomlinson, Capt Nicholas, career, 174; plan for attack, 174–6; views on Sound, 276–7; Signal No. 39, 409, 515 Mentioned, 177, 188
Totty, Rear-admiral Thomas, 196, 199, 238–9, 509
Trekroner Fort ('Crown Island'), 328–9, 332–3, 335, 346–7, 351, 364, 377, 395, 402, 404–6, 411–14, 416–17, 419–24, 428, 432, 434, 449–51, 454, 458–9
Trigge, Lt-general Thomas, 106, 286–7
Troubridge, Capt (later Rear-admiral

Troubridge, Capt—cont.
  Sir) Thomas, 23, 39–40, 44, 56, 112,
  121, 140, 169–70, 172, 179, 187, 190–1,
  193–4, 196, 220, 229, 240, 243, 305,
  340, 436, 442, 455, 476, 479, 484, 490,
  508
Troubridge, Midshipman Edward T.,
  476
Truce: and Nelson, 414, 416–25, 429;
  and Parker, 428, 435; and Crown
  Prince, 417, 420–3, 428, 454; and
  Lindholm, 454; and Fischer, 451; and
  Stewart, 417, 423–3, 429
Tuchet, Midshipman the Hon. John,
  442
Tucker, Jebediah (St Vincent's
  secretary), 137–40, 159–60, 200
Tyler, Capt (later Vice-admiral Sir)
  Charles, 225
Tyler, Lt Charles, 225

Uldall, Lt (later Capt) Johan, 390, 477–8
Union, Act of, 93, 126, 135–6

Vansittart, Nicholas, MP (later 1st
  Baron Bexley), becomes junior
  minister, 143; Hesse mission, 144–7;
  meets Hesse, 207–8; meets Bernstorff,
  208–12; sends Parker report, 259; sees
  Parker, 265–9; reports to Addington,
  275;
  Mentioned, 149, 186, 193, 202, 214–
  15, 217, 220, 249, 260–4, 281, 285,
  298, 463
Vaubois, General, 55, 59–60
Vesconte, Lt Henry de, 235
Vick, Nathaniel (King's Messenger), 105
  129, 130, 141
Villeneuve, Admiral Pierre C. de, 60
Virgin Islands, capture of St Thomas,
  St John and St Croix, see West Indies,
  Operations in

Walker, Capt James, 369, 443, 528
Wallis, Thomas (purser), 418–19, 422–3

Waltersdorff, Ernst Frederik, Count,
  254, 457, 460, 463, 465, 468–9, 473–5
Wedel-Jarlsberg, Count de (Danish
  envoy, Britain), 95, 105–6, 147, 156,
  213–14, 245, 247, 300–1, 325–6
West Indies: Operations in, 54–5, 106,
  200, 286–7; Nelson in, 24–4, 434;
  sickness in, 54–5, 102; Trade in, 54–5,
  101–2
Westcott, Capt George, 113
Westcott, Mrs, 113
Whitelocke, Maj-general John, 181
Whitworth, Charles, 1st Baron, 61, 64,
  100, 500
Wilks, Lt Thomas, 384
William Henry, Prince (later Duke of
  Clarence; William IV), 26, 41, 59, 87,
  227, 496
Williams, Samuel (Americal consul,
  London), 222
Willes, Edward (Decipherer of Letters),
  103
Willemoes, Lt Peter, 256–7, 458, 471, 524
Wleugal, Lt (later Admiral) Peter J.,
  369, 386, 420
Wleugal, Vice-admiral Johan P., 204,
  420
Worontzow, Count (Russian envoy,
  Britain), 480
Wrestler's Arms, Great Yarmouth, 172,
  185, 186
Wulff, Lt (Anton Johan) Rasmus, 343,
  392, 456
Wynne, Elizabeth, see Fremantle, Lady
  Elizabeth
Wynne, Eugenia, 228
Wynne, Richard, 228

Yelland, Lt (later Capt) John, 354, 397,
  399–400, 426–7, 442–4
York, Duke of, see Frederick
Young, Vice-admiral William, 123, 517–
  18
Youlden, Henry (master's mate), 442

DAVENPORT
MERRILLVILLE, IN 46410

P9-EDL-418

025.04 G428f
Gilster, Paul, 1949-
Finding it on the Internet
: the Internet Navigator's
Internet.

$24.95

53461

DATE			
AG 15 '96			

DAVENPORT COLL MERRILLVILLE

Finding it on the Internet.

53461

JE 26 '96

DAVENPORT COLLEGE LIBRARY
MERRILLVILLE, IN 46410

BAKER & TAYLOR

FINDING IT ON THE INTERNET

The Internet Navigator's Guide to Search Tools and Techniques

REVISED AND EXPANDED, SECOND EDITION

Paul Gilster

John Wiley & Sons, Inc.

NEW YORK • CHICHESTER • BRISBANE • TORONTO • SINGAPORE

I know of nothing more pleasant, or more instructive, than to compare experience with expectation, or to register from time to time the difference between idea and reality. It is by this kind of observation that we grow daily less liable to be disappointed.

Samuel Johnson

Publisher: Katherine Schowalter
Editor: Philip Sutherland
Assistant Editor: Allison Roarty
Managing Editor: Susan Curtin
Text Design & Composition: North Market Street Graphics, Selena Chronister

Designations used by companies to distinguish their products are often claimed as trademarks. In all instances where John Wiley & Sons, Inc. is aware of a claim, the product names appear in initial capital or all capital letters. Readers, however, should contact the appropriate companies for more complete information regarding trademarks and registration.

This text is printed on acid-free paper.

Copyright © 1996 Paul Gilster
Published by John Wiley & Sons, Inc.

All rights reserved. Published simultaneously in Canada.

This publication is designed to provide accurate and authoritative information in regard to the subject matter covered. It is sold with the understanding that the publisher is not engaged in rendering legal, accounting, or other professional service. If legal advice or other expert assistance is required, the services of a competent professional person should be sought.

Reproduction or translation of any part of this work beyond that permitted by section 107 or 108 of the 1976 United States Copyright Act without the permission of the copyright owner is unlawful. Requests for permission or further information should be addressed to the Permissions Department, John Wiley & Sons, Inc.

Library of Congress Cataloging-in-Publication Data
Gilster, Paul
     Finding it on the Internet : the Internet navigator's guide to search tools and techniques / Paul Gilster. — Rev. and expanded, 2nd ed.
          p.   cm.
     Includes index.
     ISBN 0-471-12695-0 (alk. paper)
     1. Internet (Computer network)   2. World Wide Web (Information retrieval system)   I. Title.
     TK5105.875.I57G54   1996
     025.04—dc20   95-25739
                                                                      CIP

Printed in the United States of America
10 9 8 7 6 5 4 3 2 1

Contents in Brief

FOREWORD   xv
PREFACE   xvii

Chapter 1   Tools of the Navigator   1

Chapter 2   The World Wide Web: Hypertext as Search Tool   11

Chapter 3   Gopher: Finding Resources by Menu   85

Chapter 4   Veronica: Gopher as Search Engine   127

Chapter 5   archie: Finding Files   155

Chapter 6   WAIS: Searching for Text   187

Chapter 7   HYTELNET: Finding Telnet Sites   229

Chapter 8   WHOIS, netfind, X.500: Finding People   259

Chapter 9   E-Mail: Noninteractive Searching   309

Chapter 10   The Future of Internet Searching   349

GLOSSARY   361
INDEX   369

Contents

FOREWORD   xv
PREFACE   xvii

Chapter 1   The Tools of the Navigator   **1**

A Word on Methodology   2
The Tools and Their Potential   3
   The World Wide Web   4
   Gopher   5
   Veronica   5
   archie   5
   WAIS   6
   HYTELNET   6
   Library Tools   7
   WHOIS, X.500, and More   7
   Mailing Lists   7
A Search Methodology   8
   The Realistic Search   9

Chapter 2   The World Wide Web: Hypertext as Search Tool   **11**

The Nature of Hypertext   12
The Web's Resources   13
Exploring the Web   14
   Reading a Document On-Line with the Web   14

vii

Accessing the World Wide Web   16
Using a World Wide Web Browser   19
World Wide Web Terminology   20
World Wide Web Directories   21
Scott Yanoff's Special Internet Connections   22
Using the Yahoo Directory   26
Searching with Galaxy   32
Keyword Search Methodology at a Directory Site   35
Argus—The Clearinghouse for Subject-Oriented Internet
    Resource Guides   38
BTG Hot List   39
CMC Information Sources   39
The Combined AAUP Journals Catalog   39
Commercial Sites Index   39
The Electronic Journals Database Overview   39
FTP Sites Lists   39
Global Network Navigator   40
INFOMINE   40
The Interactive Yellow Pages   40
Internet Resources Meta-Index   40
InterNIC Directory of Directories   40
The ISP Internet Yellow Pages   40
The Mother-of-all BBS   41
New Riders' Official World Wide Web Yellow Pages   41
The OTIS Index   41
Publicly Accessible Mailing Lists   41
TILE.NET   41
Web of Wonder   41
The Web Pointer   42
The World Wide Web Virtual Library   42
Worldwide Yellow Pages   42
The yellowPages.com   43
Work Software Yellow Pages   43
Robots, Spiders, and Other Search Tools   43
Running a Search with The Web Crawler   45
How The Web Crawler Works   47
The Lycos Server   49
The World Wide Web Worm   53
JumpStation   57
InfoSeek   59
Harvest   61
NIKOS—A World Wide Web Index   61
RBSE's URL Database   61
The Open Text Index   61
World Wide Web Wanderer/WANDEX   62

Other Web-Based Search Tools   63
    ALIWEB   63
    The Awesome Lists   63
    CUSI   64
    Global On-Line Directory   65
    The Internet Sleuth   65
    W3 Catalog   65
    Bookmarks—Organizing Your Search Tools   65
    Adding a Bookmark   67
    Organizing a Bookmark List   68
    Creating a New Header   69
    Adding Bookmarks under Particular Headers   69
    Headers within Headers   70
    Using Separators   70
    Viewing Bookmark Information   70
    Importing and Exporting Bookmarks   71
    Views of the Bookmark Page   72
    Keeping the Bookmark List Timely   72
    Bookmarks for the Shell Account User   73
World Wide Web Tips   73
    Choose Your Tools with Care   74
    Be Prepared to Wait   74
    Construct a Comprehensive Bookmark List   74
    Run Benchmark Searches   74
    Be Wary of Title Searches   75
    Learn How the Site Functions   75
    Picture Your Result   75
    Use Specific Search Terms   75
    Be Prepared to Change Your Terms   76
    Use Relevance Rankings with Great Caution   76
    Adjust the Number of Hits   76
    Arrange Your Results by Topic   76
    Consider Other Search Tools   77
Web Browsers and SLIP/PPP   77
Web Browsers as All-Purpose Interfaces   78
    Gopher through a Web Browser   78
    FTP through a Browser   79
    Reading USENET News with a Browser   81
    Running a Telnet Session in a Browser   83
A Mandate for Searching   84

Chapter 3   Gopher: Finding Resources by Menu   85

Searching as Process   86
The Nature of Gopherspace   86

Accessing Gopher   90
    A Choice of Clients   91
        Using Telnet to Access Gopher   92
What's Available via Gopher?   93
Learning to Use Gopher   94
Mastering the Unix Gopher Client   98
File Viewing Commands   99
    File Management Commands   100
    Using Gopher with Bookmarks   100
Gopher's Search Capabilities   107
The WSGopher Toolbar   109
    The WSGopher Menu Structure   110
Examining Gopher's Resources   112
    Using Gopher's Telnet Connection   113
    Using Gopher to Find Files   115
    Using Gopher with WAIS   119
    Using CCSO Name Servers with Gopher   120
    Gopher's Sights and Sounds   121
Keeping Up with Gopher   124
    The Future of Gopher   124

Chapter 4   Veronica: Gopher as Search Engine   127

How Veronica Works   128
Accessing Veronica   129
    Using Gopher Client to Reach Veronica   129
    Using Telnet to Reach Veronica   130
    A More Specific Search   132
    Refining the Search   135
    Using Gopher's Data Types with Veronica   136
A Sample Search for Information about CD-ROMs   138
A Veronica Strategy Emerges   141
Combining Keywords to Search   142
Summarizing Veronica's Search Options   146
Sample Veronica Search Terms   147
Occasional Frustrations of Using Veronica   148
Using Jughead   150
    Locating a Jughead Server   151
    Tips on Using Veronica   151

Chapter 5   archie: Finding Files   155

The Nature of File Transfer Protocol   155
archie Scouts the Internet Terrain   158

Using archie   160
Using Telnet to Search with archie   161
    A Sample Search Using archie with Telnet   165
    archie's Command Options Using Telnet   167
    Setting Up archie   168
    Changing Your Search Parameters   168
    Where and What archie Searches   169
    Controlling archie's Output   170
    Sorting Commands   171
Choosing an Output Format   171
    Activating the Status Line   172
    Miscellaneous archie Commands   173
The (Sometimes) Helpful whatis Command   173
archie through a Client Program   177
    Using archie's Command Switches   177
    An archie Search Methodology   185

Chapter 6   WAIS: Searching for Text   187

How WAIS Works   188
What You Can Find with WAIS   188
Accessing WAIS   189
A Sample WAIS Search Using swais   191
The Nature of Content Navigation   195
The Basic swais Commands   197
    swais Movement Commands   197
    swais Search Commands   197
    Miscellaneous swais Commands   198
    WAIS Keyword Limitations   198
    Using a Graphical WAIS Client   198
    The Basic WinWAIS Commands   207
A Routine WAIS Strategy   209
    WAIS through the World Wide Web   211
Using Gopher to Access WAIS   214
Using waissearch for Specific Servers   217
Interesting WAIS Sites   220
Keeping Up with WAIS   227

Chapter 7   HYTELNET: Finding Telnet Sites   229

Using HYTELNET   230
    HYTELNET Servers   231
    Downloading HYTELNET   231

Putting HYTELNET to Work   232
The HYTELNET Commands   237
HYTELNET as Search Tool   238
    Searching for The Well   239
HYTELNET and Library Resources   242
Using HYTELNET through the World Wide Web   243
Using HYTELNET through Gopher   244
Keeping Up with HYTELNET   246
LIBTEL: An On-Line Library Resource   247
Using LIBS to Search Remote Libraries   249
Gopher as Library Tool   251
The World Wide Web and Library Searching   254

Chapter 8   WHOIS, netfind, X.500: Finding People   259

X.500 and the Search for Addressing Standards   260
X.400: What It Is and How It Works   261
    How X.400 Differs from TCP/IP Electronic Mail   261
X.500 as a Directory Service   262
X.500 Connection Options   263
    By Telnet to an X.500 Server   263
The NameFLOW-Paradise Service: A Different Interface   266
Using Gopher to Run an X.500 Search   268
    X.500 through a Web Browser   269
WHOIS as a Search Tool   271
    Accessing WHOIS   272
    Using WHOIS through Telnet   272
    Tips on Using WHOIS by Telnet   276
netfind: Fingering the Right Person   282
    Accessing netfind   282
    Accessing netfind with Telnet   283
    How netfind Works   284
    netfind Search Strategies   289
What Is finger Information   291
Knowbots and Intelligent Searching   293
    Using the Knowbot by Telnet   293
    The Knowbot through the World Wide Web   296
    Using the Knowbot by Electronic Mail   296
CCSO Directories   298
Campus Wide Information Systems   301
Searching the USENET Archives   303
Two New Directory Services on the Web   306
Going to the Source   307

Chapter 9   E-Mail: Noninteractive Searching   **309**

    archie through Electronic Mail   309
    archie by E-Mail Commands   310
    A Sample archie Search Using Electronic Mail   311
    WAIS by Electronic Mail   312
        Constructing a WAISmail Search   313
        A Sample WAISmail Search   313
        The WAISmail Commands   315
        Binary Files through WAISmail   318
    Gopher by Electronic Mail   318
        A GopherMail Query   320
        Limiting GopherMail's Output   321
        Going Directly to a Gopher   322
        A GopherMail Search Using Veronica   322
    finger by Electronic Mail   325
    WHOIS by Electronic Mail   326
    Checking Internet IP Addresses   327
    Searching a Mailing List Archive Site   329
        A Mailing List Search Paradigm   329
        Targeting the Right Mailing List   330
        Sending for an Index   331
    Constructing the Search   333
        Requesting Messages from the LISTSERV   333
        The Typical Mailing List Search   334
        The View from Eastern Europe   335
        Automating the Search with InfoMagnet   339
        More Mailing List Sources   341
        Reading More on Mailing List Searching   342
    Finding and Using Other Mail Servers   342
    A Sample Mail Server Search   343
        Interesting Mail Server Sites   344

Chapter 10   The Future of Internet Searching   **349**

    The Emergence of CNIDR   351
    Building Search Engines   353
    Taming the Kudzu Patch   354
    The Nature of the Internet Search   355
    What the Internet Needs   356
    Growing into a Worldwide Cyberspace   358

    GLOSSARY   361
    INDEX   369

Foreword

It has been three years now since the Clearinghouse for Networked Information Discovery and Retrieval was funded by the National Science Foundation. Today I find myself reflecting on how information technology has changed and how it has affected my life. Clearly, the hardware has gotten more powerful and for much less cost. Today there is another distinction that many of us take for granted—the interactive quality of the Internet. We used to have the mail-order catalog approach to services on the network. You know, send a piece of email with a request, and then wait for something to be returned. Oh, we had telnet and ftp where you could log onto a remote computer but there was nothing like what we have now—a click and things happen—sounds, images, video, and information arrive on the desktop. It is truly amazing to be able to navigate this thing we call the Internet.

To navigate is a crucial idea. We talk about surfing or cruising the net as though we're just going around the block for a soda. The most exciting software lately has been the World Wide Web browsers that permit you to wander through home pages and remote sites. But surfing, cruising, and browsing do not bring to mind a conscious or well-defined route from the question to the answer. That is one of the challenges for new arrivals at the portals of cyberspace—how to go in, find what you need, get back out, and then return if necessary. *Finding It on the Internet Second Edition* will prove to be a welcome addition to a new adventurer's navigational kit. Although it is not a map per se, it teaches you to read the signs, and to choose which tool to do the work. You wouldn't use a magnifying glass to see objects far away, nor would you have much success with looking at the ground with binoculars. Paul Gilster's scenarios provide similar framework for the novice navigator to compare Internet tools.

Recently, I was on a flight. It was a clear day and I had a window seat at 37,000 miles somewhere over the United States. As I looked out the window I saw many different landmarks. Some were natural, while others had been built. Suddenly I had a flash of insight into why so many folks panic when introduced to the Internet, the information superhighway, or cyberspace. Below me I knew there were thousands of people, tens of thousands of television sets, and perhaps millions of socks. Those are just three examples of an almost infinite number of different things that I was moving above. As I moved along at 400 miles per hour even more objects passed under me. The larger ones I could see. The smaller ones I only imagined. My imagination ran away with me. I pulled down the window shade to give myself a rest. Wow! What an incredible amount of stuff there is in this world we live in. I was overwhelmed. Then I stopped and closed my eyes. When I opened them again all I saw was the back of the seat in front of me, my book on the small table, and the glass of ginger ale. Now that's something I can deal with.

In a similar way Paul Gilster will take you, the reader, and lead you step by step through different tool sets to develop skills and strategies to close your eyes to the worldwide Internet and focus on the burning questions you need answered. It is that attention to detail, the here and now, that will make your search for useful information much more fruitful.

George H. Brett II
Clearinghouse for Networked Information
Discovery and Retrieval
Research Triangle Park, North Carolina
George.Brett@mcnc.org

Preface

The most pleasant surprise for any Internet researcher is the development of World Wide Web search tools. In the past 18 months, we have seen the Web's evolution into a searchable information space, accessible through a wide variety of software engines. The degree of experimentation and the pace of development, however, has ensured that searchers still have their work cut out for them. Which engine to use, and for what purpose, will remain key components of any Internet search. Nevertheless, it is safe to say that we will begin to rely more and more upon the Web as the first stop on our information gathering expeditions, and the effectiveness of the new engines will help us find what we need faster than ever before.

We should not, however, make the mistake of assuming that one or two sweeps through the World Wide Web suffice as a data hunt. It was clear when the first edition of this book appeared, and remains clear today, that the Internet is populated by a huge variety of information resources, many of them poorly catalogued and difficult to locate. With any search engine, the key is to learn its limitations. We must ask: What does it access, and how thoroughly? What kind of data types can it find, and of those, how much information can it retrieve? Beyond this, how does it construct its searches; how often does it update its database? Searchers who ignore such issues are doomed to incomplete results, a fate I hope this book may deter.

Indeed, just as there is no single World Wide Web search engine that can be considered comprehensive, there is no single Internet search tool that suffices. A properly constructed search is one that takes into account the varied types of network information and proceeds accordingly. Yes, it is true that we have seen a marked slowdown in the number of new Gophers, while Web sites have multiplied in the thousands, but we cannot afford to ignore the possibility that a Gopher somewhere may contain just the text file we need. The same can be said for WAIS databases, for FTP sites, and the whole panoply of Internet-accessible materials. It would be comforting to turn all our work over to a single software tool, but ultimately, it would also be deluding; the Internet remains a tricky beast to master, one that demands a full measure of our resourcefulness.

The new structure of *Finding It on the Internet*, then, is designed to suggest a paradigm. Begin with the World Wide Web, using both directory sites and search engines. Tap these with attention to how they are constructed and how they conduct their searches. Move on if necessary to Gopher, searching it through the Veronica engine. Be ready to consult FTP sites if binary files are called for, using archie as accessible through its various clients, and don't forget to consult a directory of servers to see which WAIS databases may prove useful to the job. HYTELNET should be examined to see whether any Telnet-accessible databases can supply information, while both LIBS and LIBTEL offer library and university information. E-mail only searchers will find directions for using the majority of these tools by mail, while those hunting individuals will also find instructions on using the Internet's cumbersome, but occasionally effective, white pages directories. Development of these and other tools proceeds all over the world, and continues to be encouraged by the Clearinghouse for Networked Information Discovery and Retrieval, here in North Carolina.

My thanks go out to Joe Ragland, a friend and Internet expert who signed on to review the manuscript, as he has done for previous books. Thanks, too, to Alan Blatecky and George Brett at CNIDR, whose valuable insights have always helped me obtain an overview of the complicated game of Internet searching. The many readers who weighed in with comments of their own about the various search tools were a source of continual inspiration. Finally, the team that has always supported me at John Wiley & Sons once again proved their mettle. Phil Sutherland and Allison Roarty are easy people to work with, but always there when insight is required, and the production team, from Frank Grazioli to Janice Borzendowski, and the invaluable suggestions of Bob Ipsen and Jeff Demarais, have added materially to this book.

1

The Tools of the Navigator

When you think about it, the Internet is all about questions. A global information network is too big to use like a conventional library resource; there aren't any librarians, few catalogs exist, and you can't just wander aimlessly through thousands of World Wide Web pages, Gopher sites, WAIS databases, USENET newsgroups, mailing list archives and FTP directory listings, browsing for what you need. To make the Internet work for you requires a different model. You must find out how to harness the power of its computers, learning to run software engines designed to extract the ore from tons of network slag. It can be a frustrating experience. Consider:

- Somewhere on the Internet, there is a collection of texts and photographs of papyrus manuscripts from ancient Egypt. Over 1,000 searchable records of these papyri exist, along with 200 images, in languages ranging from Greek and Latin to Demotic (a script developed from hieroglyphs) to Coptic (ancient Egyptian written with Greek letters). You're writing a research paper for a class in ancient history and would like to have a look at this collection. How do you find it? And if you can track it down, how do you know whether it's an authoritative source or the work of a hobbyist?
- Somewhere at one of thousands of FTP sites around the globe, a personal information manager exists that can help you organize your crowded schedule and extract more productivity out of your day. It comes highly recommended, and you know that it's available at numerous locations. But how do you learn the FTP address to make the retrieval? Just as important, how do you know you've received the latest version, rather than a beta copy of shareware that was posted years ago?
- Somewhere in a major corporation an old friend from college now works as a vice president. You'd like to send electronic mail to renew the acquaintance, but you've no idea what her address is. Is there a way to track down an electronic mail address without calling up the person in question and simply asking? You know

that numerous directories are found on the Internet. Which do you use, and how? Perhaps most important, how do you know the address you finally get is accurate?

Some of these questions are relatively straightforward; this book is about finding the answers to them. We can certainly go out and find information on the Internet. In fact, the range of tools at our disposal is relatively large. We can look at Gophers around the world, navigating through their easy-to-use menu structure. We can search large numbers of these menus with Veronica. Names can be checked with WHOIS and netfind, while large-text databases can be searched with WAIS (Wide Area Information Servers). The World Wide Web, a collection of thousands of interlinked multimedia documents, is now searchable as well, through tools like Web Crawler, Lycos, and the World Wide Web Worm. We can also use topic-indexed lists of Web sites, homing in ever more precisely on the location of our information. I will show you the techniques that make all this possible, along with sample searches that will allow you to test your new skills.

Other of the questions, however, are harder to answer. Yes, we can find information, but how good is it? How do we establish its authoritativeness, or determine its age, or keep ourselves from finding the same information under different names at different sites? Just how useful is information on the Internet anyway, and how far should we trust it? Without doubt, the notion of a digital library is intriguing, but I must raise a warning flag. The Internet is far from being a satisfactory library. Networked information is in its infancy, as a generation of frustrated librarians know. We must, then, separate the hype from the reality.

You can do more with the Internet than you probably thought possible by way of finding information, but you probably can't do as much as you would like to, at least not until the tools to expand its present holdings and validate its archives become more precise. So as we take this journey, examining Internet search methods and the tools that make them fly, remember to keep your eyes on the future. This is a book about a subject that has never been in so great a state of flux. The evolution of the tools we will work with is a critical story in the future of knowledge dissemination. How it turns out depends upon us.

A Word on Methodology

The movement toward graphical client software on the Internet in the past several years has been striking. It is an outgrowth of the fact that more and more providers are making low-cost SLIP (Serial Line Internet Protocol) and PPP (Point-to-Point Protocol) connections available. This book makes no presumptions about your method of access; I will show you how to use the basic search tools in a variety of formats, from character-based Unix client programs to graphical tools like WinWAIS and WSGopher, and World Wide Web browsers like Netscape. The idea is not so much to show you keystroke by keystroke what to do, but to illustrate broader principles of searching. You will need to adapt these principles to whatever client programs best meet your needs, although I will suggest those I think are the most effective as we proceed.

Standard dial-up accounts use a modem to connect to a service provider's computer; it is the service provider's machine that is on the Internet, using the Internet's protocols and working with various client programs. The dial-up user takes advantage of whatever client programs the service provider has made available on its machine. The interface is character-based and works through terminal emulation, making the remote computer think that it is talking to a terminal rather than to a separate computer.

A SLIP (or PPP) connection, on the other hand, makes it possible for the user's desktop machine to go directly on the Internet. Rather than working with someone else's clients, the user decides which clients he or she would like to run on the computer. And because the machine is now running TCP/IP (the set of protocols that makes the Internet function) itself, it is possible to use a wide variety of client programs. In short, such a user is no longer limited to terminal emulation and character-based programs. Instead, his or her own computer is a full-fledged part of the Internet and can act like it.

What kind of access is best for searching? There is no easy answer. Some search tools, especially WAIS, are much more approachable when presented through a graphical interface. This is more a function of the weakness of the character-based client programs available for WAIS than a commentary on character-based clients in general. Other programs, Gopher being the outstanding example, are available in full-featured Unix clients that can as readily be used through a shell account as with a graphical client. But with the explosive growth of the World Wide Web showing no sign of abating, most users will want to migrate into the SLIP/PPP environment to take advantage of the graphical browsers like Mosaic and Netscape. While the character-based lynx browser is quite well designed, it cannot show the graphical features that distinguish the best Web sites. The mixture of access types and client options I will show you in this book may suggest that only rarely does a single tool suffice to handle a given job, and that the latitude offered by the Internet in this regard is wide.

The Tools and Their Potential

Just a few years ago, the Internet search problem was rarely considered. Resources were appearing at sites worldwide, from text files to programs of various kinds, from images to sound, and people went about their work within relatively small communities that shared knowledge. You knew about the local database on meteorology because you saw someone tap it from his or her terminal; perhaps you passed the information along to a colleague at a later date. The directory of campus information was useful because you could check out concert schedules; but perhaps it didn't occur to you that other campuses were building directories. In any case, you found out about such projects by word of mouth.

The great story of the Internet in the 1990s is the movement away from this anecdotal approach to data gathering and toward a rational system of organization. Not that we have arrived at this goal—the horizon is distant. But the concept that we could use networked computer power to organize an inherently chaotic sea of information has taken hold. Or perhaps an aeronautical metaphor is more apt. For we are in an era much like the early days of aviation, when it seemed that every week brought some new record set, some new design tested, and people were out building experimental aircraft in their garages. It was a time when almost anything could happen, and often did.

Thus, Gopher. This superb approach to organizing information came about not through some central plan handed down by committee but through the efforts of a team of computer programmers and system administrators who were simply thinking on their feet. The University of Minnesota was computerizing, its networks jammed with faculty and students, many of whom had questions. How to answer them, without spending all day every day as teachers, was the motivation for Mark McCahill and the team that built Gopher. How were they to know that it would catch, that soon there would be thousands of Gophers around the globe, linking together, growing, pointing to data?

The World Wide Web is an even better example. Indeed, the surge in Gopher sites is now subsiding as more and more information providers switch into the hyperlinked environment of the Web. The concept of linking multimedia information files using a hypertext system made sense to the physicists at CERN, the giant Swiss research center; it would offer them a way to keep in communication no matter where they were located around the globe. Who could have foreseen that the whole Web idea would, in the hands of talented software developers in the United States, turn into the Internet's first smash hit, a program called Mosaic, which revolutionized the way we access the network? And who would have thought that the combination of graphical browsing, intuitive commands, and lowering access costs would trigger a rush onto the Internet of such startling magnitude? But breakthroughs are so frequently unforeseen.

Search tools, then, grow up out of the needs of a small community of users attacking a specific problem. Word of the tool spreads as others find it helpful; soon it is adopted at another site, and the two begin to exchange information. Before long, the tool is worldwide; system administrators realize they need to tap its power, and its momentum becomes unstoppable. At this point, perhaps the tool's designers realize they are dealing with a commercial proposition. Gopher is now a commercial product, as is archie, as is at least one implementation of WAIS; so, too, are the legions of new Web browsers. In Chapter 10, we will examine how such commercialization may affect the continuing development of these tools in the light of the necessity for standards. Our tools, after all, must operate together.

The same is true of all of the search tools that have brought such excitement—and, let's face it—such frustration to the Internet. We will examine each in turn. This book is about these tools and how to use them.

The World Wide Web

Hypertext provides a unique take on displaying information. By adding hypertext links to a document, you are enabling your reader to jump from one item to another within the document; reading takes on a nonsequential flavor driven not by the original author's sense of organization but by the information needs of the reader. For some kinds of text, this approach is a valuable way to cut to the chase, drawing maximum benefit from a document with the least amount of time. Add in hypertext links *between* documents and you begin to create an information space with no formal pathways. You begin at one end and explore. No two paths through the labyrinth are precisely the same.

The World Wide Web was developed by Tim Berners-Lee and his colleagues at CERN; developmental work continues in the hands of Berners-Lee and the World Wide Web Consortium. Propelled by Mosaic, the first great Internet interface, the Web became a comprehensive approach to information retrieval. Its remarkable growth has propelled the creation of new access programs, like Netscape, that control how we connect to the resources of the Internet. Like Gopher, the Web connects us to numerous resources, from Telnet to FTP to WAIS and more. Material from USENET newsgroups is accessible through the Web, as are graphics images and sound files. As a browsing environment, the Web offers unparalleled access to network resources with little overhead; you can become proficient on this tool within minutes, and spend hours moving through the data sea.

For all its seductions, though, the Web and its hypertext links cannot offer everything. The price of browsing is time. Your ramblings through the Web will reveal sites and files you never dreamed existed, but the ability to cut directly to the material you need is only now being developed. We are seeing frenzied development of tools like Web Crawler, Lycos, and the World Wide Web Worm, each designed to provide keyword-driven searches of the thousands of home pages now available. Some of these tools are more accurate than others; some sacrifice comprehensiveness for speed. The point is, the Web is a great starting point for a search, but it shouldn't be your only option. Sometimes a Veronica search will serve you better, or a quick run with archie through a bank of FTP sites. Experience with each tool will suggest which is best for a given situation.

Gopher

Gopher is all about menus. Show people that they can reach your resource, not by issuing a complex command at the system prompt, but simply by moving an arrow around on the screen with their cursor keys, then pressing RETURN to examine the document. As we'll see, Gopher also opens doors. You can move to what appears to be an item of local information on a Gopher submenu, only to discover that it actually exists on a distant computer. Press a RETURN, and you activate a Telnet session to visit the site. Gopher, we will learn, is dynamic, referring to resources throughout a worldwide Gopherspace.

Veronica

Fred Barrie and Steven Foster at the University of Nevada at Reno realized that along with Gopher's powerful interface came several inherent problems. Gopher was propagating as a client/server tool throughout the Internet, but there was no way to know what was on the menus at another Gopher site without actually logging on there to look. As more and more system administrators began putting useful resources on-line, the dimensions of this problem grew. There had to be some way to identify Gopher files.

Veronica grew out of this need. Essentially an indexing system, Veronica servers regularly check Gopher sites around the globe to examine their menu titles. When you run a Veronica search, you are consulting this database and checking it against your own keywords. A Veronica search never leaves the Gopher environment, producing results that appear as Gopher menus, and which, like any Gopher items, can be accessed by pointing to them and pressing the RETURN key.

We will examine Veronica as an essential adjunct to Gopher; indeed, it's hard to imagine how you could draw maximum benefit from the Gopher system other than with the help of Veronica. Unfortunately, Veronica also illustrates a growing problem throughout the Internet: Demand is intense, the load on the limited number of Veronica servers is high, and delays and inability to connect are a common occurrence. Veronica, as we will see, demands patience, and an understanding that the tools we use and the sprawling network that supports them are still very much under construction.

archie

Think of information as Peter Deutsch and Alan Emtage once saw it. McGill University's School of Computer Science needed useful software. Examining FTP sites around the Internet was a necessity, but the process was labor-intensive, calling for the user to tap into a site and check, directory by directory, what was available. Information as fortress, with each fiefdom containing its own archives, and no link between castles but a single FTP connection. Something had to be done.

The archie tool that resulted from this dilemma automated what Deutsch and Emtage did manually; it conducted sweeps of selected FTP sites and stored the results in an indexed database. When you consult an archie server, you are checking your search term against such a database, which then produces hits showing you where to find the file you need. The public domain software program you would have spent hours locating by happenstance is now provided to you in a series of sites with appropriate directories and filenames. You have but to FTP to the site and retrieve a copy.

Now in commercial development through Bunyip Information Systems, archie is expanding in significant new directions. The critical need: bring more information to bear on the results of the typical archie search. As things now stand, your search will produce sites and filenames, but you have no way of knowing whether the program you're retrieving is the most recent version or an older implementation. Bunyip is responding to this dilemma by encouraging the implementation of *templates,* which will contain file information about the holdings at various FTP sites. The widespread use of such templates would make archie searching considerably more effective.

WAIS

Wide Area Information Servers makes large databases of information accessible. Developed through research efforts at Thinking Machines Corp. in Cambridge, Massachusetts, with the help of corporate sponsorship from Apple Computer, KPMG Peat Marwick, and Dow Jones and Co., WAIS has become a major search engine.

We will learn how to run such searches even as we cope with inherent WAIS limitations, which you, the end user, will experience. If you're using a shell account to access the Internet, you'll find the WAIS client program (called swais) is primitive and hard to manipulate. SLIP/PPP users can tap graphical clients like WinWAIS that do a much better job of displaying results and allowing you to home in on your target. Even so, WAIS suffers from a lack of databases in many fields—it's largely concentrated in the sciences at the moment—and the system shows a puzzling tendency to produce search results seemingly unrelated to your goals.

These are problems I will address because it will do you no favors to paint an over-optimistic view of Internet searching. Each search tool has powerful advantages and, as we'll see, limitations. We can find ways around some of them; for others, we will have to supplement our searching with one tool by reference to another. In many cases, we will find what we need; in some, we won't. The good news is that things are getting better. All of these tools remain under active development; in the case of WAIS, WAIS Inc. pursues new commercial applications under the guidance of Brewster Kahle, the creator of WAIS; its recent purchase by America Online points to a much broader audience for the WAIS protocols. And the Clearinghouse for Networked Information Discovery and Retrieval in Research Triangle Park, North Carolina, supports an active program of research and development, centered around a freeware program called Zdist and related issues of resource discovery.

HYTELNET

A take on hypertext that differs from that of the World Wide Web is provided by HYTELNET, a program developed by Peter Scott at the University of Saskatchewan.

Available as a standalone program as well as a networked tool, HYTELNET points to Telnet resources and can be a quick way for you to determine everything from the location of a database on agriculture to the address needed to search an on-line library in New Zealand. The program is maintained at an FTP site and is frequently updated to reflect network changes. You can also use a Web browser to search its database.

Library Tools

The library community has been fertile ground for the development of Internet tools. And no wonder. The diverse needs of those who access voluminous information through computers have prompted the widespread appearance of library catalogs on the network. We also examine the library question through such tools as LIBTEL and LIBS. We are a long way from the digital library spoken of so enthusiastically in the press, but the appearance of such tools points to a future where networks take on the task of providing high-quality reference material on-line.

WHOIS, X.500, and More

Sooner or later, the problem of how to find people on the Internet will surface. If you're used to thinking of computers as marvelous data managers, you'll presume that somewhere an Internet directory exists, allowing you to query it by name or location to determine an electronic mail address. To your astonishment, you will quickly learn that instead of a single, comprehensive directory, there exist hundreds of tiny directories. Often they cover the people at a particular organization. What's worse, you can't query them until you know the separate address for each directory.

Millions of people use the global Internet, but only a fraction of them are accessible through electronic searching. The tools we use, from WHOIS to the automated Knowbot program to the White Pages directories using the X.500 standard, compel us to master diverse techniques, search widely through distributed databases, and as often as not, come up short in our search. We will examine the frustrations and occasional breakthroughs of people-oriented searching by working through sample searches for each tool.

Mailing Lists

Your electronic mailbox provides the opportunity to listen in on specialized conversations on most any topic. By subscribing to a mailing list, you are giving permission for each posting sent to that list to be sent to your mailbox as well. Keeping up with such conversations is a great way to learn about new ideas in your line of work or to pursue a hobby. But mailing lists can also be research tools, for many of them keep archives of their postings at computer sites around the Internet. These sites are seldom tapped, since using them depends upon a knowledge of the software with which they were created. But getting up to speed on mailing list research requires mastering only a few commands; the rest is simply a matter of practice.

Many mailing lists work through automated programs like LISTSERV, Majordomo, and Listproc. These programs allow the moderators of the list to consign the basic administrative chores to computers, which handle subscription processing and other tasks by receiving and acting upon specific commands. The same software can be used to search a mailing list's archives, even if the commands to do so seem clumsy and require that every request be formatted in a precise way. We'll go through the commands for LISTSERV in these pages. Learning how to use them will make mailing list archives a handy research tool.

A Search Methodology

The truth about Internet searching is this: Both the network and its navigational instruments are in their infancy. Searching can uncover unexpected terrain, sometimes rich with promise. It can just as likely turn up parched earth, with little or no potential. You must learn how to search effectively, know where and how to look, and perhaps just as important, know when to stop. A measure of frustration simply comes with the turf.

That said, the Internet search tools we will use provide us with numerous ways to examine the network's resources. We will use each in a variety of ways, running sample searches to display their features, and to give you an example of what can be done. In each case, the searches are not prepackaged. I have not gone out on the network to verify resources and then reverse-engineered a search to make any search tool look better than it is. When our searches come up with less than we'd like, you will see the result. When they hit paydirt, that will also be obvious.

The effective Internet searcher will think in terms of building a methodology. The only way to construct one is to learn the ins and outs of the various tools and then bring this knowledge to bear upon the problem at hand. What I recommend most strongly is that you do not make the mistake of focusing upon a single tool because it seems easier to use than the rest. The quickest way to limit yourself is to become trapped inside one set of commands and a single interface. Do this and the limitations of your tool will catch up with you.

No, the correct method is to run sample searches like those shown to you in this book until you have an understanding of how the various tools work. Then, when confronted with a real-world search problem, ponder which of the tools gives you the best angle on your information. Do you need to cut to the chase, entering a keyword to pin down resources? If so, the World Wide Web is now becoming an option, through one of the search engines examined here; be careful, though, of getting lost following extraneous hyperlinks, which can take you down numerous datapaths and distract you from your purpose. Veronica is also a viable choice; it lets you search for menu items on Gophers around the Internet.

But don't stop there, for after running your Veronica search and examining the Gopher resources, you can move back to the Web for a different kind of searching. Using hypertext links, you can now browse for the less obvious data, the items that didn't appear on Gopher menus, the Telnet links and FTP sites that may have escaped the attention of Gopher compilers. Don't hesitate to mine WAIS if full text is in the picture; perhaps a WAIS database exists with information germane to your task. A swift run through the Directory of Servers database at Thinking Machines Corp. may flag unexpected treasures.

Rarely, you see, does a search reach completion through a single resource. Serious Internet work requires combining search tools, looking into issues from a variety of perspectives. None of them is complete, but each can contribute to your knowledge of the available information. One tool leads to another, if you will let it. A frustrating search in WAIS may prompt you to a solid hit with the World Wide Web, but you won't know to make the effort unless you master the rudiments of each tool now.

The Realistic Search

Research and development into Internet search tools continues through the efforts of the teams behind our current tools, other independent researchers and developers, and through the Clearinghouse for Networked Information Discovery and Retrieval in Research Triangle Park, North Carolina. Funded largely by the NSF, the Clearinghouse, known as CNIDR (pronounced snyder), is performing yeoman work on the issue of standards and the interoperability of our tools by making sure that developers from the various software communities stay in communication and address common needs.

In Chapter 10, we examine the work of CNIDR, and through the comments of its leading figures, learn about the problems of today's search tools, and how these problems can be addressed in future versions. No one would have imagined five years ago that the number of tools available for our use would grow so large in so short a time. At this point, the influx of new users to the Internet calls up the question of the quality of our data and what we can do to enhance it. Most of what is currently available on the network is freely available material, and for good reason. We have lacked until recently the necessary tools for security and intellectual property protection that would allow us to place genuinely original information on-line. This is our next challenge.

Boswell reports what Samuel Johnson said when he observed a man who had had an unhappy marriage decide to marry again after the death of his first wife. The marriage, said Johnson, was the triumph of hope over experience. No seasoned Internet searcher would deny that an element of that same phenomenon is present in working with the network today. It is easy to glorify our ready access to resources, but experience teaches that all too often what we can obtain is limited in scope and often falls short of expectations. Fortunately, the work of CNIDR and the ongoing development of network standards leads us to hope that one day the so-called digital library, an electronic Alexandria, will become a reality.

2

The World Wide Web: Hypertext as Search Tool

Most searching proceeds in a linear fashion. There is a particular path to follow, starting with entering a request for information or making a choice from a menu. The steps you take during the search are defined by the program you interact with, which uses its own protocols to consult one or more databases of information. Sometimes this information is local, that is, available on the computer you're using to search; and sometimes it's broadly distributed throughout the Internet, so that your search program moves from one location to another in its work. Whatever the case, the search has its own logic, and you learn to work within parameters laid down by the programmers who originally developed the tools you are using.

Hypertext and hypermedia are ways to transcend at least some of these limitations. Using them, you move through a set of structured information—not sequentially, but by making jumps between the various kinds of data you need. Rather than being forced to choose between gradually narrowing choices on fixed screens of menus, you have the ability to move between items that have been linked to each other by the person who set up the hyperconnections. If that person did a good job, then your information hunt proceeds more quickly and certainly more intuitively than it would using many other search tools. If the hyperlinks are less than optimum, then your browsing runs into the same frustrations inherent in any browsing process: No one can anticipate every possible link; and search methods, while ingenious, are limited by the vision of those who construct the tools.

The development of a browsing tool into a full-blown search engine has been the story of the World Wide Web's recent history. In essence, the Web has changed from a diverting way to poke around the network's resources to a dynamic search mechanism that allows you to start at the top and send out information queries for pages that meet your criteria. There are two ways to effect such a transformation: Developers can create a database of Web information, culling hyperlinks and other words on Web pages, making the whole thing searchable; or, they can set up topic-based directories, allowing the reader to work through a logical progression of information to find the site he or she needs. We have seen a remarkable increase in both activities in the past few years, to the

11

point that, today, the Web is where I recommend you start with any search. This also reflects the huge growth in Web servers; with over 30,000 sites now supplying information, and a growth rate that dwarfs all other Internet tools, the Web is the place to begin looking. Having searched it, you can turn to the entire range of other tools to fill in the gaps.

The Nature of Hypertext

Despite its information-age pedigree, hypertext as an information retrieval model has a long history. The index of any book is, in a sense, a hypertext tool, just as a judicious footnote pointing to further information on the bottom of the page or in the endnotes is a way of linking one set of data to another. You can pursue the additional information at your discretion. The idea is simple: One set of ideas may be closely related to others. If we can find a way to show these associations within the document, and make it possible for the reader, or user of information, to move between them, then we have expanded the intellectual process by making knowledge more available. And if we can link not only text-based ideas but also other forms of media—graphics, sound, moving video—in a similar way (pulling together different forms of data is called *hypermedia*), then we have found a way to make the whole range of digital resources available in an easy-to-use environment, one requiring relatively little work on the part of the information hunter, yet one that pays off with solid results. It is doubtless this ease of use that accounts for the growth in the Web over the past few years. The Internet has suddenly acquired an interface that makes older command-line implementations seem balky and obsolete.

What the computer does is hardly revolutionary—Chesterton would have understood hypertext in seconds, and doubtless produced an aphorism about it. But computer power makes it easier to access hypermedia information. Rather than noting a footnote number following a sentence, then checking the back of the book for the right reference, you are able to press a key at the marked place and instantly retrieve the linked data. And instead of setting up a single link, it's possible to create a document with numerous connections, each of which opens to other documents containing numerous connections, so that reading this material now loses its sequential nature entirely and becomes a pursuit of ideas through a forest of data.

You will understand hypertext if you realize that there is no single way to read a hypertext document. Open a textbook on physics and you read text, refer to illustrations and equations, and consult notes at the end of the chapter. Read through a hypertext book on physics and your route will be determined largely by what you need to know. Perhaps I have a weakness in understanding inertia. My reading through the relevant section would have me examining background information, choosing links that pointed to the basic concepts. Your reading might involve a hunt through the same textbook's links to mass. In an ideal world, even though we would both be using the same textbook, we would be optimizing our separate learning experiences.

The proponents of hypertext believe it is a new medium, one that transcends the limitations of standard printed books and opens up information in ways suited to the individual learner. Let's examine hypertext and hypermedia as they're available over the Internet now, to see how truly these ideals are realized. After all, there is no better example of unstructured information than the Internet itself.

The Web's Resources

The World Wide Web is the outstanding Internet implementation of hypermedia, one that gains new adherents daily as information searchers discover its power. The Web's project leaders like to refer to the Web as containing a *virtual library,* an electronic Alexandria of information. The concept is visionary; certainly the translation of intellectual archives into digital form has hardly begun in many fields of knowledge. But browse through a list of topics available through the Web and I think you'll agree that it has made the data resources of the Internet available in a useful, structured way. Figure 2.1 shows an example of how information can be structured on the Web. This home page is located at the World Wide Web Consortium's site; the organization, an industry consortium run by the Laboratory for Computer Science at the Massachusetts Institute of Technology, promotes the growth of the Web by producing specifications for future development and software to make it work.

You are looking at a directory of Internet sites broken out by category, as viewed through Netscape, a popular World Wide Web browsing program. I can select any underlined topic, say, Anthropology, click on it, and be taken to a second list that provides links to a range of servers that specialize in anthropological topics. By scrolling

Figure 2.1   The home page at the World Wide Web Virtual Library. Note the address in the Location: field.

through this second document (I can use the scroll bar to the right of the screen image), I uncover page after page of hyperlinks to sites that focus on anthropology. I can click on any one of the underlined links to go to it.

The information available through sites like this one can be viewed through various filters, for the Web makes it possible not only to read hypertext documents, but to tap a wide range of other resources. You can read USENET network news through a good browser program, examine sound and video files at Web sites, browse through the contents at Gopher sites worldwide, run WAIS searches, connect to a remote computer via Telnet to run local database programs at the site, search FTP archives and download files, and hunt for the e-mail addresses of individuals using WHOIS and X.500. Indeed, Internet resources are migrating to the Web in unprecedented numbers. As we'll see, you can find on-line journals and newspapers here, library catalogs, mailing list archives, finger information, and on-line forms that allow you to order products and become updated on services.

Realize, too, that when you access the World Wide Web, your hypermedia jumps move not only between documents but between server sites. Although the interface suggests that you have reached a single repository of information, which you are now exploring, in fact you are tapping a worldwide system of linked data whose connections have been rendered transparent to the user. Perhaps there is a server in London that could be useful to you. You could always reach it by a direct Telnet connection, but by using the Web instead, you can read the necessary document without ever worrying about how to make the underlying connection. Making the retrieval process intuitive, then, includes doing the busy work for you behind the scenes, a job at which the Web excels.

Exploring the Web

There is no one correct way to find information on the Web. In fact, the nature of its hypertext links implies that there will be multiple paths to the same information. This is both a plus and a minus: a plus in that your explorations often uncover links to information you hadn't realized were available; a minus in that finding a specific item you need often requires working through several layers of linked information, when a more targeted search could call up your data more quickly. The Web is, above all, an exploration tool, a kind of interactive library you browse at your leisure and with an eye open to discoveries. Some search tools require an analytical frame of mind, some a knack for detail. The Web requires curiosity—and patience.

Reading a Document On-Line with the Web

The deeply interlinked nature of hypertext becomes apparent with a quick browse through a text file. In Figure 2.2, I have opened a hypertext document called The Big Dummy's Guide to the Internet, published and made available on-line by the Electronic Freedom Foundation. The Big Dummy's Guide is a fine example of the Internet's self-referential nature.

Through the voluntary efforts of Adam Gaffin and Jörg Heitkötter, it has evolved into a reference guide that can answer many a thorny network question, and which, thanks to the World Wide Web, is now accessible to anyone through a few mouse clicks. The section I am reading involves electronic mail. And as you can see, various items are underlined. Each of these points to a hypertext link. I might, for example, click on the section called *E-Mail to other Networks*. Doing so produces the screen shown in Figure 2.3.

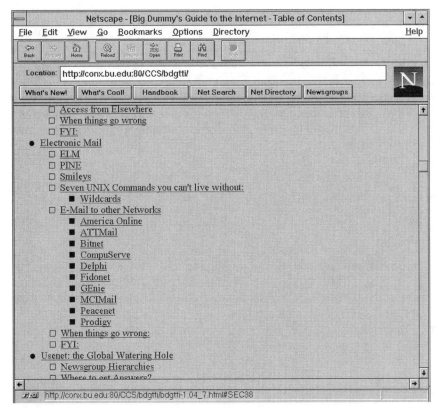

Figure 2.2   Looking over a text file with the help of hypertext.

The result is another page of linkages, allowing me to choose the kind of system I want to move mail between. I choose the underlined word GEnie to find out how to send mail to GEnie. Figure 2.4 shows the result. The hypertext link has taken me directly to that place in the text that addresses GEnie. No index, no squinting at footnotes, the information pops up by pressing a key.

In a nutshell, this is how hypertext works. One link leads you to another; you work your way through a document not sequentially, but by a series of leaps. Remember, though, the process is heavily dependent upon the links established by a human being using a hypertext editor. Usually these links are effective; you can see how helpful it is to be able to home right in on the on-line service that we need so that we can send mail to users of it. Occasionally, however, a link points to the wrong thing. Look, for example, at what The Big Dummy's Guide to the Internet shows as its link to e-mail information about CompuServe:

```
CompuServe

Our forum on CompuServe is also open. 'GO EFFSIG' to join. Many of the files on
ftp.eff.org, as well as other items of interest, are mirrored in the EFFSIG
libraries.
```

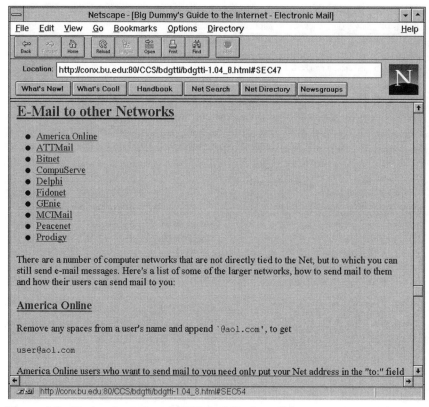

Figure 2.3   Moving deeper into the Web by following a link.

By an oversight, we have been taken to an item that is not about e-mail addressing but, instead, about the Electronic Frontier Foundation's forum on CompuServe (the link will doubtless be updated by the time you read this). The point is, we can't expect perfection from any cataloging method. As each site attracts more users, minor glitches like these tend to be discovered and fixed.

Accessing the World Wide Web

The Netscape program with which we viewed the preceding site is one of the best Internet client programs around; it offers a full range of tools within a menu-driven interface, and provides for such necessities as storing the addresses of frequently accessed sites so that you don't have to enter them every time you want to use them, but can just click on a menu item to launch your session. The World Wide Web functions through programs like Netscape, but it's important to realize that your choice of tool doesn't affect the underlying reality of World Wide Web use. Let's briefly review the ways you can access the Web.

THROUGH A CHARACTER-BASED CLIENT PROGRAM

If your access to the Internet is through a shell account, you will be placed in a character-based environment, one in which your computer is being used as a terminal on a remote computer system. Your call to your service provider gives you access to the Internet clients available on the remote machine; you can manipulate these clients (usually Unix-based programs) to perform your network tasks. The World Wide Web uses several character-based browsers; the one we focus on in this book is called lynx.

To determine whether lynx is available on your system, type **lynx** at the prompt. You should see a screen like the one in Figure 2.5. While other character-based browsers are available, lynx is clearly the best. It offers highlighting of hyperlinks and, although it cannot be used like a graphical browser to view photographs and other images, its easy movement between links makes it a powerful program to master. You can move between links using the arrow keys, pressing RETURN to call up the link in question. And as you can see in the figure, the basic commands for lynx are provided at the bottom of the screen.

THROUGH A GRAPHICAL CLIENT ON YOUR MACHINE

If your access to the Internet is through a SLIP or PPP connection or a direct network connection at your place of work, you will be able to use graphical programs like Netscape or Mosaic. These programs, by using the full power of your desktop computer's microprocessor, can display World Wide Web information in its complete range of imagery, with font changes like those in a printed publication, and spectacular visual

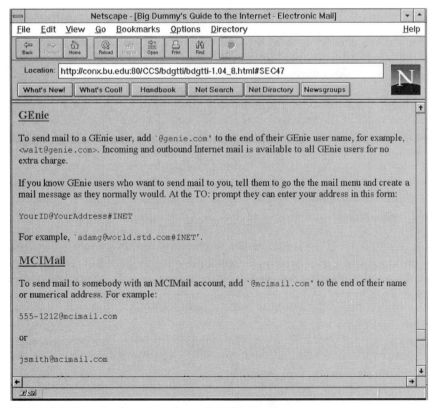

Figure 2.4   Learning how to send e-mail to GEnie addresses.

Figure 2.5 A World Wide Web home page as viewed through lynx.

effects that a character-based browser cannot make available because of the limitations of the connection. That makes SLIP/PPP desirable—though not absolutely essential— for Web work. But I have no doubt that when you see Web pages in their graphical glory, you'll want to set up a SLIP or PPP connection if at all possible.

If you're interested in the Netscape browser I use to illustrate the Web in this book, you can reach it through the server at Netscape Communications Corp. The program is free for educational and non-profit purposes; otherwise, its use is limited to a 90-day trial, after which you must pay a fee. Complete information comes with the documentation furnished with the program. Try one of the following addresses:

ftp://ftp.netscape.com/netscape1.1/

ftp://ftp2.netscape.com/netscape1.1/

But be advised that the Netscape site is a busy one, and you may have to use a *mirror site* elsewhere. Mirror sites are duplicates of the material found in the primary site; they are set up to ease the traffic congestion on the main server. For Netscape's mirrors, look into the following:

From North America:

ftp://wuarchive.wustl.edu/packages/www/Netscape/netscape1.1/

ftp://ftp.cps.cmich.edu/pub/netscape/

ftp://ftp.utdallas.edu/pub/netscape/netscape1.1/

ftp://ftp.micro.caltech.edu/pub/netscape/

ftp://unicron.unomaha.edu/pub/netscape/netscape1.1/
ftp://server.berkeley.edu/pub/netscape/
ftp://SunSITE.unc.edu/pub/packages/infosystems/WWW/clients/Netscape/
ftp://magic.umeche.maine.edu/pub/Mirrors/nscape/

From South America:

ftp://sunsite.dcc.uchile.cl/pub/WWW/netscape/netscape/

From Europe:

ftp://sunsite.doc.ic.ac.uk/computing/information-systems/www/Netscapes/
ftp://ftp.sunet.se/pub/www/Netscape/netscape1.1/
ftp://ftp.luth.se/pub/infosystems/www/netscape/netscape/

From Africa:

ftp://ftp.sun.ac.za/pub/archiving/www/mcom/netscape/

From Asia:

ftp://sunsite.ust.hk/pub/WWW/netscape/
ftp://SunSITE.sut.ac.jp/pub/archives/WWW/netscape/
ftp://bash.cc.keio.ac.jp/pub/inet/netscape/
ftp://ftp.glocom.ac.jp/pub/net/netscape/
ftp://ftp.pu-toyama.ac.jp/pub/net/WWW/netscape/
ftp://ftp.cs.titech.ac.jp/pub/net/WWW/netscape/netscape1.1/
ftp://ftp.nc.nihon-u.ac.jp/pub/network/WWW/client/netscape/
ftp://ftp.elcom.nitech.ac.jp/pub/netscape/
ftp://ftp.leo.chubu.ac.jp/pub/WWW/netscape/netscape1.1

Using a World Wide Web Browser

A *browser* is simply a client program that helps you work with the World Wide Web. Its function is to display documents and to make the links between items of information available. You can then choose which links you'd like to follow as you pursue your course through the Web. Bear in mind that a browser is a powerful tool; it is designed to tap into almost all the resources available on the Internet, from Gopher to WAIS to Telnet, from NNTP (the Internet news protocol) to file retrieval by FTP. In fact, the diverse nature of these links means we are not necessarily limited to text as we use the World Wide Web. Hypermedia refers to linking diverse resources, such as text to audio, images to text, or text to data. Depending on the browser you use, you might be able to display, for example, images or sound along with standard text files.

Why are these interfaces called browsers? Because the nature of working with the World Wide Web precludes your considering it a static information medium. Any movement through it involves making judgment calls about the kind of information you need. By necessity, your path through a series of data linkages is a kind of exploration; you don't always know where you will wind up. The concept of browsing, then, makes sense. A good browser program will enhance your Web explorations by making it easy to examine resources and move from link to link.

Many browsers are available on the Internet for a wide variety of platforms; the programs exist both in source code and in executable form. A direct TCP/IP connection to the Internet, or dial-up account with SLIP or PPP, makes browsers available that display graphics, typefaces, and complex page formats along with the basic text. Browsers like these, created for the Macintosh, Microsoft Windows, the X Window System and others, are becoming more powerful thanks to the rapid strides in the development of Internet search tools; they point to a future rich in audio and video links from or to text documents.

World Wide Web Terminology

The World Wide Web was created as a tool for physicists, who needed some way to examine resources at the European Laboratory for Particle Physics (CERN) in Geneva, Switzerland. Its creator, Tim Berners-Lee, has since moved from CERN to head up the World Wide Web Consortium at the Massachusetts Institute of Technology. You can see the home page for this site in Figure 2.6. Scouting through the information here is an

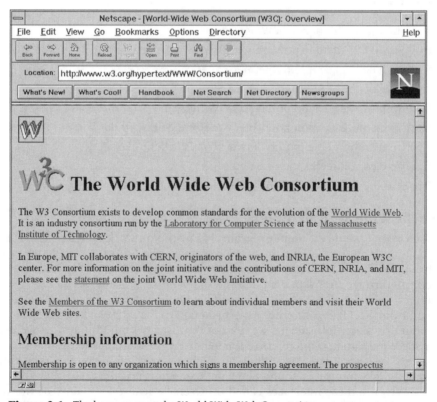

Figure 2.6   The home page at the World Wide Web Consortium.

excellent way to learn more about the Web itself and the continuing evolution of its standards.

Standards, in fact, are what make the Web possible. As we've seen, a Web cruise is a process of moving from one link to another, the exact route chosen by you as you determine what is relevant to your needs and what isn't. The fact that the Web can access so many different kinds of information in so many places means, naturally, that it must have some way of linking data, no matter what form that data may take. In his work at CERN, Berners-Lee created the techniques by which this would be accomplished. Examine, for example, the address for the page shown in Figure 2.6:

http://www.w3.org/hypertext/WWW/Consortium/

This is a URL, or Uniform Resource Locator. Anything available over the Internet can be described with a URL, which shows you not only the kind of resource that is involved, but also the address of that resource. The Web uses URLs to specify the location of its information sites. In Web parlance, we call each Web document a *page*; the primary page for a given site is called its *home page*.

To move data around on the Web, we use HTTP, which stands for HyperText Transport Protocol. While the Web actually uses numerous protocols, it is HTTP that allows us to work with so many different data types. Click on a hyperlink and your Web browser will move to the underlying URL. We can access FTP sites, calling up their directories on-screen with the same underlining of links that we see on World Wide Web pages themselves. We can also view Gopher materials, moving up and down their menu trees by using point-and-click commands (or, if we're using a character-based browser, by working with the arrow keys). The Web, as you can see, possesses not only a broad reach, but it can also hide the complexities of all these operations from you. And when you do want to see the URL that marks the page you're reading, a browser like Netscape shows that information at the top of the screen.

Creating hypermedia is no trivial matter. The links between information must be chosen with care, and the skills of the person making these critical choices will determine how useful a given hypertext document will be. The Hypertext Markup Language, or HTML, is used to produce documents in this format, using a hypertext or plain text editor that encodes the links to other documents. The result is a potpourri of hypertext materials in varying degrees of usefulness. Some are linked sparingly; you'd like to be able to follow up leads that aren't provided. Others contain a multiplicity of links to a wide range of data.

World Wide Web Directories

When the World Wide Web began to take hold, there was an explosion of new home pages being created by people captivated with the Web's potential for carrying multimedia information. This led to a problematic situation for searchers. Many of the Internet's most recent additions were in the form of Web pages, but there were few ways you could search the Web to find them. Instead, it became necessary to browse from one site to another, hoping to progressively home in on what you needed. The first major Web directory was the Virtual Library set up by CERN, and now maintained at the World Wide Web Consortium. It provided some imposition of order by breaking the Web sites it knew about into categories; if you knew in general what you were looking for, you could home in on it.

This is site-driven searching, accomplished by human indexing teams. In most cases, the directory, no matter how many entries it contains, only lists the location of sites that fit your description. It contains no detailed information about the contents at those sites, other than what is presumed from their subject matter. This limitation is obvious in the origin of these services. Like the Yahoo site we'll examine soon, many of them grew up out of what was originally a lengthy hotlist of sites maintained by one or more individuals. This list was later supplemented by others and the overall catalog grew, one site at a time. Some directories make it easy for users to add sites of their own to the list, which, again, expands the directory as more and more people tap it.

In its elemental form, directory searching is a matter of framing a query by adopting the broadest possible search parameters. You must become adept at putting yourself in the mind of a Web page designer. If you were placing Web sites into categories, where would you place a site on the Mayan ruins in the Yucatan. Under history? Tourism? Indigenous cultures? Because there are no hard and fast guidelines for making such decisions, you have to be willing to experiment. The Web quickly teaches that when a search turns up nothing, the fault may not lie in a lack of materials but in the nature of the search concept.

Think of a funnel. Top-down searching means you begin with the widest possible field. You then progress down into the funnel; each time you do, the number of choices becomes fewer, until finally, you are left with only the selections that fit your criteria. At a well-organized Web site, this will happen fairly quickly. At a poorly arranged one, it may not happen at all, and you may find yourself on a merry chase through links to information that lead to extraneous data. But Web directories are a good place to begin any search of the Internet, because they give you a good overview of what's out there. Many of them are now implementing keyword searches of their sites, which can simplify the search process. And after you've examined one or more directories, you'll want to turn your attention to search engines that let you search by keyword across various Web servers. We examine the latter later in this chapter.

Scott Yanoff's Special Internet Connections

As an example of a simple Web directory search, let's turn to a document called Special Internet Connections. It's the work of Scott Yanoff, who for years now has compiled a list of Internet sites broken into categories. Yanoff's list began as a text document, one of the few that described a wide range of Internet resources available through various access methods, everything from FTP to Telnet to electronic mail. It became even more useful because Yanoff did a thorough job of updating his material; each new addition presented new sites, as well as address changes and modifications to the older ones. Yanoff still posts this list to the USENET newsgroup news.answers.

Put such a document into the World Wide Web system and you add to its value immensely. After all, a printed document leaves you with references that you must then enter into your software to achieve a connection. A hypertext document lets you simply click on any of the resources to be taken directly to it. This makes exploring the Internet a more productive process, because you don't have to worry about such things as command syntax for FTP sessions and how to enter a World Wide Web URL to go to a specified site. Instead, your Web browser does all the work for you.

The URL for Special Internet Connections is as follows:

http://www.uwm.edu/mirror/inet.services.html

Remember how to reach such a locator. The HTTP designation tells you that this is a World Wide Web document; it is accessible through HyperText Transport Protocol. To view it, you enter the URL listed above into your browser. The address of the computer in question is:

www.uwm.edu

This is a standard Internet address. It tells us we are connecting to a World Wide Web-site (www); the .edu tells us that this Web server is located at an educational site. Following the .edu is the directory path to the home page. Notice that the file we are trying to reach is this one:

internet.services.html

The html stands for Hypertext Markup Language, and tells us that this is a document written in that format.

Reaching such an address through a browser is not difficult, but the method depends upon the kind of browser you are using:

- With a graphical browser like Netscape, you can use the program's menus. Pull down the File menu and click on the Open Location item. This pops up a dialog box that allows you space to enter the new address. A click on the Open button takes you to it. A lengthy URL like the one just given does take some time to enter, and you must be careful to type the entire URL with precision, letter-by-letter, because a single mistake will cause the browser to fail to connect. But once you've entered it and traveled to the site, you can always use the browser's bookmark feature to add the address to a hotlist, thus having it on hand for future use. With Netscape, for example, you would pull down the Bookmarks menu and choose Add Bookmark.
- With a character-based browser like lynx, the method is different. In the absence of pull-down menus, you enter the **g** command followed by the address in question. The command to go to the Yanoff site would thus be:
    g http://www.uwm.edu/mirror/inet.services.html
  Again, the address must be entered with precision. But like Netscape and Mosaic, lynx provides a bookmark feature that lets you note a page for future use by saving it to a file. You can use the **a** command to save any page to your bookmark file. The **v** command is then used to view your bookmarks.

Examine Figure 2.7, which shows the home page for Special Internet Connections. You can see the method followed by Web directories in this figure. Each broad category is set up as a hyperlink; you can tell this because hyperlinks are underlined (with the lynx browser, links are shown in highlighted form instead). When you click on one of the hyperlinks, you move to a broader set of possibilities. In Figure 2.8, I have moved through the Yanoff list to look for items about music. As a former guitarist, I am interested in reacquiring my skills, and would like to see what is available on the Internet.

It seems I'm in luck, for I've uncovered a subsection of the Yanoff list that focuses on guitars. When I move the cursor over a hyperlink, its shape will change to show that I am pointing to such a link, and at the bottom of the screen, the URL of the document in question will be shown. Here we can see the wide-ranging ability of a good Web browser to pick out resources. The material we are looking at, which is information about guitar tablature and chords, is in fact available at an FTP site. Its URL is:

file://ftp.nevada.edu/pub/guitar/

The file prefix is sometimes used instead of ftp, but the meaning is identical; we are looking at material offered at an FTP site, which is accessible through a Web browser. In this case, the address is ftp.nevada.edu, while the directory we want to examine is pub/guitar. If we click on this link, we will be taken into the FTP site, as in Figure 2.9.

The site, which calls itself OLGA—The On-Line Guitar Archive, is stuffed with material about the instrument. You can see that by using a Web browser to access it, we are placed in a graphical environment. Each subdirectory is shown as a hyperlink, so that

Figure 2.7 The home page for Special Internet Connections, still an excellent place to start a topic-driven search for information.

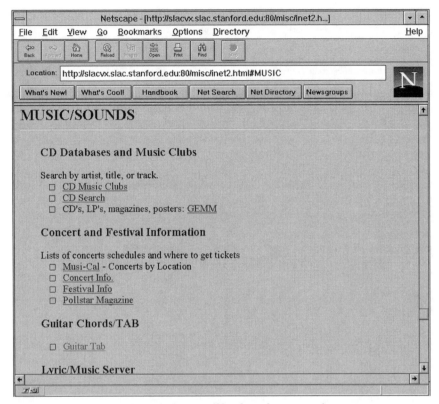

Figure 2.8 Searching through the Yanoff list for information about music.

we move around in the computer's directory structure by using mouse clicks (or, with lynx, by pressing the RETURN key after moving the highlight with the arrow keys). Documents are shown as small graphics of a page of paper; folders are shown with a folder icon. We can even download a file by clicking on it and telling our browser to save the file to disk.

I have moved to a site I wanted to see by starting with the broad overview. Had I started looking under the term guitar on the Yanoff list, I wouldn't have found it as readily as by starting with the general term music, which put me into the right category for the search in question. Having moved to the relevant part of the list, it was easy to home in on what I needed. And because of the hypertextual nature of the list, I was able to go directly to the site to explore its holdings, and then return to the Special Internet Connections document when I was finished.

It's interesting for those of us who have followed Scott Yanoff's work since he began his list in 1991 to see that so many of the links have become references to Web pages. The protocol that used to have the most clout was Gopher, which won converts because of its easy-to-use menu structure. Today, Web sites, with their distinctive http marker, predominate, although you still find e-mail, Telnet, and the occasional Gopher site on the Yanoff list. Figure 2.10, for example, shows how a Gopher site is interpreted by Netscape. As with our FTP session, the Gopher's menu structure here is translated into

Figure 2.9   Examining an FTP site through a Web browser.

hyperlink form. Each item is accessible with a mouse click, which moves us either to a document or a submenu with additional items.

While Gopher growth has slowed dramatically in the United States and, to some extent, in western Europe, the protocol continues to proliferate in much of the rest of the world. In many areas, character-based interfaces remain the primary means of access, so that the benefits of graphical Web pages are less palpable, while the ease of use that Gopher provides offers great attraction for new users. Don't assume that because the Web is becoming a major Internet tool, all other forms of accessing data will disappear. The strength of a good browser is partly its ability to access Internet information of all kinds.

Using the Yahoo Directory

One of the best directories that has appeared for World Wide Web material is Yahoo, a hierarchical index of Web sites. With a database maintained at Stanford University by David Filo and Jerry Yang, Yahoo has won converts because of its scope—its links to Web sites are numerous and continuously updated—and its reliability. Although it is always possible that a given link may become outdated, due to changes at the server site,

Yahoo doesn't yield many connection problems; if it's on the Yahoo list, it's usually a valid URL. You can find Yahoo at this URL:

http://www.yahoo.com/

You can see that a good Web directory has implications not just for you as a searcher, but for anyone who wants to get a new World Wide Web page noticed. Because Yahoo is a database that provides links to other sites, it grows through the addition of new and noteworthy home pages. The system provides an interface that allows people to suggest new sites to add, and incorporates user feedback to assist in determining when a particular URL is no longer valid. Thus the project is in many ways collaborative, an ongoing attempt to organize Web material with the help of the Internet's users. Yahoo also uses search robots—software engines that can roam the Internet looking for new material—in its work. We'll look at such automated systems later in this chapter.

Using Yahoo takes us one step deeper into the Internet, for its list of links is more extensive than that of the Yanoff document. Take a look at the home page at Yahoo, which is shown in Figure 2.11. As is now familiar, we have a list of topics, each set up as

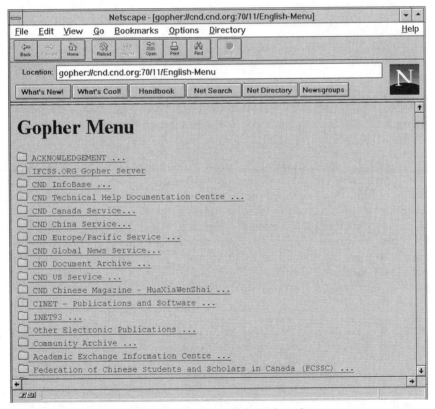

Figure 2.10 Gopher is also accessible through the Web, with its menu structure set up as a system of hyperlinks.

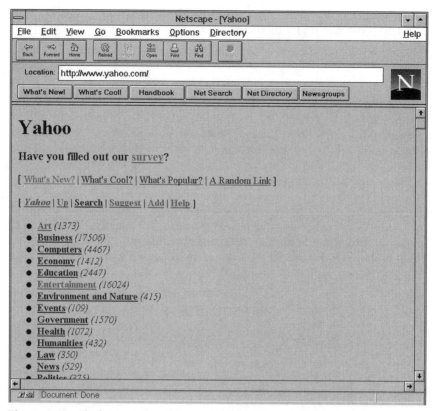

Figure 2.11   The home page at Yahoo, one of the Internet's best directory sites.

a hyperlink. We can click on any of these to go to the submenu, and so, step-by-step, proceed to what we need. In this case, I am interested in films. As a movie buff, I keep a collection of films that I've taped off the television, and enjoy going back to certain favorites again and again. One of my favorite films of more recent times is *Local Hero,* the story of an oil company executive who is sent to Scotland in search of land for a new project his company wants to build. Along the way, he is subtly and charmingly changed by the people he meets at a small Scottish village. I recall that Burt Lancaster played a wonderful role as the oil company's CEO, but the rest of the cast escapes me, as does the name of the director. To remedy this, I'll search the Internet by using Yahoo.

HINT: You should not expect to see the same topics at each Web directory site. Remember: The Web is reliant upon the organizing decisions made by the people who create these directories. Maybe you are a graduate student in anthropology and would expect to see items that fit that description on the main menu (they appear, as a matter of fact, on some directories). But Yahoo doesn't see it that way; its creators have placed links to anthropological data under the broad heading Social Science. The method, then, is to try to think the way the organizers do. If you don't find your category right away, pursue other leads, clicking on hyperlinks until the right submenu appears.

First I need to find resources involving the cinema. Paging down Yahoo's home page, I find no entry for Film or Movies, so I know I need to broaden my terms. Fortunately, the home page list is a short one, and it's easy to go through to eliminate possibilities. I'm left with two choices: Entertainment or Society and Culture. The latter seems unlikely to house information about movies, so I click on Entertainment to begin my search. Doing so, I'm presented with another menu of topics, within which I find the topic Movies and Films, along with a gratifying subnote indicating that the category contains almost 600 entries. A click takes me to the page, shown in Figure 2.12.

Here we see how Yahoo continues to nest information. Some of these items lead to still further menus; they're the ones shown in a somewhat heavier font, and followed by a number in parentheses to show how many links they contain. Others are links to specific home pages; we can verify this by moving the cursor over one and examining the underlying URL, which will always appear at the bottom of the screen.

An item called The Internet Movie Database catches my eye. Clicking on this item calls up a submenu of sites for this service, as follows:

```
The Internet Movie Database - Australia
The Internet Movie Database - Germany
The Internet Movie Database - Japan
```

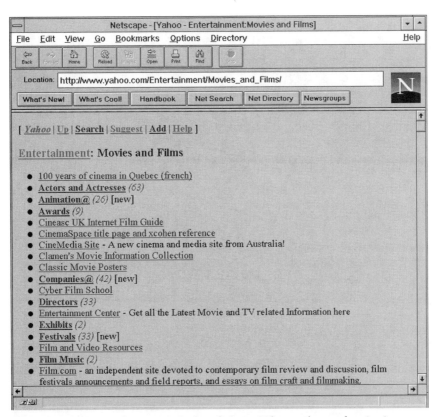

Figure 2.12 Moving deeper into the list of sites at Yahoo; we're now homing in on our topic.

```
The Internet Movie Database - Korea
The Internet Movie Database - UK [*]
The Internet Movie Database - USA
Index Mirror Sites
```

The principle, of course, is that you should always use a server that is near you, to reduce network congestion. I'll therefore choose the USA site by clicking on it. And as Figure 2.13 shows, now I've moved into an interesting situation. I seem to have a complete movie database; in the figure, I have moved to its search screen.

As you can see, I can search this database by movie title, cast, character name, genre, and a number of other variables. Note what has happened here. I have moved to a World Wide Web site by using a directory, thus using the top-down approach that directories require. Once at the directory site, however, I am able to search it using keywords, a much more concise methodology. The search screen by title is shown in Figure 2.14. I can enter my movie title, *Local Hero*, by moving the cursor to the blank field at the top of the screen and then clicking on the button marked Start Title Search.

When I do, I am presented with a screen full of information about the film. As you can see in Figure 2.15, I've found the answers to my questions about the movie right off the bat. The name of the film's star is Peter Riegert, who played the bemused Mac Mac-Intyre; much of the rest of the cast is listed here as well. Burt Lancaster played oil indus-

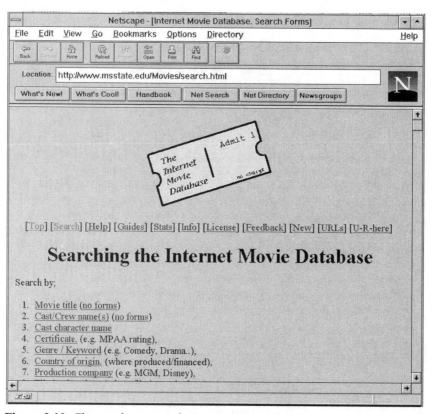

Figure 2.13   The search screen at the Internet Movie Database.

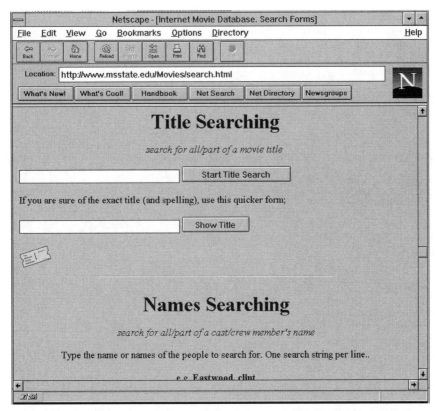

Figure 2.14 The Search by Title screen at the Internet Movie Database, which lets me search by keyword.

try tycoon Felix Happer. You will have noticed, no doubt, that each of these entries is itself a hyperlink.

I could explore the films of Bill Forsyth, the brilliant Scottish director, by clicking on his underlined name. I would learn that he also directed the low-budget but successful *Gregory's Girl,* among other films. As for star Peter Riegert, I could click on his name to learn about his other credits, such as the TV movie *Barbarians at the Gate,* where he played Peter Cohen, or the theatrical release *The Mask,* where he played Lt. Mitch Kellaway. Because each of those items, in turn, has its own link, I could call up information about the individual films as well.

But perhaps we'd like to see a review of *Local Hero.* The database is obliging. It offers an icon on the search screen that lets us look at such reviews. In Figure 2.16, I have called up the one in question. This figure shows a review that originally appeared in one of the USENET newsgroups (rec.arts.movies.review), and is now maintained in an archive with its own hypertext links.

The key fact to notice about our search of the Web for information about *Local Hero* is that we never needed to enter exacting search parameters. The directory structure that Yahoo provided was sufficient to take us to a database that allowed us to run a keyword search (although if we had wanted to home in quickly on the movies page, we could have

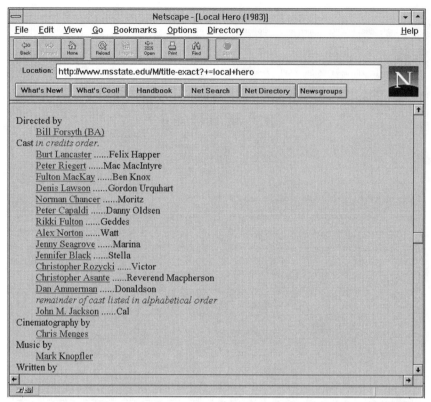

Figure 2.15 The list of characters of *Local Hero* turns out to include further hyperlinks, allowing us to call up information about each one.

run a keyword search of the Yahoo site from the top menu as well). We followed a path of most general to most specific, ending with the ability to run queries past a dedicated database. And all our movements were controlled by mouse clicks. A directory like this thus becomes a primary tool for the information hunter. Its main drawback, the fact that it can require a fair amount of browsing as we move between menus, is offset by its ease of use, and its ability to help us locate resources we didn't know existed. You will want to explore Yahoo to run sample searches of your own. You'll also quickly learn that the number of such directories is growing rapidly. Let's examine some more.

Searching with Galaxy

Using Internet directories like Yahoo and the Yanoff list can be unwieldy if we only use them as categorized lists; in that sense, they require repeated passes through their menus to uncover information. This method tends to encourage extended sessions of exploration rather than quick, targeted searches into the Web, a fascinating process, but only if you have the time to do it. But most directories now include some keyword search capability along with their directories, to allow you to home in on what you want. One such directory is Galaxy, a service of TradeWave Corporation. Its home page is shown in Figure 2.17. Galaxy's home page is at this URL:

Figure 2.16   A review of *Local Hero* as found by searching the Internet Movie Database.

http://www.einet.net/galaxy.html

I like this directory; more than any other, its topics are laid out in logical and carefully considered form, and its links are evaluated according to the caliber of the information they retrieve. Let's go hunting with Galaxy.

In ancient times, people cast sticks upon the ground to provide the numerical references by which to query the I Ching, the Chinese book of prophecy. Like its Greek counterpart in Delphi, the I Ching is an oracle of unusually cryptic language, one that requires reflection and, perhaps, the powers of the subconscious mind to untangle. The telecommunications age version of the I Ching, I have been told, is available over the Internet. The question: Where is it, and can Galaxy help us find it?

To determine the answer, the first step is to scan through the topic listings. There is no top-level listing for philosophy or religion, but both can be found under the broader heading Arts and Humanities, as you can see from Figure 2.17. While oracles raise interesting philosophical questions, I would have to consider the general topic to be religious—either you believe in oracles or you don't. Clicking on the hyperlink marked Religion, then, I am taken to another page, where things get dicey. Here I find still more hyperlinks, but none of them seems immediately connected to anything as arcane as the I Ching.

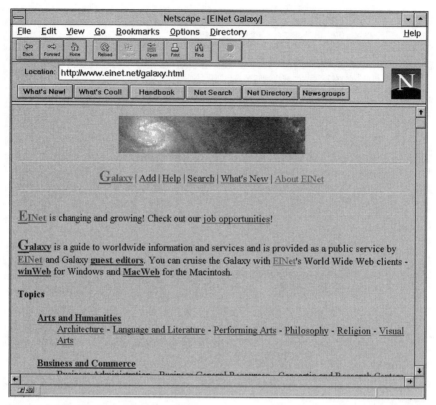

Figure 2.17   The home page for Galaxy.

This is where directory services can be both fascinating and frustrating. I spent an intriguing half hour going through the various links, discovering Internet resources I had never known existed, and profiting from the experience by adding several to my Netscape bookmark list. On the other hand, it took that long to track down the I Ching—a good thing I wasn't in a hurry! It turned up under the heading Religion-Community, where topics from Judaism to Buddhism to Shamanism also appear, along with Voodoo and Meditation. The link I wanted was called Advanced I Ching. Clicking on it called up Figure 2.18.

This is fascinating stuff. You click on a hyperlink to "cast the coins" the I Ching uses in its prognostications; actually, of course, you're setting a program in motion to perform the virtual version of the same thing. Hint: Those in the know tell me that when using the I Ching, you should place your hands upon the keyboard and concentrate on your current situation before clicking this hyperlink; otherwise, the oracle may not deliver a useful prophecy. As for understanding what the I Ching tells you, you're on your own.

If you're a sharp-eyed reader, however, you saw that Galaxy's screens include a link called Search. This directory is an intriguing example of how the Web is gradually giving over to a keyword-searchable format (Yahoo also allows us to search by keyword, as do many of the new directories sprouting up on the Internet). Click on the Search link and you will see the screen in Figure 2.19. I have already filled in the search term in the appropriate field. Notice that I can specify a fixed number of hits, and that I can choose to search World Wide Web pages either by their links or by full text, entries on Galaxy itself, or Gopher sites, or, for that matter, any combination of these.

Keyword Search Methodology at a Directory Site

Let's take a more specific look at these options, by way of illustrating how such a search can proceed. While the specific options discussed are particular to Galaxy, the principles involved are common to any directory site with a search function:

Galaxy Pages   This is an index of pages maintained within the Galaxy database itself. When you use it, you are searching for broad references to information. Thus, you might search under the term religion, or philosophy, to call up clusters of pages that fit that description.

Galaxy Entries   This is a title-only index of information references in pages at Galaxy. You could use this setting to run a highly specific information search. You might, for example, search under the term Hong Kong to call up pages that dealt with that city.

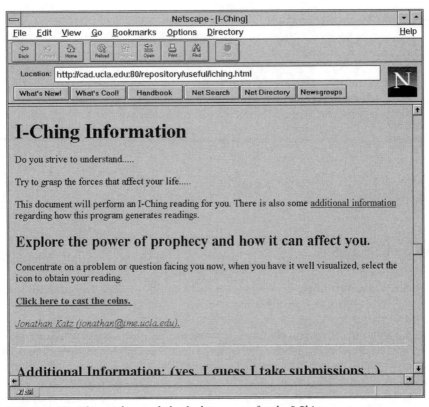

Figure 2.18   The oracle revealed—the home page for the I Ching.

Figure 2.19 Galaxy's search screen allows you to set up keyword searches and to specify unique parameters for each search.

Gopher	This is an index of Gopher menu titles. Notice that we are not referring to full-text within Gopher sites, but rather, the titles found on the Gopher menus that refer to such documents.
HYTELNET	This index contains material from the HYTELNET database, to be discussed later. HYTELNET maintains references to Telnet sites around the globe.
World Wide Web Text	This is a full-text index of all World Wide Web pages found at the Galaxy site.
World Wide Web Links	This is an index of all the links found in all the pages at the Galaxy site.

To implement such a search function, you can use single words or phrases as your keyword. Suppose, for example, that I wanted to search for information about the country of Ghana. To keep things at their simplest level, I could run a search using ghana as my search term. To run as comprehensive a search as possible, I would choose from among the preceding list, clicking on World Wide Web Text and, perhaps, Gopher. When I click on the Search button, Galaxy consults the databases I have checked and returns a list of hits in the form of hyperlinks. I wind up with four World Wide Web pages with mentions of Ghana somewhere in their text; I also get a considerably larger number of hits with Gopher.

> **HINT:** Choose carefully when you decide which resources to consult in running such a search. For example, in the Ghana search, I chose Gopher as well as World Wide Web pages. Why? Because Ghana is in a part of the world where the Internet has yet to become firmly established. While network connections to the country do exist, the full graphical capabilities of the World Wide Web are unlikely to be in use there. We're more likely to see character-based activity in the form of tools like Gopher. If I had been searching for information about a more developed economy, Germany, say, I might have run a search using the World Wide Web from the start, knowing that numerous Web pages exist in that country. The moral: always tailor your search to the kind of information you are requesting. Ask yourself which resources are *likely* to be available about your topic.

You can also use the Boolean operators AND, OR and NOT to restrict your results. These words specify a relationship between two or more search terms. Suppose what I really want to know about is education in Ghana. The way to specify a search around that topic is to use two keywords, ghana and education, in this form:

ghana and education

followed by a click on the Search button. Running this search, I come up with several Gopher references, among them these:

```
Education in West Africa: The Daily Graphic (Ghana) and the Daily Times (Nige-
ria) as mirrors of concern - Score: 1000

Community health education in rural Ghana: The Danfa project- An assessment of
accomplishments - Score: 1000
```

Notice the score of 1000 following each hit. This tells us that these items meet our criteria exactly. You can see what is happening here. The Boolean word AND is being used to specify that I want to see documents that contain both the word Ghana and the word education. An instance of each word on its own would not qualify.

It is also possible to use the OR and NOT qualifiers. NOT would be used to exclude documents from our search. Consider the following search strategy:

west africa not ghana

Here we have told the database to search for anything involving West Africa that does not include the word Ghana. This kind of operator is handy if we want to exclude something obvious. For example, suppose you are dealing with a major news story from a particular country, and want to exclude it from your search. You might, for example, be looking for something about Serbia, but you might not want information about the ongoing warfare in that area. The search term that follows might help:

serbia not bosnia

This would yield hits on Serbia itself, while excluding Bosnia; it would likely, therefore, come up with information more closely tied to, say, the Serbian economy or Serbian history than the troubled relationship between the Serbs and their neighbors.

The OR qualifier is used when you want to broaden your search. In the African example, suppose I wanted to get general information about several countries in West Africa. I might search for countries under this kind of strategy:

ivory coast or ghana

Now I would be returned a list of hits that included either the Ivory Coast or Ghana, but any one document might include one and not the other.

The ability to search a site by keyword simplifies how we use these World Wide Web directories, turning them into a prime means of tracking down hard-to-find resources. Not all directory sites offer keyword searches, but the trend is certainly in the direction of making some kind of keyword capability available. My advice when you approach any directory site is that you study it to find out whether keyword searching is an option. If it is, run a few sample searches to see how effective such a search can be at that site. You should also page through the directory structure to get a feel for how effectively the administrators have organized their material, and how often new material is added. Knowing which sites are the best to use for the kind of searching you do will save you time and effort.

Let's move on now to look at some other directory sites. It's not possible to examine them all—hundreds of directories, from the broadest to the most specific, are coming on-line. What I've tried to do here is to suggest some of the best sites that I know. These are sites I have found useful in my own work, and they constitute a good place to start for the would-be information hunter.

Argus—The Clearinghouse for Subject-Oriented Internet Resource Guides

An exceptionally useful site, this directory is available through the University of Michigan and Argus Associates. Rather than simply presenting links to various URLs, this directory includes documents that present and evaluate the various Internet information sources—it's a directory of directories. And in a major stroke for humanism in the age of the machine, the site's founders have this to say about their approach:

> The Clearinghouse was founded on the belief that in order to make the Internet a more useful information environment, human effort must be combined with searching and browsing technologies. As librarians, we believe that for the most part, language and ideas are simply too ambiguous for automated retrieval systems to properly identify and evaluate. It appears that artificial intelligence technologies will not meet this challenge in the near future, so intellectual labor is necessary to provide qualitative assessment of the Internet's information. The Clearinghouse serves as a centralized location for these efforts.

This recognition of the ambiguity of language is heartening, particularly when it comes as the backdrop to a site as useful as this one. Click on a given topic and you are whisked to a page that lists guides by various authors that evaluate Internet information about that topic. Some are in hypertext format; others are plain text. The Clearinghouse, then, is one of the most intelligently conceived guides on the Internet, and should be an early stop for any information hunter. Its URL:

http://www.lib.umich.edu/chouse/chhome.html

BTG Hot List

This site offers links to some of the Web's primary search tools and provides links arranged by category to government information and computer resources. Its URL:

http://www.btg.com/hotdir/btghot.html

CMC Information Sources

John December's work has been well known on the Internet for years; he has provided a useful gathering point for materials related to networking in general and the Internet in particular. This page can take you to links that fill in background information about almost any Internet topic, with full examination of the Internet's ramifications in the government, educational, and business environments. December updates the list frequently, so it's a good place to check frequently as the Net continues to expand.

http://www.rpi.edu/Internet/Guides/decemj/icmc/toc1.html

The Combined AAUP Journals Catalog

A useful page if you're trying to locate scholarly journals on a wide variety of topics. You can search by title, subject, press or keyword; there's even WAIS capability for full-text searching, and links to other catalogs of journals on Web pages and Gophers. Made available by the Association of American University Presses.

http://aaup.pupress.princeton.edu:70/1/journals/

Commercial Sites Index

A directory of commercial sites that includes a built-in search engine. Contains roughly 10,000 listings arranged alphabetically and by category.

http://www.directory.net/dir/directory.html

The Electronic Journals Database Overview

This is the kind of site we need more of—it's a specialized listing of electronic journals, with links to those that are readily available at Gopher or FTP sites, and full information about those only accessible through e-mail subscription. These journals differ from those in the previously described AAUP database in that they are not necessarily academic in nature. I like this site because you normally hear about on-line journals only through the occasional announcement on a mailing list or USENET newsgroup. An interactive list like this therefore does the entire network community a service.

http://fiasco.snre.umich.edu/ejournals/ej.out.html

FTP Sites Lists

A gigantic, alphabetized listing of FTP sites, with background information and hyperlinks to each.

http://hoohoo.ncsa.uiuc.edu:80/ftp/a-e.html

Global Network Navigator

This magazine-style approach to updated network information is fun to browse through, and notable for its Whole Internet Catalog, based upon Ed Krol's best-selling book. The latter offers a category-driven listing of Internet sites that is similar to Galaxy's, along with regularly updated selections of the Top 50 sites. Global Network Navigator has recently been acquired by America Online, and should attain new prominence as that network seeks to expand its Internet presence.

http://gnn.com/gnn/gnn.html

INFOMINE

If you're interested in finding out what the government makes available on-line, this is the place. INFOMINE covers U.S. federal, state, and local government resources, and provides links to broader-based Internet tools. You can look at sites by subject and title or search by keyword.

http://lib-www.ucr.edu/govpub/

The Interactive Yellow Pages

Internet information grouped by category. The pages are confusingly arranged, making searching more difficult; some appear to be advertisements, others are links to non-commercial Web information.

http://netcenter.com/yellows.html

Internet Resources Meta-Index

Made available by the National Center for Supercomputing Applications, this page categorizes the various directories and indices available to you on the Internet. As such, it's a great place to get an overview of what's happening in the realm of search tools, with convenient hyperlinks to all of them. Indices include Gopher, WAIS, FTP, and other protocols, and there is an experimental meta-index that allows you to search any number of sites from the NCSA page, similar to what is found on The Awesome Lists page.

http://www.ncsa.uiuc.edu/SDG/Software/Mosaic/Demo/metaindex.html

InterNIC Directory of Directories

A category-based listing of resources made available by InterNIC Directory and Database Services at AT&T. Includes pointers to a wide variety of sites, including white and yellow page directories, library catalogs, and computing centers.

http://ds.internic.net/cgi-bin/tochtm1/0intro.dirofdirs/

The ISP Internet Yellow Pages

Searchable by keyword or category listing. This site is full-featured and powerful, with links to thousands of Web pages.

http://www.index.org/

The Mother-of-all BBS

This site gathers home pages for companies, universities, research centers, government agencies, and product announcements for hardware and software companies. Links are listed alphabetically on a massive home page, and WAIS capabilities are available, allowing you to search by keyword.

http://www.cs.colorado.edu/home/mcbryan/bb/summary.html

New Riders' Official World Wide Web Yellow Pages

Allows you to search by category or keyword through the on-line version of New Riders' book of the same name.

http://www.mcp.com/nrp/wwwyp/

The OTIS Index

A searchable index that provides links to the major directory and search sites on the Internet. Includes a commercial sites index, a searchable FTP index, and links to newsgroups and publications.

http://www.interlog.com/~gordo/otis_index.html

Publicly Accessible Mailing Lists

For years now, Stephanie da Silva has provided an invaluable service to the Internet community by cataloging information about the various mailing lists available to e-mail users. Now her lengthy list is available in searchable form. Because mailing lists are notoriously hard to track, this site is a must for the serious user. Here is the URL:

http://www.NeoSoft.com/internet/paml/

TILE.NET

A major directory, with listings of USENET newsgroups, FTP sites, and LISTSERV-based mailing lists. In each case, the subject matter can be viewed in a variety of ways. For example, to look up an FTP site, you can examine lists sorted alphabetically, by country, by operating system, or indexed by file contents. The indices are searchable, allowing you to home in quickly on the item you need.

http://tile.net/

Notice the simple user interface in the TILE.NET page shown in Figure 2.20.

Web of Wonder

A straightforward page arranged by topic, much in the manner of Yahoo, with keyword search capability added.

http://www.digimark.net/wow/index.html

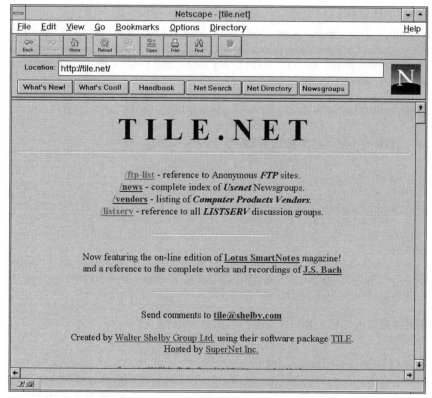

Figure 2.20 TILE.NET allows you to search FTP sites, USENET newsgroups, computer vendors, and mailing lists.

The Web Pointer

Pointers to interesting Web sites grouped by category. While not as comprehensive as Yahoo, the site is well maintained and includes links to the major pages in each category.

http://www.wam.umd.edu/~charlmac/Places/places.html

The World Wide Web Virtual Library

From the World Wide Web Consortium, this is the original Web directory page once maintained at CERN, the site of the Web's development. Arranged alphabetically by subject.

http://www.w3.org/hypertext/DataSources/bySubject/Overview2.html

Worldwide Yellow Pages

A business-oriented guide that allows you to examine commerce on the Internet. Listings are arranged by headings, name or location, and there is a forms-based search capability that lets you search by all three.

http://www.yellow.com/

The YellowPages.com

A listing of thousands of Internet sites by category.

http://theyellowpages.com/

Work Software Yellow Pages

Business organizations listed by company, product, or niche. Lists numerous sites but is not easy to search.

http://planetcom.com/workmedia/wsyp.html

Web directories like these are the tip of the iceberg. I've attempted to show you the ones I consider the most useful, but the sheer number and diversity of new directory sites means that you will use these core URLs to track down new directories that best fit your own interests. Because there are so many possibilities, it's necessary to pause now to consider how to keep up with them all. In particular, learning how to manage the World Wide Web browser's bookmark functions is a critical subject. We'll examine it later in this chapter. First, however, we must turn to the broader topic of automated search tools and how they function.

Robots, Spiders, and Other Search Tools

Using a cluster of Web directories gives you the opportunity to home in on information of interest. But have you ever wondered how the information was gathered? How, for example, do administrators at a directory site gather all the hyperlinks and organize them to fit within a searchable whole? There is no one answer to this. Some sites count on the contributions of readers, who are given the opportunity to suggest new sites of their own—this is a classic way to leverage the Internet's own user base. Others make use of automated systems to acquire new site URLs; Yahoo is well known for this type of data gathering.

It's now time to examine the automated approach to Web searching. Whereas a directory site commonly makes it possible for you to search it with keywords, your search is more or less limited to that site itself. Although it may have compiled an impressive set of listings, the directory is self-contained, and represents only a fraction of the total number of Web pages available on the Internet. What is needed to search in a more comprehensive way is a software tool that can move between sites, one that can locate documents within the entire structure of Web-space and return selected hits in the form of Web documents. We call tools like this robots, although you'll also see them referred to as spiders, or wanderers, or even worms. In essence, a Web robot is a software engine that retrieves information from Web sites and searches for text *across* Web servers. It is therefore not limited to a single server.

You can see the advantage of a good robot immediately. Rather than relying on the inevitably quirky and parochial URL lists brought in by people using your site, the robot allows you to make broad information sweeps through the Web. The data it returns can be fed into a database whose holdings can be searched with a search engine, using your Web browser's forms feature. In essence, then, the user moves from browsing the Web, looking more or less at random through huge information banks, to actively searching the Web. And because the system is automated, it can be updated at regular intervals. This is a necessary process, because the last thing a good index should include are pointers to information that has become out of date. Everyone knows this, and people at sites that are maintained solely by human update are as aware of it as anyone else, but automating the procedure means it is more likely to be handled efficiently.

NOTE: Conventional database searching usually involves Boolean operators, which, as already explained, are terms like AND, OR, and NOT that specify the relationship between the keywords used in the query. We will look at Boolean operators in greater detail later in this book as we consider their use with Veronica, a search engine that examines Gopher menu items. It is interesting to note here that the new Web search engines are not being limited to Boolean searches.

Attempting the full-text indexing of distributed sites, their authors are moving quickly into natural language approaches that redefine how we search for information. In particular, natural language (think of human, as opposed to machine, language) allows search results to be ranked according to relevancy—the computer is trying to figure out what you need, and present the results accordingly. Relevancy can be determined by anything from the number of search terms that appear in a document to the frequency of their appearance in that document, and, often, the proximity of one search term to another within the document.

We usually think of the technique of relevancy ranking as connected with the Wide Area Information Servers system we examine in a later chapter. WAIS, as a matter of fact, adopts relevancy feedback techniques, in which you can resubmit a query after you have marked certain of its results as particularly relevant; the search engine will then attempt to use the documents you have selected as the basis for a new search that finds more documents like them. Perhaps it's no surprise, then, that many of the automated systems used on the World Wide Web employ WAIS as the search engine for the databases they generate. WAIS has proven unusually flexible in the area of full-text searching.

But whatever the underlying engine, natural language searching has another ramification. It means that searchers can frame their query statements in a wider range than would be available through the more limited Boolean search syntax and its rigid parameters. While natural language approaches to textual searching are in their infancy, they promise greater ease of searching for the novice and, we can hope, a quicker route to more accurate results, thus saving the time that would have been required to go completely through a list of misleading hits, in search of the one or two items that truly fit the bill.

In this section, we will examine a number of robots that are currently conducting information sweeps on the World Wide Web. We'll also consider nonrobot alternatives for performing many of the same functions, for as we'll see, robots raise issues involving network performance—a poorly implemented robot can place a considerable strain upon a server site—and they are not good at distinguishing between categories of documentation. Is a Web page of local rather than international interest? Is it a temporary page due to be taken down? Is it the home page for a major category of information at a site, or only a link to a subsidiary document? The robot cannot tell, and therefore makes it a practice to store everything it encounters. You can see that this information-gathering method is high in network overhead and, at times, low in efficiency.

Running a Search with The Web Crawler

The Web Crawler, now owned and maintained by America Online, is a major search engine created by Brian Pinkerton at the University of Washington. The robot operates by moving through the Web and building up an index that can then be searched using the site's search page. You can find The Web Crawler at the following URL:

http://webcrawler.com

Before going too deeply into the specifics of how The Web Crawler works, let's run a sample search. This robot is exceedingly easy to use. We simply enter our keyword(s) on the query page in the appropriate field. It's necessary to click the mouse once with the pointer inside the keyword field; we can then enter the keyword(s) of our choice.

Suppose I am looking for information about the Apollo program, having been galvanized by watching a recent movie about Apollo 13. I'd like to learn more about the individual missions and who flew them. What happened, for example, on Apollo 10—what was its mission, who were the members of its crew, and how did it fit into the overall lunar program?

I can use apollo as a keyword and run the search. But rather than using a single search term, let's consider our options. It's always useful in searching to make a list of possible keywords. In this case, any of the following might do:

apollo space nasa

I can link search terms by accepting the default shown in the appropriate field on The Web Crawler's search page. By doing so, I set up an automatic AND statement between my search terms, meaning The Web Crawler will look only for those documents that contain all three of my search terms. It's as if I had written this:

apollo and space and nasa

A page that shows up with only two of the three won't qualify. While The Web Crawler uses the AND connector as a default, it's also possible to click on the box to deselect this option. If you do so, the search engine will search with an implied OR between any two consecutive words. It would, in the preceding example, find any item that contained the world apollo, or the word space, or the word nasa.

In Figure 2.21, I have entered my three search statements in the keyword field on The Web Crawler's query page. Notice that I have clicked the box that sets up an automatic AND statement between each search term. Notice, too, that The Web Crawler

Hint: Why would you want to set up a search with an AND statement between each keyword? The answer is that your search might retrieve a wide range of documents depending upon how specific your keyword is. Common keywords make for huge lists of hits, and many of the items on those lists won't be very useful. The more specific you can be, the better. Thus, combining keywords progressively narrows the possible hits; you won't receive as many possibilities, but those you do see should be much closer to what you want.

Figure 2.21   Search terms ready to use on The Web Crawler's search screen.

includes the ability to limit the number of hits you retrieve; in this case, I have accepted the default setting of 25 hits.

When I click on the Search button, The Web Crawler consults its index and returns a series of hits based upon my search statement. You can see these results in Figure 2.22.

My query resulted in 103 hits, of which 25 were presented to me. Had I run this search with a single keyword, I would have called up quite a few more hits, but my list would not have been as targeted as this one is. I can browse through the list by clicking on items that look promising. Item 1, for example, is a page maintained by the Kennedy Space Center. It contains plentiful links to Apollo, as shown in Figure 2.23. Here, I am presented with a complete listing of the Apollo missions, with hyperlinks for each. Each retrieved page contains crew rosters, crew biographies, dates of the flight, a complete history of flight activities, and hyperlinks to other pages of interest. I can call up documents, including press releases, moving video, images, and sounds from any of the Apollo missions. And this is just the first of the items recovered from my search.

Examine the results shown in Figure 2.22 with some care. Notice that each listing shows a number to the left of the item, and that these numbers are presented in descending order, starting with 1000. What you are looking at is a statement of relevance; the most relevant document is shown with the score of 1000, while less relevant items are steadily decreased in score. You can't assume that this relevance listing is accurate—a good searcher will browse through all the results—but the items at the very top of the list should, at least theoretically, be strongly related to your query.

Oh yes, the answers to my Apollo 10 questions. The crew consisted of Eugene A. Cernan, John W. Young, and Thomas P. Stafford. The mission: to demonstrate the performance of the lunar command module and the lunar excursion module while orbiting the moon, in preparation for the lunar landing that was planned for Apollo 11. In essence, Apollo 10 was what the Kennedy Space Center archive calls a dress rehearsal for the manned lunar landing; the lunar module descended to within 50,000 feet of the moon's surface.

How The Web Crawler Works

The Web Crawler contains three primary parts:

- The search engine itself.
- A database of documents found through the efforts of the search engine.
- A set of agents that retrieve documents from the network, returning them to the database for indexing and storage.

Figure 2.22 A list of hits from The Web Crawler search.

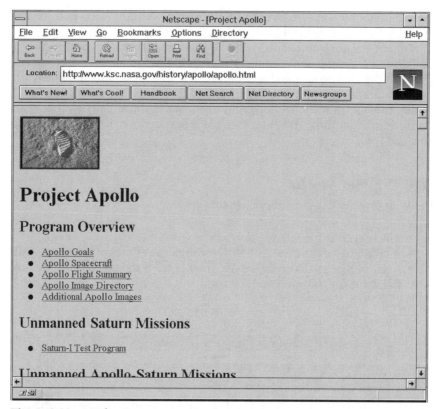

Figure 2.23   A Web page maintained by the Kennedy Space Center, loaded with information about the Apollo project.

Let's pause for a moment on the search engine. The Web Crawler searches by examining a particular set of links and then exploring the links on those documents to see where they lead. Ignoring pictures, sound, PostScript, or binary data, the system attempts to create an index of as large a part of the Web as possible. While index space is invariably limited, the algorithms used ensure as wide a coverage as possible among the numerous servers now operating on the Web. A different algorithm is used in real-time search mode. In the latter mode, The Web Crawler runs the user query against its index, notes relevant documents, and follows unexplored links from those documents. New documents thus retrieved are added to the index, after which the query is run once again, and its results are sorted for relevance. Think of this as an ongoing process that continues until a sufficient list of hits has been found, or until a preset time limit has expired.

It's important to understand just what it is you're searching with any search engine. The Web Crawler allows you to search the entire text of the documents it finds on its travels, for example, which can be a useful thing indeed. Many search engines allow only a search of the document title and its URL statement. A full-text search can ferret out an otherwise inaccessible term that may mean the difference between success and failure in a data hunt. Given the size of a full-text database, however, and the strain on system resources it must take to compile it, we would expect The Web Crawler's database to contain fewer documents than engines that index purely by document title and URL.

The Lycos engine we'll examine next contains far more documents, but it does not provide for a complete full-text search of its gigantic database.

Where does The Web Crawler fit in among the wide range of Internet search tools? Its full-text capability makes it a useful tool with which to initiate a search; The Web Crawler can turn up items buried deep within Web pages that few other search engines could find. I like to start hunting through the World Wide Web with The Web Crawler, knowing that if I fail to find what I'm looking for, I can turn to our next search engine, Lycos, for a hunt through a larger database of documents, albeit one that does not implement full-text search capabilities.

The Lycos Server

Created at Carnegie-Mellon University by Michael Mauldin, the Lycos Catalog of the Internet is one of the premier search engines available, with millions of URLs stored in its huge database. The news that Microsoft has licensed the Lycos catalog for its Microsoft Network is only one more indication of the growing importance of Web search engines (America Online's acquisition of The Web Crawler is another). We're likely to see further consolidation between the major players as companies take network positions and acquire these necessary search tools from the universities and private developers who originally built them.

Remember the principle of the search engine: The robot, or spider, or wanderer, whichever term you fancy, cruises the World Wide Web on an automated basis, gathering information that it returns to a database at its site. The database grows; it becomes a map of at least a part of the universe of connected Web sites. Just how much information is available at a particular site depends upon the methodology used in the search process. We just saw that The Web Crawler searches by full text, but most search engines don't have this capability. Lycos, for example, harvests many more URLs, and its database can thus be considered a more comprehensive source of information, provided you bear in mind what it stores and what it doesn't. Here is what Lycos gleans from a given site:

- The words in the title of the Web page.
- The words in the headings on that page and any subheadings.
- The hyperlinks used on that page.
- The 100 most significant words in the document.
- The first 20 lines of the document.
- The size in bytes and the number of words in each file.

How serious is this limitation? It depends very much upon what you're looking for. A page title is the broadest of data fields; it could easily miss links to other information, and so, for that matter, could the major headings on a Web page. But the indexing of significant words is genuinely useful, and certainly the gathering of the first 20 lines of each document provides a solid base upon which to continue your information hunt. Add to this the fact that the Lycos robot has cataloged millions of URLs—the site estimates that it has abstracted three-fourths of the documents available on the Web worldwide—and you can see that Lycos is a powerful search tool.

You can access the Lycos server at this URL:

http://lycos.cs.cmu.edu/

NOTE: How does Lycos decide which words in a particular Web page are significant and which are not? The system considers such obvious factors as word frequency (removing, of course, commonly used connectors such as and, a, the, and so on). It places extra weight on terms found in titles and headers, as well as in the first paragraph of each document. Building up a list of significant words is chancy when left to a computer; you can't assume that the Lycos engine is infallible. But if you try to think like Lycos, you'll have better luck when using it. I often imagine the ideal Web page that would fit my particular search needs, and try to visualize how its creators would set it up. I can then consider how Lycos would record such a page in its database, and try to weight my search terms toward words that would fit this description.

Figure 2.24 shows the forms-based search page at the site. Setting up the search is simple enough. You enter your search term in the Query field and click on the Start search button to run your search. The results will be returned as a series of hyperlinks, all ranked in terms of relevance.

Suppose that I am trying to find information about the tango. I've just watched the Al Pacino film *Scent of a Woman,* and remember the scene in which Al performs a memorable tango at a New York hotel. I'd like to find out whether there are servers on the

Figure 2.24   The search page at Lycos, one of the Web's best search engines.

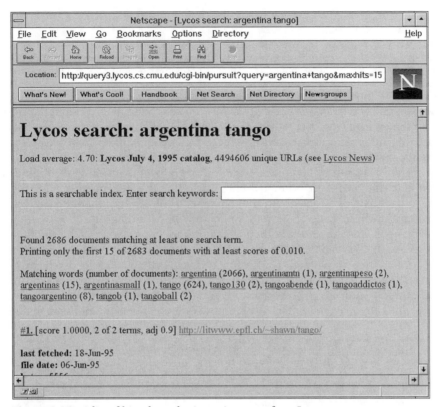

Figure 2.25   A list of hits about the Argentine tango from Lycos.

World Wide Web that hold tango information. Knowing that the tango was created in Argentina, I might set up a search using these terms:

argentina tango

I quickly retrieve a set of hits, as shown in Figure 2.25. The first of these hits, shown as #1 and listed by its URL, runs off the bottom of the page; I could see the rest of it by using the scrollbar. But when I do, I see this information:

```
#1. [score 1.0000, 2 of 2 terms, adj 0.9] http://litwww.epfl.ch/~shawn/tango/
last fetched: 18-Jun-95
file date: 06-Jun-95
bytes: 5556
links: 23

title: tango dance notation argentina argentine

keys: tangoargentino tango argentina

excerpt: tango dance notation argentina argentine REPRESENTS EPFL OR ANY OTHER
INSTITUTION OTHER THAN THAT OF PRIVATE PERSONS EXPLICITLY STATED IN THE SOURCE OF
THE HTML DOCUMENT. PLEASE CONTACT US IF YOU INTEND TO PUBLISH ANY REFERENCE HERE,
```

THANK YOU "J'en ai assez que tout le monde me dise que ce que je fais n'est pas
du tango. Moi, comme je suis fatique, je responds que je fais de la musique du
Buenos Aires. Mais la musique de Buenos Aires, qu'est-ce c'est..? Du tango. Alors
ce que je fais c'est du tango." Astor Piazzolla This server is in Switzerland, and
maintained by S. Koppenhoefer. with information-donations from contributors all
over the world.

Here, the basic fields are presented; you can see the major words in the title, keywords,
and the excerpt from the World Wide Web page. By paging through the list of hits, I can
use this information to determine which sites are most likely to prove useful. Figure 2.26
shows the one I chose as the best.

This turns out to be quite a page for tango lovers. Scrolling through it, I will find a
listing of films with great tango scenes, including the aforementioned *Scent of a Woman*,
as well as lists of books about the dance, and information about a method of notating
dance movement called labanotation, complete with diagrams.

Lycos is a gem, and it is the logical second step in your Web search, assuming you
began with The Web Crawler to get the overview. It's Lycos that can help turn up a broad
list of hits that supplement your initial queries. But you should also be aware of the way
Lycos functions. In this example query, we used two keywords: argentina and tango.
What Lycos did with those search terms is to find documents where the two terms
appeared close together. The system always prefers documents that match as many of

Figure 2.26   A tango server, discovered by Lycos.

the search terms as possible (it also looks for documents that have more occurrences of any one term). But what if we want to tinker with Lycos' functions? The following possibilities exist:

- If you want to set up a Boolean-style search using AND to connect your search terms, you can do so by resetting the field marked Min-terms. In the example shown in Figure 2.24, Min-terms is set to 1. If I had two search terms and wanted to connect them with an AND, I could reset this field to 2. Lycos would then return only documents that contained both words.
- You can use a hyphen to set up a negative statement for a query. Suppose, for example, that I wanted to find pages that included information about the tango but that did not mention Argentina. I could do this with the following search statement: tango -argentina
- Normally, Lycos does not force an exact match on your search statement. Searching under the term argentin, for example, would call up hits on Argentina, Argentinian, Argentine, and so on. If you want to force an exact match, you can use a period. Appending it to a term forces Lycos to look for the term exactly as specified. Thus, if I wanted to find any Web page that included the term Argentine, I would write my query this way:

    argentine.

Note that the period is appended to the search statement; it does not precede it.

You can see that Lycos is quite a useful tool. And as with any search tool, you should be aware of the kind of resources it checks. The Lycos search engine examines not just World Wide Web pages, but also FTP and Gopher sites on its daily excursions through the Web. Realizing this, you get an idea of the scope of this search engine. Gopher documents and files are, in many parts of the world, not yet available through World Wide Web servers. It's very possible, then, that a search engine that can return hits with Gopher will find things that other engines will not.

The World Wide Web Worm

Having read about two World Wide Web search engines, I hope you're beginning to see a methodology emerging. Always check to see what resources the search engine can make use of. Then examine how the material is indexed once it gets into the database.

NOTE: Is Lycos as slow as it seems? The answer is yes and no. Yes, because it's often true that when you try to search this system, you'll receive a message that a given server is too busy to be used right now, and suggesting that you try one of the other Lycos servers. No, because despite the size of its database, Lycos searches are run quite efficiently. The problem is solely that caused by running a system that gets hundreds of thousands of users per week through seven computers. You shouldn't be surprised to find access limited. The developers suggest that you search before 11:00 A.M. or after 6:00 PM (these are times at the Lycos site at Carnegie-Mellon in Pittsburgh, Pennsylvania). You may also want to try using the smaller catalog that is available through Lycos. Although it contains a subset of the entire database, it is nonetheless a useful search tool, and because most people who want to use Lycos ask for the large catalog, the small catalog servers are usually available.

In that way, you can determine the best strategy to use as you formulate your search terms. Using our next resource, The World Wide Web Worm, for example, it's useful to know that it does not, as opposed to The Web Crawler, index the textual content of documents. Instead, it homes in on the URLs themselves, as well as the hypertext that is underlined on a standard Web page. This has interesting ramifications, for a Web hyperlink can point to a sound file, an image, or even a moving video clip. Thus The World Wide Web Worm (WWWW) can be a handy tool if file-finding is your need. You can reach The World Wide Web Worm at this URL.

http://www.cs.colorado.edu/home/mcbryan/WWWW.html

The Worm's home page is shown in Figure 2.27. You can see at once by examining this figure that The World Wide Web Worm has a different searching hierarchy than we've encountered before. Along with a blank keyword field, we are presented with three scrollable boxes. The default is set at search all URL references, meaning we would run our keyword search past these, but if we pull down the window by clicking on the arrow here, we would find we could also search by a variety of other means. Let's run through the options in order:

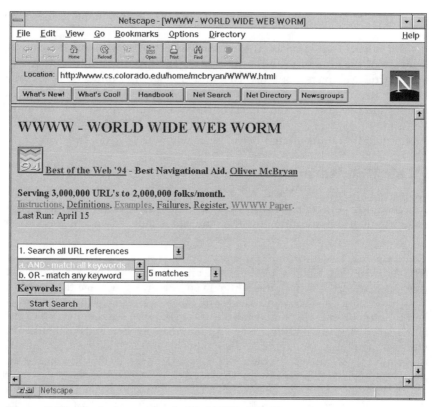

Figure 2.27   The home page for the World Wide Web Worm.

Search all URL references	Runs a search of the hypertext in the WWWW database.
Search all URL addresses	Runs a search of URLs themselves.
Search only in document titles	Runs a search against the titles of HTML documents.
Search only in document addresses	Runs a search against the address of an HTML file.

Let's restate the Worm's search methods, since they can be confusing. You have four ways to search with this tool. When the Worm works with URL references, it is looking at the text that is underlined on the typical Web page. You might see, for example, a hyperlink that said Click here for more information on Afghanistan. This text would appear on the Web page as a hyperlink:

Click here for more information on Afghanistan

It is the underlining that alerts you to the fact that this is a hyperlink. And it is the text in such hyperlinks that is available through the first type of WWWW search.

The second type of WWWW search is of the URLs themselves; these are the addresses to which the hyperlink refers. Remember that a URL is a very specific pointer to a resource, as in the following (fictitious) example:

ftp://pagels.paradox.com/pub/physics/question.zip

You can see that the URL presents all the information necessary to access a site and then refers to a particular file within that site. Because the URL contains all this information, it can be useful if, for example, we were looking for references to a particular site, or if we needed to find references to files of a particular type. While a search for files in the .zip format would be useless because of the sheer number of hits it would generate, you could run a search looking for less common filetypes. Movies in the MPEG format, for example, using the file extension .mpg, could be tracked down with such a search.

HTML titles are searchable through WWWW's engine as well. Because every HTML file includes such a title, and because the developers of Web pages usually try to be descriptive in their use of titles, the ability to search a database containing such titles can be useful. And finally, you can search through a database containing the addresses of the HTML files themselves. This could be helpful if you were trying to find documents from a particular country. Looking for information about Denmark, you might try a type 4 search and specify the dk country code for Denmark.

The World Wide Web Worm, it's clear, is a very precise engine, one that lets us home in on particular types of information, without giving us the flexibility of full-text searches of the contents of Web documents. The Worm's search techniques can be varied from the main search screen. You are offered a choice between two basic methods:

AND—match all keywords	This type of search assumes an AND connector between your keywords, and will return hits only if all the keywords you use are included.

OR—match any keyword   This type of search assumes an OR connector; it will return a hit even if it finds only one of your keywords.

You will also see that WWWW makes it possible to adjust the number of hits it returns by using the Matches: field. This field is set by default at five hits, but can be adjusted up to 5000 depending upon user preference.

As a sample search, suppose I am interested in tracking down home pages about France. One way I might approach this task would be to choose search type 3, which would let me examine the titles of HTML pages. With the single keyword of france, I could then ask for 50 hits and see what resulted. In Figure 2.28, you can see my list. By clicking on any of these items, I can move directly to them. It may not be full-text searching, but WWWW does allow me a great deal of precision in finding pages.

I can also use this tool as a file-finder. Suppose, for example, that I am looking for the WinZip utility, a Windows-based compression and decompression program developed by shareware author Nico Mak. By searching through URLs themselves, I can use the keyword winzip to generate the list shown in Figure 2.29. WWWW has provided me with a list of pages where links to WinZip appear; I can click on any of these to examine the page in question and find my file.

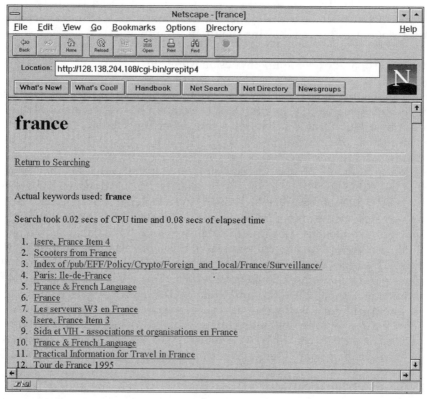

Figure 2.28   A list of Web pages referring to France, as found through The World Wide Web Worm.

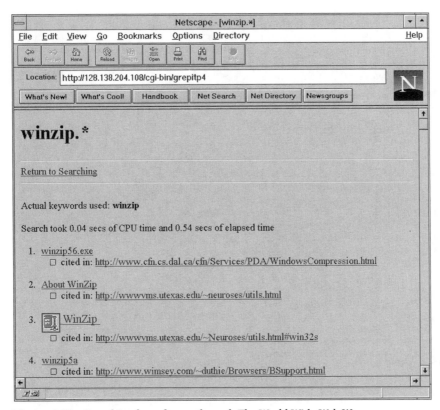

Figure 2.29   Searching for software through The World Wide Web Worm.

More than the other search tools we've examined, The World Wide Web Worm takes some getting used to; it's necessary to run a number of sample searches until you become familiar with the various options available and can straighten out the terminology. Created by Oliver McBryan at the University of Colorado, the Worm has served up several million URLs to its growing list of users, and its pinpoint searching techniques make it a tool you will want to master.

JumpStation

Another precision search tool, albeit one with a smaller database than several of the engines we've already discussed, is Jonathan Fletcher's JumpStation. Created at Stirling University in Scotland, the JumpStation is a full-text index tool, which gives you the possibility of finding terms that are not located in headers or other major parts of a Web page. Its drawback: The database is not nearly as large as those of several other engines. You can reach the JumpStation at this URL:

http://js.stir.ac.uk/jsbin/jsii

Figure 2.30 shows you the search page for this tool.

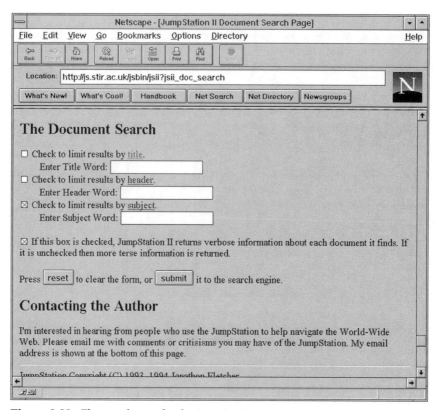

Figure 2.30 The search page for the JumpStation.

In addition to full-text searching, the JumpStation gives you several other options:

Title searching You can search for any words occurring in a document title. As always, you're dependent upon the skill of the person who created a given page's title, but this is a useful way to reduce the number of possible hits to a smaller, but more accurate, quantity.

Header searching Headers, theoretically, prove valuable sources because they break down the major content of a given page into units. Of course, a header search can't dig out text under the header that refers to your topic only peripherally.

URL searching Not yet implemented, a URL search will give you the ability to look for keywords in document URLs.

The JumpStation's search page allows you to choose between search methods by clicking on the relevant checkbox. This can provide for fruitful searching because of the degree of control it affords you. For example, you could combine types to search for every page that contained the word japan in the title and the word tourism in the content field (be advised that, when you do this, only the first word entered in each type box is used in the search).

InfoSeek

InfoSeek is one of the outstanding search tools on the Internet. A subscription-based service, it does more than collect data about World Wide Web pages; it also indexes USENET newsgroups, computer magazines, newswires, and press releases, along with company profiles, movie reviews, technical support databases, and a variety of other information sources. Several pricing options exist, including the standard plan at $9.95 per month, which includes 100 free transactions (InfoSeek defines a transaction as a query or document retrieval). Additional transactions are charged at the rate of $.10 each. Occasional users can simply pay a $.20 fee for each transaction, with no monthly fee incurred.

With information on over 350,000 Web pages, InfoSeek is a major player in the Web search game. Indexing proceeds on a full-text basis up to the first 50K of text. You can "weight" words and phrases as being required, desirable, or undesirable, giving you considerable precision over the search method. Its additional content also distinguishes InfoSeek from other search engines; where else can you search Reuters, the Associated Press, Businesswire, PR Newswire, and the Newsbytes News Network, not to mention over 10,000 USENET newsgroups? These unique commercial features make InfoSeek a

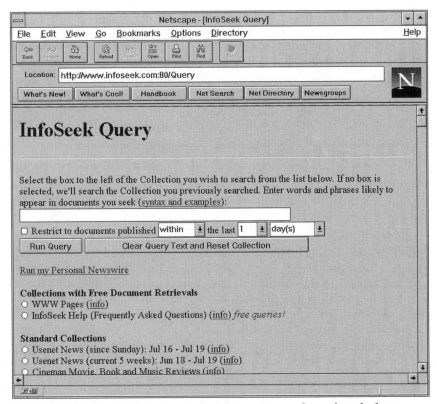

Figure 2.31 The query screen at InfoSeek, a commercial search tool of enormous capabilities.

site you'll want to examine, and you can set up a trial account for free, giving you a month to experiment on the system. You can reach it at this URL:

http://www.infoseek.com:80/doc/help/InfoSeekIntro.html

The InfoSeek query screen is shown in Figure 2.31. Notice that you search by keyword and can restrict your search by time; the database to be searched is chosen by clicking on the fields offered beneath the keyword field.

Your first move with InfoSeek, after setting up your account, should be to go to the Query Syntax, Examples, and Tips screen, which appears as a hyperlink on the search screen. Here you will be presented with the basic parameters of an InfoSeek search, such as the following:

Commas   Use a comma to separate proper names that should be found in your search document. The comma separates names so they don't appear to be part of one larger name. Proper names should be capitalized to improve your search accuracy.

Double Quotes   Use double quotes to show words that should be adjacent. For example, entering "world trade" as your search term will tell Info-Seek that the two words should appear together.

Hyphens   Use hyphens instead of double quotes if you choose; both tell InfoSeek that the two words mentioned should be adjacent to each other.

Brackets   Use brackets to show words that should be near each other in any order. Thus, [world international trade] looks for documents that contain the search terms in some proximity to each other, but not necessarily in the order presented in the query.

Plus Signs   The plus sign (+) is used to indicate a word that is required in your search (see next). No space should appear after the plus sign.

Minus Signs   The minus sign (–) is used when you want to declare a term undesired in your search. No space should appear after the minus sign.

When InfoSeek runs your search, it will try to find the best match between the terms you have given it and the documents housed in its database. But note that not all search terms will appear in every document. InfoSeek gives priority to matching the most important terms. If there is a search term that you require to be in every retrieved document, use the plus (+) key to indicate it. And remember that a minus sign (–) can be used to exclude a term. Wildcard characters, incidentally, don't work; InfoSeek will search for an asterisk (*) as part of the search term.

As you can see, using these InfoSeek operators allows you to be quite specific in tailoring a search, thus reducing the total number of hits and ending up with a highly targeted list of results. Twenty hits will be shown to any query, although up to 200 are available through the system. For ease of use, comprehensive coverage, and a well-structured query language, you won't find a better service than InfoSeek.

Harvest

Created by a team led by Michael Schwartz at the University of Colorado at Boulder, Harvest is a powerful search program that allows users to gather information with precision. A server using the Harvest software is referred to as a *broker* in this terminology, and a number of demonstration brokers are available that show off the power of the Harvest system. Interestingly, you can either use the broker itself or retrieve data from it to construct your own indices. With funding from the Advanced Research Projects Agency, the Air Force Office of Scientific Research, the National Science Foundation, Hughes Aircraft Co. and Sun Microsystems, this is a system that looks to be a long-term attempt to improve Internet data gathering.

Among current Harvest brokers available for searching are these:

SEC EDGAR	An index that lets you search documents that have been filed with the Securities and Exchange Commission.
AT&T 800 Information	An index of 800 numbers made available from AT&T.
WWW Pages	An index of close to 50,000 World Wide Web pages, indexed by content summaries.
PC Software	Indexed information about thousands of software programs.
NetNews	An index of news drawn from USENET.

You can check these and other Harvest brokers at this URL:

http://harvest.cs.colorado.edu/

NIKOS—A World Wide Web Index

Supported by Rockwell Network Systems and California State Polytechnic University, NIKOS contains a search function that supports multiple word searches and runs them through a steadily growing database. The site is poorly documented at present, but seems to be under active development.

http://www.rns.com/cgi-bin/nomad

RBSE's URL Database

This site contains a database built by an automated robot program that retrieves the full text of documents and indexes them using a powerful WAIS engine. RBSE stands for the Repository Based Software Engineering (RBSE) program, a research and development project designed to improve NASA's software capability; it is run by David Eichmann at the University of Houston, Clear Lake. The biggest drawback of the database as it is currently constituted is that its holdings are limited. You can check it out at this URL:

http://rbse.jsc.nasa.gov/eichmann/rbse.html

The Open Text Index

A powerful search engine that was just establishing itself on the Internet when this book went to press, the Open Text Index allows you to search several million World Wide Web pages by keyword(s). The index uses Open Text Corporation's server software, which automates the searching process by making continual sweeps for data. Open Text indexes every word on a page, using fourteen servers working together to make possible frequent updates. You can search in three ways:

Simple Search   A basic keyword search using words or phrases

Power Search   Allows you to define the parts of the document you want to search. Proximity searches are available (search for a word only when adjacent to another specified term), while Boolean techniques and relevance feedback are also available.

Weighted Search   Makes it possible to give certain terms greater weight than others in the search procedure.

Hits are presented with enough content to make it possible to evaluate the document; the associated hyperlink allows you to access the page. To try out Open Text, go to the following URL:

http://www.opentext.com

World Wide Web Wanderer/WANDEX

The Wanderer is, perhaps, the first of the robots to have traversed the Web, returning useful information about its size and growth. Now you can search an index generated by the Wanderer that contains thousands of home pages. The URL is:

http://www.netgen.com/cgi/wandex

Searches are case-insensitive and results are ranked in terms of possible relevance. The search engine was created by Matthew Gray at net.genesis, a software developer in Cam-

HINT: If you're interested in keeping up with robot-related issues, you may want to look into a mailing list devoted to the subject. To subscribe, send e-mail to this address:

    robots-request@nexor.co.uk

In your message, put the following on separate lines:

    subscribe
    help
    stop

You will be added to the mailing list. This site is also the home of the World Wide Web Robots, Wanderers, and Spiders page, which can be accessed at this URL:

    http://web.nexor.co.uk/mak/doc/robots/robots.html

The work of Martijn Koster, this is a page with links to a wealth of information about automated Web searching, including Koster's own articles, and Dave Eichmann's "Ethical Web Agents." If you're going to be using automated Web searching, you should get to know this page.

bridge, Massachusetts. Also available here is a listing of Web pages by geographical area, quite useful when you're trying to home in on a particular country or area. See this URL:

http://www.netgen.com/cgi/comprehensive

Other Web-Based Search Tools

The engines we've just examined are all major players, differing in the size of their databases and the way they allow you to search them. We can expect a great deal of future development in this field. Some of the Web pages shown in this section are sure to evolve into important tools for Web searching, and it would be a good idea to familiarize yourself with them. In each case, try to determine how the individual page is organized and what it allows you to do. The key to searching on the World Wide Web is to familiarize yourself with as many different tools as possible, so that you'll know where to turn with a specialized search.

ALIWEB

Here's a database of World Wide Web pages that doesn't function through a search engine. Instead, people write descriptions of the services and features of their Web pages and place them into a standard format, which the ALIWEB system retrieves. The forms are collated into a searchable database, which can be accessed at the following URL:

http://web.nexor.co.uk/public/aliweb/aliweb.html

The work of UK service provider NEXOR, ALIWEB began as a simple catalog of services, maintained on the NEXOR Web server. The growth of robots caused the site's organizer, Martijn Koster (who, as just noted, is also the organizer of the useful World Wide Web Robots, Wanderers, and Spiders page), to ponder how to create a database that would not have an adverse impact upon network resources. The ALIWEB site is the result. The result of the growing use of the system is that it is now mirrored at a number of sites worldwide, references to which can be found at the URL just listed.

The Awesome Lists

John Makulowich has gathered a number of interesting Internet materials together under the title The Awesome Lists. Topics are broken out more by site than by topic, which makes using the list as a directory more time-consuming than it might be, though the list of sites is well chosen. But what makes The Awesome Lists exceptional is Makulowich's work in building a comprehensive search page. To see it, travel to the primary URL and begin exploring from that point. The address is:

http://www.clark.net/pub/journalism/awesome.html

When you arrive, you will find a link to something called the All-in-One Search Page. This page is broken out by Internet protocol. Were you to click on the World Wide Web link, you would be taken to a page that lists all the forms-based Web search tools, the kind of engines we will be discussing later in this chapter. Click on News/Weather and you're whisked to a page that offers lists of every searchable site covering those topics.

What is more, you can enter your search term and run your search directly from Maku-lowich's pages, returning to them to easily search other sites for similar material.

CUSI

Standing for Configurable Unified Search Engine, CUSI is an interface for a great many World Wide Web resources. The idea here is that a single Web page can open up a wealth of searching tools; instead of moving back and forth between your tools, you can choose among them from a common interface. CUSI is, again, the work of Martijn Koster at NEXOR, one of the most prolific people engaged in the great enterprise of making Inter-net information more widely accessible. You can reach its home page at this URL:

http://pubweb.nexor.co.uk/public/cusi/cusi.html

Numerous mirror sites exist around the world. The method is to contact the primary site and examine the list of mirrors, to see which one makes the most sense for you to use.

Browsing through CUSI, I find searchable fields for a number of the search engines we've already discussed, as well as non-Web tools such as Veronica, WAIS, and Gopher. You can search using archie, netfind, X.500; you can also consult extensive databases of documents, from the Internet Request for Comments documents to a number of on-line

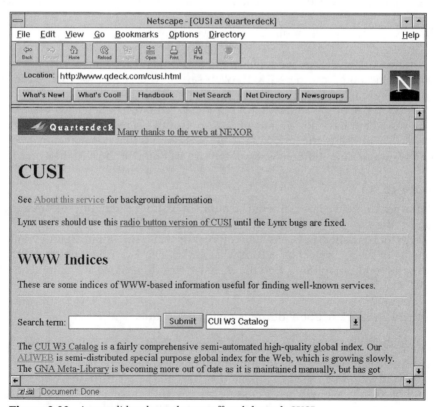

Figure 2.32   A consolidated search page offered through CUSI.

dictionaries. The extensive mirroring of this material makes putting a CUSI site on your hotlist a good idea; you'll have fast access to a wide range of search tools. You can see CUSI at one of its mirror sites in Figure 2.32.

Global On-Line Directory

CityScape Internet Services, a U.K.-based service provider, offers free on-line advertising through this directory. The database is compiled through information submitted by commercial Web-site administrators, and full-text searches are available through its search engine. Use the following URL to contact this site:

http://www.gold.net/gold/search2.html

Where the Global On-Line Directory may prove valuable is in situations where you need to search for a particular type of company in a given location. The search screen allows you to specify type of organization, field of interest, and geographical location distinguished by continent (even Antarctica is a choice!).

The Internet Sleuth

This unusual site offers keyword searching of numerous Internet databases, from the major sites like Lycos and Yahoo to obscure servers in the humanities and sciences. You can also use its directory structure to call up a list of databases by topic, running a search at any of the sites. The Internet Sleuth is available at this URL:

http://www.intbc.com/sleuth/

W3 Catalog

The Centre Universitaire d'Informatique at the University of Geneva makes available this Web search engine. Essentially, the site gathers the database resources of a number of different search tools, from NCSA's What's New and Starting Points pages to the Yanoff list and John December's Computer-Mediated Communication and Internet Tools Summary documents. The catalog can be searched at this URL:

http://cuiwww.unige.ch/cgi-bin/w3catalog

Extensively mirrored, the site can be used on servers near to you, so it's worth your time to look around the site to find such a server. You will also be interested in a comprehensive search page that provides links to many search engines and other reference tools. You can reach it at:

http://cuiwww.unige.ch/meta-index.html

Bookmarks—Organizing Your Search Tools

There was a time when using the World Wide Web was relatively simple. When you found a home page that struck your fancy, you simply made a note of it. If you needed to consult it again, you reentered its URL into your browser and did your work. The method was cumbersome—after all, it required you to enter a lengthy URL statement

> **HINT:** You shouldn't be put off by browser terminology. Although the number of browsers is rapidly multiplying, these software tools all set out to do the same thing. It doesn't much matter whether your choice is Netscape, or Spry's version of Mosaic, or perhaps Quarter-deck's Web browser. No matter what interface you use to access the Web, what you need is a method of organization. In essence, anyone who wants to take advantage of this new medium has to create his or her own information structure. Whether or not your experience at finding Web information is a successful one will depend on how effectively you do this. If you will study the following methods as they are used with Netscape, you should be able to learn enough to apply them to the browser of your choice. An hour or so spent experimenting with your browser's bookmark functions will be repaid many times over in efficiency.

each time—but on the other hand, there weren't all that many Web sites out there, and keeping them organized didn't pose too great a challenge.

Today, all that has changed with a vengeance. With Web sites in the tens of thousands, it seems that no matter how obscure your field of interest, there is likely to be a host of sites that cater to it. It becomes necessary, then, to find a way to organize information, so that you can quickly determine which of these sites is the best for your search. And, as you have just seen, the number of good directory sites that you will want to add to your bookmark list is quickly expanding.

Figure 2.33   Netscape's Bookmarks menu; note the arrangement by topic.

Fortunately, the new Web browsers make creating bookmarks a simple matter. Let's look now at how to handle this chore in Netscape, the premier graphical browser on the market. The same basic principles apply to any browser, but I will show you how to organize your material in Netscape because it has become so widely used.

Adding a Bookmark

Every browser makes it relatively simple to create bookmarks. Where things get more difficult is in organizing them. Take a look at Figure 2.33, for example, where I have moved to the INFOMINE home page. I note that this site contains links to government resources on the federal, state and local level, and I think it will be useful for my search needs. In the figure, I have pulled down Netscape's Bookmarks menu.

There are two things I want you to notice about Figure 2.33. First of all, note that the bookmark menu contains an item called Add Bookmark; you can see that I have positioned the cursor on it. When I click on that item, the bookmark is added to my bookmark list. So far, so good; we know that to add a bookmark to our list we do the following:

1. With the World Wide Web page in question on-screen, pull down the Bookmarks menu.
2. Click on Add Bookmark.

You can now look at your bookmark list to verify that the new item has appeared there. Look at the bottom of the list; new items are placed at the end unless you specify otherwise.

But this is only the first part of the story. When we add a bookmark to our list, what we have done is to make it possible for us to return to the site simply by clicking on the site name in our bookmark list. What we haven't done is to organize the information in any meaningful way. If five or six bookmarks are all you need to conduct your searches, you're in good shape. But what happens when you have hundreds of bookmarks listed, in no discernible order, and most of them not even visible without scrolling through the list on-screen? Clearly, some organizing method must be found.

CMC Magazine Index
Financial Times Group
NewsLink media list, (c) 1995
NewsPage Home Page
MediaInfo Interactive e-newspapers main
Pathfinder Home Page
TIME Magazine Home Page
Today's San Jose Mercury News
VerbWork's Virtual Den
ZD net

Figure 2.34 A submenu opens when I click on a major topic in my Netscape browser's Bookmarks page.

Organizing a Bookmark List

If you go back to Figure 2.33 again, you'll see that my bookmark list is actually a series of topics. These range from Business to Music to Search Engines to Wine and Food. Note that the list is alphabetized, and that, to the right of each topic, is a triangular pointer. This pointer indicates that, in fact, each topic contains an underlying menu of further choices. If I click on one of these, a submenu opens, which contains specific items that fit the topic description. You can see such a submenu in Figure 2.34. All I have to do to make use of one of these URLs is to click on it. Rather than inserting the complete URL statement into Netscape, I click and go to the site.

How did I organize my bookmark list this way? Take a look at Figure 2.35, which holds many of the answers. I called this screen up by clicking on the View Bookmarks item from the main Bookmarks menu in Netscape; I then clicked on the Edit button to call up the bookmark editor screen, which is what this is. It is from this screen that you can manipulate your bookmarks page to organize your data. You do this by creating headers for the broad categories of information you want to collect. You then insert bookmark items below each header, using the Up and Down buttons to control the placement of each URL.

Think in terms of hierarchies of information. The header items you create define what hierarchies you want to use in your work. Headers should always be broad categories and should be sufficiently distinct from their surrounding headers so that they will be useful to you in moving quickly to the site you're looking for. They should not, however, be so broad that their contents could be anything. Using Science as a header cuts too wide a swathe; you might be better specifying a particular science, say, Chemistry. Your individual bookmark items will be inserted beneath each header. For clarity, you should keep these organized alphabetically, which you can do by using the Up and Down buttons on the editing screen.

Figure 2.35   The screen used for editing bookmark entries in Netscape.

Creating a New Header

Once you've determined what you want to call your header, the procedure to follow to create it is straightforward:

1. Choose View Bookmarks from the Bookmarks menu, and click on the Edit button to call up the bookmark editing screen.
2. On the Bookmark List editing screen, click on New Header.
3. In the Name field, fill in the name of the header you have decided to use.
4. Using the Up and Down buttons, click until the header is properly placed on your bookmark list.
5. Click on Close to end your editing session.

At this point, if you pull down the Bookmarks menu, you should see the new header in place.

Because your header list can always be modified, either by editing or deleting particular headers, I recommend that you simply think through the kind of categories you think you will need and go ahead and set up a basic header list. You can begin adding Web sites to this list immediately. Doubtless, as you proceed, new header ideas will come to mind, or you may want to consolidate the URLs listed under several different headers under a new, single header. The only way to find out what organizing strategy works best for you is to experiment and be willing to try new combinations.

Adding Bookmarks under Particular Headers

Recall that when we created our first bookmark, it was placed at the end of the bookmark list. We then used the Up and Down buttons to move it to the place it belonged. This method works fine when you have a small number of bookmarks. New bookmarks are added to the end of the list and can be moved about as necessary. But when you begin working with large numbers of bookmarks, the method becomes unwieldy. In my case, I have hundreds of bookmarks set up through Netscape. If I were to take the default and let the bookmark be added at the end of my bookmark list, I would spend quite a lot of time clicking the Up button to place each bookmark where I wanted it to go.

To get around this problem, we can use Netscape's placement feature. This allows us to specify a header under which we want the next bookmark to be placed. I might, for example, know that I wanted the INFOMINE bookmark placed under my Search Tools-Directories header. Netscape will place it at the end of the list of URLs under that header, allowing me to use the Up button to place it more precisely (and avoiding the need to move the URL through layers of headers on my way to placing it in its proper location). Here's how to use this feature:

1. From the Bookmarks menu, choose View Bookmarks, and click on the Edit button on the ensuing window to get to the bookmark editing screen.
2. Click on the arrow in the Add Bookmarks Under field.
3. From the list of headers that appears, highlight the header under which you want to add the next bookmark.
4. Click on the Add Bookmark button at the top left of the screen to add the current Web page's URL to your bookmark list.

5. Use the Up button to move the new bookmark to its proper, alphabetical placement within your list.
6. Click on Close to end the current bookmark editing session.

Headers within Headers

Netscape's hierarchical bookmark structure allows you to embed headers within headers. When you place a bookmark under a particular header, it will appear as a submenu of the header in the menu. When you indent an item two levels deep, it will appear as a submenu of a submenu. For example, suppose you wanted to set up a broad header called Chemistry, and wanted to break it out into two subheaders, one of them called Organic and the other Inorganic. That way, when you clicked on the Chemistry item on the main Bookmarks menu, a submenu would appear listing the two choices, from which you could choose the one you needed.

To create the Organic header within the larger Chemistry header, you would do the following:

1. Create a Chemistry header using the methods just discussed.
2. Using the bookmarks editing screen, highlight the new Chemistry header.
3. Click again on New Header and create a header called Organic.
4. Use the Up button to move the Organic header so that it appears as a subheader of the Chemistry header.
5. You can create the Inorganic header in the same way. When you are through, you will be able to add bookmarks either under the broad Chemistry header, or under either of the two subheaders, Chemistry and Organic.
6. Click on the Close button to end your editing session.

Using Separators

Humans are visual creatures. When it comes to long strings of text, we need all the help we can get at sorting and organizing what we have to work with. One tool that Netscape provides in its bookmarks list is the ability to create a separator. A separator is just a line that divides one set of bookmarks, or headers, from another. Using separators, you can emphasize your organizing principles and highlight particular categories of information, or simply make sure that one set of data doesn't get confused with another.

To create a separator, take the following steps:

1. Pull down the Bookmarks menu, choose View Bookmarks, and click on the Edit button that appears to enter the editing window.
2. Highlight the bookmark after which you would like the separator to appear.
3. Click on the New Separator button.
4. A separator line will appear in your bookmark list at that point. You can move it up or down if necessary by using the Up or Down buttons on the bookmark editing window.
5. Click on the Close button to end your editing session.

Viewing Bookmark Information

The bookmark editing screen in Netscape allows you to perform various bookmark-related tasks that can be useful in your information organization. Remember that to

Figure 2.36 Full information about each bookmark can be generated by examining the bookmark editing screen.

access the complete editing screen, you first choose View Bookmarks from the Bookmarks menu, and then click on the Edit button. If you do this and take a look at the list of bookmarks that appears in the window on the left of the screen, you will see that you can use the list to check information about each bookmark. Notice in Figure 2.36 how the information is presented. Here, I have highlighted a bookmark called The ETEXT Archives from my Humanities header. And if you look to the right of the list of bookmarks, you will see that URL information about this bookmark is presented. We can see that its URL is as follows:

http://www.etext.org/

We also have information about when the URL was added to the bookmark list, and when I last took a look at it. There is also a description field in which I could add any comments I might want to make about this Web page.

Notice that the editing window also contains a button called View Bookmarks. Clicking on this button creates a new Netscape page that contains your list in HTML format. This page, in turn, can be saved by using the Save As command from the File menu.

Importing and Exporting Bookmarks

Bookmark files can be saved like any other. Suppose, for example, that you were going to be traveling and wanted to show a friend a number of interesting sites that you had found on the World Wide Web. Rather than copying all of these manually and reentering them into Netscape, it would be possible to simply save your bookmarks file and take it with you on disk to your friend's machine. There, it could be examined within his or her copy of Netscape.

To do this, we use the Export Bookmarks button. Here's the procedure:

1. Call up the bookmarks editing screen by choosing View Bookmarks from the Bookmarks file and then clicking on the Edit button.
2. Click the Export Bookmarks button.
3. In the dialog box that appears, enter a filename for your bookmark file.
4. Click OK to create the file.

This is the file you can now use to share your bookmark list with others.

From the recipient's point of view, bringing in an external bookmark file to examine is a relatively trivial exercise. Here's how to go about it:

1. Move to the bookmarks editing window using the steps detailed in the previous procedure.
2. Click on the Import Bookmarks button.
3. In the ensuing dialog box, click on the bookmark file you want to examine.
4. Click on OK. This will insert the new bookmark file as an item after the last item in the current bookmark list.

Views of the Bookmark Page

When your bookmark list gets long enough, there will be times when you want to examine it in sections. Perhaps, on a particular day, you are working on a project that involves certain kinds of Web pages. Rather than going through your entire bookmark list every time you pull it down, you could specify that, for the time being, Netscape should only show you certain segments of the list. Here's how:

1. Choose View Bookmarks from the Bookmarks menu; then click on the Edit button to call up the editing window.
2. Click on the arrow in the Bookmark Menu field.
3. Highlight the header you want to use as your main bookmark display.
4. Click on Close to close the editing window.

From now on, until you change the setting, the bookmarks you see in your bookmark list will be only those of the header you have chosen. I have found this a handy tool to use in my own work. In several recent book projects, I have isolated particular sets of information this way and have been able to work quickly, without the distractions of working through an entire, lengthy list of bookmarks.

Keeping the Bookmark List Timely

It's inevitable, given the Web's rapid pace of change, that many pages will become obsolete, or will change their address as new servers become available, people change jobs, and companies acquire Web pages belonging to other companies. I recommend that you go through your bookmark list on occasion to check your entries. You will probably find, if you have been collecting bookmarks for a while, that some of the citations have become defunct. You may click on one and be taken to a notice that the URL has changed. If it has, you can edit the URL for a given bookmark by highlighting it in the bookmark editing dialog box and then changing the listed URL on-screen.

Some pages will simply disappear; you click on the bookmark and are told that the specified address no longer exists. If this happens, you can remove a bookmark entry easily enough. To do so, follow this procedure:

1. Pull down the Bookmarks menu, choose View Bookmarks, and click the Edit button to move into the editing screen.
2. Highlight the name of the defunct bookmark.
3. Click on the Remove Item button.
4. Click on Close to exit the editing window.

Keeping your links up to date like this has a secondary benefit. It forces you to work through your bookmarks one by one on occasion, a job that will often remind you of bookmarks that you had forgotten about. Keeping your list fresh in your mind will make your research that much more effective.

Bookmarks for the Shell Account User

While graphical browsers provide the best combination of ease of use and software capability, it's also true that a Unix program operating in the shell environment can handle your bookmark chores. Because lynx is the most common—and certainly the best—browser for character-based systems, I focus here on it, although if you're using a different character-based browser, you should be able to determine its bookmark methods by studying its help system (with lynx, for example, you activate the help system by pressing the **?** key).

As far as lynx is concerned, the bookmark methodology is straightforward. Let's assume you've moved to a World Wide Web page that you'd like to save for future reference. To create the bookmark, perform the following steps:

1. Press **a** to add the current page to your bookmark file.
2. At the prompt, press **l** to save the bookmark.
3. Press **v** to call up your list of bookmarks. Here, you can verify that the link you have tried to save is indeed there.
4. Press the left arrow key to return to the current Web page.

If you run an **ls** command from your command prompt, you will discover that the bookmark file has been saved under the name lynx_bookmarks.html. This file can be edited with any text editor to make changes, such as removing links that have become out of date. While lynx's ability to manage bookmark information is a far cry from Netscape's, you can nonetheless create a basic information structure with it, and apply that structure in your future data hunting.

World Wide Web Tips

The Web is far less frustrating to use today than it used to be. In the formative era when Web pages were comparatively scarce and search engines unknown, the system's access to a broad spectrum of network technologies proved intimidating. There was no way to search from the top down, and no two searches for information seemed to turn out quite the same. The average data hunt involved clicking on hyperlinks in a more or less directed manner, depending upon the skill of the page designers, through whose work you passed. Such searches were often fascinating in their own right, and usually led to places that were off the beaten track. But they could be time-consuming and unproductive to the person who needed information on a tight schedule.

With the diversity of today's Web tools, the searcher is challenged to come up with the optimum strategy amidst a veritable sea of alternatives. Here are some tips that may help you as you master this new medium.

Choose Your Tools with Care

Remember, the major types of Web-based searches you will conduct involve either directories or search engines. The first step is to make sure you understand which is best for the kind of work you want to do. The advantage of directories is that they are easy to use; you work through structured layers of menus, each narrowing in on your destination. But directories depend upon your having the same sense of organization that the creators of the directory do, and experience has proven to me that this is often not the case. A search engine, on the other hand, lets you run your query past a broad and frequently updated database. In general, a workable method is to start with a good directory and supplement it with a search engine. If you find yourself spending too much time working through directory menus or running fruitless searches on keywords at a directory site, turn to one of the major search engines instead.

Be Prepared to Wait

The new search engines and directories are popular for a good reason; they impose a sense of order upon what was once a mass of unstructured information. That means you and I are running searches along with thousands of other people around the world on any given day, with the inevitable consequences upon response time at a given site. Don't be surprised if you can't get into a particular site, receiving instead a message that the server is overloaded and that you will have to try again later. A little practice will reveal to you that certain times of day seem to work better at particular sites. By experimenting, you can soon restrict your searching at those sites to the appropriate times.

Construct a Comprehensive Bookmark List

Nothing will help you more in your searches of the Web than to have your search tools laid out in order. I recommend strongly that you create two categories of search tool. Reserve the first for directory sites only; here put Yahoo, Web of Wonder, and the other sites we looked at in this chapter that provide topic-arranged information, often supplemented with keyword searching. Maintain the second for search engines and nothing else. When you search, examine both lists of bookmarks. Doing so will jog your memory about what's out there, and will help you to decide which directory and which search engine would make a logical starting point for your work.

Run Benchmark Searches

If information hunting is a major preoccupation or even a vocation for you, the best thing you can do is to run sample searches at the various sites just to get a feel for the material available. A relaxed, inquisitive kind of searching, not driven by immediate job or personal needs, is the approach to take when you're learning about a site for the first time. A particularly useful exercise is to work up several searches that can be run at different sites. It's instructive to see how different search tools handle the same query, and to compare the results generated at each. As new search tools become available, you can then run these benchmark searches against them, and will be able to tell which are the most likely to meet your needs.

Be Wary of Title Searches

Most developers fail to make the titles of their pages useful in the search context. These titles, found at the top of HTML documents, should clue us in as to what we can expect to find on the page. But if you were to glance through titles at random, you would be surprised at how few contain truly useful information that would help us by searching through a collection of them by keyword. If you are using a search engine that provides document text as well as title searching, you will be more likely to find what you need. A title search can be a good place to begin, but it is more than likely that it will need to be supplemented.

Learn How the Site Functions

Explore, read the Frequently Asked Questions (FAQ) documents and other background information available at the site of your search tool. Make sure to find out how the site gets its material—is the database the product of an automated search tool, or the result of information supplied by the developers of individual Web pages? What kinds of techniques can be used to search the database, and are the results ranked in terms of relevance to your search? What kinds of material does the site index? Obviously, a site that houses Gopher information is going to pull up things that won't be available at sites that limit themselves exclusively to Web documents. These and other questions should preoccupy you as you explore the capabilities of each site.

Picture Your Result

This somewhat cryptic advice suggests that when you can visualize what you're looking for, you are more likely to find it. Suppose you're looking for a home page about forestry. Given that the broad overview of your topic is what you want, a directory site may be just the ticket. Or, if you choose to search through a search engine's database, you will want to confine your search options, where possible, to HTML page titles or headers. After all, these should contain your search term, if you're looking for an entire page on a given topic.

If, on the other hand, you see your topic as obscure, you will need to turn to a full-text search engine, one that can catch that mention of Atlantic salmon on a page otherwise dedicated to trout fishing, or find a reference to the Chilean power grid on a page devoted to South American tourism. The point is, if you can form an image of what the result should look like on a typical World Wide Web page, you will know how to adjust the parameters of your search accordingly.

Use Specific Search Terms

Commonly used words are unlikely to generate hits no matter what your search engine. The idea is to isolate a search keyword or phrase that specifically identifies what you are after. In this regard, it becomes more important than ever to bear in mind the nature of the engine you are using. A search engine that automatically inserts an AND between two terms (the Web Crawler is an example) will return hits with far more specificity than one that does not. The latter, for example, would encounter a search term like nuclear physics and return as hits any documents that contained either word. The former would return only those documents that contained both the term nuclear and the term physics, increasing the likelihood of success in your search.

Be Prepared to Change Your Terms

Think of the search process as something that just begins when you receive your first page of results. In most cases, you will need to examine those results to determine how your search terms should be modified. If you receive too many hits, then it will be necessary to qualify your search terms, perhaps adding other words that will need to be found along with the original term, or using whatever operators the search engine in question makes available to restrict the search. The important thing to realize is that this is a perfectly normal process. By running a search repeatedly, each time with an adjusted set of keywords, you strengthen the possibility of finding the information you need.

Use Relevance Rankings with Great Caution

Nothing would be more foolish than to dismiss all results from your search that didn't meet the ranking criteria of a machine. While computers are getting better all the time at searching, they still aren't very good at understanding what we have in mind as we search. Using cut-and-dried techniques, such as weighing the number of times a search term appears in a document, or how close multiple search terms appear to each other on a Web page, the search engine may completely misidentify the kind of page you are looking for. It pays to go through any list of hits carefully from top to bottom, seeing for yourself whether you agree with the computer's findings. Do this a few times and you will quickly learn to take nothing for granted.

Adjust the Number of Hits

Many search tools allow you to adjust the number of hits you receive. A default, commonly 10 or 25, will be suggested, and if you make no adjustments, this is what you will receive. But if you read the results page carefully, you may find that you are looking at 25 hits out of a total of hundreds. Such a result would be a sure indication that your search terms needed to be tightened. More ominously, from the standpoint of the individual search, it would say that the hits you do see on the page are only the froth on a great wave of information, and that they may well be useless because your search terms are too common. It is far better to have a small but relevant list of hits than a huge mass of unrelated data.

Arrange Your Results by Topic

If you're working on specific projects involving World Wide Web research, be sure to set up the topic on your bookmark list. Then, as you explore your list of results, be sure to add any pages that appear particularly promising to this list. You can always delete those that don't pay off later; initially, the point is to begin building your list of resources for later reference. A bookmark list arranged by well-defined topics is one you'll use again and again; it allows you to create your own directory structure for the Internet maze of information. Be sure to arrange the home pages you collect alphabetically beneath each topic.

Consider Other Search Tools

Given the number of search tools available, you shouldn't be too quick to consider a search inconclusive. Try several different Web sites to see if any of them show promise. But also consider whether there may be other types of search tools that would better fit your search. As we'll see in the rest of this book, the Web is only the starting point for Internet searching. If it's textual documentation you're looking for, it may well be that a Gopher holds just the article you need, and it may not show up through a search on the Web. Although we haven't examined it, a tool called Veronica can search Gopher menus to find such items. Don't confine yourself to the Web just because it's the hottest Internet technology at present.

Web Browsers and SLIP/PPP

In this chapter, we've looked at both a character-based browser (lynx) and a graphical one (Netscape), but the emphasis has been heavily upon the graphical environment. This is because more and more users are finding that access to the Internet is simplified by using mouse-driven point-and-click commands, and pull-down menus supplemented by icons. While you can do your work on the Web with a character-based browser, you will not have available the range of graphical features that makes the Web today so spectacular, and your browser will not offer the functionality of a Netscape or a Mosaic, software programs with built-in capabilities like bookmark list management and links to other client programs.

But before we proceed to look at other Internet tools, a key issue must be addressed: the nature of your Internet connection. A graphical Web browser requires direct network access to perform its magic; it counts on manipulating that connection so that, working with the hardware resources on your desktop, it can bring you the entire range of graphical features we've just seen demonstrated. There are two ways to make such a connection:

- You can be part of a network that already connects directly to the Internet.
- You can use your model to call a server that offers SLIP (Serial Line Internet Protocol) or PPP (Point-to-Point Protocol) connections.

A *shell account,* by contrast, is an Internet account on a service provider's machine. It does not provide the graphical client capability inherent in SLIP/PPP. Think about what happens when you place a call to a shell account. You are calling a computer at the site of your service provider. *Your* machine is not on the network; rather, it is using the services of a computer that is. You can run client programs on your service provider's machine, but you cannot run clients on your own computer because you lack the necessary TCP/IP connection. Only your service provider's computer can run clients, sending the results to you through the telephone line. Your computer then emulates a terminal and connects through a character-oriented mode like VT-100. All of which works fine, but allows you no graphical features.

Both SLIP and PPP adopt a different model. Yes, each begins with your establishing a telephone connection through your modem to a service provider's site. But by using SLIP or PPP software on your own machine, the connection you make enables you to use TCP/IP features on your own. The result: Your computer can be an Internet host—you can have your own Internet address, rather than piggybacking through the computer at your service provider's site. In addition, you can run any client software that your own computer's operating system will allow. Programs like Mosaic, Netscape, and other graphical tools become available for use.

Think of regular shell connectivity, then (as opposed to SLIP and PPP), as offering a lowest common denominator approach to Internet browsing and searching. You have a wide range of tools but lack a graphical interface and the capabilities of a graphical client program. But if you have a SLIP/PPP connection, then the world of graphical software is open. And because prices on these connections have fallen so greatly (and show every sign of continuing to fall), you can expect interest in both SLIP and PPP to grow. Add to this the fact that setting up the necessary software is becoming an easier proposition and you can see why you may want to consider such a connection in your own network activities.

Web Browsers as All-Purpose Interfaces

In the rest of this book, I'll be looking at a number of search tools that can all be used through dedicated client programs. But it's significant to note that a good Web browser like Mosaic or Netscape can likewise be used as a platform for a number of these programs. It's possible, for example, to move into a Gopher menu and read the results with a Web browser, adding the benefits of the browser's interface to your Gopher work; FTP can be managed the same way. And while good clients exist to handle these applications, there are times when you will be running Web-based searches and would just as soon use your Web browser to access such resources. Let's look briefly at how Web browsers display them.

Gopher through a Web Browser

A great deal of information still exists solely at Gopher sites around the world; indeed, although the World Wide Web has become the tool of choice, thousands of Gophers are available, housing everything from textual documents to graphics files and executable programs. Figure 2.37 shows you the Gopher at the University of Minnesota, where Gopher was created. Note that the Gopher menu items are underlined, showing us that they are hyperlinks; as we know, a click on any underlined item will call up the information. Gopher's menu structure, of course, is intact, with everything that implies about finding our data. We move up and down menu trees to use Gopher, as we'll see in more detail when we examine this tool in Chapter 3.

To go directly to a Gopher site, you must enter the Gopher's URL in the following format:

gopher://*address*/

For example, to see the Gopher at The World (a major Gopher site from a service provider in Massachusetts), we would enter the URL this way:

gopher://world.std.com/

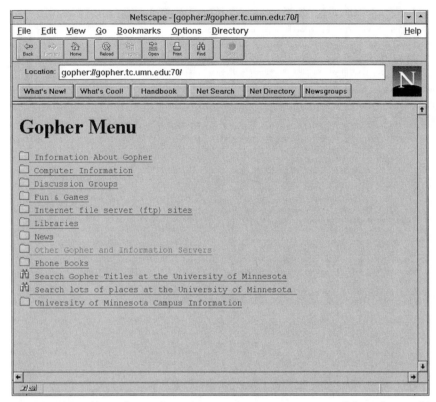

Figure 2.37   The Gopher at the University of Minnesota, as viewed through a World Wide Web browser.

Running a Gopher session in Netscape, then, involves the following procedure:

1. From the File menu, choose Open Location.
2. In the Open Location field, enter the URL of the Gopher you want to contact.
3. Click on Open to begin the session.

Of course, how you enter URLs depends on the kind of browser you use; there will be slight differences, for example, between the various versions of Mosaic. But the basic idea remains the same: enter the Gopher's URL, and your browser will take you directly to the site.

Figure 2.38 shows the beginning of Tennyson's *Ulysses*, as presented on The World's Gopher and viewed through Netscape. Notice the lengthy URL in the Document URL box. Every step of the retrieval process is encapsulated here, from the World's Gopher address down to the exact path to the file.

FTP through a Browser

And what about FTP? In Figure 2.39, we are looking at the holdings at an FTP site. To go to an FTP site, simply enter the correct URL for the site. The URL should appear in this form:

Figure 2.38   Tennyson's *Ulysses* viewed through Netscape on The World's Gopher.

file://*address*/

For example, to reach the oak.oakland.edu software repository by anonymous FTP, you would enter this as your URL:

file://oak.oakland.edu/

You may now move through the directories at the site. As you do, the Netsite window will show the URL of each item you examine. A particular file may sport quite a lengthy URL. For example:

file://oak.oakland.edu/pub/msdos/compress/comp430s.zip

Fortunately, the browser handles the anonymous FTP login for you; there is no need to insert your password or enter anonymous at a prompt. Transferring a file to your own system is likewise easy. Click on the file, then on the Save to Disk option, giving the file the name of your choice.

Here, then, is the procedure for launching an FTP session with Netscape:

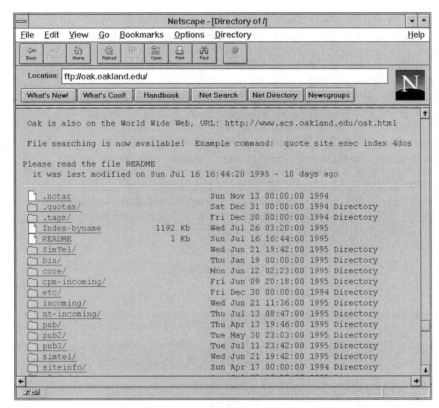

Figure 2.39 Examining a list of FTP files with Netscape.

1. From the File menu, choose Open Location.
2. In the Open Location field, enter the URL of the site you want to contact.
3. Click on Open to launch the session.

Reading USENET News with a Browser

Surprisingly, Netscape turns out to be an excellent USENET newsreader; in fact, I prefer reading newsgroups with this program to almost any of the dedicated client pro-

NOTE: Although I'm giving you directions for using the Netscape browser, it really doesn't matter which browser you use. True, each will have slight modifications to its command and menu structure, but the broad principles underlying browser use are the same. The key is to get to know your own browser, especially its bookmark features. Make sure that you know how to activate a session with a Gopher using URLs, and learn how to download files to your computer from an FTP site. By simplifying the interface at such sites, the browser makes it considerably easier to find your way around, locating files you need with a minimum of effort.

grams except Newswatcher (for the Macintosh) and Trumpet for Windows. In Figure 2.40, you can see a message from the newsgroup comp.internet.net-happenings, which records interesting new sites on the Internet. Noteworthy here are the hyperlinks embedded within the message. We can, for example, travel directly to the site mentioned in this message by clicking on its hyperlink; Netscape has correctly identified the URL within the message as a link and has made it possible for us to click on it. A variety of newsgroup tools are also presented that make USENET navigation a comparatively simple process. Other browsers also offer newsreaders, but none so fully featured as Netscape's.

Reading newsgroups with Netscape involves this procedure:

1. From the Directory menu, choose Go to Newsgroups.
2. Alternatively, you can enter the URL of a particular newsgroup by pulling down the File menu and choosing Open Location. URLs for newsgroups are set up as in the following example:

    news:comp.internet.net-happenings

Note the lack of slashes following the colon.

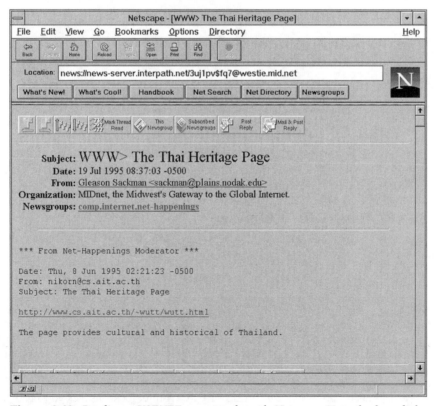

Figure 2.40 Reading a USENET message through Netscape. Note the hyperlinks embedded in the message.

Running a Telnet Session in a Browser

Activating a Telnet session through a Web browser is a workable proposition. To do so, you must have configured the browser to use a Telnet client on your system; the browser will contain options so that it can use external programs that you specify by citing a specific path to the program. When you have identified one, you can insert the URL of a Telnet site and proceed to open the connection.

In the Netscape environment, setting up the Telnet application involves the following procedure:

1. From the Options menu, choose Preferences.
2. From the Preferences screen, choose Applications and Directories.
3. Enter the path and filename of your Telnet client in the appropriate space.

You can see the Applications and Directories screen in Figure 2.41.

To activate a Telnet session, use the URL of the site you want to contact, in the following format:

telnet://*address*/

Figure 2.41 Netscape's Applications and Directories window. Entering a Telnet client here will allow you to activate Telnet sessions in the browser.

Assume, for example, that I would like to Telnet to the site sunsite.unc.edu. I would enter the URL this way:

telnet://sunsite.unc.edu/

The session, then, would proceed as follows:

1. Pull down the File menu and choose the Open Location item.
2. Enter the URL in the Open Location field.
3. Click on Open to start the session.

A Mandate for Searching

The Internet is growing larger at such a clip that keeping track of its abundant resources is a job in itself. We've just seen how World Wide Web browsers can help us to locate information from a variety of sources, allowing us to search directories and use keywords to find our data. We now embark upon a tour of other forms of Internet searching software and the commands necessary to make them function. And as we do, bear this thought in mind: no two Internet searches are going to be identical. One day you may find what you need the first time out through a directory service like Yahoo. The next day, you may go from search engine to search engine, looking for material that always seems just one hyperlink away. It will behoove you to learn, then, not just the Web-based search tools we've already examined, but the numerous other ways of searching the Internet. Not all of them are easy to use; you'll find archie troublesome if you don't like fiddling with search parameters, and you may run out of patience with directory systems like WHOIS. But proper searching, in addition to being rewarding when you find what you want, is also challenging and complicated. Stopping with the World Wide Web would be to forsake a multitude of specialized engines that can pay off by locating obscure and hard-to-reach information. Let's move on, then, step by step, starting with a look at Gopher.

3

Gopher: Finding Resources by Menu

Gopher offers, after the World Wide Web search tools we've just examined, the next easiest way to find information on the Internet. But the fact that this chapter follows the one on the Web does not imply that you should turn to Gopher only if your Web search fails. The important thing to remember is that various kinds of tools frequently access different kinds of information. It may well be that the perfect document for your search is accessible only through a Gopher, and that the Web tool you used to run your search didn't include that Gopher (or, perhaps, any Gophers at all) in its database. The only way to find your document, then, is to learn how Gopherspace works.

On a broader level, this is a statement about any kind of structured searching. What we have on the Internet is a whole series of tools that have grown up around the idea of locating information. Each has its eccentricities; each poses its own challenges and, perhaps most significantly, each accesses its own particular holdings of data to run your search against. In many cases, a thorough search will not be resolved with a single run at a particular search engine or browsing tool. Instead, you will run one search that will return a limited number of hits; you will expand the search by adjusting your keywords; you will run the revised search past other search engines. Ultimately, you will have consulted a number of possible sources, using varying Internet protocols, to find the result you need.

Intimidated? You needn't be. The point is simply that Internet searching requires patience. There is nothing bewilderingly technical about the process; instead, the key is your ability to think logically and to anticipate how the information in various databases is structured. If possible, try to learn as much as you can about any search tool, and put yourself in the mind of its creators. Ask yourself how the information you need would look from their perspective, how it might be indexed in their system, and what kind of search approaches would most readily find it. Always be willing to adjust your search as it progresses, for an initial query is usually just the beginning of an extended process of data gathering.

Searching as Process

The search process on the Internet, or anywhere else, is generally collaborative. We look for things through clues or pointers brought to our attention by other people. Those who have made it their job to create locator tools do the entire on-line community a service. They also impose a particular vision of order upon a mass of unstructured information. The key to good searching, then, is to understand the nature of their vision. Each search tool operates from within the boundaries its creators have set. No better example of this thesis exists than Gopher.

To understand Gopher, you need to realize the benefits, and drawbacks, of menued information. A menu is infinitely better than an unadorned prompt, such as the & or % symbols that confound so many new users of Unix systems. The prompt encourages action, but which one? Clueless, the novice can only type commands, learning the process through tedious trial and error. Presenting newcomers with a menu of choices simplifies their task, but it also imposes a new kind of limitation. The user is now dependent upon the developer's sense of what is important and what is not. Each menu reflects the priorities of the person who made it.

Gopher was created at the University of Minnesota in 1991, where Mark P. McCahill and an inspired team of programmers (Robert Alberti, Daniel Torrey, Paul Lindler, and Farhad Anklesaria) set about streamlining the help facilities on their campus. The problem faced by the university's Microcomputer, Workstation, and Networks Center was this: The computer systems available on campuses demanded a high degree of user sophistication. Answering the same questions over and over again took time; surely there was a way to make the basic tasks of network information gathering intuitive, so that even the first-timer could work productively and with minimal assistance.

Aware of the issues that troubled neophytes, McCahill's team designed Gopher to make campus on-line navigation simple. Their methodology worked. Soon, Gopher had begun to spread beyond its home campus, and before long, it was in use at thousands of sites around the Internet. It took the arrival of the World Wide Web, and, in particular, the Mosaic browser for the Web, to slow Gopher's growth. But even today, with so much development effort going into new Web pages, Gopher remains a viable option, and is in extensive use both in the United States and around the world.

The Nature of Gopherspace

Ponder the implications of menu-driven information. Resources must be identified and organized into sensible units—campus news items under one head, library information under another, perhaps; the developer assigns discrete items to categories as a way of creating a shape for his or her data. Menus proceed relentlessly inward. You choose item 3, from which another menu opens, from which you choose item 6, from which another menu opens, until you reach the terminus: the resource you are looking for.

HINT: Although the names of many Internet tools are actually acronyms, don't look for one lurking behind the name Gopher. It's actually a reference to the Golden Gophers of the University of Minnesota. It also refers to the software's ability to "go for" information and, in the eyes of the imaginative, to burrow through uncharted Internet terrain.

Think of menus, then, as a linear presentation of information, one in which your options are limited by the shape of the search tool. If you probe deeply into a menued structure and then change your mind, your only recourse is to retrace your steps, backing out of the menu in reverse order until you once again reach the top. Movements *across* the fields of nested data are trickier. Gopher allows you to jump to its main menu from anywhere in the environment, but you can't readily cross from a third-level menu under item 3 to a second-level menu under item 4 on the main menu. Your data hunt is a series of descents and resurfacings, dependent on an imposed structure, which we assume is logical. At first blush, this seems restrictive.

Fortunately, the creators of Gopher had something up their sleeves. They included a bookmark feature, which we'll discuss in a moment; it is your key to using Gopher wisely. Every time you see a Gopher item of interest, you can add it to your bookmark list, which becomes a kind of personal menu. At the end of your browsings, you can move to that menu and choose from the items on it. Your search has moved from a broad survey of information to a tightly focused search. Don't even think of using Gopher without bookmarks.

Gopher also involves a way of nesting information that brings a remarkable new dimension to traditional menus. Gopher's menus are dynamic; they change as the resources available to the system change, for as Gopher moves out over the Internet, it provides links to a wide variety of resources. Gopher can open the door to a Telnet session to a site; you merely press the RETURN key with the highlight bar over the item in question. Gopher can connect you to FTP archives with the help of archie, and can let you read USENET news, consult WAIS databases, probe X.500 and other white pages directories, and talk to other Gophers. These resources, of course, constantly change, and thus, so do Gopher's menus.

Figure 3.1 illustrates a typical Gopher top menu as seen by the Unix Gopher client through a shell account. This is what you see when you use the Gopher at the University

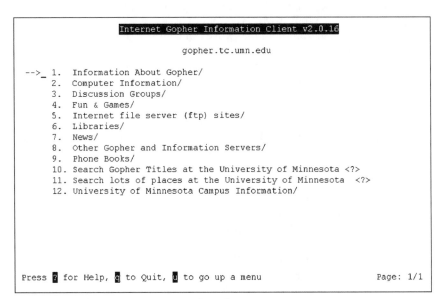

Figure 3.1   The top menu at a typical Gopher site.

of Minnesota, known whimsically as the "mother Gopher," just as the resources connected by Gopher systems worldwide have become known as "Gopherspace." In this figure, you see a mixture of resources, some of them of local interest at the University, others pointing in the direction of Internet destinations elsewhere. Gopher is anchored to its local site, providing useful tools for users in the neighborhood, but it also opens out to the worldwide flow of networked information (if you're a science fiction fan, think of wormholes as an analogy. Hit the right switch and you're in another galaxy).

Gopher isn't a search tool as much as it is a browser. True searching involves a computer performing search work at your behest; browsing is when a human is the search engine. As we'll soon see, Gopher can become a search environment with the help of Veronica, but by itself, this tool's menu structure is perhaps best likened to a library's bookshelves. Rather than searching a card catalog electronically, you wander into the stacks to browse. What you find may surprise and delight you, but it's not, strictly speaking, the result of a targeted search.

NOTE: Internet terminology can sometimes be confusing. The term browser has come to refer to a category of software, specifically, the tools we use to access the World Wide Web. But the term became popular because it is descriptive; what we are doing on the World Wide Web is browsing, in the sense that we are exploring hyperlinks and looking through hitherto unknown datapaths. In a broader sense, Gopher can be described as a browser (though not a World Wide Web-style software browser), because its menu system causes us to follow information down chains of structured pointers. Both techniques in one way or another use browsing as their central concept. By contrast, a search engine is a tool that lets us target a specific keyword and search precisely.

You'll notice how far these terms have begun to overlap. We've seen that we can use search engines, like Lycos, InfoSeek, and The World Wide Web Worm, on the Web itself. But if you draw the fundamental distinction between browsing for information by following links to see where they lead and searching for information through precise techniques and keywords, you can see that the Internet offers two large categories of retrieval tools. These categories subsume within them the entire range of Internet protocols and the actions they allow us to implement. This book will be concerned with both categories, browsers and search engines, because the two methods complement each other. Each has a place in the panoply of search methods.

A Gopher is an excellent browsing tool for a university, whose blend of academics in various fields and students without computer backgrounds makes a menu structure a natural. Students at the University of Minnesota would have no difficulty, for example, in finding out more about their school's administrative policies with this Gopher. By choosing item 12 from the main menu, *University of Minnesota Campus Information/*, they would quickly be presented with the screen shown in Figure 3.2. Notice how broad a range of campus information is presented in this submenu. Note, too, that most of these items are followed by a slash (/). The symbol indicates the presence of further menu choices beyond this item.

But item 8 on the top menu, *Other Gopher and Information Servers/*, shows us how broad Gopher's reach is. By choosing it, we find ourselves at the submenu shown in Figure 3.3, where there are options like *All the Gopher Servers in the World/*, along with more specific menu items that reduce the choice to single continents like Asia or Africa. These

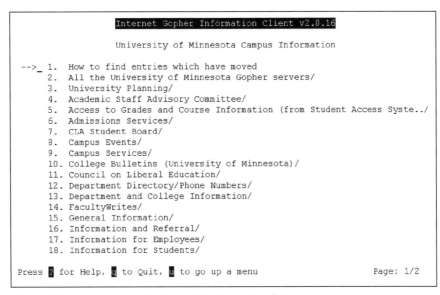

Figure 3.2   Exploring the Gopher at the University of Minnesota.

menus open to further choices, until we select a particular Gopher we would like to contact. Gopher will then make the necessary connection, and soon we have a Gopher at a distant site on our screen. Figure 3.4 displays the Gopher at the University of Edinburgh in Scotland.

The point of this quick tour is that the resources Gopher points to are not static items on a menu. Because of its dynamic linkages with other resources on the Internet, Gopher becomes a powerful interface that shields many network transactions from the

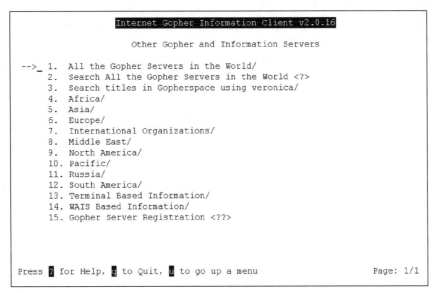

Figure 3.3   Gopher's submenus open to other Gophers around the world.

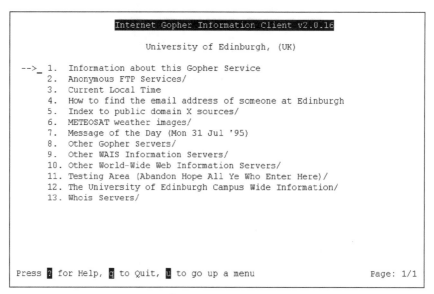

```
┌──────────────────────────────────────────────────────────────────────┐
│               Internet Gopher Information Client v2.0.16               │
│                                                                        │
│                      University of Edinburgh, (UK)                     │
│                                                                        │
│   -->_ 1.  Information about this Gopher Service                       │
│        2.  Anonymous FTP Services/                                     │
│        3.  Current Local Time                                          │
│        4.  How to find the email address of someone at Edinburgh       │
│        5.  Index to public domain X sources/                           │
│        6.  METEOSAT weather images/                                    │
│        7.  Message of the Day (Mon 31 Jul '95)                         │
│        8.  Other Gopher Servers/                                       │
│        9.  Other WAIS Information Servers/                             │
│       10.  Other World-Wide Web Information Servers/                   │
│       11.  Testing Area (Abandon Hope All Ye Who Enter Here)/          │
│       12.  The University of Edinburgh Campus Wide Information/        │
│       13.  Whois Servers/                                              │
│                                                                        │
│                                                                        │
│                                                                        │
│                                                                        │
│  Press ? for Help, q to Quit, u to go up a menu            Page: 1/1   │
└──────────────────────────────────────────────────────────────────────┘
```

Figure 3.4   Connecting to a Gopher in Scotland.

user, who would otherwise have to set up Telnet sessions, WAIS searches, and the like by entering a series of commands. As the resources contacted by Gopher themselves change, so do the menus. What we seem to lose by resorting to a framework of nested menus we regain by virtue of Gopher's ability to talk to other machines and to engage in a continuous process of updating. Coupling Gopher with the tool called Veronica (discussed in the next chapter) gives us one of the Internet's better search engines.

HINT: When you call up Gopher on your screen, the particular Gopher site you see will depend upon several factors. If you're using a shell account, you'll find that when you give the **gopher** command at the system prompt, you will see whichever Gopher site the administrator of your network has decided to use as the home Gopher for that service. Remember, a Gopher client can be set up to reference any Gopher server on the Internet. Your service provider may provide its own Gopher server, but if it doesn't, it will probably use a nearby Gopher, one containing information about the local area as well as links to other materials.

   If you're using a SLIP/PPP account to access the Internet, the same principle applies. The developer who wrote your Gopher client program will have set it up to log on automatically to a particular Gopher when you first run the program. This default setting can be overridden from within the program, so that you can choose any Gopher you please to be the one you log on to as your first stop. In general, choose a Gopher that isn't too far away from you, so as to minimize the workload on the network. For targeted information-hunting, you can use this Gopher as your home base when you do decide to venture out onto the broader Net.

Accessing Gopher

There are two ways to reach a Gopher. The first is by using a Telnet connection to a public access Gopher site. The second is to use a local client program to make the connection. Between the two, as is the case with all Internet search tools, a client program is best. It is more responsive, less demanding of system resources, and gives you the greatest flexibility in your search. Conversely, using Gopher by Telnet, while allowing you to perform most basic Gopher functions, restricts your ability to save files, and you may find that other Gopher features are unavailable as well.

Always check, then, to see if you have a client program available before relying on Telnet. If you use a shell account, you can check this by typing **gopher** at your service provider's system prompt, following it with a **RETURN.** If there is no Gopher on your system, you will see something like this:

```
gopher: Command not found.
```

Only in the absence of such a client should you use one of the Telnet addresses provided in the upcoming section on Telnet. If a Gopher is installed (as is most likely the case), you will quickly see its main menu.

If you use SLIP/PPP or a full network connection, you should examine the software available on your system. Many Internet software packages today come with a variety of tools, and it's possible that a Gopher client is already loaded on your computer. Look in your Internet program groups or folders to see which programs are there. With a SLIP/PPP connection, for example, clicking on the icon of a Gopher client will usually cause your networking software to place the telephone call to your service provider; once that call has been completed, the Gopher menu will appear.

A Choice of Clients

As with other Internet tools, the kind of client you run depends upon the kind of connection you're using. The Gopher client I've just illustrated runs on basic Unix systems using VT-100 terminal emulation; because it operates on any text-based terminal, it is the client most widely available to users of shell accounts.

But today we are moving into the graphical era, with SLIP/PPP connections proliferating, and Internet access increasingly common in businesses large and small. Numerous graphical clients exist for Gopher use. One such is xGopher, a client program for the X Window system, that allows Unix users to tap pull-down menus and scroll bars and a variety of other intuitive tools. Macintosh users can turn to TurboGopher. Developed at the home Gopher at the University of Minnesota, TurboGopher likewise provides a point-and-click interface, and in its new incarnation offers a visually exciting, virtual reality-based twist on Gopher menus, as we'll see later in this chapter.

Microsoft Windows users have the widest degree of choice; a number of freeware and shareware Gopher clients have been created for them, including Hgopher and WSGopher, not to mention commercial implementations from many providers of networking software. In this chapter, I will illustrate Gopher use predominantly with WSGopher, a freeware program developed by Dave Brooks at Lockheed Idaho Technologies Co. You can retrieve WSGopher at the following URL:

ftp://dewey.tis.inel.gov/pub/wsgopher/wsg-12.exe

And Mac users will find TurboGopher at this URL:

gopher://boombox.micro.umn.edu/11/gopher/Macintosh-TurboGopher/
    TurboGopher2.0.1.sea.hqx

Don't be too concerned about my choice of clients in this chapter. As with the World Wide Web, Gopher functions through a set of underlying protocols. All the capabilities I am going to show you with WSGopher will also be available to you through other Gopher clients, although you may have to implement them in different ways.

My advice is, learn the possibilities by studying the Gopher clients I use in this chapter (and I'll present the command set for the Unix Gopher later on in the chapter). Then, examine your own client to see how to implement these features. In the case of graphical clients, the basic functions will be readily available and, thanks to pull-down menus and icons, relatively easy to use.

HINT: If you're interested in exploring the various options for client programs, you should be aware of a World Wide Web page that can help you choose the best. This page, the Consummate Winsock Apps List, also provides hyperlinks to the home site of each client, so that you don't have to worry about where to find the software. To access this site, use the following URL:

http://cwsapps.texas.net/

Or try the mirror site at:

http://www.wilmington.net/

Using Telnet to Access Gopher

A number of public access Gopher sites have become available for those without local client programs. Their addresses and login information follows in Table 3.1. As always, choose Telnet sites as close to you as possible.

Table 3.1   Public Access Gopher Sites

Address	Location	Login
ux1.cso.uiuc.edu	Univ. of Illinois at Urbana-Champaign	gopher
panda.uiowa.edu	Univ. of Iowa	—
gopher.msu.edu	Michigan State Univ.	gopher
pubgopher.msu.edu	Michigan State Univ.	gopher
consultant.micro.umn.edu	Univ. of Minnesota	gopher
gopher.ohiolink.edu	Ohio Library and Information Network	gopher
ecosys.drdr.virginia.edu	Univ. of Virginia	gopher
gopher.virginia.edu	Univ. of Virginia	gwis
info.anu.edu.au	Australian National University	info
gopher.puc.cl	Pontificia Universidad Catolica de Chile	gopher
ecnet.ec	EcuaNet; Corporacion Equatoriana de Informacion (Ecuador)	gopher
info.brad.ac.uk	University of Bradford, U.K.	info
gopher.th-darmstadt.de	Technische Hochschule Darmstadt (Germany)	gopher
gopher.ncc.go.jp	National Cancer Center, Tokyo	gopher
gopher.uv.es	Universidad de Valencia (Spain)	gopher

HINT: Any list of Internet sites is subject to change, as greater system load is exerted on their resources by the vast number of new users coming onto the Net. If you try a Telnet site and find that you are asked for a password as well as a login, it may well be that the system administrator has decided to close the site to public access. In that case, try another site. The number of Telnet-accessible Gophers is diminishing as we move toward a much wider dispersal of client software, but the resources listed here will get you started if you do lack a client.

What's Available via Gopher?

Gopher servers house all kinds of content, and moving from one Gopher to another to explore is simple. While the World Wide Web continues to generate the lion's share of new documents on the Internet, we can expect the amount of information available through Gopher to increase as well. As of August, 1995, Steve Foster at the University of Nevada at Reno could confirm 9,046 Gopher servers in operation, using a search harvest with the Veronica tool we'll discuss in the next chapter. The benefits of Gopher have kept it in the running as a popular protocol. For anyone working with slower-speed connections or in a character-based environment, Gopher is an excellent publishing tool, one that allows any organization to make materials available in a logical and user-accessible way.

NOTE: An unregistered Gopher is simply one that you won't find on the master list at the University of Minnesota Gopher; in other words, the Gopher team doesn't know about it yet, or else the site is restricted. Be aware, then, that any list of Gopher servers you see is only a subset of the entire Gopher population. Though harder to find than registered Gophers, their unregistered brethren are growing in number.

The range of subjects covered by these servers is impressive. Consider the eclectic nature of just a few:

Armadillo, The Texas Studies Gopher. Specializes in the natural and cultural history of Texas.

> gopher://chico.rice.edu:1170/

Base de Dados Tropical. A Brazilian Gopher dedicated to biodiversity and biotechnology data.

> gopher://bdt.ftpt.br/

The Electronic Frontier Foundation. Mailing lists and archives related to the work of the EFF, which focuses on studying and clarifying issues of law and privacy on the network.

> gopher://gopher.eff.org/

The Electronic Newsstand. Magazines, reviews, and other publishing ventures on-line.

> gopher://gopher.internet.com/

The Internet Wiretap. Classical literature from Greece and Rome in digital form, plus archival information on electronic texts of all kinds.

gopher://wiretap.spies.com/

The InterNIC Gopher. Links InterNIC materials through a common interface, containing information on service providers, networking, Internet organizations, directories, and more.

gopher://gopher.internic.net/

NASA Goddard Space Flight Center Gopher. Contains NASA flight information and imagery.

gopher://gopher.gsfc.nasa.gov/

Panix Gopher. Maintained by Panix, a New York-based Internet provider. Contains the Del Rey Internet newsletter, the Tor books on-line newsletter, and archives of the Society for Electronic Access.

gopher://gopher.panix.com/

RIPE Network Coordination Centre Gopher. RIPE provides support for Internet activities in Europe. A wide range of documents on European networking.

gopher://gopher.ripe.net/

Technet Singapore Gopher. Information about Singapore, news bulletins, and the National Technology Plan of the island nation.

gopher://gopher.technet.sg/

University of Minnesota Gopher. This is the mother Gopher; it contains campus news, a listing of Gopher servers around the world, movie reviews, recipes, and more.

gopher://gopher.micro.umn.edu/

Gopher Jewels. A large list of Gopher sites divided by category. Look in the Other Gophers and Information Resources menu.

gopher://cwis.usc.edu/

The Library of Congress Machine-Assisted Realization of the Virtual Electronic Library (MARVEL) Gopher. The on-line catalog of this huge archive; information about the U.S. Congress and Federal government activities; links to information sources by subject, from the arts, social sciences, literature, and history to medicine and natural science. Abundant Internet information.

gopher://marvel.loc.gov/

This sampler is provided only to whet your appetite. To keep up with the rapidly changing list of Gophers on the Net, your only effective recourse is to learn to extract the information from Gopher itself.

Learning to Use Gopher

The Gopher interface is easy to master. The basic process is to move around the menus using your mouse, clicking on anything that you want to see. A single click highlights the item in question; a double-click takes you to it. Figure 3.5, for example, shows what the top menu looks like at the University of Illinois at Urbana-Champaign. As viewed in WSGopher, this top Gopher page is shown in a subwindow of the primary WSGopher window.

Figure 3.5 The top Gopher menu at the University of Illinois at Urbana-Champaign.

The WSGopher graphical interface simplifies your task of using the Gopher protocols. It's obvious from looking at the screen, for example, that if you need help, you can pull down the Help menu by clicking on the Help command at the top right of the screen (and, you are reminded, you could also use the F1 key, as shown at the bottom left). Most Internet search tools incorporate some kind of help facility; the Unix Gopher client, for example, lets you call up a help screen by entering a ? at the prompt. But the graphical screen of tools like WSGopher means you don't have to remember which command generates what response.

HINT: Before using any search tool, be sure to master its help system. This is the equivalent of traveling to a new city, where your first task should be to learn about the city's public transportation system. In the case of Gopher, work through whatever help function your client makes available, familiarizing yourself with the material there. A Windows-based tool like WSGopher makes help easy to find; it offers hypertext links within the help screens to help you locate what you need. Don't be hesitant to begin exploring with a new client as soon as you have loaded it. With help so close, you can usually puzzle your way out of any situation.

We can also examine the WSGopher screen to learn how to exit the program. As is common with Microsoft Windows-based software, this is accomplished by pulling down the File menu and choosing Exit. The menus provided by the program are worth exploring as you take WSGopher out for its first spin. Rather than showing you the basic com-

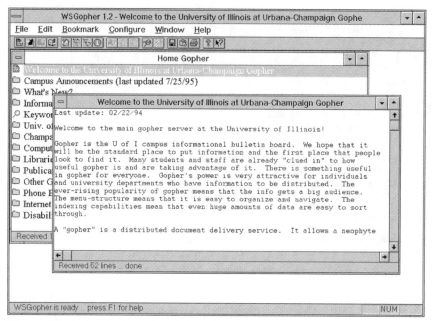

Figure 3.6 A document as viewed through WSGopher. Note that it appears inside its own window, while the main menu remains in a background window.

mands somewhere on the primary screen (the Unix Gopher client does this), a graphical client can embed them within easy-to-reach menus.

Moving through the information at the University of Illinois is a matter of point-and-click. As you can see, there is a good deal of material here, ranging from information about the university itself, complete with keyword searching of UIUC Gopher menus, to publications, libraries and other reference materials, phone books, FTP sites, and other Gophers. Most items are shown with a file folder icon to their left. The folder indicates that if we click on this item, we will encounter a nested submenu. But notice that the first item on the list contains an icon that appears to be a piece of paper with a corner turned down. This is the icon for a single document. We can click on the document to retrieve it. When we do, a new window appears housing the information, as shown in Figure 3.6; the previous window, containing the menu we have just been using, remains in the background; to move back and forth between the two windows, we simply click once on the window to which we want to move. To remove a window, we double-click in the close box at the top left of the window in question.

Notice that the active window, the one containing the document we have just asked to see, shows us only part of the document. To read the whole document, it is necessary to use the scroll bar at the right of the screen. Clicking on the downward-pointing arrow there will move the screen display down one line at a time, while clicking toward the bottom of the scroll bar (but not on the arrow itself) will move the display a screen at a time.

Perhaps we'd like to read this document off-line; computer screens are hard on the eyes where large amounts of text are involved. This is easy to accomplish when using a graphical client like WSGopher. To save a file, we simple call down the File menu by clicking on it. We can then use the Save Item command to save it to disk. Remember that

HINT: A Windows-based Gopher client like this one presents its information in a series of Windows. If you find this display difficult to read, the answer is to maximize the window you are reading by clicking on the button at the top right of the active window display. Moving back and forth between the Maximize and Minimize buttons allows you to control whether you see multiple windows on-screen or only the one you are reading at the time. You can also vary window size with standard Windows methods, clicking and dragging the window into the size and shape desired.

we are using a SLIP/PPP account with WSGopher; this means that we are moving Internet packets of information directly between our computer and the Internet. Saving a file, then, involves nothing more than telling the software to perform this action. When we do so, the window shown in Figure 3.7 will appear.

As you can see, this dialog box allows us to assign a name and a location to the file we are about to save. Clicking on OK will then save the file. The file structure in the figure reflects my own system setup; yours will doubtless be different, but you can see that you have the flexibility to assign the file to any location you choose.

HINT: If you're accessing Gopher through a Telnet connection, you won't be able to print documents or save them on a remote computer (after all, you don't have an account on that system). The best option available to you under such a circumstance is to mail the file to your address. To do so, page to the end of the file in the Unix Gopher client, where you will see the following text:

`Press <RETURN> to continue, <m> to mail, <s> to save, or <p> to print:`

Choose the **m** command. You will be given a screen that allows you to enter your e-mail address. Shortly, the document you have mailed will appear in your mailbox.

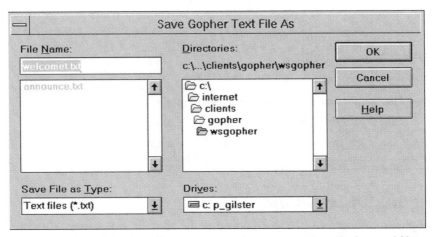

Figure 3.7 This dialog box allows you to specify a name and location for saved files.

The beauty of SLIP/PPP, as opposed to a shell account accessed through terminal emulation, is that your computer is actually on the Internet while you perform the necessary file transactions. If you were using the Unix Gopher client, you would need to save the file to your service provider's computer and then download it to your own computer (or else use the mail function to send it to yourself). SLIP/PPP, then, simplifies our lives in several ways. Although such a connection is more difficult to set up, once running, it provides you with a simpler work environment and allows you to do things you could not do with a shell account.

Printing is another example. If I wanted to print the document we've just retrieved from the University of Illinois, I could do so directly by calling down the File menu. I would then simply click on the Print command. With a shell account, the print function would not be available (after all, the service provider's computer is located at another site, so even if you could output on a printer there, you would have to retrieve the file later). The great decrease in the cost of SLIP/PPP has meant that countless new users are now experiencing these time-saving capabilities at their own desks.

As you can see, the basic Gopher commands are not difficult to master, and WSGopher even provides a toolbar with icons for easy movement between them. Browse through the Gopher commands in your own client to familiarize yourself with them. In the next section, we will look at the complete command set for the Unix Gopher client. Then I'll show what you can do with the more advanced capabilities of Gopher and its links to other protocols.

HINT: With Gophers available in such numbers, you may learn the address of an interesting one and want to go directly to it, without wading through all the Gopher menus to reach it. Any Gopher client will allow you to do this. Suppose, for example, that I want to reach the wonderful Gopher at The WELL, The Whole Earth 'Lectronic Link in Sausalito, California. I know the URL:

gopher://gopher.well.sf.ca.us/

To move directly to this Gopher, I pull down WSGopher's File menu and choose the New Gopher Item command. In the dialog box that appears, I enter the address of the site. A click on OK then opens a window to The WELL. Figure 3.8 illustrates this process.

Be advised: Some Gophers use nonstandard port numbers (Gopher usually defaults to port 70). If you see such an address, always add the port number as part of your entry. For example, to reach the Texas Studies Gopher referred to earlier, you would have to include its port number. Its URL is:

gopher://chico.rice.edu:1170/

The entry in the WSGopher dialog box, then, would be:

chico.rice.edu:1170

Note the colon between the address and the port number. Without the port number, the client will be unable to complete the transaction.

Mastering the Unix Gopher Client

Gopher's command set is not conceptually difficult, no matter which client you use. Here we examine the basic Gopher commands for the Unix client, which allows us to

Figure 3.8   Specifying a new Gopher server in WSGopher.

perform the same actions we just managed with WSGopher. Those with a character-based shell account will want to master these commands. In the following sections, we'll use Gopher to generate information, and consider the kinds of things it can do best. As with any search tool, Gopher's strengths are best utilized for particular kinds of research needs.

File Viewing Commands

Here are the basic commands for file viewing and moving about in a document with the Unix client.

<RETURN>	Allows you to view a document. Place the arrow on the document in question; then press **RETURN**.
<SPACEBAR>	Moves to the next page of the document. Note: You can also use several other keys to achieve the same result. In addition to the SPACEBAR, you can use the plus key (+), the PageDown key, or the right bracket key (>).
b	Allows you to view the previous page. You can also use the left bracket key (<), the minus key (–), or the PageUp key to do the same thing.
<number>	Enter the number of the menu item to which you wish to go, followed by a RETURN. Or you can move the arrow using the keys described in the next section to do the same thing.
Up arrow	Moves the arrow to the previous line. You can also use Ctrl-P or k to do the same thing.
Down arrow	Moves to the next line. You can also use Ctrl-N or j to do the same thing.
Left arrow	Exits the current item and moves up one level. You can also use the u command.
Right arrow	Selects the current item.
m	Returns to main menu.

HINT: You'll save time when working with long menus if you enter the number of the item to which you wish to go and follow it with a RETURN. This takes you directly to that item and bypasses the rest of the menus, saving you the need to move menu by menu until you reach the page you want.

Another tip: When dealing with several pages of data, go through the entire list all at once, jotting down the numbers of items you'd like to examine, rather than pausing to examine each document individually. It's much faster to do this and then enter, from the last page, the number of each item you want to see. Remember, Gopher can hang up due to network problems when you ask to see a given document. If this happens, and you've already compiled your entire list before you try to see a document, it's easy to go back, run the search again, and use the same numbers to find what you need.

File Management Commands

Here are the basic commands for saving and mailing files with a shell account. These commands are critical, because they allow you to bring Gopher information to your own computer for searching, printing, and other uses.

s   Saves the current item to a file. Remember: You can use this command only if you are running a Gopher client on your own system. You can't use it if you're using a Telnet session to reach a Gopher.

m   Mails the file to the address you specify. This is the route to take when you use Gopher through Telnet. The command becomes available only at the document level; i.e., as you are reading a document, and have reached its end or have given a q command to exit it.

p   Prints the file selected. This command becomes operative at the end of a document, or when you have typed a q to exit it. You can use it only if you have a direct TCP/IP connection to the Internet.

D   Downloads the item selected to your computer.

Using Gopher with Bookmarks

One handy, though often misunderstood, feature of Gopher is that it allows you to use bookmarks to keep your place. Bookmarks can help to surmount the menu limitation we discussed earlier—the fact that menu-driven searches so often have you moving deeper and deeper into layered information, then backing out one menu at a time. With bookmarks, you can jump immediately to the data you have marked, thus streamlining a complicated search.

Let's examine how this works in WSGopher. Suppose we are browsing through a Gopher looking for various kinds of information about the so-called information highway, the massive and thus far unorganized attempt to bring high-speed networking to average citizens. In Figure 3.9, I am using the Gopher at Software Tool and Die in Brookline, Massachusetts; this company runs one of the major dial-up service provider operations on the East Coast, called The World.

I have moved to a menu on its Gopher that offers government information, where I've found several items of interest. The first item, *Americans Communicating Electronically* certainly looks promising, and the folder to the left of the entry indicates another

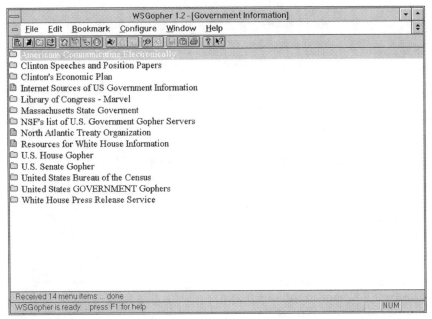

Figure 3.9   Using The World's Gopher to track development along the information highway.

menu with further choices beneath it. Also intriguing are the entries marked *NSF's List of U.S. Government Gopher Servers* (after all, the National Science Foundation has been a major player in the development of the Internet, and in the high-speed testbeds so crucial to the growth of gigabit-speed networking). And then there's *Internet Sources of U.S. Government Information*. This one is obviously a document; it's marked with a page icon rather than a folder.

Let's begin by marking the first item as a bookmark, because I plan to come back to it later. To do so, I highlight the item with a single mouse click and then pull down the Bookmark menu, choosing the Add Bookmark command. Figure 3.10 shows what happens when I do so.

As you can see, a dialog box has appeared that allows me to select a category in which to save the bookmark. WSGopher comes preconfigured with a whole range of such categories, as shown in the dialog box. You can pick one of the existing categories or create a new one. In this case, I think it would make sense to create a new category. Let's call it Government Networking. We can create it by filling in the Name: field at the top of the dialog box and then clicking on the Create button.

When we do this, the new category appears on the list of categories within the dialog box. We can then click on OK to cause the bookmark to be created within that category. In the future, when we want to examine such a bookmark, it's only necessary to pull down the Bookmark menu and choose the Fetch command. But before we do so, let's create some more bookmarks to illustrate how the process works. I'm interested in the item marked *Internet Sources of U.S. Government Information*. To make it into a bookmark, I need only highlight it on The World's menu and pull down the Bookmark menu, again clicking on Add Bookmark to repeat the process just detailed. Only now,

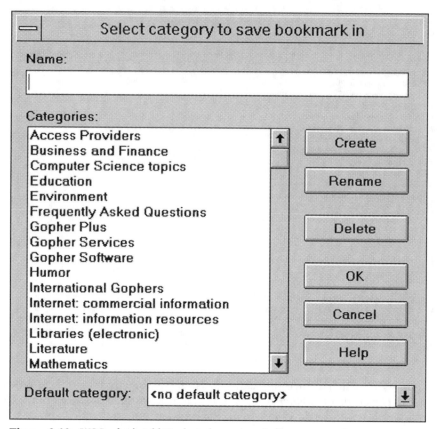

Figure 3.10 WSGopher's Add Bookmark command allows you to choose a category within which to save your bookmark.

because I already have a category in place, I need only double-click on the Government Networking category to cause the new bookmark to be inserted there.

I also note the item on The World's menu called *NSF's List of U.S. Government Gopher Servers.* Double-clicking on this item calls up a menu of Gopher sites, as shown in Figure 3.11. Within it are two items that intrigue me. The first, *National Coordination Office for HPCC (NCO/HPCC) Gopher,* is clearly related to the subject in question. HPCC stands for High Performance Computing and Communications, an integral part of the emerging National Information Infrastructure. Figure 3.12 shows what I see when I click on this Gopher.

The second item, marked *Government in General (maintained by UCI),* may also prove useful, as it should lead to other government servers, perhaps containing press releases and other information about the topic. I'll make both of these items bookmarks using the methods described.

Finally, I'll turn to the National Science Foundation Gopher itself, which should have some relevant materials. Within it, I find a compilation of documents and other

Figure 3.11   A list of Gopher servers maintained by the National Science Foundation.

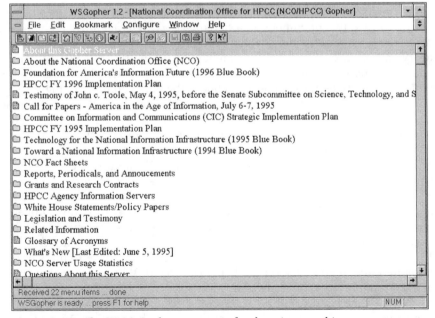

Figure 3.12   The HPCC Gopher, a resource for those interested in government communications policy.

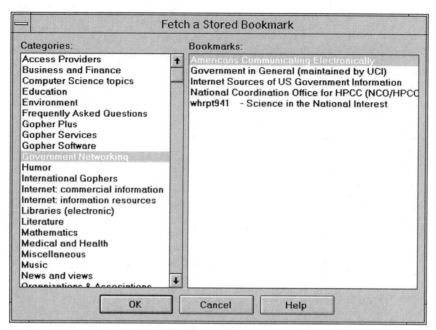

Figure 3.13 Results of clicking the Fetch command. Notice that the bookmarks I have added are now listed under the category Government Networking.

data. Among them is a document whose menu title is Science in the National Interest. I decide to save this document as a bookmark as well, again by highlighting it, calling down the Bookmark menu, clicking on Add Bookmark, and double-clicking on the category, in this case, my new Government Networking topic. Now I should have a list of bookmark items for future reference. To move to any item I have saved, I only need to pull down the Bookmark menu and choose the Fetch command. Figure 3.13 shows the screen that results when I double-click on the Government Networking topic.

I now have complete point-and-click capability, allowing me to return to any Gopher item I have set up as a bookmark with a simple mouse action. As you can see, using bookmarks has enabled me to move beyond many of the limitations of the menu structure that Gopher imposes upon its information. Without this capability, I would have had to retrace my steps each time I wanted to look again at these documents.

This set of bookmarks is as elastic as any Gopher menu. Using it, we actually point to different Gophers with it—the one at the National Coordination Office for High Performance Computing and Communications, and the National Science Foundation Gopher, along with the original Gopher at The World that we started our session with. To see the bookmark list at any time, remember, all we have to do is to pull down the Bookmark menu and click on the Fetch command. WSGopher makes the list of bookmarks available any time we need it.

Notice that it's possible to refer either to single documents or to entire Gopher menus with a bookmark list; I did just that in the list of items I saved to this list. As a search tool, the bookmark list will prove helpful. As I continue to browse through The World's Gopher looking for further insights, I can always return to my interest list without backing out through a sequence of menus. I can choose Gopher menus and menu items from Gophers all over the world, so I'm not limited in any geographical sense. Then I can examine the entire list at once and move easily between its items. Nothing shows off the dynamic nature of Gopher menus as well as the ability to use bookmarks.

HINT: The problem with tools like Gopher and the World Wide Web is that the resources they point to are so varied that keeping track of what you've found as you continue through cyberspace is extremely difficult. The best kind of Gopher session is a foraging expedition, proceeding through the menus, going ever deeper in search of data, always noting interesting destinations along the way by marking them with bookmarks. At the end of this time, you return to the bookmark screen to evaluate what you've found and to decide which of these items are now worth your closer attention.

NOTE: Can you also use bookmarks with the standard Unix client? Absolutely. While WSGopher's snazzy, category-driven interface won't be available, you can still save items of interest to a separate Gopher menu, which you can customize to reflect your own interests. Here are the relevant commands:

a   Adds the current item to your bookmark list.
A   Adds the current menu to your bookmark list.
v   Allows you to view the current bookmark list.
d   Deletes a bookmark entry.

What is really compelling about Gopher bookmarks is that you can save an entire search. For example, some Gophers maintain links to archie servers; these tools, to be discussed in Chapter 5, allow you to search FTP sites around the world for files. In Figure 3.14 you can see a Gopher menu with links to archie servers.

Now, suppose that I run archie searches relatively frequently, so as to ensure that I keep up with the latest releases of particular freeware software programs. I can set this page up as a bookmark like any other. Then, when I want to run a search, I can go directly to the archie site I need. Or I can get even fancier. The World maintains the ClariNews AP Online and Reuters Newswire Index features. Because I follow economic and political news in Latin America with some interest, I can set up a search under the terms latin american business briefs. I happen to know that UPI makes reports under this title available every day. Figure 3.15 shows you typical results of such a search; I'm viewing this time through the Unix Gopher client.

There is a lot of Latin American news here, along with much else that is business related but not specifically about Latin America. The reason for this is that this is a WAIS database, which searches by ranking items in order of what it perceives to be their relevance to your search. (More about WAIS and its eccentricities in Chapter 6.)

Further, I would like some way to check on Latin American news every day. To do so, I can enter an **A** *after* I have retrieved this search screen (that is, after the search itself has been run). This enters the search onto my list of bookmarks. When I call up the bookmark list by entering a **v**, I find the following entry:

```
-->> 1. Search ClariNews UPI newswire index: Latin American Business Brief../
```

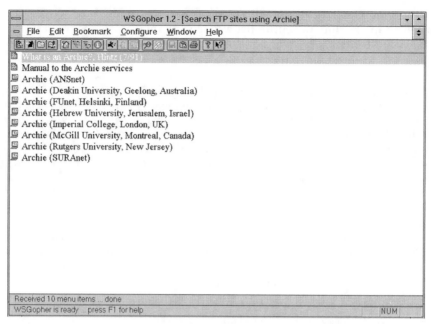

Figure 3.14   Gopher can set up links to any kind of information, including searchable archie servers.

Perhaps you're beginning to get the overview. By using bookmarks, I can go into The World's Gopher every day and, rather than wade through the menu structure, simply call up the bookmark list with a **v** command from the main menu. There I find my search,

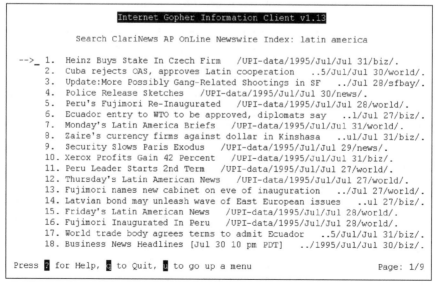

Figure 3.15   Results for a search for Latin American news. Such a search can be set up as a Gopher bookmark, and thus rerun every time you access the site.

HINT: The more you use your list of bookmarks, the more valuable it will become. If you want to start the Unix Gopher client with your bookmark list as the top menu, you can do so by entering the Gopher **-b** command at your service provider's prompt. Your bookmark menu will be the first thing you see. You will also see an additional menu item like the following:

```
    6. Root Gopher server: Gopher.interpath.net/
```

This gives you a menu choice that leads you back to the top menu of the Gopher server you normally contact when you start the program.

and all I have to do to run it is press the **RETURN** key. Voilà—updated Latin American news on a daily basis, with a minimum of fuss.

Gopher's Search Capabilities

Gopher's search capabilities are limited, but you should be aware of your ability to move quickly through extended menus of information. It is possible to search for particular menu items this way. Suppose, for example, that I happened to be dealing with a particularly long, multipage Gopher menu. A list of library catalog sites is an example; libraries from all over the United States might be listed on a single menu. If all I needed to find were library catalogs in North Carolina, I could search by pulling down WS-Gopher's Edit menu and choosing the Find command. The search window is shown in Figure 3.16; in the figure, I have already inserted my search term, and can activate the search by clicking on the Find Next button.

Take a good look at the figure so that you'll understand the search options available.

Match Case	This box, when clicked, tells the search engine to look only for words that match the keyword's letters by case. This can be useful if, for example, you're looking for proper nouns and want to distinguish between them and other terms.
Direction	By clicking on the Up or Down button, you can decide which direction you want Gopher to search. Your search will begin by moving down through the menu, but if you choose to search for a new term, you may want to click on the Up button to examine the part of the menu you've already passed over.
Find Next	This button is clicked to begin your search. If the first instance of your search term is not the menu item you want, then click on the button again, and again as necessary; each click will take you to the next appearance of your search term.

It's important to realize just what Gopher is doing here. The search tool you're using is workable only on the active Gopher menu; it does not search across Gopher's menus, or from one Gopher server to another (we'll examine two tools, Jughead and Veronica, which handle these capabilities, in a moment). Thus, bear in mind that you can use the Find command to locate menu items, but you already have to be in the right menu and have a good idea that the information you want is located on that menu. Further, the

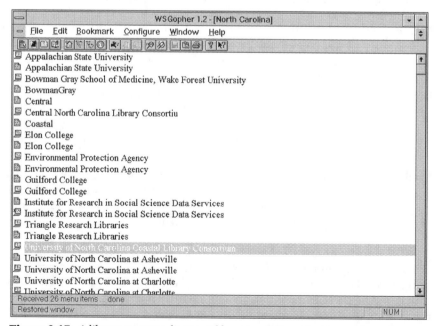

Figure 3.16 Using WSGopher's search command to find a menu item.

HINT: If you're using the Unix Gopher client, you can run searches just as easily. Here are the basic commands:

/   Searches for a particular item on a Gopher menu.

n   Searches for the next occurrence of your search term.

NOTE: Don't be alarmed if a Gopher search doesn't come off as planned. Network usage may be heavy or a node on the Net may fail; if that occurs, Gopher may simply leave you hanging. The best advice in such circumstances is to wait a while and try again, when usage may be less heavy.

Figure 3.17 A library resource discovered by using the search command.

search takes place on menu titles only; it does not extend into the actual text of the underlying Gopher documents. Figure 3.17 shows a library screen I uncovered with the preceding search command; it's loaded with North Carolina library catalogs accessible through the Internet.

The WSGopher Toolbar

The beauty of a toolbar is that once you have mastered it, you will be able to handle the major Gopher chores simply by clicking on an icon. The downside of toolbars is that their icons can be difficult to interpret, because there is no standard set of icons for Internet tasks. Doubtless your own work will be performed in much the same as my own; you'll become comfortable with certain icons and use them frequently, while you'll perform other chores through the pull-down menus. The choice is yours. Let's now take a look at what each of the WSGopher icons can do.

Calls up the Fetch Bookmark window, giving you quick access to your bookmark lists.

Adds the current item to your bookmark list. Note the plus sign as a way to remember this one.

Adds the current directory window to your list of bookmarks. Again, note the plus sign.

Calls up the bookmark editor.

Goes to the home Gopher server you have established in the software.

Moves to the top menu of the current Gopher.

Moves back one menu level in the current Gopher.

Calls up a window that provides information about the current Gopher item.

Retrieves a highlighted Gopher item.

Cancels the current transaction. Use this if a connection appears to hang.

Cancels all transactions.

Finds text in a Gopher window.

Repeats the previous search for the next occurrence of the keyword(s).

Saves the current item to disk.

Copies the current item to the Windows keyboard.

Prints the current item.

 Retrieves information about the current version of WSGopher.

 Provides context-sensitive help.

An examination of the toolbar will point out an interesting fact. WSGopher provides 18 separate icons for major chores, and four of these are related to its bookmark features. The fact that these four icons are placed as the first items on the toolbar should further drive home the point: Bookmarks are your way of organizing Gopher information, and your success at searching will depend upon how well you are able to manage your data.

HINT: To call up information about the current Gopher item with the Unix Gopher client, use the = command. You will be presented with a screen like the one in Figure 3.18. Now it may not be particularly useful to have port or path information, and we may already know the name of the service in question, but it can be handy in some cases to know the address of the service, which is provided here. It is also a good idea to check the date the file in question was last modified. This will tell you how current the information is. (Though not, of course, how accurate it might be!)

The WSGopher Menu Structure

Here is a thumbnail sketch of the WSGopher command structure, menu by menu. You can use it as a reference as you work through various Gophers (and keep in mind that the major actions can also be performed on WSGopher's toolbar). But remember that your choice of Gopher client is up to you; the important thing is that the basic com-

```
Link Info (0k)                                                           100%
+----------------------------------------------------------------------------+
#
Type=0+
Name=About Interpath
Path=0/Interpath
Host=gopher.interpath.net
Port=70
Admin=John Tomasetti +1 (919) 890-6308 <jpt@interpath.net>
ModDate=Wed Nov  2 11:20:05 1994 <19941102112005>
URL: gopher://gopher.interpath.net:70/00/Interpath


Size        Language      Document Type
----------  ------------- -----------------------------
.8k         English (USA) Text/plain


Server Information


+----------------------------------------------------------------------------+
[Help: ?]  [Exit: u]
```

Figure 3.18   Information about servers and Gopher items can be accessed by using the = command.

mands are the same, even when they're implemented in different ways in particular clients. So no matter which client you use, try to master the underlying action.

FILE MENU

New Gopher Item	Opens a dialog box that lets you enter an address to reach a new Gopher.
Home Gopher	Takes you to your home Gopher.
Fetch Item	Takes you to the highlighted menu item.
Info on Item	Shows information about the server and particular menu item.
Reload	Allows you to request that a Gopher menu be loaded again.
Cancel	Cancels the current network request.
Cancel All	Cancels all ongoing requests in all windows.
Print	Prints the current window.
Print Preview	Shows what a printout of the current window would look like.
Print Setup	Allows you to change your printer setup.
Page Setup	Allows you to change printing parameters.
Exit	Exits WSGopher.

EDIT MENU

Copy	Copies text or directory items to the clipboard.
Find	Provides a search screen that lets you search for text in the current Gopher menu.
Find again	Searches for the next occurrence of your search term.

BOOKMARK MENU

Fetch	Calls up a window within which you can choose a category and specific bookmark.
Add Bookmark	Adds a bookmark to the current category.
Add Directory Bookmark	Adds a bookmark for the entire directory.
Edit Bookmarks	Calls up an editor within which you can edit your bookmarks.
Get Bookmark Root	Goes to the top menu at the site on which your bookmark resides.
Categories	Calls up your list of bookmark categories and allows you to choose a default for subsequent actions, such as adding a new bookmark.

CONFIGURE MENU

Home Gopher Server	Allows you to choose the Gopher that will come up when you load the program.

Local Directories	Allows you to set the directory that WSGopher will use for downloaded items and temporary files.
Viewers	Presents a screen that lets you add external programs for file viewing. WSGopher will recognize the filetype by the extension on each file. A file with a .gif extension, for example, can be routed to an external file viewer.
Telnet/3270 Path	Provides a dialog box allowing you to enter a path for Telnet or 3270 connections. 3270 refers to a type of connection in which you are accessing an IBM mainframe computer; its command structure is correspondingly different from that of the normal Telnet session.
Fonts	Allows you to change the default fonts for menu and file viewing.
Extended Views	Allows you to control how WSGopher views the basic data types. You can control the order in which WSGopher attempts to read particular file information.
User Options	A set of changeable defaults that control such things as viewer prompts and the timing of the viewing of downloaded files.
WINDOW MENU	
Cascade	Arranges multiple windows in an overlapped fashion.
Tile	Arranges multiple windows so they don't overlap.
Arrange Icons	Arranges icons minimized at the bottom of the screen.
Back Track	Moves you back to the parent Gopher window of a particular menu item.
Toolbar	Controls whether you see the toolbar.
Status Bar	Controls whether you see the status bar.

Examining Gopher's Resources

As we've seen, Gopher is a flexible tool; it can show us not only where information is located and let us read it, but it can also make the necessary network connections behind the scenes. This is precisely what we'd like a good browser to do. One of the major barriers to retrieving Internet information is that it is necessary to approach data from different directions. One site offers files via FTP, another requires the interactivity of a Telnet session, while a third allows you to read key documents on-line through its own Gopher server. The ideal world is one in which we don't need to keep the various procedures and addresses straight.

One of the World Wide Web's great strengths is that it provides a common interface for many of these procedures; so, too, does Gopher. In fact, WSGopher itself can reveal how diverse are the possibilities for accessing information with this protocol. You will recall that the program uses icons to show you what kind of resource you are dealing with. We've already seen a folder icon to point to underlying menus, and a printed page icon to indicate a text document. But other kinds of information are likewise available. Here are the major icons in question:

A text file; note the turned down page motif.

Points to a Gopher directory.

A phone book, searchable by Gopher.

A DOS archive (in most cases, a file compressed using the PKZIP compression program).

A uuencoded file, in which binary data has been rendered into an ASCII format for transmission over Internet e-mail systems.

The Gopher search icon. Indicates a database available for searching.

A Telnet session.

An image, either in the GIF or JPG format.

A moving image, most likely in MPEG format.

A sound file, in any number of possible formats.

Using Gopher's Telnet Connection

Let's see what happens when we choose a Gopher item with Telnet links. In Figure 3.19, I have clicked on an item called Oceanic BBS, created by the University of Delaware College of Marine Studies as a forum for discussion. As you can see, when I click on the item, I am prompted with a hint about how to log on to the remote system. I also am provided with a button to click to launch the session. When I click on this button, the session begins, as shown in Figure 3.20.

Let's ponder for a moment what has happened here. For WSGopher to establish a Telnet connection, it has to rely on an external Telnet client to do the work. That means that we have to configure the program so that it knows where to find the client. We do this by pulling down the Configure menu and clicking on the Telnet/3270 path item. In the resulting dialog box, we insert the path to the Telnet client we have available. In my case, I use a program called Trumptel, but you can use any Telnet client of your choice, just as long as you tell WSGopher where to find it.

And remember, each Telnet session will have its own set of parameters and procedures. Once you have left the Gopher menu, the system you have accessed is the one that is calling the shots. You can explore it as you choose, or leave, but you should look carefully, no matter what the system, to make sure you know how your software handles exiting the session. When you do exit, you will be returned to WSGopher, and can proceed with further explorations.

Figure 3.19 Before logging on at a Telnet site, WSGopher presents information about how to get in.

Figure 3.20 A Telnet session launched through Gopher.

NOTE: When you press the equal sign (=) key to get information about a menu item with the Unix Gopher client, the information listed under Type is interesting. The type field is used to describe the kind of object this item represents. A 7 stands for an index search, while an 8 is a Telnet session. You may not think you'll ever have to use these numbers, but in the next chapter, when we get into Veronica searches, you'll see how important they will become.

0   A text file.

1   A directory or menu. These are marked on Gopher menus with the slash symbol (/).

2   A CCSO phone book. This is a directory service to help you find people on the Internet, about which more in a moment.

3   Error.

4   A Macintosh file in the BinHex format. These items are marked on Gopher menus as <HQX>.

5   A DOS binary file in archived form. This means the files are probably in .ZIP or .ARC format, although other types of archiving are in use. These items are found on the menus with the <PC Bin> suffix.

7   An index search. Marked with the <?> suffix on the menus.

8   A Telnet connection (<TEL>).

9   A binary file (<Bin>).

g   A GIF file.

h   An HTML file.

I   An image file, other than GIF format.

M   A MIME multipart or mixed message file.

s   A sound file.

T   A Telnet 3270 session.

Using Gopher to Find Files

Gopher works just as well at initiating an FTP session; indeed, you can use Gopher with a search tool called archie to find the files you need, and then move directly to the necessary site to retrieve them (we'll examine archie in detail in Chapter 5). The advantage of searching for and retrieving files this way is that the interface shields you from the complexities of the search. Instead of running a tricky archie session, you can let Gopher do the work.

How to find an archie site with Gopher? A Gopher menu item with the search icon in front of it is one that will take us to a searchable index. In the Unix Gopher client, an index will be shown with a question mark inside of brackets (<?>). In this section, I will use the Unix Gopher to run an FTP search, hoping to drive home the point that the difference in clients is not critical. The main thing to understand is how the search itself is run; the vehicle for running it is up to you. Here is how an archie search is presented as a menu option at The World:

HINT: If you're running the Unix Gopher client, you may run into menu items that, rather than showing <TEL> as a suffix, use <3270>, which is a version of Telnet designed to handle the various screen-drawing techniques of IBM mainframe computers. A Telnet session to one of these sites is accomplished the same way as a regular Telnet session by pressing the RETURN key with the item selected.

But note: Getting out of such a session can be problematical. As opposed to a regular Telnet session, where Ctrl-] invariably takes you back to the telnet> prompt if you get stuck, many tn3270 sessions have their own escape mechanisms. If you can't remember the system's command for exiting, and a Ctrl-] doesn't work, try a Ctrl-C. You should wind up at a tn3270> prompt. From there, you can enter quit to exit.

```
--> 1.   Exact search of archive sites on the internet <?>
    2.   Substring search of archive sites on the internet <?>
```

Notice the nature of these menu items. With archie, as we'll see in Chapter 4, there are two primary ways of searching for files. A *substring* option allows your search term to be embedded within a larger word—archie will still find it. Using an *exact* search turns up only the precise keyword you gave the search engine; this can be a problem because this kind of search might miss many files that could be of interest. Suppose we were looking for a program that helped us chart commodity prices. An exact search for a program called future.exe would pull up only that file; it would not locate futures.exe, or future2.exe, or other variants. A substring search would find them all.

So, it's best to use the substring option by choosing item 2 on the menu, and use exact searches when we know the exact filename in advance. Choosing item 2, then, we retrieve a screen box prompting us to enter a search term. As you'll recall from the previous chapter, archie searches from the command prompt can be set up with a number of options. Be aware that Gopher's interface doesn't yet give us the bells and whistles available in a straight archie search. If your search is truly complex, you'll be able to fine-tune it using the methods of Chapter 5 and a regular archie client. But for most searching, Gopher's interface will suffice.

Let's go find a file. Anyone who has used PKware Inc.'s powerful compression utilities knows how useful they are. **PKZIP** and **PKUNZIP** give you the ability to reduce a file to a fraction of its former size, or to expand it when needed. Both **PKZIP** and **PKUNZIP** run from the DOS command line, but I've heard about a Windows shareware program called **WINZIP** that gives the whole process a Windows interface. Can we find it using Gopher? Let's enter **winzip** as the search term, as shown in Figure 3.21. The results of that search are partially shown in Figure 3.22.

As you can see, we have called up several items, each of which contains an address and complete path information to a directory that looks promising. Choosing item 4, for example, I call up the following hit:

```
--> 1. winzip50.zip (188k) [Jan 26 1994] <PC Bin>
```

This, a binary file, is clearly the program we need.

We'll go much deeper into the complexities of archie in Chapter 5. For now, simply note that you can use the friendly Gopher interface to run a search in a variety of ways. Some sites, for example, offer Telnet connections to archie servers. When you press the

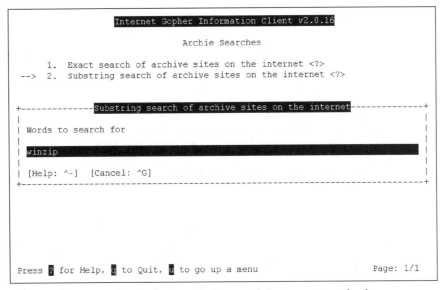

Figure 3.21   Using the search term winzip to track down a program by the same name.

RETURN key to launch a Telnet session, you will be prompted to log on with the term archie. Searching such a site for a graphics display program called lview, for example, I entered the command **find lview** and pulled up the following hits:

Figure 3.22   Results of the archie search as shown by Gopher.

```
Host ftp.actrix.gen.nz     (192.100.53.23)
Last updated 07:46 2 Aug 1995

    Location: /pub/incoming/windows
      FILE     -r--rw-r-- 250069 bytes 09:48 5 Jun 1995 lviewp16.zip

Host ftp.auckland.ac.nz    (130.216.1.1)
Last updated 08:00 2 Aug 1995

    Location: /pub/www/clients/windows/helpers
      FILE     -rw-r--r-- 304843 bytes 12:38 18 Apr 1995 lviewpla.zip
```

Notice that I'm given the FTP site address, along with the path and filename of the program I'm after. You can also search for broad categories of information, rather than individual files. Looking for material on genetics, for example, you could enter genetics

NOTE: Incorporating archie within Gopher goes a long way toward expanding Gopher's search capabilities. But my experience with Gopher also suggests that the system is not as easy to use as it might be. Running sample searches for this chapter, for example, I was forced to repeat my search on numerous occasions, delayed by the fact that archie servers are often overloaded and therefore slow to respond. The system, in other words, is in place, but using it can be frustrating. Nor does tapping archie through Gopher provide all the flexibility of a straight archie search, which allows you to run a variety of parameters along with your search terms to restrict the hits generated by your search.

Internet research work can be like this—what you seem to gain by a particular interface can be lost thanks to slow performance caused by an overloaded server or any number of other factors. You would be best to cultivate a frame of mind that accepts these deficiencies, because you will run into them no matter which search engine you employ. Someday we will all enjoy the benefits of high-speed connections and adequate network processing power to handle the growing load, but until then, we will have to master a sometimes balky and inconsistent infrastructure, hoping to coax information out of it, and succeeding often enough to keep us in the hunt. Internet searching isn't often easy.

HINT: Gopher occasionally seems to lock up. You wait interminably for a response but nothing happens. If you're using WSGopher or another graphical client, there is an easy way out. WSGopher, for example, contains a Cancel command on its File menu. Pull down the menu and click on Cancel to break you out of the loop. You'll then be presented with a box telling you what happened to your connection, as shown in Figure 3.23.

The Unix Gopher client may freeze up with this statement in the bottom right-hand corner of your screen:

```
Retrieving Directory..
```

To exit, try a Ctrl-C. The result will be the Gopher quit prompt:

```
Really quit (y/n)?
```

At this point, enter an **n** for no instead of the usual **y.** You'll then receive a box telling you what happened to your connection. At this point, you can press the **RETURN** key to return to the Gopher menu you were just using. Such hangups are not uncommon with Gopher. If they keep happening, you may want to wait and try to run your search at a later time.

Figure 3.23   Result of a hung Gopher session.

as your search term, hoping to find directories of that name, which would presumably house a variety of software related to the field.

Using Gopher with WAIS

Just as Gopher can be used to track down files with archie, it can also cope with the Wide Area Information Servers (WAIS) system. We'll examine WAIS carefully in Chapter 6, but for now, we'll consider WAIS in its simpler form as an index searchable through Gopher. While Gopher does not offer you the full power you can muster through a direct WAIS search (that is, not all WAIS options are available), it does make it possible to run a search through its relatively simple interface.

Figure 3.24   WAIS databases as displayed by Gopher.

Figure 3.24 shows a Gopher screen listing WAIS databases. From this point on, you simply select the database you would like to search and press a RETURN to activate Gopher's search screen.

Using CCSO Name Servers with Gopher

Although we'll discuss how to find people on the Internet in Chapter 8, you should be aware at this stage of another kind of Gopher resource that does that. A CSO name server is named after the Computing Services Office at the University of Illinois at Urbana-Champaign, which first developed the software. CSOs are used to find people on the Internet, and they're found in an ever-widening number of institutions. Today, you're likely to see these servers referred to as CCSO servers, which stands for Computing and Communications Services Office, the revamped name of this group. But no matter what you call them, these servers can be helpful in tracking down information about people.

In Figure 3.25, for example, we are looking at a screen of CCSO name servers, any of which is accessible through Gopher. Note that there are 274 menu items here and you'll realize how far the CCSO servers have spread in academe. (Note: Not all of the servers illustrated are CCSO name servers; others, indicated by the magnifying glass icon, are directories based on other technology.)

Clicking on any of the CCSO entries will take you to a screen in which you can set up a search. You will be asked to fill in fields of information: name, e-mail address, department, and so on. You enter whatever information you know and run the search. The fields are set up in a simple form; you move between them by clicking. This form is shown in Figure 3.26.

Figure 3.25   CCSO name servers as displayed by Gopher.

Figure 3.26 The CCSO search form.

    CCSOs are not difficult to use, and their growth addresses a key Internet problem—the need for more comprehensive directories of people and institutions. We'll examine this problem and run a sample CCSO search in Chapter 8.

> **NOTE:** You may, in your Gopher travels, run across the term Gopher+. This refers to a new set of features that the Gopher development crew added to the original Gopher protocol. A Gopher+ server, for example, can provide extended information about a particular menu item. It might be that an item was available in more than a single format; if so, this is information that Gopher+ can pass along. Based upon user preferences, WSGopher can display the item in the format of choice. This is controlled with the Configure menu by using the Extended Views command.
>
>   Gopher+ also includes interactive items. An Ask form allows you to fill information in blanks and return the completed form to the Gopher server. The server acts on this data to return the particular item you've requested. You can see that the administrators of Gopher servers can use Ask forms to support various kinds of data entry, such as registration for a conference or on-line transactions. In general, these are features that you will encounter through WSGopher that will enhance your use of the program, but the subtleties of their implementation can be left up to system administrators.

Gopher's Sights and Sounds

    Text has always been the backbone of the Internet's communications structure; in fact, RFC 822, which specifies how mail messages are to be handled over the network, limits such messages to 7-bit ASCII characters. But increased bandwidth and the efforts of network pioneers to create software tools have placed a new emphasis upon sight and sound. And Gopher is not exempt; it is now possible to retrieve photographs and other

Figure 3.27 The Gopher menu uses icons to indicate that these particular files are images.

pictures through its menus, as well as to fetch binary files that contain sounds. We will be seeing more and more of these resources as audio and video become more established on the Internet.

How do we know when we're dealing with images on a Gopher menu? The icons give the game away, as shown in Figure 3.27. Here each image is shown with a distinctive icon that flags its nature. The Unix Gopher will likewise flag images, by using the <Picture> designation after the menu item. In Figure 3.27, we're examining a collection of images from Dallas Museum of Art. Any of them can be saved to disk by pulling down WSGopher's File menu and choosing the Save Item command. Or, we can choose to view the graphics immediately.

Recall that to set up a Telnet session, we had to tell WSGopher how to find an external Telnet program; when we clicked on the Telnet item, WSGopher then let the external program run the session, returning us to the Gopher menu when Telnet was complete. Much the same thing occurs with WSGopher's display of images. By pulling down the Configure menu and choosing the Viewers option, we are able to insert a pathname for the file viewer of our choice. In Figure 3.28, for example, I have just added HiJaak Pro as my file viewer for files ending in the .gif extension; GIF is a popular graphics format used on images all over the Internet. Now, whenever I click on a Gopher menu item that houses a GIF file, WSGopher will download the file and then send it to HiJaak Pro for display on my screen. I could set up any number of viewers this way, specifying other file extensions, such as .jpg (for JPEG, another popular file format). For that matter, I could add extensions for external audio programs to play sound files.

Sound? Absolutely. Audio files are becoming ever more widely available over the Internet. You need the right hardware to be able to play such a file back, but if you own a multimedia PC, you can always download the file just as you would download an

Figure 3.28 Setting up HiJaak Pro as my file viewer for GIF files.

image file, and play it back on your own equipment. A variety of sound collections exist. The G. Robert Vincent Voice Library at Michigan State University is an example of how rich a resource sound may eventually become on the Internet. The library contains

Figure 3.29 A collection of audio files available through Gopher. Note the speaker icon.

speeches, performances, lectures and other audio files from over 40,000 people recorded over the past 100 years. Thus far, only a fraction of these are presently available over the Internet. Figure 3.29 shows a Gopher menu for this collection. Note that each sound file is followed by its length, giving you an idea of download time. The small speaker icon tells you the type of file that Gopher is dealing with.

HINT: We've already seen that WSGopher, like World Wide Web browsers, requires external programs to display certain kinds of files. One good place to locate such files is through the site at Netscape Communications. The URL:

http://home.netscape.com/assist/helper_apps/index.html

Here you'll find references to the major shareware and freeware programs that can be used as file viewers and configured either with a Web browser or with a Gopher. Here, for example, are some well-established programs for Windows:

LView	An excellent display program for graphics files in a wide range of formats. The work of Leonardo Haddad Loureiro, LView is shareware but available for free use if it is only being tapped for recreational purposes.
MPEGPLAY	A shareware program from Michael Simmons that will play moving videos in the MPEG format (it does not handle QuickTime).
WHAM	An audio player for the various kinds of sound files available through the Web and Gopher.
Trumpet Telnet	From Peter Tattam, the creator of Trumpet Winsock, this is a stable Telnet client.

Whatever your platform, Mac or Windows or Unix, you will find the software you need by consulting the pointers at this site. Another good site for searching is:

http://www.ncsa.uiuc.edu/SDG/Software/WinMosaic/viewers.html

This is the National Center for Supercomputing Applications site, where the Mosaic browser was developed.

Keeping Up with Gopher

Internet communications developments are fast breaking. You'll want to keep up with Gopher happenings if you find the tool useful. To do so, consider signing up for a Gopher newsgroup on USENET. The group is comp.infosystems.gopher. Another possibility (particularly if you're limited to e-mail access to the Internet alone) is to sign up for the Gopher-News mailing list. Send your request for a subscription to Gopher-news-request@boombox.micro.umn.edu. Finally, for a moderated mailing list containing announcements of new Gopher software and services, send to gopher-announce-request@boombox.micro.umn.edu.

The Future of Gopher

The rapid rise of the World Wide Web has recently obscured Gopher's success as a publishing tool and a vehicle for the dissemination of easily accessible information. But just when it appeared that Gopher had begun to show its age, the original Gopher team at the University of Minnesota challenged the Internet community with a new model. The creators of the popular TurboGopher client for the Macintosh now offer a virtual reality-based version of the software that presents Gopher sites as three-dimensional structures in a vividly imagined Gopherspace. The virtual landscape pictures buildings (the servers) whose contents are advertised on their sides, while a series of audio and visual cues show actions. You can hold down the mouse button and move about within this landscape. Switching Gopher sites causes your view to be elevated, as if you were taking an airplane ride to a new city; music is likewise used to cue the user to Gopherspace features. The beauty of the virtual reality modeling practiced by the University of Minnesota Gopher team is that existing databases can be made three-dimensional without any extensive rewriting of their software.

HINT: Virtual reality modeling can be eerie. The TurboGopherVR strategy may be to show Gopher information in the form of buildings, but to this researcher, the effect is of standing on some surreal plain surrounded by monoliths, something like a digital Stonehenge. Whatever the metaphor, however, virtual reality makes navigation through the resulting information space easier by relating your motions to movements of the mouse and their corresponding visual effects. TurboGopherVR takes some getting used to, but the model is ultimately fascinating as you begin to master it. I suspect VR techniques will play a large role in the future not only of Gopher, but of other Internet search tools as well.

TurboGopherVR takes a giant step at moving Gopher into a graphical world, thus challenging what had been the World Wide Web's greatest asset—its visual, intuitive dis-

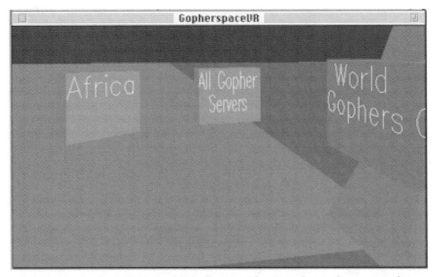

Figure 3.30 TurboGopherVR adds striking visual cues to the Gopher process, bringing electronic publishing into a three-dimensional world.

play. A version of TurboGopherVR is now available for the Macintosh at the following URL:

gopher://boombox.micro.umn.edu/11/gopher/Macintosh-
    TurboGopher/TurboGopherVR

A Unix version is also available, while versions for other platforms are under development. Figure 3.30 shows the TurboGopherVR program at work.

4

Veronica: Gopher as Search Engine

As a browsing tool, Gopher's great talent is that it simplifies the process of information retrieval by allowing us to concentrate on what we need rather than on the complexities of accessing it. On the other hand, using menued information, even with so bulletproof an interface, contains built-in obstacles. Although we have learned to put Gopher's bookmarks to work to tag items, our session remains a lengthy process of exploration, more hit and miss than targeted strategy.

We can, of course, uncover quite a bit this way, including precisely the data we need. But what we would like is a way to cut through all the unnecessary menu stops. How much simpler it would be if we could build an engine that could search Gopherspace. Such a program would take the guesswork out of our searching by returning a list of menus containing the terms we specified. We could enter information highway as our search term and a list of Gophers with that term somewhere in their menu structure would appear. Hours of search time and menu scanning could be condensed into seconds.

Such an idea came to Steven Foster and Fred Barrie at the University of Nevada at Reno's System Computing Department. archie provided a precedent; it allowed users to locate text, data, and executable files at sites throughout the Internet community. Why not create something similar for Gopher? Using Gopher's ability to create menus out of diverse information sources, this new tool would produce a customized menu based on the results of its search. And, as with any Gopher menus, each item would thereby be accessible through the usual Gopher methods.

Make no mistake about it, Barrie and Foster's work has created one of the Internet's premium search tools. Called Veronica, the new engine was developed in November 1992, and quickly sprung to prominence as users experienced its many advantages. For most of my own information gathering, Veronica is an inescapable stop. Using it, I can find out what's available on a large percentage of the world's Gopher servers, not only in the form of textual and binary files, but also Telnet-accessible information sources mentioned on Gopher menus, and references to such resources as USENET archives and even World Wide Web documents. Indeed, almost every item offered by a Gopher server is indexed by Veronica, which makes for quite a reference source. As of late July 1995,

Veronica could locate 9,046 Gopher servers. Given the range of information being fed into this base, the use of Veronica as a search tool is indispensable.

> **NOTE:** When is a Gopher not available to Veronica? In most cases, when it is a special-use server, such as one used by a corporation in the performance of its business or any other kind of private organization not wishing its Gopher materials to be made public. Such servers are often restricted to users in their own domains, and Veronica is unable, therefore, as it "harvests" its data, to acquire the necessary references to use them in its database. But Veronica does contain information on almost all the Gophers made available for the use of the general public.

> **NOTE:** Where do they dream up these names? Intriguingly, most Internet tools seem to have multiple referents. Thus, Gopher's origins as a school mascot as well as a retriever that "goes for" data. Veronica, likewise, owes a debt to several sources. Readers of the Archie comic strip or listeners to the old Archie Andrews radio show may remember Veronica as Archie's girlfriend. And we already know about archie itself, a search tool known for its software's ability to search archives (take out the v). So if Veronica is a kind of archie for Gophers, then it makes sense that it have a name associated with archie (archie, by the way, was *not* originally named after Archie Andrews).
>
> On the other hand, maybe we should give credence to the Frequently Asked Questions document about Veronica. With a straight face, it claims the name means this: **v**ery **e**asy **r**odent-**o**riented **n**et-wide **i**ndex to **c**omputerized **a**rchives. And brace yourself for another search tool, working closely with Gopher and Veronica, called Jughead. More about the meaning of its reverse-engineered acronym later in this chapter.

How Veronica Works

Menu items presented by Gopher are references to the files or services—whatever their type—found beneath them in the menu structure. Veronica is able to search these titles by consulting an index it maintains. By entering a keyword, you are able to run your search past this index. You should, therefore, think of Veronica in somewhat the same terms you think of archie. Veronica must collect data from the Gopher servers it consults and then make searches of that database available to the clients that access it. The database is updated on a monthly schedule by a Veronica server, which queries the Gopher servers it knows about and asks for their menus.

The results of the search are presented on your screen as a menu, which you can then use in the same way you use any Gopher item, pressing the cursor keys or clicking with a mouse to move to the item you wish to inspect. As you can see, Veronica is not a standalone program; there are no Veronica client programs in the same sense that Gopher clients have proliferated on the network. Rather, Veronica retains a cohesive link to Gopher, working with the Gopher client of your choice to present the results of its searches and make their connections available to you. Or, if you choose, you can use a World Wide Web browser to access this tool. For the sake of simplicity, I will use the Unix Gopher to illustrate Veronica use in this chapter.

Accessing Veronica

Veronica's tight links with Gopher mean that you can connect to it through a Gopher client, which will allow you to reach a Gopher server that provides its own link to Veronica. Chances are, your usual Gopher site will offer a Veronica link. But if it does not, many other Gopher sites are available that do. If, on the other hand, you lack access to a Gopher client, you can still use Veronica through a Telnet connection to a public Gopher client.

Using a Gopher Client to Reach Veronica

You can look for Veronica at your service provider's site by calling up Gopher, as discussed in Chapter 3. The best place to look is under any menu item that refers to other Internet information servers. For example, here is what I see when I dial in to the Gopher at Interpath, my service provider in Raleigh, and look for Gopher-related materials:

```
1. Search Gopherspace using Veronica/
```

This is obviously the menu choice I want. On the other hand, perhaps it's not a choice found on your Gopher server. In that case, look for a menu item referring to other Gopher servers. Veronica will likely be found on such a list.

If it still doesn't turn up, you can take a shortcut by going to the mother Gopher at the University of Minnesota. The URL is this:

gopher://gopher.micro.umn.edu/

Follow the menu tree and you'll wind up with ready access to Veronica. Look for the menu item labelled *Other Gopher and Information Servers/*. Veronica should appear as a menu choice like this one:

```
3. Search titles in Gopherspace using veronica/
```

Taking this menu choice will produce a list of Veronica servers currently available, along with related information. You can see the screen in Figure 4.1. Examine this menu with interest. Obviously, the Frequently Asked Questions document is of value. The date will change with updates, so keep an eye on it and whenever a new version comes out, save and print it out for reference. Item 10 is also one to watch for updates; it contains information about the proper form to use in composing your search statements for Veronica. The tool continues to change as improvements are added, and the first word you may get about these changes is in this document.

Notice, too, that you have received a list of various Veronica servers. It's possible that your own site may contain fewer server references, or even different ones. This is because the menu is reconfigured on a routine basis to reflect the currently active Veronica servers; these, obviously, will change over time. It's helpful to know about other servers, because you may connect to one and receive a message that there are too many connections in progress for your search to be carried out on that server. In that case, using a different server is necessary.

You will also note in Figure 4.1 the following line:

```
Simplified veronica chooses server - pick a search type:
```

```
         Internet Gopher Information Client v2.0.16

              Search titles in Gopherspace using veronica

  -->_

      3.  Find GOPHER DIRECTORIES by Title word(s) (via NYSERNet   ) <?>
      4.  Find GOPHER DIRECTORIES by Title word(s) (via PSINet) <?>
      5.  Find GOPHER DIRECTORIES by Title word(s) (via SUNET) <?>
      6.  Find GOPHER DIRECTORIES by Title word(s) (via U. Nac. Autonoma .. <?>
      7.  Find GOPHER DIRECTORIES by Title word(s) (via UNINETT..of Bergen) <?>
      8.  Find GOPHER DIRECTORIES by Title word(s) (via University of Koe.. <?>
      9.  Frequently-Asked Questions (FAQ) about veronica - January 13, 1995
     10.  How to Compose veronica Queries - June 23, 1994
     11.  More veronica: Software, Index-Control Protocol, HTML Pages/
     12.  Search GopherSpace by Title word(s) (via NYSERNet   ) <?>
     13.  Search GopherSpace by Title word(s) (via PSINet) <?>
     14.  Search GopherSpace by Title word(s) (via SUNET) <?>
     15.  Search GopherSpace by Title word(s) (via U. Nac. Autonoma de MX.. <?>
     16.  Search GopherSpace by Title word(s) (via UNINETT/U. of Bergen) <?>
     17.  Search GopherSpace by Title word(s) (via University of Koeln) <?>
          Simplified veronica chooses server - pick a search type:

  Press ? for Help, q to Quit, u to go up a menu              Page: 1/2
```

Figure 4.1 Veronica servers available through the Gopher at the University of Minnesota.

If you were to move to the second page of this Gopher menu, you would find two more choices:

```
19. Simplified veronica: Find Gopher MENUS only <?>
20. Simplified veronica: find ALL gopher types <?>
```

A "simplified" search is one in which the software contacts all the Veronica servers for you; this saves you the need to try them one by one until you find one that isn't busy.

As spelled out in this figure, you have the ability to search a Veronica server in two ways:

- Find GOPHER DIRECTORIES by Title word(s): This method searches only for Gopher directories whose titles contain your keywords. A directory search is broader than a more comprehensive search, because it is isolating references to large subcategories of information. If you find a Gopher directory that houses a menu item corresponding to your search term, you have probably found a site that will contain multiple files about that topic.
- Search GopherSpace by Title word(s): This method looks for words in menu titles, and can point to any kind of Gopher resource. In other words, any menu item listed on a Gopher, from a textual document to an image, a binary file, a Gopher directory, a Telnet session, or a WAIS index, can be retrieved if it appears on the menu with your keyword in it.

Using Telnet to Reach Veronica

Because Gopher and Veronica are so tightly interwoven, you know that in the absence of a Gopher client or a World Wide Web browser on your system, you will need to use Telnet to

HINT: The load on Veronica servers has become intense, as people have begun to realize how convenient their searching capabilities are. Don't be surprised to find a Veronica server unable to handle your request. The beauty of the simplified search capability is that you don't have to worry about this; the software will work behind the scenes to find a server that is free. The alternative is to go through the Veronica servers one at a time, entering your query until you find a server that can accept the request.

access a Gopher site from which you can tap into Veronica. The list of Gopher sites is the same given in Chapter 3. As always, use the site nearest to you to minimize network congestion. And as mentioned before, use a client program if at all possible. A client will provide a faster search and will take the best advantage of the equipment you have available.

A Simple Veronica Search

To illustrate the workings of Veronica, let's run two sample searches. In the first, I want to show you in particular how directory-based searches can be used to find broad collections of information. Suppose I'm interested in learning about sites on the Internet that specialize in architecture. I don't necessarily have a specific query in mind; rather, I want to browse through the holdings at such sites to see what is available. A directory-based search is useful for this because we know that it will pull up menu items that point to underlying collections of information.

Choosing a Veronica server under the category Search GopherSpace by Title word(s), I press a **RETURN** to call up the search screen (I chose the Veronica server at NYSERNet in New York, it being the only one open to run my request at the time I tried it). The search screen looks like what you see in Figure 4.2.

Figure 4.2 Searching Gopher directories with the keyword architecture.

When I press another **RETURN** to launch this search, Veronica will consult its database and return a series of hits. You can see my first screen of hits in Figure 4.3. The important thing to notice about this screen is that it consists not of individual files, but of directory materials. You can verify this by examining the items; they end with a slash, which is the Unix Gopher client's way of telling us there is an underlying menu of resources (WSGopher, on the other hand, would flag each of these with a folder icon, which tells us precisely the same thing). Notice, too, that we have 12 screens of hits, so we've uncovered quite a lot of architecturally related material. The information presented in Figure 4.3 is just another Gopher menu, although one constructed for us by Veronica. And we can use it in precisely the same way; we put the on-screen marker on the item we want to see and press a **RETURN** or, if we're using a graphical client, we simply double-click on the item in question. Doing so with item 12 on the list of hits in Figure 4.3 calls up another screen, the submenu of this particular Gopher directory. You can see it in Figure 4.4.

Here we have a single page of Gopher items, all located on the same Gopher server. Most, but not all, are additional directories of information; some are text files. If we're just browsing to gather an idea of what kind of resources are available about architecture through Gopher, we've uncovered the fact that an immense number of files exist.

A More Specific Search

You won't always want to run broadly based searches like this one; sometimes it will be necessary to home in on particular types of resources, or to search for individual data or information files. The search I'm about to show you represents the kind of activity the average user brings to Veronica. And just as you learned that using Gopher without bookmarks was ignoring the true potential of the medium, so using Veronica without

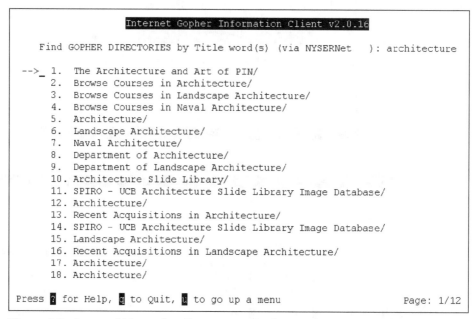

Figure 4.3 A page of hits, each a directory at a Gopher site that contains information about architecture.

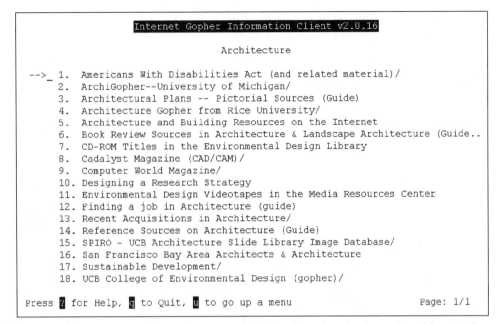

Figure 4.4   Examining a particular directory. The list of Veronica hits is used just like a Gopher menu—choose what you want to see and the software will take you to it.

proper attention to its various search options sharply reduces the effectiveness of your search. Consider what follows, then, a paradigm that is under construction; we will add to it as we go.

We'll start with the basics and gradually build a much more comprehensive search routine. First, an easy-to-answer information request. I'd like to learn about QWK mail readers, which allow various kinds of bulletin board systems to work with mail to and from the Internet. A friend is interested in establishing a bulletin board with Internet links, but doesn't know what is available that would help him download and distribute messages to his callers. He'd also like to learn more about QWK in general, not only in terms of the software programs out there, but the theory behind the data transfer.

I call this a simple request because of its narrow focus. I'm looking for information about a named subject—QWK. I can specify this knowing that everything I generate will have something to do with my topic. It's not as if I were searching under broad terms like reader or mail. The ability to focus is a key tenet in any Internet search strategy. Always ask yourself how narrowly you can specify your data needs and still retrieve what you need. Too narrow a focus pulls up no hits. Too broad a strategy results in long search times and huge numbers of hits to wade through (although, as we'll see, there are times when a broad search is essential; more on this in a moment). Each search calls upon you to juggle these possibilities. A practiced eye soon develops.

My first step in the search process is to choose how I want to use Gopher. I will begin by choosing Search GopherSpace by Title word(s), hoping to find programs and documentation about my subject. I call up the search screen as before by pressing a RETURN with the highlight on the relevant menu item (and now find that only the Veronica server at SUNET in Sweden, is available for my request). I enter my search term—QWK—in the space provided, just as in our recent architecture search. I could just as easily have used qwk, for Veronica is not sensitive to case.

HINT: Memorize what I just said: *Veronica is not sensitive to case.*

When I press a RETURN after entering my search term, the Veronica search begins. This is shown in Gopher fashion by a statement in the right-hand corner of the screen:

```
Searching..-
```

HINT: Don't be alarmed if Veronica occasionally hangs up at this point, leaving you with the searching prompt on and a seemingly frozen connection. When this occurs, it may be because a necessary network connection is congested or down. The solution is to do the same thing you would do with Gopher; remember, Veronica works *through* Gopher. Press a **Ctrl-C**, then answer **n** when you're prompted whether you want to quit Gopher. This should pop you out of cyberspace limbo and let you try again. Or, if you're using WSGopher, choose the Cancel command from the File menu.

This method works most of the time. When it doesn't, repeat **Ctrl-C** several times, which may take you back to your provider's prompt. And don't be surprised if there are times when you have no choice but to hang up to break out of the frozen system.

When the search is complete, you'll get a screen full of information or, more likely, several screens. Figure 4.5 shows one of 11 screens that this search generated. Let's

```
┌──────────────────────────────────────────────────────────────────┐
│              Internet Gopher Information Client v2.0.16            │
│                                                                    │
│          Search GopherSpace by Title word(s) (via SUNET): QWK      │
│                                                                    │
│      1.  qwkq200.zip - Display a random QWK tagline at boot-up     │
│      2.  taglx340.zip - Tag Line Xpress: Enhanced QWK Tagline manager │
│      3.  qwkp0294.zip - List of QWK format readers and mail doors  │
│  -->_ 4.  speed140.zip - Database-type QWK offline BBS mail reader  │
│      5.  mmgr136a.zip - Mail Manager v1.36a: QWK mail door for RBBS-PC │
│      6.  mnet200.zip - MNET v2.00 QWK->REP network conversion util. │
│      7.  mplus351.zip - MMGR +Plus+ v3.51 QWK mail door: RBBS/Fido │
│      8.  qwkp9405.zip - List of QWK format readers and mail doors  │
│      9.  1st-111?.zip - 1stReader v1.11, QWK offline reader        │
│     10.  blueq151.zip - Blue Wave <-> QWK BBS mail packet convertor │
│     11.  qwkp9404.zip - List of QWK format readers and mail doors  │
│     12.  qprn111.zip - Removes unwanted messages from QWK packets  │
│     13.  wr101a.zip/wr101b.zip - WIN3:WaveRider QWK/BlueWave offline reader │
│     14.  mplus352.zip - MMGR +Plus+ v3.52 QWK mail door: RBBS/Fido │
│     15.  qwkp0394.zip - List of QWK format readers and mail doors  │
│     16.  fidoq120.zip - FidoQwk v1.20, QWK <-> FidoNet converter   │
│     17.  qprn110.zip - Removes unwanted messages from QWK packets  │
│     18.  uniqwk30.zip - WIN3: Offline QWK mail reader w/multlang. supt │
│                                                                    │
│ Press ? for Help, q to Quit, u to go up a menu        Page: 1/11  │
└──────────────────────────────────────────────────────────────────┘
```

Figure 4.5   One page of results from a search throughout Gopherspace.

examine this screen with some care. As you can see, it's a regular Gopher menu, and it's clear that if we were to move the arrow to any of these items and press a RETURN, we could call up the information. But every item on this menu refers in some manner to QWK. It's important, too, to note the kinds of information we've been presented.

Item 130, aq_122.readme (not shown in the figure but available by paging through our results) is a text file; we can assume this because of its title, and because Gopher shows us no slash following the item, which would indicate an underlying subdirectory. Item 127, on the other hand, shows an .hqx suffix, indicating that we're looking at Macintosh material in the BinHex archival format. And if we were to page through the rest of the 11 screens, we would find still other kinds of information and files. Item 11 is qwkp9404.zip, a compressed binary file, which turns out to be a list of QWK format readers. A number of files also provide background information on QWK, including item 44, called QWK reader for Mac, which contains an overview of the QWK system.

Just what are we looking for? Again, we need to define our mission. It's useful to know that we can retrieve various executable files here, but we are really concentrating on text files, because we're looking for background information. This reduces the population of files to consider by quite a bit. One way to approach an overview of information is to search Gopher directories, rather than all the files in Gopherspace. To do so, we can use the Gopher directories option to run our search. When I did this on the same SUNET Veronica server, I came up with the following hits:

```
1.   qwk/
2.   QWK offline-reader information/
3.   QWK :c4/
```

In each case, we are looking at a directory with a submenu branching off from it; we are clued into this by the slash following the entry. Remember, directory searching is a good way to garner overview information; it tells you where repositories of data that fit your keyword are located. Looking through these directories, I was able to gather a list of current products, a file containing information on QWK's mail packet structure, and the addresses of people who write QWK programs. And, of course, I could use the usual Gopher methods to save these files.

Refining the Search

If you are happy with the preceding search because it tracked down the QWK information we needed, you should reexamine your search methodology. Yes, we did find what we wanted, but the search we ran was inexcusably slack. It produced 11 screens full of information, but much of the material was not what we wanted. The fact that Veronica called up so much also meant that we had to spend time sifting through all the results, a wasteful procedure when alternatives are available.

How could we home in more precisely on our search materials? By tuning up Veronica through a series of search options. To do so, we will restrict Veronica to finding certain Gopher data types (recall that we looked at these data types in Chapter 3.) Gopher marks its retrieved material through a series of official data type suffixes; there are also a number of experimental types being developed for pictures and sound. Veronica can be restricted to search for just the types you specify—the automated equivalent of going through menu after menu looking for particular kinds of files and directories.

The key is to add **-t** to our search request. PC binary files, for example, correspond to data type 5. We might want to search for these if we were looking for the actual QWK software and programs that supported it. To search for PC binary files alone, we frame our query this way: **qwk -t5**. Veronica doesn't care where we drop in the -t modifier, so we could also enter **-t5 qwk** for the same result (note that there is no space between the -t and the number following it). The result of this modified search is shown in Figure 4.6. Notice that 11 pages of material have been reduced to four, and that each item has the search term qwk in its entry.

HINT: The method we've just used can stand as an archetype for Internet searching, and for Veronica searching in particular. With millions of Internet destinations, our primary goal is to reduce the number of hits to those items that are truly useful. That can call for some exceedingly judicious choices in terms of keywords and search parameters. With each tool you master, you will want to learn, first of all, how to enter the basic keywords, but second, and more important, how to modify the search terms so that you can specify with precision what you are trying to do. This can get tricky—each search engine has its own take on parameters and how to modify them—but the time you spend acquiring a thorough knowledge of your most oft-used tools will be rewarded in solid results.

Using Gopher's Data Types with Veronica

The list of data types available to Veronica shows us that we can specify to a fair degree of precision what it is we'd like to find. Let's explore the options now within the framework of a highly targeted search. Suppose we'd like to determine what Internet databases

```
Internet Gopher Information Client v2.0.16

          Search GopherSpace by Title word(s) (via SUNET): QWK -t5

-->  1.  mt_qwk_r.lzh <PC Bin>
     2.  proqwk.zip       19KB Keep QWK packets from same source in .. <PC Bin>
     3.  cqwk14.zip     1616KB CmpQwk v1.4 Win 3.1 QWK off-line mail.. <PC Bin>
     4.  pow10.zip       149KB PowerLine offline .QWK reader   <PC Bin>
     5.  proqwk11.zip     19KB Rename .QWK packets in ProComm Plus..N <PC Bin>
     6.  uniqwk30.zip    216KB Windows .QWK Mail Reader (Multilangua.. <PC Bin>
     7.  vbrdr14.zip     104KB VBReader: .QWK format offline mail re.. <PC Bin>
     8.  winq200a.zip    282KB WinQwk: Win-based message reader for .. <PC Bin>
     9.  wr10a.zip       363KB Wave Rider, .QWK and BlueWave-format .. <PC Bin>
    10.  wr10b.zip       297KB Wave Rider, .QWK and BlueWave-format .. <PC Bin>
    11.  wr110upd.zip    248KB Update to Wave Rider BlueWave and QWK.. <PC Bin>
    12.  FIDOQ118.ZIP Toss BBS mail between Fido- and QWK-networks .. <PC Bin>
    13.  MM20B31.ZIP  MarkMail v2.00B31: QWK mail door for PCBoard .. <PC Bin>
    14.  MNET200.ZIP  MNET v2.00 QWK->REP network conversion util. .. <PC Bin>
    15.  RAMAIL20.ZIP QWK mail door for Remote Access BBS         .. <PC Bin>
    16.  RNET107U.ZIP RNet 1.07: QWK networking software for PCBoar.. <PC Bin>
    17.  PDQWK10.ZIP  QWK standard maildoor for GT-Power v17..{104KB} <PC Bin>
    18.  QWKQ200.ZIP  Display a random QWK tagline at boot-up       .. <PC Bin>

Press ? for Help, q to Quit, u to go up a menu              Page: 1/4
```

Figure 4.6 Results of a targeted search for PC binary files.

exist with information about geology. One way to do this would be to look for Telnet connections that are available on Gopher menus. Veronica is made for this kind of searching.

Remember the Telnet data type: Telnet connections are given the suffix <TEL> and correspond to data type 8. This means we can search for them using the search term **geology -t8**. We have narrowed our search to only Telnet items. The result:

```
        Search gopherspace at PSINet: geology -t8
-->>    1.  Resources on Geology, Geophys, Astron., Astrophys. (Login: 1p.. <TEL>
        2.  Resources on Geology, Geophys, Astron., Astrophys. (Login: 1p.. <TEL>
        3.  USGS Pacific Marine Geology (PMG) data catalog <TEL>
```

Does the big picture begin to emerge? We have more control over a Veronica session than we realized. The issue is not how to narrow these choices—as we're finding, Veronica is not that difficult to master—but rather how to exercise good judgment in setting up an initial search strategy and then following through to the best possible result.

Suppose, for example, that we're interested in learning about Gopher resources relating to wine. We're looking in particular for text files—not directories or programs—and would like to limit our search to that data type. We can set up a search using the keyword statement **wine -t0**. Now, when we press **RETURN** to launch the search, we should retrieve a list of any Gopher menu items that contain the word wine and exist in the form of text files. You can see the first of nine pages of hits in Figure 4.7.

Veronica's ability to limit searches by data type can be a lifesaver; it allows you to discard from the outset material you know to be valueless for your search, while telling your search engine specifically what data type you need. With that in mind, let's create several searches and consider how they can best be managed.

```
        Internet Gopher Information Client v2.0.16

        Search GopherSpace by Title word(s) (via SUNET): wine -t0

-->_  1.  Tint-in-red-wine-may-help-heart,-study-say.
      2.  Men-should-quaff-five-bottles-of-wine-a-week,-study-says.
      3.  Why-red-wine-is-apparently-good-for-you.
      4.  [ANNOUNCE] The first Wine FAQ is here!
      5.  HB0345 Regulating Sale of Wine
      6.  The Aesthetics of the Greek Banquet: Images of Wine and Ritual. F. ..
      7.  The Wine Revolution in France: The Twentieth Century. L.A. Loubere.
      8.  80D.* An Analytical View of Wines and  Wine Chemistry.
      9.  94.1.6, BMCR E-Post-It (Old Wine)
     10.  93-10-01-16: Wine Boycott for UFW
     11.  MID-ATLANTIC WINE FESTIVAL
     12.  VINIFERA WINE FESTIVAL
     13.  TENNESSEE GRAPE AND WINE NDUSTRY
     14.  TENNESSEE GRAPE AND WINE INDUSTRIES
     15.  Wine Awards
     16.  Wine Awards
     17.  margarita-wine-punch (2k)
     18.  warm-sweet-red-wine (2k)

Press ? for Help, q to Quit, u to go up a menu          Page: 1/9
```

Figure 4.7 A list of hits using the keyword wine, and limiting the data type to text files only.

HINT: It's time to refresh your memory about Gopher's data types and the numbers associated with them. Briefly:

0	A text file
1	A directory
2	A CCSO name server
3	ERROR
4	A Macintosh file in BinHex format
5	A DOS binary archive
7	A searchable index
8	A Telnet connection
9	A binary file
s	A sound file
g	A GIF image file
M	A file containing MIME data, which is an evolving method useful for sending multimedia mail communications.
h	An HTML file
I	An image file other than GIF format
T	A Telnet 3270 session

A Sample Search for Information about CD-ROMs

The goal: We'd like to learn more about Internet resources that are available on CD-ROM disks. The number of such disks seems to be growing, with providers supplying everything from TCP/IP software to disks mirroring huge shareware collections like SIMTEL20 and others. Unix public domain software is also out there, along with such implementations as Linux, a Unix system configured for the PC. We want to find out more comprehensively what's there and how to get it.

We can try a Veronica search at its widest setting simply by entering the search term **cdrom** and pressing a **RETURN**. But by doing so, we run into an immediate difficulty. The results of such a search are illustrated in Figure 4.8. True, there's much that proves useful. Paging through this material, we find a document about CD-ROM shareware, along with what seem to be numerous text files about the medium. The problem shows up when we examine the bottom right-hand corner of the screen, where we find this:

```
Page: 1/12
```

Twelve pages of material is a lot to wade through. On the other hand, it's certainly worth doing if we find what we need here. But a second problem arises if we go to that twelfth page. There, we find the final item:

```
200.   NEC CDROM Driver?.
```

Is it just chance that, in our search, we've generated precisely 200 hits? Not by a long shot. The number of hits can be regulated at the site of each Veronica server. What you see, in other words, isn't always a full set of what's available. When a search generates a

```
                Internet Gopher Information Client v2.0.16

              Search GopherSpace by Title word(s) (via SUNET): cdrom

  -->   1.  Linux/GNU/X UNIX(R) clone for PC's: beta CDROM now available
        2.        Street Maps of the U.S. on CDROM
        3.        RE: Street Maps of the U.S. on CDROM
        4.        RE: Street Maps of the U.S. on CDROM
        5.  Administrivia: New CICA Shareware CDROM for MS Windows
        6.  Re: Khoros 1.5 CDROM on LGX Linux
        7.  Re: Khoros 1.5 CDROM on LGX Linux
        8.  cdrom.inf - How to obtain SimTel files on CD-ROM
        9.  cdrom.inf How to obtain SimTel files on CD-ROM
       10.  CDROM Databases Available in the Government Docs Area
       11.  CDROM Databases Available in the General Reference Area
       12.  CDROM Databases Available in the Science/Engineering Area
       13.  CDROMLAN; CDROM-L
       14.  cdrom
       15.  CDROM
       16.  info-mac-cdrom-3.txt
       17.  cdrom/
       18.  cdrom  [ 2Jul92, 8kb]

 Press ? for Help, q to Quit, u to go up a menu          Page: 1/12
```

Figure 4.8 A Veronica search for CD-ROM materials.

large number of hits, a cutoff must be found to avoid bombarding you with thousands of entries (and, for that matter, to avoid overloading network connections). This can be seen graphically if we run the same search at a different Veronica server.

The previous search took place on the SUNET server. When I ran the search at NYSERNET's server, I generated not 200 but 201 hits. The 201st was a dandy:

```
201.  ** There are 1487 more items matching the query "cdrom" available ...
```

If 12 pages of hits totals 200 items, then 1,487 more items should mount up to roughly *89 pages* of additional Gopher items. Of course, we can use Gopher's / command to search these pages, or use the Find command with a graphical Gopher, but given that we don't yet have specific search terms to work with, this is impractical; so, too, is the idea of paging through a grand total of 101 screens of Gopher items hoping to find what we need.

First of all, we can take a look at text files; that is, we can search for any Gopher menu items that contain the term cdrom and are also text files. If we enter **cdrom -t0** as our search term, we pull up another 12 screens. They consist of entries like these:

```
19.   Data Dictionary for the 90 PUMS CDROM files
20.   About USA Counties on CDROM
21.   Users Guide to USA Counties CDROM
22.   CDROM Databases
23.   cdrom
24.   CDROM drive and sound card for sale
25.   README.HEASARC_CDROM, Size=12259
26.   cdrom_sss.lsm, Size=490
```

```
27.   cdrom.inf
28.   nascent.cdrom
29.   cdrom.1st
30.   Info-Mac_3_CDROM_NEC_Driver_Fix
31.   New Project Gutenberg CDROM
32.   CDROM Encyclopedias?
```

Paging through the list of hits, I run across a great deal of background information. In fact, item 201 on this list shows that there are an additional 2,209 items about this topic available in text format. That's far too many to page through at random!

HINT: If you're serious about the Internet, you'll have to learn to cope with its frequent frustrations. For example, in running the CD-ROM search, I also located a number of items that no longer were available. Although the Veronica search pulled them up on-screen, when I tried to access them, I retrieved a message like this one:

```
0Server error: '/netwire/files/C/CDROM.TXT ' does not exist!!
```

What has happened here is that the file that was once at this location has been moved, so that the Gopher server could not find it; in its turn, Veronica's index has become out of date, and has not yet caught the error in a new data sweep. All we can do about such problems is to understand the limitations of the medium and proceed to another item. Fortunately, Veronica indices are updated roughly once a month, so the number of such misfires is relatively low.

So let's get creative. First, we'll examine the list of data types and make a decision about what might be useful. Earlier, we used the directory data type to narrow our search for QWK readers to directories only; we found three. We might want to try that with CD-ROM materials, discovering possible archival sites that might be interesting to examine (you will see later that we could run the equivalent search using archie). And let's take a look at data type 7, which consists of indexed databases, as well. Perhaps something exists for CD-ROM in this format.

Let's run the search with the term **cdrom -t17**. Note that it isn't necessary to separate the numbers for the various data types; cdrom -t17 searches for the term cdrom in any directory (data type 1), as well as in any indexed database (directory type 7). And when we run the search, we retrieve eight pages of information, most of which consist of directories like those shown:

```
1.   cdrom/
2.   cdrom/
3.   cdrom on bramble (Jim Robb)/
4.   cdrom(a) on manitou (Carol Brown)/
5.   cdrom(b) on manitou (Carol Brown)/
6.   cdrom on quissett (Eric Schmuck) /
7.   (Soon) GLORIA mosaics and data on CDROM (with DOS graphics) /
8.   Local Woods Hole USGS WORKSTATIONS: login, anon ftp, or cdrom/
9.   cdrom Drivers for various CD ROM devices/
```

The last two items on page 8 turn out to be searchable databases, as shown by their <?> suffix:

```
140.  Life Sciences Collection CDROM List of Journals <?>
141.  CDROM Applied Science and Technology <?>
```

Eight pages, with 141 entries, is workable if we are conducting a broad sweep for background information. And indeed, we can find a substantial amount of background material by running the search in this form. We learn about the existence of several USENET newsgroups and their archives:

```
53.  comp.publish.cdrom.hard Hardware used in publishing with CD-ROM./
54.  comp.publish.cdrom.mult Software for multimedia authoring & publis../
55.  comp.publish.cdrom.soft Software used in publishing with CD-ROM./
```

We learn about CD-ROM journals:

```
92.  Online & CDROM Review--E2EO01/
```

We also find directories under various aspects of CD-ROM installation and usage:

```
31.  CDROM Installation Program/
32.  CDROM Products/
33.  CDROM Product Appearance Images/
```

And finally, we find one of the major suppliers of CD-ROM disks of Internet information:

```
37.  Walnut Creek CDROM ........................... 6 entries/
```

By combining the information we find inside key directories with the Frequently Asked Questions document we retrieved from our first search, we have built up a battery of knowledge about our subject.

Can we perform the same search tasks with a graphical Gopher client? Of course. In Figure 4.9, for example, you can see a Veronica search screen as presented by WSGopher. Note what is happening in this figure. The major data types are all laid out for us in the form of menu choices, each marked with the small magnifying glass icon that tells us we are working with a searchable index. Clicking on any of these items will call up the search field. As you can see, we can choose between files, directories, CSO servers, indices, and Telnet sessions.

A Veronica Strategy Emerges

Earlier, I said that there were times when it made sense to run a broad search first before narrowing your focus. Indeed, our search for CD-ROM materials illustrates the point; we did find such resources as a Frequently Asked Questions document and a variety of other references. Then we proceeded to focus on particular types of searching. Remember, you should always evaluate the data type possibilities as you examine the results of a Veronica search. The need for background material may compel you to limit the search to text files that might contain such information. A search for an on-line database would doubtless require you to search for Telnet sessions available through Gopher, while a directory-based search would reveal the existence of archival holdings of material about your subject.

I generally advocate that any Veronica search, save for the most simple, should consist of at least two, and possibly three, passes through the material. The first is a general

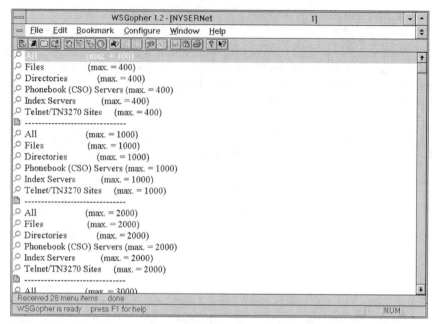

Figure 4.9 A Veronica search screen as viewed through WSGopher.

sweep for files germane to your topic, while the second builds upon the first, attempting to fill in the gaps left by that initial search, and aimed at saving you the effort of wading through page after page of Veronica hits. The third sweep, if necessary, is constructed out of a newly tightened search strategy, based upon what you have learned from the results of the first two. To summarize, then:

Step 1: The broad search, examining your initial hits to see what's relevant, or to determine whether your search needs to be more focused. The broad search may be run without any data type parameters; here, you're just scouting for information. If you find everything you need in this step, you can stop here. If not, move to step 2.

Step 2: The narrow search, examining the resources you think are the most effective in following up your query. Here, you use Veronica's data types to zero in on what you need. Evaluating the results, you determine whether you need to proceed to step 3.

Step 3: The narrowest search, in which you refine your keywords themselves to tighten up your strategy.

How do you refine your keywords? Read on.

Combining Keywords to Search

Now we can start to get crafty. Rather than using a single keyword, we'll branch out into multiple keywords with Boolean-style connections. We'll also learn to specify the number of hits we'd like to examine. Adding this level of search capability to Veronica makes it capable of finding files quickly, which otherwise might take hours of searching, if you ever found them at all.

But before you begin a new search, you should make a necessary adjustment to your Gopher menus. If you are going to use Veronica frequently, and anyone who searches the Internet with any degree of consistency should do so, then you need to make it easier to reach your search tool. To do this, use the Gopher bookmark page.

> **HINT:** The Gopher client most dial-up users will work with makes narrowing a search a simple matter. When you enter your search term into the search field, that term stays there after the search has been run. Type, for example, use **cdrom** as your search term and run the search. Then, when you want to refine the search, go back to the search screen. The term cdrom is still there, with the cursor waiting at the end of the word. Now you can add another term to it. Perhaps add **-t1**, so that your entire search term is now **cdrom -t1**. Press the **RETURN** key and the revised search is run. Adding yet another search term or modifier is done the same way.
>
> For the same reason, moving your search to another Veronica server is easy. Leave the search screen and go back to the list of Veronica servers. Change the server you want to search and press **RETURN**. Voilà! The same search strategy is fed to the new server.

As shown in Chapter 3, putting the marker arrow next to an item and entering an **a** will add that item to your bookmark page. This is how I built up the following bookmark page, which is what I see when I type a **v** from within Gopher:

```
1.   Search gopherspace using veronica (Server 1) <?>
2.   Search gopherspace at NYSERNet <?>
3.   Search gopherspace at PSINet <?>
4.   Search gopherspace at U. of Manitoba <?>
5.   Search gopherspace at UNR <?>
6.   University of Minnesota/
```

As you can see, I've compiled a list of Veronica servers, and have included the Gopher at the University of Minnesota, where I picked up the links to these Gophers in the first place. Now, when I sign on to Gopher, all I have to do is to enter a **v** and the list is ready to be used. With a graphical Gopher, the same idea holds, only you add bookmarks through the program's menus.

Remember, the Unix Gopher client stores your bookmark list in a local file called .gopherrc, which determines Gopher's configuration. The bookmarks remain in that file until you change them. WSGopher maintains its bookmarks in a more complex bookmark manager, which will be of greater value to you as you learn to add useful sites to it. Whichever client you use, bookmarks can take you back quickly to the necessary Veronica sites to run your searches.

Now, let's begin a new search. In this session, let's say we are trying to learn about current research into cancer; specifically, we want to know what treatments or research investigations are underway on the subject of breast cancer. We can begin by running a basic Veronica search under the term cancer, which will generate numerous hits. When I used the Veronica server at the University of Manitoba, in fact, I wound up with 28 pages of Gopher items on the subject. This result is what we would expect on a topic as important as cancer; and indeed, the last item on the 28th page notes that there are more than 2,000 additional entries.

Don't be put off by this. Remember the key principle: When your subject is broad, begin with a broad sweep, looking in particular for text files. Carefully search the first few screens of entries for anything germane. In this context, several good materials suggest themselves on the initial page of our sweep, as shown in this segment of our results:

```
1.    Faulty-math-heightens-fears-of-breast-cancer..
2.    Fatalismo-toward-cancer;.
3.    Fear-of-breast-cancer..
4.    Tenneco-s-chief-has-brain-cancer..
5.    U.S.-ties-secondhand-smoke-to-cancer..
6.    Study-ties-DDT-to-cancer-cases..
7.    Cancer-causing-gene-found,-with-a-clue-to-how-it-works..
8.    Coincidence-or-link-between-cancer-and-hereditary-diseases?.
9.    Colon-cancer-screening;-contradictory-results-puzzle-researchers..
10.   Little-benebit-seen-in-prostate-surgery;-study-finds-sixfold-incre...
11.   Power-lines-didn-t-cause-girl-s-rare-cancer,-jury-finds;.
12.   Report-call-simple-test-effective-in-reducing-colon-cancer-deaths..
13.   Advances-in-detection-create-dilemma-on-prostate-cancer..
14.   New-study-links-liquor,-cancer..
15.   Stories-on-cancer's-causes-are-said-to-be-misfocused;-media-overpl...
16.   Study-find-less-family-breast-cancer-risk..
17.   Cancer-victims-may-sue-over-effects-of-radiation-therapy..
18.   Study-says-some-cancer-may-be-linked-to-'junk'-DNA..
```

Later in the listing, we find interspersed entries of interest, like this one:

```
22.   Breast-cancer:-success-is-imminent-in-search-for-key-gene..
```

or this one:

```
25.   Rivalry-holds-up-discovery-of-breast-cancer-gene;-Scientists-bicke...
```

But clearly, going through the entire list is going to be a major headache because it's so big. To get around it, let's combine terms.

We're interested in breast cancer, and we can enter that as our search term. When we put two words together this way an AND connector is implied, so we would retrieve any menu items using the term breast cancer, but also such entries as "cancer of the breast," where the two words are not adjacent. So let's search under **breast cancer.** Doing so reduces our hit list to 12 pages, quite an improvement. You can see this result in Figure 4.10.

We find numerous files of interest in these screens, but again, we're wondering if there is some way to reduce our search time still further. Progressively, we are homing in on our target, and now that we know we can combine terms, let's search under the following:

cancer (breast and treatment)

By nesting the breast and treatment terms in parentheses, we are asking Veronica to search for any entry that includes the term cancer as well as the terms breast and treat-

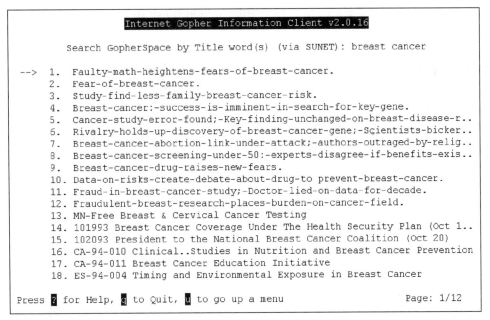

Figure 4.10 Results of a search for breast cancer materials.

ment. This turns out to be a productive search; we narrow our hit list to just over one page. Here are a few of our hits:

```
1.  P1: PA-93-083 STUDIES ON THE PREVENTION, ETIOLOGY, CONTROL, BIOLOG...
2.  PA-93-083 STUDIES ON THE PREVENTION, ETIOLOGY, CONTROL, BIOLOGY, D...
3.  Autologous Bone Marrow Transplantation in the Treatment of Breast ...
4.  Patients Needed for Clinical Trials for New Treatment for Breast C...
5.  SUPERSEDED-15. THE TREATMENT OF PRIMARY BREAST CANCER:.
6.  81. TREATMENT OF EARLY-STAGE BREAST CANCER.
```

If we choose, we could get fancier still. Perhaps we're interested in any kind of treatment *except* bone marrow transplantation. To ask for Gopher items concerning the treatment for breast cancer *not* including bone marrow methods, we could use this search statement:

cancer (breast and treatment) not (bone marrow)

When we run this search, we pull up the following hits:

```
1.  NCI Treatment Referral Center Protocol for Breast Cancer. . . .[400..
2.  P1: PA-93-083 STUDIES ON THE PREVENTION, ETIOLOGY, CONTROL, BIOLOGY..
3.  Patients Needed for Clinical Trials for New Treatment for Breast Ca..
4.  Autologous BM Transplantation in the Treatment of Breast Cancer cn..
5.  PA-93-083 STUDIES ON THE PREVENTION, ETIOLOGY, CONTROL, BIOLOGY, DI..
```

We have isolated precisely what we were after, using Veronica's ability to nest and combine search terms. As you can see, this is a very powerful tool, which has taken us from thousands of items of Gopher information down to a one-page menu with five items closely related to our topic.

Summarizing Veronica's Search Options

The Veronica search options we have discussed so far, along with several new ones, are listed here. Let's take a moment to review these before we proceed.

-t(*datatype*)   The -t type specifier tells Veronica what type of Gopher item to search for. The ones you're most likely to use are these:

-t0 for text files

-t1 for directories

-t2 for CSO phonebooks

-t7 for indexed databases

-t8 for Telnet sessions

The -t specifier can appear anywhere in your search term; it makes no difference, for example, whether you enter **mongolia -t1** or **-t1 mongolia**; you'll get the same result. Note that no spaces are allowed between the -t and the number following it. Note, too, that to specify more than one data type, you put the numbers together behind the -t. Thus, -t18 searches for directories and Telnet sessions.

1   Asks for link files containing the results of your search.

A link file? This means that Veronica will generate a file showing where all the resources it uncovers are to be found, along with the usual information generated by the = command. When I ran the search for information on breast cancer, and include the -1 statement, I received, as the first item on the list, a Gopher item containing the link file:

```
1.  *** Link info for cancer (breast and treatment) not (bone marrow) ...
```

By pressing a RETURN at this point, I was able to view a file of all the links. A snippet of this is shown:

```
Type=0
Name=NCI Treatment Referral Center Trial for Breast Cancer
Path=0/NUS-NCI CancerNet/allfiles/4060/400008
Host=nuscc.nus.sg
Port=70
#
Type=0
Name=Patients Needed for Breast Cancer Treatment Clinical Trials
Path=0/NUS-NCI CancerNet/allfiles/4060/600713
Host=nuscc.nus.sg
Port=70
```

Obviously, asking for a link file may be important if you need information about the location of the resources before proceeding.

m   Limits the number of items Veronica will retrieve.

By itself, -m requests Gopher not to limit itself to 200 items (or whatever limit has been set at the site); instead, you will retrieve the entire file list. Used with a number, -m specifies how many items you want to see. If I were looking for information about the space shuttle, for example, I could specify 500 items through the search term **space shuttle -m500**.

and   Allows you to combine search terms. Thus, **japan and history** retrieves Gopher items containing both terms.

not   Allows you to exclude a term. Thus, **germany not kohl** retrieves any Gopher item containing the word germany, but not those with the term kohl in them.

Let's drive these basics home through a series of search statements.

Sample Veronica Search Terms

To begin Veronica searches, always use a single term. Thus:

books

will retrieve any Gopher menu item with that term in it. This search pulls a huge amount of entries, as shown:

```
-->>   1.  C-New Books Women and Feminism.
       2.  Books and Literary Events/
       3.  Electronic Books/
       4.  Phone Books/
       5.  Intro Ph (phone books).
       6.  UNIX BOOKS.
       7.  Books, journals, ref's/
       8.  New books on European forest history during the eighties. .
       9.  About Phone Books.
```

At this point in the discussion, you know how to narrow a search in the following ways:

- The AND operator: **books and history** is a valid search strategy. It searches for any Gopher items containing both terms, but will not retrieve items with only one or the other term. Remember, you could also write this search term as **books history**. Veronica assumes the AND connection whenever you use more than one word as your search term. You could, therefore, retrieve menu items where the two words were not adjacent. An item called *Electronic books and journals in History/* is just as likely to appear as one called *crypto-history-books.txt/* (both of these are actual menu items).
- The OR operator: **books or e-text** tells Veronica to look for menu items containing *either* term, but not necessarily both.
- The NOT operator: **books not electronic** tells Veronica to find all menu items including the word **books** but not the term **electronic**. This rules out, for exam-

ple, electronic text archives like Project Gutenberg's, or any others that fall under the rubric "electronic books."

- Parentheses: Use parentheses when you want to nest search terms for maximum effectiveness; **electronic books and (gutenberg or wiretap)**, for example, searches for any menu items composed of both the term **electronic books** along with either the term **gutenberg** or **wiretap** (the latter being another collection of electronic text archives).
- Wildcard searching: Use an asterisk (*) in place of characters at the end of a word. For example, suppose you need books about art. You could search under the combined term **books and art**. But then you might miss anything using the term artistic, artisans, or similar terms (Veronica will not search for embedded words). To get around this, you can search for **books and art***. The asterisk tells Veronica to retrieve any Gopher menu item *beginning* with the letters **art-**.

> **HINT:** Don't make the common mistake of misunderstanding Veronica's search capabilities. Veronica is a searchable index of the titles of menu items on the various Gophers scattered throughout the network. Veronica does not run full-text searches of the files it finds; it can only tell you when there is a *menu item* that corresponds to your search term. The document or file *behind* the menu item is yours to explore; Veronica doesn't see it.

Occasional Frustrations of Using Veronica

Veronica is a useful search engine, but it has limitations. First of all, Gopher menus correspond to no universal standard. Each system administrator makes his or her own call about how to build a Gopher menu. Of necessity, this makes your searches reliant on your own ingenuity. You are forced to think not only of obvious search terms but also of less likely ones, under the theory that someone, somewhere, might have used those terms to list your data on a Gopher. We've seen this problem before, in a hundred ways, on the Internet at large. Because there is no central organization, what the network offers can surprise you. This is a major weakness of the network as a data source, yet it also makes exploring the Internet a challenging and sometimes exciting activity.

Another Veronica drawback is the fact that your hit lists contain numerous duplications as Veronica tracks down the same material made available at different Gopher sites on the network. There is no way to sift through and eliminate every instance of duplicates, because often the same file will appear under a different name. Then, too, you'll occasionally run a search that you know should generate hits, only to receive a message that there is nothing available:

```
+--------------------+--------Gopher Error--------+-------------------+
|                    |                            |                   |
| Words to search for|  Nothing available.        |                   |
|                    |                            |                   |
|                    |  [Cancel - ^G] [OK - Enter]|  [Accept - Enter] |
|                    |                            |                   |
+--------------------+----------------------------+-------------------+
```

There is little to do in this case but to try again.

Or perhaps you'll see this message:

```
1. *** Too many connections - Try again soon. ***.
```

This, however, isn't a Veronica problem; it's a result of demand exceeding supply in terms of the resources available; there just aren't that many Veronica servers out there. Trying at a different time of day may be the best approach if you run into this message frequently.

Another puzzling result can occur when you retrieve a menu of items and then try to access one in particular. Rather than calling up the file you were expecting to see, Veronica delivers something like this:

```
1. Server error: - Cannot access that directory.
```

Here the likely culprit is a change at the Gopher site in question. A menu item has changed since the last time Veronica checked its records for that site. The item still appears on the menu generated by Veronica, but it's no longer where it's supposed to be.

Finally, you may see something like this:

```
Bookmarks
      1.  Search gopherspace using veronica (Server 1) <?>
      2.  Search gopherspace at NYSERNet <?>
      3.  Search gopherspace at PSINet <?>
      4.  S+--------------------Network Error--------------------+
+----------|                                                    |---------+
|          |  Cannot connect to host comics.scs.unr.edu, port 800.  |    |
| Words to |                                                    |         |
|          |  Connection refused by host.                       |         |
|          |                                                    |         |
|          |                       [Cancel - ^G]  [OK - Enter]  |         |
+----------|                                                    |---------+
           +----------------------------------------------------+
```

Note what has happened here: From the bookmark page, I've tried to run a search at the Veronica server at the University of Nevada in Reno. The connection has been refused, for a variety of possible reasons. Wait a while and try your search again if you receive such a message, or attempt the search at another Veronica server. This is one more reason that setting up your bookmark page with multiple Veronica servers as menu items can save you time.

HINT: Given that we have so many different ways of tightening up a Veronica search, why don't we just do it immediately? In other words, doesn't it make sense to try to be as specific as possible in any search from the beginning? The answer is a qualified yes, which really means it depends upon your search tool. In the case of Veronica, we must bear in mind the limitation of what Veronica is searching. Since it can only examine Gopher menus and not any text within the files on those menus, we could easily go right past a file that might contain just what we need, just because it didn't have the title we had expected. That means it makes more sense to take a top-down approach. If you begin with a broader data search and gradually refine it, you will be more likely to catch in your net those files that might otherwise have escaped, because you will get a feel for what is out there at each step of the way. It takes longer than a more precise search, but it is much more likely to pay off in results.

Using Jughead

Veronica's ability to limit itself to certain data types and its relative flexibility in the construction of keywords and phrases makes it a helpful search tool. Certainly your ability to find your way around in the universe of Gophers would be sharply curtailed without Veronica, even if it is heavily dependent on the skills of the people who construct Gopher menus, since they have created the database upon which it relies. And we've already seen its problems: servers are frequently overloaded, and thus hard to access; Veronica cannot dig out text from within the menu items it finds; it produces redundant hits, giving us many views of the same information.

Internet search tools are like this; there is no perfect browser, no ideal engine. What we must do in each case is to learn the strengths and limitations of the tools at our disposal. Interesting in this regard is another search tool that works with Gopher. And like the whimsically named Veronica, Jughead is another clever acronym: **J**onzy's **U**niversal **G**opher **H**ierarchy **E**xcavation **a**nd **D**isplay. Jonzy is Rhett Jones, who works at the University of Utah Computer Center where Jughead made its first appearance in 1993. And like Veronica, Jughead takes an existing concept and refines it to make the tool in question more effective.

Whereas Veronica expands Gopher by allowing you to consolidate your information gathering in Gopherspace, Jughead moves in the opposite direction. Its concept is to allow you to search GopherSpace, but in a user-delimited fashion. For example, suppose you know about a great Gopher but you don't want to work through every one of its menus to find what you need. With Jughead, you can search that Gopher alone. A Jughead server maintains a database of the menu items at that site and allows users to search them.

Jughead is easier to demonstrate than to explain because, like Veronica, it is so closely linked with Gopher. This, for example, is what a Jughead item looks like at the University of Minnesota Gopher:

```
10.   Search Gopher Titles at the University of Minnesota <?>
```

Pressing a RETURN with the arrow on this item generates the search screen we've come to expect from Gopher, and allows us to enter a search term. As with Veronica, search terms can include AND, OR, and NOT; the AND is assumed unless you use one of the other terms. Case is irrelevant.

Jughead, however, does sport a few commands of its own, as follows:

?all *searchterm*   Retrieves all hits Jughead finds on a particular term. Example: **?all philos*** returns all hits at the site containing the root term **philos-**.

Note the question mark, which must be included for this strategy to work. The default number of hits is a maximum of 1,024 items; you would use **?all** *searchterm* if you anticipated a greater number and wanted to see them all. In most cases, this command will be unnecessary. If you're searching at a particular site, it is unlikely that there will be this many items corresponding to your search term unless the site is running quite a large Gopher!

?help *searchterm*   Produces the Jughead help file, along with any hits on your search term.

?limit=n *searchterm*	Limits the results of your search to the number of items (n) you designate. Thus **?limit=10 faculty** produces the first 10 hits and no more for this term.
?version *searchterm*	Returns the version number of Jughead, plus the hits on your search term.

Locating a Jughead Server

The only way to track down a Jughead server, other than by trial and error, is to use Veronica, which can tell you where many of them are operating. Remember, it would be pointless to search under the broad term Jughead, because you would wind up with such things as text files about Jughead. So limit your search to indices by using the **-t7** command. Thus, your search term would be **jughead -t7**. This will retrieve any Jughead menu item that points to a searchable index; it will not, unfortunately, find a Jughead server that has been labelled, like the one at the University of Minnesota, Search Gopher Titles at the University, or other such variants. Veronica, remember, is very precise; it's looking for the term jughead in the menu item itself.

Here are a few of the hits this search generated:

```
1.   jughead search of [acs6.acs.ucalgary.ca] 3000 <?>
2.   jughead search of [bramble.er.usgs.gov] 3000 <?>
3.   jughead search of [cscgoph2.albany.edu] 3000 <?>
4.   jughead search of [decsys.vsb.cz] 3000 <?>
5.   jughead search of [dewey.lib.ncsu.edu] 3000 <?>
6.   jughead search of [dinosaur.ums1.edu] 3000 <?>
7.   Search EECS Department Gopher using Jughead <?>
8.   Search all of Bigcat's Gopher menus using Jughead <?>
9.   Cerca amb Jughead <?>
10.  Search CUline Gopher Menus using JugHead <?>
11.  Search UB CIT Menus using jughead <?>
12.  Search directories in GopherSpace: Jughead (U.Birmingham,UK) <?>
13.  Search UMinfo Contents (JUGHEAD) <?>
14.  jughead search of [cwis.nyu.edu] 3000 <?>
15.  jughead search of [gopher.ch.ic.ac.uk] 3000 <?>
16.  jughead search of [gopher.cis.mcmaster.ca] 3000 <?>
```

Note the additional problem here. These Jughead servers aren't clearly labelled as to location. But if you have read carefully, you already know the answer to this. Use the **-1** command to create a link file showing all the addresses. Thus, a better search strategy would be **jughead -t7 -1**. Now you can access the link file and see where the Jughead servers are (at least, the ones labelled as such on their menus).

Tips on Using Veronica

It's easy enough to become stuck with a Veronica search. With so many Internet tools to choose from, keeping the various options straight is itself time-consuming. And then you run into additional blocks, such as not being able to get into multiple Veronica sites because of traffic, or an inability to frame a search in terms that will produce results. Here are a few tips to help you when things look bleak.

- Remember the top-down approach. Because Veronica only indexes items in the menu titles on each Gopher server, you can't expect that it will find everything you need the first time through. The material you are looking for about the Tennessee Valley Authority, for example, may be tucked away in a file called FDR Projects, while the list of RAF airfields you're trying to compile for a paper may be located not under airfields at all, but under Battle of Britain. So always try to think of the broadest possible search term if the one you're currently using doesn't pay off. If you can't find Madrid, try Spain.

- Choose carefully between directories and other filetypes. Remember, Veronica gives you the opportunity to search just in Gopher main menu items, or directories, which should make it possible to focus on hits that relate to collections of information about your topic. A top-level menu item called Politics may be just the place to start exploring for information about Wendell Wilkie, but you'll have to dig into that directory, once you've located it, to find out, whereas a more targeted search throughout all of Gopherspace might land directly on a file called wilkie.doc that answers your questions. Because you don't know which will happen, you will often have to run both kinds of searches.

- Use Veronica's ability to find specific kinds of files. If you are after a map of Burma, it may make sense to search for any Gopher items that include the word Burma in their title and are also image files. On the other hand, if you need a database in Sweden, looking for Telnet connections that are shown on menus with the word Sweden in their title ought to work. In particular, learn how to differentiate between the filetypes so that you can keep your list of hits manageable. Nothing is more intimidating than retrieving 1,148 hits and knowing that the only way to work through them is by paging down one page at a time.

- Use the -m command sparingly. This command allows you to specify how many hits you want to see. At first, it may seem like a good idea to use it often. You could, for example, tell Veronica to send you no more than 25 hits for a given search. But what if Veronica actually found 657 hits and returned only 25? How would you know that the material you needed was among the 25 hits the system showed you? The answer, of course, is that you wouldn't. It's far better to limit your list of hits by using the filetypes and by constructing thorough keyword strategies, rather than by setting up an arbitrary number to cover poor search technique.

- Learn to mix and match your keywords. Using keywords in combination will definitely lower the number of hits while improving their quality. In addition, using wildcards will enable you to search for variant forms of your keywords, a valuable ability when you're not sure under what title a menu item might appear. Remember that you can use parentheses, as shown earlier, to make your keyword strategies even more specific.

- Be willing to back out of searches. By this I mean that if you make a keyword strategy *too* specific, your list of hits may fall to zero. In that case, don't give up hope; just remember that you may have eliminated some promising material because you hadn't thought through how a system administrator might have decided to label particular information. Be willing to experiment with keywords until you find some that work. Doing this will make you an expert at coming up with and employing synonyms (maybe a good thesaurus should be on your desk, too).

- Keep up with Veronica documentation. We've already seen that you can call up a basic document about Veronica and how it works by downloading the material from the list of Veronica sites. This document changes frequently as the system is tweaked and improved. Make sure you are always armed with the latest documentation to take advantage of any new features.
- Use text files for background information. Remember, you can specify that Veronica show you only textual files by using option 0. If you do this, you will often find a great deal of material that focuses on providing broad background data about your topic. It is often the case that an initial Veronica search designed to call up textual information can give way to a more targeted search for other filetypes, once you have determined what you need by examining the relevant text files.
- Recall the basic Veronica parameters. The system is not case-sensitive, so you needn't worry about case in proper names, for example. The system inserts an AND between two statements; thus, searching for internet navigator is the same as searching for navigator AND internet; for that matter, the statement could be phrased navigator internet; Veronica will find menu items that contain both specified words, but not necessarily in any order.
- Be skeptical. Too many people think their search tools are infallible; when they retrieve few hits, they assume the network is devoid of information that pertains to them. You should always consider running your Veronica search in conjunction with other Internet search tools if it finds less than you were hoping for. With so much activity now shifting onto the World Wide Web, it may well be that a search there could supplement the Gopher materials that Veronica finds. But remember, too, that Veronica's menu title system means that it can't examine individual documents within those menus. There will be times when the only way to find what you need, even with Veronica, is to examine one Gopher directory after another. In cases like those, you just hope that Veronica can home in as close as possible, and you'll have to take manual control of the search from that point forward.

5

archie: Finding Files

The Internet is by its nature a system in which information is "distributed." This means that there is no central site, no archival storage place for all of its riches. We can see why this must be. After all, the data packets that carry the traffic moving across and through the Internet have no single source, move along no fixed pathway, and arrive at sites determined entirely by the header information they carry. To ask that such a system be centralized is to misunderstand the nature of networking.

A constant tension is maintained, then, between the virtual anarchy of thousands of data "conversations" between the computers that route the Internet's data and the needs of individuals to find particular computer files. The big three Internet applications—electronic mail, FTP, and Telnet—function to help us communicate and exchange information. We can use both electronic mail and Telnet if we have an address, and the same is true of FTP. The question for Internet explorers is, how do I get the critical address?

In this chapter, we examine a key Internet tool, and one with a long history. archie is in many ways representative of the networks it serves. The idea of using the Internet as a vast repository of software, from executable programs to graphics to textual documents, grew out of the archie concept. Yet the program, command-driven and intimidating to the newcomer, places its own demands upon the user. What you will need here and with other Internet tools is a willingness to learn a set of commands and their options. No, the average archie command isn't intuitive. But neither is it difficult to understand once you comprehend how archie goes about its job. Using archie, you begin to make the Internet a genuine resource, and once you've mastered it, you can use a graphical archie client to simplify the process.

The Nature of File Transfer Protocol

File Transfer Protocol, or FTP, is a way of moving computer files from one site to another. We are concerned here with a particular variant of FTP called *anonymous FTP*. The reason: Anonymous FTP is open to anyone. The administrators at computer sites around the world make directories full of information available to anyone who logs in as anonymous (the convention is to use your Internet address as your password). Because you need no special permission to get into these sites, they constitute a kind of Internet "swap box," where everything is freely available. The range of programs available at these sites is staggering and growing every day.

Consider the number of networks alone. Mark K. Lottor's Internet Domain Survey found 61,000 as of late summer 1995 (compared to the 16,000-plus found by the same survey in October 1993, and the 30,000 available when the first edition of this book appeared). Then realize that each site differs according to the wishes of its administrators. One may specialize in Macintosh software, as does ftp://mac.archive.umich.edu. Another may focus on a broad range of computer platforms, as does the huge site at Washington University in St. Louis, ftp://wuarchive.wustl.edu. A third may collect textual information, such as the valuable ftp://rtfm.mit.edu, which houses background documents called Frequently Asked Questions (FAQs); these supply information about topics discussed in USENET newsgroups.

Obviously, software is also duplicated at many sites; you can imagine a popular public domain or shareware program appearing on anonymous FTP directories around the globe: thousands of sites, some large, some small, with new ones appearing daily. No wonder estimates of the number of files available over the Internet go as high as 6 terabytes, or 6,000 gigabytes, of stored programs, text files, and data. Directory follows directory, subdirectories branch into still more subdirectories, and soon the file you need is buried six layers deep at a site whose name you've never heard of in a country half a world away.

Where to begin? Even before you start using Internet tools, one place to check is a listing of FTP sites. The best single place I can send you for FTP site lists is an address on the World Wide Web. The URL is:

http://hoohoo.ncsa.uiuc.edu:80/ftp-a-e-.html

This is Perry Rovers' Monster FTP Sites List, and it's a priceless collection of information (old hands will remember that this list was once maintained by Tom Czarnik and Jon Granrose). You can also retrieve it in a host of other ways. Here's the URL for an FTP session; look in the directory shown for the multiple files of the complete list. At last examination, there were 20.

ftp://rtfm.mit.edu/pub/usenet/new.answers/ftp-list/sitelist/

European readers should try this URL:

ftp://garbo.uwasa.fi/pc/doc-net/ftp-list.zip

And those in Asia will want to try this one:

ftp://ftp.edu.tw/documents/networking/guides/ftp-list/

The home page for the Monster FTP Sites List is shown in Figure 5.1. As you can see, each of the list documents is set up as a hyperlink.

You may also want to try an experimental service provided by the Computing and Communications Services Office of the University of Illinois at Urbana-Champaign. This

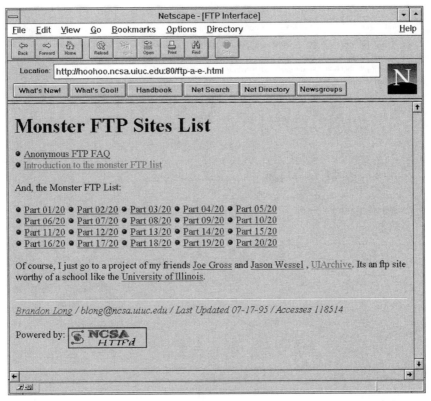

Figure 5.1 A listing of sites set up with hyperlinks provides an overview of FTP activity.

excellent site allows you to search several major collections, including the huge SimTel and CICA software archives. When you go to the site, you can choose the collection you want to search and enter your keyword. In Figure 5.2, for example, I have just run a search under the keyword recipe and have called up a collection of hits. To retrieve any of these, I simply double-click on the item, which is presented with a hypertext link to its home site.

Joe Gross and Jason Wessel created this excellent search tool, which can be found at this URL:

http://uiarchive.cso.uiuc.edu/

While its search capabilities are limited to several major collections, it also provides links to archie searches through a World Wide Web page; using archie, you can consult servers worldwide to run the same search.

And that is the key to archie—rather than being limited to two or three data repositories, it's a worldwide system that can search computers at over a thousand sites. The challenge faced by the people who developed archie was to find a way to sort through the Internet's embarrassment of riches in order to track down particular computer files. Ideally, the search system would allow the user to specify a keyword and the system

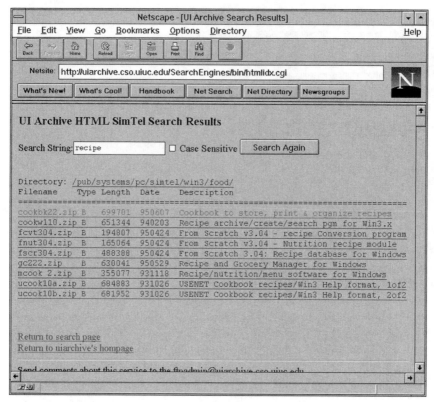

Figure 5.2 Results of a search under the keyword recipe at the University of Illinois at Urbana-Champaign.

would then hunt it down. This posed considerable problems of logistics, given the Internet's constantly changing landscape. The solution they came up with, as you'll see, is an ingenious one.

archie Scouts the Internet Terrain

archie was developed at McGill University's School of Computer Science by Alan Emtage, Bill Heelan, and Peter Deutsch. Like many good computer tools, the program developed out of a university's need to save money. Looking for public domain software, the McGill team began searching anonymous FTP archive sites, and eventually began to automate the process of scanning their findings. From this evolved an information tool that is among the most widely used on the Internet. Deutsch and Emtage, as we'll see shortly, went on to found Bunyip Information Systems of Montreal, which licenses the archie server system and provides upgrades and support. There is every indication that Bunyip Information Systems plans to continue enhancing archie. The system has been expanded, for example, to handle Gopher search capabilities. And the company is also working on a number of other information-gathering techniques. In addition to archie, its products include The Internet Prospector, which offers further collections of information and access methods.

HINT: Hoping to keep up with archie developments? The best way to do so is to use the World Wide Web site at Bunyip Information Systems. The URL is:

http://www.bunyip.com/

Here you will find an excellent background document about archie, which answers questions about how information is indexed, how to perform a basic search, and how to acquire an archie server. You can also keep up with the latest news on other Bunyip products, including The Internet Prospector.

You may also want to look into FTP holdings at various archie server sites. For example, a look at Bunyip's own server will indicate several interesting files in the pub/bunyip-docs directory. Try this URL:

ftp://ftp.bunyip.com/

You will find a list of archie servers worldwide here. A list of public access servers is likewise provided later in this chapter.

An aside on money: The fact that archie is now being offered as a commercial system, with support and enhancements, does not mean that you, the end user, will suddenly have to pony up hard cash to use it. Bunyip Information Systems has added functionality to the original tool and marketed it to the sites that want to carry it. A public domain implementation remains available. The people who deal with the commercial aspects of archie, then, are the system administrators who are putting archie on-line at their site. The end user's job is simply to figure out the best ways to use this powerful resource.

Consider archie a set of related functions. The software maintains a list of Internet FTP sites known as the Internet Archives database (the term archie, as you're doubtless beginning to realize, is a play on "archive" (the subsequent appearance of the tool called Veronica reminds us that it's also the name of a memorable cartoon character). The database is searchable by a variety of servers across the Internet. Note, then, that archie does not make data sweeps across the entire Internet; rather, it targets specific sites, with the permission of their administrators, and searches them.

Going through the directories at these sites manually would, obviously, take 24 hours per day for the individual user, who would, in any case, constantly be falling behind as new files and directories were added to one or another site. By automating the process, archie can make its own sweep of FTP directories, compiling them and storing the results in its database; such sweeps are conducted roughly twice per month. Each site's holdings therefore stay relatively up to date at any given moment, although there may be a slight overlap; an archie search could, for example, point to a file that had been removed shortly after the last archie database update. And, of course, a new file that a given archie server doesn't yet know about could be added to the holdings at a specific site.

Although the system began at McGill University, the need to spread the wealth soon became apparent. By late 1992, 20 public access archie servers were available to the Internet community; by mid-1993, that number approached 30, and today, over 60 servers operate in some 20 countries. Three copies are being operated by the InterNIC, along with U.S. sites, SURAnet, Rutgers University, the University of Nebraska at Lincoln, and the Clearinghouse for Networked Information Discovery and Retrieval (the last is not publicly accessible).

These server computers query database listings from over 1,000 sites, which are scattered through corporations, government agencies, and a variety of other organizations. Within the archie system alone, some 230 gigabytes of files are available for searching; and remember, archie covers only a subset of the files available throughout the entire network. archie servers are averaging 30,000 queries every day.

If you like doing things the hard way, you could always retrieve and examine the listings that archie creates for its database; they're available at the individual server sites. In doing so, and in finding a way to search these materials, you would be re-creating the original process that led to archie. But fortunately, there is no reason to reinvent the wheel. And as useful as it is in terms of searching FTP directories, archie is no longer limited to making directory searches alone. Indeed, the technology behind archie is adaptable to any kind of database, which is how the whatis database, cataloguing descriptions of software, came to be made available in 1991.

To go to the source for archie information, contact its developers. The address is:

Bunyip Information Systems
310 St-Catherine St West, Suite 300
Montreal, Quebec H2X 2A1
Voice: 514-875-8611
Fax: 514-875-8134
mailto: frontdesk@bunyip.com

You can expect more such databases using the archie system and other methodologies from Bunyip in the near future. Be aware, too, that archie's popularity has led to its being incorporated into a variety of other Internet tools, including Gopher and the World Wide Web. The convergence of search technology makes it possible to work with many tools in a range of formats, allowing you to choose the user interface best suited to your needs.

Using archie

There are three ways to access archie directly (that is, without going through the medium of one of the other search tools). Here are your options:

1. Use Telnet to contact an archie server. Suppose, for example, that I want to contact the SURAnet archie server; its URL is:

   ```
   telnet://archie.sura.net
   ```

   At the login prompt, enter **archie**.
2. Use a client program to access archie. Your choice of client will depend upon the kind of connection you are using. A shell account user can reach an archie client by typing **archie**, followed by a **RETURN**, at the system command prompt (if no client is available at your provider, you'll have to use Telnet or the third option). A SLIP/PPP user has several clients available that bring archie into the graphical arena. We'll examine these clients shortly.
3. Contact archie by electronic mail. To do so, send a message with your search commands to one of the archie servers. The address is easy to construct—just add the term **archie@** to the server address. Thus, to send electronic mail to the archie server at SURAnet, I would send my message to **archie@archie.sura.net**.

As we'll see, there are reasons why you may want to take the electronic mail route even if you have Telnet capabilities or the services of a local client program. But when choosing between Telnet and a local client, the local program is best because you are less likely to run into difficulties. The traffic load on the server can be intense, particularly at peak periods during business hours. Using your own system's client program to forward your query can save you time, and it is also the best way to conserve network resources. We'll encounter this principle again with other Internet search tools.

Using Telnet to Search with archie

A list of archie servers is presented in Table 2.1. If you examine this list, you'll see that there are servers throughout the world. Bear in mind this fundamental principle: It is less demanding on network resources to use Telnet to a location near to you. Resist the temptation to contact an archie server in Australia if you happen to live in the southern United States, where BBN Planet's server at SURAnet would do just as well. International traffic can be heavy and there is no need to cause further congestion on already crowded circuits.

Table 5.1   archie Servers Worldwide

archie.au	University of Melbourne	Australia
archie.univie.ac.at	University of Vienna	Austria
archie.bunyip.com	Bunyip Information Systems, Inc.	Canada
archie.cs.mcgill.ca	McGill University	Canada
archie.uqam.ca	University of Quebec	Canada
archie.funet.fi	Finnish University and Research Network	Finland
archie.univ-rennes1.fr	—	France
archie.th-darmstadt.de	Technische Hochschule, Darmstadt	Germany
archie.ac.il	Hebrew University, Jerusalem	Israel
archie.unipi.it	University of Pisa	Italy
archie.wide.ad.jp	WIDE Project, Tokyo	Japan
archie.kornet.nm.kr	KORNET	Korea
archie.sogang.ac.kr	Sogang University	Korea
archie.uninett.no	Trondheim	Norway
archie.icm.edu.pl	Warsaw University	Poland
archie.rediris.es	RedIRIS, Madrid	Spain
archie.luth.se	University of Lulea	Sweden
archie.switch.ch	SWITCH, Zurich	Switzerland
archie.ncu.edu.tw	National Central University, Chung-li	Taiwan
archie.doc.ic.ac.uk	Imperial College, London	United Kingdom
archie.hensa.ac.uk	University of Kent at Canterbury	United Kingdom
archie.sura.net	BBN Planet Southeast	USA
archie.internic.net	AT&T InterNIC	USA
archie.rutgers.edu	Rutgers University, NJ	USA
archie.ans.net	Advanced Network & Services; Elmsford, NY	USA

Remember that the ranks of archie servers are likely to be supplemented by the time you read this. Many of the archie sites update you when you log on, with a list of alternative server sites presented on-screen. More servers will take some of the load off the existing sites, but you should continue to target only those sites nearest you. And, as we'll see, doing so isn't always an intuitive process.

If you are using a commercial online service, for example, consider the nature of your connection before you log on to archie. CompuServe routes its traffic through a central site in Columbus, Ohio. This is true no matter where its customers happen to live. So if you are based in, say, Portland, Oregon, but are using CompuServe to send an electronic mail query to an archie server, it should be the server nearest to Columbus rather than the one nearest to Portland. The same is true of DELPHI and BIX (Massachusetts), America Online (Virginia), and any other commercial on-line service. Keeping your provider's location in mind will keep you within the bounds of proper network etiquette.

Once you've chosen your server, the command **telnet** *server_name* takes you there with a shell account, while SLIP/PPP users can simply enter the address; log in as **archie**. Be advised that, as the traffic load on these systems increases, users more frequently encounter busy signals. These occur in the form of a message when you attempt to log on, telling you that due to the number of Telnet connections already in place, you are unable to use the system at this time. An example of this kind of message is shown in Figure 5.3.

As you can see, this server, the one at archie.sura.net, provides you with alternative server sites after it informs you that there are too many users currently logged on for you to use the system. You are also given the opportunity to use a login of qarchie, which activates a much simplified archie capability that is limited to queries only. We'll concentrate, though, on the full-bore archie search as mediated through Telnet to a different site.

The archie search screen you'll receive when you do make the connection is a spare one; it's illustrated in Figure 5.4. Certain relevant information is presented immediately. Terminal type we can assume; it's set to VT-100, which is the standard for character-based terminal emulation. Pay particular attention to the cryptic comment *'search' (type string) has the value 'sub'*. At this juncture, it doesn't make much sense, but as we'll see, the values set in this field can be changed and have great bearing on how we conduct an archie search.

The basic search command for archie is **find** *keyword*. When you enter this information followed by a **RETURN**, archie will search the directories and files in its database for items that match. For example, **find astronomy** is a search statement that will likely retrieve a number of directories named astronomy. When I entered this search at the archie site just mentioned, two things happened. First, I received information about the status of the search and my own position in the queue of those waiting to use archie.

```
archie> find astronomy
# Search type: sub.
# Your queue position: 1
# Estimated time for completion: 00:05
working... \
```

Soon after, archie delivered the information I needed. A portion of this material is shown in Figure 5.5.

Examine this result with care. We're looking at one of several screens of hits. Each of the hits shown is a directory; the site is shown immediately above the directory path. Thus the directory pub/mac/umich/misc/astronomy/ is to be found at the FTP address

```
SunOS UNIX (yog-sothoth.sura.net)

login: archie
ALL ARCHIE SESSIONS IN USE

I'm sorry. This archie server is currently at the limit of its
interactive login sessions. Please use another archie server or try again
later.
                    -archie administration
So far        16 > 15 (max)
-------------------< List of active archie servers >-----------------
                                          Last Update: Mar 14th 1995

        archie.au                 139.130.23.2       Australia
        archie.univie.ac.at       131.130.1.23       Austria
        archie.belnet.be          193.190.248.18     Belgium
        archie.bunyip.com         192.77.55.2        Canada
        archie.cs.mcgill.ca       132.206.51.250     Canada
        archie.uqam.ca            132.208.250.10     Canada
        archie.funet.fi           128.214.6.102      Finland
        archie.univ-rennes1.fr    129.20.254.2       France
        archie.th-darmstadt.de    130.83.22.1        Germany
        archie.ac.il              132.65.16.8        Israel
        archie.unipi.it           131.114.21.10      Italy
        archie.wide.ad.jp         133.4.3.6          Japan
        archie.hana.nm.kr         128.134.1.1        Korea
        archie.kornet.nm.kr       168.126.63.10      Korea
        archie.sogang.ac.kr       163.239.1.11       Korea
        archie.uninett.no         128.39.2.20        Norway
        archie.icm.edu.pl         148.81.209.2       Poland
        archie.rediris.es         130.206.1.2        Spain
        archie.luth.se            130.240.12.23      Sweden
        archie.switch.ch          130.59.1.40        Switzerland
        archie.switch.ch          130.59.10.40       Switzerland
        archie.ncu.edu.tw         192.83.166.12      Taiwan
        archie.doc.ic.ac.uk       146.169.16.11      UK
        archie.doc.ic.ac.uk       146.169.17.5       UK
        archie.doc.ic.ac.uk       146.169.2.10       UK
        archie.doc.ic.ac.uk       146.169.32.5       UK
        archie.doc.ic.ac.uk       146.169.33.5       UK
        archie.doc.ic.ac.uk       146.169.43.1       UK
        archie.doc.ic.ac.uk       155.198.1.40       UK
        archie.doc.ic.ac.uk       155.198.191.4      UK
        archie.hensa.ac.uk        129.12.43.17       UK
        archie.sura.net           192.239.16.135     USA (MD)
        archie.unl.edu            129.93.1.14        USA (NE)
        archie.internic.net       192.20.225.200     USA (NJ)
        archie.internic.net       192.20.239.132     USA (NJ)
        archie.internic.net       198.49.45.10       USA (NJ)
        archie.rutgers.edu        128.6.18.15        USA (NJ)
        archie.ans.net            147.225.1.10       USA (NY)


-------------------------------------------------------------------------
The current time is Thu Aug 10 14:59:59 EDT 1995
```

Figure 5.3   Trying to log on at an archie site when there are too many connections.

```
Escape character is '^]'.

SunOS UNIX (yog-sothoth.sura.net)

login: archie

                        Welcome to Archie!
                          Version 3.3

                    BBN Planet Southeast Region

For Information or questions about this archie server,
please send mail to:

            archie-admin@sura.net


# Bunyip Information Systems, Inc., 1993, 1994, 1995

# Terminal type set to `vt100 24 80'.
# `erase' character is `^?'.
# `search' (type string) has the value `sub'.
archie> _
```

Figure 5.4 Logging on to archie at SURAnet
(BBN Planet Southeast Region).

ftp.loria.fr, while /pub/mirror/mac/misc/astronomy is located at pereiii.uji.es, and so forth. Keep in mind your ability to search for directories; doing so can help you locate archives you'll want to return to for particular types of software in the future.

Having located the file or directory we're interested in, we can then use FTP to move directly to that site, where we can explore and retrieve files as we please. All of which makes archie seem like a simple search tool that homes in on exactly what we need. But, in fact, the kind of files we're looking for, and the methods we use to search for them, are highly variable. archie contains numerous options that can modify the search you run and make it more precise. These commands can also help reduce congestion on the networks, so using archie effectively involves learning what they are.

```
Host ftp.loria.fr     (152.81.10.10)
Last updated 02:21  5 Aug 1995

    Location: /pub/mac/umich/misc
       DIRECTORY     drwxr-xr-x     1024 bytes   09:28 30 Jul 1995   astronomy


Host pereiii.uji.es    (150.128.1.2)
Last updated 05:41  6 Aug 1995

    Location: /pub/mirror/mac/misc
       DIRECTORY     drwxr-xr-x     1024 bytes   06:10 26 Jul 1995   astronomy


Host nic.switch.ch    (130.59.1.40)
Last updated 03:39  6 Aug 1995

    Location: /mirror/umich-mac/misc
       DIRECTORY     drwxrwxr-x     1024 bytes   03:05 25 Jul 1995   astronomy


Host ftp.sunet.se    (130.238.127.3)
:_
```

Figure 5.5 Partial results from an archie search using the term astronomy.

> **NOTE:** An aside on names: The Internet changes faster than most things in this transitory world, so it's no surprise that the standard archie search command, which was once **prog,** has been renamed **find. prog** had a certain elegance, in that it named the type of resource—programs—it was looking for. But **find** is easier to remember and more accurate, since many of the items turned up by a standard archie search are not, in fact, programs, but directories, documents, and other kinds of information. If you've become accustomed to the **prog** command, however, you can still use it.

A Sample Search Using archie with Telnet

Let's illustrate how you can adapt archie to meet more precise needs by setting up a search for a software program. I've been told by a friend about a shareware package called 2Do, developed by William P. Anderson and made available on bulletin board systems and at FTP archive sites around the world. 2Do is a handy program that sets up lists of necessary tasks—to-do lists, in other words. Not only does it sort them using a variety of different, user-defined methods, but it also tags items with different colors depending on their priority. Clearly, this is a handy program to evaluate and, if it proves its mettle, to register for use.

The basic archie search, then, would be **find 2do**. But this time, let's think about limiting the results of the search. After all, the astronomy hunt we just concluded actually retrieved numerous screensful of information. We could use many hits if we were looking for directories of general information, as we would assuredly find in directories called astronomy. But when searching for a particular program, we don't need to pull in screenful after screenful; we just need a few good sites.

archie allows us to do this with a modified command. Before entering **find 2do**, we'll enter a command that changes the way archie does business: **set maxhits 10** tells archie that we only want a maximum of 10 hits; the search should stop after reaching that point. This command should be given before the **find 2do** command because it sets archie to search under these constraints. There are a variety of other commands that we can use the same way; for now, let's see what happens when we run the search.

```
archie> set maxhits 10
archie> find 2do
# Search type: sub.
# Your queue position: 1
# Estimated time for completion: 00:06
working... |
```

And soon we have our information, as shown partially in Figure 5.6.

We've also got a problem, because if you examine the results, looking in each case at both the directory and the name of the file we've generated, you can see that none of these is likely to be the 2Do program we're hoping to find. In fact, we seem to have wandered into a number of selections having to do with images. And while archie has indeed found the search term we gave it, which was 2do, that search term is embedded in a longer word, pln2dot.

Two lessons emerge from this result. First, when you limit archie's maximum number of hits, you always have to bear in mind that you may set the number too low, and thus retrieve only material that doesn't meet your needs. You would then have to go back

```
Host ftp.cc.utexas.edu     (128.83.40.1)
Last updated 02:57 22 Jul 1995

    Location: source/X11R6/contrib/test/InsPEX/refimages
        FILE     -r--r--r--    2464 bytes  21:00 12 Feb 1991  pln2dot


Host ftp.sunet.se    (130.238.127.3)
Last updated 14:34 29 Jun 1995

    Location: /pub/X11/R6untarred/contrib/test/InsPEX/refimages
        FILE     -r--r--r--    2206 bytes  20:00 12 Feb 1991  pln2dotdash
        FILE     -r--r--r--    2464 bytes  20:00 12 Feb 1991  pln2dot


Host ftp.uoknor.edu     (129.15.91.50)
Last updated 02:51 16 Jul 1995

    Location: /mirrors/X/X11Rx/R6untarred/contrib/test/InsPEX/refimages
        FILE     -r--rw-r--    2464 bytes  15:00 12 Feb 1991  pln2dot
        FILE     -r--rw-r--    2206 bytes  15:00 12 Feb 1991  pln2dotdash

archie> _
```

Figure 5.6   Searching for the 2Do program.

and reset this number. The second lesson is that archie is clearly searching not just for the standalone term we gave it—2do—but also for that sequence of three characters as found inside any other words. We get pln2dot as a result because the search term is nestled inside the larger expression. Surely there must be some way to avoid retrieving such unnecessary material.

And, of course, there is. Recall the introductory archie screen we retrieved when we first opened the Telnet connection into this site. It contained the statement *'search' (type string) has the value 'sub'*. The time has come to disentangle this arcane expression and put it to work. Search values within archie can be set by another set of commands. The archie software defaults to the search type *sub*, for substring. Upper- and lowercase are ignored. This means that the program will hunt just as it did in the 2do example, looking for any name that contains the search string we specify.

Of course, that value can be changed. If we want to find only the exact program name as we look for the 2Do program, we can do so by setting the search type to *exact*. The syntax is **set search exact**. This would seem to solve our problem, but in fact, it actually opens up another can of worms, because programs aren't listed this way in file archives. We would be unlikely to find 2Do under that precise name; more likely it would be 2do.exe, or 2do.zip, and any number of other variations.

Can we also search using wildcard characters, so we might be able to locate any file that *begins* with the term 2do, no matter what its ending? The answer is yes. The way to do this is through a Unix *regular expression,* which is the way many archie clients search by default. When you're using a Telnet client, you have to specify that you want to **set search regex**, for regular expression. A regular expression in Unix terminology is a way of fine-tuning your search. Here I've already set the search type to regex, and am now entering a command that specifies how I want archie to search for the file.

```
archie> find ^2do.*
# Search type: regex.
```

```
# Your queue position: 1
# Estimated time for completion: 00:07
working...
```

The command is cryptic, as regex statements tend to be. We'll untangle it in a moment. If you look at the results as they appear in Figure 5.7, you'll see that I've isolated only those files *beginning* with the term 2do. Now we're in business. We've located something called 2dov10.zip, a file which, as we would find out upon unpacking it, contains 2Do version 1. This is the file we need, and our only remaining task is to go to the site using FTP and retrieve the file. The actual set of hits I received for this search was limited to eight, whereas if I had left the search type at sub, I would have generated a large number of hits, most of them irrelevant. By focusing our search using the search type regex, then, we've saved ourselves time and reduced the network's workload.

The principle is this: Although you can achieve many successful searches simply by using the **find** *keyword* command at the archie prompt, you will search more effectively and certainly more efficiently if you learn to use archie's search options. In a moment, we'll examine the structure of a Unix regular expression, so that the oddball cryptography of my preceding search statement will make more sense. But first, let's examine the range of archie options and try to formulate an effective search strategy.

archie's Command Options Using Telnet

archie is loaded with command-line options that allow you to tune up your search. The software actually functions by means of a set of variables, the values of which can be changed to reflect the kind of search you want to run. Some variables are *Boolean*, meaning you simply choose to turn them on or off. Others are *numeric;* you enter a number with them. The third kind of variable is a *string* variable; this just means you enter a "string," or sequence of characters to set the variable as needed.

```
        FILE    -rw-r--r--  847427 bytes  19:00 28 Apr 1993  2dov10.zip


Host ftp.sunet.se    (130.238.127.3)
Last updated 14:34 29 Jun 1995

    Location: /pub/pc/windows/mirror-cica/util
        FILE    -r--r--r--  847427 bytes  19:00 28 Apr 1993  2dov10.zip


Host ftp.icm.edu.pl    (148.81.209.3)
Last updated 04:17 14 Jun 1995

    Location: /pub1/cica/util
        FILE    -r--r--r--  847427 bytes  19:00 28 Apr 1993  2dov10.zip


Host joker.optics.rochester.edu    (128.151.240.1)
Last updated 03:09 17 Jul 1995

    Location: /mac/sounds/prisoner
        FILE    -rw-r--r--   27647 bytes  20:00 20 Oct 1991  2door.hqx

archie> _
```

Figure 5.7 Tightened search strategies allow us to track down only those files that begin with our search statement.

Don't be put off by all this talk of variables. archie doesn't require that you do high-level programming to make it work. I will present the major variables in a moment. Each is typed at the command prompt before you begin your search. We use the **set** command to change the settings for each variable.

Setting Up archie

To learn what the current settings are, type the command **show**. Here is the result of entering such a command when using Telnet to the archie server at archie.sura.net.

```
archie> show
# 'autologout' (type numeric) has the value '60'.
# 'compress' (type string) has the value 'none'.
# 'encode' (type string) has the value 'none'.
# 'language' (type string) has the value 'english'.
# 'mailto' (type string) is not set.
# 'match_domain' (type string) is not set.
# 'match_path' (type string) is not set.
# 'max_split_size' (type numeric) has the value '51200'.
# 'maxhits' (type numeric) has the value '25'.
# 'maxhitspm' (type numeric) has the value '100'.
# 'maxmatch' (type numeric) has the value '100'.
# 'output_format' (type string) has the value 'verbose'.
# 'pager' (type boolean) is not set.
# 'search' (type string) has the value 'sub'.
# 'server' (type string) has the value 'localhost'.
# 'sortby' (type string) has the value 'time'.
# 'status' (type boolean) is set.
# 'term' (type string) has the value 'vt100 24 80'.
archie>
```

This is, in fact, a pocket list of the archie variables, many of which we'll be dealing with in the upcoming list. We'll now examine some of these parameters to explain how they function. In each case, we'll change the variable by using the **set** command, followed by the name of the variable and the value we have chosen for it. When I refer to giving the command **set pager**, I could just as easily have stated "set the pager variable." We are changing the values by which archie operates to make our search work.

Changing Your Search Parameters

set search sub   This is the default for Telnet searches with archie version 3.x. The search will retrieve any file or directory name containing your search term within it, regardless of case. This is why a search under 2do retrieved the pln2dot hits. 2do is a "substring" of pln2dot. Searching for tin would retrieve bulle*tin* and s*tin*g, among other hits.

set search subcase   This is a case-sensitive substring search. It works like the regular substring search, except that it differentiates between upper- and lowercase letters. A search for 2DO with search type set to subcase would ignore any files named 2do because of the difference of case.

set search exact   Here archie looks for an exact match. This works well if you are looking for directories, as we saw when we asked archie for information about astronomy. But it can be a problem when you search for individual files, since they may often have extensions that would cause the exact search to miss them. A search for astronomy would not flag the text file astronomy.txt or the compressed file astronomy.Z. But an exact search is a quick one, and if you know the exact listing of the file you need, this is how to get it.

set search regex   This uses Unix regular expressions to conduct the search. Used without further specification, a regex search becomes a substring search, because regular expressions assume a wildcard character at the beginning and end of the search term. You can, however, specify that the search term should only appear at the beginning of the retrieved file or directory name by using the caret (^) character. A dollar sign ($) specifies that the search term is to appear at the end of the retrieved file or directory name.

Confused? Don't worry. I'll have more on regex searches at the end of this section.

You should also be aware of three other options that combine the search strategies just listed.

set search exact_sub   Here you are searching for an exact hit, but if archie finds no matches, it will then try the substring search strategy.

set search exact_subcase   The search begins using the exact strategy, but if it fails, it switches to a subcase or case-sensitive substring search.

set search exact_regex   This begins with the exact search method, but switches to regex if no matches are found.

As you can see, the range of options under search terms is broad. Shortly, we'll put the search strategies to work to find files, changing our search types as we go. For now, though, concentrate on another set of options that determines the particular place archie should run its search.

Where and What archie Searches

You can tell archie to search particular places for a specified search term, again using the **set** command.

set match_domain *string*   This means that you can determine a particular domain that you want to search. Perhaps you want to limit your search to universities. If so, you could use the command **set match_domain edu** to limit archie to edu sites. Or you could take a geographical slant on things. Perhaps you need a file from Switzerland. Your command **set match_domain ch** would limit the search to that domain.

set match_path
Here you are able to restrict your search by examining the directories archie will look in for your search term. This would make sense if you had a fair idea that your files fit into a general category. If you were looking for a file that compiled statistics on the planets, and you knew its name was planet.zip, you could restrict your search to directories called astronomy by entering the command **set match_path astronomy**. If you needed a particular graphics tool, you might use **set match_path graphics**.

The search pays no attention to case. If you want to use multiple terms, you can separate them with colons. Thus, **set match_path beer:brewing** will retrieve files with one or both of these components—beer or brewing—in the names of the directories that lead to them.

Controlling archie's Output

Fortunately, archie allows you a great deal of control over what it sends you. You should consider the output commands among the most important in your archie repertoire. Using them properly will save you time.

set maxhits *number*
Depending on what you're searching for, an archie hunt can rack up quite a few hits. This is particularly true if you are looking for a fairly common shareware program or a text document that has been receiving wide circulation. Your need is to find a good, preferably nearby site from which to download this file. What you don't need is a huge list of file sites, all of them offering the same file. In fact, the archie system will function much better if you reduce its workload. Why not call up just a few hits, assuming your search terms are tightly chosen?

The command **set maxhits 25** reduces the number of matches to 25 (and, of course, you can set the number where you choose, providing it is between 0 and 1,000). Once archie hits the upper limit, the search stops. You will see quite a difference between this search limitation and the default, which is 1,000 matches (individual servers, of course, may set the default at whatever value they choose).

HINT: As with Veronica, you should be careful when setting up a maximum number of hits with archie. Your first temptation may be to limit the number of hits so as to have a manageable set of files to work with. But if your search terms are so slack in the first place that you are generating too many hits, then it's likely that keeping the number of retrieved hits at a low number will simply cause you to miss files that might be useful if displayed. If your searches are retrieving too many hits, the best way to reduce the number is to tighten up your search methods and play closer attention to your use of keywords.

set maxhitspm *number*
Two other output variables are associated with the **maxhits** command. The statement **set maxhitspm 10** will return 10

files for each filename that archie matches. The reason that there is a separate **maxhitspm** command has to do with the way the archie database works. A filename can have several files associated with it, each of them sharing the same name; the name of the file in the database points to the location of each of the other files throughout the FTP sites on the Internet that share the same name.

set maxmatch *number*   The associated command **set maxmatch** *number* sets a maximum number of matching files that archie will find.

Think of the output commands this way: The number you use with **set maxhits** determines the total number of hits returned by archie; **set maxmatch** determines the total number of filenames that match the search term; **set maxhitspm** determines the number of files returned for each filename that archie is able to match. These distinctions can be useful in cases where you are trying to search for a common filename, one that the archie database shows occurring at numerous sites. In most cases, however, simply restricting your search with **maxhits** is a sufficient way to limit your search output.

Sorting Commands

Perhaps you prefer to see archie's output sorted alphabetically or by file size. A number of sorting commands are available.

set sortby *filename*   Sorts archie's output alphabetically by the name of the files it retrieves.

set sortby *hostname*   Sorts alphabetically by the name of the host computer.

set sortby *none*   Does not sort the output.

set sortby *size*   Sorts archie's output by largest to smallest files.

set sortby *times*   Sorts by time, with the most recent files listed first.

Important note: All the sorting commands can be run in reverse order by prefixing the **sortby** statement with the letter **r**. To sort in reverse order by size, for example you would enter **set sortby rsize**. To sort by reverse alphabetical order of filenames, enter **set sortby rfilename**, and so on.

Choosing an Output Format

The normal results of an archie search are in *verbose* mode, as illustrated in Figure 5.7; they provide host name and IP number, the date of the file's last updating, its directory location, and associated file information. You may, on the other hand, prefer to look at the output in *terse* mode, which reduces the information for each file into a single line. Here, for example, is what the output looks like when restricted to terse mode. I've entered a search for the shareware communications program Qmodem, from Mustang Software, Inc. I've restricted the number of hits to 10 (**set maxhits 10**) and have requested terse mode:

```
ftp.unicamp.br 16:56 16 Jul 1995 512 bytes /pub/simtel/msdos/qmodem
ftp.uoknor.edu 14:52 13 Jul 1995 1024 bytes /mirrors/SimTel/msdos/qmodem
```

```
ftp.sunet.se 14:40 25 Jun 1995 8192 bytes /pub/pc/mirror/SimTel/msdos/qmodem
nic.switch.ch 03:51 23 Jun 1995 512 bytes /mirror/simtel/msdos/qmodem
plaza.aarnet.edu.au 04:57 20 Jun 1995 512 bytes /micros/pc/SimTel/msdos/qmodem
ftp.icm.edu.pl 15:17 5 Jun 1995 512 bytes /pub3/msdos/qmodem
medusa.k12.ar.us 18:40 11 Apr 1995 2048 bytes /pub/simtel1/disc1/qmodem
ftp.iij.ad.jp 10:14 26 Feb 1995 512 bytes /pub/msdos/qmodem
ftp.uoknor.edu 14:00 21 Apr 1994 1024 bytes /src/pc/comm/qmodem
ftp.std.com 21:00 1 Mar 1993 1024 bytes /customers2/src/pc/comm/qmodem
```

As you can see, the output is now reduced to a single line for each hit. The commands needed to achieve this result follow.

set output_format terse For terse output as just shown.

set output_format verbose For standard, full-length archie output.

set output_format machine Useful when you want to manipulate the archie results through another program.

Activating the Status Line

archie's status line shows the progress of your search as it's running. You can activate it with the command **set status**.

MAILING YOUR RESULTS

Rather than examining your results during the Telnet session, you may prefer to have them sent to you via electronic mail. To do so, you can use the **mailto** variable. Once you have set this variable, you can then use the **mail** command to have the output of your last command sent to you.

set mailto *username* Entering **set mailto vprice@eapoe.com**, for example, sends the output of your search to the specified address. You can also specify more than one address in case you want to forward your results to someone else. You can use the **mail** command to mail your results without setting the **mailto** variable, but if you do, you will need to enter an address each time you invoke the mail function.

set pager One problem with an archie search is that your results can scroll past before you have the chance to examine them. Using the **mail** command to send the output to your mailbox is one option. Another is to change the way archie displays material on the screen. The **pager** variable allows you to slow archie down. With it, you can cause the system to display your results in single screens of information; you move between screens by pressing the SPACEBAR. To do this, give the command **set pager**. After you have read the material in question on-screen, you exit the pager program (it's called less, by the way) by entering a **q**, followed by a **RETURN**.

Miscellaneous archie Commands

Although you'll use the **set** command more than any other, because it functions to change the key variables that determine how archie works, there are a number of other commands that can make your work with archie easier.

list   This command can be used by itself to indicate all the sites in the database at the server site, or in conjunction with a Unix regular expression to limit the search to particular domains. I could, for example, use **list** to search for all sites in the United Kingdom, using a regex term:

        list.*uk$

This command returns any site with the uk domain name and excludes all others. The $ sign at the end of the statement specifies that no text should follow the search term; the .* allows any text to exist in front of the search term.

The (abbreviated) output of a **list** command looks like this:

```
bells.cs.ucl.ac.uk              128.16.5.31      19:32 12 Jul 1995
ccp4.dl.ac.uk                   148.79.160.77    14:06 29 Jun 1995
colonsay.dcs.ed.ac.uk           129.215.160.5    12:55 29 Jun 1995
cs6400.mcc.ac.uk                     0.0.0.0     04:11 10 Jun 1995
ftp.tex.ac.uk                   128.232.1.87     08:32 29 Jun 1995
ftp.wcmc.org.uk                 192.26.45.200    17:46 13 Jul 1995
lune.csc.liv.ac.uk              138.253.42.172   03:39 27 Jun 1995
ftp.warwick.ac.uk               137.205.192.14   04:06 12 Jun 1995
micros.hensa.ac.uk              194.80.32.51     03:51 12 Jun 1995
ftp.bath.ac.uk                  138.38.32.34     03:50 12 Jun 1995
pluto.ulcc.ac.uk                193.63.88.3      12:33 29 Jun 1995
edif.cs.man.ac.uk               130.88.13.226    03:50 12 Jun 1995
scitsc.wlv.ac.uk                134.220.4.1      12:38 29 Jun 1995
```

help   Don't overlook archie's extensive help system. While it's impenetrably written and as terse as any Unix manual page, it nonetheless can bail you out of a jam while you're still on-line. Having given the **help** command, you can use a **?** at the help prompt to list the available subtopics. To exit help, type **done** at the help prompt.

quit   Use this command to exit from archie. You can also use **exit** or **bye**.

servers   Enter the **servers** command to generate a list of publicly available archie servers known to the site you are currently using. This is a good way to keep up to date as new archie servers come on-line.

The (Sometimes) Helpful whatis Command

Any method of specifying a search presupposes certain constraints. archie, for example, allows you to search for files with particular names, or to specify parts of those names and retrieve any files that match your specifications. The method works when you have one of two things: a reasonable expectation of what the filename is or a more general term that can be used to search for directories at the various sites that may contain the software or documents you need. Where the method fails is in those instances when you have a rough idea of what you need but not the faintest idea of what its name might be.

To work around such problems, archie maintains a second set of data called the Software Description Database, in which are found short descriptions and the names of numerous files stored around the Internet. As with archie's Internet Archives Database, you should realize that not all these files are executable programs; many are documents, and some are simply stored data. Whatever the case, using the Software Description Database through the **whatis** command can help you find what you need.

To search the database, use **whatis** followed by the term you are looking for. I might, for example, want to find programs or text files relating to satellites.

```
archie> whatis satellite
RFC             346                 Postel, J.B. Satellite consider.
RFC             357                 Davidson, J. Echoing strategy f.
RFC             829                 Cerf, V.G. Packet satellite tech
n3emo-orbitf    Track earth satellites
```

A useful list; we have three Requests for Comments (RFCs) documents involving satellites and one file, apparently a program, that tracks earth satellites. Since we are returned to the archie prompt after this search, we can now simply enter the **find** command to track down one of these files. Alas, entering **find n3emo-orbitf** produces no hits and reveals a major limitation of the whatis database. Because the database is not updated regularly, it's often possible to find a file within it that has been removed from the holdings of the various FTP sites.

Be advised, too, that you are at the mercy of the indexers when you use the **whatis** command. Suppose you were looking for a program that would catalog your collection of rare wines. You could try the **whatis wine** command. But note the result:

```
archie> whatis wine
RFC             109                 Winett, J.M. Level III Server P.
RFC             110                 Winett, J.M. Conventions for us)
RFC             147                 Winett, J.M. Definition of a so)
RFC             167                 Bhushan, A.K.; Metcalfe, R.M.; .
RFC             183                 Winett, J.M. EBCDIC codes and t.
RFC             393                 Winett, J.M. Comments on Telnet.
RFC             466                 Winett, J.M. Telnet logger/serv.
```

The database has looked for the term wine and has found it—within the name of the author of the RFCs listed here, J.M. Winett. As you can see, **whatis** searches for the substring exactly as you enter it (ignoring case).

On the other hand, there are times when **whatis** can home in directly on what you're after. Suppose we were looking for a program that would help us catalog audio tapes. The **whatis** command now produces quite a few hits, many of them clearly oriented toward computer storage.

```
archie> whatis tape
ansitape        ANSI tape program
arch            Let users archive and unarchive files to tape in a bat
buffer          Helps write remote tapes *fast*
cassette        Generate a label for a cassette tape or compact disc c)
cktar           Compare tar tape against file system
```

cmstape	Read and write IBM VM/SP CMS dump tapes
copytape	Magtape copy program
cpio	Various public domain program to read "cpio" format ts
exebyte_toc	Table of Contents for Exebyte 8mm tapes
magtape	Read and write ANSI labeled tapes, copy tapes even wis
magtapetools	Magtape handling package
makeddtape	Reads a tape and produces a shell script to read the s
mdump	Multiple dump per tape utility
multivol	Multi-volume tape utility. Splits its input across ms
pdtar	A PD tar(1) replacement. Writes P1003 (POSIX) standa.
read-vms-backs	Read VMS backup tapes
read20	Read TOPS-20 "DUMPER" tapes on UNIX
remote	Remote mag tape routines
remote-magtape	Library routines to handle reading tapes from remote s
remtape	Remote magtape library for 4.3BSD
rename	Rename files from their inode numbers after using ress
rmtlib	Remote magtape library for BSD
rtar	Diffs to tar to use a remote system's tape drive
tape	An audio tape database program
tapetest	Test magnetic tapes by writing a test pattern and thek
tar	PD versions of the tar(1) (Tape ARchive) program
tar_aids	Tools to read damaged tar tapes
tarfix	Fix and convert tape archives
vms-backup	Read VMS BACKUP tapes
whichtape	Simple database tools to help find files on backup tas

We might be interested in the one listed as:

```
tape An audio tape database program
```

To track it down, we simply type the command **find tape** at the archie> prompt. But wait; since **find tape** will generate many hits with the default search variable **sub**, let's change the setting to regex. Entering **set search regex**, I then give the command **find ^tape.***, which should narrow the list considerably. Soon we have a number of possibilities, including this one:

```
Host audrey.sait.edu.au (130.220.16.88)
Last updated 09:46 29 Jun 1995

    Location: /linux/slackware/rootdsks.144
        FILE -rw-r--r-- 588729 bytes 19:00 3 Nov 1994 tape144.gz
```

Is this the file we need? Unfortunately, we won't know without going to the site to check it out. Neither the Internet Archives Database nor the Software Description Database can verify which of the possibilities is ours.

Keep the limitations of the **whatis** command in mind as you use it. The most important is the fact that any **whatis** search you run does not search the entire set of FTP sites available through the standard archie database. Instead, it searches the separate Software Description Database. This sharply limits its ability to run a comprehensive search. Second, remember that the Software Description Database itself is limited by the fact that the people who created the file you need may not have penned a description of it, and therefore could not have sent their description to the database administrators at Bunyip Information Systems. All in all, this remains an extremely limited database.

A Brief Aside on regex

Unix regular expressions can be complicated, but you don't have to master every nuance of their usage to put them to work. The idea is that regular expressions allow you to search for specific patterns. If you're familiar with wildcards as used in MS-DOS, you'll find some of what follows familiar, although regular expressions go far beyond what DOS wildcards allow. Here are some basic principles:

- Using a search term without further regex expressions causes the search to be treated as a hunt for substrings; the effect is as if you entered **set search sub**. Thus, **find geotype** is the same as entering the regex expression **find.*geotype.***. Why? Read on.
- In a regular expression, the period (.) stands for *any single character*. In the regex expression **.*geotype.***, the period at the beginning means the search term can be preceded by any one letter. The same principle holds at the end, only in reverse. Any one letter can follow the search term geotype.
- In regular expressions, an asterisk (*) stands for *zero or more occurrences of the preceding regular expression*. Thus, in the statement **.*geotype.***, the period lets the search term be preceded by any one letter, while the asterisk means that any number of letters can occur before the geotype string occurs. (In other words, the asterisk looks to the preceding expression, which is a period, and determines that it can occur any number of times). At the end of the statement, the asterisk has the same meaning. Any number of letters can follow the basic search string geotype.
- A caret (^) in the first position sets the search term at the beginning of the word. The statement **find ^geotype**, then, would return only hits that *began* with the term geotype. Always use the caret if you know the search string begins the filename.
- A dollar sign ($) means that the search term may occur *only at the end of a word*. Thus, **find geotype$** would retrieve 123geotype, but not geotype.exe. Always use the dollar sign if you know that the search string ends the filename.
- Use brackets to show a set of characters you want to match. Thus, **find [djrt]une** will retrieve dune, june, rune, and tune, matching any of the four bracketed characters to the string that follows. It will also find june-92-meeting.tar.Z, thesis.june29.ps, and system-7-tune-up. This is because regular expressions have .* at the beginning and at the end, unless the caret (^) or dollar sign ($) appears. This is why I said earlier that a search under **find geotype** is the same as a search using the term **find .*geotype.***.
- If you want to exclude particular characters, you can do so by using brackets and the caret character combined. Thus, **find [^tj]une** will retrieve dune and rune, but not tune and june.
- You can use a special character (that is, one that would normally be treated as part of a regex expression) in your search term if you use a backslash (\) in front of it. For example, if I were searching for a file about faxing with a particular extension, such as .001, I could search this way: **find .*fax\.001**. The .* at the beginning would allow the term fax to occur with any number of letters in front of it. The backslash would indicate that the period (.) following it is to be treated as part of the search term, and not in its normal regex manner (matching any single letter).

As you can see, regular expressions are complicated, and these notes barely scratch the surface. Bear in mind, however, that basic substring searches, or a combination of exact and substring, as in the setting **set search exact_sub**, will handle most of the work you need to accomplish. Use regex searching when your needs are extremely specific and you wish to exclude as many options as possible from your results. Used properly, a regex search is your most precisely tuned tool for using archie. I doubt, though, that you'll need to use it often.

If you want to learn more about regular expressions, I recommend Harley Hahn's *Unix Unbound* (Osborne-McGraw Hill, 1994) as the best single text covering the subject.

archie through a Client Program

Using archie through Telnet to an archie server works well, but you will find that some servers are getting a lot of work these days, and the load on their systems often means they must limit the number of simultaneous users. Therefore, you may run into a screen advising you to try again later, along with a list of alternative sites. This complication needn't trouble you if you have access to an archie client on your system. The client programs are not limited by the same restrictions that hold Telnet sites to only a few users, and they're fast, too.

To find out whether your shell account offers access to an archie client, type **archie** at your command prompt. If the client is available, you should receive a list of commands. If not, you will see something like this:

```
archie: Command not found.
```

Numerous graphical archie clients exist, for the SLIP/PPP environment as well, and for users with a dedicated network connection. Among the most popular are Wsarchie for PCs running Microsoft Windows and Anarchie for the Macintosh. Let's take a look at both types of client program.

Using an archie Client with a Shell Account

If archie is available on your system, running a search with it is simplicity itself. The basic command is simply **archie** *keyword*. Thus, **archie chess** searches for files with the string chess contained within them. It will also, of course, pull up any directories that use the name chess. The results of this search are shown in Figure 5.8. This figure shows one screen of several that scrolled past when I ran this search.

But wait. Just as we used variables, changing their values as necessary, to alter the way we worked with Telnet, archie client programs also provide ways of modifying your search. Rather than doing so through **set** commands, however, the archie client uses *command switches*. A switch is simply an optional letter you enter after the archie command; adding it causes the client program to search in the specified way. Let's now examine the primary archie options.

USING ARCHIE'S COMMAND SWITCHES

By typing archie at my system's command prompt, I receive the set of command switches available, preceded by a line that reads more like nuclear physics than computing:

```
Usage: archie [-acelorstvLV] [-m hits] [-N level] string
```

But don't be put off by the imposing brackets and dashes. The statement means that the **archie** command is to be followed by any of the switches shown, in the order shown, fol-

```
Host krynn.efd.1th.se

    Location: /pub/hp-calc/educalc/horn_disk_6/games
          FILE -rwxrwxr-x        9165   Jun  3 1992  chess

Host ftp.luth.se

    Location: /pub/386BSD/386bsd-0.1/filesystem/usr/othersrc/games
       DIRECTORY drwxr-xr-x         512  Apr 12 00:00   chess
    Location: /pub/misc/lyrics/c
       DIRECTORY drwxr-xr-x         512  Apr 15 00:00   chess
    Location: /pub/unix/4.3bsd/net2/games
       DIRECTORY drwxrwxr-x        512  Mar 13 1993    chess

Host nctuccca.edu.tw

    Location: /Operating-Systems/Coherent/mwcbbs
       DIRECTORY drwxr-xr-x         512   Jul 23 00:00   chess
    Location: /Operating-Systems/bsd-sources/games
       DIRECTORY drwxr-xr-x         512   Jul 23 00:00   chess
    Location: /UNIX/bsd-sources/games
       DIRECTORY drwxr-xr-x         512   Jul 23 00:00   chess
    Location: /USENET/FAQ/news/answers/games
```

Figure 5.8   Using an archie client to search for chess files.

lowed by the search term or "string" that you choose. A command, for example, might read as follows:

archie -c -m15 laserjet

This would tell archie to search for the term laserjet, matching only files listed in lowercase, and retrieving no more than 15 matches. Build your query with care, using the correct command switches, and you'll save yourself time. Here are the switches:

-a	Lists all matches as Alex filenames. Alex is a tool that allows you to read files at remote sites.
-c	Sets up a case-sensitive substring search. You could, for example, differentiate between files labeled dsck3.exe and DSCK3.EXE or, for that matter, DSck3.exe and dscK3.exe. This is the same as entering **set search subcase** with a Telnet connection.
-e	Matches the search term exactly. This is the default setting for the line-oriented archie Unix client. The equivalent command with an archie server is **set search exact**.
-r	Sets up a Unix regular expression search. The command to do this with an archie server through Telnet would be **set search regex**.
-s	Creates a case-insensitive substring search. The equivalent command is **set search sub**, which is the default setting for archie version 3.x when accessed by Telnet.

-l	Lists one match per line. This is the same command as **set output_format machine** with a Telnet connection to archie. It produces output that you can then use for further processing with a variety of Unix tools.
-t	Sorts the results by time and date, with the most recent date first. It is the equivalent of **set sortby time**.
-m *number-of-hits*	Sets the number of items the archie search will return. Thus, **-m15** returns 15 hits. It is the equivalent of the server command **set maxhits**. If you fail to specify a maximum number of hits, archie will default to an exact search and provide a maximum of 95 matches.
-o *filename*	Stores the results of your search in the file whose name you specify; thus, **archie graphics -o graphics.txt**. This can be handy when you're retrieving a large number of hits and don't want to scroll through all the material on-screen.
-h *hostname*	Allows you to specify a server host for your search. Thus, **archie -h archie.sura.net** tells the client to use the server at SURAnet to run its search.
-L	Lists the servers known to the archie client, as well as the server the client defaults to when it searches. When archie is set up at your site, the system administrator decides to which archie server the client will connect. As shown, you can always use the -h switch to search a different server site. Here is the output from this command at my site:

```
% archie -L
Known archie servers:
    archie.ans.net (USA [NY])
    archie.rutgers.edu (USA [NJ])
    archie.sura.net (USA [MD])
    archie.unl.edu (USA [NE])
    archie.mcgill.ca (Canada)
    archie.funet.fi (Finland/Mainland Europe)
    archie.au (Australia)
    archie.doc.ic.ac.uk (Great Britain/Ireland)
    archie.wide.ad.jp (Japan)
    archie.ncu.edu.tw (Taiwan)
 * archie.sura.net is the default Archie server.
 * For the most up-to-date list, write to an Archie server and give it the
   command
'servers'.
```

-N   Allows you to adjust how fast your search proceeds. The archie system refers to this as the *query niceness level,* which is in itself a nice touch. It means that if your search isn't urgent, you can choose to inform the system of this fact in order to give more urgent requests priority. You can choose a niceness level between 0 and 35,765, with the default at 0. The higher the number, the nicer you are.

         Ponder the **-N** option with care. If you insert no value, your job simply joins the queue and moves on through. But choose a value of **-N 1000,** and you are allowing the system to handle your request with a little less urgency. You may want to avoid the highest settings, however. Setting **-N 32765** tells archie to run your job only after the queue is empty. Nobody is that nice.

-V   A long archie search can be baffling; your screen seems to be frozen, and you don't know for sure whether the system is still responding. You can fix this with the **-V** command, which causes archie to insert a statement on occasion. What you'll see is this:

```
Searching...
```

Note several things about these command options. First, if you compare this list with the extensive set of server commands available through a Telnet connection, you'll see that your choices are relatively limited, although the major features certainly are available. And be aware that we didn't even explore many of the lesser-traveled byways of server site commands; the list of possibilities through an archie client can seem rather limiting when compared to the Telnet option.

Another thing to remember is that the **whatis** command is not available through a client program like the line-oriented archie client for Unix. **whatis** is of very limited utility, of course, so that may not strike you as a major limitation.

On the other hand, the client approach is easy to use, with the command switches available at your system prompt merely by typing archie. For most searches, using a client when one is available is the preferred method of access.

Using archie with a Graphical Client Program

A SLIP/PPP connection will allow you to use graphical client programs like Wsarchie, my personal favorite of the archie clients for Microsoft Windows, or Anarchie for the Macintosh. A graphical client places the archie commands in the context of a menu-driven environment with mouse-click commands, and the major functions made readily available in the form of buttons and dialog boxes. In Figure 5.9, you can see the Wsarchie search screen.

Wsarchie provides three fields that bear immediate scrutiny in terms of running a search:

Search for   This is where you put your keyword. The usual archie constraints apply; that is, the system will search for your keyword on the basis of how you have defined the search. The type of search you will run is determined by the buttons that appear at the top right of the screen.

Archie Server   This box lets you choose which archie server should run your search. Note the scroll arrow to the right of the dialog box. By clicking on this, you call down a list of the archie servers known to Wsarchie, and can choose among them. Notice that archie.internic.net is set up as the default, but as with any archie default, you can change the setting.

Domain   This allows you to specify how you want to restrict your search by domain. You might, for example, choose to restrict your search to sites in Britain. By entering uk in the domain field, you ensure that archie will only provide hits from that domain.

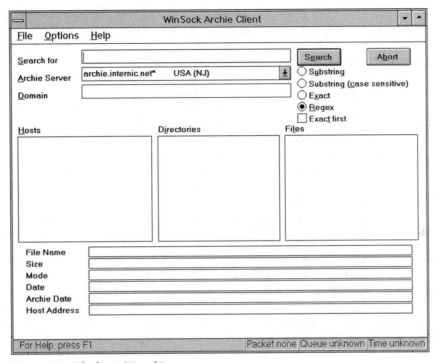

Figure 5.9   The basic Wsarchie screen.

Notice also the five buttons to the right of the screen. These control how your keywords are to be interpreted.

Substring	Sets up a regular substring search, meaning that archie will search for your keyword even if it occurs within a larger word.
Substring (case-sensitive)	Creates a case-sensitive substring search.
Exact	Sets up archie to search for the exact keyword you specify, disallowing substring matches.
Regex	Sets up a Unix regular expression search. This is the default with Wsarchie.
Exact first	Searches first for an exact match, then goes to whatever other option you have set up. This can be useful if you are pretty sure that you know the exact filename you need, but want to check via other search methods just in case.

You can see from examining these options that using Wsarchie is like using any other archie client. What you are doing is tweaking the way your keywords will be treated by the system. What differs is primarily the way the software looks and the methods you use to change its settings. Some clients will provide you with more options than others; you may have noticed, for example, that the line-oriented Unix client we looked at previously gave you a great deal more control over a variety of issues, such as display of your results and the number of hits to be retrieved, than does Wsarchie. But Wsarchie is considerably easier to use.

Let's run an archie search with Wsarchie. Suppose I am trying to track down a good program to manage recipes. I have thousands of recipes I've gathered over the years from my collection of cookbooks and food-related notes. How do I go about putting them in some sort of coherent, computer-organized order? To find out, I'll try the keyword recipe out on archie. I choose a substring search for this, because my keyword may appear inside a larger term; remember, archie searches for filenames and directories, so we want to be able to pick up a reference to a file that might be called something like recipemgr.zip or something similar. I submit the request to archie.internic.net, and soon the results pour in, as shown in Figure 5.10.

Notice how Wsarchie displays them; the highlighted address, which is shown on the left of the screen, contains the directories and files shown to the right. As I move the highlight down, going from one FTP site to another, the information in the directories and files windows changes to reflect what's at the site. Full information on each particular highlighted file is also shown at the bottom of the screen, where we learn not only the file's name, but also its size, date, and host address.

Now, however, we run into a typical archie problem. As you would imagine, many of the cookbook-type software programs out there on the Internet don't necessarily have the string recipe in their names. I did find one program, recipe2.ob.cpt.hqx, a Macintosh

Figure 5.10   Results of a Wsarchie search looking for recipe manager programs.

program, that looked promising, but in this search, I'm trying to retrieve a program for Microsoft Windows. And while I retrieved a lengthy list of hits, most of the material refers to actual recipes posted on-line, in the form of archives, many of them from the USENET newsgroups related to cookery.

What to do? Clearly, a change of keyword is called for. There are several possibilities. By searching under the keyword cooking, I looked for directories of that name that, presumably, would include database programs to hold recipes. For this search, I could use the exact setting, since I was only looking for directories, not filenames. Bearing in mind that some of my previous search's hits were likewise directories, I soon had compiled a list of sites that seemed to have extensive holdings in the food area. I could then use my FTP client to examine the holdings at those sites and determine the program I needed.

Such a method is indirect; it requires two search sweeps, one using archie, another using an FTP client. But in some cases, there is no other choice. I searched again under the keyword cookbook, searching with a substring setting to see what I might find. An extensive list of hits appeared, but many of them referred to files unrelated to the preparation of food, as in a "cookbook" of network sign-on techniques, for example. When you hit this kind of brick wall, you have to remember that archie can only consult its database to find the names of the files that have been placed within it. And if the kind of file you are looking for has a difficult-to-locate name, archie can be challenging to use. Sometimes searching through an FTP site's directories is the best you can do, but archie can help you to locate the site and the directory in question.

I did eventually find the recipe manager program I was looking for. And an examination of the options available may show why archie can be frustrating, at times, to use. Just take a look at some of the filenames I located, mostly through browsing at FTP sites. They included mcookn.zip (a program called MicroCook), cook.zip (SoftCook for Windows), rpw12.zip (Recipe Processor for Windows), and komp4.exe (Komputer Kitchen). As you can see, the actual filename for each of these programs is, according to MS-DOS conventions, compressed into the familiar constraints of the system. This means a name of no more than eight letters, followed by an extension of no more than three.

The problem, of course, is that archie can't search for anything but these filenames. That means that even if I knew to look for a program called SoftCook for Windows, I would have to guess at the way it would be represented in a filename. Maybe I would get lucky and find cook.zip, but I would be very unlikely to find Recipe Processor for Windows, with its rpw12.zip filename, unless I knew in advance exactly what the filename was. We're dealing with the limitations of file-naming conventions and the archie system itself, at least, as it's presently constituted.

So what would you do in such a case? You could do what I did, and locate directories that led to holdings on the subject of food and recipes. Or you could sidestep archie at this point and run a search with one of the World Wide Web-based search tools. The advantage of this method would be that you could fairly quickly locate several home pages that focused on cooking, and it's likely that on at least one of these, links to an FTP site with software would be made available. The point is, you could use any of these methods to generate the information you needed, but you'd have to think on your feet the whole way. Searching the Internet is rarely a cut-and-dried process.

If you're interested in Wsarchie, you can find the program at the following URL:

ftp://ftp.demon.co.uk/pub/ibmpc/winsock/apps/wsarchie/

As of this writing, the filename was wsarch08.zip. The program is the work of David Woakes.

Macintosh users will want to examine a program called Anarchie, which provides full archie capability in the Mac environment. Created by Peter Lewis, Anarchie is available at Macintosh-related sites all over the Internet. A recent search using Anarchie itself turned up hits like these:

ftp://freebsd.cdrom.com/

ftp://ftp.univie.ac.at/

ftp://nic.switch.ch/

ftp://ftp.iro.montreal.ca/

At the time of this writing, the filename was anarchie-15.hqx. You can see the results of my search for the program in Figure 5.11.

You may be wondering why the Anarchie hits show only the site address and not the full pathname. The reason is that Anarchie contains full FTP capability within the program; you don't need to know the pathname if you want to retrieve one of these files, because all you have to do is to double-click on any of them to send Anarchie itself out to run your FTP session and download the file. This is useful stuff, I think you'll agree; the combination of capabilities saves you time. Interestingly, Wsarchie can also be con-

Figure 5.11 A search for the Anarchie program using Anarchie itself.

figured to do much the same, although it will turn to an external client program like WS_FTP to perform the task. But in either case, the FTP session and the archie search are melded into a single operation. Saving time and simplifying operations is the goal of any properly constructed Internet search tool.

An archie Search Methodology

The wealth of variables and switches that archie makes available through server sites and local clients allows you to tailor your search to virtually any specification. As you begin to use archie to gather information and find the files you need, however, there are certain key precepts that will enable you to search more effectively. They involve setting up a basic set of defaults that can save you time and trouble.

The archie Unix client, for example, defaults to a maximum of 95 hits and an exact search, unless you specify otherwise. Using archie through Telnet results in a default search type of sub, rather than an exact search. A server default of a maximum of 100 hits is common, but the number may go as high as 1,000. Server sites allow you to send the results of your search to yourself in the form of a mail message, while archie clients let you save the output of your search in a file. Both allow you to sort the output in a variety of ways (although the Telnet option clearly gives you a wider range). In other words, paying attention to how each system is set will allow you to search either with the same set of parameters.

To search effectively, ask yourself these questions:

1. What are the current options at the system I'm using? You can check them at a server site by using the **show** command. If you're using the archie Unix client, simply type **archie** at the system prompt. The resulting list will remind you that the default search type is exact, and that the maximum number of hits is 95. You can check the current server with the **archie -L** command. If you're using a graphical client be sure to examine your software's configuration options.
2. How do I want to view the results? You'll waste time if you construct a careful search and then lose the results as most of them scroll off your screen. If using Telnet, consider setting the pager variable (**set pager**), which allows you to read one screen at a time. Alternatively, send the results to your mailbox, using the **mailto** variable and the **mail** command. If you're using the Unix archie client, consider directing the output of your search to a file using the **-o** *filename* switch.
3. How do I establish my search type? This can be the hardest decision you'll have to make with archie. How you search depends upon what you're after. Consider the following possibilities:
   - Use an exact search when you know the name of the file as it is stored. If you are sure there is a sam.johnson.txt file out there, then the exact setting should take you right to it, provided it's available at one of archie's FTP sites.
   - Use an exact search when you're looking for directories of information about general topics. If, for example, I want to know where I can find directories labelled chemistry, I could search under that term, knowing that I would retrieve numerous directories but few filenames that matched.
   - Use a sub search when you know the name of the program you're after but don't necessarily know how it's packaged. I might want to find a program called switch.exe, but I know it could be available as switch.zip, or switch20.exe, or

any number of possible variations. A sub search can help you ferret out such materials.

- Consider an exact_sub search. The command **set search exact_sub** lets the system look for the precise search term you enter; if it fails to find it, it looks using substring methods. The advantage is that you may get lucky and land your file right off the bat; if you don't, you don't need to run a separate substring search for it. You can enable this option in Wsarchie with a mouse click.
- Use a regex search if you feel confident of only part of the name of the file you're searching for. Although a substring search would also reveal your search term buried inside a larger string, it may be that you're sure the search term appears at the beginning or the end of the filename. Searching for a program called pqx, for example, I might suspect that it's labelled with its version number, as in pqx13.exe, or some such. I can use a regex search to look for the pqx search term and to specify that it appear only at the beginning of any matches.

4. How many hits am I willing to work with? One hundred may be more than you need, so why not speed up the search with a **set maxhits 15** command or its client equivalent, **archie -m15**? If your search is properly constructed, you shouldn't be receiving huge numbers of hits in any case. If you are, tighten your search terms.

5. Should I sort my output to show the most recent files first? Doing so, you are ensuring that you're getting the latest version of the program or text file in question. The server command is **set sortby time**; the Unix archie client command is **archie -t**.

6. Should I use the "niceness level settings"? By all means, if you're not in a hurry to get your results, use these settings. Set your niceness level high and, even if your request takes longer, you'll have helped reduce the workload at the server site. This is particularly applicable if you're submitting a long search. Another possibility is to submit your archie query by mail. We'll talk about how to do that in Chapter 9.

6

WAIS:
Searching for Text

A close look at the World Wide Web search engines, Gopher, and Veronica shows how versatile all these tools are at finding files on the Internet. In fact, given the riches we can uncover through their combined efforts, it seems churlish to raise any doubts about their effectiveness. But technology is always redefining itself, and each new advance leads invariably to the next question. There are things, for example, that Gopher and Veronica simply cannot do; we must consider what they are and how a totally different networking concept addresses them.

When you run a Veronica search, you are retrieving information from Gopher menus scattered throughout the worldwide Internet. But this information is, in a sense, surface-level; it produces the titles of individual programs, graphics images, text files, and directories, but it does not tell us what is inside them. A file labelled "A New Approach to Networking," for example, might be about Rupert Murdoch's dealings with MCI, or it might be an examination of ATM switching technology. The point is, we can't tell from the title alone what it is, and thus must rely on the people who choose these titles to do their jobs well. A similar limitation affects many Web-based search engines.

What's missing is the ability to search the contents of a database for specific text. Perhaps I want to know something about Alfred the Great. I can search in a variety of ways for articles and even directories about the great king of Wessex, but using Veronica, I would miss a directory called /medieval, which could, for all I know, contain a lot about him. But if I could find a database stuffed with textual information with an appropriate search engine, I could then descend to the document level, searching for words within the text. And if the database were designed to handle the task, I could retrieve a list of hits which would be ranked in order of importance.

The system I am describing is called WAIS—**W**ide **A**rea **I**nformation **S**ervers. The brain child of Brewster Kahle, the concept was refined by him while working at Thinking Machines Corp., a producer of massive parallel computers and information retrieval engines. Apple Computer also played a role, as did KPMG Peat Marwick and Dow Jones and Co. The result is a public domain implementation as well as a series of more sophisticated versions, which bring these powerful capabilities to computers of all descriptions. Kahle himself, meanwhile, founded his own firm, WAIS Inc., to focus on WAIS and the future of data retrieval. America Online recently acquired WAIS Inc., an indication of how one major company sees the significance of this technology.

How WAIS Works

To understand WAIS (pronounced ways) and its improvement on prior search methodologies, you need to know something about its history. Driving the enterprise was the need to make text-based information systems more accessible to corporate executives (this accounts for the heavy corporate sponsorship of the original project). A key to the concept is that a good search interface must be usable by nontechnical people. (We might wish, given the success of WAIS, that all search tools were designed for executives and others not proficient with computer technology. The interface industry would doubtless improve!)

Another key: A good retrieval engine must be able to address a wide variety of data through a *single* interface. We can see why this would be so in business, where numerous sources are important, yet frequently accessed by different types of software. The WAIS project sought to circumvent that obstacle by bringing a new search method to database access, one that not only provided an easy-to-use interface, but that produced its results in a way strikingly different from conventional database methods.

Graft these needs into the network environment and you get a system that can draw information from widely dispersed databases through a common front end. The client/server relationship of the network is the key. When you decide to search a WAIS database, you set up a search by choosing key terms, which are then sent to the appropriate server computer. The WAIS system will return a list of documents that contain the keywords you've specified. The WAIS servers are linked to databases that can reside anywhere on the Internet. WAIS clients exist for a wide variety of computers, from DOS to Unix, the Macintosh and Microsoft Windows.

The answers to your initial query are only the beginning of the process. Once the remote server has sent the results of its search, the client program displays these hits in a sequence that is ranked by the number of occurrences of the search terms in the files in question. Thus, a document that contains numerous examples of your search term ranks high on the list, while one containing a single reference ranks at the bottom. You then can refine your query by noting which of the search results is closest to what you need, and run a new search. This process is called *relevance feedback*.

What You Can Find with WAIS

Unlike Gopher, which offers collections of local information as well as links to remote files and services of a diverse nature, WAIS servers are specialized. The nature of the Internet means they may be located anywhere in the network; each will focus on particular topics. We find, for example, servers dealing with specialties like mathematics, or physics, or astronomy. Because WAIS allows textual searching (and finely tuned textual searching at that), bringing USENET newsgroups, as well as archived BITNET and Internet mailing lists, into the system is a natural. We also find binary data. Although WAIS searches for text, the element downloaded can be a program, an image, a sound file, or a moving video.

Given the background of the Internet as a research and communications tool within the academic and scientific communities, it is no surprise to learn that a research slant permeates the current crop of servers. The network itself is a prime area for WAIS to catalog. Michael Strangelove's Directory of Electronic Journals and Newsletters, for example, can be consulted through a WAIS database called elec_journ_newslett.src (src is the WAIS server suffix; it stands for source. When you see a file with the .src suffix, you are looking at a WAIS database). For Your Information documents, provided as background tools for Internet users, are available through another server (fyis.src), while articles from the monthly Matrix News newsletter are available as matrix_news.src. Whimsy has its place as well. The USENET cookbook, drawn from recipes posted by cooking aficionados all over the world, is available as usenet-cookbook.src. So, too, are Internet standards documents (internet-standards.src) and network information for newcomers (internet-intros.src).

Chris Christoff has compiled a listing of WAIS sources that demonstrates the system's range. We find servers holding documents on everything from aeronautics and astronomy to music, food, and robotics. Although sources in the humanities are comparatively rare, their number will grow as WAIS expands. From specialized items like the *Bryn Mawr Classical Review* (bryn-mawr-classical-review.src) to the *Journalism Periodicals Index* (journalism.periodicals.src), servers in arts and letters today merely suggest the possibilities. The on-line poetry server (poetry.src) is perhaps a better gauge of what is to come; it contains the complete works of Shakespeare and Yeats. The notion of a distributed literature available for keyword search throughout the network is an exciting one. So, too, is the concept of a comprehensive on-line encyclopedia, a project whose potential can be gauged by examining the *Encyclopaedia Britannica* page on-line; the encyclopedia's search engine was provided by WAIS, Inc. You can examine a number of WAIS publishing projects at the WAIS, Inc. home page. Its URL is:

http://www.wais.com.

Brewster Kahle likes the idea of WAIS as a publishing tool; its beauty is that it can provide the necessary vehicle that enables anyone with information to contribute that knowledge to the network. "Everybody has something to say," Kahle notes. "Everybody has a newsletter, a piece of expertise, a favorite recipe. Maybe they're an expert on car types or IBM PC clones. If we can make a system that helps people share that expertise, we as a societal organism become richer." And because WAIS is interactive, you don't compile information only to have it molder away in an attic. You get the data you need when you need it. Kahle considers WAIS a new medium for publishing. (True to his interests, the founder of the technology keeps a printing press in his basement.)

Accessing WAIS

To tap WAIS resources, four methods are available:

- You can access the system through a local client program. Clients exist for most operating systems. Microsoft Windows users can try the excellent EINet Win-WAIS, while WAIS for Macintosh (formerly WAIStation) is available for the Mac. A character-based interface is provided through swais on Unix machines, while

HINT: If you're interested in seeing a current list of WAIS databases, there are several possibilities. The first is to log on to the WAIS home page on the World Wide Web, at the address previously mentioned:

http://server.wais.com/

There you'll find a list of WAIS databases as one of the hyperlinked destinations; you can search from this page as well, as we'll see later in this chapter.
    Another method is to use the WAIS, Inc. FTP site:

ftp://wais.com/pub/directory-of-servers/wais-sources.tar.Z

Here you will also find a WAIS source description document in two parts, one listing WAIS databases and their descriptions by category, the other listing them in alphabetical order. These documents are maintained by Chris Christoff. European users should try a different URL:

ftp://nic.funet.fi/pub/networking/services/wais/

And users in the Pacific should try:

ftp://archive.orst.edu/pub/doc/wais/

Another method is to set up a Telnet session to the following URL:

telnet://wais.wais.com

By logging on as **wais**, you will be placed in the directory of servers and shown a list of WAIS databases for perusal.
    Background documents about WAIS are likewise available on the Internet. Perhaps the best concentration of such resources is through WAIS, Inc.'s FTP server. If you will start in the /pub directory and work out from there, you will find information about the WAIS system in several subdirectories. This material includes a Frequently Asked Questions document, a list of relevant books, and background information about how WAIS came to be.

xwais is the preferred interface for X Window systems. Other options include mxqwais (OSF-Motif), olwais (Open Windows), waisserver (VMS), and os2wais (OS/2).

- You can access WAIS by Telnet to a remote site. Connect to one of the following URLs, and use **wais** as your username:

      telnet://sunsite.unc.edu
      telnet://wais.wais.com

These sites operate with the swais client. We will begin this chapter with a discussion of how to use swais, but will spend the balance of the chapter using the EINet WinWAIS client, thus illustrating both methods of access.

- You can run a WAIS search through a non-WAIS client. Gopher, for example, can search WAIS databases, and you can also use a World Wide Web browser to perform the same feat. For those with a shell account, the Gopher interface is considerably easier to work with than swais, while those with a SLIP/PPP connection may prefer to stay within the familiar terrain of their Web browser rather than mastering a dedicated WAIS client like EINet WinWAIS.

- You can run a WAIS search through e-mail. We discuss how to perform an e-mail search in Chapter 9.

```
% telnet wais.wais.com
Trying 192.216.46.98 . . .
Connected to wais.wais.com.
Escape character is ' ^ ]'.

SunOS UNIX (wais)

login: wais
Last login: Wed Aug 16 06:25:40 from bubble.yonsei.ac
Welcome to swais, the text-terminal telnet client to WAIS.
Please type user identifier (optional, i.e user@host): gilster@interpath.net
TERM = (vt100)
Starting up. This may take awhile . . .
```

Figure 6.1   Logging in to WAIS at WAIS, Inc.

A Sample WAIS Search Using swais

Let's begin a WAIS session now by setting up a Telnet connection to one of the publicly available WAIS clients. To do so, we use the following URL:

telnet://wais.wais.com

This takes us to the server at WAIS, Inc. The logon sequence is shown in Figure 6.1. Pressing a RETURN when you see the message TERM = (vt100) will set the default terminal emulation.

Figure 6.2 shows the opening screen at wais.wais.com, once you get past the logon material. The screen displays a listing of WAIS databases in alphabetical order and beginning with numbered sources. As you can see by referring to the top right of the screen, some 549 of these databases were available when I logged on. The server for each is listed, along with the name of the database, and any pricing information. A highlight is currently atop the first database on the list; this can be moved by using the arrow keys. Although the databases we're looking at here are available for free, WAIS includes pricing capabilities that will allow commercial users to make information available for a fee. Indeed, the WAIS system should be a significant player in the dissemination of fee-based information from content providers of all kinds.

With 549 databases to search, how do we proceed to home in on our information? The answer is that there are directories of WAIS databases that are themselves searchable. Indeed, if we were to scroll through the list shown in Figure 6.2, we would find the entry for one:

```
205:  [   quake.think.com]  directory-of-servers        Free
```

This entry is just another WAIS database, only its content is a master list of all the WAIS sources known to the server. That means we have a searchable resource that can tell us which WAIS databases are best suited to our actual search. Thus we see the beginnings of a WAIS search paradigm. WAIS searches occur in two major stages:

- The first search examines a directory of servers to see which databases are most applicable to our needs.

```
SWAIS                              Source Selection              Sources: 549
    #           Server                            Source              Cost
001:   [ wais.access.gpo.gov]  103_cong_bills                         Free
002:   [ wais.access.gpo.gov]  104_cong_bills                         Free
003:   [ wais.access.gpo.gov]  1992_cri                               Free
004:   [ wais.access.gpo.gov]  1993_cri                               Free
005:   [ wais.access.gpo.gov]  1994_cri                               Free
006:   [ wais.access.gpo.gov]  1994_hob                               Free
007:   [ wais.access.gpo.gov]  1994_record                            Free
008:   [ wais.access.gpo.gov]  1994_register                          Free
009:   [ wais.access.gpo.gov]  1994_unified_agenda                    Free
010:   [ wais.access.gpo.gov]  1995_cri                               Free
011:   [ wais.access.gpo.gov]  1995_hob                               Free
012:   [ wais.access.gpo.gov]  1995_record                            Free
013:   [ wais.access.gpo.gov]  1995_register                          Free
014:   [ wais.access.gpo.gov]  1995_unified_agenda                    Free
015:   [           archie.au]  aarnet-resource-guide                  Free
016:   [ndadsb.gsfc.nasa.gov]  AAS_jobs                               Free
017:   [ndadsb.gsfc.nasa.gov]  AAS_meeting                            Free
018:   [     munin.ub2.lu.se]  academic_email_conf                    Free

Keywords:

<space> selects, w for keywords, arrows move, <return> searches, q quits, or ?_
```

Figure 6.2   The opening WAIS screen at wais.wais.com.

HINT: Don't be put off by the interface you see in Figure 6.2. swais is not user-friendly, but neither is it downright hostile. The commands I will provide will show you how to use the system. We'll then move to using WAIS through a graphical client, where the value of the rich interface that EINet WinWAIS provides will become obvious. The important point to remember, however, is that even if you are using a shell account and have no access to graphical tools, swais can allow you to search the WAIS database of your choice. It will simply require you to master a larger set of commands.

- The second search targets the databases the first search uncovered, searching them for specific keyword information.

I'll provide the basic swais movement commands in a moment; for now, however, we need a quick way to get to the directory of servers entry, which is item 205 on this list. To do so, we use the **J** key (it must be a capital J). This will move us through the list of WAIS databases one screen at a time, allowing us to quickly get to the directory. The number attached to it may well have changed by the time you read this; just remember that the databases are listed alphabetically and you will be able to find it.

Because many WAIS databases exist that contain information about the Internet itself, let's run a quick search using internet as a keyword. The first thing we have to do is to tell swais which of the 549 databases we want to search. This turns out to be simple. The method is to highlight the database in question and then press the SPACEBAR. An asterisk will appear next to the database entry, telling us that the server has been selected for searching. We can then use the **w** key to run the search. This will produce an immediate result at the bottom of the screen. The help information there has been replaced with information about the keyword entry field, as shown here. Note that I have already entered the search term: internet.

```
Keywords: internet
Enter keywords with spaces between them; <return> to search; ^C to cancel
```

We can enter more than one search term; for now, however, we will keep things simple. We press a RETURN to begin the search. swais queries the server and produces a screen full of hits, as shown in Figure 6.3. Examine this screen with some care. You are looking at a listing of WAIS servers that specifically address themselves to Internet issues. There are actually several screens, as can be seen in the top right-hand corner of the figure, where the following appears:

```
Items: 40
```

We can move between the screens using a variety of possible keys, which I'll discuss in a moment; for now, we'll simply pick a source on this screen. Let's assume we are interested in searching the server called internet_services. To do so, we move the highlight down using the arrow keys. At this point, the going gets more difficult. If we press a RETURN here, we get background information about the server, as shown in Figure 6.4.

Remember, the database we are searching is a reference to all WAIS servers; we should therefore expect that the entries within it will be descriptive documents about these databases. This can be valuable information; it helps us to determine whether a particular database is going to be useful in our searching. But obviously, the screen shown in Figure 6.4 provides no method allowing us to search the internet_services database itself. What to do?

The answer is, we must return to the original screen by entering the **q** command. When we do this, we are returned to our screen of 40 hits from the search on the keyword internet. Pressing an **s** from this screen will take us back to the initial screen, showing all 549 WAIS databases. We know now that we want to search internet_services,

```
SWAIS                           Search Results              Items: 40
   #    Score    Source                      Title            Lines
001:   [1000]  (          19950105) ANU-SocSci-Internet-Rscrces    -1
002:   [ 834]  (          19950105) internet_services              -1
003:   [ 751]  (          19950105) ANU-Internet-Voyager-Guide     -1
004:   [ 697]  (          19950105) Internet-user-glossary         -1
005:   [ 614]  (          19950105) ripe-internet-drafts           -1
006:   [ 563]  (          19950105) internet-intros                -1
007:   [ 542]  (          19950105) internet-standards-merit       -1
008:   [ 540]  (          19950105) internic-internet-drafts       -1
009:   [ 517]  (          19950105) internet-rfcs-europe           -1
010:   [ 514]  (          19950105) internet_info                  -1
011:   [ 499]  (          19950105) SURAnetGuide-All               -1
012:   [ 498]  (          19950105) comp.internet.library          -1
013:   [ 492]  (          19950105) internet-mail                  -1
014:   [ 401]  (          19950105) internet-standards             -1
015:   [ 338]  (          19950105) nsfnet-rfcs                    -1
016:   [ 337]  (          19950105) rfcs                           -1
017:   [ 323]  (          19950105) netinfo                        -1
018:   [ 323]  (          19950105) isoc                           -1


<space> selects, arrows move, w for keywords, s for sources, ? for help_
```

Figure 6.3   A list of hits using the search term internet.

```
(:source
   :version  3
   :ip-address "130.235.162.11"
   :ip-name "munin.ub2.lu.se"
   :tcp-port 210
   :database-name "internet_services"
   :cost 0.00
   :cost-unit :free
   :maintainer "anders@munin.ub2.lu.se"
   :description "Server created with WAIS release 8 b5 on Aug 19 11:38:54 1992 b
y anders@munin.ub2.lu.se

Various documents describing services available on the internet:
* INTERNET DATABASES By Billy Barron,
  University of North Texas VAX System Manager
* Internet mailservers
* The Internet Resources Guide is compiled by the
  NSF  Network Service  Center (nnsc@nnsc.nsf.net) at BBN Systems
* NOT JUST COWS - A Guide to Internet/Bitnet Resources in Agriculture
  and  Related Sciences
  Written and compiled by Wilfred Drew. May 8, 1992

and more to come.
:_
```

Figure 6.4 Generating background information about a server in swais.

so we want to move to its entry on the master list. But first, there is an important piece of housekeeping to be performed. The directory of servers database that we searched originally is still marked as one of the databases to be searched; we can verify this by noting that an asterisk still appears by its entry. Naturally, we don't want to include it in our search of internet_services; it would do nothing but produce redundant hits. So, with the highlight on that entry, press the SPACEBAR again. This will remove the directory from our list of searchable databases; the asterisk will disappear.

Now we can move through the list of servers until we reach the entry for internet_services. We place the highlight over the internet_services entry and press the SPACEBAR. This places internet_services on a list of servers that we have chosen for searching (more than one WAIS database, you see, can be searched simultaneously; although in this search we are using only one database, we could theoretically search many in a single search sweep). Now, with just one WAIS database selected for searching, we should be ready to run our search.

NOTE: Although I've selected only one server to search in this example, we'll soon see that the ability of WAIS to search multiple servers at once is a key to its power. The idea is to use a single interface for a wide variety of distributed information. In this area, WAIS reminds us that the Internet's great push in recent months has been toward a common interface, a lesson driven home by the success of the World Wide Web.

The **w** key is always our keyword command. Pressing it calls up the keyword field, which still contains our original search statement: internet. Let's extend that now by including the word library, assuming we are looking for servers that deal with library materials available over the Internet. Thus, we now have two search words in action:

```
SWAIS                        Search Results                    Items: 40
  #     Score     Source               Title                      Lines
001:    [ 559] (internet_servic)  *   Bibliographical Databases -- Dozens     5
002:    [ 543] (internet_servic)  -Library Catalogs      ftp dla.ucop.edu     8
003:    [ 323] (internet_servic)  -Internet Resrce Guide ftp nnsc.nsf.net     3
004:    [ 313] (internet_servic)              INTERNET DATABASES              8
005:    [ 313] (internet_servic)  -Library of Congress    telnet dra.com o    3
006:    [ 310] (internet_servic)  Cleveland Public Library Catalog           61
007:    [ 310] (internet_servic)  University of Utah Library Card Catalog     61
008:    [ 310] (internet_servic)       * SPECIAL INTERNET CONNECTIONS         4
009:    [ 300] (internet_servic)     library@cme.nist.gov            Manufact
010:    [ 294] (internet_servic)  -Music Newsletter     mail listserv@vm.mari
011:    [ 288] (internet_servic)     service@nic.ddn.mil        Internet RFCs an
012:    [ 287] (internet_servic)  -Dante Project         telnet library.d     3
013:    [ 268] (internet_servic)  Boston University Library Catalog (TOMUS   121
014:    [ 251] (internet_servic)  -FTP Sites/Archives    ftp ocf.berkeley.e   13
015:    [ 243] (internet_servic)  Chapter 2: Library Catalogs               118
016:    [ 242] (internet_servic)  URSUS, University of Maine System Librar   121
017:    [ 241] (internet_servic)     info-server@sh.cs.net       Internet commun
018:    [ 228] (internet_servic)  *  NETLIB -- Netlib is a library of publ     7


<space> selects, arrows move, w for keywords, s for sources, ? for help
```

Figure 6.5   Results of a search using the terms internet and library.

internet and library. When we press the RETURN key to run this search, we produce the results shown in Figure 6.5.

All of these are library-related items maintained at the internet_services WAIS server. We can move the highlight bar between them to choose the ones we want to view. Pressing the SPACEBAR with an item highlighted causes that item to be chosen, and its contents displayed on the screen. We can use the SPACEBAR repeatedly to page through the file. Or, if we decide to read no more of this particular document, we can use a **q** to leave the pager program. Figure 6.6 shows an article on library catalogs as displayed by swais.

Be aware that the **q** command is pesky. Not only does it get us out of the pager program, it also is used when we want to leave swais at the end of a search. More than a few times I've hit the **q** at the wrong moment, only to have swais end my session abruptly. There is no remedy but to be careful.

Let's run through the procedure one more time. We're using the directory of servers initially to search for WAIS servers that pertain to our topic. Once we have determined what they are, we can select one or more of them in which to search. We deselect the directory-of-servers so that we don't run a redundant search including it, and then proceed to search the other servers. We can then view any of our results by pressing the SPACEBAR with the highlight over the item we wish to see.

The Nature of Content Navigation

The simple search just shown tells us much about how WAIS handles information, and also reveals the differences between it and more conventional methods of database retrieval. Brewster Kahle calls the WAIS methodology *content navigation*, a method of searching that allows us to move between large collections of documents and search them using simple English questions. Rather than working with complex Boolean

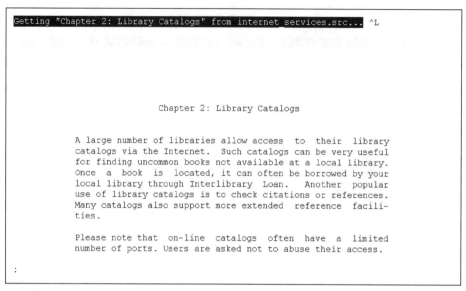

```
Getting "Chapter 2: Library Catalogs" from internet services.src...  ^L




                        Chapter 2: Library Catalogs


          A large number of libraries allow access  to  their  library
          catalogs via the Internet.  Such catalogs can be very useful
          for finding uncommon books not available at a local library.
          Once  a  book  is  located, it can often be borrowed by your
          local library through Interlibrary  Loan.   Another  popular
          use of library catalogs is to check citations or references.
          Many catalogs also support more extended  reference  facili-
          ties.


          Please note that  on-line  catalogs  often  have  a  limited
          number of ports. Users are asked not to abuse their access.

      :
```

Figure 6.6   An article on display through swais.

NOTE: The nature of the swais interface is perhaps the least important part of a WAIS discussion. You should be aware that interface design is in constant flux as new ways of approaching Internet resources are realized. The underlying WAIS engine is what drives your research, not the particular interface you are using at the time. The basic principle of choosing your databases first, then running the search against them, will apply whether you're running swais through a shell account or EINet WinWAIS or WAIS for Macintosh through a SLIP/PPP or a dedicated network connection. As with so many things on the Internet, your own ingenuity will frequently be called into play as modifications to the various interfaces are made. But the time you spend mastering the underlying system and understanding basic WAIS concepts will result in better and more efficient searching, no matter what display you see.

search strategies, as is common with database searches, the user simply enters words that seem germane as the search terms, and then examines a list of resulting documents (Boolean searching, however, remains possible and, in some databases, preferable).

Now the method becomes interesting and innovative. The documents thus retrieved are themselves the user's key to finding further, still more applicable documents. WAIS examines the number of words that the documents have in common with the search terms. Those with many hits appear at the top of the list; they have the highest score. If you examine the screen in Figure 6.5 again, you will see that all these items have been given a ranking, beginning with the number 559 as the highest rank. This ordered list of documents represents stage 1 of our search. We can now use it to refine the search for stage 2.

How? By choosing from among this list those documents that most nearly meet our criteria. Although WAIS has identified numerous documents that contain our search words, it has no way of knowing at this point which of these are most apropos. We can, however, select documents that we like and then ask WAIS to run the search again (provided both server and search engine support the process). Through the technique known as relevance feedback, WAIS will apply itself to locating other documents more nearly like the ones we've chosen. In an ideal world, this would result in a progressive process, narrowing each search until the documents we retrieve are precisely what we want. As we'll see, however, the relevance feedback process is limited by the design of the database and the search engine itself.

Dow Jones News/Retrieval implemented relevance feedback technology when it established its DowQuest service, although DowQuest uses a different search engine than WAIS. Dow Jones users typically place a call by modem to the DJN/R computers, running the search there. Over the Internet, of course, WAIS takes a different approach. Here, the client/server structure of networking comes to the fore. The most exciting aspect of WAIS is that it can query, through its protocols, servers of information at diverse sites, established as data repositories by anyone who wants to set up a server.

The Basic swais Commands

The swais interface we have been dealing with so far provides basic WAIS features, and it is your route into the WAIS database environment. Clearly, an expanded network connection through SLIP, PPP, or a full-fledged Internet connection at work would allow you to use a variety of client software, incorporating pull-down menus, mouse-driven commands, and other graphical features. But swais is what shell account users have available when they contact WAIS through a Telnet connection, and a great deal can be done with it.

The basic swais commands follow. Note that swais works in what is known as *cbreak mode,* which means that, when using a single character command, you don't have to press the RETURN key to activate the command. Look through these commands, and then we'll go onto the network to run some sample swais searches.

swais Movement Commands

Down arrow	Moves the highlight down to the next source (this can also be achieved through a **j** or a **Ctrl-n** command).
Up arrow	Moves up one source (or you can use **k** or **Ctrl-p**).
Ctrl-d	Moves down one screen at a time. You can also use **J** or **Ctrl-v**.
Ctrl-u	Moves up one screen at a time. You can also use **K**.
number	By entering a number, you can move directly to the source number you've specified.
/pattern	Allows you to move directly to the source that begins with your pattern. Thus, you could go directly to eff.documents.src by typing **/eff**, and so on.

swais Search Commands

SPACEBAR	Selects or deselects the current source for use in a search. At the article level, displays the current item.
=	Deselects all sources. This is handy when you want to begin a new search and choose your sources from scratch.

r	Marks the current item as a relevant document. Used in relevance feedback sweeps.
R	Shows you a list of documents you have marked as relevant.
s	Shows you the list of sources and allows you to select new ones.
u	Marks an item to be added to the list of sources for your search.
v	Enables you to view information about the current source or article.
w	Lets you select keywords.
RETURN	Performs the search (after you enter keywords). Or, at the article level, displays the current item. Also can also be used after selecting your sources to ask for a new keyword.

Miscellaneous swais Commands

m	Mails the current item. This is a handy command; you can mail swais results to yourself or to any Internet address.
o	Sets swais options.
h	Produces a basic help display. You can also use the **?** command.
H	Shows the history of the program.
q	Quits the article you are reading. Or, at the main menu, quits swais.
S	If you are using a WAIS client on your own computer, this command saves the text you are reading to a file. But you can't use this command on a public WAIS host. Telnet users should use **m** instead.

WAIS Keyword Limitations

As powerful as it is, WAIS imposes a structure upon database searching that you must keep in mind; otherwise, your results may be startling. Most database searchers are familiar with Boolean logic, which we looked at briefly in Chapter 4. Boolean logic allows you to use a series of terms like AND or OR in a search statement. The search term shortstop AND ozzie, for example, sets off a search looking for documents containing both statements. The term shortstop OR ozzie searches for documents containing one or the other of the terms, and so on. Boolean logic can become quite complicated, which is why information brokers exist and how they earn their fees.

Not all WAIS servers support Boolean logic. If you enter shortstop AND ozzie as your WAIS keywords, these servers will find documents containing the term shortstop, documents containing the term ozzie, and documents containing both. Bear this in mind when you run a search with multiple terms and retrieve hits that don't include one of your terms.

Using a Graphical WAIS Client

We've examined the swais client available to users of shell accounts, and have found that, while the primary WAIS functions are all available through it, many of them are far from intuitive. A graphical client can make the process of using WAIS much simpler, and can drastically shorten search times by letting us concentrate more on our strategies than on the intricacies of using the program itself. The program I recommend for this purpose is EINet WinWAIS, a full-featured WAIS client that includes a graphics file viewer. EINet stands for Enterprise Integration Network, an operation once managed by the Microelectronics and Computer Technology Corporation, a computer consortium based in Austin, Texas. The EINet technology was acquired from MCC by SunRiver Corporation in 1995; among its leading products is the Galaxy directory service we examined in Chapter 2. The EINet enterprise is now known as TradeWave Corporation.

You can retrieve the WinWAIS software at the following URL:

ftp://ftp.einet.net/einet/pc/ewais204.exe

There is also a "zipped" version, and it makes no difference which you choose to use. The WinWAIS program was once shareware but has since been made available as freeware. Full installation instructions are provided in the form of a text file that accompanies the software.

To demonstrate WAIS in a graphical setting, let's examine how we might run a session, including the use of relevance feedback to tighten up our results. I'm interested in learning more about issues of privacy and network communications. One of the great boons of the network environment is our ability to move quickly between widely distributed sites of data. But of course the counterweight is the question of how much information we are making available about ourselves and our businesses in the network environment. Certain WAIS databases seem likely to contain information that could help us understand these issues, and what current thinking about them is.

For this search, we will use four WAIS databases: risks-digest.src compiles the postings on the USENET newsgroup comp.risks, which discusses the problems and dangers associated with computing technology; eff-talk.src is an archive of the comp.org.eff.talk newsgroup, in which discussions relating to the Electronic Frontier Foundation take place. The EFF is an activist organization that is attempting to establish basic principles of law as they apply to computer networking. The isoc.src database contains material collected by The Internet Society, which promotes the study of key network issues, while computers-freedom-and-privacy.src contains the text of the proceedings from the Conference on Computers, Freedom and Privacy II, courtesy of the Association of Computing Machinery in New York.

HINT: How did I decide which sources to use in this search? The selection of sources is always a key issue, and it remains one of the most frustrating aspects of WAIS use. The first thing I did was to run keywords like privacy and freedom past a directory of servers, to determine which WAIS databases contained useful material. Unfortunately, while WAIS works excellently with the documents within such databases, its directory system is poorly indexed, and you often miss key sources because a particular database has not been thoroughly annotated. In the real world, it's often necessary to work through the list of databases, scanning down the list to see if any catch your eye by virtue of their title. This is an inelegant way to conduct Internet searching, but in some cases, it's the only recourse.

STEP 1: SELECTING OUR SOURCES

We can't search WAIS without telling our client program which sources we want to examine. I have begun this session by calling up EINet WinWAIS. The initial screen is shown in Figure 6.7. You can see that we have moved a long way from the sparse swais

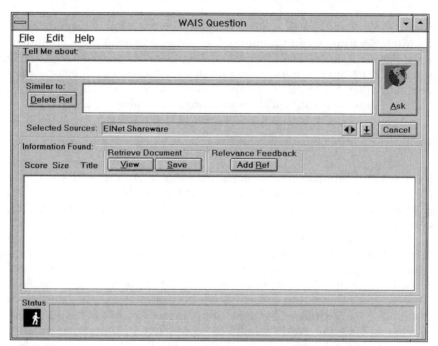

Figure 6.7 The primary screen for EINet WinWAIS, a graphical WAIS client.

client. Here, we are in the presence of pull-down menus and mouse-driven commands. The search screen provides a keyword field, and another field that lets us set up relevance feedback searches, as we'll do in a moment. Launching the search is simply a matter of clicking on the Ask button, which displays results in the lower box.

But first, let's take a look at how to choose a database to search. By default, the program arrives with two sources already selected. One is a database of information about EINet software; the other is a directory of servers. These sources are available for searching by first pulling down the Edit menu, then choosing the Select Sources option. You will see the screen shown in Figure 6.8.

As you can see, two databases are available; one of them, the EINet Shareware database, has been selected for searching. Were we to run a search at this point, that is the database we would search. The first choice, then, is to deselect the EINet database by highlighting its entry in the Selected Sources field and then clicking on the Remove button. Doing this empties the Selected Sources field. We must then highlight the directory of servers and click on the Select button to use it. Its name will then appear in the Selected Sources field. The graphical WinWAIS client starts out with the assumption that to locate other servers, you will go through the directory of servers, which contains proper address information about each. So getting the directory of servers selected for use is the critical step.

We have already made our choices about which sources to use, in the form of the four WAIS databases previously mentioned. Now what we need to do is to tell WinWAIS to use those four sources. This involves searching the directory of servers for those four databases, so it can acquire the necessary address information and place the databases in the WinWAIS source collection. Perhaps the easiest method to acquire a source is to

Figure 6.8 Examining WinWAIS' sources screen to see which databases are available for searching.

enter its name in the keyword field. In Figure 6.9, for example, I have entered the term eff in the Tell Me about field that WinWAIS offers, hoping to find the database called eff-talk.src. And, as you can see, this database appears at the top of the list.

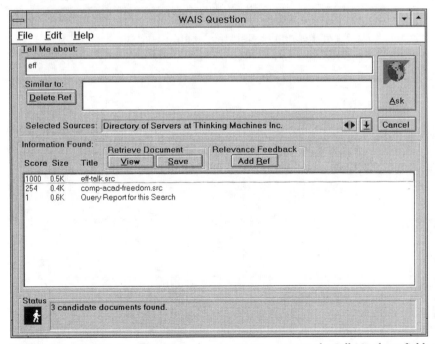

Figure 6.9 Finding the eff database by entering its name in the Tell Me about field. This is a quick way to acquire the necessary information to use a particular database.

This method will find any database as long as we know its name, and will supply WinWAIS with the information it needs to use that database in any subsequent search.

STEP 2: SELECTING PARTICULAR SERVERS FOR THE SEARCH

Keep in mind what's happening here. We are searching a directory of servers to locate the specific servers we want to use in the search. We have discovered that we can find each server, one at a time, by using its name in the keyword field as we search the directory. Now we must tell WinWAIS that we want to add each of these sources to its own list.

To do so with the eff-talk.src database, I simply highlight its entry on the results screen and click on the View button. The screen shown in Figure 6.10 will appear. Notice what has happened. First, information about the database itself is presented. Second, we are given the option of saving this database by clicking on a button. And we have three save options:

- We can save the source but not select it for immediate use.
- We can save the source and select it for use.
- We can save the source, select it, and run the same query past it.

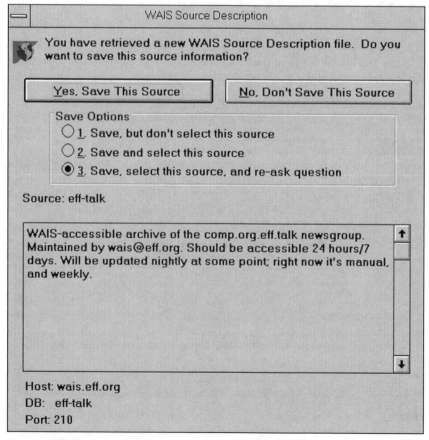

Figure 6.10 Background information about the eff-talk database, along with options for its use.

The correct option for adding the eff-talk.src database to our list is the first; we save the source and but do not select it for immediate use (after all, the source we want to keep using until we have located all four WAIS databases is the directory of servers; only then will we deselect the directory and proceed to search the other four). We will follow this method for all four of the databases that we want to search, first finding them in the directory and then saving the source information to our WAIS client.

When the process is complete, we should have all four servers available to Win-WAIS. Now we need to return to the Select WAIS Sources screen to deselect the directory of servers, which we no longer need, and select the four we want to use. When the process is complete, the Select WAIS Sources screen should look like Figure 6.11. All four databases are now ready to be searched.

STEP 3: RUNNING THE INITIAL SEARCH

We now are ready to select a keyword and run our search. To do so, we must enter our keywords in the Tell Me about field on the main WinWAIS screen. Let's use the term privacy and see what we get. Entering that term and clicking on the Ask button, we get a series of results, as shown in Figure 6.12.

You can see that we've retrieved quite a few hits; it's necessary to use the scroll bar to the right of the results column to see all of them. As with swais, each of the results is ranked according to what the WAIS system assumes to be its significance to it. Thus the top item is marked with a perfect 1000; WAIS thinks it is precisely what we need, based upon word counts. As the list continues, the relevance ranking of each item progressively diminishes.

We must not, however, accept these results at face value. Remember, WAIS is making a guess at what we'll find useful, based upon a specific set of algorithms. What we want to do is to hunt through the entire list to find any items that may be close to what

Figure 6.11   The revised sources screen, showing the new servers we have added to the list.

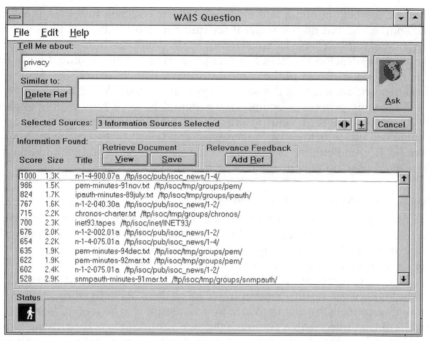

Figure 6.12 Results of searching in WinWAIS under the term privacy.

we want, no matter how WAIS may rank them. We will then use these items to run a revised search using relevance feedback.

HINT: If you have sharp eyes, you may have noticed that Figure 6.12 lists three information sources as selected, rather than four. What has happened is that one of the four databases we have chosen to search is temporarily unavailable. You will often find this to be the case, as servers are shut down for maintenance and upgrading. Some WAIS databases are more reliable than others, so don't be surprised if you wind up searching on a subset of your original choice of sources. In any case, we have been able to run our search on privacy past three of our four sources. We could probably run the same search the following day and find that the missing database was available again.

STEP 4: MARKING ITEMS FOR OUR NEXT SWEEP

Using the list of documents we have retrieved, we have several options. We could highlight any specific item we wanted to see and click on the View button to examine it; a RETURN does the same thing. In most cases, this is how we will use WinWAIS—we'll run a single search and then examine the results. Figure 6.13 shows a document as viewed in this way.

However, we want to use relevance feedback this time around to make our list of hits still closer to what we want. To do so, we must mark those items on our initial list of hits

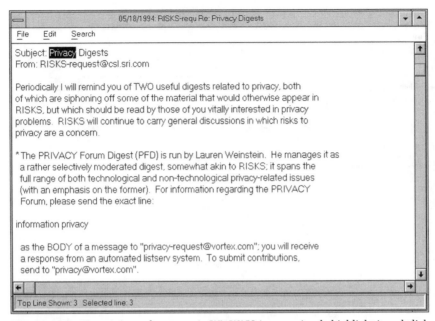

Figure 6.13 Examining a document in WinWAIS is easy; simply highlight it and click on the View button.

that most closely match what we are after. We do this by moving the highlight bar to the item in question and then clicking on the Add Ref button. This selects that document as a relevant document, and adds it to the list for the subsequent sweep through the data using relevance feedback.

HINT: No matter which client you're using, the principles we're examining here apply in any WAIS search. The swais client, for example, allows you to select an item as relevant for a relevancy feedback sweep by using the **r** key. Highlight the item in question and press the **r** key; swais will keep a list of all such items and, when you run the second search, will look for documents that are like the ones you have marked. You can use the **R** command with swais to see the list of relevant documents. The beauty of WinWAIS, of course, is that it puts the entire process into a more visually obvious environment.

For the purposes of our search, I have selected certain items from the list of hits that I think are particularly useful. I have moved through the list and clicked the Add Ref button with the highlight over each item I want to use. In Figure 6.14, I have chosen a number of items for relevance feedback. Note that several appear in the Similar to field in WinWAIS, while others could be seen by using the scroll arrow to the right of the Similar to box. We can now use these items to run a second search using the same keyword.

Step 5: Putting Relevance Feedback to Work

To run the second search, all we need to do is to resubmit our query by clicking on the Ask button. Our original search term is still there and we can leave it where it is. What we are doing, after all, is running the same search, but this time we have specified to WinWAIS

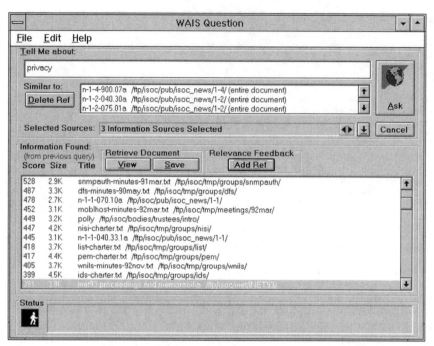

Figure 6.14 Note the inset items selected for the relevance feedback search. WinWAIS will use these to find new documents that match our preferences.

that certain items are more likely to be what we want than others. WinWAIS will take this information into account as it goes to work on our behalf. The new list of results will, theoretically, represent a more accurate search. You can see these results in Figure 6.15.

Again, we have a list of hits. But compare this list to the previous one and you will see that the two are not the same. Using the information we supplied it, WinWAIS has searched again for documents that are closer to those we want. The second list is, theoretically, a more accurate search result.

I say theoretically because, in this case, the WAIS servers behind the WinWAIS client are not a terribly powerful implementation of WAIS. Yes, we can run relevance feedback searches with them, but in practice, the results turn out to be not much different from our initial screen of results (and remember, not all servers support relevance feedback). More sophisticated WAIS servers and clients, however, can perform exceedingly focused searches using the WAIS techniques. The WAIS implementation that searches the *Encyclopaedia Britannica* on-line, for example, is a remarkable example of a full-featured WAIS engine at work. Whereas most CD-ROM based encyclopedias can provide you with articles that include hyperlinks, the Britannica on-line edition can search the full text of the encyclopedia for your search term. You will thus retrieve hits that would be invisible to any other form of search engine, and will not be reliant upon the skills of an indexer to determine what you should see. You can check this out for yourself at the following URL:

http://www.pathfinder.com/

There is a link here to the *Encyclopaedia Britannica* pages.

Figure 6.15 Results of a relevance feedback search; notice that, while many of the items are identical, we have a new sorting order, reflecting WinWAIS' attempt to home in on what we want.

HINT: How many relevance feedback searches should you run? Theoretically, by continuing to use relevance feedback until the results you are generating stay roughly the same, you will have exhausted the system's ability to refine the search any further. In practice, your search will most likely include only a single relevance feedback sweep. To do more will be counterproductive, using up valuable search time for little in the way of significant results.

The Basic WinWAIS Commands

The WinWAIS screen, like that of Wsarchie, presents the primary commands necessary for using the client, while more specialized parameters can be adjusted through the program's menus. Let's briefly review the primary data entry points on the main WinWAIS screen.

Tell Me about   The keyword entry field. You can search any WAIS database by entering your keyword(s) in this field; the search will be run past whichever WAIS databases you have selected.

Similar to   Relevancy feedback items are shown in this box. When you choose an item to use in a relevancy feedback search, it will be listed here, with the addition of a scroll arrow if the list gets too long to appear in its entirety in the box.

Delete Ref	Removes the highlighted item from your relevancy feedback list.
Ask	This button is used to submit your keyword query to the WAIS system.
Cancel	Cancels the current WAIS request.
Selected Sources	This box tells you how many WAIS databases you have selected for the search. Using the scroll arrow, you can view the current sources.
View	By clicking this button with a particular item highlighted in the box below, you are asking to see the item in question. It will appear in a separate window. WinWAIS will launch the appropriate application for viewing the file.
Save	Allows you to save a particular item to disk.
Add Ref	Allows you to add an item to your relevancy feedback list. Highlight the item in question and push this button.
Status	Displays messages describing the progress of the current search.

The key to using WinWAIS successfully is understanding that the choice of WAIS databases is critical. The WinWAIS model is designed so that your initial search is on a directory of servers, which allows you to uncover specific databases that will serve in your second search. Thus we have a basic WAIS model:

- An initial search of a directory of servers that allows you to choose one or more databases.
- A second search of the databases you've thus uncovered.

And, as we've likewise seen, when you already know about databases that can be useful, you can simply enter their names in the search field when searching the directory of servers, and then save them as sources for your search. The WinWAIS menu commands are listed in the following sections.

THE FILE MENU

New Question	Produces a dialog box allowing you to choose sources for a new search.
Open Question	Each WAIS question is actually a combination of keywords and selected sources of information; these are saved as files with the .ask extension. You can save a question for later use, including its keywords and sources. The Open Question command lets you use or edit a previously saved question.
Save Question	Choosing this option saves the current question. You might do this, for example, if you were trying to maintain a regular watch on a particular database's holdings, scanning it periodically for updates. By saving the question, you could simply choose it from a list of saved questions and run it again, without having to reenter all the source and keyword information.

Delete Question	Produces a dialog box that allows you to delete a question.
Exit	Exits WinWAIS.

THE EDIT MENU

Select Sources	Produces a dialog box allowing you to choose which source(s) you want to use for a search.
Clear Query Info	Clears the keyword screen of all information.
Preferences	Produces a user preferences screen, allowing you to establish in which directories you want WinWAIS to save information, questions, and other information. Also allows you to set up system defaults, such as the initial database to be searched.

HINT: If you're a Macintosh user, you'll want to look into a Macintosh version of the Win-WAIS software we've just examined. The program is available at numerous sites around the Internet. Try this URL:

> ftp:// ftp:/wais.com/pub/freeware/mac/mac-wais-129.hqx

Bear in mind that if you can't track down a client at a site I've mentioned, it may be because of changes at the site. In that case, an archie search will doubtless turn up other download sites for your program. And remember that complete client information for a variety of operating systems is provided through the Frequently Asked Questions document that covers WAIS. You can get it from this URL:

> ftp://wais.com/pub/wais-doc/waisfaq.txt

A Routine WAIS Strategy

As with other Internet search tools, you should consider developing a strategy you will use whenever you approach WAIS. By keeping a particular format of searching in mind, you ensure that your search remains focused. Moreover, given the fact that each of the search tools we've examined makes particular demands upon your memory and patience, it's helpful to have a strategy blocked out no matter what your search subject matter might be. Later in the search, you can depart from the canned approach to refine and tweak your strategy as the need arises.

Here, then, are the basic components of a suggested WAIS strategy:

1. **Download and use a list of WAIS servers.** We've already examined how to get two different text files listing current WAIS servers, and you should keep updating these files as new servers come on-line.

   But wait. Can't you just jump into WAIS and search a directory of servers? The answer is yes, but my experience on the system has proven to me that there is no substitute for a methodical, off-line survey of available servers before you attempt your search. As good as WAIS is—and at times it is quite good—it won't always find the best servers for the topic you need. When I ran the previous search past the directory of servers, for example, and searched it under the term privacy, it came up with exactly one hit: the computers-freedom-and-privacy.src server. The other sites, so useful in our search, did not appear.

The reason is obvious: The computers-freedom-and-privacy.src server is the only one that contained the search term privacy in its title, or as a keyword in the .src file. The lack of effective indexing, then, keeps us from making optimum use of the directory of servers. To keep up with WAIS events and to stay on top of new server sites as they come on-line, download and use the text files listing these sites. And periodically browse through one of the Telnet sites, like that at wais.wais.com, which lists all the servers. Believe me, there is nothing more frustrating than realizing *after* a lengthy search that there was a different server you could have included in your search that contained exactly what you needed.

2. **Use as few servers as you can.** True, one of the beauties of WAIS is that you can search multiple servers; in fact, this ability is crucial for some kinds of searches. But highly focused searches may require only one server; adding others only limits the number of hits from the one most likely to meet your requirements. Suppose, for example, that I were searching for the meaning of the acronym IEEE. The server acronyms.src would be all I would need to solve this search puzzle, quickly giving me the result (Institute of Electrical and Electronics Engineers).

3. **Think on your feet about which server to use.** The choice of servers is by no means intuitive; I could have found the preceding information as well, for example, in the internet-user-glossary.src server. WAIS often requires experimentation and a hefty dose of common sense to generate what you need. After a while, you will learn to stop looking for an immediately obvious solution and start casting about for more subtle ways to solve your problem.

4. **Begin your search with broad terms; narrow as necessary.** You might think that the quickest way to run a search is to be extremely precise. But all too often, the results of such an approach are hits that seem to have no bearing on what you need. Examine, for instance, what happens when I search the directory of servers for WAIS sites dealing with cooking. An amateur chef, I want to find out what recipes my fellow network denizens have been contributing to the gastronomic world. I set up a WAIS search under a series of keywords, reasoning that the more terms I use, the more precise the result will be. Thus my search terms are recipes, food, cooking, and online. The result is shown in Figure 6.16.

At first glance, I seem to have hit pay dirt; after all, I've retrieved 40 hits, 12 of which are shown in the figure. But actually, most of these items are inconsequential for my search, as WAIS itself attests by giving them low rankings. Nonetheless, I know by now that regardless of what ranking WAIS has assigned, I must go through the list with care to ensure that something doesn't slip past that I can use. And all this takes up time.

I can do better by going to a single search term, and keeping it broad enough to take in my topic. The term is recipes. The result is a single server, a precise hit in the form of the recipes.src database.

Remember: Your time is valuable; anything you can do that both keeps your search targeted and relieves you of the obligation to sift through long lists of irrelevant material is all to the good. Stay flexible, and think of single concepts that encapsulate your search needs.

Figure 6.16   Using multiple search terms for precise results.

5. **Use relevance feedback sparingly.** We've already seen that relevance feedback can produce a reordered list of documents, with some items that were ranked low on the scale now given higher ranking, and vice versa. But in its present state of development, relevance feedback is comparatively awkward to use, while the benefits of employing it are relatively minor. We still have to work through each screen of information to be sure that WAIS hasn't misassigned a document that we really do want to read. In terms of conserving our search time, then, relevance feedback adds little value. Refinements of the WAIS model and an ever-widening pool of servers will eventually change this; for now, however, consider relevance feedback no more than an option.

6. **Mail documents to yourself.** If you're using swais, you can send any relevant documents from your search to yourself by mail. Use the **m** command to do so. The advantage of this is that you can then print the documents for later study.

WAIS through the World Wide Web

One of the easiest ways to run a quick WAIS search is through the World Wide Web. WAIS, Inc., for example, makes numerous WAIS databases available through an intuitive Web page that can be found at this URL:

http://www.wais.com/newhomepages/wais-dbs.html

The methodology is simple. You scroll through a list of WAIS databases and choose the one you want to search. Then you enter your keyword in the Find field and click on the Search button to launch the operation. You can see the primary search page at WAIS, Inc. in Figure 6.17. Not shown in the figure, but available by scrolling down through this page, is a lengthy list of hyperlinks, each to a WAIS database. A click on one of these hyperlinks reveals background information about any of the WAIS sources.

Using WAIS through the Web actually involves two possibilities. If you proceed from the primary search screen, as shown in Figure 6.17, you will be searching a directory of servers, looking for sources that fit your keywords. If you choose a hyperlink to go directly to a source, you will be searching within that particular database. This matches the two parts of the WAIS search that we've already discussed, the first being the sweep through a directory, the second being a targeted search of a particular database. The only disadvantage of using a Web client to run such a search is that you are limited to searching one database at a time, rather than multiple ones, as you could do with Win-WAIS and even swais.

Let's examine how a typical search might run using the Web to tap WAIS. I would like to learn about the Mabinogion, the great medieval Welsh text based upon the region's mythology and heroic legend. This collection is preserved in a manuscript called *The Red Book of Hergest,* dating from the fourteenth century. What can I find out about it, and are there any digital versions of this fascinating work available on the Internet?

The first step is to query the directory of servers, which, in this case, means searching from the Web page whose URL I just gave you. And because I'm curious about what

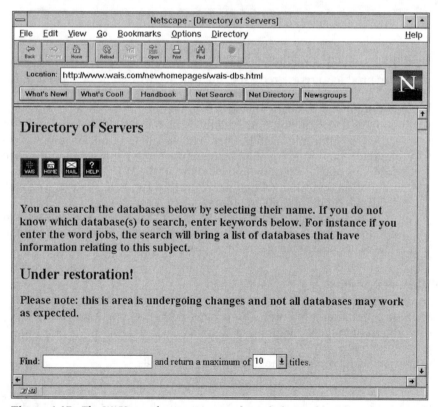

Figure 6.17 The WAIS search screen as seen through the World Wide Web.

Figure 6.18 Results of a search using the keyword language.

kind of language databases might be available in general, I'll use the keyword language just to see what happens. I soon retrieve a set of hits, as shown in Figure 6.18.

Most of the hits concern computer languages, which is no surprise, since so much of the WAIS database work has been on behalf of technologically oriented enterprises. But if we page through the list, a variety of other things appear. There are databases about languages in the Pacific, and one that covers Tibet. Another focuses on French, and yet another on the endangered aboriginal languages of Australia. Mixed among these hits is one that fits the bill for this search. It's a WAIS source that collects postings from the WELSH-L mailing list. You can see its description in Figure 6.19. All that's necessary to look at such a description is to click on the hyperlink for the database in question.

And as you can see in Figure 6.19, we are presented with a keyword field in which we can enter our search term, along with a button to launch the query. By entering the search term mabinogion and clicking on the Submit Query button, I launch the search, and soon pull up numerous hits from the mailing list archives here. A sample, which answers the question about the Mabinogion, is shown in Figure 6.20.

Remember, the one drawback of the seemingly effortless Web interface is that you can't search multiple databases at the same time. The method, if you needed to search more than one, would be to move from one database to the next, running the same search each time. It's more cumbersome than using WinWAIS, but as we've seen, search-

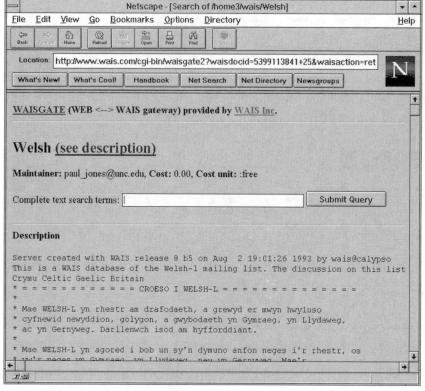

Figure 6.19 Examining the description of a database; this one specializes in Welsh literature.

ing in this environment is quite easy to do, and you can run useful WAIS searches using these methods.

Using Gopher to Access WAIS

Using WAIS with a client like WinWAIS can be a joy, as the client takes much of the difficulty out of our navigation. And we've just seen how easy it is to use WAIS with a World Wide Web browser. Users of shell accounts, however, are limited to the swais interface to do their work. swais can be a powerful tool, but no one would accuse it of elegance or ease of use.

My view, then, is that swais users should master the program to acquire a thorough grounding in WAIS fundamentals. From there on, however, they may want to consider using WAIS through the Gopher interface, if their searching needs are relatively straightforward. I restrict this statement to simple searches because, unlike swais, Gopher does not allow you to select multiple WAIS servers to search with a single sweep through the data. This means you must accurately target your databases one at a time, adding to your search time if you are trying to cover much ground. On the other hand, many of the databases we'd like to examine are unique; perhaps half of my own search time is con-

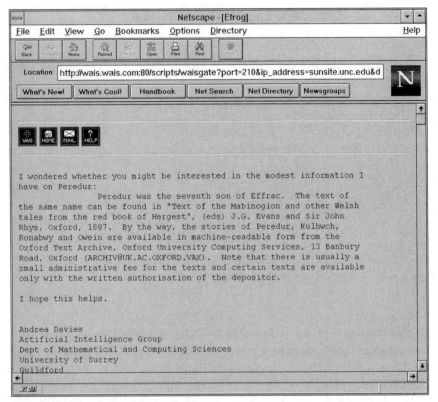

Figure 6.20 A sample of the hits I generated while searching for information about the Mabinogion.

centrated within a single database at a time. For these searches, Gopher allows me to use a familiar interface and run my searches quickly.

For this example, I am going to use the Gopher at the University of Minnesota. The URL is:

gopher://gopher.micro.umn.edu/

And because I'm using a character-based Gopher client for this search, I'll use the command **gopher gopher.micro.umn.edu** at the system prompt. From the opening Gopher screen, I'll look for a relevant item, like this:

```
8.  Other Gopher and Information Servers/
```

This one seems the most likely, as it points to a wide range of services. Taking it, I move on to a submenu item:

```
14. WAIS Based Information/
```

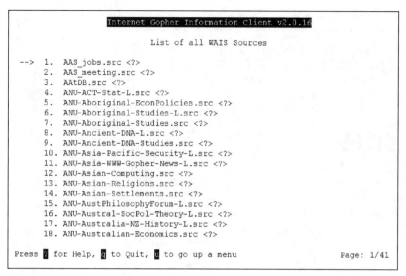

```
┌──────────────────────────────────────────────────────────────────┐
│              Internet Gopher Information Client v2.0.16            │
│                                                                    │
│                      List of all WAIS Sources                      │
│                                                                    │
│  -->  1.  AAS_jobs.src <?>                                         │
│       2.  AAS_meeting.src <?>                                      │
│       3.  AAtDB.src <?>                                            │
│       4.  ANU-ACT-Stat-L.src <?>                                   │
│       5.  ANU-Aboriginal-EconPolicies.src <?>                     │
│       6.  ANU-Aboriginal-Studies-L.src <?>                        │
│       7.  ANU-Aboriginal-Studies.src <?>                          │
│       8.  ANU-Ancient-DNA-L.src <?>                                │
│       9.  ANU-Ancient-DNA-Studies.src <?>                         │
│      10.  ANU-Asia-Pacific-Security-L.src <?>                     │
│      11.  ANU-Asia-WWW-Gopher-News-L.src <?>                      │
│      12.  ANU-Asian-Computing.src <?>                             │
│      13.  ANU-Asian-Religions.src <?>                             │
│      14.  ANU-Asian-Settlements.src <?>                           │
│      15.  ANU-AustPhilosophyForum-L.src <?>                       │
│      16.  ANU-Austral-SocPol-Theory-L.src <?>                     │
│      17.  ANU-Australia-NZ-History-L.src <?>                      │
│      18.  ANU-Australian-Economics.src <?>                        │
│                                                                    │
│  Press ? for Help, q to Quit, u to go up a menu      Page: 1/41   │
└──────────────────────────────────────────────────────────────────┘
```

Figure 6.21   Using WAIS through Gopher.

Moving through these screens, I am able to generate a screen of WAIS servers, as shown in Figure 6.21. We are looking at a long list of WAIS servers. If you examine the bottom right-hand side of the screen, you will see that this is 1 screen out of 41 possibilities. In fact, some 726 WAIS servers are listed here. With so many servers, the problem is to track down which servers you need without spending half the day doing it.

As we did at the WAIS, Inc. site, then, we need to consult a directory of servers. And, in fact, there are numerous server directories from a number of sites. The one I urge you to use is directory-of-servers.src, which is likely to be the most up to date and comprehensive. As of this writing, it was found on the menu at the gopher.micro.umn.edu site as item 410:

```
410.  directory-of-servers.src <?>
```

Of course, these numbers will change (on the Internet, change is a daily and even hourly phenomenon). But to shorten our search, we can always use the Gopher search function from the main screen. To do so, we use this command:

/ directory-of-servers

The slash tells Gopher that we're searching; we could, of course, have searched under directory, or even dir, but this search takes us precisely to where we need to be.

I'm interested in tracking down a poem by William Butler Yeats. I know that it had something to do with the sea and with white birds. To find it, I will need to locate a server that specializes in literature. Thus, with the arrow pointing to the directory-of-servers.src server, I press the RETURN key to set WAIS to work. Soon I have a list of servers that fit my search term literature, as shown in Figure 6.22.

From here, I choose the most likely candidate, which is called poetry.src. Putting the arrow on it, I press the RETURN key again, calling up the search screen. Now I enter my

Figure 6.22   Servers found searching under the term literature.

term; I'll use white birds, since I remember the term from the poem I read so long ago. WAIS ponders this request and then generates a screen of hits, as shown in Figure 6.23.

In this screen, we find that Yeats used the term in other poems, most particularly in the early "Wanderings of Oisin" (a lovely poem laced with Celtic echoes); we also see hits from Shakespeare and Sylvia Plath. But my poem is found as item 5, where it is listed as *WhiteBirds*. I move the pointer to this item and press another RETURN to see the poem. Figure 6.24 shows the result.

If you find this kind of literary excavation as exciting as I do, ponder both the implications of the technology and the current liabilities it possesses. Yes, we can find poetry by keyword searches using a distributed database; we have no idea where the server for poetry.src is and it really doesn't affect our search. You can imagine a future in which vast quantities of library information are made available in similar fashion, extending literacy and opening opportunities for research throughout the world.

On the other hand, we run up against the fact that the Internet in its present form contains only the smallest smattering of such information. We're out of luck, for example, if we're searching for most poets; we've got Yeats and Shakespeare, but where are Milton and Eliot, Herrick and Wyatt, Hopkins and Tennyson? What we need is further growth of the basic WAIS infrastructure. More libraries need to be built along the information highway.

Using waissearch for Specific Servers

What do you do if you know about a specific WAIS server that you'd like to search? As we've seen, you have several options. The first is to query a directory of servers, like the one at wais.wais.com, using the name of your server as the search term to call it up; you then add it to your list of sources and search. Another is to use Gopher, which presents

```
┌─────────────────────────────────────────────────────────────────┐
│              ▐Internet Gopher Information Client v1.11▌            │
│                                                                   │
│                     poetry.src: white birds                       │
│                                                                   │
│  --> 1.  WanderingsOfOisin   /mas/library/Poetry/currently-waised/Yeats/. │
│      2.  The_Rape_of_Lucrece   ../currently-waised/Shakespeare/Various_Poems/. │
│      3.  DramaticPoem   /mas/library/Poetry/currently-waised/Yeats/. │
│      4.  Venus_and_Adonis   ..try/currently-waised/Shakespeare/Various_Poems/. │
│      5.  WhiteBirds   /mas/library/Poetry/currently-waised/Yeats/. │
│      6.  FatherOHart   /mas/library/Poetry/currently-waised/Yeats/. │
│      7.  BaileAndAillinn   /mas/library/Poetry/currently-waised/Yeats/. │
│      8.  QueenMaeve   /mas/library/Poetry/currently-waised/Yeats/. │
│      9.  The Snowman on the Moor          Sylvia Plath.           │
│     10.  Sonnet-98   ..s/library/Poetry/currently-waised/Shakespeare/Sonnets/. │
│     11.  Commendatory_Poems_and_Prefaces   ..aised/Shakespeare/Various_Poems/. │
│     12.  The_Phoenix_and_the_Turtle   ..tly-waised/Shakespeare/Various_Poems/. │
│     13.  CivilWar   /mas/library/Poetry/currently-waised/Yeats/. │
│     14.  GiftOfHarun   /mas/library/Poetry/currently-waised/Yeats/. │
│     15.  Dream with Clam-Diggers          Sylvia Plath.          │
│     16.  Spinster          Sylvia Plath.                         │
│     17.  Sonnet-A_Lovers_Complaint   ../currently-waised/Shakespeare/Sonnets/. │
│     18.  Silences                        Gilbert Sorrentino.     │
│                                                                   │
│  Press ▐ for Help, ▐ to Quit, ▐ to go up a menu      Page: 1/3    │
└─────────────────────────────────────────────────────────────────┘
```

Figure 6.23   Searching the works of Yeats for the term white birds.

NOTE: Gopher is an easy way to use WAIS, especially after we've dealt with the relatively unintuitive swais interface. But Gopher does possess two major drawbacks. Using it, you can't tap more than a single WAIS database at a time; nor can you use relevance feedback techniques to refine your search. Since both of these can be helpful WAIS features, it's clear that a Gopher search is best when your needs are highly targeted. Even then, you must be willing to sift through the resultant screens with great care to find what you need. WAIS will be unable to reshape the output through subsequent searching and relevance techniques.

you with a list of servers. But there is a third alternative, which allows you to go directly to a server. It is a handy, text-based client program called waissearch. You use it through a shell account.

The command structure of waissearch is simple enough. You enter the **waissearch** command and follow it with this information: the WAIS host server, the WAIS source you want to access, the port number (if it is other than 210, which is the standard port for WAIS), the WAIS database you are trying to reach, and the keyword for your search. The syntax, then, is as follows:

waissearch -h *source* **-p** *portnumber* **-d** *database keyword*

This is clumsy, but it works. I'll search the weather.src server to see if I can get today's weather forecast as an example. To do so, I enter the following command at my system's command prompt:

% waissearch -h wais.wais.com -d weather weather

```
cap{THE WHITE BIRDS}

I WOULD that we were, my beloved, white birds on the
foam of the sea!
We tire of the flame of the meteor, before it can fade
and flee;
And the flame of the blue star of twilight, hung low
on the rim of the sky,
Has awaked in our hearts, my beloved, a sadness that
may not die.
A weariness comes from those dreamers, dew-dabbled,
the lily and rose;
Ah, dream not of them, my beloved, the flame of the
meteor that goes,
Or the flame of the blue star that lingers hung low in
the fall of the dew:
For I would we were changed to white birds on the
wandering foam: I and you!
I am haunted by numberless islands, and many a
Danaan shore,
Where Time would surely forget us, and Sorrow come
near us no more;
--More--(82%)[Press space to continue, 'q' to quit.]
```

Figure 6.24 Yeats' poem "The White Birds" displayed on screen. Note that the search terms are highlighted.

Note the form this request takes. I've specified the wais.wais.com site for my search. I haven't entered a port number, because waissearch will default to port 210, which is standard for WAIS servers. I've entered -d weather to name my database (I can leave off the .src suffix and waissearch will understand). I've followed the database name with my search word, which is itself weather. The response comes through quickly; here's a sample:

```
Search Response:
NumberOfRecordsReturned:   40
1:  Score: 1000, lines: 473 'WX-TALK.INFO'
2:  Score:  885, lines:  39 'weather.help'
3:  Score:  500, lines: 335 'Interior-British-Columbia.txt'
4:  Score:  346, lines: 137 'US-National-Summary.txt'
5:  Score:  308, lines:  31 'Atlanta-GA.txt'
6:  Score:  308, lines: 125 'Austin-TX.txt'
7:  Score:  308, lines:  34 'Baltimore-MD.txt'
8:  Score:  308, lines:  31 'Boston-MA.txt'
9:  Score:  308, lines:  44 'Charlotte-NC.txt'
10: Score:  308, lines:  40 'Chicago-IL.txt'
11: Score:  308, lines:  34 'Cincinnati-OH.txt'
12: Score:  308, lines:  32 'Cleveland-OH.txt'
13: Score:  308, lines: 160 'Coastal-British-Columbia.txt'
14: Score:  308, lines:  65 'Detroit-MI.txt'
15: Score:  308, lines: 125 'Houston-TX.txt'
16: Score:  308, lines:  32 'Knoxville-TN.txt'
```

waissearch lets me choose which forecast I want by selecting its number and then pressing the RETURN key. I choose item 4, which seems to be a summary of weather across the United States. Soon a lengthy forecast scrolls across my screen.

HINT: waissearch can be helpful if you have a specific site you'd like to query and want to go right to it, without going through the rigamarole of dealing with a directory of servers first. But be sure to turn on your capture buffer when you're dealing with this program, or the results of your search may scroll past you before you know it.

Interesting WAIS Sites

I wouldn't even try to give you a comprehensive list of WAIS servers in this book. The medium is changing so fast that any such listing becomes obsolete almost immediately. If you do want to see a list of currently available sources, the best procedure is to download server site information in a text file from the address given earlier, or to study it on-line.

Certain WAIS servers are, however, of more than passing interest to the generalist. I found myself building a list of servers that I regularly consulted, because although it is possible to search a directory of servers, many of my own searches wound up being run on servers that I stumbled upon by chance. And as my list grew, I realized that tailoring such a list for my own use was a good idea. If you become an active WAIS searcher, I would advise you to maintain a list of sites that particularly meet your own needs or pique your interest. Be sure to keep your list updated! To get you started, the following are some sites that have proven useful to me.

aarnet-resource-guide.src
The AARNET Resource Guide, containing Internet background materials.

acronyms.src
A database of acronyms and abbreviations.

alt.wais.src
News from the alt.wais newsgroup. A handy way to check the archives of an active USENET newsgroup dealing with WAIS.

ANU-Buddha-L.src
Postings from the Buddhist Academic Discussion group about Buddhism and related philosophical issues.

ANU-Internet-Voyager-guide.src
The social scientist's handbook to using the Internet.

ANU-Pacific-History.src
The Pacific History Journal Bibliography, citing journal articles on the subject.

ANU-Socsci-Netlore.src
This server is a good one to know about. It contains information about network resources of particular interest to academic researchers in the social sciences, arts, and humanities. New material is added every two weeks.

ANU-Taoism-Listserv.src
Postings on the taoism-l listserv.

ANU-ZenBuddhism-l.src
Postings on Zen Buddhism history, lore, writings, and practice.

bit.listserv.pacs-l.src
The archives of the PACS-L list established by the University Libraries and the Information Technology Division of the University of Houston. PACS-L deals with computer systems in libraries, including CD-ROM databases, computer-assisted instruction, expert systems, hypermedia programs, library microcomputer facilities, locally mounted databases, on-line catalogs, and remote end-user search systems.

bryn-mawr-classical-review.src
Archives of the *Bryn Mawr Classical Review.*

bryn-mawr-medieval-review.src
Full text of the *Bryn Mawr Medieval Review.*

cica-win3.src
Provides an index to the Microsoft Windows archive at the Center for Innovative Computing Applications (ftp://ftp.cica.indiana.edu), which contains thousands of Windows programs.

cicnet-directory-of-servers.src
A directory of servers at CICNet, The Committee on Institutional Cooperation Network in Ann Arbor, Michigan. This site contains a directory of servers and information about servers at CICnet and elsewhere.

cnidr-directory-of-servers.src
A Directory of Servers is operated by CNIDR, The Clearinghouse for Networked Information Discovery and Retrieval.

college-email.src
Information on finding e-mail addresses for university students.

com-priv.src
Contains the com-priv mailing list archive. Updated nightly, com-priv discusses issues related to the commercialization and privatization of the Internet.

comp.archives.src
Archives of the comp.archives newsgroup.

comp.binaries
Executable programs from the newsgroup comp.binaries.

comp.internet.library.src
An index for the newsgroup comp.internet.library, which focuses on issues involving the computerization of library resources.

comp.risks.src
Archives of the comp.risks newsgroup, discussing issues related to computer security and the impact of technology on society.

cool-directory-of-servers.src
A top-level directory for Conservation OnLine (COOL), a collection of WAIS databases containing information on the conservation of library, archives, and museum materials. Users should query the cool-directory-of-servers.src to determine which COOL database will best meet their needs. To see a list of all the COOL databases, use the word source as your search term. New databases will be added to COOL so it will be a good idea to search this server regularly.

cs-journal-titles.src
Contains an index of article titles and authors from some 600 journals, books, and other publications relating to computing.

current.cites.src
Current Cites is a monthly publication of the Library Technology Watch Program—The Library, University of California at Berkeley. Over 30 journals in librarianship and computer technology are scanned for selected articles on electronic publishing, optical disk technologies, computer networks and networking, information transfer, expert systems and artificial intelligence, and hypermedia and multimedia. Brief annotations accompany most of the citations.

disco-mm-zenon-inria-fr.src
A database of compact discs, containing ASCII text descriptions and graphics files of their covers, along with audio sampler files.

earlym-l
Medieval and renaissance music, as discussed on the EARLYM-L mailing list and the rec.music.early newsgroup.

educom.src
EDUCOM documents, including archives, project updates, summaries, and a calendar of events.

eff-documents.src
Documents from the Electronic Frontier Foundation, including the EFF newsletter. This site mirrors the EFF ftp archives at ftp://ftp.eff.org.

elec_journ_newslett.src
Information on electronic journals, a fast-growing area of Internet development.

Eric-Digests.src
Short reports on educational topics.

ftp-list.src
A list of anonymous FTP sites.

fyis.src
The For Your Information documents (a subset of RFCs that provides general background information about Internet topics).

homebrew.src
Indexed archives of the homebrew mailing list and the rec.crafts.homebrew newsgroup from USENET. Files date from 1989, and are reindexed weekly.

hst-weekly-summary.src
Weekly summary of Hubble Space Telescope (HST) completed observations.

hytelnet.src
All the information that is stored in the HYTELNET package by Peter Scott, of the University of Saskatchewan. This includes library OPACs, BBSs, CWISs, and any other TELNET accessible sites.

inet-libraries.src
Internet access to library catalogs is the subject, with information from a variety of directories and lists.

info-mac.src
Information from the info-mac newsgroup from USENET.

internet_info.src
Introductory material and guides for using the Internet.

internet-mail.src
Contains Scott Yanoff's internetwork mail guide, which provides information on addressing e-mail to networks connecting to the Internet.

internet_services.src
Various documents describing services available on the Internet. Includes Billy Barron's list of Internet Databases, a list of Internet mail servers, The Internet Resources Guide, and "Not Just Cows—A Guide to Internet/Bitnet Resources in Agriculture and Related Sciences."

Internet-user-glossary.src
Based on the FYI document called the Internet Users' Glossary, this server includes basic terms and acronyms you'll encounter around the network. Produced by the User Glossary Working Group of the User Services Area of the Internet Engineering Task Force, which is itself known by its acronym IETF.

internic-whois.src
A WAIS implementation of the WHOIS database at the InterNIC. WHOIS is composed of root-level domains, networks, DNS servers, autonomous system numbers, organizations, and points of contact for the domains, networks, servers, and autonomous system numbers.

isoc.src
Documents from the Internet Society.

journalism.periodicals.src
A WAIS-accessible version of the Journalism Periodicals Index, made available at no charge as an experiment by the Graduate School of Journalism at The University of Western Ontario. The Index to Journalism Periodicals is a cross-referenced subject index produced on microfiche. It contains more than 10,000 citations to articles from about 40 trade, professional, and academic journals related to journalism and mass communication. Most of the titles indexed are from Canada or the United States, but some international journals are also indexed. References cover subjects such as business aspects of the media, ethics, freedom of information, government regulation, labor relations, medicine coverage, technology, and women in the media. Practical topics such as editing, investigative reporting, photojournalism and reporting are also included.

lawrence-obrien-interview.src
I include this one as a demonstration of what WAIS can do. This server provides a focused look at former Democratic Party leader Lawrence O'Brien, with much information about his work in the Johnson and Kennedy administrations. We can envision future databases, equally focused, containing the memoirs of people in the news, a wonderful resource for scholarship.

macintosh-news.src
Publications of interest to Macintosh users. Includes the info-mac digest (info-mac@sumex-aim.stanford.edu), Michael Kelly's comp.sys.mac.programmer digest, and Adam Engst's TidBITS, an electronic magazine for the Macintosh.

mailing-lists.src
Listings of Internet and BITNET mailing lists, along with electronic serials and journals and USENET newsgroups.

matrix_news.src
Articles, columns, and more from *Matrix News*, a monthly electronic newsletter on networking.

midwest-weather.src
National Weather Service forecasts for the states of Michigan, Ohio, Indiana, Illinois, Wisconsin, Iowa, and Minnesota. Updated hourly from the Gopher weather server at the University of Minnesota.

movie-lists.src
Contains the latest releases of the USENET rec.arts.movies lists. The lists provide current references to TV and film credits. Includes lists of actors, actresses, cinematographers, composers, directors, and writers.

network-bibliography.src
Network-related bibliographies, including: Computer Networking Bibliography, Libraries and Information Resources, and the Networks bibliography compiled by Deidre E. Stanton.

news.answers-faqs.src
Contains all Frequently Asked Questions (FAQs) from the USENET newsgroup news.answers. It is updated daily.

Omni-Cultural-Academic-Resource.src
Internationally oriented materials drawn from a variety of sources including databases and newsgroups.

online@uunet.ca.src
If you search on-line databases like DIALOG or Dow Jones News/Retrieval, you'll find much of interest here. This is a compilation of material from a mailing list that focuses on information brokering.

poetry.src
The intention of this server, its compilers say, is to collect as many poems as possible. Contains the complete poems of Shakespeare and Yeats, as well as a smattering of other poets.

proj-gutenberg.src
Mirrors the documents produced by Project Gutenberg. The documents themselves are at ftp://mrcnext.cso.uiuc.edu:etext/*. The purpose of Project Gutenberg is to encourage the creation and distribution of English language electronic texts.

rec.gardens.src
Articles from the USENET newsgroup rec.gardens.

rfcs.src
Contains the Internet Request for Comments documents. Very handy for those in need of technical information.

risks-digest
Archive of postings to the mailing list that focuses on Internet problems and the risks of using computers in general.

roget-thesaurus.src
An on-line version of *Roget's Thesaurus*, provided by Project Gutenberg. This database is also available in the Gopher at gopher://gopher.micro.umn.edu, and for anonymous FTP from ftp://mrcnext.cso.uiuc.edu.

sample-books.src
Various on-line electronic texts.

sf-reviews.src
An archive of the USENET newsgroup rec.arts.sf.reviews, which is a forum for reviews of works of interest to fans of science fiction, as well as related genres like fantasy and horror.

smithsonian-pictures.src
Image files produced by the Smithsonian Institution's Office of Printing & Photographic Services, made available through a grant from the Apple Library of Tomorrow Program. These images cover topics ranging from air and space to science, technology, history, and current events. Photographs from Smithsonian museums on the Mall in Washington, D.C., plus other Smithsonian bureaus such as the National Zoo and the Smithsonian Astrophysical Observatory.

sunsite-ftp.src
An index of all the index and "readme" files in the anonymous FTP directory of Sunsite at the University of North Carolina in Chapel Hill.

SURAnetGuide-All.src
The SURAnet Guide to Selected Internet Resources.

US-Congress-Phone-Fax.src
Telephone and fax numbers for members of the U.S. Senate and House of Representatives.

US-State-Department-Travel-Advisories.src
The U.S. State Department Counsular Information Sheets and Travel Warnings. This can be a handy server to know about, and you can couple it with the CIA World Factbook server discussed shortly to obtain an overview of a particular country for travel purposes.

usenet-addresses.src
One-line entries consisting of names and e-mail addresses culled from the Reply To or From lines of USENET postings, as well as a last-seen date associated with each address.

usenet-cookbook.src
The USENET Cookbook.

usenet.src
Periodic informational postings (including FAQ postings) from various USENET newsgroups. Contains all entries that are cross-posted to *.answers newsgroups, as well as all postings (except those in comp.mail.maps) included in the List of Periodic Informational Postings, which appears monthly in news.announce.newusers.

wais-discussion-archives.src
Access to the wais-discussion mailing list's archives.

wais-docs.src
Contains the text of all the current documentation for WAIS.

weather.src
A weather information server. Search for weather, and you will get the day's satellite weather maps. You can also retrieve textual weather forecasts.

White-House-Papers.src
Press releases and other documents from the Clinton White House.

world-factbook93.src
The CIA World Factbook 1993; this document has been slightly modified (table of contents removed, dashed lines placed between countries, and more) from Project Gutenberg.

zipcodes.src
A WAIS index of U.S.A. Zip Code database.

Keeping Up with WAIS

Like most moving targets, WAIS can be tracked through USENET newsgroups. Two now exist: comp.infosystems.wais and alt.wais. If you want the latest on commercial WAIS client and server software, contact WAIS Inc. The address is:

WAIS Inc.
690 Fifth St.
San Francisco, CA 94107
Voice: 415-356-5400
Fax: 415-356-5444
E-mail: frontdesk@WAIS.com

For information on a freely available WAIS server, contact the Clearinghouse for Networked Information Discovery and Retrieval. You can examine the Zdist software (formerly known as freeWAIS) at this URL:

http://cnidr.org/cnidr_projects/freewais1.0.html

Chapter 10 of this book focuses on, among other things, the work of CNIDR.

7

HYTELNET:
Finding Telnet Sites

We've examined a wide range of Internet tools, from the browsing capabilities of World Wide Web directories to the targeted search engines such as Lycos and InfoSeek that allow us to run keyword searches of resources. WAIS is a powerful search engine, hampered at this juncture primarily because of the limited range of the databases available in its format. We can expect that to change as the advantages of full-text searching suggest themselves to more and more content providers. But if you ponder the kinds of resources we've put through their paces thus far, one glaring omission should stand out. We have as yet considered no way to hunt down interesting Telnet sites.

Telnet is a way of setting up interactive sessions with remote computers. As one of the original "big three" Internet protocols, it allows the user to log on to a remote site, sign on through whatever logon procedure is in effect, and use databases or whatever other resources the system administrator at the site has made available. Perhaps the most common Telnet application for the average Internet user today is the on-line library catalog. Using Telnet, people can log on at libraries around the globe—hundreds are now on-line—and search their card catalogs. You can even search the Library of Congress. A wide range of databases are also available, although most are relatively specialized in particular scientific and educational disciplines. The trick with Telnet is knowing what's out there, and the goal is to find a way to search such services.

We'd like, in other words, a concise way to use a directory of Telnet resources. Such a tool would allow us to explore connections off-line, thus avoiding the delays created by actually logging on at each site only to find that the information there isn't useful. It should also include login information at each site, so that we wouldn't have to pause each time and look up this information in a separate text. And when the time came to log on to a given computer, the tool would make the process as painless as does the Web.

Couch these parameters within a hypertext context and you've described HYTEL-NET, a hypertext browser that charts many sites on the Internet that are accessible by Telnet. This includes not only Telnet-accessible databases and other interactive sites, but also Telnet connections to information available at Gopher, WAIS, and World Wide Web sites, as well as library catalogs and Campus Wide Information Systems (CWISs). Created by Peter Scott of Northern Lights Internet Solutions in Saskatoon, Saskatchewan, the earliest versions of the program were developed for MSDOS-compatible equipment, but subsequent versions have now appeared. The Macintosh adaptation was created by Charles Burchill of the University of Manitoba, while a Unix/VMS client has been prepared by Earl Fogel, of the Computing Services Department at the University of Saskatchewan, and a Microsoft Windows version was created by Bruce Clouette.

If you plan to become an accomplished searcher of the Internet, HYTELNET needs to be in your bag of tricks. Like other search tools, the program offers its own particular slant on the navigation process. By downloading the software and running it on your own machine, any user (and this includes those using a shell account to access the Internet) can take advantage of its useful index of resources. And while those without a direct network connection can't take advantage of HYTELNET's ability to connect directly to the sites it displays, anyone with a SLIP/PPP or dedicated connection can run the whole connection process through the HYTELNET software.

Using HYTELNET

HYTELNET is useful to any category of Internet user. We can tap its resources in four ways:

- Using HYTELNET is easiest with a SLIP/PPP or a dedicated network connection. By downloading the software, we make available on our machines a database that, with the pressing of a key, takes us directly to the sites it describes. As opposed to other Internet search tools, the browsing process is completed on our own machines before a network connection is made. It is only when we have made the decision about a site we'd like to explore that we press the RETURN to begin the Telnet session. At that point, we use HYTELNET's login information to begin our exploration of the remote computer. This login information is one of the primary benefits of HYTELNET.
- HYTELNET is available over the World Wide Web. To examine it on-line, check the following URL:

      http://www.usask.ca/cgi-bin/hytelnet/

- For those with shell account connections only, HYTELNET is also useful, because the program not only describes Telnet sites but also provides login and instructions for each. Thus, tracking the addresses you need in your next Internet session becomes a trivial task, providing they are indexed by HYTELNET. You simply jot down what you need to know (or, if you're running a multitasking session, just keep HYTELNET running in a window for easy reference) and then supply the necessary information to make the Telnet connection.
- Finally, HYTELNET is available through Telnet, although the number of sites offering such access is limited. Use them only if you have no other means of access. You can log on to a HYTELNET server and use the system on-line, checking the addresses you need for later Telnet sessions. Although the Unix version accessible through Telnet is capable of making direct Telnet connections to remote sites, this feature may not be available when you access the system through one of the Telnet addresses I give in the next section.

HYTELNET Servers

The following is a list of the HYTELNET Telnet sites that I know about.

Server	Address	Login
Columbia Law School	lawnet.law.columbia.edu	lawnet
El Paso Community College	laguna.epcc.edu	library
Manchester Computing Centre, UK	info.mcc.ac.uk	hytelnet
National Chiao Tung University, Taiwan	nctuccca.edu.tw	hytelnet
Oxford University, UK	rsl.ox.ac.uk	hytelnet
University of Adelaide, Australia	library.adelaide.edu.au	access
University of California, San Diego	pubinfo.ucsd.edu	Log in as infopath. Select Internet-Navigation and Search Tools from main menu. Select Hytelnet from the next menu.

In the figures in this chapter, I use both a standalone implementation of HYTEL-NET as well as a SLIP/PPP connection to illustrate how the program works.

Downloading HYTELNET

The HYTELNET database is frequently updated as Telnet addresses change and new ones are added, which makes keeping up with new versions a critical matter. You can always find the latest version of the program at the University of Saskatchewan, where Peter Scott first created it. The URL is:

ftp://ftp.usask.ca/pub/hytelnet/

Use anonymous FTP to connect and download the software. Here, you will find a listing of the subdirectories for the various operating platforms. Note that there is even an Amiga implementation of HYTELNET.

```
drwxr-xr-x  2 1033     system       512 Aug 27 1993 amiga
drwxr-xr-x  3 1033     system       512 Jun 12 11:43 mac
drwxr-xr-x  5 1340     system      4608 Jun 11 10:17 pc
drwxr-xr-x  3 1033     system       512 Jun 12 11:27 unix
drwxr-xr-x  3 1033     system       512 Mar 16 16:09 vms
drwxr-xr-x  2 1340     system       512 May  9 13:22 windows
```

To reach any of these directories, enter **cd *directory_name***. In other words, to get the PC version, you would type **cd pc**. To get the Macintosh version, it's **cd mac**, and so on.

The archival file for HYTELNET is located within each directory. At the time of this writing, the software had reached version 6.9. The filename for the PC was hyteln69.zip, a zipped file containing the necessary executable program and support files. While the version number will change as HYTELNET undergoes updating (the software is made available in new versions on a frequent basis), the format isn't likely to vary, so look for hytelnxx.zip, where *xx* stands for version numbers. If you're a Mac user, the file is HYTELNET6.9.sit.bin.

> **HINT:** Don't forget that whatever platform you're going to use HYTELNET on, the program you're downloading is a compressed file. If you're using a shell account, you must enter the **binary** command at the ftp> prompt before you start the actual download. After logging in at ftp.usask.ca, enter **binary** followed by a **RETURN** before changing directories. Doing so will ensure an accurate download. The file transfer command itself is standard FTP—**get hyteln69.zip** (for MS-DOS machines). Once unpacked and installed, the program creates numerous subdirectories and individual files.

If you intend to use HYTELNET through a Telnet session, choosing, for whatever reason, not to run it on your PC, you certainly can, and we'll see in a moment how to invoke the program through Telnet. But I recommend that you consider downloading this admittedly gigantic database anyway. For one thing, using the Telnet solution places a greater strain upon thinly stretched network resources, so only use it if you have no other choice. For another thing, having a wealth of Internet destinations available for your off-line browsing can be extremely useful, and it is guaranteed to give you ideas about future sessions you'd like to try. At the very least, consider downloading the software, unpacking it, and running it just to get the feel of the interface. Like most of the World Wide Web browsers, HYTELNET is an easy program to master.

> **NOTE:** Although versions of HYTELNET exist for various platforms, the Mac, Unix, Windows, and VMS versions of the database all use the information files included in the PC version. This means that if you plan to download one of the other versions, you will need to also download these text files. Further information about installation and use is available at the FTP site.

Putting HYTELNET to Work

Now let's put HYTELNET through its paces to examine how the system works. I will illustrate the procedures using the Windows version of the program, but the underlying structure remains the same no matter which platform you put the software on. The same holds true if you access HYTELNET through a Telnet session—the basic principles of moving around the system and retrieving information remain the same no matter what the platform.

You can see the initial HYTELNET screen in Figure 7.1. As you can see, in the center of the screen below the menu bar is a menu of items, each with a bracketed abbreviation to its right. A highlight sits atop <*WHATIS*>, which is the abbreviation for the item *What is HYTELNET?*

Like Gopher and the World Wide Web, HYTELNET poses few conceptual difficulties for the new user. You move about the screen by using the Previous Item or Next Item buttons shown at the bottom of the screen. To select an item after you have moved to it,

Figure 7.1   The primary HYTELNET screen, using the Windows version of the program.

you can use the Backward or Forward buttons adjacent to the other buttons. Alternatively, you can click on an item to move directly to it. The item you have selected will then appear on the screen. Figure 7.2 shows what happened when I clicked on the Forward button with the highlight on the *<WHATIS>* item. To move back to the original screen, I would simply click on the Backward button.

The range of HYTELNET information is also suggested, though imperfectly, by the opening menu (Figure 7.1). Library catalogs are certainly a major feature of HYTELNET's listings (remember that HYTELNET's developer has a background as a library specialist). You should also be aware that the program draws extensively on the University of North Texas directory of Telnet-accessible library catalogs, maintained by Billy Barron. The *raison d'etre* of the UNT list is to serve as a directory of on-line bibliographic databases with accompanying Telnet site information, so the library-oriented slant of HYTELNET is understandable.

Browse down the list. There are items marked *Other resources <SITES2>* and *Catalog interfaces <SYS000>*. A world of information can lurk behind the simplest menu entry. Choosing the *<SITES2>* item, for example, reveals a powerful submenu, as shown in Figure 7.3.

Notice the range here. We have links to everything from archie, our FTP file finder, to CWIS systems, which list university personnel and students. We also have major entries such as *<FUL000>*, which points to databases, and *<FRE000>*, pointing at Free-Net systems worldwide. *<DIR000>* covers various white pages directory systems, while

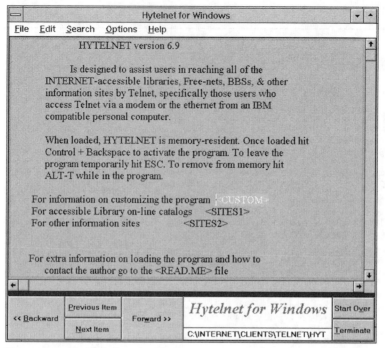

Figure 7.2 Using the Forward button to move deeper into the HYTELNET database.

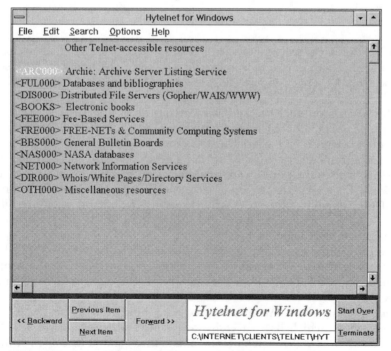

Figure 7.3 An extensive list of sites opens up when you move deeper into the HYTELNET program.

NOTE: If we were using HYTELNET through a Telnet session in the shell environment, we wouldn't be able to launch the actual Telnet session to a remote site. But even using HYTELNET for reference only, we could check on any item to retrieve the information we needed to log in. In cases where HYTELNET can't make the connection, it can still provide us the necessary data. We learn from Figure 7.5, for example, that the address for this HYTELNET server is news.janet.ac.uk. We also learn that the login here is news. If we wanted to contact the JANET server, we would simply have to return to our shell account prompt and launch a Telnet connection from there, thus achieving the same result.

Be aware, too, as you move from one HYTELNET server to another via Telnet, you won't necessarily see the identical set of information or, depending on your access method, even the same interface. But the underlying program is HYTELNET. Check into HYTELNET at the University of Arizona and you get the basic HYTELNET package. Try Columbia Law School and you get this menu:

```
CU-LawNet Info System
    ---------------------------------------------------------------------
    1 - Law Library Catalog PEGASUS
    2 - University Catalog CLIO
    3 - Project JANUS experimental textual search interface
    4 - Law School Academic Services
    5 - Law School Career Services
    6 - ColumbiaNet
    7 - Advanced World wide library access (HYTELNET)
    h - Help message
    ---------------------------------------------------------------------

Please make a selection or enter Q to quit.
```

Don't expect every HYTELNET implementation to look the same then; certainly, as Gopher has spread around the Internet, the variety of individual Gophers has become more and more apparent. The same thing seems to be happening with HYTELNET, although the process hasn't gone nearly as far.

<NET000> shows us the location of a variety of network information sources. Let's take the <NET000> option for a moment. Here, we find contact information for prominent sites all over the Internet, as shown in Figure 7.4.

By moving the highlight to any one of these items and clicking on the Forward button, we can learn more about it. Figure 7.5, for example, shows us the opening screen at the Joint Academic Network, known as JANET, in the United Kingdom. Notice that we are not only given information about what we will find when we log on at JANET, but are also told just how the logon should proceed. We have both a Telnet address and a logon ID.

Now HYTELNET gets truly intriguing. In front of us, we have all the information needed to make a Telnet connection to JANET. We can proceed to do just that by double-clicking on the word telnet in the screen shown in Figure 7.5. HYTELNET will pass the necessary information to the Telnet program of our choice, enabling the connection to be made. In Figure 7.6, I have logged on at JANET, using the logon ID HYTELNET has supplied.

Notice that the session itself is running in an external Telnet program. To use such a program, HYTELNET requires that the Telnet client be running at the time we click on

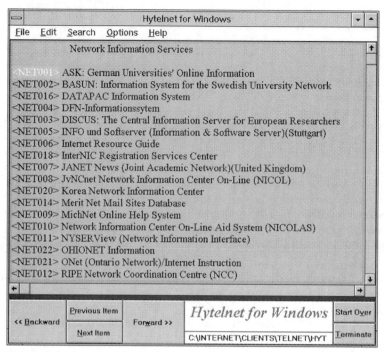

Figure 7.4 Contact information for sites around the Internet.

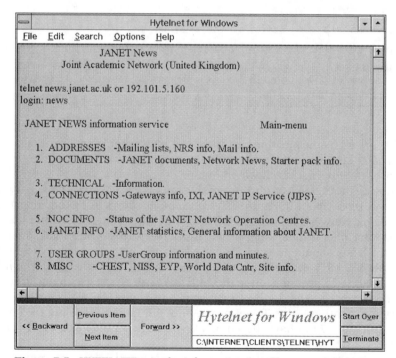

Figure 7.5 HYTELNET provides information that allows you to log on to a wide range of sites.

```
┌─────────────────────────────────────────────────────────────────────┐
│ JANET news information service.                          Main-menu    │
│                                                                       │
│     1.  ADDRESSES    -JANET Addresses, NRS info, Mail info.           │
│                                                                       │
│     2.  DOCUMENTS    -JANET documents, Network News, Starter pack, NRS Guide. │
│                                                                       │
│     3.  TECHNICAL    -Information on IP, Ether, Rainbow, X.29/Telnet, X25/TCP. │
│                                                                       │
│     4.  CONNECTIONS -Gateways info, IXI, JANET IP Service (JIPS).     │
│                                                                       │
│     5.  NOC INFO     -Status of the JANET Network Operation Centres.  │
│                                                                       │
│     6.  JANET INFO   -JANET stats, CERT Info, General JANET Information. │
│                                                                       │
│     7.  USER GROUPS -User Group information and minutes.              │
│                                                                       │
│     8.  MISC         -CHEST, NISS, World Data Cntr.                   │
│                                                                       │
│     9.  JANET.NEWS   -Server help and information, Reporting faults.  │
│ . . . . . . . . . . . . . . . . . . . . . . . . . . . . . . . . . . . │
│     Help                          Main-menu  Suggestion  Redisplay    │
│     Contents                                             Quit         │
│  Command?                                                             │
└─────────────────────────────────────────────────────────────────────┘
```

Figure 7.6 The actual logon at the remote JANET site, through an external Telnet program.

the screen information to launch the session; if it is not, the program will display a message asking us to start the Telnet program.

The HYTELNET Commands

There are few commands to master with the Windows version of HYTELNET, and here they are, along with their variations. Bear in mind as you work through the HYTELNET menus that what you are doing is working with hypertextual links. Click on a highlighted item and you move to that underlying file, which may itself contain nested files, and so on.

Next Item	Highlights the next hypertext file, which will then appear highlighted.
Previous Item	Highlights the previous hypertext file, which will appear highlighted.
Forward	Moves directly to the highlighted link. The easiest way to do this, however, is to double-click on the item with your mouse.
Backward	Restores the previous file.
ESC	Moves to the previous Windows application.
Start Over	Takes you back to the primary HYTELNET screen.
Terminate	Ends the program.

And, as we've seen, you can move directly to a Telnet site by double-clicking on the word Telnet (or, depending upon the nature of the site, the term tn3270, which indicates a special kind of Telnet connection to an IBM mainframe computer). Your Telnet program must be running at the time for the connection to be made.

If you are using other implementations of HYTELNET, including the Unix and Telnet-accessible ones, you will have a different set of commands to achieve the same results. Here they are, along with their variations:

HINT: As configured by its author, HYTELNET's database contains only Telnet or tn3270 connections. The program can optionally be set up to include any FTP, Gopher, Finger, or World Wide Web sites that you would like to add, and these can likewise be launched by double-clicking on the reference, assuming it is followed by a valid Internet address. In that case, the program would launch the client program of your choice to run the individual session. HYTELNET clients can be chosen from its Options menu. SLIP/PPP users, however, will probably not want to follow this course. HYTELNET for Windows, for example, assumes you are using a character-based interface through a commercial provider like DELPHI, to which the program will pass its commands; configuring it for different types of clients therefore means entering a new program name each time you want to use a particular client. It is far easier to save HYTELNET for Telnet and tn3270 sessions only, while using other tools for Gopher, FTP, and the World Wide Web.

Down arrow	Selects the next menu item.
Up arrow	Selects the previous menu item.
Right arrow	Moves to the next menu page (this is the same as pressing the RETURN key).
Left arrow	Moves back to the previous menu page.
+	Scrolls down to the next menu page.
−	Scrolls up to the previous menu page.
m	Returns you to the main screen.
?	Produces a help screen.
q	Quits HYTELNET.

HYTELNET as Search Tool

HYTELNET's resemblance to the World Wide Web is the result of its hypertext linkages. Using a Web browser, you move about a site by choosing items, delving deeper into subjects that interest you. The same positive aspects of World Wide Web that we have already discussed—its ability to let you discover information by following your nose down virtual pathways, its excellence as a browsing tool—apply to HYTELNET. And so, of course, do some of the defects that made Web searching so difficult in the early days. HYTELNET for Windows can be searched by pulling down the Search menu, but the search will take place only on the current screen. To go deeper, we must manage the process ourselves, by choosing menu item after menu item and checking out what we find.

HINT: If you are a shell account user, you can save the network considerable traffic if you download HYTELNET and run your search on it off-line before trying anything else. This way, you can explore the pathways to the information you need without tying up network resources. You can then access your service provider and run the necessary Telnet session to reach the site you require. Using Telnet to access the HYTELNET servers is helpful in understanding how the program works, but if you keep the program on your system and only use Telnet for a particular search need, you minimize network workload.

Searching for The WELL

Established in Sausalito, California, in 1985, The WELL has established itself as one of the on-line world's more interesting destinations. Its ancestry as a resource of the *Whole Earth Catalog* community has ensured it an active base of users and system operators who are concerned with using technology to advance the social welfare. Having heard interesting things about this system, I decided to find it on-line to learn more. HYTEL-NET, I assumed, could help with this search.

The most obvious place to begin such a search is under the *Other resources <SITES2>* heading from the main menu (Figure 7.1). Highlighting it, I press a RETURN to access the list of Internet destinations previously shown. I'm interested in checking several of these. *<FEE000> Fee-Based Services* is a possibility; without knowing whether a fee is involved in accessing The WELL, it would be wise to put this on our list for future reference. *<FRE000> FREE-NETs & Community Computing Systems* is also a possibility; after all, The WELL has made quite a name for itself as a community service system, bringing the benefits of worldwide networking to an active local as well as international community.

And then there's *<BBS000> General Bulletin Boards;* again, it's a possibility, depending on how we stretch the definition of bulletin board. *<NET000> Network Information Services* may have something on The WELL, but it doesn't seem likely; these tend to be network-affiliated sites such as NICs (Network Information Centers); the InterNIC is a good example. Let's go ahead and check *<NET000>* just to be on the safe side. When I click on this item, I call up the screen we already looked at in Figure 7.4. I search this screen by pulling down HYTELNET's Search menu and taking the Find option, but the search turns up nothing. True, HYTELNET has provided loads of useful information about various network connections. It's helpful, for example, to know that you have quick access to the InterNIC and RIPE, the European Network Information Centre in Amsterdam, through the HYTELNET connection. No mention of The WELL, however; we're in the wrong category of material.

<BBS000> General Bulletin Boards is another possibility. Here, I generate a second multipage list containing bulletin board systems accessible on the Internet. Some examples follow:

```
<BBS001> Advanced Technology Information Network (Calif Ag Tech Institute)
<BBS039> AfterFive BBS
<BBS095> American Institute of Physics Careers Bulletin Board
<BBS089> Automated Library Information Xchange (ALIX)
<BBS043> Badboy's Better Bulletin Board System (BBBBS)
<BBS002> Bergen By Byte A/S - Bergen - Norway
<BBS051> Bulletin Board of the ProMAX Users Group
<BBS052> CAPPnet: California Academic Partnership Program
<BBS071> Classroom Earth!
<BBS005> Cosy at Victoria, British Columbia, Canada
<BBS007> Delft University Bulletin Board System (Netherlands)
<BBS104> Dentistry-On-Line
<BBS038> Edinburgh University Computing Service - EUCS
<BBS074> Electric Ideas Clearinghouse bulletin board system (EICBBS)
<BBS058> European Southern Observatory Bulletin Board
```

```
<BBS087> Federal Bulletin Board U.S. Government Printing Office (GPO)
<BBS090> Federal Highway Administration Electronic Bulletin Board System
<BBS068> FedWorld: National Technical Information Service
```

It's an interesting list, to be sure; these are bulletin board systems that contain Internet hooks to allow users to log on via Telnet. Public access Unix sites are available, as are a number of specialized bulletin boards like Classroom Earth! and the American Institute of Physics Careers Bulletin Board. But The WELL doesn't make the list; it's much more of a full-service system as well as an Internet access provider than a bulletin board per se.

<FRE000> FREE-NETs & Community Computing Systems is next on our list. Here we're looking at regional and community-based systems. Free-Nets in particular are interesting; they're public access computer systems created by local activists whose vision of socially conscious telecommunications has extended many benefits of the Internet to people who would otherwise not have them. The WELL isn't exactly a Free-Net, but let's see what else is on this menu. Here's a snippet:

```
<FRE051> Alachua Free-Net
<FRE048> Arizona Telecommunication Community (AzTeC)
<FRE013> Big Sky Telegraph
<FRE059> Blue Sky Freenet of Manitoba
<FRE012> Buffalo FREE-NET
<FRE064> Calgary Free-Net
<FRE022> CapAccess: National Capital Area Public Access Network
<FRE044> Central Virginia's Free-Net (CeVaNet)
<FRE042> Chebucto Community Net
<FRE050> Chesapeake Free-Net
<FRE036> CIAO! Free-Net
<FRE001> Cleveland FREE-NET
<FRE023> Columbia Online Information Network (COIN)
<FRE029> Dayton FREE-NET
<FRE011> Denver FREE-NET
<FRE072> De Digitale Stad, Amsterdam
<FRE069> EASTMAN FreeNet (Manitoba)
<FRE055> Edmonton FreeNet
```

There are plenty of interesting systems here (Big Sky Telegraph in Montana, in particular, is one of the most creative networking projects in the United States), but no WELL.

We fall back on our final possibility: *<FEE000> Fee-Based Services*. Double-clicking with the highlight on the item takes us to a multipage listing of systems that charge for access. Here's a sample of what we find there:

```
<FEE089> The Power Exchange
<FEE093> PUCnet Computer Connections (Edmonton,Canada)
<FEE091> Resudox Online Services (Ottawa, Canada)
<FEE079> Sate1NET
```

```
<FEE094> Silicon Valley Public Access Link
<FEE023> STN (Scientific and Technical Information Network)
<FEE057> Techbook
<FEE022> Telerama
<FEE063> TelLink Networking - An Internet access service
<FEE028> Texas Department of Commerce Bulletin Board
<FEE064> Texas Innovation Network
<FEE032> Texas Metronet
<FEE045> Universal Access Online Communications Service
<FEE080> UUNorth Incorporated, Guest Information Service
<FEE083> The VILLAGE(R) of Cambridge
<FEE036> Vnet Internet Access - Charlotte North Carolina
<FEE027> Web - The Network for social change
<FEE007> The WELL, Sausalito, California
<FEE015> The World
<FEE070> WorldClassroom (Guest Login)
```

The WELL is listed as *<FEE007>*. I can now double-click on this item to see the necessary Telnet information, as shown in Figure 7.7. Here we are given complete informa-

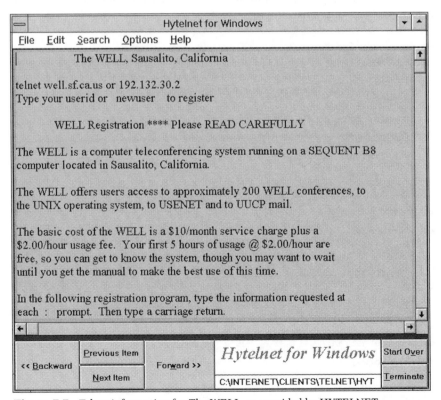

Figure 7.7   Telnet information for The WELL, as provided by HYTELNET.

NOTE: You can see from the preceding search that HYTELNET lacks an ability to search across its menu structure. It could use its own equivalent of Veronica, but in the absence of such a tool, users can search across directories with an external utility program. On the other hand, no search tool is devoid of context. HYTELNET exists to provide as comprehensive as possible a directory of Telnet-accessible resources, as opposed to Gopher, which attempts to establish a local menu structure with links to the rest of the Internet. HYTEL-NET is a valuable resource because it compresses a wide range of information in a small space; there is no other directory of Telnet resources that comes close. I turn to it often to uncover sources I otherwise wouldn't have known existed.

tion about the system, which allows us to make the Telnet connection, log on, and, if we choose, establish an account.

HYTELNET and Library Resources

Library catalogs are the reason HYTELNET was created; it shouldn't surprise us that they remain its strongest suit. The main menu item, *Library Catalogs <SITES1>*, takes us to a submenu offering a choice of libraries in the Americas, Europe and Scandinavia, and Asia, the Pacific region, and South Africa. Within each, the library listings are broken down by country, as shown:

```
Europe/Scandinavia

<AT000> Austria

<BE000> Belgium

<HR000> Croatia

<CZ000> Czech Republic

<DK000> Denmark

<FI000> Finland

<FR000> France

<DE000> Germany

<GR000> Greece

<HU000> Hungary

<IS000> Iceland

<IE000> Ireland

<IL000> Israel

<IT000> Italy

<LT000> Lithuania

<NL000> Netherlands

<NO000> Norway

<PL000> Poland

<RO000> Romania

<SI000> Slovenia
```

Pressing a RETURN on one of these items produces site information for various systems. Here, for example, is the listing for the University of Budapest:

```
Technical University of Budapest

TELNET TULIBB.KKT.BME.HU or 152.66.114.1
Username: aleph
At the CCL> prompt, type ?/eng for English version

To exit, hit the Telnet escape key
```

Now, all this is well and good, but isn't this what HYTELNET does with all its resources? The answer is yes, but there's more to the story. The great profusion of searchable library catalogs on the Internet presents us with a useful tool, but library systems abound in utter profusion. Sure, we can use Telnet to get into a particular site, but what do we do when we're there? Perhaps the library in question is running software called **CLSI**, or **DOBIS/LIBIS**, or **DYNIX**, or **GALAXY**. Then again, maybe its librarians work with **GEAC**, **GEAC ADVANCE**, **GvB**, or **INLEX**. The list can be extended quite a way, to **NOTIS** systems, to the **OCLC** interface, to **PALS**. Each of these systems provides access to a library catalog, but with its own interface and command structure. What's a user to do?

HYTELNET is a handy tool for addressing this problem; if your needs include library searching, you should have it in your arsenal. From the main menu, take the item marked *Help files for catalogs <OP000>;* a click of the mouse leads you to a listing of all the mentioned library software systems. Clicking the mouse on NOTIS, for example, calls up several screens, such as the following:

```
Using NOTIS
Title searches:      To search for a particular title, use the t= search command
                     followed by the title. Example: t=foundation

Author searches:     To search for a particular author, use the a= search command
                     followed by the author's name. Example: a=asimov

Subject searches:    To search for a particular subject, use the s= search com-
                     mand followed by the subject. Example: s=tennis

Keyword searches:    To search for a particular keyword, use the k= search com-
                     mand followed by a string. Example: k=cry wolf

                     You may use the logical operator (AND, OR, NOT) andparenthe-
                     sis to group the operators. Also, $ is a wildcard character.
                     Examples: k=car and fast k=computer and not ibm k=comp$ and
                     (toy or game)
```

As you can see, HYTELNET has delivered the basic tools for getting around the system. Keeping HYTELNET ready for use as you engage in a Telnet session with a remote library may be one of the best moves you can make. It's hard to imagine taking full advantage of the Internet's library resources without it.

Using HYTELNET through the World Wide Web

Perhaps the easiest way to get acquainted with HYTELNET is through a World Wide Web browser. As mentioned earlier, the URL is http://www.usask.ca/cgi-bin/hytelnet/. When you travel to the site, you will see the screen in Figure 7.8.

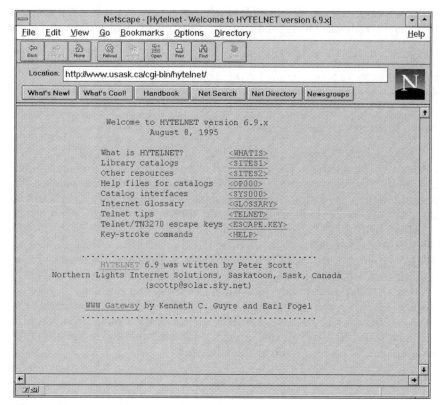

Figure 7.8   HYTELNET as viewed through a World Wide Web browser.

As you can see, the basic implementation of HYTELNET remains the same as always. You move to the item you want to see and click on it to call it up. When you choose a site for examination, you are presented with the usual contact information. Figure 7.9 illustrates that the Web version sets up the actual Telnet address as a hyperlink, so that you can use your browser to go straight to the site. In the figure, we're looking at background information on the American Bibliography of Slavic & East European Studies. The Telnet address, alexia.lis.uiuc.edu, is underlined, illustrating its status as a hyperlink.

Using HYTELNET through Gopher

A helpful implementation of HYTELNET through Gopher is available at Washington and Lee University. The URL is:

gopher://liberty.uc.wlu.edu

A SLIP/PPP user can go directly to this site using client software. If you are using a shell account, your command would be **gopher liberty.us.wlu.edu**. Alternatively, you could find this Gopher by using Telnet to one of the Gopher sites available thusly, and then follow menus to access remote Gopher sites from there. But the client approach is easier.

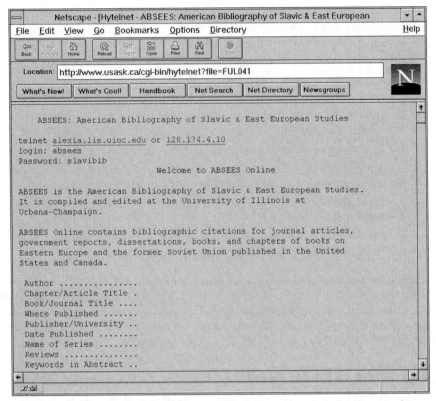

Figure 7.9 The Web version of HYTELNET allows addresses to be set up as hyperlinks.

At the Washington and Lee Gopher, look for a menu item like the following:

```
4. Explore Internet Resources/
```

From there, the following submenu will take you to the HYTELNET options:

```
3. Telnet Login to Sites (HYTELNET) /
```

The Gopher implementation of HYTELNET is helpful because it brings a search capability into play that HYTELNET would otherwise lack. Examine the following screen to see what I mean. The Gopher has broken down HYTELNET's menued information into separate branches, and includes a search option under item 1.

```
Telnet Login to Sites (Hytelnet)

--> 1.  Hytelnet (word search) <?>
    2.  Library Catalogs /
    3.  Library Catalogs, By System Type /
    4.  Library Catalogs, Help Files /
    5.  New or Revised Hytelnet Entries      [updated: Tuesday 7:10]/
    6.  Other Resources /
```

By pressing a RETURN at this point, we call up a search screen in the usual Gopher format. I tried out this feature by entering the term nasa in the search field and pressing another RETURN. I retrieved the list below:

```
Hytelnet (word search): nasa

-->  1.   NASA Goddard Space Flight Center
     2.   NASA Goddard Space Flight Center <TEL>
     3.   NASA Mid-continent regional technology transfer center BBS
     4.   NASA Mid-continent regional technology transfer center BBS <TEL>
     5.   NASA Science Internet (NSI) Online Network Data
     6.   NASA Science Internet (NSI) Online Network Data <TEL>
     7.   NASA Spacelink <TEL>
     8.   NASA Spacelink
     9.   NASA/IPAC Extragalactic Database
     10.  NASA/IPAC Extragalactic Database <TEL>
```

By allowing us to cluster various references from HYTELNET and to search across its menu structure, Gopher thus provides a Veronica-style boost to the program. Of course, the actual boost is provided by WAIS, which underlies the Gopher engine in this case. It's an example of how integrated search engines change the way we work on the Internet, often functioning behind the scenes to do so.

Keeping Up with HYTELNET

HYTELNET is expanding, with frequent updates and ever-widening coverage, and it remains the only viable way to keep up with Telnet sites across the whole spectrum of Internet activity. You should make it a point to keep up with HYTELNET and update your software as frequently as possible. To do so, consider joining the HYTELNET mailing list, which is simple. Send mail to the following address:

listserv@kentvm.bitnet

or

listserv@kentvm.kent.edu

In your message, include the following line:

subscribe hytel-l *your_name*

Insert your own name in the statement, and leave the Subject: field blank.

The archive site for the HYTELNET list is at listserv@kentvm.bitnet. Send the command **index hytel-l** to retrieve the index. You can search for material by using the methods outlined in Chapter 9 on mailing list archives.

And, if you're interested in retrieving an article by HYTELNET creator Peter Scott, you can do so by sending mail to this address:

listserv@uhupvm1.uh.edu

The message body should contain the following line:

get scott prv3n4 f=mail

LIBTEL: An On-Line Library Resource

Two other menu-driven systems exist to provide access to library materials, as well as bulletin board systems, CWIS implementations, databases, and other resources. Both provide active links to Telnet so that you can find what you need and access it immediately. LIBTEL was developed by Dan Mahone, of the University of New Mexico in Albuquerque; it is available in Unix and VMS versions, as well as through a Telnet connection. LIBS comes from Mark Mesmer at Sonoma State University in California. Let's take a quick look at both.

LIBTEL was designed to provide access through menus to libraries and public access database sites around the world. Once you've found the resource you're interested in, LIBTEL proceeds to make the connection for you. An inherent problem in library searching remains, however—you can easily move between library collections in a wide variety of areas, but you don't necessarily know which is the most likely site for what you need. Fortunately, Gopher once again springs to the rescue, as we'll see shortly. For now, we'll use LIBTEL to make the connection.

To access LIBTEL, use Telnet to connect to the following site:

telnet://bbs.oit.unc.edu

Log in as **launch**. You will be greeted with a menu and asked to set up a new account, which you can do by entering your name and choosing a password. From this point, follow the menu structure to reach LIBTEL. The software currently appears as menu item 3.

```
3. On-line Information Systems (LIBTEL)
```

Choose this item and you will be taken to the primary LIBTEL menu:

```
Internet Accessible Libraries and Information Systems
─────────────────────────────────────────────────────

(NA) North American Region      (MISC) Miscellaneous Services

(EUR) European Region           (BBS) Other Bulletin Boards

(ANZ) Pacifica Region           (NOT) Notes on LIBTEL (Please Read)

(ASA) Asian Region              (CTP) Contemporary Poetry

(ME) Middle-Eastern Region      (EXIT) Go Back to the BBS

To return to this screen during search press 'ctrl G'

Where would you like to go?
```

Like HYTELNET, LIBTEL is easy to use. In this case, the idea is to choose one of the terms in parentheses, which will take you to a submenu for the particular library region you are interested in. I will choose (NA) for North American libraries, and retrieve the following menu:

```
North American Region Libraries and Information Systems
-----------------------------------------------------------------
(AL)Alabama                (ME)Maine              (OH)Ohio
(AK)Alaska                 (MB)Manitoba           (OK)Oklahoma
(AB)Alberta                (MD)Maryland           (ON)Ontario
(AZ)Arizona                (MA)Massachusetts      (OR)Oregon
(AR)Arkansas               (MI)Michigan           (PA)Pennsylvania
(BC)British Columbia       (MN)Minnesota          (PE)Prince Edward I.
(CA)California             (MS)Mississippi        (QB)Quebec
(CO)Colorado               (MO)Missouri           (RI)Rhode Island
(CT)Connecticut            (MT)Montana            (SA)Saskatchewan
(DE)Delaware               (MX)MEXICO             (SC)South Carolina
(DC)Washington DC          (NE)Nebraska           (SD)South Dakota
(FL)Florida                (NV)Nevada             (TN)Tennessee
(GA)Georgia                (NB)New Brunswick      (TX)Texas
(HI)Hawaii                 (NF)Newfoundland       (UT)Utah
(ID)Idaho                  (NH)New Hampshire      (VT)Vermont
(IL)Illinois               (NJ)New Jersey         (VA)Virginia
(IN)Indiana                (NM)New Mexico         (WA)Washington
(IA)Iowa                   (NY)New York           (WV)West Virginia
(KS)Kansas                 (NC)North Carolina     (WI)Wisconsin
(KY)Kentucky               (ND)North Dakota       (WY)Wyoming
(LA)Louisiana              (NS)Nova Scotia
Where would you like to go? [RETURN to exit]
```

All of the available areas are shown with the necessary commands in parentheses. A native of Missouri, I'll choose that state by entering **MO** followed by a **RETURN**. I am then presented with a submenu of possible sites there:

```
Missouri
                University of Missouri
                     1. Columbia Campus
                     2. Rolla Campus
                     3. St. Louis campus
                     4. Washington University in St. Louis
Pick a number [RETURN exits]
```

When I choose item number 1, for the University of Missouri at Columbia, something interesting happens. I am presented with the necessary login information to get me into the system there, a sequence I wouldn't have been able to duplicate without this helpful screen:

```
Columbia Campus
                Press TAB to get to the COMMAND prompt and type
                DIAL VTAM. At the next prompt, type LUMIN
                To quit, type #LOGOFF and then UNDIAL.
Connect? [y]
```

Note the last item. By entering a **y**, followed by a **RETURN**, at this point, I tell LIBTEL to make the Telnet connection for me. Like the Macintosh, Unix, and VMS versions of HYTELNET, LIBTEL can take you directly to the site. Figure 7.10 shows the result, the login screen at the University of Missouri at Columbia.

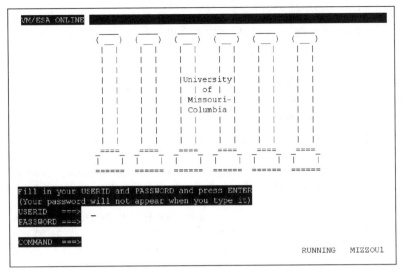

Figure 7.10   Logging on at the University of Missouri.

LIBTEL is clearly a simple and accessible system. Given the large number of library catalogs now on the Internet, having a concentration of possible sites in one place is extremely useful, as is the sign-on information. LIBTEL's disadvantage is that it is not a program but a simple script. It houses no external database or file; to modify the information requires editing the actual script materials. LIBTEL is also limited in being offered only through the overworked UNC site. Were good library tools to spread to numerous additional sites, using library catalogs would become much easier.

HINT: As with all Internet tools, you must be wary of generalizations. LIBTEL occasionally blips; in fact, when running a recent session, I discovered that the login information required had been changed at the remote site I was trying to access. If this happens to you, consider changing sites for your search, and be aware that some libraries are beginning to restrict access to their catalogs. Or, if the site in question is important to you, wait a day or two for LIBTEL to be updated to reflect the change.

Using LIBS to Search Remote Libraries

LIBS (**L**ibrary **I**nternet **B**rowsing **S**oftware) is a Telnet-based network access tool that helps users find and log on to library catalog systems. The program became available in June 1991, reaching what creator Mark Mesmer considered a stable version 1.0 in July of that year. Originally crafted to run under the VMS operating system, LIBS became available in 1992 in a Unix version. The system also grew in size, connecting to numerous on-line library catalogs as well as Campus Wide Information Systems (CWIS), information services, and a variety of databases. Mesmer, who is Director of Computing, Media and Telecommunications at Sonoma State University in California, continues to refine and extend the software.

How can you use LIBS? If your site does not make it available locally, you can evaluate the program through a Telnet session. Here are several sites that handle LIBS.

Address	Site	Login
nic.csu.net	California State University	libs
rsl.ox.ac.uk	Menuegesteuerter hierarchischer Bibliothekszugang	libs
oavax.csuchico.edu	CSU Chico LIBS Information Service	libs

As you can see, the standard login for a LIBS system is libs. After using Telnet to reach one of these sites, and entering libs at the login prompt, you will see a menu like the one shown in Figure 7.11.

The menu is straightforward. Note that, like HYTELNET, LIBS includes links to a wide variety of information. We'll begin our examination by asking to see library catalogs in the United States (menu item 1). The menu of states gives us the ability to pick one. Let's choose Hawaii.

```
University of Hawaii

Note the following instructions carefully

Once you are connected:

The UH Computing Center greeting will display, which concludes with the prompt:
"enter class". Then type LIB.

Select VT100 as your terminal type from the menu (option 5)

To exit the system, simply type //EXIT,
or press Control-C Q <return> to exit at any time

Do you want to connect now? (Y or N):
```

```
         LIBS - Internet Access Software
         Mark Resmer, Sonoma State University

On-line services available through the Internet:

1 United States Library Catalogs
2 Library Catalogs outside the United States
3 Campus-wide Information Systems
4 Databases and Information Services
5 Wide-area Information Services
6 Free-Net's
7 Information for first time users

Press RETURN alone to quit

Press Control-] Q (return) to exit at any time

Enter the number of your choice:
```

Figure 7.11 The basic LIBS screen, showing its menu of information.

We have all the information we need to log on at the University of Hawaii, and a prompt asking whether we want to proceed with the connection.

LIBS also provides a handy menu for CWIS systems. These come in handy when we are trying to locate people in a university setting. Figure 7.12 shows this menu. And a glimpse at LIBS' range is shown by its menu of miscellaneous resources, all of them accessible by Telnet:

```
The following services are available:

        1 CHAT Information System

        2 FEDIX/MOLIS

        3 Geographic Name Server

        4 HP Calculator BBS

        5 Library of Congress - DRA

        6 Library of Congress - Washington D.C.

        7 UMD Database

        Press RETURN alone to see previous menu

        Press Control-C Q <return> to exit at any time

        Enter the number of your choice:
```

CHAT is an intriguing information retrieval technology developed by Communications Canada (one part of which lets you engage in conversation with a computer), while the *UMD Database* contains a variety of information about computer, government, and economic data. Note, too, that we have access to U.S. Federal sites such as FEDIX/MOLIS, not to mention the Library of Congress. LIBS clearly boasts quite a range.

Gopher as Library Tool

We have already seen that Gopher includes library catalogs; it's possible to tap into holdings from Singapore to Sacramento using its powers. But several Gophers deserve spe-

```
Campus-wide Information Systems are accessible in the following places:

      1 Arizona                         2 Arkansas
      3 Colorado                        4 Indiana
      5 Illinois                        6 Iowa
      7 Massachusetts                   8 Missouri
      9 Texas                          10 Nebraska
     11 New Brunswick                  12 New Hampshire
     13 New Jersey                     14 New Mexico
     15 New York                       16 North Carolina
     17 Ohio                           18 Pennsylvania
     19 Quebec                         20 South Carolina
     21 Switzerland                    22 United Kingdom
     23 Vermont

            Press RETURN alone to see previous menu
            Press Control-C Q <return> to exit at any time

            Enter the number of your choice: _
```

Figure 7.12 Using LIBS to locate information on campus.

cial mention for anyone interested in exploring libraries. They are the sites containing the most current lists of library catalogs available on the Internet. The list of connections was originally drawn from the data files of HYTELNET and converted to Gopher format by Michigan State University. The list was then checked against Billy Barron's *Accessing On-line Bibliography Databases* document, compiled by him when he was at the University of North Texas, as well as a comparable list published by Art St. George at the University of New Mexico and Ron Larsen at the University of Maryland.

The result? Useful Gopher information about libraries that can help us answer the fundamental library problem. It's very useful, of course, to be able to search a HYTEL-NET or a LIBTEL to find the information we need to log in at a given library, but what do we do when we know the nature of the collection we're interested in examining, but don't know where it is? Suppose, for example, that I wanted to track down libraries with a stronger than usual emphasis on a particular subject, such as southern historical literature?

Gopher, you'll recall, allows connections to databases. Let's see what we can find at the Yale University Gopher. Figure 7.13 gives you an idea. We find a Gopher menu full of library catalog items; indeed, Yale maintains a current list of all library catalogs accessible on the Internet (kudos to the team that maintains this site—Marie-Christine Mahe at Yale, Lou Rosenfeld at the University of Michigan, and Billy Barron himself). You can see that the eighth item, *Paper List* (*BBarron's Accessing Online Bib Dbases*) may be useful; it's the document just referred to, containing an excellent introduction to on-line libraries and information about connections worldwide. And above it are library catalogs broken into global areas. By double-clicking on one of these items, I call up a list of

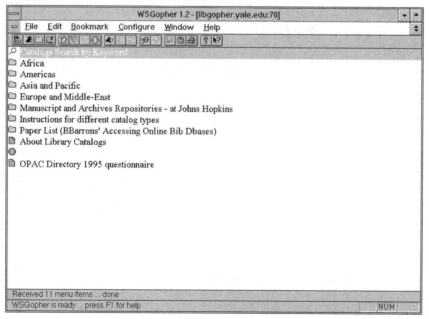

Figure 7.13 The Yale University Gopher maintains extensive library resources.

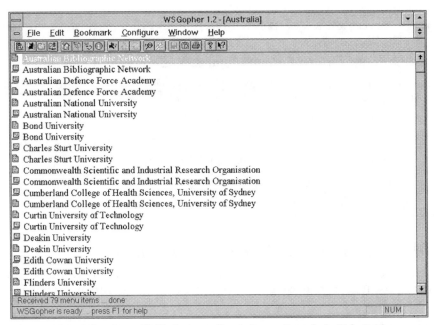

Figure 7.14   Libraries available in Australia as shown through the Yale Gopher.

libraries broken down, first by country, and then by individual connection. Figure 7.14 shows the libraries available in Australia. Now I have all the information I need to home in on libraries that can help me in a given region, and I can use Gopher's links to data to move to them automatically.

But note in Figure 7.13 that we also have a search field that allows us to enter keywords to search the library catalog database for particular kinds of information. It would be possible, for example, to enter a search term like southern historical, if our interest were in collections of such material, and retrieve a list of libraries specializing in that field.

There are several Gophers you should be aware of that specialize in library science. Here are their URLs:

gopher://squirrel.utdallas.edu	If you're using a shell account enter **gopher squirrel.utdallas.edu** or, in the absence of a client program, work through Gopher menus by Telnet to reach it. A client program through **SLIP/PPP** is the easiest route. This site is at the University of Texas in Dallas.
gopher://libgopher.yale.edu	The Yale University library site. Provides useful instructional material for searching the different types of catalogs.
gopher://gopher.sunet.se	For European users, a mirror of much of this material.

HINT: You can also retrieve Billy Barron's guide by FTP, if you prefer to have it in paper format. The URL is:

> ftp://ftp.utdallas.edu/pub/staff/billy/libguide

You can also check a World Wide Web page where Barron contributes articles he has written about library research on the Internet. Its URL is:

> http://www.utdallas.edu/acc/billy-bib.html

A fine World Wide Web page highlighting Internet library resources is found at:

> http://www.lib.utexas.edu/Libs/World_Libraries.html

as shown in Figure 7.15. And another is at:

> http://www.lib.washington.edu/~tdowling/libweb.html

The World Wide Web and Library Searching

We've already seen that HYTELNET can be searched over the World Wide Web, and it's no surprise that an increasing number of library resources are now moving into the Web

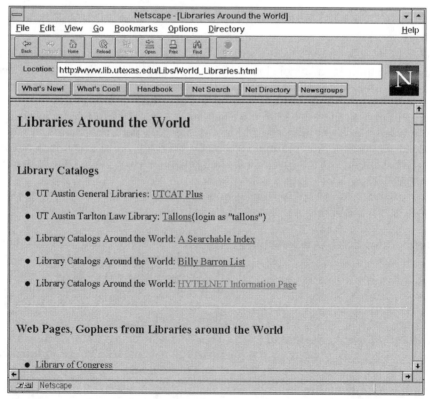

Figure 7.15 The World Wide Web also provides useful pages devoted to library resources.

environment. When a library goes onto the Web, the interface issue gets interesting. In Figure 7.16, you can see the Brown University Library home page.

A number of interesting links are usually established at such sites, but when we turn to the actual catalog search at Brown, as at most universities, the connection remains via Telnet. However, there is more to the library story on the World Wide Web than this. Z39.50 is a standard for defining information retrieval between one computer and another (we've already examined one implementation of Z39.50—WAIS). The most useful thing about Z39.50 is that it makes it possible to search a remote database without knowing anything about the kind of search system implemented at that site. As we've seen, libraries use a wide variety of software; indeed, one of the helpful things about HYTELNET is its ability to include the various systems in its help database. Approved by the National Information Standards Organization in 1988, Z39.50 is gaining increasing attention as a way of hooking up the enormous library resources now on the Internet.

The Clearinghouse for Networked Information Discovery and Retrieval makes available a public domain program called ZClient which can be implemented in such information searches. The Library of Congress, for example, allows searching of its books file through a WWW/Z39.50 gateway, and includes a number of other servers that can be

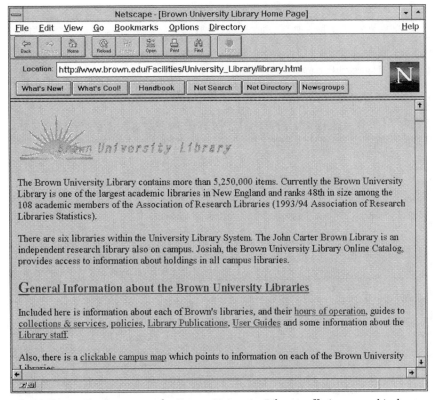

Figure 7.16 The home page for Brown University Library, offering a graphical entry point to the on-line catalog and other information.

searched through a World Wide Web browser, many of them at university libraries. You can see a form from the Library of Congress Web page in Figure 7.17. Here we can search for books by title or personal name. In Figure 7.18, you can see the results of a search using the keyword fleet, which turned up some 217 hits at Amherst College.

The moral of this chapter is that you can't be too committed to a single interface when you're searching for information. As we've seen, Telnet sources can get us plenty of information, but we can also tap into useful Web and Gopher implementations for particular sets of information, while the trend in library cataloguing seems to favor continued development of World Wide Web gateways. Fortunately, the Web search directories and engines we examined in Chapter 2 make it relatively simple to find such resources.

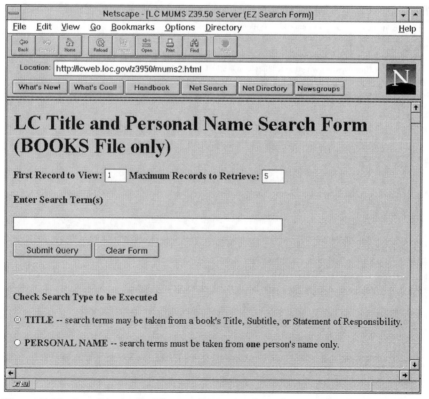

Figure 7.17 Searching at the Library of Congress through a World Wide Web browser.

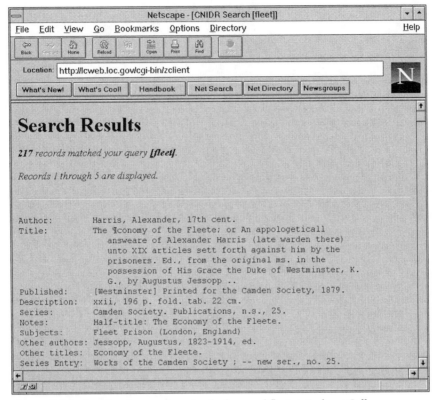

Figure 7.18   Results of a search under the keyword fleet at Amherst College.

NOTE: Z39.50 and WAIS are not synonymous. When Thinking Machines Corp. set about creating WAIS, they turned to the existing Z39.50 implementation to serve as the protocol behind it. This version of Z39.50, established in 1988, became the basis for the software produced by WAIS, Inc.; it included a number of extensions suited for WAIS. But the Z39.50 standards body produced a new version in 1992, adding considerable new functionality. The original 1988 version of Z39.50 is not interoperable with the 1992 version, which means that a Z39.50-1992-based client cannot communicate with a WAIS server. Meanwhile, a number of organizations now offer products based upon the 1992 iteration of Z39.50, including Research Libraries Group, AT&T, and the Clearinghouse for Networked Information Discovery and Retrieval itself. In fact, the protocol has been selected as the basis for the federal government's Government Information Locator Service. While both WAIS and Z39.50-1992 software can be used to search extensive collections of information, they are definitely not based upon the same protocol.

8

WHOIS, netfind, X.500: Finding People

Notwithstanding the popularity of the World Wide Web, electronic mail is the most widely used resource on the Internet. That it should be is no surprise; one-to-one communication, whether global or local, is quick and easy to manage using even the simplest mail programs, like Unix mail or more adaptive readers like pine and, in the SLIP/PPP environment, the full-featured Eudora. Mastering the addressing scheme behind TCP/IP shouldn't present any problem either, because an Internet address can be typed in as is—the Domain Name System is responsible for making the necessary conversions into IP (Internet Protocol) numbers, while the network's routers see to it that the message is delivered.

Where we run into problems is in finding the address in the first place. Newcomers find themselves in the awkward position of having access to a powerful communications medium without knowing to whom they can talk. Typically, they begin their mail excursions by sending messages to people on their local network or other users of their dial-up service provider, perhaps responding to a welcome message or to a posting they think relevant. Their list of potential correspondents increases as they begin signing on to mailing lists and reading the postings on USENET.

Inevitably, though, the day comes when you know the name of a person but don't know how to reach him or her. In this chapter, we will discuss how to cope with this dilemma. It is, perhaps, the most widely asked question on the Internet: How do I find a particular mailing address? And surprisingly, the Internet's directory tools make the job an extremely difficult proposition. We'll take a look at present directory schemes and show how they can help; their limitations may surprise you. We'll then examine the range of options to try when your first search doesn't work. In no other area of Internet research is the finding process more accumulative than here. It may take numerous tools and multiple searches with each to find the address you need. And even with all that firepower, you may still come up empty.

X.500 and the Search for Addressing Standards

We'd like to have something on the order of a telephone book, albeit an electronic one: Insert the name in the specified place, and out comes a list of possible people; choose the one you want, and the address appears. The analogy to telephone directories is so obvious that Internet directory tools are often referred to as "yellow pages" and "white pages," with the same distinction as between the paper versions. Yellow pages are the directories to search for business addresses; the white pages contain the names of individuals. But, as we'll see, the two areas frequently overlap, and in many cases, a white pages search will require a business or organization name to make it work. In addition, the multiplicity of directory options makes any Internet name search far more complicated than searching through standardized telephone directories.

X.500 is an attempt to create directories in a format useful to network users. Because there is no central site running the Internet, the information available on it is distributed widely throughout the world. A directory system that hopes to reach people will have to be able to extend into many different locations, searching throughout a broad spectrum of possibilities. To do this, X.500 uses a so-called *distinguished name*, which allows the system to search flexibly for a given person and, having found him or her, to map that person's name into a standard format called X.400.

Let's untangle the terminology. Terms like X.400 and X.500 refer to standards developed by the International Organization for Standardization (known by its French acronym, ISO). ISO was founded in 1947 as a voluntary organization (which means no treaties are involved) that would meet to foster international agreements on standards for many different technologies. The national standards organizations of participating countries comprise the membership of ISO, which, in turn, certifies them to carry out standards-making activities. Each of these bodies can participate in ISO discussions and vote on any ISO technical committee. Membership now includes some 100 different countries. The organization is currently divided into over 2,700 technical committees, subcommittees, and working groups.

Another term you've doubtless encountered as you waded into the Internet is Open Systems Interconnection (OSI). OSI is a reference model, a set of protocols, used for making sure that the various data communications functions that have to work together to make a worldwide network operate do indeed function as planned. After all, with thousands of networks feeding into the Internet, the variety of equipment passing packets of data is immense. OSI, then, is designed to help these different machines work together; its goal is open systems, keeping the products of a multitude of manufacturers transparent to each other and working. The system grew out of the work of several standardization committees that began work in the early 1980s on nonproprietary standard protocols; both the ISO and the International Telecommunications Union have been heavily involved in subsequent OSI developments.

The results of this effort appeared as a reference model to networking that defined the so-called OSI Reference Model—called ISO 7498. The model divides the communications process between any two applications into seven layers, each of which provides a service to the next highest layer. These layers can include everything from the physical devices that make the connection work to the operating system and application software that round out the connection process. Thus OSI defines an application layer, a presentation layer, a session layer, a transport layer, a network layer, a data link layer, and a physical layer. The physical layer includes such items as the specification of the wire or other medium and the connectors that hook it up. The data link layer includes such features as error correction and detection, and so on.

If this sounds familiar, it's because open systems and the integration of varied resources are what the Internet's TCP/IP protocols are all about. And despite the efforts of OSI adherents, the present-day Internet has been largely defined by TCP/IP. OSI's problem has been the glacial pace of its implementation, as its adherents have focused on developing their protocols by committee while TCP/IP was being engineered and perfected in real-time networking situations. And even as the idea of multiprotocol networking gathered steam, OSI has remained more of a goal than a working environment, far outstripped by TCP/IP at network sites worldwide.

But if there is one area in which the impact of OSI has made itself felt, it is in the realm of directory tools, largely because this is one area where existing Internet methods have failed to coalesce. ISO has had limited success in the area of electronic mail (almost all Internet mail traffic now moves using the Simple Mail Transfer Protocol), but we need to examine OSI mail handling briefly to pave the way for its directory services. Read on.

X.400: What It Is and How It Works

X.400 (also known as Message Handling System) is a mail transfer standard that can serve as a gateway protocol between different kinds of mail systems. Think of X.400 as an alternative way to specify a network address. The method was developed by another group with a French acronym, the Comite Consultatif Internationale de Telegraphique et Telephonique (International Telephone and Telegraph Consultative Committee). This group, known as the CCITT is, in turn, an organ of the International Telecommunications Union (ITU), which formulates recommended standards and procedures. The ITU was involved in the original development of OSI. Out of this bureaucratic swirl came a new set of e-mail standards, X.400, which would be incorporated into OSI.

How X.400 Differs from TCP/IP Electronic Mail

X.400 addresses are different from standard Internet addresses. Recall that the addressing strategy used by TCP/IP works with names and domains. A computer on the Internet can be referred to by a name or a number. In fact, its address can be presented as a sequence of either. Thus, library.dartmouth.edu can also be expressed as 129.170.16.11, while info.ccit.arizona.edu can also be written as 129.196.76.201. When the network address is expressed numerically, it is called an IP (Internet Protocol) address. Type in the name of the computer you hope to reach, and the translation of that name into the appropriate IP address is handled for you by a computer within the domain in question. The transaction is thus transparent to the end user.

X.400 addresses consist of more than a name and a domain. They are constructed from a list of attributes, allowing them to be broken down in great detail and making them much more specific than any IP address. When you construct an X.400 address, you specify the attributes to create the entire address. Each attribute is given along with an equal sign (=) and a value; slashes separate one attribute from the next. Unwieldy? Indeed. Consider the following example of an X.400 address:

/G=John/S=Dryden/O=Whitehall/C=UK/ADMD=TELEMAIL/@sprint.com

Here's how to untangle these elements:

G   Given name. The recipient's first name.

S   Surname. The recipient's last name.

O   The organization at which the recipient works or is affiliated.

C   Country code.

ADMD   The name of the mail system the recipient is using.

You can add a huge number of qualifiers to your field of attributes, including the following:

DDA   Domain-defined attribute. This is a code that identifies the recipient. It could be an account name or any other number specific to the individual.

I   An initial, as in /G=William/I=F/S=Buckley/.

PRMD   A private system with a gateway into the public mail system.

Because there are so many possible attributes, and because you won't necessarily know which attributes you need to specify in a given address, piecing together an X.400 address from information you already know is probably pointless. The very complexity of the X.400 address conventions makes it necessary for us to fall back on some kind of organizing structure—which is precisely what X.500 is all about.

X.500 as a Directory Service

Think of X.500 as a directory service that organizes the information tied up inside unwieldy X.400 addresses. Rather than needing to know an entire X.400 address, we're able to feed the directory a few of the terms we do know and it will accomplish the search for us. But we have to specify where we're looking. Using Telnet to reach a specific X.500 site, for example, I could type in a name, but in the absence of an organization, the system would simply search its local directories for the person in question. But because X.500 searches are interactive, I can then narrow the search with further specifications. The beauty of X.500 is that it allows local directory services to be connected in order to form a distributed global directory; to the end user, the entire directory is accessible from a local server.

In its totality, X.500 can be considered a worldwide directory project that currently holds data for some 2,800 organizations. As you consider using X.500, remember that most of the information in its directories has been supplied by the individual organizations involved. And remember, too, that this directory system is by no means universally accepted; numerous organizations in various countries have opted not to participate, so there is no guarantee that the organization or the person you are looking for will be available through X.500. Many corporations, for example, prefer to keep their database information private, although some do offer a subset of the data to public scrutiny.

NOTE: Where does the term X.500 come from? In true bureaucratic fashion, it's named after the number of the CCITT document that contains its specification. Rumors of a more glamorous name for the enterprise have yet to be realized.

X.500 Connection Options

A variety of methods are available for using an X.500 database. They include the following:

- Connect to X.500 Using Telnet. X.500 searches by Telnet are generally run through several different software programs. You will encounter line-oriented clients called de, dish, or fred, and there is a menu-driven client called sd. Unfortunately, X.500 is an evolving system, and the software that runs your searches is as likely to crash as not, so be prepared to be patient as you explore it. A number of sites are available, including those listed in Table 8.1.

Table 8.1   X.500 Servers Available by Telnet

Address	Country	Login
jethro.ucc.su.oz.au	Australia	fred
sun1.iihe.ac.be	Belgium	dua
x500.denet.dk	Denmark	de
login.dkuug.dk	Denmark	ds
x500.tu-chemnitz.de	Germany	x500
ashe.cs.tcd.ie	Ireland	de
x500.ieunet.ie	Ireland	de
jolly.nis.garr.it	Italy	de or fred
zoek.nic.surfnet.nl	Netherlands	no login required
elc1.mat.torun.edu.pl	Poland	de or dish
chico.redires.es	Spain	directorio
hypatia.umdc.umu.se	Sweden	de
nic.switch.ch	Switzerland	dua
dir.ulcc.ac.uk	United Kingdom	dua
paradise.ulcc.ac.uk	United Kingdom	dua
ds.internic.net	United States	x500

- Use a local client. A variety of clients are available—in the world of X.500, they are known as Directory User Agents, or DUAs. Personal computer users can choose between programs like Windows Directory User Agent, Swix, waX.500, and piXie, all of them freeware. The easiest client implementation is to use a World Wide Web browser like Netscape to handle an X.500 search in a fully graphical environment. For the purposes of this chapter, I will illustrate basic X.500 procedures through a Telnet session to a remote server, and then show samples of both a Gopher-driven search and one conducted using a Web browser.

By Telnet to an X.500 Server

Because the fred interface can be accessed from any kind of computer, let's use it to examine X.500. For this session, I'll access the Italian Directory Service Project, which makes both the fred and de programs available as alternative interfaces. The URL is:

telnet://jolly.nis.garr.it

Log in as fred; no password is required. What you'll see when you sign on is shown in Figure 8.1.

Searching with fred's help is fairly basic. You type **whois** followed by the name you're looking for and the name of the organization where the person is employed. (WHOIS, by the way, is a separate protocol; it's not part of X.500). A typical search, then, might appear in this form:

whois dryden -org whitehall

There are numerous commands to use with fred, and be warned, they are by no means easy to remember. In fact, the manual page for fred makes this comment: "The command syntax, while meant to be intuitive, is tedious." In my part of the world, this is known as an understatement.

Some of the commands that fred will accept are shown here:

whois *name*	Searches for entries with this name in the default area. The "area" is set by the system administrator at the directory site. Thus, searching with the command **whois jones** pulls up anyone named Jones at, in this case, the Italian site.
whois surname *name*	Allows you to specify a particular surname. This can be different from the preceding command, because fred uses a namesearch variable that will match either surnames or full names depending on how it's set. **whois surname jones** searches only for a surname of jones.
whois *name* **-org** *organization*	Specifies a particular organization along with a name. I could, for example, search using **whois**

```
Escape character is '^]'.

SunOS UNIX (jolly)

login: fred
Last login: Thu Aug 24 12:42:44 from 193.204.68.168
SunOS Release 4.1.3_U1 (JOLLY-X25) #1: Wed Jan 5 19:39:49 MET 1994




Welcome to the Italian Directory Service Project (DIR-ITA)

Try   "help" for a list of commands
      "whois" for information on how to find people
     "manual" for detailed documentation
      "report" to send a report to the white pages manager

To find out about participating organizations, try
     "whois -org *"

  accessing service, please wait...

fred> _
```

Figure 8.1 Logging on at an X.500 site using Telnet.

jones -org abc to specify a search for someone named jones at ABC Corporation, presuming ABC Corp. was participating in X.500. Alternatively, searching under **whois jones -org a*** would cause fred to run through all the organizations beginning with **a** one at a time, asking whether I wanted to search in each one.

whois -org *

Presents the registered organizations in the default geographical area.

whois -org * -geo @*countrycode*

Generates a report of all registered organizations in a particular country. For example, the command **whois -org * -geo @c=it** will generate a list of organizations in Italy. A sample of this list is shown in Figure 8.2.

The limitations of using X.500 for searching should by now be obvious. Your search will be successful only if the organization to which the person is affiliated is using X.500. You can, of course, check this by using the **whois -org *** command, but that adds another step to your search method; in any case, it frequently results in your finding that your target's firm isn't involved in X.500. Using X.500 is clearly a hit or miss proposition.

fred does provide help functions, although they're about as intuitive as fred itself. Nevertheless, the help system does let you focus in on the major commands. Enter **help** and you'll receive a list of commands. But a better idea is to enter **manual**, which will produce the manual page for fred, along with the great variety of command options available. I recommend you capture this material and print it for future reference.

```
fred> whois -org * -geo @c=it
393 matches found.
   1. Accent                                              +39-39-6899857
   2. Achab s.r.l.                                         +39-2-55182169
   3. Aerimpianti                                          +39-2-54971
   4. Agenzia Spaziale Italiana                            +39-6-85671
   5. Agic s.r.l.                                          +39-10-3313325
   6. Aitek s.r.l.
   7. Alenia S.p.A. - Laboratorio di Tecnologie dell' Informazione +39-6-41503411
   9. Alias S.r.l.                                         +39-432-69417
  10. Alpa Srl                                             +39-2-26141480
  11. Altair Data System                                   +39-2-6422057
  12. Anit                                                 +39-10-466137
  13. Ansaldo Ricerche                                     +39-10-6551
  14. Ansaldo Sistemi Informatici                          +39-10-655 1
  15. Ansaldo Spa                                          +39-10-5501
  16. Anthropos s.a.s.                                     +39-2-48403634
  17. Apogeo s.r.l.                                        +39-2-89404722
  18. Arcadia S.r.l.                                       +39-2-76009529
  19. Area di Ricerca
  20. ARS                                                  +39-2-52025327
  21. Ars S.r.l.                                           +39-2-4390853
--More--
```

Figure 8.2 Finding organizations in Italy that participate in the X.500 directory project.

The NameFLOW-Paradise Service: A Different Interface

As we've seen, fred is but one interface to X.500 services. The NameFLOW-Paradise Service provided by the European network called DANTE is a case in point. There, an X.500 directory is provided through a more intuitive interface called Directory Enquiries, or de, which was developed by Paul Barker at University College under the auspices of the European Commission's COSINE PARADISE Project funding. Directory Enquiries draws the same information—electronic mail addresses, postal addresses, telephone and fax numbers—out of the database as fred does: You provide information and the directory service then searches both local and remote databases to try to match it.

To reach the NameFLOW-Paradise Service, use the following URL:

telnet://paradise.ulcc.ac.uk

Log on as **dua**. You will see the screen shown in Figure 8.3.

Space does not permit a thorough explication of the NameFLOW-Paradise Service's commands. But note that entering an **i** will produce several pages of instructions, while using the **?** key will take you into the system's help functions.

The system works by asking you a sequence of questions. You are prompted for name, department, organization, and country. You need not answer them all, of course, and outcomes vary depending upon how you approach the search. Entering a single name, even a surname alone, will get the program started trying to match entries with similar names. It even attempts to handle common misspellings (don't ask fred to do that). Entering precise information about an organization or department will help you home in on the person you need. Entering an asterisk (*) will cause the system to list all people in the selected department or organization.

```
NameFLOW-Paradise Directory Service.

Select the mode you would like:

S Simple queries - if you know the name of the organisation you want to search
  (this is how the interface always used to behave)

P Power Search - to search many organisations simultaneously

B  Browser - best suited for exploring the Directory

Y Yellow Pages - power searching but allows user to search for an entry
   based on criteria other than the entry name

U Enter search string in form of User-Friendly Name - e.g,
   p barker, ucl, uk

I Brief instructions explaining the program modes and how to use the program

? The help facility - usage and topics

Q To quit the program

Enter option:
```

Figure 8.3 Logging on at the NameFLOW-Paradise Service in the United Kingdom.

You can even leave the name field blank and search for broader information about the people in various departments and organizations. To produce the results shown in Figure 8.4, I entered an asterisk instead of a name, doing the same under the department field. When prompted for an organization, I entered ulc, for University College London. I was then prompted for which group within the University of London Computer Centre I would like to search. Choosing the User Services Group from a short menu, I retrieved the information shown.

Although easier to work with than fred, the NameFLOW-Paradise Service's interface remains daunting, and you'll have to practice to get the hang of it. The system's initial menu offers simple lookups, by which it means searches for a specific person, department, or organization. Entering an **s** at the command prompt sets this mode. Another route is a multiple organization search, which should be chosen when you know the name of a person and the country in which they work but don't know the name of the organization. The command for this mode is **p** (it stands for power search). A **q** quits the program entirely.

It will be interesting to see how the NameFLOW-Paradise Service develops. The origin of the service was in the PARADISE Pilot Project, which was in the process of building a coordinated international directory service for the European Research Community. The next phase transforms the pilot project into a fully operational service. NameFLOW currently provides access to national directory services in countries throughout Europe, as well as Australia, Brazil, the United States, and more. If you're interested in learning more about this directory project, here is the address:

DANTE
Lockton House
Clarendon Road
Cambridge CB2 2BH

```
    User Services Group

Found the following entries.  Please select one from the list
by typing the number corresponding to the entry you want.

United Kingdom
   University of London Computer Centre
     User Services Group
         1   Julie Altmann        +44-171-405-8400 x 358   J.Altmann@ulcc.ac.uk
         2   Margaret Barfield    +44-171-405-8400 x 403   M.Barfield@ulcc.ac.uk
         3   Linda Hawkins        +44-171-405-8400 x 366   L.Hawkins@ulcc.ac.uk
         4   James Henderson      +44-171-405-8400 x 359   J.Henderson@ulcc.ac.uk
         5   Chris Howarth        +44-171-405-8400 x 362   C.Howarth@ulcc.ac.uk
         6   Allan Hume           +44-171-405-8400 x 367   A.Hume@ulcc.ac.uk
         7   Malcolm Keech        +44-171-405-8400 x 357   M.Keech@ulcc.ac.uk
         8   Minaz Punjani        +44-171-405-8400 x 330   M.Punjani@ulcc.ac.uk
         9   Andy Quick           +44-171-405-8400 x 438   A.Quick@ulcc.ac.uk
        10   Rosa Quick           +44-171-405-8400 x 342   R.Quick@ulcc.ac.uk
        11   Steven Self          +44-171-405-8400 x 372   S.Self@ulcc.ac.uk
        12   David Winstanley     +44-171-405-8400 x 397   D.Winstanley@ulcc.ac.uk

Simple query mode selected
Person's name, q to quit, * to browse, ? for help
:- _
```

Figure 8.4 A search for users at University College, London.

United Kingdom
Voice: +44 223 302 992
Fax: +44 223 303 005
mailto:V.Berkhout@dante.org.uk
http://www.dante.net/nameflow.html

Using Gopher to Run an X.500 Search

Gopher provides an intuitive and easily accessed route to X.500, allowing you to search X.500 directories by moving through a series of menus. Many Gophers will have an entry labeled *Phone Books* or something similar, leading you to a submenu of choices. Figure 8.5 shows a typical X.500 menu as shown by the Gopher at The World.

Note that, with the exception of the first three items, the rest of the entries show individual countries. Each leads you to a submenu. Choosing Australia, for example, opens up a list of organizations offering X.500 directories in that country, as shown in Figure 8.6. As you see, I can now choose to search an individual organization, or I can take the broader search option to search within the entire country. The actual search is run by double-clicking on the search icon and entering a keyword in the ensuing field.

HINT: The X.500 search method should be apparent by now. You begin at the upper level within a given country, searching for an organization. If the organization you are looking for is available, you can then search within it for the person you are trying to find. Obviously, you have to know where your person is working for this method to work, which is a major drawback of this kind of directory.

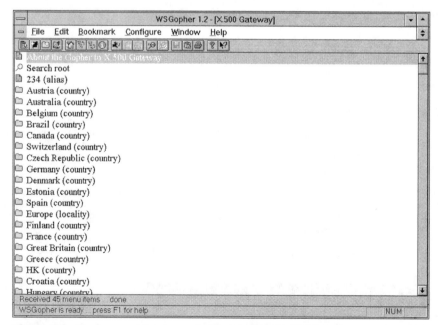

Figure 8.5 Gopher provides an easy-to-use interface for X.500 work.

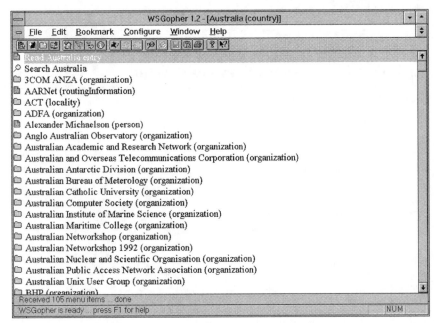

Figure 8.6   A display of organizations in Australia that are involved with X.500 directories.

X.500 differentiates between the levels you choose to search on. At its upper levels, which means when you search from the root or country level, searches are assumed to be for organizations or localities; at the lower levels (searching within an individual organization), searches are assumed to be for people. The Gopher implementation isn't perfect, but it is an easy way to use X.500, and the ubiquity of Gopher means you'll be able to run such searches whenever you choose, without worrying about the more problematical interfaces posed by programs like de or fred. As we'll soon see, Gopher gateways to WHOIS, netfind, CCSO servers, and more are now available.

X.500 through a Web Browser

As it has in so many other areas, the World Wide Web allows us to use X.500 with a minimum of fuss. In Figure 8.7, you can see the White Pages page at the InterNIC, which offers a Web interface to X.500 as well as WHOIS and netfind. You can explore this page at the following URL:

http://www.internic.net/ds/dspgwp.html

Figure 8.8 shows the actual X.500 search screen. As you see, we have a keyword field in which we can enter the first our our queries, along with a button that can launch the search. As with Gopher, the top-level search looks for broad information; in this case, countries (or you can simply page down the list and click on the country in which you want to search). At the country level, individual organizations are listed, and in typical Web fashion, can be clicked upon to retrieve information about the people within them,

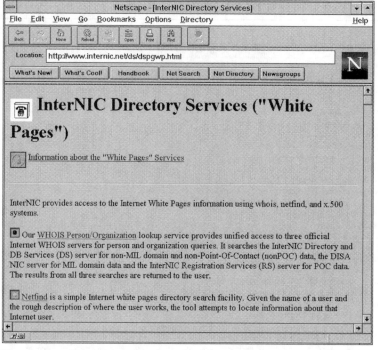

Figure 8.7 The InterNIC's White Pages services as seen through a Web browser.

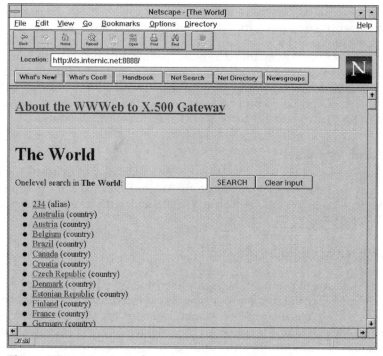

Figure 8.8 An X.500 search screen in the World Wide Web environment.

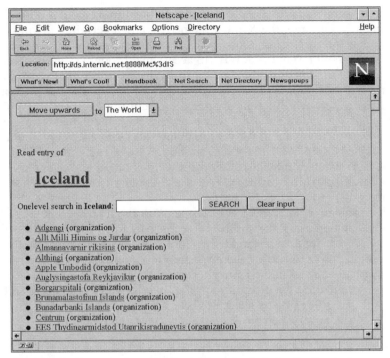

Figure 8.9 Preparing to search for information in Icelandic directories.

and to set up searches on their database contents. Figure 8.9 shows the country screen for Iceland.

I can click on any of these organizations (some 106 are listed) and, finally, home in on the individuals I want to examine by clicking on their separate entries. Using a Web browser, it's clear, makes the X.500 process about as transparent as it can get.

HINT: The Internet's people-hunting tools bring out a key fact about the network. Those interfaces that provide you with the greatest ease of use often allow you limited functionality. In the case of the X.500 system, searching through a World Wide Web browser is much easier than searching with de or fred, but the two Telnet-accessible client programs give you a greater degree of control over your search by allowing you to specify exactly what you are looking for, and thus homing in on it. If you master one of the latter client programs, you will be able to dispense with some of the browsing through menus that is inherent in both the Gopher and World Wide Web implementations of X.500, which is fine if you are sure about the name of the organization you are looking for. Both Gopher and the Web, however, make it easier to use X.500 if you aren't quite sure, let's say, of the complete name of the organization or its spelling.

WHOIS as a Search Tool

A white pages directory works by letting you insert a keyword; the information contained in the directory that is associated with that term then appears. By offering a variety of search commands (especially with the full-featured, though difficult-to-use, de and fred client programs), the X.500 system we studied certainly fits this description. But so do other Internet search tools, perhaps the most prominent of which is WHOIS. Servers around the Internet make WHOIS accessible through a variety of techniques.

But again we run into the organization trap. The average WHOIS server lets you run your queries past a database of names and addresses for a particular organization. You can move easily between different organizations and their respective WHOIS servers, but the result is typical of the Internet's problems with individual name searches: We need to know something about the person in question *before* we can mount the search. In addition, the various WHOIS servers are not aware of each other, which means that each must be consulted individually, and software changes at one site may not reflect changes at another. Think of these servers as allowing isolated searches for specific information.

Another problem with WHOIS is its scope. With the Internet reputed to be home to as many as 30 million users, the number of people contained within WHOIS databases is a tiny fraction of the total. You should, therefore, consider WHOIS within the larger context of other directory tools; after all, any search for a given person has a limited chance of success with directories in their current state of development. Any search may require that you use several different directory tools to find the person you need, and after using them all, you may still come up short. It's been said before and it's still true, that sometimes the best way to get a person's e-mail address is to call them on the phone and ask.

Accessing WHOIS

As with other Internet search tools, there are a variety of ways to tap into a WHOIS server.

- Using Telnet. Shell account users can reach a WHOIS server with a simple command: **telnet** *server-name*. Thus, **telnet indiana.edu**, or **telnet whois.adelaide.edu.au**. Log in as **whois**. SLIP/PPP users can take advantage of a graphical Telnet client.
- Using a local client. The character-based Unix client is called whois. There is also a Microsoft Windows client called WinWhois; for information about this shareware program, check this URL: http://www.biddeford.com/~jobrien/tidewater.html.
- Using electronic mail. The mail address is mailserv@ds.internic.net.

Using WHOIS through Telnet

The first thing to do when you want to use WHOIS with Telnet is to locate a public access server. For purposes of illustration, I'll use the server at the InterNIC, which contains the names of many people who have been involved with the Internet's registration procedures, including system administrators and technical contacts at major sites. The InterNIC is reachable at the following URL:

telnet://whois.internic.net

However, a wide variety of servers are out there; in fact, the latest list, which is collected and compiled by Matt Power of M.I.T., shows close to 200 sites, ranging from the Royal Institute of Technology in Sweden to the Faculty of Electronic Engineering at

Warsaw University, although the great majority of the sites are in the United States. Power's list does not include sites that provide directory services exclusively through finger or by electronic mail, so the actual number of directory sites is higher still. Here's a snippet of Power's list:

indiana.edu	Indiana University C=US
kean.edu	Kean College C=US
acad.csv.kutztown.edu	Kutztown University C=US
whois.rsmas.miami.edu	University of Miami, Rosentiel School of Marine and Atmospheric Sciences C=US
mit.edu	Massachusetts Institute of Technology C=US
whois.msstate.edu	Mississippi State University C=US
vax2.winona.msus.edu	Minnesota State University - Winona C=US
nau.edu	Northern Arizona University C=US
whois.ncsu.edu	North Carolina State University C=US
nd.edu	University of Notre Dame C=US
earth.njit.edu	New Jersey Institute of Technology C=US
acfcluster.nyu.edu	New York University, Courant Institute C=US
sun1.mcsr.olemiss.edu	University of Mississippi C=US

Don't be misled by naming conventions. Although it is common to choose WHOIS as the first part of the domain name, as in whois.msstate.edu, many sites don't do this. California State University in Sacramento, for example, runs its WHOIS service from the host csus.edu, reflecting the fact that some sites have chosen to put their WHOIS servers high up in the organization's domain hierarchy. The thing to do, then, is to retrieve Power's complete list of WHOIS servers and proceed from there. Its URL is:

ftp://rtfm.mit.edu/pub/whois/whois-servers.list

As we'll see in a moment, there are differences between the way servers handle the user interface for WHOIS. For now, our practice will involve the InterNIC WHOIS server as accessed by Telnet. Later, I'll show you how to log on to other servers on the list.

Using WHOIS is relatively simple. Having given your Telnet command, you'll encounter a prompt, at which point you type in the search information you need. The system default is to run a broad search which attempts to match your search term in a variety of fields, from name to net address. The results are then displayed; in the case of a single hit, you get the detailed information: in the case of multiple hits, you'll receive short summaries. Figure 8.10 shows the login screen at the InterNIC's WHOIS server.

Typing **whois** then takes us to the system prompt.

```
Whois:
```

To proceed from this prompt, we simply type in the name we are looking for. Figure 8.11 shows what happens when we type the name **bradley** at the prompt. As you can see,

```
*****************************************************************
* -- InterNIC Registration Services Center --
*
* For wais, type:                    WAIS <search string> <return>
* For the *original* whois type:     WHOIS [search string] <return>
* For referral whois type:           RWHOIS [search string] <return>
*
* For user assistance call (703) 742-4777
# Questions/Updates on the whois database to HOSTMASTER@internic.net
* Please report system problems to ACTION@internic.net
*****************************************************************
Please be advised that use constitutes consent to monitoring
(Elec Comm Priv Act, 18 USC 2701-2711)

6/1/94
We are offering an experimental distributed whois service called referral
whois (RWhois). To find out more, look for RWhois documents, a sample
client and server under:
gopher: (rs.internic.net) InterNIC Registration Services ->
        InterNIC Registration Archives -> pub -> rwhois
        anonymous ftp: (rs.internic.net) /pub/rwhois
Cmdinter Ver 1.3 Fri Aug 25 10:13:26 1995 EST
[vt100] InterNIC >
```

Figure 8.10   The login screen at the InterNIC.

we've retrieved a number of bradleys; the system will pause partway through the list to ask if we want to see the rest of the hits.

Most records in a WHOIS database include a name field. If you're trying to find a particular person, bear in mind that the name field is presented last name first. Searching for Bill Bradley, then, we would type **bradley, bill** as our search term. Entering **bradley, b** would include anyone with a first initial of B.

```
Bradley, Mike (MB648)           MBRADLEY@IGC.APC.ORG              510-482-1712
Bradley, Mitch (MB361)          wmb@FORTHWARE.COM               (415) 961-1302
Bradley, Nigel (NB126)          nigel@BRADLEY1.DEMON.CO.UK   011 44 1635 38605
Bradley, Patrick (PB313)        postmaster@ESCORTSERVICES.COM    213-666-6642
Bradley, Paul (PB415)           sysadmin@ACCIDENT-ATTORNEYS.COM  503-343-1473
Bradley, Randy (RB683)          bradley@MARCVM.MARC.USDA.GOV   (402) 762-4156
Bradley, Randy (RB543)          root@MCSTUL.COM                (918) 491-8000
Bradley, Richard M. (RMB)       richardb@SPIDER.CO.UK          +44 31-554-9424
Bradley, Robert (RB426)         postmaster@CANADA-IMMIGRATE.COM (604) 669-0389
Bradley, Robert (RB806)         admin@WEB-SEARCH.COM             207-773-0147
Bradley, Rolie (RB409)                                        +1(416)947-6042
Bradley, Samuel (SB142)         SBradley@powersoft.com           508-287-2323
Bradley, Seth J. (SJB4)         sbradley@SCIC.INTEL.COM        (503) 531-5045
Bradley, Steven (SB227)         steven@SGB.OAU.ORG             (407) 862-7226
Bradley, Tom (TB416)            tomb@PRIMERETAIL.COM             410-234-1768
Bradley, William P. (WPB3)      postmaster@WBRADLEY.COM          916 395 0709
Christofferson, Bradley J. (BJC)bradley@PEPPER.COM             (415) 525-3325
Horowitz, Bradley (BH94)        bradley@MEDIA.MIT.EDU          (619) 658-0179
Rogers, Brad (BR242)            bradley@METRONET.COM             817-277-5806
Rotter, Bradley N. (BNR2)       bradley@ROTTER.COM             +1 702 832 2252
Schauf, Brad (BS397)            bradley@NCGROUP.COM              614-436-2962
Thornton, Bradley (BT74)        bradley@WORF.INFONET.NET       (310) 379-2170
Zimmer, Bradley (BZ8)           bradley@ZIMNET.COM             (910) 763-0488
Whois:
```

Figure 8.11   A search using the keyword bradley.

Any part of a name up to a space or a comma can be specified as the search term. You can also run a *partial search*, which lets you search for everything starting with the target term. Putting a period (.) after the text indicates the partial search is in effect. Thus, **john.** will retrieve not only people whose last name is John, but also Johns, Johnson, Johnston, and so on. When we try this at the InterNIC, this is what we get:

```
Whois: john.
[No name] (JOHNS-HST)          JOHNSON.JVNC.NET              192.67.236.10
(Johnson, Bob) (B())           johnson@CENTCON.COM          (818) 879-9992
Ackley, John (JA188)           john@SOFTSPACE.COM           (614) 873-3907
Action Title (JOHN-W-MAX-DOM)                               JOHN-W-MAX.COM
Adams, John (JA73)             johna@A-K.BOSTON.MA.US
                                    407 735 3248 (FAX) 1 407-732-8552
There are 1782 more matches. Show them?
```

The system has flagged several people whose name matches our specifications. Faced with displaying over 1,700 matches, it asks us whether we want to continue.

We should, however, be able to narrow down our search further than this. When there is only a single match found for our search term, we will get the full record. Thus, a search on the name Kosters brings the following record of InterNIC employee Mark Kosters:

```
Whois: kosters
Kosters, Mark A. (MAK21) markk@INTERNIC.NET
        Network Solutions, Inc.
        505 Huntmar Park Drive
        Herndon, VA 22070
        (703) 742-4795

        Record last updated on 30-Aug-94.
```

Here the record includes postal address, phone number, electronic mail address, and the date of last update.

Sometimes, though, you will have to search broadly and then tell the system which name you need. Let's assume we're searching for someone with the surname Jones; we know the first name begins with a c, but that is all. We can set up such a search using the search term **jones, c***. The results are shown in Figure 8.12.

Examine the list closely. At the left, each name is followed by an expression in parentheses. Look at the first entry for Charles Jones, for example. It is followed by the term CJ23. This is a field in the database called the *handle*; it's a unique identifier to the person in question. We can now tell the system which of these entries we want to see in detail by specifying the handle. Here is what happens:

```
Whois: !cj23
Jones, Charles (CJ23)      charliej@TELTRUST.COM
    Teltrust Data Services
    Teltrust Data Services
    221 North Charles Lindbergh Dr.
    Salt Lake City, UT 84116
    (801) 535-2200

    Record last updated on 31-Aug-94.
```

```
Jones, Charles (CJ23)           charliej@TELTRUST.COM              (801) 535-2200
Jones, Charles (CJ111)                                            714-675-1695
Jones, Charly (CJ35)            charly@NETCOM.COM                 (206) 851-9876
Jones, Chris (CJ458)            jcj@visual.com                    508 836-4400
Jones, Chris (CJ76)             cjones@GW.GIGASD.COM        (617) 982-9500 x168
Jones, Chris (CJ2-AU)           Collsen@Info.tas.gov.au
                                        +61 02211 934 FAX +61 02231 526
Jones, Chris (CJ141)            chris@NET-CONNECT.NET             (318) 234-4396
Jones, Chris (CJ147)            chris.jones@CLEAT.ORG             (713) 852-9596
Jones, Christopher (CJ129)      cwjones@IX.NETCOM.COM             619-581-2297
Jones, Chuck (CJ124)            cjones@ACUTRAC.COM                619-670-6141
Jones, Clay (CJ153)             clay@telos.com                   (719) 632-4004
Jones, Clayton (CJ44)           crjones@MINDSPRING.COM           (404) 621-8300
Jones, Cliff (CJ12)             root@ECRAAA.ARMY.MIL
                                        (410) 787-1188 (DSN) 923-7742/7743
Jones, Cory A. (CAJ)            cory_jones@VORTEX.VDT.COM         (503) 754-2806
Jones, Cory A. (CJ19)           jonesc@WORLDACCESS.COM
                                        (360) 253-9730 (360) 263-8000
Jones, Craig (CJ27)             Craig.M.Jones-1@UMN.EDU
                                        (507) 433-8804 (507) 433-9654
Jones, Curtis (CJ41)                    (714) 736-5240 (DSN) 933-5240
Jones, Cyle (CJ66)                                              502 651-5741
Jones, Cynthia (CJ115)          eskimo.joe@ICON.NET      (405) 624-3210 ext. 27
Whois:
```

Figure 8.12 We can use wildcards to produce results when we don't know a person's exact name.

Using an exclamation point (!) before the handle, and following it with the handle itself (with no space in between) has retrieved the record we need. As we'll see shortly, we can do the same thing with a client-based search of a WHOIS server.

Tips on Using WHOIS by Telnet

As illustrated, asking WHOIS for a broad search term like john. is asking for plenty of responses and, in the process, stressing the system (as well as the user's patience). It would make more sense, then, to work out a search strategy to minimize time and system resources. Fortunately, there are ways of doing so. Perhaps the most significant of these is the ability to search by field.

Each record in a WHOIS database contains a field specifying the kind of record it is. Because the main database holds records for individuals, domains, groups, hosts, networks, and organizations, you can search by these criteria. The result is fewer matches from WHOIS, but matches that more closely meet your search terms. An additional bonus is that this method of searching allows you to perform searches on fields not normally searched during a general query, such as the one we just did for names beginning with john.

SEARCHING BY DOMAIN

To search a database by domain, you simply use the keyword do before your search term. For example, entering **do std** at the WHOIS prompt produces the following hits:

```
Whois: do std
STD Systems (STD2-DOM)                                   STD.NET
STD Technology Inc. (STDGROUP-DOM)                   STDGROUP.COM
Software Tool & Die (STD-DOM)                            STD.COM
```

You can see any one of these by entering its full domain name:

```
Whois: std.com
Software Tool & Die (STD-DOM)
   1330 Beacon Street
   Brookline, MA 02146

   Domain Name: STD.COM

   Administrative Contact, Technical Contact, Zone Contact:
       Shein, Barry (BS25) netadmin@WORLD.STD.COM
       617-739-0202

   Record last updated on 03-Nov-94.

   Domain servers in listed order:

   WORLD.STD.COM              192.74.137.5
   NS.UU.NET                 137.39.1.3

Whois:
```

This list includes not only the usual address information, but also the server machines within the std domain.

SEARCHING BY HOST

Perhaps you'd like to see which hosts, or computers, are available at a specific site or within a given area. To do so, use the ho keyword, followed by your search term. To list hosts in Indiana, for example, you would use **ho indiana** as the search statement.

```
Whois: ho indiana
Indiana Cooperative Library Services Authority (OAK3-HST) OAK.PALNI.EDU
                                                            198.62.84.36
Indiana Higher Education Telecommunications Systems (JEFFERSON-HST) JEFFERSON.IT
                                                            157.91.128.2
Indiana Higher Education Telecommunications Systems (WASHINGTON-HST) WASHINGTONT
                                                            157.91.128.1
Indiana Sports Corporation (DNS29-HST) DNS1.INSPORTSCORP.COM  198.133.236.4
Indiana University (CALIBAN-HST) CALIBAN.IUS.INDIANA.EDU      149.160.3.175
There are 8 more matches. Show them? y
Indiana University (GRENDEL-HST) GRENDEL.IUS.INDIANA.EDU      149.160.18.2
Indiana University (VITA1) IUGATE.UCS.INDIANA.EDU               129.79.1.9
Indiana University (WOLFGATE-HST) WOLFGATE.WOLFNET.ORG          199.5.228.1
Indiana University of Pennsylvania (ACORN-IUP) ACORN.GROVE.IUP.EDU  144.80.128.8
Indiana University-Purdue University at Indianapolis (HUMMER) HUMMER.IUPUI.EDU
                                                               134.68.1.9
Indiana University (CICA-HST) CICA.CICA.INDIANA.EDU           129.79.20.27
Indiana Wesleyan University (BARNABUS-HST) BARNABUS.INDWES.EDU    199.8.20.2
Indiana Wesleyan University (DORCAS-HST) DORCAS.INDWES.EDU        199.8.20.1
Whois:
```

This retrieves records of host computers with the word indiana somewhere in their records. Note that the search term does not have to appear in the actual computer name. It does in a record like iuvax.cs.indiana.edu, but the hosts at Indiana Wesleyan University appear despite the fact that the term indiana does not show up in the machine name.

If you wanted to get more specific, you could ask for computers at a particular location by specifying a unique search term. Thus, **ho university of montana** would produce the following result:

```
Whois: ho university of montana
University of Montana (SELWAY)        SELWAY.UMT.EDU 150.131.14.2
University of Montana (UMT)    UMT.UMT.EDU    150.131.14.1
```

SEARCHING BY NETWORK

You can also use WHOIS to search by network records, using the ne keyword. Here, I've asked the WHOIS server for information about Infonet, a major packet switching network.

```
Whois: ne infonet
INFONET (NET-INFOLAN-C)        INFOLAN-C      192.92.20.0
INFONET (NET-INFOLAN-C1)       INFOLAN-C1     192.92.21.0
INFONET (NET-INFOLAN-C10)      INFOLAN-C10    192.92.30.0
INFONET (NET-INFOLAN-C11)      INFOLAN-C11    192.92.31.0
INFONET (NET-INFOLAN-C12)      INFOLAN-C12    192.92.32.0
There are 106 more matches. Show them?
```

Again, because of the length of the reply, I'm asked whether I want to see the entire list. Although I've searched for Infonet by using the network name, it's also possible to search by network number. Thus, **ne 192.92** would also retrieve the Infonet information, along with a great deal more, as shown in the following result:

```
Whois: ne 192.92
A.B. Dick Company (NET-ABDCPREPRESS) ABDCPREPRESS   192.92.84.0
AMCAST Industrial Corporation (NET-AMCAST) AMCAST   192.92.98.0
Abekas Video Systems (NET-ABEKRD) ABEKRD           192.92.109.0
Allegheny Ludlum Corporation (NET-ALCNET) ALCNET   192.92.159.0
Applied Computing Systems (NET-ACS) ACS            192.92.123.0
There are 168 more matches. Show them?
```

SEARCHING BY INDIVIDUAL NAME

To search by person, you can simply use the pe keyword. The effect is the same as if you had entered the name directly at the WHOIS prompt. Here, I'm searching for anyone with the name holland.

```
Whois: pe holland
Holland, Adrian (AH306)       aholland@ACTIONCOM.COM              (905) 477-3222
Holland, Anthony R. (TONY)    TONY@KL.SRI.COM                    (415) 859-4246
Holland, Art (AH272)          art@STUDIO.DISNEY.COM              (818) 558-2324
Holland, Barry (BH285)        hostmaster@PIPEX.NET +44 181 759 5511 [081]-562-4150
Holland, Carl D. (CDH10)                301-826-4908 (DSN) 312-326-4908
There are 37 more matches. Show them? y
```

SEARCHING BY MAILBOX

A general WHOIS search checks the mailbox field for matches. You can also home in on mailboxes by using a set of further keywords.

user@   Specifies that the system should search the username part of mail
              addresses for your target. You could, for example, use a search term of
              @billg, if you knew that your target's username was billg.

@host   Pulls in all mailboxes on a given host. This is what I retrieved when I used
              @unc as my search term:

```
Whois: @unc
Adams, Robert (RA106)      Robert_Adams@UNCG.EDU      (910) 334-1048
Beil, Bill (BB2)           beil@UNCECS.EDU           (919) 841-9196
Cancro, Art (AC11)         ajc@UNCNSRD.ORG           (914) 761-0632
Caston, David (DC17)       dcaston@UNCECS.EDU        (919) 770-3315
Curry, Chuck (CC242)       chuck_curry@UNCG.EDU      (919) 334-5350
There are 25 more matches. Show them?
```

user@*host*   Searches for an exact mailbox address. This would be useful if you knew
              the mailing address but wanted further information, such as a phone
              number, about the person.

SEARCHING OTHER SERVERS

As you've seen, Matt Power's list contains quite a few WHOIS servers that can be
accessed by Telnet. However, many of these machines are not set up as public access
WHOIS servers, and they're often not easy to use. When you set up a Telnet connection
to the address listed on Power's list, you may be asked to log in and provide a password.
To prevent this, be advised that WHOIS servers usually run on port 43 of the computer.
When you Telnet directly to the machine, in other words, you should use the port number in your address. Thus, if you want to use the WHOIS server at Indiana University,
you would enter the command **telnet indiana.edu 43**, rather than just **telnet indi-
ana.edu**. The proper form for the URL of the same service is telnet://indiana.edu:43.

   This is an important fact to keep in mind. If I try to reach the WHOIS server at
North Carolina State University, using the whois.ncsu.edu address given by Power, I
wind up being asked to log in. But if I add the port number, I can enter the system. It is
not, however, set up to make use easy. Note in the following login that once I am
accepted into the system, I am given no prompt. The system is simply waiting for me to
enter a search term, as I do here.

```
% telnet whois.ncsu.edu 43
Trying 152.1.1.23 ...
Connected to floyd.cc.ncsu.edu.
Escape character is '^]'.
willis, william
Name            : Willis, William E.
Campus address  : M-2 Hillsborough Bldg., Box 7109
Campus phone    : 5-2516 5-3787
Department      : Computing Center
Position        : Associate Provost/Academic Computing
E-mail address  : BILL_WILLIS@NCSU.EDU
Connection closed by foreign host.
```

USING **WHOIS** WITH A LOCAL CLIENT PROGRAM

With a local client on your system, you can quickly search a WHOIS database with a few
simple commands. The basic strategy is to use the command **whois [-h *host*] 'name'**

(note that the name in question should be surrounded by single quotation marks); use this command from your system prompt. Here again, it's necessary to have the list of WHOIS servers that we retrieved earlier in this chapter. Setting up a search at the Inter-NIC, for example, I would enter the following command:

whois -h whois.internic.net 'johnson'

to find anyone named Johnson in the InterNIC database (there are quite a few). Likewise, to search the server at whois.ncsu.edu, I would proceed with this command:

whois -h whois.ncsu.edu 'johnson'

By using a client, I don't need to specify the port address, as I would have to do if I were trying to reach this site by Telnet. Here is an example: I'm searching the WHOIS server at North Carolina State University for network guru William Willis, the person whose information I retrieved in the previous example. The result follows:

```
% whois -h whois.ncsu.edu 'willis, william'
Name            : Willis, William E.
Campus address  : M-2 Hillsborough Bldg., Box 7109
Campus phone    : 5-2516 5-3787
Department      : Computing Center
Position        : Associate Provost/Academic Computing
E-mail address  : BILL_WILLIS@NCSU.EDU
```

Note several things about this search. First, I'm using a full name, and have entered the last name first, followed by the first name. Second, I enclosed the name with single quotation marks. Without them, the search may not work.

If you fail to specify a host site, the system defaults to whichever WHOIS server your system administrator has specified. It may well be the InterNIC server, because it contains so many major Internet figures. Otherwise, it may be a server within your own organization, or one that is geographically close to you. For European users, it is likely to be the server at RIPE, the Reseaux IP Europeens, in Amsterdam. To perform searches comparable to those we've been running with the InterNIC, then, Europeans should use the address whois.ripe.net.

Bear in mind as you search that the WHOIS databases may contain different references to the same person. In the preceding example, I found Dr. Willis at North Carolina State University's WHOIS server; using the WHOIS server at the InterNIC also located him, but with a different result:

```
Whois: whois -h whois.internic.net 'willis, william'
Willis, William E. (WEW) willis@EOS.NCSU.EDU
        X Engineering Software Systems Corporation
        1001 Brothwell Court
        Raleigh, NC 27606
        (919) 859-2466
        Record last updated on 10-Sep-91.
```

Same person, but a different reference, this time to a company he is involved in rather than to the university (and note how old the information is). The InterNIC's WHOIS server is, in fact, a good place to begin a WHOIS search. Its database contains many of the major figures in the Internet community. The WHOIS server at nic.ddn.mil, which used to contain civilian as well as military addresses, is now reduced to MILNET people only, and won't help you if you're looking for a civilian. It is, obviously, the place to go for military people.

When a search retrieves more than a single name, you are presented with a list of possibilities, just as when using a Telnet connection to a WHOIS server. The following output resulted from my search for someone whose last name is Smith, with a first name beginning with the letter s.

```
% whois -h whois.internic.net 'smith, s*'
Smith, S.w. (SS724)          stevesw@ENET.NET                    602 870-5468
Smith, Sam (SS105)           72570.2411@COMPUSERVE.COM       (501) 320-1446
Smith, Samuel A. (SAS7)      ssmith@IQUEST.COM               (205) 883-4493
Smith, Scott (SS374)         netadmin@WORMS-GIIS.ARMY.MIL011-49-6241-487003
Smith, Scott (SS48)                                          (602) 287-4977
Smith, Scott (SS219)         POSTMASTER@SMITHWARE.COM        (615) 386-3100
Smith, Scott (SS483)         ssmith@PRIMENET.COM             (209) 255-1447
Smith, Scott (SS562)         admin@ISERVE.COM               +1 812 945-1200
Smith, Scott (SS644)         sdsmith@NETCOM.COM              (408) 977-7030
Smith, Scott (SS675)         smiths@VXCONSULT.COM              303-530-5345
Smith, Scott (SS681)         sdsmith@NEWSCAST.COM              801-584-2800
Smith, Scott (SS813)         postmaster@GNOMES.ORG          +1 408 264 6541
Smith, Scott A. (SAS8)       wizard@CROSSLINK.NET              703-569-2874
Smith, Scott D. (SDS7)       ggh@NESTNET.COM                +1 408 977 7030
Smith, Shabina (SS616)       ati@CRIS.COM                    (334) 661-5770
Smith, Sharleen (SS247)                                      (212) 408-3647 FAX
```

To choose one of these entries, I must send another **whois** command. This time I specify the handle:

```
% whois -h whois.internic.net 'ss724'
Smith, S.w. (SS724) stevesw@ENET.NET
   Ping Manufacturing Corp.
   2201 W. Desert Cove
   Phoenix, AZ 85029
   602 870-5468

   Record last updated on 27-Jul-95.


The InterNIC Registration Services Host contains ONLY Internet Information
(Networks, ASN's, Domains, and POC's).
Please use the whole server at nic.ddn.mil for MILNET Information.
```

As you can see, using a Telnet connection is in this case easier than working with a client; there is less to type. Any client program that handles WHOIS can be used to search these databases; and remember that you can also search, as with X.500, through Gophers and World Wide Web sites, thus adding to ease of use but limiting somewhat your search options. Do bear in mind the limitations of WHOIS, though, so you don't expect too much from the system. All of these directories together are only approximations of the network-wide directory we really need.

netfind: Fingering the Right Person

A WHOIS search is tightly focused; you choose the database to examine and then use the WHOIS program to find your target. Obviously, this involves knowledge of, or at least an educated guess about, where your person is located. The netfind program suffers from the same limitation. You enter a name and any other information you have, such as organization or location, and turn netfind loose. The program then scours the network looking for what you need. It can turn up a name and mailing address, as well as finger information about the person you're trying to find. What it can't do is to search comprehensively for a name alone; it must have a reasonable description of where the target person works to be successful. Within those admittedly narrow parameters, however, netfind can be a useful tool.

Accessing netfind

There are two ways to run a netfind search:

- Using Telnet to log on to a remote computer. The current list of netfind servers is shown in Table 8.2. As always, remember that, by the time you read this, the list

Table 8.2 netfind Servers Available by Telnet

Server Address	Location	Country
archie.au	AARNet, Melbourne	Australia
netfind.if.usp.br	University of Sao Paulo, Sao Paulo	Brazil
netfind.ee.mcgill.ca	McGill University, Montreal, Quebec	Canada
malloco.ing.puc.cl	Catholic University of Chile, Santiago	Chile
netfind.vslib.cz	Liberec University of Technology	Czech Republic
netfind.fnet.fr	Association FNET, Le Kremlin-Bicetre	France
netfind.uni-essen.de	University of Essen	Germany
netfind.elte.hu	Eotvos Lorand University, Budapest, Hungary	Hungary
netfind.icm.edu.pl	Warsaw University, Warsaw	Poland
lincoln.technet.sg	Technet Unit, Singapore	Singapore
nic.uakom.sk	Academy of Sciences, Banska Bystrica	Slovakia
krnic.net	Korea Network Information Center, Taejon	South Korea
netfind.mgt.ncu.edu.tw	National Central University	Taiwan
monolith.cc.ic.ac.uk	Imperial College, London	United Kingdom
mudhoney.micro.umn.edu	University of Minnesota, Minneapolis, MN	USA
bruno.cs.colorado.edu	University of Boulder, CO	USA
ds.internic.net	InterNIC Directory and Database Services, South Plainfield, NJ	USA
eis.calstate.edu	California State University, Fullerton, CA	USA
netfind.sjsu.edu	San Jose State University, San Jose, CA	USA
dino.conicit.ve	Consejo Nacional de Investigaciones Cientificas y Technologicas, Caracas	Venezuela

will likely have been expanded. The best way to keep up with new server sites is to log on to the server at bruno.cs.colorado.edu (log in as **netfind**); alternate servers are listed on the opening screen.

- Using a client program. To determine whether you have one available on your system, type **netfind** at the system prompt. netfind clients are available only for systems running Sun Microsystem's SunOS 4.x operating system. However, you can run a netfind search with a World Wide Web browser as well.

Accessing netfind with Telnet

Let's use netfind to run a basic search routine. Out of curiosity, I've decided to hunt for a known target: myself. Let's see if netfind can track me down. We'll use Telnet to reach the netfind server at the University of Colorado in Boulder. The URL is:

telnet://bruno.cs.colorado.edu

The login is **netfind**.

When the connection is established, you'll see a screen of alternate server information (if too many people are using netfind at the same time, you may be given instructions to try one of the other sites). This is followed by the login prompt:

```
I think that your terminal can display 24 lines. If this is wrong, please enter
the "Options" menu and set the correct number of lines.

Top level choices:
        1. Help
        2. Search
        3. Seed database lookup
        4. Options
        5. Quit (exit server)
-->>
```

The help system for netfind is relatively comprehensive, and I recommend that you work your way through it with your capture buffer on so that you can print it for later reference. But for now, let's work our way through the system doing a sample search. I enter **2** to tell the system I want to search, and the following prompt appears. Note how I've answered it:

```
Enter person and keys (blank to exit) -->> gilster interpath north carolina
```

I've given netfind some basic information about myself—my last name, the name of the network I used when preparing this chapter, and a geographical location. Remember, netfind needs—at minimum—a name and a rough description of where the search target works; that is, where he or she is likely to have an account from which to access the Internet. The information you give netfind can consist of a state, a city, a company, an educational institution, or a domain from a DNS address. When I entered the preceding information, I was quickly prompted as follows:

```
Enter person and keys (blank to exit) --> gilster interpath north carolina
Please select at most 3 of the following domains to search:
```

```
       0. interpath.com (interpath, a division of capitol information systems,)
       1. interpath.net (interpath, raleigh, north carolina)
       2. pdial.interpath.net (interpath, raleigh, north carolina)
Enter selection (e.g., 2 0 1) -->
```

What has happened is that netfind has located several possible targets within which to run its search, and is offering me the choice of which to search. I can choose up to three of these targets for any single search. I enter a **1**, and get this response:

```
( 1) got nameserver dns2.interpath.net
( 1) got nameserver dns1.interpath.net
( 1) SMTP_Finger_Search: checking domain interpath.net
( 2) SMTP_Finger_Search: checking nameserver dns2.interpath.net
( 3) SMTP_Finger_Search: checking nameserver dns1.interpath.net
SYSTEM: dns1.interpath.net
        Login name: gilster                In real life: Paul A Gilster - s
        Directory: /interpath/users/gilster    Shell: /bin/csh
        On since Aug 28 08:35:48 on ttyp3 from stargazer.interp
        48 seconds Idle Time
        No unread mail
        No Plan.

FINGER SUMMARY:
- "gilster" is currently logged in from
  stargazer.interpath.net, since Aug 28 08:35:48.
- The most promising email address for "gilster"
  based on the above finger search is
  gilster@stargazer.interpath.net.

Continue the search ([n]/y) ? -->
```

I've retrieved a lot of data. netfind has pulled finger information from my account at Interpath, which includes a directory and path statement. My full name is listed, the name of the host computer (stargazer) that I was using when I wrote this, and the fact that I was currently logged on, not to mention that I had no unread e-mail as of the time of this search. The suggested address, according to netfind, is gilster@stargazer.interpath.net.

This looks great, and is very close to the right answer. In fact, the address I commonly use is gilster@interpath.net, which reflects a mail-forwarding arrangement inside Interpath that takes any mail sent to that address and sends it to my account. netfind has brought us into the system I use, and has even found the name of the host, but its best guess at the address fell short. The moral: When you retrieve a netfind result, examine it carefully and be willing to experiment. The correct address is included in the finger information given, but netfind can't unravel every possible forwarding arrangement.

How netfind Works

netfind works with several different search tools. First, it maintains its own *seed database* of sites, including information on the names of computers, organizations, and Internet domains. netfind determines the best matches for your search terms there and then checks into these sites using tools like finger and WHOIS to find a match. When you are given a list of domains to choose from, netfind will search the domain(s) you select, looking for *nameservers*, which are the computers that manage machine addresses. Having done this, it searches all computers in the domain. netfind looks for the last time the user logged in and the computer on which he or she last read mail in an attempt to isolate the most likely address. Many people, after all, have multiple accounts.

Your keywords should include a name and one or more locations. A name can be a first or last name; it can even be a user ID. A location can be a geographical place or a domain from an Internet address, which is why we were able to use interpath as well as north carolina, as our search terms in the preceding search. But think geography rather than domain names. Although you can use a domain name in your search, you must specify it without the dots. The domain std.com, for example, would be entered as std com in a netfind search. And, in a netfind quirk, it would be best to enter it as com std, reversing the word order; netfind will start with the last term in the list and, if it is a common term like com, will simply advise you that there are too many hits to provide a manageable list. But if you reverse the terms, the search will run. When I entered com std as my search term, the following list appeared:

```
Please select at most 3 of the following domains to search:
     0. cri-std.dk (unspecified)
     1. std.com (software tool and die, brookline, massachusetts)
     2. stdgroup.com (std technology inc, california)
     3. std.caci.com (caci, arlington, virginia)
     4. std.comsat.com (communications satellite corporation, clarksburg, ma)
     5. std.ida.org (united states institute for defense analysis, alexandri)
     6. std.sri.com (stanford research institute international, menlo park, )
     7. std.teradyne.com (teradyne, inc, agoura hills, california)
     8. world.std.com (software tool and die, brookline, massachusetts)
     9. std.u-ryukyu.ac.jp (university of the ryukyus, sembaru, nishiharacho)
Enter selection (e.g., 2 0 1) -->
```

When it receives your search terms, netfind returns a list of the domains it has found. If there are more than 100 such domains, the system will list some of these and ask you to create a more specific search. The following, for example, is what happened when I was trying to find a particular address in Palo Alto. I knew that an on-line friend, Paul Pease, lived in the city, and I also knew that he had an account with a service provider called Netcom. But I had forgotten his specific address. What to do?

First, I tried a purely geographical search, coupled with his last name, using the keywords pease palo alto:

```
Enter person and keys (blank to exit) --> pease palo alto
Netfind: your search covers more than 150 domains
Partial list of domains that matched your search:
     1dc.net (first data resources, inc, palo alto, california)
     3do.com (the 3do company, palo alto, california)
     42ndst.com (42nd street, palo alto, california)
     abitare.org (abitare internet access, palo alto, california)
     acknosoft.com (acknosoft inc, palo alto, california)
     adaworks.com (adaworks, palo alto, california)
     admin.stanford.edu (administration office, stanford university, palo al)
     adnovum.com (adnovum software, palo alto, california)
     advice.com (advice marketing communications, palo alto, california)
     aegisstar.com (aegis star corporation, palo alto, california)
     affymax.com (affymax research institute, palo alto, california)
```

```
affymetrix.com (affymetrix, inc, palo alto, california)
ahi.com (artificial horizons, inc, palo alto, california)
air-ca.org (american institutes for research, palo alto, california)
airsoft.com (airsoft, inc, palo alto, california)
ako.dec.com (digital equipment corporation, western research laboratory)
al.org (atlantean league, palo alto, california)
aladdin.com (aladdin enterprises, palo alto, california)
alderaan.com (hinden designs, palo alto, california)
amix.com (amix corporation, palo alto, california)
amt.ako.dec.com (digital equipment corporation, western research labora)
anagram.com (anagram laboratories, palo alto, california)
analogical.com (analogical systems, palo alto, california)
angel.org (angel, palo alto, california)
animated.com (animated systems & design, palo alto, california)
animatrix.com (animatrix, inc, palo alto, california)
animorphic.com (animorphic systems, palo alto, california)
```

The list of domains went on for several screens, and I was asked to come up with a better strategy. Using a tool like netfind, you have to think on your feet. My previous search generated plenty of sites in Palo Alto, but of course, my target's service provider might not be physically located in that city; he could be accessing the Internet through a packet connection to the server site. So I looked up Netcom's domain name, which turned out to be, not surprisingly, netcom.com. I incorporated that information into the search as follows (note that no periods separate the domain names):

```
Enter person and keys (blank to exit) --> pease netcom com
Please select at most 3 of the following domains to search:
    0. netcom.com (netcom online communication services, san jose, californ)
    1. ix.netcom.com (netcom online communication services, san jose, calif)
    2. net.netcom.com (netcom online communication services, san jose, cali)
    3. netcom.netcom.com (netcom online communication services, san jose, c)
    4. slip.netcom.com (netcom online communication services, san jose, cal)
    5. uucp.netcom.com (netcom online communication services, san jose, cal)
    6. daren.slip.netcom.com (netcom online communication services, san jose)
Enter selection (e.g., 2 0 1) -->
```

Now I'm getting somewhere. The list of domains contains only one that's relevant, which I have selected; I now see that Netcom is located in San Jose, California. Having entered the number (0) for the search to focus on the most likely menu choice, I let netfind generate a new set of information:

```
( 1) SMTP_Finger_Search: checking domain netcom.com
------
Domain search completed. Proceeding to host search.
------
( 1) SMTP_Finger_Search: checking host mail.netcom.com
( 2) SMTP_Finger_Search: checking host netcom2.netcom.com
( 3) SMTP_Finger_Search: checking host netcom4.netcom.com
( 4) SMTP_Finger_Search: checking host netcom3.netcom.com
( 5) SMTP_Finger_Search: checking host uucp4.netcom.com
( 5) do_connect: Finger service not available on host uucp4.netcom.com -> cannop
( 5) SMTP_Finger_Search: checking host netcomsv.netcom.com
( 1) do_connect: Finger service not available on host mail.netcom.com -> cannotp
```

```
( 1) SMTP_Finger_Search: checking host gator.netcom.com
( 5) do_connect: Finger service not available on host netcomsv.netcom.com -> cap
( 5) SMTP_Finger_Search: checking host ns.netcom.com
( 2) SMTP_Finger_Search: checking host ftp.netcom.com
( 3) SMTP_Finger_Search: checking host uucp2-b.netcom.com
( 5) do_connect: Finger service not available on
( 5) SMTP_Finger_Search: checking host netcompa.netcom.com
( 2) do_connect: Finger service not available on host ftp.netcom.com -> cannot p
( 2) SMTP_Finger_Search: checking host nfs-serv.netcom.com
( 3) get_host_addr: gethostbyname for uucp2-b.netcom.com failed
( 3) SMTP_Finger_Search: checking host netcompl.netcom.com
( 3) get_host_addr: gethostbyname for netcompl.netcom.com failed - no such host
( 3) SMTP_Finger_Search: checking host uucp2.netcom.com
( 1) SMTP_Finger_Search: checking host mork.netcom.com
( 3) do_connect: Finger service not available on host uucp2.netcom.com -> cannop
( 3) SMTP_Finger_Search: checking host office.netcom.com
( 1) do_connect: Finger service not available on host mork.netcom.com -> cannotp
( 1) SMTP_Finger_Search: checking host netcomsj2.netcom.com
( 1) get_host_addr: gethostbyname for netcomsj2.netcom.com failed
( 1) SMTP_Finger_Search: checking host netcomsj.netcom.com
( 1) get_host_addr: gethostbyname for netcomsj.netcom.com failed
( 1) SMTP_Finger_Search: checking host uucp5.netcom.com
( 1) do_connect: Finger service not available on host uucp5.netcom.com -> cannop
( 5) get_host_addr: gethostbyname for netcompa.netcom.com failed - no such host
( 3) connect timed out
( 2) connect timed out

NOTE: Received no responses, and some host or network failures occurred.
      Maybe try this search again later.
Enter person and keys (blank to exit) -->
```

And here we're confronted with a classic Internet problem. We've run what seems to be an exhaustive search, using the sites that seem to be correct, yet netfind can't come up with anything; indeed, the program advises us that it received no responses to our query. What to do? The most important thing is to understand how netfind works.

The program actually searches in two waves. First, it searches into the domain in question, looking for mail-forwarding information; it will then try to use finger to retrieve data about the search target at whatever hosts it finds. In its second phase, the system performs finger searches into other host computers in its main database. It then summarizes its search results, generating screensful of information tracking its progress. Entering Ctrl-C will interrupt any search in progress and cause netfind to summarize what it has found so far. And, because this program is extremely specific in what it does, we may have to know, or guess, the user identification that our target uses when he or she signs in. I have assumed that Paul Pease used pease as his login name, but perhaps I was wrong; netfind can't find anything. So I'll gamble by trying a search under the keyword ppease, figuring he may have run his initial into his last name to create a login ID. Many people, after all, take this common strategy when creating a login. When I run this search, I finally retrieve something.

```
( 1) SMTP_Finger_Search: checking domain netcom.com
Mail for Paul Pease is forwarded to ppease@netcom.netcom.com
NOTE:  this is a domain mail forwarding arrangement - so mail intended for
```

"ppease" should be addressed to "ppease@netcom.com" rather than "ppease@netcom.netcom.com".

```
( 1) SMTP_Finger_Search: checking host netcom.netcom.com
------
Domain search completed. Proceeding to host search.
------
( 1) SMTP_Finger_Search: checking host mail.netcom.com
( 2) SMTP_Finger_Search: checking host netcom2.netcom.com
( 3) SMTP_Finger_Search: checking host netcom4.netcom.com
( 4) SMTP_Finger_Search: checking host netcom3.netcom.com
( 5) SMTP_Finger_Search: checking host uucp4.netcom.com
( 1) do_connect: Finger service not available on host mail.netcom.com -> cannotp
( 1) SMTP_Finger_Search: checking host netcomsv.netcom.com
( 1) do_connect: Finger service not available on host netcomsv.netcom.com -> cap
( 1) SMTP_Finger_Search: checking host gator.netcom.com
( 5) do_connect: Finger service not available on host uucp4.netcom.com -> cannop
( 5) SMTP_Finger_Search: checking host ns.netcom.com
( 5) do_connect: Finger service not available on host ns.netcom.com -> cannot dp
( 5) SMTP_Finger_Search: checking host ftp.netcom.com
( 5) do_connect: Finger service not available on host ftp.netcom.com -> cannot p
( 5) SMTP_Finger_Search: checking host uucp2-b.netcom.com
( 5) get_host_addr: gethostbyname for uucp2-b.netcom.com failed
( 5) SMTP_Finger_Search: checking host netcompa.netcom.com
( 5) get_host_addr: gethostbyname for netcompa.netcom.com failed - no such host
( 5) SMTP_Finger_Search: checking host nfs-serv.netcom.com
( 1) SMTP_Finger_Search: checking host netcompl.netcom.com
( 4) SMTP_Finger_Search: checking host uucp2.netcom.com
( 2) SMTP_Finger_Search: checking host mork.netcom.com
( 3) SMTP_Finger_Search: checking host office.netcom.com
( 1) get_host_addr: gethostbyname for netcompl.netcom.com failed - no such host
( 1) SMTP_Finger_Search: checking host netcomsj2.netcom.com
( 2) do_connect: Finger service not available on host mork.netcom.com -> cannotp
( 2) SMTP_Finger_Search: checking host netcomsj.netcom.com
( 4) do_connect: Finger service not available on host uucp2.netcom.com -> cannop
( 1) get_host_addr: gethostbyname for netcomsj2.netcom.com failed
( 2) get_host_addr: gethostbyname for netcomsj.netcom.com failed
( 5) connect timed out
( 3) connect timed out

FINGER SUMMARY:
- The most promising email address for "ppease"
  based on the above finger search is
  ppease@netcom.com.
Enter person and keys (blank to exit) -->
```

And indeed, it turns out that ppease@netcom.com is the correct address. netfind has pulled out the address for me, but the problem is that I had to guess at the login name to find it. You can see that, by the time you factor in all the things you have to already know to make netfind work, you are already close to identifying the address you need.

netfind Search Strategies

By now, you can see that netfind is at its best when you already have most of the information you need. Let me illustrate this with one more search, and conclude with some general thoughts on netfind search strategies.

My target in this case is Michael March, president of a firm called Internet Direct, Inc. in Phoenix. To home in on Mr. March, I have asked netfind to search for michael internet direct. I retrieve a list of people whose first name is Michael, a snippet of which is shown here:

```
Login: kraken                       Name: Michael Stephen
        Directory: /users/k/kraken      Shell: /bin/bash
        Never logged in.
        No Plan.


        Login: images                   Name: Michael Blum
        Directory: /users/i/images      Shell: /bin/bash
        Last login Thu Aug 24 13:12 (MST) on ttyr7 from lsvl4.la.asu.edu
        No Plan.


        Login: bach                     Name: Michael Olcott
        Directory: /users/b/bach        Shell: /bin/bash
        Last login Fri Aug 25 18:54 (MST) on ttyp1 from phx-ts2
        No Plan.
```

This material is followed by netfind's search into various hosts:

```
Domain search completed. Proceeding to host search.
------
( 1) SMTP_Finger_Search: checking host slip149.indirect.com
( 2) SMTP_Finger_Search: checking host slip138.indirect.com
( 3) SMTP_Finger_Search: checking host id1.indirect.com
( 4) SMTP_Finger_Search: checking host blueberry.indirect.com
( 5) SMTP_Finger_Search: checking host slip208.indirect.com
( 3) get_host_addr: gethostbyname for id1.indirect.com failed - no such host
( 3) SMTP_Finger_Search: checking host slip186.indirect.com
```

Finally, a summary statement appears:

```
FINGER SUMMARY:
- Found multiple matches for "michael" in finger output, so unable to
  determine most recent/last login information or most promising
  electronic mail information. Please look at the above finger search
  history and decide for yourself which is best.

Continue the search ([n]/y) ? -->
```

Now it's necessary to scroll through the list of results to see if any of them correspond to the person we want to find. And by doing so, I locate him:

```
SYSTEM: indirect.com
        Login: march                    Name: Michael Swinson March
        Directory: /users/m/march       Shell: /bin/bash
```

```
Office: Hmmmm.. time for pie!      Office Phone: (602) 274-0100
Home Phone: (602) 274-0100
Last login Sun Aug 27 04:35 (MST) on ttyp3 from roux
No Plan.
```

As you can see, I have found the person I was after. And the search has reiterated these core principles about netfind:

- You can search for a person's first, last, or username.
- You can specify one or more locations, which can be geographical names or domain names from an Internet address.
- You can use any of the parts of an organization's name or any parts of its domain name as keywords in your searches.
- Using too many keywords will frequently cause your search to fail.
- If netfind locates more than one domain that meets the criteria of your search, it will display a list of matching domains, and ask you to choose up to three for your search. If more than 100 domains match your search, netfind will ask you to form a more specific query.
- netfind works best the more you know. The optimum search occurs when you can specify the bulk of a mailing address; in other words, when what you lack is the username at the site.
- netfind may take you close to your target but fail to go the last mile. Its attempt to determine which is the best address will rely on such factors as when and how many times the person has logged on to multiple accounts and so forth. As with any Internet search tool, you have to be able to turn on a dime when you use netfind.

As with many other Internet search tools, netfind can also be accessed via the World Wide Web. You can see one search screen in Figure 8.13; I tracked this one down at the following URL:

http://www.nova.edu/Inter-Links/netfind.html

And as you can see, the Web page in question leads to a Gopher search for netfind information, reminding us that both a World Wide Web client and a Gopher client could be used to access a netfind server. In practice, I find little difference between using these methods and running a netfind search through Telnet; the search still demands that you master the basic netfind methodology in order to be successful.

netfind is an evolving tool; future plans call for it to support WHOIS, X.500, and other directory information, so you should plan to keep up with it if finding people on the network is important to you. Its creator, Michael F. Schwartz, has estimated that netfind can reach over 10 million individuals. I verified this by checking with Schwartz, after running a netfind search to get his e-mail address. The search strategy schwartz boulder colorado turned it up (although not without considerable digging): schwartz@cs.colorado.edu. And if you're interested in tracking netfind-related issues, you can use a mailing list. Send mail to netfind-users-request@cs.colorado.edu. In the body of your message, enter this: **subscribe netfind-users**.

Figure 8.13 A netfind search can be run through a World Wide Web browser.

What Is finger Information?

netfind, as we've seen, works with finger information to tell you something about the person in question. Let's refresh our memories about what this involves. finger is a program that will display public information about a user on an Internet host computer. A growing number of sites restrict finger searches, but most do not. The service generates a user ID for the person you're asking about, the person's full name, and more. Here's an example, taken by fingering my own address:

```
% finger gilster
Login name: gilster                    In real life: Paul A Gilster - Computers
Directory: /interpath/users/gilster    Shell: /bin/csh
On since Aug 29 09:32:44 on ttyp4 from stargazer.interp
No unread mail
Project: Freelance Technology Writer
Plan:
Available 8:00 AM to 6:00 PM EST weekdays.
```

We've retrieved my home directory, the Unix shell I use (csh), and information about when I was last logged on, and when I've received new mail. Also listed are two other categories. Project and plan are both fields established to allow users to communicate something about themselves. Both are based on files: The project field contains the contents of the file .project, and the plan field contains whatever is in .plan. Both these files can be created and are maintained in the user's home directory. Mine show my occupation and a snippet of information about when I work.

Because of the availability of project and plan fields, finger information can be very interesting. Here, for example, is what you would retrieve if you fingered netfind's creator, Michael F. Schwartz:

```
% finger mfs@latour.cse.ogi.edu
[latour.cse.ogi.edu]
Login name: mfs                      In real life: Mike Schwartz
Directory: /home/latour/schwartz     Shell: /bin/tcsh
On since Aug 18 10:35:32 on console  7 days 13 hours Idle Time
No unread mail
Project: Resource Discovery and Internet Information Systems
Plan:
Department of Computer Science
University of Colorado
Boulder, CO 80309-0430
Voice: +1 303 492 3902
Email: schwartz@cs.colorado.edu
WWW: http://rd.cs.colorado.edu/~schwartz/Home.html


Office: ECOT 7-11


On sabbatical May 1995-August 1996. From July-December 1995 will be at:
        Department of Computer Science and Engineering
        Oregon Graduate Institute of Science & Technology
        P.O. Box 91000
        Portland, OR 97291-1000


Research efforts:
        - scalable resource discovery
        - interoperable information systems
        - agile integration of information
        - scalable information provisioning through distributed object caching
          and topology-adaptive replication
        - Internet measurement


Travel/Meetings:
    Aug 28-29       SIGCOMM Middleware Infrastructure Workshop, Cambridge, MA
    Aug 30-Sep 1    SIGCOMM Conference, Cambridge, MA
    Sep 17-18       Cannon Beach, OR
    Sep 23-24       Los Angeles, CA
    Sep 25          Internet Catalogers Workshop, Mich. State Univ., East Lansing
    Sep 26          Sun Microsystems Laboratories, Mountain View, CA
    Sep 27          University of California, Berkeley, CA
    - 1996 -
    Jan 24-26       USENIX Conference, San Diego, CA
    Apr 2           SIGCOMM '96 program committee meeting, ISI, Los Angeles, CA
    Aug 28-30       SIGCOMM '96 conference, Stanford, CA
```

```
Login name: mfs                          In real life: Mike Schwartz
Directory: /home/latour/schwartz         Shell: /bin/tcsh
On since Aug 18 10:35:59 on ttyp0 from :0.0
7 days 13 hours Idle Time

Login name: mfs                          In real life: Mike Schwartz
Directory: /home/latour/schwartz         Shell: /bin/tcsh
On since Aug 18 10:35:59 on ttyp1 from :0.0
7 days 14 hours Idle Time
```

Note that the project information is limited to a single line, but the plan information is comprehensive; it can contain whatever you choose to put in its file. All of this is by way of illustrating that finger can hold plenty of information if the person in question has chosen to add such information to his or her .plan and .project files. What you will see, then, depends on the site in question and the person's own preferences. You may want to consider manipulating your own .plan and .project files to update them or, if they don't yet exist, creating them with a text editor like pico or vi.

Knowbots and Intelligent Searching

A Knowbot is the sort of creation science fiction tempted us with, an automated program that not only searches for information by itself, but does so with a fair degree of intelligence. Given the complexity of the Internet, this is exactly the sort of tool we'd like to employ. Rather than having to figure out every possible route through the data highway, we want to specify our needs and then do something else while our intelligent agent scours the data paths. We haven't yet reached that goal, but the first Knowbot, created by the Corporation for National Research Initiatives, is available, providing a tantalizing glimpse of what future developments may bring.

Using the Knowbot by Telnet

To access the Knowbot, use Telnet. The URL is:

telnet://info.cnri.reston.va.us:185

185 is the *port* number, a software specification that routes traffic to the right destination on the server computer (it has nothing to do with hardware serial ports). No login is required. Here is what you will see when you log in:

```
% telnet info.cnri.reston.va.us 185
Trying 132.151.1.15 ...
Connected to info.cnri.reston.va.us.
Escape character is '^]'.

                  Knowbot Information Service

KIS Client (V2.0).   Copyright CNRI 1990.   All Rights Reserved.


KIS searches various Internet directory services
to find someone's street address, email address and phone number.
```

```
Type 'man' at the prompt for a complete reference with examples.
Type 'help' for a quick reference to commands.
Type 'news' for information about recent changes.

Backspace characters are '^H' or DEL

Please enter your email address in our guest book...
(Your email address?) > gilster@interpath.net


>
```

The prompt is inscrutable, but the basic command is **query**. You use it in combination with the search term you're after. Let's use **query daniel dern** for this example. Dern is a highly regarded author of Internet books and magazine articles. Let's see if the Knowbot can find him.

```
> query daniel dern
Trying whois at ds.internic.net...

The ds.internic.net whois server is being queried:

No match for "DERN and DANIEL"

The rs.internic.net whois server is being queried:

Dern, Daniel (DD129)              ddern@DERN.COM
    Daniel Dern, Internet analyst
    PO Box 309
    Newton Centre, MA 02159
    (617) 969-7947

The nic.ddn.mil whois server is being queried:
No match for name "DERN,DANIEL".
Trying mcimail at cnri.reston.va.us...
Name:       Daniel Dern
City:       Belmont
State:      MA
Country:    US
(Press RETURN to continue)
```

The results are interesting on several levels. First, notice what is happening as the search proceeds. The Knowbot is running a search through the InterNIC (the WHOIS servers at ds.internic.net and rs.internic.net) before proceeding to the Defense Data Network's Network Information Center (now known as the DISA NIC, though still referred to here by its old title, the DDN NIC). Finding no matches there, the Knowbot suddenly pulls up a hit, an address at MCI Mail, part of the entry shown here.

Clearly, the Knowbot can search far afield for information. In fact, the InterNIC and MCI Mail are just two of its possible sources; the Knowbot maintains no address lists of its own, but relies on others. To find out what other possibilities exist, enter **services** at the bracket (>>) prompt. As of late 1995, the Knowbot was aware of the WHOIS server run by the InterNIC, MCI Mail, RIPE (Reseaux IP Europeens—in effect, the European InterNIC), the Latin American NIC, finger, WHOIS (servers at various Internet sites), X.500, quipu-country (an X.500 listing of country abbreviations), quipu-org (an X.500 listing of known organizations and site-contacts, allowing X.500 searches for Internet addresses).

Be aware that when the Knowbot begins its work, only some of these sources are selected as defaults for searching. The defaults are the InterNIC, MCI Mail, and RIPE. These services are defaults because the only thing they require is a name to search for. The other services require further information before they can be run. To provide such information, you can use a variety of commands. Here are the basic ones:

country	Allows you to specify a particular country.
help	Prints the basic commands.
man	Prints the manual page for the Knowbot.
news	Prints updated information about the Knowbot.
org	Allows you to specify an organization at which your target works. This is important for X.500, finger, and WHOIS searching, which must use a specified organization name. The organization name should be the title of the organization, or at least enough of it to provide a unique identifier for the Knowbot. You can use part of a hostname here; thus, org ncsu.edu could be used instead of org north carolina state.
print	Shows you the name, organizations, and services you have set up.
query	Searches for the person in question. You can use a first, middle, or last name. When you enter two names, the Knowbot assumes they are first and last names, in that order.
quit	Leaves the service.
service	Adds the specified service to the list of sources to check.
services	Prints the services the Knowbot will examine.

These commands must be entered one to a line, but you can use as many commands as you wish. The **print** command will then remind you of the organizations and services you have chosen up to this point in the search.

The following, for example, is how I would search for Brewster Kahle, the man behind the creation of the Wide Area Information Servers concept, and now president of WAIS, Inc. Note that I give the commands on separate lines: **org wais.com** tells the server to look for this organization, and enables it to search X.500, WHOIS, and finger services because we have been specific about the organization. I follow this with the query command:

```
> org wais.com
> query kahle
Trying whois at ds.internic.net...

The ds.internic.net whois server is being queried:
--------------------
Kahle, Brewster (BK28) kahle@THINK.COM
    Thinking Machines Corporation
    245 First Street
    Cambridge, MA 02142-1264
    (617) 234-1000

    Record last updated on 15-Apr-91.
```

```
The rs.internic.net whois server is being queried:
Kahle, Frank (FK14)        frank@IGS.NET          613-592-5619
Kahle, Warren (WK21)       warren@SCCSI.COM       (713) 681-8897

The nic.ddn.mil whois server is being queried:

Kahle, Richard P., Jr. (RPK2) rkahle@WSMR-EMH82.ARMY.MIL
                              (505) 678-2209 (DSN) 258-2209

(Press RETURN to continue)
```

Note that we have retrieved one record for Kahle, but that it is out of date, a common problem with InterNIC directory tools, whose database references are often ill-maintained. In fact, as the Knowbot search proceeds, we find another reference to Kahle:

```
Name:          Brewster M Kahle
Organization:  Thinking Machin
City:          Menlo Park
State:         CA
Country:       US
E-Mail:        482-0486@mcimail.com
Source:        mcimail
Ident:         482-0486
Last Updated:  unknown
```

But, as you can see, it too is out of date, for Kahle has moved on from Thinking Machines Corp. to become president of WAIS, Inc. The moral of the tale is that you should always regard Internet directory information with suspicion until it has been confirmed. There is no area of networking activity so in need of upgrade.

The Knowbot through the World Wide Web

If Telnet searching is more complex than you prefer, you can also search the Knowbot through a new World Wide Web page. The URL is:

http://info.cnri.reston.va.us/kis.html

You can see the Knowbot search page in Figure 8.14.

Using the Knowbot by Electronic Mail

You can also send mail to the Knowbot to generate the information you need. To do so, send to one of two possible addresses:

kis@cnri.reston.va.us

or

netaddress@regulus.cs.bucknell.edu

Place your search request in the body of the message, using the same format as for a Telnet session. This is a sample e-mail message I sent to the Knowbot to retrieve information about network figure Tony Rutkowski:

Figure 8.14 A Knowbot search screen on the World Wide Web.

```
% mail kis@cnri.reston.va.us
Subject:
query rutkowski
```

The results quickly appear in my mailbox (I display only a section of them):

```
The rs.internic.net whois server is being queried:

Rutkowski, Anthony M. (AMR25)  amr@ISOC.ORG        +1 703 648 9888
Rutkowski, Jan (JR73)          irek@NASK.ORG.PL        +48 24 626061
Rutkowski, John (JR243)        jr@BDESIGNS.COM      (610) 583-9887
Rutkowski, Kathleen M. (KMR)   kmr@CHAOS.COM        (703) 471-0593
Rutkowski, Stas (SR305)        stas@SIRIUS.COM      (415) 665-8869
Rutkowski, Tom (TR5)           root@EXELE.COM       (716) 385-9740
Rutkowski, Tom (TR44)          trutk@IBSOLUTIONS.COM (716) 224-2575
Rutkowski, Tony (TR96)         tonyrt@MCS.COM       (312) 443-9300
```

The great benefit of the Knowbot is that it allows you to search a wide variety of white pages for information without learning the particular search syntax of each one. The same search terms that you use for MCI Mail, for example, are applicable to your search in the other databases. This alone makes the Knowbot a tool you'll want to keep an eye on. For additional information about this intriguing search tool, you may want to join a mailing list where questions and problems are addressed. To subscribe to the

Knowbot Information Service mailing list, send mail to kis-users-request@cnri. reston.va.us. Leave the subject field blank. The message should read **subscribe kis-users** *your name*.

CCSO Directories

We've already seen that many of the search tools discussed in this chapter can be used through a variety of different interfaces. WHOIS, for example, can be tapped through Gopher or a Web browser, while WAIS provides a useful search tool for the USENET address server discussed in a moment; it is accessible either through a local WAIS client or via a World Wide Web gateway. Generally, I've addressed the search tools themselves in this chapter, with reference to the capability of using them in other formats in the relevant chapters. But one tool deserves special treatment, because it is explicitly designed as a white pages directory front end and can be used easily through the medium of Gopher.

This tool is the CCSO. Unlike most Internet terms, this acronym doesn't explain much about itself when unravelled. It stands for Computing and Communications Services Office, and refers to the entity at the University of Illinois at Urbana-Champaign where this tool was first developed. You will find Gopher entries marked CCSO at many academic sites; they'll appear on a graphical client's screen with whatever search or phonebook icons your client uses, as shown with WSGopher in Figure 8.15.

As you can see, we are presented with a long list of CCSO directories at their respective institutions (these are shown by the telephone icon). Other entries are also searchable, as shown by the magnifying glass icon preceding them. Some of these directories are based on WHOIS servers, some on X.500 and various other search tools. We'll con-

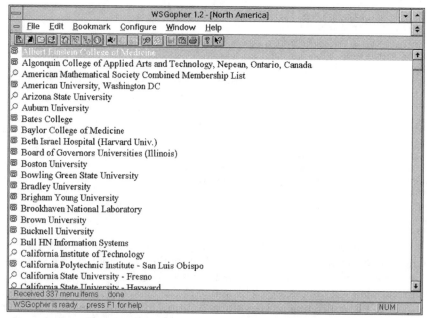

Figure 8.15   CCSO entries as shown through a graphical Gopher client.

Figure 8.16 The search screen at the CCSO serving Bucknell University.

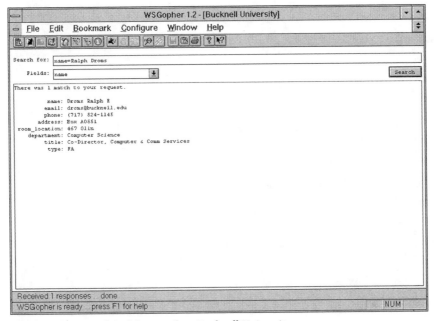

Figure 8.17 Results of the search at Bucknell University.

centrate on CCSOs by trying to find a person at Bucknell University, which is home to the developer of the Knowbot, Ralph Droms. Let's see if we can get the right address. Figure 8.16 shows what happens when I click on the entry for Bucknell. I am given a screen with fields of information. In Figure 8.17, you can see the results of running a search. To run it, all I had to do was to click on the name field in the pull-down menu and insert the name, in this case, Droms. I then clicked on the Search button.

By moving through the drop-down menu, I could have chosen from among a number of fields, everything from name to e-mail address, class year, fax number, home address, and department. I used a full name in my search, but I could also have used an asterisk to serve as a wildcard in my statement. Thus, entering **r* droms** would have retrieved anyone whose last name was droms and whose first name began with an r.

You can also search CCSO directories through the World Wide Web. In Figure 8.18, I have moved to the following URL:

http://www.uiuc.edu/cgi-bin/ph/lookup?

Here, I am examining a list of CCSO servers known to the University of Illinois at Urbana-Champaign. Figure 8.19 shows a typical search screen, this one at the University of Otago in Dunedin, New Zealand. Keywords are entered in the field at top right; a RETURN launches the search.

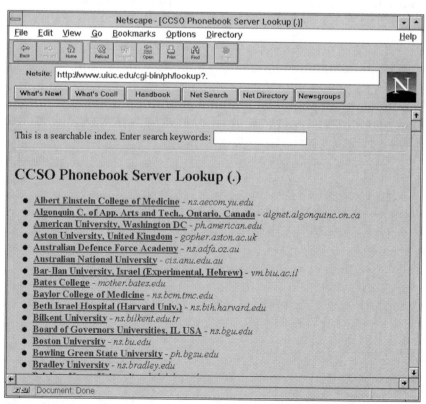

Figure 8.18   A CCSO directory search screen as viewed on the World Wide Web.

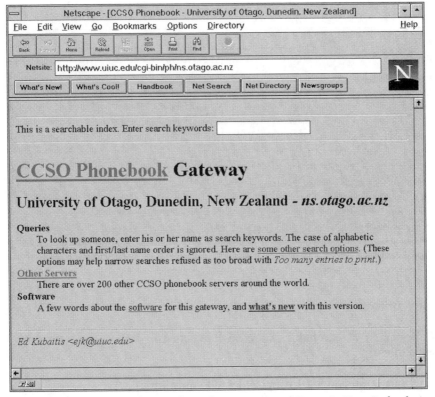

Figure 8.19 Searching for people at the University of Otago in New Zealand via CCSO.

Campus Wide Information Systems

If you know the object of your search works at a particular university, but that university does not maintain a CCSO, you still have a good chance of finding him or her through a Campus Wide Information System, or CWIS. These depositories of campus information frequently include directories of faculty and students, along with information on campus events, class schedules, library information, job opportunities, and anything else related to campus life. Figure 8.20 shows the opening screen for a Campus Wide Information System at the University of Pennsylvania. Notice item 7, labelled *Directories*.

Suppose I am looking for someone on the staff at the university's library. Using this CWIS, I can simply move through a series of menus to find him or her. In Figure 8.21, I have moved through directory listings for various departments and have found the appropriate screen. I now have the information needed to contact my target.

Obviously, Campus Wide Information Systems can zero in directly on our targets. But first, we have to know which systems are available; after all, despite their recent proliferation, CWIS services haven't spread onto every campus, and certainly are more easily found at larger schools. There are two ways around this dilemma. First, CWIS entries are available on many Gopher menus, which can take you right into the system in question. Second, there are several useful World Wide Web sites that emphasize university and college connectivity. Check the following URLs:

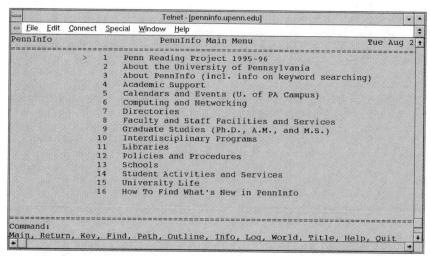

Figure 8.20 A Campus Wide Information System at the University of Pennsylvania.

http://www.unival.com/cn/collegenet.html

CollegeNET, a searchable database that lets you browse by geography, tuition and enrollment.

http://www.mit.edu:8001/people/cdemello/univ.html

A listing of colleges and universities by home page.

```
┌─                     Telnet - [penninfo.upenn.edu]               ▼ ▲
│ ⊝  File  Edit  Connect  Special  Window  Help                      ◆
│ PennInfo                      SEAS Library                  Tue Aug 2 ↑
│ ================================================================
│
│ Library Staff
│
│ Name                      ROOM        PHONE   Electronic mail addres
│ ────────                  ────        ─────   ──────────────────────
│ Revathy Iyer              217 Towne   7266    iyer@seas
│ Marilyn Brown             217 Towne   7266    marilyn@seas
│ Gretchen Sneff            217 Towne   7267    sneff@seas
│ Iren Sokolova             203 Moore   8135    sokolova@seas
│ Hugh Turner               203 Moore   8135    turner@seas
│
│
│ ────────────────── END OF DOCUMENT ──────────────────
│
│
│ ================================================================
│ Command:
│ Main, Return, Key, Find, Path, Outline, Info, Log, World, Title, Help, Quit
│ ◆                                                                  ▼
```

Figure 8.21 Results of a search at the University of Pennsylvania; I simply followed menu choices to pull up this directory of names.

http://www.clas.ufl.edu/CLAS/american-universities.html

A complete listing of university home pages.

So many academic institutions have put their CWIS systems onto the World Wide Web that these URLs should prove extremely useful. Look first for your school at one of these sites; then move into Gopher servers and consider Telnet connections. Bear in mind that if you plan to do frequent searches with CWIS systems, the search methods may vary from one site to another. But these systems are maintained for on-campus use, which means that they are explicitly designed to be easy to use. So follow through with the commands suggested on-line, and you should be able to search the available directories. Figure 8.22 shows the home page for the University of North Carolina at Wilmington. Note the search item at the bottom left, which calls up a search screen.

Searching the USENET Archives

USENET, that worldwide assemblage of newsgroups on every conceivable topic, provides yet another database that can be searched for name and address information. Figure 8.23

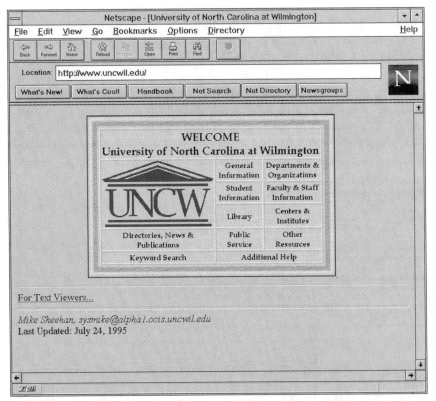

Figure 8.22 The home page for the University of North Carolina at Wilmington. More and more universities are moving onto the World Wide Web.

shows a typical USENET message. Notice at the top that the Internet address of the sender, along with a full name, is provided. Clearly, being able to search an archive of such material for a mailing address could provide a useful way to track someone down, provided he or she were a user of USENET newsgroups.

At the Massachusetts Institute of Technology is a computer whose network address you need to know. It's rtfm.mit.edu. This machine serves as a repository of archives for USENET at large; here, a variety of documents including the complete collection of Frequently Asked Questions (FAQs) for USENET newsgroups is stored. For our purposes, the most interesting thing about this machine is the white pages directory on it, which stores the address information from USENET postings in a database. There is a strong likelihood that the name and address of a recent poster to USENET will be found here, making this a prime hunting ground for address searchers.

To reach the USENET address server, send electronic mail to the following address:

mail-server@rtfm.mit.edu

You can leave the subject field blank. The body of the letter should contain your search terms in the following format:

send usenet-addresses/*name*

Here is how I sent a request to this server when I was checking to determine the address of Jonathan Kamens, a familiar network figure who has contributed a great deal to the Internet through his work at MIT:

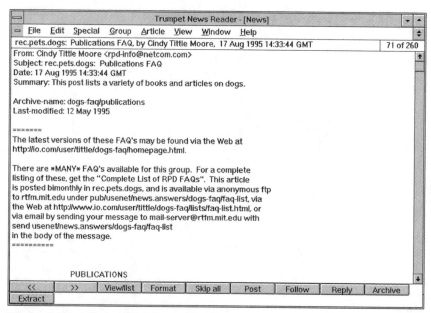

Figure 8.23 A typical USENET message, containing name and address information that can be used in a search for e-mail addresses.

```
% mail mail-server@rtfm.mit.edu
Subject:
send usenet-addresses/kamens
```

The result was quick to arrive, as shown:

```
Date: Tue, 29 Aug 1995 10:57:25 -0400
From: mail-server@bloom-picayune.MIT.EDU
To: gilster@interpath.net (Paul A. Gilster)
Subject: mail-server: "send usenet-addresses/kamens"
Reply-To: mail-server@bloom-picayune.MIT.EDU
Precedence: junk
X-Problems-To: owner-mail-server@rtfm.mit.edu
X-UIDL: 809785098.010


-----cut here-----
steve.kamens@channel1.com (Steve Kamens)    (Apr 17 95)
Jonathan.I_.Kamens@holt-systems.com (Jonathan I. Kamens)    (Dec 7 94)
jonathan.i..kamens@unkbbs.iac.net (JONATHAN I. KAMENS)      (Feb 5 95)
snk@tpsinc.com (Sam Kamens)    (Dec 7 94)
"Lauren Kamens" <p00273@psilink.com>    (Sep 10 94)
HARRYK@avs.kent.edu (Harry Kamens)      (Dec 13 94)
jik@cam.ov.COM (Jonathan I. Kamens)      (Feb 22 95)
kamens69@futures.wharton.upenn.edu (JOSHUA KAMENS)    (Jan 4 95)
fb758@cleveland.Freenet.Edu (Samuel N. Kamens)      (Jul 19 94)
jik@cam.ov.com (Jonathan I. Kamens)    (Jun 22 95)
HARRYK@lms.kent.edu (Harry Kamens)      (Jun 21 95)
kamens69@futures.wharton.upenn.edu (Joshua Kamens)    (May 3 95)
kamens69@futures.wharton.upenn.edu (Josh Kamens)    (May 1 95)
snk@metro.tpsinc.com (Sam Kamens)    (May 24 95)
kamens69@futures.wharton.upenn.edu (Josh"MAMOON"Kamens)    (Apr 3 95)
jik@ANNEX-1-SLIP-JIK.CAM.OV.COM (Jonathan I. Kamens)    (Apr 29 95)
jik@annex-1-slip-jik.cam.ov.COM (Jonathan I. Kamens)    (Apr 30 95)
jik@annex-1-slip-jik.cam.ov.com (Jonathan I. Kamens)    (Apr 30 95)
jik@annex-1-slip-jik.cam.ov.com (Jonathan Kamens)    (Jun 19 95)
-----cut here-----
```

Numerous hits show up, including a variety of addresses for the indefatigable Kamens. These are all drawn from postings on USENET; you simply have to go through the hits to determine which is the address you need. Incidentally, a WAIS database called usenet-addresses is also accessible for keyword-driven searching. You can find it by checking a directory of servers using your WAIS client or a Telnet session to a swais client.

For a long time, Kamens maintained an extremely useful document about finding people on the network. Development of this text file, which includes a number of ingenious methods for tracking people down on the Internet, has now been taken over by David Lamb. To get it, use anonymous FTP to this URL:

ftp://rtfm.mit.edu/pub/usenet/news.answers/finding-addresses

Or read it on-line on the World Wide Web at:

http://www.qucis.queensu.ca/FAQs/email/finding.html

Lamb also maintains a Web site devoted to finding people on college and university campuses:

http://www.qucis.queensu.ca/FAQs/email/college.html

Two New Directory Services on the Web

LookUP! and Four11 are two new directory services that provide extensive database searching for network addresses. LookUP! offers free basic searching for anyone who can use a forms-based World Wide Web browser. If you become a member at the site, you can take advantage of a number of additional features, including Unix regular expression searching and the ability to add names to the database. What's more, membership is currently free. You can check out LookUP! at this URL:

http://www.lookup.com/

When I ran a search for Howard L. Funk, an Internet consultant and on-line acquaintance, I came up with a number of hits through LookUP!, as shown in Figure 8.24. Note that each hit is presented as a hyperlink, so that I can send e-mail to Mr. Funk just as soon as I've located his Internet address.

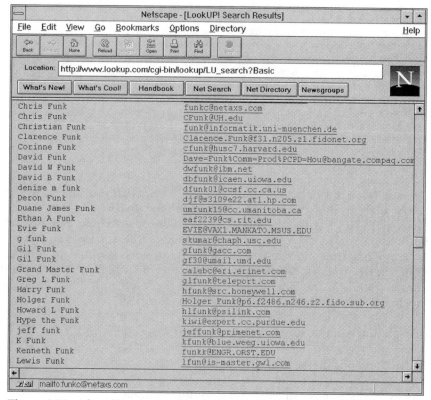

Figure 8.24   A list of hits produced by the LookUP! service.

Figure 8.25   The basic search screen used by the Four11 service.

Another worthwhile directory project is Four11, which you can reach at the following URL:

http://www.four11.com/

Four11 offers what it calls the Internet's largest white pages directory, with over 1.2 million listings and 150,000 registered users. You can list yourself in the database by completing a simple on-line form when you first log on at the site; extensive listing options are available. The Four11 search screen is shown in Figure 8.25.

Going to the Source

As we've seen, finding a particular person on the Internet is no easy task, unless you already know a great deal about that person. Aware of the problem, researchers and programmers are already working hard on the solution. In many respects, creating a satisfactory directory structure remains one of the greatest challenges of the Internet.

Today, even if you do know a few things about your target, it may still prove impossible to learn more. Some commercial on-line services, for example, don't make information about their members available. This will continue to be a problem, for the number of dial-up users coming into the Internet from sources like America Online and

CompuServe is growing daily. Thus the odds increase that your Internet person hunt may come up short. There is, however, one solution we haven't yet examined.

If you still can't find the person you're looking for, consider asking a live person. If you know the address of the machine your person uses but don't know his or her user name, you can always send a request to the administrator responsible for that machine. Every domain accepts the electronic mail address **postmaster**. Therefore, if you know that your contact uses the machine chaos.sbh.edu, you could send a message to the following address:

postmaster@chaos.sbh.edu

A polite request ought to get the e-mail name you need.

9

E-Mail: Noninteractive Searching

Approximately seven million people use one or another of the commercial on-line services like CompuServe or America Online, and for many, this is their only link to the Internet. While some services are now moving beyond electronic mail to offer other Internet features, including full SLIP/PPP access, it is nonetheless true that huge numbers of modem users can reach the Internet only by mail. We must factor in the growing number of local bulletin board systems (BBS) with Internet links; until recently, they have provided access to electronic mail and (sometimes) USENET newsgroups alone.

Clearly, an interactive Internet account is preferable, because it allows us to use such crucial features as FTP, Telnet, and the World Wide Web. But the people who use networks are ever ingenious, and a wide (some would say wild) variety of fixes have appeared, allowing users to tap most of the Internet search tools in some fashion through electronic mail. Some of these methods are efficient and relatively straightforward; others are complex and frequently unstable. But I think you will be surprised at how many sources you can search through an electronic mail connection. Let's examine them.

archie through Electronic Mail

Without interactive FTP, archie would seem to be the kind of tool we could do without. After all, searching for files on the Internet will do us little good if we can't retrieve them. But a service called ftpmail has appeared that allows mail users to send requests for files to designated sites; the results are then mailed to the user in 7-bit ASCII format, according to standard Internet conventions regarding e-mail. Even executable files may be sent this way in uuencoded form. Decode the file using a software tool called uudecode and you have a working program. The intricacies of ftpmail are beyond the scope of this book (for a complete discussion of ftpmail and sample sessions showing how to use it, see my book *The New Internet Navigator*, John Wiley & Sons, Inc., 1995).

For now, though, the question becomes, how do we activate archie and search FTP sites by electronic mail? Actually, those of us with fully interactive Internet connections frequently find that using the system by mail is beneficial, even if the methodology seems cumbersome. People accessing archie through Telnet sessions already know that the load on archie servers has become intense, enough so that it's frequently difficult to log on. An electronic mail message can save you the trouble of repeatedly trying the same server looking for an open slot.

For that matter, the timing of many archie searches isn't necessarily critical. When you don't have a pressing need to review the results immediately, why not consider the e-mail route? Your list of hits will appear in your mailbox in short order, and in the meantime, you can proceed with other work. Not all of archie's search capabilities are available through mail, just as many of the advanced Telnet settings are unusable through a local Unix client, but certainly the major commands can be driven through mail.

archie by E-Mail Commands

The way to use a mail server is to send a message to the site with your command inside. You can send mail to any of the archie server sites listed in Chapter 5. The address to use is:

archie@*server*

where *server* is the name of the archie site. This can result in an awkward-sounding address. For example, if I choose to send my e-mail request to the server at archie.ans.net, I would send to the address archie@archie.ans.net. As you can see, the idea is simply to prefix the archie@ sequence to the server address.

The message you send should contain the appropriate archie commands and nothing else. You are not limited to a certain number of commands, but do note that *each command must begin in the first column of a line, or it will not be processed correctly.* We'll see this principle applied when dealing with any mail server, so commit it to memory now.

The major archie commands you're likely to use in an electronic mail search follow. Within your message, the basic archie-by-Telnet commands are available (and it would be a good idea, if you plan to use archie by mail, to review those commands as listed in Chapter 5). And note, some servers may still be using older software. Alternative commands for using them are also listed here.

compress	Causes archie to send your reply in compressed and encoded form.
find	The familiar search command, which supplanted the older **prog** command with archie version 3.0 (although you can still use **prog**). But note: Your electronic mail search presumes a search strategy based on Unix regular expressions (regex). This is opposed to the line-oriented Unix client program (which presumes an exact search unless you change its settings) and Telnet to an archie server, which defaults in version 3.0 to sub (substring). You will probably want to set a different search type before proceeding. Use the usual Telnet search type commands to do so.
help	Put this in your message and archie will return the basic help document, listing the e-mail commands and providing further information. Acquiring and studying the help document for all of these electronic mail services is an excellent idea.

set mailto	You can set a path statement that tells archie to return your search results to an address different from the one on your e-mail. The older version of this command is **path**. Thus, entering **path plorre@casa-blanca.com** instructs the system to send results to that address, as does **set mailto plorre@casablanca.com**. It's a good idea to include the path statement in any case to ensure accuracy.
set maxhits	Determines the maximum number of hits archie will recover for any particular search. Using the statement **set maxhits 50**, for example, limits your results to 50 possible hits.
set search	Allows you to choose the type of search you want to run. A **set search sub** statement, for example, sets up a subcase search that will look for your search term inside longer filenames.
quit	Closes your archie request.
servers	This is another way of generating an updated list of archie servers. The server site will return a list of all servers known to it at the time.
whatis	Allows you to supply a keyword for a search of the Software Description Database. This is another reason to use electronic mail. The Unix client program for archie does not support **whatis** searches (although using Telnet to reach an archie server does).

A Sample archie Search Using Electronic Mail

Assume I am interested in searching for files having to do with fax software. I can set up an archie search as shown in the following message (note that I've left the Subject: field blank).

```
% mail archie@archie.sura.net
Subject:
set mailto gilster@interpath.net
set search sub
set maxhits 50
find fax
whatis fax
quit
```

Let's take the search statement apart. I've begun with my electronic mail address, inserted here simply as a precaution against any mix-up in the header of my message. The next statement is familiar; it sets the search type as sub, so that my search will find any example of the search term, fax, within the file or directory name. I've limited the maximum number of hits to 50, and then inserted the find command, **find fax**. I've also included **whatis fax**, because I'd like to have a look at what's in the Software Description Database under this heading. I haven't sorted the output by time because I'm exploring in general for fax files; I'm not worried at this point about which is most recent. The **quit** command closes my request.

The message is then sent on its way. Depending on how busy the server is, I will find the results waiting in my mailbox in a reasonable amount of time. Figure 9.1 shows one screen's worth of what I retrieved. I can now use ftpmail to retrieve any file I'm interested in.

Figure 9.1   archie search results as sent by e-mail.

NOTE: One final note about archie: Servers respond to requests made upon them by lining up the searches. The smaller requests are taken care of more quickly than the larger ones, which means that when you send a large query to archie, or make your queries frequent, you're creating a longer waiting period for everyone. The principle is to avoid asking for big jobs during busy times of day. If you're using an archie client program, setting the -N option for "niceness" reflects well upon your attitude toward your fellow on-line citizens. According to the archie manual page, an -N setting of 5000 ranks as "very nice." Surely we can all afford to wait a few extra minutes by being so.

WAIS by Electronic Mail

WAIS hardly suggests itself as a satisfactory vehicle for electronic mail. The nature of a WAIS search, after all, is to query an electronic database, receiving a set of hits that we can then tune up with relevance feedback. But as we saw in Chapter 5, relevance feedback isn't always effective, even if we're running a sophisticated WAIS client program. And because we can do a great deal without using it, the ability to search through e-mail becomes more interesting. The WAIS mail server we are about to discuss isn't elegant, but it can return the results you need.

Once again, we can offer thanks to Thinking Machines Corp. in Cambridge, Massachusetts, where WAIS was initially developed. There Jonny Goldman developed the mail server program called WAISmail. The procedure for tapping WAISmail is common to any mail server. You send a message to the appropriate address specifying what you are looking for and where to look for it. WAISmail runs the search and sends back a list of hits. You can then examine the list, choosing items you'd like to see, and request them.

HINT: There are times when the mail server approach to an Internet search seems very compelling, even to those with a dedicated network connection. Perhaps it's late on a Friday afternoon and you're ready to head for a well-deserved weekend break. But you also need to track down a document or two on the Internet. You could stop packing your briefcase and do it now. Or you could send the search to WAISmail and let the mail server handle it for you. On Monday morning, presumably refreshed, you would return to your office to find the results of your search waiting.

Constructing a WAISmail Search

The address for WAISmail is waismail@sunsite.unc.edu (the WAISmail server at Thinking Machines Corp. is no longer available). The vital thing about using the system is that the message must be formatted precisely as shown. Here is the format:

search *source-name keywords*

A Sample WAISmail Search

Let's search the CIA World Factbook looking for information about Zambia. World copper prices have been volatile, and I have heard that Zambia is rich in copper. What more can we learn about Zambian ore deposits, in case we have an interest in investing at this point in the market cycle?

First, we need to learn what WAIS databases are available. To find out, we can send the following command to the WAISmail server:

search xxx

This command should appear in the body of the message, not the Subject: field. What we are doing is sending a bogus database name to the server so that it will respond with a list of the servers it actually has available. The list that will soon appear in our mailbox will show the databases we can search through WAISmail. In our case, the database called world-factbook seems relevant. To use it, we construct a search statement:

search world-factbook zambia

Then we send the message to waismail@sunsite.unc.edu. The result, which soon arrives as a message in our mailbox, is shown in Figure 9.2.

The results are interesting. As you can see, WAISmail has restricted itself to 10 responses. As with a standard, interactive WAIS search, the hits have been given numerical rankings. Thus, item 1 shows a ranking, or score, of 1000, while number 2 shows a score of 957. Clearly, WAIS has chosen correctly, because as we examine the list, we see that the first entry is indeed the main entry for Zambia. Other entries are articles about other countries, in which Zambia is mentioned but probably doesn't play a major role.

We want to retrieve document 1. To do so, we consult the WAISmail information again. The procedure for requesting a document is to send another message to WAISmail@sunsite.unc.edu. This time, the message will have but a single line containing the word retrieve along with the identifier for the document we want. We can find this by

```
Searching: world-factbook
Keywords: zambia

Result # 1 Score:1000 lines:  0 bytes:  10625 Date:920120 Type: TEXT
Headline: Zambia  Geography Total area: 752,610 km2; land area: 740,720 km2
DocID: 0000000244CIA :cmns-moon.think.com@cmns-moon.think.com:210%TEXT

Result # 2 Score: 957 lines:  0 bytes:  11466 Date:920120 Type: TEXT
Headline: Namibia  Geography Total area: 824,290 km2; land area: 823,290 km2
DocID: 0000000153CIA :cmns-moon.think.com@cmns-moon.think.com:210%TEXT

Result # 3 Score: 957 lines:  0 bytes:  10988 Date:920120 Type: TEXT
Headline: Malawi  Geography Total area: 118,480 km2; land area: 94,080 km2
DocID: 0000000134CIA :cmns-moon.think.com@cmns-moon.think.com:210%TEXT
Result # 4 Score: 935 lines:  0 bytes: 151677 Date:920120 Type: TEXT
Headline:     Appendix C: International Organizations and Groups
DocID: 0000000250CIA :cmns-moon.think.com@cmns-moon.think.com:210%TEXT

Result # 5 Score: 935 lines:  0 bytes:  10992 Date:920120 Type: TEXT
Headline: Zimbabwe  Geography Total area: 390,580 km2; land area: 386,670 km2
DocID: 0000000245CIA :cmns-moon.think.com@cmns-moon.think.com:210%TEXT

Result # 6 Score: 935 lines:  0 bytes:  13174 Date:920120 Type: TEXT
Headline: Zaire  Geography Total area: 2,345,410 km2; land area: 2,267,600 km2
DocID: 0000000243CIA :cmns-moon.think.com@cmns-moon.think.com:210%TEXT

Result # 7 Score: 935 lines:  0 bytes:   8384 Date:920120 Type: TEXT
Headline: World  Geography Total area: 510,072,000 km2; 361,132,000 km2
(70.8%) is water and
DocID: 0000000240CIA :cmns-moon.think.com@cmns-moon.think.com:210%TEXT
Result # 8 Score: 935 lines:  0 bytes:  10422 Date:920120 Type: TEXT
Headline: Botswana  Geography Total area: 600,370 km2; land area: 585,370 km2
DocID: 0000000028CIA :cmns-moon.think.com@cmns-moon.think.com:210%TEXT

Result # 9 Score: 914 lines:  0 bytes:  13224 Date:920120 Type: TEXT
Headline:    Appendix B: Abbreviations for International Organizations and
Groups
DocID: 0000000249CIA :cmns-moon.think.com@cmns-moon.think.com:210%TEXT

Result #10 Score:    1 lines:  0 bytes:  21384 Date:930616 Type: TEXT
Headline: *** HELP for the Public CM WAIS Server ***
DocID: 0000000000HELP:cmns-moon.think.com@cmns-moon.think.com:210%TEXT
```

Figure 9.2 Results of a WAISmail search for information about Zambia.

examining the results in Figure 9.2; we are looking for the line marked DocID. This is how the first of our hits appeared:

```
Result # 1 Score:1000 lines: 0 bytes: 10625 Date:920120 Type: TEXT
Headline: Zambia Geography Total area: 752,610 km2; land area: 740,720 km2
DocID: 0000000244CIA :cmns-moon.think.com@cmns-moon.think.com:210%TEXT
```

The document identifier is lengthy:

```
0000000244CIA :cmns-moon.think.com@cmns-moon.think.com:210%TEXT
```

To request this document, then, we must send this message:

retrieve 0000000244CIA :cmns-moon.think.com@cmns-moon.think.com:210%TEXT

Before long, the document appears in our mailbox. Here is the first part of it, showing the retrieval mechanism at work:

```
Retrieving "0000000244CIA :cmns-moon.think.com@cmns-moon.think.com:210%TEXT"
 DocID: 0000000244CIA
 Database: cmns-moon.think.com
 Host: cmns-moon.think.com
 Port: 210
 Type: TEXT
```
```
0000244CIA
920120
CIA World Factbook 1991
Zambia
```

This material is followed by a lengthy document, with information about Zambia's natural resources, political leadership, population, and more. Along with this potpourri of information comes the material we are seeking, relating the country's copper deposits to its economy:

```
Economy
Overview: The economy has been in decline for more than a decade with falling
imports and growing foreign debt. Economic difficulties stem from a sustained
drop in copper production and ineffective economic policies. In 1990 real GDP
stood only slightly higher than that of 10 years before, while an annual popula-
tion growth of more than 3% has brought a decline in per capita GDP of 25% dur-
ing the same period. A high inflation rate has also added to Zambia's economic
woes in recent years.
```

Clearly, if we plan to take a position in Zambian copper resources now, we're the adventurous kind of investor! It should be noted, of course, that this is relatively old information; a more updated world-factbook93 database is also available, but contains less by way of background material than this source. As in many Internet situations, we're forced to rely upon a combination of search results from various sources to draw lasting conclusions.

The WAISmail Commands

The following are the commands you can use to make WAISmail work. Notice that it is possible to change various parameters if you want, for example, to see more than the default number of responses. Invoke one command per line.

maxres *\<number>*	Sets the number of hits returned by the number you select. This command should be set before you issue your **search** command.

HINT: The document identifiers for the WAISmail system are quite lengthy, and a single error in the request will cause the system to bounce your request entirely. Even the spaces between items must be accurately transcribed. Therefore, you may find it easier to simply use the reply function in your mail program when you request a document. By doing so, and including the text of the WAISmail document in your response, you can then edit the message to eliminate everything but your **retrieve** command and the document identifier itself. WAISmail will also accept and act on the DocID by itself (with no **retrieve** command). If you do this, be sure that there are nothing but blank spaces between the beginning of the line and the DocID keyword.

search *<source-name> <keywords>*	The source name you insert in your **search** command is the name of the source as listed in the directory of servers; you don't need to include the .src suffix. Note: You can search through more than one source at a time if you wish. To do so, enclose the source names in quotations. For example, to search usenet-cookbook.src and usenet.src for messages involving Thai cuisine, you would enter the command **search "usenet-cookbook usenet" thai**.
retrieve *<DocID>*	Retrieves a document. Note that you must include the identifier for each item you wish to retrieve. Enter the identifier with great care.

HINT: WAISmail makes it possible to retrieve more than one item at a time. To do so, separate your retrieval commands with a blank line. And note this statement in Jonny Goldman's help document for WAISmail: "Most 'Bad DocID' errors are the result of lost spaces in transmission."

DocID: *<DocID>*	Also retrieves a document. Here, the DocID stands by itself and generates the necessary retrieval.

To retrieve, for example, one of the Thai recipes I found in the multiple source search I just ran, I would send this command:

DocID: 0000000417WWP :cmns-moon.think.com@cmns-moon.think.com:210%TEXT

I can do this simply by using the reply function in my mail reader and editing out all the other WAISmail DocIDs. Again, multiple retrievals are possible within a single message; just separate the ID numbers with a blank line. Figure 9.3 shows part of the resulting file as read through the pine mail reader program.

And, if you think the DocIDs we've been using are lengthy, you haven't seen anything yet. Consider this one:

Figure 9.3   A Thai recipe as retrieved through WAISmail.

```
DocID: 0 1760
/proj/WAIS/db/weather/weather.help:/proj/WAIS/WAIS-sources/weather@quake.quake.t
hink.com:210%TEXT
```

I show you this to illustrate not only how unwieldy a DocID can be, but also to point out that WAISmail can handle DocID statements that take up more than a single line. When this happens, the important thing to remember is not to insert any extra spaces into the DocID statement. Some mailers force you to use 80 character lines, which is where this problem may arise.

HINT: WAISmail is more than a little bit finicky! When using the DocID command to retrieve a document, you must type the word DocID exactly as shown. Case matters.

like *<DocID>*   Allows you to set up a relevance feedback search by telling WAIS-mail that a particular document is the kind you're looking for. While it is possible to use relevance feedback by mail (which is in itself intriguing), the results are not likely to be worth the time it takes to construct the query with multiple "like" documents. If you do use like, be aware that all like commands must go before the search command.

Binary Files through WAISmail

If you're interested in retrieving nontextual information through WAISmail, you're in luck; such files will be sent to you in uuencoded form. The basic mail protocols used on the Internet specify that mail must travel as 7-bit ASCII characters, as we saw in the section on using archie by mail. A program called uuencode is used to translate a binary file, such as an executable program or a graphics file, into ASCII. On your end, you need a copy of the uudecode program, which can sort out the resulting ASCII tangle and make the file back into a program.

> **HINT:** uudecode can be run from the system prompt in a Unix environment. Or, if you need to run it on your own computer, you can find versions of the program all over the Internet. Run an archie search to find abundant listings. From the system prompt, enter the command **archie uudecode**, or use uudecode as your keyword with any archie client. The site you choose will depend on your system. For MS-DOS users, for example, a major source is the huge FTP archive at ftp://oak.oakland.edu (the Oak Software Repository at Oakland University, Rochester, Michigan). Look in the directory pub3/simtel-win3/encode for a variety of implementations (although the directory may have changed by the time you read this—software sites are always in a state of evolution). Macintosh users will want to check out sites like ftp://mac.archive.umich.edu.

Let's test the system by looking for a satellite image of today's weather. I'll search the weather.src server through WAISmail with the following command:

search weather gif

Here I am using gif as one of my keywords because I want to find images, which are often made available in so-called **G**raphics **I**nterchange **F**ormat. This is the quickest way to get recent satellite images through the weather.src server.

Files retrieved through this process look like a mess in their uuencoded form, a sea of apparently random ASCII characters. But after turning the uudecode program loose on it, I retrieve the image shown in Figure 9.4.

> **HINT:** WAISmail is flaky; more often than not, it returns an empty screen. Oddly enough, the same search run the next day produces hits. The only advice I can give you is to keep trying. WAIS by mail is a daunting exercise in many respects, and using it may test the limits of your patience. Needless to say, a fully interactive Internet account, using a graphical WAIS client like WinWAIS, can make WAISmail seem antiquated.

Gopher by Electronic Mail

Gopher by electronic mail? Surely I jest. But in fact, there is a way to access Gopher through e-mail, believe it or not. GopherMail, created by Fred Bremmer (with help from Nick Hengeveld and Matt Ranney), does the trick. It's an ingenious solution to the problem of using Gopher by mail, although one that's byzantine enough that it will probably convince you of the virtues of getting a full Internet connection. Whereas WAISmail is comparatively straightforward—you run a search, identify one or more documents, and

Figure 9.4   A satellite image retrieved through WAISmail and subsequently decoded.

then request to see them—GopherMail's challenge is to adapt to the e-mail format of the menued information structure that the underlying client uses.

This is no easy matter, but Gopher by mail is certainly better than no Gopher at all. To access GopherMail, send mail to one of the addresses shown in Table 9.1. Clearly, your choice should be dictated by whichever is closest to you, under the principle that we always want to use the smallest number of system resources possible. If you send a message with no subject and nothing in the text field, GopherMail will respond with a help document that explains how to use the system.

Table 9.1   GopherMail Servers

Address	Country
gophermail@cr-df.rnp.br	Brazil
gophermail@eunet.cz	Czech Republic
gopher@ftp.technion.ac.il	Israel
gopher@join.ad.jp	Japan
gopher@ncc.go.jp	Japan
gopher@nig.ac.jp	Japan
gopher@nips.ac.jp	Japan
gopher@dsv.su.se	Sweden
gophermail@calvin.edu	USA
gopher@ucmp1.berkeley.edu	USA

A GopherMail Query

Your first move with GopherMail is to take a look at the main Gopher menu at a Gopher-Mail site. To do so, send mail to one of the GopherMail addresses in Table 9.1 with no subject and no message. GopherMail will respond with a Gopher menu that will be the basis for everything that happens next. In Figure 9.5, you can see the basic response.

> **HINT:** Services like GopherMail aren't designed from the ground up to handle heavy traffic loads (Fred Bremmer concocted the system as a way to keep in touch with Gopher after he left the college). So when the server at Calvin College began to experience a load factor of some 5,000 to 6,000 hits per day, it put a considerable strain on the system. I am listing the Calvin site (gophermail@calvin.edu) as a viable address because it still is at the time of this writing, but the powers that be at the college are considering shutting the server down because of the load. If you attempt to use GopherMail through the Calvin College address and get no response, you'll have to explore the other GopherMail sites.

Examine this screen. Notice that it is structured as a standard Gopher menu, including local information about the National Cancer Center (in this case, I have gone through a GopherMail site in Tokyo) and various cancer resources, as well as menu links to worldwide information. Nothing, in other words, is unusual about the menu save for the way we'll access individual items. Also included in the returned document, along with the menu, is a list of the links to the various Gopher items (these links are not visible in Figure 9.5, but can be seen by scrolling through the complete document). We discussed links in Chapter 3 on Gopher; they provide information about where each item is found, including address and port number.

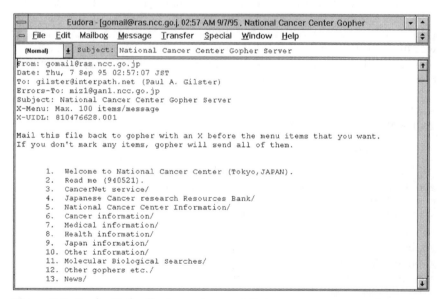

Figure 9.5 GopherMail will return a document that you can use as a search template for your Gopher work by mail.

You might, for example, choose to find out more about the National Cancer Center itself. To do so, heed the instructions above the Gopher menu and place an **x** before the items you want to see. The easiest way to do this is to simply edit the incoming mail file in your mail reader. Tell your mail reader that you want to insert the original message in your reply. Then, place the **x** directly in front of item 1, *Welcome to National Cancer Center (Tokyo, JAPAN),* and you have alerted the server to send you this document. The next step is simply to mail the entire message back to the original address.

HINT: When marking items with an **x**, remember to place the **x** at or near the beginning of the line. It should appear *before* the menu numbers for the options you choose. Figure 9.6 shows my request when I have told the GopherMail server that I want to see choice 1. I've also requested the second item, a readme file. Note: It is not necessary to edit out the rest of the original message; marking the items you need is sufficient.

Limiting GopherMail's Output

Some electronic mail gateways restrict the size of the messages they can handle; therefore, GopherMail provides two ways to break its output into several smaller messages when they become too big. First, you can tell GopherMail the maximum number of menu items it should send in a single message. Alternatively, you can specify the maximum size for incoming messages by including the necessary information in the Subject: field of your message.

For example, to restrict the number of menu items to 10, you would send the command **Menu=10** in the Subject: field. To restrict the size of incoming messages to 49,000 bytes, you would enter the command **Split=49000**. You can place either or both of these responses in the Subject: field.

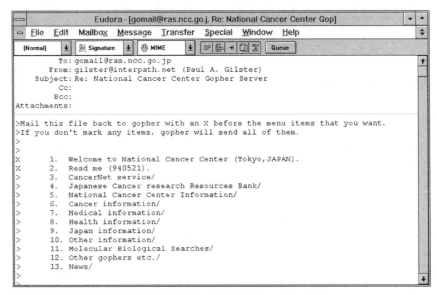

Figure 9.6   Editing the GopherMail file. The Xs indicate the file(s) you want to retrieve.

The alternative is to place the same commands in the body of your message, in which case they should appear on separate lines. This information is already included in the basic GopherMail reply to your initial query. It is placed after the menu items and before the link information that accompanies them. The material looks like this:

```
Split=27K bytes/message <- For text, bin, HQX messages (0 = No split)
Menu=100 items/message <- For menus and query responses (0 = No split)
```

To change any of these values, simply edit them in your mail program as a part of your response to the GopherMail server.

Going Directly to a Gopher

We now have the basic principle down—placing an **x** in front of the item we want to see, and then mailing the menu back to the GopherMail server. But what if we simply want to go directly to a site? We could work our way through the Gopher menu structure at the GopherMail site, but this would take up unnecessary amounts of time, for we would be using e-mail to go ever deeper into a Gopher menu. A better way is to specify to the GopherMail server that we want to see the menu at a particular site.

To do so, I need only send the address of the Gopher I want to see in the Subject: line of my message. Wanting to see the Gopher at the University of Minnesota, I entered its address, gopher.micro.umn.edu, directly in the Subject: field of a message to a Gopher-Mail server (in this case, the one at Calvin College). The menu was retrieved and sent back to me as an e-mail message. I can now use this menu to move to any of its items by placing an **x** before them and returning the message.

HINT: Notice that when I entered the address in the Subject: field of my message, I did not use the URL. The URL for this Gopher would be:

gopher://gopher.micro.umn.edu/

But what GopherMail wants to work with is an address. If you enter the URL instead, you will retrieve only an error message.

A GopherMail Search Using Veronica

To prove that GopherMail works, let me demonstrate how you can use it to search for information with Veronica. I am interested in tracking down Gopher sites containing material on flying, hence my Veronica search term will be aviation. The first thing I need to do is to examine the menu I just retrieved from the University of Minnesota. When I get the menu back, I put an **x** by the appropriate item. In this case, it is item 8:

```
8. Other Gopher and Information Servers/
```

I return the message with an **x** in front of this item and soon receive a return message, which is the submenu found by choosing item 8:

```
1.  All the Gopher Servers in the World/
2.  Search All the Gopher Servers in the World <?> (Send keywords in Subject:)
3.  Search titles in Gopherspace using veronica/
4.  Africa/
```

```
 5.  Asia/
 6.  Europe/
 7.  International Organizations/
 8.  Middle East/
 9.  North America/
10.  Pacific/
11.  Russia/
12.  South America/
13.  Terminal Based Information/
14.  WAIS Based Information/
15.  Gopher Server Registration.
```

Now I can choose item 3, again placing an **x** by it and mailing the message back to GopherMail. This will allow me to access the Veronica servers. The return message is shown in Figure 9.7. Note that this response includes the instruction, critical for our purposes, to search by putting our keywords in the Subject: field. I choose one of the Veronica sites by putting an **x** in front of it and then send the message, inserting the keyword aviation into the Subject: field.

The response is broken into two messages, each quite lengthy. A sample is shown in Figure 9.8. As you can see, the method now simply repeats what we have been doing. The basic GopherMail procedure remains the same at all levels. You select the menu item that you wish to see, place an **x** by it, and return the message to the GopherMail server. Keep this process going until you get the information you need.

And here's a final tip: GopherMail, as mentioned earlier, provides links to the various menu items it finds. Links look like this:

```
Name=Find GOPHER DIRECTORIES by Title word(s) (via NYSERNet )
Numb=3
Type=7
```

Figure 9.7 Veronica can be searched by electronic mail using GopherMail.

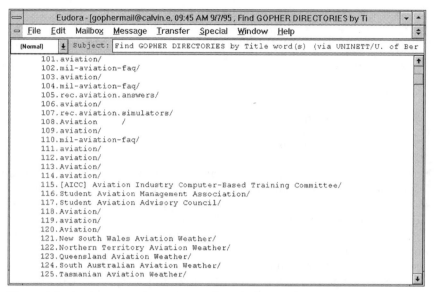

Figure 9.8   Responses to a Veronica search on the keyword aviation.

HINT: If you plan to use GopherMail with any regularity, keep the basic strategy in mind. And because everything is based on the original Gopher menu that GopherMail sends you, keep a copy of that document at hand for subsequent use. If you use a mail program like pine or a client like Eudora, you can save the document in a folder and reuse it whenever the need arises. If you are using GopherMail through a mail-only service like a local bulletin board (which is more likely, because if you had full Internet access you would probably be using Gopher interactively), then maintain a copy of the document as an ASCII file, which you can reedit for subsequent searches.

```
Port=2347
Path=-t1
Host=empire.nysernet.org
```

This example is the link to the NYSERNet Veronica server; link information for every menu item is provided below the menus returned by GopherMail. If you decide to use a particular tool, like Veronica, on a regular basis, you can clip out this link information and use it as the text of a new message, sending it to the GopherMail server, and including your search term in the Subject: field, thus saving you the time of having to go through the entire Gopher menu tree once again. Be sure to include the GopherMail housekeeping information regarding message size and menu items. Thus your complete clip should look like this:

```
Split=27K bytes/message <- For text, bin, HQX messages (0 = No split)
Menu=100 items/message <- For menus and query responses (0 = No split)
Name=Find GOPHER DIRECTORIES by Title word(s) (via NYSERNet )
Numb=3
```

```
Type=7
Port=2347
Path=-t1
Host=empire.nysernet.org
```

finger by Electronic Mail

finger is a useful Internet tool that allows us to access various information servers and to retrieve data about people connected to the Net. As with GopherMail and WAISmail, it is also possible to use electronic mail to query a finger site. And, as before, the results are returned to us in the form of a mail document.

For fun, let's see if we can generate a list of trivia questions about movies and television. A finger server exists to provide just this service. The address is cyndiw@magnus1.com, and we would normally reach it using the command **finger cyndiw-@magnus1.com**. In this case, however, we want to send mail to a different address:

infobot@infomania.com

We'll send mail to this address with the following subject line: **finger cyndiw@magnus1.com**. Sending this message, I quickly receive a response, as shown in Figure 9.9 through the Eudora e-mail program.

Of course, finger can also be used to generate information about individuals, which is how the service evolved in the first place. To do so, we use the same technique. For example, if I want to finger my own user ID at my alternate account on The World, I would use the command **finger pag@world.std.com**. As before, I would put this command in the Subject: field of my message and leave the message body blank. Soon I would receive a response:

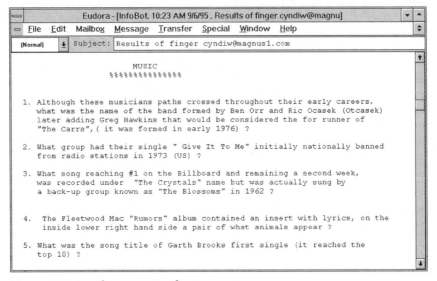

Figure 9.9   A mail response to a finger request.

```
[world.std.com]
world -- IP19 IRIX release 5.3 version 11091811

pag     . Paul A Gilster     Login Fri 18-Aug-95 11:01AM from mercury.interpath.net
  [4597,4597] </home/ie/pag>; Group: pag
  Groups: pag

  pag has new mail as of Wed 23-Aug-95 7:51AM
  last read Fri 18-Aug-95 11:02AM
```

This is not terribly useful information, although, as discussed in Chapter 8, I could supplement it by creating a .plan and/or a .project file.

WHOIS by Electronic Mail

Mail-only users of the Internet have the ability to conduct a WHOIS search. Some WHOIS servers will handle mail queries. To use the important server at the InterNIC, you would send mail to mailserv@ds.internic.net. Through this means, you can access the WHOIS databases of the InterNIC, including the MILNET server, the server at Inter-NIC Registration Services (for nonmilitary personnel), and the local server at Directory and Database Services. The server at this addresses accesses all three of these databases.

Assuming I want to retrieve information about network writer Ed Krol, I could send the following mail to the mailserver:

```
% mail mailserv@ds.internic.net
Subject:
whois .krol
```

It's important to note the conventions for constructing the message here. First, no subject is necessary. Second, the mail server recognizes the leading period (.) I have placed before Krol's name; this tells it I am making a query for a person rather than an organization. Notice, too, that I have begun the message in the far left column. If I fail to do this, the automated mail server function won't work. Soon a message will appear with the result, as shown in Figure 9.10.

I could also use mail to look for organizations. Suppose I wanted to know which computers were on-line at the University of Wisconsin. Constructing a mail request would be simple. In this case, I would leave out the leading period (.), which would tell the server this is not a request for a person. The server will then search for any information regarding the university. Here is my command:

```
% mail mailserv@ds.internic.net
Subject:
whois university of wisconsin
```

A snippet of what I receive is shown in Figure 9.11. As you can imagine, this query generated quite a few hits.

If you use mail as your primary access to the Internet and need to find people, I would suggest you get the complete list of WHOIS mail server commands from the InterNIC. To do this, send mail to the same address, mailserv@ds.internic.net, with the command **whois help** as your message.

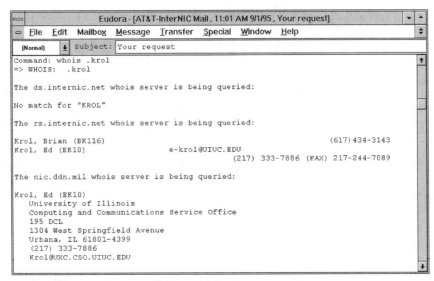

Figure 9.10 Results of a WHOIS search by electronic mail.

Checking Internet IP Addresses

Perhaps you already know an Internet address and would like to know the IP address at that site. The difference between a Domain Name System (DNS) address like world.std. com and an IP address is that the DNS address, which uses words to describe computers, works in opposite fashion to the numerical IP addressing scheme. Whereas the DNS sets up addresses with the most specific information at the far left (as in gilster@inter-

Figure 9.11 Searching for active addresses at the University of Wisconsin through WHOIS.

path.net, where the most specific item, my name, is on the left, and the most general, .net, is on the right), IP addresses present their most general information at the left and work progressively to the right, ever tightening their specificity.

If you're wondering why you would need an IP address in the first place, given the fact that the Domain Name System has become so widespread, the answer is that IP numbers are how the network's computers do their work. A name server computer in the appropriate domain actually translates the names you use in your address into the corresponding IP numbers for routing. And there are times when a given site may have the IP numbers for various destinations but not the DNS names. This can occur particularly at military sites; many use IP addresses exclusively for their addressing. Persons at such a site might need the IP address for a computer for which they had only a DNS address. To find it, it is possible to use an IP Address Resolver. As of this writing, there are two available. The addresses are as follows:

resolve@cs.widener.edu

dns@grasp-insa-lyon.fr

Use the first of these if you're based in North or South America; use the second if you're in Europe or Asia, to minimize network overhead.

The usage is straightforward. Send a mail message to either site with the query **site address.** For example, if I want to find out the IP address for the machine mercury.inter-path.net, I can do so by sending this query: **site mercury.interpath.net.** Shortly, I receive a response:

```
Date: Wed, 6 Sep 95 10:55:24 EDT
From: resolve@cs.widener.edu (Address Resolver)
Subject: Response for address(es)
To: gilster@interpath.net (Paul A. Gilster)
Sender: resolve@cs.widener.edu (Address Resolver)
Reply-To: resolve-request@cs.widener.edu (Resolve Maintainer)
Precedence: bulk
X-UIDL: 810399315.002

The address(es) for your request:

        mercury.interpath.net               199.72.1.1


--
Contact sven@cs.widener.edu with problems or comments.
Please note: no guarantees come with this, it's just a hack.
```

At the dns@grasp.insa-lyon.fr site, you can get a help file by sending the command **help** as the text of your message. This site has a different set of commands:

ip *host*   Retrieves the IP address of the computer specified. Thus my command might be **ip mercury.interpath.net.**

name *ip#*   Retrieves the hostname from the IP address you supply.

ns *host*   Retrieves the name servers at the host you specify.

help   Sends the help file.

HINT: Take note of the comment at the end of the message from the IP resolver. "No guarantees come with this," says the message, "it's just a hack." In a broader sense, you should bear in mind that many interesting network tools are like this; they grow out of the work of individuals and small groups at various network sites, and sometimes have a brief life. Others grow out of similar circumstances to become key network tools; archie is a case in point.

So, as you use Internet tools and learn of new ones, you should realize that it is possible that some of them will have changed considerably by the time you try them out. If this is the case, be patient. The network is in a state of continuous evolution. Ultimately, changes to its tools can only occur through experimentation and a willingness to try, and to support, new ideas.

Searching a Mailing List Archive Site

Mailing lists provide a mother lode of valuable information, but in many ways they remain one of the most unexploited resources on the Internet. Because of their origins at academic sites through the pioneering work of BITNET, mailing lists are often highly specific and sometimes arcane, but there are few subjects worthy of serious investigation that are not reflected in them. These lists, heavily subscribed to by the academic departments in whichever specialty is being discussed, often maintain archives of previous postings that can prove useful to the intellectually curious. And many new lists, covering every conceivable topic, have begun to appear as the mailing list concept has spread into the realm of general computing, its traffic flowing over the broader Internet.

The reason mailing lists and their archives are not more commonly considered a part of Internet search strategies is that they are so difficult to use. Mailing lists are often controlled by programs called LISTSERVs (although other automatic mailing list programs, such as Listproc and Majordomo, are growing in use). LISTSERVs automate the mailing process and control what happens when you ask to search an archive site.

The noninteractive nature of the connection—BITNET mail, for example, flows through gateways to and from the Internet, because the underlying computer protocols differ—means that searching is a multistep process. You can think in terms of Gopher-Mail as a precedent, although even its complicated back-and-forth messaging is relatively straightforward compared to the demands of using a mailing list archive.

A Mailing List Search Paradigm

The mailing lists that grew up in the LISTSERV environment use a tool called the Command Job Language Interpreter (CJLI) to manage searches of their archives. Each search must be run with exceeding care so as not to violate the conventions of the CJLI. Those conventions are based on a basic search template, which is shown below. Your job is to fill out this template and send the result to the LISTSERV in question.

```
//
Database Search DD=Rules
//Rules DD *
command 1
```

command 2

. . .

/*

We will insert our own commands into the relevant parts of the template to make our search work. Stay with me now as we go through the procedures.

Targeting the Right Mailing List

Searching a LISTSERV is a highly targeted enterprise; you must know which LISTSERV and which mailing list you are going to search. The question is, how do you make that determination? The way to begin is to query the BITNET Network Information Center (BITNIC) to receive a list of mailing lists. To do so, send electronic mail to the following address:

listserv@bitnic.bitnet

The text of your message should be **list global** (the Subject: field can be left blank), which will send a compilation of all lists known to BITNIC at the time. This list will be a subset of the total number of lists available through the Internet, but it will offer an excellent place to start in your search for mailing lists.

We can also focus on particular topics if we choose. To search the global list on-line, we need to send another command to the same address: listserv@bitnic.bitnet. The command should be **list global** */topic*. For example, let's assume I am trying to learn something about Admiral Nelson and the great naval engagements of the Napoleonic wars. It would interest me to hear what specialists in the field were saying, but I don't know which mailing lists to sign on to. I can send the command **list global/history** to BITNIC.

In response, I receive a message containing the desired information. In fact, there are numerous history mailing lists; each is shown with its name to the left, followed by the letter L, for list. The results shown in Figure 9.12 represent only a fraction of the output of this search command. But you can see that by searching the global list, we have quickly reduced our range of choices, and can now look among these lists for the ones most appropriate for our search.

For the purposes of our search, let's choose the Military History list (MILHST-L). We can always try another list if this one doesn't pay off.

HINT: Not all sites can work with the .bitnet suffix in an address. If you try to reach BITNIC and your mail bounces, try the "percent hack," a solution named after one of the characters used to direct mail. For example, instead of sending to listserv@bitnic.bitnet, you could try this:

listserv%bitnic.bitnet@mitvma.mit.edu

We are routing our mail through a known BITNET gateway. Doing so should resolve the problem. The gateway's mail program will forward the message properly.

More than one BITNET/Internet gateway exists. You can try cunyvm.cuny.edu, for example, or pucc.princeton.edu. The format remains the same:

name%node.bitnet@*gateway.address*

Thus, I could route my BITNIC mail as follows:

listserv%bitnic.bitnet@pucc.princeton.edu

```
 ───                Eudora - [1.8a, 10:38 AM 9/1/95 , File: "LISTSERV LISTS"]    ▼ ▲
 ═  File  Edit  Mailbox  Message  Transfer  Special  Window  Help              ▲
                                                                               ▼
 [Normal]      ↕  Subject: File: "LISTSERV LISTS"
 ─────────────────────────────────────────────────────────────────────────── ↑
 KYROOTS          KYROOTS@UKCC.BITNET
                  Kentucky Genealogy & History Discussions

 MAPHIST          MAPHIST@HARVARDA.BITNET
                  Map History Discussion List

 MEDART-L         MEDART-L@UTORONTO.BITNET
                  MEDART-L - Medieval Art History

 MEDIEV-L         MEDIEV-L@UKANVM.BITNET
                  Medieval History

 MENA-H           MENA-H@ULKYVM.BITNET
                  History of the Mideast and North Africa

 MILHST-L         MILHST-L@UKANVM.BITNET
                  Military History

 MISSIONS         MISSIONS@YALEVM.BITNET
                  Missions History Discussion Group (MISSIONS)

 MUS330A          MUS330A@LISTSERV.ARIZONA.EDU                                 ↓
                  Music 330a - Music History
```

Figure 9.12   You can search for mailing lists by topic by querying BITNIC.

Sending for an Index

Having determined which mailing list we want to search, we now need to determine whether an archive is maintained by the mailing list in question. We already have an address for the Military History list; it's milhst-1@ukanvm.bitnet. And because we need to send our commands to the LISTSERV rather than the list itself, we must use the term listserv in the address. Consequently, the proper address will be listserv@ukanvm.bitnet.

HINT: Note the principle here. When you're dealing with a BITNET mailing list address, substitute the term listserv for the name of the mailing list. Suppose I want to query a mailing list called sharp-l@iubvm.bitnet. I substitute listserv for sharp-l. Thus, my address for the query is listserv@iubvm.bitnet. This is the address I would need to use for any searches of this list's archives.

To retrieve any index at this site, we send the command **index milhst-l** to the address we've already specified: listserv@ukanvm.bitnet. If there is an archive there (and at this point, we don't know whether there is, since not all mailing lists maintain such archives), we will receive a return message giving us the news. And indeed, a message quickly appears. Figure 9.13 shows a sample of what it contains.

Examine this figure for a moment, and you will see that the discussions of the Military History list have been broken down into monthly segments, each with a statement indicating who can access them. If we chose, we could retrieve any one (or more) of these monthly files. To retrieve the last one shown in the figure, for example, we would send the command **get milhst-l log9509**, and send it to the list address at listserv@ukanvm.bitnet. We would then have a record of all the messages that appeared on that mailing list during the month of September 1995.

```
Date:          Fri, 1 Sep 1995 09:42:02 -0500
From: BITNET list server at UKANVM (1.7f) <LISTSERV@UKANVM.CC.UKANS.EDU>
Subject:       File: "MILHST-L FILELIST"
To: gilster@MERCURY.INTERPATH.NET
X-UIDL: 809982480.008


*   MILHST-L FILELIST for LISTSERV@UKANVM.
*
*   Archives for list MILHST-L (Military History)
*
*  ::::::::::::::::::::::::::::::::::::::::::::::::::::::::::::::::::::::::
*
*   The GET/PUT authorization codes shown with each file entry describe
*   who is authorized to GET or PUT the file:
*
*      ALL = Everybody
*      OWN = List owners
*
*  ::::::::::::::::::::::::::::::::::::::::::::::::::::::::::::::::::::::::

*
*   NOTEBOOK archives for the list
*   (Monthly notebook)
*                           rec              last - change
* filename filetype    GET PUT -fm lrecl nrecs   date     time     Remarks
* -------- --------    --- --- --- ----- ----- -------- -------- ---------------
  --------------
  MILHST-L LOG9503    ALL OWN V      86 20482 95/03/31 21:51:36 Started on Wed,
  1 Mar 1995 00:18:55 -0700
  MILHST-L LOG9504    ALL OWN V      87 28480 95/04/30 23:56:25 Started on Fri,
  31 Mar 1995 22:49:47 -0800
  MILHST-L LOG9505    ALL OWN V      87 27931 95/05/31 23:11:04 Started on Mon,
  1 May 1995 01:20:21 -0400
  MILHST-L LOG9506    ALL OWN V      80 17342 95/06/30 23:21:29 Started on Thu,
  1 Jun 1995 02:10:53 -0400
  MILHST-L LOG9507    ALL OWN V      84 24204 95/07/31 22:14:30 Started on Sat,
  1 Jul 1995 04:41:18 -0500
  MILHST-L LOG9508    ALL OWN V      84 15092 95/08/31 23:59:44 Started on Tue,
  1 Aug 1995 07:55:26 -0400
  MILHST-L LOG9509    ALL OWN V      80   230 95/09/01 08:20:42 Started on Fri,
  1 Sep 1995 00:20:11 CST
```

Figure 9.13 An archival index obtained from the Military History list.

Why do we have to query an individual mailing list about whether it maintains an archive? Because many do not, and others restrict their use of their archives to members of the list. We can't assume that a given list maintains an archive. If you ever want to know which databases of information are available through a particular LISTSERV computer, send the command **database list** to that server. A given LISTSERV might make several different archives available for a variety of mailing lists. If you attempt to query a mailing list whose archives are available only to its members, you will receive a message informing you of the need to subscribe.

But we're after more specific game than a monthly collection of messages. We want to know what is being said about Admiral Nelson. So let's search across the collected archives for any messages referring to the hero of the Battle of Trafalgar, the man who said, before sailing into the engagement in which he would die, "England expects every man will do his duty."

Constructing the Search

We know now that to search this archive, we must establish a search template containing our search terms. Setting up the search is simple enough; we simply plug the term nelson into the template. We also include the command **index** so that we will have a list of the messages that meet our criterion (without this command, we would run the search but receive no results!). Here is what the search statement looks like:

```
//
Database Search DD=Rules
//Rules DD *
Search Nelson in milhst-l
Index
/*
```

We send this message in the same manner we send any command to the LISTSERV; that is, we use no entry in the Subject: field and send the command as the text of our message.

By return mail, we will receive the answers to our query. As you can see by consulting Figure 9.14, the list contains, on the far left, item numbers for each message in the archive, followed by other information, including the date and time of posting and the subject posted on the message itself. We will use the Subject field here to help determine which of these messages we want to examine. We can request the LISTSERV to send one or more messages by once again using the CJLI.

Requesting Messages from the LISTSERV

As always, we use mail to send our request to the LISTSERV. Again, we need to construct a workable template, but this time, we want to add a second command, which tells the LISTSERV which messages we want to see. Examining Figure 9.14, we might ask, for example, to look at messages 1124, 2057, and 2507. Here is how I have structured the template, with a request to examine these messages.

```
//
Database Search DD=Rules
//Rules DD *
Search Nelson in milhst-l
Print all of 1124 2057 2507
/*
```

Figure 9.14   Results of a search of the Military History archives.

Notice that the template follows the identical format as before, but this time with a request to print (or send) the messages we want. Sending this template to the LISTSERV, we will soon receive the requested messages.

HINT: You don't always have to be a member of a mailing list to search its contents. These commands will work with many of the mailing lists that maintain an archive. If they do not, it may be necessary for you to join the list long enough to run the necessary search. To join a mailing list, send the command **subscribe** *listname your_name*. Thus, to sign on to the Media-L list (a discussion of education and technology issues for people who work in media services), I would send the command **subscribe media-l paul gilster** to the relevant LIST-SERV address, which happens to be listserv@bingvmb.bitnet.

The Typical Mailing List Search

We have now established a search paradigm for searching a LISTSERV archive:

1. Find the right mailing list.
2. Translate the mailing list address into the appropriate LISTSERV address.
3. Query the LISTSERV to see if an archive is available. If necessary, join the mailing list to enable yourself to access its archives (you can always unsubscribe at any time).
4. Search the archive using keywords inserted into the CJLI template.
5. Request the files you would like to see.

We will now put the paradigm to work on a quick practice search that involves further manipulation of the search commands, and thus, more refined searching.

The View from Eastern Europe

I enjoy studying the stock market, and, in particular, the workings of emerging markets around the globe. One that interests me more than most is that of the Czech Republic. Made up of the regions of Bohemia and Moravia, along with part of Silesia, the Czech Republic was created when the former Czechoslovakia broke into two parts in 1993. From the perspective of investment, the country is interesting to me because it has continued a number of key market reforms instituted by the previous government, including massive privatization of industry and industrial restructuring. Unemployment has remained low, while the currency, the koruna, seems undervalued. All in all, this sounds like an interesting place for an investor with a taste for speculation.

Can the Internet offer up any information investment possibilities in the Czech Republic? To find out, I turn first to BITNIC, to see whether there are any mailing lists that fit the bill. The address, as before, is listserv@bitnic.bitnet; the command is **list global/europe**. In keeping with the search paradigm, I am simply trying to uncover any relevant lists; note that I cast my net as broadly as possible, not knowing just what to expect. And soon I have a result:

```
Excerpt from the LISTSERV lists known to LISTSERV@BITNIC on 11 Sep 1995 08:36
Search string: EUROPE
**********************************************************************
* To subscribe, send mail to LISTSERV@LISTSERV.NET with the following *
* command in the text (not the subject) of your message:             *
*                                                                    *
*                   SUBSCRIBE listname                               *
*                                                                    *
* Replace 'listname' with the name in the first column of the table.  *
**********************************************************************
Network-wide ID  Full address and list description
---------------  --------------------------------
BIOREP-L         BIOREP-L@HEARN.BITNET
                 Biotechnology Research in the European Union
CEPES-L          CEPES-L@HEARN.BITNET
                 CEPES UNESCO (European Centre for Higher Education)
CERRO-L          CERRO-L@AEARN.BITNET
                 Central European Regional Research Organization
CESSDA-L         CESSDA-L@HEARN.BITNET
                 Council of European Social Science Data Archives (CESSDA)
CETEFL-L         CETEFL-L@CSEARN.BITNET
                 list for Central-European teachers
CLARKEURO        CLARKEURO@LISTSERV.CLARK.NET
                 ClarkNet European Networking
CND-EP           CND-EP@IUBVM.BITNET
                 China News Digest - Europe/Pacific
COAST-EU         COAST-EU@HEARN.BITNET
                 Rotterdam Architecture Academy/European Coast/tourism/internat+
E-EUROPE         E-EUROPE@PUCC.BITNET
                 Eastern Europe Business Network
```

I've found no list specifically targeting the Czech Republic, but the last item on this list, the Eastern Europe Business Network, looks promising. We know enough from this information to construct the necessary address. To query the automated system that runs the mailing list, we must substitute the term listserv for the name of the list. Thus, the address is listserv@ pucc.bitnet.

Now we need to find out if the list uses an archive. Our message to the LISTSERV handing the Eastern Europe list is as follows: **index e-europe**. The result appears in partial form here:

```
* E-EUROPE FILELIST for LISTSERV@PUCC.
*
* Eastern Europe Business Network Filelist
*
* This filelist may be sorted in columns 47 to 63 to get a list of
* files in the order of their updates. Sorting in descending order
* shows the most recently updated files at the top.
*
*
* *************************************************************************
*                              rec              last - change
* filename filetype GET PUT -fm 1rec1 nrecs   date     time    File description
* -------- --------  --- --- --- ----- -----  -------- -------- ----------------
* :::::::::::::::::::::::::::::::::::::::::::::::::::::::::::::::::::::::::::
*
* The GET/PUT authorization codes shown with each file entry describe
* who is authorized to GET or PUT the file:
*
*    ALL = Everybody
*    OWN = List owners
*
* :::::::::::::::::::::::::::::::::::::::::::::::::::::::::::::::::::::::::::
  E-EUROPE INTRO      ALL OWN .    .     0 ........ ........ Introduction to E-EUROPE,
basic commands for file subscription

*
* NOTEBOOK archives for the list
* (Weekly notebook)
*                              rec              last - change
* filename filetype GET PUT -fm 1rec1 nrecs   date     time    Remarks
* -------- --------  --- --- --- ----- -----  -------- -------- ----------------
-----
  E-EUROPE LOG9201    ALL OWN V     80  2693 93/01/07 09:44:35 Started on Sat,
18 Jan 1992 09:44:12 EST
  E-EUROPE LOG9202    ALL OWN V     80  5313 93/01/07 09:44:44 Started on Sat,
1 Feb 1992 10:23:01 EST
  E-EUROPE LOG9203    ALL OWN V     80  4007 93/01/07 09:44:54 Started on Mon,
2 Mar 1992 09:56:43 EST
  E-EUROPE LOG9204    ALL OWN V     80  2657 93/01/07 09:45:02 Started on Thu,
2 Apr 1992 08:14:39 EST
  E-EUROPE LOG9205    ALL OWN V     80  3472 93/01/07 09:45:17 Started on Fri,
1 May 1992 11:17:52 EDT
  E-EUROPE LOG9206    ALL OWN V     80  1627 93/01/07 09:45:22 Started on Wed,
3 Jun 1992 07:45:56 EDT
  E-EUROPE LOG9207    ALL OWN V     80  2815 93/01/07 09:45:30 Started on Thu,
2 Jul 1992 09:14:51 EDT
```

```
    E-EUROPE LOG9208    ALL OWN V      80   1545 93/01/07 09:45:37 Started on Mon,
3 Aug 1992 18:21:42 EDT
    E-EUROPE LOG9209    ALL OWN V      80   1166 93/01/07 09:45:44 Started on Mon,
7 Sep 1992 07:43:33 EDT
    E-EUROPE LOG9210    ALL OWN V      80    977 93/01/07 09:45:48 Started on Mon, 5
Oct 1992 07:33:26 EDT
    E-EUROPE LOG9211    ALL OWN V      80   2525 93/01/07 09:45:55 Started on Mon,
2 Nov 1992 12:36:40 EST
```

The content of the entire list is immaterial; what we have done is verify that there is indeed an archive at this site. Our next step is to search it.

We are interested in the Czech Republic, so I will construct the following search template and send it:

//

Database Search DD=Rules

//Rules DD *

Search czech in e-europe

Index

/*

At this juncture we will learn whether we are given access to the archives; if not, we will have to join the mailing list by sending a **subscribe e-europe your_name** message to the LISTSERV address. Instead, we quickly receive a list of hits:

```
> Search czech in e-europe
--> Database E-EUROPE, 370 hits.

> Index
Item #     Date      Time     Recs     Subject
------     ----      ----     ----     -------
000001  92/01/18   09:44     160     E-EUROPE Communication January 18, 1992
000018  92/01/24   11:10     153     E-EUROPE Jan 24, 1992
000027  92/01/28   10:33     196     E-EUROPE Jan 28, 1992
000028  92/01/29   10:48     227     E-EUROPE JAN 29, 1992
000030  92/01/30   09:25     176     E-EUROPE JAN 30, 1992
000032  92/02/01   10:23     148     E-EUROPE FEB 1, 1992
000036  92/02/05   10:01     198     E-EUROPE 02/05/92
000042  92/02/13   10:24     221     E-EUROPE 02/13/92
000048  92/02/24   09:38     247     E-EUROPE 02/24/92
000050  92/02/26   10:38     225     E-EUROPE 02/26/92
000052  92/02/28   10:25     281     E-EUROPE 02/28/92
000057  92/03/09   09:12     324     E-EUROPE 03/09/92
000061  92/03/17   06:22     360     E-EUROPE 03/17/92
```

The list goes on; we have 370 hits all told, meaning that 370 messages on the Eastern Europe mailing list have used the search term czech at least once.

Now that I have determined that this mailing list contains a good deal of information about my subject, I would like to tighten up the search. To do so, I will add a second term, and search using the following paradigm:

```
//
```

Database Search DD=Rules

//Rules DD *

Search czech AND invest in e-europe

Index

```
/*
```

My search has simply added the AND operator to look for messages containing both my search terms. Sending this message to the LISTSERV, I retrieve more targeted hits, some of which are shown here:

```
000500 94/05/03 14:21      68     Foreign investment in the Czech Republic
000522 94/05/05 08:32      42     Re: Foreign investment in the Czech Republic
000527 94/05/05 08:34      33     Re: Foreign investment in the Czech Republic
000531 94/05/05 13:19      45     Re: Foreign investment in the Czech Republic
000536 94/05/06 08:14      22     Re: Foreign investment in the Czech Republic
000545 94/05/08 11:12     103     Investment in Russia
000554 94/05/10 13:34      21     Looking for publisher
000557 94/05/10 15:12      36     Re: Looking for publisher
000589 94/05/16 09:06      50     CERRO
000817 94/06/21 12:26     241     Invitation to Investment symposium (fwd)
001047 94/08/14 12:36      14     foreign investment data?
001049 94/08/15 08:28      24     Re: foreign investment data?
001063 94/08/16 13:38     116     Europe: Resources for the Curious
001075 94/08/19 07:29      79     Czech News
001100 94/08/22 09:41      28     Re: Czech PTT info
001107 94/08/23 11:06      96     Czech Business News
001113 94/08/23 15:49     132     Re: Czech Business News
001120 94/08/24 17:53     383     Re: Business News (fwd)
001177 94/09/06 09:39     148     Eastern European News
001206 94/09/09 09:13     153     Havel in Chicago
001292 94/09/22 15:59     250     ACCESS Czech Republic Business Bulletin
001339 94/10/01 08:22      21     NEW INVESTMENTS
001371 94/10/13 13:01     142     Prague Energy & Environment Conference
001380 94/10/18 10:15      27     Czech Investment fund on NYSE
```

Clearly, this mailing list is going to pay off. Paging through the hits, I find a number of them to be of interest. I can now construct the final search paradigm including the numbers of the messages I want to see:

```
//
```

Database Search DD=Rules

//Rules DD *

Search czech AND invest in e-europe

Print all of 500 522 527 1049 1380

```
/*
```

The relevant messages will soon appear in my mailbox. From these, I learn several disturbing things. First, the Czech government seems to offer few incentives to foreign companies, such as tax breaks or discounted areas for doing business. A number of barriers exist that make it extremely difficult for foreigners to invest directly in the Prague Stock Exchange; for example, it's necessary to acquire local representation from a Czech citizen to make such a purchase and, in any case, the price of traded shares is confusing, while purchases themselves can only be made in the local currency. All in all, the general take on investing here among members of the Eastern Europe list is that it's too early in the game to get involved, and they may be right.

Automating the Search with InfoMagnet

The problem with mailing list searching is that it can require such exact keyword entry, as you've seen when I constructed CJLI search statements. One way around this difficulty is a program called InfoMagnet, which takes mailing lists into a graphical environment and allows you to perform most of these chores with point-and-click commands. The program allows you to isolate specific mailing lists that meet your requirements, send them basic commands to subscribe, and suspend, mail delivery or search, either a group at a time or by multiple groups at once. Automatic search capabilities available through InfoMagnet let you run the same search on a periodic basis to keep up with timely postings. Available through the Walter Shelby Group in Bethesda, Maryland, InfoMagnet is shareware and can therefore be tried out before you purchase it. Its URL:

http://www.shelby.com/pub/shelby/imag.html

Figure 9.15 shows you an example of InfoMagnet at work. Here I am examining mailing lists that InfoMagnet clusters around the general heading Literature. I can quickly join or search the archives of any of these mailing lists by clicking on the appropriate icon; results will be returned by standard e-mail. You can see what a difference this is from the laborious CJLI search statement that we've been using up to now. InfoMagnet even knows when a particular mailing list maintains private archives, meaning that joining the list is required before the archives can be searched. In Figure 9.16, I have set up a search for information about St. Augustine in the mailing list called Elenchus, which focuses on the history of the Christian Church in late antiquity. All I need to do to run the search is to click on the Search button.

I can also get a glimpse of the particulars of each list by clicking directly on it. In Figure 9.17, I have done this for a mailing list that specializes in mystery fiction. Notice that I can ask InfoMagnet to tell me what recent topics of conversation have been popular in the list in question; the results will be sent to me by e-mail. Figure 9.18 shows the list.

I generally recommend that searchers learn the primary search commands for all their tools, but I have seen that many Internet users simply don't take advantage of mailing list archives because they are perceived as being so difficult to search. For people in that situation, InfoMagnet is a natural; it allows them to run sophisticated searches and, just as important, locate the best mailing lists for those searches, with no complicated command syntax of the sort that can so easily lead to error messages. Users of the registered version can take advantage of the software's ability to update mailing list entries; the latter is no small consideration given how hard it is to stay current on what's available.

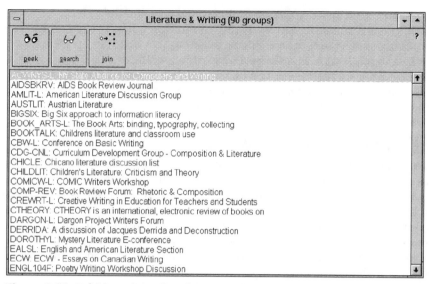

Figure 9.15 InfoMagnet's results when I searched for mailing lists about literature. Notice the icons at the top, which allow me to quickly join, search, or get more information about a particular list.

Figure 9.16 The search screen from InfoMagnet simplifies access to mailing list archives and allows you to set up quick searches like this one.

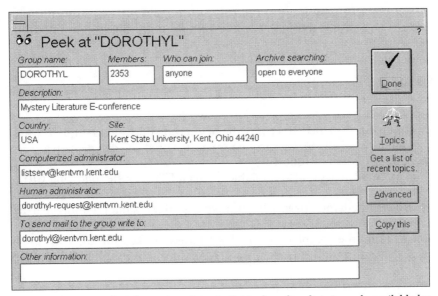

Figure 9.17 Specific information about individual mailing lists is made available by InfoMagnet.

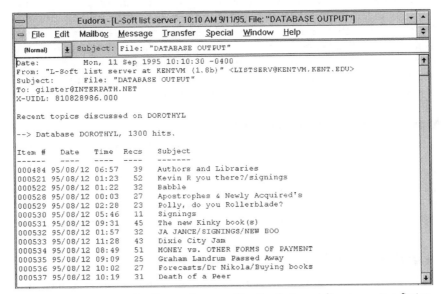

Figure 9.18 Recent topics discussed on a mailing list that specializes in mystery fiction.

More Mailing List Sources

I've shown you the systematic search of LISTSERVs as one possibility for mailing list searches; it's the one that's workable through an e-mail connection. But bear in mind that a wide variety of mailing lists exists, wider than is shown through the BITNIC's global list. The best directory of mailing lists is the one maintained by Stephanie da Silva. You can get the da Silva list in several ways. One possibility is to join a USENET newsgroup where it is regularly posted in multiple parts. Try one of the following:

news.lists

news.announce.newusers

news.answers

I recommend the latter, since it is the newsgroup on which Frequently Asked Questions documents from all the newsgroups are posted, and you can pick up a great deal of interesting information by following it.

The da Silva list is also available through FTP. Try the following URL:

ftp://rtfm.mit.edu/pub/usenet-by-group/news.answers/mail/mailing-lists/part1

You will find the complete list at this address, broken into its constituent parts, from part1 through, as of this writing, part17. And if you have a World Wide Web browser, try:

http://www.neosoft.com/internet/paml

These mailing lists use a variety of automated software, and some of them are maintained solely by humans, which means that to join them, you simply send a message asking the moderator to add you to the list. The most interesting development in terms of list archives is that many lists are making their holdings available on the World Wide Web. The da Silva list contains information about how to sign up for lists and the methods each uses to maintain its archives. I must add that there is no better way to learn about mailing list resources on the Internet than to page through the da Silva list noting the range of what is available. The diversity is nothing short of astonishing.

Reading More on Mailing List Searching

A number of other search options are available to the dedicated mailing list searcher in a huge document that provides all the necessary commands. Searching mailing lists isn't for the timorous, but if you find that these archives contain information that is valuable to you, you'll want to acquire this document. It is called Revised LISTSERV Database Functions, and it is available through the BITNIC. To get it, send mail to listserv@bitnic.bitnet. In the body of your message, send the command **info database**.

Finding and Using Other Mail Servers

We know now that a mail server is a computer that is programmed to accept e-mail requests for files, with greater or lesser human intervention, depending on the system. A remarkable amount of information is available through such servers, much of it specialized in nature. We can break our use of mail servers into two parts. First, it pays to send for the mail server's help documents, which give you specific information about how to use it. Second, we'll send another message to the server requesting a specific file. Whether it's a text file or an executable program, the result will appear as an ASCII file in our mailbox.

What's available through such a mail server? Stock quotes, for one thing, as made available through the QuoteCom service. You can retrieve the e-mail addresses of members of Congress, or retrieve Frequently Asked Questions documents from various USENET newsgroups. The USENET Oracle is a different kind of mail server; you send it questions about absolutely anything at all and receive Delphic replies, which are actually generated by networked individuals far and wide who are joining the fun. ACE, Americans Communicating Electronically, offers government documents by mail, while OSS-IS offers FTP lists, library and service lists, and other government information.

A Sample Mail Server Search

Let's run a sample query past a mail server. We'll choose the Amateur Radio mail server at info@arrl.org. The first step, remember, is always to send for the help message. We do so by sending mail to the Amateur Radio address and enclosing the single command **help** in the body of the message. The response is shown in Figure 9.19.

We learn from the help message that we can retrieve an index of files by sending the command **index** to the mail server. The index soon appears, with a listing of files. The basic layout is shown here:

```
#RULES AND REGULATIONS - FCC MATTERS
ALLOCATE.TXT      5k 950706 Amateur Frequency Allocations
RIB.TXT           1k 950626 ARRL Reg. Info. Branch functions services and infor-
                            mation - list
BANDPLAN.TXT     11k 950626 ARRL Recommended Band Plans
3RDPRTY.TXT       1k 950527 Countries that the US has 3rd Party Agreements with
RECIPOP.TXT       2k 950527 US/ worldwide reciprocal operating countries list
ADDRESSE.FCC     16k 950410 FCC Field Office addresses - by state/county
```

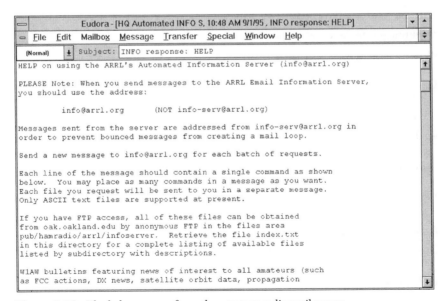

Figure 9.19 The help message from the amateur radio mail server.

```
CONTACT.FCC      4k 950626 How and WHEN to contact FCC - phone #s and addresses
610INSTR.TXT    10k 950411 Using FCC Form 610 - license changes - renewal - lost
                           etc.
PART97.TXT     136k 950812 FCC Rules Part 97
FCCCMNTS.TXT     5k 950527 How to submit comments on an NPRM to the FCC
CALLSYS.TXT      4k 950527 FCC Fact Sheet 206 - call sign assignment system
VANITY.TXT      19k 950410 FCC NPRM 93-305 - Rules to implement a vanity call-
                           sign system.
VANITY.NEW       2k 950410 FCC news release on Vanity call signs
```

To retrieve one of these files, we need only to specify the filename, along with the **send** command. Thus, to receive an article about amateur radio frequency allocations, we would use the command **send allocate.txt**. The method is simple; the only thing to bear in mind is that many mail servers implement their own variations on these methods, and you should always get the help file and read it before you try to use the server.

Interesting Mail Server Sites

The following are some mail servers that may pique your interest.

ALMANAC

USDA government news and information about the use of computers in agriculture. Sites:

almanac@esusda.gov

almanac@ecn.purdue.edu

almanac@oes.orst.edu

almanac@ces.ncsu.edu

almanac@silo.ucdavis.edu

almanac@joe.uwex.edu

almanac@wisplan.uwex.edu

Command: Use the command **send guide** in the body of your message to get started.

AMATEUR RADIO

Text files about amateur radio and shortwave subjects. Site:

info@arrl.org

Command: Send mail with the **help** command in the body of the message to get started.

AMERICANS COMMUNICATING ELECTRONICALLY

Government documents by e-mail. Site:

info@ace.esusda.gov

Command: Use the **send help** command in body of message.

CANCERNET

Cancer information available through electronic mail. Site:

cancernet@icicb.nci.nih.gov

Command: **help** or **Spanish** in the body of the message.

CAREER CENTERS ONLINE

A resume service and jobs database offering search by location and other features. Site:

occ-info@occ.com

Command: **help** in the body of the message.

THE ELECTRONIC NEWSSTAND

Material from a wide range of general interest and more specialized magazines. Site:

gophermail@enews.com

Command: send a blank message for help.

GENETICS BANKS

A database of genetic material information. Sites:

gene-server@bchs.uh.edu
retrieve@ncbi.nlm.nih.gov
blast@ncbi.nlm.nih.gov
genmark@ford.gatech.edu
blocks@howard.fhcrc.org
mail cbrg@inf.ethz.ch
quick@embl-Heidelberg.DE
netserv@embl-Heidelberg.DE

Command: Send the **help** command in the Subject: field to all these addresses except blast@ncbi.nlm.nih.gov and cbrg@inf.ethz.ch; to these, send the **help** command in the body of the message.

INFOMANIA

A variety of e-mail services including weather updates and a music catalog. Site:

infobot@infomania.com

Command: Send **help** in the Subject: field of your message.

OSS-IS

Government documents, FTP lists, Frequently Asked Questions documents, and more. Site:

info@soaf1.ssa.gov

Command: Send **index** in the message field.

NetLib

Mathematical programs via e-mail. Sites:

netlib@ornl.gov
netlib@uunet.uu.net

Command: Place the **send index** command in the body of the message.

StatLib Server

Statistical information and datasets for researchers. Site:

statlib@lib.stat.cmu.edu

Command: **send index** in body of message.

Stock Market

Quotes on current issues and information about commercial services related to the market. Site:

services@quote.com

Command: Place **help** in the Subject: field.

The USENET Oracle

Answers all questions about your life and fortunes. Site:

oracle@cs.indiana.edu

Command: Send mail with the command **help** in the subject field.

U.S. Congress

Electronic mail addresses for members of the House and Senate. Site:

congress@hr.house.gov

Command: send a blank message for a list of addresses.

UUCP Map Entries

UUCP map information by mail. Site:

dns@grasp.insa-lyon.fr

Command: **help** in body of message.

White House Summaries

Summaries of daily White House press releases. Site:

almanac@esusda.gov

Command: Send **subscribe wh-summary** in the body of the message.

10

The Future of Internet Searching

Curiously, the future of Internet searching may not consist of a completely new set of tools, at least not for the time being. The development of today's tools was not evolutionary but rather sudden and quirky. Four years ago, little was available that allowed you to run searches or browse effectively for Internet material. Then, after several years of concentrated activity at a number of sites, the key tools emerged: Gopher, WAIS, archie, Veronica, and, perhaps most significantly, the World Wide Web and the whole cluster of browsers that have sprung up around it. The immediate future is likely to consist of numerous adjustments to these existing tools to make them more powerful.

Numerous enhancements to today's technology are now being addressed. Gopher has been tuned to handle a greater variety of filetypes and to work with clients that can understand which items they can access and which they cannot. archie is likewise in a state of flexibility and growth, as Bunyip Information Systems moves toward adding new data-gathering and front-end serving components beyond the current harvesting of FTP sites. Indeed, archie seems to be leaving its file-specific roots behind to grow into a general database maintenance engine. Meanwhile, a flurry of activity persists with the World Wide Web, including the widespread acceptance of browsing engines like Mosaic and Netscape. It is here that the greatest change is occurring, with new directories appearing in profusion, and a variety of approaches to search engines being developed.

All this growth makes it clear that the paradigm for the development of navigation tools has undergone a sea change. Gopher and archie both grew out of the perceived need to organize large collections of data; essentially, they were responses to a problem whose dimensions were, at that time, only beginning to become clear. Today, these tools, developed within the academic community and tuned for its audience of university users, students, and scholars, have become commercialized. Bunyip Information Systems provides archie to various sites under a subscription system, with discounts for educational institutions. Gopher, likewise, has moved to the commercial model (although free versions will remain available). WAIS continues its commercial track under the auspices of WAIS Inc., with ownership ultimately in the hands of America

Online, while the Clearinghouse for Networked Information Discovery and Retrieval provides a non-commercial software engine using the Z39.50 protocols called Zdist.

It was inevitable that the need for better navigation tools would become a money-making proposition, and only right that the people who had put in so much time and effort creating these tools would receive compensation for their work. Unfortunately, the effect of this today, in some quarters, is that rival camps are actively developing independent solutions to common problems. Is the World Wide Web a better venue for network searching than the worldwide system of Gophers? Is the Veronica solution for Gopher menu searching superior to WAIS and its distributed databases? Such questions may stir debate among partisans, but the nature of network data implies that these tools serve us best when they work together; each has its strengths in its own niche of the Internet. No tool is an island, to paraphrase John Donne, in a worldwide distributed cyberspace.

Although it will be fascinating to observe developments in each of the search tools, not to mention the growth of additional software, it has been gratifying to see a healthy move in the direction of user interface issues. Gopher, of course, grew into prominence because it addressed the need of the technologically unsophisticated to benefit from the computing resources of a university. By attaching itself to Gopher's browsing engine, Veronica benefits from the same relatively undemanding interface, although it now struggles with access problems—too many users are trying to take advantage of too few servers. The World Wide Web offers an inherently nontaxing way to move about a wide cluster of information, jumping between items as the need arises. The Web, indeed, appears to be the most likely arena for future growth in that a good browser makes complicated tasks easy to accomplish through the use of mouse-driven commands and pull-down menus.

With the Internet growing into commercial environments and—through new service providers including the major long-distance carriers—into the home, we are likely to see this trend accelerate. Watch for providers to offer interfaces unique to their services, front ends that can simplify complex Internet tasks; even the pesky configuration options of a SLIP/PPP account can be automated. Watch too for search engines to evolve in the direction of more refined clients, programs that users can put to work immediately because the programs lead them through the search process step by step. The benefits of a good client program are no more keenly felt than with WAIS, as we saw when comparing the use of swais with the graphical WinWAIS client. It is no exaggeration to say that the average user may find swais so difficult as to be unusable, while the same network newcomer can master WinWAIS and be running searches in short order.

What can be done with future searching programs? For one thing, the model of Internet searching, which has been largely based upon Boolean search techniques, is now moving in the direction of natural language approaches and software that can recognize links between concepts. Natural language software can create a relevancy ranking, much like the one we've seen used in WAIS, that is based upon such things as the number of times a particular keyword appears in your document, or how close your terms appear to each other in the documents in question. We've already seen that relevancy feedback is a less than overwhelming application with many WAIS databases, but when run through a good server, as is the case with the *Encyclopaedia Britannica* site examined earlier, it can produce an excellent series of results, and can reduce your search time.

As Web search tools become more numerous, we'll see relevancy ranking as implemented by various companies spreading. Concept searching is a different notion altogether; it allows you to extract information in less conspicuous ways. By building topic trees, the administrator of a database can cluster information, so that your query on one concept calls up hits from related groupings of data. At the moment, concept searching appears to be less accurate than older Boolean models, but it's clear that advances in this field hold great promise. Our goal, after all, is to search effectively massive databases of binary information in ways that don't exhaust the time of the researcher. Finding effective ways to limit the number of possible hits is a major goal of programmers.

The ability to search across multiple databases is likewise destined to expand. We've already seen just how many sites exist that contain potentially useful information. It would be useful to be able to apply a single interface to the search task and have it consult all applicable databases. Perhaps even more useful, and certainly more futuristic, is the growth of intelligent agent software that will run searches for us, and customize itself according to the information needs we specify. Such software could run repeated searches, finding new material and updating our knowledge base, perhaps in the form of daily or weekly news summaries that will someday be as common as newspapers today.

All of these tools are under active development today. And the convergence between the demands of new users for solutions they can understand and the market reality of a burgeoning Internet industry intent on tapping the public dollar will continue to drive our search engines forward. Already, the price of a SLIP/PPP account is competitive with that of the older VT-100 shell account model. Whereas the traditional dial-up user had no way to work with mice and pull-down menus in a graphical environment, SLIP/PPP users now take these things for granted. Their growth has caused a groundswell in client software development that continues unabated, one that has changed the look and feel of almost all Internet client programs. The great development of the next five years will be the gradual shift from interface issues, many of them already resolved for the better, to power issues—the need to improve the efficiency of the underlying search engines.

The Emergence of CNIDR

The Internet has always benefited from the tension between its underlying anarchy and the need to impose structure upon its operations. Consider that the worldwide metanetwork contains some 50,000 participating networks within its matrix, and you realize that an imposed organizational structure is both problematic and at the same time desirable. We revel in the Net's wide open spaces and seemingly limitless freedom of expression, but we chafe when we can't find the file we want; we long for order.

Out of this tension has arisen the wide variety of search and browsing tools we have examined in this book. From archie to Gopher to WAIS and beyond, Internet search tools spring out of our need to organize cyberspace just enough to allow our computers to pass along information to each other. It should be no surprise, then, that the need to track down resources has prompted the growth of an organization whose charter is broad enough to encompass all our search tools: the Clearinghouse for Networked Information Discovery and Retrieval, or CNIDR. Located in Research Triangle Park, North Carolina, CNIDR exists to promote the use of these tools and to foster their future development.

Numerous organizations have contributed to the emergence of CNIDR as a center for the development of distributed discovery and retrieval tools. Early support came from the Center for Communications at MCNC in North Carolina; MCNC itself is a research consortium involved in microelectronics, communications, and supercomputing in a nonprofit environment. Other early backers included Apple Computer, Inc., Digital Equipment Corporation, IBM, NeXT, and the University of North Carolina at Chapel Hill, whose Office of Information Technology has been an active player in the development of networked research tools.

CNIDR was conceived as a more specific institution than the one into which it has evolved. The notion was of a support center promoting the Wide Area Information Servers (WAIS) retrieval concept that we discussed in Chapter 6. Developers, implementers, and users of the initial public domain WAIS software were among its first participants, and the idea of a clearinghouse for Internet navigation and search and retrieval systems was what initially caught the eye of the National Science Foundation, a crucial funder of the center's projects.

The Clearinghouse was able to hold a WAIS workshop in February 1992, with the help of funding from a National Science Foundation cooperative agreement, and the energetic efforts of CNIDR director George Brett and assistant director Jane Smith. Even before the workshop, both Brett and Smith had been active proponents of search and retrieval tools, speaking at numerous conferences and aligning their fledgling organization with such groups as the Internet Engineering Task Force (IETF), the Coalition for Networked Information (CNI), and the Reseaux Associes pour la Recherche Europeenne (RARE), which fosters network growth in Europe (RARE has since merged with EARN, the European Academic Research Network, to form a new organization called TERENA, the Trans-European Research and Education Networking Association).

In October 1992, CNIDR received a three-year grant from the NSF, which it has used to increase its network activities. CNIDR's server was brought on-line to provide pointers to the various client and server implementations of WAIS, Gopher, and any other Internet search tools that have been developed for use in the public domain. By creating and promoting such a site, CNIDR thus simplifies the task for anyone who is hoping to establish a server or use a search tool for any kind of information resource.

But such a site has broader implications as well. By providing a central focus, it encourages developers of new tools to work within established frameworks that will ensure compatibility and interoperability between their tools. As tools are created, CNIDR can play a key role in generating news of their existence on the network and promoting their use. The site also provides pointers to documentation and project information, ideally stimulating future growth in those areas that need development most.

"Our major focus," says CNIDR director George Brett, "is the research and education environment; but in that light, following the public library model, what we're trying to do is to create a level paying field, a baseline for the entry points of these tools. We have a tradition of building consensus, of bringing diverse communities together." Building such a consensus among developers, Brett believes, will ensure robust tools in the future.

A January 1992 meeting in Denver, attended by prominent members of the library and networking communities, makes Brett's point. Brett's focus was on the creation of a common vocabulary. Some people talk about *templates*, others talk about *records*; some database-oriented researchers discuss *fields*, others talk about *data elements*. How is it possible to be sure they are all talking about the same thing? The group spent three hours working out a consensus on a list of seven basic terms, and then went on to hammer out another 23. Similar meetings have occupied CNIDR's attention in the areas of medical networking and K-12 education.

The Global Schoolhouse Project was one such project. Sponsored by the National Science Foundation, the project was designed to showcase the convergence of technology and education, teaching educators and students how to use client software to extract information from networked computers. The methods included, in addition to the kind of software we've examined in this book, videoconferencing and distance learning tools. In one session, CNIDR used Cornell University's CU-SeeMe software in conjunction with MUSH 2.0, a virtual environment conferencing system, to engage in a live dialog with students in several states. The project ended officially in December 1994, but not before demonstrating the potential of Internet connectivity in the public school classroom.

Ongoing work at CNIDR includes the maintenance of the freeWAIS program, a public domain implementation. Development efforts on freeWAIS have, however, been supplanted by work on Zdist, which uses the 1992 version of the Z39.50 standard (see Chapter 6 for a refresher on Z39.50; for the moment, suffice it to say that freeWAIS and the original WAIS implementations from Thinking Machines Corp. used an earlier version of the Z39.50 protocol, which is not interoperable with the improved, later version). Isite is an integrated software tool developed by CNIDR that includes a search engine, a text indexer and the Z39.50 tools needed to access remote databases; Isite includes the Zdist engine. Other CNIDR tools: The Gopher Book, a Winsock-compatible Gopher client for Microsoft Windows, and WAIS Manager, a WAIS client.

Building Search Engines

Not many years ago, funding for network developments came from various agencies of the federal government. The mission was broad, but the notion of connecting significant resources, such as universities, research centers and laboratories, and defense establishments was critical. Underlying this expansion was the NSFNET, funded by the government, and aimed at furthering the expansion of regional networks by connecting universities to the nation's supercomputer sites. Indeed, we could say that in many respects the Internet as a research tool grew into maturity during this period.

We are now moving into a new era, one in which the old notion of free exchange—George Brett calls it the "circle of gifts"—is giving way to the hard realities of the marketplace. Under the old paradigm, the academic user saw no real costs to networking. Hard cash was subsumed in taxes and federal grants; it took the eye of an accountant to follow the connection. "We built up this notion that everything is for free," Brett says. "It still gets a lot of play. As we move into the commercialized marketplace, increasingly, people realize there is financial value to be gained from various aspects of the network."

Case in point: Gopher. Call it a presentation tool, a browser; whatever the description, Gopher met the needs of university computer science departments that were simply overloaded with requests for information. The question is: How to keep end users connected and productive, without tying up every system administrator's time? Mark McCahill's answer at Minnesota was to create a menu structure that would be easy to understand yet powerful enough to house the primary tools needed by his users.

But the success of Gopher brought with it a surprise. User demand for the resource outstripped the expectations of everyone on the original design team. A similar response happened with archie at McGill University, where an indexing concept designed to reduce search time for a limited pool of users took on a life of its own, and quickly began to spread across the network. A circle of gifts? Certainly, in the sense that voluntary effort produced a useful network tool out of thin air. But no matter how useful, such tools pushed hard against the charter granted their creators by their respective university administrations. Budgetary restrictions and heavy demand on the tools inevitably raised the question of whether they could continue to be supported at that level.

CNIDR grows out of such concerns, and the need to support and encourage continued development within the networking community. But it also runs headlong into a growing, and sharpening, sense of competition between the tool providers. In the early 1990s, the rush of technology was producing navigation tools that couldn't interoperate as efficiently as they should. The need for some kind of organizing structure was keen, but it has always been difficult to implement within the virtual anarchy of the Internet community.

"We were concerned that there be some kind of interoperability and protocol compliance," says CNIDR assistant director Jane Smith. "It was critical to get these guys talking to each other, because they were all doing good things but in very different ways." CNIDR can point to positive results in this regard, such as a standard description of the Gopher protocol that is published as a Request for Comments (RFC), and a similar description for the World Wide Web. The development of WHOIS++, which will combine information from a variety of Internet resources into an integrated directory system, points to an emerging consensus about how our tools should interoperate.

Taming the Kudzu Patch

Kudzu is a vine, indigenous to Japan, that proliferated upon transplantation to the southeastern United States. Anyone driving the highways of North Carolina will find great thickets of the stuff growing uncontrollably over everything in its path. Throughout the South, kudzu is a blight, Dylan Thomas' "green fuse that drives the flower" in its elemental form. But in Japan, the root is carefully maintained, its leaves fed to cattle, its stems used for cloth making, its taproot used as a thickener in cooking. The difference could not be more obvious: The plant can be a pestiferous nuisance or a powerful natural resource.

It is said that kudzu can manage 12 to 18 inches of new growth every day, which may explain why CNIDR's logo is an interlinked wreath of kudzu leaves. Like kudzu, the Internet is managing growth rates that boggle the imagination. Also like the prolific plant, the network, properly cultivated, offers the potential for resource development of the kind educators and intellectuals dream about. Think of CNIDR, then, as the overseer of a potential garden. "We consider NIDR tools promising cultivators and harvesters," says CNIDR's brochure, "and the developers of these tools among the master gardeners."

There is much gardening to be done; indeed, pruning back the kudzu is an ongoing mission. Central to the forward movement of search tools is a broad conception of their interoperability. Is WAIS better than Gopher? Is the World Wide Web through a good browser the ultimate Internet search engine? Can Gopher talk to the Web? Does it need to? These issues become the stuff of long debate at networking meetings, where partisans of the rival camps engage in a kind of religious war, not so dissimilar in tone and content from the bitter exchange of religious tracts that swept Europe during the Reformation.

CNIDR's role is ecumenical. The idea is to get at resources through tools, not to promote the merits of a single approach in a network as diverse as the Internet. Says Jane Smith, "With clients like Mosaic that use URLs, you have a way to describe the location of a resource. So within the Mosaic client you can get to FTP, Telnet, Gopher, and Web resources. With that single common element you begin to break out of the religious wars." The acceptance of that model, as shown through the diversity of new browsers and the spectacular advent of Netscape, points to a future in which the older character-based environment has been completely replaced by all-inclusive Internet front ends.

The Nature of the Internet Search

We would like to think of computer networks as tools that lighten our workload. But in the realm of searching, the Internet poses as many challenges as it resolves. The level of knowledge that the user must attain to use the basic search tools is high, and the results from any given search are always susceptible to improvement. For instance, suppose we would like to find Gopher servers that mention the word music. The search is straight-forward enough; we move to the Veronica screen on our Gopher and enter the search term. We retrieve multiple pages of hits, seemingly an inexhaustible supply of information. But as we start going through the list, we begin to notice that many of the titles are duplicates, the same information posted on different Gophers. Veronica does not cross-check them for redundancy (although this problem is being worked on).

Gopher itself is a problem. Because there is no standard for Gopher menus, a system administrator can create a Gopher item and give it whatever name seems appropriate at the time. The same file may appear on 11 different Gophers under 11 different names. How do you determine whether you're dealing with duplicate information or not? For that matter, how do you know if the file you read is from the site which authored it and therefore maintains it? If you're thorough, the only way is to check each item. And that takes time.

The scope of this problem is staggering. One sweep of Gopher titles by CNIDR's Veronica machine turned up 10 million items. But upon closer examination, those 10 million files and connections showed a remarkable level of redundancy. According to George Brett, only 1.5 million unique items were actually available. And Jane Smith says, "There seems to be this notion that there's a whole lot more information out there now that we have electronic networks, but there probably really isn't."

And what of the World Wide Web? We can send automated search engines out on the Internet to locate information at Web sites, but the degree of redundancy in their lists of results is likewise discouraging. Many of them contain links to the same core set of Web servers; what appears to be 100 hits on your topic turns out to include only five servers worth examining, yet because our search tools remain relatively undeveloped, we can't find out which sites will be valuable and which will not without actually trying many of them out. Thus time is lost as the researcher clicks on hyperlink after hyperlink, hoping to find the most effective source for the information needed.

And that information may not be beyond reproach. Anyone can put information into a World Wide Web site, for example, yet random checks at such sites reveal a disturbing willingness to post items without attribution. Fortunately, there is movement on this issue. We are moving in the direction of style guides, which include the last date a given page was updated, and the name of a person who is responsible for its presence. Gopher, too, can link information about contact people at a site that is built into its links.

Surveying Internet sites, one comes to a reluctant conclusion: Many of the sources that appear so useful on the surface turn out to be examples of self-publishing, the electronic equivalent of the vanity press. The gap between those who are originating information and those who are making it available will have to be bridged. Information *maintenance* is an issue that is seldom considered in our rush to commercialize cyberspace. The updating of posted information is all too often random and capricious, and there is often no way to authenticate resources without sending e-mail to the site.

What are we looking for in terms of the quality of our information? Smith points to the current academic model. People get a Ph.D by finding specific information about a specific topic, a time-consuming process that advances their overall level of knowledge. "I don't see why we should consider that it's not going to take some special effort to get information into the electronic environment," she adds. "I still contend that's why we need the librarians. We need people with a mindset toward information management and information science. Technical people can build the structure underneath that allows that management to take place in the electronic environment."

Librarians? But aren't we living in the age of the so-called digital library? The popular media would have us believe so, but information professionals know better. In an eloquent article in *Internet World* magazine (Sept./Oct. 1993), Smith summed up her view: "If CNIDR's message has been so unclear as to promote the notion that the library as we know it is now extinct and that librarians are expendable, then we have failed in one of our critical missions."

And just as high-quality information must be available for the Internet to live up to its promise, so too must the technology of the network support that information's retrieval. Anyone who has worked with the Internet over the past several years will know how difficult it has become to reach certain sites by Telnet or FTP, while popular Web sites can present a genuine challenge even for those with high-speed network connections. Solving the problem of growing congestion awaits a broadening of the access pipe as we move toward gigabit networks capable of handling multimedia datastreams.

What the Internet Needs

Alan Blatecky is vice president of MCNC, whose Information Technologies Division houses and has provided financial support to the CNIDR team. Blatecky is concerned with how we process and filter information. An electronic mailbox, for example, might receive 200 messages on a given day. How does the user allocate time efficiently, answering significant mail, discarding the rest? How does a person search Internet information to avoid the time-killing redundancy of retrieving the same file 40 times? Of such issues is the life of an information specialist made. There is no shortage of new developments as we make the transition into a multimedia research environment.

"The World Wide Web is where the growth is," Blatecky says, "but we need better search engines. The validity and authentication of information are still major problems. There are a huge number of sites, but how many would you want to visit more than once? So we need some way to codify what's out there. As it is, you might get 600 hits from a given search, but most of them won't prove useful. What we need are better filters."

Blatecky recalls using a Web search engine to hunt for data about pollution in Russia. The item that appeared at the top of the list? A Web site with a link to information about a 1990 Sean Connery film called *The Russia House*, in which the actor portrays a publisher who becomes tangled up in espionage in the Gorbachev-era Soviet Union. Of such bogus hits are ulcers made, especially for those who seek data for a living.

For in spite of our best efforts at technology, it's an amusing but inescapable fact that in many respects the information filters we trust the most are not digital but human. I might readily disregard any one of 600 hits a particular search engine generated on my topic, figuring it would take me all day to work through them, and that in any case, most of them would prove disappointing. But if a person I trusted advised me that a good Web page was available on that topic, I would seek it out immediately. Low-tech word of mouth is trustworthy; we rely upon those with whom we've formed relationships. Nonetheless, Blatecky knows today's search tools backward and forward. Appreciative of their powers, he is likewise clear-eyed about what they lack. Consider these thoughts:

> On Gopher: "If you know what you want and where you want to go, Gopher takes care of all the interim stuff for you; you don't have to type FTP or Telnet to get there. But it doesn't really let you surf the Internet. That's the biggest criticism I have of all the search tools. They're all aimed at someone who already knows where he or she is going."
>
> On Veronica: Because it harvests Gopher menu items, Veronica is dependent upon the perceptions of the people who built the Gopher menus in the first place. Gopher menus lack standardization, which is why menu items may not be usefully descriptive. "Descriptions are something we haven't done well. In libraries, there is a common way to mark and understand things; it can be arcane but at least it gives you a commonality. That's clearly missing in today's tools."
>
> On archie: "The FTP site browser culls data without regard for its currency." Blatecky returns to the library analogy. "You can quickly go to a volume in a library that is most current. Searching for files on the Internet is more problematic. We need to know more about what we can retrieve before we retrieve it."
>
> On WAIS: Blatecky finds WAIS and Z39.50 search tools intriguing because they allow you to search thoroughly and retrieve hits ranked by relevance. What's needed next, in his opinion, is the addition of visual data. "If you were sitting at your desktop and had a photo album, you could flip through hundreds of images in minutes. But how can I do that over the Net?"

All these tools have changed with the Internet environment in the past two years, but only the World Wide Web can be said to have truly been transformed. The Web has grown so fantastically because it solves a basic problem of data integration. It provides hypertext linking, handles images, and unites methods of data retrieval from Telnet to FTP. But the Web's downside, at least in the early days of its development, has been significant. As useful as hyperlinks are, they reflect their creator's idea of what is important. "Somebody made the decision about where the links go on any World Wide Web page," Blatecky notes, "and what seems obvious to me may not be to you."

But the Web is evolving. New search engines in the form of automated software robots now allow us to build and use databases that map this worldwide information space. And around the Internet, in both commercial and non-commercial form, a wide variety of databases, searchable by keyword under a variety of strategies, has emerged to deal with the needs of researchers. Blatecky thinks the Web is headed in a significant direction, one which is exemplified by Sun Microsystems' HotJava product. HotJava is the new programming language that allows small software programs, called "applets" in Sun's terminology, to be transferred to your computer when you access the Web page in question. Today's browsers require that a wide range of necessary support applications—text editors, Telnet clients, spreadsheets, graphics viewers—be available on your machine. HotJava will allow them to be transferred only when and if they are needed.

What's more, such applets needn't be gigantic programs capable of handling any task the user throws at them. Instead, they can be small, precisely tuned tools that are designed to handle the specific task the designer of the Web page had in mind. This model flies directly against the trend of modern software development, but there are those, Sun Microsystems' Scott McNealy among them, who believe that it points to the future of the industry. We can imagine HotJava applets precisely tuned for Internet searching of particular kinds of databases, customized tools that allow us to extract the most out of unique information resources. Updates would be handled transparently to the user, who would download the latest software automatically each time he or she accessed the site.

Given these developments, what is it that the Internet needs most? Blatecky sees three major areas for improvement:

- Authentication: How do you really know to whom you're talking on the Internet?
- Security: How do you protect valuable proprietary data?
- Data Integrity: How do you safeguard your data from alteration and misrepresentation?

No one who has "surfed" the Internet for long can miss the obvious: much of the material available over the network is freely available or in the public domain. The reason for this is obvious. The Internet lacks the kind of security barriers that would allow vendors of proprietary data to place their wares on-line safely. For research-oriented networking to thrive, there must be provision for commercial growth. Making it possible for companies to make money by offering high-quality information over the network is critical.

Provisions for on-line billing, along with security to prevent unauthorized access, will make the network into a more useful repository of information; secure transactions, as a matter of fact, form a major part of development efforts at the major Internet companies. Right now, to search back issues of newspapers, the information professional turns to commercial database vendors like DIALOG, BRS, and Dow Jones News/Retrieval. These companies have implemented security measures by controlling access to their systems through passwords and by maintaining their services over dial-up packet providers like MCI's Xstream and SprintNet. Why not move such operations onto the worldwide Internet, providing that the network evolves in the direction of Blatecky's big three?

Ultimately, we are talking about encouraging the dissemination of massive databases of information. CNIDR's role is to drive debate on such issues. "If we're going to do our job right, we need to continue to push the tools," said Blatecky. "So whether it's working with the Mosaic folks developing and pushing security or some other project with a different developer, we want to be pushing these issues so they're being addressed by somebody. We focus primarily on the public domain material, but there is no reason why industry can't take some of this, add its own value to it, and market it."

Growing into a Worldwide Cyberspace

If our tour through the Internet has proven anything, it's that the notion of an information highway is idle daydreaming without the ongoing development of our research tools. Make what you will of hundreds of video channels on demand, interactive games playing, home banking, and all the rest; what will count is the ability of a person with a computer to access high-quality information in a variety of formats, from text to audio to moving video, and to translate acquired data into greater productivity. Too much speculation about our future assumes that the Internet will become nothing more than a new form of television with interactive push buttons, a prospect that chills the committed networker.

What we need is clear:

- A movement of genuinely useful data—including commercially available materials of unquestioned value—onto the network.

- A concomitant movement to ensure intellectual property rights. Before the best of our intellectual heritage can become available, there must be a way for people to get paid for their work. The availability of networked information may also require changes in copyright law.
- A new focus on data maintenance as the most crucial aspect of preserving the integrity of our on-line data centers.
- A solution to the problem of authentication, so that electronic transactions of any stripe can take place with unquestionable authority.
- The growth of network security systems to provide firewalls between data and those who are not supposed to have access.
- A means of securing the integrity of information so that electronic alteration cannot distort the intent of posted materials.
- Better search systems and tools, so that searchers can rely upon comprehensive databases of current materials as they run their sweeps through the data.
- Direct linkages between data and its creators, along with posted information on the contact person for the data in question and the date of the most recent updates.

People sometimes compare the Internet today to the telephone system as it grew into a nationwide communications service. But perhaps a better analogy is to the power companies. The nation's power grid eventually brought electricity to the farthest reaches of the United States, allowing the transformation that made high technology possible. Networking a planet requires similar infrastructure projects on a massive scale, the laying of fiber-optic cable to business and homes, the introduction of new tools in the workplace environment, and user training.

The Internet is a precursor of such a worldwide network. It will grow through expanded data pipes and increasingly powerful computing tools, but no one would imagine that transforming our intellectual base into the electronic environment will be easy. We have barely begun this process. The tools we have examined here remind us that we need a coalition of information professionals, librarians, computer scientists, and independent scholars to help us refine our model. We are creating the electronic counterpart to the Dewey decimal system, an information tool that, if we are prescient enough to build it right, may one day lay rightful claim to the extravagant title of "digital library."

Glossary

anarchie A Macintosh-based archie client that also contains FTP functions.

anonymous FTP Entering **anonymous** as your login at an FTP site allows you to use resources that the system administrator has made available to the public. See FTP.

ANSI American National Standards Institute. This body is responsible for standards like ASCII (q.v.).

archie A system of distributed computers that tracks the holdings at FTP sites throughout the world. You can use archie to search for files.

ARPA Advanced Research Projects Agency (formerly DARPA). This agency funded the original research that resulted in ARPANET, the network that validated the concept of packet switching through TCP/IP.

ARPANET Funded by ARPA to study how to make computer networks secure in the event of nuclear war, this network later split its functions, with MILNET breaking off in 1983. ARPANET was retired in 1990.

ASCII The American Standard Code for Information Interchange, which creates a standard for representing computer characters.

asynchronous The transmission of information without reference to timing factors on the receiving end.

ATM Asynchronous Transfer Mode. Perhaps the hottest news in network technology, it allows networks to move vast amounts of data, such as live video, on a switched, as opposed to a point-to-point, basis.

backbone The system of high-speed connections that routes long-haul traffic, connecting to slower regional and local data paths.

bandwidth The size of the data pipeline. The higher the bandwidth, the faster information can flow.

BBS A bulletin board system. The term usually refers to a small, dial-up system designed for local users, although some BBSs are now widely available over public data networks.

BITNET An academic network containing mailing lists on a wide variety of subjects, often populated by scholars and experts in their various fields. Used a different protocol than the Internet to move its data. BITNET traffic now moves almost entirely over the Internet.

browser   A program used to navigate the World Wide Web. Browsers like Mosaic and Netscape allow you to click on a link to another document, and move to a different computer where that resource is stored.

CNIDR   The Clearinghouse for Networked Information Discovery and Retrieval, in Research Triangle Park, North Carolina. Its mission is to support the development of network search tools.

client   Software that requests services from another computer (called the server). This model is known as client/server computing.

CMC   Computer Mediated Communication, an acronym you will occasionally encounter that refers to the entire range of networking activities.

compression   The process of squeezing data to eliminate redundancies and allow files to be stored in less disk space.

CSO or CCSO   An acronym (Computing Services Office) for a system that allows you to search for students and faculty members at a given school. Now found as CCSO—Computing and Communications Service Office—following a name change at the site.

CWIS   Campus Wide Information Systems serve universities and colleges with local news, directories, library connections, and databases.

cyberspace   The universe of networked computers. Your electronic mail could be said to flow through cyberspace.

dial-up user   A person who accesses the Internet through a modem. This can refer either to a shell account—the user connects to a machine that is on the Internet and uses its resources, rather than having his or her machine actually on the network—or a SLIP/PPP account (q.v.), in which the user's computer exchanges data packets directly with the Internet.

domain   A part of the DNS name. The domain to the far right is called the top-level domain. In the following example, this is .com.

Domain Name System   The system that locates the IP addresses corresponding to named computers and domains. A DNS name consists of a sequence of information separated by dots. Thus mayer.hollywood.com. The Domain Name Service is a program that resolves domain names into IP addresses.

downloading   Moving a file from one computer to another.

e-mail   Electronic mail involves sending and receiving messages over the network. You use a mail program like mail or pine to compose and read your messages.

FAQ   A Frequently Asked Questions list is a document that covers basic information from a particular USENET newsgroup or mailing list.

finger   A program that can display information about users on a particular system. Can also be used for other kinds of data.

Free-Net   A community-based, volunteer-built network. Free-Nets are springing up in cities around the world, as citizens work to provide free access to selected network resources, and to make local information available on-line.

FTP   File Transfer Protocol is your tool for moving files from any one of thousands of computer sites to your service provider's machine. From there, you can download them to your own computer.

ftpmail   A way to retrieve binary files through electronic mail.

FYI   The acronym for For Your Information. Refers to a series of Internet documents containing basic material for beginners.

gateway   A computer that handles moving data from one network to another.

Gopher   A tool developed at the University of Minnesota that creates menus that allow you to access network resources by moving an on-screen pointer. The idea behind Gopher is to simplify the process of using network information. Gopher can point to text files, Telnet sites, WAIS databases, and a wide range of other data.

GopherMail A way to retrieve Gopher information by sending e-mail to a mail server.

Gopherspace A play on cyberspace. Gopherspace is a whimsical term for the worldwide system of Gophers.

header A header appears as the first part of a data packet, and contains addressing information and provides provisions for error-checking. The word is also used to refer to the part of an e-mail message preceding the body of text.

hits In network parlance, the term for results as applied to a database search. You might say, for example, that Veronica returned 65 hits when you searched under a particular keyword.

home directory The directory on the service provider's computer that shell account users are allocated for their accounts. This is the directory you are in when you log on.

host A computer directly connected to the network.

hostname The name of a computer on the Internet. Can be almost anything that the system administrator can dream up.

HTML Hypertext Markup Language. HTML is used to prepare documents that can be displayed by World Wide Web browsers. The document displays formatting, graphics, and links to other documents.

HTTP HyperText Transport Protocol. HTTP enables hypertextual browsing through the World Wide Web; the user clicks on links that are established in a Web document and moves to that document, even though it may be located on a different computer. HTTP provides for the specification of resources through Uniform Resource Locators, or URLs.

hypermedia The ability to display a range of different media through hyperlinks. A World Wide Web page, for example, may contain photographs or drawings, textual formatting, and links to audio and video sources.

hypertext Data that provides links between key elements, allowing you to move through information nonsequentially.

HYTELNET A hypertextual program that offers a database of Telnet sites.

Internet The worldwide matrix of connecting computers using the TCP/IP protocols. Does not include, but often moves traffic for, other networks like BITNET and UUCP. If you see the term internet (with a lowercase i), you are dealing with a TCP/IP network that is separate from the worldwide Internet.

Internet Architecture Board (IAB) Formerly the Internet Activities Board. Coordinates research and development of the TCP/IP protocols and oversees standards for the Internet Society.

Internet Engineering Task Force (IETF) A task force working as part of the IAB that develops standards for protocols and architecture on the Internet.

Internet Society Promotes the growth of the Internet and works to assist those groups involved in its use and evolution.

InterNIC Internet Network Information Center. Your first place to ask questions about the network itself. Maintains a wide variety of data, which it makes accessible to all users.

interoperability The ability of diverse computer systems to work together by using common protocols. Without it, the Internet could not exist.

IP Internet Protocol defines the packet structure of a datagram; it functions at the network layer of the protocol stack. IP also defines the addressing mechanism used to deliver data to its destination.

IP Address A network address expressed in numbers.

ISO The International Standards Organization. Creates standards for international use, not all of which take hold (see OSI).

Knowbot   A network tool that allows you to search several different databases consecutively to find network addresses and information.

LAN   A local area network, usually in a business office, connecting multiple computers to a server computer.

LIBS   A Telnet-accessible library search tool.

LIBTEL   A search engine for library catalogs and university resources.

LISTSERV   A program that manages mailing lists on BITNET by responding automatically to e-mail requests and distributing new messages.

lynx   A character-based World Wide Web browser that allows access to the World Wide Web for people with shell accounts.

mail server   A computer that responds to electronic mail requests for information. You could ask a mail server, for example, to send you a particular file by giving a precise command, such as **send index**, and so on.

mailing list   A group discussion carried on through electronic mail. BITNET is home to numerous mailing lists on a huge range of topics. Its traffic, and that of other mailing lists, now flows over the broader Internet.

metanetwork   A network that is made up of numerous other networks. The Internet is the prime example.

MIME   Multipurpose Internet Mail Extensions; the system for providing graphics and other nontextual data through e-mail.

Mosaic   A graphical tool that allows you to access World Wide Web information in a point-and-click environment. Can be used effectively only if you have direct network or SLIP/PPP access.

multicast   As opposed to broadcasting, which would send data to everyone, multicasting means moving data from one point to multiple, specified network points. The term is used in connection with the operational procedures of the MBONE.

nameserver   A computer that manages Internet names and numeric addresses.

netfind   A network search tool that allows you to track down user information.

netiquette   The etiquette of using the network. Not a trivial issue, especially now that the rise in commercial Internet sites is raising questions about advertising and other business uses of the Net.

Netscape   A popular World Wide Web browser created by many of the original team members who developed Mosaic.

network   Computers connected to communicate information.

newsgroup   A USENET discussion about a particular topic. Some 11,000 newsgroups now exist.

NIC   Network Information Center. An organization charged with maintaining a particular network.

NNTP   Network News Transfer Protocol. The standard for the exchange of USENET messages across the Internet.

node   Any computer attached to a network can be called a node.

OSI   Open Systems Interconnection is a standard for networking developed by the ISO (q.v.). Its use has given way almost completely to TCP/IP.

packet   The basic unit of Internet data. A message sent across the Net is broken into packets, each marked with the address and other pertinent information, such as error-checking data. The TCP/IP protocols see to it that the packets are rebuilt at their destination.

packet switching   The process of sending packets through the network, allowing for alternate routing if a particular network link fails.

pico   An easy-to-use text editor operating under Unix.

pine   A program used to read and create electronic mail. Uses the pico text editor and provides on-line help as well as an intuitive interface and an address book.

ping   A utility that lets you check whether a given host is reachable.

POP   Post Office Protocol allows electronic mail messages to be stored on your service provider's computer until you log in to retrieve them. The protocol then downloads the messages to your computer. You use a client program like Eudora or Pegasus Mail to read and reply to messages.

port   The designation identifying the location of a particular program on an Internet host computer.

postmaster   The person who takes care of the mail system at a given site. The postmaster responds to queries about users on the system and makes sure the mail gets through.

PPP   One of two methods (the other being SLIP) for exchanging data packets with the Internet over a telephone line. Point-to-Point Protocol offers data compression and error correction, and remains under active development.

protocol   A protocol defines how computers communicate; it is an agreement between different systems on how they will work together. The set of TCP/IP protocols defines how computers on the Internet exchange information (a set of protocols is commonly called a suite).

public data network   A network providing local numbers by which you can access computer services in different cities, using X.25 protocols to move data.

RARE   The Reseaux Associes pour la Recherche Europeenne, an association of network organizations in Europe. Serves a function similar to that of the IETF. Now incorporated into TERENA.

resolution   The process of translating an Internet name into its corresponding IP address.

RFCs   Requests for Comments. A series of documents that describe the protocols driving the Internet, along with diverse information about its operations.

RIPE   The Reseaux IP Europeens is an organization of European Internet providers. RIPE has now been incorporated into TERENA.

router   A computer system that makes decisions about which path Internet traffic will take to reach its destination.

server   A computer that provides a resource on the network. Client programs access servers to obtain data.

service provider   A company that offers access to the Internet. Dial-up users obtain an account on the service provider's system and use its computers to log on to the Net.

shell   A program that provides the interface users work with on Unix systems. A variety of shells are available.

shell account   A dial-up account to a Unix-based service provider's machine. Using a shell account, you use whatever resources the provider has made available on his or her machine, but do not exchange data packets directly with the Internet. You cannot run client programs like Netscape and Eudora over a shell account; they demand a SLIP/PPP connection.

signature   A short note, usually containing your name, address, and other information (and including, often, a favorite quotation) that appears at the end of mail or newsgroup messages you send. A signature is set up by creating a special file in your home directory.

SLIP   Serial Line Internet Protocol. As opposed to regular dial-up accounts, a SLIP account allows your computer to receive an IP address. FTP sessions are thus handled directly between remote computers and your system, without going through your service provider's computers first. A SLIP account also allows you to run graphical front-end programs like Mosaic or Netscape.

SMTP   Simple Mail Transfer Protocol is the Internet standard protocol for handling electronic mail messages between computers.

synchronous   The process of sending data communications at a fixed rate. Both sender and receiver must operate at the same rate to achieve synchronous communications.

T1   1.544 Megabits per second data transfer over a leased line.

T3   45 Mbps data transfer over a leased line.

tar   A method of file archiving.

TCP/IP   Transmission Control Protocol/Internet Protocol. This is the set of protocols that drives the Internet, regulating how data is transferred between computers.

Telnet   An Internet protocol that allows you to log on to a remote computer. Used, for example, in searching remote databases.

terminal emulation   The process of communicating with a remote computer as if your computer were actually a terminal connected to that computer. By treating it as a terminal, the remote machine is seldom able to tap the full processing power built into your computer, thus limiting the interface you work with. VT-100 is the most common form of terminal emulation.

tn3270   Works like Telnet, but designed to handle IBM systems, which require full-screen operations.

TurboGopher   A Macintosh Gopher client.

Unix   An operating system used by most service providers. Shell account users usually encounter Unix when they log on to a service provider's system, and must use Unix commands to handle routine chores like file management. Berkeley Unix comes with the TCP/IP protocols already built in.

URL   Uniform Resource Locator. A standard way to refer to resources that specifies the type of service as well as the exact location of the directory or file in question.

USENET   A worldwide network of newsgroups on thousands of subjects, which can be accessed by newsreader programs like Trumpet for Windows or WinVN.

UUCP   Unix to Unix Copy Program is a method of transferring files between computers that includes electronic mail. Thousands of computers around the world use the UUCP network to exchange mail over dial-up telephone lines.

Veronica   A program that allows you to search Gopher menus for particular keywords.

vi   A text editor with an inscrutable interface that is widely distributed over the Internet. pico is much easier to use.

VMS   An operating system used by Digital Equipment Corporation VAX computers.

WAIS   Wide Area Information Servers is a system that allows you to search databases by keyword and refine your search through relevance feedback techniques.

WAIS for Macintosh   The best Macintosh client for using WAIS.

WAISMail   A method of searching WAIS databases by electronic mail.

WAN   A Wide Area Network can be any network whose components are geographically dispersed.

WHOIS   A program that allows you to search a database for people or network addresses.

Winsock   A dynamic link library, or DLL, file that contains the procedures for making Microsoft Windows work with TCP/IP. A Winsock is needed to run client programs like Mosaic or WinWAIS on a Windows-based system via SLIP/PPP.

WinWAIS   A Microsoft Windows-based WAIS client.

workstation   Workstations are generally more powerful than desktop IBM-compatible or Apple computers, and usually run Unix as their operating system.

World Wide Web   A series of protocols that work through hypertext links to data, allowing you to explore network resources from multiple entry points.

Wsarchie   A Microsoft Windows-based archie client.

WSGopher   A graphical Gopher client for the Microsoft Windows environment.

X.25   An older standard that defines how connection-based services operate. X.25 requires a connection to be made before data is transmitted.

X.500   A directory standard based on OSI (q.v.).

Index

AAUP, 39
Accessing On-line Bibliography Databases,
    252
  URL for, 254
Addresses, 259–260, 327–328
  (*See also* People-oriented searching)
ALIWEB, 63
All-in-One Search Page, 63
America Online, 6, 40, 45, 49, 162, 188, 307,
    309, 350
Anarchie, 177, 180, 184
Anderson, William P., 165
Anonymous FTP (*see* FTP)
archie, 4, 5–6, 155–186, 349, 353
  accessing, 160
  background of, 128, 157–160
  case sensitivity in, 166, 168–169, 170
  and client systems, 177–186
  command switches, 177–180
  commands, 162, 165–177
  determining search method in, 185–186
  via e-mail, 160, 172, 309–312
  and Gopher, 115–119, 160
  and graphical client programs, 180–186
  and HYTELNET, 233
  and regex, 166–167, 169, 176–177, 186
  sample search with, 165–167, 311
  servers, list of, 161, 173
Argus (Clearinghouse for Subject-Oriented
    Internet Resource Guides), 38

Association of American University Presses
    (*see* AAUP)
AT&T 800 Information, 61
Audio files, accessing, 122–124
Automated searching (*see* Robots)
Awesome Lists, 63–64

Backslash symbol, use of, 176
Barrie, Fred, 5, 127
Barron, Billy, 233, 252
Benchmark searches, 74–75
Berners-Lee, Tim, 4, 20–21
The Big Dummy's Guide to the Internet, 14,
    15
Binary files, 122, 309, 318
BITNET, 188, 224, 329, 330, 334
BIX, 162
Blatecky, Alan, 356–357, 358
Bookmarks, 23, 65–73, 74, 76
  in character-based systems, 23, 73
  in Gopher, 100–107
Boolean operators, 37–38, 44, 62, 350
  in archie searches, 167
  vs. content navigation, 196
  in Jughead searches, 150
  and Lycos, 53
  in Veronica searches, 142, 147, 153
  and WAIS servers, 198
Bremmer, Fred, 318, 320

Brett, George, 352, 353, 355
Brokers, 61
Brooks, Dave
Browser(s), 19–20, 77–78, 81
    character-based, 77–78
    for FTP sessions, 79–81
    Gopher as, 88
    graphical, 3, 4, 23, 77–78
    for Telnet sessions, 83–84
    as USENET newsreader, 81–82
    and Veronica, 128
    (*See also* Mosaic, Netscape; Web
        browsers)
BTG Hot List, 39
Bunyip Information Systems, 6, 158, 159,
    160, 349
Burchill, Charles, 230

Campus Wide Information Systems (*see*
    CWIS)
Case sensitivity:
    and Gopher, 107
    and Veronica, 134
    and WAISmail, 317
    and the Wanderer, 62
CCITT (International Telephone and
    Telegraph Consultative Committee),
    261
CCSO (Computing and Communications
    Services Office):
    data type, 138
    directories, 298–300
    name servers, 120–121
CERN, 4, 20–21
Character-based systems, 77
    to access WAIS, 189, 215
    to access the Web, 16–17, 26
    bookmarks in, 73
    and browsers, 21, 73
    and Gopher, 93, 98
    vs. graphical, 2–3
    and WHOIS, 272
    (*See also* Shell accounts; Unix)
Christoff, Chris, 189
CityScape Internet Services, 65
CJLI (Command Job Language Interpreter),
    329, 333, 339
Clearinghouse for Networked Information
    Discovery and Retrieval (*see* CNIDR)

Client programs, 2–3
    to access archie, 160, 177–186
    to access Gopher, 90–91
    to access netfind, 283
    to access WAIS, 189
    to access WHOIS, 272, 279–281
    and Hypernet, 238, 244
    selecting, 92
Client/server relationship, 188, 197
CMC Information Sources, 39
CNIDR (Clearinghouse for Networked
        Information Discovery and Retrieval),
        6, 9, 159, 221, 255, 257, 350, 351, 354,
        358
Combined AAUP Journals Catalog, 39
Command Job Language Interpreter (*see*
        CJLI)
Commercial Sites Index, 39
Commercial systems, 4
    (*See also* Fee-based information)
Compression utilities, 116
    and Hytelnet downloading, 232
CompuServe, 15, 16, 162, 308, 309
Computer Networking Bibliography,
        Libraries and Information Resources,
        225
Concept searching, 350–351
Configurable Unified Search Engine (*see*
        CUSI)
Conservation Online (COOL), 222
Consummate Winsock Apps List, 92
Content navigation, 195–197
Corporation for National Research
        Initiatives, 293
COSINE PARADISE project, 266
CUSI (Configurable Unified Search Engine),
        64–65
CWIS (Campus Wide Information Systems),
        301–303

DANTE network, 266, 267
da Silva, Stephanie, 41, 341
Data types:
    for Gopher, 138
    with Veronica, 136–138, 146, 152
December, John, 39
DELPHI, 162
Deutsch, Peter, 5–6, 158
Dial-up accounts, 2–3

Directory Enquiries (de), 263, 266–268
Directory of directories, 38
Directory of Electronic Journals and
    Newsletters, 189
Directory of Telnet-accessible library
    catalogs, 233
Directory searching, 11, 21–43
    automated approach (robots), 43–44
    and Galaxy, 32–38
    limitations of, 22
    and name servers, 120–121
    vs. search engines, 74
    site-driven, 22
    with Special Internet Connections, 22–26
    tips for, 74–77
    top-down approach to, 22, 30
    use of keywords in, 22, 32, 34
    with Veronica, 135
    and WAIS databases, 191
    with Yahoo, 26–32
    (*See also* People-oriented searching)
Directory sites (list of), 38–43
Directory User Agents (OVAs), 263
Distinguished name, 260
Domain Name System (DNS), 259, 327–
    328
Dow Jones News/Retrieval, 197, 358
DNS (*see* Domain Name System)
Droms, Ralph, 300

EINet WinWAIS, 189, 198–199
    advantages of, 198, 205
    basic commands, 207–209
    and relevance feedback, 199, 205–207
    sample WAIS search, 199–207
    URL for, 199
    and using keywords, 203–205, 207
Electronic Frontier Foundation (EFF), 199,
    222
Electronic journals, 39, 222
Electronic mail (*see* E-mail)
E-mail, 155, 259, 309
    to access archie, 160, 172, 309–312
    to access Gopher (*see* GopherMail)
    to access WHOIS, 272, 326
    and binary files, 318
    finding mail servers, 342–344
    and finger, 325–326
    Gopher newsgroup addresses, 124

and IP addresses, 327–328
and Knowbot, 296
list of mail server sites, 344–347
locating addresses for, 272, 326
and mailing lists, 7–8, 41, 329–342
and OSI, 261
postmaster for, 308
sample searches using, 311, 343
and saving Gopher documents, 97
and WAIS, 190, 198, 211
    (*See also* WAISmail)
X,400 vs. TCP/IP
E-mail addresses:
    for archie, 310
    for BITNET Network Information Center
        (BITNIC), 330
    for Bunyip Information Systems, 160
    for Da Silva directory of mailing lists,
        342
    for finger server, 325
    for Gopher newsgroups, 124
    for GopherMail, 319
    for HYTELNET mailing list, 246
    for InterNIC server, 326
    for Knowbot, 296
    for mail server sites, 344–347
    for netfind, 290
    for postmaster, 308
    for Revised LISTSERV Database
        Functions, 342
    for robot-related issues, 62
    for USENET address server, 304
    for WAIS, Inc., 227
    for WAISmail, 313
Emtage, Alan, 5–6, 158
Enterprise Integration Network (*see* EINet)
Eudora, 259, 324, 325

FAQs, 75, 129, 141, 225
    for USENET newsgroups, 304
Fee-based information, 239, 240, 349–350,
    353
    and archie, 159
    and WAIS, 191, 349
    (*See also* Commercial systems)
File Transfer Protocol (*see* FTP)
Filo, David, 26
Finding people (*see* People-oriented
    searching)

finger information, 291–293
  and e-mail, 325–326
  and Knowbot, 295
Fletcher, Jonathan, 57
Fogel, Earl, 230
For Your Information documents, 189, 223
Foster, Steven, 5, 93, 127
Four11, 306, 307
fred interface, 263–265, 266
Free-Nets, 240
  (*See also* Public access systems)
Frequently Asked Questions (*see* FAQs)
FTP (File Transfer Protocol), 1, 4, 22, 24,
    155–156
  anonymous, 155, 223, 231
  and archie, 5–6, 115, 159, 164, 184–185
  and Gopher, 115–116
  and netscape, 19–20, 80–81
  site lists for, 39, 41, 156
ftpmail, 309, 311
Full-text searching, 75, 229
  and Global On-Line Directory, 65
  and InfoSeek, 59
  and JumpStation, 57
  and Veronica, 148
  and WAIS, 206
  and Web Crawler, 48–49

Galaxy, 32–38, 199
GIF (Graphics Interchange Format), 122,
    318
Global Network Navigator, 40
Global On-Line Directory, 65
Global Schoolhouse Project, 352–353
Goldman, Johnny, 312
Gopher, 2, 3–4, 5, 25–26, 85–126, 349, 353,
    355
  accessing, 78, 90–93, 127
  and archie, 105, 115
  bookmark feature in, 87, 100–107, 143
  as browser, 88
  and CCSO, 120–121
  and character-based systems, 93, 98
  commands for Unix client, 98–100
  and CWIS, 301
  via e-mail, 318–325
  and FTP sessions, 115–119
  graphical clients for, 91
  history of, 86, 350

  and HYTELNET, 244–246
  and library resources, 251–253
  limitations of, 357
  list of data types for, 138
  and Lycos, 53
  mailing list addresses for, 124
  multimedia capabilities, 121–124, 135
  in Netscape, 25–26, 79
  and network connections, 112
  as publishing tool, 124
  via Telnet, 92, 113–115, 116–117
  typical menu in, 87–88
  and Veronica, 44, 90, 127–128
  and virtual reality modeling, 125–126
  and WAIS searches, 119–120, 214–217
  and Web browsers, 78, 85
Gopher+, 121
The Gopher Book, 353
GopherMail, 318–325, 329
Gopherspace, 86–88, 125, 127
Government involvement in networks, 353
Government resources (INFOMINE), 40
Graphical-based systems, 3, 4, 17–19, 77
  and archie, 180–186
  browsers, 3, 4, 77–84
  vs. character-based, 2–3, 17–18, 77
  and Gopher, 91
  and WAIS, 198
Graphics Interchange Format (*see* GIF)
Gray, Matthew, 62
Gross, Joe, 157

Harvest, 61
Heelan, Bill, 158
Help systems, 95
  for archie, 173, 310
  for fred, 265
  for HYTELNET, 238
  for Knowbot, 295
  for netfind, 283
  for swais, 198
Hgopher, 91
Hierarchies of information, 68
High Performance Computing and
    Communications (*see* HPCC)
Home pages, 21, 41
HotJava, 357
HPCC (High Performance Computing and
    Communications), 102

HTML (Hypertext Markup Language), 21, 75, 138
HTTP (HyperText Transport Protocol), 21
Hyperlinks, 11, 55
  and Gopher, 78
  and HYTELNET, 237, 238, 244
  limitations of, 11, 14–15, 21, 28
  and Lycos, 50
  in Special Internet Connections, 23–24
  and Yahoo, 29–31
Hypermedia, 11, 12, 19
Hypertext, 4, 11, 12, 14–15, 21, 28, 237, 238
HYTELNET, 6–7, 223, 229–258
  accessing, 230, 238, 244
  as browsing tool, 238, 242
  via Gopher, 244–246
  and library resources, 233, 242–243, 247–257
  list of servers, 231
  procedures for using, 231–237
  sample search, 239–241
  updating, 246–247
  via World Wide Web, 243–244

Icons, for WSGopher toolbar, 109–110
Image file formats, 122, 124, 138
  (*See also* GIF)
InfoMagnet, 339–340
INFOMINE, 40, 67
InfoSeek, 59–60
Intellectual property protection, 9, 359
Intelligent agent software, 351
Interactive Yellow Pages, 40
International Organization for Standardization (*see* ISO)
International Telecommunications Union (*see* ITU)
International Telephone and Telegraph Consultative Committee (*see* CCITT)
Internet, 1, 3, 8, 14, 155, 165, 183, 260, 351, 354
  background of, 189, 353
  demand on, 5
  e-mail access to, 309, 313
  guides to, 38, 223
  and information maintenance, 2, 9, 355–356, 359
  and intellectual property issues, 359
  limitations of, 217, 271

  and mailing, 261
  mailing lists for, 224
  relationship to World Wide Web, 13–14
  and security issues, 358–359
Internet Archives database, 159, 174
The Internet Prospector, 158
Internet Protocol (*see* IP)
Internet Request for Comments, 64
Internet Resources Meta-Index, 40
Internet Sleuth, 65
Internet Society, 199, 224
Internet Users' Glossary, 223
InterNIC Directory of Directories, 40, 239
  White Pages, 269
IP (Internet Protocol), 259, 261
  finding addresses for, 327–328
Isite, 353
ISO (International Organization for Standardization), 260
ISP Internet Yellow Pages, 40
ITU (International Telecommunications Union), 260, 261

Joint Academic Network (JANET), 235
Jones, Rhett, 150
Journalism Periodicals Index, 224
Journals, electronic, 39, 222
Jughead, 107, 128, 150–151
JumpStation, 57–58

Kahle, Brewster, 6, 187, 189, 195, 295–296
Keyword searches, 5, 8, 22, 31–32, 35–38, 75–76, 136, 357
  with archie, 116, 162, 183
  and Boolean operators, 37–38
  and InfoSeek, 60
  and Internet Sleuth, 65
  and JumpStation, 58
  materials available for, 189
  and name searches, 274, 276–279
  and Open Text Index, 61–62
  and titles, 75
  types of, 62
  and USENET, 305
  and Veronica, 128, 142–146, 152
  and Web Crawler, 45–46
  and white pages, 271
  and World Wide Web Worm, 55–56

Knowbots, 7, 293–298
Koster, Martijn, 62, 63, 64
Krol, Ed, 40, 326

Language, ambiguity of, 38
Lewis, Peter, 184
Library Internet Browsing Software (*see*
    LIBS)
Library resources, 7, 233, 242–243, 247–257
    using Gopher, 251–253
    using the Web, 254–257
    (*See also* LIBS; LIBTEL)
LIBS (Library Internet Browsing Software),
    247, 249–251
LIBTEL, 7, 247–249
Linux, 138
Listproc, 7, 329
LISTSERV, 7, 329–339
    requesting messages, 333–334
    Revised LISTSERV Database Functions,
        342
    searching, 333, 335–339
    search template, 329–330
LookUP!, 306
Lycos, 2, 5, 49–53, 65
lynx, 3, 17, 23, 73

Mahone, Dan, 247
Mail handling, 261
    (*See also* E-mail)
Mailing lists, 7–8, 329–342
    directory of, 341
    (*See also* LISTSERV)
Majordomo, 7, 329
Mak, Nico, 56
Makulowich, John, 63
Mauldin, Michael, 49
McBryan, Oliver, 57
McCahill, Mark, 3, 86, 353
Menu-driven information, 5, 86–87, 88, 90
    (*See also* Gopher)
Mesmer, Mark, 247, 249
Message Handling System (*see* X.400)
Mirror sites, 18, 64
Monster FTP Sites List, 156
Mosaic, 3, 4, 17, 349, 354
    and Gopher, 86
Mother Gopher, 88, 129
Mother-of-all BBS, 41

Multimedia, 122–124
mxqwais (for OSF-Motif), 190

NameFLOW-Paradise Service, 266
Name servers, 120–121, 138, 285
National Center for Supercomputing
    Applications, 40
National Science Foundation (*see* NSF)
Natural language approach, 44, 350
netfind, 282–291
    accessing, 282–283
    e-mail address for
    keywords for, 285, 290
    list of servers via Telnet, 282
    methodology of, 284–288, 290
    sample searches, 283–284, 285–288,
        289–290
NetNews, 61
Netscape, 2, 3, 4, 13, 16, 17, 21, 23, 349, 354
    addresses for, 18–19
    and bookmarks, 67
    and file viewing programs, 124
    and Gopher, 25–26, 79
    mirror sites for, 18, 64
    for Telnet sessions, 83–84
    as USENET newsreader, 81–82
    and X.500, 263
Network Information Centers (NICs), 239
New Riders' Official World Wide Web
    Yellow Pages, 41
NEXOR, 63, 64
NIKOS (World Wide Web Index), 61
NNTP (Internet news protocol), 19
NSF, 9, 352
NSFNET, 353
Numeric variables, 167

olwais (for Open Windows), 190
Open Systems Interconnection (*see* OSI)
Open Text Index, 61–62
OSI (Open Systems Interconnection),
    260–261
OSI Reference Model, 260–261
os2wais (for OS/2), 190
OTIS Index, 41

Page (for World Wide Web), 21
PC Software, 61

People-oriented searching, 7, 260–309
  with CCSO, 298–300
  with CWIS, 301–303
  with finger information, 291–293, 325
  with Four11, 306, 307
  with Knowbot, 293–298
  with LookUP!, 306
  with netfind, 282–291
  with WHOIS, 271–281
  with X.500, 262–271
Pinkerton, Brian, 45
piXie, 263
Point-to-Point Protocol (*see* PPP)
Port number, 98, 293
  and accessing WHOIS servers, 279
Power, Matt, 272–273, 279
PPP (Point-to-Point Protocol), 2
prog, 165, 310
Protocols, 260–261
  (*See also* TCP/IP)
Public access systems, 92, 240, 247, 279,
    349, 353, 358
Publicly Accessible Mailing Lists, 41

qarchie (*see* archie)

RBSE's URL Database, 61
regex (Unix regular expression), 166–167,
    169, 176–177, 306
Relevance feedback, 46, 76, 350
  with EINet WinWAIS, 199, 205–207
  with WAIS, 188, 197, 198, 211
  with WAISmail, 312, 317
Repository Based Software Engineering (*see*
    RBSE)
Requests for Comments (*see* RFCs)
Revised LISTSERV Database Functions,
    342
RFC 822, 121
RFCs (Requests for Comments), 64, 174,
    225, 354
Robots, 43, 49, 62, 357
  disadvantages of, 44
  mailing list for, 62
  and RBSE, 61
  and Web Crawler, 45
  and World Wide Web Wanderer, 62
  and Yahoo, 27
Rovers, Perry, 156

Schwartz, Michael, 61, 290, 292–293
Scott, Peter, 6, 230, 231, 246
Search engines, 85, 349
  vs. directories, 74
  future trends in, 350–351, 356–357
  humans as, 88
  integration of, 246
  and name servers, 120–121
  organization of, 65–66
  tips for using, 74–77
  Web-based, 45–65
  (*See also* Browsers; Robots)
Search methodology, 8, 53–54
  and ambiguity of language, 38
  and benchmark searches, 74–75
  and combining tools, 8
  concept searching as, 351
  content navigation as, 195–197
  directory vs. search engines, 74
  and full-text searching, 49, 55, 57, 61
  and human limitations, 11, 38, 44
  across multiple databases, 351
  narrowing the focus of, 133
  and natural language approach, 44, 350
  and precision tools, 55, 56, 57, 60, 61
  site-driven, 22
  and top-down approach, 22, 149
  across Web servers, 43
  (*See also* Directory searching; Keyword
    searches; People-oriented searching;
    Search engines)
SEC EDGAR, 61
Serial Line Internet Protocol, 2, 3
Shell accounts, 77
  and archie, 160, 162, 177
  file management commands for, 100
  and Gopher, 3, 90, 91, 98
  and HYTELNET, 230
  and WAIS, 6, 190, 197, 214
  and waissearch, 218–219
  and Web access, 16–17
  and WHOIS, 272
  (*See also* Character-based systems; Unix)
Simple Mail Transfer Protocol, 261
Site-driven searching, 22
slash symbol, use of, 88
SLIP (*see* Serial Line Internet Protocol)
SLIP/PPP, 3, 77–78, 350, 351
  and archie, 162, 177
  and browsers, 20
  and Gopher, 90, 91, 98

SLIP/PPP (*Cont.*)
    and HYTELNET, 230, 244
    and WAIS, 190
    and World Wide Web, 17, 18
    and WHOIS, 272
Smith, Jane, 352, 354, 355, 356
Software Description Database, 174, 175, 311
Special Internet Connections, 22–26
Spiders (*see* Robots)
Standards, 260
Strangelove, Michael, 189
String variables, 167
Subscription-based services, 59
SURAnet Guide to Selected Internet
    Resources, 226
swais, 6, 190–195, 350
    to access WAIS, 189
    basic commands for, 197–198
    vs. Gopher interface, 214
    and sample WAIS search, 191–195
    Swix, 263

TCP/IP, 3, 261
    and addresses, 259
    and use of browsers, 20, 77–78
Telnet, 155, 229
    to access archie, 160, 161–162, 165
    to access Gopher, 90–91, 92, 97, 112,
        113–115
    to access HYTELNET, 230, 231, 235, 237
    to access Knowbot, 293
    to access LIBS, 250
    to access LIBTEL, 247
    to access netfind, 282–284
    to access Veronica, 129, 130–131
    to access WAIS, 190
    to access WHOIS, 272–279
    activating sessions with a browser, 83–84
    Gopher data type for, 138
    and network traffic, 238
    and qarchie, 162
    table of X.500 servers, 263
Templates, 6, 329–330
terse mode (*see* archie, output format)
Textual searching (*see* WAIS; Full-text
    searching)
Thinking Machines Corp., 6, 187, 312, 353
    Directory of Servers, 8
TILE.NET, 41

Toolbar, for WSGopher, 109–112
Traffic loads on systems, 30, 74, 161, 162
    and archie, 310
    and HYTELNET, 238
Trumptel, 113
TurboGopher, 91, 125–126
2do, 165

Uniform Resource Locator (*see* URL)
Unix, 2
    and bookmarks, 73, 105
    and Gopher, 91, 95, 98–99, 105, 110, 115,
        128
    and HYTELNET, 230, 237–238
    prompts in, 86
    regular expression (regex) in, 166–167,
        169, 176–177, 306
    TurboGopher for, 126
    and uudecode, 318
    and WAIS, 189
    and WHOIS, 272
    (*See also* Character-based systems; Shell
        accounts; Unix commands)
Unix commands:
    for compression utilities, 116
    for file viewing, 99
    for Gopher searches, 108, 118
    for saving and mailing, 100
URL (Uniform Resource Locator), 21
URLs:
    for ALIWEB, 63
    for Anarchie, 184
    for Awesome Lists, 63
    for Billy Barron's guide to on-line
        bibliography databases, 254
    for BTG Hot List, 39
    for Bunyip Information Systems, 159
    for CCSO Web site, 300
    for Clearinghouse for Subject-Oriented
        Internet Resource Guides, 38
    for CMC Information Sources, 39
    for Combined AAUP Journals Catalog, 39
    for Commercial Sites Index, 39
    for CUSI (Configurable Unified Search
        Engine), 64
    for CWIS, 302–303
    for DANTE, 268
    for Da Silva directory of mailing lists, 342
    for EINet WinWAIS, 199

for Electronic Frontier Foundation, 93
for Electronic Journals Database
    Overview, 39
for finding people on the Internet,
    305–306
for Four11, 307
for FTP site lists, 39
for FTP sites, 156
for Galaxy, 33
for Global Network Navigator, 40
for Global On-Line Directory, 65
for Gopher at The Well, 98
for GopherMail, 322
for Gophers (various), 93–94
for Harvest brokers, 61
for HYTELNET, 230, 231
for HYTELNET through Gopher, 244
for InfoMagnet, 339
for INFOMINE, 40
for InfoSeek, 60
for Interactive Yellow Pages, 40
for Internet Resources Meta-Index, 40
for Internet Sleuth, 65
for InterNIC, 272
for InterNIC Directory of Directories, 40
for InterNIC White Pages, 269
for ISP Internet Yellow Pages, 40
for Italian Directory Service Project (for
    fred and de interfaces), 263
for JumpStation, 57
for Knowbot via Telnet, 293
for Knowbot Web site, 296
for library-oriented gophers, 253
for LookUP!, 306
for Lycos, 49
for mother Gopher, 129
for Mother-of-All BBS, 41
for NameFLOW-Paradise Service, 266
for National Center for Supercomputing
    Applications, 124
for netfind server at University of
    Colorado, 283
for netfind via WWW, 290
for Netscape, 18
for Netscape communications, 124
for Netscape mirror sites, 18–19
for New Riders' Official World Wide Web
    Yellow Pages, 41
for NIKOS, 61
for Open Text Index, 62

for OTIS Index, 41
for Publicly Accessible Mailing Lists, 41
for RBSE's URL database, 61
for Special Internet Connections, 23
for SURAnet archie server, 160
for TILE.NET, 41
for TurboGopher, 91
for TurboGopherVR, 126
for University of Minnesota Gopher, 215
for uudecode, 318
for WAIS databases, 211
for WAIS FAQ, 209
for WAIS home page, 189
for WAIS via Telnet, 190
for Web Crawler, 45
for Web of Wonder, 41
for Web Pointer, 42
for WHOIS servers (list), 273
for WinWAIS for Macintosh, 209
for WinWHOIS, 272
for Work Software Yellow Pages, 43
for World Wide Web Consortium, 21
for World Wide Web Virtual Library, 42
for World Wide Web Wanderer/WANDEX,
    62
for World Wide Web Worm, 54
for Worldwide Yellow Pages, 42
for Wsarchie, 183
for WSGopher, 91
for W3 Catalog, 65
for Yahoo, 27
for YellowPages.com, 43
for Zdist software, 227
USENET, 4, 14, 59, 223, 226, 303–306
    and activating sessions with a browser,
        81–82
    and archives searches, 303–304
    e-mail address for, 304
    FAQs, 304
    and keyword searching, 305
    and WAIS, 188, 227
uudecode, 309, 318

verbose mode (*see* archie, output format)
Veronica, 2, 44, 77, 127–153, 350
    accessing, 129–131
    background of, 128
    and bookmarks, 143
    Boolean operators in, 142, 147, 153

Veronica (*Cont.*)
    canceling, 134
    case sensitivity in, 134, 153
    and data types, 136–138, 146, 152
    directories search with, 135, 152
    and Gopher, 5, 127–129
    and GopherMail, 322–325
    limitations of, 148–149, 357
    and link files, 146
    and multiple keywords, 142–146, 152
    sample searches with, 138–141, 147–148
    search methods of, 131–136, 141–149
    tips for using, 152–153
    and wildcard searching, 148
Virtual library, 13, 42

WAIS (Wide Area Information Servers), 2, 3,
        4, 6, 44, 105, 187–227, 349, 353
    accessing, 189–190
    and CNIDR, 352
    as content navigation, 195–197
    database directories for, 191
    and e-mail, 190, 312–318
    and fee-based information, 191
    and Gopher, 119–120, 190, 214–217
    and interfaces, 3, 188, 189–190, 196
    keyword command for, 194
    and multimedia files, 188
    as publishing tool, 189
    and relevance feedback, 188, 197, 198,
        199, 205–207, 211, 312, 317
    sample searches with, 191–195, 199–207,
        313–315
    search methodology, 191–192, 209
    servers for, 220–227
    updates on, 227
    URL for home page, 189
    and waissearch, 218–219, 220
    and Web interface, 211–214
    and Z39.50, 257
WAIS for Macintosh (*see* WAIStation)
WAIS Manager, 353
WAISmail, 312–318
waissearch, 218–219, 220
waisserver (for VMS), 190
WAIStation, 189
Wanderers (*see* Robots)
waX.500, 263

Web browsers, 19–20, 43–65, 66, 77, 349
    and bookmarks, 67–73
    as interfaces, 78–84
Web Crawler, 2, 5, 45–49
Web of Wonder, 41, 74
Web Pointer, 42
Well, The, 98, 239–241
Wessel, Jason, 157
White pages directories, 7, 260, 269
    and CCSO, 298
    and Knowbot, 297
    and USENET, 304
WHOIS, 7, 224, 265, 271–281
    accessing, 272
    disadvantages of, 272
    via e-mail, 326
    and Knowbot, 295
    list of servers, 273, 279
    search method, 271–272
    via Telnet, 272–279
    tips for using, 276–279
    use with local client program, 279–281
WHOIS++, 354
Whole Earth 'Lectronic Link (*see* Well, The)
Whole Internet Catalog, 40
Wide Area Information Servers (*see* WAIS)
Wildcard searching:
    and archie, 166, 169
    and CCSO, 300
    and InfoSeek, 60
    and Veronica, 148
    and WHOIS, 276
Windows formats, 97
WinWAIS, 2, 6, 350
WinZip utility, 56
Woakes, David, 184
Work Software Yellow Pages, 43
World, The, 100, 115, 268
World Wide Web, 2, 4–5, 11, 13, 14, 112
    accessing, 16–19
    and archie, 160
    directories for, 21–43
    future of, 350, 355, 356
    and keyword searches, 34, 75–76
    and library searches, 254–257
    pages for, 21
    protocols for, 21
    searching, 45–65, 211–214
    tips for using, 74–77

World Wide Web Consortium, 4, 13, 20, 21, 42
World Wide Web Robots, Wanderers, and Spiderspage, 62
World Wide Web Virtual Library, 42
World Wide Web Wanderer/WANDEX, 62–63
World Wide Web Worm (WWWW), 2, 5, 53–57
Worldwide Yellow Pages, 42
Worms (*see* Robots)
Wsarchie, 177, 180, 207
WSGopher, 2, 91, 94–98
   and bookmarks, 100–104, 110, 111
   canceling, 118
   icons list for, 109–110, 113
   image display in, 122
   menu structure in, 110–112
   and network connections, 112–114
   saving files in, 96–97
   searching in, 107
   use of toolbar, 109–112
   and Veronica search, 141, 143
WWW Pages, 61
W3 Catalog, 65

xGopher, 91
xwais (for X Windows), 190
X.400 (Message Handling System), 260–262
X.500, 7, 260, 262–271
   connection options, 263
   and de, 266–268
   and directory user agents, 263
   and fred, 264–265
   and Gopher, 268–269
   and Knowbot, 295
   pc programs for, 263
   search method, 268–269
   table of servers via telnet, 263
   using a Web browser, 269–271

Yahoo, 26–32, 65, 74
Yang, Jerry, 26
Yanoff, Scott, 22, 25
yellow pages, 260
yellowPages.com, 43

ZClient, 255
Zdist, 6, 350, 353
Z39.50, 255, 257, 350, 353

CATCH THE

Technology Wave

WILEY COMPUTER PUBLISHING

The New Internet Navigator
Totally Revised and Expanded
PAUL GILSTER

"Paul Gilster's *The Internet Navigator* is the new champ."
—*Internet World*

"Everything nontechies need to know"
—*U.S. News & World Report*

The New Internet Navigator rises to the challenge of keeping pace with all of the new developments on the Internet. This revised and expanded edition includes coverage of the Web and Slipp/PPP with traditional UNIX platforms, the World Wide Web and Web browsers such as Netscape and Mosaic and expanded coverage of commercial online services like CompuServe, AOL and others.

ISBN# 0-471-12694-2
Price $24.95 US/$34.95 CAN
paper 784 pp. 1995

Online Resources for Business
ALFRED GLOSSBRENNER and JOHN ROSENBERG

Whether you are doing market research or sizing up the competition, you won't want to venture online without this resource. This guide helps you find the information your company needs to stay competitive without wasting any time or thousands of dollars. Online experts Glossbrenner and Rosenberg give you the bottom line on the business services — DIALOG, Lexis/Nexis, Dow Jones, and NewsNet: the consumer services—Compuserve, America Online and Prodigy: and the Internet. They tell you what type of information is available from each service, how much it costs and sophisticated search strategies, tools and techniques.

ISBN# 0-471-11354-9
Price $24.95 US/$34.95 CAN
paper 348 pp. 1995

The SLIP/PPP Connection
PAUL GILSTER

You need this book to access the World Wide Web and to use graphical Internet tools. This is the first complete, step-by-step guide to getting, using, and maintaining a SLIP or PPP connection. Dozens of money saving coupons inside entitle you to free or reduced-rate SLIP accounts from leading service providers.

ISBN# 0-471-11712-9
Price $24.95 US/$32.50 CAN
paper 480 pp.

The New Internet Business Book
Second Edition
JILL ELLSWORTH

"...a critical resource that you can't afford to be without."
—*Entreprenuer magazine*

This is the comprehensive book about doing business on the Internet...from doing market research and obtaining competitive information, to announcing products and making sales. Totally revised and updated, this bestselling guide gives you clear answers to all of your Internet buisness questions, including: who is on the Internet, what are business and organizations doing on the Internet and WWW, and why are so many business, from one person start-ups to large corporations, getting connected to the Internet?

ISBN# 0-471-14160-7
Price $24.95 US/$32.50 CAN
paper 512pp 1996

WILEY
Publishers Since 1807

Available at Bookstores Everywhere
For more information check out the **Wiley Computer Publishing Web site** at
http://www.wiley.com/compbooks/

Prices are subject to change

DAVENPORT COLLEGE LIBRARY
MERRILLVILLE, IN 46410